D&AD11

TASCHEN

About D&AD

The annual D&AD Awards – the creative industry's most highly-regarded – celebrate creativity, originality and technical excellence in design and advertising. Launched in 1962 by a group of London-based designers and art directors, D&AD is a nonprofit educational charity with the world's most feted professionals featuring on both its judging panels and winners lists. By celebrating creative communication and rewarding its practitioners, D&AD raises standards across the industry, and provides inspiration to the next generation of creative people everywhere.

Über den D&AD

Die jährlichen D&AD Awards sind die Auszeichnungen mit dem höchsten Renommee in der Kreativbranche. Hier werden Kreativität, Originalität und hervorragende technische Ausführung im Bereich Design und Werbung gefeiert. D&AD wurde 1962 von einer Gruppe Designer und Art Directors in London gegründet. Diese nicht kommerzielle Bildungs- und Wohltätigkeitsorganisation besteht aus den weltweit besten Profis der Branche – sowohl auf Seiten der Jury als auch auf Seiten der Gewinner. Durch die Würdigung kreativer Kommunikation und die Auszeichnung praktischer Arbeiten erhöht D&AD die Standards in der Branche und sorgt weltweit bei der nächsten Generation kreativer Menschen für Inspiration.

À propos de D&AD

Les prix annuels D&AD – les plus prestigieux du secteur de la création – récompensent la créativité, l'originalité et l'excellence technique en matière de design et de publicité. D&AD, une organisation à vocation pédagogique et à but non lucratif, a été créée en 1962 par un groupe de designers et de directeurs artistiques londoniens. D&AD compte parmi ses jurés et ses lauréats les professionnels les plus réputés au monde. En célébrant la communication créative et en primant les spécialistes de cette discipline, D&AD établit des critères d'excellence pour tout le secteur et inspire les générations futures dans le monde entier.

Contents

Sanky, D&AD President

President's Introduction

I grew up in a house FULL of books. Books change the sound of a room, the smell, the light and most importantly what could happen in the room. Books, we need them. So I knew at the start of my presidency that I would make a physical version of the Annual. But we now produce over 11,000 Annuals per year – books that have to wing it to far-flung corners... I wondered to what cost. I decided that my task was to make the Annual as sustainable as possible, with the intention to have the process carry on for years to come. This commitment is one that TASCHEN are truly passionate about too. The journey needed companions, as I didn't know enough about the practicalities of sustainable design. I also needed a designer who would be sympathetic to the cause but not let quality suffer. Nat Hunter (Airside) and Harry Pearce (Pentagram) were the easy choices. Fast forward 8 months... The result you hold in your hand. Importantly, the cover idea stems from wanting to celebrate the wonderful graphic quality of the original D&AD mark, created in 1962 by Fletcher Forbes Gill. We have rigorously fiddled with other things (stock, stock sourcing, glue, ink, etc.) to the point that we feel that at this moment we have a version of the book that is as sustainable as it could get... with a visual design that lets the work sing. I am very proud of what we've done... At D&AD's 49th year it's good to look forward; this is an indication of how we all should behave as designers and creatives, with belief in our hearts and commitment in our minds. Dedicated to the memory of my mother, Alison Kate Sankarayya.

Einleitung des Präsidenten

Ich wuchs auf in einem Haus VOLLER Bücher. Bücher verändern den Klang eines Raumes, seinen Geruch und das Licht – und vor allem das, was in diesem Raum möglich wird: Dazu brauchen wir Bücher. Mir war zu Beginn meiner Präsidentschaft klar, dass ich eine materielle Version des Annuals herausbringen wollte. Wir produzieren jährlich 11.000 Exemplare unseres Annuals, und diese Bücher müssen auch in den entlegensten Ecken der Welt landen… da fragte ich mich, was das wohl kostet? Ich beschloss, das Annual so nachhaltig wie möglich zu gestalten – mit der Idee, dass dieser Prozess in den nächsten Jahren weitergehen wird. Diese Verpflichtung geht auch TASCHEN voller Leidenschaft ein. Ich brauchte einige Mitstreiter, weil ich mich beim Einsatz von nachhaltigem Design nicht wirklich gut auskannte. Ich benötigte zudem einen Designer, der sich auch für diese Sache engagiert, ohne Abstriche bei der Qualität. Nat Hunter (Airside) und Harry Pearce (Pentagram) waren meine Wahl. Acht Monate später… Das Ergebnis halten Sie in Händen. Die Coveridee entstammt im Wesentlichen dem Wunsch, die Qualität des originalen D&AD-Markenzeichens zu feiern, das 1962 von Fletcher Forbes Gill geschaffen wurde. Wir haben alles so lange optimiert (das Papier und dessen Herstellung, Leim, Druckfarbe etc.), bis wir den Eindruck hatten, dass unsere Version des Buches so nachhaltig ist wie irgend möglich… mit einem großartigen visuellen Design. Ich bin sehr stolz auf das, was wir erreicht haben. Im 49. Jahr des D&AD ist es gut, nach vorn zu schauen. Dies ist ein Hinweis darauf, wie wir uns als Designer und Kreative verhalten sollten: mit Glauben in unseren Herzen und der Entschlossenheit im Geiste. Gewidmet dem Andenken an meine Mutter: Alison Kate Sankarayya.

Introduction du président

J'ai grandi dans une maison PLEINE de livres. Les livres modifient la sonorité d'une pièce, son odeur, sa lumière et, chose plus importante encore, ce qui peut s'y passer. Nous avons besoin des livres. Je savais donc dès le début de mon mandat présidentiel que je ferais une version physique de l'Annuel. Mais nous produisons désormais quelques 11 000 Annuels par an, livres qui sont acheminés jusqu'aux quatre coins du monde… Je me demandais à quel prix. Je décidais que mon devoir était de produire un Annuel aussi écologique que possible, avec l'intention d'établir un processus qui continuerait dans les années à venir. C'est là un engagement que TASCHEN partage aussi avec passion. Cette entreprise devait être un travail d'équipe, car je n'en savais pas assez sur les aspects pratiques du design durable. J'avais aussi besoin d'un designer acquis à la cause mais qui saurait préserver la qualité. Nat Hunter (Airside) et Harry Pearce (Pentagram) étaient des choix évidents. Huit mois plus tard… Le résultat que vous tenez entre vos mains. L'idée de la couverture, c'était important, découle du désir de rendre hommage à la merveilleuse qualité graphique du logo original de D&AD, créé en 1962 par Fletcher Forbes Gill. Nous avons ajusté avec rigueur d'autres éléments (stocks, approvisionnement, colle, encre, etc.) jusqu'à ce que nous ayons enfin le sentiment de tenir une version du livre aussi durable que possible… et une conception visuelle qui laisse le travail s'exprimer. Je suis très fier de ce que nous avons fait… En cette 49e année de D&AD, il est bon de regarder vers le futur ; cela donne une idée du comportement que nous devrions tous adopter, designers et créatifs : la conviction au cœur et l'engagement à l'esprit. Dédié à la mémoire de ma mère, Alison Kate Sankarayya.

D&AD's 49th year was a good one. The relevance, difficulty of achievement and resulting desirability of the Pencils was underscored by a very strong entry from myriad nations.
Our presence in the land of 1s and 0s went from strength to strength: we launched a brand-new, content-rich website. Traffic doubled. We introduced a critically acclaimed iPad application for the Annual, and saw our 30,000th Twitter follower come through the digital doorway. We launched our first new Pencil since we started: the White Pencil. If you don't know about it, now's the time to find out... We welcomed new commercial partners, attracted to us by the steadily increasing buzz around the D&AD community in recent years. Because we were commercially successful, we were able to re-commit fulsomely to our real purpose: perpetuating brilliance in commercial creativity, across disciplines and around the world.
We renewed our vows with more than one hundred colleges and their tutors, to whom D&AD provides a vital resource (especially since the current government doesn't seem to feel that education for creative people deserves funding).
We are now, at last, in a position to bring a more complete version of D&AD, combining awards, education and community, to many more parts of the world than before. These have been challenging years for everyone. But we've emerged in great shape, fully-energized, and committed to fighting the good fight for creativity everywhere, 365 days a year. We have reason to believe that our 50th year will be a big step towards a very, very exciting future.
Thank you all for your continued support and, in the words of Tim Riley: 'Keep the faith'.

Tim O'Kennedy
CEO

Das 49. Jahr des D&AD war ein gutes Jahr. Welche Bedeutung die Pencils haben, wie schwierig es ist, diesen Preis zu erhalten, sowie die daraus entstehende Begehrlichkeit kann man an den vielen Einreichungen aus unzähligen Nationen erkennen.
Unsere Präsenz im Lande der Einsen und Nullen hat sich immer weiter entwickelt: Wir haben eine brandneue Website gestartet, die viel zu bieten hat. Der Traffic hat sich verdoppelt. Für das Jahrbuch haben wir eine von der Kritik gefeierte iPad-App veröffentlicht und können den 30 000. Twitter-Follower begrüßen. Seit unserer Gründung verleihen wir zum ersten Mal einen neuen Pencil: den White Pencil. Wenn Sie den nicht kennen, wird es Zeit, mehr darüber zu erfahren ... Wir durften neue Geschäftspartner begrüßen, die von der stetig zunehmenden Begeisterung um die Community von D&AD in den letzten Jahren angezogen wurden. Weil wir kommerziell so erfolgreich waren, konnten wir uns für unsere wahre Aufgabe engagieren: die Förderung einer brillanten kommerziellen Kreativität, spartenübergreifend und weltweit umgesetzt.
Wir erneuerten dieses Gelübde mit über Hundert Hochschulen und ihren Tutoren, für die D&AD eine unerlässliche Quelle darstellt (vor allem, seitdem die gegenwärtige Regierung den Eindruck vermittelt, die Weiterbildung kreativer Menschen verdiene keine zusätzlichen finanziellen Mittel).
Schließlich befinden wir uns nun in einer Position, aus der heraus wir D&AD umfassender und in viel mehr Bereiche der Welt als vorher bringen und dabei Awards, Weiterbildung und Community kombinieren können.
Diese Jahre waren für jeden eine Herausforderung. Doch nun sind wir wieder da – in großartiger Form, voller Energie und bereit, den guten Kampf für Kreativität überall voranzutreiben, 365 Tage im Jahr! Wir sind sicher, dass unser 50. Jahr ein großer Schritt in Richtung einer spannenden Zukunft sein wird. Dank an alle für die anhaltende Unterstützung und mit den Worten von Tim Riley: „Keep the faith."

Tim O'Kennedy
CEO

La 49e année de D&AD aura été un bon millésime. L'importance, l'exigence de nos Crayons, et donc la convoitise qu'ils suscitent, ont été accentuées par la très forte participation d'une myriade de pays. Notre présence sur Internet, royaume des 1 et des 0, n'a cessé de croître : nous avons lancé un nouveau site riche de contenus ... et la fréquentation a doublé. Nous avons introduit pour l'Annuel une application iPad qui a été applaudie par la critique, et notre 30 000e fan nous a rejoints sur Twitter.
Nous avons lancé notre premier nouveau Crayon depuis nos débuts : le Crayon Blanc. Si vous ne savez pas de quoi je parle, le moment est venu de vous mettre au courant ... Nous avons accueilli de nouveaux partenaires commerciaux, attirés par l'ébullition qui ne cesse de croître autour de la communauté de D&AD depuis quelques années.
Cette réussite commerciale nous a mis en mesure de prendre un nouvel engagement envers ce qui constitue notre raison d'être : perpétuer le brio en matière de créativité commerciale, internationalement et dans toutes les disciplines.
Nous avons renouvelé nos liens avec plus de cent collèges et leurs professeurs, auxquels D&AD fournit une ressource vitale (notamment depuis que le gouvernement actuel semble estimer que l'enseignement destiné aux créatifs ne mérite pas d'être subventionné).
Nous sommes enfin capables de proposer une version plus complète de D&AD, une version associant remises de prix, enseignement et communauté, et d'atteindre des régions du monde bien plus nombreuses qu'auparavant. Ces années ont été un défi pour tous, mais nous en sommes sortis en grande forme, pleins d'énergie et bien décidés à nous battre au service de la créativité, où qu'elle soit, 365 jours par an. Nous avons des raisons de penser que notre 50e année sera un grand pas vers un avenir très, très prometteur.
Merci à tous pour votre soutien continu et, comme dirait Tim Riley : « Gardez la foi ».

Tim O'Kennedy
PDG

D&AD Executive Committee

Digital Advertising
Foreman
Mark Chalmers
Perfect Fools

Fernando Barbella
BBDO Argentina
Chris Beckles
Five by Five Digital
Andy Cameron
Wieden+Kennedy London
Paul Clements
TBWA\Copenhagen
Paul Collins
KBS+P
Andy Cutbill
R/GA London
Matt Dyke
AnalogFolk
Dirk Eschenbacher
DDB China
Nancy Hartley
SapientNitro
Dawna Henderson
henderson bas
Alessandra Lariu
McCann Erickson New York
Robert Lund
Forsman & Bodenfors
Fernanda Romano
Euro RSCG Worldwide
Gregory Titeca
Happiness Brussels

Direct
Foreman
Dave King
M&C Saatchi Auckland

Bernd Fliesser
Draftfcb Partners
Iain Hunter
CMW
Paul Kitcatt
Kitcatt Nohr Alexander Shaw
Michael Koch
gkk DialogGroup
Victor Ng
DDB Shanghai
Justin Wright
TBWA\Hunt\Lascaris
Johannesburg

Integrated & Earned Media
Foreman
Craig Davis
Publicis Mojo Australia
& New Zealand

Philip Andrew
Clemenger BBDO
Rosie Bardales
Wieden+Kennedy Amsterdam
Christoph Becker
GyroHSR
Matthew Bull
Lowe Worldwide
Gustav Martner
CP+B Europe
Eco Moliterno
Africa
Satoshi Takamatsu
Ground Tokyo
Steve Vranakis
VCCP

Mobile Marketing
Foreman
Patrick Moorhead
Draftfcb North America

Jon Carney
Marvellous
mills
ustwo™
Hiroki Nakamura
Dentsu Tokyo
Scott Seaborn
Ogilvy & Mather London
Despina Tapaki
Joule Worldwide
Scott Witt
Apple

Music Videos
Foreman
James Hackett
EMI

Jules Dieng
El Niño
Nabil Elderkin
RSA Films
Joceline Gabriel
Freelance Music Video
Representative
Svana Gisla
Black Dog Films
Jake Nava
Cherry Films
Andreas Nilsson
Blink Productions

Outdoor Advertising
Foreman
David Nobay
Droga5 Australia

Richard Denney
DDB UK
Susan Hoffman
Wieden+Kennedy Portland
Darren Spiller
Fallon Minneapolis
Damon Stapleton
TBWA\Hunt\Lascaris
Johannesburg

Press Advertising
Foreman
Russell Ramsey
JWT London
Florence Bellisson
BETC Euro RSCG
Robin Fitzgerald
CP+B Los Angeles
Luiz Sanches
AlmapBBDO
Ben Tollett
adam&eve
Stephan Vogel
Ogilvy & Mather Frankfurt

Radio Advertising
Foreman
Mike Schalit
Net#work BBDO

Mike Blunt
WAM London
Tony Hertz
Hertz:Radio
Ralf Heuel
Grabarz & Partner Hamburg
Stuart Outhwaite
Creature London
Stef Selfslagh
Boondoggle
Munzie Singh Thind
Grand Central Recording Studios

TV & Cinema Advertising
Foreman
Ben Priest
adam&eve

Colin Hickson
Publicis London
Danny Hunt
Dare London
Carol Lam
McCann Erickson Shanghai
Simon Learman
Creative Consultant

TV & Cinema Communications
Foreman
Karin Fong
Imaginary Forces

Darius Ghanai
Lichtrausch
Adam Jenns
Mainframe
Sophie Lutman
Lambie-Nairn
Richard Morrison
Fig Productions
Matt Scarff
BSkyB
Olivier Schaack
CANAL+

Book Design
Foreman
Jim Stoddart
Penguin Books
Lucas Dietrich
Thames & Hudson
Simon Elliott
Rose Design

David Pearson
David Pearson Design
Miriam Rosenbloom
Scribe Publications
Paul Sahre
Office of Paul Sahre (O.O.P.S.)
Astrid Stavro
Studio Astrid Stavro

Branding
Foreman
Stephen Doyle
Doyle Partners

Andy Audsley
Ziggurat Brand Consultants
Lisa Carrana
The Brand Union
Jason Gregory
GBH
Heinrich Paravicini
Mutabor
Richard Scholey
The Chase
Jane Wentworth
Jane Wentworth Associates

Digital Design
Foreman
Andy Sandoz
Work Club

Gavin Bates
Fudge Studios
Conor Brady
Organic US
Benjy Choo
Kilo Studio
Belén Coca
La Despensa
Mike John Otto
BlackBeltMonkey
Ted Persson
Great Works
Nicolas Roope
Poke London

Graphic Design
Foreman
Michael Bierut
Pentagram Design

Nick Eagleton
The Partners
Mark Farrow
Farrow Design
Keren House
Aricot Vert
Dylan Kendle
Tomato
Claire Warner
Browns

Magazine & Newspaper Design
Foreman
Ruth Ansel
Ruth Ansel Design

John Belknap
Belknap+Co
Michael Bojkowski
ok interrupt
Matt Curtis
Eureka Magazine at The Times
Fernando Gutiérrez
The Studio of Fernando Gutiérrez
Sónia Matos
Público
Richard Spencer Powell
Monocle Magazine

Packaging Design
Foreman
Jonathan Ford
Pearlfisher

Jean Berrisford
Union Swiss
Tina Chang
Little Fury Design/
Start Here
Martin Grimer
Aesop
Yoji Nobuto
Shiseido
Daniela Nunzi-Mihranian
Jones Knowles Ritchie
Craig Oldham
Music

Product Design
Foreman
Adam White
Factorydesign

Paul Bradley
Frog
Allan Chochinov
Core 77
Lars Holme Larsen
Kibisi
Dorian Kurz
Kurz Kurz Design
Yosuke Watanabe
Ab Rogers Design
Ben Watson
Seymourpowell

Spatial Design
Foreman
Peter Higgins
Land Design Studio

Jussi Ängeslevä
ART+COM
Tim Greenhalgh
Fitch
Owain Roberts
Gensler
Daniel Weil
Pentagram Design
Isay Weinfeld
Isay Weinfeld
Lies Willers
Opera

Art Direction
Foreman
Alexandra Taylor
Mrs McGuinty Ltd

Tim Ashton
Antidote
Nils Leonard
Grey London
Lotta Marlind
Garbergs
Dave Towers
Rapier
Götz Ulmer
Jung von Matt Hamburg
Yoshihiro Yagi
Dentsu Tokyo

Film Advertising Crafts
Foreman
Barnaby Spurrier
Tomboy Films

James Bradley
750mph
Matt Buels
Hungryman
James Hagger
Troublemakers.tv
Jonathan Kneebone
The Glue Society
Rich Orrick
Work Film Editors

Illustration
Foreman
Paul Davis
Big Orange

Tom Brown
TBA+D
Linda Burrows
Style Magazine at
The Sunday Times
Maxine Hose
Leo Burnett London
James Joyce
Artist & Designer
Shailesh Khandeparkar
Illustrator & Graphic Designer
Kevin Lee
Ogilvy & Mather Shanghai

Photography
Foreman
Terry Jones
i-D Magazine

Martin Brent
Advertising Photographer
Dimitri Daniloff
Freelance Photographer
Julia Fullerton-Batten
Fine Art & Advertising
Photographer
Choi Liu
M&C Saatchi London

Michael Schnabel
Studio Schnabel
Keith Terry
DLKW Lowe

Typography
Foreman
Ben Stott
Graphic Designer

Gail Anderson
Spotco
Sara De Bondt
Sara De Bondt Studio
Guy Featherstone
Wieden+Kennedy London
Justus Oehler
Pentagram Design
Si Scott
Si Scott Studio

Writing for Advertising
Foreman
Dave Trott
CST The Gate

Jim Elliot
Goodby, Silverstein & Partners
Ted Heath
RKCR/Y&R
Judy John
Leo Burnett Toronto
David Kolbusz
BBH London
Mike McKay
BBDO San Francisco

Writing for Design
Foreman
Dan Germain
innocent

Sarah Brownrigg
Freelance Copywriter
Sarah McCartney
Little Max
Mike Reed
Reed Words
Tim Rich
Freelance Writer
Neil Taylor
The Writer

President's Award

Neville Brody is simply one of those individuals you can't imagine the world of design without. Undoubtedly, without him all creative industries would look, feel, act and behave differently, and truly to their detriment. From his tales of living in a squat, annoying his college in the 70s, to now, as Dean of Communications helping the RCA through what may be its toughest times due to the government's lack of support for the arts, it goes without saying that Neville has been one step ahead of us all... Fighting the good, difficult fight. Fighting sometimes for exploration, sometimes for (re)education, sometimes for professionalism... but always fighting. Neville teaches us all that we need actions not words. There are three reasons why I became a designer; he's at least two of them.

Sanky
D&AD President

Auszeichnung des Präsidenten

Neville Brody ist einer jener Menschen, ohne die man sich die Welt des Designs einfach nicht vorstellen kann. Zweifelsohne würde sich ohne ihn die gesamte kreative Branche ganz anders anfühlen, sie würde anders aussehen und sich anders verhalten – und das definitiv zu ihrem Nachteil. Von seinen Geschichten, als er noch in einem besetzten Haus wohnte, über den Ärger, den er in den 1970ern seinem College bereitete, bis heute, wo er als Dean of Communications dem RCA durch dessen bisher schwierigste Zeit half, weil die Regierung der Kunst die Mittel gestrichen hat, kann man zweifellos sagen, dass Neville uns stets einen Schritt voraus war ... Er kämpfte den guten, schwierigen Kampf. Er kämpfte manchmal für Erforschung, manchmal für Bildung und Umschulung und so manches Mal für Professionalität ... aber gekämpft hat er immer. Von Neville können wir alle lernen, dass nicht geredet, sondern gehandelt werden muss. Es gibt drei Gründe, warum ich Designer wurde: Mindestens zwei davon sind er.

Sanky
Präsident des D&AD

Prix du président

Neville Brody fait tout simplement partie des personnes sans lesquelles le monde du design serait inimaginable. S'il n'existait pas, c'est certain, tous les secteurs de la création seraient différents, à l'intérieur comme de l'extérieur, et s'en porteraient à coup sûr plus mal. Depuis le squat où il a vécu un temps et ses exploits de trublion à l'université dans les années 1970, jusqu'à aujourd'hui, où, en qualité de recteur du département de communication, il aide le Royal College of Art à traverser ce qui constitue peut-être sa période la plus dure en raison du manque de soutien gouvernemental accordé aux arts, il va sans dire que Neville a toujours été à l'avant-garde, un pas avant nous tous ... Se battant pour la bonne et difficile cause. Se battant parfois pour l'exploration, parfois pour la (ré)éducation, parfois pour le professionnalisme ... mais se battant, toujours. Neville nous apprend, à tous, que nous avons besoin d'actions, pas de mots. Je suis devenu designer pour trois raisons ; Neville est au moins deux d'entre elles.

Sanky
Président de D&AD

Student of the Year

Advertising
for Oxfam

A Better Life Without Oxfam
The brief was to encourage support for Oxfam. Our campaign 'A Better Life Without Oxfam' proposes an ideal world where Oxfam wouldn't need to exist. We ask people to consider the lives of Oxfam volunteers all over the world who long to return to their homes. The online platform allows users to follow the volunteers and the dreams they would like to pursue after completing their mission. By engaging people with the workers in action, and asking them to help with individual projects, global problems such as hunger or poverty seemed easier to face.

Students
Christian Asmar
Manu Manceda
Virginia Feito
Tutor
Elvio Sanchez
College
Miami Ad School, Madrid

Without poverty we wouldn't need Oxfam, and everyone's lives would be better.
A Better Life
INDIA
Works on building school in mumbai.
Patricia Sirera
Wants to write a series of children's books
Works on promoting girls' education.
Robert Ericksen
Share: Status Photo Link Video
What's on your mind?
Patricia Sirera
Hey guys! please sign this petition and pass it around. We need 10 000 signatures to get these girls a new school!!!
Mumbai School Petition.
Please sign and pass!
February 21 at 2:16pm via iPhone · Like · Comment · Share
Write a comment...

Student First in Graphics

Packaging Design
for The Body Shop

We're Still Body Shop Underneath
The brief was to design a contemporary range of packaging for The Body Shop that unites their brand values with the premium nature of the products. Our solution uses a patterned paper wrap to dress up the existing packaging, The Body Shop's famous little bottles. The wrap is origami folded to give the product the status of something special, a treat. The reverse reads 'we're still Body Shop underneath', with a short description of the ethics and values the brand has upheld in manufacturing that particular product. They are not trying to be anything they are not, they still believe in the same values, they are still Body Shop, but they are dressed to impress.

Student
Emma Hayes
Tutor
Catharine Slade-Brooking
College
University for the Creative Arts, Farnham

WE'RE STILL BODYSHOP UNDERNEATH.
THIS TEA TREE OIL WAS SOURCED FROM FAIRTRADE FARMERS IN KENYA
THIS BOTTLE IS PET PLASTIC
THIS PAPER IS 100% RECYCLED
WE DIDN'T TEST ON ANIMALS TO MAKE THIS MOISTERISER
WE DON'T DO THIS BECAUSE ITS FASHIONABLE. WE DO IT BECAUSE WE CARE
RECYCLE EDITION BOTTLE.
THIS BOTTLE IS RECYCLABLE. RETURN IT TO A BODYSHOP STORE AND HELP KEEP OUR PACKAGING SUBSTAINABLE
THE BODY SHOP
RECYCLE EDITION BOTTLE.
TEATREE LOTION
SUITABLE FOR BLEMISHED SKIN.
LIGHTWEIGHT HYDRATION WITH SHINE CONTROL.
ARBRE A THE LOTION
CONVIENT AUX PEAUX A IMPERFECTIONS.
LIGHTWEIGHT HYDRATION WITH SHINE CONTROL.
250ml (8.4 US FL OZ)
TEA TREE LOTION
RECYCLE
BOTTLE
150ml
LIQUID
SPF 15
RECYCLE
BOTTLE
30ml

Student First in Advertising

Copywriting for D&AD

Write it Like You Mean it
The brief was to create a copy-based campaign to promote D&AD's 'refreshed' edition of The Copy Book. A creative team at BMB once told us to think Target Audience, Target Audience, Target Audience. This is exactly what we did. The target audience in this brief was students and lecturers, so we decided to add adapted signs alongside existing ones in universities and colleges. The disguised adverts aimed to entertain, surprise and inform.

Students
Stephanie Marie Flynn
Olivia Shortland
Tutor
David Anderson
College
Leeds College of Art

Toilets closed for refurbishment Apologies for the inconvenience
I'd give it a while if I were you.
Write it like you mean it. Read
The Copy Book
dandad.org
No admittance authorised personnel only
Important people only, including The Queen, The Pope and Dizzy Rascal.
Write it like you mean it. Read
The Copy Book
dandad.org
218
No entry
218
No go, mo fo
218
Write it like you mean it.
Read
The Copy Book

Student First in Advertising

Copywriting for D&AD

It Takes Work to Make it Work
The brief was to create a copy-based campaign to promote D&AD's 'refreshed' edition of The Copy Book. Our solution was to deconstruct the most recognisable tag lines from global brands by imagining where they had begun. We tried to demonstrate both the effort and process involved in coming up with smooth and meaningful copy. This print campaign for a book on copywriting aims to be a wry comment on the very fact that it takes a lot of work to make it work.

Students
Alexandra Hickmott
Ryan Purcell
Tutor
Lyn Clarke
College
RMIT University

NOKIA
Joining two or more individuals together for the purpose of communication
it takes work to make it work.
D&AD's Refreshed edition of The Copy Book
Great advertising ideas. Put in writing.
dandad.org
i am currently experiencing a strong positive emotion of affection
It takes work to make it work.
D&AD's Refreshed edition of The Copy Book
Great advertising ideas. Put in writing.
dandad.org
AT THIS EXACT MOMENT ENGAGE IN ACTIVITY.
It takes work to make it work.
D&AD's Refreshed edition of The Copy Book
Great advertising ideas. Put in writing.
dandad.org

Student First in Advertising

Digital Direct for E-ON

The E-ON Plugin
The brief was to encourage Generation Y to reduce their energy consumption. Our research gave us insight into the existence of a 'new' energy villain in the world that no one is talking about: the Internet, where our audience spends much of their time. We learned that within 10 years the Internet will use as much power as a whole new continent. Our solution was a plugin for your browser that helps to reduce your energy consumption on the web.

Students
Kaspar Prinz
Robin Wiman
Tutor
Annika Berner
College
Beckmans School of Design

e·on
The Internet
Tube

Student First in Advertising

Advertising Open Brief

ISHR Typewriter
For this brief set by D&AD, students were invited to show their creative excellence in whatever way they wished. We chose to support the ISHR (International Service for Human Rights), by talking about the right to freedom of expression, which is still strongly restricted in many countries. Journalists are tortured, even killed, because of the content they publish. In short, every keystroke can mean death. In our film, a man in a dark warehouse is typing using a typewriter. With each keystroke he makes, a shot is heard. The more he writes, the more shots rain down on him from all sides. At the last keystroke, he is shot dead. Freedom of speech means death for many journalists.

Students
Christian Hergenröther
Andreas Roth
Tutor
Michael Rösel
College
Filmakademie Baden-Württemberg

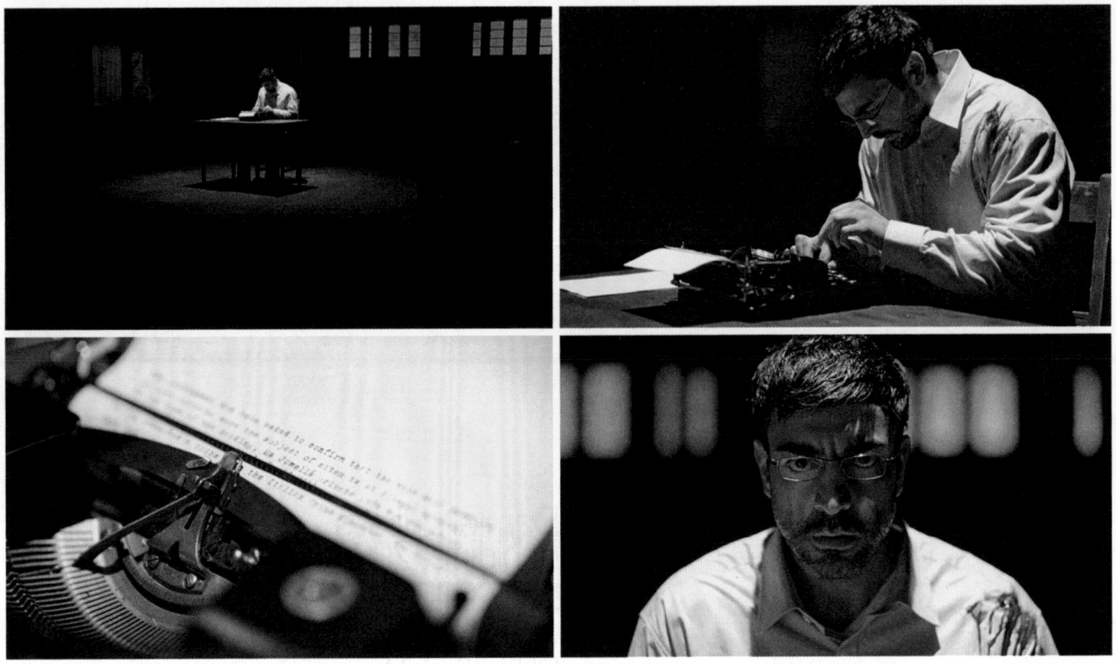

Student First in Advertising

Advertising for Umbro

Umbro 1350
The brief was to launch 'A Frame', Umbro's lifestyle footwear collection, to a young, football inspired, audience. Our campaign for the 1350 lifestyle footwear range shows football and lifestyle, the two sides of the UMBRO brand. The TV spot does this with a series of dynamic split screens. Shoeboxes show the two sides through black and white colouring. They can be stacked to create the Umbro logo at point of sale. The website splits its content between football and lifestyle and the two sides can be accessed separately.

Students
Andy Shrubsole
Scott Taylor
Tutor
Marion Morrison
College
Kingston University

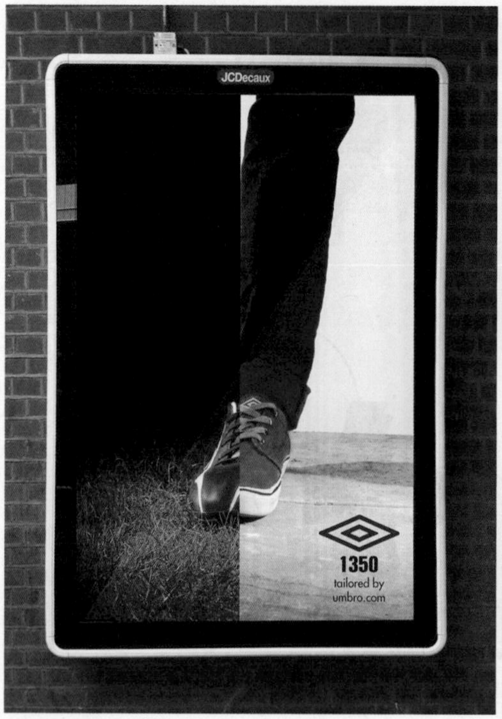
JCDecaux
1350
tailored by
umbro.com

Student First in Graphics

Branding for The Partners

Temporarily Admitted
The brief, set by The Partners, was to create the identity for an art gallery to tour hospitals. This solution shows the exhibits themselves being temporarily admitted. Working in partnership with the UK's most contemporary galleries would generate media interest across the country. The directional element of the exhibition uses a tape system which links the exhibits. The captions and tape will be printed on a yellow vinyl and will run along the floor. The main element of the brand is a yellow overlay that appears on existing printed media, website pages and gallery spaces. The brand will temporarily take over the websites of the exhibiting artists. The yellow overlay will create a link to the Temporarily Admitted web page.

Student
Catherine Perrott
Tutor
Michael Evidon
College
University of Hertfordshire

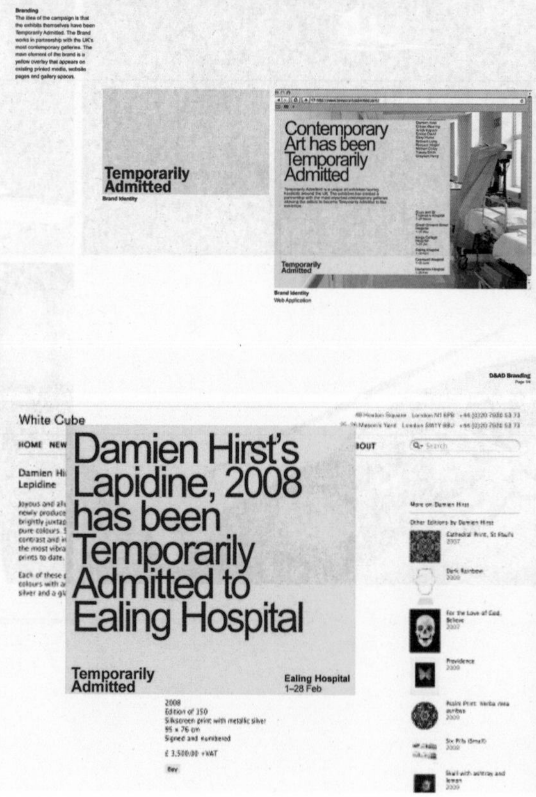
Temporarily Admitted
Contemporary Art has been Temporarily Admitted
White Cube
Damien Hirst's Lapidine, 2008 has been Temporarily Admitted to Ealing Hospital
Temporarily Admitted
Ealing Hospital
1–28 Feb

HELP

Student First in Graphics

Integrated Communications for McDonald's

Mc Royale
The brief was to create an integrated campaign that celebrates the inherent democracy of the McDonald's brand. We decided to invite someone 'of the people' who had never been to McDonald's: Her Royal Majesty Queen Elizabeth II. The campaign would start with a billboard outside Buckingham Palace. The idea is to create a democratic movement with lots of PR in a truly British manner, and to show that there is a McDonald's for everyone.

Students
Alexander Hernesten
Egle Vilutyte
Tutor
Jo Hodges
College
LCC University of the Arts London

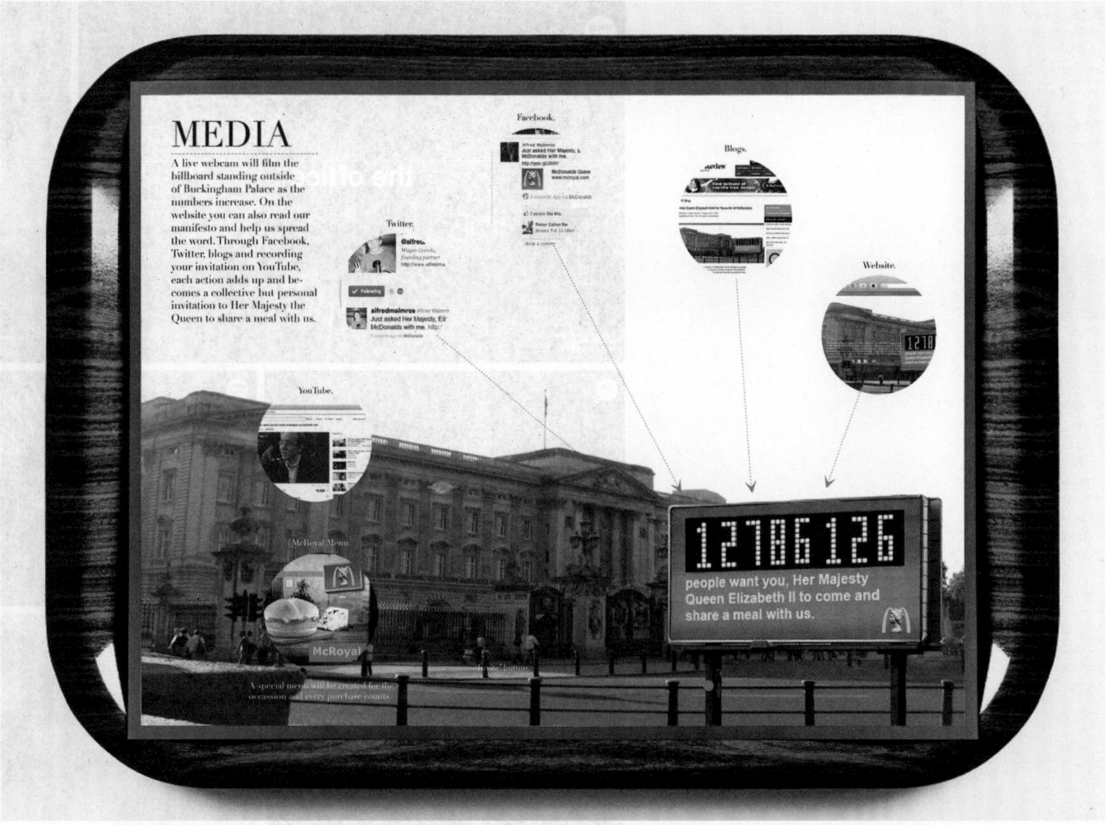
MEDIA
A live webcam will film the billboard standing outside of Buckingham Palace as the numbers increase. On the website you can also read our manifesto and help us spread the word. Through Facebook, Twitter, blogs and recording your invitation on YouTube, each action adds up and becomes a collective but personal invitation to Her Majesty the Queen to share a meal with us.
Facebook.
Twitter.
Blogs.
Website.
YouTube.
McRoyal
12786126
people want you, Her Majesty Queen Elizabeth II to come and share a meal with us.

Student First in Graphics

Integrated Communications for McDonald's

UK Expressions
The brief was to create an integrated campaign that celebrates the inherent democracy of the McDonald's brand. Our solution celebrates the diversity of expressions in the UK. We discovered just how rich the English language is, and chose to embrace this throughout the campaign. Expressions deviated, even within the same room: is it a napkin or a serviette? Getting people to interact with the various phrases triggers healthy debate. We enjoyed how passionate people were about their own language and wanted this passion to be conveyed within the McDonald's brand.

Students
Becky Fuller
Anna Gladwin
Tutor
Gyles Lingwood
College
University of Lincoln

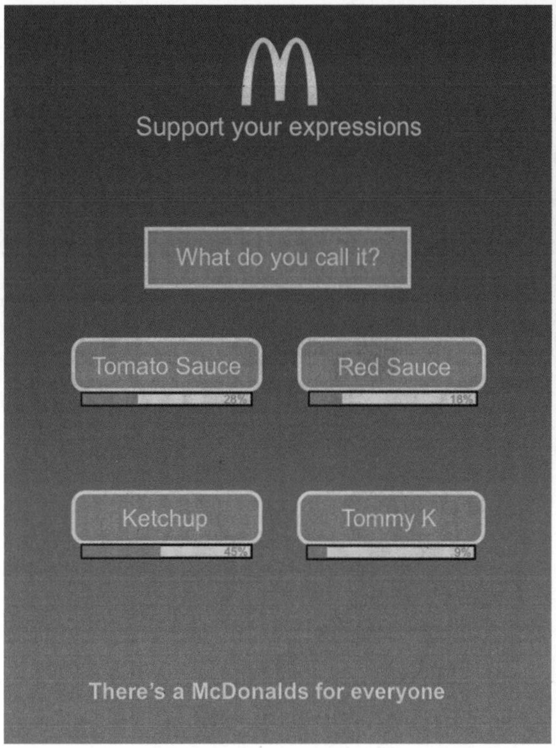
Support your expressions
What do you call it?
Tomato Sauce
28%
Red Sauce
18%
Ketchup
45%
Tommy K
9%
There's a McDonalds for everyone

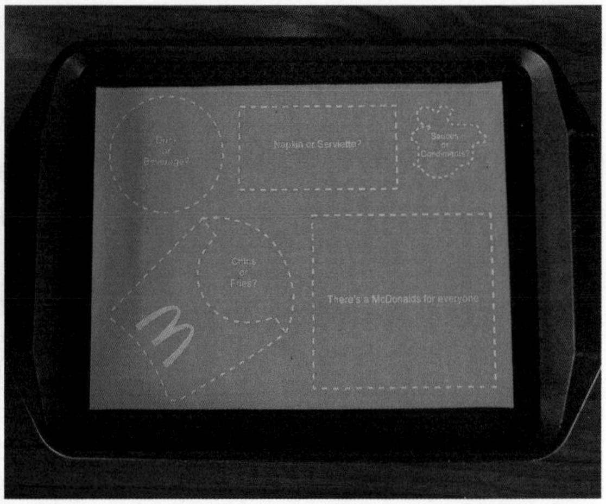
Napkin or Serviette?
There's a McDonalds for everyone

HEINZ
TOMATO KETCHUP
HEINZ
TOMATO SAUCE
HEINZ
RED SAUCE
HEINZ
TOMMY K
There's a McDonalds for everyone

Student First in Graphics

Interactive Design for the BBC

Timewheels
The brief was to design a platform that brings to life the cultural riches within the BBC Archive. My re-envisioning of the online BBC Archive is more reflective of the real archival vaults. It uses existing BBC databases and puts them in one easy to navigate place. Users can search through any show, person, channel, or year and see an entire history complete with information and multimedia content. These histories are then presented on timewheels, to allow more information on the screen at once while paying homage to the BBC's visual identity – something that is also done during the 30 second introduction comprising past and present channel idents.

Student
Sam Morris
Tutor
Bryan Clark
College
University College Falmouth

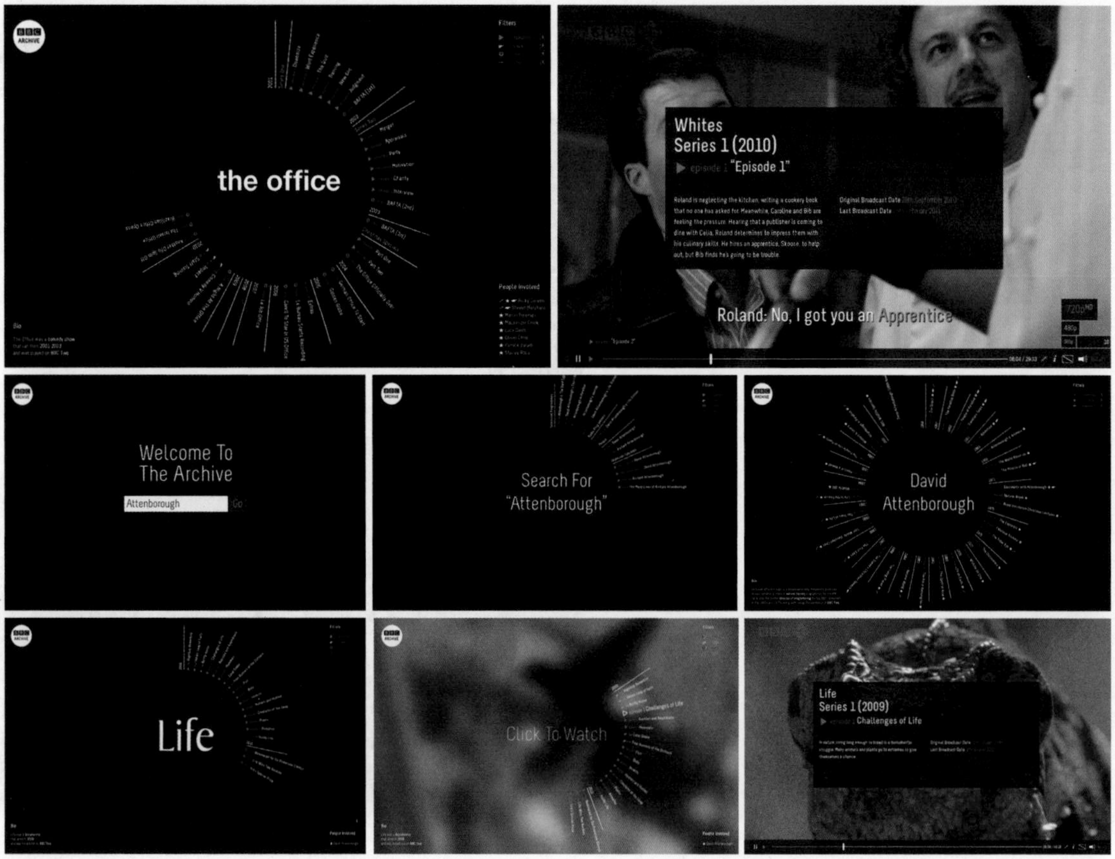
the office
Whites
Series 1 (2010)
"Episode 1"
Roland: No, I got you an Apprentice
Welcome To
The Archive
Attenborough
Search For
"Attenborough"
David
Attenborough
Life
Click To Watch
Life
Series 1 (2009)
Challenges of Life

Student First in Graphics

Open Graphics for Arjowiggins Creative Papers

Walk'n'Paint
The brief was to create a viral movement amongst designers that unbreakably links Arjowiggins Creative Papers with creativity and the creative design process. Our solution was Walk'n'Paint: imagining the world as an endless blank sheet of paper, we created an app for users to design the largest painting mankind could ever imagine. The app uses GPS to trace the user's movements and transform them into a painting, as if the streets were the canvas. This kind of street art can be shared with friends and other users, to learn skills, earn fame, and get more features and goodies.

Students
Jenne Genser
Christian Grelich
Tutor
Michael Hoinkes
College
Design Factory International

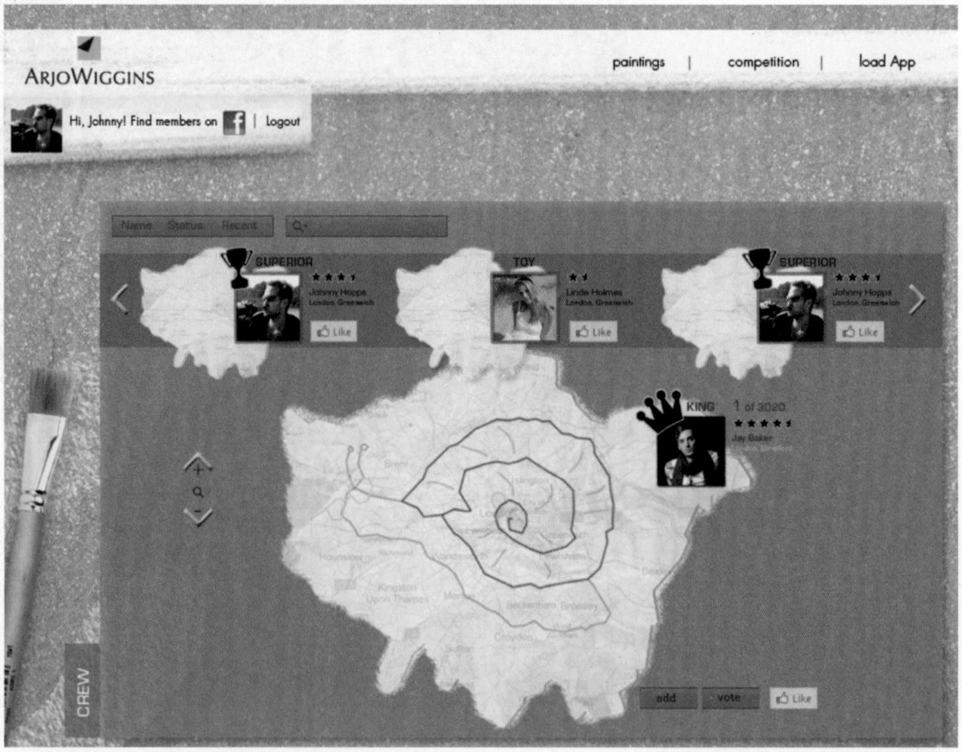
ArjoWiggins
paintings | competition | load App
Hi, Johnny! Find members on | Logout
Name Status Recent
SUPERIOR
TOY
KING
1 of 3020
Like
add
vote
CREW

Student First in Crafts

Animation for The Walt Disney Company

Student
Jonathan Mckee
Tutor
John McMillan
College
University of Ulster

The Dreamcatcher
This is a piece of animation in response to Disney's brief to create a lead character, infused with personality and depth, for a narrative-driven comedy cartoon.
The series is based around Baku, a dreamcatcher who spends each night catching and foiling members of a vicious group, The Nightmares.
The animation, entirely hand-drawn and painted, depicts a battle between Baku and one of these Nightmares, as it breaks into his owner's home intent on eating the children's dreams. Fortunately, Baku has a clever plan to stop it.

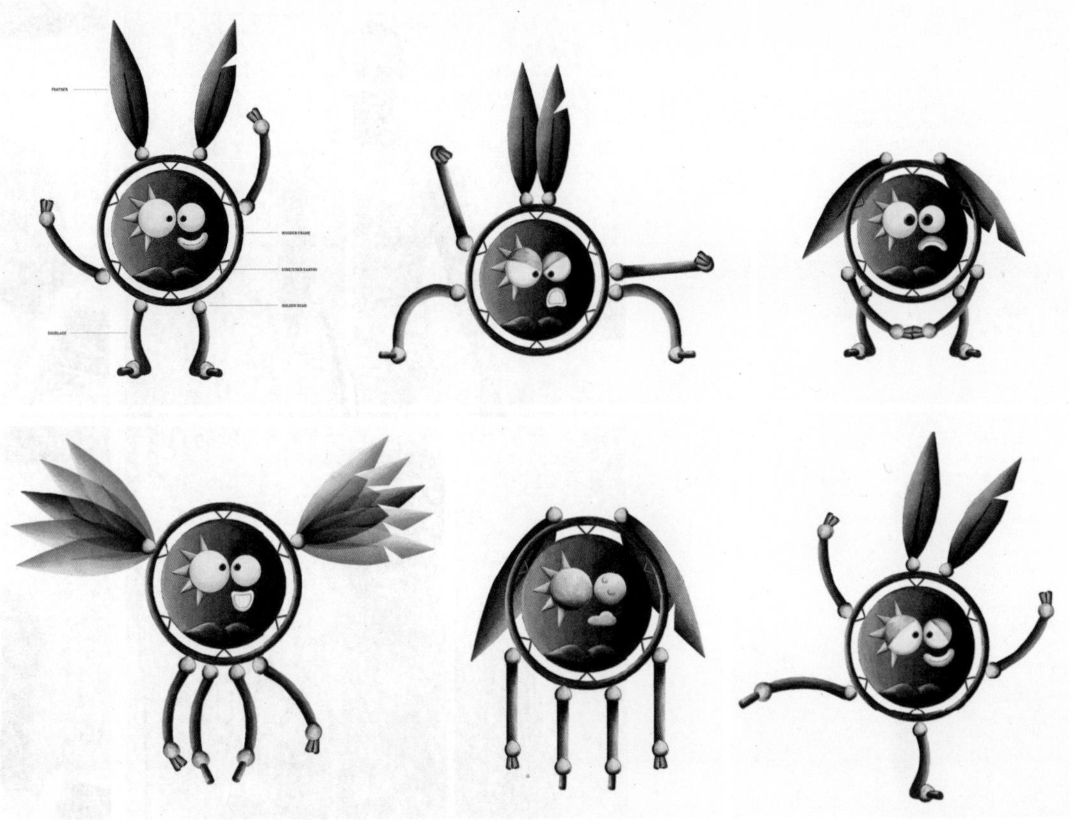

Student First in Crafts

Illustration for Diesel

Student
Helena Bradbury
Tutor
Geoff Grandfield
College
Kingston University

Movie Star / Pandora
The brief was to explore and illustrate 'Movie Star' and 'Pandora', two musical tracks by Roisin Murphy. Movie Star is about a girl's ambition to become a star. The song describes the seedy aspects of show business, with one lyric being about showing 'a little leg'. With our life-sized confectionary leg, we illustrated the idea of a movie star as a commodity to be consumed by the masses. For the other song, we illustrated the intriguing nature of Pandora. She is represented with just an outline and no features. Sections of a female form are printed on semi transparent paper, layered on top of each other and bound into a book. All the pages are bound together in order to create an obsessive desire leading one to tear each page. In the words of Roisin Murphy, 'where does the love of Pandora not leave destruction in its wake?'

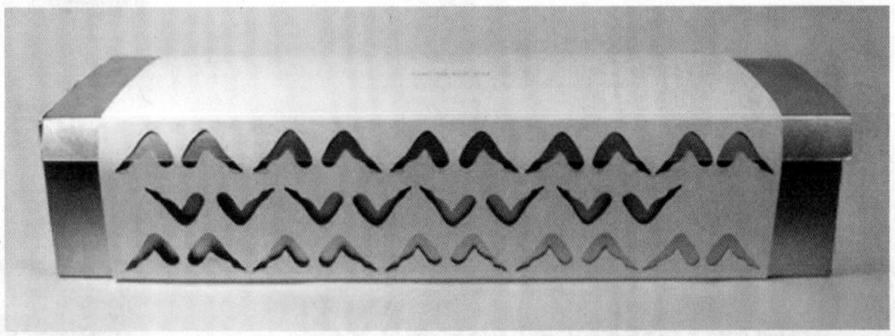

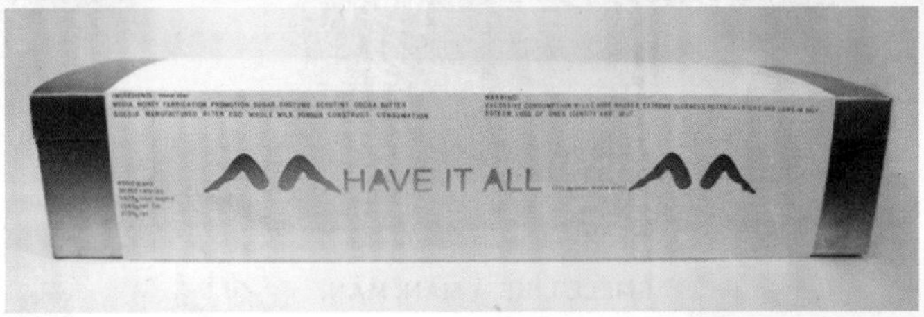
HAVE IT ALL

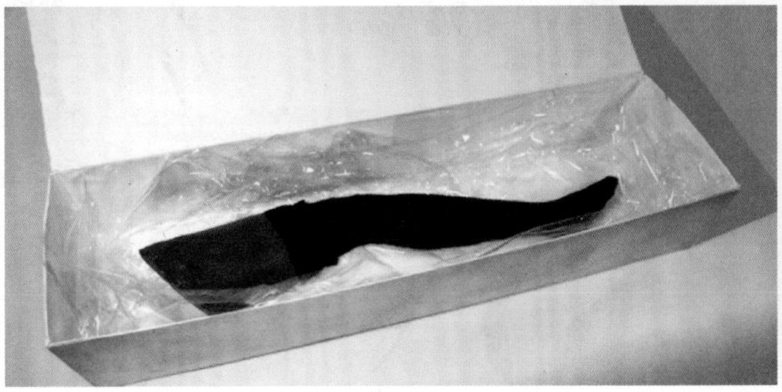

PANDORA

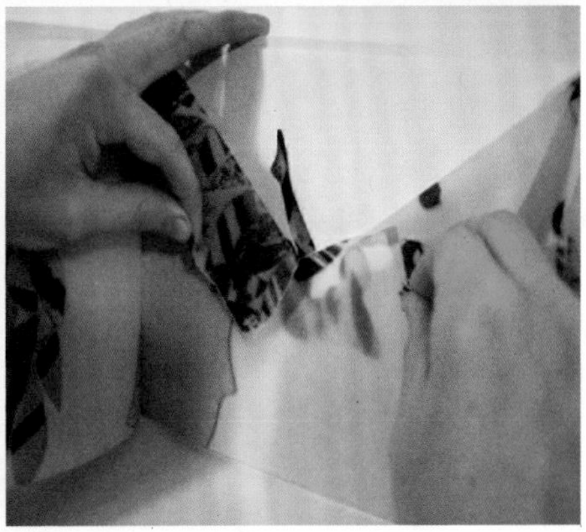

Black Pencil in TV & Cinema Advertising

TV Commercial Campaigns
Wieden+Kennedy Portland for Old Spice

The Man Your Man Could Smell Like / Did You Know / Questions / Boat
'The Man Your Man Could Smell Like' and 'Did You Know?' were created to appeal to men, as well as the women in their lives who do the majority of male body wash purchasing, to show how great a man can smell when they use Old Spice body wash. 'Questions' and 'Boat' built on the success of 'The Man Your Man Could Smell Like'. They continued the story and celebrated what's possible when a man smells like Old Spice. 'The Man Your Man Could Smell Like' was also awarded a Black Pencil as a single execution in TV Commercials 21-40 Seconds. 'Boat' was nominated in TV Commercials 1-20 Seconds. 'Did You Know' was selected in TV Commercials 1-20 Seconds and 'Questions' was selected in TV Commercials 21-40 Seconds.

Director
Tom Kuntz
Art Directors
Craig Allen
Eric Kallman
Copywriters
Craig Allen
Eric Kallman
Creative Directors
Jason Bagley
Eric Baldwin
Executive Creative Directors
Mark Fitzloff
Susan Hoffman
Executive Producer
Jeff Scruton
Agency Producer
Erin Goodsell
Agency Executive Producer
Ben Grylewicz
Post Executive Producer
Saima Awan
Line Producer
Scott Kaplan
Visual Effects Producer
Arielle Davis
Visual Effects Supervisor
Phil Crowe
Editor
Carlos Arias
Director of Photography
Neil Shapiro
Production Company
MJZ
Advertising Agency
Wieden+Kennedy Portland
Planner
Britton Taylor
Account Handler
Diana Gonzalez
Brand Manager
Carl Stealey
Assistant Brand Manager
Shanan Sabin
Client
Old Spice

SMELL LIKE A MAN, MAN.
Old Spice
The Man Your Man Could Smell Like

SMELL LIKE A MAN, MAN.
Old Spice
Boat

You're Beautiful
SMELL LIKE A MAN, MAN.
Old Spice

Questions

SMELL LIKE A MAN, MAN.
Old Spice
AQUA REEF
SHOWTIME
AFTER HOURS
Swagger

Did You Know

● Black Pencil in
Digital Advertising

Web Films
B-Reel for Google
Creative Lab

The Wilderness Downtown
This interactive interpretation of Arcade Fire's song 'We Used to Wait' was built entirely with the latest open web technologies, including HTML5 video, audio, and canvas. The story is told in multiple choreographed browser windows that pop up revealing new scenes as the song unfolds. The video also borrows from Google's database of street images, personalising the experience for each viewer. By entering the address of their childhood homes before the song begins, viewers are treated to a narrative that takes place on the very streets where they grew up. Viewers are also able to control onscreen elements.

Director
Chris Milk
Art Direction
B-Reel
Writer
Chris Milk
Lead Developer
Mr.doob
Creative Directors
Chris Milk
Aaron Koblin
Executive Producers
Jennifer Heath
Jon Kamen
Frank Scherma
Line Producer
Ari Palitz
Colourist
Dave Hussey
Visual Effects Designer
Scott Bravo
Editor
Livio Sanchez
Cinematographers
Shawn Kim
Chris Milk
Information Architect
Aaron Koblin
Interactive Design
B-Reel
Interactive Production
B-Reel
Production Company
@radical.media
3D Design
Magoo 3D Studios
Music & Sound
Arcade Fire
Client
Google Creative Lab
Brands
Google
HTML5

ARCADE FIRE
THE WILDERNESS DOWNTOWN
An interactive film by Chris Milk
Featuring "We Used To Wait"
Built in HTML5
Enter the address of the home where you grew up
SEARCH
[?]

http://www.thewildernessdowntown.com/container.html

Black Pencil in Spatial Design

Installations
JWT New York for Human Rights Watch

Burma
In 2010, Burma held its first elections in 20 years. But elections are meaningless when more than 2,100 political prisoners remain locked up in Burma's squalid prisons. Human Rights Watch created a campaign calling for the release of these innocent prisoners. A giant installation was built at New York's Grand Central Terminal. The installation featured a mock prison with 200 miniature cells and 2,000 pens in lieu of cell bars. Visitors could remove the pens to symbolically free the prisoners, and then use the pens to sign an onsite petition calling for their release.

Executive Creative Director
Andrew Clarke
Chief Creative Officers
Harvey Marco
Peter Nicholson
Art Director
Roy Wisnu
Head of Art
Aaron Padin
Copywriter
Chris Swift
Photographers
Bill Bramswig
Platon
Director of Photography
Izzy Levine
Producers
Paul Charbonnier
John Minze
Tadd Ryan
Director of Production
Kit Liset
Director of Integrated Production
Clair Grupp
Advertising Agency
JWT New York
Production Company
Cigar Box Studios
Project Managers
Elaine Barker
Jessie Hoyt
Art Buyer
Elizabeth Corkery
Account Executive
Lindsay Gash
Client
Human Rights Watch

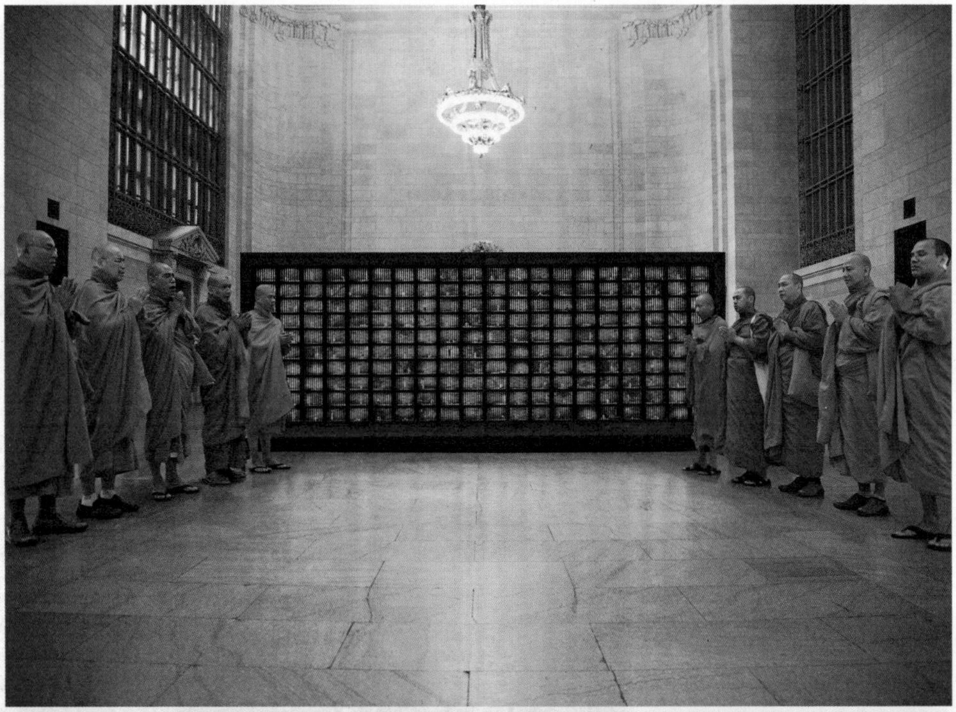

Black Pencil in Product Design

Consumer
Product Design
Apple Industrial Design Team for Apple

iPad
The iPad, at just half an inch thick and 1.5lbs, is a revolutionary device for web, email, photos, videos, music, games, e-books, and more. The iPad's 9.7-inch LED-backlit, Multi-Touch™ display lets users physically interact with applications and content. It has a recyclable aluminium enclosure and an energy-efficient LED display with arsenic-free glass, and contains no brominated flame retardants or PVC.

Designers
Jody Akana
Bart Andre
Jeremy Bataillou
Daniel Coster
Evans Hankey
Julian Hönig
Richard Howarth
Daniele De Iuliis
Jonathan Ive
Steve Jobs
Duncan Kerr
Shin Nishibori
Matthew Rohrbach
Peter Russell-Clarke
Christopher Stringer
Eugene Whang
Rico Zörkendörfer
Manufacturer
Apple
Design Group
Apple Industrial Design Team
Client
Apple

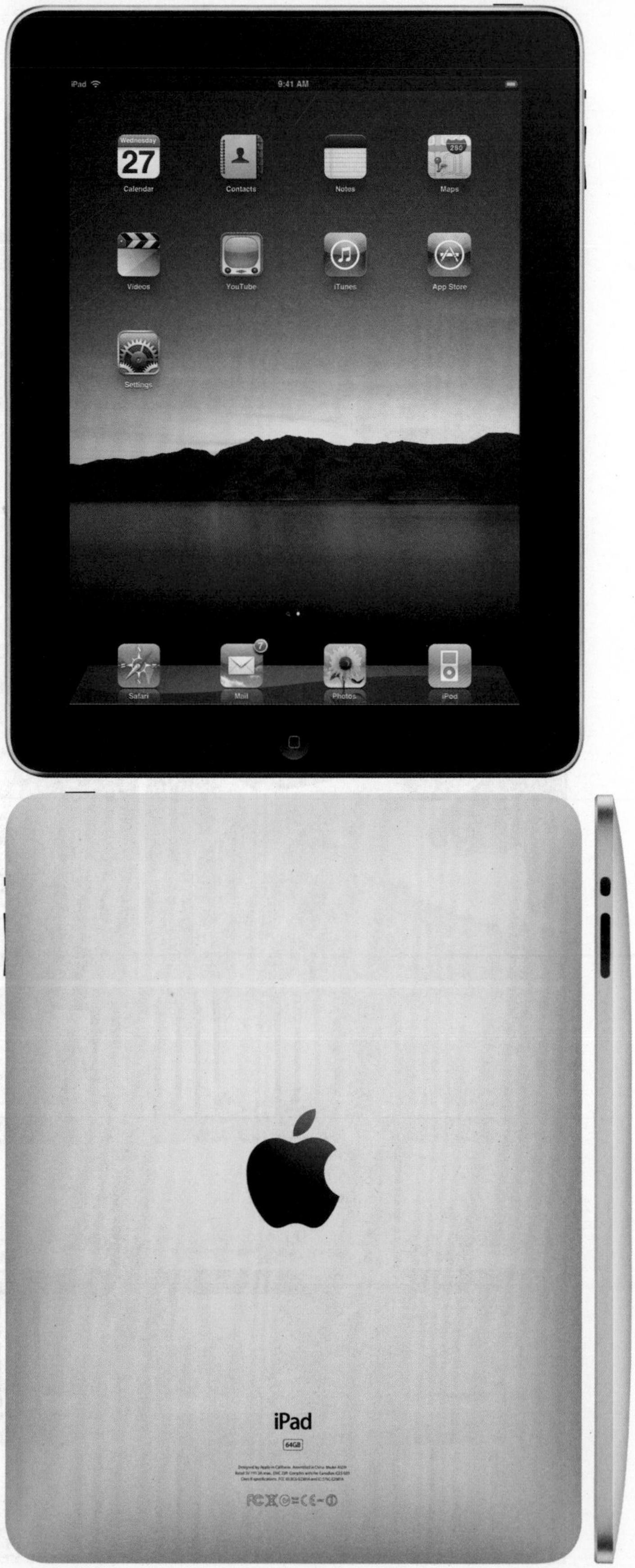
iPad
9:41 AM
Wednesday
27
Calendar
Contacts
Notes
Maps
Videos
YouTube
iTunes
App Store
Settings
Safari
Mail
Photos
iPod
iPad
64GB

● **Black Pencil in Product Design**

Consumer Product Design
Samuel Wilkinson Design for Hulger

Plumen 001
Rather than hiding the unappealing traditional compact fluorescent light behind boring utility, Plumen 001 was designed as an object the owner would want to show off. The glass tubes take an irregular yet harmonious form. The two organic shapes of the tubes mirror each other to create symmetry. The silhouette changes with every perspective, creating new interest at every angle. The Plumen bulb uses 80 per cent less energy and lasts eight times longer than incandescent bulbs. It is sold as a design object rather than a commodity, allowing premium materials and processes to be used to give the best possible quality of light.

Designer
Samuel Wilkinson
Design Director
Nicolas Roope
Technical Designer
Michael-George Hemus
Manufacturer
Hulger
Design Agency
Samuel Wilkinson Design
Technical Design
Hulger
Client
Hulger
Brand
Plumen

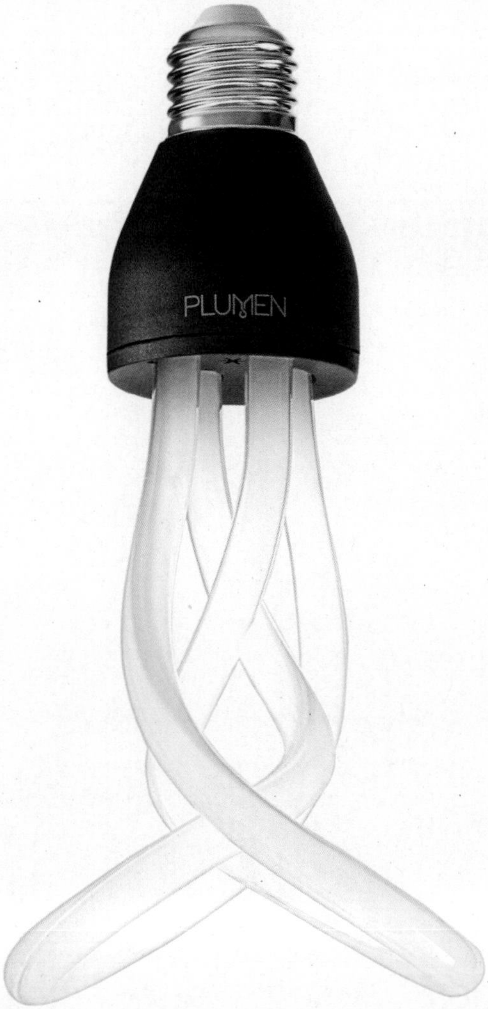
PLUMEN

PLUMEN

PLUMEN

Yellow Pencil in Digital Advertising

Integrated Digital Campaigns
BBH New York
for Google

Google Chrome Fast
The Chrome Fast integrated campaign established Google Chrome as the fastest browser on the web. We demonstrated Chrome's speed through 'Speed Tests', a viral video that matched Chrome against a potato gun, sound waves and lightning. We extended the Chrome Fast message online through web films, rich media banners and a contextualised banner blitz. Lastly, we challenged people to be Chrome Fast by launching FastBall, an interactive YouTube game that turned everyday sites into a race around the web. The campaign helped expand Chrome's marketshare to overtake Apple's Safari as the world's second most popular browser.

Executive Creative Directors
Calle Sjoenell
Pelle Sjoenell
Robert Wong
Chief Creative Officer
Kevin Roddy
Creative Technologist
Richard Schatzberger
Head of Interactive
Suzanne Molinaro
Art Directors
Erik Holmdahl
Steve Peck
Copywriters
Jared Elms
Jeff Johnson
Beth Ryan
Agency Producer
Orlee Tatarka
Director
Aaron Duffy
Advertising Agencies
BBH New York
Google Creative Lab
Production Company
1st Avenue Machine
Interactive Production Companies
B-Reel
Bajibot
Editorial Company
Lost Planet
Head of Broadcast
Lisa Setten
Client
Google

CHROME BY GOOGLE
GOOGLE.COM/CHROME

PANDORA

CBS
The Internet. Chrome fast.
Get Chrome

Yellow Pencil in
Digital Advertising

Digital Solutions &
Use of Social Media
Wieden+Kennedy
Portland for
Old Spice

Old Spice
Response Campaign
'The Man Your Man Could Smell Like' made a big splash in early 2010, and we wanted to use that success to have a more direct, engaging conversation with fans. The result was the 'Response' campaign, an experiment in real-time branding in which the Old Spice guy personally responded to fans online. Over 186 messages were created in just over two-and-a-half days of production; the work went on to record more than 65 millions views, making it one of the fastest growing and most popular online campaigns in history.

Creative Directors
Jason Bagley
Eric Baldwin
Executive Creative Directors
Mark Fitzloff
Susan Hoffman
Global Interactive Creative Director
Iain Tait
Interactive Designer
Matthew Carroll
Developers
John Cohoon
Trent Johnson
Art Directors
Craig Allen
Eric Kallman
Copywriters
Craig Allen
Jason Bagley
Eric Baldwin
Eric Kallman
Producer
Ann-Marie Harbour
Advertising Agency
Wieden+Kennedy
Portland
Production Company
Don't Act Big
Digital Strategist
Josh Millrod
Account Handler
Diana Gonzalez
Brand Manager
James Moorhead
Assistant Brand Manager
Shanan Sabin
Client
Old Spice

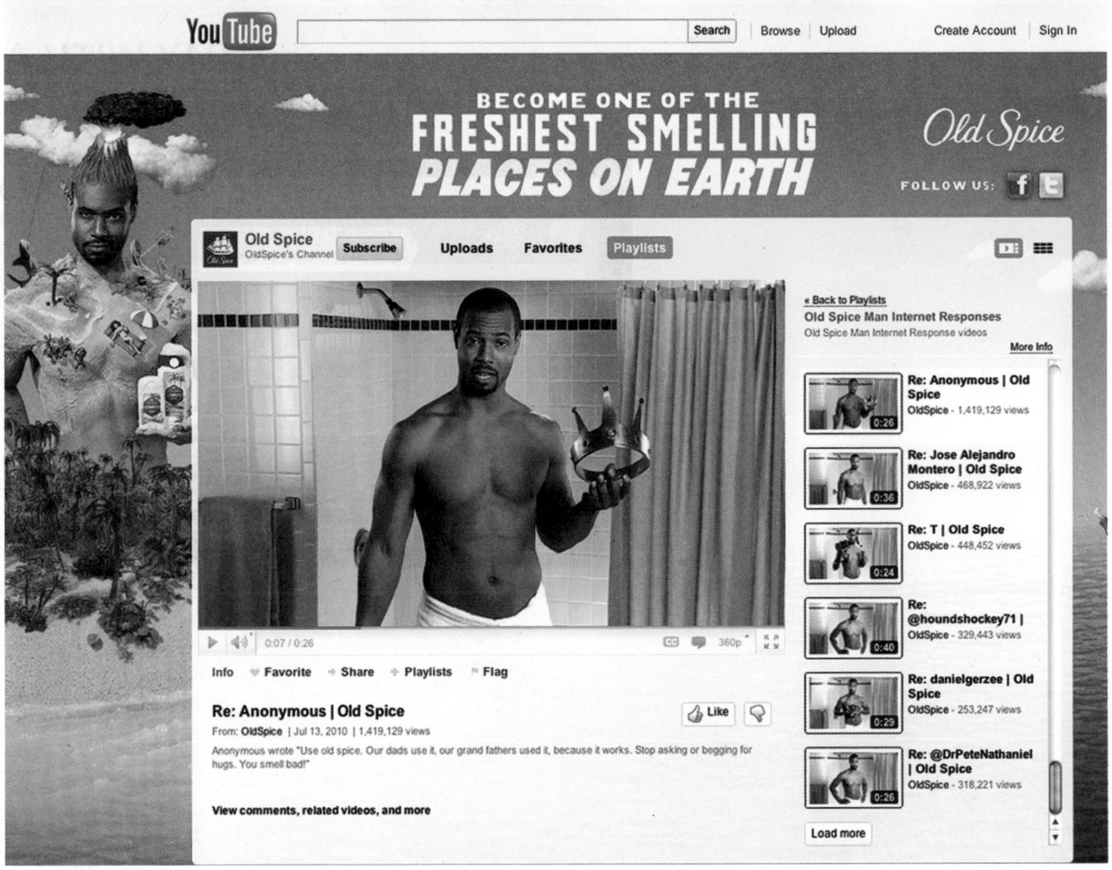
YouTube
Search
Browse
Upload
Create Account
Sign In
BECOME ONE OF THE
FRESHEST SMELLING
PLACES ON EARTH
Old Spice
FOLLOW US:
Old Spice
OldSpice's Channel
Subscribe
Uploads
Favorites
Playlists
« Back to Playlists
Old Spice Man Internet Responses
Old Spice Man Internet Response videos
More Info
Re: Anonymous | Old Spice
OldSpice - 1,419,129 views
Re: Jose Alejandro Montero | Old Spice
OldSpice - 468,922 views
Re: T | Old Spice
OldSpice - 448,452 views
Re: @houndshockey71 |
OldSpice - 329,443 views
Re: danielgerzee | Old Spice
OldSpice - 253,247 views
Re: @DrPeteNathaniel | Old Spice
OldSpice - 318,221 views
Load more
0:07 / 0:26
360p
Info
Favorite
Share
Playlists
Flag
Re: Anonymous | Old Spice
From: OldSpice | Jul 13, 2010 | 1,419,129 views
Like
Anonymous wrote "Use old spice. Our dads use it, our grand fathers used it, because it works. Stop asking or begging for hugs. You smell bad!"
View comments, related videos, and more

Yellow Pencil in Digital Advertising

Digital Solutions & Use of Social Media
R/GA New York for Innovative Thunder

Pay with a Tweet
How do you promote a book that no one knows exists? The writers of 'Oh My God What Happened and What Should I Do?' had a dilemma. How would they reach the masses? Pay with a Tweet is the first social networking payment system, where people pay with the value of their social network. People who have something to sell simply add the Pay with a Tweet button to their site, and people who want the product simply click on the button and tweet about it. So Pay with a Tweet became a whole new way to trade content online.

Associate Creative Directors
Leif Abraham
Christian Behrendt
Programmers
Alexander Milde
John Tubert
Advertising Agency
R/GA New York
Client
Innovative Thunder

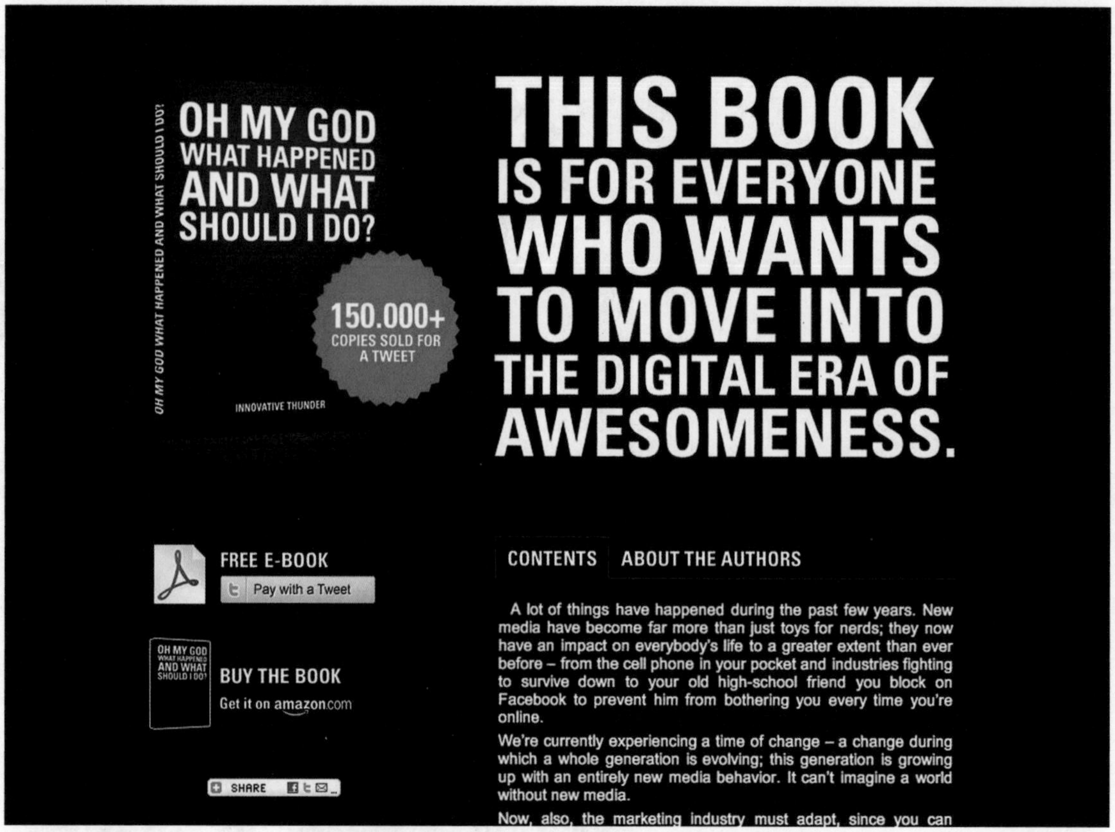
OH MY GOD WHAT HAPPENED AND WHAT SHOULD I DO?
150.000+ COPIES SOLD FOR A TWEET
INNOVATIVE THUNDER
THIS BOOK IS FOR EVERYONE WHO WANTS TO MOVE INTO THE DIGITAL ERA OF AWESOMENESS.
FREE E-BOOK
Pay with a Tweet
BUY THE BOOK
Get it on amazon.com
SHARE
CONTENTS
ABOUT THE AUTHORS
A lot of things have happened during the past few years. New media have become far more than just toys for nerds; they now have an impact on everybody's life to a greater extent than ever before – from the cell phone in your pocket and industries fighting to survive down to your old high-school friend you block on Facebook to prevent him from bothering you every time you're online.
We're currently experiencing a time of change – a change during which a whole generation is evolving; this generation is growing up with an entirely new media behavior. It can't imagine a world without new media.

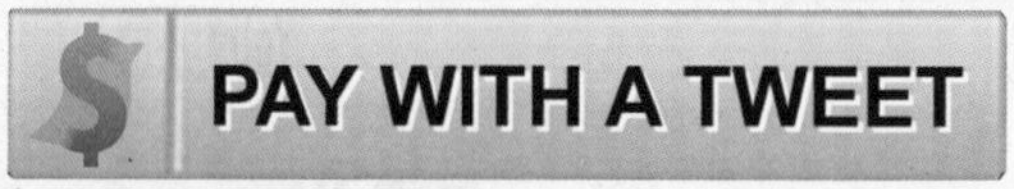
PAY WITH A TWEET

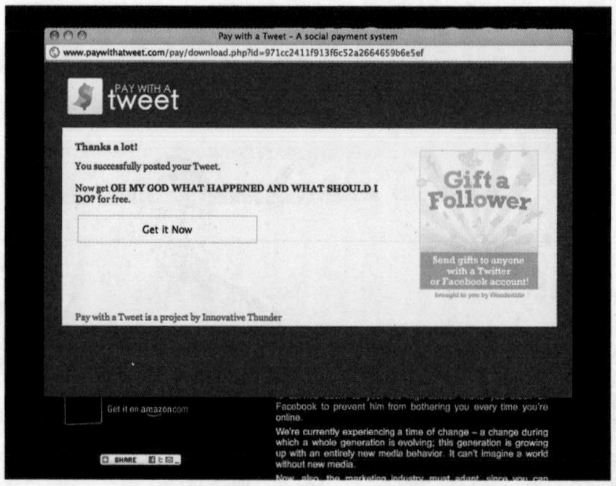
Pay with a Tweet - A social payment system
PAY WITH A tweet
Thanks a lot!
You successfully posted your Tweet.
Now get OH MY GOD WHAT HAPPENED AND WHAT SHOULD I DO? for free.
Get it Now
Gift a Follower
Pay with a Tweet is a project by Innovative Thunder

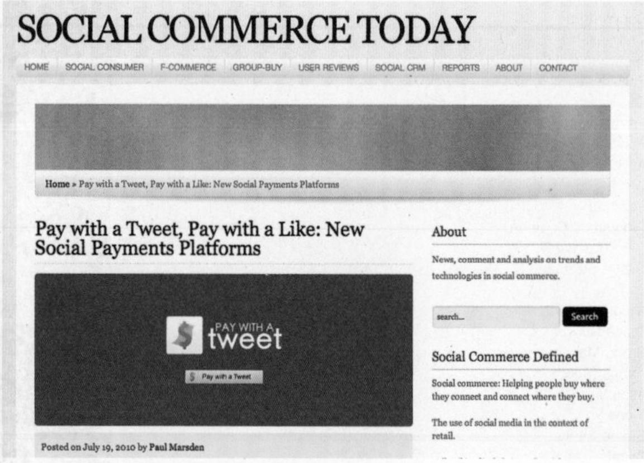
SOCIAL COMMERCE TODAY
Pay with a Tweet, Pay with a Like: New Social Payments Platforms
About
News, comment and analysis on trends and technologies in social commerce.
Social Commerce Defined
Posted on July 19, 2010 by Paul Marsden

Nomination in Digital Advertising

Integrated Digital Campaigns
Google Creative Lab
for YouTube

YouTube Life in a Day
This campaign fuelled YouTube's 'Life in a Day', a global experiment to craft the first user-generated feature film shot on a single day, July 24th 2010. This mass digital call-to-action built a crescendo to filming day, enticing people to submit footage. It spanned all digital channels, sparking YouTube's biggest mass participation (80k uploads) with over 4,500 hours of footage submitted. The best contributors were credited as co-directors in Ridley Scott and Kevin Macdonald's final cut, which premiered at Sundance and on YouTube, re-defining the editorial ambitions of the internet.

Creative Directors
Tim Rodgers
Tom Uglow
Technical Director
Jurgen Prause
Interactive Producer
Susan Agliata
Flash Programmers
John Chips-Harding
Tom Dunn
Josh Noble
Art Directors
Jordan Fisher
Aidan Sharkey
Ross Warren
Producers
Jack Arbuthnott
Liza Marshall
Tim Partridge
Senior Digital Producers
Christophe Taddei
Michael Veitch
Project Creators
Google Creative Lab
YouTube
Lead Digital Agency
Google Creative Lab
Digital Creative Agency
rehabstudio
Creative Agency
Toaster
Production Companies
rehabstudio
Scott Free
Design Studio
Toaster
Marketing Director
Anna Bateson
Product Marketing Manager
Nate Weinstein
Entertainment Marketing Manager
Sara Pollack Darsky
Head of Consumer Marketing
Lee Hunter
Global Communications Manager
Anna Richardson
Client
YouTube

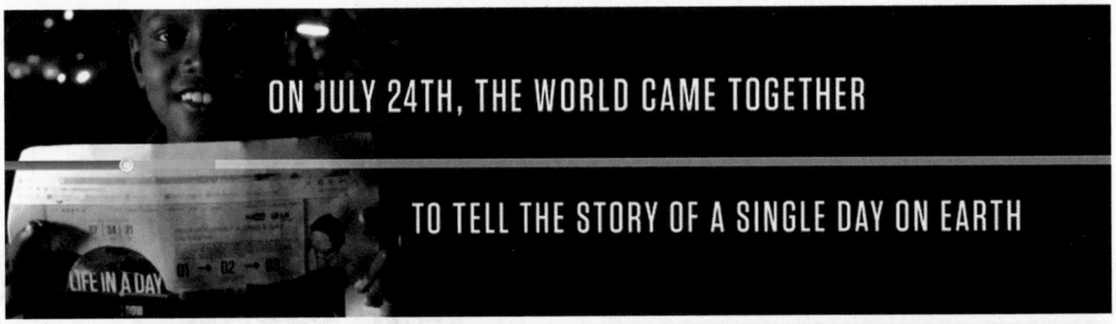
ON JULY 24TH, THE WORLD CAME TOGETHER
TO TELL THE STORY OF A SINGLE DAY ON EARTH
LIFE IN A DAY

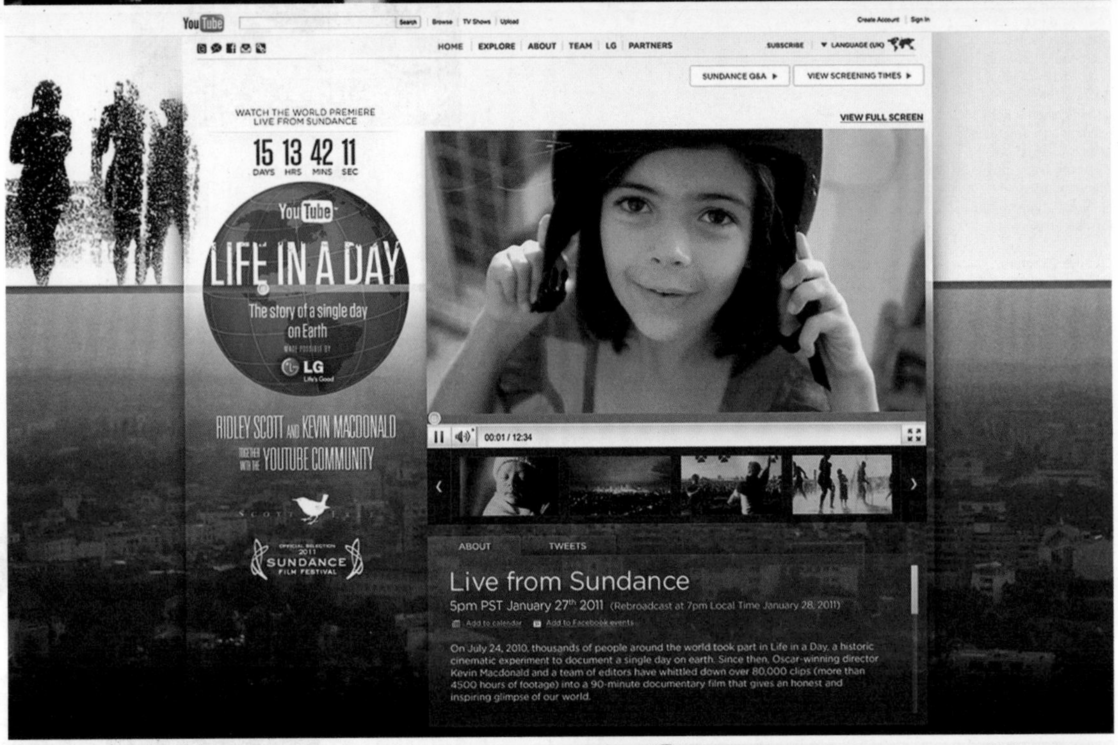
HOME
EXPLORE
ABOUT
TEAM
LG
PARTNERS
SUNDANCE Q&A
VIEW SCREENING TIMES
WATCH THE WORLD PREMIERE LIVE FROM SUNDANCE
15 13 42 11
DAYS HRS MINS SEC
VIEW FULL SCREEN
YouTube
LIFE IN A DAY
The story of a single day on Earth
LG
RIDLEY SCOTT AND KEVIN MACDONALD
TOGETHER WITH THE YOUTUBE COMMUNITY
SUNDANCE FILM FESTIVAL
00:01 / 12:34
ABOUT
TWEETS
Live from Sundance
5pm PST January 27th 2011 (Rebroadcast at 7pm Local Time January 28, 2011)
On July 24, 2010, thousands of people around the world took part in Life in a Day, a historic cinematic experiment to document a single day on earth. Since then, Oscar-winning director Kevin Macdonald and a team of editors have whittled down over 80,000 clips (more than 4500 hours of footage) into a 90-minute documentary film that gives an honest and inspiring glimpse of our world.

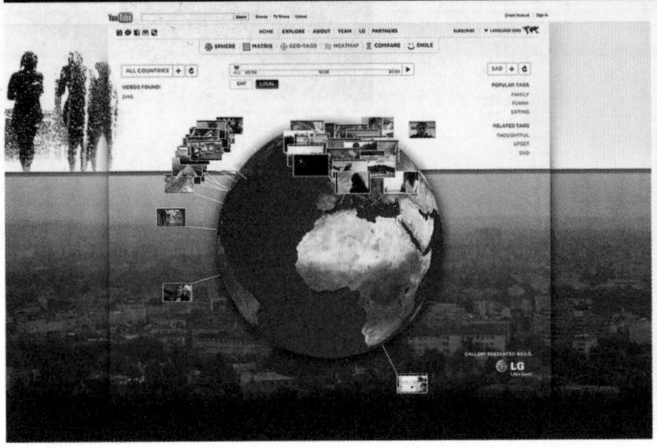

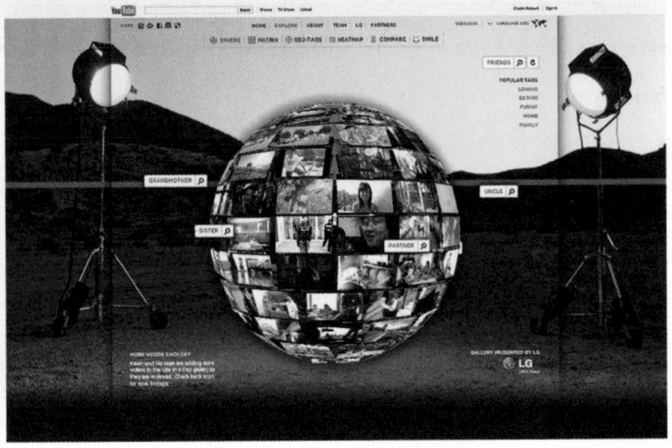

Nomination in Digital Advertising

Campaign Sites
Hello Monday for Google

Google Demo Slam
Technology rocks! Especially when it's available to the world and doesn't cost a thing. But learning about it? That's not so great. What the world really needs is a few brave souls willing to tech demo like no one has dared demo before, so everyone can benefit from this stuff. That's Demo Slam, a competition website where users can upload video tech demos that visitors then vote on. A stage where amazing tech demonstrations battle for your enjoyment.

Creative Directors
Jeppe Aaen
Jon Koffler
Executive Creative Directors
Jan Jacobs
Leo Premutico
Robert Wong
Designer
Ed Kim
Lead Developer
Anders Jessen
Interactive Developers
Kasper Bøttcher
Mike Fey
Art Directors
Anthony Alvarez
Phillip Bonnery
Emmie Nostitz
Dave Tomkins
Copywriters
Jason Ashlock
Ben Clare
Bipasha Mookherjee
Iain Nevill
Alex Romans
Producer
Amy Chuang
Agency Producer
Matthew Mattingly
Digital Agency
Hello Monday
Advertising Agency
Johannes Leonardo
Creative Agency
Google Creative Lab
Project Manager
Amanda Kelly
Account Directors
Andreas Anderskou
Dean Rubinstein
Client
Google

Google Demo Slam
Slams
Champs
The Tech
All Demos
Make your own demo
Choose the champ:
WHAT?
Vs.
Video Chat Magic by Eliza and Joel
Anything
Extra Spicy Slam by Candace, Dana, and Alana
Google Translate
Choose me
Choose me
Share this slam:
Share:
Terms of Service
Privacy Policy
About Demo Slam
FAQ
©2010 Google

Google Voice Search
Google voice allows you to search by speaking. Simply say the word or phrase into your mobile phone and the search results will appear.
Try it now
0:55 / 1:30
480p
Maria Sharapova
by Dan and Jonny
Choose me
Share this video:

Nomination in Digital Advertising

Grouek for BIC

A Hunter Shoots a Bear
The challenge was to promote Tipp-Ex's Pocket Mouse online, so the product was demonstrated directly and for the first time on YouTube. After using the product to erase the title of the YouTube video he is featured in, a hunter encourages viewers to rewrite the title. Each new title gets a video response so the possibilities are infinite for viewers. The ad received over 46 million YouTube views and over one million Facebook shares. It earned media worth €3.2 million, while sales in Europe from September to October 2010 increased by 30 per cent.

Creative Director
Georges Mohammed-Chérif
Flash Programmer
Yoann Gueny
Art Director
Louis Audard
Copywriter
Tristan Daltroff
Digital Producers
Laurent Marcus
Mélanie Rohat-Meheust
Digital Assistant
Bastien Chanot
Agency Producer
Elodie Jonquille
Interactive Producer
Emmanuel Saccocini
Film Director
Olivier Bennoun
Film Producer
Willy Morence
Digital Agency
Grouek
Advertising Agency
Buzzman
Community Manager
Xavier Le Boullenger
Account Handler
Antoine Ferrari
Senior Account Executive
Thomas Granger
Brand Manager
Delphine Dreuillet
Marketing Manager
Alexis Vaganay
Client
BIC
Brand
Tipp-Ex

YouTube
Rechercher
Parcourir
Ajouter une vidéo
Créer un compte
Connexion
A hunter shoots a bear
Join us on Facebook
Tipp-Ex White and rewrite
Pocket Mouse
00:08 / 00:22
AndyTheHunter | 17 August 2010
Huge bear attacks after being shot by a hunter!
9213586 views
Like
Save to
Share
<Embed>
Hungry grizzly#3
32678 views
Titan&Louie75
Tod's hunting in North Carolina
34587 views
Buzzmanthebossss
Polar bear in danger
123997 views
Grangerthebiatch

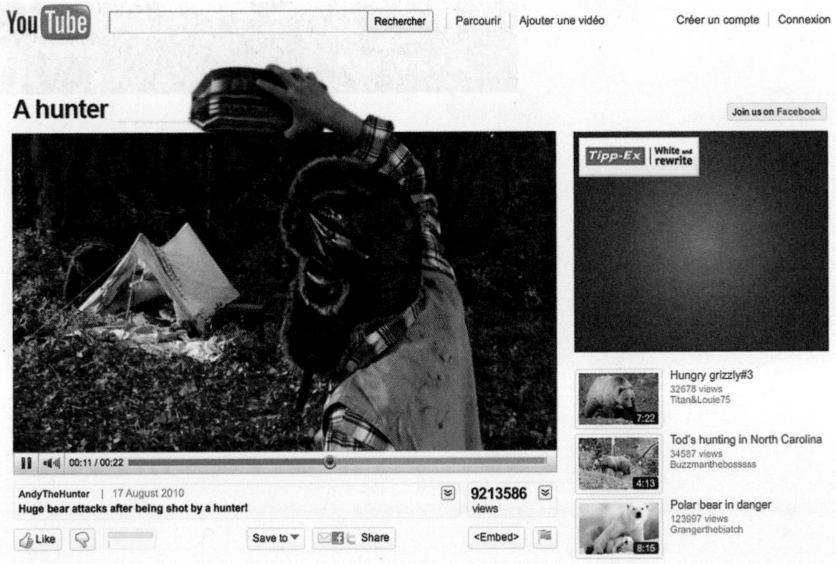
YouTube
Rechercher
Parcourir
Ajouter une vidéo
Créer un compte
Connexion
A hunter
Join us on Facebook
Tipp-Ex White and rewrite
00:11 / 00:22
AndyTheHunter | 17 August 2010
Huge bear attacks after being shot by a hunter!
9213586 views
Like
Save to
Share
<Embed>
Hungry grizzly#3
32678 views
Titan&Louie75
Tod's hunting in North Carolina
34587 views
Buzzmanthebossss
Polar bear in danger
123997 views
Grangerthebiatch

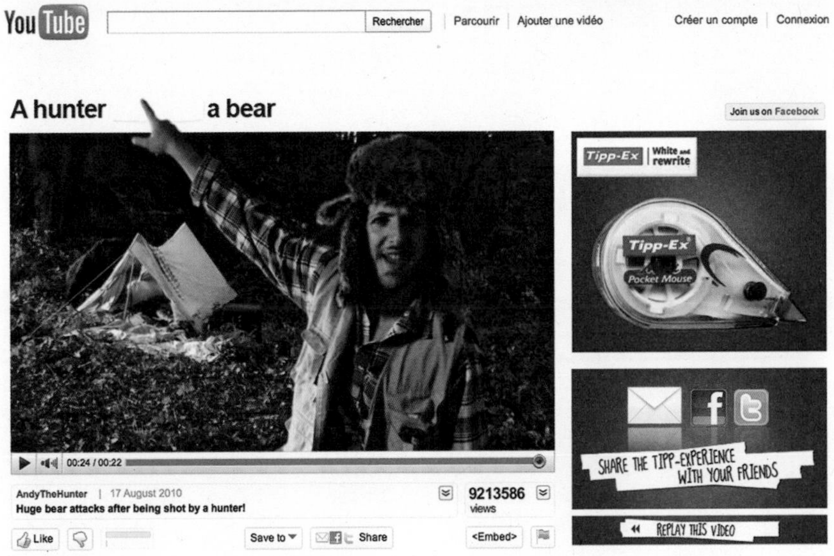
YouTube
Rechercher
Parcourir
Ajouter une vidéo
Créer un compte
Connexion
A hunter a bear
Join us on Facebook
Tipp-Ex White and rewrite
Pocket Mouse
SHARE THE TIPP-EXPERIENCE WITH YOUR FRIENDS
REPLAY THIS VIDEO
00:24 / 00:22
AndyTheHunter | 17 August 2010
Huge bear attacks after being shot by a hunter!
9213586 views
Like
Save to
Share
<Embed>

● Nomination in Digital Advertising

Web Films
Pool Worldwide
for TomTom

Darth Vader & Master Yoda Record their Voices for TomTom GPS
The brief was simple: let the world know that everybody's favourite Star Wars voices are available for TomTom devices. In two virals, we see Lord Vader and Master Yoda recording their voices for TomTom. Each, in their own way, makes the lives of the sound engineers a living hell. We tried to explain the product in the most logical, natural and entertaining way possible, by simply showing how it was made. Nothing is more compelling and funny to watch than the Dark Lord and his green nemesis struggling to fit into our mortal world.

Director
Willem Gerritsen
Producer
Michel de Goede
Editor
Brian Ent
Lighting Cameraperson
Daan Nieuwenhuijs
Design Studio
Pool Worldwide
Advertising Agency
Pool Worldwide
Production Company
Czar.nl
Special Effects
The Ambassadors
Sound Design
The Ambassadors
Brand Manager
Jean-Francois Perron
Client
TomTom

Darth Vader

Master Yoda

Nomination in Digital Advertising

Web Films
Milk+Koblin for American Recordings & Lost Highway Records

The Johnny Cash Project
This project was a global collective artwork. Beginning with a single video frame as a template, and using a custom drawing tool embedded in the site, viewers create their own personal portraits of the Man in Black. Their work is combined with art from participants around the world, and integrated into a collective whole: a crowd-sourced, interactive music video for the song 'Ain't No Grave'. Strung together and played in sequence over the song, the portraits create a moving, evolving homage to a beloved musical icon. As people discover and contribute to the project, this living portrait continues to transform and grow.

Director
Chris Milk
Design Director
James Spindler
Technical Director
Aaron Koblin
Interactive Designer
Frank Campanella
Creative Directors
Chris Milk
Aaron Koblin
Lead Flash Developer
Jesse Freeman
Lead Developer
Mr.doob
Lead Software Engineer
Avery Brooks
Producers
Chris Milk
Aaron Koblin
Executive Producers
Jennifer Heath
Jon Kamen
Rick Rubin
Evan Schechtman
Associate Producer
Naomi Gilbert
Senior Interactive Producer
James Calhoun
Visual Effects Designer
Simon Brewster
Editor
Akiko Iwakawa
Digital Creative Agency
Milk+Koblin
Production Companies
@radical.media
Milk+Koblin
Record Companies
American Recordings
Lost Highway Records
Video Commissioner
Retta Harvey
Clients
American Recordings
Lost Highway Records

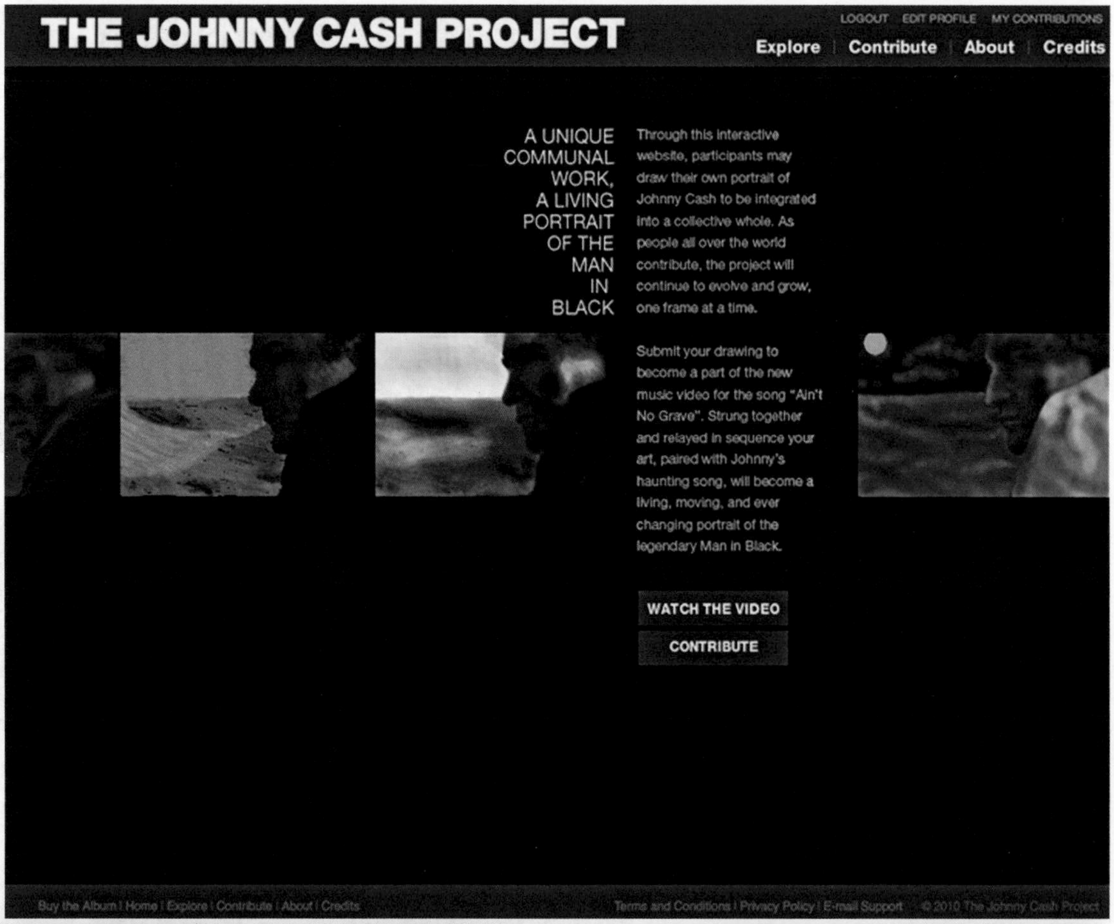
THE JOHNNY CASH PROJECT
LOGOUT EDIT PROFILE MY CONTRIBUTIONS
Explore | Contribute | About | Credits
A UNIQUE COMMUNAL WORK, A LIVING PORTRAIT OF THE MAN IN BLACK
Through this interactive website, participants may draw their own portrait of Johnny Cash to be integrated into a collective whole. As people all over the world contribute, the project will continue to evolve and grow, one frame at a time.
Submit your drawing to become a part of the new music video for the song "Ain't No Grave". Strung together and relayed in sequence your art, paired with Johnny's haunting song, will become a living, moving, and ever changing portrait of the legendary Man in Black.
WATCH THE VIDEO
CONTRIBUTE
Buy the Album | Home | Explore | Contribute | About | Credits
Terms and Conditions | Privacy Policy | E-mail Support © 2010 The Johnny Cash Project

CASH PROJECT
Explore | Contribute | About | Credits
Frame #583
PREV FRAME
NEXT FRAME
BACK TO VIDEO
DRAW THIS FRAME
SHARE
FRAME: 583

Nomination in
Digital Advertising

Web Films
agencytwofifteen
for Microsoft Xbox

Bright Falls
The psychological action thriller 'Alan Wake' represented a new depth of storytelling for Xbox 360 and the video game industry, with a rich, engaging plot that played like a television series. Rather than creating a marketing campaign, we created an episodic prequel to that TV series, named after the town the game is set in. This way, instead of trying to describe, distil, or repurpose the game's fiction, we became part of it. With 'Bright Falls' ending right as the game begins, the handover was seamless. All viewers had to do to continue our story was play the game.

Director
Phillip Van
Art Directors
Nate Able
Ben Wolan
Copywriters
Mat Bunnell
Phillip Van
Executive Creative Directors
Scott Duchon
John Patroulis
Associate Creative Directors
Nate Able
Mat Bunnell
Ben Wolan
Producers
Tomer Devito
Rhea Scott
Agency Producer
Joyce Chen
Advertising Agency
agencytwofifteen
Production Company
Little Minx
Visual Effects
Beast San Francisco
Music & Sound Design
Black Iris
Client
Microsoft Xbox
Brand
Alan Wake

Oh Deer

EMBRACE ME OR FEAR ME
IT IS HUNGRY FOR MORE
THANK YOU FOR MY SUFFERING
I HAVE ALREADY ARRANGED MY LEGACY

Time Flies

Lights Out

Local Flavour

Off the Record

Clearcut

● **Nomination in Digital Advertising**

Web Films
AKQA Amsterdam
for Nike

Write the Future
Every four years, the keys to football heaven are dangled in front of the international elite. One goal, one pass, one game saving tackle can be the difference between fame and forgotten. And what happens on the pitch in that split second has a ripple effect that goes beyond the match and the tournament. The 'Write the Future' film was launched via Nike Football's Facebook page, propelling it to over 40 million views, with more likes on Facebook and more mentions on Twitter than any other campaign, making Nike the most shared brand online in 2010.

Director
Alejandro González Iñárritu
Art Directors
Stuart Harkness
Freddie Powell
Copywriters
Stuart Harkness
Freddie Powell
Creative Directors
Mark Bernath
Eric Quennoy
Executive Creative Director
Jeff Kling
Producers
Greg Cundiff
Dominic Freeman
Executive Producers
Jani Guest
Richard Packer
Post Executive Producer
Jane Dilworth
Agency Producers
Olivier Klonhammer
Elissa Singstock
Visual Effects Executive Producer
Stephen Venning
2D & 3D Designer
Tom Busel
2D & 3D Artist
Neil Davies
Editors
Ben Jordan
Stephen Mirrione
Charlie Moreton
Rick Orrick
Lighting Cameraperson
Emmanuel Lubezki
Director of Photography
Jeroen van der Poel
Sound Designer
Raja Sehgal
Digital Agency
AKQA Amsterdam
Advertising Agency
Wieden+Kennedy Amsterdam
Production Company
Independent Films
Visual Effects
The Mill London & New York
Editing
Mirrione Work
Sound Design
Grand Central Studios
Phaze UK
Music Remix
MassiveMusic Amsterdam
Planners
Graeme Douglas
Dan Hill
Account Handlers
David Anson
Jordi Pont
Head of Broadcast
Erik Verheijen
Global Advertising & Content Manager
Colin Leary
Brand Communications Director
Enrico Balleri
Global Brand Communications Director
Todd Pendleton
Client
Nike

RONALDO
7

Nomination in
Digital Advertising

Digital Solutions & Use of Social Media
TBWA\London
for Wrigley

Updater
We took something our fans were doing every day on Facebook and added some rainbow power to it. We built a live call centre/online film factory that sucked in their status updates and turned them into Super Mega Rainbow Updates. A fan just typed in his update, then our call centre staff recorded it as an awesome film and posted it back to the fan's wall in mere minutes. Our fans created 21,000 Super Mega Rainbow Updates in just two weeks. Very super.

Creative Directors
Johan Dahlqvist
Lee Tan
Executive Creative Director
Mark Hunter
Art Director
Andrew Bloom
Copywriter
Eric Tell
Director
Jakob Marky
Producer
James Cunningham
Web Producer
Sara-Lee Rost
Agency Producer
Trudy Waldron
Production Manager
Cathy Buchanan
Editor
James Norris
Advertising Agency
TBWA\London
Digital Production Company
Perfect Fools
Production Company
Academy Films
Sound Design
Wave
Planner
David Fryman
Account Manager
Justin Martin
Brand Leader
Emma Massey
Client
Wrigley
Brand
Skittles

facebook
Search
Home
Skittles Transform your Monday blues into Monday multi-coloured, mega awesome! Hit the 'UPDATER update and we'll do the rest! about an hour ago
Wall
Info
Updater
Giveaway
Phoenix vs...
Terms and C...
Suggest to friends
Subscribe via SMS
Information
Founded:
1974
11 friends like this.
6 of 11 friends
See all
Melissa Smith
Sarah Brown
Dick Dunford
Mel Nicolaou
Missy Blackford
Kris Samyui-Adams
1,650,924 people like this
SHARE
UPDATE THE RAINBOW
WHAT'S ON YOUR MIND?
Matt Smart is eating a ham sandwich.
GET MY CURRENT UPDATE
CREATE MY UPDATE

facebook
Search
Home
Profile
Matt Smart
Edit My Profile
News Feed
Messages
Events
Friends
Uber clique
Create Group...
See All
Game Requests
Apps
More
Friends on Chat
News Feed
Top News · Most Recent 300+
Share: Status Photo Link Video
What's on your mind?
Matt Smart is eating a ham sandwich.
0:06 / 0:27
Matt Smart – Super Mega Rainbow Update
www.youtube.com
The Super Mega Rainbow Updater from Skittles turns your normal update into an awesome film about you! Try it today at http://updatetherainbow.co.uk
November 12 at 12:55am via Update The Rainbow · Like · Comment · SuperMega Rainbow Updater
Events
What are you planning?
4 event invitations
Red Lion Pub Quiz
Thursday 8:00pm
Erik Tell's birthday. See All
Sponsored
Grow your business
Requests
4 group invitations
17 Page suggestions
2 game requests
Pokes
Daniel Colledge · Poke Back
Jonathan Colledge · Poke Back

Nomination in Digital Advertising

Digital Solutions & Use of Social Media
Berghs School of Communication

Don't Tell Ashton
How could 22 interactive students from Berghs School of Communication make themselves known to the industry, and attract people from all over the world to study at Berghs? We invited people to join a project: the world's first artwork made by Twitter users. Three days after launch the artwork was completed, reaching over four million people from 151 countries. Major industry press and media picked up the project and people all over the world wrote about it, from Japanese blogs to Russian printed press. On Google the phrase 'Don't tell Ashton' produced 130,000 results in the first week.

Digital Creatives
Jonas Åhlen
Maja Folgerö
Olle Isaksson
Felipe Montt
Dinny Zerge
Production Manager
Lina Appelgren
Creative Team
Berghs School of Communication
Digital Strategists
Johan Gerdin
Victoria Nyberg
Public Relations Consultants
Sara Eriksson
Maria Sandberg
Marketing Director
Åsa Marklund
Client
Berghs School of Communication

DON'T TELL
ASHTON
A PROJECT FROM BERGHS INTERACTIVE 2010

FINALLY ASHTON TWEETED...
Why am I the last one to find out about everything http://brizzly.com/pic/2PE5. #donttellashton
11:57 PM Jun 8th via Brizzly
Retweeted by 86 people
aplusk
ashton kutcher

AND WROTE ABOUT IT ON FACEBOOK
Ashton Kutcher the students from #donttellashton found me yesterday. great story about the power of Social Media. amazing result.
skewed magazine » THEY FINALLY TOLD ASHTON | Don't tell Ashton
www.skewedmagazine.com
Last month we ran a post about the student project Don't tell Ashton from Berghs School of Communication, and yesterday we got an update. Who would've known they would actually fly to LA, meet with Kutcherhimself and show him the completed artwork.
June 10 at 12:26am · Hide Feedback (1,989) · Share · Report
1,691 people like this.
View all 298 comments

Nomination in Digital Advertising

Digital Solutions & Use of Social Media
Masashi+Qanta+Saqoosha+Hiroki
for Zenith Co.

SOUR/MIRROR
This is an interactive music video for the Japanese band SOUR. The song 'Mirror' is about the fact that everything around you is a mirror that reflects who you are. This gave us the idea of a journey to find yourself through your connections with people online. By connecting to their Facebook, Twitter, and webcam, the video is customised for every viewer based on their personal data and social networking status. We also raised the production budget through Kickstarter, and allowed @SOUR_official's Twitter followers to become part of the colour pixels in the video.

Creative Director
Masashi Kawamura
Design Director
Masashi Kawamura
Technical Director
Qanta Shimizu
Flash Programmers
Yuma Murakami
Saqoosha
Qanta Shimizu
Designer
Masashi Kawamura
Art Director
Masashi Kawamura
Directors
Masashi Kawamura
Hiroki Ono
Saqoosha
Qanta Shimizu
Film Producers
Hisaya Kato
Yasuhito Nakae
Film Project Manager
Hidetoshi Nagamine
Artist
SOUR
Digital Agency
Masashi+Qanta+Saqoosha+Hiroki
Client
Zenith Co.
Brand
SOUR

File Edit View History Bookmarks Window Help
Hi-hat
Drum stick
Bass
Ken's forearm
's thigh

SOUR / MIRROR

SOUR / MIRROR
facebook
Hiroki Ono

● Nomination in Digital Advertising

Digital Solutions & Use of Social Media
1-10design & The Strippers for UNIQLO

UNIQLO Lucky Line
Our aim was to set the mood for the next UNIQLO special sale and to lead people from the web to real stores. We created a queue – the UNIQLO Lucky Line – on the UNIQLO website to wait for the sale, using Twitter and Facebook. If people tweeted, they could join the line and get discount coupons from real stores. The world's first queue on the web created a big buzz. In total 2.2million people in the world joined the line, and UNIQLO set a single day sales record of more than 10billion yen.

Creative Director
Yasuharu Sasaki
Interactive Designer
Yoshihiro Yasuda
Flash Programmer
Kenichi Nagai
Programmers
Takakuni Matsuishi
Tomohiro Otsuka
System Engineer
Jun Kuriyama
Designers
Arata Kobayashi
Momoko Takaoka
Noriko Watanabe
Art Director
Shoko Watanabe
Copywriters
Kazuomi Goto
Yasuharu Sasaki
Agency Producer
Shinsaku Ogawa
Directors
Keigo Nakanishi
Hisayoshi Tohsaki
Illustration
eBoy
Digital Agencies
1-10design
The Strippers
Advertising Agency
Dentsu Tokyo
Marketing Manager
Yoshihisa Watanabe
Client
UNIQLO

UNI QLO
UNIQLO LUCKY LINE
634355 PEOPLE
UNIQLO IN TAIPEI'S HANKYU DEPARTMENT STORE
GRAND OPENING IN
JOIN
ABOUT
COPYRIGHT(C) UNIQLO CO., LTD. ALL RIGHTS RESERVED.
RULES, PRIVACY POLICY
FAQ
SUBSCRIBE TO UNIQLO MAIL MAGAZINE
CONTACT US
繁体中文 / ENGLISH
SOUND

UNI QLO
634354
GRAND OPENING IN
JOIN
ABOUT
JOIN UNIQLO LUCKY LINE
SELECT AVATAR AND INPUT YOUR COMMENTS.
W's premium down light hooded vest
W's tweed mini skirt
COMMENTS (80 characters max.)
Hello!
獲得號碼?????!
http://www.uniqlo.com/tw/#line #luckyline
Text will be inserted automatically after you input your comments. These comments along with your place in the queue will be automatically sent to Facebook/Twitter. After this, your comments on Facebook/Twitter will be shown in the queue along with your ID.
SEND COMMENTS AND JOIN THE QUEUE
COPYRIGHT(C) UNIQLO CO., LTD. ALL RIGHTS RESERVED.
RULES, PRIVACY POLICY
FAQ
SUBSCRIBE TO UNIQLO MAIL MAGAZINE
CONTACT US
繁体中文 / ENGLISH
SOUND

Nomination in Digital Advertising

Digital Solutions & Use of Social Media
BBH New York
for Google

Google Chrome FastBall
To promote a browser to people immune to banners, we created Chrome FastBall, a race across the internet. This first YouTube game of its kind showed how the web is faster and easier with Google Chrome. Over one million visitors moved a ball through our series of linked YouTube videos. When the ball stopped they solved a challenge using Google Maps, Search and Translate, Twitter and Last.fm that tested their wits and reflexes, and proved the browser's speed.

Executive Creative Directors
Calle Sjoenell
Pelle Sjoenell
Robert Wong
Chief Creative Officer
Kevin Roddy
Creative Technologist
Zach Blank
Art Director
Erik Holmdahl
Copywriter
Beth Ryan
Interactive Producers
Sandra Nam
Jennifer Usdan McBride
Head of Interactive
Suzanne Molinaro
Sound Designer
John Wilkinson
Advertising Agencies
BBH New York
Google Creative Lab
Interactive Production Company
B-Reel
Executive Director of Innovation
Ben Malbon
Account Handlers
Jessica Bigarel
Rossa Hsieh
Business Director
Ben Malbon
Client
Google

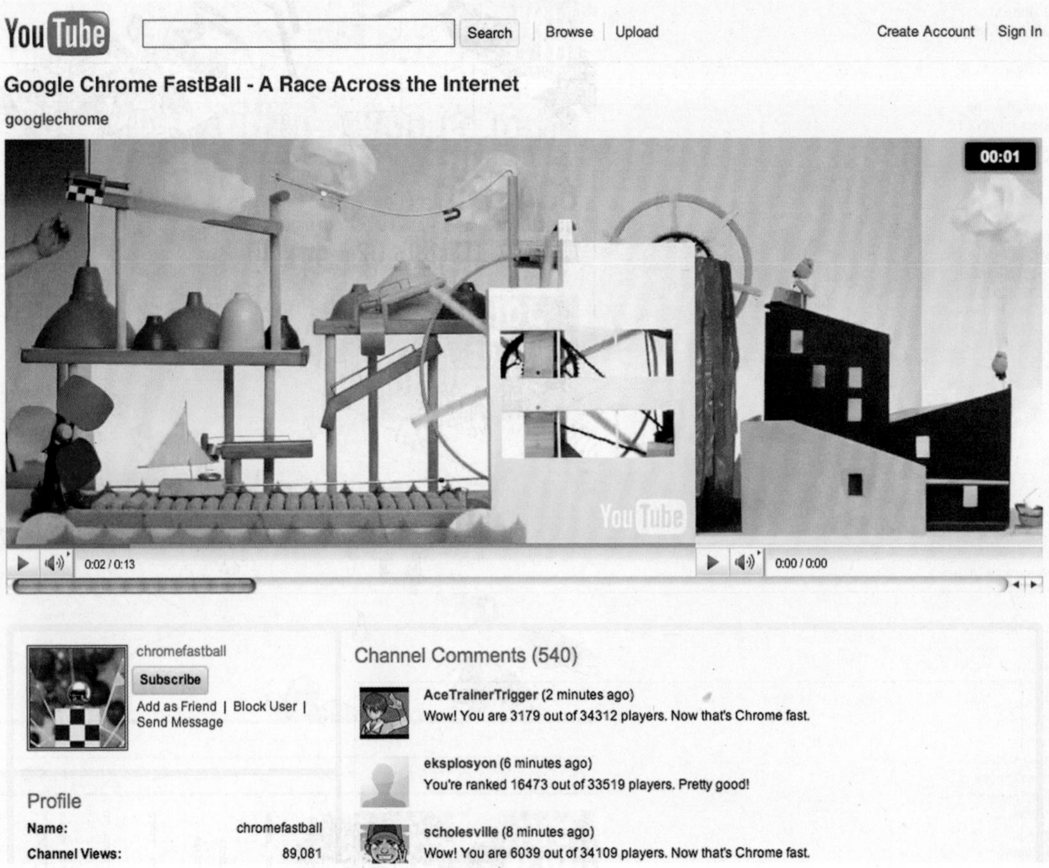
Search
Browse
Upload
Create Account
Sign In
Google Chrome FastBall - A Race Across the Internet
googlechrome
00:01
0:02 / 0:13
0:00 / 0:00
chromefastball
Subscribe
Add as Friend | Block User | Send Message
Profile
Name: chromefastball
Channel Views: 89,081
Channel Comments (540)
AceTrainerTrigger (2 minutes ago)
Wow! You are 3179 out of 34312 players. Now that's Chrome fast.
eksplosyon (6 minutes ago)
You're ranked 16473 out of 33519 players. Pretty good!
scholesville (8 minutes ago)
Wow! You are 6039 out of 34109 players. Now that's Chrome fast.

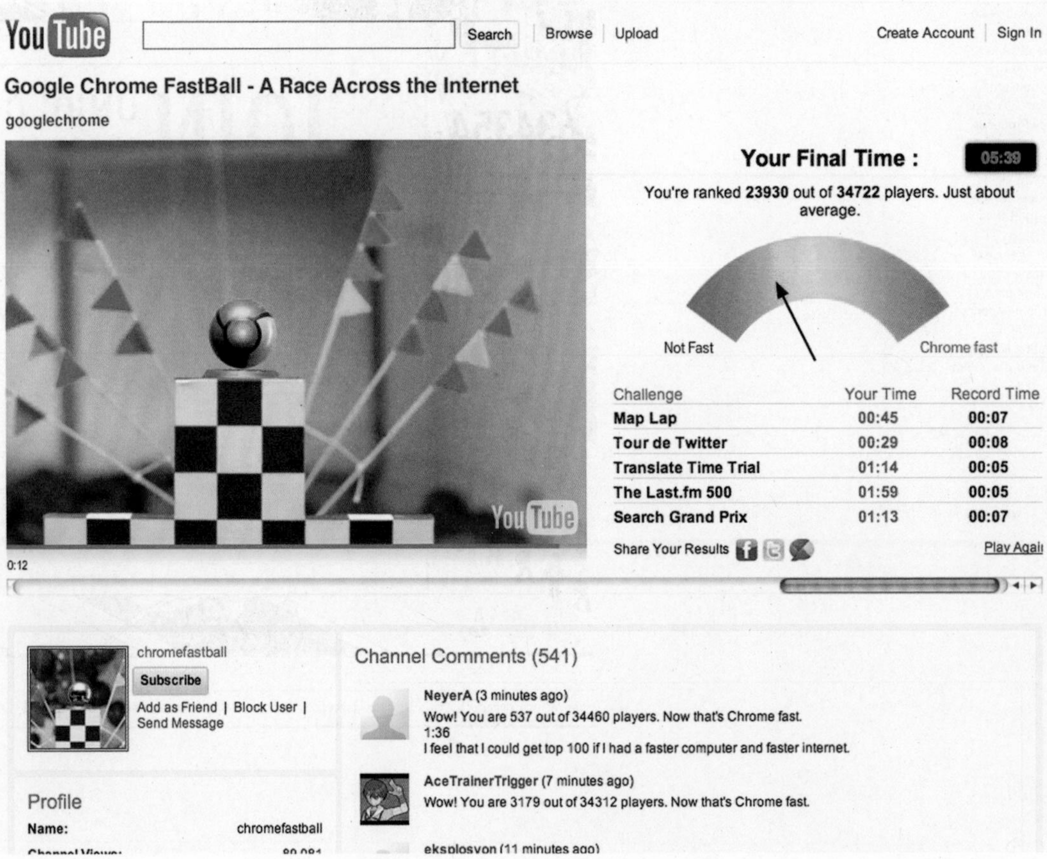
Search
Browse
Upload
Create Account
Sign In
Google Chrome FastBall - A Race Across the Internet
googlechrome
Your Final Time :
05:39
You're ranked 23930 out of 34722 players. Just about average.
Not Fast
Chrome fast
Challenge
Your Time
Record Time
Map Lap 00:45 00:07
Tour de Twitter 00:29 00:08
Translate Time Trial 01:14 00:05
The Last.fm 500 01:59 00:05
Search Grand Prix 01:13 00:07
Share Your Results
0:12
chromefastball
Subscribe
Add as Friend | Block User | Send Message
Profile
Name: chromefastball
Channel Comments (541)
NeyerA (3 minutes ago)
Wow! You are 537 out of 34460 players. Now that's Chrome fast.
1:36
I feel that I could get top 100 if I had a faster computer and faster internet.
AceTrainerTrigger (7 minutes ago)
Wow! You are 3179 out of 34312 players. Now that's Chrome fast.

Nomination in Digital Advertising

Animation & Illustration for Digital Advertising
Studio 4C for INPES

Attraction
Attraction is an anti-smoking interactive anime commissioned by the French health education institute INPES, to raise awareness about tobacco companies manipulating today's youth. As France is the second largest market in the world for Japanese animation, Attraction speaks in a familiar voice to French adolescents, without being a patronising or stern government communication. To meet the expectations of teens who grew up with anime, we worked with Koji Morimoto, one of the directors of 'The Animatrix' and animation director of the infamous film 'Akira'.

Animator
Koji Morimoto
Director
Koji Morimoto
Creative Directors
Alexander Kalchev
Siavosh Zabeti
Executive Creative Director
Alexandre Hervé
Technical Director
Yates Buckley
Interactive Directors
Anrick Bregman
Takayoshi Kishimoto
Lead Developer
David Hartono
Art Directors
Alexander Kalchev
Siavosh Zabeti
Copywriters
Alexander Kalchev
Siavosh Zabeti
Integrated Producer
Guillaume Cossou
Executive Producers
Piero Frescobaldi
Eiko Tanaka
Sound Engineer
Clement Reynaud
Music Composers
Fred Avril
Danger
Sound Mixer
Raphael Fruchard
Animation Studio
Studio 4C
Advertising Agency
DDB Paris
Interactive Production
Unit9
Sound Production
THE
Account Executive
Mathieu Roux
Board Account Director
Orane Faivre de Condé
Client
INPES

PRÉSENTEZ UN OBJET DE LA
COULEUR DEMANDÉE À LA CAMÉRA.
注意

Integrated Digital Campaigns
Grow Interactive
for FedEx

Changing World
FedEx knows how much the world is changing, so it created a website (experience.fedex.com) that shows where these changes are taking place. The images are made possible by a system that animates maps according to different sets of information, allowing users to interact with the data that affects their lives and business. This stimulates thinking about global trading opportunities – which FedEx is ideally placed to help with. Subjects include population, investment, education and even beer drinking. The site operates in eight languages, and is supported by banners, rich media and augmented reality.

Creative Directors
Dale Lopez
Pia Roxas-Ocampo
Interactive Creative Director
Drew Ungvarsky
Executive Creative Directors
Brandie Tan
Simon Welsh
Chief Creative Officer
David Guerrero
Flash Programmers
Darius Penano
Jeff Penano
Ricky Williams
Art Directors
Joe Branton
Dale Lopez
Brandie Tan
Copywriters
David Guerrero
Pia Roxas-Ocampo
Simon Welsh
Animator
Jason Levesque
Agency Producer
Doug Stivers
Interactive Producer
Eric Green
Interactive Director
Benjamin Mace
Digital Agency
Grow Interactive
Advertising Agencies
BBDO Guerrero
BBDO New York
Digital Strategist
Mark Himmelsbach
Account Directors
Michaela Skelly
Peter McCallum
Senior Vice President
Peter McCallum
Client
FedEx

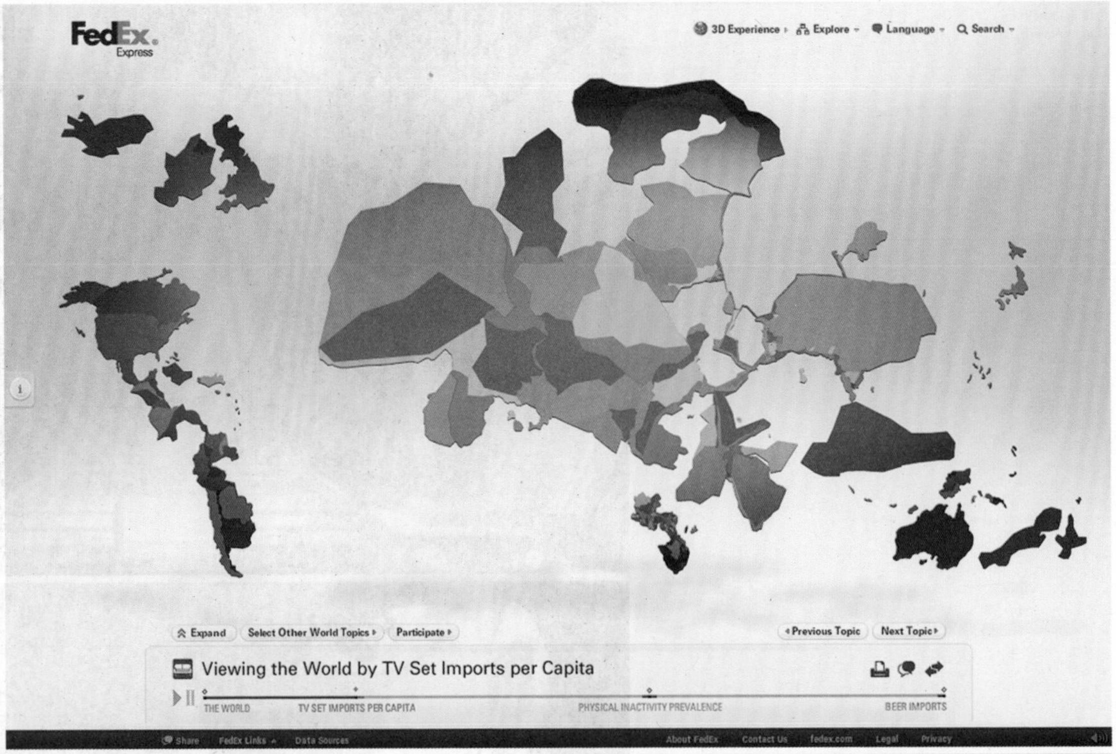
FedEx
Express
3D Experience
Explore
Language
Search
Expand
Select Other World Topics
Participate
Previous Topic
Next Topic
Viewing the World by TV Set Imports per Capita
THE WORLD
TV SET IMPORTS PER CAPITA
PHYSICAL INACTIVITY PREVALENCE
BEER IMPORTS
Share
FedEx Links
Data Sources
About FedEx
Contact Us
fedex.com
Legal
Privacy

FedEx
Foreign Investments
Log in | Register
HOME NEWS SPORT FINANCE COMMENT BLOGS CULTURE TRAVEL LIFESTYLE FASHION TECH
Jobs Dating Offers
Travel
TRAVEL LATEST
The Big Picture
Where in the world?
TRAVEL PRESS AWARDS 2010
Online Publication of the Year
Stay connected on Acela Express with AmtrakConnect
acela
Sign Language
TRAVEL OFFERS
The rising cost of global
Deals of the day: cruises

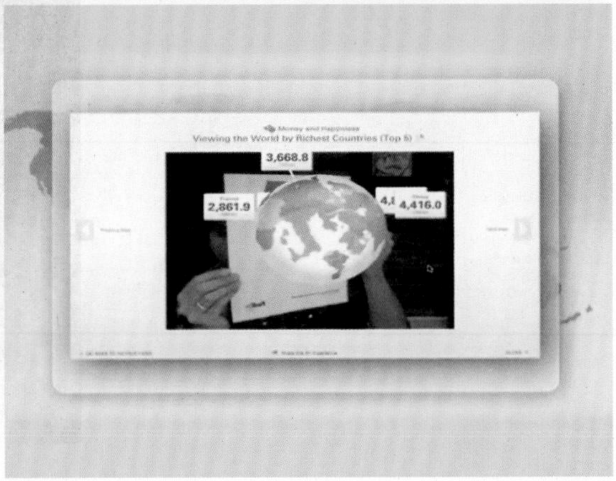
Viewing the World by Richest Countries (Top 5)
3,668.8
2,861.9
4,416.0

Integrated Digital Campaigns
Droga5 New York
for Bing & Jay-Z

Decode Jay-Z with Bing
We teamed up with Microsoft's Bing and Jay-Z to launch his autobiography, 'Decoded'. Leading up to the book's release, each page was placed in a location relevant to its specific content. Pages appeared in hundreds of locations, using billboards and bus shelters, and creating innovative new media to tell the story. In total 200 executions were placed around the world, each a story in itself. Fans frantically searched to find all the pages of the book through an experience built on Bing Maps. By solving Jay-Z clues using Bing Search, they assembled the book online before it hit the stores.

Creative Directors
Kevin Brady
Neil Heymann
Duncan Marshall
Ted Royer
Nik Studzinzki
Creative Chairman
David Droga
Designer
Jon Donaghy
Art Director
Jon Kubik
Copywriters
Spencer Lavellee
Adam Noel
Digital Producer
Toph Brown
Senior Digital Producer
Andrew Allen
Head of Integrated Production
Sally-Ann Dale
Director of Photography
Paul McGeiver
Print Producers
Mea Cole-Tefka
Cliff Lewis
Advertising Agency
Droga5 New York
Public Relations
Sunshine, Sachs & Associates
Head of Print Services
Rob Lugo
Director of Digital Strategy
Hashem Bajwa
Account Handler
Shawn Mackoff
Chief Executive Officer
Andrew Essex
Marketing Managers
Ryan Cameron
Eric Hadley
Clients
Bing
Jay-Z
Brand
Decode Jay-Z with Bing

320 PAGES RELEASED
320 PAGES LOCATED
320 PAGES DECODED
SHARE
PAGE 150 & 151
DECODED BY KELLY B.
10:59 AM | OCT 20, 2010
MANHATTAN BRIDGE, BROOKLYN
SHARE ON FACEBOOK
POLITICS AS USUAL
DECODE
JAY-Z
WITH BING
Jay-Z and his fans created history. Every single page of 'Decoded' was released into the world and recompiled before the book hit stores. See how it all unfolded.
SEE THE STORY
BUY THE BOOK
THANKS FOR HELPING TO MAKE HISTORY.
bing

DE
CO
DED

DECODE JAY-Z

THE Best DJ
In the US of A

Integrated Digital Campaigns
Euro RSCG London
for Akzo Nobel

Dulux Let's Colour Project
Our aim was to get people to think of Dulux as soon as they think of colour. So the 'Let's Colour' project was born. Together with local communities, we painted places in four cities around the world. The events were shot as a brand film where everything we see is real. The project left behind a real transformation. After the first four countries we received thousands of requests from around the world to host events. 'Let's Colour' became an ongoing campaign that positioned Dulux as the colour authority in the paint market.

Creative Director
Fernanda Romano
Executive Creative Director
Mick Mahoney
Art Director
Braulio Kuwabara
Digital Art Director
Mariana Costa
Copywriter
Fabio Abram
Digital Copywriter
Rebecca Campbell
Producer
Ben Croker
Agency Producer
Jodie Sibson Potts
Director
Adam Berg
Advertising Agency
Euro RSCG London
Production Company
Stink
Account Handler
Ken Mulligan
Global Chief Marketing Officer
Sucheta Govil
Client
Akzo Nobel
Brand
Dulux

Blue colour symbolises nothingness

Let's Colour project
Home
Our Project
Our Blog
Get Involved
Tell Your Friends
Events
Press
Our Blog
Rooms with colour confidence
Posted 09:10 AM by Rebecca Campbell
0
Digg
5
retweet
There's nothing quite like walking into a room that makes a statement. A room that says "here I am" or "look at me" standing proud and tall for you to look at. Here is a selection of some of our favourites. The thing they all have in common is the single minded boldness of our old friend… colour! We especially like the wall colour extension to the ceiling of the final four. Who said colour had to be vertical?
Blog Editor
There are many ways everyone can be part of the project
Get Involved
Spread some colour with everyone in your world
Tell Your Friends
FOLLOW US
BRAZIL
INDIA
FRANCE
UNITED KINGDOM
NETHERLANDS
SOUTH AFRICA
Subscribe to RSS feed
Subscribe via email
LATEST TWEETS
@tinalovespinot thanks for the RT :)
Colouring Cairo: http://bit.ly/eae7Pj #letscolour #egypt #akzonobel
Rooms with colour confidence: http://bit.ly/jykmrq #letscolour #color
Horizontal colour: http://bit.ly/jykmrq #letscolour #color

Campaign Sites
Poke for
Orange UK

GlastoTag
To build awareness of Orange's sponsorship of Glastonbury and celebrate the festival's 40th anniversary, we decided to take a huge photo of all 350 metres of the Pyramid Stage field with everyone in it. GlastoTag was born. We stitched together 36 photos, presented the image online and invited visitors to find and tag themselves in the crowd using Facebook Connect. With 1.3 million visits to the site, 7,000 tags and 7,000 Facebook likes, GlastoTag was lauded as an example of the 'golden age of the industry' and achieved an official Guinness world record for the most tagged photo.

Creative Directors
Emma Cakehead
Jason Fox
Nicolas Roope
Ben Tomlinson
Technical Director
Tom Quick
Flash Programmer
Jamie Ingram
Designers
Matt Booth
Katie Marcus
Copywriter
Liam Nicholls
Agency Producers
Lauren Matthews
Ollie Wright
Creative Agency
Poke
Client
Orange UK

Glastonbury home
GlastoTag
GlastoNav app
Chill 'n' Charge tent
GlastoBlog
Glastonbury 2010
help
share
get link
full screen
music
Glastonbury
musicstore
monkey
David Coe
add friend

Campaign Sites
Soon in Tokyo
for Elisava

I Am Not an Artist
'I Am Not an Artist' is an animated .gif paranoia about nonstop design workers. A platform to engage with and spread fun and content to young designers and creatives all over the world. It was conceived for Elisava, the Barcelona design school for future design workers, to communicate the school's philosophy of hard daily work, challenging the perception that designers live out their inspirations.

Creative Directors
Javi Donada
Angelo Palma
Designer
Thiago Monteiro
Developer
Jesus Gollonet
Art Director
Javi Donada
Copywriter
Angelo Palma
Animation Directors
Matt Cooper
Johnny Kelly
Sound Designer
Cristiano Nicollini
Advertising Agency
Soon in Tokyo
Account Handler
Nuria Guinovart
Brand Manager
Anna Salvador
Marketing Manager
Martha Carrio
Client
Elisava

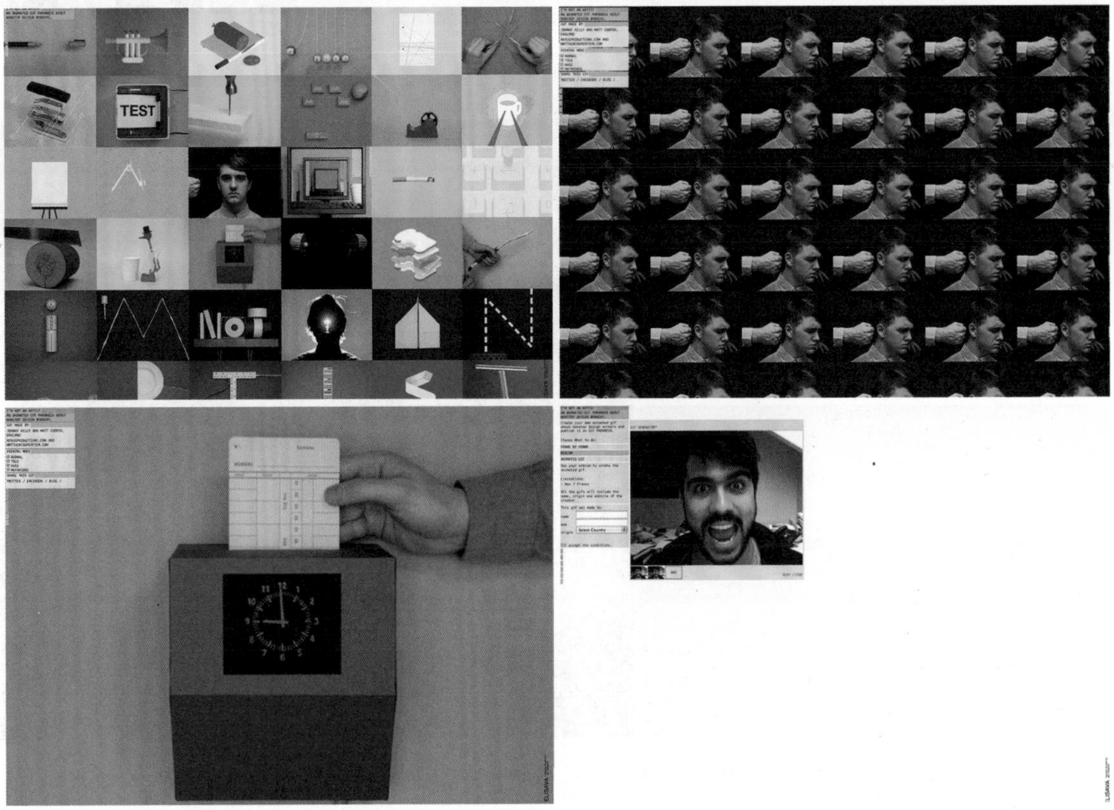
TEST
NoT

Web Films
krow for
Fiat Professional

The Fleet
To position Fiat Professional as the people who understand how difficult it can be to end up with the right vans, and as the people with the right answers, we created a ten-part comedy dramatising the trials and tribulations of being a fleet manager, and placed it on the website of a made-up company, Lightfoot Logistics.

Art Director
David Chidlow
Copywriters
Ali Crockatt
David Scott
Creative Director
Nick Hastings
Producer
Glynis Murray
Agency Producer
Emma Rookledge
Editor
Nick Arthurs
Sound Designer
James Cobbald
Music Composer
Alan Hawkshaw
Advertising Agency
krow
Interactive Design
Relish
Production Company
Tomboy Films
Account Handlers
John Gallagher
John Quarrey
Brand Manager
Gerry Clarke
Marketing Manager
Paul Godden
Client
Fiat Professional

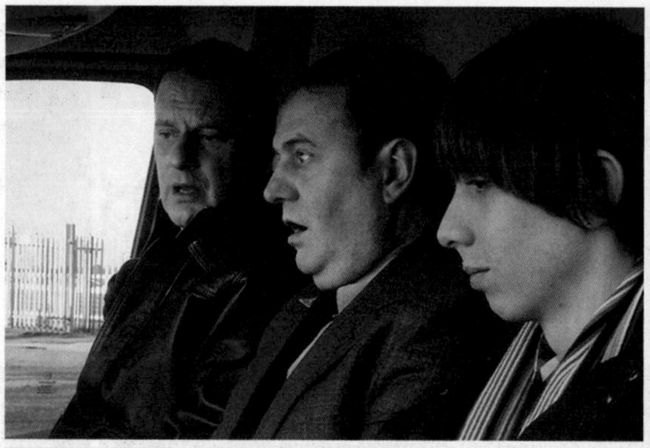

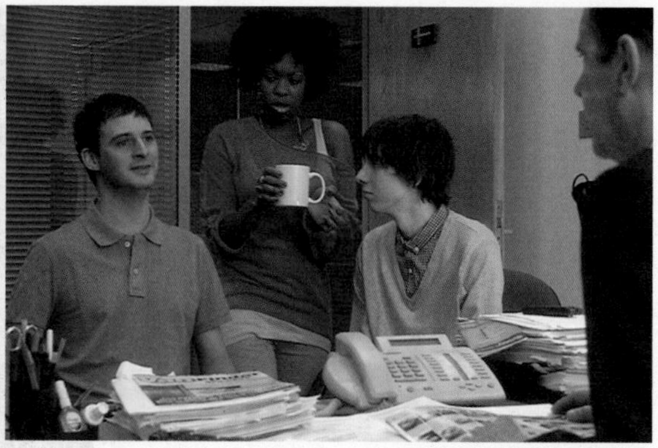

LIGHTFOOT LOGISTICS
HOME
MEET THE TEAM
THE FLEET
MAKE CONTACT
ABOUT LIGHTFOOT
THE DRIVE, THE DRIVERS, AND THE VANS TO GIVE YOU WHAT YOU NEED, WHEN YOU NEED IT.
'The Fleet'
THE FUNNY SIDE OF FLEET MANAGMENT
Watch Now
EPISODE 1 Salesman
EPISODE 2 Rival
EPISODE 3 Scary Doug
EPISODE 4 McCain
EPISODE 5 Mopeds
EPISODE 6 Loved up
EPISODE 7 Nice tie
EPISODE 8 Big switch
EPISODE 9 Lost
EPISODE 10 Kofi Annan
Click here and we'll let you know when the new episode is out.
HOW BIG IS YOUR PACKAGE?
Size (m³):
Weight (kg):
don't mind
don't mind
CALCULATE NOW
THE FLEET
We've chosen our vans carefully to guarantee that you get what you need, when you need it.
SEE THE FLEET
MEET THE TEAM
Click on one of the buttons to find out more about key members of the team.
MEET PETE
MEET GERRY
MEET THE TEAM
MAKE CONTACT
Sally is waiting to answer all your questions. Simply click the contact button below to get in contact.
MAKE CONTACT

Web Films
Made in Valby for
the Danish Road
Safety Council

The Family: The Party
This is an online traffic campaign targeted at young men, showing that even the Mafia takes road safety seriously and finds traffic the most stupid place to die.

Director
Adam Hashemi
Copywriters
Brian Lykke
Jesper Rofelt
Creative Director
Jesper Rofelt
Producer
Tanja Paik
Cinematographer
Lasse Frank
Set Designer
Peter Grant
Advertising Agency
Made in Valby
Production Company
Made in Valby
Client
Danish Road
Safety Council

Web Films
Pereira & O'Dell for
LEGO Systems

**The Brick Thief:
A LEGO Short Film**
'The Brick Thief' unites and excites former LEGO kids to rediscover the brand once their children reach the brick-building age. LEGO CL!CK is a site devoted to creativity, innovation, and the moment when ideas just CL!CK. The mischievous and moustachioed Brick Thief is a man of good intentions, and an excellent creative problem-solver, if he can just borrow a few of your LEGO bricks. The short film sparks nostalgia by recalling when the art of play fostered our imagination and our knack for invention.

Direction
Blue Source
Art Director
Jason Apaliski
Copywriter
Jaime Robinson
Creative Directors
PJ Pereira
Kash Sree
Agency Producers
Jeff Ferro
Sara Krider
Special Effects
Andy Hall
Andy McKenna
Editor
Damion Clayton
Advertising Agency
Pereira & O'Dell
Brand Managers
Michael McNally
Julie Sterne
Client
LEGO Systems
Brand
LEGO

Web Films
Droga5 New York
for PUMA

Hardchorus
We open with a small group of hardcore football fans, also known as hooligans. Suddenly, one of them starts singing the first words of 'Truly, Madly, Deeply' by Savage Garden. Another hooligan joins in, and as the camera pulls out, we see that the whole pub is packed with hooligans. They all sing together with the power of an entire stadium of fans during a football game, turning the cheesy love song into something big, beautiful and romantic. After the last chorus, a super appears: 'It's match day. It's Valentine's Day. Let your better half know how you feel'.

Director
Ben Gregor
Art Director
Petter Hernmarck
Copywriter
Erik Hogfeldt
Designer
Jon Donaghy
Executive Creative Directors
Duncan Marshall
Ted Royer
Creative Chairman
David Droga
Associate Creative Director of Digital
Neil Heymann
Producer
Ben Mann
Executive Producers
Matthew Brown
Tim Katz
Agency Producer
Dana May
Head of Integrated Production
Sally-Ann Dale
Editor
Alaster Jordan
Director of Photography
John Lynch
Advertising Agency
Droga5 New York
Production Company
Knucklehead
Post Production
The Mill New York
Music Conducting
Red Rhythm
Client
PUMA
Brand
Love=Football

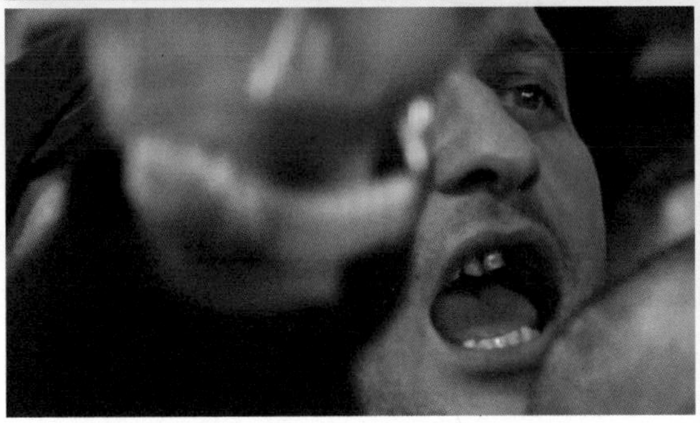

PUMA
IT'S MATCH DAY.
IT'S VALENTINE'S DAY.

Digital Solutions & Use of Social Media
AlmapBBDO for Volkswagen do Brasil

Twitter Zoom
The Volkswagen Fox sponsored São Paulo's biggest music festival, Planeta Terra. Our task was to spread the Fox's message beyond the event, reaching every youngster in São Paulo. We hid a series of tickets within the city and launched an online platform where visitors could see Google Maps. The mechanism was simple: the more tweets #foxatplanetaterra received, the closer the zoom on the map. The first one to get to the ticket won it. This went on for four days in a row. As a result, the tweet became a topic trend in São Paulo in less than two hours.

Creative Directors Sergio Mugnaini, Luiz Sanches
Technical Director João Lopes
Interactive Designer Vanessa Marques
Art Director Guiga Giacomo
Copywriter Ricardo Wolff
Art Assistant Ricardo Pocci
Advertising Agency AlmapBBDO
Development On Interactive
Account Handlers Fernão Cosi, Carla Magro, Ana Beatriz Porto, Vanessa Previero
Marketing Manager Herlander Zola
Client Volkswagen do Brasil
Brand Volkswagen Fox

Looking for tickets? Just tweet #foxatplanetaterra
It's simple: the more you tweet, the closer you get to the hidden tickets for the Planeta Terra Festival. All you have to do is tweet #foxatplanetaterra and wait for the zoom to get closer and close. Then, just rush to the appointed spot and grab your pair of tickets!
How to win? Winners Planeta Terra Terms Share:
São Paulo
Today's Tweets: 00258
Stay Tuned. Follow us on Twitter.
How to win?
Follow us on twitter
Come on everyone, we're only 1200 away. #foxatplanetaterra
I need'em so bad. #foxatplanetaterra
Everyone unite! #foxatplanetaterra
A Tweet
Each tweet #foxatplanetaterra makes the map zoom in. Basically, the more tweets, the bigger your chance to find out where the lost tickets are at.
B Find
When the total ammount of tweets is reached, a password will appear over the map. The next step is to rush to the appointed place.
C Win
The first ones to arrive at the appointed spot with the correct password will win a pair of tickets. Important: participants must be over 18 years old.

Digital Solutions & Use of Social Media
Jung von Matt/next for WWF Deutschland

Save as WWF
Millions of square metres of rain forest are cleared every year, for paper on which pointless documents are printed out. To raise global awareness of the destruction this causes, we invented the WWF – a file format that cannot be printed out. Every individual, company and organisation can join in by simply downloading, using and sharing WWF files. Our message: Save as WWF, save a tree. After four weeks, 200,000 users from 183 countries had visited the website and downloaded the software over 30,000 times.

Creative Directors Sven Loskill, Jan Rexhausen
Technical Directors Simone Bitzer, Susanne zu Eicken
Art Directors Alexander Norvilas, Michael Seifert
Copywriter Lisa Glock
Web Designer Tom Schallberger
Agency Producer Lana Nugent
Sound Designer Rose Tribble
Digital Agency Jung von Matt/next
Advertising Agency Jung von Matt/Fleet
Account Handler Benjamin Wenke
Brand Manager Dr Dirk Reinsberg
Client WWF Deutschland

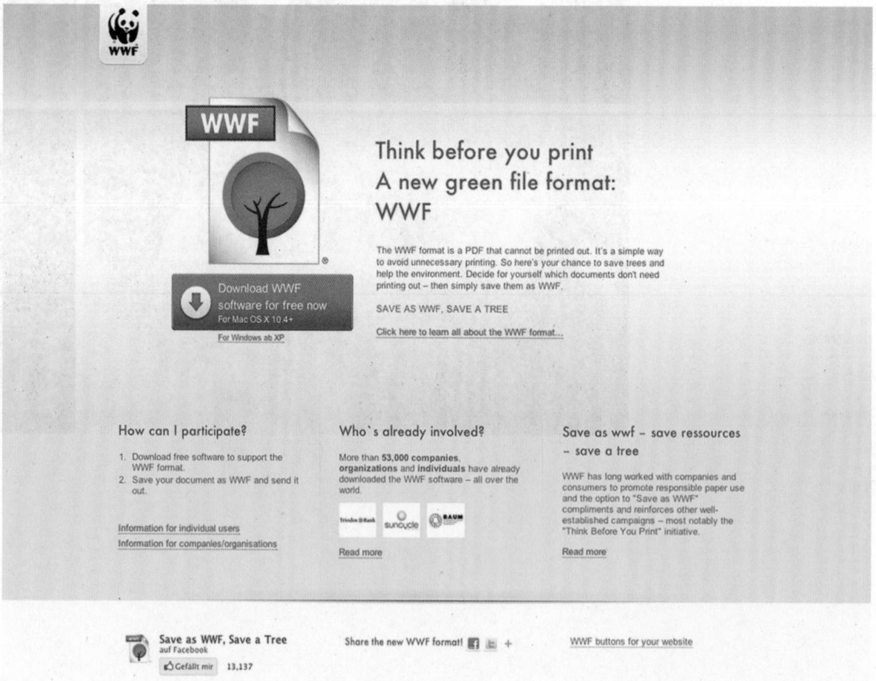
WWF
Think before you print
A new green file format: WWF
The WWF format is a PDF that cannot be printed out. It's a simple way to avoid unnecessary printing. So here's your chance to save trees and help the environment. Decide for yourself which documents don't need printing out – then simply save them as WWF.
SAVE AS WWF, SAVE A TREE
Click here to learn all about the WWF format...
Download WWF software for free now
For Mac OS X 10.4+
For Windows ab XP
How can I participate?
1. Download free software to support the WWF format.
2. Save your document as WWF and send it out.
Information for individual users
Information for companies/organisations
Who`s already involved?
More than 53,000 companies, organizations and individuals have already downloaded the WWF software – all over the world.
Read more
Save as wwf – save ressources – save a tree
WWF has long worked with companies and consumers to promote responsible paper use and the option to "Save as WWF" compliments and reinforces other well-established campaigns – most notably the "Think Before You Print" initiative.
Read more
Save as WWF, Save a Tree
auf Facebook
Gefällt mir 13,137
Share the new WWF format!
WWF buttons for your website

Digital Solutions &
Use of Social Media
JWT New York
for Microsoft

Brand Journalism
IT decision-makers are a particularly resistant target; they are not swayed by advertising alone. We produced content by creating a dedicated agency 'news team' to monitor everything said about Microsoft Enterprise Software on the Internet. They identify which conversations to be a part of and activate a blogger to speak on Microsoft's behalf. We tapped into topics our geeks care about, published in places where crucial decision-making conversations happen.

Creative Director
Louis-Philippe Tremblay
Executive Creative Directors
Walt Connelly
Justin Crawford
Chief Creative Officer
Ty Montague
Creative Director of Global Integration
Jim Consolantis
Copywriter
Chiyong Jones
Advertising Agency
JWT New York
Production Company
JWTwo
Experiential Messaging Executive Director
Brian Clark
Content Strategy Director
Kyle Monson
Director of Brand Production
Sergio Lopez
Business Director
Tina Galley
Group Business Director
Beth Waxman-Arteta
Account Managers
Michael McKloskey
Michael Page
Client Global Marketing & Communications Strategist
Deana Singleton
Client Senior Advertising Manager
Kevin Basch
Client Senior Product Manager
Larry Grothaus
Client
Microsoft

Geek
AD
AGENCY

Digital Solutions &
Use of Social Media
Wieden+Kennedy London for Nokia

Own Voice
To advertise the sat nav on Nokia phones, we invented a new product feature, called Own Voice, that lets people record the voices of friends and family to be a constantly changing chorus of guides on their Nokia sat nav. Through a mobile app, our website and Facebook, millions invited loved ones to record a few commands. It permanently improved the product experience and helped the brand to live out its motto: Connecting People.

Creative Directors
Sidney Bosley
Rob Perkins
Executive Creative Directors
Tony Davidson
Kim Papworth
Graphic Designer
Seppo Palo
Senior Designer
Tom Haswell
Senior Concept Designer
Mihael Cankar
Head of Design
Dan Griffiths
Director of Creative Technology
Antti Kilpelä
Development Director
Rob Gibson
Head of Development
Chris Blackburn
Interactive Art Director
Zaid Al-Asady
Producer
Jeanne Bachelard
Software Development Agency
Starcut
Advertising Agency
Wieden+Kennedy London
Communications Agency
Glue Isobar
Strategist
Josh Millrod
Information Architect
Jonathan Godsell
Account Director
Minni Lakotieva
Head Project Manager
Marko Laitinen
Client
Nokia

OWN VOICE
NOKIA
Connecting People
Start creating your Own Voice pack
Search
Rob Steiner
Selected (9 friends)
Fern Trelfa
John Kirkham
Mathew Kramer
Sidney Bosley
My voice packs
How it works

OWN VOICE
NOKIA
Connecting People
Dan's best mates
100%
My voice packs
How it works
Publish now

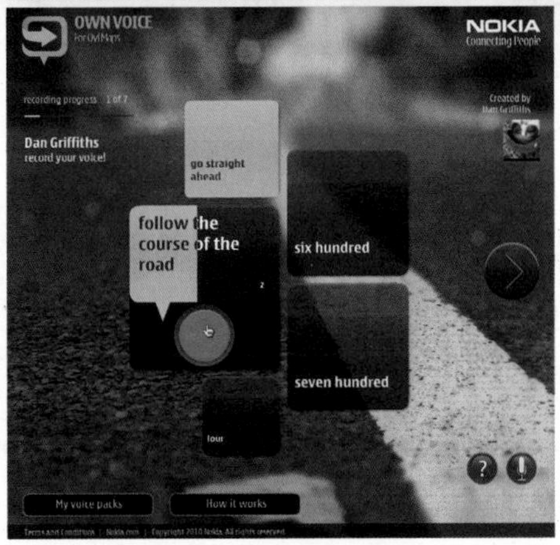
OWN VOICE
NOKIA
Connecting People
Dan Griffiths
record your voice!
go straight ahead
follow the course of the road
six hundred
seven hundred
My voice packs
How it works

Digital Solutions & Use of Social Media
Ogilvy Guatemala for Claro

Ringtowns
More than 30 Ringtowns were created using the Mayan names of some of the 1,500 Guatemalan towns and cities with coverage from mobile phone operator Claro. Ringtowns were launched through a nationwide radio campaign, inviting people to get them for free, to share them through social media and use them on their mobile phones, turning every incoming call or message into a commercial for Claro's nationwide mobile coverage. Ringtowns were available to consumers through MMS or from Claro's website.

Creative Directors Jose Contreras, Ramiro Eduardo, Ruben Leyton, Miguel Mayen
Design Director Desiree Cojulun
Technical Director Soizic Freyschmidt
Interactive Designers Desiree Cojulun, David Galdamez
Flash Programmer David Galdamez
Mobile Designer David Galdamez
Designer Francisco Coutiño
Mobile Developer Monica Ruiz
Developer Soizic Freyschmidt
Art Director Francisco Coutiño
Copywriter Jorge Perez
Producer Juan Carlos Flores
Animator Polo Uribio
Sound Designer Ender Barrientos
Mobile Marketing Agency TPP
Advertising Agency Ogilvy Guatemala
Account Handler Gustavo Alejos
Brand Manager Eduardo Muniz
Marketing Manager Wellyngton Da Silva
Client Claro

RINGTOWNS
Claro

Chiquimula
San Pedro
Esquipulas
SOME EXAMPLES
RINGTOWNS

TOP 10 RINGTONES
DOWNLOADS
Ringtowns- CLARO
70152
1
Manos al aire - NELLY FURTADO
65078
2
Poker face - LADY GAGA
59304
3
Loba - SHAKIRA

Digital Solutions & Use of Social Media
Dentsu Tec for UNIQLO

UNIQLO Lucky Counter
The aim was to improve UNIQLO's brand presence as the company renewed its online store. The campaign, 'UNIQLO Lucky Counter', enabled users to knock down prices of UNIQLO's bestselling products. Every time a user tweeted about a product through the site, its price went down. So users could get a better price in exchange for spreading the campaign via Twitter. In this way, UNIQLO was very successful at promoting and branding without any extra ad budget.

Creative Director Hiroki Nakamura
Technical Director Hideo Matsumoto
Flash Programmer Hiroshi Kozuma
HTML Engineer Yuma Murakami
System Engineer Takuho Yoshizu
Designer Sumiyo Miki
Art Director Kohei Kawasaki
Agency Producer Hajime Yakushiji
Digital Agencies Dentsu Tec, IMG SRC, RYDEN, S2 Factory
Advertising Agency Dentsu Tokyo
Project Managers Hideo Matsumoto, Ryuta Ohara
Product Manager Kanami Yamaguchi
Marketing Manager Yoshihisa Watanabe
Client UNIQLO

LUCKY COUNTER SPECIAL SALE 9/24 – 9/26
> FAQ
TWEET해 주셔서 감사합니다. 이하의 상품은 9/24~9/26 동안, 표시된 스페셜 가격으로 구입하실 수 있습니다.
※기간중에 링크처의 세일상품이 매진될 경우가 있습니다. 양해해 주시기 바랍니다.
24,900원 40.16% OFF!! 014,900원 SPECIAL SALE!!
24,900원 40.16% OFF!! 014,900원 SPECIAL SALE!!
79,900원 25.03% OFF!! 059,900원 SPECIAL SALE!!
29,900원 33.44% OFF!! 019,900원 SPECIAL SALE!!
29,900원 33.44% OFF!! 019,900원 SPECIAL SALE!!
49,900원 40.08% OFF!! 029,900원 SPECIAL SALE!!
29,900원 33.44% OFF!! 019,900원 SPECIAL SALE!!
29,900원 33.44% OFF!! 019,900원 SPECIAL SALE!!
49,900원 30.06% OFF!! 034,900원 SPECIAL SALE!!
149,000원 20.13% OFF!! 119,000원 SPECIAL SALE!!

Digital Solutions & Use of Social Media
Johannes Leonardo
for Daffy's

Daffy's Underground
We knew our client, Daffy's, wasn't at the forefront of young consumers' minds. But we knew where the consumers were, what they carried with them, and what would get them engaged. So we created an image too explicit for traditional media. We cut it into 40 pieces and posted those pieces in subway stations with a cryptic call to action of #undergroundpuzzle. By using Twitter to unite contributions, our idea resonated with a select group.

Creative Directors
Johannes Jacobs
Leo Premutico
Designers
Emmie Nostitz
Ferdinando Verderi
Art Directors
Emmie Nostitz
Ferdinando Verderi
Agency Producer
Matthew Mattingly
Photographer
Tom Hines
Advertising Agency
Johannes Leonardo
Account Handlers
Matt Ahumada
Frederique Nahman
Brand Manager
Will Bracker
Client
Daffy's

twitpic
Twitter username
Remember me
Login
Rotate photo
View full size
Posted on April 7, 2010
More photos
Put this photo on your website
Size and perspective are tricky, but here are two good chunks. #undergroundpuzzle
@ugpuzzle

MORE BANG LESS BUCK
WOMEN'S DENIM
ORIGINALLY: $188
DAFFY'S: $39.99
SILK PURPLE DRESS
ORIGINALLY: $98
DAFFY'S: $23.99
DAFFY'S

Sound Design & Use of Music for Digital Advertising
Red Urban
for Volkswagen

Anyone for a Sunday Drive
To launch the all-new Volkswagen Golf, we set about resurrecting the romance of the Sunday drive to remind people that driving can still be fun. The campaign included two broadcast commercials, national newsprint, and an interactive microsite that invited users to take a musical Sunday drive.

Sound Designer
Jonas Hurtig
Music Composer
Alec Harrison
Music Arranger
Alec Harrison
Creative Director
Christina Yu
Designer
John Thai
Flash Programmer
Heung Lee
Art Directors
Joel Pylypiw
John Thai
Copywriter
Jon Murray
Agency Producer
David Isaac
Advertising Agency
Red Urban
Account Director
Nicole Milette
Brand Manager
Lynne Piette
Director of Marketing
Bruce Rosen
Client
Volkswagen
Brand
Golf

MENU
Anyone for a Sunday Drive?
Remix Road
Give it a go
The 2011 Golf
See it from all sides
Build & Price

MENU
Remix Road
Switch the loops on and off and see how the scenery changes. Click and grab the record to get busy with some scratching.
Start

MENU
SHARE

MENU
SHARE

Yellow Pencil in Direct

Direct Integrated Campaign
AlmapBBDO
for Billboard

Music. See What it's Made of.
To advertise Billboard Magazine, we created print ads featuring stars like Bono, Eminem and Marilyn Manson, with each image composed of their respective influences, plus a touch of humour. We then created subway posters and digital panels that allowed consumers to take their photo, enter their favourite artists, and see their image recreated instantly. They could also upload images to Flickr. Finally, online, we sent Last.fm users a link to a website which recreated their profile images based on their favourite artists' images. Those who subscribed to Billboard magazine received the ultimate gift: a free poster of their own image. This campaign was also nominated in Direct Response/Ambient.

Art Directors
Danilo Boer
Marcos Kothlar
Marcos Medeiros
Copywriter
Andre Kassu
Creative Directors
Dulcidio Caldeira
Luiz Sanches
Illustrators
Marcos Kothlar
Marcos Medeiros
Typographer
José Roberto Bezerra
Advertising Agency
AlmapBBDO
Marketing Manager
Antonio Camarotti
Client
Billboard

Música
Entenda do que é feito.
Billboard BRASIL
www.billboardbr.com
Bob Dylan
David Bowie
Madre Teresa

Billboard BRASIL

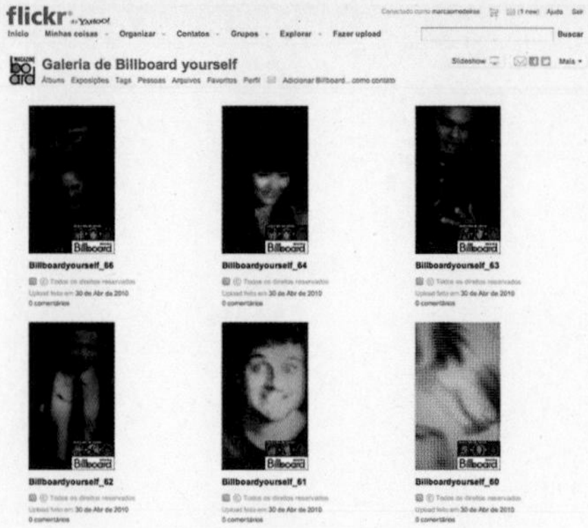
flickr
Galeria de Billboard yourself

Yellow Pencil in Direct

Direct Integrated Campaign
Saatchi & Saatchi Sydney for the Toyota Motor Corporation

Country Australia Border Security: Nothing Soft Gets In
To remind country Australians that Toyotas are the only 4WDs as tough as they are, we built a border post between the outback and the city, and established Country Australia Border Security to defend it from 'soft' city folk with their 'soft' city ways and their 'soft' city stuff. We equipped the team with Toyota 4WDs, the only vehicles up to the task. Our propaganda campaign was designed to intimidate and interrogate city people, while giving country folk a new champion. 'Tofu, hair gel, small fluffy dogs, roller blades, soy decaf lattes. Not on our watch.'

Art Director
Vince Lagana
Digital Art Director
Simon Jarosz
Copywriter
Steve Jackson
Creative Director
Dave Bowman
Executive Creative Director
Steve Back
Director
Tim Bullock
Producer
Julianne Shelton
Agency Producer
Kate Gooden
Advertising Agency
Saatchi & Saatchi Sydney
Production Company
Prodigy Films
Planner
Simon Bird
Business Director
Amy Turnbull
Group Business Director
Ben Court
Brand Manager
Scott Thompson
Client
Toyota Motor Corporation
Brand
Toyota

COUNTRY AUSTRALIA BORDER INSPECTION STATION
AY 91 ZR

COUNTRY AUSTRALIA BORDER SECURITY NOW TARGETING:
DOOF DOOF MUSIC
TOYOTA
NOTHING SOFT GETS IN

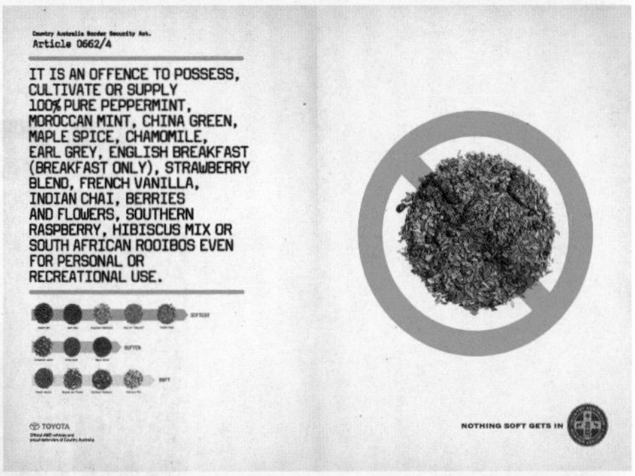
Article 0662/4
IT IS AN OFFENCE TO POSSESS, CULTIVATE OR SUPPLY 100% PURE PEPPERMINT, MOROCCAN MINT, CHINA GREEN, MAPLE SPICE, CHAMOMILE, EARL GREY, ENGLISH BREAKFAST (BREAKFAST ONLY), STRAWBERRY BLEND, FRENCH VANILLA, INDIAN CHAI, BERRIES AND FLOWERS, SOUTHERN RASPBERRY, HIBISCUS MIX OR SOUTH AFRICAN ROOIBOS EVEN FOR PERSONAL OR RECREATIONAL USE.
TOYOTA
NOTHING SOFT GETS IN

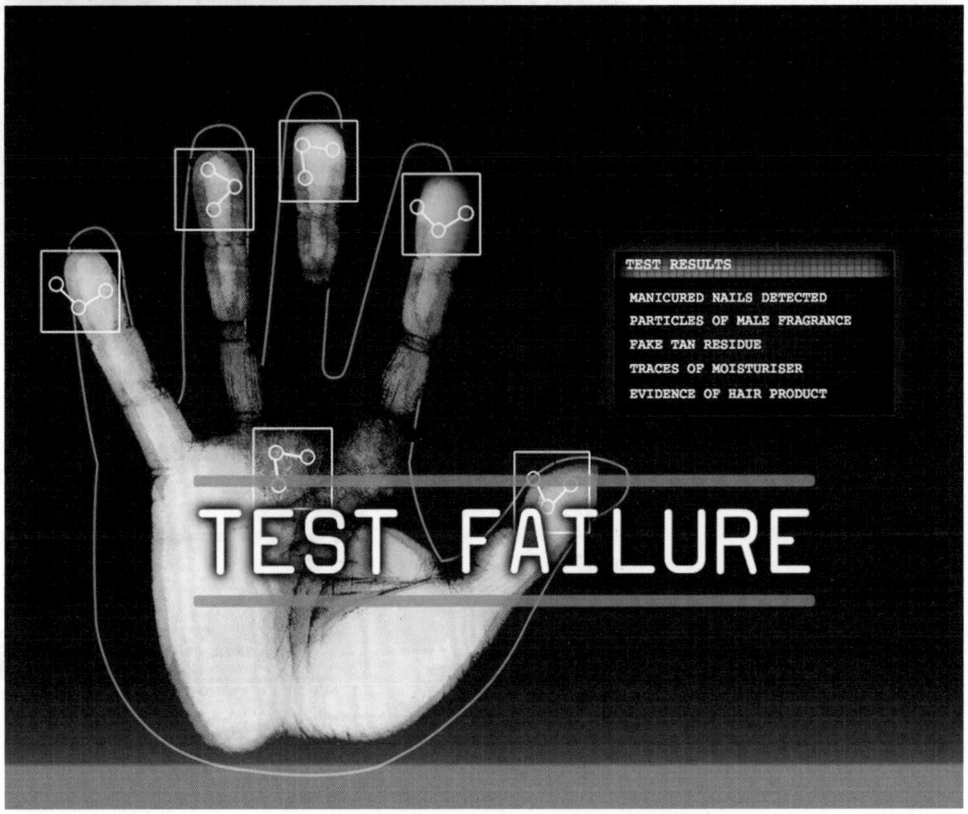
TEST RESULTS
MANICURED NAILS DETECTED
PARTICLES OF MALE FRAGRANCE
FAKE TAN RESIDUE
TRACES OF MOISTURISER
EVIDENCE OF HAIR PRODUCT
TEST FAILURE

Yellow Pencil in Direct

Direct Response/Digital
TBWA\London
for Wrigley

Updater
Skittles believe life's better inside the Rainbow. So we invited our Facebook fans to harness some of its power with the Super Mega Rainbow Updater. We built a live call centre and online film factory and asked our fans to supply it with their status updates. Here our staff recorded the updates as awesome films and posted them back onto our fans' Facebook walls in mere minutes. The whole assembly line was driven by the fans' input and willingness to be Rainbow-fied. In just two weeks, they created and shared over 21,000 films.

Art Director
Andrew Bloom
Copywriter
Eric Tell
Creative Directors
Johan Dahlqvist
Lee Tan
Executive Creative Director
Mark Hunter
Director
Jakob Marky
Producer
James Cunningham
Editor
James Norris
Agency Producer
Trudy Waldron
Web Producer
Sara-Lee Rost
Production Manager
Cathy Buchanan
Advertising Agency
TBWA\London
Production Company
Academy Films
Web Production
Perfect Fools
Sound Design
Wave
Planner
David Fryman
Account Director
Emma Massey
Account Manager
Justin Martin
Client
Wrigley
Brand
Skittles

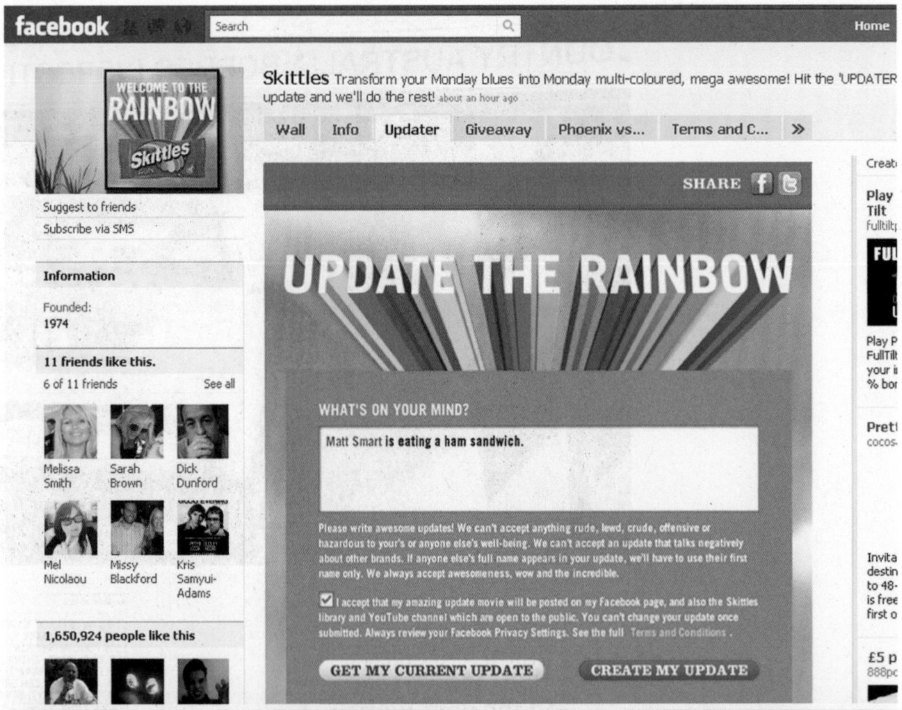
facebook
Search
Home
Skittles Transform your Monday blues into Monday multi-coloured, mega awesome! Hit the 'UPDATER update and we'll do the rest! about an hour ago
Wall
Info
Updater
Giveaway
Phoenix vs...
Terms and C...
WELCOME TO THE RAINBOW
Suggest to friends
Subscribe via SMS
Information
Founded:
1974
11 friends like this.
6 of 11 friends
See all
Melissa Smith
Sarah Brown
Dick Dunford
Mel Nicolaou
Missy Blackford
Kris Samyui-Adams
1,650,924 people like this
SHARE
UPDATE THE RAINBOW
WHAT'S ON YOUR MIND?
Matt Smart is eating a ham sandwich.
GET MY CURRENT UPDATE
CREATE MY UPDATE

Drinking Water

facebook
Search
Home
Profile
Matt Smart
Edit My Profile
News Feed
Messages
Events
Friends
Uber clique
Create Group...
See All
Game Requests
Apps
More
Friends on Chat
News Feed
Top News · Most Recent 300+
Share: Status Photo Link Video
What's on your mind?
Matt Smart is eating a ham sandwich.
0:06 / 0:27
Matt Smart – Super Mega Rainbow Update
www.youtube.com
The Super Mega Rainbow Updater from Skittles turns your normal update into an awesome film about you! Try it today at http://updatetherainbow.co.uk
November 12 at 12:55am via Update The Rainbow · Like · Comment · SuperMega Rainbow Updater
Events
What are you planning?
4 event invitations
Red Lion Pub Quiz
Thursday 8:00pm
Erik Tell's birthday. See All
Sponsored
Grow your business
Requests
4 group invitations
17 Page suggestions
2 game requests
Pokes
Daniel Colledge · Poke Back
Jonathan Colledge · Poke Back

Nomination in Direct

Direct Response/
Press & Poster
Leo Burnett Toronto
for James Ready

James Ready
Billboard Coupons
James Ready is always doing what it can to help people afford beer. This year James Ready invented billboard coupons, a way for people to save money on necessities like food, dry cleaning and grooming, leaving them with more money to buy James Ready beer. By partnering with local retailers we created a programme that allowed people to take a picture of our billboard, show the picture to the corresponding retailer and receive savings on items. Saving money means more beer money! Everyone wins.

Art Directors
Anthony Chelvanathan
Paul Giannetta
Copywriters
Sean Barlow
Steve Persico
Creative Directors
Lisa Greenberg
Judy John
Group Creative Director
Paul Giannetta
Print Producer
Gladys Bachand
Advertising Agency
Leo Burnett Toronto
Account Director
Natasha Dagenais
Group Account Director
David Buckspan
Account Executive
Jordan Lane
Client
James Ready

J.R. 5.5
JAMES READY 5.5
MUST BE LEGAL DRINKING AGE.
†Coupon expires July 3, 2010. See store for details. *Plus deposit.
15% OFF COUPLES HAIR REMOVAL.†
TAKE A PICTURE OF THIS COUPON.
SHOW IT TO NEFERTITI SALON, 1277 OTTAWA ST.
CLICK!
HELPING YOU SAVE $26.10* FOR JAMES READY BEER.

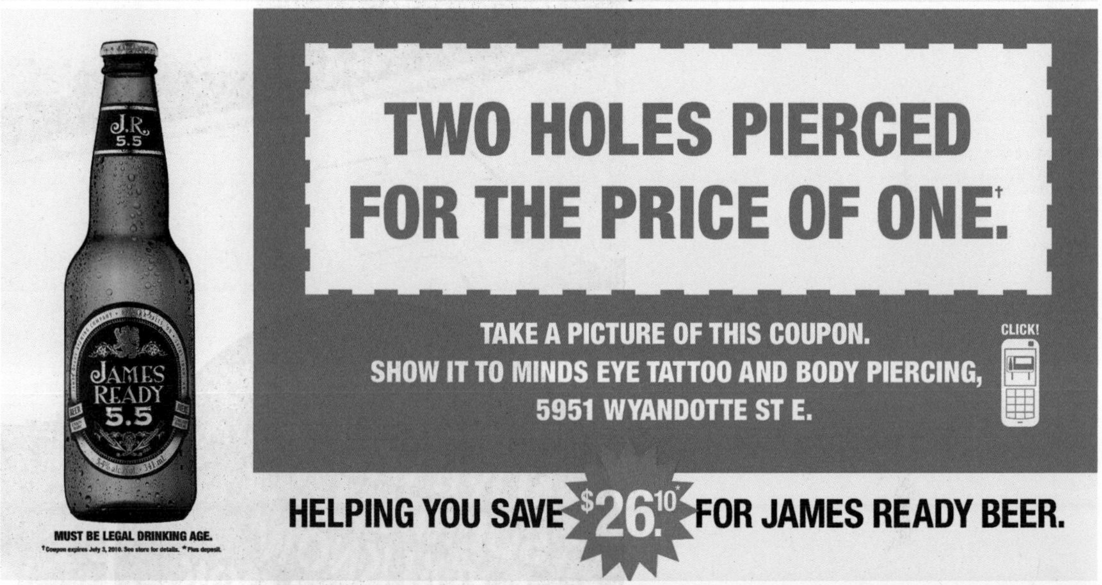
J.R. 5.5
JAMES READY 5.5
MUST BE LEGAL DRINKING AGE.
†Coupon expires July 3, 2010. See store for details. *Plus deposit.
TWO HOLES PIERCED FOR THE PRICE OF ONE.†
TAKE A PICTURE OF THIS COUPON.
SHOW IT TO MINDS EYE TATTOO AND BODY PIERCING,
5951 WYANDOTTE ST E.
CLICK!
HELPING YOU SAVE $26.10* FOR JAMES READY BEER.

J.R. 5.5
JAMES READY 5.5
MUST BE LEGAL DRINKING AGE.
†Coupon expires July 3, 2010. See store for details. *Plus deposit.
SAVE $2.26 ON STAIN REMOVAL FROM PANTS.†
(SOME STAINS EXCLUDED)
TAKE A PICTURE OF THIS COUPON.
SHOW IT TO MENA'S CLEANERS, 4606 TECUMSEH RD. E
CLICK!
HELPING YOU SAVE $26.10* FOR JAMES READY BEER.

Direct Integrated Campaign
Leo Burnett Hong Kong
for Zoo Records

Hidden Sound Campaign
Zoo Records champions the hidden sounds of alternative music. To promote the company, we took 14 local indie bands and embedded their songs into QR codes assembled into the shapes of animals that live hidden in the city. Scanning the codes reveals the songs and allows you to buy the CDs. This campaign was also nominated in Direct Response/ Press & Poster.

Art Directors
Kenny Ip
Leo Yeung
Copywriters
Joey Chung
Cyrus Ho
Wen Louie
Creative Directors
Brian Ma
Alfred Wong
Executive Creative Director
Connie Lo
Advertising Agency
Leo Burnett Hong Kong
Account Handler
Matthew Kwan
Client
Zoo Records

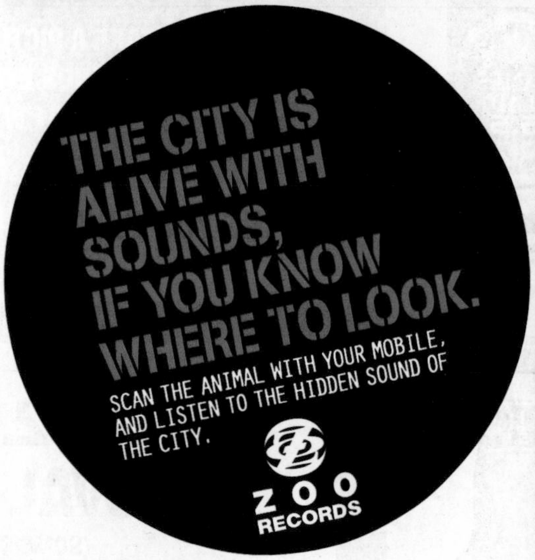
THE CITY IS ALIVE WITH SOUNDS, IF YOU KNOW WHERE TO LOOK.
SCAN THE ANIMAL WITH YOUR MOBILE, AND LISTEN TO THE HIDDEN SOUND OF THE CITY.
ZOO RECORDS

PL 8169

Direct Integrated Campaign
Colenso BBDO
for Yellow Pages
New Zealand

Yellow Chocolate
In February 2010 we launched the fastest selling chocolate bar in New Zealand. But we weren't selling chocolate. Five months earlier we had given an average New Zealander, Josh, a task: to create a chocolate bar that tasted of yellow. He could only use businesses from the Yellow Pages to help. He needed to sort out the flavour, packaging, distribution and marketing, and then launch it. He succeeded. It outsold favourite brands like Snickers two to one. People queued to pay $2 for our piece of Yellow Pages direct marketing. And it became the most talked about campaign in New Zealand.

Art Directors
Steve Cochran
Aaron Turk
Copywriters
Steve Cochran
Aaron Turk
Creative Directors
Steve Cochran
Dave King
Aaron Turk
Digital Creative Director
Aaron Goldring
Executive Creative Director
Nick Worthington
Director
Chris Graham
Producer
Tanya Haitoua-Cathro
Digital Producer
Amanda Theobold
Agency Producer
Paul Courtney
Editor
Paul Maxwell
Photographer
Stephen Langdon
Retoucher
Kevin Hyde
Advertising Agency
Colenso BBDO
Production Company
Good Life Films
Sound Design
Native Audio
Planner
James Hurman
Account Manager
Katya Urlwin
Account Directors
Terri Cumiskey
Rachel Turner
Group Account Director
Andrew Holt
Marketing Director
Kellie Nathan
Client
Yellow Pages
New Zealand

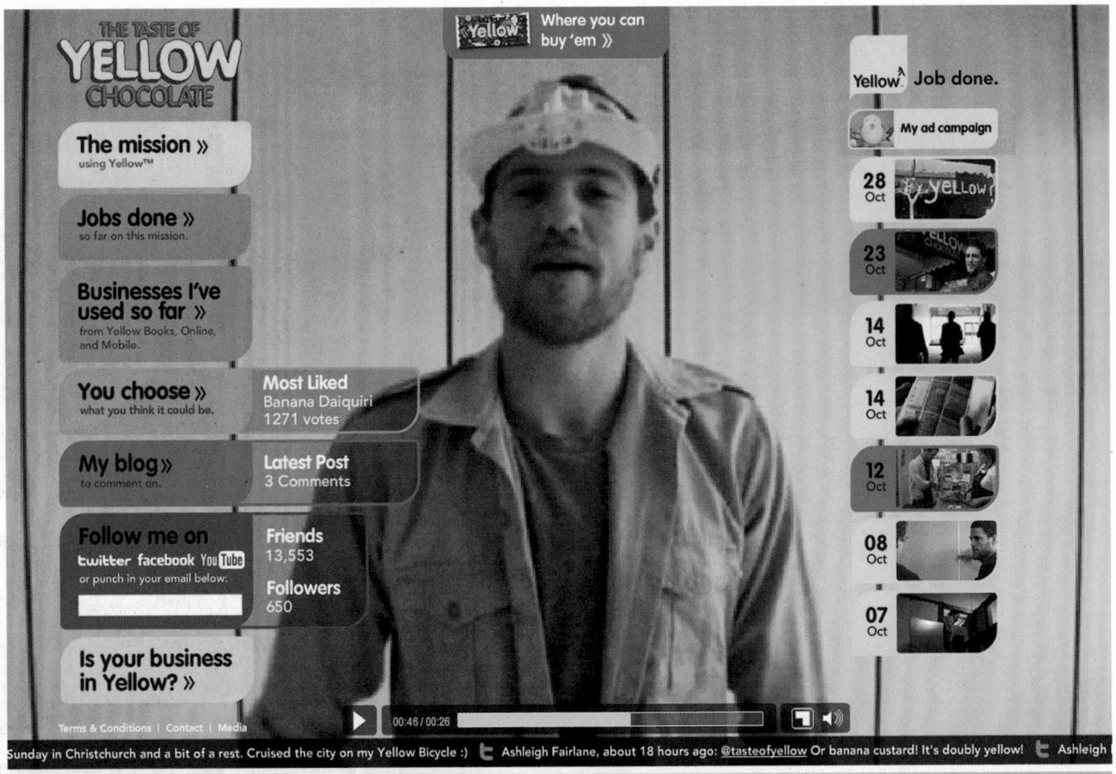
THE TASTE OF YELLOW CHOCOLATE
Where you can buy 'em »
Yellow Job done.
My ad campaign
The mission »
using Yellow™
Jobs done »
so far on this mission.
Businesses I've used so far »
from Yellow Books, Online, and Mobile.
You choose »
what you think it could be.
Most Liked
Banana Daiquiri
1271 votes
My blog »
to comment on.
Latest Post
3 Comments
Follow me on
twitter facebook YouTube
or punch in your email below:
Friends
13,553
Followers
650
Is your business in Yellow? »
Terms & Conditions | Contact | Media
00:46 / 00:26
28 Oct
23 Oct
14 Oct
14 Oct
12 Oct
08 Oct
07 Oct
Sunday in Christchurch and a bit of a rest. Cruised the city on my Yellow Bicycle :) Ashleigh Fairlane, about 18 hours ago: @tasteofyellow Or banana custard! It's doubly yellow! Ashleigh

APN
Latest tweet from Josh as he uses businesses in Yellow to create a yellow tasting chocolate bar.
TASTEOFYELLOW: ...SORTED! I HAVE A TEMPORARY PERSONAL
yellowchocolate.co.nz

Direct Integrated Campaign
Clemenger BBDO Melbourne for Guide Dogs Australia

Support Scent
Guide Dogs Australia's sole purpose is ending the isolation that can result from being blind. So when creating marketing support for its cause, we thought it absolutely vital not to exclude the blind. Anything requiring sight, such as ribbons, was considered unacceptable. Therefore we created something that appeals to another sense entirely – smell. A unisex fragrance called Support Scent was born, which actually allows the blind to recognise support around them. Priced at $5, all proceeds from the scent go to the charity. Now a whole new support base for the blind has emerged, with a 33 per cent lift in fundraising upon launch.

Art Director
Tom Martin
Copywriter
Julian Schreiber
Designer
Beci Orpin
Interactive Designer
Sam Hodgson
Digital Creative Director
Damian Royce
Executive Creative Director
Ant Keogh
Creative Chairman
James McGrath
Directors
Micca Delaney
Amy Gerbhardt
Producers
Jane Liscombe
Allison Lockwood
Agency Producer
Sevda Cemo
Editors
Micca Delaney
Jack Hutchings
Megan Voevodin
Advertising Agency
Clemenger BBDO Melbourne
Production Company
Exit Films
Sound Design
Flagstaff Studios Melbourne
Strategic Planner
Mike Hyde
Account Directors
Nici Henningsen
Ricci Meldrum
Project Managers
Sevda Cemo
Jo Currie
Client
Guide Dogs Australia

SUPPORT SCENT
SUPPORT SCENT
Guide Dogs
Australia
kit

We've partnered with Guide Dogs Australia to create Support Scent:
HOW DO YOU SHOW SUPPORT FOR SOMEONE WHO CAN'T SEE?
SUPPORT SCENT
$5
SUPPORT SCENT

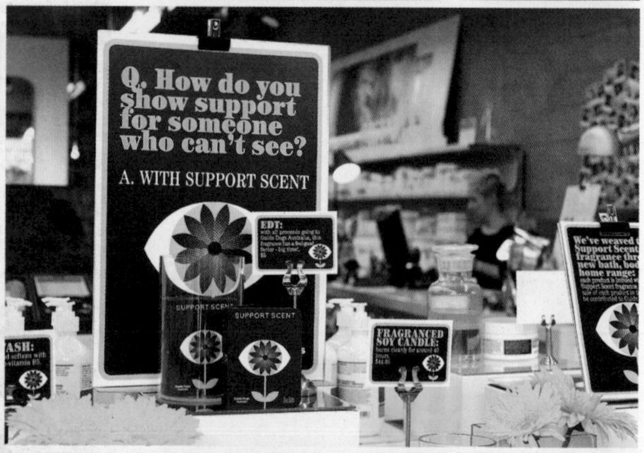
Q. How do you show support for someone who can't see?
A. WITH SUPPORT SCENT

Beauty with the feel-good factor.

Direct Integrated Campaign
Happy Soldiers for Pacific Brands

Dated Pillows
Tontine is Australia's largest manufacturer of pillows. It had a problem. People weren't changing their pillows often enough. This was due to the fact that they didn't have a good reason to change their pillows, and they had no idea how old their pillows actually were. We came up with the idea of printing a best before date on all Tontine pillows. We then gave people a reason why they should have a pillow with this best before date. It wasn't just a campaign; it was a permanent product innovation.

Art Director
John Kane
Copywriter
Ben Sampson
Designer
Tim Haynes
Creative Director
John Kane
Director
Rey Carlson
Producer
Bonnie Fay
Agency Producer
Meredyth Judd
Advertising Agency
Happy Soldiers
Planners
Sophie Price
Mark Sareff
Account Handler
Emma DiGiacomo
Business Director
Lindsey Evans
Brand Manager
Adam Heathcote
Marketing Manager
Lucinda Kew
Client
Pacific Brands
Brand
Tontine

You have had more sleeping partners than you think.
Your pillow grows over time, made up of your dead skin cells and the things that feed on them. The older it is the worse it gets. It's why we stamp our pillows with the date we think you should change it.
THIS IS A TONTINE FRESH PILLOW.
WITH NORMAL USE WE SUGGEST CHANGING IT BY
OCTOBER 2012
TONTINE
www.tontine.com.au

As you grow to love your pillow, it just grows.
Your pillow grows over time, made up of your dead skin cells and the things that feed on them. The older it is the worse it gets. It's why we stamp our pillows with the date we think you should change it.
OCTOBER 2012
TONTINE
www.tontine.com.au

TONTINE FRESH
This fresh pillow is made with treated filling and date stamped so you'll know when to change it.
www.tontine.com.au
SEE BACK OF PACK

Direct Integrated Campaign
Happy Soldiers
for Virgin Money

On the Card
The challenge was to launch Virgin Money's new Virgin Flyer Credit Card. A credit card that gave you points to fly on Virgin every time you used it. We discovered that people were wary of the promises of flyer reward cards. So instead of telling people the card worked, we proved it. We paid for the entire campaign for the new Virgin Flyer Credit Card, with the Virgin Flyer Credit Card. This earned us hundreds of flights, which we gave away to the public. It was a product demonstration, a promotion and a generous brand act in one.

Art Director
John Kane
Copywriter
Ben Sampson
Designer
Tim Haynes
Creative Director
John Kane
Director
Ben Lawrence
Producer
Michael Cook
Agency Producer
Helen Hendry
Editor
Stuart Morley
Sound Designer
Rafael May
Advertising Agency
Happy Soldiers
Production Company
The Feds
Planner
Mark Sareff
Media Planner
Sophie Price
Account Handler
Emma DiGiacomo
Managing Director
Lindsey Evans
Business Director
Sasha Firth
Brand Manager
Ryan Dinsdale
Marketing Manager
Nathan Wilson
Client
Virgin Money

We paid for our advertising with our new Virgin Flyer Credit Card and earned over 200 flights.
We'd like to give them to you at virginmoney.com.au
Virgin money

Direct Integrated Campaign
Scholz & Friends Berlin for Daimler Mercedes-Benz Vertrieb Deutschland

Meister vs. Meister
Germany, year of the Football World Cup 2010. Mercedes-Benz Vito initiates a different kind of competition: master craftsmen are personally challenged to a football game by a selection of legendary football world and European champions. It's Meister versus Meister. The legendary team, which includes the world champions from 1954, 1974 and 1990 (Horst Eckel, Sepp Maier and Andreas Brehme), sets out on a road trip in a Mercedes-Benz Vito and competes against four teams on their local football pitches.

Art Directors
Stefan Schuster
Joerg Waschescio
Copywriters
Christian Brandes
Tobias Deitert
Stefan Lenz
Creative Directors
Robert Krause
Martin Pross
Matthias Spaetgens
Philipp Woehler
Directors
Johannes Grebert
Philipp Stoelzl
Editors
Rain Kencana
Daniel Klessig
Marty Schenk
Lighting Cameraperson
Felix Leibert
Photographers
Tino Pohlmann
Nikolas Schmidt-Burgk
Advertising Agency
Scholz & Friends Berlin
Production Company
Bigfish
Account Handlers
Anna Gabriel
Vera Krausse
Stefanie Wurst
Brand Manager
Lutz Wienstroth
Marketing Manager
Nicole Baldisweiler
Client
Daimler Mercedes-Benz Vertrieb Deutschland
Brand
Mercedes-Benz Vito

Meister vs. Meister
DFB-ALLSTARS
GERÜSTBAU J. MOTZKAU
Sonntag, 30. Mai, ab 11 Uhr – Stadion Sonnenblume, Velbert
Mercedes-Benz

Meister vs. Meister
IRGENDWANN MACHT JEDER DAS SPIEL SEINES LEBENS
„Der ultimative Wettkampf 2010."
Mercedes-Benz

Mercedes-Benz
Der Wettkampf
Die Meister
Für Fans
Video & Fotos
Der Vito
Newsletter
Kontakt
DFB-Allstars, aufgepasst!
Wir nehmen die Herausforderung an!
FC Birbaum & CO
Die Weltmeister...
Deinzerteam
Rennert - Kicker
Die Flintstones
Bald fertig
Mehr zum Team
Torjäger-Meister
Die Bunzelmänner
Himmelsstürmer
The Hammers
Gauchos 1
1. FC Boymann L...
Der Schalkner M...
1.FC Maria hilf
Die Billis
Lacklerprofis
Polymold GmbH &...
Scherrer

Direct Response/Digital
Grabarz & Partner for
IKEA Deutschland

Unbox the Banner
IKEA asked us to promote its discounted products and motivate the target group to visit the online store. Our solution was to create banners that can be assembled by the web user. For the first time visitors could experience online what they knew from IKEA offline: saving money by assembling something themselves. Each of the three banners showed the IKEA flatpack containing all the parts along with assembly instructions for putting it together. Once the assembly was completed, the price of the item dropped and the visitor could go to buy it directly from the IKEA online store.

Art Directors
Per Wolter
Oliver Zboralski
Copywriter
Constantin Sossidi
Creative Director
Tom Hauser
Executive Creative Director
Ralf Heuel
Graphic Artists
Eike Fietje
Milena Pfannkuche
Digital Animator
Matthias Mach
Advertising Agency
Grabarz & Partner
Technical Project Manager
Holger Knauer
Project Manager
Jan Luebcke
Client
IKEA Deutschland

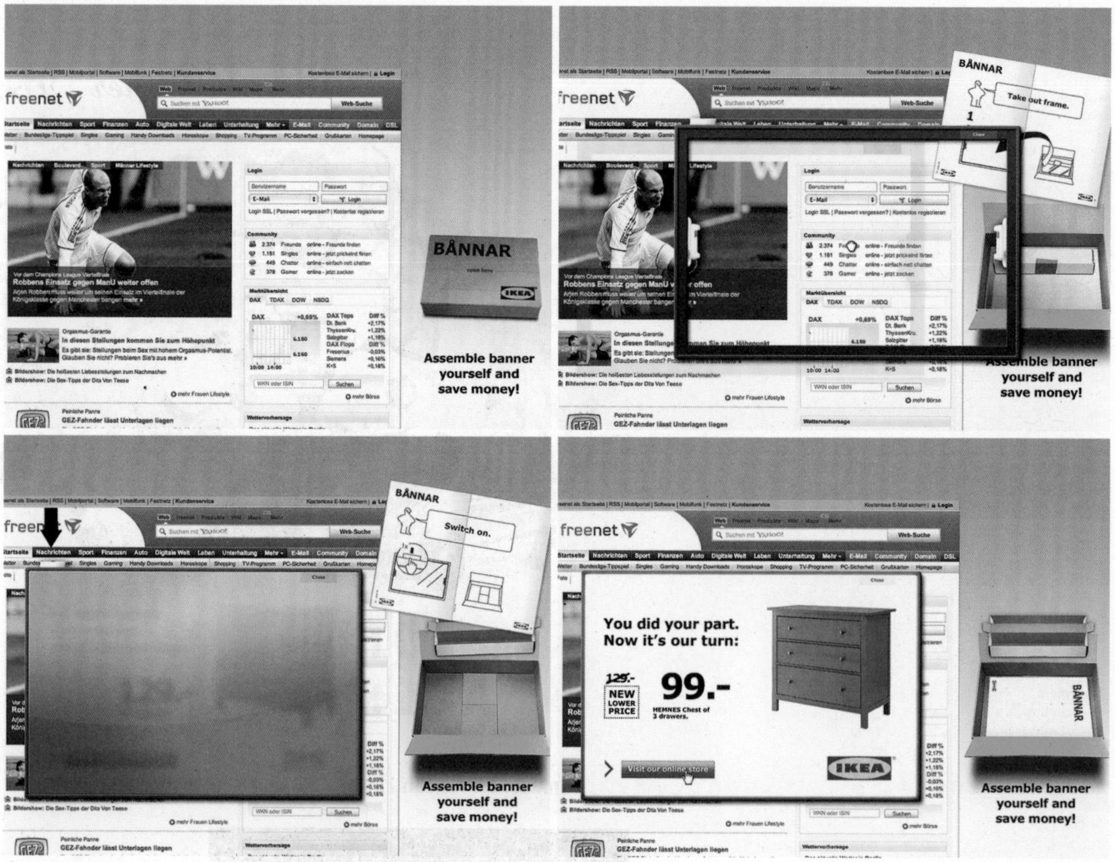
freenet
BÅNNAR
IKEA
Assemble banner yourself and save money!
Take out frame.
Switch on.
You did your part.
Now it's our turn:
129.-
NEW LOWER PRICE
99.-
HEMNES Chest of 3 drawers.
Visit our online store

Direct Response/Digital
Droga5 Sydney for CUB

VB Profile Intervention
We developed a way for people to challenge their friends' superficiality in social media, and call out the double life they lead on Facebook. Profile Intervention allows people to burst the superficial bubbles their mates have been living in. Using their over-the-top profile page as ammunition, mates can formulate an online video diagnosis to send to their friends and bring them back to reality.

Art Directors
Andy Fergusson
Guybrush Taylor
Copywriter
Chris Berents
Creative Directors
Cam Blackley
Matty Burton
Executive Creative Director
Duncan Marshall
Creative Chairman
David Nobay
Digital Producer
Sora Nobari
Executive Digital Producer
Brett Mitchell
Agency Producer
Paul Johnston
Advertising Agency
Droga5 Sydney
Production Company
Jungle Boys
Digital Production Company
Resn
Account Handlers
Esther Knox
Lucy McBurney
Business Director
Jamie Clift
Marketing Director
Peter Sinclair
Senior Brand Manager
Craig Maclean
Group Marketing Manager
Paul Donaldson
Client
CUB
Brand
VB

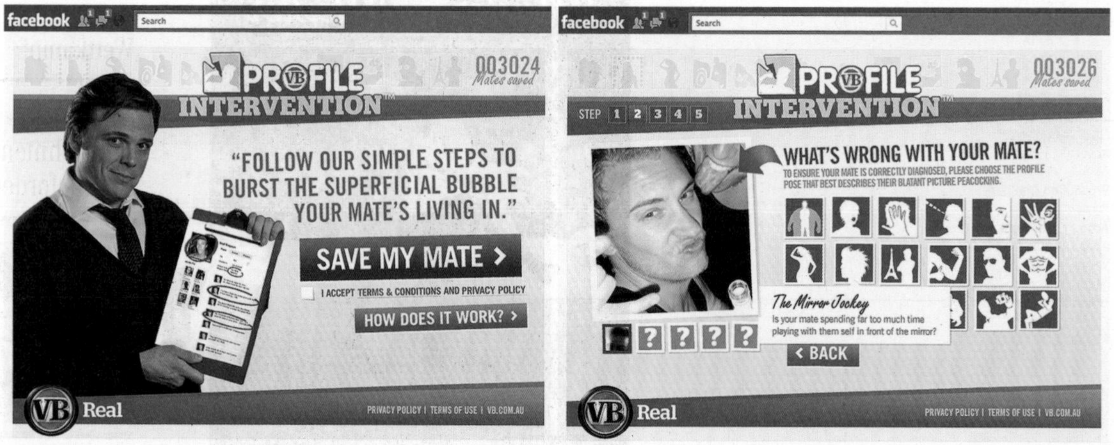
facebook
PROFILE INTERVENTION
003024 Mates saved
"FOLLOW OUR SIMPLE STEPS TO BURST THE SUPERFICIAL BUBBLE YOUR MATE'S LIVING IN."
SAVE MY MATE >
I ACCEPT TERMS & CONDITIONS AND PRIVACY POLICY
HOW DOES IT WORK? >
VB Real
PRIVACY POLICY | TERMS OF USE | VB.COM.AU
003026 Mates saved
STEP 1 2 3 4 5
WHAT'S WRONG WITH YOUR MATE?
TO ENSURE YOUR MATE IS CORRECTLY DIAGNOSED, PLEASE CHOOSE THE PROFILE POSE THAT BEST DESCRIBES THEIR BLATANT PICTURE PEACOCKING.
The Mirror Jockey
Is your mate spending far too much time playing with them self in front of the mirror?
< BACK
VB Real
PRIVACY POLICY | TERMS OF USE | VB.COM.AU

Direct Response/Digital
DDB Paris for Bouygues Telecom

When Facebook Becomes a Book
When Bouygues Telecom was launching its Facebook platform, it asked us to create something that would go beyond using your profile picture in a funny way, or entertaining your friends with a joke. We decided to look at the way we use Facebook and found that even though we use the social networking site every day, we forget the favourite moments we share online. So we created an app that could change that, and keep your Facebook in a book.

Art Directors
Alexander Kalchev
Siavosh Zabeti
Copywriters
Alexander Kalchev
Siavosh Zabeti
Executive Creative Director
Alexandre Hervé
Advertising Agency
DDB Paris
Development
Perfect Fools
Strategic Planner
Fabien Leroux
Account Directors
Marie-Laure Dangeon
Antoine Gilbert
Client
Bouygues Telecom

facebook
Home
Profile
Account
CHOISIR le CONTENU
LES AMIS qui feront partie du livre.
Période et STATISTIQUES
Septembre 2008
Février 2011
28 09 2008
21 02 2011
Date de début du livre
Date de fin du livre
Je veux inclure:
Statuts
Photos
1757 / 1803 statuts
594 / 614 photos
CONTINUER
RETOUR
APERÇU
Bouygues
Create an Ad
Play SocialCity
Immerse yourself in the utopian world of SocialCity. Play now!
Like
Earn up to 5.50% p.a.
ANZ
ANZ Online Saver – access your funds 24/7, no minimum balance and earn up to 5.50% p.a. until 30 Jun 2010. Apply online by 30 Mar 2010.
Like
Sydney 1-Day Coupons
1 huge Sydney coupon emailed daily.
Like
Contact Report
About Advertising Developers Careers Terms • Find Friends Privacy Mobile Help Center

Direct Response/Digital
McCann Worldgroup Hong Kong for Metro Publishing Hong Kong

Future Daily on April Fool
Thirteen years after the handover to China, Hong Kong is facing increasing threats to press freedom. To alarm the public about this, we created a website and asked people to write what they thought would make the headlines in 18 years. We then published the most voted-for stories, word for word, in a special edition paper that we distributed on April Fool's Day. The futuristic theme and April Fool's launch acted as a smokescreen for people to express their heartfelt opinions.

Art Directors
Gary Lam
Joseph Mok
Copywriters
April Fang
Law Chi Hang
Spring Liu
Creative Directors
Law Chi Hang
Joseph Mok
Stanley Wong
Executive Creative Director
Nick Lim
Chief Creative Officer
Spencer Wong
Production Programmers
Keat Mok
Anna Tsang
Interactive Content Director
Zoe Kuo
Content Production Director
Paul Swee
Technical Director
Henry Chu
Publication Editors
Jeff Lee
Jeff Wong
Advertising Agency
McCann Worldgroup Hong Kong
Integrated Communications Planner
Penelope Yau
Account Handlers
Yen Lee
Chris Tam
Winson Wong
Marketing Manager
Fey Wong
Client
Metro Publishing Hong Kong
Brand
Metro Daily

Contact Us | Terms & Conditions
metro in 18years 18年後 都市日報
2028
26 February
10 : 32
41°C
Home-used tanks at Tiananmen Square exhibit on 10th Anniversary of June 4th Apology
Hong Kong with 41°C Average Temperature.
Winters disappear amid relentless global warming.
Housing price hits new high. Parents sell kids to buy property
Pandas extinct Public fooled by state costumed cover-up
China introduces tax on "dirty money". Forecast 634 billion in new income
YOUR HEADLINE HERE
Taiwan troops pour into China
Animal lovers drool over new Apple 'iPet'.
Genetically-modified footballer sets new trend. FIFA considers legislation.
China stops censorship, Google returns to China
Hottest
Latest
Local
China
World
Business
Sports
Entertainment
Health
Lifestyle
Classified Ads

Direct Response/Digital
Publicis London for
Renault UK

The Mégane Experiment
Our challenge was to raise awareness of the Renault Mégane and position the car as ‘anti-bland’. Statistical research pointed to a powerful thought: Mégane was a bringer of joy. Towns with more Méganes had more joie de vivre. And the most powerful way to promote this thought was to put it to the test through a real experiment: could an English town with no Mégane vehicles embrace the French way of life and the car that epitomises it?

Art Directors
Robert Amstell
David Hillyard
Digital Art Director
Christian Horsfall
Copywriter
Matthew Lancod
Digital Copywriter
Ian Sweeney
Creative Director
Ed Robinson
Digital Creative Director
Alix Pennycuick
Executive Creative Directors
Tom Ewart
Adam Kean
Designer
Paul Belford
Director
Henry-Alex Rubin
Producer
Drew Santarsiero
Agency Producers
Joe Bagnall
Colin Hickson
Digital Producer
Ken Blake
Photographers
Paul Murphy
Mark Wesley
Digital Agency
Publicis Modem
Advertising Agency
Publicis London
Account Handler
Selina Osborn
Client
Renault UK
Brand
Mégane

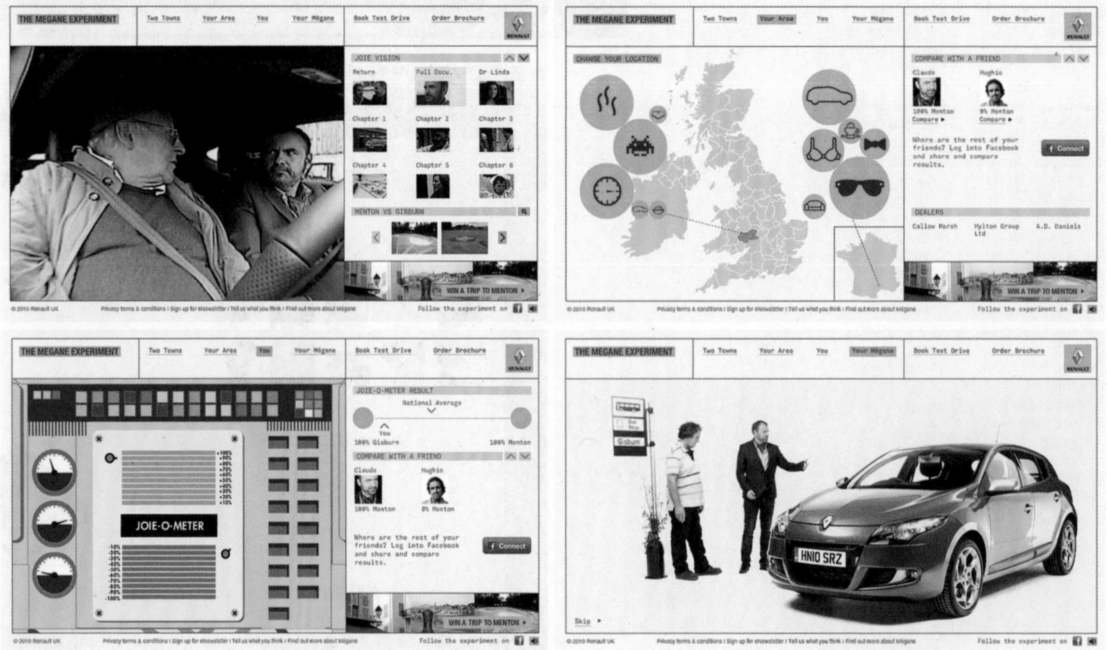
THE MEGANE EXPERIMENT
JOIE-O-METER
HNI0 SRZ

Direct Response/TV
& Cinema Advertising
The Red Brick Road
for Thinkbox

Dogs’ Home
This ad for Thinkbox, the marketing body for commercial TV in the UK, aimed to show the power of TV advertising. A couple are walking down a row of kennels in a dogs’ home when they come across a scruffy mongrel. Knowing he doesn’t stand a chance against the cuter dogs, he plays them his very own TV commercial. Once they’ve seen his household credentials, the couple are left in no doubt as to which dog to choose.

Art Director
Mark Slack
Copywriter
Gemma Phillips
Director
Andy McLeod
Creative Director
Justin Tindall
Producer
Kirsty Dye
Agency Producer
Charles Crisp
Set Designer
Mike Gunn
Special Effects
Jim Allen
Editor
Andy McGraw
Lighting Cameraperson
Stuart Graham
Music Composer
Randy Bachman
Music Arranger
Randy Bachman
Sound Designer
Parv Thind
Advertising Agency
The Red Brick Road
Production Company
Rattling Stick
Planner
Paul Hackett
Account Handlers
Lisa Pilbeam
Barbara Waite
Brand Manager
Lindsey Clay
Marketing Manager
Jamie Maskall
Client
Thinkbox

Introducing Harvey
Every home needs a Harvey

Direct Response/TV & Cinema Advertising
Jung von Matt/Spree for NBC Universal Global Networks Deutschland

Last Call
This interactive horror film for TV channel 13th Street is controlled by a member of the cinema audience. To participate, audience members submit their mobile phone numbers to a dedicated hotline when they buy their ticket. The moment the female protagonist finds a phone to call someone who might be able to help her, the film's controlling software contacts one of the submitted mobile phone numbers. Once the viewer picks up, he or she has to help her escape by choosing a path through an old sanatorium. Specially developed software transforms the participant's answers into specific instructions and launches an appropriate follow-up scene.

Art Directors
Marius Bell
Daniel Leverenz
Director
Milo
Creative Directors
Peter Gocht
Andreas Henke
Christian Kroll
Executive Creative Directors
Wolfgang Schneider
Mathias Stiller
Producers
Glenn Bernstein
Stephan Pauly
Katharina Strauss
Agency Producer
Julia Cramer
Sound Designer
Julian Holzapfel
Software Developer
Alexandra Ion
Post Production Producers
Simone Legner
Tim Tibor
Advertising Agency
Jung von Matt/Spree
Account Managers
Carlo Blatz
Jürgen Day
Brand Manager
Elmar Krick
Marketing Manager
Dirk Böhm
Client
NBC Universal Global Networks Deutschland
Brand
13th Street

NOTAUFNAHME

Direct Response/TV & Cinema Advertising
Three Drunk Monkeys for Guide Dogs NSW/ACT

The Guide Dog Interviews
We held a series of interviews with real candidates applying for a role that requires the same job dedication that is expected of a successful guide dog: working 24/7, never taking holidays, training for ten years and foregoing financial payment. We cut together the best moments for this ad and posted the most entertaining interviews on a Guide Dogs YouTube channel. The project made national news.

Art Director
Becky Alperstein
Copywriter
Henry Kember
Director
Paola Morabito
Creative Director
Noah Regan
Executive Creative Directors
Justin Drape
Scott Nowell
Producers
Susie Douglas
Tara Riddell
Executive Producer
Peter Grasse
Agency Producer
Helen Willis
Editor
Dan Lee
Sound Designer
Abigail Sie
Advertising Agency
Three Drunk Monkeys
Production Company
Curious Film
Recording Studio
Song Zu
Planner
Fiona Lake
Account Handler
Jill Large
Group Account Director
Carolyn Contois
Marketing Manager
Charles Ulm
Client
Guide Dogs NSW/ACT

We've found the perfect candidate

Direct Response/
Ambient
Del Campo Nazca Saatchi & Saatchi
for AbInbev

Andes Teletransporter
Andes is the leading beer in Mendoza, Argentina. Whilst men love to go to the bar to drink beer and have fun with friends, their girlfriends hate it when they do so. Our solution was Andes Teletransporter, a soundproof booth with a sound panel that recreates noises from lots of different environments. Men could sound like they were in a traffic jam or looking after their baby nephew, therefore being 'out' of the bar without actually leaving it. Meaning more happy men and fewer broken-up couples.

Art Director
Carlos Muller
Copywriter
Patricio del Sante
Designers
Juan Pedro Porcaro
Bruno Tortolano
Creative Director
Javier Campopiano
Executive Creative Directors
Maxi Itzkoff
Mariano Serkin
Direction
Nico & Martin
Producer
Caro Cordini
Agency Producers
Adrian Aspani
Patricio Martinez
Camilo Rojas
Director of Photography
Leandro Filloy
Advertising Agency
Del Campo Nazca
Saatchi & Saatchi
Production Company
Primo Buenos Aires
Sound Design
Supercharango
Editing
Cinecolor
Account Handler
Maria Lorena Pascual
Account Executive
Jaime Vidal
Regional Brand Managers
Pablo Firpo
Eduardo Palacios
Vice President of Marketing
Ricardo Fernandez
Client
AbInbev
Brand
Andes

ANDES
TELETRANSPORTER

Direct Response/
Ambient
Y&R Johannesburg
for Xbox

Need for Speed?
People who love speed are often caught by speed cameras, receiving their fines in the post. To take advantage of this, we designed banners reading 'Need for speed?' with the Xbox logo, which we placed opposite selected speed cameras. When drivers were caught by the cameras our banners appeared within the photos on the fines. This innovative use of the media, combining the ambient hijacking of the speed cameras and the commandeering of direct mail via the postal fines, perfectly isolated our target audience, allowing us to urge them to only put the pedal to the metal with Xbox.

Art Directors
Mbuso Ndlovu
Rory Welgemoed
Copywriter
Leon Kotze
Creative Directors
Michael Blore
Clinton Bridgeford
Liam Wielopolski
Photographer
Gerry Jennings
Producers
Gerry Jennings
Tracy Morton
Advertising Agency
Y&R Johannesburg
Planner
Sarah Britten
Account Handler
Lynton Asbury
Brand & Marketing Manager
Yvette van Rooyen
Client
Xbox
Brand
Xbox 360

Need for speed?
XBOX

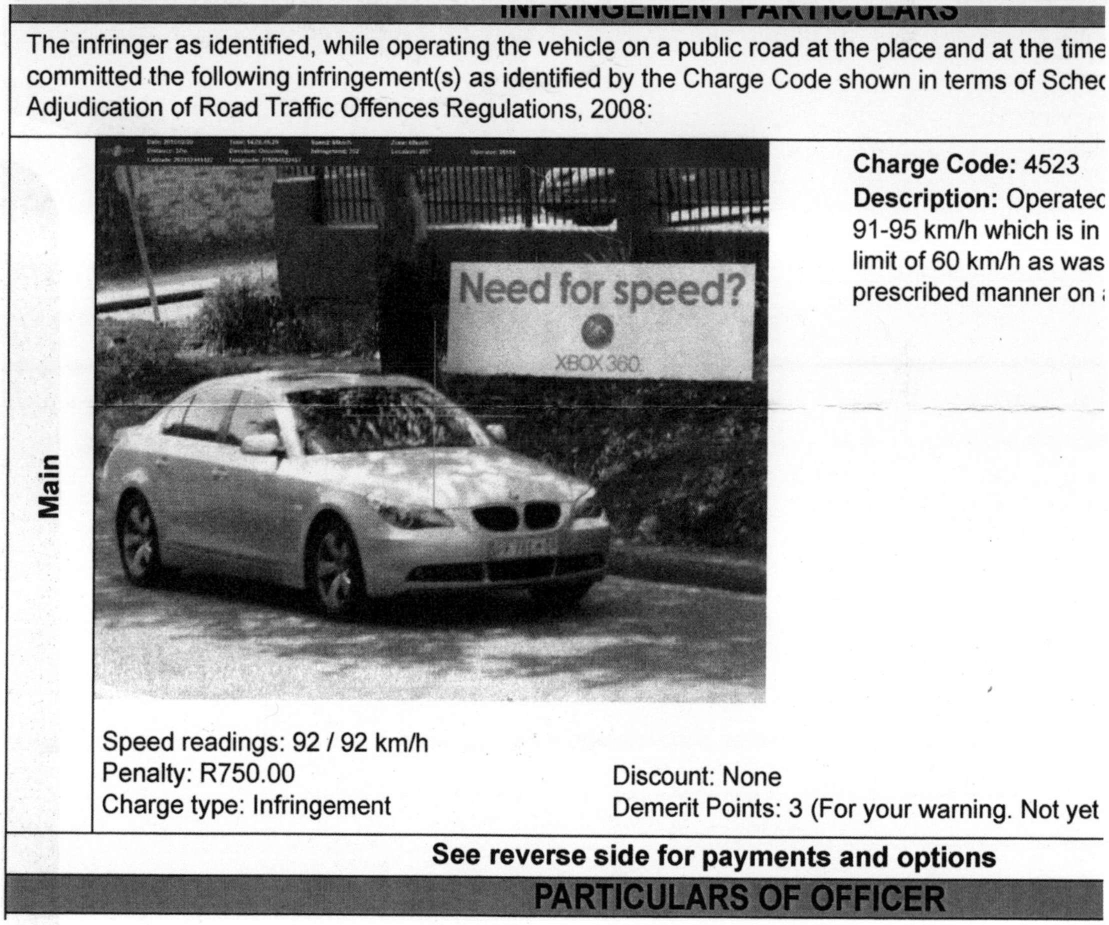

INFRINGEMENT PARTICULARS

The infringer as identified, while operating the vehicle on a public road at the place and at the time
committed the following infringement(s) as identified by the Charge Code shown in terms of Schec
Adjudication of Road Traffic Offences Regulations, 2008:

Main

Need for speed?
XBOX 360

Charge Code: 4523
Description: Operatec
91-95 km/h which is in
limit of 60 km/h as was
prescribed manner on a

Speed readings: 92 / 92 km/h
Penalty: R750.00
Charge type: Infringement
Discount: None
Demerit Points: 3 (For your warning. Not yet

See reverse side for payments and options

PARTICULARS OF OFFICER

Direct Response/
Ambient
iris worldwide
for Quit UK

The End
Smokers are increasingly immune to conventional anti-smoking approaches. The task was to reach them in a surprising way with a powerful and motivating message. Research showed that sedentary leisure activities indexed highly against long-term smokers, especially reading. Inserts were placed in the back pages of novels and electronically on Kindle. The insert looked like a page from the book and was placed in bookstores, second-hand book shops, charity shops, vending machines and Kindle-based publications.

Art Director
Silvia Sella
Copywriter
Nick Clement
Creative Director
Shaun Mcilrath
Deputy Creative Directors
Si Mannion
Ant Melder
Advertising Agency
iris worldwide
Marketing Manager
Glyn Mcintosh
Client
Quit UK

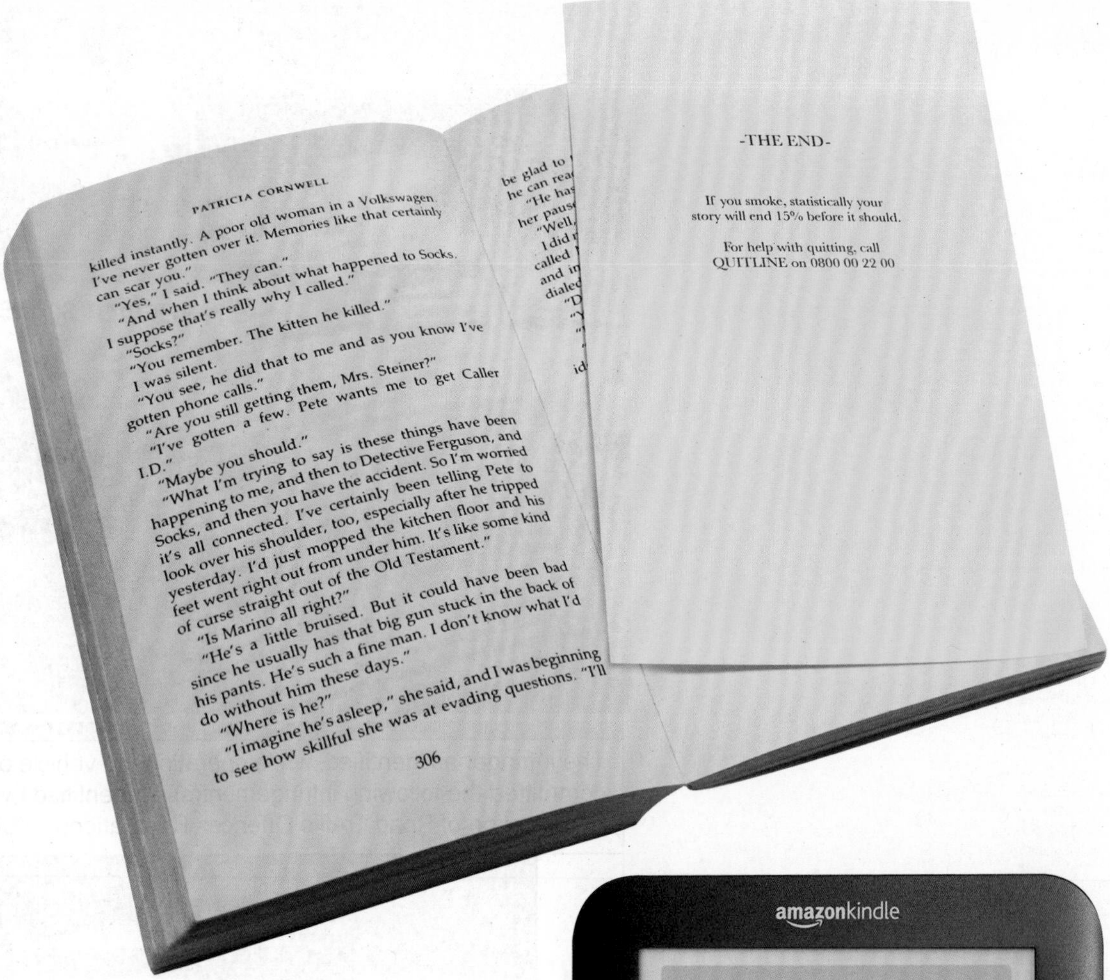
PATRICIA CORNWELL
killed instantly. A poor old woman in a Volkswagen.
I've never gotten over it. Memories like that certainly
can scar you."
"Yes," I said. "They can."
"And when I think about what happened to Socks.
I suppose that's really why I called."
"Socks?"
"You remember. The kitten he killed."
I was silent.
"You see, he did that to me and as you know I've
gotten phone calls."
"Are you still getting them, Mrs. Steiner?"
"I've gotten a few. Pete wants me to get Caller
I.D."
"Maybe you should."
"What I'm trying to say is these things have been
happening to me, and then to Detective Ferguson, and
Socks, and then you have the accident. So I'm worried
it's all connected. I've certainly been telling Pete to
look over his shoulder, too, especially after he tripped
yesterday. I'd just mopped the kitchen floor and his
feet went right out from under him. It's like some kind
of curse straight out of the Old Testament."
"Is Marino all right?"
"He's a little bruised. But it could have been bad
since he usually has that big gun stuck in the back of
his pants. He's such a fine man. I don't know what I'd
do without him these days."
"Where is he?"
"I imagine he's asleep," she said, and I was beginning
to see how skillful she was at evading questions. "I'll
306
-THE END-
If you smoke, statistically your
story will end 15% before it should.
For help with quitting, call
QUITLINE on 0800 00 22 00

amazonkindle
-THE END-
If you smoke, statistically your
story will end 15% before it should.
For help with quitting, call
QUITLINE on 0800 00 22 00
87%
Locations 3604-6
4135
Menu
Del
Sym
Alt
Home
Back

Direct Response/
Ambient
JWT New York for
Human Rights Watch

Burma
In 2010, Burma held its first elections in 20 years. But these elections are meaningless with more than 2,100 political prisoners remaining locked up in Burma's squalid prisons. Human Rights Watch created a campaign calling for the release of these innocent prisoners. A giant installation was built at New York's Grand Central Terminal. The installation featured a mock prison with 200 miniature cells and 2,000 pens in lieu of cell bars. Visitors could remove the pens to symbolically free the prisoners, and then use the pens to sign an onsite petition calling for their release.

Art Director
Roy Wisnu
Copywriter
Chris Swift
Photographers
Bill Bramswig
Platon
Executive Creative Director
Andrew Clarke
Head of Art
Aaron Padin
Chief Creative Officers
Harvey Marco
Peter Nicholson
Producers
Paul Charbonnier
John Minze
Tadd Ryan
Director of Production
Kit Liset
Director of Integrated Production
Clair Grupp
Director of Photography
Izzy Levine
Advertising Agency
JWT New York
Production Company
Cigar Box Studios
Account Executive
Lindsay Gash
Project Managers
Elaine Barker
Jessie Hoyt
Art Buyer
Elizabeth Corkery
Client
Human Rights Watch

Direct Response/ Ambient
TBWA\Hunt\Lascaris Johannesburg for the International Organisation for Migration

A Campaign Designed to Drop Sales
Like human traffickers, we targeted our most vulnerable people: children at school or just walking the streets of townships and impoverished urban slums. And just like the criminals, our most powerful weapon was deception. On the streets of their own neighbourhoods, we made men, women and children disappear. We created tunnels with false walls that precisely matched the real walls behind them, so that when people walked through, they disappeared – leaving onlookers wondering what had happened to them. Once people were informed of our anti-human trafficking message and given a toll-free number, they could pass the information on.

Art Director
Miguel Nunes
Copywriter
Charles Pantland
Photographers
Des Ellis
Rob Wilson
Creative Director
Vanessa Gibson
Executive Creative Director
Damon Stapleton
Producers
Sharon Cvetkovski
Sandra Gomes
Advertising Agency
TBWA\Hunt\Lascaris Johannesburg
Production Company
E-Graphics
Planner
Leigh-Anne Kazantzas
Account Handler
Sandra Chapman
Marketing Manager
Wambui Gititu
Client
International Organisation for Migration

UP TO
4 MILLION
PEOPLE
DISAPPEAR
EVERY
YEAR

UP TO
4 MILLION
PEOPLE
DISAPPEAR

Direct Response/
Ambient
Fallon Minneapolis
for H&R Block

Never Settle for Less
At a time of serious economic hardship, we wanted to prove that H&R Block gets people more money back on their tax returns; that, unlike in so many other parts of their lives, with us they didn't have to settle for less. So we journeyed to Greenback, Tennessee, and a diner in Los Angeles, and offered to redo the taxes of everyone there. Twenty days, 1,500 man-hours, and a few thousand cups of coffee later, we brought nearly $25,000 back to the people there – money they didn't even know they were owed.

Art Director
Scott O'Leary
Copywriter
Ryan Peck
Director of Photography
Salvatore Totino
Chief Creative Officer
Darren Spiller
Director
Mark Romanek
Editors
Erik Carlson
Michael Heldman
Producers
Ted Knutson
Lauren May
Aristides McGarry
Executive Producers
SueEllen Clair
Dave Morrison
Director of Integrated Production
Corey Esse
Sound Designer
Jeff Payne
Advertising Agency
Fallon Minneapolis
Production Company
Anonymous Content
Account Handlers
Chris Lawrence
Pete Leacock
Business Managers
Brent Larson
Brendan Lawrence
Client
H&R Block

$5344.

Direct Mail/Very Low Volume
Leo Burnett Guangzhou
for Haomei Aluminum

Noisy Outside Campaign
To promote Bucalus' reliable soundproof window systems, special musical cards were created in order to arouse interest in an engaging way. The fronts of the cards resemble Bucalus windows, and upon opening, noises commonly heard on the streets of China on a daily basis – from construction sites, crowds and traffic jams – hit the audience. Once they 'close the window', they shut out the urban noise completely.

Art Director
Chanson Li
Copywriter
Chong Kin
Photographer
Shiyuan Gao
Designer
Chanson Li
Creative Directors
Well Tan
Jennifer Wang
Darren Zhang
Executive Creative Director
Chong Kin
Advertising Agency
Leo Burnett Guangzhou
Account Handlers
Jon Leung
Nikko Zeng
Client
Haomei Aluminum
Brand
Bucalus

Reliable soundproof systems.
BUCALUS 贝克洛
BUCALUS 贝克洛

Reliable soundproof systems.
BUCALUS 贝克洛
BUCALUS 贝克洛

Direct Mail/Very Low Volume
TAXI Canada for Hazco

Blueprint
Authentic architectural drawings in authentic architectural tubes were sent to architectural firms to keep Hazco's demolition services 'front of mind' in prospective clients from the planning stage.

Art Director
Kelsey Horne
Copywriters
Nick Asik
Trent Burton
Photographer
Jason Stang
Designer
Kelsey Horne
Creative Director
Trent Burton
Print Producer
Marsha Walters
Advertising Agency
TAXI Canada
Account Handler
Ginny Wetmore
Client Business Developer
Amy Vizina
Client
Hazco

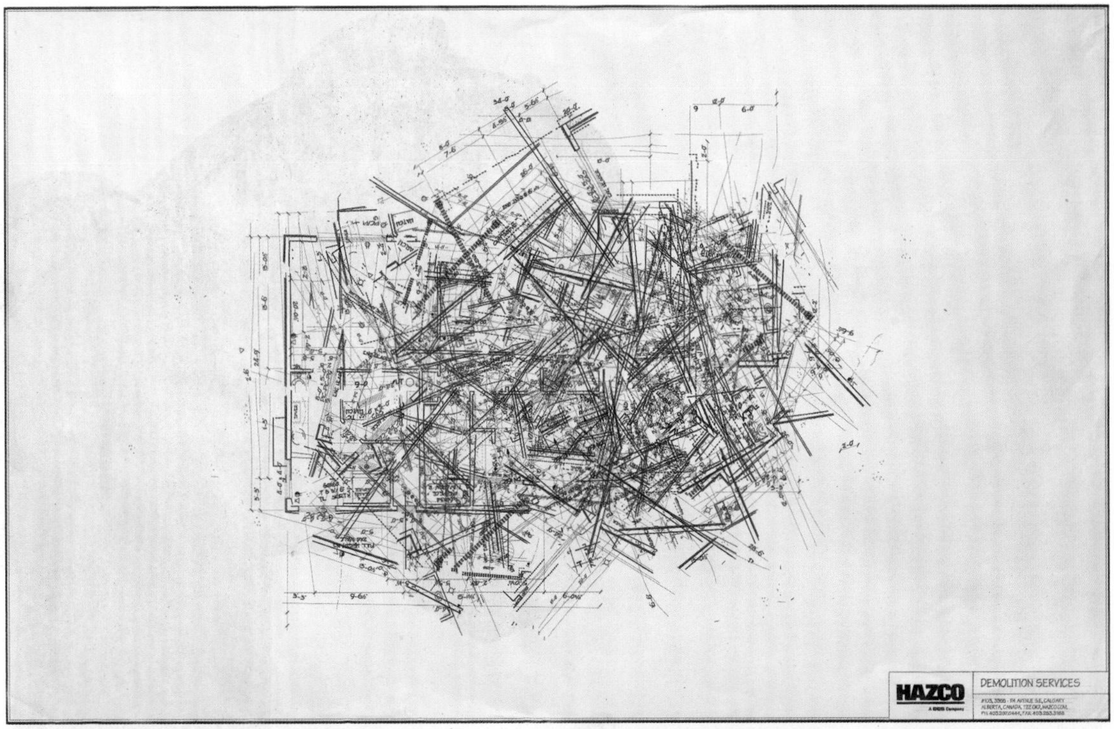
HAZCO
DEMOLITION SERVICES

HAZCO

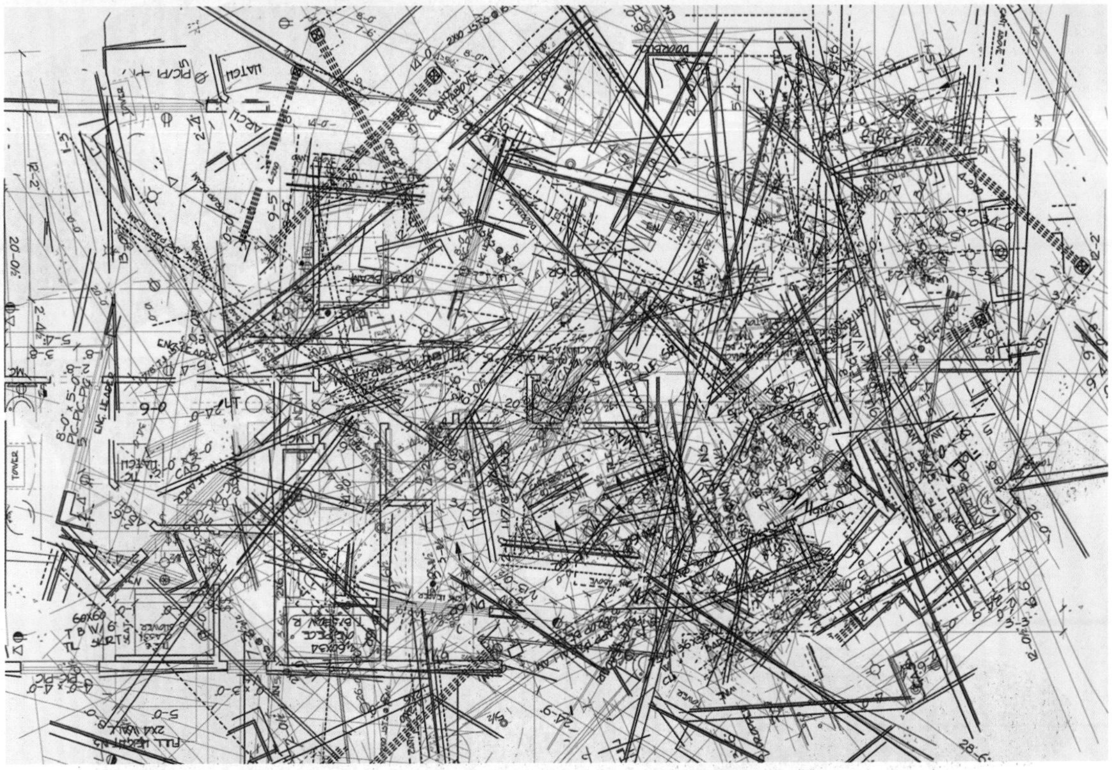

Direct Mail/
Very Low Volume
DDB Brasil
for Saxsofunny

Imaginary Musical Instruments
To make Saxsofunny the most well-known sound production company that produces advertising campaigns, we wanted to engage creative people in the market and create buzz. The target was Saxsofunny clients and prospects that had never experienced the company's services. The solution was to create cases for imaginary musical instruments conveying the message 'we play the sound you need', and reinforcing the idea that Saxsofunny complies with any client's sound needs. Inside the instrument's case was the company's portfolio, showing its vast experience in advertising campaigns.

Art Director
Max Geraldo
Copywriter
Aricio Fortes
Creative Directors
Guilherme Jahara
Marcelo Reis
Cassiano Saldanha
Sergio Valente
Advertising Agency
DDB Brasil
Marketing Manager
Zezinho Mutarelli
Client
Saxsofunny

WE PLAY THE SOUND YOU NEED.
Saxsofunny

Direct Mail/Low Volume
RMG Connect for
American Express

Mailing with a Novel
A Platinum Card owner read a novel in a hotel far from home, the last page of which was missing. She called American Express, and after a little while she received the page. To give Gold Card owners a taste of this fantastic service, we have sent them the page from the novel. It is from Daniel Kehlmann's bestseller 'Measuring the World'. The last word could not be more fitting: America.

Art Directors
Angela Brinkmann
Simone Werdel
Copywriter
Wolfgang Zimmerer
Creative Director
Wolfgang Zimmerer
Advertising Agency
RMG Connect
Senior Account Director
Kevin Bakracevic
Marketing Director
Andreas Krick
Marketing Manager
Marc Nägel
Client
American Express

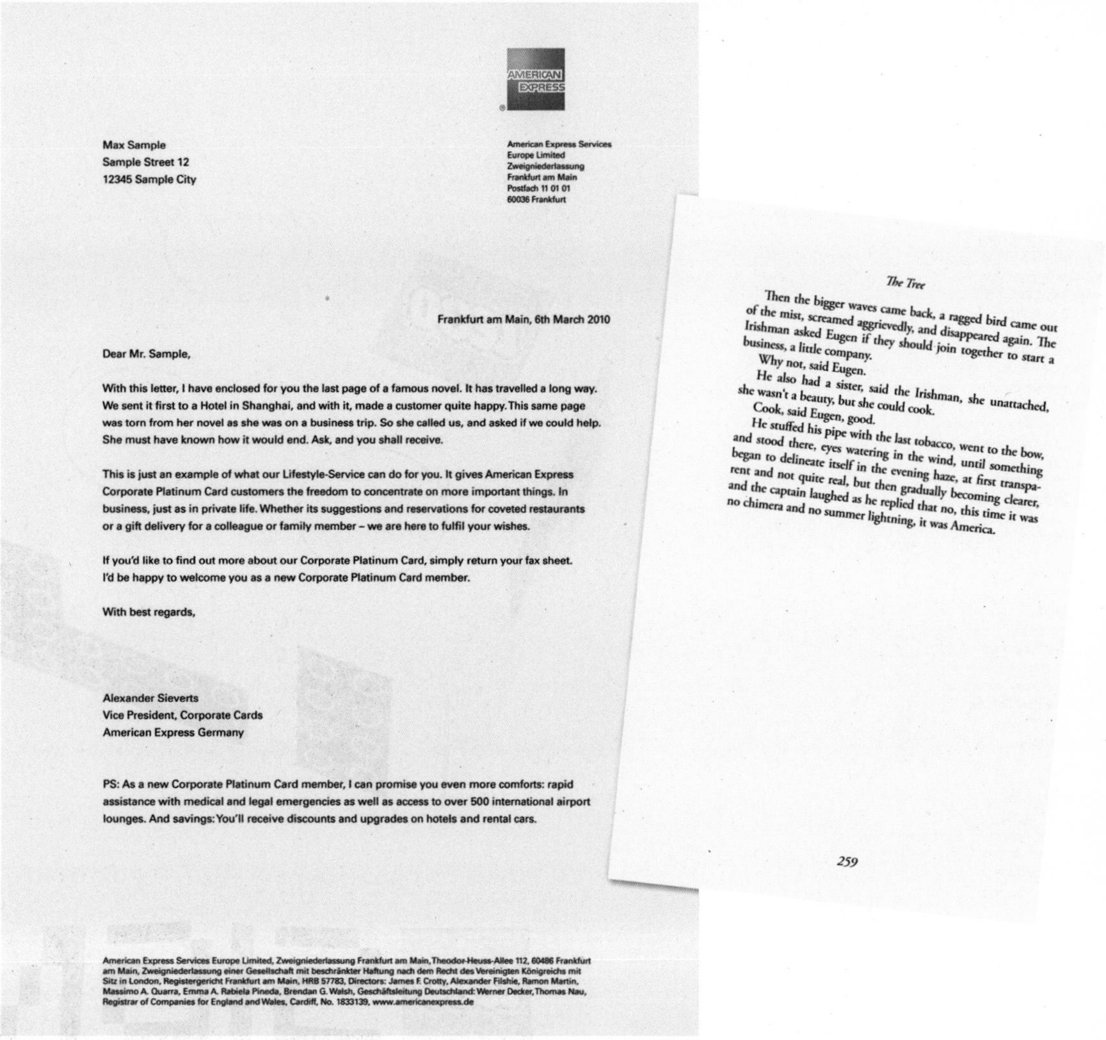

AMERICAN EXPRESS

Max Sample
Sample Street 12
12345 Sample City

American Express Services
Europe Limited
Zweigniederlassung
Frankfurt am Main
Postfach 11 01 01
60036 Frankfurt

Frankfurt am Main, 6th March 2010

Dear Mr. Sample,

With this letter, I have enclosed for you the last page of a famous novel. It has travelled a long way. We sent it first to a Hotel in Shanghai, and with it, made a customer quite happy. This same page was torn from her novel as she was on a business trip. So she called us, and asked if we could help. She must have known how it would end. Ask, and you shall receive.

This is just an example of what our Lifestyle-Service can do for you. It gives American Express Corporate Platinum Card customers the freedom to concentrate on more important things. In business, just as in private life. Whether its suggestions and reservations for coveted restaurants or a gift delivery for a colleague or family member – we are here to fulfil your wishes.

If you'd like to find out more about our Corporate Platinum Card, simply return your fax sheet. I'd be happy to welcome you as a new Corporate Platinum Card member.

With best regards,

Alexander Sieverts
Vice President, Corporate Cards
American Express Germany

PS: As a new Corporate Platinum Card member, I can promise you even more comforts: rapid assistance with medical and legal emergencies as well as access to over 500 international airport lounges. And savings: You'll receive discounts and upgrades on hotels and rental cars.

American Express Services Europe Limited, Zweigniederlassung Frankfurt am Main, Theodor-Heuss-Allee 112, 60486 Frankfurt am Main, Zweigniederlassung einer Gesellschaft mit beschränkter Haftung nach dem Recht des Vereinigten Königreichs mit Sitz in London, Registergericht Frankfurt am Main, HRB 57783, Directors: James F. Crotty, Alexander Filshie, Ramon Martin, Massimo A. Quarra, Emma A. Rabiela Pineda, Brendan G. Walsh, Geschäftsleitung Deutschland: Werner Decker, Thomas Nau, Registrar of Companies for England and Wales, Cardiff, No. 1833139, www.americanexpress.de

The Tree

Then the bigger waves came back, a ragged bird came out of the mist, screamed aggrievedly, and disappeared again. The Irishman asked Eugen if they should join together to start a business, a little company.

Why not, said Eugen.

He also had a sister, said the Irishman, she unattached, she wasn't a beauty, but she could cook.

Cook, said Eugen, good.

He stuffed his pipe with the last tobacco, went to the bow, and stood there, eyes watering in the wind, until something began to delineate itself in the evening haze, at first transparent and not quite real, but then gradually becoming clearer, and the captain laughed as he replied that no, this time it was no chimera and no summer lightning, it was America.

259

Direct Mail/Low Volume
Serviceplan Gruppe
for LEGO

LEGO Signs
It is hard for LEGO fans to keep track of existing and new products. So we sent out boxes in the shape of a LEGO brick containing some bricks and a plate. On an information sheet we explained to the recipients what they should do: take the plate and arrange the black and white bricks as any sign they could think of. Every possible sign represents a certain LEGO model. Then they were directed to go to www.lego-signs.com, turn on their webcam and hold the plate into the camera. They could then view the product in 360°.

Art Director
Till Diestel
Copywriter
Rudolf Novotny
Creative Directors
Maik Kaehler
Christoph Nann
Chief Creative Officer
Alexander Schill
Programmers
Gabriel Cuedo
Florian Feiler
Benjamin Heeb
Markus Mrugalla
Advertising Agency
Serviceplan Gruppe
Account Handlers
Tim Schnabel
Patrick Stehle
Marketing Manager
Katharina Sutch
Client
LEGO

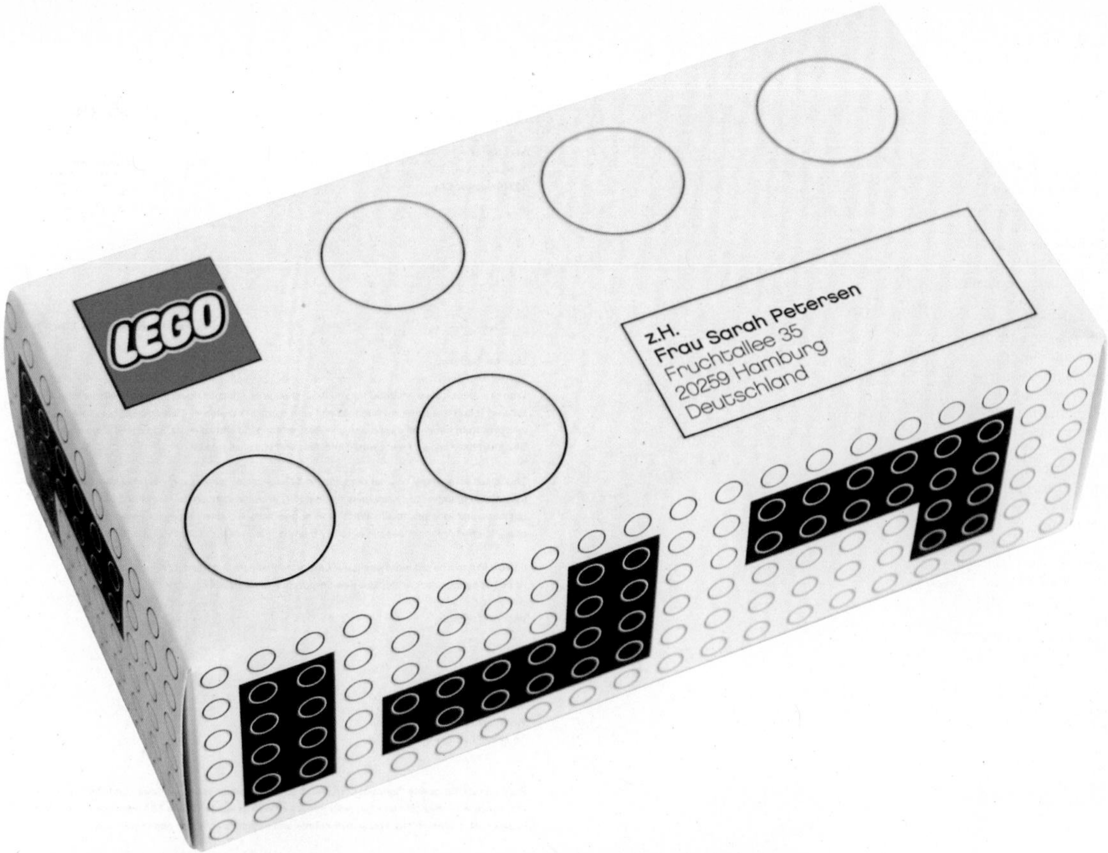
LEGO
z.H.
Frau Sarah Petersen
Fruchtallee 35
20259 Hamburg
Deutschland

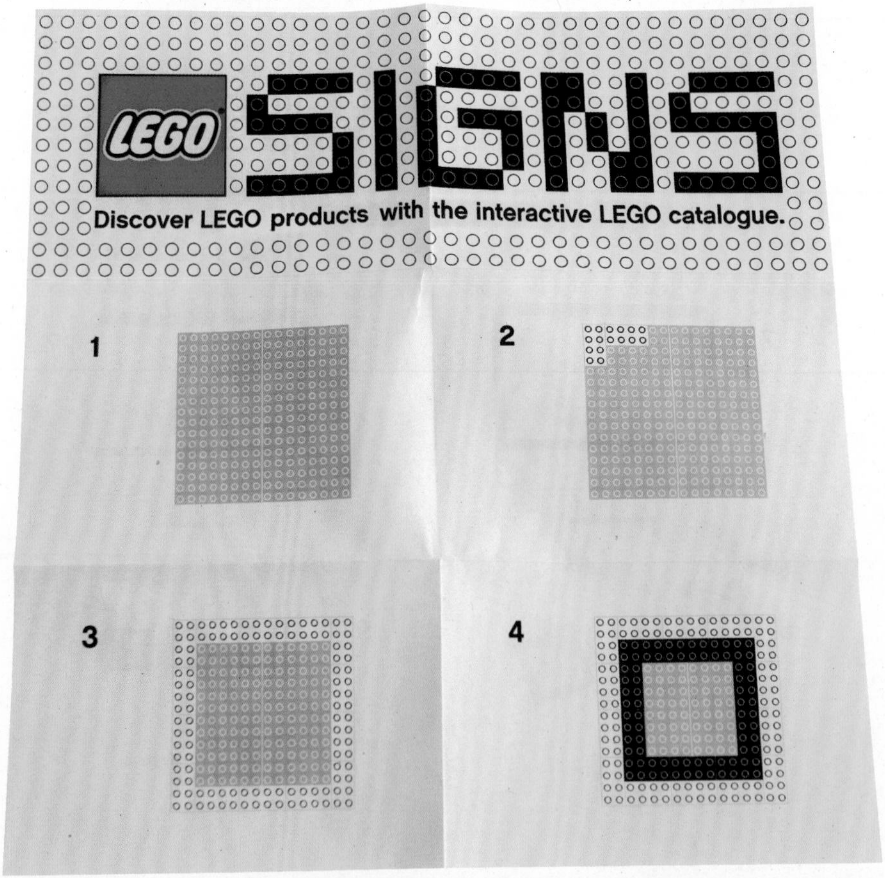
LEGO
SIGNS
Discover LEGO products with the interactive LEGO catalogue.
1
2
3
4

Direct Response/
Press & Poster
Grey Group Kuala Lumpur for the Malaysia Nature Society (MNS)

Belum Petition Campaign
Malaysia's Temengor Forest Reserve is over 130 million years old. Unfortunately only one-third is protected, which leaves the rest open to further destruction. To ensure that action is taken, the Malaysian Nature Society (MNS) and Body Shop Malaysia created a signature petition. We developed posters featuring signatures designed to look like animals. Displayed at Body Shop and MNS, they encouraged immediate participation as well as directing people to the website, where they could make a further difference.

Art Directors
Richard Chong
David Sin
Copywriter
Nadia McDonald
Illustrators
Vince Low
Jack Wong
Creative Director
David Sin
Print Producer
Peter Soo
Advertising Agency
Grey Group Kuala Lumpur
Client
Malaysia Nature Society (MNS)

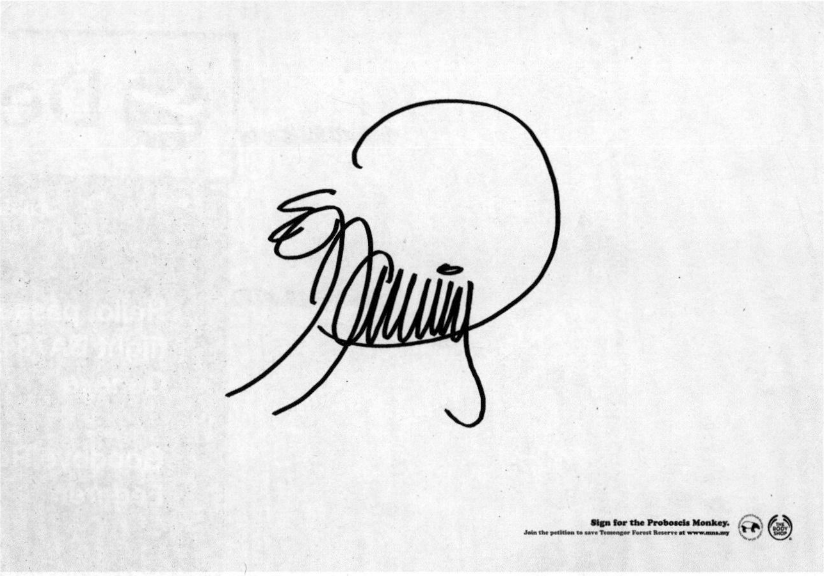
Sign for the Proboscis Monkey.

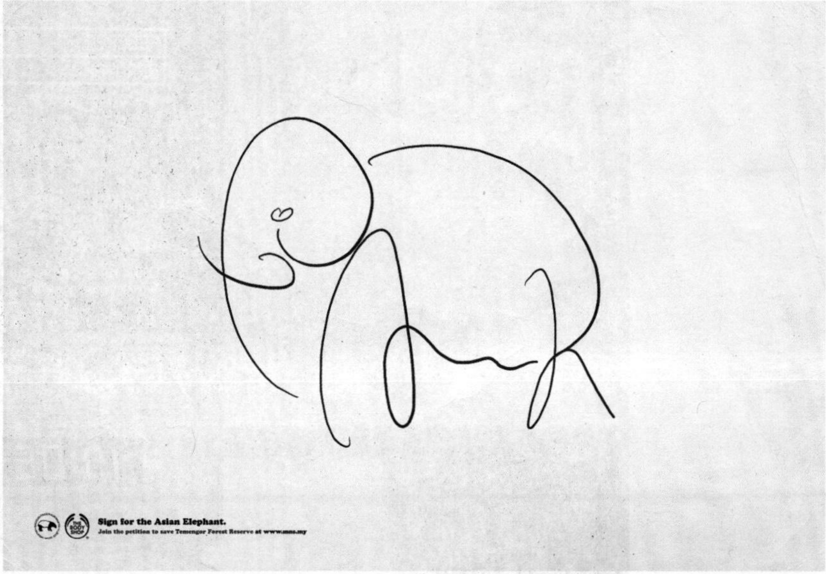
Sign for the Asian Elephant.

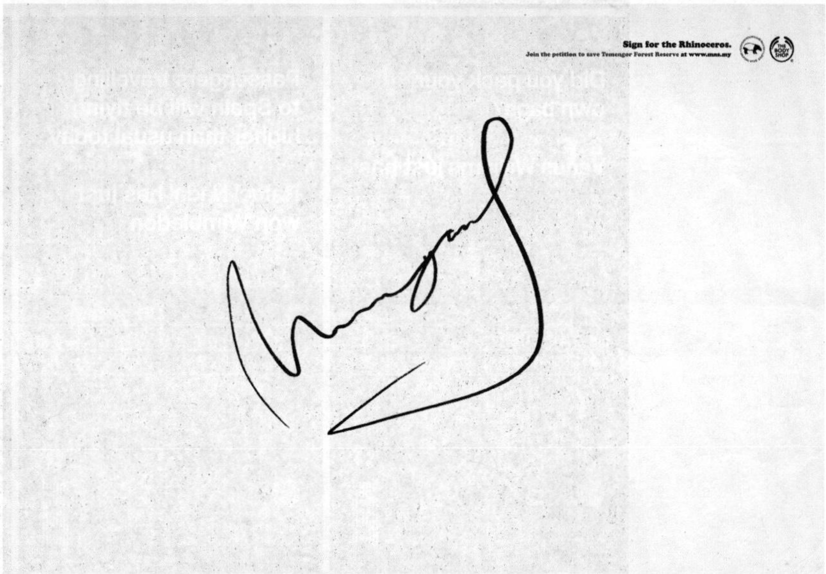
Sign for the Rhinoceros.

Direct Response/
Press & Poster
OgilvyOne London
for Lotus

Lotus T5
People thought that Lotus was just an email program. To demonstrate its ability to connect multiple sources of live data, we connected Heathrow's live air traffic control data and live scores from the Wimbledon Tennis Championship. We then mashed it up with players' nationalities to create live, useful, customised messages for departing passengers at Heathrow's Terminal Five. Over 300 different headlines appeared on 73 digital airport screens during the two weeks of the Wimbledon Tennis Championships.

Art Director
Kristal Knight
Copywriter
Katriona Gordon
Creative Directors
Emma de la Fosse
Charlie Wilson
Head of Digital Creative
Pavlos Themistocleous
Head of Technology
Mark Sweatman
Producer
Rosemary Faulkner
Advertising Agency
OgilvyOne London
Planner
Nina Mynk
Account Handler
Kieran Bradshaw
Account Director
Phil White
Brand Manager
Rosemary Brown
Client
Lotus
Brand
IBM

Departure
JCDecaux
Hello, passengers on flight BA734 to Geneva
Goodbye Roger Federer
Final score: Sets
FEDERER 1
BERDYCH 3
Lotus Knows more than you think
ibm.com/lotusknows/uk
IBM
SAMSUNG
17:06

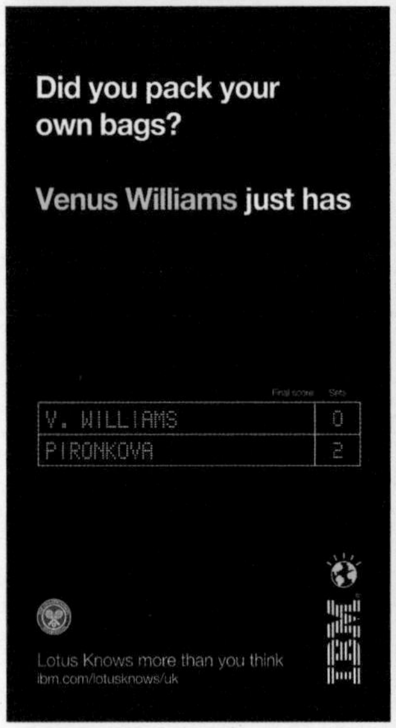
Did you pack your own bags?
Venus Williams just has
V. WILLIAMS 0
PIRONKOVA 2
Lotus Knows more than you think
ibm.com/lotusknows/uk
IBM

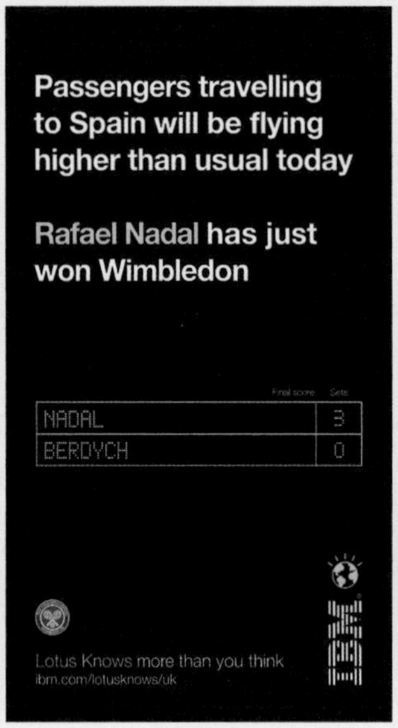
Passengers travelling to Spain will be flying higher than usual today
Rafael Nadal has just won Wimbledon
NADAL 3
BERDYCH 0
Lotus Knows more than you think
ibm.com/lotusknows/uk
IBM

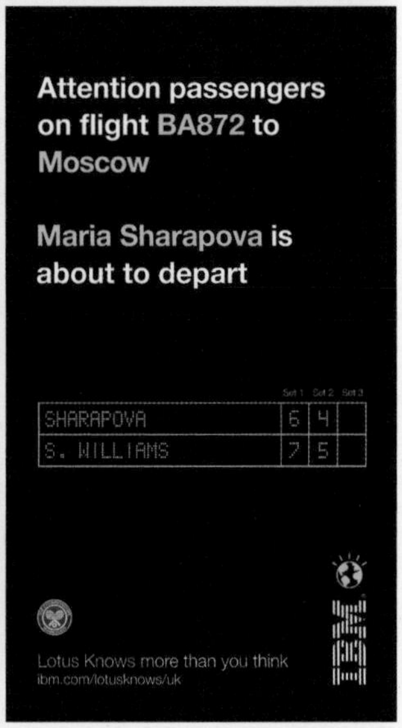
Attention passengers on flight BA872 to Moscow
Maria Sharapova is about to depart
SHARAPOVA 6 4
S. WILLIAMS 7 5
Lotus Knows more than you think
ibm.com/lotusknows/uk
IBM

Direct Response/
Press & Poster
Leo Burnett Toronto
for James Ready

James Ready Fall Billboard Campaign
In 2010 James Ready launched a billboard campaign in beer store parking lots to help its loyal drinkers save money for beer. The billboards promoted services like free stylish haircuts and free semi-professional portraits. On the specified dates, James Ready gave free haircuts to and took free portraits of all those who showed up. The money our drinkers saved on a haircut or a portrait could then be spent on James Ready Beer. Everybody wins and everybody drinks more James Ready beer.

Art Director
Anthony Chelvanathan
Copywriter
Steve Persico
Illustrator
Kimberley Pereira
Creative Directors
Lisa Greenberg
Judy John
Group Creative Directors
Sean Barlow
Paul Giannetta
Chief Creative Officer
Judy John
Print Producer
David Eades
Advertising Agency
Leo Burnett Toronto
Account Executive
Jordan Lane
Account Director
Natasha Dagenais
Group Account Director
David Buckspan
Client
James Ready

J.R. 5.5
JAMES READY 5.5
HELPING YOU SAVE $26.10 FOR J.R. BEER.
FREE ON OCT. 2
STYLISH HAIRCUTS!
RIGHT HERE
MUST BE LEGAL DRINKING AGE.

J.R. 5.5
JAMES READY 5.5
HELPING YOU SAVE $26.10 FOR J.R. BEER.
FREE ON SEPT. 25
SEMI-PROFESSIONAL PORTRAITS!
RIGHT HERE
MUST BE LEGAL DRINKING AGE.

Art Direction for Direct
TBWA\Hunt\Lascaris Johannesburg for
City Lodge Hotels

Cassette
To celebrate City Lodge's 25th anniversary as the agency's client, we took their customer-focused promise of 'Feel at Home' a step further and made City Lodge feel like we're all one family. We collected memories the same way a family would have 25 years ago – on home video. A scuffed and aged VHS sleeve contained a moulded cassette, which opened up to reveal two DVDs containing a reel of all the ads we'd done together, plus old, embarrassing photos from parties and other interactions the agency and client had had over the years.

Art Director
Adam Weber
Copywriter
Kamogelo Sesing
Designer
Bronwen Bridgeford
Creative Director
Adam Weber
Executive Creative Director
Damon Stapleton
Agency Producer
Sandra Gomes
Videographer
Fausto Becatti
Advertising Agency
TBWA\Hunt\Lascaris Johannesburg
Account Handler
Jenny Trenchard
Marketing Manager
Peter Schoeman
Client
City Lodge Hotels

E-180
TBWA\HUNT\LASCARIS
HLCL
HUNT LASCARIS CITY LODGE
VHS
E-180
25 YEARS OF MEMORIES
HIGH QUALITY VIDEO
HLCL
HUNT LASCARIS CITY LODGE
VHS
E-180
HISTORY REEL
HIGH QUALITY VIDEO
HLCL
HUNT LASCARIS CITY LODGE
HIGH QUALITY VIDEO
CITY LODGE
25 YEARS OF MEMORIES
E-180
VHS
Renee's Graduation
A-TEAM
M*A*S*H
Magnum P.I.
City Lodge 1985
TEAR HERE TO OPEN

Art Direction for Direct
M&C Saatchi London
for Transport for London

Heritage Campaign
There are hundreds of interesting stories about the tube. Our brief was to bring a few of them to life. We did this by weaving facts (and a bit of fiction) into the designs of historical seat covers. We then asked passengers to guess: Tube or False?

Art Director
Ned Corbett-Winder
Copywriter
Martin Latham
Typographer
Gareth Davies
Executive Creative Director
Graham Fink
Advertising Agency
M&C Saatchi London
Planner
Cressida O'Shea
Account Handler
Tom Vaughan
Group Marketing & Communications Manager
Nigel Hanlon
Director of Group Marketing
Chris MacLeod
Client
Transport for London
Brand
London Underground

The ghost of actor
William Terris is thought to
haunt Covent Garden station
MAYOR OF LONDON
Tube or False?
Find out at tfl.gov.uk/tubeorfalse
Transport for London
UNDERGROUND

ONE NIGHT DURING WW2
177,500 LONDONERS
SLEPT IN TUBE STATIONS
MAYOR OF LONDON
Tube or False?
Find out at tfl.gov.uk/tubeorfalse
Transport for London
UNDERGROUND

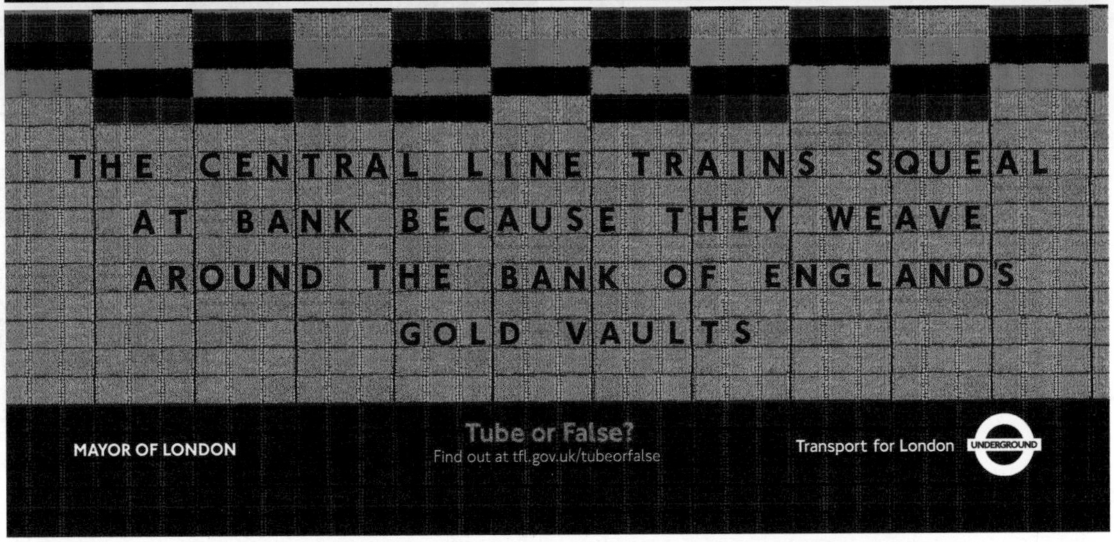
THE CENTRAL LINE TRAINS SQUEAL
AT BANK BECAUSE THEY WEAVE
AROUND THE BANK OF ENGLAND'S
GOLD VAULTS
MAYOR OF LONDON
Tube or False?
Find out at tfl.gov.uk/tubeorfalse
Transport for London
UNDERGROUND

Art Direction for Direct
Syfy

Being Human Press Kit
In Syfy's new drama series, 'Being Human', viewers are introduced to Aidan, Josh and Sally – three seemingly normal 20-somethings just trying to live normal lives. No small feat considering that they're actually a werewolf, a vampire and a ghost. It's an unusual series that posed an unusual challenge: getting members of the press to grasp the premise of the drama without defaulting to preconceptions of supernatural beings. To introduce 'Being Human' to the media, Syfy released a premium 'Guide to Being Human', a book with step-by-step instructions on how to fit in in the normal world.

Art Director
Edward Sherman
Copywriter
Diana Davis
Photographer
Jill Greenberg
Creative Director
William Lee
Executive Creative Director
Michael Engleman
Vice President, Creative Director
James Spence
Production Company
Syfy
Client
Syfy

BEING HUMAN
IS HARDER THAN IT LOOKS
TIPS, TRICKS & TOOLS FOR LIVING A NORMAL LIFE
Syfy Imagine Greater

MEND YOUR WAYS!
Don't let your WILD SIDE ruin another shirt!

B.Y.O.B.
BRING YOUR OWN BLOOD (JUST IN CASE)
BH
VOLUNTEER VICTIM

Writing for Direct
Ace Saatchi & Saatchi
for 2211 Works

Our Ride
Vespas are touring bikes. They are therefore specifically designed for the comfort of both the driver and the passenger, throughout the journey. So we created a campaign to position the bike as a genuine alternative to cars for all drivers and passengers. Hence 'Our Ride'. We then explored the journey two riders go on together, not just on the bike, but throughout life.

Copywriters
Andrew Petch
Tony Sarmiento
Art Directors
Gelo Lico
Andrew Petch
Biboy Royong
Creative Directors
Raoul Floresca
Andrew Petch
Advertising Agency
Ace Saatchi & Saatchi
Photography
Getty
Photolibrary
Brand Manager
Nani Juarez
Marketing Manager
Migs Oca
Client
2211 Works
Brand
Vespa

She was behind me when I started the band.
Behind me when I won my first fight.
Behind me when I aced my exams.
Behind me when I turned down college.
Behind me when I got our record deal.
Behind me when I chose not to fight.
Behind me when I quit the band.
Behind me when I took the job.
Behind me when her parents weren't.
Behind me when I wanted a small wedding.
Behind me when I wanted a big party.
Behind me when I wanted a 52" screen.
Behind me when I mortgaged the house.
Behind me when I started the company.
Behind me when I had the operation.
Behind me when my father died.
Behind me when my partners split.
Behind me when I nearly quit.
Behind me when I restored the business.
Behind me when I re-formed the band.
Behind me when I overtook the bus.
Vespa
Our ride

Visit our showroom at 2211 Works • 2211 Leon Guinto, Malate • Tel. 521-9581

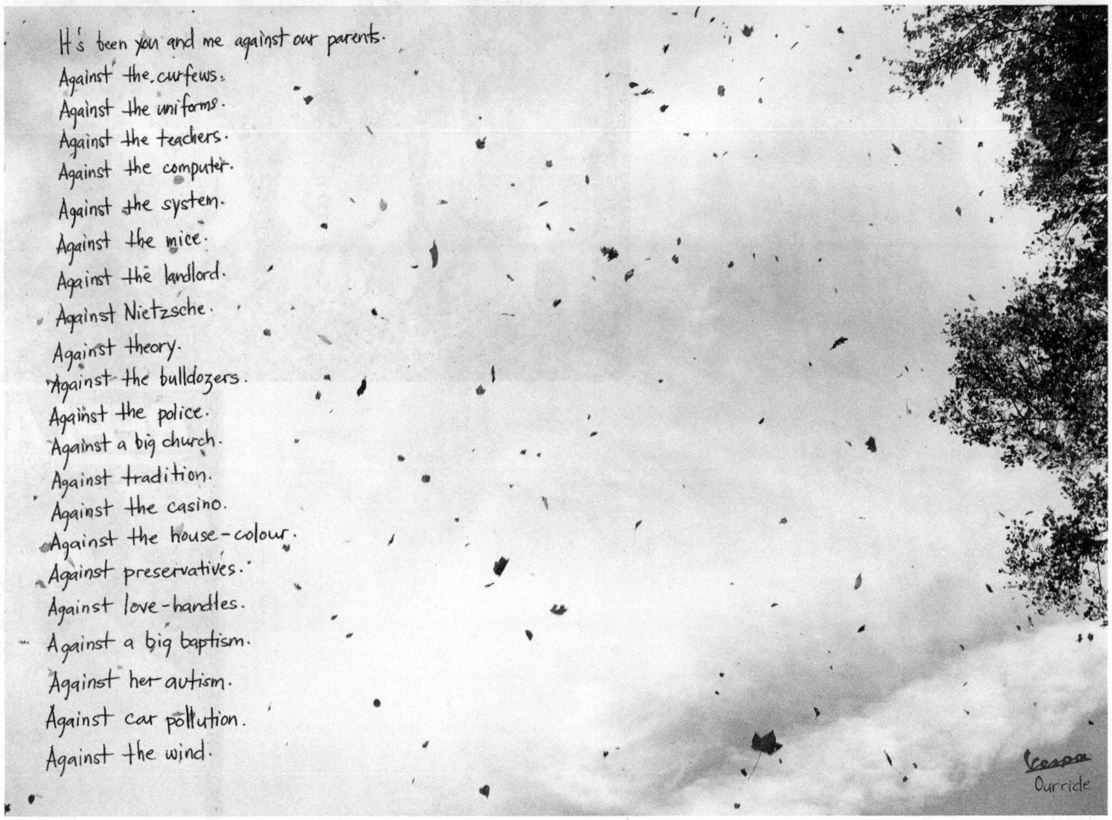
It's been you and me against our parents.
Against the curfews.
Against the uniforms.
Against the teachers.
Against the computer.
Against the system.
Against the mice.
Against the landlord.
Against Nietzsche.
Against theory.
Against the bulldozers.
Against the police.
Against a big church.
Against tradition.
Against the casino.
Against the house-colour.
Against preservatives.
Against love-handles.
Against a big baptism.
Against her autism.
Against car pollution.
Against the wind.
Vespa
Our ride

Visit our showroom at 2211 Works • 2211 Leon Guinto, Malate • Tel. 521-9581

● Yellow Pencil in Integrated & Earned Media

Integrated
TBWA\Chiat\Day Los Angeles for Gatorade

Gatorade REPLAY
Once athletes graduate from high school, their competitive activity declines significantly, as does their Gatorade consumption. We wanted to reignite the competitive spark among these athletes, extending Gatorade loyalty beyond their teen years. So we fuelled an opportunity every athlete dreams of – a second chance – by reuniting former high school teams to replay their original games five, ten, even 15 years later. There were thousands of submissions from teams nationwide, resulting in the formation of the Replay League. Due to demand, Replay goes international in 2011. The campaign was also selected in Earned Media.

Art Director
Brent Anderson
Copywriter
Steve Howard
Creative Directors
Brent Anderson
Steve Howard
Worldwide Creative Director
Lee Clow
Director
Loren Mendell
Producers
Graham Hughes
Tim Newfang
Senior Producer
Laura Mickelson
Executive Producers
H Read Jackson
Brian O'Rourke
Jimmy Smith
Editor
Curtis Roen
Web Content Editor
Greg Young
Advertising Agency
TBWA\Chiat\Day Los Angeles
Event Marketing
Paragon Marketing Group
Public Relations
Fleishman-Hillard
Group Planning Director
Scott MacMaster
Account Director
Amy Farias
Account Supervisor
Magdalena Huber
Worldwide Communications Director
Jeremy Miller
Client Manager of Branded Entertainment
Lauren Fritts
Client Senior Manager of Entertainment Marketing
Jill Kinney
Client
Gatorade

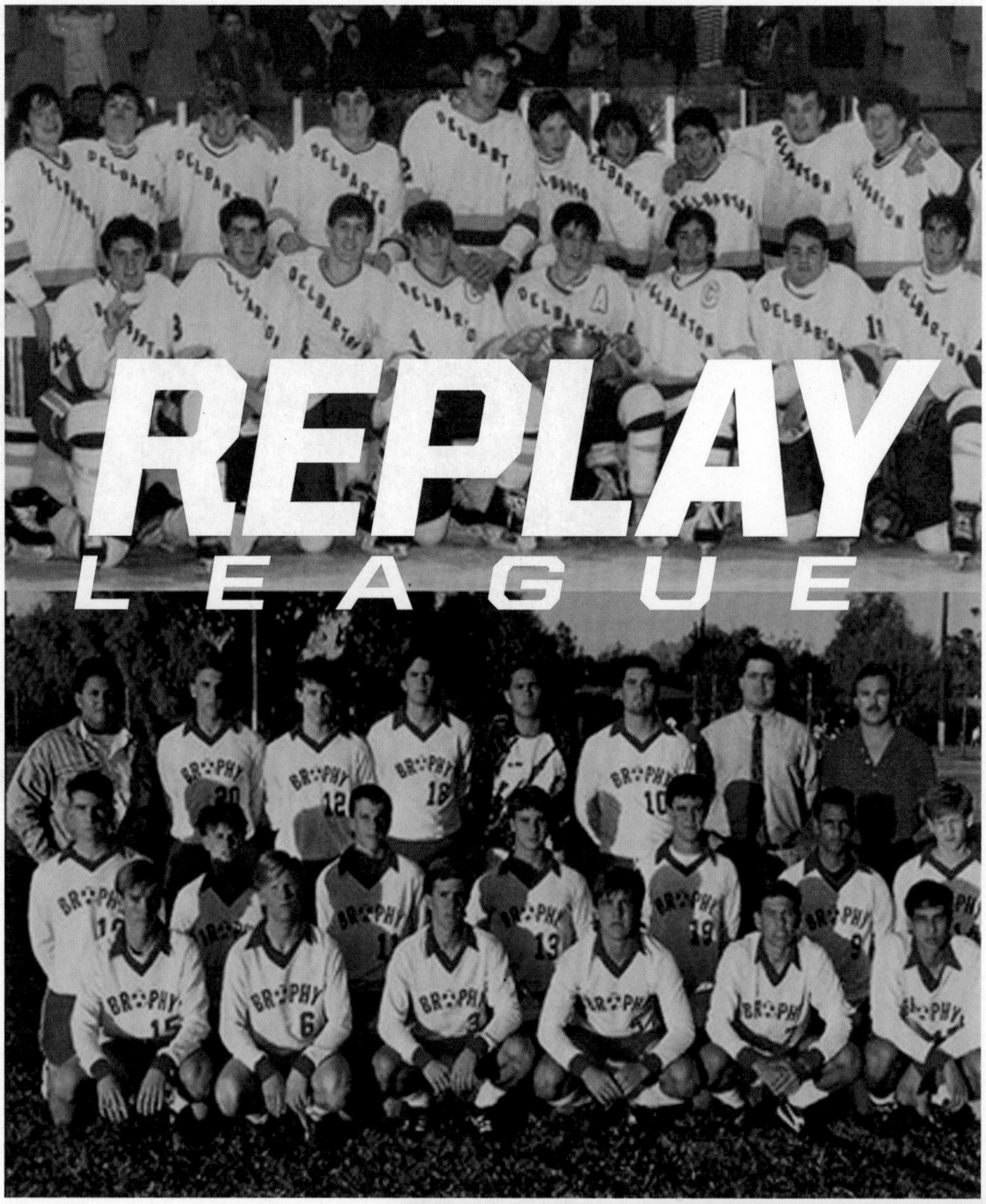
REPLAY
LEAGUE

REPLAY
FUELED BY G
WATCH
COMPETE
TRAIN
FACEBOOK
WORKOUTS
THE
REWIND YOURSELF
WORKOUTS
WARM UP
Remember high school? No? Well, you've at least seen pictures of your former self, right? Now we're talking. Your body was so much different then: Slimmer. Stronger. Sexier. Reclaim what was once yours and Rewind Yourself. Choose a workout that best matches your goals

REPLAY FUELED BY G
14
REPLAY
50
12

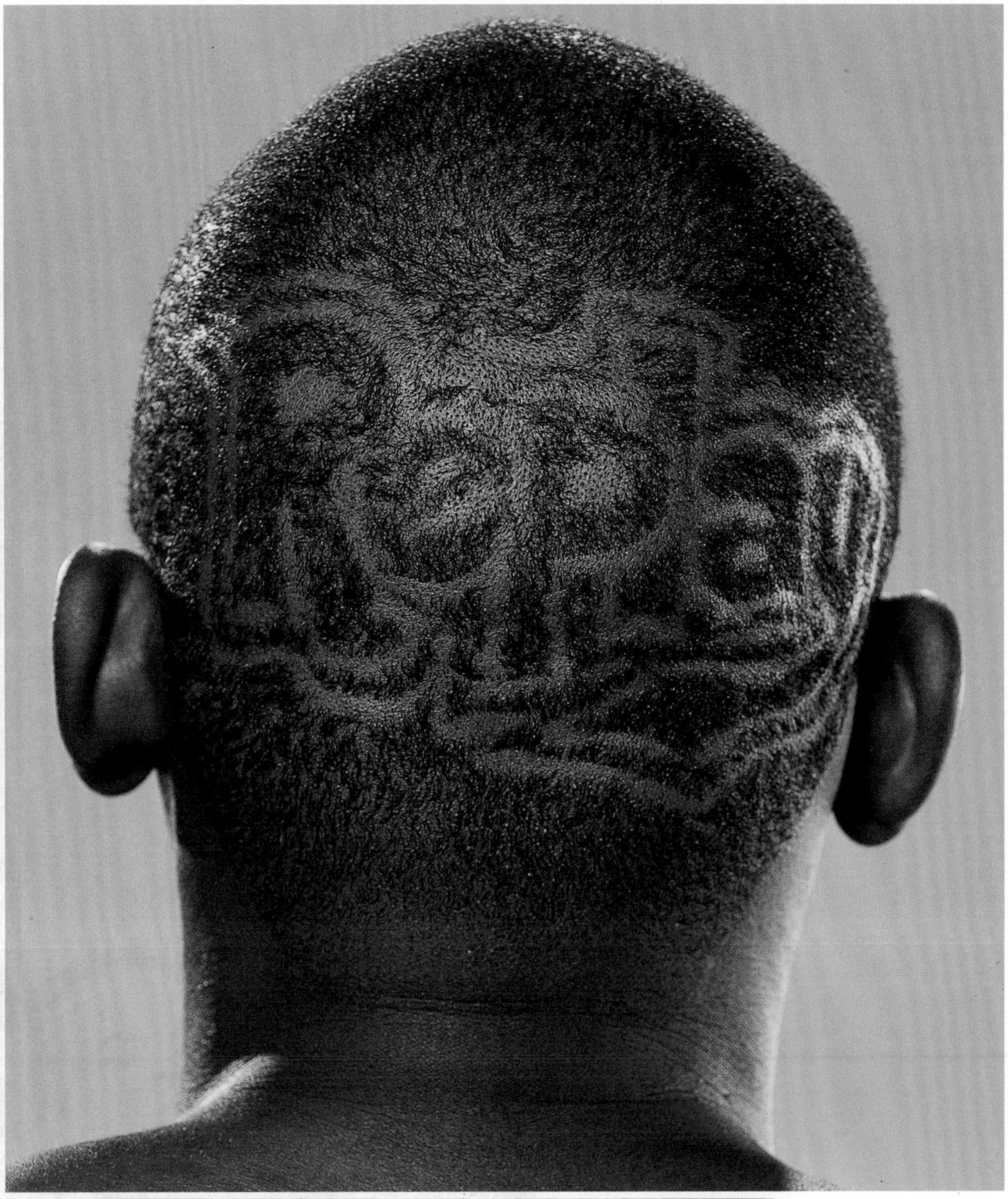

FUELED BY G

Yellow Pencil in Integrated & Earned Media

Integrated
Wieden+Kennedy Amsterdam for Nike

Write the Future
Every four years, the keys to football heaven are dangled in front of the international elite. One goal, one pass, one game saving tackle can be the difference between fame and forgotten. And what happens on the pitch in that split second has a ripple effect that goes beyond the match and the tournament. How could Nike dominate the world's biggest football tournament without being a sponsor? By owning the conversation around the event through a carefully orchestrated mix of social media, film, outdoor, retail and print. Nike achieved its goal by becoming the most shared online brand in 2010.

Advertising Agency
Wieden+Kennedy Amsterdam
Digital Agencies
AKQA Amsterdam
Wieden+Kennedy Amsterdam
Media Agencies
MindShare
Razorfish
Wieden+Kennedy Amsterdam
Client
Nike

NIKEFOOTBALL.COM

HOME
GALLERY
T&Cs
#NIKEFUTURE
WHO WILL WRITE THE FUTURE?
WRITE THE HEADLINE FOR THE PLAYER YOU THINK WILL WRITE THE FUTURE
CHOOSE YOUR PLAYER
COUNTRY
PLAYER
FILTER BY

CHANGE HISTORY WITH JUST ONE STRIKE
WRITE THE FUTURE
NIKEFOOTBALL.COM

Yellow Pencil in Integrated & Earned Media

Integrated
Wieden+Kennedy Portland for Old Spice

The Man Your Man Could Smell Like
The integrated 'Smell Like a Man, Man' campaign was created to spark a conversation about body wash and convince ladies that Old Spice is the only way to help their man truly smell like a man.

Art Directors
Craig Allen
Eric Kallman
Copywriters
Craig Allen
Eric Kallman
Creative Directors
Jason Bagley
Eric Baldwin
Executive Creative Directors
Mark Fitzloff
Susan Hoffman
Director
Tom Kuntz
Agency Producer
Erin Goodsell
Interactive Producer
Ann-Marie Harbour
Visual Effects Producer
Arielle Davis
Photographer
Danielle Levitt
Global Interactive Director
Iain Tait
Advertising Agency
Wieden+Kennedy Portland
Production Company
MJZ
Visual Effects Company
The Mill Los Angeles
Digital Strategist
Dean McBeth
Account Handlers
Michael Dalton
Diana Gonzalez
Jess Monsey
Art Buyer
Heather Smith-Harvey
Brand Manager
James Moorhead
Client
Old Spice

SMELL LIKE A MAN, MAN.
Old Spice

MAKE SURE
YOUR MAN SMELLS LIKE A MAN.
Old Spice

MAKE SURE
YOUR MAN SMELLS LIKE A MAN.
Old Spice

Yellow Pencil in Integrated & Earned Media

Integrated
Droga5 New York
for Bing

Decode Jay-Z with Bing
We teamed up with Microsoft's Bing and Jay-Z to launch his autobiography, 'Decoded'. Leading up to the book's release, each page was placed in a location relevant to its specific content. Pages appeared in hundreds of locations, using billboards and bus shelters, and sometimes innovative new media to tell the story. In total 200 executions were placed around the world, each a story in itself. Fans frantically searched to find all the pages of the book through an experience built on Bing Maps. By solving Jay-Z clues using Bing Search, they assembled the book online before it hit stores.

Art Director
Jon Kubik
Copywriters
Spencer Lavellee
Adam Noel
Designer
Jon Donaghy
Creative Directors
Kevin Brady
Neil Heymann
Duncan Marshall
Ted Royer
Nik Studzinski
Creative Chairman
David Droga
Digital Producer
Toph Brown
Senior Digital Producer
Andrew Allen
Director of Photography
Paul McGeiver
Print Producers
Mea Cole Tefka
Cliff Lewis
Advertising Agency
Droga5 New York
Public Relations
Sunshine, Sachs & Associates
Head of Print Services
Rob Lugo
Head of Integrated Production
Sally-Ann Dale
Director of Digital Strategy
Hashem Bajwa
Agency Chief Executive Officer
Andrew Essex
Account Handler
Shawn Mackoff
Marketing Managers
Ryan Cameron
Eric Hadley
Clients
Bing
Jay-Z
Brand
Decode Jay-Z with Bing

DECODE JAY-Z bing
DECODE THIS PAGE OF JAY-Z'S BOOK 'DECODED.' TEXT JYZCANOPY120 TO 44144 OR GO TO BING.COM/JAY-Z.

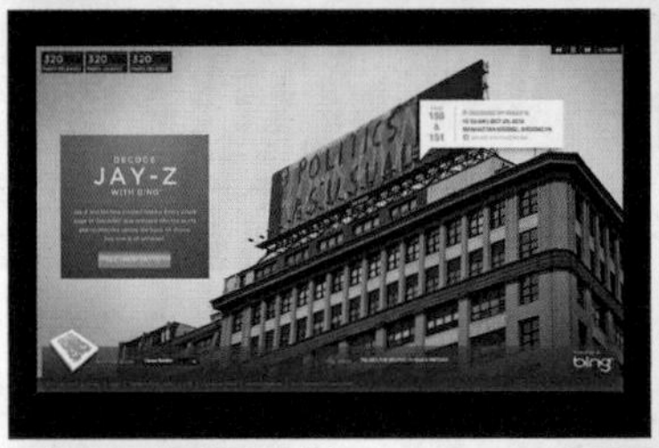

GUCCI for DECODED

Yellow Pencil in Integrated & Earned Media

Earned Media
CP+B for Domino's Pizza

Pizza Turnaround
Domino's came to us with a new pizza that scored better in taste tests than any they'd ever made. But 50 years of pushing speed and efficiency had eroded the brand's reputation for taste. We had a great new product our battered brand couldn't credibly announce. Our solution: come clean. Admit we'd made bad pizza in the past, prove we'd listened to people's complaints, and give them a reason to believe in us again. The resulting campaign yielded the largest quarterly same store sales increase in fast food history.

Art Directors
Brian Lambert
Andrew Lincoln
Copywriters
Roberto Lastra
Matt Talbot
Creative Directors
Tony Calcao
Mark Moll
Associate Creative Directors
Matt Denyer
Craig Miller
Chief Creative Officers
Jeff Benjamin
Andrew Keller
Rob Reilly
Director
Henry Alex Rubin
Experience Director
Matt Walsh
Interactive Technical Directors
Scott Prindle
Brian Skahan
Interactive Producers
Erica de Rozario
Chris Mele
Agency Producers
Christina Carter
Julie Vosburgh
Group Executive Producer
Ivan Perez-Armendariz
Advertising Agency
CP+B
Client
Domino's Pizza

Totally void of flavor.
Karen Kaiser
Marketing Director

Domino's Pizza
At the Door of Our Harshest Critics

THE BIG MONEY msnbc.com

Domino's learns Twitter, Facebook lessons

When you change product and ask people about it, they actually tell you

By Caitlin McDevitt
THE BIG MONEY
updated 1/20/2010 7:51:32 AM ET

Domino's Pizza recently launched the "Pizza Turnaround," a campaign in which it sought feedback from customers on how to improve its pizza recipe. It was a self-deprecating endeavor. The company paid to create a commercial featuring someone who says, "Domino's pizza crust to me is like cardboard." But through admitting that its product wasn't perfect, Domino's was promising to make it better. The campaign got lots of attention, so on the PR front, it seemed like it was relatively successful.

Nomination in Integrated & Earned Media

Earned Media
TBWA\London
for Wrigley

Updater
In 2010, Skittles had no TV budget, but still needed to reach its audience. So we detonated the brand on Facebook with the Super Mega Rainbow Updater. When a fan wrote his or her status update, it got sent to our live call centre and online broadcast station. Our staff recorded the update as an awesome film, then posted it back to the fan's wall in mere minutes. A total of 21,000 films were created in two weeks. And with every fan's update potentially seen and shared by all their Facebook friends – and viewable on our library and YouTube channel – the reach was immense.

Art Director
Andrew Bloom
Copywriter
Eric Tell
Creative Directors
Johan Dahlqvist
Lee Tan
Executive Creative Director
Mark Hunter
Director
Jakob Marky
Producer
James Cunningham
Agency Producer
Trudy Waldron
Web Producer
Sara-Lee Rost
Production Manager
Cathy Buchanan
Editor
James Norris
Advertising Agency
TBWA\London
Digital Production Company
Perfect Fools
Production Company
Academy Films
Sound Design
Wave
Planner
David Fryman
Account Manager
Justin Martin
Account Director
Emma Massey
Client
Wrigley
Brand
Skittles

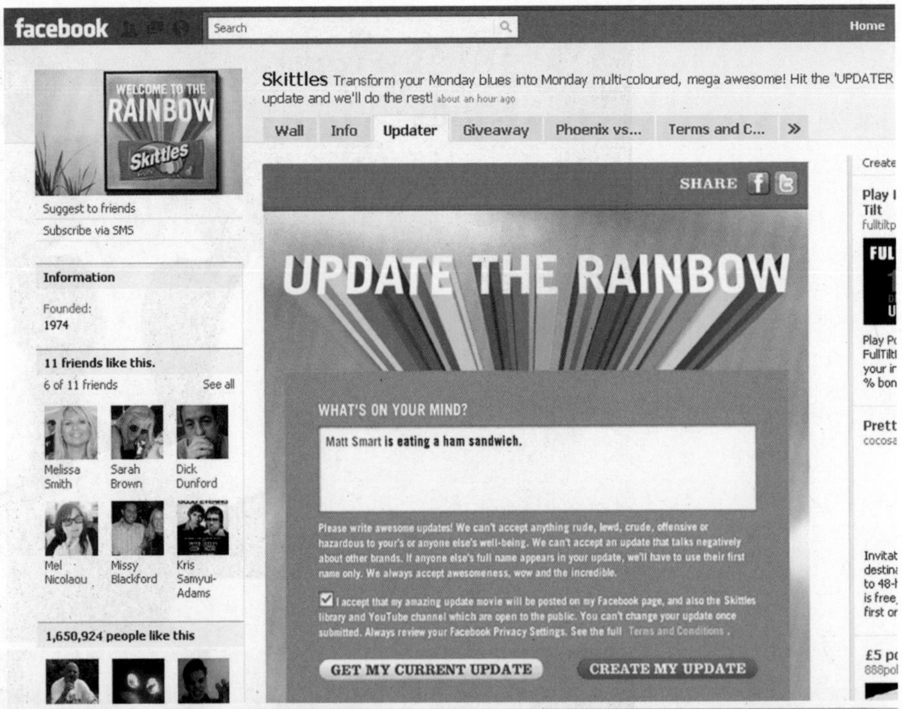
facebook
Search
Home
WELCOME TO THE RAINBOW
Skittles
Skittles Transform your Monday blues into Monday multi-coloured, mega awesome! Hit the 'UPDATER update and we'll do the rest! about an hour ago
Wall
Info
Updater
Giveaway
Phoenix vs...
Terms and C...
Suggest to friends
Subscribe via SMS
Information
Founded:
1974
11 friends like this.
6 of 11 friends
See all
Melissa Smith
Sarah Brown
Dick Dunford
Mel Nicolaou
Missy Blackford
Kris Samyui-Adams
1,650,924 people like this
SHARE
UPDATE THE RAINBOW
WHAT'S ON YOUR MIND?
Matt Smart is eating a ham sandwich.
GET MY CURRENT UPDATE
CREATE MY UPDATE

Drinking Water

facebook
Search
Home
Profile
Matt Smart
Edit My Profile
News Feed
Messages
Events
Friends
Uber clique
Create Group...
See All
Game Requests
Apps
More
Friends on Chat
News Feed
Top News · Most Recent 300+
Share: Status Photo Link Video
What's on your mind?
Matt Smart is eating a ham sandwich.
0:06 / 0:27
Matt Smart – Super Mega Rainbow Update
www.youtube.com
The Super Mega Rainbow Updater from Skittles turns your normal update into an awesome film about you! Try it today at http://updatetherainbow.co.uk
November 12 at 12:55am via Update The Rainbow · Like · Comment · SuperMega Rainbow Updater
Events
What are you planning?
4 event invitations
Red Lion Pub Quiz
Thursday 8:00pm
Erik Tell's birthday. See All
Sponsored
Grow your business
Requests
4 group invitations
17 Page suggestions
2 game requests
Pokes
Daniel Colledge · Poke Back
Jonathan Colledge · Poke Back

● Nomination in Integrated & Earned Media

Earned Media
R/GA New York for Innovative Thunder

Pay with a Tweet
How do you promote a book that no one knows exists? The writers of 'Oh My God What Happened and What Should I Do?' had a dilemma. How would they reach the masses? Pay with a Tweet is the first social networking payment system, where people pay with the value of their social network. People who have something to sell simply add the Pay with a Tweet button to their site, and people who want the product simply click on the button and tweet about it. So Pay with a Tweet became a whole new way to trade content online.

Associate Creative Directors
Leif Abraham
Christian Behrendt
Programmers
Alexander Milde
John Tubert
Advertising Agency
R/GA New York
Client
Innovative Thunder

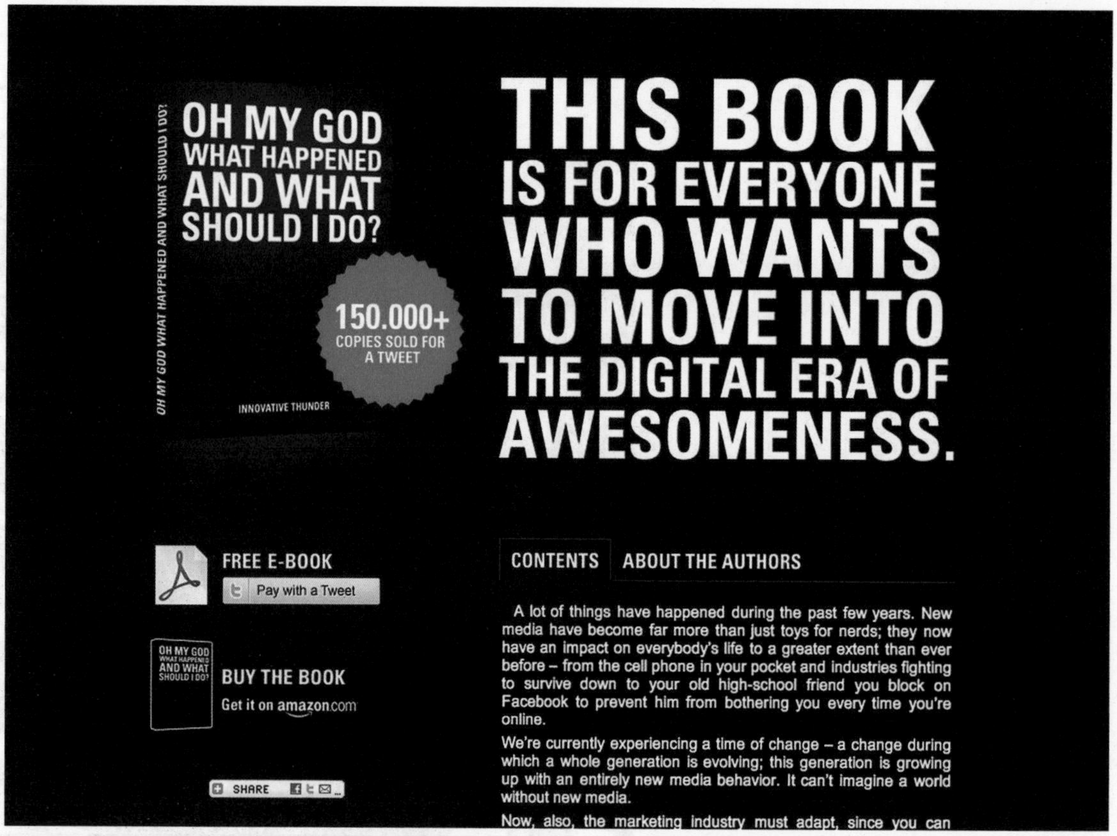
OH MY GOD WHAT HAPPENED AND WHAT SHOULD I DO?
OH MY GOD WHAT HAPPENED AND WHAT SHOULD I DO?
150.000+ COPIES SOLD FOR A TWEET
INNOVATIVE THUNDER
THIS BOOK IS FOR EVERYONE WHO WANTS TO MOVE INTO THE DIGITAL ERA OF AWESOMENESS.
FREE E-BOOK
Pay with a Tweet
BUY THE BOOK
Get it on amazon.com
SHARE
CONTENTS
ABOUT THE AUTHORS
A lot of things have happened during the past few years. New media have become far more than just toys for nerds; they now have an impact on everybody's life to a greater extent than ever before – from the cell phone in your pocket and industries fighting to survive down to your old high-school friend you block on Facebook to prevent him from bothering you every time you're online.
We're currently experiencing a time of change – a change during which a whole generation is evolving; this generation is growing up with an entirely new media behavior. It can't imagine a world without new media.
Now, also, the marketing industry must adapt, since you can

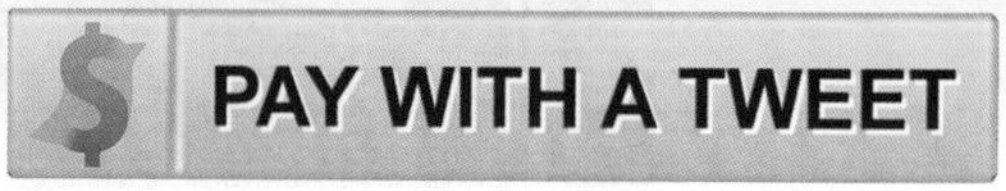
PAY WITH A TWEET

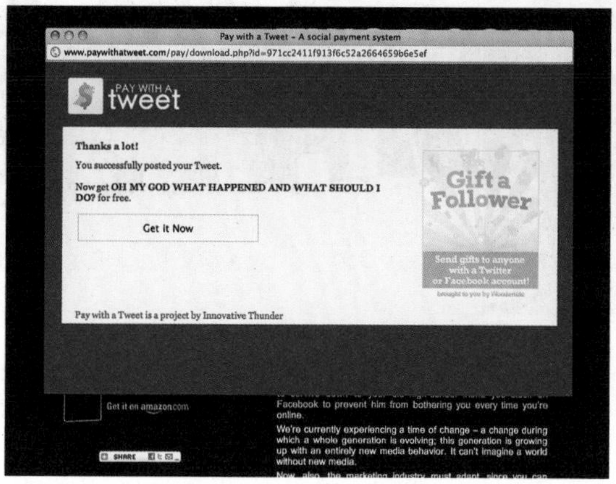
Pay with a Tweet - A social payment system
PAY WITH A tweet
Thanks a lot!
You successfully posted your Tweet.
Now get OH MY GOD WHAT HAPPENED AND WHAT SHOULD I DO? for free.
Get it Now
Gift a Follower
Send gifts to anyone with a Twitter or Facebook account!
Pay with a Tweet is a project by Innovative Thunder

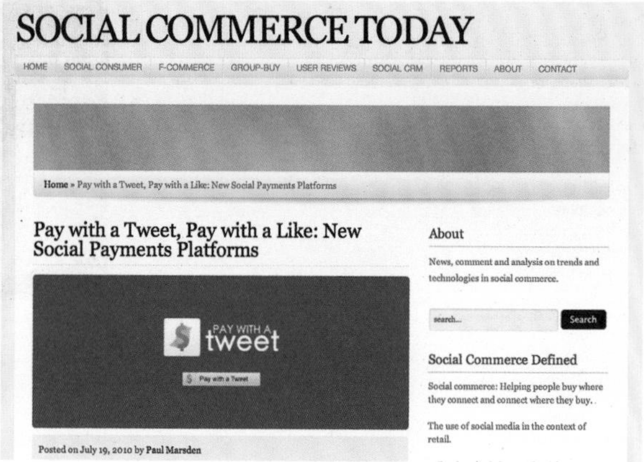
SOCIAL COMMERCE TODAY
HOME
SOCIAL CONSUMER
F-COMMERCE
GROUP-BUY
USER REVIEWS
SOCIAL CRM
REPORTS
ABOUT
CONTACT
Home » Pay with a Tweet, Pay with a Like: New Social Payments Platforms
Pay with a Tweet, Pay with a Like: New Social Payments Platforms
PAY WITH A tweet
About
News, comment and analysis on trends and technologies in social commerce.
Search
Social Commerce Defined
Social commerce: Helping people buy where they connect and connect where they buy.
The use of social media in the context of retail.
Posted on July 19, 2010 by Paul Marsden

Integrated
Clemenger BBDO Melbourne for Guide Dogs Australia

Support Scent
Guide Dogs Australia's sole purpose is ending the isolation that can result from being blind. So when creating marketing support for its cause, we thought it absolutely vital not to exclude the blind. Anything requiring sight, such as ribbons, was considered unacceptable. Therefore we created something that appeals to another sense entirely – smell. A unisex fragrance called Support Scent was born, which actually allows the blind to recognise support around them. Priced at $5, all proceeds from the scent go to the charity. Now a whole new support base for the blind has emerged, with a 33 per cent lift in fundraising upon launch.

Art Director
Tom Martin
Copywriter
Julian Schreiber
Designer
Beci Orpin
Interactive Designer
Sam Hodgson
Digital Creative Director
Damian Royce
Executive Creative Director
Ant Keogh
Creative Chairman
James McGrath
Directors
Micca Delaney
Amy Gerbhardt
Producers
Jane Liscombe
Allison Lockwood
Agency Producer
Sevda Cemo
Editors
Micca Delaney
Jack Hutchings
Megan Voevodin
Photographer
David Rosendale
Advertising Agency
Clemenger BBDO Melbourne
Production Companies
Exit Films
Kit Cosmetics
Sound Design
Flagstaff Studios Melbourne
Project Manager
Sevda Cemo
Strategic Planner
Mike Hyde
Account Directors
Nici Henningsen
Ricci Meldrum
Client
Guide Dogs Australia

SUPPORT SCENT
SUPPORT SCENT
Guide Dogs
Australia
kit

Beauty
with the
feel-good
factor.

HOW DO YOU SHOW
SUPPORT FOR SOMEONE
WHO CAN'T SEE?
SUPPORT SCENT

Integrated
Colenso BBDO
for Yellow Pages
New Zealand

Yellow Chocolate
In February 2010 we launched the fastest selling chocolate bar in New Zealand. But we weren't selling chocolate. Five months earlier we had given an average New Zealander, Josh, a task: to create a chocolate bar that tasted of yellow. He could only use businesses from the Yellow Pages to help. He needed to sort out the flavour, packaging, manufacturing, distribution and marketing, and then launch it. He succeeded. It outsold favourite brands like Snickers two to one. People queued to pay $2 for our piece of Yellow Pages direct marketing. And it became the most talked about campaign in New Zealand.

Art Directors
Steve Cochran
Aaron Turk
Copywriters
Steve Cochran
Aaron Turk
Creative Directors
Steve Cochran
Dave King
Aaron Turk
Executive Creative Director
Nick Worthington
Digital Creative Director
Aaron Goldring
Director
Chris Graham
Producer
Tanya Haitoua-Cathro
Digital Producer
Amanda Theobold
Agency Producer
Paul Courtney
Editor
Paul Maxwell
Photographer
Stephen Langdon
Retoucher
Kevin Hyde
Advertising Agency
Colenso BBDO
Production Company
Good Life Films
Sound Design
Native Audio
Planner
James Hurman
Account Directors
Terri Cumiskey
Rachel Turner
Group Account Director
Andrew Holt
Account Manager
Katya Urlwin
Marketing Director
Kellie Nathan
Client
Yellow Pages
New Zealand
Brand
Yellow

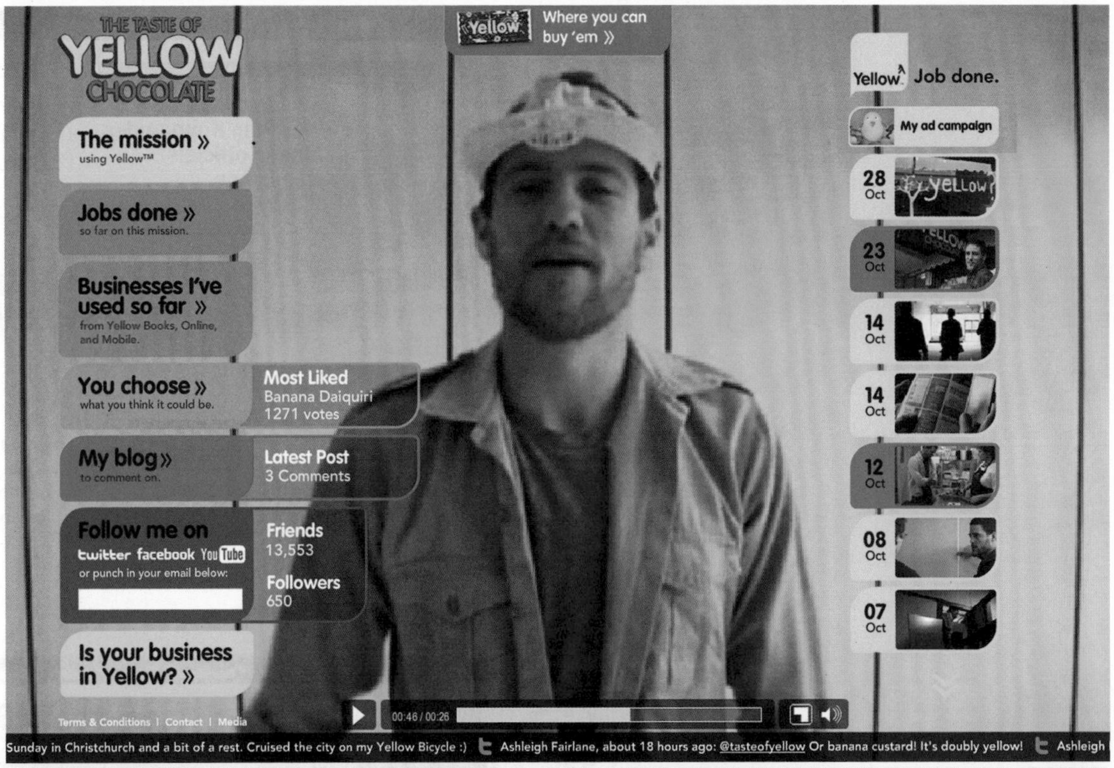
THE TASTE OF YELLOW CHOCOLATE
Where you can buy 'em »
Yellow Job done.
My ad campaign
The mission » using Yellow™
Jobs done » so far on this mission.
Businesses I've used so far » from Yellow Books, Online, and Mobile.
You choose » what you think it could be.
Most Liked Banana Daiquiri 1271 votes
My blog » to comment on.
Latest Post 3 Comments
Follow me on twitter facebook YouTube or punch in your email below:
Friends 13,553
Followers 650
Is your business in Yellow? »
28 Oct
23 Oct
14 Oct
14 Oct
12 Oct
08 Oct
07 Oct
Terms & Conditions | Contact | Media
00:46 / 00:26
Sunday in Christchurch and a bit of a rest. Cruised the city on my Yellow Bicycle :) Ashleigh Fairlane, about 18 hours ago: @tasteofyellow Or banana custard! It's doubly yellow! Ashleigh

Yellow

APN
Latest tweet from Josh as he uses businesses in Yellow™ to create a yellow tasting chocolate bar.
TASTEOFYELLOW: ...SORTED! I HAVE A TEMPORARY PERSONAL
yellowchocolate.co.nz

Integrated
McCann Worldgroup Hong Kong for Metro Publishing Hong Kong

Future Daily on April Fool
Thirteen years after the handover to China, Hong Kong is facing increasing threats to press freedom. This campaign was designed to alarm the public about the worrying decline of freedom of speech in Hong Kong. We created a website and asked people to write what they thought would make the headlines in 18 years. We then published the most voted-for stories, word for word, in a special edition paper that we distributed on April Fool's Day. The futuristic theme and April Fool launch acted as a smokescreen for people to express their heartfelt opinions.

Art Directors
Gary Lam
Joseph Mok
Copywriters
April Fang
Law Chi Hang
Spring Liu
Creative Directors
Law Chi Hang
Joseph Mok
Stanley Wong
Executive Creative Director
Nick Lim
Chief Creative Officer
Spencer Wong
Publication Editors
Jeff Lee
Jeff Wong
Interactive Content Director
Zoe Kuo
Content Production Director
Paul Swee
Technical Director
Henry Chu
Production Programmers
Keat Mok
Anna Tsang
Advertising Agency
McCann Worldgroup Hong Kong
Integrated Communications Planner
Penelope Yau
Account Handlers
Yen Lee
Chris Tam
Winson Wong
Marketing Manager
Fey Wong
Client
Metro Publishing Hong Kong
Brand
Metro Daily

Contact Us | Terms & Conditions
Harbour disappears as HK & Kowloon linked by landfill.
New Law passed: 99% Hong Kong under Chinese officials' surveillance.
Taiwan National Party takes Chinese rule from Communists
Increasing wealth gap. Hong Kong introduces Communism
Tiananmen Square renamed as June 4 Memorial Square
50°C Christmas. Construction worker dies from heatstroke.
2 million march in streets Chief Executive announces martial law.
HK issues new $5k, $10k banknotes.
China admits Tiananmen mistake after 40 years.
First gay US president. All male US Congress.
China demolishes "One Country Two Systems", blames Hong Kong people for abusing freedom
Pleas for Hong Kong universal suffrage fail again. Moon now hottest new home for HKers.
Hottest Latest Local China World Business Sports Entertainment Health Lifestyle Classified Ads

ANIMAL LOVERS DROOL OVER NEW APPLE 'iPET'
MAHJONG DEBUTS AT 2028 OLYMPICS
2ND-GENERATION STARS SWEEP MUSIC AWARDS
metro in 18years 18年後 都市日報 2028 1st April www.newsin18yrs.com
HARBOUR GONE
HK & KOWLOON LINKED BY LANDFILL
18 YEARS FROM NOW... IT'S IN YOUR HANDS!

metro Local News
Housing price hits new high
Parents sell kids to buy property
HK auto passion: School of Motoring gains Uni status
Stray animals now thing of the past
Acid attacker caught after 20 years

Integrated
BBH New York
for Google

Google Chrome Fast
The Chrome Fast integrated campaign established Google Chrome as the fastest browser on the web. We demonstrated Chrome's speed through 'Speed Tests', a viral video that matched Chrome against a potato gun, sound waves and lightning. We extended the Chrome Fast message online through web films, rich media banners and a contextualised banner blitz. Lastly, we challenged people to be Chrome Fast by launching FastBall, an interactive YouTube game that turned everyday sites into a race around the web. The campaign helped expand Chrome's marketshare to overtake Apple's Safari as the world's second most popular browser.

Art Directors
Erik Holmdahl
Steve Peck
Copywriters
Jared Elms
Jeff Johnson
Beth Ryan
Executive Creative Directors
Calle Sjoenell
Pelle Sjoenell
Robert Wong
Chief Creative Officer
Kevin Roddy
Director
Aaron Duffy
Agency Producer
Orlee Tatarka
Creative Technologist
Richard Schatzberger
Advertising Agencies
BBH New York
Google Creative Lab
Production Company
1st Avenue Machine
Interactive Production Companies
B-Reel
Bajibot
Editing
Lost Planet
Head of Interactive Production
Suzanne Molinaro
Head of Broadcast
Lisa Setten
Client
Google
Brand
Chrome

CHROME BY GOOGLE
GOOGLE.COM/CHROME

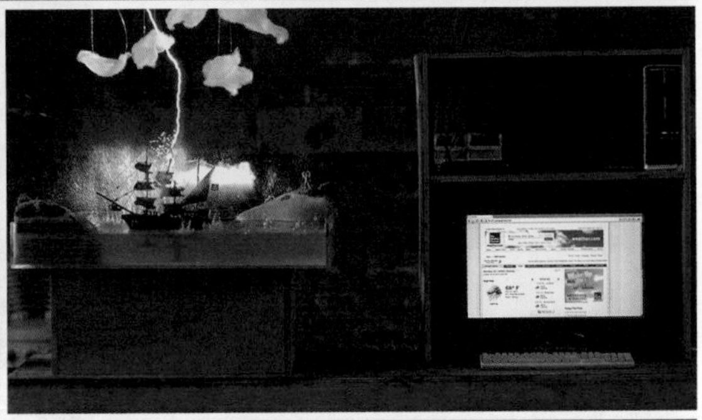

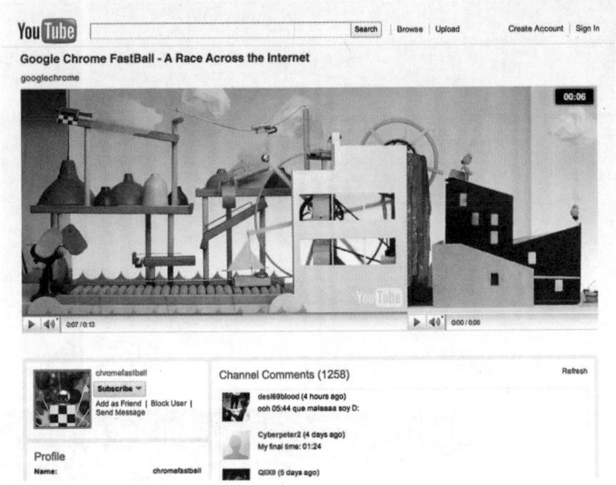
YouTube
Google Chrome FastBall - A Race Across the Internet
googlechrome
Channel Comments (1258)
Profile

CBS
The Internet. Chrome fast.
Get Chrome
Home
Video
Community
Photos
Episodes
Cast
About
Ultimate Fan

Integrated
Wieden+Kennedy Portland for Levi Strauss & Co.

Ready to Work
In 2010, Levi's was launching its new Workwear range of clothing during a time of recession in America. To highlight Levi's pioneering spirit, the campaign brought the real, ambitious rebuilding efforts of the citizens of a run-down old steel town, Braddock, PA, to life. By rolling up its sleeves and joining in with the town's efforts, Levi's authentically showcased its Workwear range – worn by Braddock citizens – and showed all of us that there are pioneering frontiers to be found everywhere, no matter who we are or where we live.

Art Directors
Julia Blackburn
Mike Giepert
Copywriter
Nathan Goldberg
Designer
Steve Denekas
Creative Directors
Don Shelford
Tyler Whisnand
Executive Creative Directors
Mark Fitzloff
Susan Hoffman
Director
John Hillcoat
Producers
Matt Factor
Shelly Townsend
Agency Producers
Ben Grylewicz
Sarah Shapiro
Editor
Tommy Harden
Director of Photography
Harris Savides
Sound Designer
Richard Wagner
Advertising Agency
Wieden+Kennedy Portland
Production Company
Skunk
Planner
Andy Lindblade
Account Handlers
Tamera Geddes
Andrew Schafer
Jessie Young
Marketing Managers
Len Peltier
Doug Sweeny
Client
Levi Strauss & Co.
Brand
Levi's

Levi's
GO FORTH
EVERYBODY'S WORK
IS EQUALLY
IMPORTANT
BRADDOCK, PA
LEVI.COM

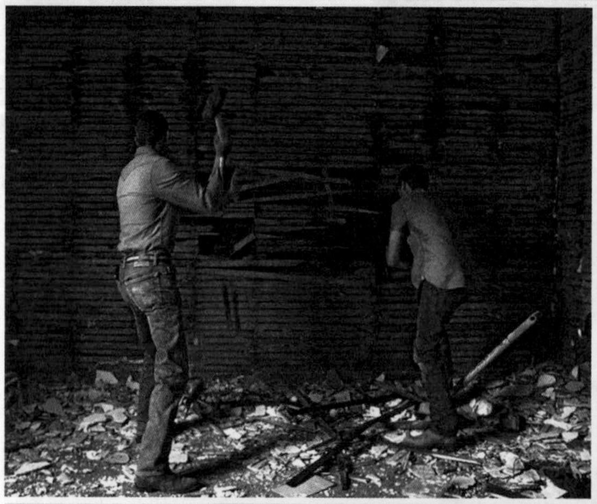

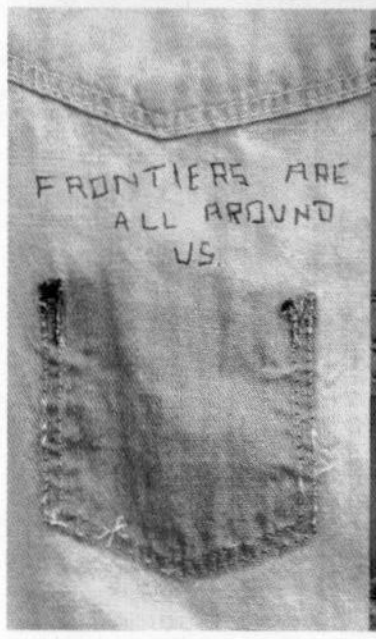
FRONTIERS ARE ALL AROUND US

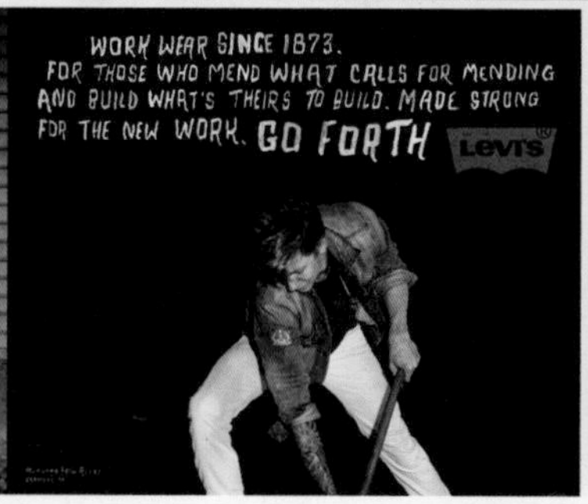
WORK WEAR SINCE 1873.
FOR THOSE WHO MEND WHAT CALLS FOR MENDING AND BUILD WHAT'S THEIRS TO BUILD. MADE STRONG FOR THE NEW WORK. GO FORTH
Levi's

Integrated
CHE*CHE & TBWA\Berlin for
Pernod Ricard Germany

MADE
MADE is a space in Berlin created by Absolut vodka to foster creative collaborations. These are conducted on the principle of 'creative clashes', where various creative visionaries create something new and outstanding together. This principle was applied to everything, from the architectural design of the space, to the art performances, as well as all levels of communication. The creative clashes were the basis for posters and trailers, which ran in the creative crowd's favourite bars on art installations containing monitors. All content was featured on the MADE blog, a forum for artists all over the world.

Art Directors
Philip Borchardt
Philipp Migeod
Copywriters
Dirk Henkelmann
Felicitas Olschewski
Designers
Chehad Abdallah
Andrew Morgan
Ricardo Mueller
Design Director
Alexis Dornier
Creative Directors
Philip Borchardt
Dirk Henkelmann
Executive Creative Directors
Kurt Georg Dieckert
Stefan Schmidt
Tatjana Stein
Nico Zeh
Producers
Luise Biesalski
Philip Gaedicke
Agency Producer
Johannes von Liebenstein
Audio Producers
Crada
Valerie Goodman
Miki
Advertising Agencies
CHE*CHE
TBWA\Berlin
Planner
Christina Keller
Account Managers
David Barton
Alexis Mardon
Client
Pernod Ricard Germany
Brand
Absolut

ANYTHING CAN HAPPEN
WHEN CREATIVE MINDS CLASH AT MADE.
www.made-blog.com

ANYTHING CAN HAPPEN
WHEN CREATIVE MINDS CLASH AT MADE.
www.made-blog.com

MADE

Integrated
DDB UK for Philips

Parallel Lines
There are millions of ways to tell a story, there's only one way to watch one. To dramatise the cinematic qualities of Philips TVs and demonstrate the brand's passion for film, we created the 'Parallel Lines' campaign. We wrote a single, short piece of dialogue and challenged directors from Ridley Scott Associates to come up with their interpretation of it. The result was six very different, highly cinematic short films, including a 3D film. The films can be viewed online and play within a virtual Philips cinema-proportion (21:9) TV. A competition open to the public resulted in 637 films being made. The campaign was also selected in Earned Media.

Art Director
Shishir Patel
Digital Art Directors
Antonia Costa
Iain Robson
Copywriter
Sam Oliver
Digital Designers
Maximiliano Chanan
Nelleke van der Maas
Bart Mol
Robert Northam
Wijbrand Stet
Interactive Designer
Christine van Rossum
Chief Creative Officer
Neil Dawson
Producer
Natalie Powell
Advertising Agency
DDB UK
Production Company
RSA
Project Manager
Ivelle Jargalyn
Account Handlers
Zoë Hinckley
Sandra Krstic
Neill Robb
Client
Philips

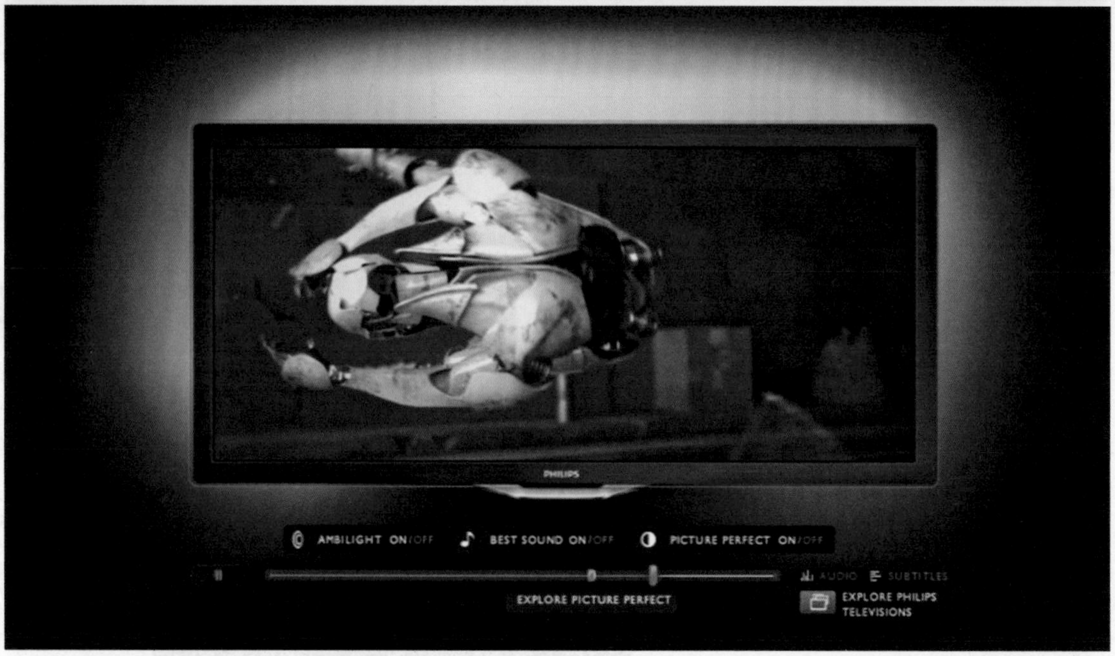
PHILIPS
AMBILIGHT ON/OFF
BEST SOUND ON/OFF
PICTURE PERFECT ON/OFF
AUDIO
SUBTITLES
EXPLORE PICTURE PERFECT
EXPLORE PHILIPS TELEVISIONS

Integrated
Saatchi & Saatchi
Sydney for Lion
Nathan Australia

Beer Economy
The Tooheys 'New' campaign was built on a simple and indisputably Australian truth: beer is constantly used as a currency between mates. So we made Tooheys New the Official Currency of the Beer Economy. This integrated campaign showed that whatever a mate asks you to do, there's always a fair price in beer. We gave the country its first ever comprehensive price guide to the Beer Economy.

Art Director
Peter Galmez
Copywriters
John McKelvey
James Ross-Edwards
Creative Director
Dave Bowman
Executive Creative Director
Steve Back
Director
Justin Kurzel
Producer
Michelle Bennett
Agency Producer
Jules Jackson
Editor
Gabriel Muir
Lighting Cameraperson
Adam Arkapaw
Photographer
Chris Searl
Sound Designer
Simon Lister
Advertising Agency
Saatchi & Saatchi
Sydney
Production Company
Cherub Pictures
Planner
Neal Fairfield
Account Handler
Alex Carr
Brand Manager
Todd Atkinson
Client
Lion Nathan Australia
Brand
Tooheys New

MasterCard
VISA
TOOHEYS NEW
ACCEPTED HERE

I.O.U.
I JAMES certify that you are entitled to: Schooner/s 6-Pack/s 2 Carton/s
of Tooheys New/Tooheys New White Stag in return for helping you move in the RAIN
Sign Date 21-12-09
For the Love of Beer

HOME
THE BEER ECONOMY
SPONSORSHIP
HISTORY
PRODUCT INFO
HOT OFFERS
TOOHEYS NEW WHITE STAG
THE BEER ECONOMY
Lending your mate a hand when it's needed is just a part of being mates. The deal is that when the jobs done, it's his shout at the bar or the bottle shop. It doesn't matter if you've mowed his lawn or helped him re-tile his roof he owes you a beer. The question is: how many? Find out what it's worth with the Tooheys™ Beer Economy.
Tooheys New - Grass
0:00 / 0:15
NOT SURE WHAT IT'S WORTH? TRY OUR HANDY BEER ECONOMY CALCULATOR
4
TASK: HELPING MATE MOVE
DURATION: 4 HOURS
CONDITIONS: TREACHOROUS
= 8 CASES OWED
TOOHEYS NEW – LIVE TRADING
GET INVOLVED
I OWE YOU
Your mate has bailed you out of a tight spot. You owe him a beer or two... write him an I.O.U.
WANT TO WORK FOR BEER?
Start trading in the Tooheys New™ beer economy!

Integrated
JWT Mexico for the
Mexican Red Cross

Coin-op Kiddie Rides
After the 2009 financial crisis, we couldn't just do the same old-fashioned fundraising drive. We needed to get people involved, interested and inspired, so we built coin-operated rides featuring Red Cross vehicles for kids to play on, while serving as collection boxes. The importance of every single donation was now easy to see. Children and their parents could give coins and instantly see the effect of their donation: the ambulance, the helicopter and the boat moved just as the Red Cross moves. And the Red Cross gave you something back immediately: a moment of joy.

Art Directors
Victor Rojas
Esteban Sacco
Copywriter
Rodrigo Rothschild
Creative Directors
Gabriel Bello
Miguel Brito
Enrique Codesido
Manuel Techera
Director
Nicolas Caicoya
Agency Producers
Gilberto Amezquita
Damiana Marin
Advertising Agency
JWT Mexico
Production Company
Colectivo Cine
Brand Manager
Rafael Hernandez
Client
Mexican Red Cross

CRUZ ROJA MEXICANA
COLECTA NACIONAL 2010
CON TU AYUDA PODEMOS SEGUIR ADELANTE
CRUZ ROJA MEXICANA

YOUR HELP CAN KEEP US GOING

YOUR HELP CAN KEEP US GOING

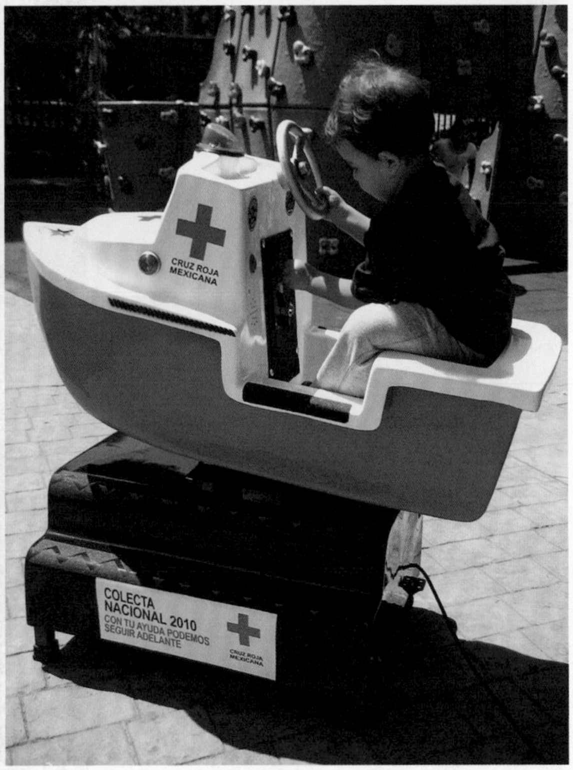
CRUZ ROJA MEXICANA
COLECTA NACIONAL 2010
CON TU AYUDA PODEMOS SEGUIR ADELANTE
CRUZ ROJA MEXICANA

Earned Media
Del Campo Nazca Saatchi & Saatchi
for AbInbev

Andes Teletransporter
Andes is the leading beer in Mendoza, Argentina. Whilst men love to go to the bar to drink beer and have fun with friends, their girlfriends hate it when they do so. Our solution was Andes Teletransporter, a soundproof booth with a sound panel that recreates noises from lots of different environments. Men could sound like they were in a traffic jam or looking after their baby nephew, therefore being 'out' of the bar without actually leaving it. Meaning more happy men and fewer broken-up couples.

Art Director
Carlos Muller
Copywriter
Patricio del Sante
Designers
Juan Pedro Porcaro
Bruno Tortolano
Creative Director
Javier Campopiano
Executive Creative Directors
Maxi Itzkoff
Mariano Serkin
Direction
Nico & Martin
Producer
Caro Cordini
Agency Producers
Adrian Aspani
Patricio Martinez
Camilo Rojas
Director of Photography
Leandro Filloy
Advertising Agency
Del Campo Nazca Saatchi & Saatchi
Production Company
Primo Buenos Aires
Editing
Cinecolor
Sound Design
Supercharango
Account Handler
Maria Lorena Pascual
Account Executive
Jaime Vidal
Regional Brand Managers
Pablo Firpo
Eduardo Palacios
Vice President of Marketing
Ricardo Fernandez
Client
AbInbev
Brand
Andes

ANDES
TELETRANSPORTER

Earned Media
Taproot India for Bennett & Coleman India

Aman Ki Asha:
Hope for Peace

The first anniversary of the horrific Mumbai terror attacks saw India and Pakistan inflamed by fundamentalist jingoism once again. Aman ki Asha (Hope for Peace) was a cross-border peace initiative by the two largest media groups on both sides, calling for peace in the face of intense hostility. This was launched with the most courageous headline in the history of the world's largest democracy – 'Love Pakistan' – on the front page of the world's most-read English newspaper. The movement became a rallying call and a platform for one of the bravest peace initiatives in the modern world.

Art Director
Abhishek Sawant
Copywriter
Chintan Ruparel
Creative Director
Santosh Padhi
Director
Shoojit Sircar
Producer
Swadha Kulkarni
Cameraman
Vijay Kartik
Advertising Agency
Taproot India
Production Companies
Footcandles
Rising Sun
Account Handler
Priyank Misra
Brand Manager
Priya Gupta
Marketing Manager
Rahul Kansal
Client
Bennett & Coleman India
Brand
The Times of India

THE TIMES OF INDIA
THE TIMES OF INDIA
aman ki asha
AN INDO-PAK PEACE PROJECT
THE FIRST STEP
MUSIC CAN NEVER TAKE SIDES
Lines are meant to divide. But melodies always pull us closer. So let's open our hearts and ears for the love of music. As maestros from either side of the border lend their voice to move us, yet again, towards each other.
Date Day City Artists Venue
Jan 16 Saturday Delhi Kailash Kher/Rahat Fateh Ali Khan Qila Rai Pithora, Saket
Jan 17 Sunday Mumbai Shubha Mudgal/Abida Parveen Bandra Fort
Jan 19 Tuesday Kolkata Euphoria/Strings Nicco Park
Date Day City Artists Venue
Jan 22 Friday Hyderabad Parvathy Baul/Arif Lohar Chowmahalla Palace
Jan 23 Saturday Bangalore Hariharan/Ghulam Ali Jayamahal Palace
Jan 24 Sunday Ahmedabad Wadali Brothers/Abu Muhammad Vastrapur Lake

LOVE
PAKISTAN
Feels odd to see those two words side by side doesn't it?
Terror, hatred and fanaticism somehow sit more comfortably in our minds when we think of the other side of the border.
Words that we've been fed in daily doses over the last six decades. And in greater doses over the last one year.
Shutting our minds to the undeniable truth that people across the border are, above all, people. Like us.
So here's the question. Is there any chance at all, that we could still raise a hand, not in anger but in greeting?
Depends on who raises his hand first, some of us would say. Also how, whisper a few others. But mostly, it all boils down to one simple question.
Why?
Why must we do it? Why do we need them? Why don't they first say sorry for what they've done? And the answer is simple.
It's easier to say Hi than to say Sorry. It's shorter too. Besides, there is no rule that says a book has to be closed before a new one is opened. Not even if it's a history book.
So on the first day of this new year, we're going to make a start. Again.
With Aman Ki Asha. A brave, new people-to-people initiative by The Times of India and Pakistan's Jang Group to bring the people of two fine nations closer together. Culturally, emotionally and peacefully.
Starting with a series of cross-border cultural interactions, business seminars, music & literary festivals and citizens meets that will give the bonds of humanity a chance to survive outside the battlefields of politics, terrorism and fundamentalism.
In the hope that one day, words like Pakistan, India and Love will not seem impossible in the same sentence.
aman ki asha
AN INDO-PAK PEACE PROJECT
THE FIRST STEP

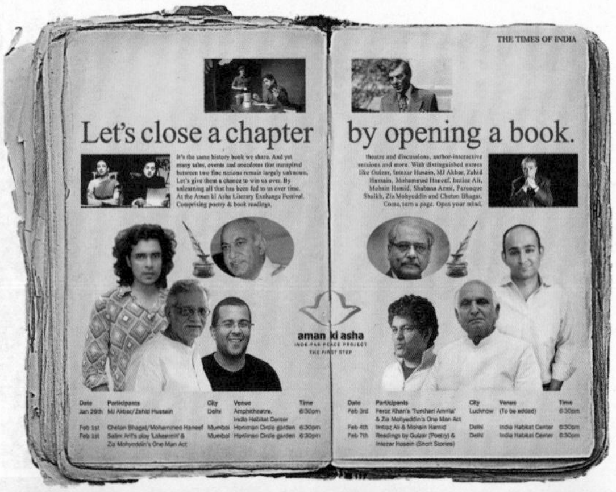
THE TIMES OF INDIA
Let's close a chapter
by opening a book.

EXCLUSIVE
aman ki asha
A HOPE FOR PEACE ACROSS BORDERS
BREAKING NEWS
PROBE AGAINST COPS
TIMES NOW
Rathore throws law book at Ruchika's

Earned Media
Prime PR for Electrolux

Vac from the Sea
In 2010, Electrolux launched its Green Range vacuum cleaners, made from 55–70 per cent recycled plastic. Electrolux's green quest is to produce 100 per cent recycled vacuum cleaners, but there isn't enough recycled plastic on land to do this. In the oceans, there are plastic patches the size of Texas. 'Vac from the Sea' was launched to collect plastic from oceans with environmental organisations, make vacuum cleaners out of it, and exhibit them. Part of the Green Range revenue was donated to plastic research. The campaign reached 175.2 million people and increased Green Range sales distribution by 300 per cent.

Art Directors
Carl Fredrik Holtermann
Fredrik Olsson
Copywriters
Devi Brunson
Carl Fredrik Holtermann
Creative Director
Jonas Bodin
Executive Creative Director
Tom Beckman
Production Manager
Vanja Bajc
Public Relations
Prime PR
Planner
Kerem Yazgan
Head of Planning
Marcus Wenner
Project Managers
Karin Schollin
Mattias Ström
Media Strategist
Sakari Pitkanen
Issues & Crisis Management Expert
Charlie Stjernberg
Media Relations Manager
Claes Nyströmer
Digital Communications Manager
Antti Laukkanen
Business Segment Manager
Jonas Magnusson
Product Marketing Manager
Niklas Melin
Public Relations Assistant
Linda De Giuseppe
Client Public Relations Manager
Julia Emmerich
Client Project Manager
Robert Perrakoski
Client Vice President of Sustainability
Cecilia Nord
Client
Electrolux
Brand
Electrolux Green Range

treehugger
A Discovery Company

Vacuum Cleaners Made from Ocean Plastic Highlight Ugly Pollution, Beautiful Design
by Jaymi Heimbuch, San Francisco, California on 10.26.10
DESIGN & ARCHITECTURE

Photos via Electrolux

This summer we let you know about a really cool project from Electrolux, a company that wanted to make a series of their well-known vacuum cleaners out of plastic collected from the ocean. Well, they've done it -- and the vacuums turned out way cooler than we'd have imagined. The company just announced five unique vacuum cleaners each made from plastics collected from a different sea. Check them out, and a video on the process of collecting, processing, and manufacturing the new models.

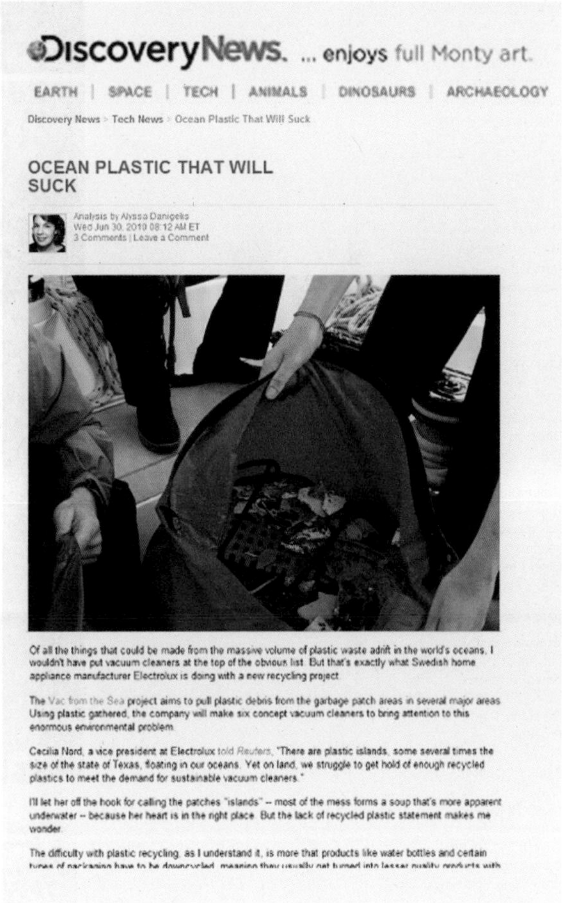
DiscoveryNews. ... enjoys full Monty art.

EARTH | SPACE | TECH | ANIMALS | DINOSAURS | ARCHAEOLOGY

Discovery News > Tech News > Ocean Plastic That Will Suck

OCEAN PLASTIC THAT WILL SUCK

Analysis by Alyssa Danigelis
Wed Jun 30, 2010 08:12 AM ET
3 Comments | Leave a Comment

Of all the things that could be made from the massive volume of plastic waste adrift in the world's oceans, I wouldn't have put vacuum cleaners at the top of the obvious list. But that's exactly what Swedish home appliance manufacturer Electrolux is doing with a new recycling project.

The Vac from the Sea project aims to pull plastic debris from the garbage patch areas in several major areas. Using plastic gathered, the company will make six concept vacuum cleaners to bring attention to this enormous environmental problem.

Cecilia Nord, a vice president at Electrolux told Reuters, "There are plastic islands, some several times the size of the state of Texas, floating in our oceans. Yet on land, we struggle to get hold of enough recycled plastics to meet the demand for sustainable vacuum cleaners."

I'll let her off the hook for calling the patches "islands" -- most of the mess forms a soup that's more apparent underwater -- because her heart is in the right place. But the lack of recycled plastic statement makes me wonder.

The difficulty with plastic recycling, as I understand it, is more that products like water bottles and certain

Earned Media
Ogilvy New York for IBM

Watson
IBM built a computer, Watson, which understands human language. As a test of its ability, Watson competed on the quiz show 'Jeopardy!' against the world's two greatest champions. We created an avatar as the public face of Watson and took people behind the scenes, documenting Watson's progress for two years. We explained the science behind the machine and educated the world about its possibilities. The campaign resulted in 10,000 media stories, $50million in earned media, and one billion impressions. Seventy per cent of Americans were aware of Watson, while traffic to ibm.com increased by 556 per cent.

Art Directors
Miles Gilbert
Michael Paterson
Copywriters
Mark Girand
Steven Schroth
Senior Copywriter
Niels West
Creative Directors
Mark Girand
Michael Paterson
Executive Creative Directors
Tom Godici
Greg Ketchum
Group Creative Directors
David Korchin
Jason Marks
Chief Creative Officer
Steve Simpson
Director
Paul Bozymowski
Executive Producer
Lee Weiss
Senior Producer
Jenn Pennington
Executive Digital Producer
Pierre Wendling
Agency Producer
Erika Tribble
Music Producer
Karl Westman
Advertising Agency
Ogilvy New York
Production Company
@radical.media
Editing
@radical.media
Go Robot
Client Worldwide Executive Creative Director
Susan Westre
Client
IBM

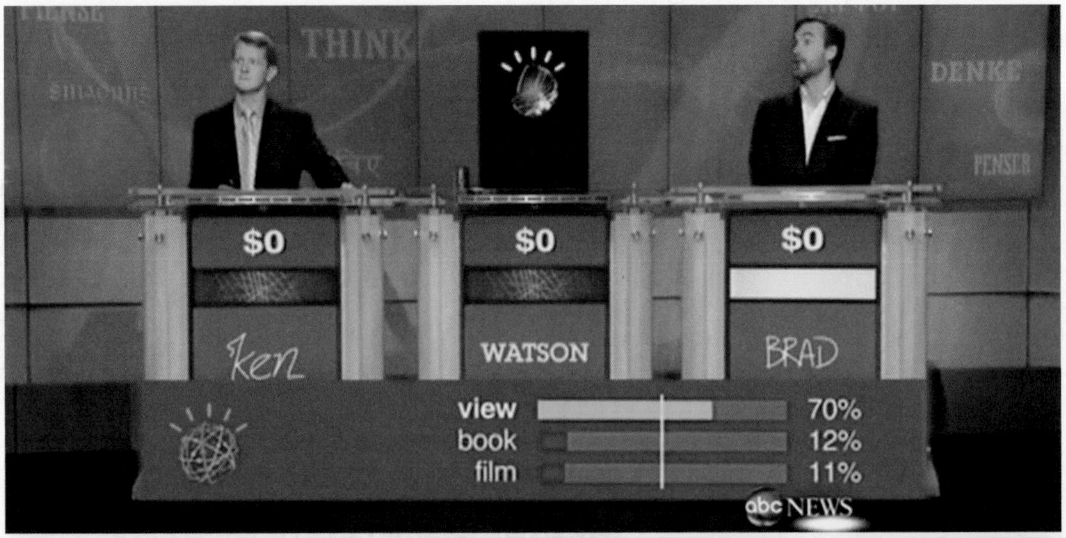
THINK
DENKE
PENSER
$0
$0
$0
Ken
WATSON
BRAD
view 70%
book 12%
film 11%
abc NEWS

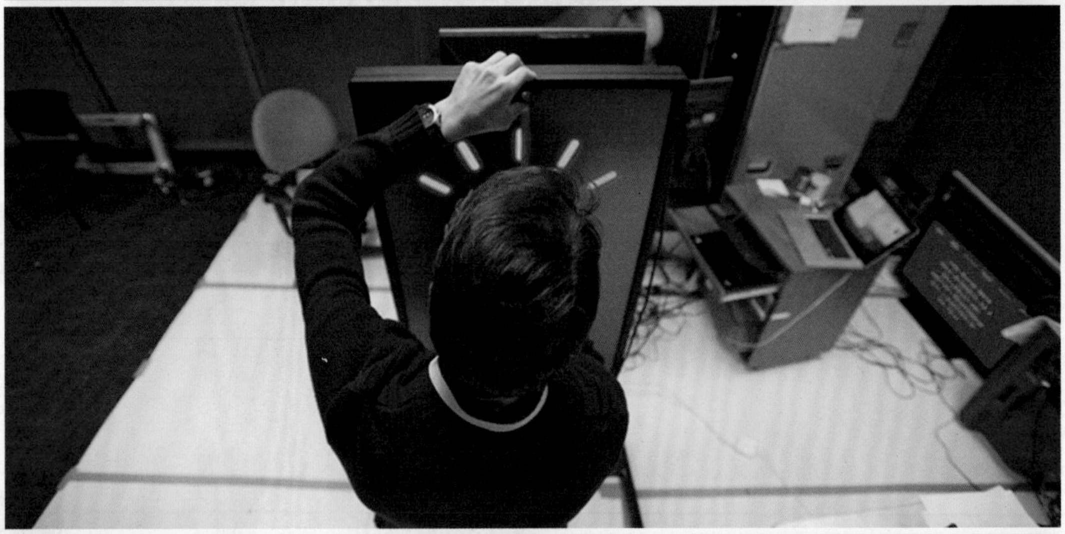

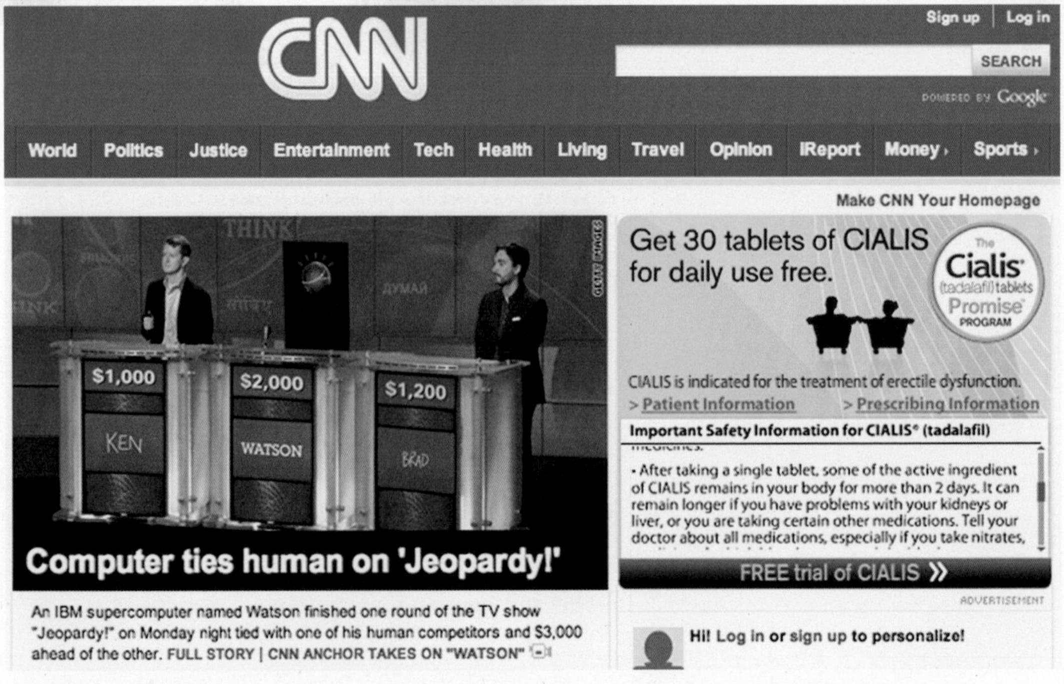
Sign up | Log in
CNN
SEARCH
POWERED BY Google
World Politics Justice Entertainment Tech Health Living Travel Opinion iReport Money › Sports ›
Make CNN Your Homepage
THINK
$1,000
$2,000
$1,200
KEN
WATSON
BRAD
Computer ties human on 'Jeopardy!'
An IBM supercomputer named Watson finished one round of the TV show "Jeopardy!" on Monday night tied with one of his human competitors and $3,000 ahead of the other. FULL STORY | CNN ANCHOR TAKES ON "WATSON"
Get 30 tablets of CIALIS for daily use free.
The Cialis (tadalafil) tablets Promise PROGRAM
CIALIS is indicated for the treatment of erectile dysfunction.
> Patient Information
> Prescribing Information
Important Safety Information for CIALIS® (tadalafil)
• After taking a single tablet, some of the active ingredient of CIALIS remains in your body for more than 2 days. It can remain longer if you have problems with your kidneys or liver, or you are taking certain other medications. Tell your doctor about all medications, especially if you take nitrates,
FREE trial of CIALIS »
ADVERTISEMENT
Hi! Log in or sign up to personalize!

Earned Media
Shalmor Avnon
Amichay/ Y&R
Interactive Tel Aviv
for AIDS Task Force

Get Tested Project
The AIDS Task Force's main goal was to encourage more people to get tested and increase awareness of World AIDS Day. Our radio campaign had a radical idea: radio presenters took HIV tests and got their results live on air. 'Get Tested' was an open idea platform; presenters made the campaign their own. More than 20 hours of original branded content were created. The open idea platform was a collaboration between advertising, media, content and PR for one goal and message: get tested.

Art Director
Shirley Eva Bahar
Copywriter
Orit Bar Niv
Creative Director
Amit Gal
Executive Creative Director
Tzur Golan
Chief Creative Officer
Gideon Amichay
Advertising Agency
Shalmor Avnon Amichay/ Y&R Interactive Tel Aviv
Planners
Hila Tamir
Niva Ziv
Head of Strategic Planning
Yoni Lahav
Account Handler
Inbal Stern
Account Supervisor
Shiran Chen Gross
Executive Client Director
Adam Polachek
Client
AIDS Task Force

102FM
102FM
רדיו תל אביב

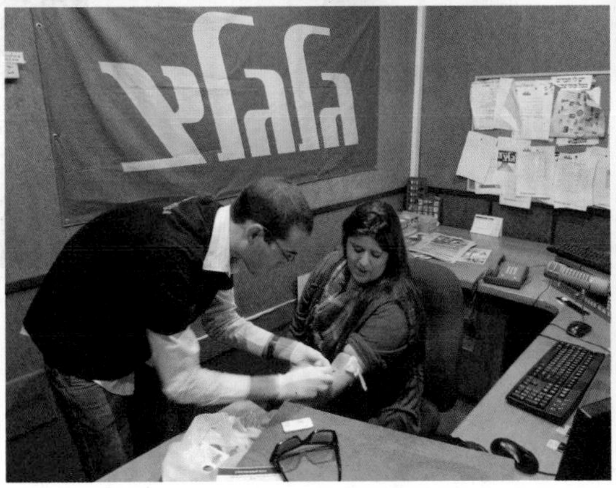
גלגלצ

שידור חי 11:11
FM 97.8, 105.5
יום האיידס הבינ"ל
מגיש רשת ג', מנחם פרי, עורך
בדיקת HIV בשידור חי
שידור ישיר
ערוץ 2 החדשות

Earned Media
TBWA\Chiat\Day
New York for Keep a Child Alive

Digital Death
The AIDS epidemic in Africa isn't the prime issue it once was. To raise money for Keep a Child Alive, we had to do something that would really get people talking. Our idea was simple: if the millions dying weren't getting the world's attention, perhaps losing the lives of those we idolise would. So on 1 December, World AIDS Day, Hollywood died...digitally. The world's top celebrity tweeters vowed to stay off all social media until $1million was raised to buy their digital lives back. The goal was reached in less than six days.

Art Director
Isabella Castano
Copywriter
Ani Munoz
Creative Director
Lisa Topol
Chief Creative Officer
Mark Figliulo
Producer
Viet-An Nguyen
Agency Producers
Josh Morse
Robert Valdes
Print Producers
Joni Adams
Katherine D'Addario
Editor
Sonejuhi Sinha
Advertising Agency
TBWA\Chiat\Day
New York
Project Manager
Rayna Lucier
Account Supervisor
Keiko Kurokawa
Account Director
Nikki Maizel
Client
Keep a Child Alive

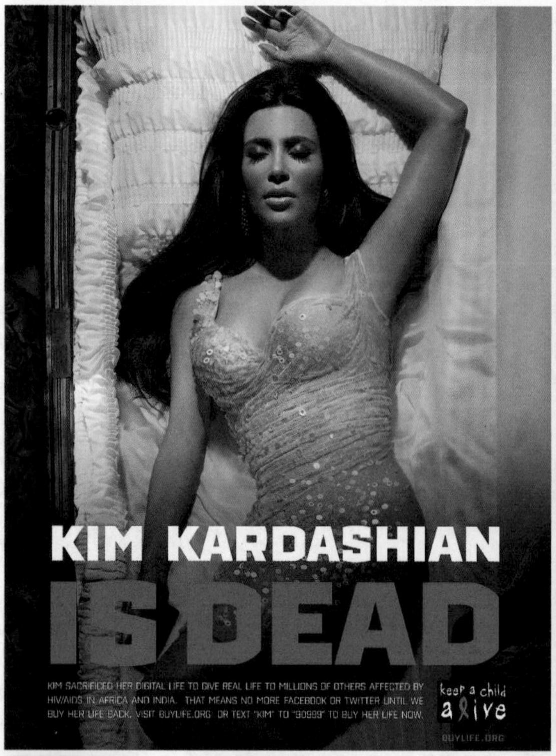
KIM KARDASHIAN
IS DEAD
KIM SACRIFICED HER DIGITAL LIFE TO GIVE REAL LIFE TO MILLIONS OF OTHERS AFFECTED BY HIV/AIDS IN AFRICA AND INDIA. THAT MEANS NO MORE FACEBOOK OR TWITTER UNTIL WE BUY HER LIFE BACK. VISIT BUYLIFE.ORG OR TEXT "KIM" TO "90999" TO BUY HER LIFE NOW.
keep a child alive
BUYLIFE.ORG

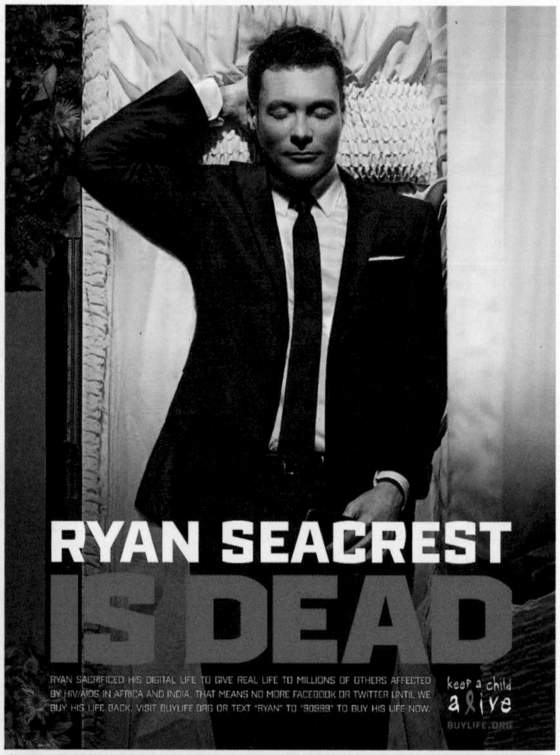
RYAN SEACREST
IS DEAD
RYAN SACRIFICED HIS DIGITAL LIFE TO GIVE REAL LIFE TO MILLIONS OF OTHERS AFFECTED BY HIV/AIDS IN AFRICA AND INDIA. THAT MEANS NO MORE FACEBOOK OR TWITTER UNTIL WE BUY HIS LIFE BACK. VISIT BUYLIFE.ORG OR TEXT "RYAN" TO "90999" TO BUY HIS LIFE NOW.
keep a child alive
BUYLIFE.ORG

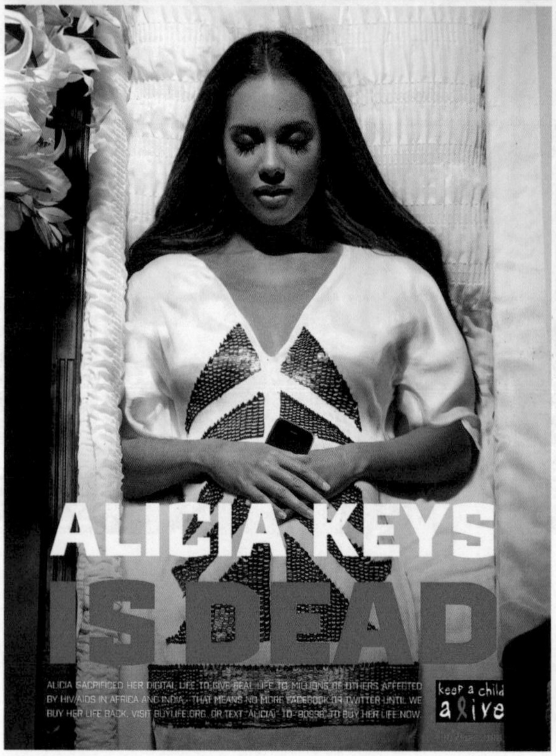
ALICIA KEYS
IS DEAD
ALICIA SACRIFICED HER DIGITAL LIFE TO GIVE REAL LIFE TO MILLIONS OF OTHERS AFFECTED BY HIV/AIDS IN AFRICA AND INDIA. THAT MEANS NO MORE FACEBOOK OR TWITTER UNTIL WE BUY HER LIFE BACK. VISIT BUYLIFE.ORG OR TEXT "ALICIA" TO "90999" TO BUY HER LIFE NOW.
keep a child alive

keep a child alive
DIGITAL DEATH

DIGITAL DEATH
ALICIA KEYS IS ALIVE
$1,000,000
BUY LIFE NOW
VIEW THE DIGITAL DEAD

Earned Media
4th Amendment Wear

Metallic Ink Printed Underclothes
4th Amendment Wear is specifically designed to broadcast messages to TSA X-ray officers just when they are peeking at your privates. The Fourth Amendment to the Constitution of the United States, which is meant to prevent unwarranted search and seizure, is readable on TSA body scanners, as these underclothes have it printed in metallic ink. Now there's a way to protest against those intrusive TSA X-ray body scanners without saying a word. Let them know they're spying on the privates of a private citizen.

Art Director
Matthew Ryan
Copywriter
Tim Geoghegan
Designer
Matthew Ryan
Industrial Designer
Matthew Ryan
Creative Directors
Tim Geoghegan
Matthew Ryan
Retoucher
Matthew Ryan
Client
4th Amendment Wear

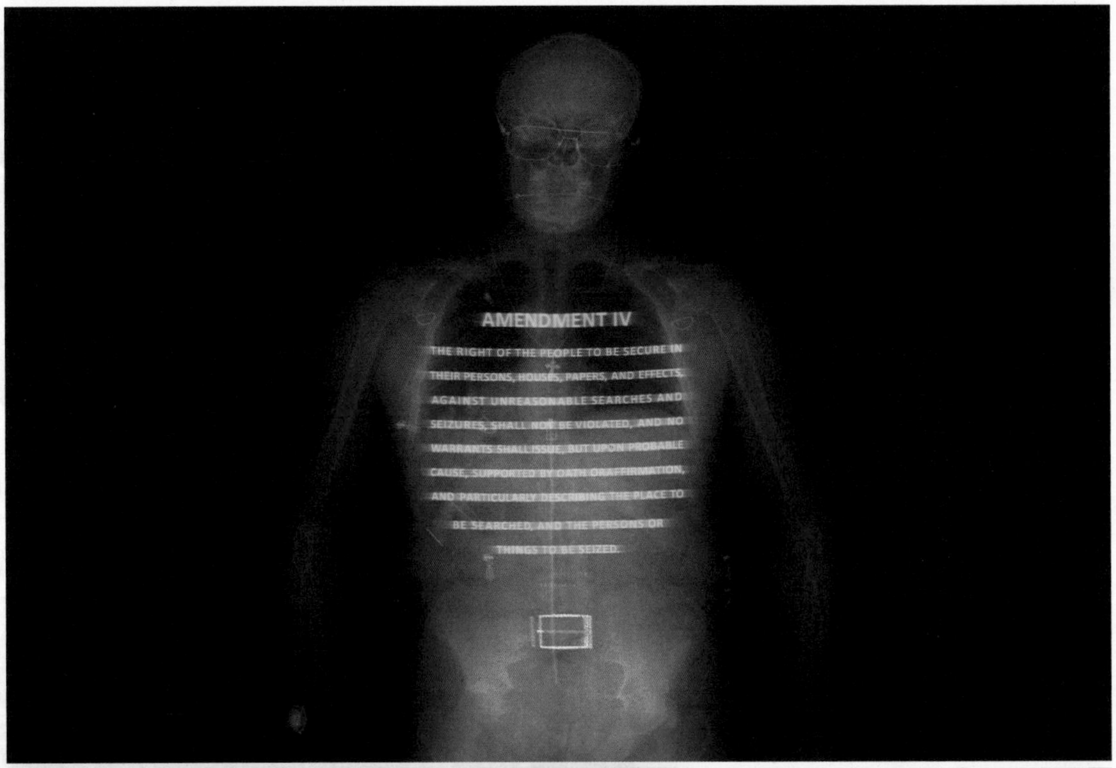
AMENDMENT IV
THE RIGHT OF THE PEOPLE TO BE SECURE IN THEIR PERSONS, HOUSES, PAPERS, AND EFFECTS, AGAINST UNREASONABLE SEARCHES AND SEIZURES, SHALL NOT BE VIOLATED, AND NO WARRANTS SHALL ISSUE, BUT UPON PROBABLE CAUSE, SUPPORTED BY OATH OR AFFIRMATION, AND PARTICULARLY DESCRIBING THE PLACE TO BE SEARCHED, AND THE PERSONS OR THINGS TO BE SEIZED.

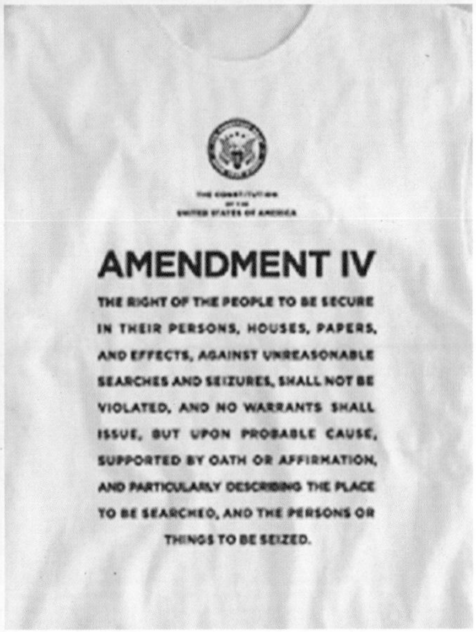
AMENDMENT IV
THE RIGHT OF THE PEOPLE TO BE SECURE IN THEIR PERSONS, HOUSES, PAPERS, AND EFFECTS, AGAINST UNREASONABLE SEARCHES AND SEIZURES, SHALL NOT BE VIOLATED, AND NO WARRANTS SHALL ISSUE, BUT UPON PROBABLE CAUSE, SUPPORTED BY OATH OR AFFIRMATION, AND PARTICULARLY DESCRIBING THE PLACE TO BE SEARCHED, AND THE PERSONS OR THINGS TO BE SEIZED.

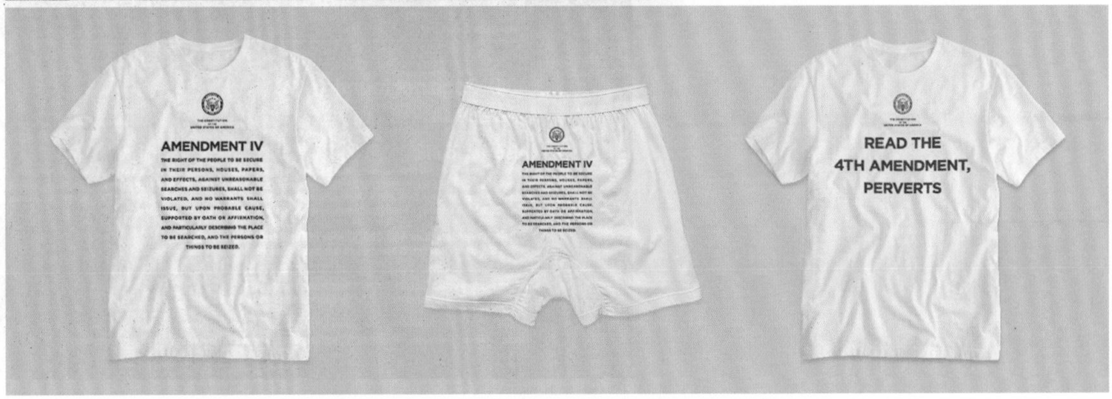
AMENDMENT IV
AMENDMENT IV
READ THE
4TH AMENDMENT,
PERVERTS

Earned Media
kempertrautmann for Initiative Vermisste Kinder (Missing Children's Initiative)

Germany's Biggest Search for Missing Children

Every year in Germany more than 100,000 children are reported missing. On behalf of Initiative Vermisste Kinder (Missing Children's Initiative), we launched a campaign where everybody can play an active role in the search, by reinventing the way we search for missing children. Under the title 'Deutschland findet euch' (Germany will find you), we used Facebook to launch Germany's first and largest-ever search campaign. In order to make the search party faster and more effective, we used a whole range of measures to raise awareness of the 'Deutschland findet euch' platform.

Art Directors
Leif Johannsen
Bruno Luglio
Copywriter
Sebastian Merget
Creative Directors
Marcell Francke
Patrick Matthiensen
Advertising Agency
kempertrautmann
Digital Agency
BlueMars
Production Company
nhb video
Public Relations
fischerAppelt
Account Handlers
Marcell Francke
Patrick Matthiensen
Marketing Manager
Lars Bruhns
Client
Initiative
Vermisste Kinder

VERMISST
DEUTSCHLAND-FINDET-EUCH.DE
LIGA total! Mit persönlicher Konferenz!

WWW.DEUTSCHLAND-FINDET-EUCH.DE
ZEUGEN GESUCHT!
SEIT FREITAG, 3. SEPTEMBER - 21:30 UHR WIRD MIRCO SCHLITTER (10) AUS GREFRATH VERMISST.
HINWEISE AN: 02162-377-1400
DEUTSCHLAND FINDET euch
INITIATIVE VERMISSTE KINDER

facebook
Deutschland findet euch
Pinnwand
Info
Willkommen
Suchen
Helfen
Karte
ERKENNST DU JEMANDEN?
HOTLINE:

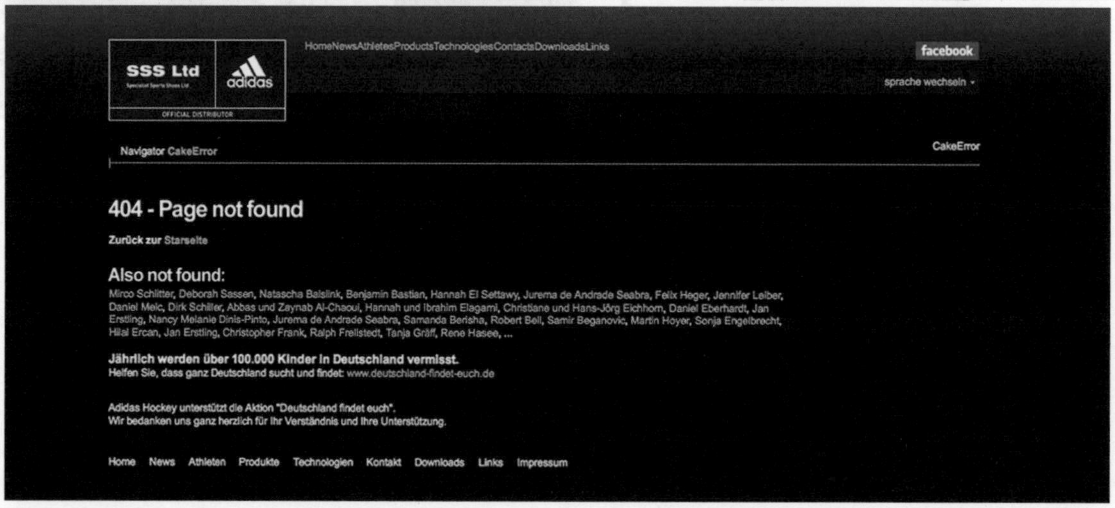
SSS Ltd
adidas
OFFICIAL DISTRIBUTOR
HomeNewsAthletesProductsTechnologiesContactsDownloadsLinks
facebook
sprache wechseln
Navigator CakeError
CakeError
404 - Page not found
Zurück zur Starseite
Also not found:
Mirco Schlitter, Deborah Sassen, Natascha Balslink, Benjamin Bastian, Hannah El Settawy, Jurema de Andrade Seabra, Felix Heger, Jennifer Leiber, Daniel Meic, Dirk Schiller, Abbas und Zaynab Al-Chaoui, Hannah und Ibrahim Elagami, Christiane und Hans-Jörg Eichhorn, Daniel Eberhardt, Jan Erstling, Nancy Melanie Dinis-Pinto, Jurema de Andrade Seabra, Samanda Berisha, Robert Bell, Samir Beganovic, Martin Hoyer, Sonja Engelbrecht, Hilal Ercan, Jan Erstling, Christopher Frank, Ralph Freilstedt, Tanja Gräff, Rene Hasee, ...
Jährlich werden über 100.000 Kinder in Deutschland vermisst.
Helfen Sie, dass ganz Deutschland sucht und findet: www.deutschland-findet-euch.de
Adidas Hockey unterstützt die Aktion "Deutschland findet euch".
Wir bedanken uns ganz herzlich für Ihr Verständnis und Ihre Unterstützung.
Home News Athleten Produkte Technologien Kontakt Downloads Links Impressum

Earned Media
Alec Brownstein

The Google Job Experiment

The Google Job Experiment was a $6 Google search ad intended to help copywriter Alec Brownstein connect with an audience of just five creative directors in New York City. When they Googled their names, the top result was a message from Alec, asking for a job. The experiment worked. We then turned it into a viral YouTube video with over a million hits, followed by a PR blitz that resulted in 9.4 million social media impressions, 15 million print impressions, 240 million web impressions, and 4.8 billion broadcast impressions. In the process, we ushered in an age of truly targeted, unique advertising messaging. All told, we garnered 5.1 billion impressions. And the total cost? Just the initial $6.

Art Director
Alec Brownstein
Copywriter
Alec Brownstein
Executive Creative Directors
Ian Reichenthal
Scott Vitrone
Agency Producer
Jona Goodman
Editor
Travis Kopach
Advertising Agency
Y&R New York
Communications Agency
DiGennaro Communications
Publicists
Kristen Bryan
Samantha DiGennaro
Nora Lyon
Client
Alec Brownstein

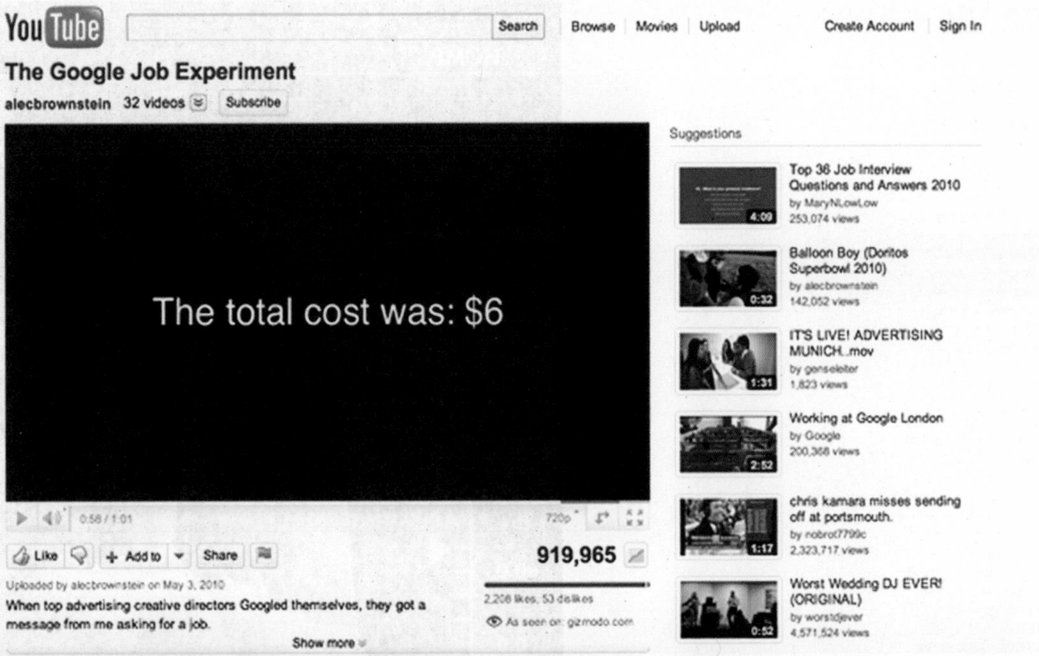

YouTube
Search
Browse
Movies
Upload
Create Account
Sign In
The Google Job Experiment
alecbrownstein 32 videos
Subscribe
Suggestions
The total cost was: $6
Top 36 Job Interview Questions and Answers 2010
Balloon Boy (Doritos Superbowl 2010)
IT'S LIVE! ADVERTISING MUNICH..mov
Working at Google London
chris kamara misses sending off at portsmouth.
Worst Wedding DJ EVER! (ORIGINAL)
Like
Add to
Share
919,965
Uploaded by alecbrownstein on May 3, 2010
When top advertising creative directors Googled themselves, they got a message from me asking for a job.
Show more

CBS News.com
CBS Evening News
The Early Show
48 Hours Mystery
60 Minutes
the early show
HOME
SHOWBIZ
RECIPES
HEALTH
MONEY
FASHION
TECH
LIFESTYLE
LIVE PREPARATIONS FOR FINAL LAUNCH OF SPACE SHUTTLE ATLANTIS AT
VIDEO
Sexy Dance Appropriate for Little Girls?
WORLD
Crash Survivor Family's Safari Blog Posted
Home > The Early Show > Leisure > Gizmos & Gadgets
NEW YORK, May 14, 2010
Google Ads Help Job Seeker Find Work
Alec Brownstein Bought Ad Execs' Names on Google; Execs Google Their Names, Find His Resume, Portfolio

FAST COMPANY
EATON
Switch ON to Eaton
Google Experiment Gets Creative Job Seeker an Agency Post
Facebook-Google Privacy PR Smear Is A Campaign In An Epic, Escalating War
CHICAGO BOOTH

GOOGLE EXPERIMENT
Adwords Land Dream Job

Alec Brownstein
GETS JOB THROUGH $6 GOOGLE CAMPAIGN
CNN

Yellow Pencil in Mobile Marketing

Mobile Campaigns & Mobile Advertising
HAKUHODO for the Japan Maritime Self-Defense Force

Salute Trainer
The Japan Maritime Self-Defense Force is an organisation that maintains peace in Japan. To refocus young people's attention on the Self-Defense Force, we created a mobile training application, Salute Trainer. A salute is a very important action expressing the spirit of the Self-Defense Force. We took accurate measurements from the perfect salute and programmed the results into the Salute Trainer. The app teaches users the salute, then sends those who achieved excellent results a recruitment email, thereby doubling up as a recruitment tool.

Creative Directors
Shota Hatanaka
Kenta Ikoma
Programmers
Hideyuki Aida
Satoru Higa
Art Director
Junichi Kurata
Copywriter
Kenta Ikoma
Producers
Hirofumi Nobuta
Toru Suzuki
Photographer
Hiroki Oguri
Director of Photography
Takahiro Kojima
Photographic Producer
Hisako Sudo
Photo Retoucher
Yosuke Mochizuki
Director
Waki Rokutan
Assistant Director
Yukako Nomura
Editor
Ryusuke Fukushima
Gaffer
Hiroyasu Sakaguchi
Second Camera Operator
Hiroki Oguri
Casting Director
Natsumi Sakuma
Advertising Agency
HAKUHODO
Production Company
HAKUHODO PRODUCTS
Production Managers
Hayato Arakawa
Tomohiro Oguchi
Planner
Yukako Nomura
Public Relations Planners
Takeshi Muro
Tatsuya Yoshio
Account Supervisor
Shota Hatanaka
Client
Japan Maritime Self-Defense Force

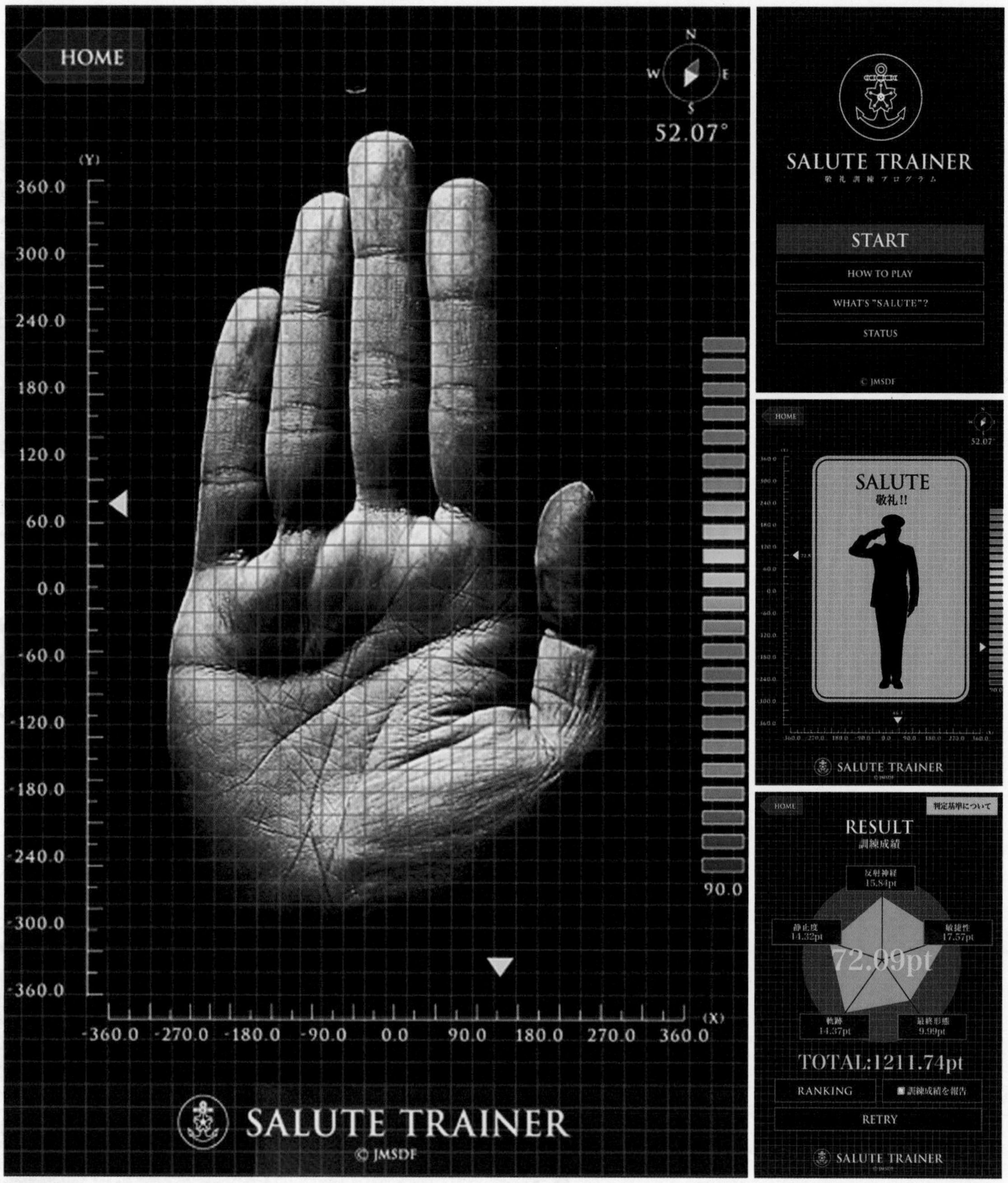
HOME
N
W
E
S
52.07°
(Y)
360.0
300.0
240.0
180.0
120.0
60.0
0.0
-60.0
-120.0
-180.0
-240.0
-300.0
-360.0
90.0
(X)
-360.0 -270.0 -180.0 -90.0 0.0 90.0 180.0 270.0 360.0
SALUTE TRAINER
© JMSDF
SALUTE TRAINER
START
HOW TO PLAY
WHAT'S "SALUTE"?
STATUS
© JMSDF
SALUTE
敬礼!!
SALUTE TRAINER
RESULT
訓練成績
72.09pt
TOTAL:1211.74pt
RANKING
RETRY
SALUTE TRAINER

Yellow Pencil in Mobile Marketing

Mobile Applications & Sites
Dentsu Tokyo

iButterfly Coupon Entertainment!
The iButterfly is an entertaining iPhone application using augmented reality, a motion sensor, and GPS functions to collect coupons. Through the iButterfly, we deliver not only coupons but also a variety of information and content. Several types of iButterflies will fly in any place at once. By using the motion sensor, people can enjoy physically catching the iButterflies.

Creative Director
Kana Nakano
Executive Creative Director
Masataka Hosogane
Programmer
Takeshi Tsuchiya
Art Director
Yoshio Hiramoto
Mobile Copywriters
Toru Oyama
Kana Nakano
Producers
Takatoshi Kamiya
Yoshikazu Nagashima
Executive Producer
Takeshi Mizukawa
Movie Director
Takeshi Kanamaru
Assistant Directors
Noriko Osumi
Takuya Shiomi
Illustrators
Yoko Hanafusa
Noriaki Onoe
Kimiaki Yaegashi
Technical Advisor
Tomonori Kagaya
Technical Supervisor
Akira Sasaki
Advertising Agency
Dentsu Tokyo
Sales Producers
Masashi Igarashi
Hiroshi Saito
Mariko Shitara
Client
Dentsu
Brand
iButterfly

Catch!
Map
Catch
Collection
Information

× 45
おみくじちょう
ビールちょう
ゴーヤちょう
ご当地キャラちょう
宣伝部ちょう
アプリちょう
幸せの青いちょう
ヲタ芸ちょう
東海道-品川
Map
Catch
Collection
Information

Collection
AD BURGER ちょう
× 25
2009.08.31 15:25 Shibuya Station
AD BURGER
ドリンクMサイズ全品通常価格より
¥100 OFF!
10/20(火)~11/20(土)まで有効
Map
Catch
Collection
Information

Nomination in Mobile Marketing

Mobile Campaigns & Mobile Advertising
TPP for Claro

Ringtowns
More than 30 Ringtowns were created using the Mayan names of some of the 1,500 Guatemalan towns and cities with coverage from mobile phone operator Claro. Ringtowns were launched through a nationwide radio campaign, inviting people to get them for free, to share them through social media and use them on their mobile phones, turning every incoming call or message into a commercial for Claro's nationwide mobile coverage. Ringtowns were available to consumers through MMS or from Claro's website.

Creative Directors
Jose Contreras
Ramiro Eduardo
Ruben Leyton
Miguel Mayen
Technical Director
Soizic Freyschmidt
Mobile Developer
Monica Ruiz
Developer
Soizic Freyschmidt
Art Director
Francisco Coutiño
Copywriter
Jorge Perez
Mobile Designer
David Galdamez
Designer
Francisco Coutiño
Design Director
Desiree Cojulun
Interactive Designers
Desiree Cojulun
David Galdamez
Flash Programmer
David Galdamez
Producer
Juan Carlos Flores
Animator
Polo Uribio
Sound Designer
Ender Barrientos
Mobile Marketing Agency
TPP
Advertising Agency
Ogilvy Guatemala
Account Handler
Gustavo Alejos
Brand Manager
Eduardo Muniz
Marketing Manager
Wellyngton Da Silva
Client
Claro

RINGTOWNS
Claro

Chiquimula
San Pedro
Esquipulas

Nomination in Mobile Marketing

Mobile Applications & Sites
Marcel & Publicis Conseil for Renault

360 Degrees
We developed an iPad application that offers consumers a 360-degree view around the inside of the Renault Espace from the comfort of their own homes. The consumer can choose from ten destinations, thereby discovering the world's most beautiful scenery through the windows of a Renault Espace. The consumer can navigate freely around the inside of the Renault Espace, enjoying the true benefit of the superior nature of the glass surface before trying it for real.

Creative Directors
Julien Benmoussa
Florent Imbert
Emmanuel Lalleve
Chief Creative Officers
Olivier Altmann
Sebastien Vacherot
Technical Director
Sylvain Bernardi
Art Directors
Thibaud Cartigny
Miguel Mantilla
Benedicte Potel
Mobile Copywriters
Sylvain Chailloux
Thierry Lebec
Cedric Leplat
Producer
Laurent Sequaris
TV Producer
Frederique Le Goff
Direction
Egocentric
Advertising Agencies
Marcel
Publicis Conseil
Account Handlers
Stephane Gaillard
Pascal Gaveriaux
Florent Moignard
Pascal Nessim
Arthur Trarieux-Lumiere
Brand Manager
Frederic Nicolaïdis
Marketing Manager
Isabelle Fossecave
Client
Renault
Brand
Espace

Mobile Campaigns
& Mobile Advertising
BBDO New York for GE

GE Ecomagination iAd
GE sought to demonstrate how Ecomagination technology can benefit everyone. We aimed to position GE at the forefront of solutions for cleaner energy and greater energy efficiency, resulting in greater good for both people and planet.
In the Ecomagination iAd, GE demonstrated this through a cool experience with a simple message. Using innovative new media and rich interactions – while also pushing the boundaries of HTML5 and video integration – the iAd allows users to explore a world where they can shake, swipe and spin to discover how Ecomagination is working to help people, the Earth and industry coexist in harmony.

Creative Director
Ron Lent
Executive Creative Directors
Mathias Appelblad
Don Schneider
Chief Creative Officer
David Lubars
Art Director
Rob Seale
Copywriter
Michael Aimette
Designer
Lea Baran
Content Producer
Nicholas Gaul
Senior Producer
David Ross
Head of Interactive Production
Niklas Lindstrom
Director of Music & Radio Production
Rani Vaz
Advertising Agency
BBDO New York
Production Company
Stardust
Client
GE

Drag to charge
your first electric car.
56%

Mobile Campaigns
& Mobile Advertising
Wieden+Kennedy London for Nokia

Own Voice
To advertise the sat nav on Nokia phones, we invented a new product feature, called Own Voice, that lets people record the voices of friends and family to be a constantly changing chorus of guides on their Nokia sat nav. Through a mobile app, our website and Facebook, millions invited loved ones to record a few commands. It permanently improved the product experience and helped the brand to live out its motto: Connecting People.

Creative Directors
Sidney Bosley
Rob Perkins
Executive Creative Directors
Tony Davidson
Kim Papworth
Interactive Art Director
Zaid Al-Asady
Graphic Designer
Seppo Palo
Senior Designer
Tom Haswell
Senior Concept Designer
Mihael Cankar
Head of Design
Dan Griffiths
Development Director
Rob Gibson
Head of Development
Chris Blackburn
Director of Creative Technology
Antti Kilpelä
Information Architect
Jonathan Godsell
Producer
Jeanne Bachelard
Advertising Agency
Wieden+Kennedy London
Software Development
Starcut
Communications Agency
Glue Isobar
Head Project Manager
Marko Laitinen
Strategist
Josh Millrod
Account Director
Minni Lakotieva
Client
Nokia

OWN VOICE
For Ovi Maps
NOKIA
Connecting People
Start creating your Own Voice pack
Search
stein
Rob Steiner
Selected (9 friends)
Add up to 11 voices. Don't forget to include yours!
Fern Trelfa
John Kirkham
Mathew Kramer
Sidney Bosley
Create my Own Voice pack
My voice packs
How it works
OWN VOICE
For Ovi Maps
NOKIA
Connecting People
Dan's best mates
Created by Dan Griffiths
You've completed
100%
My voice packs
How it works
Publish now

Mobile Campaigns & Mobile Advertising
Goodby, Silverstein & Partners for The Dalí Museum

Dalí Museum iPhone App
To build awareness of The Dalí Museum's fantastical new building, we developed a customised picture-editing app that creates dreamy surrealist overlays for photos. With zero budget, we turned to the style-makers at Hipstamatic to help bring it to life. They liked the idea so much that they waived their fees and pledged to donate any product sales income to the museum. We're proud to have built a modern-day tribute to the brilliance of Mr Dalí that not only isn't costing the museum money, but is also bringing in much-needed funds.

Creative Director
Lucas Buick
Technical Director
Ryan Dorshorst
Mobile Copywriter
Jody Horn
Mobile Designer
Brian Gunderson
Producer
Alex Burke
Director of Digital Production
Carey Head
Advertising Agency
Goodby, Silverstein & Partners
Director of Brand Strategy
Gareth Kay
Client
The Dalí Museum

DALÍ MUSEUM & Hipstamatic
Hipstamatic Presents: The Dalí Museum GoodPak, the first of Hipstamatic's GoodPak Series. Capture a surreal world through the Salvador Lens. Proceeds from the GoodPak go directly to the Dalí Museum, St. Petersburg, Florida.
App Store
DALÍ MUSEUM GOODPAK
CONTEST
THE DALÍ MUSEUM
CLICK INTO
HIPSTASURREALIST STYLE
Characterized by surrealist overlays, Salvador's glowing color palette, and a 'randomness' unlike anything ever offered by Hipstamatic, the new Dalí Museum GoodPak is a modern day ode to the brilliance of the leader of the surrealist movement. Also included is the painterly Salvador Film and custom plastic camera body for your Hipstamatic. Proceeds from the GoodPak go directly to The Dalí Museum, St. Petersburg, Florida.
GALLERY
Salvador
Salvadór
84
200

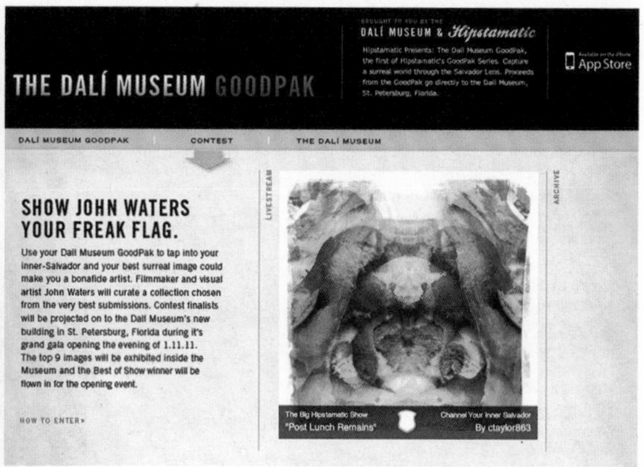
THE DALÍ MUSEUM GOODPAK
DALÍ MUSEUM & Hipstamatic
Hipstamatic Presents: The Dalí Museum GoodPak, the first of Hipstamatic's GoodPak Series. Capture a surreal world through the Salvador Lens. Proceeds from the GoodPak go directly to the Dalí Museum, St. Petersburg, Florida.
App Store
DALÍ MUSEUM GOODPAK
CONTEST
THE DALÍ MUSEUM
SHOW JOHN WATERS
YOUR FREAK FLAG.
Use your Dalí Museum GoodPak to tap into your inner-Salvador and your best surreal image could make you a bonafide artist. Filmmaker and visual artist John Waters will curate a collection chosen from the very best submissions. Contest finalists will be projected on to the Dalí Museum's new building in St. Petersburg, Florida during it's grand gala opening the evening of 1.11.11. The top 9 images will be exhibited inside the Museum and the Best of Show winner will be flown in for the opening event.
HOW TO ENTER»
LIVESTREAM
ARCHIVE
The Big Hipstamatic Show
"Post Lunch Remains"
Channel Your Inner Salvador
By ctaylor863

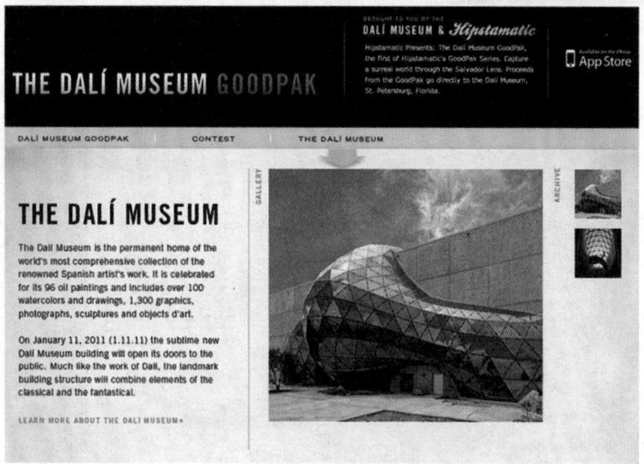
THE DALÍ MUSEUM GOODPAK
DALÍ MUSEUM & Hipstamatic
Hipstamatic Presents: The Dalí Museum GoodPak, the first of Hipstamatic's GoodPak Series. Capture a surreal world through the Salvador Lens. Proceeds from the GoodPak go directly to the Dalí Museum, St. Petersburg, Florida.
App Store
DALÍ MUSEUM GOODPAK
CONTEST
THE DALÍ MUSEUM
THE DALÍ MUSEUM
The Dalí Museum is the permanent home of the world's most comprehensive collection of the renowned Spanish artist's work. It is celebrated for its 96 oil paintings and includes over 100 watercolors and drawings, 1,300 graphics, photographs, sculptures and objects d'art.
On January 11, 2011 (1.11.11) the sublime new Dalí Museum building will open its doors to the public. Much like the work of Dalí, the landmark building structure will combine elements of the classical and the fantastical.
LEARN MORE ABOUT THE DALÍ MUSEUM»
GALLERY
ARCHIVE

Mobile Applications & Sites
AMV BBDO for PepsiCo

Late Night
We created a fully interactive 360-degree music video for the track 'Comin' to get me', written by MOBO award-winner Professor Green exclusively for Doritos. Using the iPhone's accelerometer, the app enables people to navigate their way through the 360-degree video, by moving their arms up and down or tilting the handset left and right.

Creative Director
Mark Fairbanks
Executive Creative Director
Paul Brazier
Application Developer
Neil Mendoza
Art Director
Jeremy Tribe
Copywriter
Prabs Wignarajah
Director
Chris Cairns
Producers
Suzy MacGregor
Martin Poyner
Advertising Agency
AMV BBDO
Global Creative Agency
Goodby, Silverstein & Partners
Production Company
Partizan
Post Production
The Mill Los Angeles
Account Handler
Benedict Pringle
Marketing Manager
Sam Hinchcliffe
Client
PepsiCo
Brand
Doritos

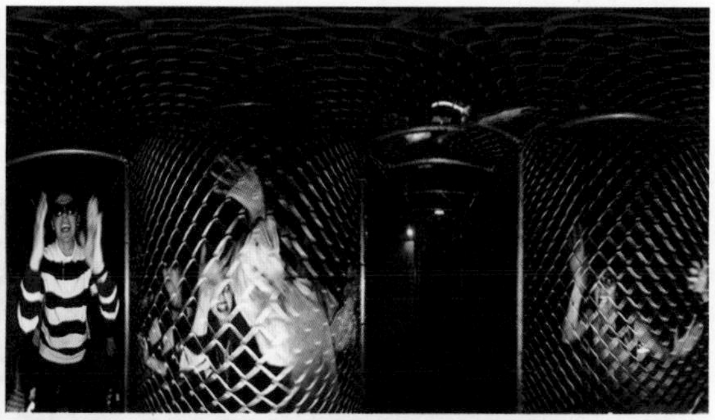

Mobile Applications & Sites
Brothers and Sisters for the Museum of London

Streetmuseum
The Museum of London wanted a digital idea to create buzz about the opening of its new Galleries of Modern London. So we created Streetmuseum, an augmented reality iPhone app that brings the museum's extensive collections to the streets. The app uses geotagging and Google Maps to guide users to sites around London, where historical images appear via the iPhone screen. Click on the '3D view' button and the app will recognise your location then use augmented reality to overlay the historic image over the current view. The museum wanted 5,000 downloads. By January 2011, we'd hit 160,000.

Creative Director
Steve Shannon
Executive Creative Director
Andy Fowler
Mobile Developers
Gavin Buttimore
Robin Charlton
Art Directors
Lisa Jelliffe
Kirsten Rutherford
Copywriters
Lisa Jelliffe
Kirsten Rutherford
Mobile Designer
Mateus Wanderley
Producer
Tanya Holland
Image Geotagger
Jack Kerruish
Advertising Agency
Brothers and Sisters
Head of Digital
Kevin Brown
Account Handler
Emma Simmons
New Business Director
Helen Kimber
Marketing Manager
Vicky Lee
Client
Museum of London

DIG FOR VICTORY

Mobile Applications & Sites
Dentsu London

Penki
Penki is Japanese for 'paint'. Penki is a light painting app for iPhones and iPads, using the same technique created for the film 'Making Future Magic: iPad Light Painting'. Pulling Penki through the air and capturing the results on long exposure lets people create their own 3D imagery and words. There are examples from Penki users on the Penki group page on Flickr. 'Making Future Magic' is Dentsu London's creative philosophy.

Creative Director
Matt Jones
Technical Director
Nick Ludlam
Designers
Camille Bozzini
Campbell Orme
Advertising Agency
Dentsu London
Design Consultancy
BERG
Strategic Director
Beeker Northam
Client
Dentsu London
Brand
Penki

FUTURE

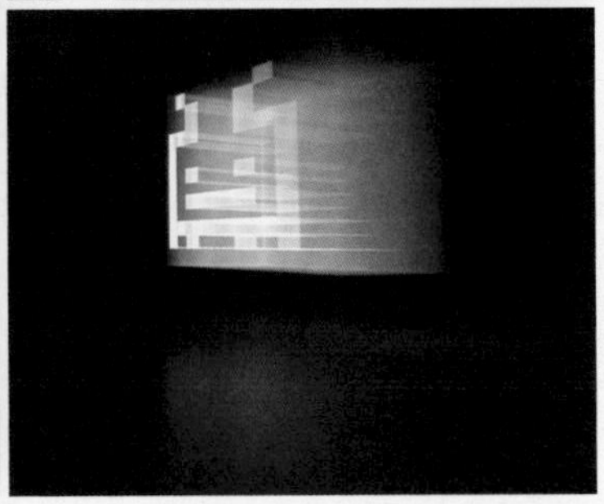

Mobile Applications & Sites
ustwo™

Granimator™
Granimator™ is a graphic wallpaper creator for the iPad. It allows the user to remix graphical pack assets, styles and backgrounds onto the stage to create multiple abstract designs. Wallpapers are posted, shared and viewed on the Granimator.com website and the Grallery iPhone app. ustwo™ has collaborated with Granimator™ pack designers from around the world, transforming the wallpaper-creating experience for users. We've collaborated with 53 pack designers to date, including James Joyce, Jon Burgerman, Kate Moross, Airside, Moving Brands, Non Format, Buro Destruct, Pete Fowler, Research Studios, Ded, Gasbook, IdN, Hush and Creative Review.

Creative Director
mills
Technical Director
Victor Essnert
Lead Developer
Kenny Lovrin
Developer
Adam Evans
Lead Designer
Andy Lafferty
Digital Design Studio
ustwo™
Project Manager
Sam Rooker Roberts
Marketing Director
Steve Bittan
Client
ustwo™

Tools
Shape Size
Draw
Erase
Clear All
Interact
Current pack
Multicity
By Kate Moross
Pack Store
My packs
Shapes
Styles
Backgrounds
Granimator
Pack Store
My Packs

Mobile Applications & Sites
Duo Blau for MINI

MINI Getaway
MINI launched the new Countryman with the 'Getaway' concept. For seven days, everybody with an iPhone was invited to hunt and catch a virtual MINI in Stockholm. You used an app where you could see the location of the virtual MINI, all other players and yourself. If you got within 50 metres of the virtual MINI, you could grab it with your iPhone. Then you had to get away, because anyone within 50 metres could take the MINI from you. The person with the virtual MINI in their iPhone when the game finished won a real MINI Countryman.

Creative Director
Johan Jäger
Art Director
Daniel Wahlgren
Mobile Copywriter
Magnus Andersson
Mobile Designer
Jon Palmqvist
Producer
Ida Modin
Mobile Marketing Agency
Duo Blau
Advertising Agency
Jung von Matt Stockholm
Media Agency
Carat
Planner
Leon Phang
Account Handler
Jan Casserlöv
Brand Manager
Fredrik Ellsäter
Marketing Manager
Stefan Ljung
Client
MINI

YOU
MINI
Regeringsgatan
Norrlandsgatan
Kungsgatan
Lästmakargatan
Lästmakargatan
Jakobsbergsgatan
Jakobsbergsgatan

Mobile Applications & Sites
Publicis London
for Depaul UK

iHobo
Depaul UK is a charity that aims to keep young people off the streets and off hard drugs. It needed more donations from affluent, socially conscious 30-somethings, so we put a young homeless person in their pockets for three days. Or, more accurately, on their iPhones. For three days, the fate of 'iHobo' is in their hands. Treated well, he thrives. Left alone and uncared for, his inevitable decline into hard drugs usage plays out on their screens. After building a sense of responsibility for him, the app prompted users to donate with a revolutionary one-click mechanism.

Executive Creative Directors
Tom Ewart
Adam Kean
Developer
Scott Walsh
Programmer
Simon Whitty
Art Director
Robert Amstell
Copywriter
Matthew Lancod
Live Action Director
Ned Miles
Animator
Matthew Osbourne
Agency Producers
Colin Hickson
Sharon Joyce
Production Assistant
Sam Holmes
Advertising Agency
Publicis London
Managing Director
Phil Mundy
Client
Depaul UK

DEPAUL UK
YOUTH·COMMUNITY·OPPORTUNITY
DONATE
REPLAY

DO NOT IGNORE iHobo

Mobile Applications & Sites
Herraiz Soto & Co
for Camper

Have a Camper Day
Why are weather applications so boring? 'Extraordinary craft' is how Camper understands technology: half imagination, half craft. To communicate this concept in a friendly, original and non-intrusive manner, we thought about how we receive weather forecasts today (boring and lifeless interfaces and icons). We created new meteorological elements made from prêt-à-porter materials and turned them into musical instruments that react to touch. Haven't got an iPad? Enjoy it on the web!

Creative Directors
Vicente Reyes
Rafa Soto
Esteve Traveset
Technical Director
Cay Garrido
Art Director
Esteve Traveset
Copywriter
Vicente Reyes
Designers
Sergio Puertas
Esteve Traveset
Vicky Walker
Sound Designer
Carlos Torrecilla
Advertising Agency
Herraiz Soto & Co
Planner
Oliver Henares
Account Handler
Robert Aran
Account Executive
Paulina Arana
Marketing Manager
Pere Quintana
Client
Camper

HAVE A CAMPER DAY

Barcelona 14°

Barcelona 14°

Mobile Interaction & Experience
Y&R New York
for Airwalk

Invisible Pop Up Store
When Airwalk decided on a limited edition relaunch of its classic sneaker, the Jim, we came up with a new way to do it: the world's first invisible pop-up stores. Bringing together mobile phones, GPS technology and augmented reality, customers could only buy the Jim if they downloaded the app, went to a pre-determined location, held up their phones, and took a photo of the augmented reality Jim floating there. That allowed them to purchase the sneaker there and then. This was an exclusive product, sold to an exclusive audience, for an entirely new retail experience.

Creative Directors
Graeme Hall
Menno Kluin
Steve Whittier
Executive Creative Directors
Ian Reichenthal
Scott Vitrone
Production Creative Directors
Shailesh Rao
Vivian Rosenthal
Art Director
Alexander Nowak
Copywriter
Feliks Richter
Designers
Austin Bone
Tiffany Ng
Executive Directors of Content Production
Nathy Aviram
Lora Schulson
Agency Producers
Devon Dentler
Jo Kelly
Global Director of Creative Content
Kerry Keenan
Advertising Agency
Y&R New York
Mobile Production
Goldrun
Brand Manager
Eric Dreyer
Client Vice President
Eric Dreyer
Client
Airwalk
Brand
Airwalk Jim

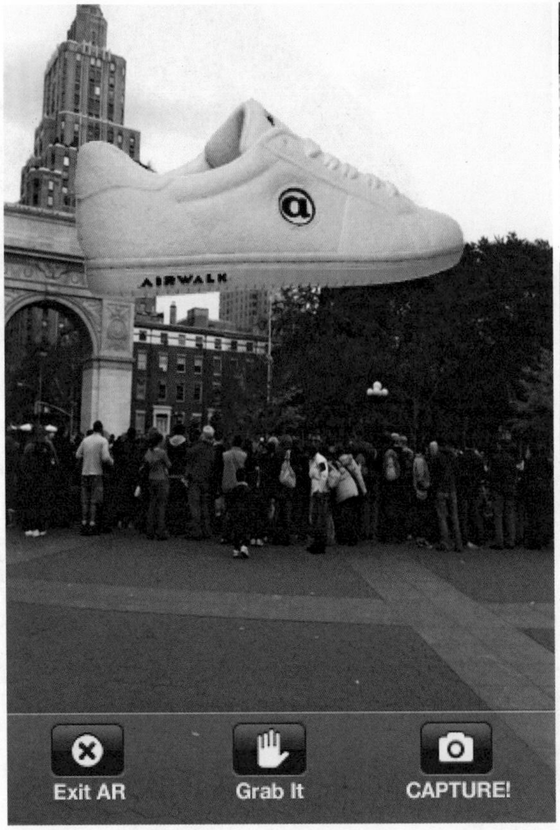
AIRWALK
Exit AR
Grab It
CAPTURE!

CONGRATS!
YOU FOUND THE JIM.

Mobile Interaction & Experience
McCann London
for Xbox

Kingmaker
Kingmaker was a multiplayer mobile phone game preceding the launch of Fable III on Xbox.The game played as a hybrid between Foursquare and the board game Risk, where players used GPS on their mobiles to battle for territory and earn gold that they could later spend in Fable III. By awarding bonus gold to players for linking their Kingmaker account to social media, we encouraged gamers to spread news for us while also providing a pre-release incentive to buy Fable III. We created an economy where we paid gamers to do our marketing for us.

Lead Creative
Pete Bardell
Executive Creative Directors
Brian Fraser
Simon Learman
Creative Technologist
Lewis Taylor
Technical Director
Stefan Feissli
Art Director
Lewis Plummer
Senior Art Director
Matt Statham
Copywriter
Mark Rowbotham
Senior Copywriter
Chris McDonald
Programmer
Stuart Lodge
Producer
Myles Hocking
Advertising Agency
McCann London
Strategist
Pete Bardell
Content Strategist
Tom Rothenberg
Account Handler
Pip Shepherd
Marketing Manager
Michael Flatt
Client
Xbox
Brand
Fable III

EUROPA NEEDS
YOU
JOIN UP AT FABLE3KINGMAKER.COM
FABLE III KINGMAKER

FABLE III KINGMAKER
THE BATTLE BEGINS THIS OCTOBER

FABLE III KINGMAKER

Yellow Pencil in Music Videos

Colonel Blimp for Infectious Music

Love Lost
Some children go for a cross-country run. Hilarity ensues.

Director
Dougal Wilson
Producer
Matt Fone
Artist
The Temper Trap
Production Company
Colonel Blimp
Editor
Joe Guest
Special Effects
Simon Tayler
Lighting Cameraperson
Lasse Frank Johannessen
Record Company
Infectious Music
Video Commissioner
Richard Skinner

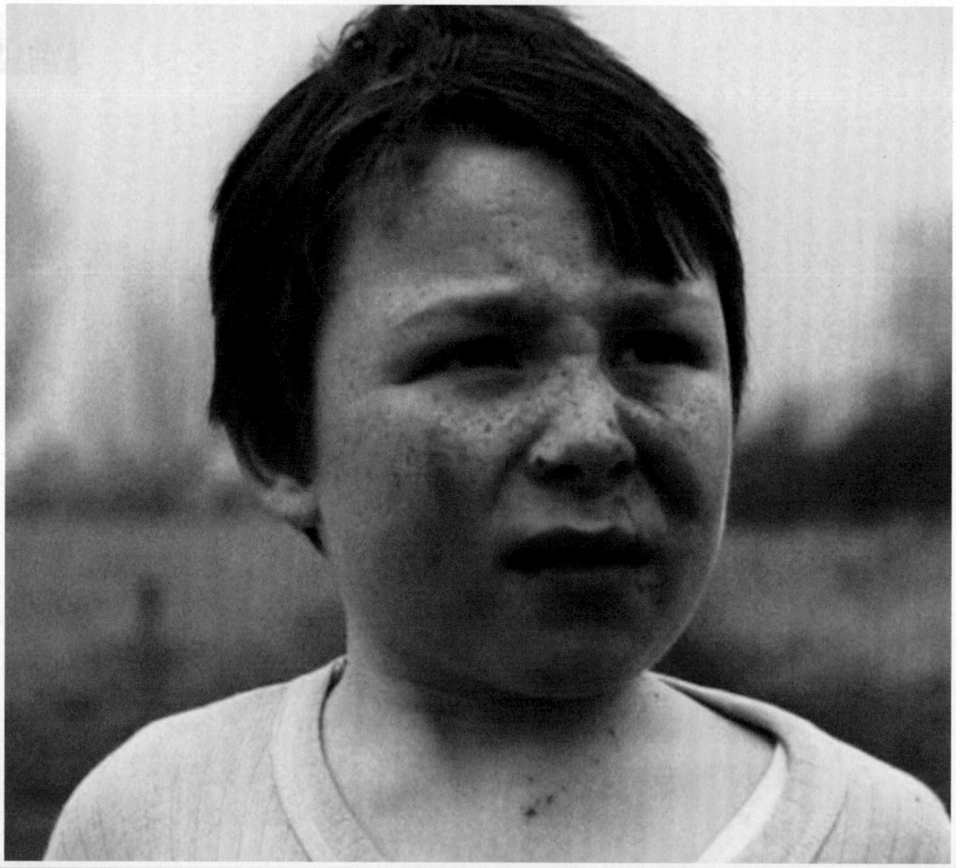

Yellow Pencil in
Music Videos

Harry & Co
for Interscope

Zef Side
This is the short film that currently has over ten million YouTube hits, which launched an unknown Die Antwoord into sudden, worldwide fame. The rest is history. Zef Side.

Director
Sean Metelerkamp
Producer
Pendra Dissel
Artist
Die Antwoord
Production Company
Harry & Co
Editor
Eben Smal
Lighting Cameraperson
Caleb Heymann
Video Producer
Pendra Dissel
Record Company
Interscope

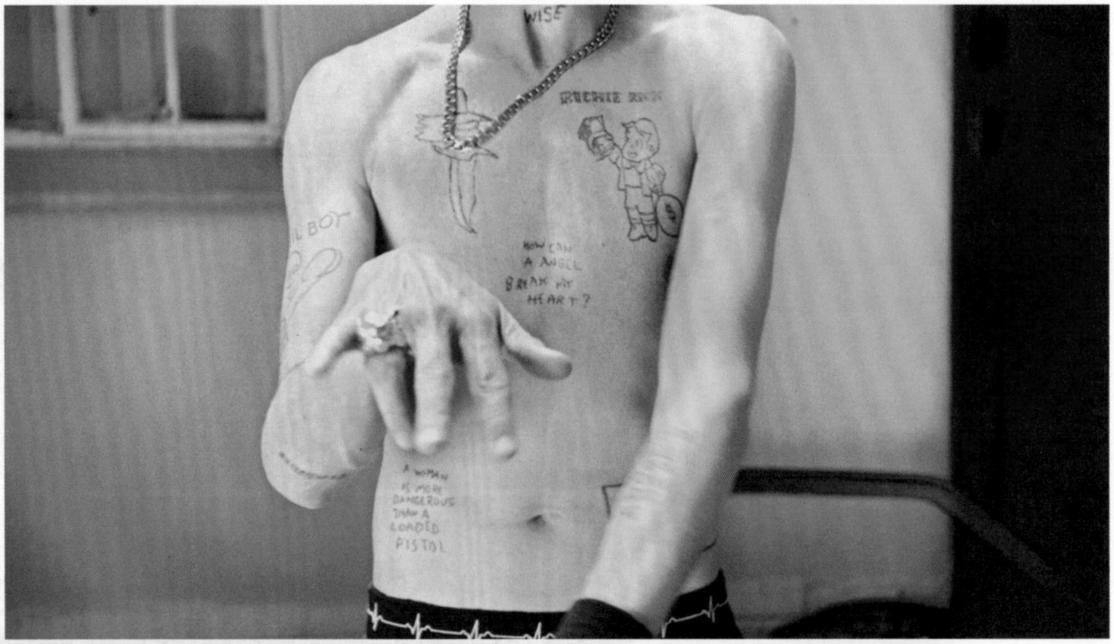
WISE
HOW CAN A ANGEL BREAK MY HEART?
A WOMAN IS MORE DANGEROUS THAN A LOADED PISTOL

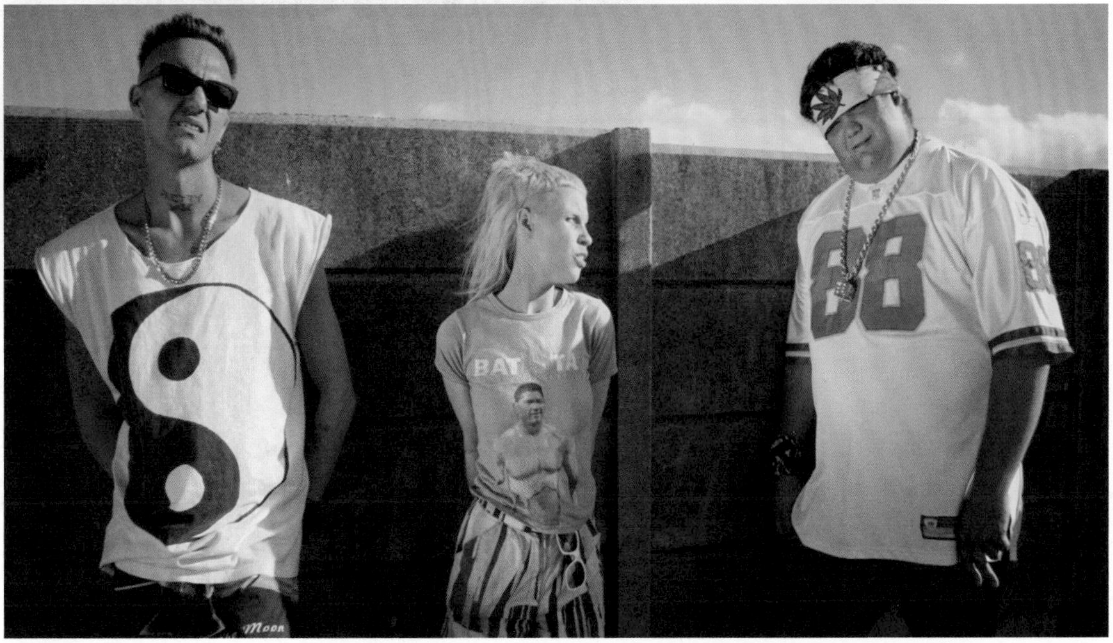

Yellow Pencil in
Music Videos

Editing for Music Videos
Partizan for
679 Recordings
& Atlantic Records

Prayin'
This is the follow-up to She Said and part of the series of videos by Plan B showing the decline of the star Strickland Banks. Prayin' was also nominated in the Music Videos category.

Editor
Tom Lindsay
Director
Daniel Wolfe
Producer
Tim Francis
Artist
Plan B
Production Company
Partizan
Lighting Cameraperson
Robbie Ryan
Set Designer
Sam Tidman
Record Companies
679 Recordings
Atlantic Records
Video Commissioner
Tim Nash

Nomination in
Music Videos

Somesuch & Co
for Mercury Records

Blind Faith
Manchester. 1991.
Five friends go
to their first rave.

Director
Daniel Wolfe
Producer
Tim Francis
Artist
Chase and Status
Feat. Liam Bailey
Production Company
Somesuch & Co
Editor
Dom Leung
Lighting Cameraperson
Lol Crawley
Set Designer
Sami Khan
Record Company
Mercury Records
Video Commissioner
Dan Curwin

Nomination in
Music Videos

El Niño for
XL Recordings

Born Free
Born Free depicts US officers rounding up ethnic minorities – redheads – and driving them to a remote area, then killing them. Born Free was also nominated in Cinematography for Music Videos.

Director
Romain Gavras
Producer
Mourad Belkeddar
Artist
M.I.A.
Production Company
El Niño
Editor
Walter Mauriot
Lighting Cameraperson
Andre Chemetoff
Record Company
XL Recordings

OUR DAY WILL COME

● Nomination in
Music Videos

Streetgang Films
for Sony Music UK

Rabbit

For this remixed single of 'Rabbit', Andreas Nilsson creates a mythological story of a living god. Our young bearded Kumari is raised and protected by a powerful guerrilla force of Amazon women. The boy is called upon by the government to explain a miraculous occurrence at the beach. Upon seeing the magical vision, the boy channels its energy and transforms himself into an all-powerful being. The video was shot in Kingston, Jamaica.

Director
Andreas Nilsson
Producer
Jason Botkin
Artist
Miike Snow
Production Companies
Furlined
Streetgang Films
Editor
Andreas Nilsson
Animator
Andreas Nilsson
Telecine Operator
Marshall Plante
Video Producer
Just Diener
Record Company
Sony Music UK
Video Commissioner
Dan Millar

Nomination in Music Videos

Partizan for XL Recordings

Bombay
Bombay was the breakthrough video for directing collective Canada, which began drawing them worldwide attention and recognition. Their style, somewhere between glamorous photography and European cinema, is a constant exploration of the search for beauty and truth. Hailing from Spain, the trio's imaginative use of bold imagery and non-linear narrative was what made this video for El Guincho one of the most memorable music videos of 2010.

Direction
Canada
Producer
Alba Barneda
Artist
El Guincho
Production Company
Partizan
Editing
Young Turks
Lighting Cameraperson
Marc Gomez del Moral
Set Designer
Maruxa Alvar
Record Company
XL Recordings

Nomination in Music Videos

Cinematography for Music Videos
Academy Films
for Polydor

Limit to Your Love
This video takes the commonplace and makes it extraordinary – in this case, subtly subjecting James's apartment to mysterious, time-space continuum-warping galactic forces.

Lighting Cameraperson
Kasper Tuxen
Director
Martin de Thurah
Artist
James Blake
Production Companies
Academy Films
Bacon Films
Editor
Peter Brandt
Special Effects
Marta Julia Johansen
Kristine Køster
Grading
Sophie Borup
Video Producer
Maria Schou Andersen
Record Company
Polydor

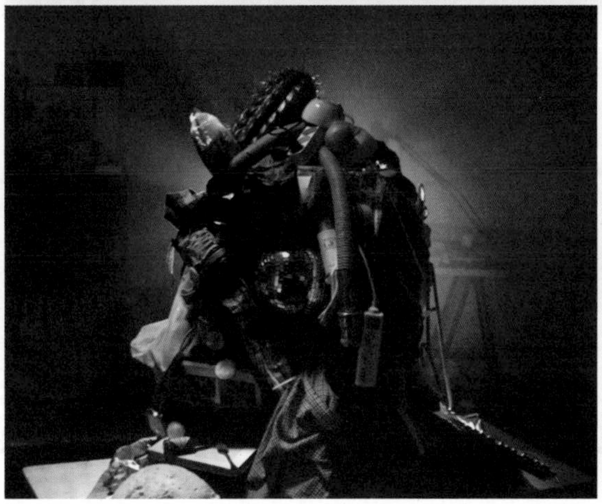

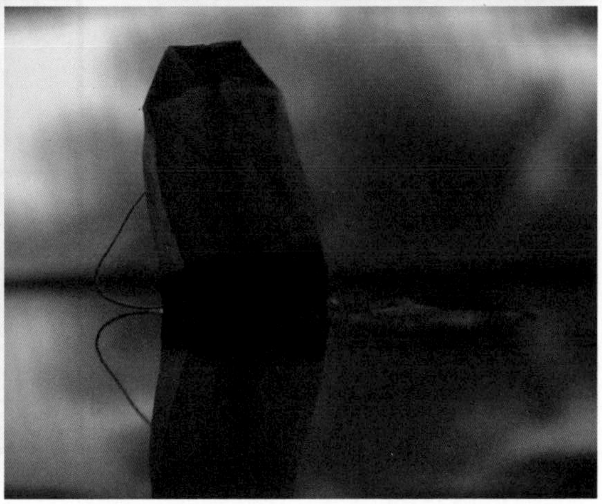

Nomination in
Music Videos

Editing for Music Videos
Final Cut for
Atlantic Records

On to the Next One
Hip-hop can be oddly conservative, with dyed in the wool conventions that are very rarely broken. Ultimately the goal of this video was to break down those conventions. It was not a narrative or straightforward performance/hip-hop video, so we had to find creative ways to make these seemingly random images work together. As tricky as it was to create a relationship between a shot of a Samurai fighter and a flaming basketball for instance, we endeavoured to achieve just that in such a way that the viewer doesn't question those juxtapositions.

Editor
Amanda James
Director
Sam Brown
Producer
Jeremy Sullivan
Artist
Jay-Z Ft. Swizz Beatz
Production Company
DNA
Post Production
Final Cut
Special Effects
The Mill London
Lighting Cameraperson
Chris Probst
Record Company
Atlantic Records

Nomination in Music Videos

Animation for Music Videos
Milk+Koblin for American Recordings & Lost Highway Records

The Johnny Cash Project
This project was a global collective artwork. Beginning with a single video frame as a template, and using a custom drawing tool embedded in the site, viewers create their own personal portraits of the Man in Black. Their work is combined with art from participants around the world, and integrated into a collective whole: a crowd-sourced, interactive music video for the song 'Ain't No Grave'. Strung together and played in sequence over the song, the portraits create a moving, evolving homage to a beloved musical icon. As people discover and contribute to the project, this living portrait continues to transform and grow.

Director
Chris Milk
Creative Directors
Aaron Koblin
Chris Milk
Design Director
James Spindler
Interactive Designer
Frank Campanella
Producers
Jennifer Heath
Aaron Koblin
Chris Milk
Associate Producer
Naomi Gilbert
Executive Producers
Jennifer Heath
Jon Kamen
Rick Rubin
Evan Schechtman
Artist
Johny Cash
Production Companies
@radical.media
Milk+Koblin
Editor
Akiko Iwakawa
Visual Effects Designer
Simon Brewster
Lead Flash Developer
Jesse Freeman
Lead Developer
Mr.doob
Lead Software Engineer
Avery Brooks
Technical Director
Aaron Koblin
Senior Interactive Producer
James Calhoun
Digital Creative Agency
Milk+Koblin
Record Companies
American Recordings
Lost Highway Records
Video Commissioner
Retta Harvey

● **Nomination in Music Videos**

Animation for Music Videos
Black Dog Films
for EMI Music

Atlas Air
Previous Massive Attack video 'Splitting the Atom' was smooth exposition. 'Atlas Air' is a different story – it's hyper-kinetic, focused on the symbolic, shape-shifting, death-bringing beast, rampaging through an increasingly recognisable landscape. 'Atlas Air', released in aid of UK charity War Child, revealed the back-story, with a video that's just as remarkable as its predecessor. 'I decided to make a prequel to the 'Splitting the Atom' clip, while leaving interpretation to the viewer to a certain extent, but mixing it with the real sense of the song and the text of Robert Del Naja', explains Edouard Salier.

Animators
Rémi Gamiette
Edouard Salier
Animation Art & Compositing
Damien Martin
Julien Michel
Xavier Reye
Director
Edouard Salier
Producers
David Danesi
Svana Gisla
Edouard Salier
Artist
Massive Attack
Production Companies
Black Dog Films
Digital District
Special Effects
Emilie Caudroit
Romuald Caudroit
Jim Cave
Jean Lamoureux
Thomas Marquet
Kevin Monthureux
Record Companies
EMI Music
Virgin Records
Video Commissioner
Svana Gisla

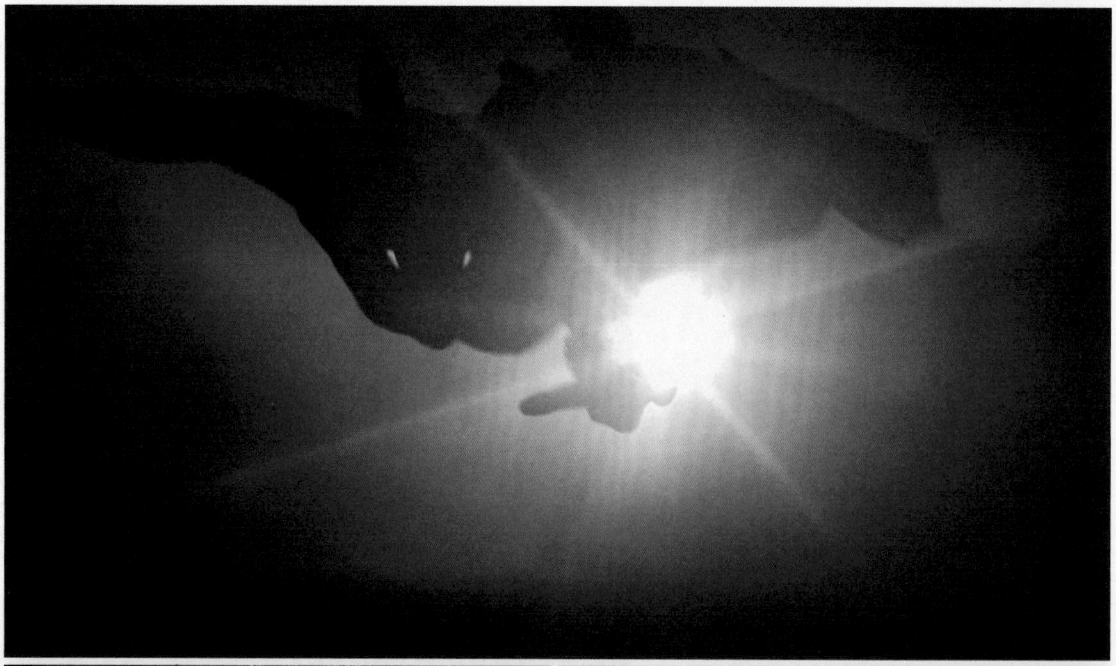

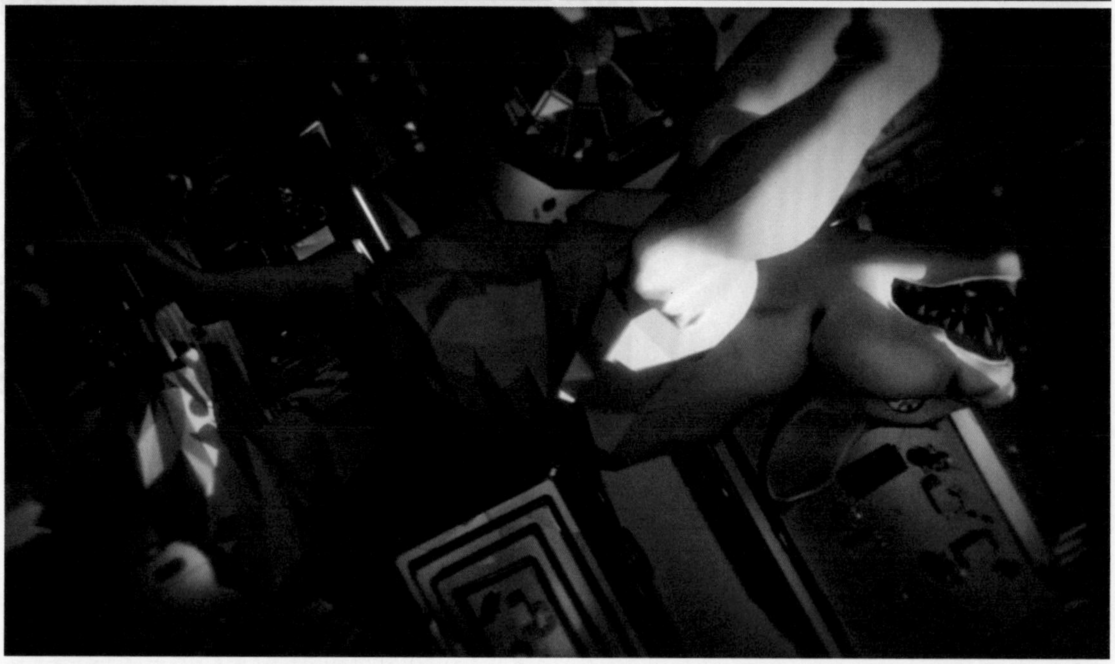

Nomination in Music Videos

Animation for Music Videos
Mathematic for Cooking Vinyl

Only Man
Parisian directing duo Jonas & François went wild with sneakers. The Audio Bullys and a number of dancers stand on a sheet of plate glass and are filmed from below. Throughout the video you get to see a lot of colourful shoe soles. The video cleverly plays off the obsession with custom sneakers in urban culture. Every single one of them has been custom designed to include pop culture references – excerpts of the lyrics looking like spoof logos, parodies of existing logos, tributes to classic album covers and film posters, weapons and tools, 3D glasses, Lego blocks, and other assorted items. What at first sight looks like an energetic dance-off turns out to be a brutal beating of the Audio Bullys. Only Man was also nominated in Special Effects for Music Videos.

Animator
Guillaume Marien
Animation
Mathematic
Directors
Jonas & François
Producer
Jules Dieng
Artist
Audio Bullys
Production Company
El Niño
Editor
Vincent Vierron
Special Effects
Guillaume Marien
Special Effects Company
Mathematic
Lighting Cameraperson
Julien Meurice
Set Designer
Laure Girardeau
Video Producer
Jules Dieng
Record Company
Cooking Vinyl

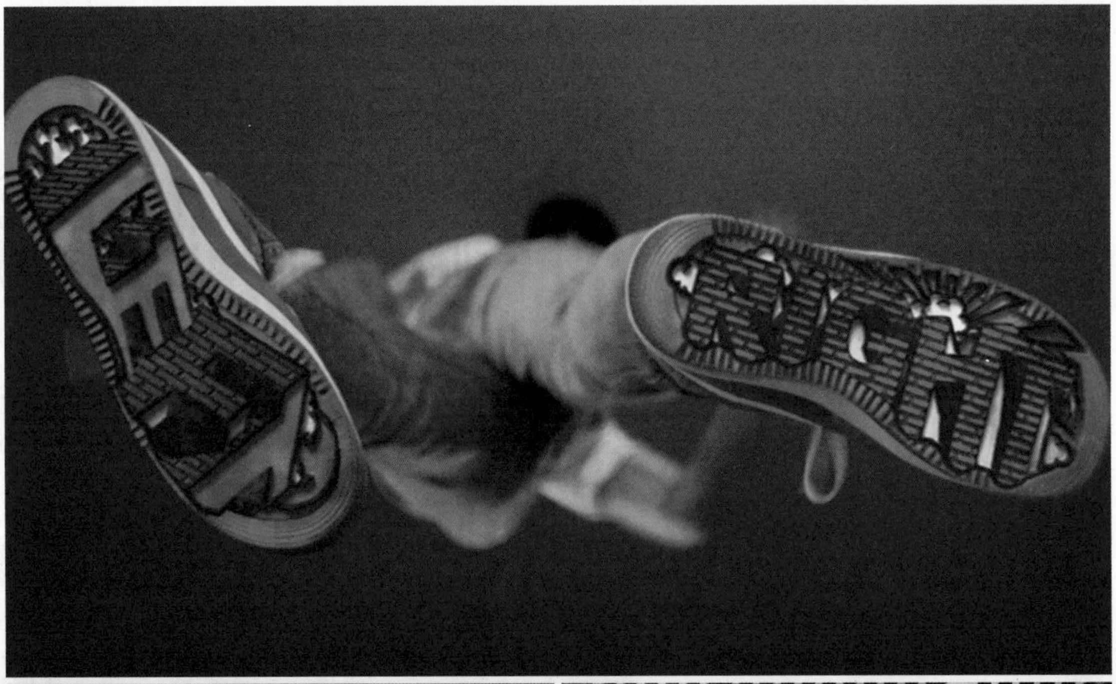

ONLY MAN
AUDIO BULLYS

- Nomination in Music Videos

Special Effects
for Music Videos
The Mill Los Angeles
for The Null Corporation

The Space in Between
Nine Inch Nails' front man Trent Reznor has taken on a new musical endeavour with his wife, Mariqueen Maandig, called How to Destroy Angels. To launch the track 'The Space in Between' the band looked to MJZ's Rupert Sanders and The Mill Los Angeles to create a striking video of bloodshed and gore. The showcase piece of the video is the devouring flames that ignite the hotel room. As Mariqueen passively sings, the luminous glow ravishes her, until she is consumed by flames. Plates of the live fire and singer were composited to create the Joan of Arc-like moment.

Visual Effects Producer
Arielle Davis
Visual Effects Company
The Mill Los Angeles
Lead 2D Artists
Andy Bate
Gareth Parr
Director
Rupert Sanders
Producer
Laurie Boccaccio
Executive Producer
Sue Troyan
Artist
How to Destroy Angels
Production Company
MJZ
Editor
Patrick Murphree
Shoot Supervisors
Phil Crowe
Cedric Nicolas-Troyan
Record Label
The Null Corporation

Music Videos
B-Reel for
Google Creative Lab

The Wilderness Downtown
This interactive interpretation of Arcade Fire's song 'We Used to Wait' was built entirely with the latest open web technologies, including HTML5 video, audio, and canvas. The story is told in multiple choreographed browser windows that pop up to reveal new scenes as the song unfolds. The video also borrows from Google's database of street images, personalising the experience for each viewer. By entering the address of their childhood homes before the song begins, viewers are treated to a narrative that takes place on the very streets where they grew up. Viewers are also able to control onscreen elements.

Director
Chris Milk
Creative Directors
Aaron Koblin
Chris Milk
Executive Producers
Jennifer Heath
Jon Kamen
Frank Scherma
Artist
Arcade Fire
Editor
Livio Sanchez
Visual Effects Designer
Scott Bravo
Cinematographers
Shawn Kim
Chris Milk
Colourist
Dave Hussey
Creative Direction
B-Reel
Production Company
@radical.media
Interactive Production & Design
B-Reel
Lead Developer
Mr.doob
3D Design
Magoo 3D Studios
Line Producer
Ari Palitz
Information Architect
Aaron Koblin
Client
Google Creative Lab
Brands
Google Chrome
HTML5

Music Videos
Nice Shoes
for Def Jam

Power
Marco Brambilla's music video painting depicts Kanye West as a doomed emperor presiding over a sensual yet apocalyptic spectacle. Gradually each figure, with its own distinct movement, creeps into the screen; the piece ends with a crescendo of fireworks and impending doom.

Director
Marco Brambilla
Producers
Jonathan Lia
Anna Smith
Artist
Kanye West
Production Company
Stink
Visual Effects Creative Director
Aron Baxter
Visual Effects
Nice Shoes
Colourist
Ron Sudul
Record Company
Def Jam

Music Videos
El Niño for
Modular People

Solitude is Bliss
There's a guy and an accident. He wants to see, but cops are blocking him. He seems ravaged. Then he is alone, and happy. Then there is a crowd, walking against him. He seems annoyed. Then he is alone again. He dances for a while. Later there will be a dog, begging for friendship, but he will knock him out. And the crowd will come back again.

Direction
Megaforce
Art Director
Natalia Makhovskaya
Producer
Jules Dieng
Artist
Tame Impala
Production Company
El Niño
Editor
Walter Mauriot
Lighting Cameraperson
Mathieu Plainfosse
Wardrobe Stylist
Svetlana Berejnaya
Record Company
Modular People

Music Videos
Partizan for
Sony Music
Entertainment UK

Somebody to Love Me
The video shows the life of a young Boy George, at the height of his fame during the 80s, through old home videos.

Director
Saam Farahmand
Producer
Leanne Stott
Artist
Mark Ronson & The Business Intl. Feat. Boy George & Andrew Wyatt
Production Company
Partizan
Editor
Tom Lindsay
Lighting Cameraperson
Florian Hoffmeister
Set Designer
Ben Ansell
Record Company
Sony Music
Entertainment UK
Video Commissioner
Mike O'Keefe

Music Videos
Screampark for
Virgin Records

Splitting the Atom
'The fixed moment of the catastrophe. The instant the atom bursts on the beast, the world freezes into a vitrified chaos. And we go through the slick and glistening disaster of humanity in distress. Man or beast? The responsibility of this chaos is still to be determined.' – Edouard Salier on 'Splitting the Atom'.

Director
Edouard Salier
Producer
Anne Lifshitz
Artist
Massive Attack
Production Company
Screampark
Animator
Rémi Gamiette
Special Effects
Jean Lamoureux
Compositor
Xavier Reye
Designer
Julien Michel
Set Designer
Damien Martin
Post Producer
David Danesi
Post Production Company
Digital District
Video Producer
Anne Lifshitz
Record Company
Virgin Records
Video Commissioner
Svana Gisla

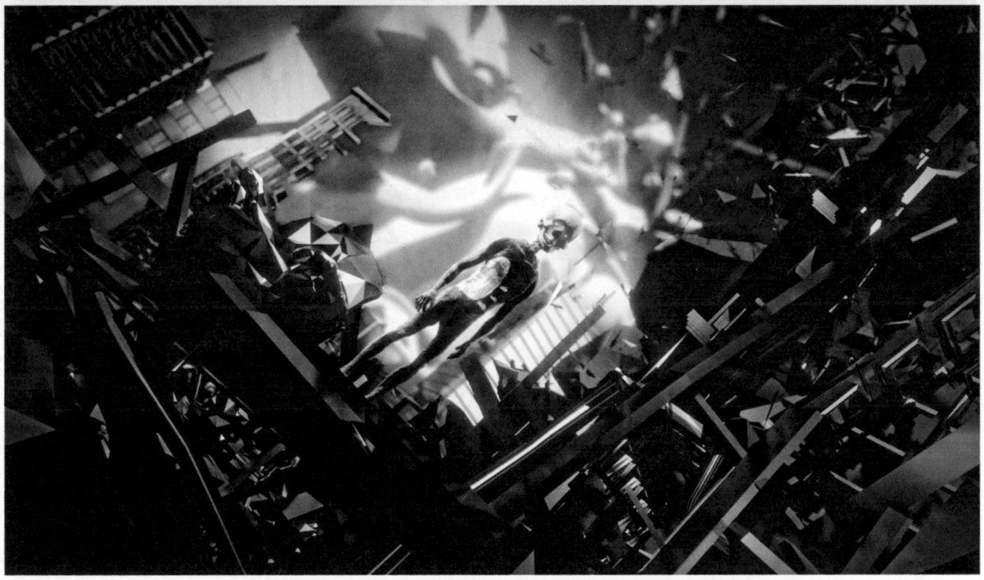

Animation for
Music Videos
Division Paris for
Record Makers

Look
This is the animated story of an ass.

Animators
Aurelie Bruneaux
Julien Chavepayre
Guillaume King
Direction
Mzyrk & Moriceau
Producer
Jules de Chateleux
Head of Post Production
Guillaume Marien
Artist
Sébastien Tellier
Production Company
Division Paris
Post Production House
Mathematic
Record Company
Record Makers

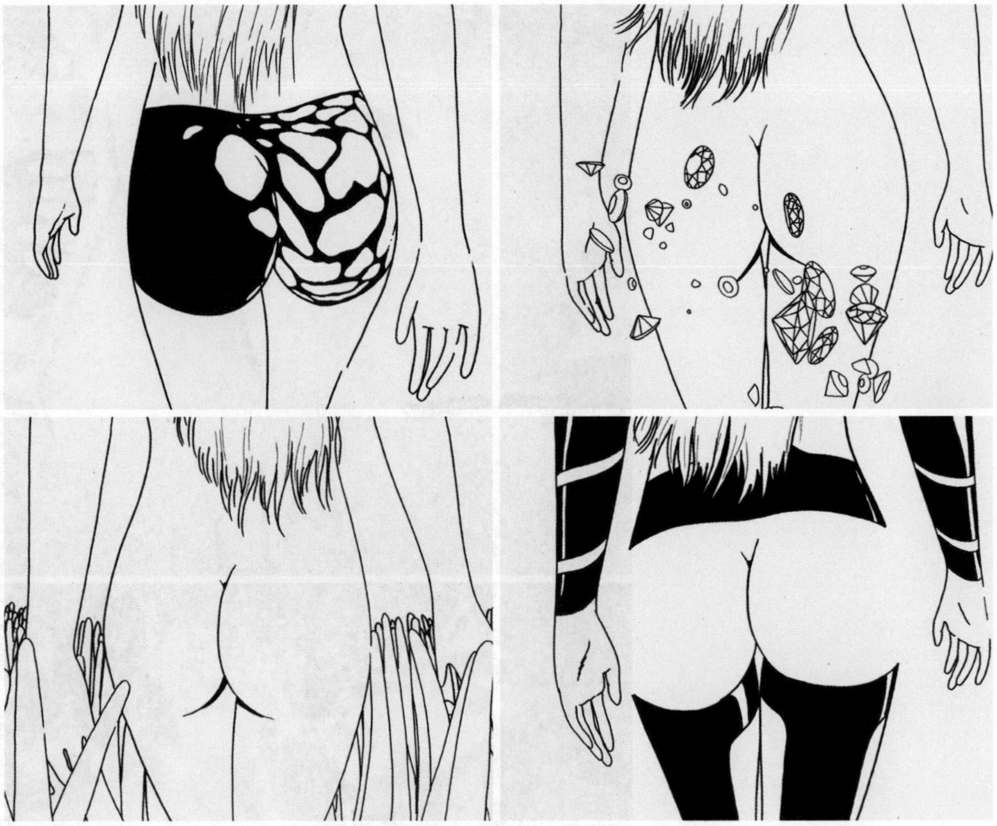

Animation for
Music Videos
Colonel Blimp
for EMI Music

Let Go
This is the music video to accompany the Japanese Popstars' new track 'Let Go'. It features techno artist Green Velvet on vocals, and follows on from the band's 'Destroy' EP. The entire video was created over an intensive 20-day period in September 2010.

Animators
Malcolm Draper
Toby Jackman
Matt Lloyd
Ed Suckling
Illustrators
Andres Guzman
Keaton Henson
David Wilson
Director
David Wilson
Producers
Tamsin Glasson
Serena Noorani
Artist
Japanese Popstars
Production Company
Colonel Blimp
Record Companies
EMI Music
Virgin Records
Video Commissioner
Nicola Brown

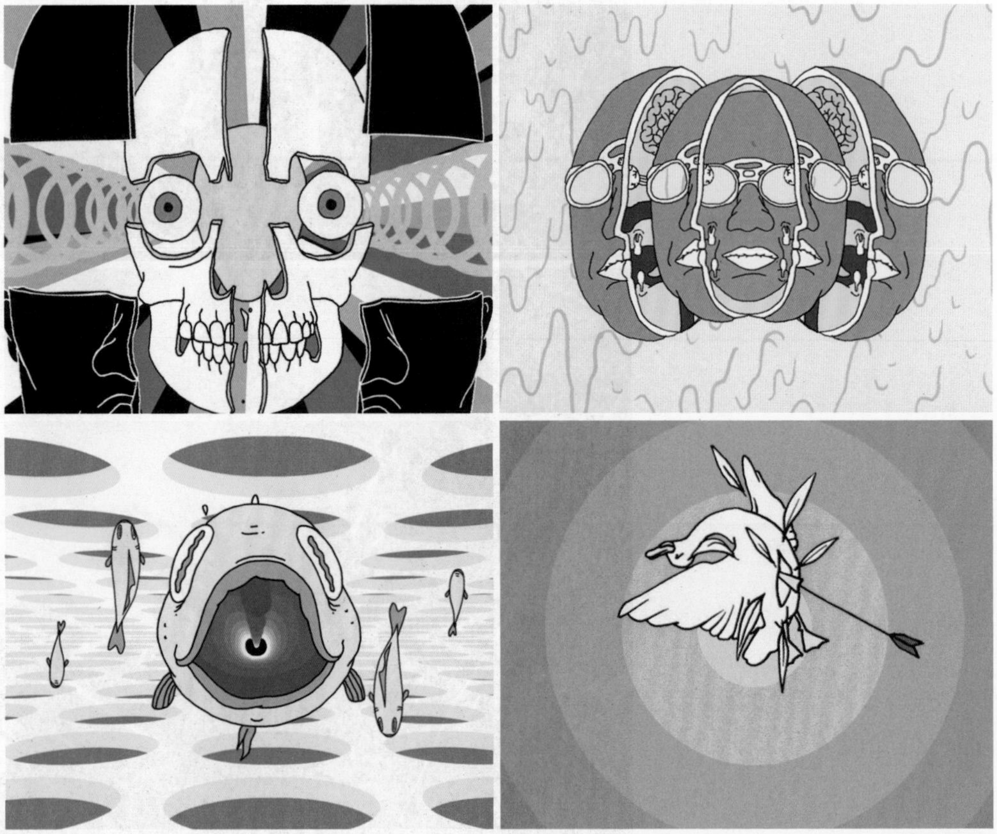

Cinematography
for Music Videos
Partizan for 679
Recordings &
Atlantic Records

The Recluse
Part three of the Plan B
videos, 'The Recluse'
shows Strickland Banks
imprisoned, after
being convicted.

Lighting Cameraperson
Robbie Ryan
Director
Daniel Wolfe
Producer
Tim Francis
Artist
Plan B
Production Company
Partizan
Editor
Dominic Leung
Set Designer
Sam Tidman
Record Companies
679 Recordings
Atlantic Records
Video Commissioner
Tim Nash

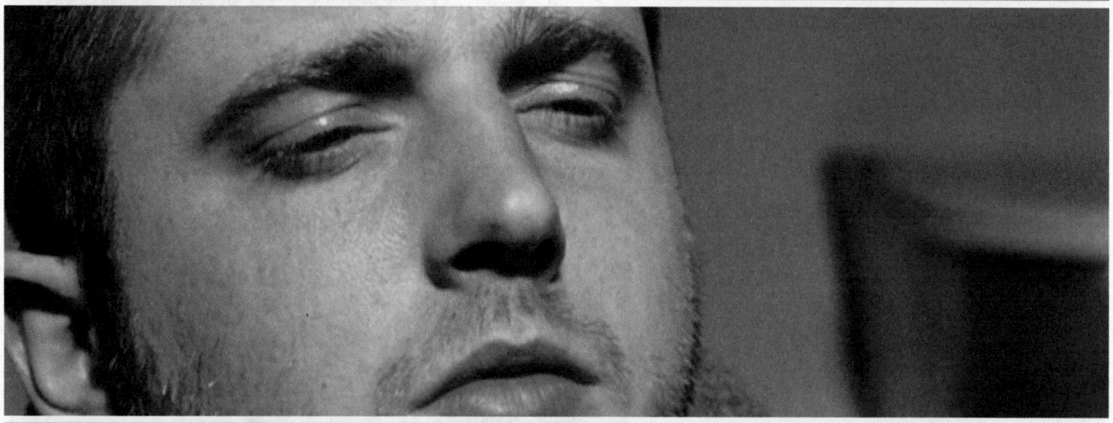

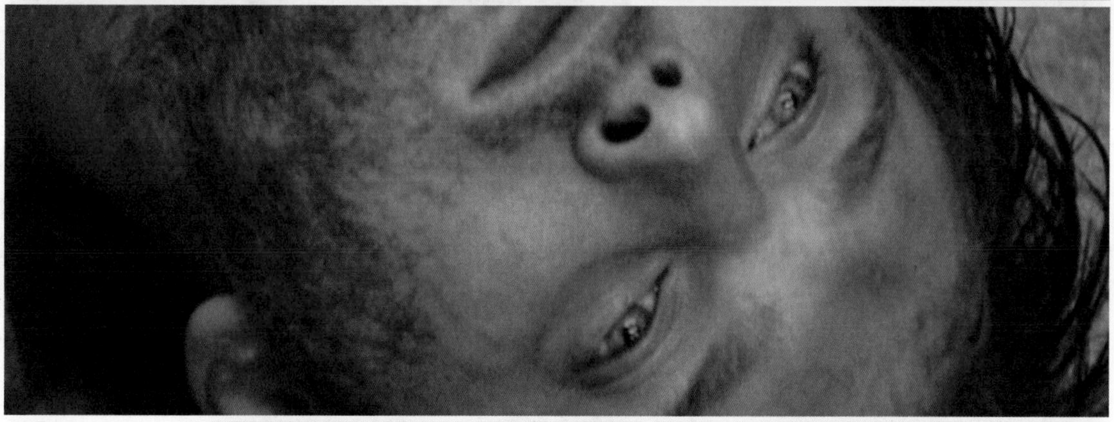

Yellow Pencil in
Outdoor Advertising

Ambient
AMV BBDO for PepsiCo

Sandwich
Our idea was to prove Walkers can make any sandwich more exciting, even the town of Sandwich, Kent. Through a series of surprise events, we turned the sleepy town of Sandwich into the most exciting town in Britain. Each event featured a celebrity: JLS took the sixth form college assembly; Frank Lampard coached the college football team; Jenson Button got behind the wheel of a black cab; Marco Pierre White sold gourmet sandwiches from a market stall; and Pamela Anderson pulled pints at the local pub while Al Murray hosted the quiz. There was something for everyone.

Art Director
Colin Jones
Copywriter
Steve Coll
Creative Directors
Steve Coll
Colin Jones
Executive Creative Director
Paul Brazier
Director of Photography
Ray Coates
Director
Declan Lowney
Producer
Simon Monhemius
Trish Russel
Advertising Agency
AMV BBDO
Production Company
HSI
Planners
Bridget Angear
Tom White
Account Handlers
Kate Gault
Justin Pahl
Adam Tucker
Brand Manager
Peter Charles
Client
PepsiCo
Brand
Walkers

Yellow Pencil in Outdoor Advertising

Ambient
Droga5 New York
for Bing & Jay-Z

Decode Jay-Z with Bing
We teamed up with Microsoft's Bing and Jay-Z to launch his autobiography, 'Decoded'. Leading up to the book's release, each page was placed in a location relevant to its specific content. Pages appeared in hundreds of locations, using billboards and bus shelters, and creating innovative new media to tell the story. In total 200 executions were placed around the world, each a story in itself. Fans frantically searched to find all the pages of the book through an experience built on Bing Maps. By solving Jay-Z clues using Bing Search, they assembled the book online before it hit the stores.

Art Director
Jon Kubik
Copywriters
Spencer LaVallee
Adam Noel
Photographer
Paul McGeiver
Designer
Jon Donaghy
Creative Directors
Kevin Brady
Neil Heymann
Duncan Marshall
Ted Royer
Nik Studzinski
Creative Chairman
David Droga
Digital Producer
Toph Brown
Senior Digital Producer
Andrew Allen
Print Producers
Mea Cole Tefka
Cliff Lewis
Head of Integrated Production
Sally-Ann Dale
Head of Print Services
Rob Lugo
Studio Artist
Chris Thomas
Advertising Agency
Droga5 New York
Public Relations
Sunshine, Sachs & Associates
Director of Digital Strategy
Hashem Bajwa
Account Handler
Shawn Mackoff
Chief Executive Officer
Andrew Essex
Marketing Manager
Eric Hadley
Client Marketing Manager
Ryan Cameron
Clients
Bing
Jay-Z
Brand
Decode Jay-Z with Bing

PAGE 2 & 3
I saw the circle before I saw the kid in the middle. I was nine years old, the summer of 1978, and Marcy was my world. The shadowy bench-lined inner pathways that connected the twenty-seven six-story buildings of Marcy Houses were like tunnels we kids burrowed through. Housing projects can seem like labyrinths to outsiders, as complicated and intimidating as a Moroccan bazaar. But we knew our way around.
DECODE JAY-Z powered by bing
DECODE THIS PAGE OF JAY-Z'S BOOK 'DECODED'.
TEXT JYZSHADOWY2 TO 44144 OR GO TO BING.COM/JAY-Z.

THE Best DJ in the US of A
JAM MASTER JAY 1965-2002

Yellow Pencil in Outdoor Advertising

Poster Advertising/
Free Format
DDB Brasil for FedEx

Neighbours: America
Our objective was to reinforce the message of FedEx's quick delivery and its global reach for a growing number of small, medium and large Brazilian companies that export products to the rest of the world. FedEx's speed of delivery to another country makes sending a package there as easy as sending it to your neighbour. The campaign featured in monthly business magazines, and economy and business newspaper supplements. 'America' was awarded a Yellow Pencil as a single execution and the campaign as a whole was nominated.

Art Director
Max Geraldo
Copywriter
Aricio Fortes
Photographer
Manolo Moran
Creative Directors
Rodrigo Almeida
Renata Florio
Moacyr Netto
Sergio Valente
Advertising Agency
DDB Brasil
Brand Manager
Guilherme Gatti
Client
FedEx

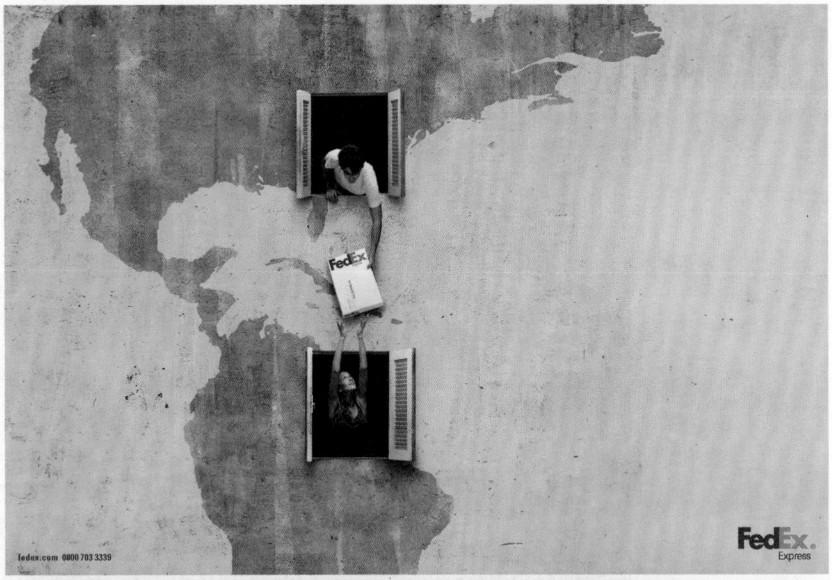
fedex.com 0800 703 3339
FedEx.
Express

fedex.com 0800 703 3339
FedEx.
Express

fedex.com 0800 703 3339
FedEx.
Express

Yellow Pencil in Outdoor Advertising

Poster Advertising Campaigns
CHI & Partners for News International

The Sunday Times Rich List
Published every year by The Sunday Times, 'The Rich List' charts the wealth of the richest people in the UK and around the world. A simple poster campaign celebrated their fortunes, playing them off each other to make visually arresting equations that compare their relative wealth. 'Cowell' was also nominated as a single execution in Poster Advertising/ Existing Sites.

Art Directors
Matt Collier
Wayne Robinson
Copywriters
Matt Collier
Wayne Robinson
Creative Director
Micky Tudor
Advertising Agency
CHI & Partners
Account Handler
Ben Etheridge
Brand Manager
Will Handley
Client
News International
Brand
The Sunday Times

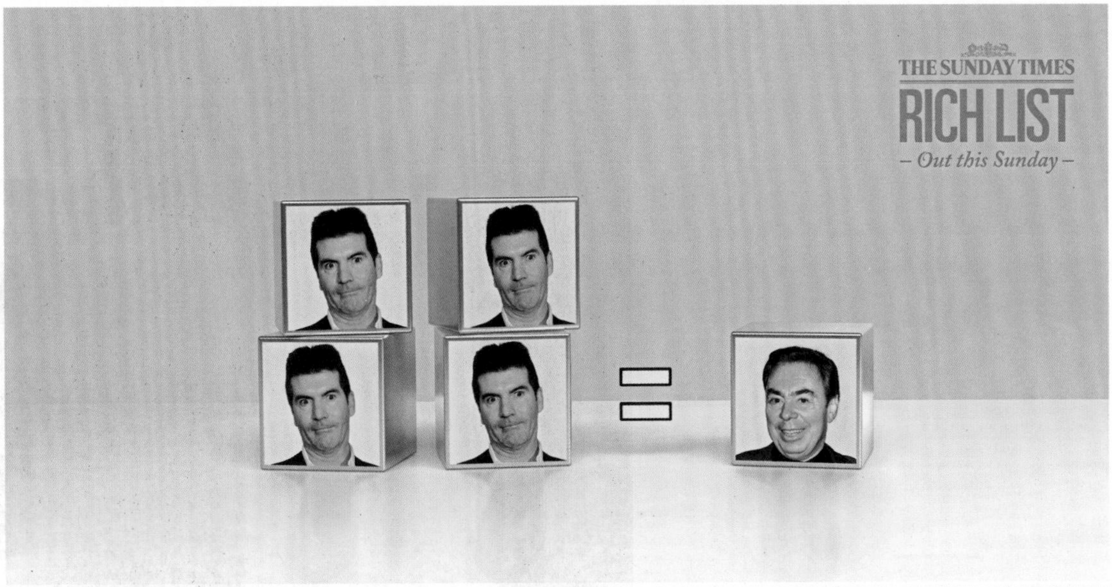
THE SUNDAY TIMES
RICH LIST
– Out this Sunday –

THE SUNDAY TIMES
RICH LIST
– Out this Sunday –

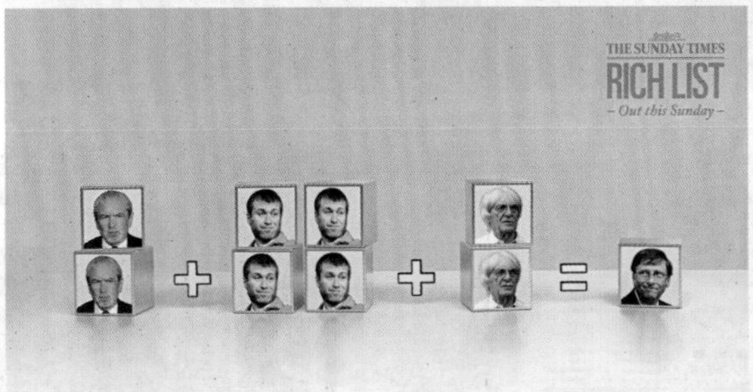
THE SUNDAY TIMES
RICH LIST
– Out this Sunday –

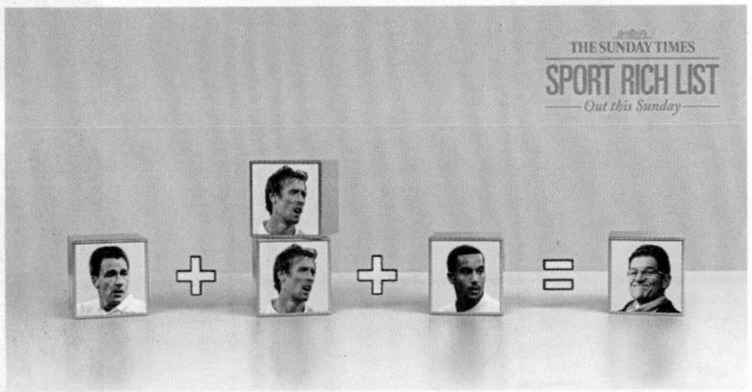
THE SUNDAY TIMES
SPORT RICH LIST
Out this Sunday

THE SUNDAY TIMES
RICH LIST
– Out this Sunday –

● Nomination in
Outdoor Advertising

Ambient
AlmapBBDO
for Billboard

Music. See What it's Made of.
In this digital installation created for Billboard Magazine, a digital panel allowed consumers to choose their favourite stars. They could then see their own photos recreated using the stars' images, enlarged on a big screen. In addition, by pressing a button, consumers could turn the panel into a photo booth, take a picture, and upload it to their Flickr accounts.

Art Directors
Danilo Boer
Marcos Kothlar
Marcos Medeiros
Copywriter
Andre Kassu
Creative Directors
Dulcidio Caldeira
Luiz Sanches
Typographer
José Roberto Bezerra
Illustrators
Marcos Kothlar
Marcos Medeiros
Advertising Agency
AlmapBBDO
Marketing Manager
Antonio Camarotti
Client
Billboard

Billboard

Billboard

Nomination in Outdoor Advertising

Ambient
Mother New York
for Target

Target Kaleidoscopic Fashion Spectacular
On 18 August 2010, after a month of rehearsals, Target presented a fashion show featuring 66 dancers, an original score, 44,640 LED bulbs, and 155 rooms in New York's Standard Hotel. Named the Target Kaleidoscopic Fashion Spectacular, the event reinvented the catwalk by using all the windows of the hotel's 18 floors to showcase the brand's upcoming autumn fashion, while providing a 20-minute light, sound and dance spectacle for the thousands of spectators on the streets below. It received 160 million media impressions and has been shared online over 12.6 million times.

Choreographer
Ryan Heffington
Music Composer
Sam Spiegel
Stylist
Mel Ottenberg
Advertising Agency
Mother New York
Lighting Design
Bionic League
Content & Show Direction
LEGS
Client
Target

● Nomination in
Outdoor Advertising

Ambient
TBWA\Hunt\Lascaris Johannesburg for the International Organisation for Migration

A Campaign Designed to Drop Sales
Like human traffickers, we targeted our most vulnerable people: children at school or just walking the streets of townships and impoverished urban slums. And just like the criminals, our most powerful weapon was deception. On the streets of their own neighbourhoods, we made men, women and children disappear. We created tunnels with false walls that precisely matched the real walls behind them, so that when people walked through, they disappeared – leaving onlookers wondering what had happened to them. Once people were informed of our anti-human trafficking message and given a toll-free number, they could pass the information on.

Art Director
Miguel Nunes
Copywriter
Charles Pantland
Photographers
Des Ellis
Rob Wilson
Creative Director
Vanessa Gibson
Executive Creative Director
Damon Stapleton
Producers
Sharon Cvetkovski
Sandra Gomes
Advertising Agency
TBWA\Hunt\Lascaris Johannesburg
Production Company
E-Graphics
Planner
Leigh-Anne Kazantzas
Account Handler
Sandra Chapman
Marketing Manager
Wambui Gititu
Client
International Organisation for Migration

UP TO
4 MILLION
PEOPLE
DISAPPEAR
EVERY
YEAR

UP TO
4 MILLION
PEOPLE
DISAPPEAR

Nomination in
Outdoor Advertising

Poster Advertising
Campaigns
TBWA\Istanbul
for IKEA Turkey

IKEA Shoe Cabinet
The brief was to communicate how IKEA shoe cabinets save space and help organise shoes. We created three different ads demonstrating how shoes can get in cramped up spaces. Accompanying these visuals, the simple tag line 'Need space?' conveyed our message clearly.

Art Directors
Orkun Onal
Can Pehlivanli
Copywriter
Volkan Yanik
Creative Director
Volkan Karakasoglu
Executive Creative Director
Ilkay Gurpinar
Advertising Agency
TBWA\Istanbul
Planners
Tugyan Celik
Toygun Yilmazer
Account Handlers
Melis Inceer
Burcu Ozdemir
Ayse Senunver
Marketing Manager
Ozge Kocaoglu
Client
IKEA Turkey

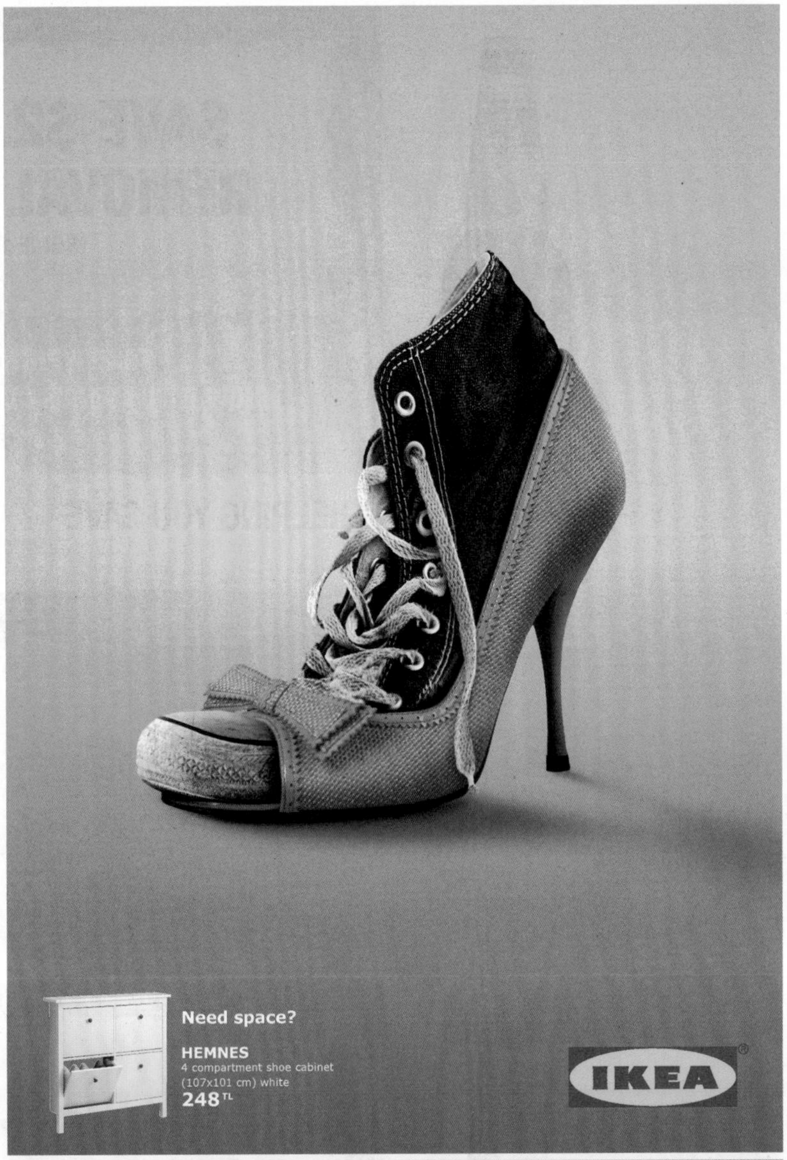
Need space?
HEMNES
4 compartment shoe cabinet
(107x101 cm) white
248 TL
IKEA

Need space?
HEMNES
248
IKEA

Need space?
HEMNES
248
IKEA

- Nomination in Outdoor Advertising

Poster Advertising Campaigns
Leo Burnett Toronto
for James Ready

James Ready Fall & Coupon Billboards
In 2010 James Ready set out to help their drinkers save money on food, dry cleaning, grooming and more. Saving money on this stuff meant drinkers would have more money for James Ready Beer. The campaign included 'Billboard Coupons' (billboards that drinkers could take a picture of and then show local establishments for deals on stuff) and a 'Beer Store Parking Lot' programme that offered free haircuts and semi-professional portraits. Drinkers could then go next door and spend their saved cash on James Ready Beer. The campaign was also nominated in Ambient.

Art Directors
Anthony Chelvanathan
Paul Giannetta
Copywriters
Sean Barlow
Steve Persico
Illustrator
Kimberley Pereira
Creative Directors
Lisa Greenberg
Judy John
Group Creative Directors
Sean Barlow
Paul Giannetta
Chief Creative Officer
Judy John
Print Producers
Gladys Bachand
David Eades
Advertising Agency
Leo Burnett Toronto
Account Executive
Jordan Lane
Account Director
Natasha Dagenais
Group Account Director
David Buckspan
Client
James Ready

J.R. 5.5
JAMES READY 5.5
SAVE $2.26 ON STAIN REMOVAL FROM PANTS.†
(SOME STAINS EXCLUDED)
TAKE A PICTURE OF THIS COUPON.
SHOW IT TO MENA'S CLEANERS, 4606 TECUMSEH RD. E
CLICK!
MUST BE LEGAL DRINKING AGE.
HELPING YOU SAVE $26.10* FOR JAMES READY BEER.

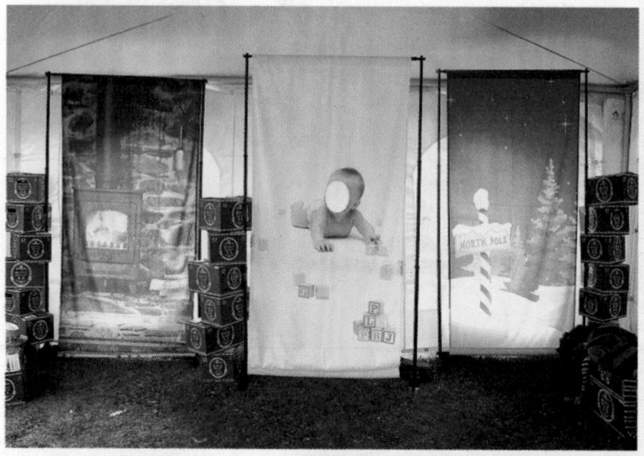
NORTH POLE

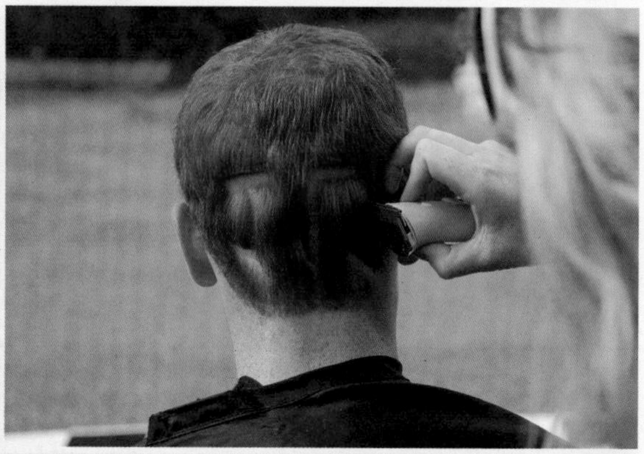

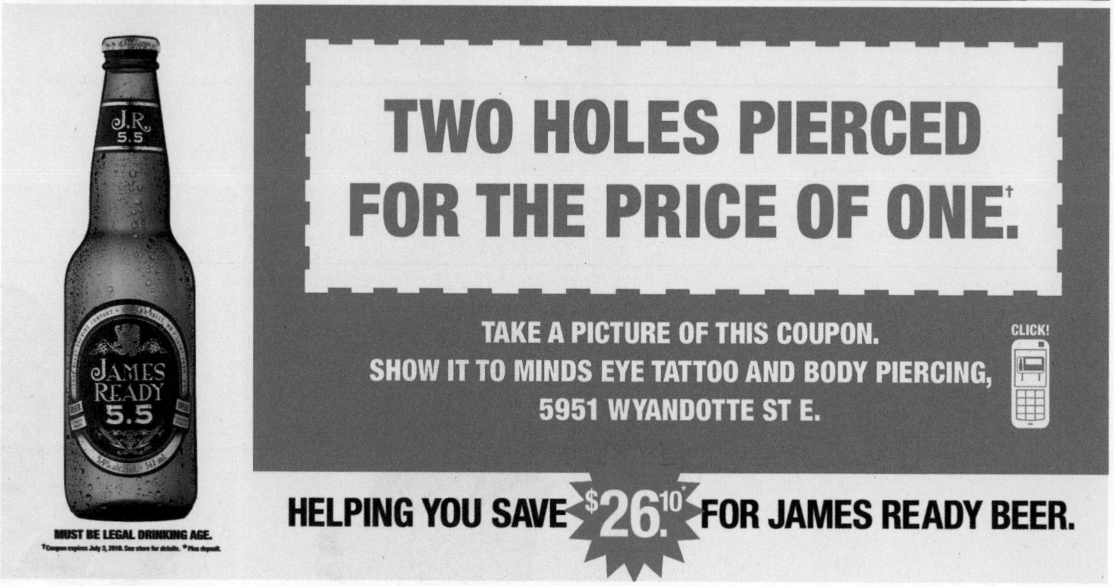
J.R. 5.5
JAMES READY 5.5
TWO HOLES PIERCED FOR THE PRICE OF ONE.†
TAKE A PICTURE OF THIS COUPON.
SHOW IT TO MINDS EYE TATTOO AND BODY PIERCING,
5951 WYANDOTTE ST E.
CLICK!
MUST BE LEGAL DRINKING AGE.
HELPING YOU SAVE $26.10* FOR JAMES READY BEER.

Nomination in
Outdoor Advertising

Poster Advertising
Campaigns
Fallon London for
French Connection

French Connection
Spring/Summer 2010
This campaign launched French Connection's Spring/Summer 2010 collection, highlighting the brand's design credentials and the quality of its clothes.

Art Director
Selena McKenzie
Copywriter
Toby Moore
Photographer
Tariel Meliava
Creative Directors
Dirk van Dooren
Richard Flintham
Advertising Agency
Fallon London
Account Handler
Katharine Easteal
Brand Manager
Stephen Marks
Client
French Connection

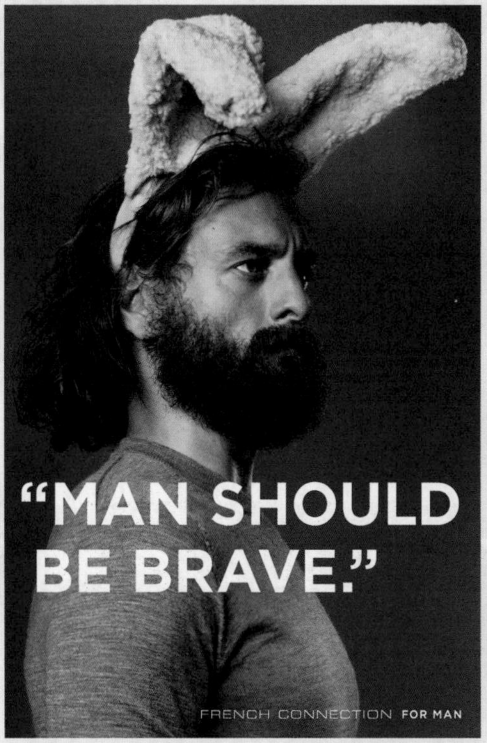
"MAN SHOULD BE BRAVE."
FRENCH CONNECTION FOR MAN

"EAT MEAT. DRESS WELL."
FRENCH CONNECTION FOR MAN

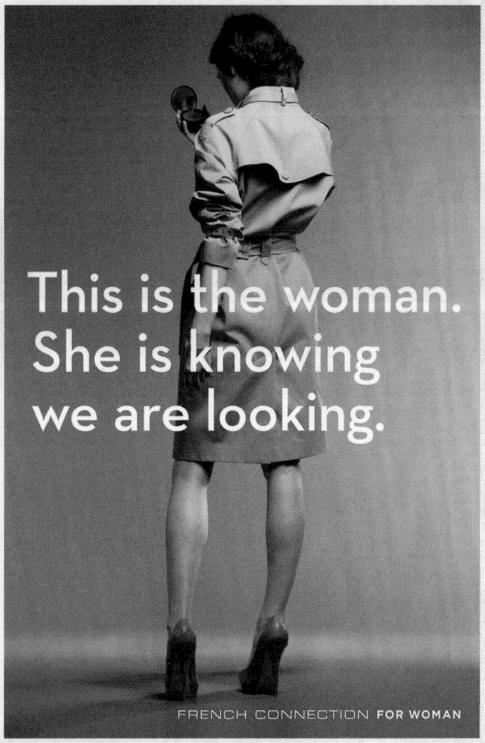
This is the woman. She is knowing we are looking.
FRENCH CONNECTION FOR WOMAN

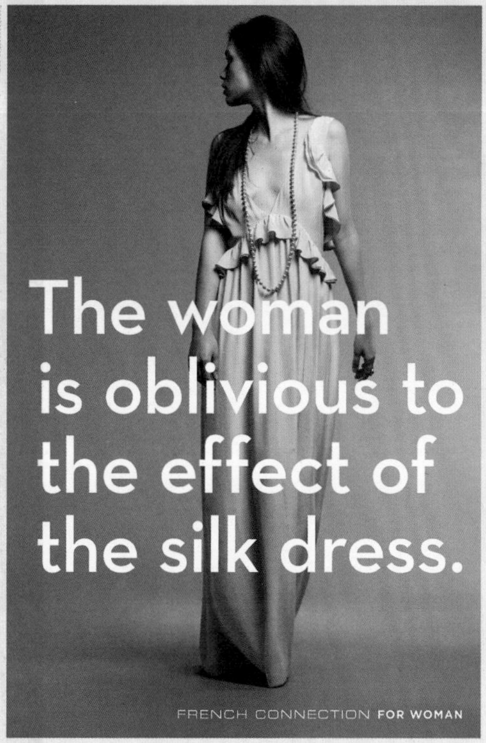
The woman is oblivious to the effect of the silk dress.
FRENCH CONNECTION FOR WOMAN

Ambient
Leo Burnett Hong Kong
for IKEA

Trailer
IKEA is known in Hong Kong as the best place for home furnishing solutions such as sofas, living room sets, bedroom suites and so on. However, the Swedish furniture giant also has an impressive range of curtains. We created a special rig to install several curtains behind the original red curtain that is usually in every cinema. The tone in which we showed off the curtains was very much like a Hollywood trailer, with proper Hollywood-style soundtrack and voice over, announcing the premiere of the new 2010 range of curtains.

Art Director
Tik Lau
Copywriter
Wilson Ang
Executive Creative Director
Victor Manggunio
Advertising Agency
Leo Burnett Hong Kong
Account Handlers
Margaret Chan
Emmie Tse
Client
IKEA

IKEA
Presents

Curtains
2010 Range

Ambient
Ogilvy Brasil for
Burger King

Whopper Face
One laptop, one hidden camera, one printer. That's all we needed to prove that Burger King sandwiches are made to order, exactly your way. When customers ordered Whopper burgers, they had their picture taken without noticing it. Customers then got their made-to-order burgers with their faces on the wrappers. That way, Burger King reinforced their 'Have it your way' positioning, proving that each sandwich is made to order, especially for the customer.

Art Director
Douglas Kozonoe
Copywriter
Eduardo Marques
Photographer
Giuliano Saade
Creative Director
Anselmo Ramos
Producer
Mauricio Granado
Advertising Agency
Ogilvy Brasil
Production Company
Bossa Nova Films
Planner
Priscila Cerutti
Account Handler
Evandro Guimarães
Brand Manager
Paul Davis
Marketing Manager
Fernanda Bare
Client
Burger King
Brand
Whopper

Feito na hora pra você
BURGER KING
ORIGINAL
WHOPPER
WITH CHEESE
1 2 3 4 5 6 7 8 9 10 11 12

Feito na hora pra você
BURGER KING
A GENTE FAZ DO SE

Ambient
Ogilvy Johannesburg
for Exclusive Books

Peepholes
With little money, we wanted to maximise our front windows and floor space to create an intriguing experience that goes to the heart of what makes biographies great: what really goes on inside celebrities' minds? We chose four celebrities represented in the biography section and worked with three local artists to bring to life some interpretations of their inner worlds. Customers were drawn to peepholes that appear on the foreheads of our famous four, through which vivid worlds were revealed. The peep boxes were set on wheels so they could form a travelling installation between stores.

Art Directors
Ian Broekhuizen
Mike Martin
Copywriters
David Krueger
Molefi Thulo
Photographer
Pierre Peters
Creative Directors
Bridget Johnson
Fran Luckin
Mike Martin
Set Designer
Greg Pentopolous
Producer
Tsakane Mhlangwane
Advertising Agency
Ogilvy Johannesburg
Production Company
Oaktree Studio
Account Handler
Caree Ferrari
Marketing Manager
Fred Withers
Client
Exclusive Books

TAKE A LOOK INSIDE
EXCLUS1VE BOOKS
BIOGRAPHIES

Ambient
Ogilvy Amsterdam
for Allsecur

Little Accident?
The Allsecur 'little accident?' upside-down car has been driven around big cities during fairs and events, including car races and motor shows.

Art Director
Darre van Dijk
Copywriter
Piebe Piebenga
Creative Directors
Darre van Dijk
Piebe Piebenga
Advertising Agency
Ogilvy Amsterdam
Planner
Michel MacDonald
Account Handlers
Tom Ijzer
Annelotte Pera
Brand Manager
Ron Adams
Client
Allsecur

's-Hertog
A little accident?
You don't pay a penny
with Allsecur car insurance.
AllSecur

073-6100
78-MJK-1
2 Conta

Ambient
BDDP Unlimited for
Solidarités International

Water Talk
Contaminated water is still the primary cause of death in the world. Each year, it leads to deadly illnesses, such as cholera, typhoid and malaria, for some eight million people, including 1.5 million children. To speak out against this tragedy in a totally new way, the humanitarian aid organisation Solidarités International put together a revolutionary public event, featuring a talking wall of water. This temporary installation conveyed poignant messages specifically intended to capture the attention of passers-by, just before World Water Day on 22 March 2010.

Art Director
David Derouet
Copywriter
Emmanuel de Dieuleveult
Creative Director
Guillaume-Ulrich Chifflot
Advertising Agency
BDDP Unlimited
Production Company
Cosa
Technological Group
Use
Account Handler
Marco de la Fuente
Brand Manager
Alain Boinet
Client
Solidarités International

DAS RAVALEMENT
I KILL

DRINKING

Poster Advertising/
Existing Sites
DDB Singapore for
Atlas Sound & Vision

Crying Kid
Bose is a brand known for clean lines, simplicity, and design that is made for life. When we were asked to promote its range of noise-cancelling headphones, we drew inspiration from the brand's design ethos. The ad demonstrates the prowess of Bose noise-cancelling technology with a simple graphic icon – the volume bar.

Art Director
Khalid Osman
Copywriter
Lester Lee
Photographer
Allan Ng
Creative Directors
Joji Jacob
Neil Johnson
Thomas Yang
Retoucher
Chew Peng
Advertising Agency
DDB Singapore
Account Handlers
Rowena Bhagchandani
Vivien Foo
Marketing Manager
Tammy Chan
Client
Atlas Sound & Vision
Brand
Bose

BOSE
Noise-cancelling headphones

Ambient
Ogilvy México for Mattel

Big Boy
This piece of outdoor advertising was installed over a pedestrian bridge in Mexico City. When people passed under it, they felt trapped, like a child traps a Hot Wheels car.

Art Directors
Iván Carrasco
Jaime González Díaz de Cossío
Mario Salgado
Copywriter
Abraham Quintana
Photographer
Diego Arrigoni
Creative Directors
Miguel Angel Ruiz
José Montalvo
Abraham Quintana
Producers
Ereth Bolaños
Alejandra Díaz
Advertising Agency
Ogilvy México
Account Handler
Pilar Troconis
Brand Manager
Roberto Guzmán
Marketing Manager
Giancarlo Melloni
Client
Mattel
Brand
Hot Wheels

Hot Wheels

Poster Advertising/
Enhanced Posters
Y&R Dubai for
Paras Pharma

Splitting Ahmed
To communicate the effectiveness of Stopache in putting an end to migraines, this ambient campaign visually demonstrated the extreme suffering of someone with a migraine. Split posters featuring portraits of people in great pain were placed outside clinics and pharmacies, drawing attention to the perfect solution: Stopache.

Art Directors
Daniel Botezatu
Kalpesh Patankar
Umran Shaikh
Copywriters
Parixit Bhattacharya
Kalpesh Patankar
Photographers
Daniel Botezatu
Umran Shaikh
Chief Creative Officer
Shahir Zag
Advertising Agency
Y&R Dubai
Creative Coordinator
Suhel Anwar
Planner
Nadine Ghossoub
Account Handler
Matthew Collier
Marketing Manager
Prabhu Kartikeyan
Client
Paras Pharma
Brand
Stopache

MIGRAINE?
Stopache

MIGRAINE?
Stopache
PARAS

Poster Advertising/
Free Format
Y&R Jakarta for
LG Electronics

Mystery Novel
The LG GX200 mobile phone boasts a superior talk time of 13.5 hours, perfect for those who appreciate the art of conversation. The campaign features speech bubbles as books with titles that announce the beginnings of some of these conversations.

Art Director
Yerry Indrajaya
Copywriter
Gloria Martie
Photographers
Handri Karya
Heru Suryoko
Typographer
Yerry Indrajaya
Illustrator
Budiman Raharjo
Designer
Flora Marcella
Executive Creative Director
Sachin Ambekar
Associate Creative Director
Ahmad Fariz
Regional Chief Creative Officer
Marcus Rebeschini
Retoucher
Alex Reagan
Advertising Agency
Y&R Jakarta
Account Handlers
Wolga Satyanto
Hendra Suryakusuma
Marketing Manager
Dony Munaf
Client
LG Electronics
Brand
LG GX200

LG
Life's Good
HONEY,
WHAT'S THAT
RED MARK
ON YOUR COLLAR?
MORE BATTERY MORE TALK
LG GX200 with 13.5 hours of talk time
and 1700 hours of standby battery life.

Poster Advertising Campaigns
Dentsu Brasil for L'Univers de Chocolat

Funny Babies
Chocolate with whisky truffles are one of L'Univers de Chocolat's bestsellers. This poster campaign was a funny and unexpected way to promote this adult-only product.

Art Director
Adriano Alarcon
Photographers
Cadu Maya
Rogerio Miranda
Creative Directors
Felipe Cama
Alexandre Lucas
Producer
Ricardo Lopez
Advertising Agency
Dentsu Brasil
Planner
Flavia Faust
Account Handlers
Fabio Britto
Tiago Lara
Art Buyer
Ana Luiza Rodrigues
Brand Manager
Nicolas Galland
Client
L'Univers de Chocolat

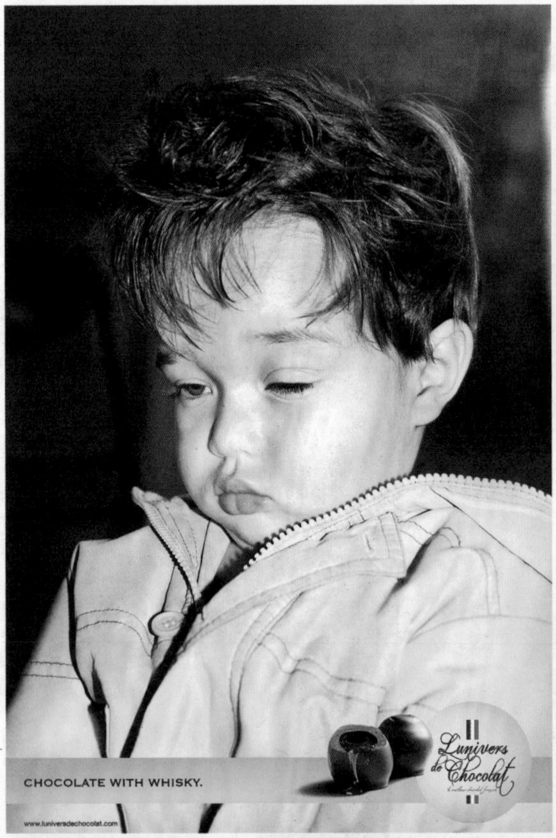
CHOCOLATE WITH WHISKY.
www.luniversdechocolat.com

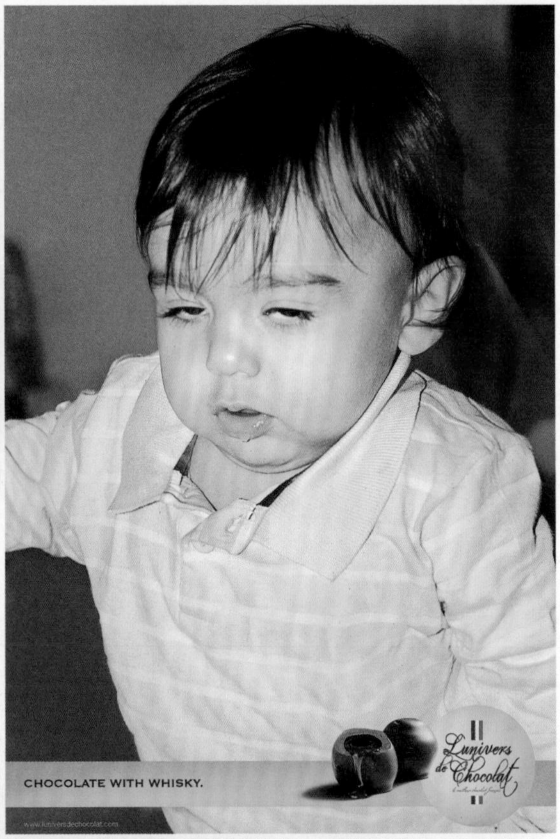
CHOCOLATE WITH WHISKY.

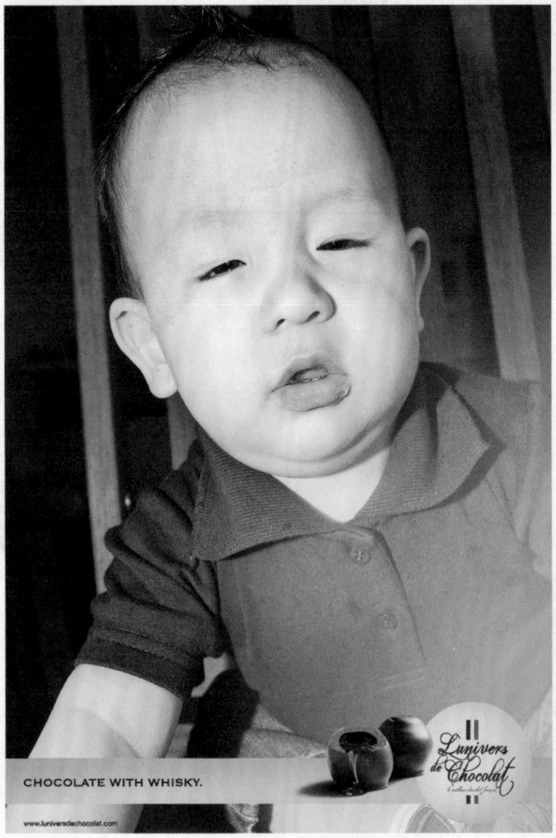
CHOCOLATE WITH WHISKY.
www.luniversdechocolat.com

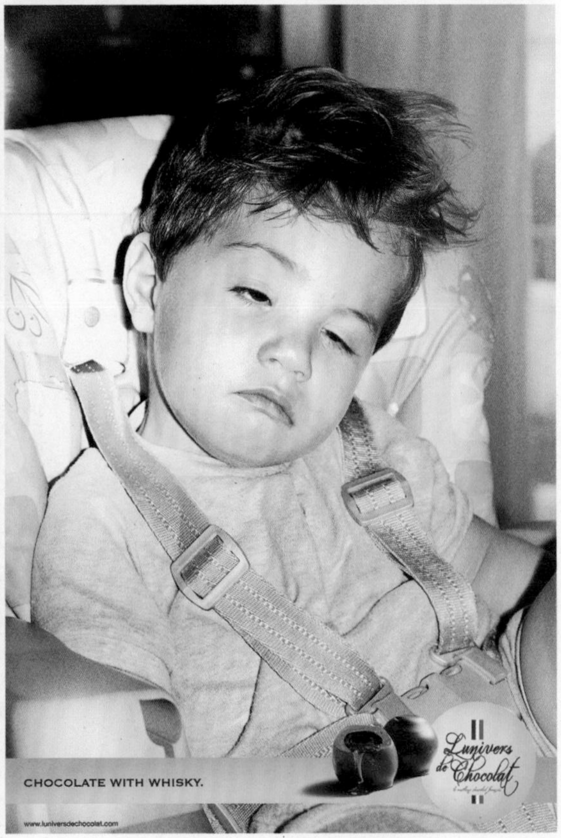
CHOCOLATE WITH WHISKY.
www.luniversdechocolat.com

Poster Advertising Campaigns
DDB Tribal Group, Düsseldorf for Volkswagen

Safety Barriers
This campaign is all about Volkswagen's technology leadership and the great benefit for its customers: safe cars. We show that only extreme passion, hard work and the permanent quest for better results lead to this success.

Art Director
Dan Strasser
Copywriter
Mihai Botarel
Creative Directors
Oliver Kapusta
Alex Reiss
Advertising Agency
DDB Tribal Group, Düsseldorf
Post Production
The Scope
Account Handlers
Marie-Louise Jakob
Silke Lagodny
Brand Managers
Hartmut Seeger
Veronika Ziegaus
Marketing Manager
Luca de Meo
Client
Volkswagen
Brand
Golf

More late nights for us, less danger for you.
Five star safety rating. The Golf.

More brainstorming for us, less danger for you.
Five star safety rating. The Golf.

More meetings for us, less danger for you.
Five star safety rating. The Golf.

Poster Advertising Campaigns
Jung von Matt/Fleet
for SPIEGEL-Verlag Rudolf Augstein

Perspective
'The Spiegel' is a respected institution in the international press. It is a serious magazine renowned for its unbiased journalistic approach. By examining every angle of each story 'The Spiegel' is qualified to give its readers a clearer, more balanced insight into the themes and events that shape Germany and the world. In these ads, we use visuals to demonstrate that there are many sides to the same story.

Art Director
Jan Rexhausen
Copywriter
Fabio Straccia
Illustrator
Noma Bar
Creative Director
Jan Rexhausen
Advertising Agency
Jung von Matt/Fleet
Account Handler
Jose Luis Carretero Lopez
Marketing Manager
Sabine Krecker
Client
SPIEGEL-Verlag Rudolf Augstein

/Different points of view
shape a better picture/
DER SPIEGEL
www.spiegel.de/international/

/Different points of view
shape a better picture/
DER SPIEGEL
www.spiegel.de/international/

/Different points of view
shape a better picture/
DER SPIEGEL
www.spiegel.de/international/

Poster Advertising
Campaigns
Y&R Beijing for
Land Rover

World's End
The brief was to effectively showcase the rugged prowess of the Land Rover Discovery 4 in a way that truly communicated its ability to go beyond. Our solution was a series of print and outdoor executions that literally took it to the end of the road, to the end of the horizon – to the world's end.

Art Directors
A S Anam
Nils Andersson
Copywriters
A S Anam
Nils Andersson
Photographers
Sebastian Siah
Kerry Wilson
Typographers
Lee Aldridge
Raul Pardo
Creative Directors
Nils Andersson
Graham Lang
Marcus Rebeschini
Mike Shackle
Retoucher
Raul Pardo
Advertising Agency
Y&R Beijing
Account Handlers
Lucy Harries
Bryce Whitwam
Brand Manager
Les Knight
Marketing Manager
Scott Dicken
Client
Land Rover

www.landrover.com
LAND-ROVER
GO BEYOND

www.landrover.com
LAND-ROVER
GO BEYOND

www.landrover.com
LAND-ROVER
GO BEYOND

Poster Advertising Campaigns
TBWA\Paris for Nissan

Symmetry
In 2010 Nissan launched its new Cube car in Europe, the very first car conceived as much as a design product as a car. To promote the launch of the car, a series of three ads demonstrated how symmetry is boring in order to dramatise one of the most iconic design aspects of the car, the asymmetry of its back. The aim of the campaign was to set people thinking about the individuality of the Cube, which flies in the face of standard car design.

Art Director
Ingrid Varetz
Copywriter
Glen Troadec
Photographer
Cindy Gravelat
Creative Directors
Eric Holden
Alasdhair MacGregor-Hastie
Remi Noel
Advertising Agency
TBWA\Paris
Account Handler
Ewan Veitch
Art Buyer
Carine Gallufo
Marketing Manager
Bruno Mattucci
Client
Nissan
Brand
Cube

Symmetry sucks.
cube
design by nissan

Symmetry sucks.
cube

Symmetry sucks.
cube

Poster Advertising Campaigns
BBDO Düsseldorf
for Spuk Pictures

The Unseen
Stock pictures are often boring and unimaginative – it's like you have seen them a million times before. Spuk Pictures offers an alternative. Its collection is not the largest, but it does offer truly exciting pictures. We demonstrated this to media professionals by giving them examples of extremely unusual pictures.

Art Director
Jake Shaw
Copywriter
Florian Birkner
Photographer
Matt Barnes
Executive Creative Director
Carsten Bolk
Chief Creative Officers
Toygar Bazarkaya
Wolfgang Schneider
Advertising Agency
BBDO Düsseldorf
Account Handler
Liselotte Schwenkert
Marketing Manager
Stefan Kranefeld
Client
Spuk Pictures

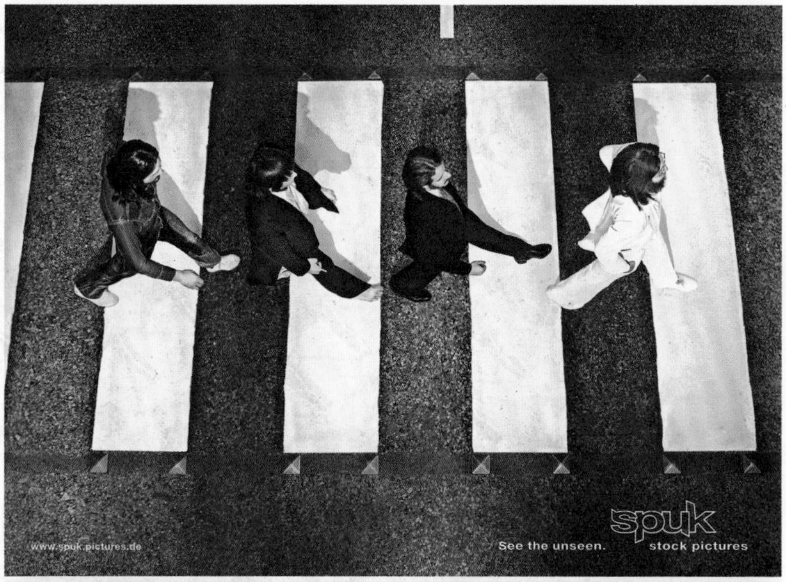
www.spuk.pictures.de
spuk
See the unseen.
stock pictures

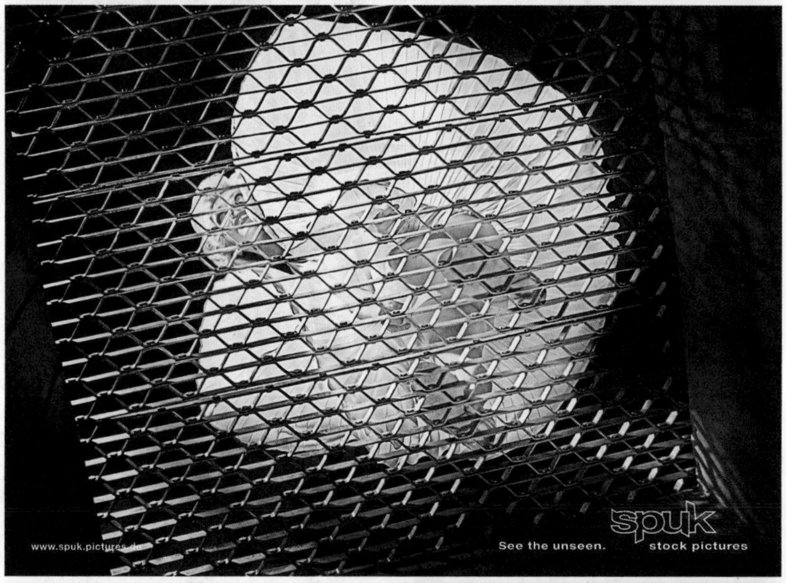
www.spuk.pictures.de
spuk
See the unseen.
stock pictures

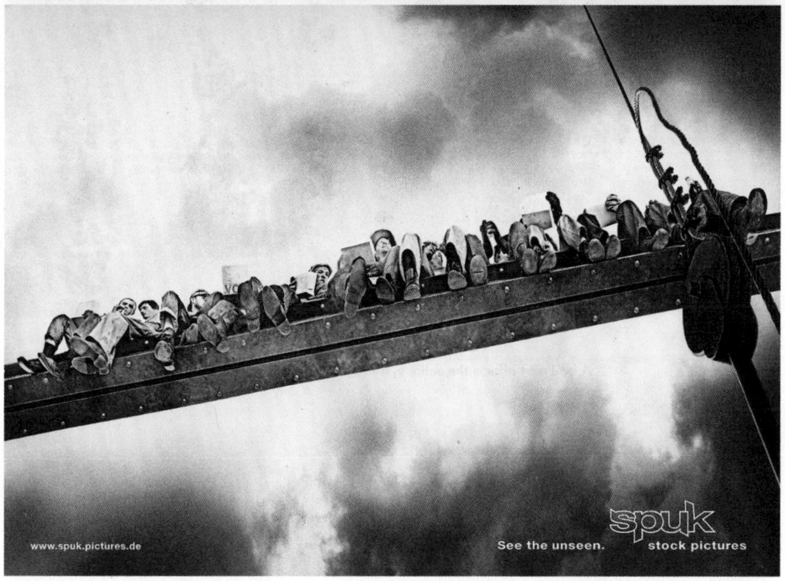
www.spuk.pictures.de
spuk
See the unseen.
stock pictures

Poster Advertising
Campaigns
AlmapBBDO
for Volkswagen

A Bad Part Affects
the Entire System
Our goal was to stress the importance of using original Volkswagen parts. To achieve this, we created a campaign showing that one single part can compromise the whole system.

Art Director
Bruno Prosperi
Copywriter
Renato Simões
Typographer
José Roberto Bezerra
Creative Director
Luiz Sanches
Advertising Agency
AlmapBBDO
Planners
Fernanda Barone
Renata Bonilha
Cintia Gonçalves
Marketing Manager
Herlander Zola
Client
Volkswagen

A bad part affects the entire system.
Volkswagen original parts.
Das Auto.

A bad part affects the entire system.
Volkswagen original parts.
Das Auto.

Poster Advertising
Campaigns
AlmapBBDO
for Volkswagen

Get a Volkswagen with Parking Sensor
To highlight the importance of parking sensors, these ads feature an image of a manual gearshift pattern. In one the reverse gear is running over a fire hydrant; in the other, a garden gnome.

Art Director
Marco Monteiro
Copywriter
Cesar Herszkowicz
Typographer
José Roberto Bezerra
Creative Director
Luiz Sanches
Advertising Agency
AlmapBBDO
Planners
Fernanda Barone
Renata Bonilha
Cintia Gonçalves
Marketing Manager
Herlander Zola
Client
Volkswagen

1
3
5
2
4
R
Get a Volkswagen with parking sensor.
Das Auto.

1
3
5
2
4
R
Get a Volkswagen with parking sensor.
Das Auto.

Poster Advertising Campaigns
AlmapBBDO
for Billboard

Music. See What it's Made of.
Magazines are made of dots. Artists are made of influences. 'Music. See What it's Made of' was a campaign for Billboard that showed how much the magazine knows about the pop music universe. In these ads featuring music stars, the images are composed of smaller images of the stars' respective musical influences.

Art Directors
Danilo Boer
Marcos Kothlar
Marcos Medeiros
Copywriter
Andre Kassu
Typographer
José Roberto Bezerra
Illustrators
Marcos Kothlar
Marcos Medeiros
Creative Directors
Dulcidio Caldeira
Luiz Sanches
Advertising Agency
AlmapBBDO
Marketing Manager
Antonio Camarotti
Client
Billboard

Music.
See what it's made of.
Billboard MAGAZINE
Kiss
Ozzy
The Cure
Cher

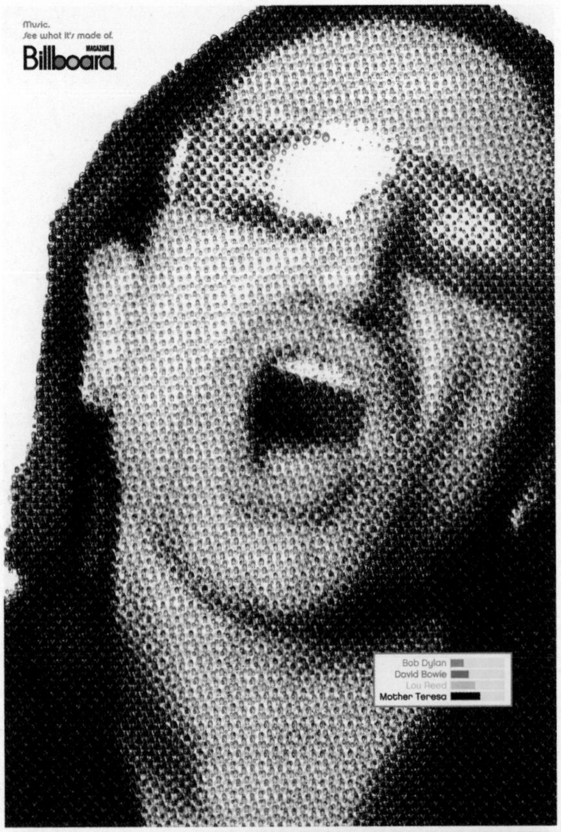
Music.
See what it's made of.
Billboard MAGAZINE
Bob Dylan
David Bowie
Lou Reed
Mother Teresa

Music.
See what it's made of.
Billboard MAGAZINE
Madonna
Madonna
Madonna
Paparazzi

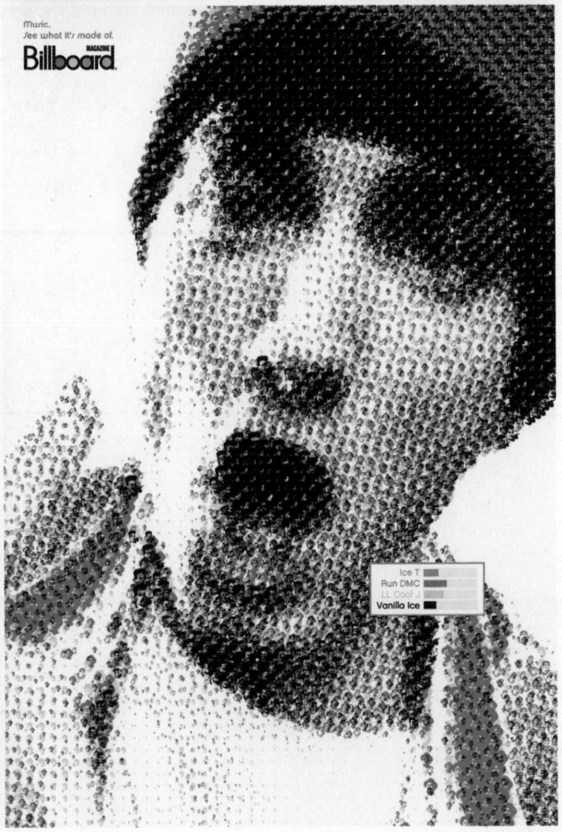
Music.
See what it's made of.
Billboard MAGAZINE
Ice T
Run DMC
LL Cool J
Vanilla Ice

Poster Advertising
Campaigns
Euro RSCG España
for Reckitt Benckiser

Screams
Strepsils, for healing
sore throats.

Art Director
Jacobo Concejo
Copywriter
Luis Munné
Creative Directors
Ekhi Mendibil
Haitz Mendibil
Germán Silva
Advertising Agency
Euro RSCG España
Photography
Grupo Rafael
Client
Reckitt Benckiser
Brand
Strepsils

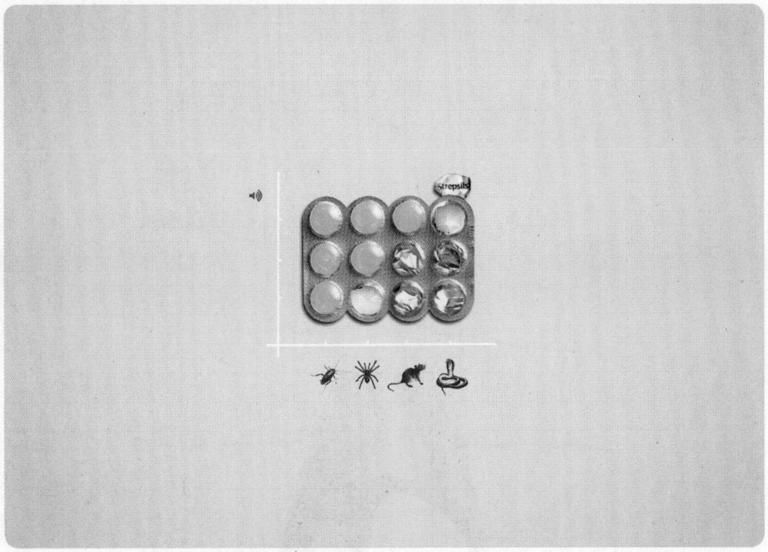

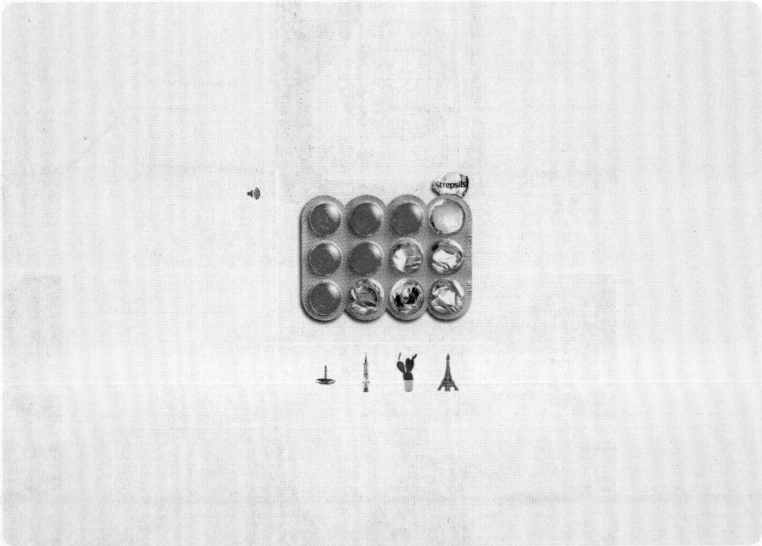

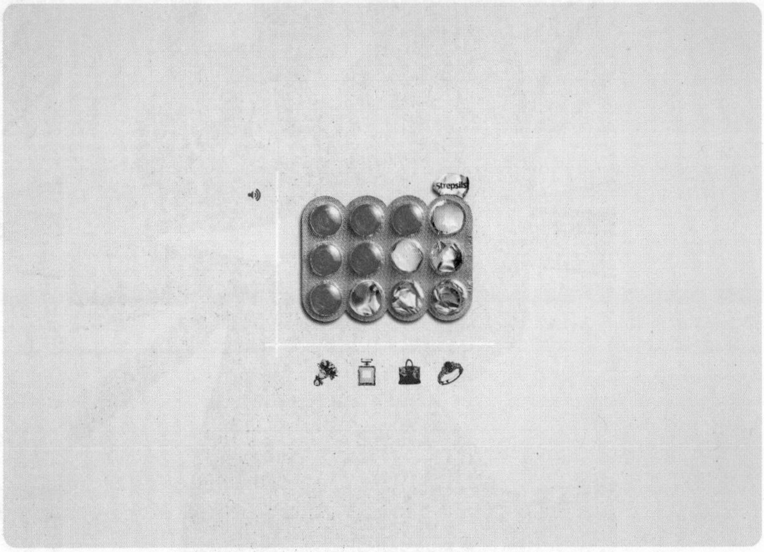

Poster Advertising
Campaigns
DDB UK for Unilever

Marmite Cereal
Bar Campaign
With this teaser-revealer campaign, we tried to fool customers into thinking that Marmite was making some totally outlandish products. That way the world's first savoury cereal bar might seem like a slightly more attractive proposition.

Art Director
Victor Monclus
Copywriter
Will Lowe
Photographer
Sarah Maingot
Designer
Pete Mould
Executive Creative Director
Jeremy Craigen
Retouchers
Greg Chapman
Steve Sanderson
Andrew Walsh
Head of Art
Grant Parker
Advertising Agency
DDB UK
Planner
Georgia Challis
Project Manager
Jon Dewart
Account Directors
Matt Bundy
Paul Mitcheson
Account Manager
Jon Busk
Art Buyer
Sarah Thomson
Client
Unilever
Brand
Marmite

Unilever
BURSTING WITH YEAST!
MARMITE
softener
LEAVES CLOTHES SOFT AND SAVOURY
2Le
STANDARD WASHES 28

Unilever
BURSTING WITH YEAST!
MARMITE
softener
LEAVES CLOTHES SOFT AND SAVOURY
2Le
STANDARD WASHES 28
That may be too far, but how about this?
MARMITE
CEREAL BAR

Unilever
MARMITE

Unilever
MARMITE
That may be too far, but how about this?
MARMITE
CEREAL BAR

Poster Advertising Campaigns
M&C Saatchi London for Transport for London

Heritage Campaign
There are hundreds of interesting stories about the tube. Our brief was to bring a few of them to life. We did this by weaving facts (and a bit of fiction) into the designs of historical seat covers. We then asked passengers to guess: Tube or False?

Art Director
Ned Corbett-Winder
Copywriter
Martin Latham
Typographer
Gareth Davies
Executive Creative Director
Graham Fink
Advertising Agency
M&C Saatchi London
Planner
Cressida O'Shea
Account Handler
Tom Vaughan
Group Marketing & Communications Manager
Nigel Hanlon
Client Director of Group Marketing
Chris MacLeod
Client
Transport for London
Brand
London Underground

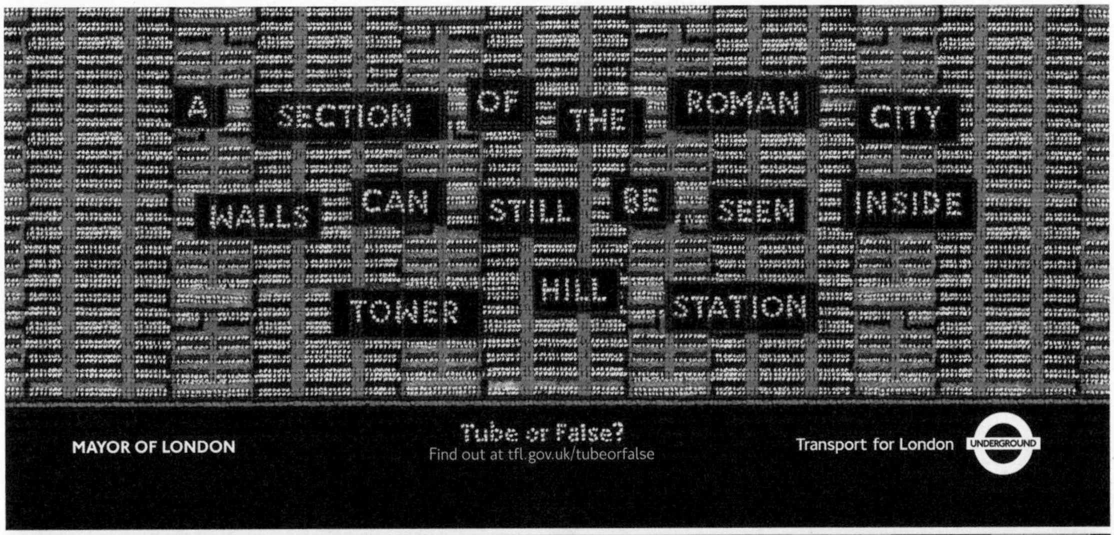
A SECTION OF THE ROMAN CITY WALLS CAN STILL BE SEEN INSIDE TOWER HILL STATION
MAYOR OF LONDON
Tube or False?
Find out at tfl.gov.uk/tubeorfalse
Transport for London
UNDERGROUND

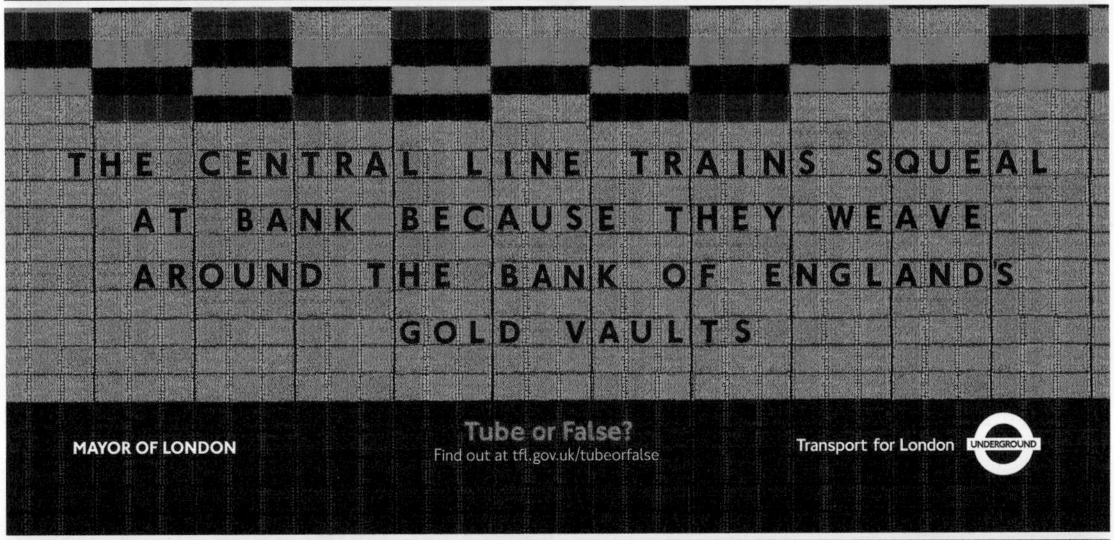
THE CENTRAL LINE TRAINS SQUEAL AT BANK BECAUSE THEY WEAVE AROUND THE BANK OF ENGLAND'S GOLD VAULTS
MAYOR OF LONDON
Tube or False?
Find out at tfl.gov.uk/tubeorfalse
Transport for London
UNDERGROUND

The ghost of actor William Terris is thought to haunt Covent Garden station
MAYOR OF LONDON
Tube or False?
Find out at tfl.gov.uk/tubeorfalse
Transport for London
UNDERGROUND

Poster Advertising Campaigns
BETC Euro RSCG
for Evian

Baby Inside
This poster campaign communicates youth as a universal and inspirational attitude that can be adopted by everyone. This 'live young' attitude is embodied through a gallery of portraits of men and women, from varied ages and ethnic backgrounds, wearing T-shirts with a baby's body printed on them. Refreshing, accessible and trendy, simple and minimal, this campaign describes youth in a universal language that is easily understood, whatever one's age, gender or nationality.

Art Director
Agnès Cavard
Copywriter
Valérie Chidlovsky
Photographer
Nathaniel Goldberg
Creative Director
Rémi Babinet
Advertising Agency
BETC Euro RSCG
Client
Evian

evian.
Live young
evian

evian.
Live young
evian

Poster Advertising Campaigns
DDB Group Hong Kong
for Freshlock China

Freshlock Campaign
When Freshlock seals in the freshness, it's like having a fresh pack every time.

Art Director
Sum Leung
Copywriter
Paul Chan
Photographer
Steve Wong
Illustrator
Thomas Ho
Creative Directors
Paul Chan
Jeffry Gamble
Advertising Agency
DDB Group Hong Kong
Client
Freshlock China

CORN FLAKES
freshLock

CHEEZ
CRACKERS
NET WT 12OZ (340g)
freshLock

Poster Advertising Campaigns
BBDO Toronto for smart Canada

Alcina Avenue / One Way / Stop Sign
We were tasked with creating a campaign to reinforce smart's positioning as the perfect vehicle for urban living. We dramatised smart's incredible manoeuvrability, by portraying ludicrously tight alleyways as streets the smart car could use.

Art Director
Jaimes Zentil
Copywriter
Craig McIntosh
Photographer
Shanghoon
Typographer
Evan Dermit
Creative Director
Ian MacKellar
Retouchers
Jano Kirijian
Sam Robbins
Jaimes Zentil
Advertising Agency
BBDO Toronto
Account Handler
Steve Groh
Brand Manager
Richard Trevisan
Client
smart Canada
Brand
smart fortwo

ALCINA AV
1
smart

smart

smart

● **Yellow Pencil in Press Advertising**

Press Advertising Campaigns
BBH London for St John Ambulance

Life Lost
This campaign launched the new positioning of St John Ambulance: The Difference. The 'Life Lost' executions demonstrate day-to-day situations where first aid could have made a difference, but didn't. The role of this campaign was to create a reappraisal of first aid, and consequently of St John Ambulance, positioning it as a life saving charity.

Art Directors
Victoria Daltrey
Mark Reddy
Adrian Rossi
Copywriters
Will Bingham
Alex Grieve
Photographer
Nadav Kander
Typographer
Dave Wakefield
Designer
Rich Kennedy
Creative Directors
Alex Grieve
Adrian Rossi
Retouchers
Antony Crossfield
Gary Meade
Print Producer
Sarah Pascoe
Advertising Agency
BBH London
Account Planner
Jude Lowson
Account Handlers
Lou Addley
Mehdi Benali
Art Buyer
Sarah Pascoe
Brand Manager
Scott Jacobson
Client
St John Ambulance

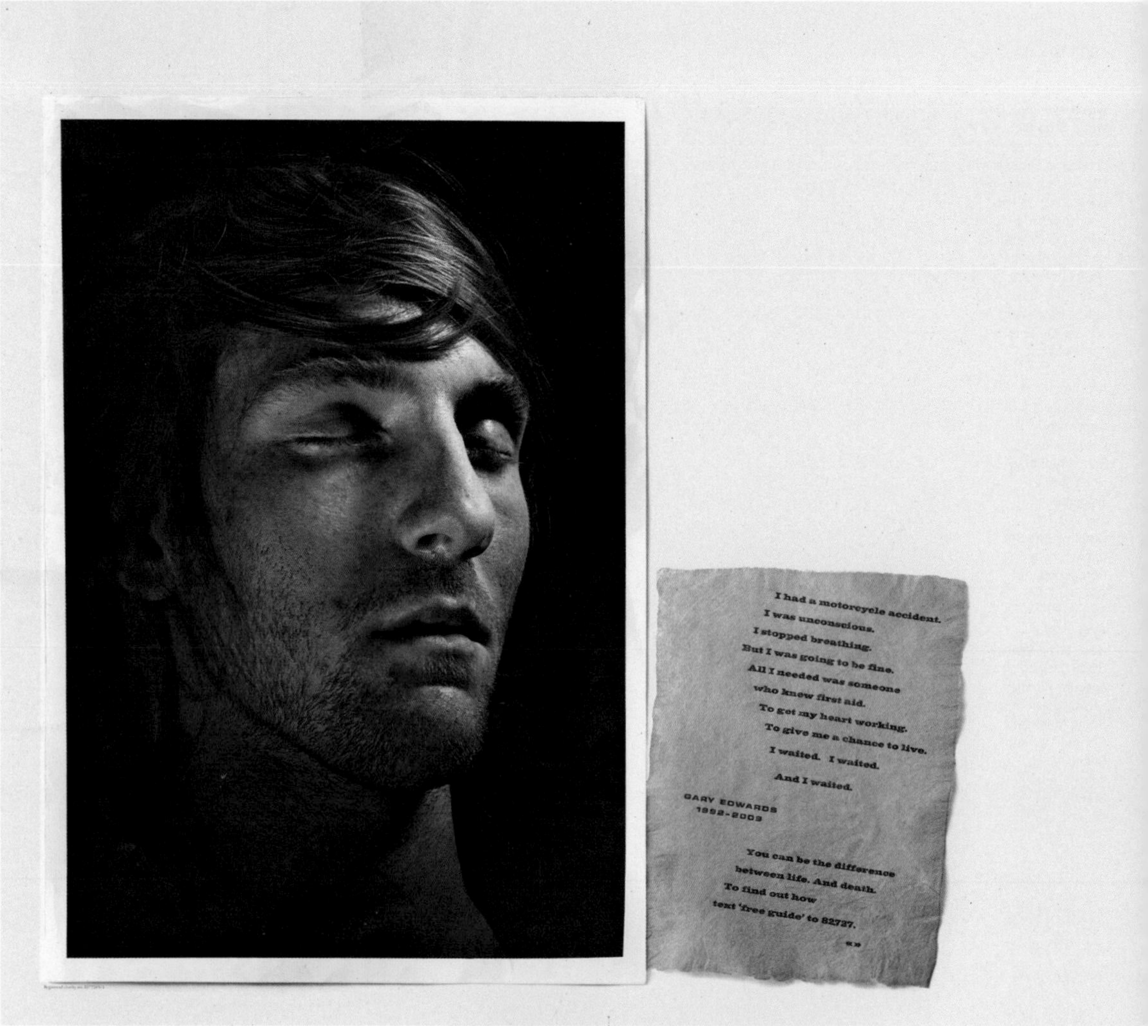
I had a motorcycle accident.
I was unconscious.
I stopped breathing.
But I was going to be fine.
All I needed was someone
who knew first aid.
To get my heart working.
To give me a chance to live.
I waited. I waited.
And I waited.
GARY EDWARDS
1992-2009
You can be the difference
between life. And death.
To find out how
text 'free guide' to 82727.

A grape stuck in my throat. I couldn't breathe. It was really scary. But I knew a grown-up would help me. Who was clever at first aid. Who knew that all I needed was some hard slaps on the back. Because grown-ups always know what to do. Don't they?
You can be the difference between life. And death. To find out how text 'free guide' to 82727.
St John Ambulance
The difference.

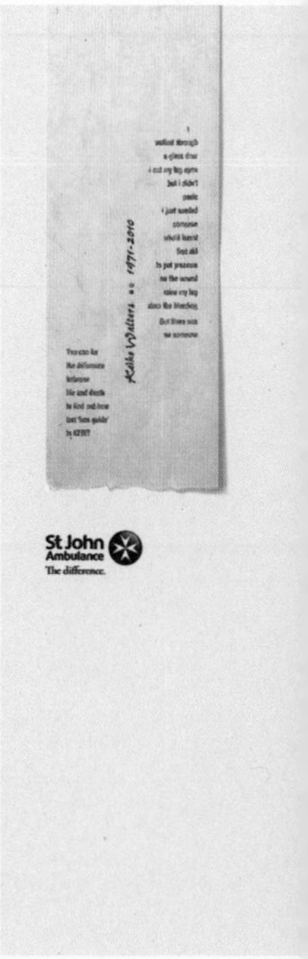
St John Ambulance
The difference.

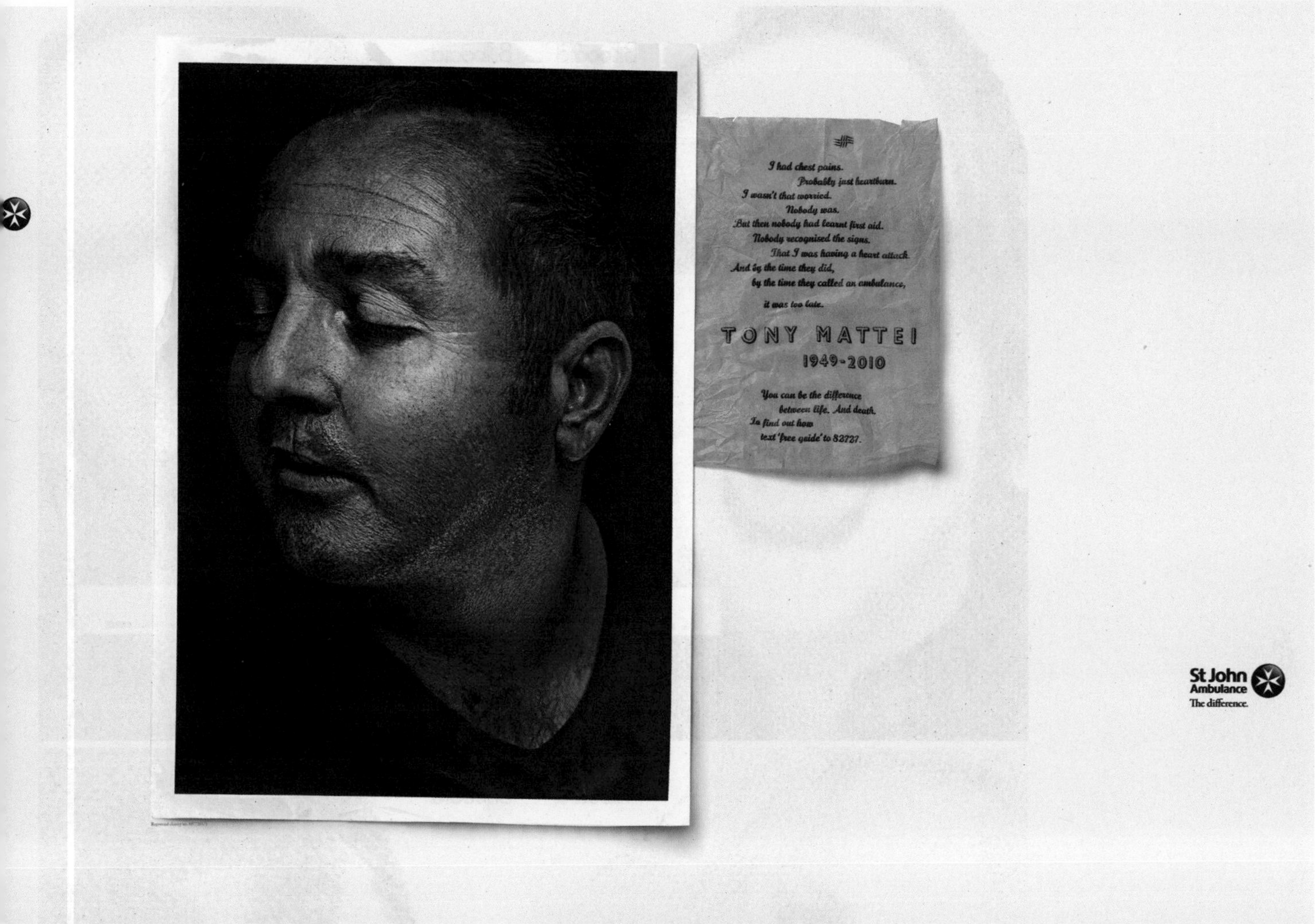
I had chest pains.
Probably just heartburn.
I wasn't that worried.
Nobody was.
But then nobody had learnt first aid.
Nobody recognised the signs.
That I was having a heart attack.
And by the time they did,
by the time they called an ambulance,
it was too late.
TONY MATTEI
1949-2010
You can be the difference
between life. And death.
To find out how
text 'free guide' to 83727.
St John Ambulance
The difference.

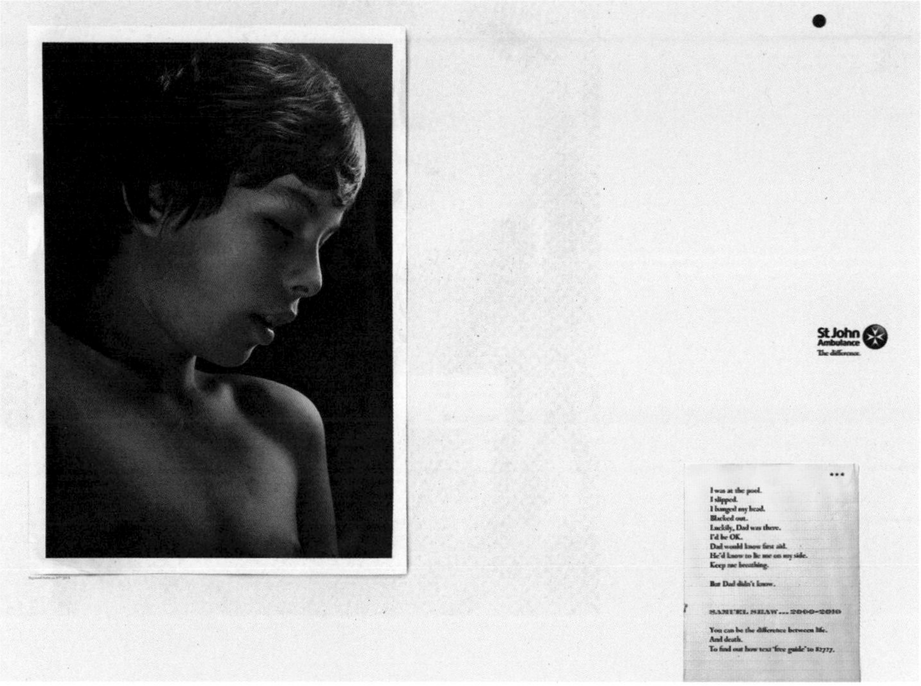
St John Ambulance
The difference.
I was at the pool.
I slipped.
I banged my head.
Blacked out.
Luckily, Dad was there.
I'd be OK.
Dad would know first aid.
He'd know to lie me on my side.
Keep me breathing.
But Dad didn't know.
SAMUEL SHAW 2000-2010
You can be the difference between life.
And death.
To find out how text 'free guide' to 82727.

Yellow Pencil in Press Advertising

Press Advertising Campaigns
AlmapBBDO
for Billboard

Music. See What it's Made of.
Magazines are made of dots. Artists are made of influences. 'Music. See What it's Made of' was a campaign for Billboard that showed how much the magazine knows about the pop music universe. We created print ads featuring stars like Bono, Eminem and Marilyn Manson, with each image composed of the stars' respective influences.

Art Directors
Danilo Boer
Marcos Kothlar
Marcos Medeiros
Copywriter
Andre Kassu
Typographer
José Roberto Bezerra
Illustrators
Marcos Kothlar
Marcos Medeiros
Creative Directors
Dulcidio Caldeira
Luiz Sanches
Advertising Agency
AlmapBBDO
Marketing Manager
Antonio Camarotti
Client
Billboard

Music.
See what it's made of.
Billboard
Kiss
Ozzy
The Cure
Cher

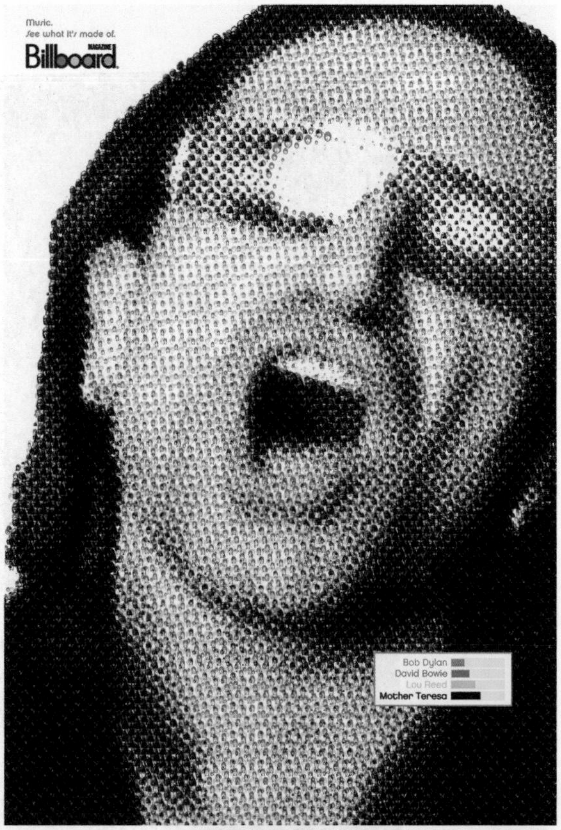
Music.
See what it's made of.
Billboard
Bob Dylan
David Bowie
Lou Reed
Mother Teresa

Music.
See what it's made of.
Billboard
Madonna
Madonna
Madonna
Paparazzi

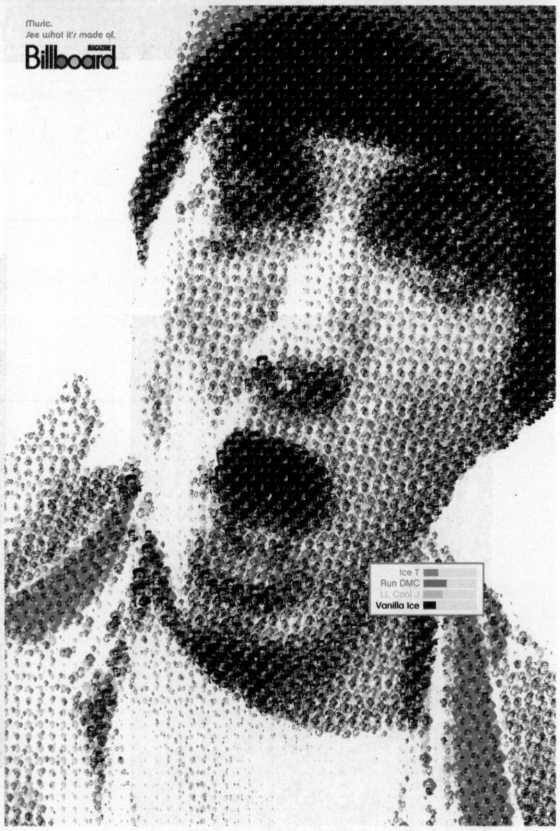
Music.
See what it's made of.
Billboard
Ice T
Run DMC
Vanilla Ice

Nomination in
Press Advertising

AlmapBBDO
for Volkswagen

A Bad Part Affects the Entire System
To stress the importance of using original Volkswagen parts, we created a campaign showing that one single part can compromise the whole system.

Art Director
Bruno Prosperi
Copywriter
Renato Simões
Typographer
José Roberto Bezerra
Creative Director
Luiz Sanches
Advertising Agency
AlmapBBDO
Planners
Fernanda Barone
Renata Bonilha
Cintia Gonçalves
Marketing Manager
Herlander Zola
Client
Volkswagen

A bad part affects the entire system.
Volkswagen original parts.

Das Auto.

- **Nomination in Press Advertising**

Press Advertising Campaigns
Ogilvy Cape Town
for Volkswagen

For Any Business
The brief was to create a print campaign demonstrating the versatility of Volkswagen Crafters across a range of commercial applications. Our idea was to tell stories using line-ups of Crafters from different companies. In this way, the campaign communicates the fact that Crafters are perfect for any business.

Art Director
Jennifer MacFarlane
Copywriter
Cuanan Cronwright
Photographer
Guy Neveling
Creative Director
Chris Gotz
Advertising Agency
Ogilvy Cape Town
Account Handler
Greg Tebbutt
Marketing Manager
Graeme Birch
Client
Volkswagen
Brand
Crafter

PROFESSIONAL WAITERS AND BARTENDERS
THE WEDDING STAFF CO.
Curry Palace Catering
EMERGENCY PLUMBING
For any business. Crafter.
Commercial Vehicles

For any business. Crafter.
Commercial Vehicles

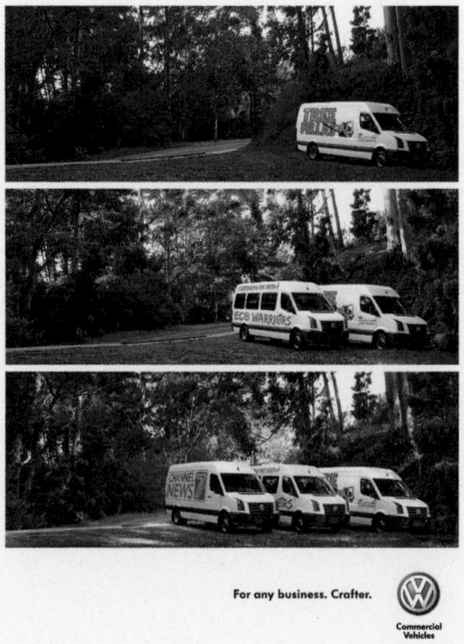
For any business. Crafter.
Commercial Vehicles

Nomination in
Press Advertising

Press Advertising
Campaigns
AlmapBBDO for PepsiCo

Drops of Sweat
Our aim was to show that Gatorade replaces the fluids and minerals lost by the body during physical activity. We assigned numbers to each of the sweat drops on the bodies of different athletes, starting at 1ml and going up to 500ml, which is the content of a Gatorade bottle.

Art Director
Andre Gola
Copywriter
Pernil
Photographer
Hugo Treu
Typographer
José Roberto Bezerra
Creative Director
Luiz Sanches
Advertising Agency
AlmapBBDO
Planners
Valter Bombonato
Cintia Gonçalves
Marketing Manager
Gustavo Siemsen
Client
PepsiCo
Brand
Gatorade

1ml
500ml

1ml
500ml

1ml
500ml

Press Advertising
Creative Juice\Bangkok
for 3M

Marble
The 3M cushion wrap, made of plastic and with many small, round, air-filled cushions, is ideal for protecting your valuable items during shipping.

Art Directors
Damisa Ongsiriwattana
Thirasak Tanapatanakul
Copywriter
Taya Soonthonvipat
Photographer
Surachai Puthikulangkura
Illustrators
Surachai Puthikulangkura
Supachai U-Rairat
Executive Creative Director
Thirasak Tanapatanakul
Retouchers
Surachai Puthikulangkura
Supachai U-Rairat
Advertising Agency
Creative Juice\Bangkok
Corporate Marketing & Public Affairs Manager
Suchinda Prasongtunskul
Client
3M

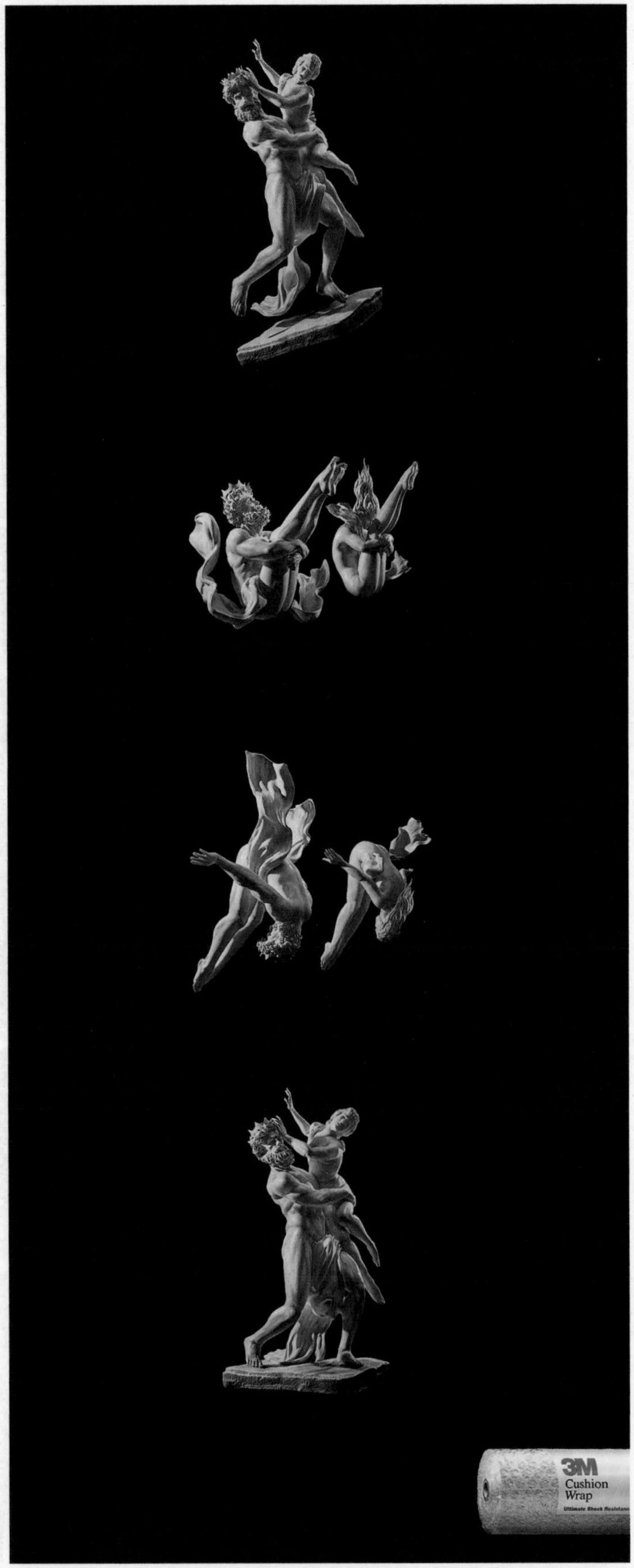
3M
Cushion
Wrap

Press Advertising
Ogilvy Cape Town
for Volkswagen

Sell Your Car
The Volkswagen Polo is so desirable yet affordable that when you see one, you want one. Targeting potential car buyers, we ran a cheeky double-sided newspaper ad in the motoring section. The front created desire, while the back allowed an unusual response, helping readers sell their current car. Our print ad became an ambient one. We turned our target market's own car windows into a new medium. Toyotas and Fords (our competitors) advertised the Polo's desirability. With an approximately three per cent response rate, this simple, low-cost idea generated thousands in earned media.

Art Director
Prabashan Gopalakrishnan Pather
Copywriter
Sanjiv Mistry
Typographers
Sanjiv Mistry
Prabashan Gopalakrishnan Pather
Creative Director
Chris Gotz
Advertising Agency
Ogilvy Cape Town
Account Handler
Jason Yankelowitz
Brand Manager
Bridget Harpur
Marketing Manager
Carrin Merkel
Client
Volkswagen
Brand
Polo

Why would you drive anything else?
New Polo.
Das Auto.

FOR SALE
I really really want a New Polo so please buy my car.
R
Call

FOR SALE

Press Advertising
DDB DM9 JaymeSyfu
for Pharex
Health Corporation

Opera
Give your cough the attention it needs before it attracts the attention you don't.

Art Director
Miko Quiogue
Copywriter
EJ Galang
3D Artist
Pinoy Reyes
Creative Directors
Jerry Hizon
Louie Sotto
Executive Creative Director
Eugene Demata
Chief Creative Officer
Merlee Jayme
Retoucher
Allan Montayre
Producers
Jess Ramo
Sheila Villanueva
Advertising Agency
DDB DM9 JaymeSyfu
Account Director
Ria Buenafe
Account Supervisor
Ronald Barreiro
Account Executive
Ina Vargas
Client Chief Executive Officer
Tomas Luke Marcelo G Agana III
Client
Pharex Health Corporation
Brand
Pharex Carbocisteine

PHAREX
Carbocisteine
COUGH SYRUP 60 mL

Press Advertising
Young & Rubicam Paris for the Surfrider Foundation Europe

The Fossil Bag
It takes hundreds of years for most pieces of rubbish to dissolve in the ocean. Throwing things into the ocean will affect the Earth long into the future.

Art Directors
Guillaume Auboyneau
Cedric Quissola
Copywriter
Pierre-Philippe Sardon
Photographer
Laziz Hamani
Creative Directors
Jorge Carreno
Robin de Lestrade
Retoucher
Pierrick Guen
Advertising Agency
Young & Rubicam Paris
Account Handlers
Brice Garcon
Aure Tessandier
Brand Manager
Stephane Latxague
Client
Surfrider Foundation Europe

Surfrider Foundation
HELP US KEEP THE OCEAN CLEAN
WHEN WE POLLUTE THE SEA, WE POLLUTE FOR A LONG TIME.
WWW.SURFRIDER.EU

Press Advertising
Shalmor Avnon
Amichay/ Y&R
Interactive Tel Aviv
for Stella Artois

Security Camera
This ad conveys the brand idea of Stella Artois: perfection has its price. Camera surveillance is how the rich protect and guard their most prized possessions. Stella Artois is obviously one of them.

Art Director
Nathan Freifeld
Copywriter
Oz Frenkel
Creative Director
Yaneev Avital
Executive Creative Director
Tzur Golan
Chief Creative Officer
Gideon Amichay
Advertising Agency
Shalmor Avnon
Amichay/ Y&R
Interactive Tel Aviv
Planners
Yoni Lahav
Zohar Reznik
Account Supervisor
Shiran Chen Gross
Account Handlers
Moran Miller
Esti Smilg
Executive Client Director
Adam Avnon
Client
Stella Artois

CAM_1 02:48:17
CAM_2 02:48:17
CAM_3 02:48:17
CAM_4 02:48:17
CAM_5 02:48:17
STELLA ARTOIS
CAM_6 02:48:17
CAM_7 02:48:17
CAM_8 02:48:17
Perfection has its price
STELLA ARTOIS

Press Advertising
Y&R Jakarta for
LG Electronics

Autobiography
The LG GX200 mobile phone boasts a superior talk time of 13.5 hours, perfect for those who appreciate the art of conversation. In this ad, we see a speech bubble in the shape of a book. The book title announces the beginning of one of these long conversations.

Art Director
Yerry Indrajaya
Copywriter
Gloria Martie
Photographers
Handri Karya
Heru Suryoko
Typographer
Yerry Indrajaya
Illustrator
Afi Kafi
Designers
Flora Marcella
Budiman Rahardjo
Associate Creative Director
Ahmed Fariz
Executive Creative Director
Sachin Ambekar
Regional Chief Creative Officer
Marcus Rebeschini
Retoucher
Alex Reagan
Advertising Agency
Y&R Jakarta
Account Handlers
Wolga Satyanto
Hendra Suryakusuma
Marketing Manager
Dony Munaf
Client
LG Electronics
Brand
LG GX200

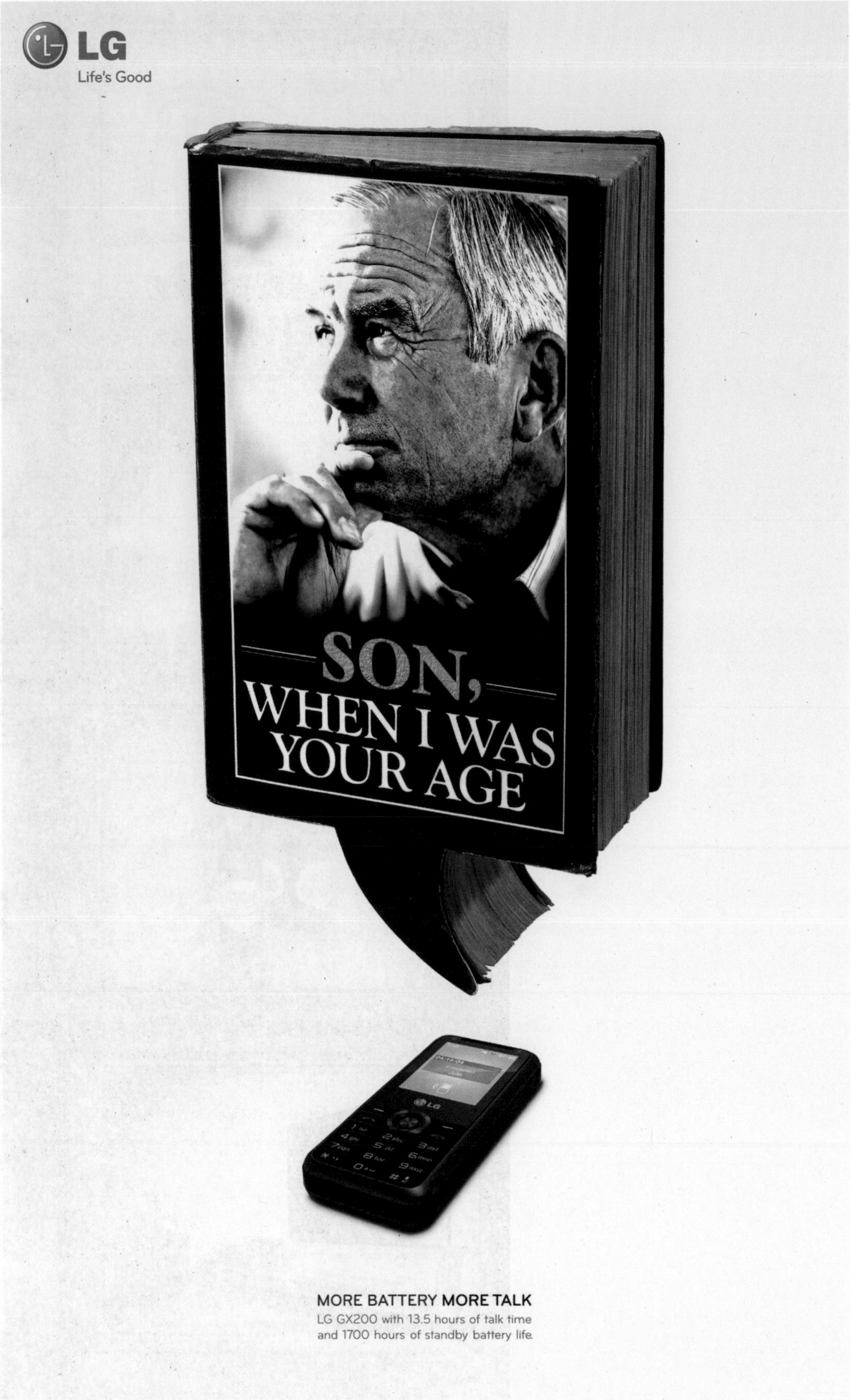
LG
Life's Good
SON,
WHEN I WAS
YOUR AGE
MORE BATTERY MORE TALK
LG GX200 with 13.5 hours of talk time
and 1700 hours of standby battery life.

Press Advertising
Grey Group Singapore
for Wildlife
Reserves Singapore

Teacher
Wildlife Reserves Singapore (WRS) felt that the general public, especially parents, were either unaware of its educational programme or did not realise the wonderful wildlife education opportunity it provides for children. We needed to heighten awareness. During programme sessions, animals play the important role of special teachers. Based on this insight, we combined a well-known school image – a class photo – together with one of the zoo's most popular residents, the orangutan. The message: WRS' education programme delivers a learning experience beyond the ordinary.

Art Director
Tan Zi Wei
Copywriter
Dunstan Lee
Photographer
Teo Chai Guan
Creative Director
Joseph Tay
Advertising Agency
Grey Group Singapore
Marketing Manager
Leow Neng Li
Client
Wildlife Reserves
Singapore
Brand
Singapore Zoo

A LEARNING EXPERIENCE BEYOND THE ORDINARY
Wildlife Reserves
SINGAPORE
EDUCATION PROGRAMMES AT WWW.ZOO.COM.SG

Press Advertising
AlmapBBDO
for Volkswagen

Crossfox. The Compact Off-road
An off-road car. A compact. And an ad that advertises these two characteristics in a concise, straightforward way.

Art Directors
Marcos Medeiros
Bruno Prosperi
Leonardo Rua
Caio Tezoto
Copywriter
Renato Simoes
Typographer
José Roberto Bezerra
Creative Director
Luiz Sanches
Advertising Agency
AlmapBBDO
Marketing Manager
Herlander Zola
Client
Volkswagen

Crossfox. The compact off-road.
Das Auto.

Press Advertising
TBWA\NEBOKO for
Heineken Netherlands

Social Networks
Every day we spend more and more time on social media, making new Facebook friends or twittering away. Heineken wants to remind us not to forget to do some real social networking once in a while. In the pub, with a cold Heineken.

Art Directors
Niels Bredemeijer
Bert Kerkhof
Copywriter
Ivar van den Hove
Creative Directors
Jorn Kruijsen
Jeroen van de Sande
Advertising Agency
TBWA\NEBOKO
Planner
Daan Remarque
Account Handler
Patritia Pahladsingh
Brand Manager
Annelotte Palthe
Marketing Manager
Ralph Rijks
Client
Heineken Netherlands
Brand
Heineken

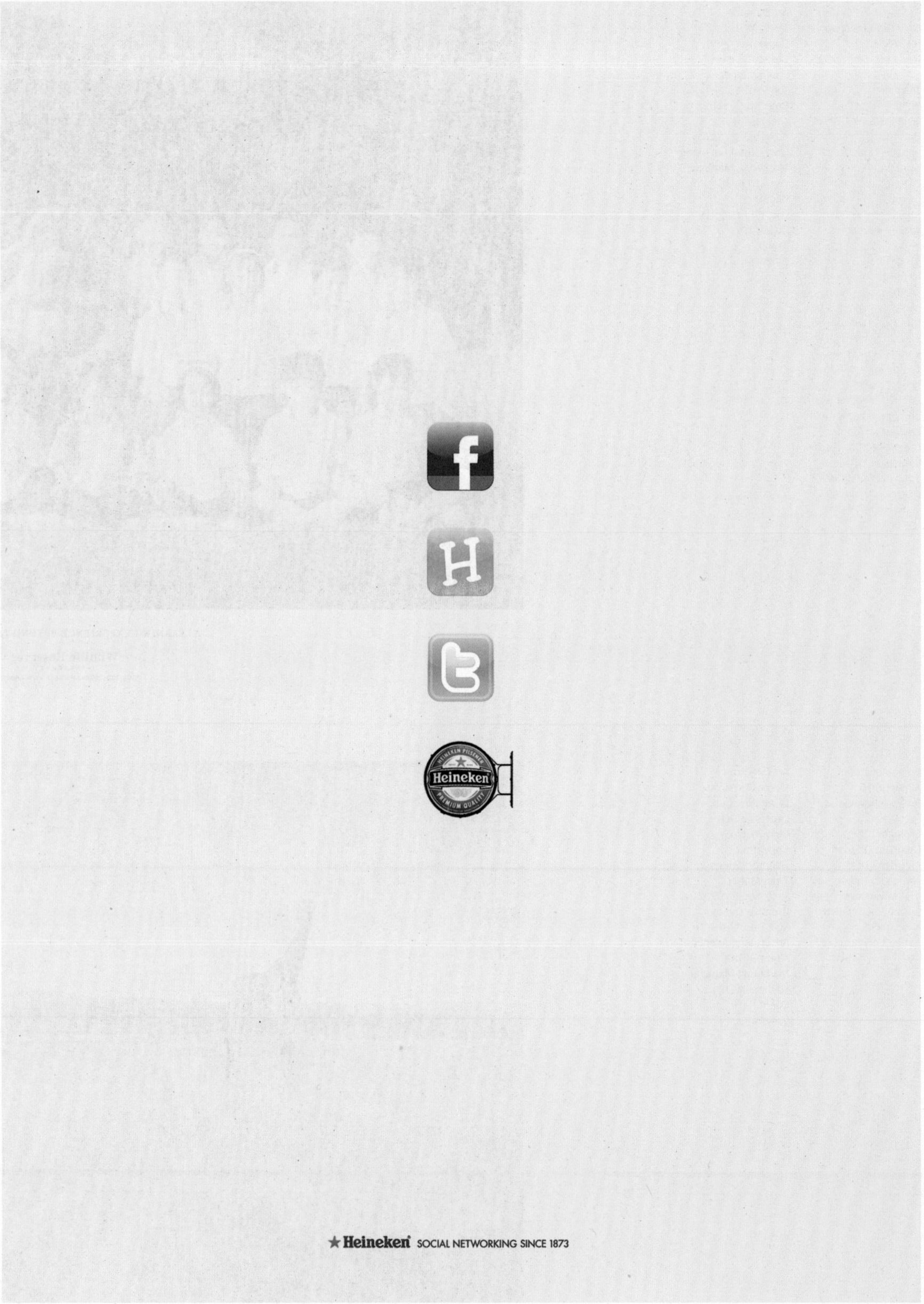
Heineken SOCIAL NETWORKING SINCE 1873

Press Advertising
AlmapBBDO for the
Escola de Arte e Design

How Far Does Your Creativity Go?
In this ad for Brazil's School of Art and Design, we wanted to show that colours may have multiple meanings (in this case, the colour yellow). The ad featured some examples, and stimulated readers to come up with new meanings through a challenging concept: how far does your creativity go?

Art Director
Andre Gola
Copywriter
Pernil
Typographer
José Roberto Bezerra
Creative Director
Luiz Sanches
Advertising Agency
AlmapBBDO
Marketing Manager
Enrique Lipizyc
Client
Escola de Arte e Design

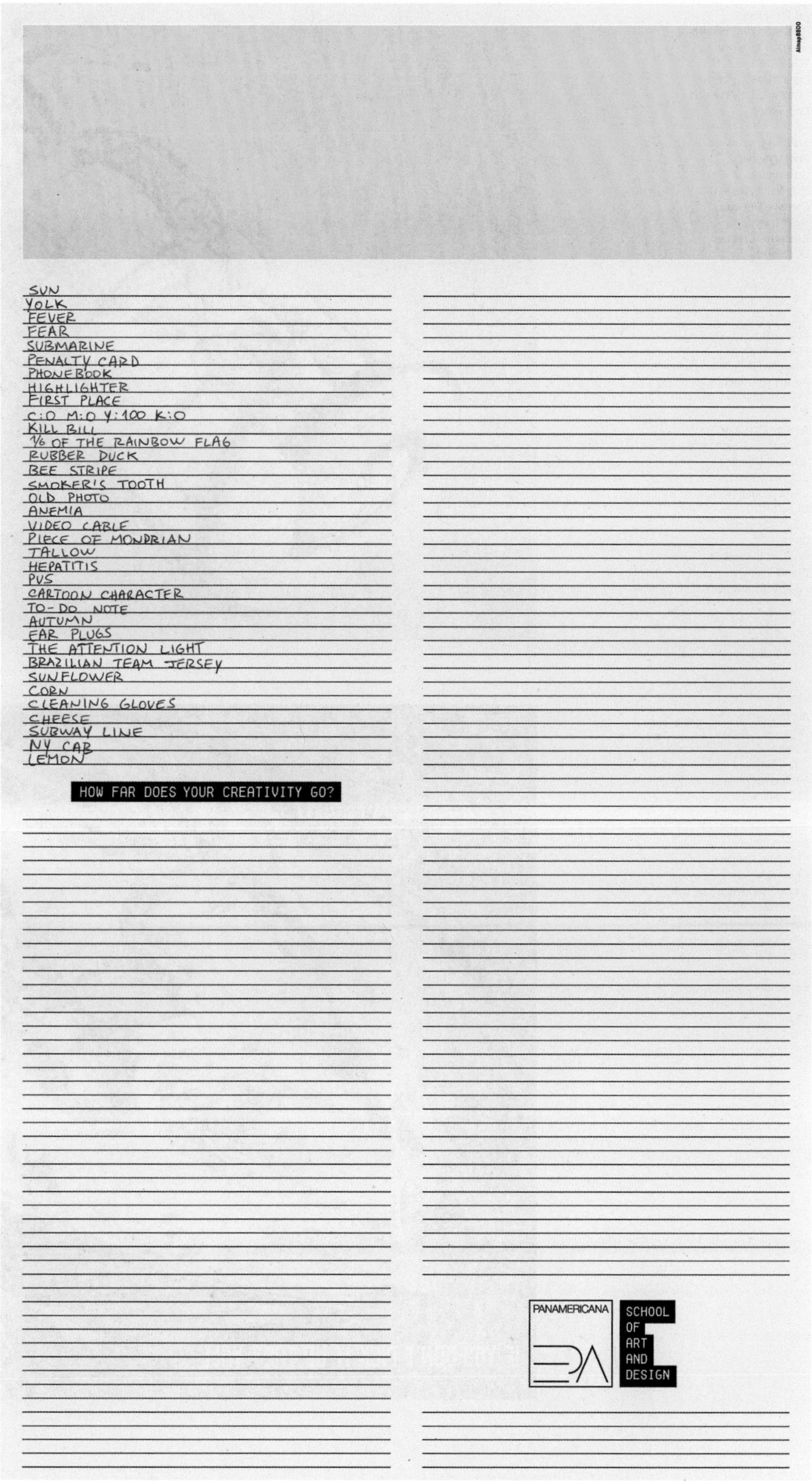
AlmapBBDO
SUN
YOLK
FEVER
FEAR
SUBMARINE
PENALTY CARD
PHONEBOOK
HIGHLIGHTER
FIRST PLACE
C:0 M:0 Y:100 K:0
KILL BILL
1/6 OF THE RAINBOW FLAG
RUBBER DUCK
BEE STRIPE
SMOKER'S TOOTH
OLD PHOTO
ANEMIA
VIDEO CABLE
PIECE OF MONDRIAN
TALLOW
HEPATITIS
PUS
CARTOON CHARACTER
TO-DO NOTE
AUTUMN
EAR PLUGS
THE ATTENTION LIGHT
BRAZILIAN TEAM JERSEY
SUNFLOWER
CORN
CLEANING GLOVES
CHEESE
SUBWAY LINE
NY CAB
LEMON
HOW FAR DOES YOUR CREATIVITY GO?
PANAMERICANA
SCHOOL OF ART AND DESIGN

Press Advertising
Ogilvy & Mather Thailand for Outdoor Innovation

Rolled Up Bed: Steel Bed
While people love travelling, they often still want home comforts. From this insight, we came up with the following proposition for Karana Travelgear: comfort like your bed at home while taking part in the outdoor activity you love. We chose a background adventurers love that goes beautifully with a steel bed. Finally, we changed the shape of the bed to look like the client's product.

Art Directors
Ratapon Huayhongtong
Gumpon Laksanajinda
Wisit Lumsiricharoenchoke
Nopadol Srikieatikajohn
Copywriter
Rudee Surapongraktrakool
Photographer
Surachai Puthikulangkura
Creative Director
Paruj Daorai
Executive Creative Directors
Wisit Lumsiricharoenchoke
Nopadol Srikieatikajohn
Retouchers
Surachai Puthikulangkura
Supachai U-Rairat
Advertising Agency
Ogilvy & Mather Thailand
Agency Producer
Paiboon Suwansangroj
Account Handler
Woorawit Yoosawat
Client Managing Director
Wasit Sirodom
Client
Outdoor Innovation
Brand
Karana Travelgear

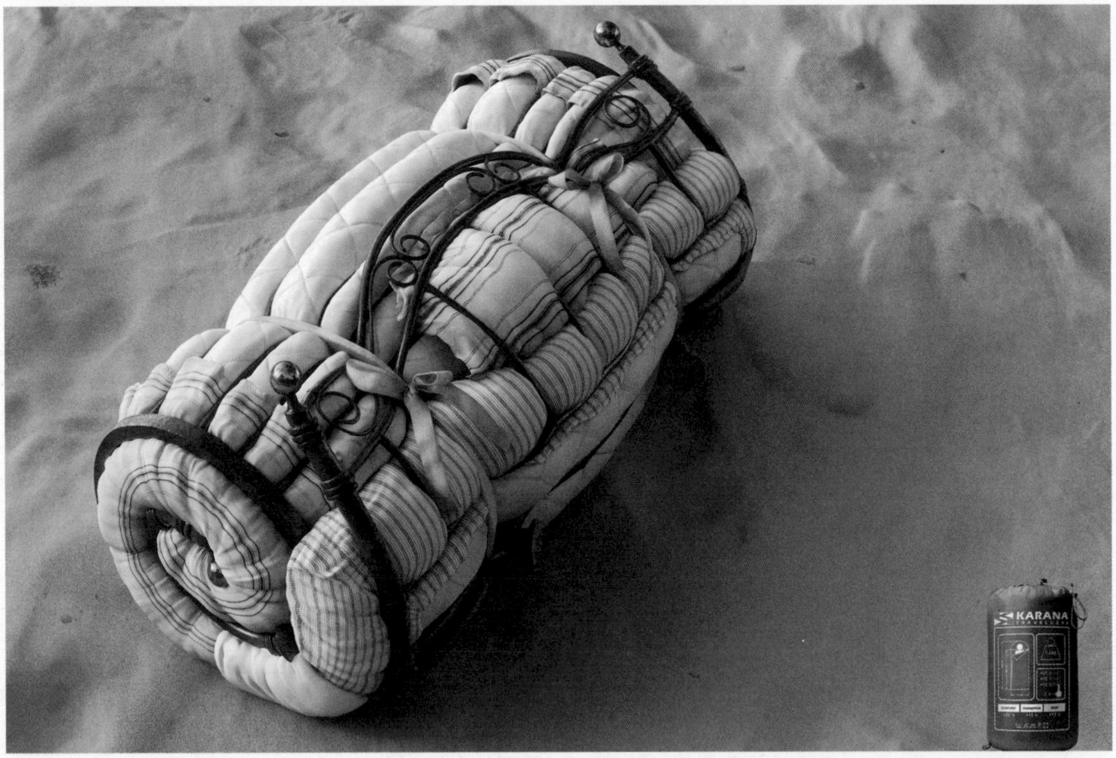
KARANA

Press Advertising
TBWA\Hunt\Lascaris Johannesburg for The Endangered Wildlife Trust

Golf Ball
The Endangered Wildlife Trust wanted to take preventative action against increased littering during the 2010 World Cup. To alert South Africans and tourists to the plight of coastal birds, TBWA\Hunt\Lascaris Johannesburg conceptualised a press campaign highlighting the effect of this pollution. The advertisements show birds that have been killed by litter they have ingested. The birds' bodies are decaying around the rubbish inside them, demonstrating how litter outlasts wildlife. Readers were driven to www.ewt.org.za to find out more.

Art Director
Wihan Meerholz
Copywriter
Jared Osmond
Photographer
Chris Jordan
Creative Directors
Damon Stapleton
Adam Weber
Executive Creative Director
Damon Stapleton
Advertising Agency
TBWA\Hunt\Lascaris Johannesburg
Account Handler
Bridget Langley
Brand Manager
Vanessa Bezuidenhout
Client
The Endangered Wildlife Trust

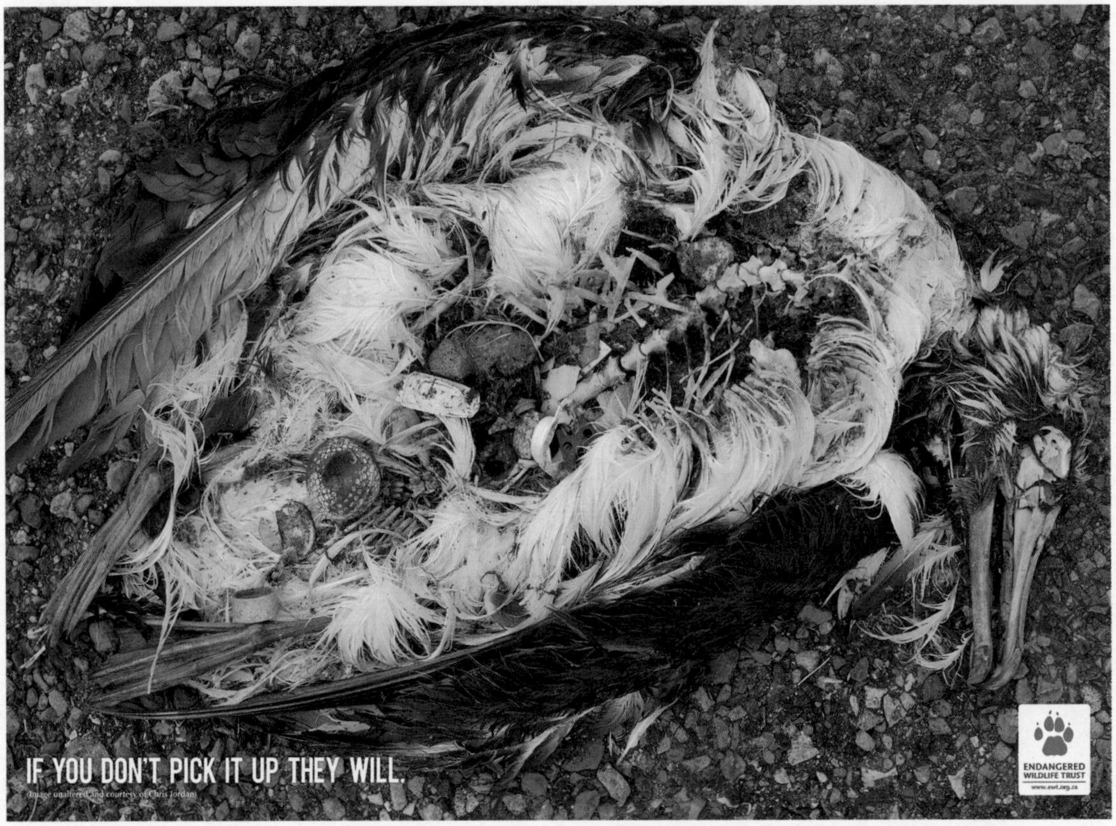
IF YOU DON'T PICK IT UP THEY WILL.
(Image unaltered and courtesy of Chris Jordan)
ENDANGERED WILDLIFE TRUST
www.ewt.org.za

Press Advertising
Forsman & Bodenfors
for Volvo

Pedestrian Detection
The all-new Volvo S60 came with a unique feature: pedestrian detection, a system that detects humans on the street and stops the car if the driver does not brake in time. Like a never-ending pedestrian crossing.

Art Director
Johan Eghammer
Copywriter
Jacob Nelson
Photographer
Peter Gherke
Designer
Mikko Timonen
Advertising Agency
Forsman & Bodenfors
Retouching
Tutch Me
Production Companies
Adamsky
F&B Factory
Account Supervisor
Anders Bothén
Account Manager
Anna Levegård
Client Advertising Manager
Bengt Junemo
Client
Volvo

THE ALL-NEW VOLVO S60 WITH PEDESTRIAN DETECTION.
DMZ 054
VOLVO

Press Advertising
DDB Singapore for
Atlas Sound & Vision

Construction /
Crying Kid
Bose is a brand known for clean lines, simplicity, and design that is made for life. When we were asked to promote its range of noise-cancelling headphones, we drew inspiration from the brand's design ethos. The campaign demonstrated the prowess of Bose noise-cancelling technology with a simple graphic icon: the volume bar.

Art Director
Khalid Osman
Copywriter
Lester Lee
Photographer
Allan Ng
Creative Directors
Joji Jacob
Neil Johnson
Thomas Yang
Retoucher
Chew Peng
Advertising Agency
DDB Singapore
Account Handlers
Rowena Bhagchandani
Vivien Foo
Marketing Manager
Tammy Chan
Client
Atlas Sound & Vision
Brand
Bose

BOSE
Noise-cancelling headphones

BOSE
Noise-cancelling headphones

Press Advertising
DDB Singapore
for the Breast Cancer Foundation

Pimple
Each year, over 280 Singaporean women succumb to breast cancer. In a majority of these cases, the tragedy could have been avoided with early detection. Less vital activities like spa treatments take approximately 45 minutes, while mammograms take just 20 minutes. To encourage women to get their breasts screened and to promote early detection, we challenged them to rethink their priorities. What is more deserving of your time: a pimple or breast cancer? We brought this insight to life with a novel body painting technique.

Art Directors
Andrea Kuo
Thomas Yang
Copywriters
Joji Jacob
Khairul Mondzi
Photographer
Allan Ng
Typographer
Andrea Kuo
Illustrator
Andy Yang
Creative Directors
Joji Jacob
Neil Johnson
Thomas Yang
Advertising Agency
DDB Singapore
Retouching
Digitalist
Account Handlers
Rowena Bhagchandani
Ng Ling Kai
Dominic Lee
Brand & Marketing Manager
Elaine Tan
Client
Breast Cancer Foundation

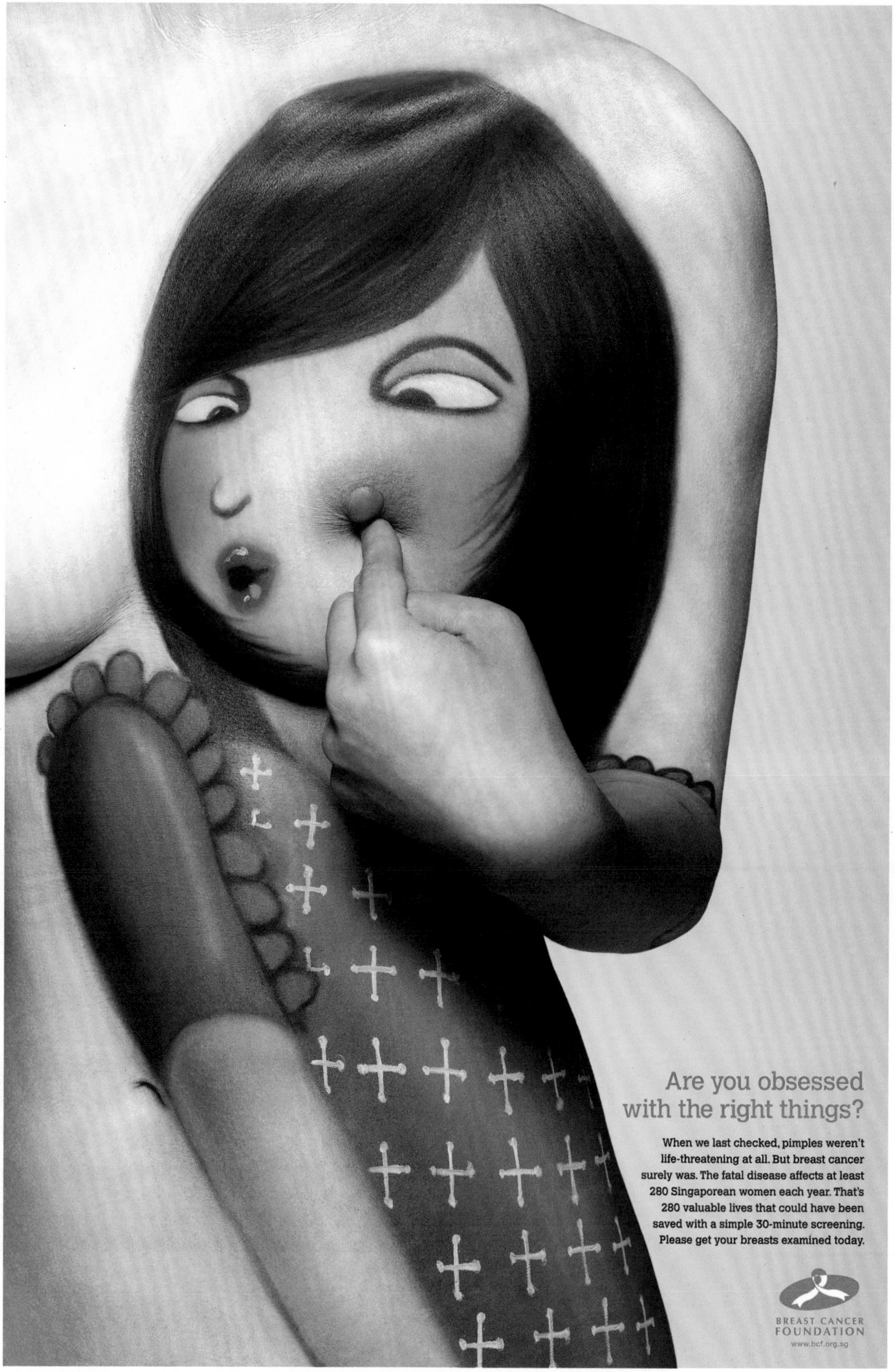
Are you obsessed with the right things?
When we last checked, pimples weren't life-threatening at all. But breast cancer surely was. The fatal disease affects at least 280 Singaporean women each year. That's 280 valuable lives that could have been saved with a simple 30-minute screening. Please get your breasts examined today.
BREAST CANCER FOUNDATION
www.bcf.org.sg

Press Advertising
Lowe Bull Cape Town
for Independent Newspapers

George Bush, Shoe / Tiananmen Square, Tank
The objective was to demonstrate how the Cape Times reports on world events from every angle in order to deliver balanced and unbiased information. Cape Times readers possess above-average general knowledge, and are well educated and discerning when it comes to news. The solution was to show a well-known news story from a less well-known perspective. There's always another side to every story and the ads demonstrate that in a simple, engaging way. 'Shoe' shows how it must have felt to be on the receiving end of Iraqi journalist Muntadhar Al-Zeidi's shoe. The focus in 'Tank' is on what and how the driver of a tank on Tiananmen Square must have been thinking, bringing a more human dimension to the event.

Art Director
Cameron Watson
Copywriter
Simon Lotze
Photographers
Michael Lewis
Nick Van Reenen
Creative Director
Kirk Gainsford
Retoucher
Juliet White
Advertising Agency
Lowe Bull Cape Town
Account Handler
Vicki Hey
Marketing Manager
Michael Vale
Client
Independent Newspapers
Brand
Cape Times

In-depth news investigated from every angle.
CAPE TIMES
Know all about it.

In-depth news investigated from every angle.
CAPE TIMES
Know all about it.

Press Advertising
Draftfcb South Africa
for Lexus

Green Handbag /
Pink Handbag

The brief was to communicate one of the many 'minor' features on the Lexus IS250. These features, like traction control, rear-view camera and keyless entry, are often overlooked when creating a selling proposition. To illustrate keyless entry, we worked with the following insight: when fumbling through a handbag for your keys, the inside of that bag can often feel like a surreal universe where certain things are familiar and others seem completely alien. We wanted to create that sense of vastness and chaos, an endless, bizarre universe where keys seem to disappear.

Art Director
Alan Lewus
Copywriter
Morne Strydom
Typographer
Alan Lewus
Illustration
Carioca
Creative Director
Grant Jacobsen
Chief Creative Officer
Brett Morris
Advertising Agency
Draftfcb South Africa
Account Handler
Struan De
Bellelay-Bourquin
Marketing Manager
Lisa Mallett
Client
Lexus
Brand
Lexus IS250

Keyless entry standard on the IS250. Thankfully.
LEXUS
The pursuit of perfection

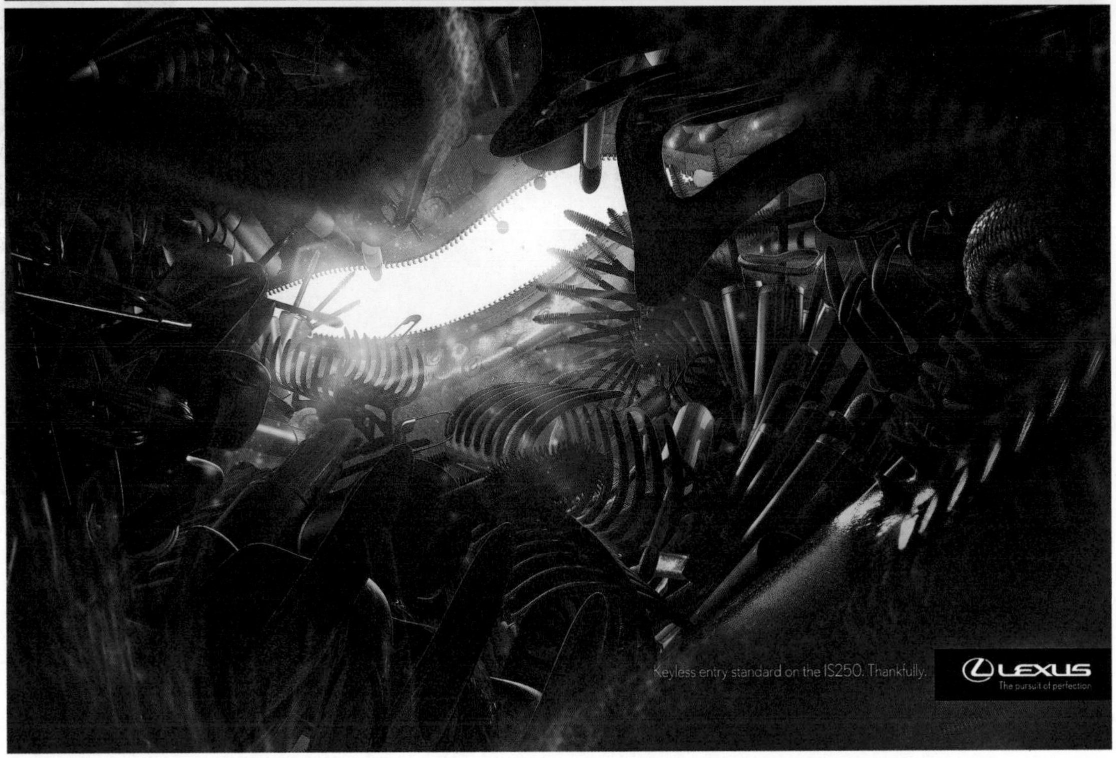
Keyless entry standard on the IS250. Thankfully.
LEXUS
The pursuit of perfection

Press Advertising
Baumann Ber Rivnay Saatchi & Saatchi for Procter & Gamble Israel

Coffee
We have numerous encounters with food and drink every day. This print ad reveals Ariel as the remedy for those inevitable stains that are just waiting to happen.

Art Directors
Aia Bechor
Noam Laist
Photographer
Yoram Aschheim
Creative Directors
Yoram Levi
Eran Nir
Retoucher
Alex Malik
Advertising Agency
Baumann Ber Rivnay Saatchi & Saatchi
Planner
David Kosmin
Senior Planner
Guy Gordon
Account Handler
Idit Zuckerman
Account Executive
Noa Sherf
Account Supervisor
Inbal Rov
Brand Manager
Nirit Hurwitz
Marketing Manager
Or Ellensweig
Client
Procter & Gamble Israel
Brand
Ariel

COFF
SU
There's always
a stain waiting
to happen
ARIEL

Press Advertising
BBDO Chile for
Mitsubishi Motors Chile

Porcupine
The challenge for our client was to boost sales of replacement parts. The challenge for BBDO Chile was to find an engaging, informative and funny way to explain that a bad decision when choosing a replacement part for your car can be very risky.

Art Directors
Sebastian Caceres
Emerson Navarrete
Silvio Vildosola
Copywriter
Marcelo Correa
Illustrator
Silvio Vildosola
Creative Directors
Marcelo Correa
Emerson Navarrete
Advertising Agency
BBDO Chile
Account Handler
Cesar Araya
Brand Manager
Cecilia Unanue
Marketing Manager
Francisca Valenzuela
Client
Mitsubishi Motors Chile
Brand
Mitsubishi

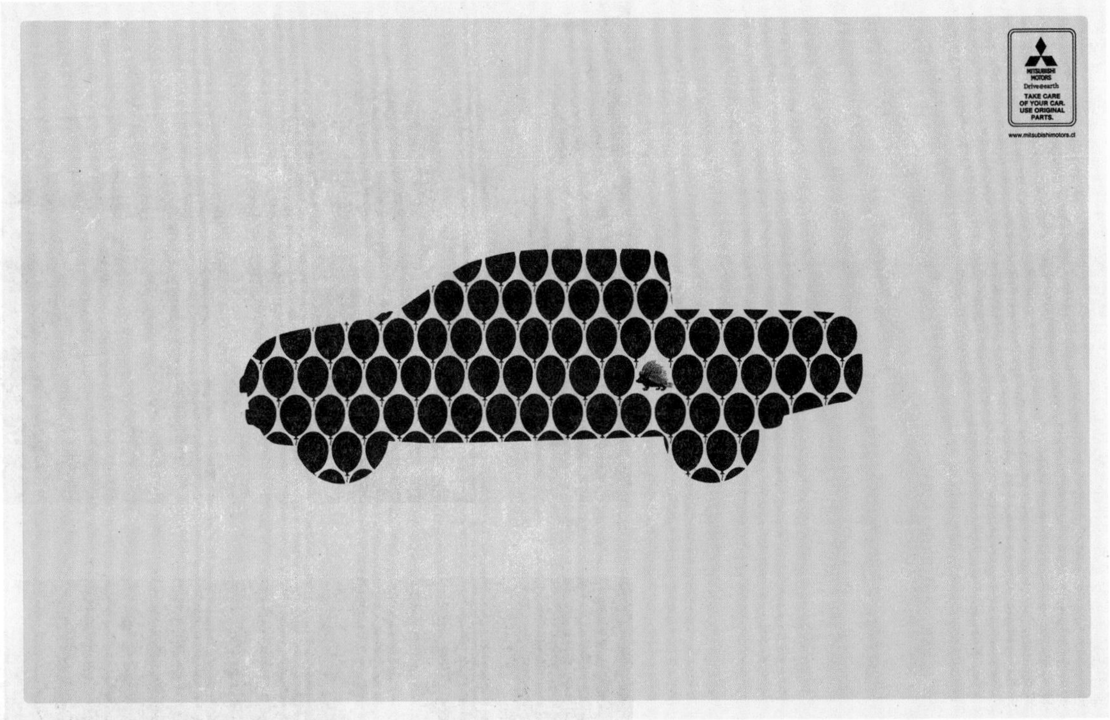
MITSUBISHI
MOTORS
Drive@earth
TAKE CARE
OF YOUR CAR.
USE ORIGINAL
PARTS.
www.mitsubishimotors.cl

Press Advertising Campaigns
AMV BBDO for Tower Hamlets Council

Mums / Girls / Boys
To coincide with a road safety initiative in the borough of Tower Hamlets, the brief was to help raise awareness of the dangers of texting while driving. A recent study showed that writing or reading a text message while driving increases the chances of having an accident by up to 23 times. To illustrate the statistic at the core of the idea, each protagonist is seen 23 times, conveying the message that when a driver texts behind the wheel, an accident is almost unavoidable.

Art Director
Ant Nelson
Copywriter
Mike Sutherland
Photographer
Trevor Ray Hart
Typographer
James Townsend
Creative Directors
Ant Nelson
Mike Sutherland
Executive Creative Director
Paul Brazier
Retoucher
Mark Deamer
Print Producer
Simon Pedersen
Advertising Agency
AMV BBDO
Project Manager
Linda Carlos
Planner
Martin Beverley
Account Handler
James Drummond
Client
Tower Hamlets Council

TEXT WHILE YOU'RE DRIVING
AND YOU'RE 23 TIMES MORE LIKELY
TO HAVE AN ACCIDENT

TEXT WHILE YOU'RE DRIVING
AND YOU'RE 23 TIMES MORE LIKELY
TO HAVE AN ACCIDENT

TEXT WHILE YOU'RE DRIVING
AND YOU'RE 23 TIMES MORE LIKELY
TO HAVE AN ACCIDENT

Press Advertising Campaigns
Ogilvy Cape Town
for Volkswagen

The Donated Ad Space Campaign
For BlueMotion, Volkswagen's more eco-sensitive range, we asked our client to put its money where its mouth was by donating part of its expensive advertising space to small, eco-focused not-for-profit organisations. It was a win-win initiative. The non-profits got their message out there, and BlueMotion proved itself as a brand that doesn't just talk, but also takes action.

Art Director
Prabashan Gopalakrishnan Pather
Copywriter
Sanjiv Mistry
Creative Director
Chris Gotz
Advertising Agency
Ogilvy Cape Town
Account Handlers
Greg Tebbutt
Jason Yankelowitz
Brand Manager
Bridget Harpur
Marketing Manager
Carrin Merkel
Client
Volkswagen
Brand
BlueMotion

DONATED AD SPACE
Dyer Island Conservation Trust
Dyer Island Conservation Trust delivers unique conservation and research programmes in the fragile and critically important marine eco-system at the southern-most tip of Africa.
Here we strive to protect the largest surviving colonies of the endangered African Penguin;
the globally important breeding and calving grounds of the Southern Right Whale;
and, one of the world's largest populations of the mysterious Great White Shark.
To learn more visit www.dict.org.za
BlueMotion
It's all about giving a little bit back. Eco-conscious BlueMotion technology.
Das Auto.

DONATED AD SPACE
SUPPORT HARVEST OF HOPE
BlueMotion
Das Auto.

DONATED AD SPACE
Help keep the Vaal River free from pollution.
BlueMotion
Das Auto.

DONATED AD SPACE
BlueMotion
Das Auto.

Press Advertising Campaigns
Lowe Indonesia for UNICEF Indonesia

Kids
Most Indonesian children spend an average of five hours glued to the TV every day. That's more than double the duration recommended by the American Academy of Paediatrics. This campaign for UNICEF Indonesia is to promote healthier television-watching habits for children.

Art Director
Tania Huiny
Copywriter
Ferly Novriadi
Photographer
Anton Ismael
Creative Director
Ferly Novriadi
Executive Creative Director
Din Sumedi
Retoucher
Alexander Loppies
Advertising Agency
Lowe Indonesia
Retouching
Magic Cube
Account Handler
Joseph Tan
Client
UNICEF Indonesia
Brand
UNICEF

See what you can switch on,
when the screen is off.
unicef

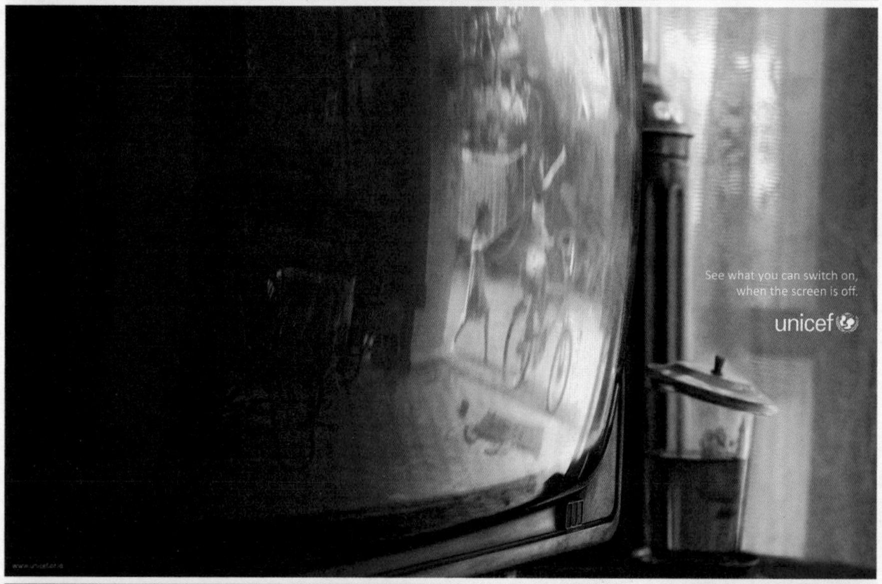
See what you can switch on,
when the screen is off.
unicef

See what you can switch on,
when the screen is off.
unicef

Press Advertising
Campaigns
DDB Tribal
Group Düsseldorf
for Volkswagen

Safety Barriers
This campaign was all about Volkswagen's technology leadership and the great benefit for its customers – safe cars. We show that only extreme passion, hard work and the permanent quest for a better result lead to this success.

Art Director
Dan Strasser
Copywriter
Mihai Botarel
Creative Directors
Oliver Kapusta
Alex Reiss
Advertising Agency
DDB Tribal Group
Düsseldorf
Post Production
The Scope
Account Handlers
Marie-Louise Jakob
Silke Lagodny
Brand Managers
Hartmut Seeger
Veronika Ziegaus
Marketing Manager
Luca de Meo
Client
Volkswagen
Brand
Golf

More late nights for us, less danger for you.
Five star safety rating. The Golf.

More brainstorming for us, less danger for you.
Five star safety rating. The Golf.

More meetings for us, less danger for you.
Five star safety rating. The Golf.

Press Advertising
Campaigns
Naga DDB Malaysia
for Star
Publications Malaysia

Too Long
We were asked to get people to log onto MyStarJob.com and search for new jobs. Our solution was to plant seeds of doubt in people's minds, giving them reasons to question their current positions. We advised them that if work was starting to take over all aspects of life, maybe it was time to change jobs.

Art Director
Wong Shu Kor
Copywriters
Grenville Francis
Ted Lim
Photographer
Jesse Choo
Creative Director
Ted Lim
Retouchers
Lim Chiew Ling
Sammax
Advertising Agency
Naga DDB Malaysia
Account Handlers
Grenville Francis
Wong Lian Hwa
Brand Manager
Ivy Leong
Client
Star Publications
Malaysia

Been in the job too long?
My Star Job.com

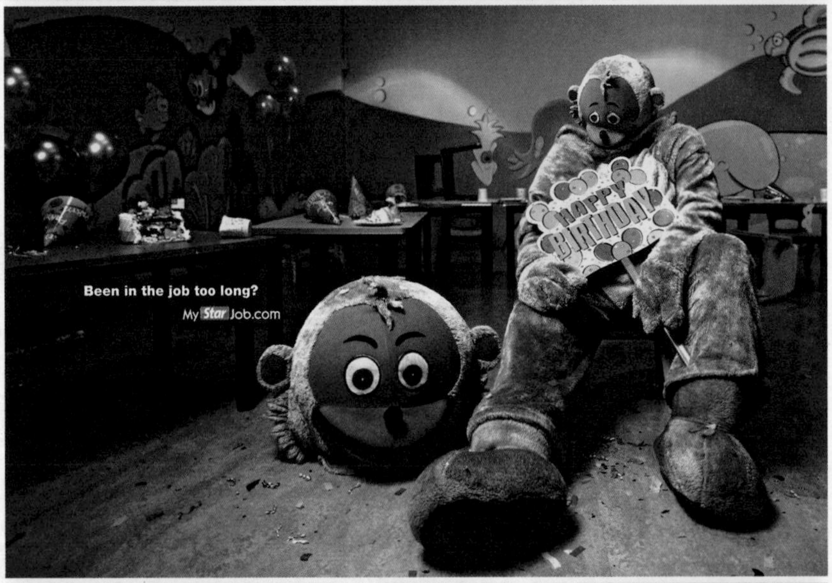
HAPPY BIRTHDAY
Been in the job too long?
My Star Job.com

Been in the job too long?
My Star Job.com

Press Advertising
Campaigns
JWT Italy for MUF
(Museo Nazionale
del Fumetto)

Comic Strips
To encourage people who go to traditional museums to visit the National Comics Museum, a number of famous paintings were presented using cartoon strips, turning the original content of the paintings into a humorous storyboard. The campaign was issued in the local free press and in magazines for tourists, who visit the Tuscan towns of artistic interest looking for museums and cultural events.

Art Director
Flavio Mainoli
Copywriter
Paolo Cesano
Illustrator
Manlio Truscia
Creative Directors
Paolo Cesano
Flavio Mainoli
Advertising Agency
JWT Italy
Marketing Manager
Angelo Nencetti
Client
MUF (Museo Nazionale
del Fumetto)

THE FART by Velasquez
©Velasquez 1666
comics are art. just funnier.
.muf
Comics
Museum
Lucca

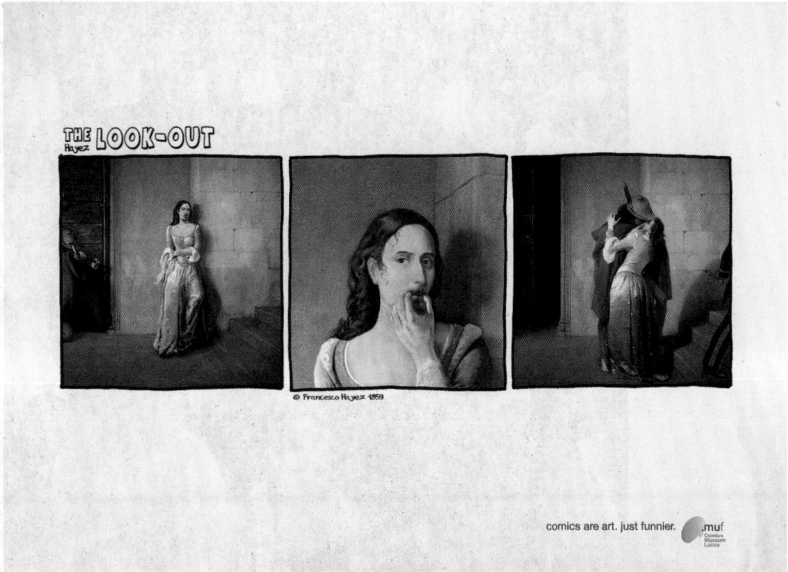
THE LOOK-OUT
Hayez
© Francesco Hayez 1859
comics are art. just funnier.
.muf

THE STRIP POKER
BY: MANET
©MANET 1862
comics are art. just funnier.
.muf

Press Advertising Campaigns
Colenso BBDO for Amnesty International

Ignore
So many of us haven't signed up to be members of Amnesty, and by ignoring membership calls and street collectors, we are in turn ignoring serious human rights issues. In this campaign we see crowds gathering around execution, beating and brutality scenarios. But instead of facing inward as a crowd normally would, they are facing outward, turning their backs on human rights.

Art Directors
Lisa Fedyszyn
Jonathan McMahon
Copywriters
Lisa Fedyszyn
Jonathan McMahon
Photographer
Henry Jen
Designer
Lachlan Palmer-Hubbard
Executive Creative Director
Nick Worthington
Deputy Creative Director
Karl Fleet
Retoucher
Kevin Hyde
Agency Producer
Phil Newman
Advertising Agency
Colenso BBDO
Account Manager
Kate Smart
Group Account Director
Angela Watson
Client Development Director
Cyrille Koolhaas
Client
Amnesty International

IGNORE US
IGNORE HUMAN RIGHTS
AMNESTY
INTERNATIONAL

IGNORE US
IGNORE HUMAN RIGHTS
AMNESTY
INTERNATIONAL

IGNORE US
IGNORE HUMAN RIGHTS
AMNESTY
INTERNATIONAL

Press Advertising
Campaigns
BBDO Proximity
Singapore for Daimler
South East Asia

Speed Camera:
Lizard / Bird / Leaf
BlueEFFICIENCY is Mercedes-Benz's holistic approach to eco-friendly motoring. And since such ecological concern is deserving of good karma, nature reciprocates by staging a timely intervention between the car and a speed camera.

Art Director
Brad Wilson
Copywriters
Boyd Champness
Ravi Eshwar
Photographers
Eric Ng
Stryke
Andy Wee
Typographer
Brad Wilson
Creative Director
Danny Searle
Retoucher
Marvin Yang
Advertising Agency
BBDO Proximity
Singapore
Account Handlers
Jin Ooi
Edwin Tay
Brand Manager
Patricia Ho
Client
Daimler South East Asia
Brand
Mercedes-Benz

The eco-sensitive BlueEFFICIENCY C-Class.
One day, nature will return the favour.
NEVADA HIGHWAY PATROL ROUTE 95
Mercedes-Benz

The eco-sensitive BlueEFFICIENCY E-Class.
One day, nature will return the favour.
MECKLENBURG-VORPOMMERN AUTOBAHNPOLIZEI ORT: GINGST-KLUIS 604
GESCHWINDIGKEIT: 065KM/H 00027-33 DATUM: 11.07.2009 ZIET: 14:15
Mercedes-Benz

The eco-sensitive BlueEFFICIENCY B-Class.
One day, nature will return the favour.
VICTORIA POLICE
0000453920 72922
SPEED: 083KPH
LOC: GREAT ALPINE ROAD
TIME: 04:45PM
DATE: 06-05-09
Mercedes-Benz

Press Advertising Campaigns
CHI & Partners for News International

The Sunday Times Rich List
Published every year, 'The Sunday Times Rich List' charts the wealth of the richest people in the UK and around the world. This print campaign celebrated their fortunes, playing them off each other to make visually arresting equations that compare their relative wealth.

Art Directors
Matt Collier
Wayne Robinson
Copywriters
Matt Collier
Wayne Robinson
Creative Director
Micky Tudor
Advertising Agency
CHI & Partners
Account Handler
Ben Etheridge
Brand Manager
Will Handley
Client
News International
Brand
The Sunday Times

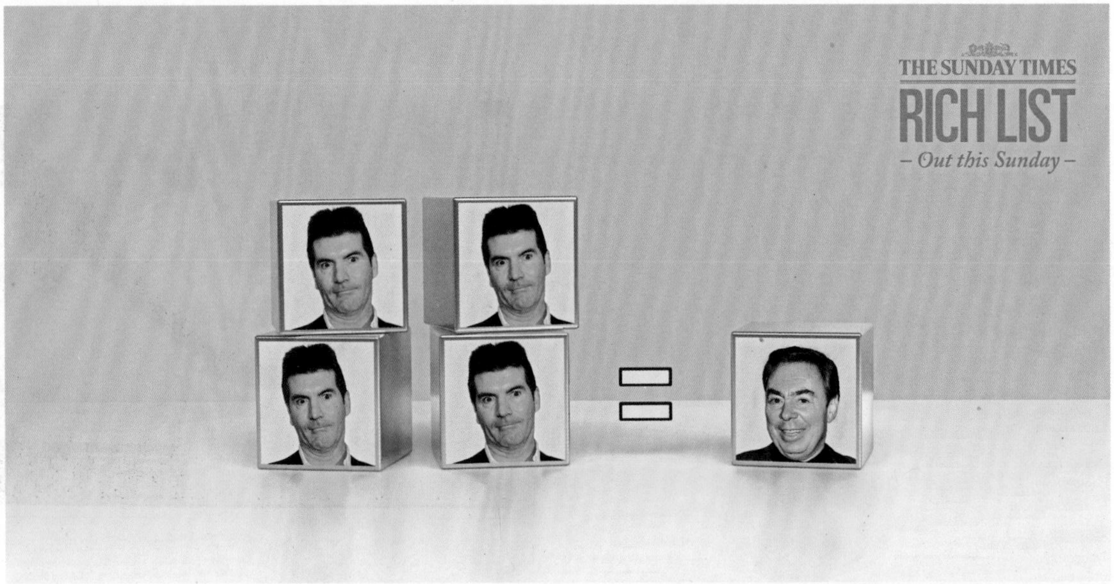
THE SUNDAY TIMES
RICH LIST
– Out this Sunday –

THE SUNDAY TIMES
RICH LIST
– Out this Sunday –

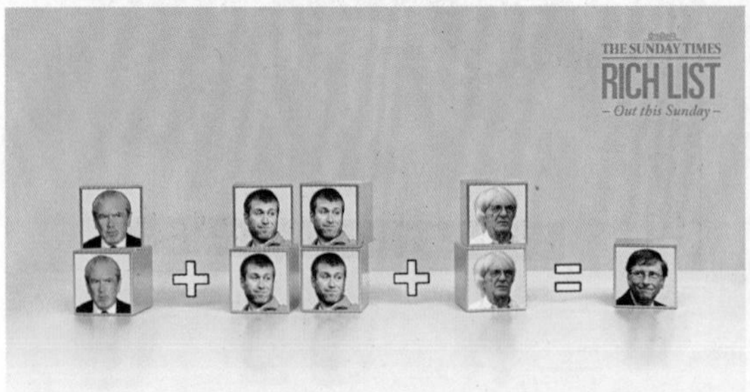
THE SUNDAY TIMES
RICH LIST
– Out this Sunday –

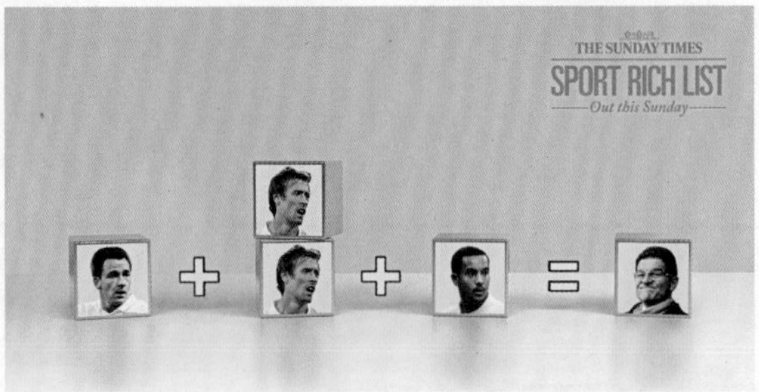
THE SUNDAY TIMES
SPORT RICH LIST
Out this Sunday

THE SUNDAY TIMES
RICH LIST
– Out this Sunday –

Press Advertising
Campaigns
BBDO Düsseldorf
for Spuk Pictures

The Unseen
Stock pictures are often boring and unimaginative – it's like you have seen them a million times before. Spuk Pictures offers an alternative. Its collection is not the largest, but it does offer truly exciting pictures. We demonstrated this to media professionals by giving them examples of extremely unusual pictures.

Art Director
Jake Shaw
Copywriter
Florian Birkner
Photographer
Matt Barnes
Executive Creative Director
Carsten Bolk
Chief Creative Officers
Toygar Bazarkaya
Wolfgang Schneider
Advertising Agency
BBDO Düsseldorf
Account Handler
Liselotte Schwenkert
Marketing Manager
Stefan Kranefeld
Client
Spuk Pictures

www.spuk.pictures.de
spuk
See the unseen.
stock pictures

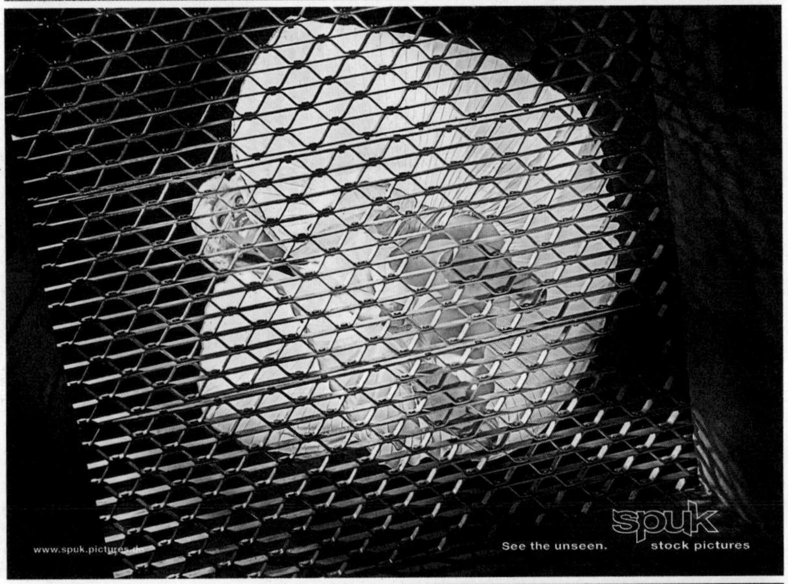
www.spuk.pictures.de
spuk
See the unseen.
stock pictures

www.spuk.pictures.de
spuk
See the unseen.
stock pictures

Press Advertising
Campaigns
Publicis Conseil
for Samusocial

Asphaltisation
For Samusocial, the French emergency service helping the homeless, Publicis Conseil created a shock press and display campaign based on the concept of 'asphaltisation'. The word means all the physical and mental symptoms developed by people living on the street: loss of orientation in time and space, loss of identity, etc. Publicis created this campaign to breathe life into the word and get everyone to understand that urgent action is needed, as the street sucks a little more life from the homeless every day.

Art Director
Alexandra Offe
Copywriter
Veronique Sels
Photographer
Marc Paeps
Creative Director
Veronique Sels
Head of Art
Frederic Royer
Print Producers
Gael Cheval
Charly Forin
Advertising Agency
Publicis Conseil
Account Handlers
Debora Guarachi
Emmanuelle Henry
Art Buyer
Jean-Luc Chirio
Client Founding President
Xavier Emmanuelli
Client General Secretary
Stefania Parigi
Client
Samusocial

THE LONGER YOU LIVE ON THE STREET
THE HARDER IT IS TO GET OFF IT samusocial
SUPPORT US AT WWW.SAMUSOCIAL.FR

THE LONGER YOU LIVE ON THE STREET
THE HARDER IT IS TO GET OFF IT samusocial

THE LONGER YOU LIVE ON THE STREET
THE HARDER IT IS TO GET OFF IT samusocial

Press Advertising
Campaigns
AlmapBBDO
for Volkswagen

Volkswagen Trucks
This campaign highlights the main feature of Volkswagen trucks: they are tailor-made. We created a measuring tape that was a replica of a truck cab. Each of the ads featured the tape measuring the exact size of different types of cargo.

Art Directors
Julio Andery
André Gola
Luiz Sanches
Copywriter
Pernil
Typographer
José Roberto Bezerra
Creative Director
Luiz Sanches
Advertising Agency
AlmapBBDO
Marketing Manager
Herlander Zola
Client
Volkswagen

Volkswagen Trucks.
The right size for your needs.

Volkswagen Trucks.
The right size for your needs.

Volkswagen Trucks.
The right size for your needs.

Volkswagen Trucks.
The right size for your needs.

Volkswagen Trucks.
The right size for your needs.

Press Advertising
Campaigns
AlmapBBDO
for Volkswagen

Handsfree Parking System
Owners of the Volkswagen Tiguan with Park Assist can park their cars without using their hands. So we asked ourselves: what would people do with their hands while the car parallel parked by itself?

Art Director
Bruno Prosperi
Copywriter
Renato Simoes
Typographer
José Roberto Bezerra
Creative Director
Luiz Sanches
Advertising Agency
AlmapBBDO
Marketing Manager
Herlander Zola
Client
Volkswagen

Hands-free parking system. Available on the Tiguan.
Das Auto.

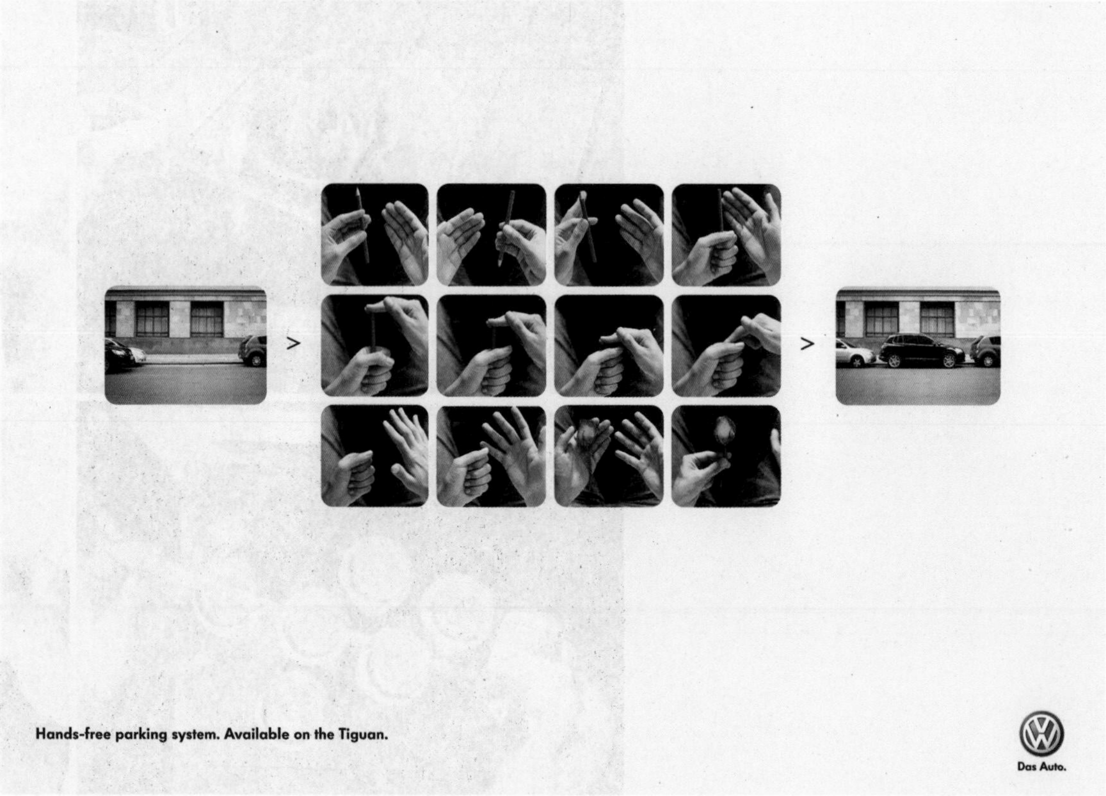
Hands-free parking system. Available on the Tiguan.
Das Auto.

Press Advertising
Campaigns
DDB Singapore
for Penguin
Books Singapore

Coin Landscapes
How do we tell budget-conscious travellers that Rough Guides are the best way to find inexpensive travel deals? The solution is to combine small change with the joy of travelling, by creating interesting landscapes – the kind that the traveller is likely to encounter – using coins from countries around the world.

Art Director
Thomas Yang
Copywriter
Joji Jacob
Photographer
Louis Chew
Creative Directors
Joji Jacob
Neil Johnson
Thomas Yang
Retoucher
Chew Peng
Advertising Agency
DDB Singapore
Account Handler
Rowena Bhagchandani
Marketing Manager
Loi Zhi Wei
Client
Penguin Books
Singapore
Brand
Rough Guides

ROUGH GUIDES

ROUGH GUIDES

ROUGH GUIDES

Press Advertising
Campaigns
Ogilvy Frankfurt
for Axel Springer
Mediahouse Berlin

Copy on
Today, for every legal music download, there are six illegal downloads. Internet piracy and illegal copying are destroying musicians' livelihoods. Young artists in particular are concerned about the impact on their income, as well as their entire existence as musicians. We took covers of legendary music albums and copied them with a standard photocopier – over and over again – until the well-known album covers were only barely recognisable. This technique demonstrates the effect of copying: the more you copy, the more music will disappear.

Art Director
Eva Stetefeld
Copywriters
Taner Ercan
Dr Stephan Vogel
Creative Director
Helmut Meyer
Advertising Agency
Ogilvy Frankfurt
Account Handler
Dr Stephan Vogel
Account Consultants
Georg Fechner
Peter Heinlein
Marketing Manager
Rainer Schmidt
Client
Axel Springer
Mediahouse Berlin
Brand
Rolling Stone

Copy on.
And one day all those legendary albums will disappear. And the great bands. And all the gifted young musicians. How are they supposed to make a living when everyone downloads their work for free? Support us: money-for-music.de
Rolling Stone

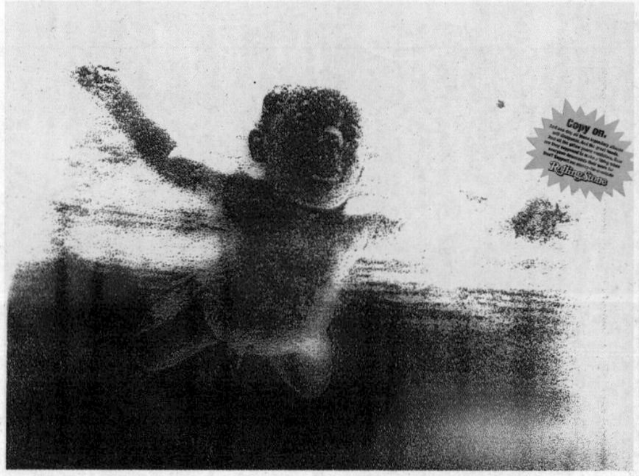
Copy on.
Rolling Stone

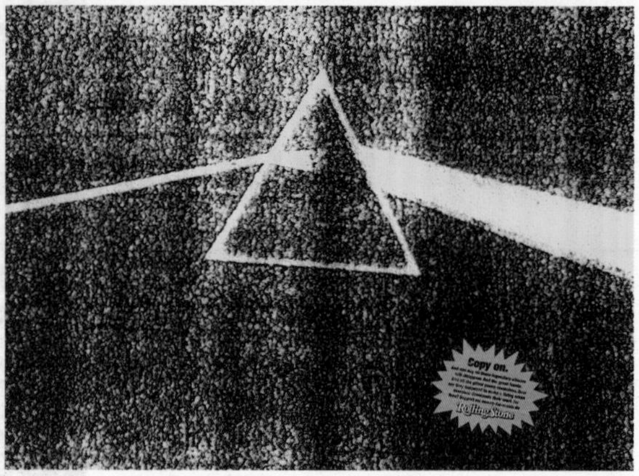
Copy on.
Rolling Stone

Press Advertising Campaigns
Young & Rubicam Buenos Aíres for ACNUR

Celebs
World Refugee Day is celebrated on 20 June. We needed to create a strong and simple message to inform people about this issue that affects 40 million people around the world. ACNUR, the UN refugee agency, takes care of ten million of those 40. We discovered that Einstein and Freud, besides being Einstein and Freud, were also once refugees. We wanted to communicate that refugees can be forced into abandoning their homes but with our help, they can never be forced into abandoning their dreams.

Art Director
Paulina Ordas
Copywriter
Juan Ignacio Galardi
Photographer
El Negro Pizzorno
Creative Director
Hernan Damilano
Executive Creative Director
Martin Mercado
Retoucher
Daniel Romanos
Advertising Agency
Young & Rubicam Buenos Aires
Account Handlers
Giselle Boyer
Eugenia Slosse
Client
ACNUR
Brand
World Refugee Day

FREUD, BESIDES BEING FREUD, WAS A REFUGEE.
There are refugee from over 70 countries living in Argentina who also have plenty to give.
UNHCR ACNUR
The UN Refugee Agency

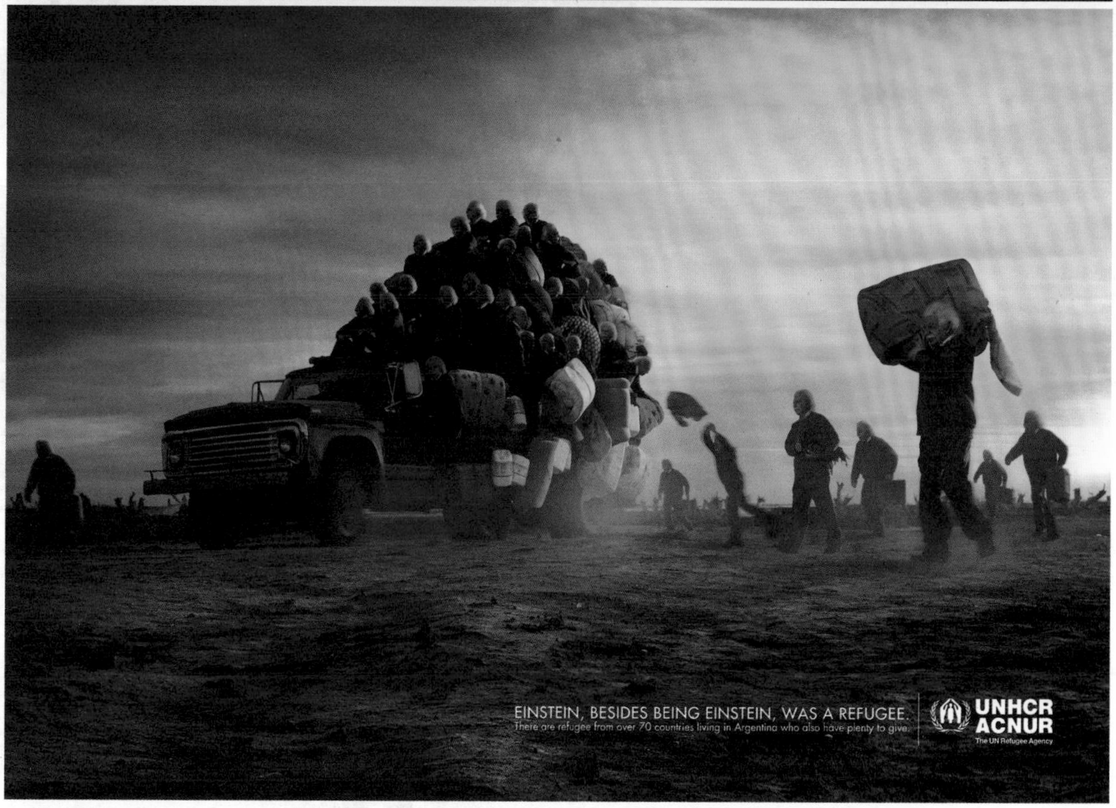
EINSTEIN, BESIDES BEING EINSTEIN, WAS A REFUGEE.
There are refugee from over 70 countries living in Argentina who also have plenty to give.
UNHCR ACNUR
The UN Refugee Agency

Press Advertising
Campaigns
DDB Brasil for FedEx

Neighbours
The aim of this campaign was to reinforce the message of FedEx's quick delivery and its global reach for a growing number of small, medium and large Brazilian companies that export products to the rest of the world.

Art Director
Max Geraldo
Copywriter
Aricio Fortes
Photographer
Manolo Moran
Creative Directors
Rodrigo Almeida
Renata Florio
Moacyr Netto
Sergio Valente
Advertising Agency
DDB Brasil
Brand Manager
Guilherme Gatti
Client
FedEx

FedEx
fedex.com 0800 703 3339
FedEx Express

FedEx
fedex.com 0800 703 3339
FedEx Express

FedEx
fedex.com 0800 703 3339
FedEx Express

Press Advertising
Campaigns
Anomaly for Diesel

Be Stupid Print
Stupid is a way of life. It's how we, Diesel, think you should live. The world would be a much better place if we were all listening to our hearts instead of our heads. 'Be Stupid' is not an advertising campaign, it's a movement. And these print ads represent many of the philosophies of being stupid.

Art Director
Coral Garvey
Copywriter
Sean McLaughlin
Photographers
Magnus Haukdal Jonsson
Kristin Vicari
Creative Directors
Mike Byrne
Kevin Lyons
Ian Toombs
Advertising Agency
Anomaly
Retouching
Tag New York
Account Handler
Paul Graham
Brand & Marketing Manager
Lucinda Spera
Client
Diesel

SMART HAD ONE GOOD IDEA AND THAT IDEA WAS STUPID.
BE STUPID DIESEL

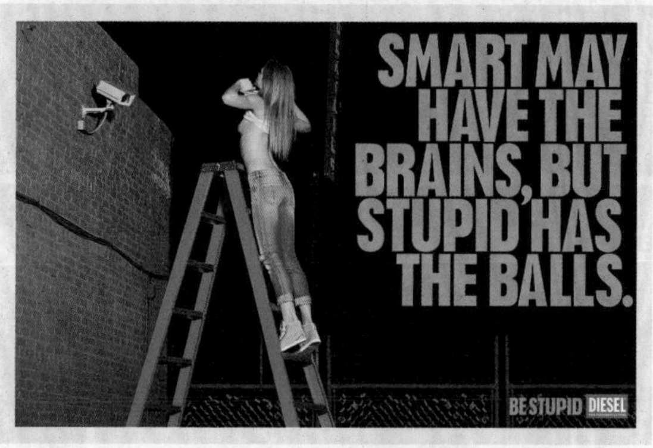
SMART MAY HAVE THE BRAINS, BUT STUPID HAS THE BALLS.
BE STUPID DIESEL

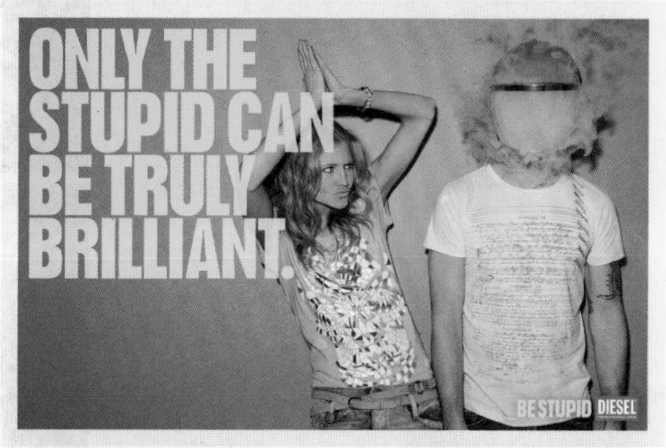
ONLY THE STUPID CAN BE TRULY BRILLIANT.
BE STUPID DIESEL

STUPID CREATES.
SMART CRITIQUES.
BE STUPID DIESEL

SMART LISTENS TO THE HEAD.
STUPID LISTENS TO THE HEAR
BE STUPID DIESEL

Press Advertising
Campaigns
Elephant Cairo for
Sima Food Industries

Out of This World
We were asked to develop a print and poster campaign for Lika Gum, a new brand of chewing gum. People don't really read ads anymore in Egypt, so we opted for a visual solution that says: this gum tastes great and blows big bubbles.

Art Directors
Ali Ali
Maged Nassar
Copywriters
Ali Ali
Maged Nassar
Photographer
Ali Ali
Advertising Agency
Elephant Cairo
Client
Sima Food Industries
Brand
Lika Gum

OUT OF
THIS WORLD
SIMA
LIKA
GUM
BUBBLE GUM

OUT OF
THIS WORLD

OUT OF
THIS WORLD

Press Advertising Campaigns
Y&R Colombia for Ofixpres Highlighter

Books
With the concept that everybody reads the same story differently, Y&R Colombia developed three graphic pieces: 'Moby Dick', 'Le Petit Prince' and 'Don Quixote'. This work was done for Ofixpres Highlighter and it shows the importance of a reader's perspective and their different points of view.

Art Directors
Oscar Muñoz
Juan Sebastian Otoya
Copywriters
Juan Camilo Valdivieso
Andres Celis
Illustrator
Juan Felipe Sierra
Creative Directors
Juan Camilo Valdivieso
Oscar Muñoz
Executive Creative Directors
Tito Chamorro
Victor Osorio
Chief Creative Officer
Mauricio Rocha
Advertising Agency
Y&R Colombia
Client
Ofixpres Highlighter

Read by a widow
Read by a Greenpeace Activist
Read by a poet
Read by a Cuban
Read by a librarian
Read by an antique shop proprietor
Everybody reads the same story differently

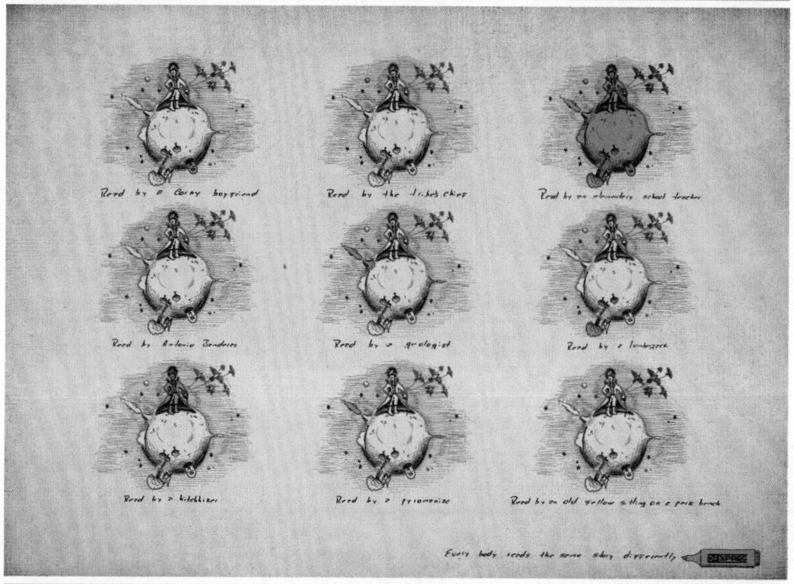
Read by a Corny boyfriend
Read by an elementary school teacher
Read by Antonio Banderas
Read by a geologist
Read by a hitchhiker
Read by an old fellow sitting on a park bench
Every body reads the same story differently

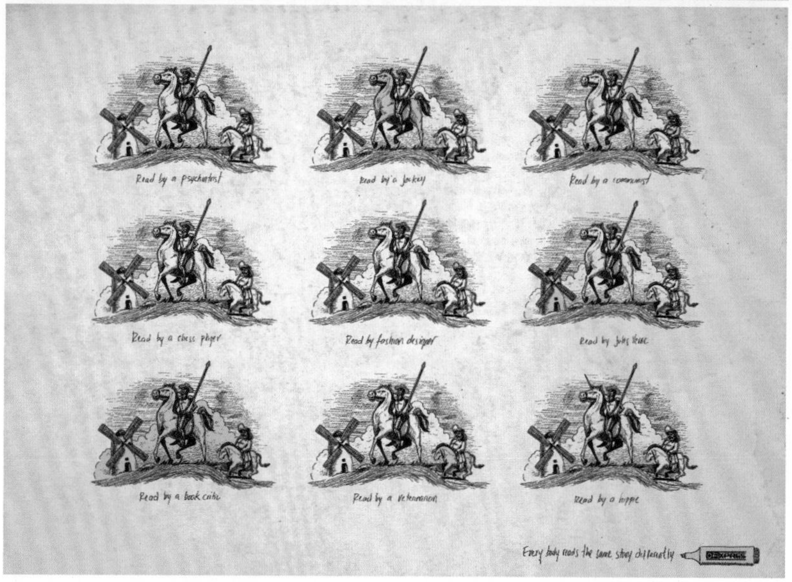
Read by a psychiatrist
Read by a jockey
Read by a communist
Read by a chess player
Read by fashion designer
Read by a book critic
Read by a veterinarian
Read by a hippie
Every body reads the same story differently

Press Advertising
Campaigns
Leo Burnett Brasil
for CVV (Centro de
Valorização da Vida)

Search
CVV offers a phone line service for people in desperation, suffering from depression, alcoholism, troubles in school or at work. These problems are overwhelming, making the person feel alone. And feeling alone always makes difficulties harder to face and overcome. Our aim was to prove that no problem is unique, and we chose to do so by showing true numbers.

Art Director
Daniel Kalil
Copywriters
Martim Baffi
Michel Zveibil
Creative Director
Ruy Lindenberg
Advertising Agency
Leo Burnett Brasil
Planner
Amanda Felicio
Account Handlers
Renato Barros
Renato Broggin
Brand Manager
André Lorenzetti
Marketing Managers
Antonio Carlos
Milton Gabbai
Client
CVV (Centro de
Valorização da Vida)

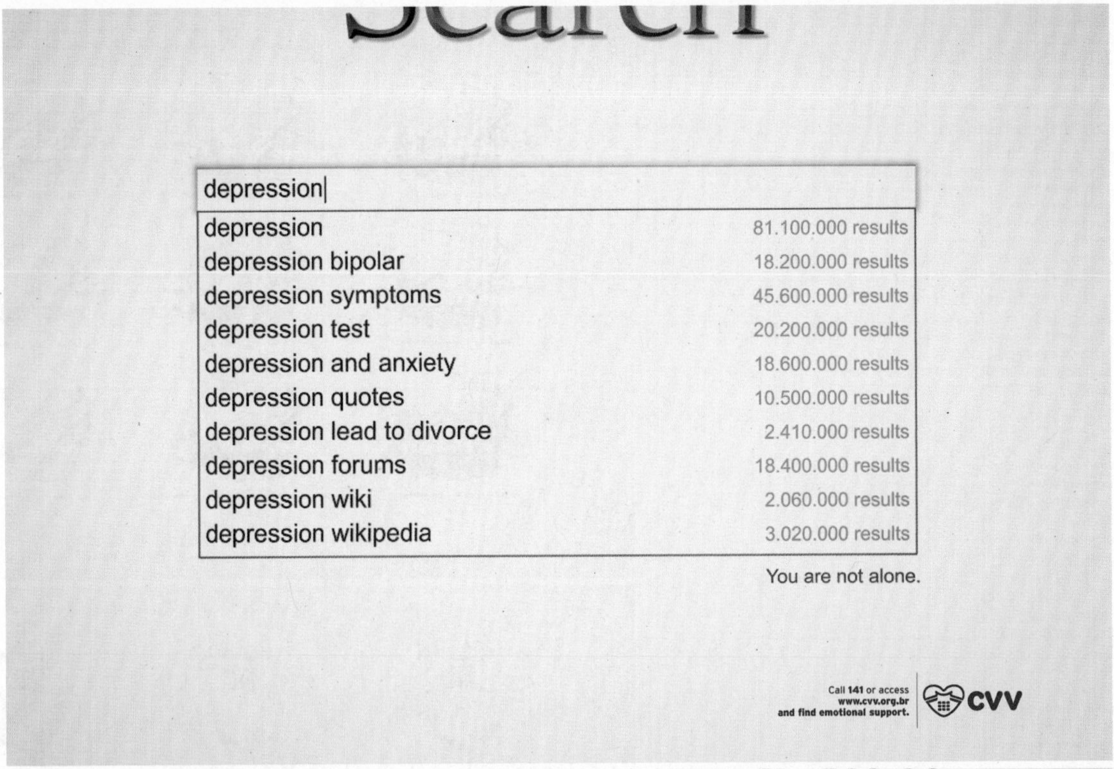
depression|
depression 81.100.000 results
depression bipolar 18.200.000 results
depression symptoms 45.600.000 results
depression test 20.200.000 results
depression and anxiety 18.600.000 results
depression quotes 10.500.000 results
depression lead to divorce 2.410.000 results
depression forums 18.400.000 results
depression wiki 2.060.000 results
depression wikipedia 3.020.000 results
You are not alone.
Call 141 or access
www.cvv.org.br
and find emotional support.
CVV

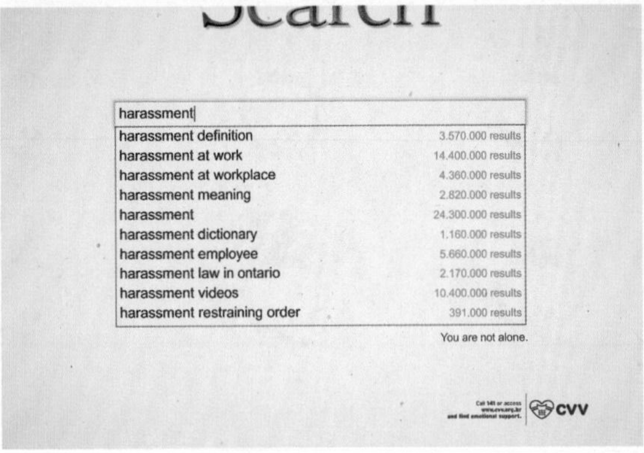
harassment|
harassment definition 3.570.000 results
harassment at work 14.400.000 results
harassment at workplace 4.360.000 results
harassment meaning 2.820.000 results
harassment 24.300.000 results
harassment dictionary 1.160.000 results
harassment employee 5.660.000 results
harassment law in ontario 2.170.000 results
harassment videos 10.400.000 results
harassment restraining order 391.000 results
You are not alone.

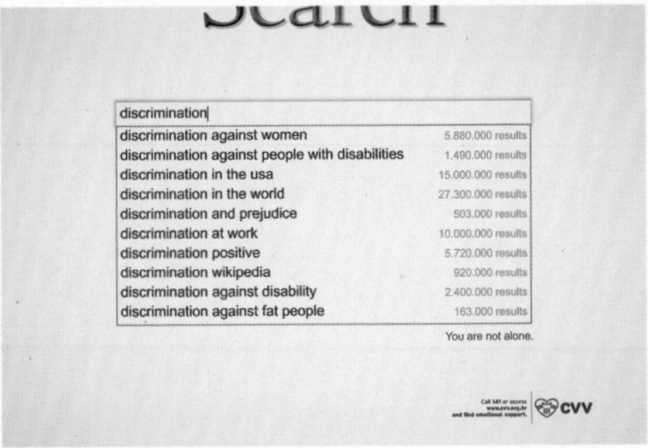
discrimination|
discrimination against women 5.880.000 results
discrimination against people with disabilities 1.490.000 results
discrimination in the usa 15.000.000 results
discrimination in the world 27.300.000 results
discrimination and prejudice 503.000 results
discrimination at work 10.000.000 results
discrimination positive 5.720.000 results
discrimination wikipedia 920.000 results
discrimination against disability 2.400.000 results
discrimination against fat people 163.000 results
You are not alone.

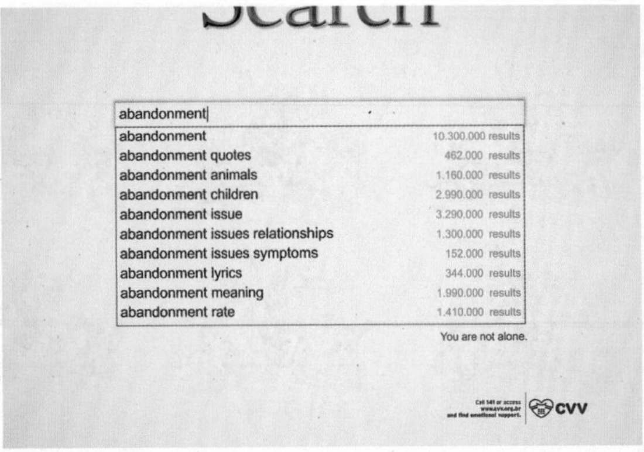
abandonment|
abandonment 10.300.000 results
abandonment quotes 462.000 results
abandonment animals 1.160.000 results
abandonment children 2.990.000 results
abandonment issue 3.290.000 results
abandonment issues relationships 1.300.000 results
abandonment issues symptoms 152.000 results
abandonment lyrics 344.000 results
abandonment meaning 1.990.000 results
abandonment rate 1.410.000 results
You are not alone.

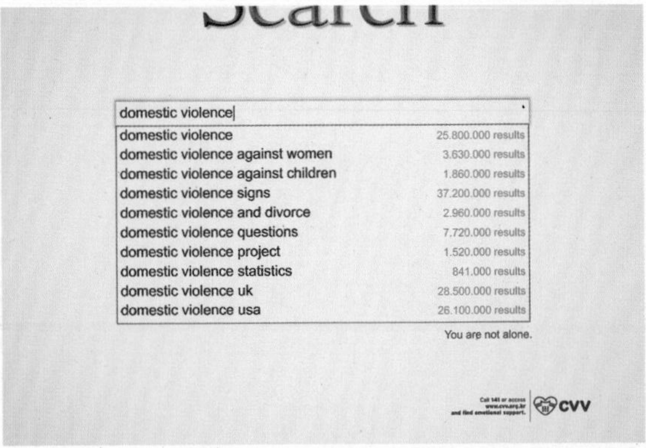
domestic violence|
domestic violence 25.800.000 results
domestic violence against women 3.630.000 results
domestic violence against children 1.860.000 results
domestic violence signs 37.200.000 results
domestic violence and divorce 2.960.000 results
domestic violence questions 7.720.000 results
domestic violence project 1.520.000 results
domestic violence statistics 841.000 results
domestic violence uk 28.500.000 results
domestic violence usa 26.100.000 results
You are not alone.

Inserts & Wraps for
Press Advertising
AlmapBBDO
for Volkswagen

EOS. The Convertible from Volkswagen.
To highlight the benefits of having a convertible car, a sunscreen sachet was printed with the image of the EOS' roof and then glued to the ad. Removing the sachet caused the roof to be removed too.

Art Director
Marco Monteiro
Copywriter
Cesar Herszkowicz
Typographer
José Roberto Bezerra
Creative Directors
Dulcidio Caldeira
Luiz Sanches
Advertising Agency
AlmapBBDO
Marketing Manager
Herlander Zola
Client
Volkswagen

EOS. The convertible from Volkswagen.
Das Auto.

EOS. The convertible from Volkswagen.
Das Auto.

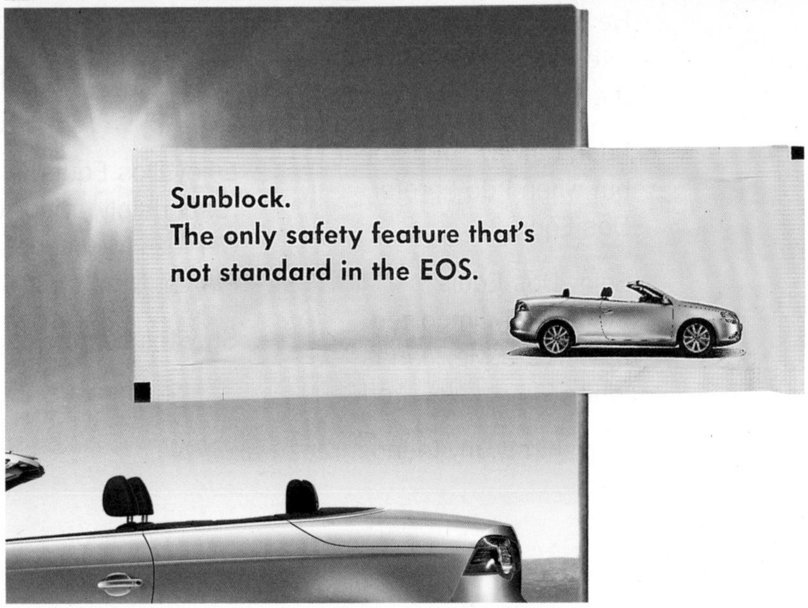
Sunblock.
The only safety feature that's
not standard in the EOS.

Yellow Pencil in Radio Advertising

Radio Advertising Campaigns
Euro RSCG New York
for Dos Equis

The Most Interesting Man in the World
Beer advertisers often assume a fairly low degree of intelligence amongst their audience, but our research revealed that our target actually had a brain and was rather irked by the clichés and sophomoric humour employed by the category. They felt misrepresented and wanted to be seen as interesting. Inspired by this insight, we created the Most Interesting Man in the World (MIM). We used his dashing attire and exotic, intriguing locales to imply that all drinkers could and should be living an interesting life. The campaign was awarded a Yellow Pencil. Standard 1, Cinco, and Holiday were all nominated as single executions in Writing for Radio Advertising.

Copywriters
Robert Cuff
Andy Currie
Jason Sweeten
David Weinstock
Art Director
Kevin Jordan
Creative Directors
Andy Currie
David Weinstock
Agency Producer
Holly Butler
Advertising Agency
Euro RSCG New York
Recording Studio
Pomann Sound
Account Handler
Katy Milmoe
Client
Dos Equis

Standard 1

VO Signs that say 'This is Not an Exit' don't apply to him.

His two cents have overruled Supreme Court decisions.

If he rode in your car, its resale value would instantly increase.

He likes the word 'fog'.

Were you to pass him on the street and he didn't see you, you would still feel like he said hello and asked you about your day.

If you were stuck in an elevator with him you wouldn't want to be saved.

Even his treehouses have finished basements.

His business card just says 'I'll Call You'.

He is… The most interesting man in the world.

MIM I don't always drink beer, but when I do I prefer Dos Equis.

VO Enjoy Dos Equis responsibly, imported by Cerveza Mexicanas White Plains, New York.

MIM Stay thirsty, my friends.

Standard 2

VO He has served as best man to grooms he's never met.

He strongly abides by the motto 'Safety Third'.

If he were to build a garden maze it would be responsible for more missing persons than the Bermuda Triangle.

Were he to say something costs an arm and a leg, it would.

His to-do lists have won Pulitzers.

Even watching him sleep has been described as breathtaking.

He's never needed lip balm.

He went to a psychic once, to warn her.

He is… The most interesting man in the world.

MIM I don't always drink beer, but when I do I prefer Dos Equis.

VO Enjoy Dos Equis responsibly, imported by Cerveza Mexicanas White Plains, New York.

MIM Stay thirsty, my friends.

Cinco

VO The Aztec calendar has his Cinco de Mayo party chiseled in.

The front of his house looks like it was built by the Mayans, because it was.

The contents of his tacos refuse to fall from the shell.

He can open a piñata with a wink and a smile.

If you were to see him walking a Chihuahua it would still look masculine.

Several saints share his likeness, or vice-versa depending on who you ask.

Dicing onions doesn't make him cry, it only makes him stronger.

He has never filled up on chips.

He is… The most interesting man in the world.

MIM I don't always drink beer, but when I do I prefer Dos Equis.

VO Enjoy Dos Equis responsibly, imported by Cerveza Mexicanas White Plains, New York.

MIM Stay thirsty, my friends.

Holiday

VO His snow globe gets 24 inches of fresh powder annually.

Regardless of temperature you can never see his breath.

His turducken consists of a duck inside a chicken inside a turkey back inside the original duck.

He has never relied on mistletoe.

His New Year's resolutions would blow your mind, that's why he doesn't tell anyone.

He's the reason those nine ladies are dancing.

One should never shake his gifts, just trust me on this one.

He is… The most interesting man in the world.

MIM I don't always drink beer, but when I do I prefer Dos Equis.

VO Enjoy Dos Equis responsibly, imported by Cerveza Mexicanas White Plains, New York.

MIM Stay thirsty, my friends.

Nomination in Radio Advertising

Radio Advertising over 30 Seconds
Wong, Doody, Crandall, Wiener for the Washington State Department of Health

Dear Me: Robert
Despite declining smoking rates, tobacco use among Washington State's working poor remained relatively unchanged. And as the US faced a deep recession, the idea of convincing smokers to give up what is often their only stress-relief tool became almost ridiculous. So we stepped aside and let them convince themselves. We followed genuine smokers as they read aloud 'Dear Me' letters they'd written to themselves about how they felt about their habit. 'Dear Me: Robert' was nominated as a single execution. The campaign was selected in Radio Advertising Campaigns.

Copywriter
Matt McCain
Art Director
Tony Zimney
Creative Director
Matt McCain
Executive Creative Director
Tracy Wong
Director
David Turnley
Agency Producer
Steph Huske
Sound Designer
John Buroker
Editor
Alan Nay
Advertising Agency
Wong, Doody, Crandall, Wiener
Production Company
Furlined
Client
Washington State Department of Health

Robert

Robert Dear Me. When you were eight, you begged Mom to stop smoking. Four years later, you started. Now Jack is seven and he begs you to quit. You hate it when you step outside and Jack and Nate see you through the sliding glass door. You know what you're doing to them and yet you go. Now Mom is dying of lung cancer and all you've told the boys is that Grandma is sick. Shame on you. Sincerely, Me.

My name is Robert and no one can make me quit but me.

FVO When you're ready to quit smoking, there's help out there.

MVO To talk to a quit coach, call 1-800-QUIT-NOW.

FVO Or go to quitline.com.

Vance

Vance Dear Me. You've been through a rough life. You ran on the streets. You went to war. You were locked up. But you pulled yourself up. You married the woman of your dreams. And now you're doing what you can to give back. Now you can help people who need to pull themselves up, too. You've got so many reasons to live now. Why not quit smoking, and save yourself one more time. Sincerely, Me.

My name is Vance, and no one can make me quit but me.

FVO When you're ready to quit smoking, there's help out there.

MVO To talk to a quit coach, call 1-800-QUIT-NOW.

FVO Or go to quitline.com.

Shanin

Shanin Dear Me. You're a good mom. You know second hand smoke is toxic to Justice and Kelsey, so you smoke outside. But how about when you freeze them in the back of the car when you have your cigarette when you're driving? And how could you tell Kelsey you won't chaperone her class outing to Mt St Helens because you can't smoke there? It is awful to think you are choosing cigarettes over your children's feelings. They are right. It's not fair. Love always, Me.

My name is Shanin, and no one can make me quit but me.

MVO When you're ready to quit smoking, there's help out there.

FVO To talk to a quit coach, call 1-800-QUIT-NOW.

MVO Or go to quitline.com.

Nomination in Radio Advertising

Radio Advertising over 30 Seconds
Newhaven Communications for the Scottish Government

Difficult Call
Women suffering from domestic abuse find it really hard to pick up the phone and talk about what they're going through. We wanted to show them that we understand and that we can help them no matter how many attempts it might take them to open up. That's why we created an ad that replicated the difficulty of one of these scenarios. To do so, we broke up a 60-second ad into three parts and aired them at different times during the same ad break, with random ads played in between.

Copywriters
Marcus Culloty
Troy Farnworth
Art Directors
Marcus Culloty
Troy Farnworth
Creative Directors
Chris Watson
Rufus Wedderburn
Agency Producers
Helen Clyne
Paula Poveda
Advertising Agency
Newhaven Communications
Account Handler
Campbell Ferguson
Client
Scottish Government

First Part

SFX Phone ringing, then getting picked up.

Joan Hello.

SFX Sniffling.

Joan Are you OK?

SFX Still sniffling.

Joan Just take your time.

SFX Door creaks open. Sudden gasp.

Joan Is he there right now?

SFX Rustling.

Joan That's OK. I understand.

SFX Phone being hung up.

Second Part

SFX Phone ringing and getting picked up.

Joan Is he gone?

SFX Sniffle.

Joan Do you want to make sure? I'll stay on the line.

SFX Phone placed on table.

Third Part

SFX Phone being picked up.

Claire Hello?

Joan It's OK. I'm still here. There's no rush. I'm here to help you. We can talk about whatever you want.

(Pause)

Claire (Sigh) Thank you.

VO If you're experiencing abuse, we understand that picking up the phone can feel like one of the hardest things you'll ever do. So when you're ready to talk, we're ready to listen. Call us on 0800 027 1234.

Domestic abuse. There's no excuse.

Nomination in Radio Advertising

Radio Advertising Campaigns
Y&R New York
for Sears

Never Ending Projects
Craftsman makes tools for projects. And when you have tools that last forever, you can work on projects that take forever. Universe Diorama was nominated in Radio Advertising over 30 Seconds and Writing for Radio Advertising. The campaign was also selected in Writing for Radio Advertising.

Copywriter
David Canning
Creative Director
Jon Eckman
Executive Creative Directors
Ken Erke
Ian Reichenthal
Scott Vitrone
Agency Producer
Jona Goodman
Executive Directors of Content Production
Nathy Aviram
Lora Schulson
Voice Over Artist
Howard Ross
Advertising Agency
Y&R New York
Recording Studio
Sonic Union
Account Manager
Priya Bordia
Client General Manager
Kris Malkoski
Client
Sears
Brand
Craftsman

Universe Diorama

SFX Tools clanging throughout.

VO Tim is building a diorama of the universe. To scale. The job is hard, but Tim's will is strong, because Tim has Craftsman hand tools. With their lifetime warranty, his tools can last forever. So Tim can build something that takes forever. Hence the universe diorama thing, which is nowhere near completion, or ever will be. But as Tim says, it's getting there. Of course it is, Tim. Keep bolting on sections to your seven rings of Saturn; they're only seventy four million miles long each. After that, keep chipping away at the rest of space, which is constantly expanding, in every direction, forever. Good thing your Craftsman hand tools will let you keep working, forever.

Craftsman. Trust in your hands.

Available at Sears hometown stores.

Bottomless Pit

SFX Tools clanging throughout.

VO Bill's digging a bottomless pit. It's a job that takes an infinite amount of dedication, but infinity is exactly what Bill has, because Bill has Craftsman hand tools. With Craftsman's lifetime warranty, Bill's tools can last forever, so he can build something that takes forever. And for Bill, that something is a bottomless pit. It has a beginning, kind of a middle, but surely, will not have an end. When concerned loved ones ask Bill how his hole is going, Bill says he's just beginning, because when you're digging a pit with no ending, you're always just beginning. Only quitters will say you can't dig a bottomless pit forever into infinity. And Bill's no quitter.

Craftsman. Trust in your hands.

Available at Sears hometown stores.

Knowledge Shelf

SFX Tools clanging throughout.

VO Dennis is building a shelf to hold all the knowledge in the world. It takes a long time, but time is on Dennis' side. Dennis has Craftsman hand tools, and with Craftsman's lifetime warranty, Dennis' tools can last forever. So he can build something that takes forever. Like a shelf filled with all the knowledge in the world. As Dennis nails another section of shelving to his never-ending row of shelving, researchers are teaching an ape named Susan how to sign her name. That's more shelf. Meanwhile, a man in a restaurant is learning how to pronounce chipotle: chi–pot–le. More shelf. But that's okay; with Craftsman hand tools, Dennis' shelf can take forever.

Craftsman. Trust in your hands.

Available at Sears hometown stores.

Ladder to Heaven

SFX Man breathing heavily and tools clanging throughout.

VO Gary's building a ladder to heaven. It's hard work and it takes a long time, but Gary has Craftsman hand tools. With Craftsman's lifetime warranty, Gary's tools can last forever. So he can build something that takes forever. Like a ladder to heaven. Step by step, nail by nail, aeon after aeon, Gary puts his tools to the test. And while some might see it as an eternal wake up at dawn horror fest of frustration and infinite sadness, Gary just knows he'll be working the weekend. When Gary's glorious ladder is complete, which will be forever from now, he will notice he read the ladder to heaven instruction manual incorrectly, and will have to start all over again. But that's okay; Craftsman hand tools will let Gary start all over again. Forever.

Craftsman. Trust in your hands.

Available at Sears hometown stores.

Radio Advertising
over 30 Seconds
Leo Burnett India
for Bajaj Electricals

Pleasure of Mixing
Radio listeners change channels every few seconds. So when we were creating a radio spot for the Bajaj hand blender, the task was to overcome this limitation and use radio effectively. We joined up with two popular radio stations and aired two different, but complementary music pieces simultaneously. Before the music began, an announcer on both channels urged listeners to switch between these channels and create their own mix of the music. As listeners switched between these channels, they enjoyed a new mixing experience, all thanks to the Bajaj hand blender.

Copywriter
Vikram Pandey
Art Director
Brijesh Parmar
Creative Directors
KV Sridhar
Nitesh Tiwari
Producer
Manohar Nayak
Agency Producer
Kevin Affonso
Advertising Agency
Leo Burnett India
Production Company
Lingo India
Account Handlers
Samarjit Choudhry
Nitin Sharma
Brand Manager
Beena Koshy
Client
Bajaj Electricals

Radio Station 1 (My FM)

Radio Announcer OK, now I am gonna play a tune for you. At the same time another one will be played for you on Big FM. Now here's what you have to do. Switch between this channel and Big FM. Mix both the tunes to make your own. Here we go.

(Music piece A)

RA Hope you have enjoyed the pleasure of mixing. Brought to you by Bajaj hand blenders.

Radio Station 2 (Big FM)

RA OK, now I am gonna play a tune for you. At the same time another one will be played for you on My FM. Now here's what you have to do. Switch between this channel and My FM. Mix both the tunes to make your own. Here we go.

(Music piece B)

RA Hope you have enjoyed the pleasure of mixing. Brought to you by Bajaj hand blenders.

Radio Advertising
over 30 Seconds
140 BBDO for
Mars Foods

Would You Rather
Snickers gives you
the energy to keep
doing what you're
doing, even if it's just
playing silly buggers.

Copywriter
Ross Nieuwenhuizen
Creative Director
Mike Schalit
Producer
Carla Bokombe
Advertising Agency
140 BBDO
Production Company
Sydney & Seymour
Studios
Account Handler
Andrew Watson
Brand Manager
Lillian Henderson
Client
Mars Foods
Brand
Snickers

MVO1 Would you rather be a giant hamster or a midget elephant?

MVO2 Elephant. Would you rather be the tallest man in the world who can't look down, or the shortest man in the world who can't look up?

MVO1 Jees. The shortest. The shortest. Would you rather eat a handful of hair or lick a public telephone.

MVO2 Um. The phone. Do you want a Snickers?

MVO1 Or?

MVO2 A Snickers.

MVO1 What's the difference?

MVO2 There's no difference.

MVO1 Why?

MVO2 They're the same.

MVO1 Why's there no choice?

MVO2 No, no, there's no choice.

MVO1 Why?

MVO2 It's a Snickers, you know, you're hungry, you want a Snickers, you eat a Snickers, duh.

MVO1 Oh, ja thanks, man. Would you rather be invisible or a mind reader?

MVO2 Oh, um. Invisible. Would you rather hit every red robot for the rest of your life, or always be wrong?

MVO1 Hmmm.

ANNCR Snickers. Don't stop.

SFX Snickers jingle.

Radio Advertising
over 30 Seconds
DDB Canada, Toronto
for Subaru Canada

Condition
When it comes to sports car ads, everyone touts the benefit of speed and performance. We decided to look at the potential downside to having a car that's fast. Namely, that the Subaru WRX will cause you to 'come too soon' to your destination. This was a tongue-in-cheek approach to talking about performance in a cluttered medium that requires attention to break through.

Copywriter
David Ross
Art Director
Paul Wallace
Creative Director
Andrew Simon
Associate Creative Directors
David Ross
Paul Wallace
Director
Terry O'Reilly
Producer
Terry O'Reilly
Agency Producers
Caroline Clarke
Andrew Schulze
Recording Engineer
Jared Kuemper
Advertising Agency
DDB Canada, Toronto
Production Company
Pirate Radio & Television
Toronto
Sound Design
Pirate Group
Account Handlers
Peter Brough
Michael Davidson
Brian Tod
Marketing Manager
Geoff Craig
Client
Subaru Canada
Brand
Subaru WRX

SFX PSA music throughout.

Woman (Soft voice and earnest) This is Brad.

Brad Hi, I'm Brad.

Woman Brad has a problem.

Brad I have a problem.

Woman He comes too early.

Brad It's true. I do.

Woman Brad is a recent patient of our clinic. He's a Subaru WRX driver burdened with excessive speed. Speed that causes him to come early on a regular basis.

Brad I came early last night.

Woman And although there is no outright cure for his condition, there are ways to mitigate the symptoms.

Brad I want to mitigate my symptoms.

Woman Using scientifically proven techniques like 'Loafing Around' and 'Dawdling', our technicians can show Brad how to delay his departure so he doesn't come so soon.

Brad Coming not so soon would be nice.

Woman In just four weeks we can guarantee Brad will be coming later than he ever thought possible.

Brad Really?

Woman Yes, Brad. Really.

Woman If you're a WRX driver who suffers from this condition, call us today and experience the joy of a 265 horse power Subaru WRX.

Radio Advertising
over 30 Seconds
JWT Melbourne
for Chemmart

Hoarse Whisperer
On Monday 17 May, Jim Jacques, the voice of harness racing in South Australia, went to work with a sore throat. He became a national talking point and internet sensation when his voice gave out during the first event on the card. By the next day, we'd turned his call of the race into an ad for Chemmart, a nationwide pharmacy chain in Australia.

Copywriters
Chris Andrews
Scott Glennon
Harsh Kapadia
Keith Nicolas
Creative Director
Richard Muntz
Producer
Catherine Warner
Agency Producer
Justine Kubale
Sound Designer
Stephen Renfree
Advertising Agency
JWT Melbourne
Production Company
Bang Bang Studios
Planner
Anuj Mehra
Account Handler
Kylie Payne
Marketing Manager
Sally Gesmundo
Client
Chemmart
Brand
Strepsils

Race Caller Going with Aalyah Rose on the inside Cop An Eyefull can't go with them then in turn 9 those between runners is Weowna Tesian on the inside, Linvel Daintee at the turn in the field. We're looking at about five or six metres to Booborowie Boy I think we're gone here in front leading the way it's Aalyah Rose, leads by two metres. In second placing...

Woman Feeling hoarse?

RC I don't think I'll get through this, in front Aalyah Rose...

SFX Race call fades as caller completely loses his voice.

Woman Strepsils cool throat lozenges. Available at Chemmart pharmacies.

Radio Advertising Campaigns
McCann Erickson Madrid for the Asefa Estudiantes Basketball Club

King's Cup
Asefa Estudiantes is one of the most modest basketball clubs in the ACB (Spanish Association of Basketball Clubs). In its entire 62-year history, it has never won the league. This year, ten years after the team last made it to a cup final, they just managed to qualify for the King's Cup in their last match. Would people still keep up their faith in this team? To find out, we set up real candid cameras to record the victims (players and fans) being baited by people in their close circle. The latter were offering an irresistible plan whose schedule just happened to coincide with the cup final.

Copywriters
Isidro Casanova
Jon Lavin
Art Director
David Fernandez
Creative Director
Jon Lavin
Executive Creative Directors
Pablo Colonnese
Monica Moro
Pablo Stricker
Chief Creative Officer
Leandro Raposo
Producer
Diego Mañas
Agency Producer
Luis Felipe Moreno
Advertising Agency
McCann Erickson Madrid
Production Companies
Media Sound
Ovideo
Account Handlers
Jesus Martinez Soria
Nuria Rosello
Jesus Vazquez
Client
Asefa Estudiantes Basketball Club

Azofra

VO Asefa Estudiantes, one of the most modest clubs in the ACB. They have never won the league. This year, they are through to the King's Cup. Albeit in last position. Will there be any faith in this team? We plan to find out.

The victim: Nacho Azofra. The team's Sports Director.

The co-conspirator: his sister-in-law.

The bait: an amateur bullfight with the pro Nacho has always wanted to meet, José Tomás. As luck would have it, the Sunday they will be playing the final... if they get that far.

Conversation between Nacho Azofra and his sister-in-law.

Nacho Azofra Yes, hello?

Sister-in-law Nacho, it's me, Pilar. Listen, Nacho...

NA Yeah...

S-I-L Listen, it's a pain in the neck. Look, sorry to have been chasing you around. I called the club, and they told me you were there. It's a real rush job, I have to get back to Gibé. She just called me. She said that on Sunday... she's spoken to José Tomás who's going to set up a bullring, I dunno, privately I suppose... and they've told her she can take someone along.

NA This Sunday?

S-I-L Yeah?

NA Yeah, the problem is I can't say, because I may be tied up in the King's Cup.

S-I-L Oh, sure! But... we'll never reach the final, surely?

NA Do I have to say now?

S-I-L Yes. Well, she was calling me and she said: tell your brother-in-law... You know, because you're always there, saying you want to see the bulls, that's all...

NA Shit! It wouldn't be half bad!

S-I-L Yeah...

NA On Sunday morning?

S-I-L Yeah... What time's the match?

NA At, er... the match is in the afternoon.

S-I-L Oh...

NA And the bulls are when? Sunday morning?

S-I-L Mmm... I'm not sure if it's morning or afternoon, but... yes, Sunday.

NA Well, I can't do that... No, no, tell her to take Matilde, don't worry... I'll tell Gibé some other time...

VO Asefa Estudiantes. That inexplicable faith.

It is travelling to the Cup.

Go with it.

Jasen

VO Asefa Estudiantes, one of the most modest clubs in the ACB. They have never won the league. This year, they are through to the King's Cup. Albeit in last position. Will there be any faith in this team? We plan to find out.

The victim: Pancho Jasen. The team's captain.

The co-conspirator: his wife.

The bait: a London concert with Metallica, Pancho's favourite band. As luck would have it, the Sunday they will be playing the final... if they get that far.

Conversation between Pancho Jasen and his wife:

Pancho Jasen Hello?

Wife Hello, dear...

PJ Who's that?

Wife It's me, dear, don't worry, it's me, Giselle.

PJ You what?

Wife Listen, I got a call from my friend, do you remember Rafa, who recorded those videos of Canto del Loco?

PJ Yes.

Wife Well, he's in London, he lives and works there... And he's got me tickets to go to the Metallica concert. The thing is it's on Sunday, and I have to let him know now whether we can go or not.

PJ But... are you mad? We can't go on Sunday! How can you go on Sunday if we've got the Cup?

Wife Well, we probably won't get there, right? It's the final, I shouldn't have thought...

PJ How can you think of going to a concert or anything else?

Wife Well, I... I just thought... I don't know, it's Sunday... you know... are you sure?

PJ Just leave me alone.

Wife Hey, listen, it's Metallica...

PJ But... for Christ's sake, what are you saying?

Wife Okay, okay... But I've already booked the flights and everything... We were going to Bilbao... and from Bilbao to London and all, you know. It was all planned, you know...

PJ But... leave me alone! Cancel all that, don't be such a bitch! I mean it... how can you do that? Don't get me worked up!

Wife Are you sure?

PJ Just leave me alone.

Wife Hey, listen, it's Metallica...

VO Asefa Estudiantes. That inexplicable faith.

It is travelling to the Cup.

Go with it.

Suárez

VO Asefa Estudiantes, one of the most modest clubs in the ACB. They have never won the league. This year, they are through to the King's Cup. Albeit in last position. Will there be any faith in this team? We plan to find out.

The victim: Carlos Suárez. The team's small forward.

The co-conspirator: his little brother.

The bait: a present from a brother he never denies anything. As luck would have it, for the Sunday they will be playing the final… if they get that far.

Conversation between Caros Suárez and his little brother:

Brother Hey, what's up? Listen…

Carlos Suárez Why are you calling me here?

Brother You remember I owed you that dinner… from Christmas?

CS Ummm…

Brother Well, on Sunday… I thought we could meet. I'm playing on Sunday, if you want you can come and watch, and then we could go for a meal and from there go to see a stand-up comedian's show. What do you think?

CS But… but you know…

Brother Yeah…

CS Listen, don't be stupid, will you? We play Valencia on Thursday, man… and then we play Barcelona, well, in theory, anyway.

Brother You have to beat Valencia first and then you have to beat Barcelona…

CS Yeah, but you know… Imagine we do win, then what?

Brother Well, if we win, I don't know…

CS Fuck, man! Maybe you should've asked me before! You can't just turn up and say…

Brother I didn't think you would beat Valencia and then beat Barcelona and play in the final…

CS Okay, fine, fine, great…

Brother If you're going to win the Cup… that's different…

CS Well if we do win the Cup, I'll take you wherever you want to go.

VO Asefa Estudiantes. That inexplicable faith.

It is travelling to the Cup.

Go with it.

Radio Advertising Campaigns
DDB Group New Zealand for SKY Television

Arts Channel: Pollock / Rothko / Van Gogh
SKY Television asked us to promote the newly discounted price of its Arts Channel. For just $2.95 a week, SKY subscribers could sign up to the Arts Channel and enjoy the lives and works of some of history's greatest artists. The most talented artists are usually the most tortured; the ones who lose their sanity and often their lives in the pursuit of artistic brilliance. With this in mind, we created radio ads that put into perspective the enormous price these artists paid to create their work, and the comparative pittance SKY subscribers pay to enjoy it.

Copywriter
Simon Vicars
Art Director
James Tucker
Group Executive Creative Director
Toby Talbot
Agency Producers
Tania Jeram
Judy Thompson
Audio Producer
Tamara O'Neill
Recording Engineers
Jon Cooper
David Liversidge
Advertising Agency
DDB Group New Zealand
Production Company
Liquid Studios
Planners
David McIndoe
Lucinda Sherborne
Account Handlers
Brad Armstrong
Danielle Richards
Scott Wallace
Marketing Executive
Amber Brown
Marketing Manager
Chaz Savage
Director of Marketing
Mike Watson
Client
SKY Television
Brand
Arts Channel

Pollock

VO Jackson Pollock wouldn't like you.

That being said, he didn't like many people.

He was an angry man.

Expelled from art school and prone to irrational violence, Pollock sought solace in a world of abstract expressionism.

But there was little refuge to be found.

Furious at an industry devoid of originality, he threw a canvas on the floor, splashed it with paint and became an overnight sensation.

Not that that was his intention.

As fame enveloped from all angles, Pollock discovered that the art he'd truly mastered, was hatred.

He hated the critics who sought meaning where there was none, and he hated the fans who fuelled his fame.

But the person he loathed more than anyone, was himself.

So he downed a bottle of vodka and sped his Oldsmobile into a tree.

Jackson Pollock didn't like many people, but he especially wouldn't have liked you.

And when you consider you can enjoy every drop of the man's artistic legacy for a trivial $2.95, you can hardly blame him.

The Arts Channel on SKY, just $2.95 a week. Art for an insultingly low price.

Rothko

VO Lucky for you, you're not brilliant.

Brilliant people have an unhealthy disposition for depression.

Take Mark Rothko.

He was brilliant.

And depressed.

In the Great Depression, no less.

Depressed when his art wouldn't sell.

And depressed when it sold to the wrong people.

Depressed when his wife left him.

And depressed when his second wife did the same.

While critics busily tore at his self-belief, accountants studiously siphoned his money away.

For 66 years, he journeyed towards inescapable sadness; a victim of anti-Semitism, commercialism and sexual impotence.

In his final hour, he sat alone at his kitchen table with a razor blade and no reason left to live.

And as the last drop of blood emptied out of him, he would have come to the grim realisation that his life's work had cost him everything.

Good thing he didn't know, 39 years later, it would only cost you $2.95.

Then he really would have been down.

The Arts Channel on SKY, just $2.95 a week. Art for an insultingly low price.

Van Gogh

VO After having his application to the clergy denied, Vincent Van Gogh decided to take it up with management. He wandered out into a field, pulled a revolver from his pocket and shot himself in the chest.

The man was mad.

And rightly so.

His first love loved someone else.

His second love was his first cousin.

And his third love was a syphilis-riddled prostitute who proved to be embarrassingly fertile.

Suffering from malnutrition and extreme paranoia, he fled to a brothel and sliced off his earlobe.

Despite creating some of art's most enduring masterpieces, he never received the respect he deserved.

And now you can carry on that fine tradition by paying the equivalent of a small potato top pie to enjoy every soul destroying piece of work he ever produced.

The Arts Channel on SKY, just $2.95 a week. Art for an insultingly low price.

Yellow Pencil in TV & Cinema Advertising

TV Commercials over 120 Seconds
Wieden+Kennedy Amsterdam for Nike

Write the Future
Every four years, the keys to football heaven are dangled in front of the international elite. One goal, one pass, one game saving tackle can be the difference between fame and forgotten. Nike's epic 'Write the Future' film showed us what the players were really playing for, in their own lives and in the lives of those who follow them. Our goal was to weave the brand into conversations about this major tournament in a way that celebrated the participating teams and athletes, and engaged football fans around the world. This was also selected in Cinema Commercials over 120 Seconds.

Director
Alejandro González Iñárritu
Art Directors
Stuart Harkness
Freddie Powell
Copywriters
Stuart Harkness
Freddie Powell
Creative Directors
Mark Bernath
Eric Quennoy
Executive Creative Director
Jeff Kling
Producers
Greg Cundiff
Dominic Freeman
Agency Producers
Olivier Klonhammer
Elissa Singstock
Executive Producers
Jani Guest
Richard Packer
Post Executive Producer
Jane Dilworth
Visual Effects Executive Producer
Stephen Venning
2D & 3D Designer
Tom Busel
2D & 3D Artist
Neil Davies
Editors
Ben Jordan
Stephen Mirrione
Charlie Moreton
Rick Orrick
Sound Designer
Raja Sehgal
Director of Photography
Jeroen van der Poel
Lighting Cameraperson
Emmanuel Lubezki
Production Company
Independent Films
Advertising Agency
Wieden+Kennedy Amsterdam
Digital Agency
AKQA Amsterdam
Visual Effects
The Mill London & New York
Editing
Mirrione
Work
Sound Design
Grand Central Studios
Phaze UK
Music Remix
MassiveMusic Amsterdam
Planners
Graeme Douglas
Dan Hill
Account Handlers
David Anson
Jordi Pont
Head of Broadcast
Erik Verheijen
Brand Communications Director
Enrico Balleri
Global Brand Communications Director
Todd Pendleton
Global Advertising & Content Manager
Colin Leary
Client
Nike

RONALDO
7

Yellow Pencil in
TV & Cinema
Advertising

Long Form
Branded Content
TBWA\Chiat\Day Los Angeles for Gatorade

Gatorade REPLAY Season 2
Once athletes graduate from high school, their competitive activity declines significantly, as does their Gatorade consumption. We wanted to reignite the competitive spark among these athletes, extending Gatorade loyalty beyond their teen years. So we fuelled an opportunity every athlete dreams of – a second chance. We reunited the original players from two Detroit high schools to replay a 1999 hockey game that was stopped in the third period after a life-threatening injury to a player's jugular.

Director
Loren Mendell
Art Director
Brent Anderson
Copywriter
Steve Howard
Creative Directors
Brent Anderson
Steve Howard
Worldwide Creative Director
Lee Clow
Producers
Graham Hughes
Tim Newfang
Senior Producer
Laura Mickelson
Executive Producers
H Read Jackson
Brian O'Rourke
Jimmy Smith
Editor
Curtis Roen
Web Content Editor
Greg Young
Advertising Agency
TBWA\Chiat\Day Los Angeles
Public Relations
Fleishman-Hillard
Event Marketing
Paragon Marketing Group
Group Planning Director
Scott MacMaster
Worldwide Communications Director
Jeremy Miller
Account Director
Amy Farias
Account Supervisor
Magdalena Huber
Manager of Branded Entertainment
Lauren Fritts
Senior Manager of Entertainment Marketing
Jill Kinney
Client
Gatorade

REPLAY
1
VAUGHN

Reebok

Nomination in TV & Cinema Advertising

TV Commercials 21-40 Seconds
BBDO New York for Mars Chocolate North America

Road Trip
'You're Not You When You're Hungry' is a campaign idea based on the insight that hunger can drastically change your personality. 'Road Trip' features Aretha Franklin and Liza Minnelli as the hunger-induced alter-egos of a group of guys on a long car trip. 'Game', which launched the campaign, debuted during the 2010 Super Bowl. It features Betty White and Abe Vigoda as the hunger-induced alter-egos of a group of guys playing football. The campaign was also selected in TV Commercial Campaigns, while 'Game' was selected as a single execution in TV Commercials 21-40 Seconds.

Director
Craig Gillespie
Art Director
Gianfranco Arena
Copywriter
Peter Kain
Creative Directors
Gianfranco Arena
Peter Kain
Chief Creative Officer
David Lubars
Executive Producer
Amy Wertheimer
Editor
Ian Mackenzie
Colourist
Tim Masick
Director of Photography
Emmanuel Lubezki
Production Company
MJZ
Advertising Agency
BBDO New York
Editing
Mackenzie Cutler
Visual Effects
Company 3
Mass Market
Sound Effects
Sound Lounge
Account Director
Kathryn Brown
Client
Mars Chocolate North America
Brand
Snickers

Road Trip

Game

Nomination in
TV & Cinema
Advertising

TV Commercials
41-60 Seconds
FoxP2 for Brandhouse

Love to Meet You
South Africa has one of the highest drink-driving accident rates in the world. We were briefed to create a campaign targeted at male drivers who are statistically more likely to drive under the influence of alcohol. Our research showed that they were not fazed by advertising featuring gory accidents, so we tried a different approach. We created a TV commercial featuring outtakes from what appears to be a dating show in which men describe the partner they are looking for. As the ad progresses, we realise that the men talking are prisoners and the partners they want are men on the outside.

Director
Robin Goode
Art Director
Ryan Barkhuizen
Copywriters
Mimi Cooper
Simon Lotze
Creative Directors
Justin Gomes
Andrew Whitehouse
Producer
Laura Sampson
Agency Producer
Katherine Tripp
Editor
Anthony Lee Martin
Sound Designer
Arnold Vermaak
Production Company
Fundi Films
Advertising Agency
FoxP2
Account Handlers
Kaylin Mendes
Morgan Tomes
Brand Manager
Phumza Rengqe
Client
Brandhouse
Brand
Drive Dry

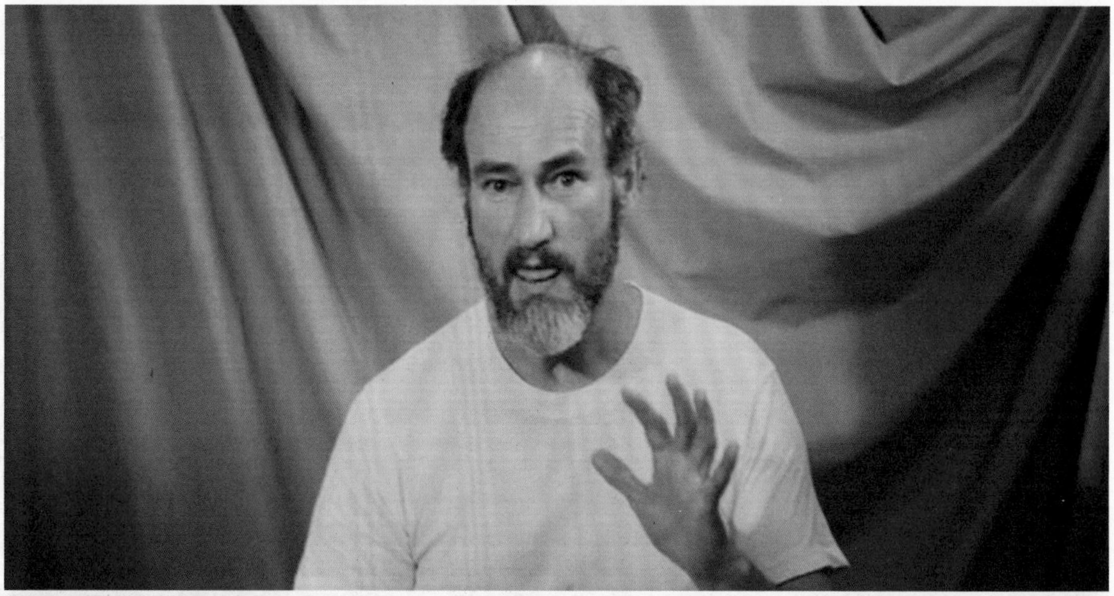

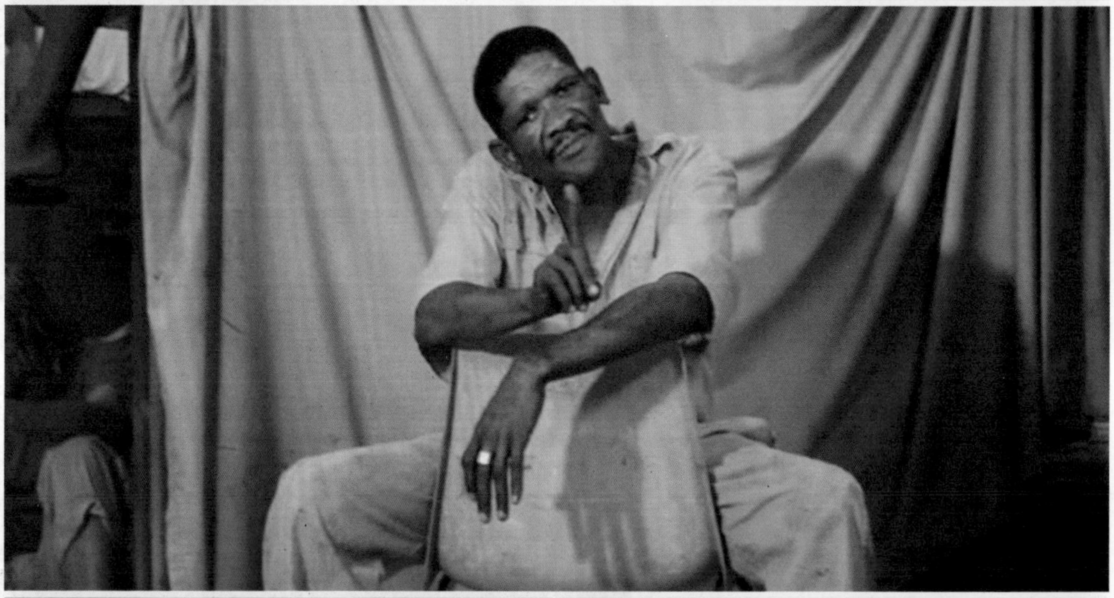

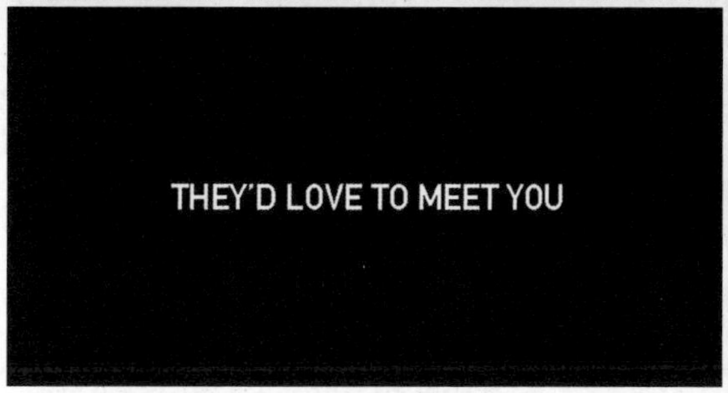
THEY'D LOVE TO MEET YOU

DRIVE DRY
A brandhouse INITIATIVE
DRIVEDRY.CO.ZA

Nomination in
TV & Cinema
Advertising

TV Commercials
61-120 Seconds
Clemenger BBDO
Melbourne for Fosters

Slo Mo

This story is a collision of men's two greatest loves – the pub and anything shot in super slow motion. Whether it's sport, wildlife documentaries or highbrow advertisements, super slow motion vision accompanied by really important music has permeated every facet of television. Which is why Carlton Draught decided it was the perfect time to turn this high precision camera on something a little less spectacular: men in pubs. The result is a celebration of beer and men, and the latest instalment in Carlton Draught's long-running 'Made from Beer' campaign.

Director
Paul Middleditch
Art Director
Anthony Phillips
Copywriter
Richard Williams
Creative Director
Ant Keogh
Creative Chairman
James McGrath
Executive Producer
Peter Masterton
Agency Producers
Sonia Von Bibra
Pip Heming
Production Manager
Paul Ranford
Editor
Peter Whitmore
Director of Photography
Daniel Ardilley
Sound Engineer
Cornel Wilczek
Production Company
Plaza Films
Advertising Agency
Clemenger BBDO
Melbourne
Music Production
Electric Dreams
Level Two Music
Melbourne
Account Manager
Phoebe Farquharson
Account Director
Mick McKeown
Group Account Director
Paul McMillan
Assistant Brand Manager
Shencia Formenton
Group Marketing Managers
Richard Oppy
Vincent Ruiu
General Manager of Marketing & Commercial Development
Peter Sinclair
Client
Fosters
Brand
Carlton Draught

TV Commercials
1-20 Seconds
Dare Vancouver for Amour

Shakespeare
This ad shows a casting session for adult movies, and through bad acting reinforces our campaign idea – you won't be watching for the acting.

Director
Richard Farmer
Art Director
Rob Sweetman
Copywriter
Bryan Collins
Creative Directors
Bryan Collins
Rob Sweetman
Producer
Ahnee Boyce
Executive Producers
Suzanne Allan
Rick Fishbein
Rich Pring
Agency Producer
Mike Hasinoff
Editors
Rob Doucet
Matthew Griffiths
Director of Photography
Richard Henkels
Production Companies
Greendot Films
Imported Artists
Advertising Agency
Dare Vancouver
Post Production Company
Cycle Media
Sound Design
Koko Productions
Account Handlers
Tamara Bennett
Colby Spencer
Client
Amour

AMOUR
You won't watch for the acting.
AMOUR
Adult movies. Direct to your TV.
amouronline.ca

Long Form
Branded Content
TBWA\Chiat\Day Los Angeles for Gatorade

Gatorade REPLAY Season 3
Once athletes graduate from high school, their competitive activity declines significantly, as does their Gatorade consumption. We wanted to reignite the competitive spark among these athletes, extending Gatorade loyalty beyond their teen years. So we fuelled an opportunity every athlete dreams of – a second chance – by reuniting former high school teams to replay their original games five, ten, even 15 years later. The season showcased a 1999 Detroit-area hockey rematch and a 2000 Chicago-area basketball rematch. There were thousands of submissions from teams nationwide, resulting in the formation of the Replay League.

Director
Loren Mendell
Art Director
Brent Anderson
Copywriter
Steve Howard
Creative Directors
Brent Anderson
Steve Howard
Worldwide Creative Director
Lee Clow
Producers
Graham Hughes
Tim Newfang
Senior Producer
Laura Mickelson
Executive Producers
H Read Jackson
Brian O'Rourke
Jimmy Smith
Editor
Curtis Roen
Web Content Editor
Greg Young
Advertising Agency
TBWA\Chiat\Day Los Angeles
Public Relations
Fleishman-Hillard
Event Marketing
Paragon Marketing Group
Group Planning Director
Scott MacMaster
Worldwide Communications Director
Jeremy Miller
Account Director
Amy Farias
Account Supervisor
Magdalena Huber
Manager of Branded Entertainment
Lauren Fritts
Senior Manager of Entertainment Marketing
Jill Kinney
Client
Gatorade

REPLAY
REPLAY
50

TV Commercials
1-20 Seconds
Wieden+Kennedy Portland for Procter & Gamble

Bear
This humorous spot, which features American football player Ray Lewis, shows him interacting with a talking bear during a game.

Director
Steve Miller
Art Director
Jimm Lasser
Copywriters
Andrew Dickson
David Neevel
Creative Directors
Jason Bagley
Eric Baldwin
Mark Fitzloff
Susan Hoffman
Producers
Donna Portaro
Frank Scherma
Agency Producers
Ben Grylewicz
Jeff Selis
Special Effects
Asher Edwards
Editor
Adam Schwartz
Music Composer
Alison Ables
Sound Designer
Jeff Sudakin
Sound Mixer
Jeff Payne
Production Company
@radical.media
Advertising Agency
Wieden+Kennedy
Portland
Account Handler
Jordan Muse
Client
Procter & Gamble
Brand
Old Spice

52

Riddell
RAVENS
52

TV Commercials
1-20 Seconds
Saatchi & Saatchi New York for Procter & Gamble

Not for You
Instead of overtly exhorting guys with thinning hair to try our product, we decided to let the product speak for itself, in terms our audience appreciates. We enlisted two-time Super Bowl Champion Troy Polamalu to be our walking, talking demo. Using humour and a sports setting, guys with thinning hair were entertained while being educated about Head & Shoulders Hair Endurance. They came away thinking that if it could help make Troy Polamalu's already full, thick head of hair even more impressive, just what could it do for their thinning hair?

Director
Gregg Popp
Art Director
Michael Vaughn
Copywriter
Neil Levin
Creative Director
Daniel Mailliard
Chief Creative Officers
Gerry Graf
Con Williamson
Executive Producer
Tim Case
Agency Producer
Peter Ostella
Editor
Tom Sherma
Production Company
Supply & Demand
Advertising Agency
Saatchi & Saatchi
New York
Editing
Cosmo Street
Client
Procter & Gamble
Brand
Head & Shoulders

100% FLAKE FREE
THICKER-LOOKING HAIR WITH HAIR ENDURANCE SHAMPOO.
head & shoulders
NFL
Official Shampoo of the NFL
NFL PLAYERS
Free of visible flakes with regular use. Vs. unwashed hair. www.troyshair.com
head & shoulders
hair endurance for men

TV Commercials
21-40 Seconds
TBWA\London
for Heineken

Diner
You're a no-nonsense man. Your wife is asking you who you'd choose if you could sleep with any woman in the world. At first you play the good husband and resist. But she keeps probing. And probing. And probing! After all, it's just a game, right? A harmless spot of fantasy? Not if your dream woman is Clare from work it's not. A woman you see every single day. Well, she did ask.

Director
Danny Kleinman
Art Directors
Marcello Bernardi
Fernando Perottoni
Copywriters
Craig Ainsley
Gabriel Miller
Creative Directors
Mark Hunter
Al Young
Producer
Johnnie Frankel
Agency Producer
Jason Ayers
Editor
Eve Ashwell
Production Company
Rattling Stick
Advertising Agency
TBWA\London
Planner
David Fryman
Account Handler
Simon Alexander
Client
Heineken
Brand
John Smiths

JOHN SMITH'S
No Nonsense
drinkaware.co.uk

TV Commercials
21-40 Seconds
TBWA\Chiat\Day New York for Wrigley

Bus
As a Scotch Korean boy enjoys some Starburst, his father takes the opportunity to extol the virtues of being a contradiction; of being solid yet juicy. The zombie sitting behind them is not impressed. Nor should he be. After all, he's alive and dead at the same time.

Director
Hank Perlman
Art Director
Jonathan Mackler
Copywriter
Jim LeMaitre
Creative Director
Jonathan Mackler
Chief Creative Officer
Mark Figliulo
Producer
Kevin Byrne
Agency Producer
Alison Gottlieb
Editor
Tom Scherma
Production Company
Hungry Man
Advertising Agency
TBWA\Chiat\Day
New York
Client
Wrigley
Brand
Starburst

It's a juicy contradiction.

TV Commercials
41-60 Seconds
Mother London for IKEA

Kitchen Party
IKEA isn't known for kitchens in the UK. We needed to change this and make IKEA kitchens famous. So we looked for a cultural truth that we could use, that would fit with our 'happy inside' campaign idea. This truth was that you always end up in the kitchen at parties, a truth immortalised by Jona Lewie's 80s hit song, 'You'll always find me in the kitchen at parties'.

Director
Kim Gehrig
Art Directors
Erik Hedman
Daniel Mencak
Erik Nordenankar
Julia Steinus
Copywriters
Erik Hedman
Daniel Mencak
Erik Nordenankar
Julia Steinus
Creative Directors
Stephen Butler
Robert Saville
Feh Tarty
Mark Waites
Producer
Laura Hegarty
Agency Producer
Craig Keppler
Editor
Joe Guest
Production Company
Academy Films
Advertising Agency
Mother London
Planner
Jacob Wright
Account Handler
Niki Manley
Client
IKEA

TV Commercials
41-60 Seconds
Mother London
for Match.com

Piano
The online dating market has a tendency to come over all scientific, functional and logical. But we all know it's not about that. For Match.com it had to be about an unequivocal belief in love. We wanted to inspire people to start their own love stories; to shift Match.com from a technical position to an emotional one. To stay away from the cliché of Hollywood happy ever afters and to capture the indescribable moment when you both just know. This is 'boy meets girl' the way we really dream about it happening.

Direction
Si & Ad
Art Directors
David Colman
Nick Hallberry
Daniel Mencak
Erik Nordenankar
Copywriters
David Colman
Nick Hallberry
Al MacCuish
Daniel Mencak
Erik Nordenankar
Creative Directors
Stephen Butler
Al MacCuish
Robert Saville
Mark Waites
Ed Warren
Producer
Lucy Gossage
Production Company
Academy Films
Advertising Agency
Mother London
Planners
Matt Andrews
Katie Mackay
Client
Match.com

TV Commercials
41-60 Seconds
Fallon London for Skoda

Made of Meaner Stuff
Filmed in Skoda's native Czech Republic, the advert opens with a shot of a television screen playing the original famous 'Cake' ad. The 'lovely' bakers are, however, soon replaced as the story unfolds to reveal a much tougher, darker and more technologically enhanced production team, who are creating the 'meaner' Fabia vRS.

Director
Nick Gordon
Art Directors
John Allison
Chris Bovill
Copywriters
John Allison
Chris Bovill
Creative Directors
John Allison
Chris Bovill
Producer
Sally Campbell
Agency Producer
Angus Smith
Editor
Dominic Leung
Director of Photography
Mathias Montero
Advertising Agency
Fallon London
Account Handlers
Katrien De Bauw
Lulu Skinner
Marketing Director
Heidi Cartledge
Client
Skoda
Brand
Fabia vRS

TV Commercials
41-60 Seconds
Ponce Buenos Aires for Unilever

Premature Perspiration
Premature perspiration is a disorder that affects millions of guys. To help them overcome this difficult problem, we developed Axe Full Control. We created a TV ad to let everyone know that the problem that embarrassed them now has a solution.

Direction
Nico & Martin
Art Director
Juan Manuel Montero
Copywriter
Rafael Santamarina
Creative Director
Hernan Ponce
Executive Creative Directors
Ricardo Armentano
Joaquin Cubria
Analia Rios
Producer
Carolina Cordini
Agency Producers
Roberto Carsillo
Brenda Morrison Fell
Editor
Pablo Colella
Production Company
Primo Buenos Aires
Post Production
Pickle
Advertising Agency
Ponce Buenos Aires
Music Composition
Swing Musica
Sound Design
La Casa Post
Planner
Marina Pen
Account Supervisor
Luciano Landajo
Client Services Director
Vanina Rudaeff
Global Brand Director
Tomas Marcenaro
Client
Unilever
Brand
Axe

TV Commercials
41-60 Seconds
Mother London for IKEA

Cats
To launch IKEA's 2011 catalogue and its new brand positioning, 'Happy Inside', we conducted an experiment to put IKEA products to the test. We released 100 cats into IKEA's Wembley store to see what furniture made them happy inside. 'Cats' was a commercial that brought 'Happy Inside' to life. The campaign has had millions of views on YouTube and has generated tens of thousands of tweets.

Director
Adam Berg
Art Director
Tim McNaughton
Copywriter
Freddy Mandy
Creative Directors
Stephen Butler
Robert Saville
Feh Tarty
Mark Waites
Producer
Ben Croker
Agency Producer
Alessia Small
Editor
Joe Guest
Director of Photography
Richard Stewart
Music Composers
Mara Carlyle
Ian Fuller
Production Company
Stink
Advertising Agency
Mother London
Planner
Jacob Wright
Account Handlers
Jon Clarke
Niki Manley
Marketing Director
Anna Crona
Client
IKEA

TV Commercials
41-60 Seconds
The Red Brick Road
for Magners

Catch
In the Magners orchards, they don't pick their apples, they wait for them to fall. Not only has this helped make Ireland's finest cider, it has also helped create Ireland's finest cricket team.

Director
Ivan Zacharias
Art Director
Peter Heyes
Copywriter
Matt Lee
Creative Director
Justin Tindall
Producer
Nick Landon
Agency Producer
Charles Crisp
Editor
Filip Malasek
Music Composers
Mark Campbell
Robert Taggart
Music Arranger
James Saunders
Sound Designer
James Saunders
Production Company
Stink
Advertising Agency
The Red Brick Road
Special Effects
The Mill London
Planner
David Hackworthy
Account Handler
Oliver Clark
Brand Manager
Rob Calder
Marketing Manager
Paul Bartlett
Client
Magners
Brand
Magners Original

Enjoy Magners sensibly
THERE'S METHOD IN THE MAGNERS
MAGNERS
MAGNERS

TV Commercials
41-60 Seconds
Wieden+Kennedy Portland for Levi Strauss & Co.

To Work
This spot conveys the reawakening of the pioneer spirit in Braddock, PA. As the town's citizens start their day and go about their inspired rebuilding efforts, we see Levi's Workwear clothing being put to good use, and understand that no matter who we are or where we live, there is always work to be done to make the world a better place.

Director
John Hillcoat
Art Directors
Julia Blackburn
Mike Giepert
Copywriter
Nathan Goldberg
Creative Directors
Don Shelford
Tyler Whisnand
Executive Creative Directors
Mark Fitzloff
Susan Hoffman
Producers
Matt Factor
Shelly Townsend
Agency Producers
Ben Grylewicz
Sarah Shapiro
Editor
Tommy Harden
Director of Photography
Harris Savides
Music Composer
Richard Wagner
Production Company
Skunk
Advertising Agency
Wieden+Kennedy
Portland
Planner
Andy Lindblade
Account Handlers
Tamera Geddes
Andrew Schafer
Jessie Young
Marketing Managers
Len Peltier
Doug Sweeny
Client
Levi Strauss & Co.

TV Commercials
41-60 Seconds
BBDO Toronto for PepsiCo Canada

Arctic Sun
When Tropicana launched the idea of bringing people a brighter morning, we created a giant artificial sun that emitted 100,000 lumens of light, literally bringing a brighter morning to Inuvik, the Arctic town whose 3,500 residents live without a sunrise for weeks each winter. Filmmakers captured the monumental raising of the sun in Inuvik for this commercial that was featured in the new campaign.

Director
Samir Mallal
Art Director
John Terry
Copywriter
Adam Bailey
Creative Director
Ian MacKellar
Producer
Michael Haldane
Agency Producer
Dena Thompson
Editor
Ross Birchall
Lighting Cameraperson
Chris Mably
Music Composer
Patrick Watson
Music Arranger
Patrick Watson
Sound Designer
Ross Birchall
Production Company
Radke Film Group
Advertising Agency
BBDO Toronto
Planner
Dino Demopoulos
Account Handler
Tim Welsh
Brand Manager
Dale Hooper
Marketing Manager
Shirley Mukerjea
Client
PepsiCo Canada
Brand
Tropicana

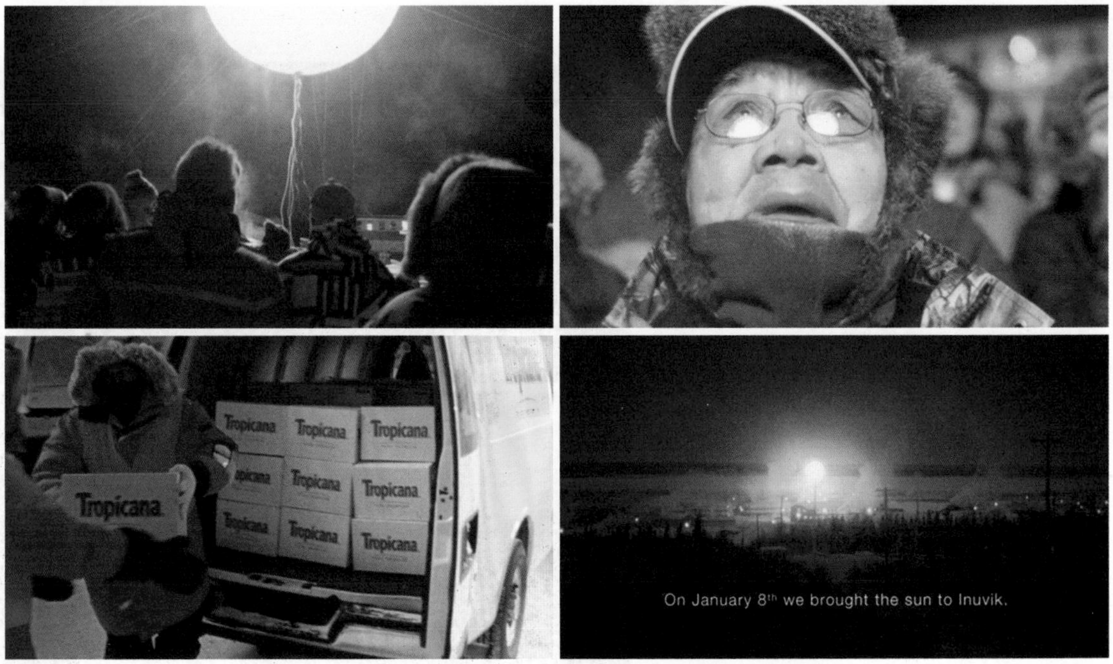
Tropicana
On January 8th we brought the sun to Inuvik.

TV Commercials
41-60 Seconds
Goodby, Silverstein & Partners for Logitech

Ivan Cobenk
The Revue uses Google TV to bring shows, movies, web videos and more right to your television. So who better to represent the enormous breadth of content available than the ubiquitous Kevin Bacon? With a little effects magic, we turned him into Ivan Cobenk, a Kevin-obsessed super fan, and created an amusing demo of the Revue and its ability to instantly access all the Kevin that Ivan could ever want.

Director
Ringan Ledwidge
Art Director
Croix Gagnon
Copywriter
Nat Lawlor
Creative Director
David Kolbusz
Producer
Alison Kunzman
Agency Producer
Elizabeth O'Toole
Editor
Rich Orrick
Director of Photography
Alwin Kuchler
Production Company
Smuggler
Advertising Agency
Goodby, Silverstein & Partners
Visual Effects
Woodshop
Special Effects Makeup
Legacy Effects
Account Handler
Leslie Barrett
Client
Logitech
Brands
Google TV
Logitech Revue

TREMORS

TV Commercials
61-120 Seconds
Droga5 New York for PUMA

Hardchorus
We open with a small group of hardcore football fans, aka hooligans. One of them starts singing 'Truly, Madly, Deeply' by Savage Garden. Another one joins in. As the camera pulls out, we see the whole pub packed with hooligans all singing with the power of an entire stadium of fans during a game. The super reads: 'It's match day. It's Valentine's Day. Let your better half know how you feel'.

Director
Ben Gregor
Art Director
Petter Hernmarck
Copywriter
Erik Hogfeldt
Executive Creative Directors
Duncan Marshall
Ted Royer
Associate Creative Director of Digital
Neil Heymann
Creative Chairman
David Droga
Producer
Ben Mann
Digital Producer
Andrew Allen
Agency Producer
Dana May
Head of Integrated Production
Sally-Ann Dale
Graphic Designer
Jon Donaghy
Editor
Alaster Jordan
Director of Photography
John Lynch
Production Company
Knucklehead
Advertising Agency
Droga5 New York
Post Production
The Mill New York
Music Conducting
Red Rhythm
Managing Directors
Matthew Brown
Tim Katz
Client
PUMA

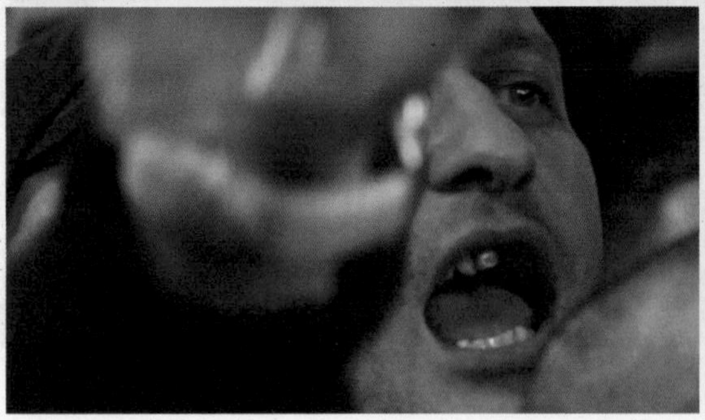

PUMA
IT'S MATCH DAY.
IT'S VALENTINE'S DAY.

TV Commercials
61-120 Seconds
Droga5 New York
for PUMA

After Hours Athlete

The brief was to differentiate PUMA's sports lifestyle brand in an ultra-competitive market by bringing back the joy. So we sponsored the largest group of unsponsored athletes out there: the After Hours Athletes. PUMA Social reminds us that we are all athletes, even if the only time we run is to catch a cab home. We know it's just as difficult to stay out till 6am as it is to get up at 6am. 'After Hours Athlete' was also selected in Cinema Commercials 61-120 Seconds.

Director
Ringan Ledwidge
Art Directors
Amanda Clelland
Jesse Juriga
Copywriters
Kevin Brady
Tim Gordon
Executive Creative Director
Ted Royer
Creative Chairman
David Droga
Producer
Sally Humphries
Agency Producer
Dana May
Head of Integrated Production
Sally-Ann Dale
Editor
Rich Orrick
Director of Photography
Ben Seresin
Music Composer
Phil Kay
Sound Mixer
Philip Loeb
Sound Designer
Jay Nierenberg
Voice Over Artist
Nash Kato
Production Company
Smuggler
Advertising Agency
Droga5 New York
Post Production
The Mill New York
Editing
Work
Planner
Chet Gulland
Client
PUMA

PUMA
puma.com

TV Commercials
61-120 Seconds
Droga5 Sydney for CUB

VB Real Cry

Recently, something fundamental has shifted in Australian society: men have become far more interested in their image. But while superficiality engulfs them, there's still a desire to be authentic. VB has always been an honest brand – the REAL beer. And for guys who've strayed too far from their real selves, VB is the perfect way back, as we ask men to look at themselves and ask, 'Have I gone too far?'

Director
Steve Rogers
Art Director
Matty Burton
Copywriter
Cam Blackley
Creative Directors
Cam Blackley
Matty Burton
Executive Creative Director
Duncan Marshall
Producer
Michael Ritchie
Agency Producer
Paul Johnston
Editor
Jack Hutchings
Production Company
Revolver
Advertising Agency
Droga5 Sydney
Music Composition
Nylon
Planner
Sudeep Gohil
Account Handlers
Esther Knox
Lucy McBurney
Creative Chairman
David Nobay
Marketing Director
Peter Sinclair
Group Marketing Manager
Paul Donaldson
Business Director
Jamie Clift
Senior Brand Manager
Craig Maclean
Assistant Brand Manager
Ashely Barton
Trade Marketing Manager
Michael Ismailoglu
Client
CUB
Brand
VB

TV Commercials
61-120 Seconds
adam&eve for
John Lewis

Always a Woman
This ad promoting the UK department store John Lewis is shot in a single, seamless camera move. Charting the life of a woman from birth through to old age, it shows that John Lewis offers a lifelong commitment to its customers.

Director
Dougal Wilson
Copywriters
Emer Stamp
Ben Tollett
Steve Wioland
Matt Woolner
Creative Directors
Ben Priest
Emer Stamp
Ben Tollett
Producer
Matthew Fone
Agency Producer
Leila Bartlam
Editor
Joe Guest
Lighting Cameraperson
Dan Landin
Music Arranger
Abi Leland
Music Supervisor
Mat Goff
Sound Designer
James Saunders
Production Company
Blink Productions
Advertising Agency
adam&eve
Planner
David Golding
Account Handler
Tammy Einav
Marketing Director
Craig Inglis
Client
John Lewis

John Lewis
johnlewis.com

Cinema Commercials
61-120 Seconds
Fallon London
for Orange

A-Team
Orange has pushed the Film Funding Board concept one step further and takes a leading role in what appears to be a genuine film trailer. With an all-star cast, including Hollywood actors Liam Neeson and Bradley Cooper (from 'The Hangover'), the Orange Gold Spot actors reference blatant Orange branding in typically tongue-in-cheek, comical scenarios as they take on the bad guys.

Director
Joe Carnahan
Art Directors
Phil Cockrell
Graham Storey
Copywriters
Phil Cockrell
Graham Storey
Creative Director
Tony McTear
Producers
Jules Davey
Kai Hsiung
Agency Producer
Tracy Stokes
Editor
John Smith
Director of Photography
Mauro Fiatore
Advertising Agency
Fallon London
Account Handler
Katrien De Bauw
Marketing Director
Spencer McHugh
Client
Orange

THE
-TEAM
orange™
IN CINEMAS THIS SUMMER

TV Commercials
over 120 Seconds
Nike Brand
Communications
Portland for Nike

Fresh Air
Launched on April Fool's Day to celebrate the 25th anniversary of the Air shoe, this ad reveals the secret behind Nike Air: Nike has been collecting the air of some of the world's top athletes such as Maria Sharapova, Sanya Richards, Paula Radcliffe, P-Rod, Troy Polamalu and John McEnroe for use inside the trainers. Take care as they may cause excessive performance.

Director
Paul Shearer
Art Director
Paul Shearer
Copywriters
Rob Burleigh
Paul Shearer
Creative Directors
Manny Bernadez
Adam Collins
Paul Shearer
Producer
Laura Gregory
Agency Producer
Alana Spears
Editor
Will Judge
Lighting Cameraperson
Angus Hudson
Production Company
Great Guns
Post Production
Rushes
Advertising Agency
Nike Brand
Communications
Portland
Music Composition
IPP Music
Brand Creative Manager
Manny Bernadez
Global Advertising
Director
Adam Collins
Client
Nike
Brand
Nike Air

MILE

TV Commercials
over 120 Seconds
Grey Melbourne
for the Transport
Accident Commission

The Ripple Effect
The Transport Accident Commission needed a new way to get young drivers to slow down. This campaign tells the stories of some of the many people affected by the crash that killed Luke Robinson on 28 March 2010. They include passengers in the car, witnesses, Luke's family and friends, local people, the mortician and the emergency services. A minimal crew filmed the entirely unscripted stories that appeared as 26 separate commercials and then as this compilation. It shows the ripple effect of one moment of recklessness.

Director
Mark Molloy
Art Director
Peter Becker
Copywriter
Nigel Dawson
Creative Director
Nigel Dawson
Executive Creative
Director
Ant Shannon
Producer
Wilf Sweetland
Agency Producer
Sandi Gracin
Editors
Jack Hutchings
Peter Sciberras
Rohan Zerna
Directors of
Photography
Adam Arkapaw
Ryley Brown
Germaine McMicking
Ari Wegner
Sound Designer
Phil Kenihan
Production Company
Exit Films
Advertising Agency
Grey Melbourne
Account Handler
Randal Glennon
Brand Manager
John Thompson
Marketing Manager
Jodi Gubana
Client
Transport Accident
Commission

The eyewitness.
The mortician.
The friend from work.

TV Commercial
Campaigns
DDB Chicago
for AB InBev

Amy / Entrance
This was part of a campaign for Bud Light that dramatically illustrated its product difference – that Bud Light is neither too heavy nor too light, and is always perfectly balanced.

Director
Tom Kuntz
Art Director
Galen Graham
Copywriters
Jason Karley
Jeb Quaid
Creative Directors
Chuck Rachford
Chris Roe
Group Creative Director
Mark Gross
Producers
Mark Hall
Jeff Scruton
Agency Producers
Liat Ebersohl
Will St Clair
Special Effects
Sean Faden
Helen Hughes
Editor
Kevin Zimmerman
Production Company
MJZ
Advertising Agency
DDB Chicago
Executive Director of Integrated Production
Diane Jackson
Account Handler
JT Mapel
Brand Manager
Gregg Billmeyer
Marketing Manager
Keth Levy
Client
AB InBev
Brand
Bud Light

AMY
©2010 Anheuser-Busch, Inc., Bud Light® Beer, St. Louis, MO
Amy

THE ARRIVAL
©2009 Anheuser-Busch, Inc., Bud Light® Beer, St. Louis, MO
Entrance

TV Commercial Campaigns
Leo Burnett Chicago
for Allstate

Mayhem Campaign
All the other insurance companies want to talk about is saving money. But what about the protection you get? When you cut your price, you cut your coverage. And if you don't have Allstate, you might not be protected... from mayhem.

Director
Phil Morrison
Art Directors
Greg Nobles
Chris Rodriguez
Copywriters
Matt Miller
Josh Mizrachi
Creative Directors
Britt Nolan
Jo Shoesmith
Executive Creative Directors
Jeanie Caggiano
Charley Wickman
Chief Creative Officer
Susan Credle
Executive Producer
Lisa Margulis
Agency Producer
Bryan Litman
Agency Executive Producer
Veronica Puc
Editors
Haines Hall
Matthew Wood
Production Company
Epoch Films
Advertising Agency
Leo Burnett Chicago
Visual Effects
Mass Market
Client
Allstate

LP 527

Teen Driver

GO STATE!

Flag

Douglas Fir

Lawn Game

TV Commercial
Campaigns
Arnold Worldwide
Boston for Legacy
for Health

Stop Me / Offer
Why would we hire a fake recruiter, set up a fake recruiting office and use hidden cameras to secretly film 60 candidates going through fake job interviews? Well, to answer one very real question: do you have what it takes to be a tobacco exec? In the past, truth has exposed the public to Big Tobacco and its questionable practices. This time we wanted to know if, even in the worst economy in 79 years, regular people could do what tobacco execs do. Could you be the executive, making decisions about a product that kills millions each year?

Director
Henry-Alex Rubin
Art Director
Rob Kottkamp
Copywriter
Will Chambliss
Creative Director
Meg Siegal
Producer
Drew Santarsiero
Agency Producer
Carron Pedonti
Editor
Lawrence Young
Production Company
Smuggler
Advertising Agency
Arnold Worldwide
Boston
Client
Legacy for Health
Brand
truth

1
1200

truth
thetruth.com

Stop Me

HIDDEN CAMERA INTERVIEW
DUSTIN H.
APRIL 16, 10:18 AM

truth
thetruth.com

Offer

Cinema Commmercial Campaigns
Fallon London for French Connection

The Man / The Woman
The aim of this campaign was to highlight French Connection's design credentials and the quality of its clothes. The adverts launching the Autumn/Winter 2010 collection carried on the theme of The Man and The Woman introduced in Spring/Summer 2010. The Man and The Woman Spring/Summer ads were both also selected as separate single executions in Cinema Commercials 41-60 Seconds.

Directors
Damien & Leila de Blinkk
Art Director
Selena McKenzie
Copywriter
Toby Moore
Creative Directors
Dirk van Dooren
Richard Flintham
Producer
Abi Hodson
Agency Producer
Gemma Knight
Editor
Ben Campbell
Production Company
onesix7
Post Production Company
MPC
Advertising Agency
Fallon London
Account Handler
Katharine Easteal
Brand Manager
Stephen Marks
Client
French Connection

The Man Spring/Summer

The Woman Spring/Summer

The Man Autumn/Winter

The Woman Autumn/Winter

Yellow Pencil in TV & Cinema Communications

Channel Branding & Identity
Animatório for Cartoon Network Latin America

Toy Soldier
Directed and produced by Animatório, Toy Soldier is the tale of a little plastic soldier's heroic journey through a child's bedroom. Surrounded by broken toys in what appears to be a battlefield, he drags himself towards the remote, in an effort to turn on the TV set and save the toys from destruction. From the moment Cartoon Network sent us the script we had two months for production until the online delivery. The biggest challenge we faced, storytelling-wise, was how to build anticipation without revealing the soldier's goal and the spot's conclusion.

Directors
Gabriel Nobrega
PG Santiago
Direction
Animatório
Lobo
Designers
Gabriel Nobrega
PG Santiago
Creative Directors
Eduardo Bragança
Hernán La Greca
Daniel Xavier
Producer
Ana Mendonça
Executive Producer
Luis Carlos Reis
Head of Production
Loic Francois Marie Dubois
Animator
Alexandre Martins
Cinematographer
Will Etchebehere
Computer Graphics Supervisor
Paulo Pinho
Render
Paulo Pinho
Digital Compositing
Paulo Ferreira
Guilherme Ferreirinha
Paulo Pinho
Riggers
Daniel Ho
Richard Maegaki
Rogerio Miyagi
Tracking
Henrique de Freitas
Audio Company
Soapbox Studios
Client
Cartoon Network Latin America

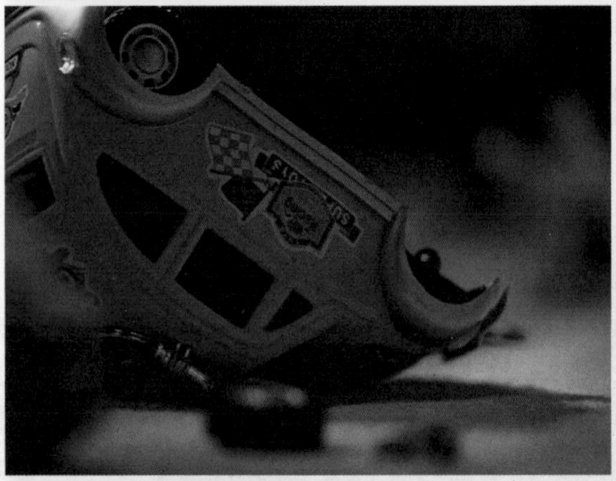

Yellow Pencil in
TV & Cinema
Communications

Channel Branding
& Identity
Meindbender Animation
for Cartoon Network

Cartoon Network
Duplicators
This is a set of 3D animated channel logo idents to fit the Cartoon Network refresh. We used our brand promise and values as the starting point and took it from there. The CN brand values can be summed up in four words: playfully irreverent, fun and adventurous. Our brand promise is: pushing the limits of fun and excitement. CN is a place where normal rules do not apply. It's a place where reality is suspended, and a home for everyone with an imagination.

Director
Olov Burman
Designer
Olov Burman
Creative Director
Rafal Gasak
Animator
Olov Burman
Lighting
Michael Bengtsson
Render
Michael Bengtsson
Modeller
Michael Bengtsson
Production Company
Meindbender Animation
Client
Cartoon Network

CN

Press the Button

Evolution

It's Magic

Duplicators

0
1
0
JUDGES

Audition

Pirate

Nomination in TV & Cinema Communications

Channel Branding & Identity
VCCP for Standard Life

Reality Check
Standard Life wanted to engage a new, younger audience in its pensions. But how could we talk to a group of people whose retirement is an unthinkably long way off, and who reject the clichéd image of old age? Instead of frightening them about their distant future, we reflected their attitudes today, using humorous situations showing how we're all guilty of trusting in financial daydreams – like writing a bestseller or marrying someone rich – rather than concrete plans. Our idents encouraged our audience to take a reality check, to find out how they could build a smarter financial future.

Direction
Si & Ad
Art Directors
Ed Kaye
Steve Vranakis
Copywriter
Alex Mavor
Creative Director
Steve Vranakis
Producer
Lucy Gossage
Agency Producer
Larissa Miola
Production Company
Academy Films
Advertising Agency
VCCP
Planner
Andrew Perkins
Account Handler
Andrew Peake
Brand & Marketing Manager
Jo Coomber
Client
Standard Life

Author

Entrepreneur

Artist

Footballer

Millionairess

Anglo-Saxon Gold

Nomination in TV & Cinema Communications

TV Promotions & Programme Junctions
McCann Erickson London for MasterCard

BRITs My Priceless Gig
We needed to use our sponsorship of the BRIT Awards in a way that went beyond the typical bolt-on association that many brands have been guilty of in the past. We offered a fan the priceless opportunity to have a past BRIT Award winner perform a gig in their living room. The competition launched with idents, online and social media, while the performance from the fan's living room was broadcast during the BRITs show and online. This put MasterCard at the heart of the buzz of the BRITs, with more than 374.6 million views across 121 countries.

Director
Matt Kirkby
Art Director
Simon Hepton
Copywriter
Matt Crabtree
Creative Director
Simon Hepton
Executive Creative Directors
Brian Fraser
Simon Learman
Producer
Garfield Kempton
Agency Producer
Jeri Low
Editor
Ben Harrex
Director of Photography
David Matches
Sound Designer
Tim Sutton
Production Company
RSA Films
Advertising Agency
McCann Erickson London
Planner
Dave Clements
Account Manager
Hatty Day
Account Executive
Kate Wood
Account Director
Jon Armstrong
Managing Partner
Jamie Copas
Brand Manager
Shaun Springer
Client
MasterCard

mypricelessgig.co.uk
MasterCard
mypricelessgig.co.uk
BRINGING THE BRIT AWARDS TO YOUR LIVING ROOM: PRICELESS.
Sponsors of The BRIT Awards
MasterCard
Opener

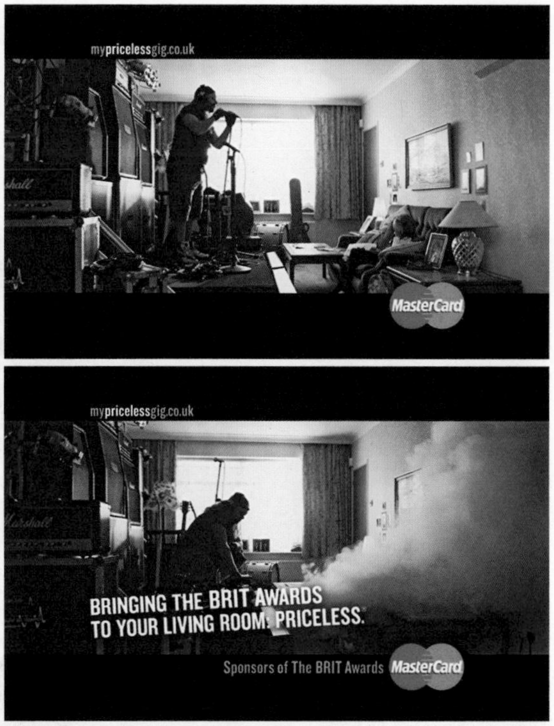
mypricelessgig.co.uk
MasterCard
mypricelessgig.co.uk
BRINGING THE BRIT AWARDS TO YOUR LIVING ROOM: PRICELESS.
Sponsors of The BRIT Awards
MasterCard
Smoke Opener

mypricelessgig.co.uk
MasterCard
mypricelessgig.co.uk
MasterCard
Guitar Opener

mypricelessgig.co.uk
MasterCard
mypricelessgig.co.uk
BRINGING THE BRIT AWARDS TO YOUR LIVING ROOM: PRICELESS.
Sponsors of The BRIT Awards
MasterCard
Lights Closer

● Nomination in TV & Cinema Communications

TV Title Sequences
Imaginary Forces for HBO & Playtone

The Pacific
This main title sequence for HBO's Second World War mini-series 'The Pacific' was inspired by the wartime sketch artists who captured the fighting on the front lines. The sequence features charcoal sketches of portraiture, as if completed in the field. The subjects are the young men whose stories unfold throughout the series, conveying the horrors of the war in the Pacific. Over 60 actual charcoal drawings were created and used as subtle transitions to the footage, which introduces each of the characters. Macro, high-speed photography captures the charcoal drawing process, creating an editorial counterpoint to the portraits.

Art Directors
Ahmet Ahmet
Peter Frankfurt
Stephen Fuller
Designer
Lauren Hartstone
Producers
Kathy Kelehan
Cara McKenney
Illustrators
Ahmet Ahmet
Stephen Fuller
Editors
Corey Weisz
Danielle White
Director of Photography
Stacy Toyama
Flame Compositor
Eric Mason
Supervising Inferno Artist
Rod Basham
Production Company
Imaginary Forces
Clients
HBO
Playtone

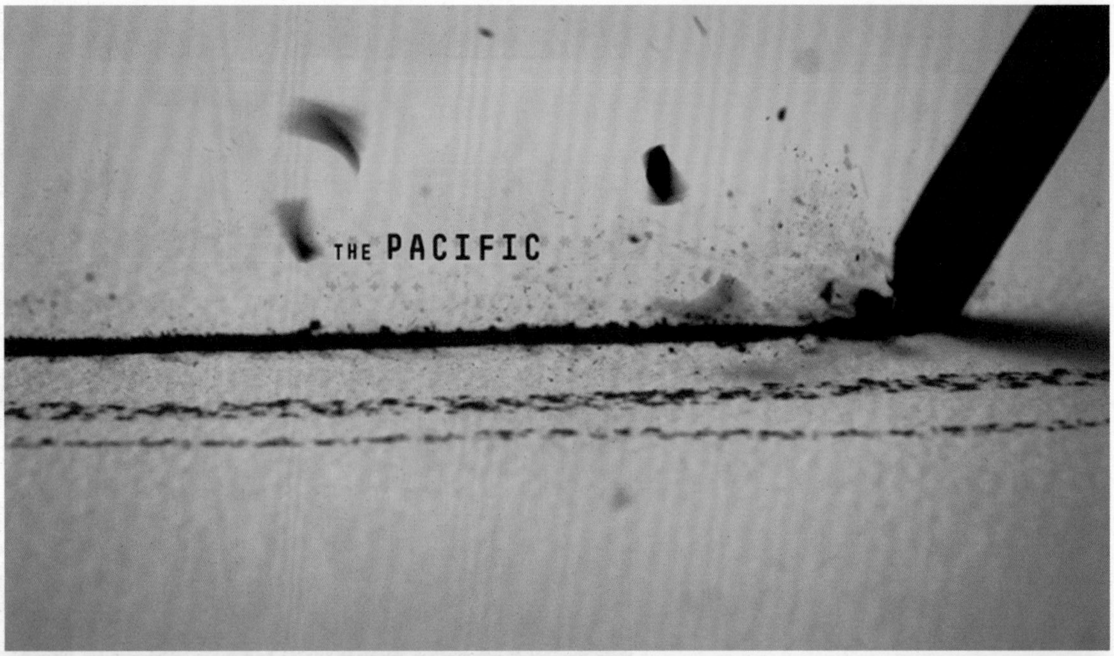
THE PACIFIC

ASHTON HOLMES
KEITH NOBBS
JACOB PITTS

MUSIC BY
HANS ZIMMER
BLAKE NEELY
GEOFF ZANELLI

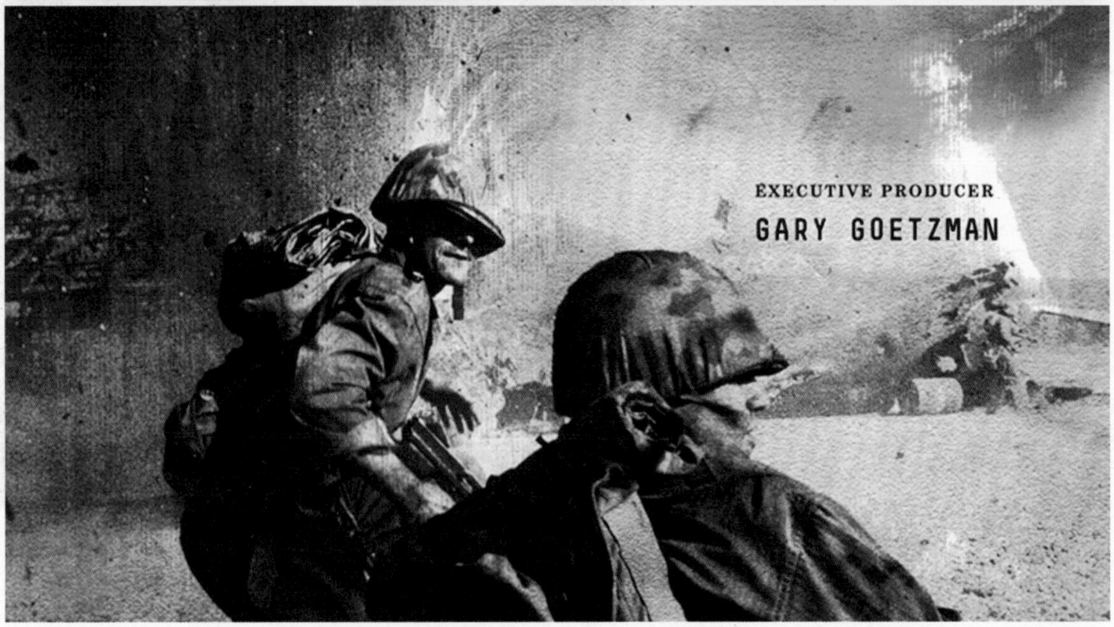
EXECUTIVE PRODUCER
GARY GOETZMAN

Multi Platform Branding & Promotions
Ireland/Davenport
for Fox International Channels & Top TV

The Walking Dead
We approached 'The Walking Dead' not as a series about zombies, but as a series about people. This allowed us to develop a sense of immediacy with the audience that added intrigue, and allowed the audience to develop empathy with the characters. We did this by bringing the challenges and dilemmas faced by the characters to life. Our approach integrated a range of traditional media with online and experiential executions to create hype and interest. The process was topped off with a launch event that immersed selected individuals in the action.

Director
Jason Fialkov
Art Directors
Lida Fourie
Chloe Jourdan
Natalie Urban
Jean Pierre de Villiers
Copywriters
Jenna Smith
Anthea Weber
James Winder
Creative Directors
John Davenport
Philip Ireland
Producer
Leanne Sanders
Agency Producer
Liesl Lategan
Editor
Zama Jolobe
Sound Designer
Louis Enslin
Advertising Agency
Ireland/Davenport
Clients
Fox International Channels
Top TV

THE
WALKING DEAD
02.11.10 FOX
toptv
EXIT

THE
WALKING DEAD
02.11.10 FOX
toptv

STORAGE
SHELVING
HOW FAR WOULD YOU GO TO SURVIVE?
WALKING DEAD

Channel Branding
& Identity
Kaktus Film for
the TV4 Group

TV4 Comedy
Identity Package
Sweden's largest comedy channel had to update its identity in order to meet the viewers' expectations and to fit with its core values: edgy, accessible, hilarious and surprising. The channel hosts a wide variety of comedic entertainment, which made boiling it all down to a strong visual identity a challenge. The animated idents function as transitions between different categories of comedy, without leaving the realm of comedy itself. Additionally, a story about an unusually tenacious little logotype takes place between programmes.

Director
Andreas Wicklund
Art Director
Bjorn Svensson
Creative Director
Mikael Holmstrom
Producer
Sigfrid Soderberg
Animators
Sten Holmberg
James Hunt
Jan Johansson
Light & Render Artists
Anton Ljungdahl
Kim Nicosia
3D Modellers
Esther Ericsson
Dan Lindqvist
Compositor
Andreas Wicklund
Sound Engineers
Magnus Andersson
Mattias Eklund
Johan Isaksson
Production Company
Kaktus Film
Design Studio
Kaktus Film
In-house Design
TV4 Group
Sound Design
Riviera
Project Manager
Helena Tonelli
Client
TV4 Group
Brand
TV4 Comedy

Penguin

Bulldozer

4
KOMEDI

Toad

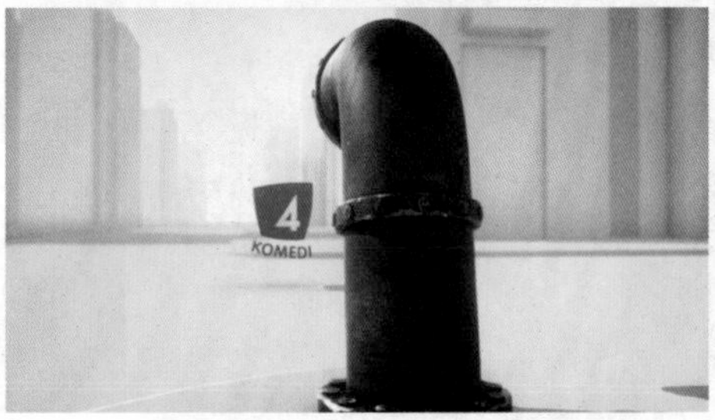
4
KOMEDI

Fan

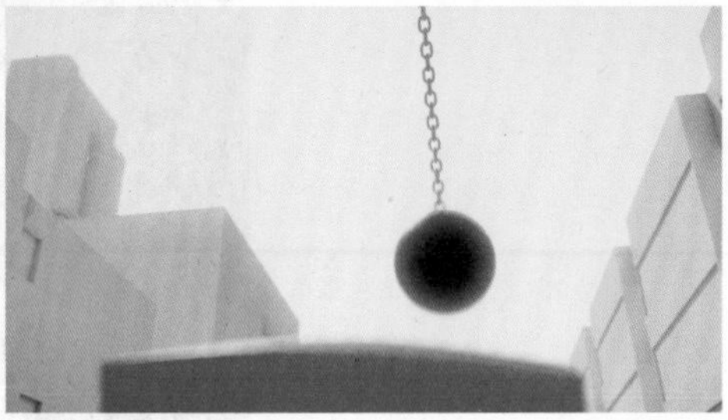

Wrecking Ball

4
KOMEDI

Ostriches

Channel Branding
& Identity
MTV World Design
Studio Milan for MTV
Networks International

MTV ROCKS Rebrand
Following the introduction of a global look and feel for MTV1 in 2009, our next task was to align MTV UK's genre-specific music channels. Embracing our mantra of 'Pop x 1000%', a set of idents was created to amplify the 'MTV ROCKS' niche sound and aesthetic. Rather than developing ideas from familiar indie music iconography, these idents explore the energy, spirit and attitude of the channel. Filmed on location in Spain and dosed with a huge amount of post production, we created an epic landscape populated with intriguing characters and events that encapsulate 'ROCKS'.

Director
Mischa Rozema
Art Directors
Carlos Carrasco
Dylan Griffith
Creative Director
Roberto Bagatti
Associate Creative Director
Anna Caregnato
Executive Producers
Ania Markham
Jules Tervoort
Director of Photography
Steve Walker
Sound Design & Music Production
MassiveMusic Amsterdam
Production Company
PostPanic
Advertising Agency
MTV World Design Studio Milan
Client
MTV Networks International
Brand
MTV ROCKS

ROCKS
Centipede

ROCKS
Fire Dish

Loop

Hallway

Bugs

Desert Drive

Channel Branding
& Identity
ManvsMachine
& One Size for Syfy

Chiller Redesign
In 2010, Chiller unveiled its exciting new redesign. To fuse its new visual language with its celebrated tagline, Chiller created a series of logo idents that emphasised one simple, undeniable message: 'scary good' is what's on Chiller. Literally. In these 5 to 10 second narratives, environments, forms and textures are used as powerful storytelling devices that connect the Chiller logo to the emotional essence of scary good: adrenaline, suspense, tension, mystery and fun.

Directors
Mike Alderson
Rogier Hendricks
Tim Swift
Kasper Verweij
Art Director
Brian Everett
Creative Director
Shea Pepper
Executive Creative Director
Michael Engleman
Producers
Bill Ikin
Kathleen Leonard
Agency Producer
Pepijin Padberg
Production Companies
ManvsMachine
One Size
Syfy
Client
Syfy
Brand
Chiller

Web

Acid

Forest

Urban

Vertigo

TV Promotions &
Programme Junctions
4creative for Channel 4

Shameless 8: Space, Tundra & Arctic
In the new season of 'Shameless', Frank Gallagher goes missing, which was very big news for the target audience. A teaser campaign that was non-storyline specific was required. With Frank as the central character of the series, it was not an option to have him missing from the promotions. So some non-storyline specific options had to be created to tease the viewers into watching.

Director
Phil Lind
Creative Director
Tom Tagholm
Producer
Louise Oliver
Set Designer
Adam Zoltowski
Special Effects Supervisor
Marcus Dryden
Editor
Dan Sherwen
Director of Photography
Magni Agustsson
Sound Designer
Rich Martin
Production Company
4creative
Client
Channel 4
Brand
Shameless

TEL 08000 858 444
PLEASE - INFORMATION NEEDED

> WHERE'S FRANK?

Space

WHERE'S FRANK?

Tundra

WHERE'S FRANK?

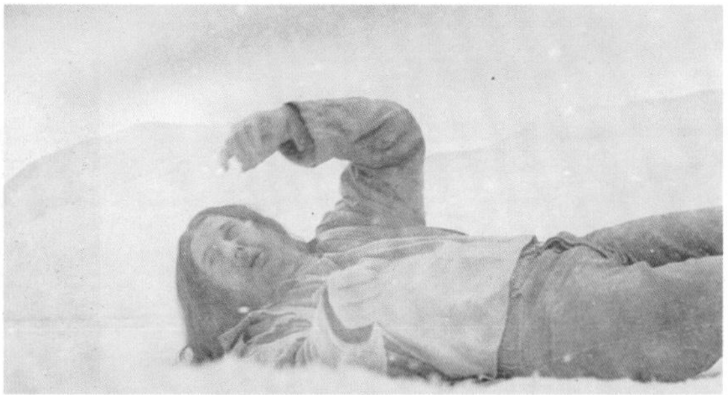

Arctic

TV Promotions &
Programme Junctions
Discovery UK
Creative for the
Discovery Channel

Bear Grylls –
Only on Discovery
For the first time Bear's new series was exclusively available on Discovery, so the brief for this project was straightforward: to 'own' Bear Grylls. A 360-degree campaign was created to present him as the dynamic face of the channel, using the brand values that Bear embodies – adventure, intelligence and a pioneering spirit – to produce a specially shot brand piece (available in stereoscopic 3D) and an innovative clip-based execution for core 'Born Survivor' fans. The campaign saw record ratings for the series, as well as increased brand recognition and spontaneous awareness of both Bear Grylls and Discovery Channel.

Directors
Meriem Adib
Ceri Payne
Art Director
Lee Healy
Copywriters
Meriem Adib
Lee Healy
Designer
Matt Beese
Creative Director
Robin Garnett
Executive Creative Director
Federico Gaggio
Producer
Bruce Meier
Production Manager
Caroline Taylor
Visual Effects Producer
James Alexander
Editor
Ceri Payne
Offline Editor
Tim Millard
Smoke Editor
Dean Wyles
Director of Photography
Alex Metcalf
Sound Designers
Arge
Rich Martin
Grader
Nick Sze
3D Production
ENVY Post Production
Creative Agency
Discovery UK Creative
Marketing Director
Tim Hughes
Client
Discovery Channel

TV Title Sequences
RKCR/Y&R for the BBC

Winter Olympics
This is an animated film advertising the BBC's coverage of the 2010 Winter Olympics in Vancouver. It tells the story of an Inuit warrior who has been tasked with rescuing a piece of an ancient ceremonial Inukshuk statue, which has been stolen by an evil bear spirit. The warrior braves death-defying arctic conditions and uses his sporting prowess to recapture the missing stone, thus restoring peace and balance to the world.

Director
Marc Craste
Art Directors
Freddy Mandy
Tim McNaughton
Copywriters
Freddy Mandy
Tim McNaughton
Creative Director
Damon Collins
Producers
Deborah Stewart
Sharon Titmarsh
Animators
Norm Konyu
Florian Mounie
Max Stoehr
Lucas Vigroux
Editor
Nic Gill
Sound Designer
Anthony Austin
Production Companies
Red Bee Media
Studio AKA
Advertising Agency
RKCR/Y&R
Planner
Ben Kay
Account Handler
David Pomfret
Client
BBC
Brand
BBC Sport

● Nomination in Book Design

Entire Books
Murray & Sorrell FUEL
for FUEL Publishing

Drawings from the Gulag
'Drawings from the Gulag' consists of material discovered in Russia by the designers. It is a definitive example of designers expanding their role to include the editing, research and design of content to produce a serious graphic novel. The material contained in the book is of great historical value, being the only known drawn history of the Gulag system, told from the perspective of a prison guard. The publication has been recognised as historically accurate by both the Centre for Holocaust and Genocide Studies in the Netherlands, and the Centre of History and New Media, George Mason University, Virginia.

Designers
Damon Murray
Stephen Sorrell
Publishers
Damon Murray
Stephen Sorrell
Illustrator
Danzig Baldaev
Editors
Damon Murray
Stephen Sorrell
Design Group
Murray & Sorrell FUEL
Client
FUEL Publishing

DRAWINGS
— FROM THE —
GULAG
FUEL
DANZIG BALDAEV

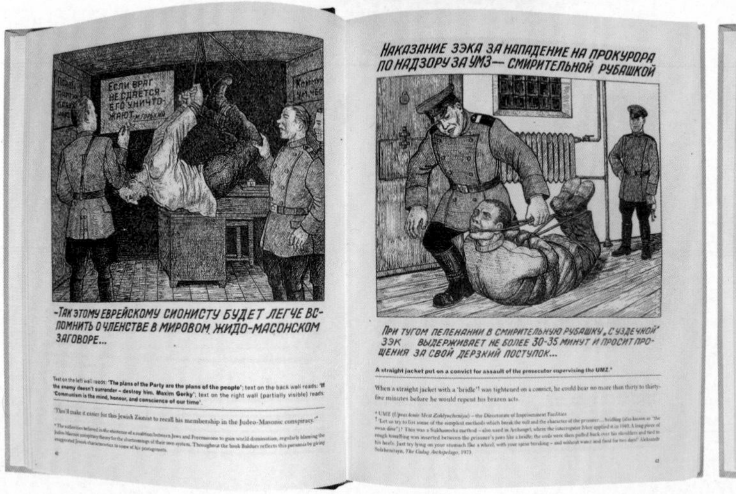
НАКАЗАНИЕ ЗЭКА ЗА НАПАДЕНИЕ НА ПРОКУРОРА ПО НАДЗОРУ ЗА УМЗ— СМИРИТЕЛЬНОЙ РУБАШКОЙ

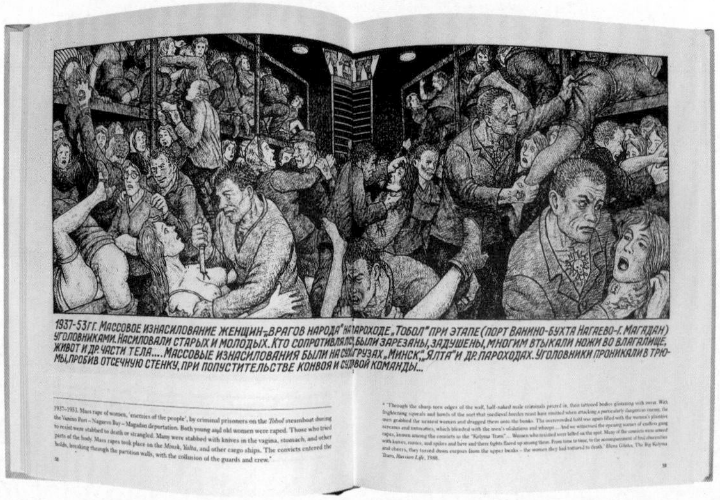

Nomination in
Book Design

Entire Books
Here Design for
Macmillan Publishers

The Geometry of Pasta
How do you know which pasta shape goes with which sauce? As any Italian will tell you, this makes the difference between pasta dishes that are merely ordinary, and the truly sublime. In this book, simple, geometric, actual-size black-and-white drawings of pasta shapes were used to demonstrate their differences and help identify the individual characteristics that make them suited to particular sauces. Also provided are dimensions of each shape, a brief history of its evolution and the perfect sauce recipe for it.

Art Director
Caz Hildebrand
Designer
Caz Hildebrand
Publisher
Jon Butler
Illustrator
Lisa Vandy
Author
Jacob Kenedy
Design Group
Here Design
Client
Macmillan Publishers

THE PERFECT SHAPE + THE PERFECT SAUCE =
THE GEOMETRY
OF PASTA
CAZ HILDEBRAND & JACOB KENEDY

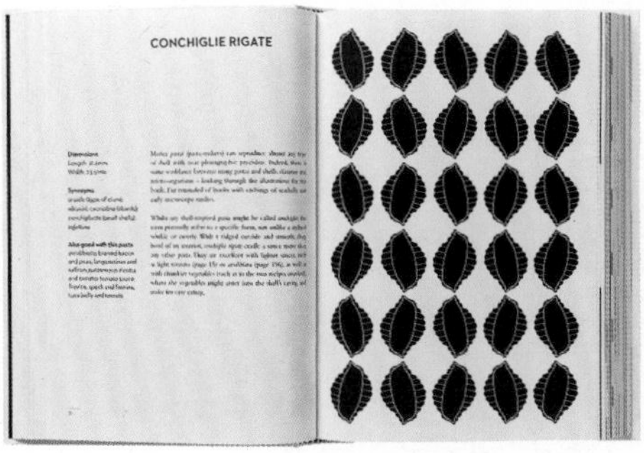
CONCHIGLIE RIGATE

THE GEOMETRY
OF PASTA

Entire Books
Oliver Helfrich for
Post Editions

The Book of Paper
From tissues to take-away coffee cups and milk cartons, paper plays an integral role in our lives, yet we often take it for granted. Through a series of sculptures, The Book of Paper elevates the aesthetic value of this most ubiquitous of materials. A collaboration between designer/sculptor Oliver Helfrich and photographer Antje Peters, The Book of Paper also features a series of essays written by artists, architects and scientists, all of whom have different approaches to paper – from adopting origami to fold space telescopes, to creating earthquake-resistant cardboard architecture.

Art Director
Oliver Helfrich
Designer
Oliver Helfrich
Publisher
Nina Post
Photographer
Antje Peters
Copy Editor
Steven Bateman
Editor
Oliver Helfrich
Client
Post Editions

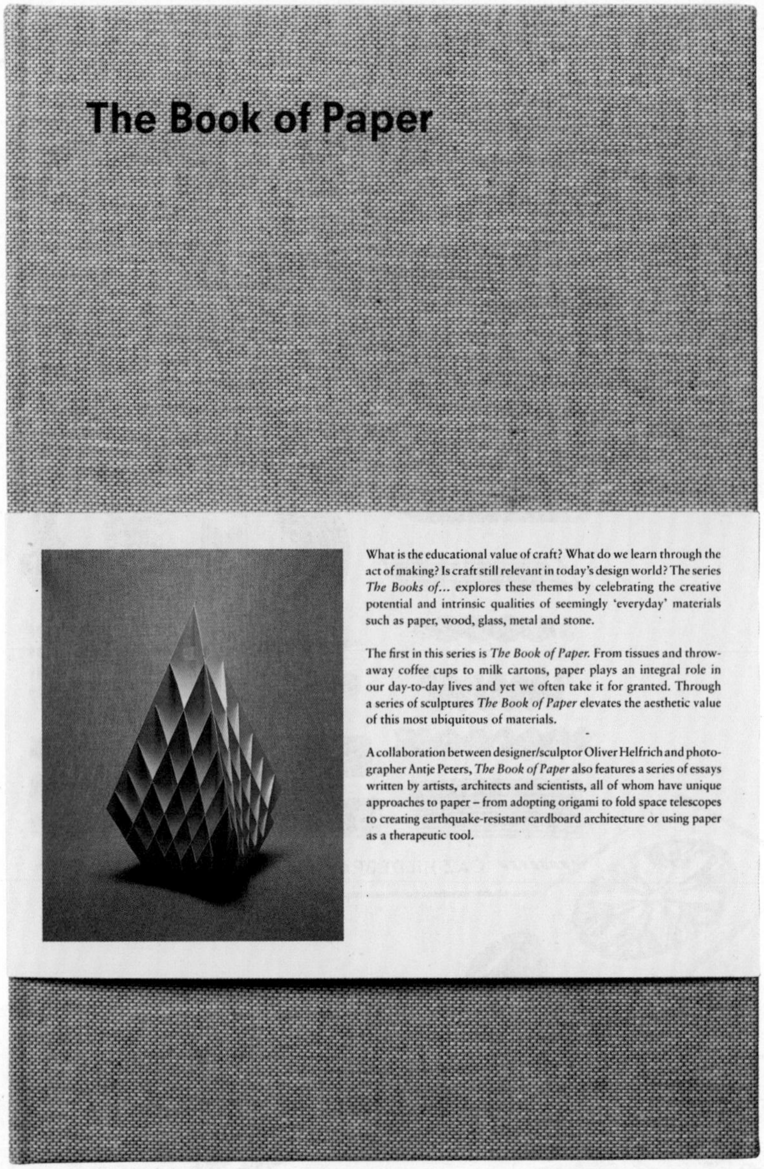
The Book of Paper
What is the educational value of craft? What do we learn through the act of making? Is craft still relevant in today's design world? The series The Books of... explores these themes by celebrating the creative potential and intrinsic qualities of seemingly 'everyday' materials such as paper, wood, glass, metal and stone.
The first in this series is The Book of Paper. From tissues and throw-away coffee cups to milk cartons, paper plays an integral role in our day-to-day lives and yet we often take it for granted. Through a series of sculptures The Book of Paper elevates the aesthetic value of this most ubiquitous of materials.
A collaboration between designer/sculptor Oliver Helfrich and photographer Antje Peters, The Book of Paper also features a series of essays written by artists, architects and scientists, all of whom have unique approaches to paper – from adopting origami to fold space telescopes to creating earthquake-resistant cardboard architecture or using paper as a therapeutic tool.

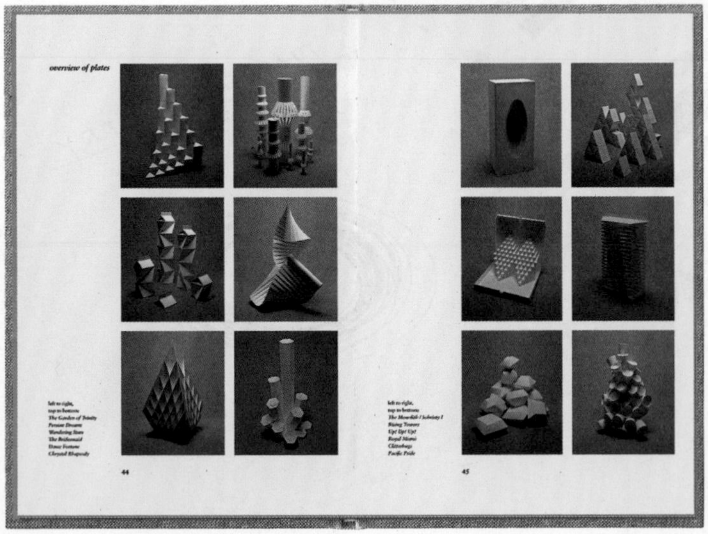
overview of plates
44
45

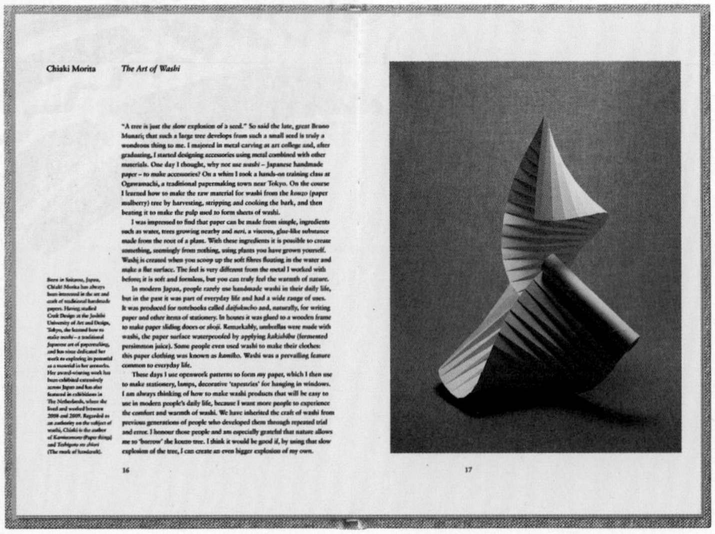
Chiaki Morita
The Art of Washi
16
17

Entire Books
Puffin Books

Puffin Designer Classics
These books are part of the Puffin Designer Classics series – limited edition books of world-famous classic stories created by leading design figures. They were published to mark the 70th anniversary of Puffin Books. Each designer chose their favourite children's classic. 'Around the World in 80 Days' was designed by David Adjaye, and 'The Secret Garden' was designed and illustrated by Lauren Child. We created bespoke books that are also beautiful objects, which look and feel wonderful and evoke the amazing stories they contain.

Art Director
Anna Billson
Designers
David Adjaye
Ama Ofeibea Amponsah
Anna Billson
Lauren Child
Publishers
Puffin Books
Brand
Puffin Classics

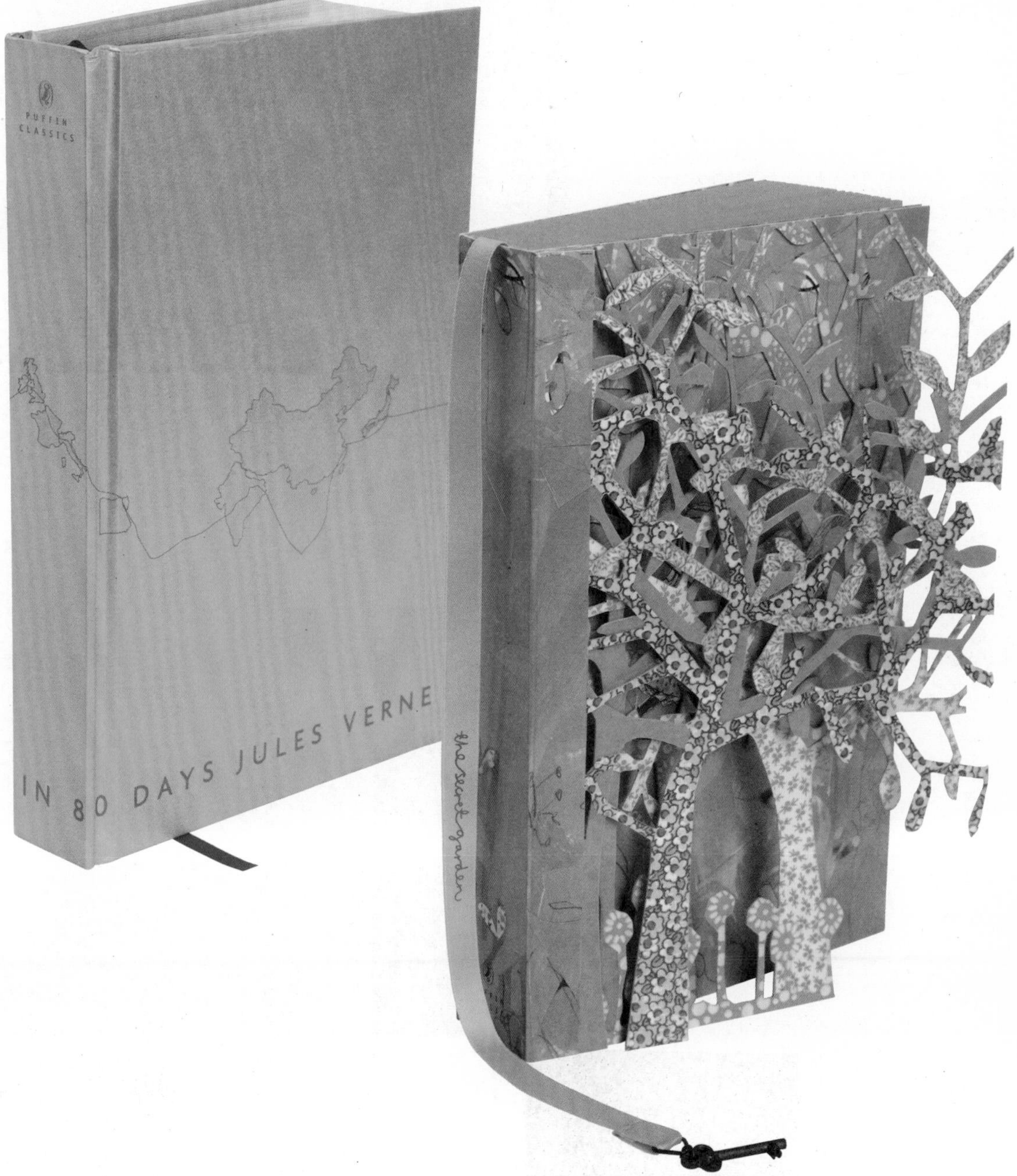
PUFFIN CLASSICS
IN 80 DAYS JULES VERNE
the secret garden

Entire Books
Pentagram Design for the Barbican Art Gallery

Surreal House Exhibition Catalogue
Angus Hyland was commissioned to design the graphic identity for 'The Surreal House', the 2010 blockbuster exhibition at the Barbican Art Gallery in London. The show examined the relationship between Surrealism and architecture and was mounted in an atmospheric, house-like series of rooms. The structure of the catalogue echoes the exhibition design; Hyland and his team created a series of typographic illustrations that are used to demarcate both areas of the exhibition and chapters or 'maisons' in the catalogue. The cover features an impossible house, an icon derived from Penrose's impossible triangle.

Art Director
Angus Hyland
Designers
Masumi Briozzo
Angus Hyland
Alex Johns
Publisher
Sally Salvesen
Design Group
Pentagram Design
Publishers
Yale University Press
Exhibition Curator
Alona Pardo
Senior Exhibition Curator
Jane Alison
Client
Barbican Art Gallery

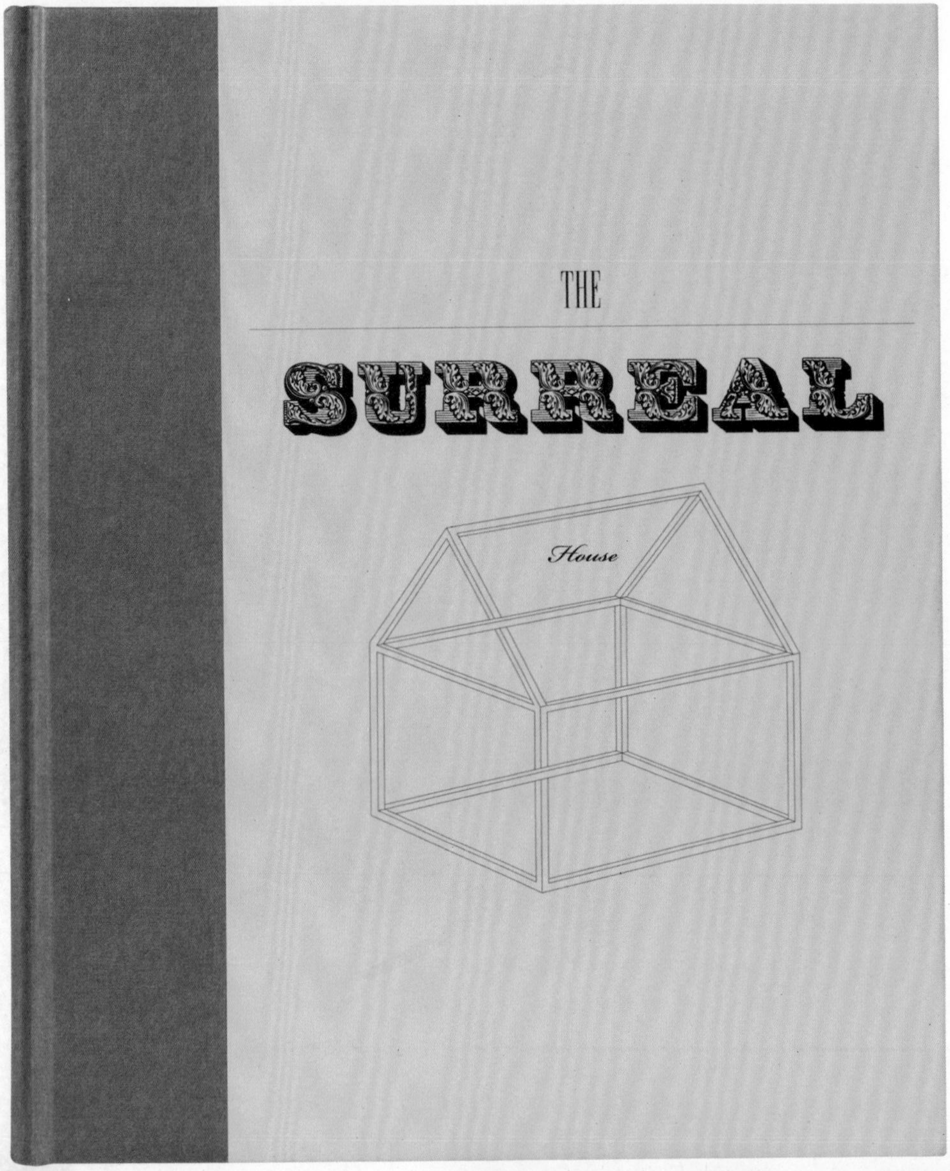
THE
SURREAL
House

mad
love

Entire Books
Sara De Bondt for
Visual Editions

Tree of Codes
In 'Tree of Codes', author Jonathan Safran Foer wrote a new narrative by carving it out of an existing book. The design brief was to make the die-cut text obvious, workable and readable, while maintaining an element of surprise to draw in literary, design and art audiences. Sara De Bondt worked closely with Foer to create a book that has the familiarity of a typical paperback, yet allows for a unique, tactile, and almost sculptural reading experience.

Designer
Sara De Bondt
Cover Designer
Jon Gray
Publishers
Visual Editions
Client
Visual Editions

Jonathan Safran Foer
Tree of Codes

see no farther.
desperately

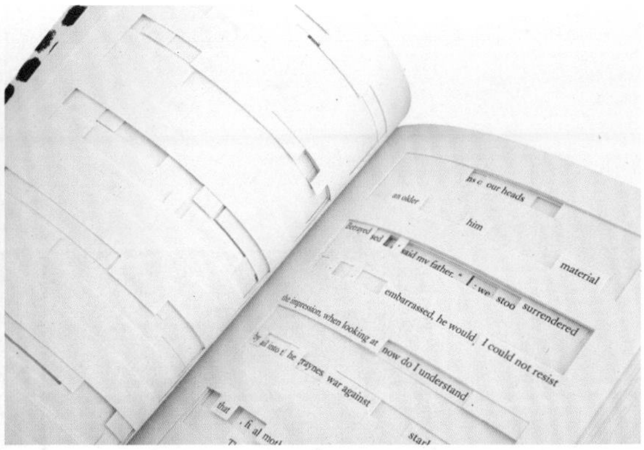

Entire Books
Forsman & Bodenfors
for IKEA

Homemade is Best
This book was designed as part of a campaign about IKEA's kitchen appliances. While it's hard to get people excited about fridges and fans, if you talk about all the tasty things you can make with them, like cookies and cakes, you have people's attention. That's why we made a baking book, with kitchen appliances in it. The idea of the book was to tone down the actual cakes and focus on the ingredients. Recipes are presented as graphic still-life portraits; when you turn the page you see the result.

Art Directors
Staffan Lamm
Christoffer Persson
Copywriters
Anders Hegerfors
Fredrik Jansson
Photographer
Carl Kleiner
Retoucher
Henrik Lagerberg
Stylist
Evelina Bratell
Publishers
Title Books
Advertising Agency
Forsman & Bodenfors
Planner
Tobias Nordström
Account Manager
Ewa Edlund
Account Supervisor
Susanna Fagring
Marketing Project Manager
Joel Idén
Client
IKEA

HEM-
BAKAT
ÄR
BÄST
Recept på 30 klassiska bakverk. Allt från små kakor till stora tårtor.

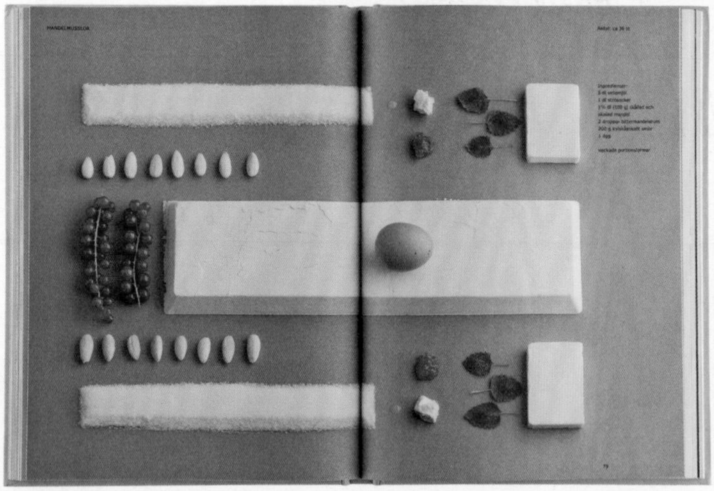

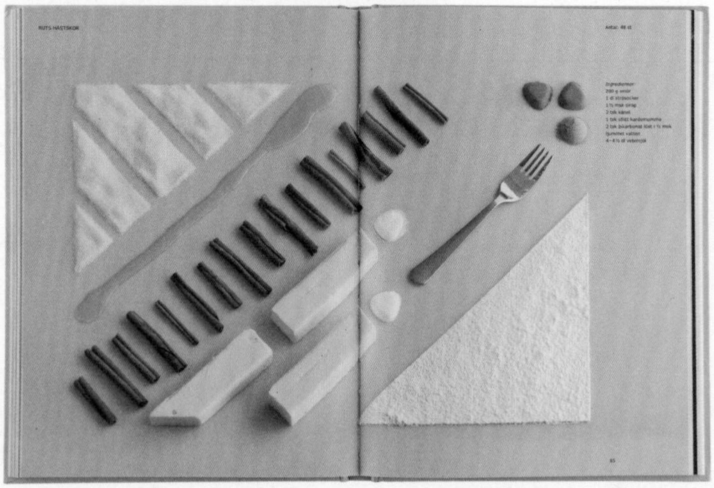

Entire Books
Music

Stuff We Really Like
We wanted to design a piece of self-promotion that could be mailed to potential clients. So we produced a 784-page book filled with stuff we really like, which was intended to resonate with people and attract like-minded personalities.

Designers
Craig Oldham
Jordan Stokes
Creative Directors
David Simpson
Anthony Smith
Creative Artworker
Jon Hatton
Copywriters
Matthew Beardsell
Paolo Carniel
Jon Hatton
Alison Johnson
Craig Oldham
James Quail
David Simpson
Phil Skegg
Anthony Smith
Jordan Stokes
Shelley Wood
Design Group
Music
Production Managers
Matthew Beardsell
Shelley Wood
Client
Music

DRINK A PINT
BLOOD A DAY
TASTE THE
BLOOD OF
CHRISTOPHER LEE

BECAUSE THE WORLD IS ROUND, IT TURNS ME ON.
[Lennon, McCartney]
2:46
STUFF WE REALLY LIKE
VOL. I

Entire Books
Irma Boom for Grafische Cultuurstichting

Irma Boom: Biography in Books
'Irma Boom: Biography in Books – Books in reverse chronological order, 2010–1986, with comments here and there' is a miniature book measuring only 50 x 38 mm. It provides an overview of book designer Irma Boom's career through more than 450 full colour illustrations across 704 pages. The book was designed by Boom herself for her retrospective exhibition at the Special Collections of the University of Amsterdam Library. Boom creates tiny models of all her books as part of the design process. This inspired the size of this miniature catalogue.

Art Director
Irma Boom
Designers
Irma Boom
Sonja Heller
Authors
Irma Boom
Mathieu Lommen
Publishers
Alwin van Steijn
Garrelt Verhoeven
Illustrator
Rem Koolhaas
Translator
John A Lane
Publishing Company
Grafische Cultuurstichting
Client
Grafische Cultuurstichting

BOOM
BOOM
BIJZONDERE COLLECTIES

HOPE
18

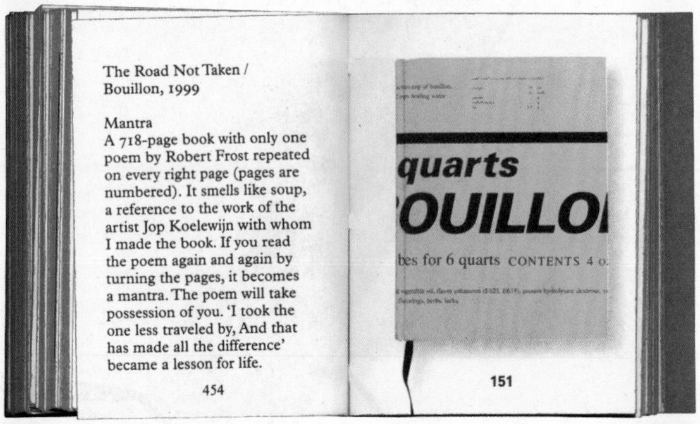
The Road Not Taken / Bouillon, 1999
Mantra
A 718-page book with only one poem by Robert Frost repeated on every right page (pages are numbered). It smells like soup, a reference to the work of the artist Jop Koelewijn with whom I made the book. If you read the poem again and again by turning the pages, it becomes a mantra. The poem will take possession of you. 'I took the one less traveled by, And that has made all the difference' became a lesson for life.
454
quarts
OUILLO
bes for 6 quarts CONTENTS 4 o.
151

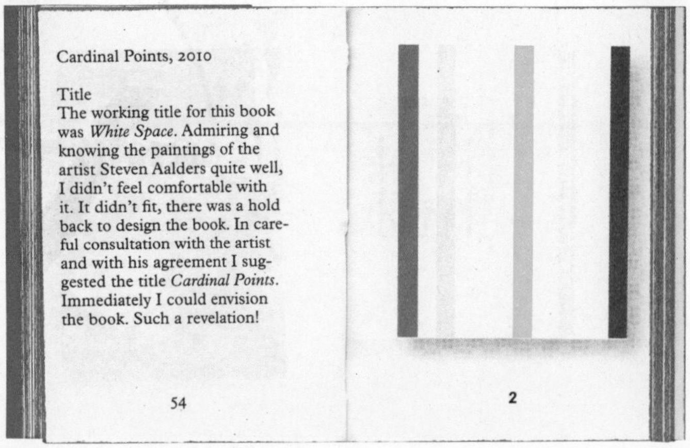
Cardinal Points, 2010
Title
The working title for this book was *White Space*. Admiring and knowing the paintings of the artist Steven Aalders quite well, I didn't feel comfortable with it. It didn't fit, there was a hold back to design the book. In careful consultation with the artist and with his agreement I suggested the title *Cardinal Points*. Immediately I could envision the book. Such a revelation!
54
2

Book Front Covers
Penguin Group UK
for Penguin

F. Scott Fitzgerald
To mark the 70th anniversary of F. Scott Fitzgerald's death, Penguin Classics planned to publish hardback editions of six titles. The patterns evoke the jazz age of Fitzgerald's stories, giving these books the elegance and glamour of the Art Deco period: the sense of ornate detail fused with the modernist aesthetic of mechanical repetition. The combination of metallic foil and matt paper gives a tactile enhancement to the reading experience. The type panel fits with the deco theme and is echoed on the detachable bookmarks.

Art Director
Jim Stoddart
Designer
Coralie Bickford-Smith
Illustrator
Coralie Bickford-Smith
Design Group
Penguin Group UK
Client
Penguin
Brand
Penguin Classics

F. SCOTT FITZGERALD
THE BEAUTIFUL AND DAMNED
F. SCOTT FITZGERALD
THE LAST TYCOON
F. SCOTT FITZGERALD
THIS SIDE OF PARADISE
F. SCOTT FITZGERALD
TENDER IS THE NIGHT
F. SCOTT FITZGERALD
FLAPPERS AND PHILOSOPHERS
F. SCOTT FITZGERALD
THE GREAT GATSBY
F. SCOTT FITZGERALD
THE GREAT GATSBY
SO·WE·BEAT·ON, BOATS·AGAINST THE·CURRENT, BORNE·BACK CEASELESSLY INTO·THE·PAST
BOOKMARK

Book Front Covers
Keenan for
Canongate Books

The Good Man Jesus and the Scoundrel Christ
In 'The Good Man Jesus and the Scoundrel Christ', Philip Pullman takes the accepted story of the Son of God and reinterprets it, so that Jesus Christ is split into two separate characters: Jesus (a good man) and his twin brother, Christ (a scoundrel). To echo this idea, the book was produced in good and scoundrel editions. Just as the book subverts the existing story, the design takes the typefaces, bookmarks and gold foil that you'd associate with the Bible and employs them in a new way.

Art Director
Mark Ecob
Designer
Keenan
Publishers
Canongate Books
Editor
Francis Bickmore
Client
Canongate Books

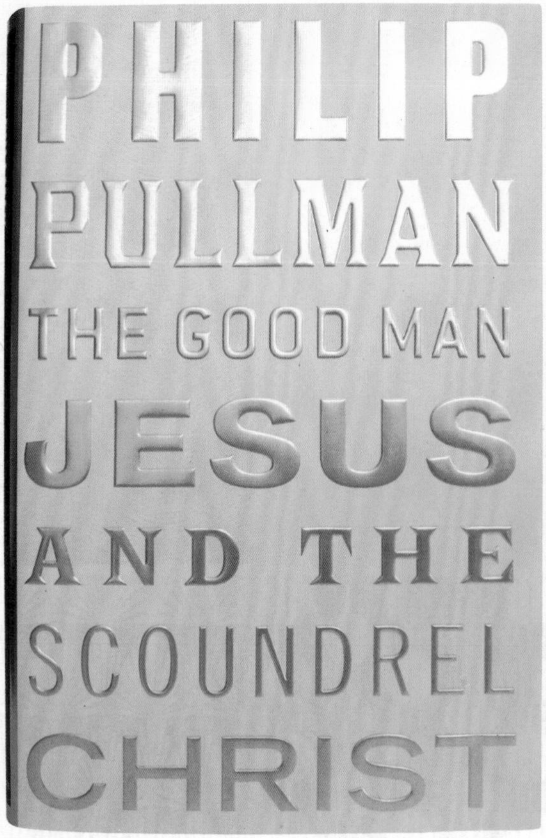
PHILIP
PULLMAN
THE GOOD MAN
JESUS
AND THE
SCOUNDREL
CHRIST

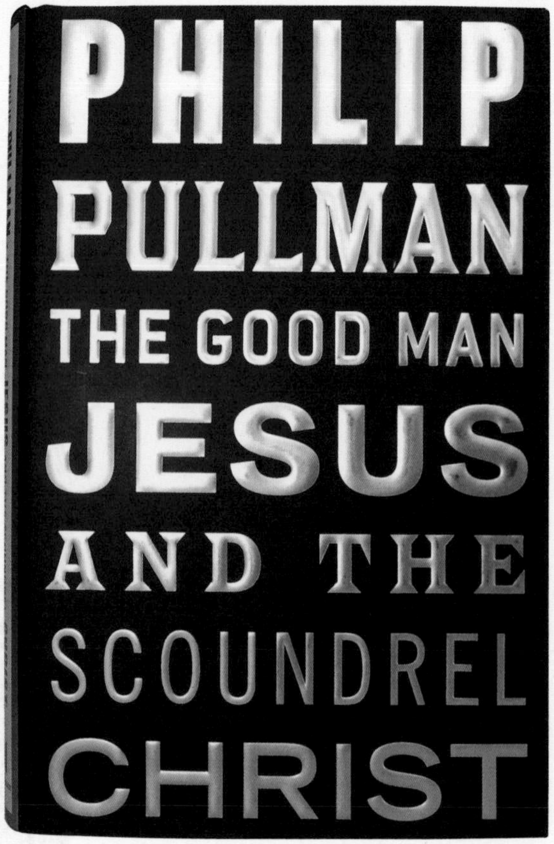
PHILIP
PULLMAN
THE GOOD MAN
JESUS
AND THE
SCOUNDREL
CHRIST

Book Front Covers
David Pearson Design
for Pan Macmillan

Cormac McCarthy
Series Style
These books are part of an ongoing series style which uses type as image.

Designer
David Pearson
Design Director
Fiona Carpenter
Design Agency
David Pearson Design
Client
Pan Macmillan

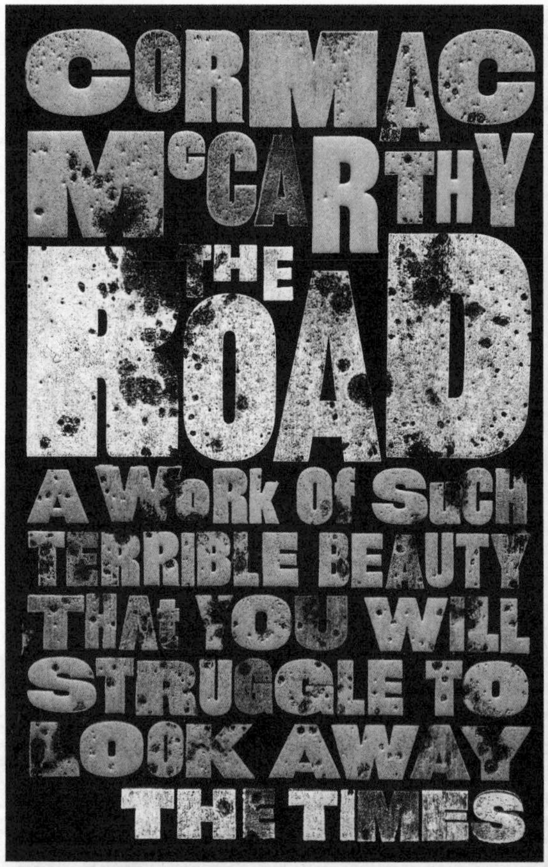
CORMAC
McCARTHY
THE
ROAD
A WoRk Of SUCH
TERRIBLE BEAUTY
THAT YOU WILL
STRUGGLE TO
LOOK AWAY
THE TIMES

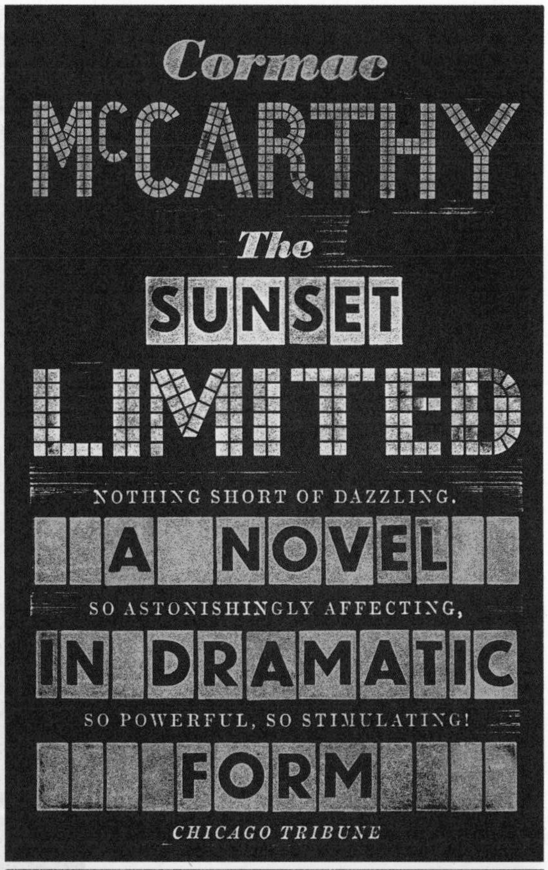
Cormac
McCARTHY
The
SUNSET
LIMITED
NOTHING SHORT OF DAZZLING.
A NOVEL
SO ASTONISHINGLY AFFECTING,
IN DRAMATIC
SO POWERFUL, SO STIMULATING!
FORM
CHICAGO TRIBUNE

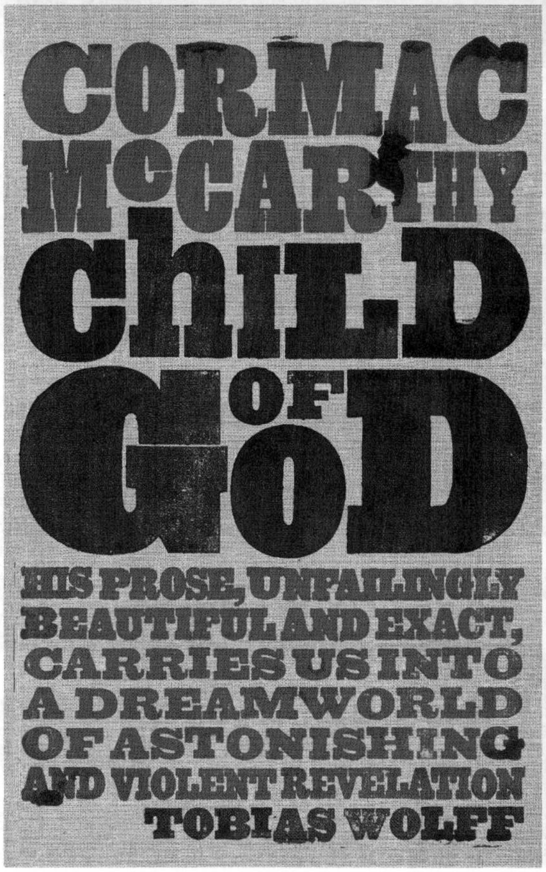
CORMAC
McCARTHY
CHILD
OF
GOD
HIS PROSE, UNFAILINGLY
BEAUTIFUL AND EXACT,
CARRIES US INTO
A DREAMWORLD
OF ASTONISHING
AND VIOLENT REVELATION
TOBIAS WOLFF

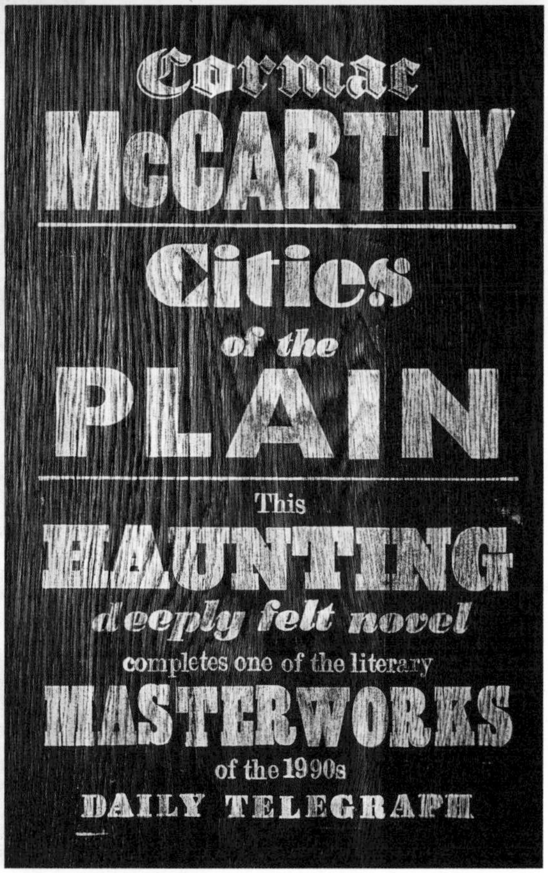
Cormac
McCARTHY
Cities
of the
PLAIN
This
HAUNTING
deeply felt novel
completes one of the literary
MASTERWORKS
of the 1990s
DAILY TELEGRAPH

Yellow Pencil
in Branding

Digital Brand Expression
GBH for PUMA
International

The PUMA Phone
The aim was to bring PUMA's brand personality to life via a mobile device. PUMA is a sports lifestyle company, which is right at the heart of the phone, with its sporty and playful sides. It even boasts the world's first solar panel on a mobile phone to make the most of the outdoors. The PUMA phone is designed to engage with you emotionally and charm you by the way it works. It talks to you like a friend, not a digital device. Every level of communication has been looked at with fresh eyes. Some of these changes are very subtle, some quite profound.

Designers
Harry Edmunds
Peter Hale
Sophie Paynter
Russell Saunders
Design Director
Peter Hale
Creative Directors
Mark Bonner
Jason Gregory
Peter Hale
Copywriters
Peter Hale
Russell Saunders
Design Studio
GBH
Brand Managers
Antonio Bertone
Nina Wolf
Director of Marketing & User Experience
Jerome Nadel
Clients
PUMA International
Sagem Wireless
Brand
PUMA

02-UK
15:37
HAPPY
I'M NOT LIKE ALL THOSE OTHER PHONES
PUMA

SOMETHING WENT WRONG I DON'T THINK IT'S MY FAULT
GET ME TO A CHARGER I DON'T HAVE LONG LEFT
MUST BE ABOUT...

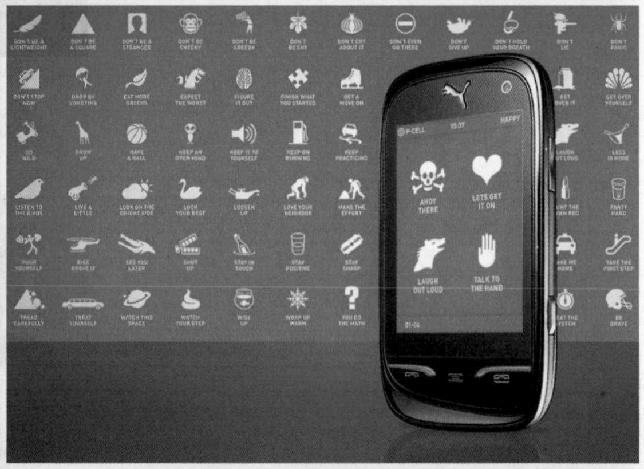

1432
MESSAGES POWERED BY THE SUN

Yellow Pencil
in Branding

Brand Experience
& Environments
GBH for PUMA
International

The PUMA
Unity Initiative
The 2010 World Cup in Africa inspired PUMA to physically convey one continent's unity through one exclusive kit. The Unity kit used the African sun, sky and soil as its inspiration, and all proceeds went to the United Nations Environmental Programme (UNEP). The initiative culminated in the African Football and Music Festival in Paris where Ivory Coast, Cameroon and Ghana joined together to play a match as a Unity XI team versus an Africa XI team. In a football first, players from all three nations were united by the special kit, while their former team mates wore their respective national kits.

Designers
Darren Barry
Phil Bold
Mark Bonner
Jason Gregory
Sebastien Thiney
Sven Tobschall
Jacob Vanderkar
Design Director
Mark Bonner
Creative Directors
Johan Adamson
Mark Bonner
Jason Gregory
Peter Hale
Filip Trulson
Photographer
Harald Loos
Typographer
Paul Barnes
Design Studio
GBH
Advertising Agency
Syrup
Events Agency
Brandon Life
Corporate Social
Responsibility Agency
Droga5
Public Relations Officer
Sara Gottman
Brand Managers
Johan Adamsson
Filip Trulsson
Client
PUMA International
Brand
PUMA

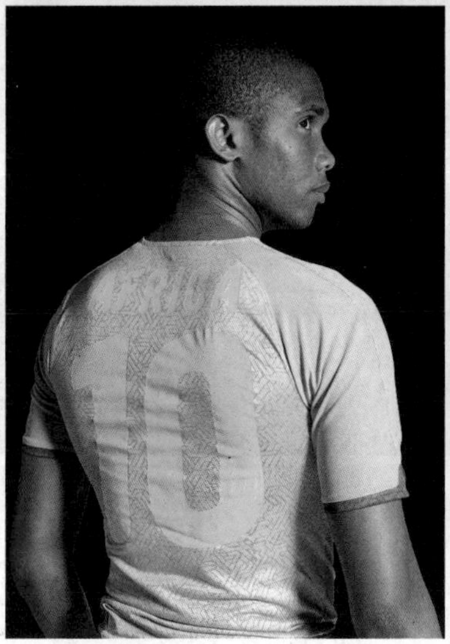

Yellow Pencil
in Branding

Brand Experience
& Environments
Mother New York
for Target

Target Kaleidoscopic Fashion Spectacular
On 18 August 2010, after a month of rehearsals, Target presented a fashion show featuring 66 dancers, an original score, 44,640 LED bulbs, and 155 rooms in New York's Standard Hotel. Named the Target Kaleidoscopic Fashion Spectacular, the event reinvented the catwalk by using all the windows of the hotel's 18 floors to showcase the brand's upcoming autumn fashion, while providing a 20-minute light, sound and dance spectacle for the thousands of spectators on the streets below. It received 160 million media impressions and has been shared online over 12.6 million times.

Stylist
Mel Ottenberg
Choreographer
Ryan Heffington
Music Composer
Sam Spiegel
Advertising Agency
Mother New York
Content & Show Direction
LEGS
Lighting Design
Bionic League
Client
Target

● Nomination in Branding

Digital Brand Expression
Jung von Matt/Limmat
for Caritas

One Minute of Silence
On 23 January 2010, after the earthquake in Haiti, Caritas and Universal Music launched a song: 'One Minute of Silence for Haiti'. It was 60 seconds of silence: 60 seconds to reflect on the victims, 60 seconds so we wouldn't forget too quickly. Priced at 97 cents, it was a micro-donation designed to keep the disaster in people's minds for as long as possible. It was spread via traditional and social media channels, promoted by pop stars, and aired by radio stations. It kept the focus on Haiti, and it still does, every time your MP3 player plays it.

Designer
Christina Baeriswyl
Art Director
Fernando Perez
Copywriter
Livio Dainese
Creative Director
Lukas Frei
Executive Creative Director
Alexander Jaggy
Developer
Pascal Beyeler
Agency Producer
Ilonka Galliard
Advertising Agency
Jung von Matt/Limmat
Film Production
Südlich-t
Record Company
Universal Music
Account Handlers
Remo Brunner
Daniel Nessler
Brand Directors
Sebastian Durband
Andrea Gnädinger
Martin Samsel
Client Head of Communication
Andriu Deflorin
Client Head of Fundraising
Jörg Arnold
Client
Caritas

One Minute of Silence
Caritas
1152 von 1732
00:30
-00:30
ONE
MINUTE
of silence
MENU

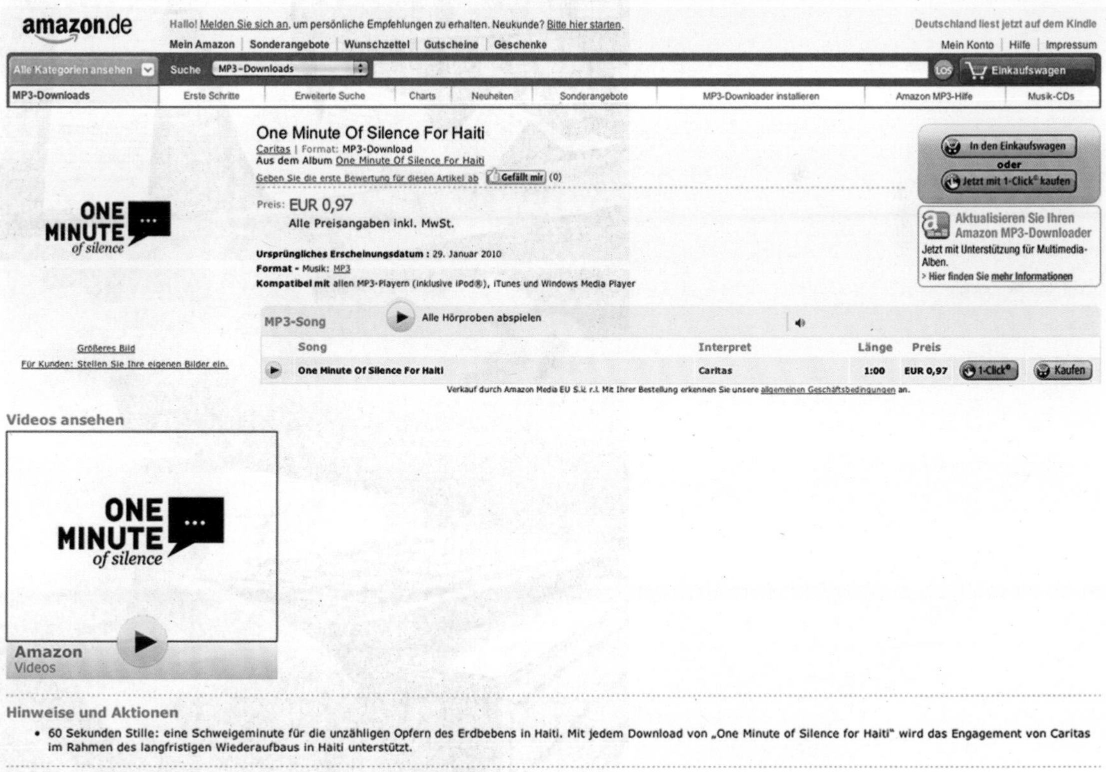
amazon.de
Hallo! Melden Sie sich an, um persönliche Empfehlungen zu erhalten. Neukunde? Bitte hier starten.
Deutschland liest jetzt auf dem Kindle
Mein Amazon | Sonderangebote | Wunschzettel | Gutscheine | Geschenke
Mein Konto | Hilfe | Impressum
Alle Kategorien ansehen
Suche
MP3-Downloads
LOS
Einkaufswagen
MP3-Downloads
Erste Schritte
Erweiterte Suche
Charts
Neuheiten
Sonderangebote
MP3-Downloader installieren
Amazon MP3-Hilfe
Musik-CDs
One Minute Of Silence For Haiti
Caritas | Format: MP3-Download
Aus dem Album One Minute Of Silence For Haiti
Geben Sie die erste Bewertung für diesen Artikel ab
Gefällt mir (0)
Preis: EUR 0,97
Alle Preisangaben inkl. MwSt.
Ursprüngliches Erscheinungsdatum : 29. Januar 2010
Format - Musik: MP3
Kompatibel mit allen MP3-Playern (inklusive iPod®), iTunes und Windows Media Player
In den Einkaufswagen
oder
Jetzt mit 1-Click® kaufen
Aktualisieren Sie Ihren Amazon MP3-Downloader
Jetzt mit Unterstützung für Multimedia-Alben.
> Hier finden Sie mehr Informationen
ONE
MINUTE
of silence
Größeres Bild
Für Kunden: Stellen Sie Ihre eigenen Bilder ein.
MP3-Song
Alle Hörproben abspielen
Song
Interpret
Länge
Preis
One Minute Of Silence For Haiti
Caritas
1:00
EUR 0,97
1-Click®
Kaufen
Verkauf durch Amazon Media EU S.à r.l. Mit Ihrer Bestellung erkennen Sie unsere allgemeinen Geschäftsbedingungen an.
Videos ansehen
ONE
MINUTE
of silence
Amazon
Videos
Hinweise und Aktionen
60 Sekunden Stille: eine Schweigeminute für die unzähligen Opfern des Erdbebens in Haiti. Mit jedem Download von „One Minute of Silence for Haiti" wird das Engagement von Caritas im Rahmen des langfristigen Wiederaufbaus in Haiti unterstützt.

Nomination in Branding

Brand Experience & Environments
McCann Erickson Malaysia for BookXcess

Receipt Stories
Independent bookstore BookXcess wanted to create a distinctive reading and writing experience for customers, which would connect the shop to story lovers across the country. Resources were limited, so a campaign with minimal expenditure yet the ability to generate viral-like user interest was needed. Customers were asked to participate in the process via a call for entry on store receipts. This invited aspiring authors to contribute a really short story on the Receipt Stories website. The most popular receipt stories of the week were published weekly on receipts printed at the store.

Designer
Douglas Goh
Art Director
Douglas Goh
Executive Creative Directors
Ean-Hwa Huang
Szu-Hung Lee
Copywriters
Szu-Hung Lee
Bee-Nee Ng
Photographer
Heng-Weng Bay
Typographer
Douglas Goh
Print Producer
Jimmy Ong
Advertising Agency
McCann Erickson Malaysia
Account Handler
Chee-Hung Goon
Client Managing Director
Andrew Yap Thiam Leng
Client
BookXcess

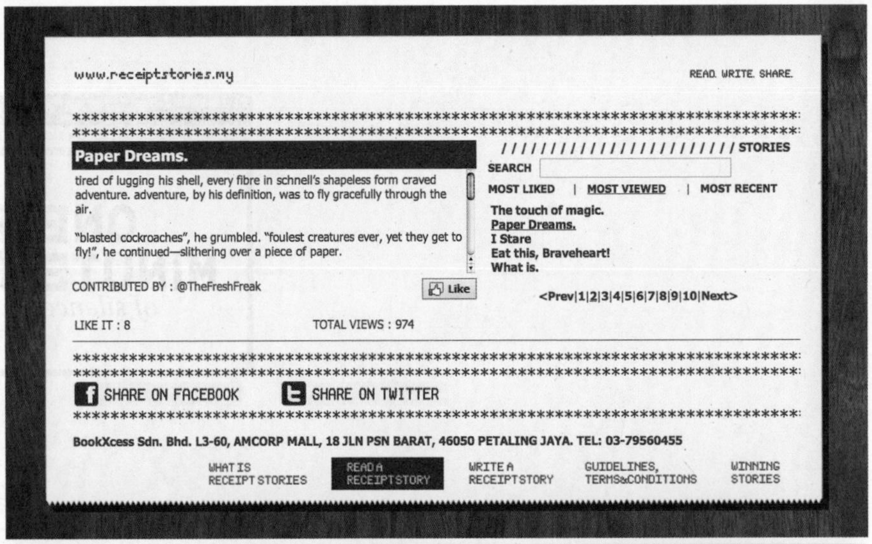
www.receiptstories.my
READ. WRITE. SHARE.
Paper Dreams.
tired of lugging his shell, every fibre in schnell's shapeless form craved adventure. adventure, by his definition, was to fly gracefully through the air.
"blasted cockroaches", he grumbled. "foulest creatures ever, yet they get to fly!", he continued—slithering over a piece of paper.
CONTRIBUTED BY : @TheFreshFreak
Like
LIKE IT : 8
TOTAL VIEWS : 974
STORIES
SEARCH
MOST LIKED | MOST VIEWED | MOST RECENT
The touch of magic.
Paper Dreams.
I Stare
Eat this, Braveheart!
What is.
<Prev|1|2|3|4|5|6|7|8|9|10|Next>
SHARE ON FACEBOOK
SHARE ON TWITTER
BookXcess Sdn. Bhd. L3-60, AMCORP MALL, 18 JLN PSN BARAT, 46050 PETALING JAYA. TEL: 03-79560455
WHAT IS RECEIPT STORIES
READ A RECEIPT STORY
WRITE A RECEIPT STORY
GUIDELINES, TERMS&CONDITIONS
WINNING STORIES

HOW TO BE A PUBLISHED WRITER IN 100 WORDS OR LESS.
READ. WRITE. SHARE.
20% DISCOUNT

BIXOLON

Branding Schemes/
Large Business
johnson banks for
the Science Museum

Science Museum Identity
A museum with a world-class collection of science-related objects and exhibitions, the Science Museum needed to define a clear identity for its visitors. After a long audit and design investigation, a visual route began to take shape that took the two-word name and created a distinctive arrangement of the characters into a four-line block that took its cue from code and digital typefaces. We then swiftly extrapolated the logo into a house-style that gave the museum immediate presence in London's highly competitive marketing environment.

Designers
Miho Aishima
Michael Johnson
Kath Tudball
Creative Director
Michael Johnson
Design Group
johnson banks
Client Head of Design
Tim Molloy
Brand Manager
Katy Hack
Marketing Manager
Andrea Dearden
Client
Science Museum

SCIENCE MUSEUM

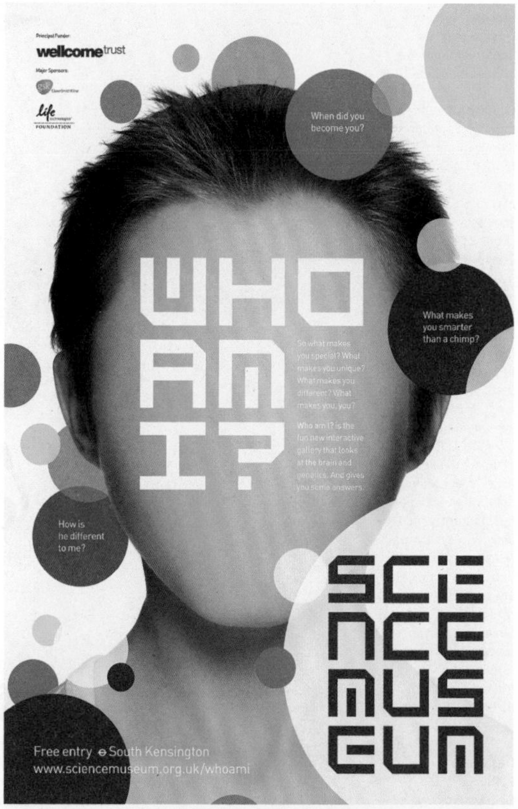
wellcome trust
WHO AM I?
When did you become you?
What makes you smarter than a chimp?
How is he different to me?
SCIENCE MUSEUM
Free entry South Kensington
www.sciencemuseum.org.uk/whoami

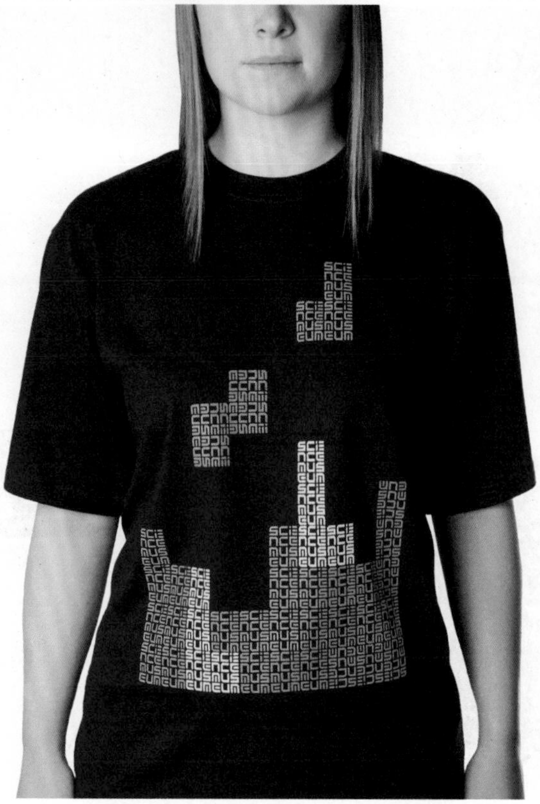

SCIENCE MUSEUM
astonishing science. spectacular museum.

Branding Schemes/
Large Business
Construct London for
Maybourne Hotel Group

Claridge's Identity
Construct London's identity and branding for Claridge's describes a luxury hotel that has played host to stars, socialites and crowned heads of Europe. Construct's strategic framework identified an Art Deco heritage, timeless glamour, and attentive, traditionally English service as the hotel's distinguishing features. The redrawn crest and logotype complement elements of an Art Deco-influenced palette of confident jade, gold, white and black, architecturally inspired chevrons, typefaces resonant of the 20s, and archive-inspired imagery. The unusual diversity and extensive range of applications reflects Maybourne Hotel Group's absolute trust in Construct as brand guardian of its properties.

Designers
Peter Bell
Georgia Fendley
Kim Hartley
Ramon Marin
Radek Wojcik
Creative Directors
Georgia Fendley
Kim Hartley
Design Agency
Construct London
Client
Maybourne Hotel Group
Brand
Claridge's

CLARIDGE'S
CLARIDGE'S
CLARIDGE'S

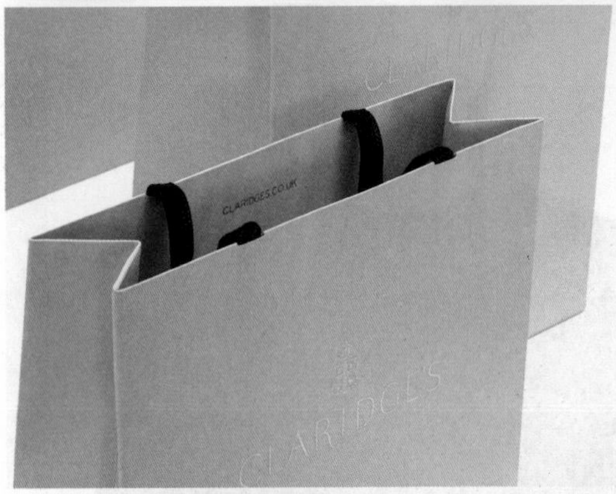
CLARIDGES.CO.UK
CLARIDGE'S

CLARIDGE'S

J'ADORE
CLARIDGE'S AND DIOR
CELEBRATE THE RETURN
OF THE GLAMOROUS
DRESSING TABLE

Branding Schemes/
Small Business
Neue Design Studio
for Visit Nordkyn

Where Nature Rules
Nordkyn Peninsula, the furthermost part of Europe, accommodates two municipalities in the county of Finnmark, Norway. A joint marketing strategy was developed for their investment in tourism. Nordkyn offers exotic outdoor experiences in an arctic climate with striking weather conditions. The identity is inspired by the shape of a snowflake and the strapline: 'Where nature rules'. A feed of weather statistics from the Norwegian Meteorological Institute alters the logo according to wind direction and temperature changes. We developed a generator where Visit Nordkyn can download its logo to match the exact weather conditions of that particular moment.

Designers
Lars Håvard Dahlstrøm
Øystein Haugseth
Benjamin Stenmarck
Art Directors
Lars Håvard Dahlstrøm
Øystein Haugseth
Benjamin Stenmarck
Design Group
Neue Design Studio
Account Handler
Gørill Kvamme
Brand Director
Gørill Kvamme
Brand Manager
Charlotte Schytte
Client
Visit Nordkyn

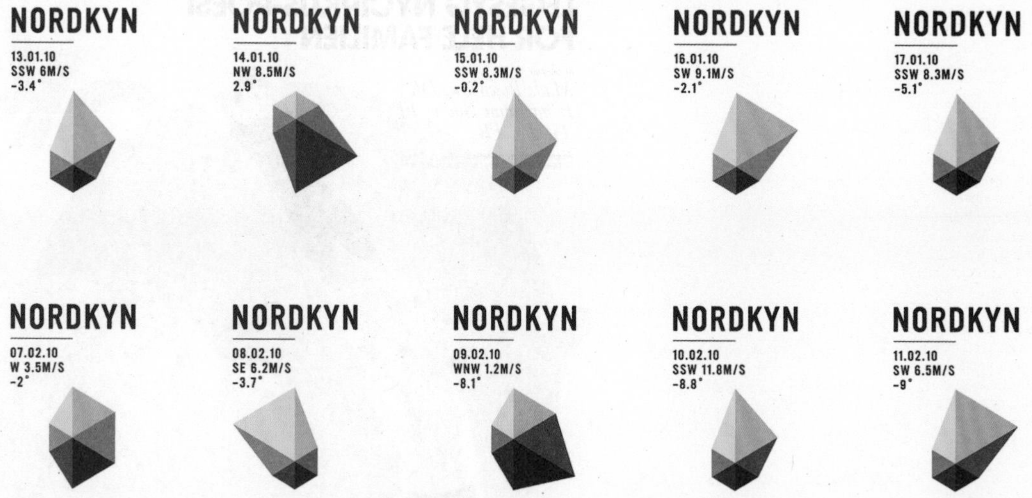
NORDKYN
13.01.10
SSW 6M/S
-3.4°
NORDKYN
14.01.10
NW 8.5M/S
2.9°
NORDKYN
15.01.10
SSW 8.3M/S
-0.2°
NORDKYN
16.01.10
SW 9.1M/S
-2.1°
NORDKYN
17.01.10
SSW 8.3M/S
-5.1°
NORDKYN
07.02.10
W 3.5M/S
-2°
NORDKYN
08.02.10
SE 6.2M/S
-3.7°
NORDKYN
09.02.10
WNW 1.2M/S
-8.1°
NORDKYN
10.02.10
SSW 11.8M/S
-8.8°
NORDKYN
11.02.10
SW 6.5M/S
-9°

NORDKYN
23.02.10
ESE 12.1M/S
-10.6°

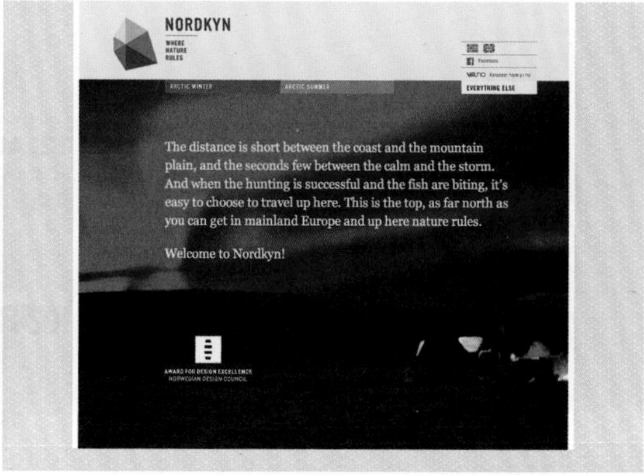
NORDKYN
WHERE
NATURE
RULES
The distance is short between the coast and the mountain plain, and the seconds few between the calm and the storm. And when the hunting is successful and the fish are biting, it's easy to choose to travel up here. This is the top, as far north as you can get in mainland Europe and up here nature rules.
Welcome to Nordkyn!

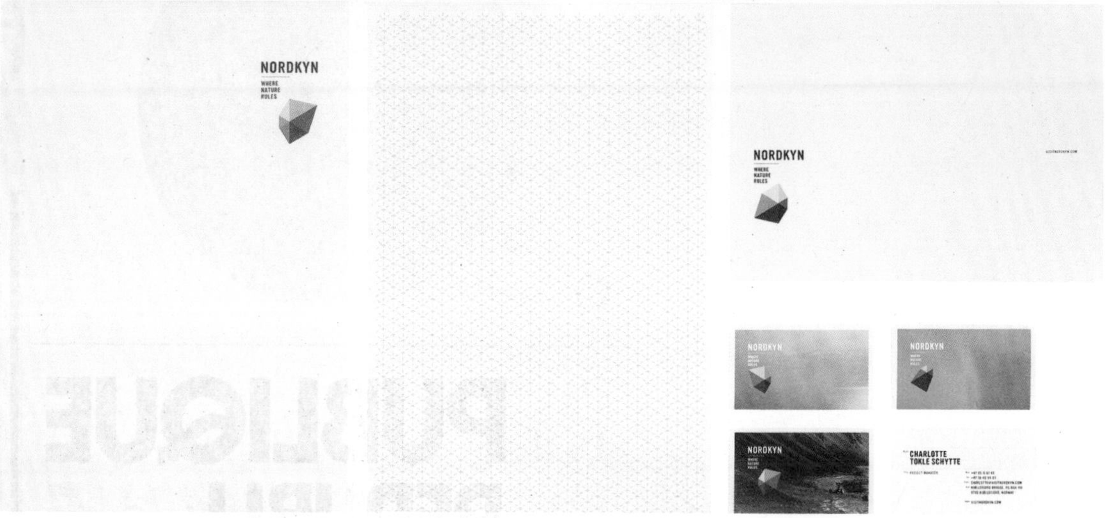
NORDKYN
WHERE
NATURE
RULES
NORDKYN
NORDKYN
NORDKYN
NORDKYN
CHARLOTTE
TOKLE SCHYTTE

Branding Schemes/
Small Business
Scandinavian DesignLab
for Republique Theatre

Republique Theatre
Season 02
How do you create continuity for a one-year-old identity, while still expressing that this is an extremely dynamic and experimental theatre? Republique's first season was successful, both in terms of performances and visibility, so it would have been tempting to let the second be more of the same, but that is not what Republique is about. The second season programme was definitely not the same, and consequently, the identity had to be taken to the next level too. Building on the simple yet distinctive design elements added an edge that suited a programme even more interesting than the previous one.

Designers
Per Madsen
Robert Daniel Nagy
Creative Director
Per Madsen
Design Agency
Scandinavian DesignLab
Account Handler
Christina Orth
Account Director
Anne-Mette Højland
Marketing Managers
Hans Christian Gimbel
Charlotte Sejer Pedersen
Client
Republique Theatre

LEGESYG NYCIRKUS-POESI
FOR HELE FAMILIEN
AF OG MED
Mads Rosenbeck, DK
Bonaventure Gacon, FR
Titoune, FR
PRÆSENTERES UNDER KØBENHAVNS INTERNATIONALE TEATERS NY CIRKUS FESTIVAL
VOLCHOK
I eget telt nær REPUBLIQUE
12. AUGUST - 10. SEPTEMBER
Billetter: 70 20 10 31, www.republique.dk og www.billetbillet.dk
REPUBLIQUE
KØBENHAVNS NYE TEATER
Østerfælled Torv 37 / 2100 Kbh Ø
www.republique.dk

REPUBLIQUE
REPERTOIRE BILLETTER OM TEATRET NYHEDER PRESSE KONTAKT
Nyheder
ABONNEMENT
Kalender 2011 - jan
Modtag nyheder
Hotel Europa
Othello
Isabella's Room
KØB BILLET
Hold dig opdateret om REPUBLIQUE på facebook.com/republique.dk

RE
MEM
BER
REPUBLIQUE
KØBENHAVNS NYE TEATER

MONARCHY
REPUBLIQUE
THEATRE
REPUBLIQUE
THEATRE
LABORATORY
REPUBLIQUE

OTHELLO
5
OTHELLO
REPUBLIQUE

Branding Schemes/
Small Business
Studio No.10
for Tygverket

Identity for Tygverket
Our mission was to design a brand new, strict identity, to create order in the Tygverket shop and in the overall communication. In order to establish the identity of Tygverket's area of expertise, we used an emblem and colours that show Tygverket is partly a fabric shop and partly a tailoring atelier. The tape measure is the key element; it represents the company and permeates the whole identity. The colours and scale are also important elements and are present in all pieces of communication.

Designers
Björn Carlsson
Henrik Naessén
Design Group
Studio No.10
Client
Tygverket

TYGVERKET
→Tyger →Sömnad →Tapetsering

TYGVERKET

TYGVERKET®
→Tyger →Sömnad →Tapetsering
→SENASTE NYTT
NYINKOMMET: ITALIENSKA MODETYGER
VANLIGA ÖPPETTIDER I SOMMAR!
VÄLKOMMEN TILL TYGVERKET!
KONTAKT

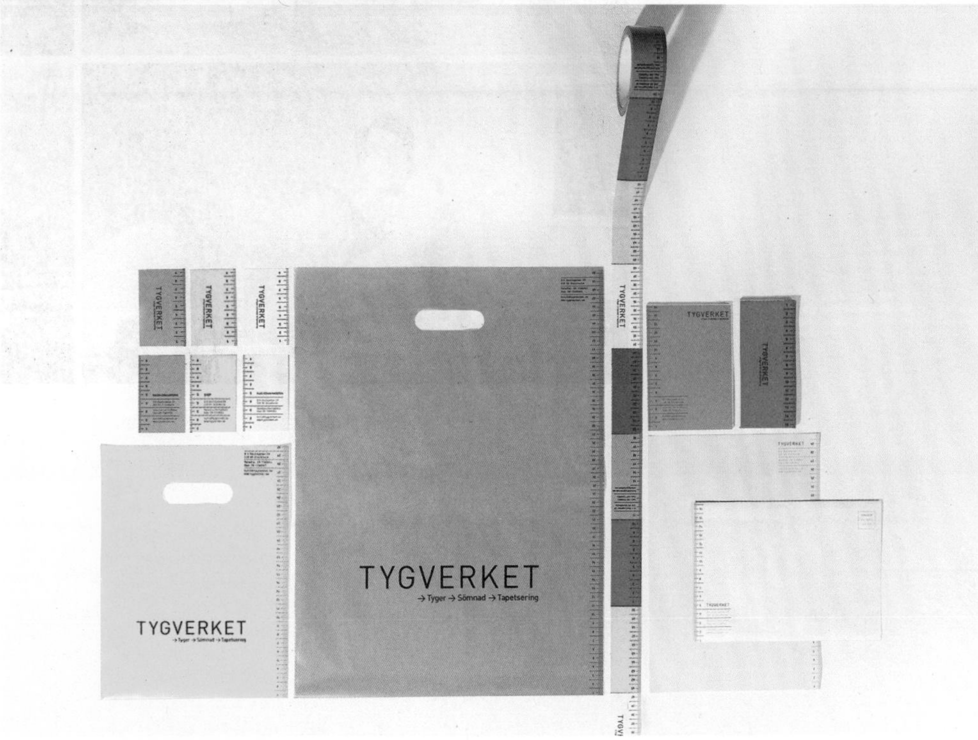
TYGVERKET
→Tyger →Sömnad →Tapetsering
TYGVERKET

Brand Expression in Moving Image
GBH for PUMA International

PUMA Phone Web Films
Each of these eight short films focuses on the inspiration for a single application on the PUMA phone, including being able to send PUMA icon messages to all your friends, track your run, and charge your phone with the power of the sun. There's even Dylan, a real puma, living, playing and sleeping in your phone. The films were created to be extremely 'analogue' in feel in order to reflect the charm and experience of using the phone. The films were used online and at trade fairs to launch the PUMA phone.

Designers
Peter Hale
Russell Saunders
Jacob Vanderkar
Design Director
Peter Hale
Creative Directors
Mark Bonner
Jason Gregory
Peter Hale
Direction
12foot6
Animation
12foot6
Design Studio
GBH
Global Brand Manager
Antonio Bertone
Clients
PUMA International
Sagem Wireless
Brand
PUMA

LET'S GET
IT ON

152

TOP

Brand Expression in Moving Image
Arc Worldwide & Leo Burnett Chicago for Symantec

Black Market
Black Market is a video featuring a fictional cybercriminal by the name of CJ Nielsen. CJ takes the viewer through the various devious techniques used by cybercriminals to steal money and the identities of their victims. The video was part of an international promotional tour sponsored by Norton, educating people about cybercrime.

Director
Alex Fendrich
Art Director
Chris von Ende
Executive Creative Directors
Dave Loew
Jon Wyville
Chief Creative Officer
Susan Credle
Copywriter
Tohru Oyasu
Editor
Meg Kubica
Producer
Matt Abramson
Agency Producer
Rob Tripas
Advertising Agencies
Arc Worldwide Chicago
Leo Burnett Chicago
Production Company
Cap Gun Collective
Editing
The White House
Senior Account Executive
CJ Nielsen
Account Supervisor
Antoniette Wico
Client
Symantec
Brand
Norton

CYBERCRIME
PAYS!
LET'S GET RICH

Digital Brand Expression
Brothers and Sisters
for the Museum
of London

Streetmuseum
The Museum of London wanted a digital idea to create buzz about the opening of its new Galleries of Modern London. We created Streetmuseum, an augmented reality iPhone app that brings the museum's extensive collections to the streets. The app uses geotagging and Google Maps to guide users to sites around London where, via the iPhone screen, historical images appear. Click on the '3D view' button and the app will recognise your location then use augmented reality to overlay the historic image over the current view. The museum wanted 5,000 downloads. By January 2011, we'd hit 160,000.

Art Directors
Lisa Jelliffe
Kirsten Rutherford
Creative Director
Steve Shannon
Executive Creative Director
Andy Fowler
Copywriters
Lisa Jelliffe
Kirsten Rutherford
Digital Designer
Mateus Wanderley
Digital Director
Kevin Brown
Developers
Gavin Buttimore
Robin Charlton
Image Geotagger
Jack Kerruish
Advertising Agency
Brothers and Sisters
Digital Project Manager
Tanya Holland
Account Handler
Emma Simmons
New Business Director
Helen Kimber
Marketing Manager
Vicky Lee
Client
Museum of London

DIG FOR VICTORY

Digital Brand Expression
TBWA\London
for Wrigley

Updater
Skittles believes life is better when you add a little colour and fun. So we took something our fans were doing every day on Facebook and added some rainbow power to it. We built a live call centre/online film factory that sucked in their status updates and turned them into Super Mega Rainbow Updates. A fan just typed in his update, then our call centre staff recorded it as an awesome film and posted it back to the fan's wall in mere minutes. Our fans created 21,000 Super Mega Rainbow Updates in just two weeks. Very super.

Art Director
Andrew Bloom
Creative Directors
Johan Dahlqvist
Lee Tan
Executive Creative Director
Mark Hunter
Copywriter
Eric Tell
Director
Jakob Marky
Producer
James Cunningham
Agency Producer
Trudy Waldron
Web Producer
Sara-Lee Rost
Editor
James Norris
Advertising Agency
TBWA\London
Production Company
Academy Films
Web Production
Perfect Fools
Sound Design
Wave
Production Manager
Cathy Buchanan
Planner
David Fryman
Account Manager
Justin Martin
Account Director
Emma Massey
Client
Wrigley
Brand
Skittles

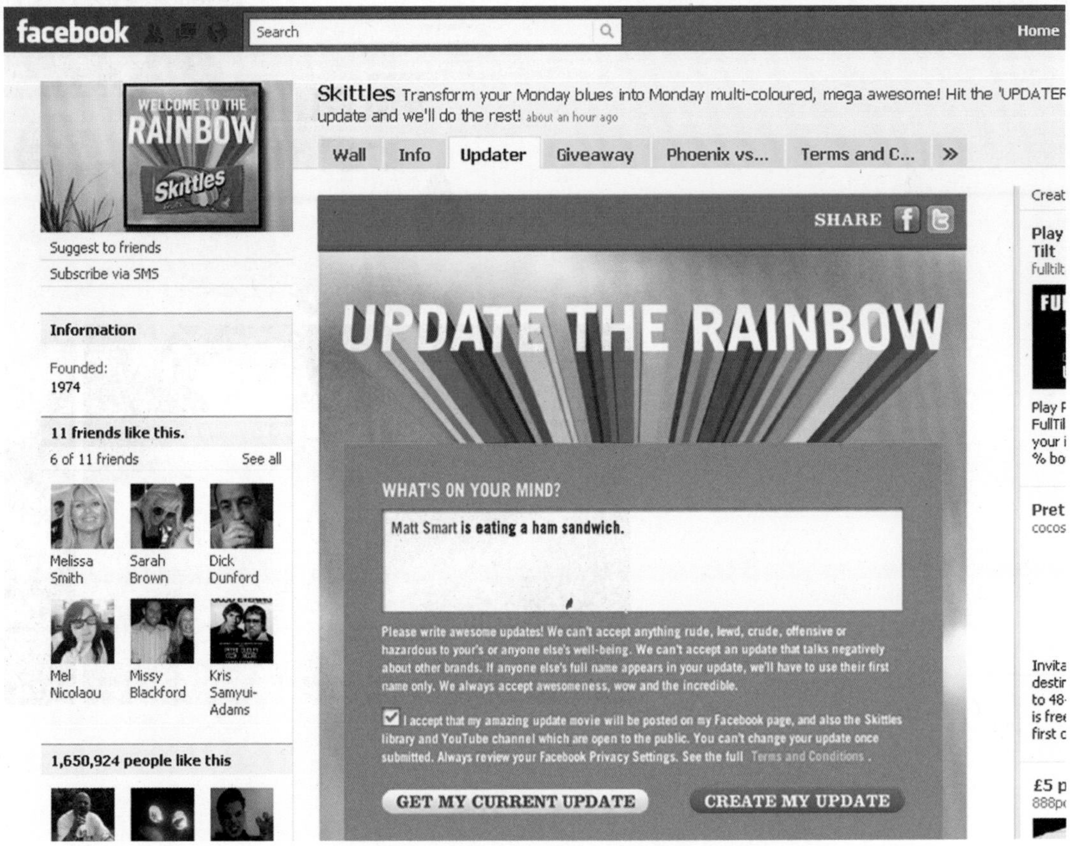
facebook
Search
Home
WELCOME TO THE RAINBOW
Skittles
Skittles Transform your Monday blues into Monday multi-coloured, mega awesome! Hit the 'UPDATER
update and we'll do the rest! about an hour ago
Wall
Info
Updater
Giveaway
Phoenix vs...
Terms and C...
SHARE
Suggest to friends
Subscribe via SMS
Information
Founded:
1974
11 friends like this.
6 of 11 friends
See all
Melissa Smith
Sarah Brown
Dick Dunford
Mel Nicolaou
Missy Blackford
Kris Samyui-Adams
1,650,924 people like this
UPDATE THE RAINBOW
WHAT'S ON YOUR MIND?
Matt Smart is eating a ham sandwich.
Please write awesome updates! We can't accept anything rude, lewd, crude, offensive or hazardous to your's or anyone else's well-being. We can't accept an update that talks negatively about other brands. If anyone else's full name appears in your update, we'll have to use their first name only. We always accept awesomeness, wow and the incredible.
I accept that my amazing update movie will be posted on my Facebook page, and also the Skittles library and YouTube channel which are open to the public. You can't change your update once submitted. Always review your Facebook Privacy Settings. See the full Terms and Conditions.
GET MY CURRENT UPDATE
CREATE MY UPDATE

Digital Brand Expression
Happiness Brussels
for Cascade

Talking Tree
Everyone has an opinion on environmental issues. But what about nature's opinion? Cascade, publishers of science magazine EOS, launched the EOS Talking Tree, a 100-year-old tree in Brussels that shared its daily life with the world on social media. To let the tree talk, it was equipped with sensors that monitored what it went through every day. Those sensors were connected to custom made software that translated the data into words on Facebook and Twitter, videos on YouTube, photos on Flickr, and sound on SoundCloud. People could follow and subscribe to its feeds on www.talking-tree.com.

Art Directors
Ramin Afshar
Tom Galle
Head of Art
Cecilia Azcarate Isturiz
Creative Directors
Karen Corrigan
Gregory Titeca
Copywriters
Ramin Afshar
Tom Galle
Film Directors
Gabriele Trapani
Federico Zanghì
Agency Producer
Bart Vande Maele
Advertising Agency
Happiness Brussels
Website Development
Bliss Interactive
Installation & Programming
Fisheye
Account Manager
Alan Cerutti
Client
Cascade
Brand
EOS Magazine

23°
2
Monday
WINDSPEED
3
km/h
My Facebook
Hello!
I'm a tree
and this is my feed.
Go
POOR AIR QUALITY
Rather sad
0
mm/h
Low Impact Month

7°
16
Wednesday
WINDSPEED
9
km/h
My Facebook
Ouch! Lots of pollutants in the air right now
12:30 PM Mar 09th 2011
POOR AIR QUALITY
Follow me on Twitter!
Add me as friend!
16708 friends
Hello!
I'm a tree and this is my feed.
ADD ME TO YOUR BLOG!
I'm ok...
0
mm/h
Low Impact Month
My everyday tracks on soundcloud:

Digital Brand Expression
Draftfcb Sweden
for Radiotjänst

The Star
Radiotjänst administers the broadcasting fee in Sweden, financing politically and commercially independent radio and TV. Blistjarna.se is a web application that lets you record yourself on webcam while reading text presented on cue cards. Your spoken words are transformed into a song through auto tune, and your visual recording is treated to make you look like the star you are – for paying the TV fee. You can share the video and download your own song as a sound file. You can also register for the TV and radio fee directly in the application – earning your star status for real.

Art Director
Andreas Englund
Copywriter
Jesper Eronn
Director
Andreas Öhman
Agency Producer
Markus Ahlm
Sound Designers
Mathias Nilsson
Christian Olsson
Advertising Agency
Draftfcb Sweden
Production Company
ACNE Production
Account Handler
Johan Gernandt
Marketing Manager
Per Leander
Client
Radiotjänst

Read the signs and it'll be just super!
SKIP INTRO

I'M A STAR
1/7
START OVER

DU ÄR EN STJÄRNA SOM BETALAR
Your support makes you a star

Digital Brand Expression
Proximity Canada for
Mars Canada

M&M's Find Red
When we heard the Google Street View camera car was coming to Toronto, we had an idea. What if we hid large M&M's inside Google Street View and challenged Canadians to find them? The result was a first-of-its-kind, multi-channel, digital treasure hunt. For four weeks, players could track down the missing candies through clues from the website, Twitter, Facebook, YouTube, Foursquare, Stickybits and QR code posters. In 630 square km, we provided over 100 clues to help players find three red M&M's and win one nifty little smart car.

Art Director
Jeffrey Da Silva
Copywriters
Rene Rouleau
Jon Ruby
Executive Creative Director
John Gagné
Associate Creative Directors
Ari Elkouby
Rene Rouleau
Jon Ruby
Jeffrey Da Silva
Jeff Vermeersch
Programmers
Iftikhar Ahmed
Edwin Locke
Technical Lead
Darrin Patey
Advertising Agency
Proximity Canada
Production Company
Hard Citizen
Animation
Topix
Account Executive
Jesse Abrams
Account Manager
Priyanka Goswami
Client
Mars Canada
Brand
M&M's

HOW TO PLAY
PRIZES
GAME STATISTICS
CLUES
MAP VIEW
I FOUND
FIND RED
LOGIN REGISTER

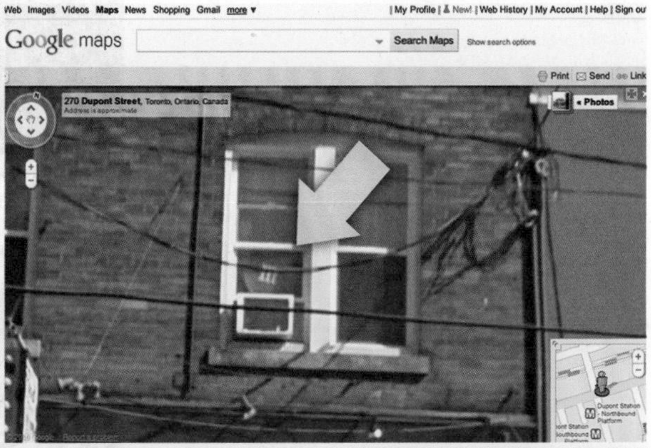
Web Images Videos Maps News Shopping Gmail more
Google maps
Search Maps
270 Dupont Street, Toronto, Ontario, Canada

Brand Experience
& Environments
TBWA\HAKUHODO
for adidas Japan

adidas Sky Comic
Sky Comic was intended to support the Japan Football Team on its journey to the 2010 FIFA World Cup in South Africa. We created thirteen 300-square metre comic strip panels, totalling approximately 3,900 square metres (42,000 square feet), a Guinness World Record. Each panel was based on a player and created in his hometown. 63,000 schoolchildren, parents and fans nationwide helped paint the panels or supported the effort online. Aerial photographs were put online along with behind-the-scenes videos, photos and fan messages. The players could view the entire giant comic strip from their plane as they departed Tokyo.

Designer
Keisuke Shimizu
Technical Director
Keitaro Takahashi
Art Directors
Hirofumi Nakajima
Haruhito Nisawadaira
Katsuhiro Shimizu
Interactive Art Director
Jun Ino
Creative Directors
Kazoo Sato
Hideyuki Tanaka
Copywriter
Masaharu Kumagai
Lead Illustrator
Shuhei Kaminaga
Illustrator
TERU
Flash Developer
Shunsuke Ohba
Sound Designer
Atsushi Shimomura
Producers
Kentaro Kinoshita
Makiko Okada
Production Managers
Hideki Harada
Mona Yamamoto
Advertising Agency
TBWA\HAKUHODO
Digital Planner
Shintaro Takeuchi
Account Director
Taro Sato
Client
adidas Japan
Brand
adidas

俊輔
左足を振り抜いたー!!

長谷部 競り勝っ太

Brand Experience & Environments
DDB China Group Shanghai for the China Environmental Protection Foundation

Green Pedestrian Crossing

The China Environmental Protection Foundation wanted to encourage people to walk more and drive less. We decided to use a busy pedestrian crossing where both pedestrians and drivers meet. We covered the crossing with a giant canvas of a large, leafless tree. Placed on either side of the road were sponge cushions soaked in green, environmentally friendly paint. As people walked across and stepped onto the sponges, they created green footprints. Each green footprint added to the canvas like leaves growing on a bare tree, conveying the message that walking helps create a greener environment.

Design Director
Jody Xiong
Art Director
Jody Xiong
Chief Creative Officer
Michael Dee
Copywriter
Jason Jin
Typographers
Jerry Cao
Jody Xiong
Print Production Director
James Chen
Advertising Agency
DDB China Group Shanghai
Planner
Jenny Liu
Client
China Environmental Protection Foundation

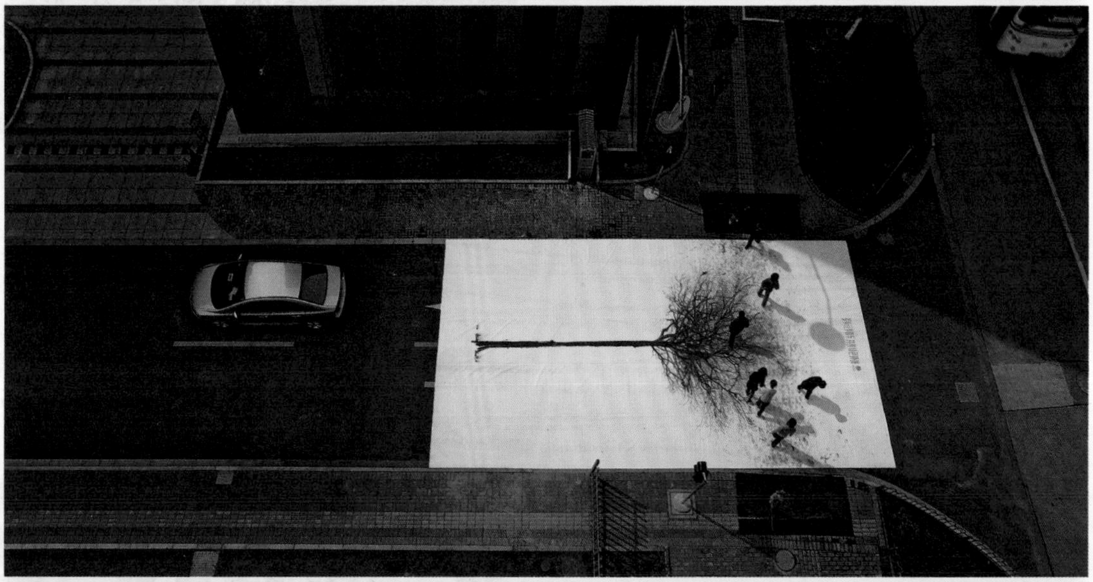

Brand Experience
& Environments
hat-trick design
for Land Securities

Land Securities
London A–Z Maps
We were asked to create environmental office graphics and a relocation campaign for the Land Securities London team, which had moved into a new space. It spanned two floors, and we could decorate any wall, pillar, roller rack or internal window. We wanted to express the company's extensive knowledge of London, its history and modern developments. The tone required was corporate and sophisticated but with a touch of humour, showing a softer side. The business is London-centric, so a focus on its core business, association with London's history, and in-depth understanding of the city, was required.

Designers
Tim Donaldson
Adam Giles
Gareth Howat
Jim Sutherland
Mark Wheatcroft
Design Directors
Gareth Howat
Jim Sutherland
Illustrator
Rebecca Sutherland
Typographers
Tim Donaldson
Adam Giles
Gareth Howat
Jim Sutherland
Writer
Samuel Pepys
Design Group
hat-trick design
Brand Manager
Anna Chapman
Client
Land Securities

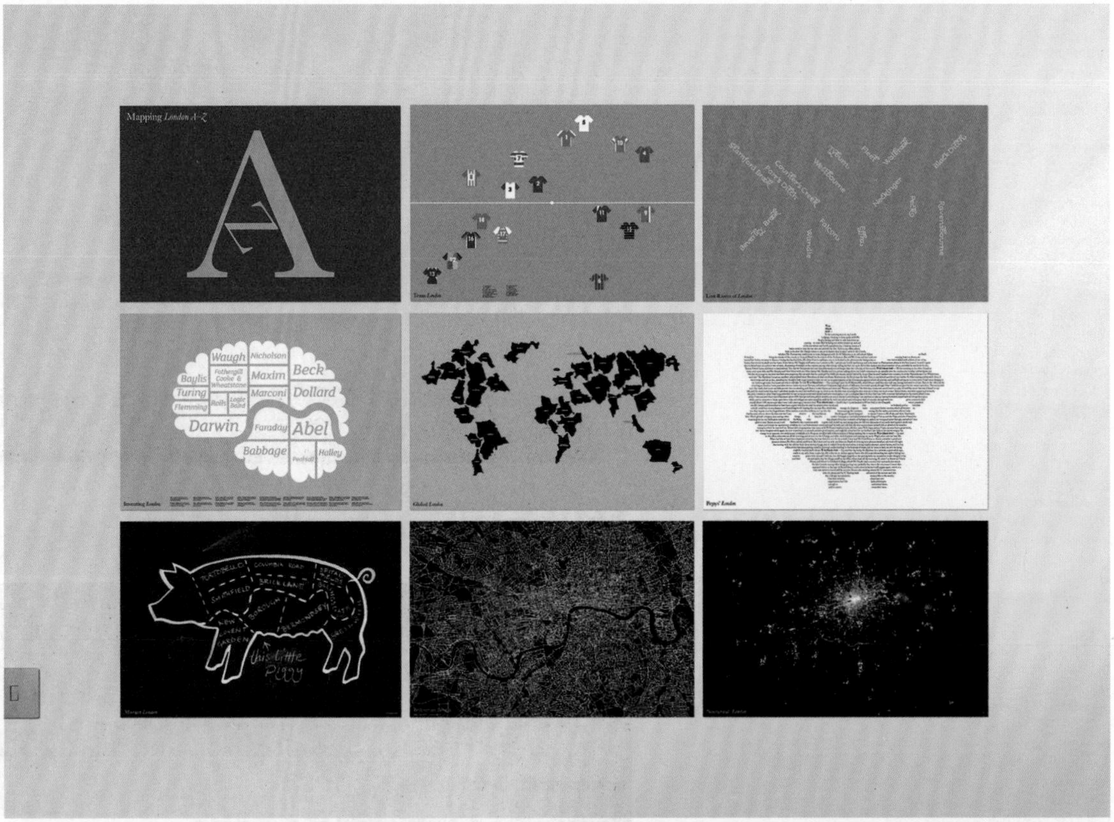
Mapping London A–Z
A
Waugh
Nicholson
Baylis
Maxim
Beck
Turing
Marconi
Dollard
Darwin
Faraday
Abel
Babbage
Holley
this little Piggy

Brand Experience
& Environments
R/GA New York for Nike

The Nike Film Room
Nike sets out to teach today's signature basketball moves to the next generation of young basketball hopefuls. We were challenged with designing an experience that gave players hands-on education on the court. The result was the Nike Film Room: part half-court, part green screen, 100 per cent education. Using a combination of green screen technology, HD cameras, and a custom-built computer program to analyse the footage, the Film Room deconstructed the kids' movements, separating the player with the ball from the background. After performing their move, kids were presented with their own Nike poster starring themselves.

Senior Visual Designer
Ted Angelilli
Interactive Designers
Tim Allen
Xavier Gallego
Art Directors
Colin Kim
Saulo Rodrigues
Creative Directors
Tim Allen
Noel Billig
Executive Creative Director
Taras Wayner
Associate Creative Directors
Jason Hoff
Colin Kim
Technical Creative Director
Josh Balik
Technical Director
Vincent Dibartolo
Copywriters
Jason Hoff
Taras Wayner
Flash Developers
David Hitchings
James Hulsizer
Programmer
Noel Billig
Producer
Nigel Goodman
Senior Open Standards Developer
Mike Brennan
Senior Presentation Code Developer
Peter Knif
Advertising Agency
R/GA New York
Group Account Director
David Fuller
Agency Vice President
Taras Wayner
Client
Nike

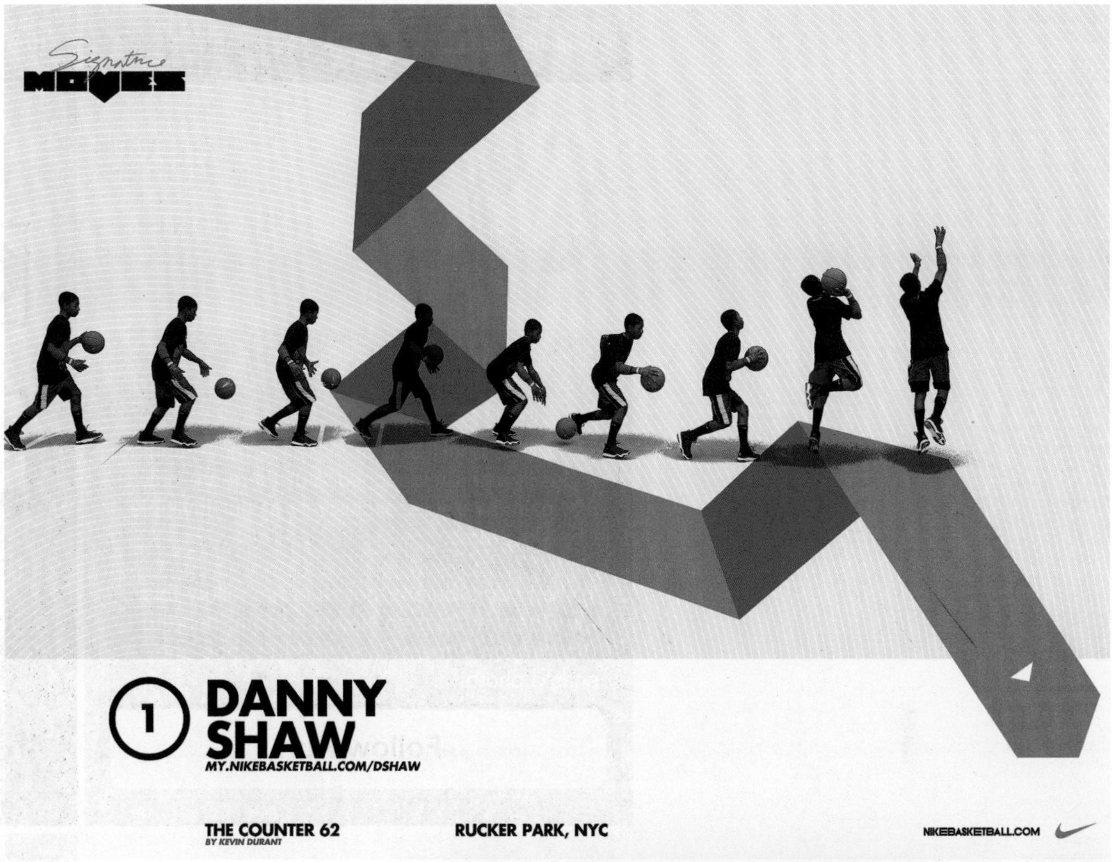
1
DANNY SHAW
MY.NIKEBASKETBALL.COM/DSHAW
THE COUNTER 62
BY KEVIN DURANT
RUCKER PARK, NYC
NIKEBASKETBALL.COM

Yellow Pencil in Digital Design

Y&R New York
for Airwalk

Invisible Pop Up Store
When Airwalk decided on a limited edition relaunch of their classic sneaker, the Jim, we came up with a new way to do it: the world's first invisible pop-up stores. Bringing together cell phones, GPS technology and augmented reality, customers could only buy the Jim if they downloaded the app, went to a pre-determined location, held up their phones, and took a photo of the augmented reality Jim floating there. That allowed them to purchase the sneaker there and then. This exclusive product was sold to an exclusive audience for an entirely new retail experience.

Designers
Austin Bone
Tiffany Ng
Art Director
Alexander Nowak
Creative Directors
Graeme Hall
Menno Kluin
Steve Whittier
Executive Creative Directors
Ian Reichenthal
Scott Vitrone
Production Creative Directors
Shailesh Rao
Vivian Rosenthal
Copywriter
Feliks Richter
Agency Producers
Devon Dentler
Jo Kelly
Global Director of Creative Content
Kerry Keenan
Executive Directors of Content Production
Nathy Aviram
Lora Schulson
Advertising Agency
Y&R New York
Mobile Production
Goldrun
Brand Manager
Eric Dreyer
Client Vice President
Eric Dreyer
Client
Airwalk
Brand
Airwalk Jim

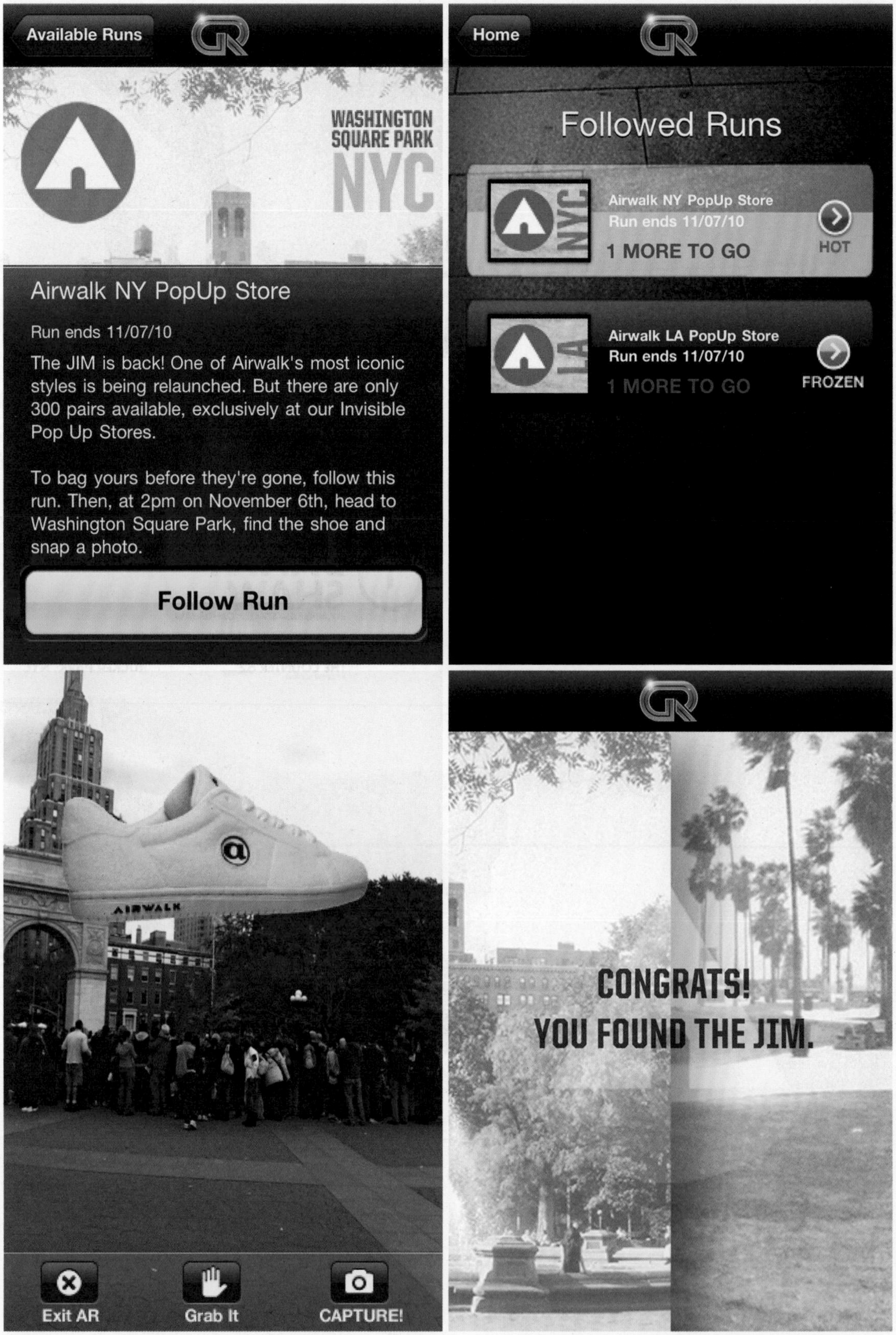
Available Runs
WASHINGTON SQUARE PARK
NYC
Airwalk NY PopUp Store
Run ends 11/07/10
The JIM is back! One of Airwalk's most iconic styles is being relaunched. But there are only 300 pairs available, exclusively at our Invisible Pop Up Stores.
To bag yours before they're gone, follow this run. Then, at 2pm on November 6th, head to Washington Square Park, find the shoe and snap a photo.
Follow Run
Home
Followed Runs
Airwalk NY PopUp Store
Run ends 11/07/10
1 MORE TO GO
HOT
Airwalk LA PopUp Store
Run ends 11/07/10
1 MORE TO GO
FROZEN
AIRWALK
Exit AR
Grab It
CAPTURE!
CONGRATS!
YOU FOUND THE JIM.

Yellow Pencil in Digital Design

B-Reel for Google Creative Lab

The Wilderness Downtown
This interactive interpretation of Arcade Fire's song 'We Used to Wait' was built entirely with the latest open web technologies, including HTML5 video, audio, and canvas. The story is told in multiple choreographed browser windows that pop up to reveal new scenes as the song unfolds. The video also borrows from Google's database of street images, personalising the experience for each viewer. By entering the address of their childhood homes before the song begins, viewers are treated to a narrative that takes place on the very streets where they grew up. Viewers are also able to control on-screen elements.

Creative Directors
Aaron Koblin
Chris Milk
Lead Developer
Mr.doob
Executive Producers
Jennifer Heath
Jon Kamen
Frank Scherma
Line Producer
Ari Palitz
Director
Chris Milk
Cinematographers
Shawn Kim
Chris Milk
Editor
Livio Sanchez
Colourist
Dave Hussey
Information Architect
Aaron Koblin
Interactive Production & Design
B-Reel
Production Company
@radical.media
3D Design
Magoo 3D Studios
Music & Sound
Arcade Fire
Client
Google Creative Lab
Brands
Google Chrome
HTML5

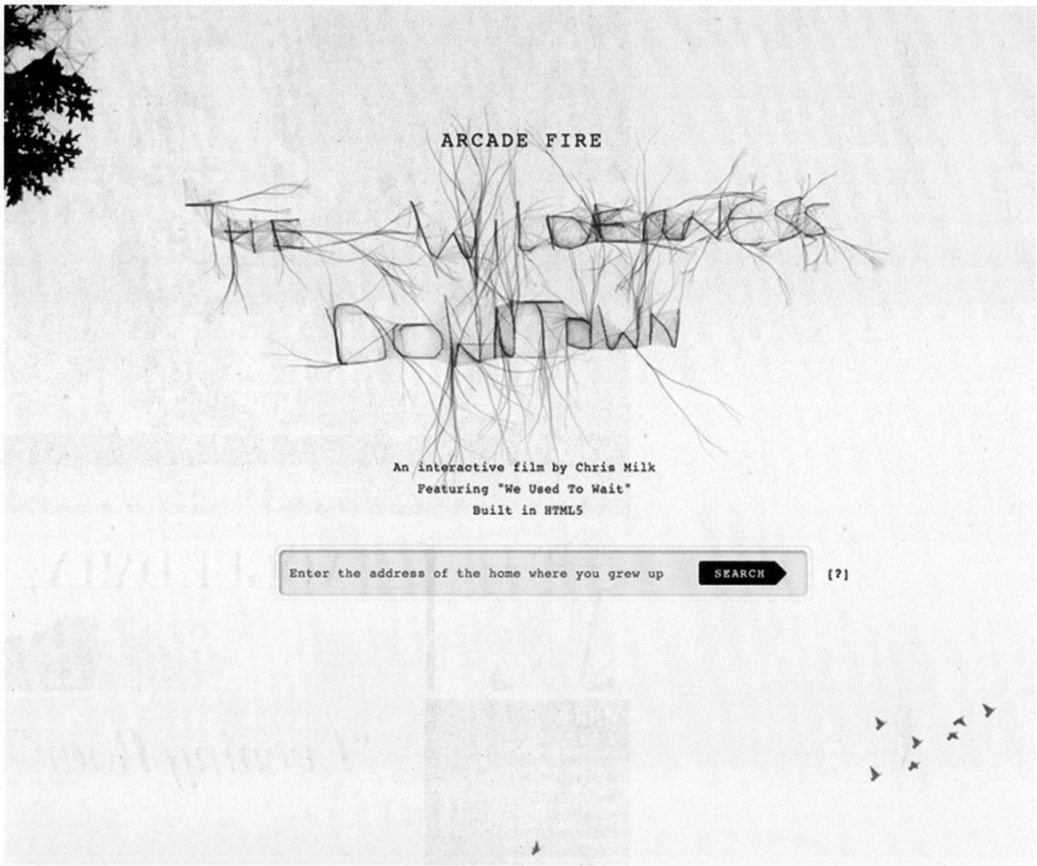
ARCADE FIRE
THE WILDERNESS DOWNTOWN
An interactive film by Chris Milk
Featuring "We Used To Wait"
Built in HTML5
Enter the address of the home where you grew up
SEARCH
[?]

Yellow Pencil in Digital Design

Graphic Design for Websites
Code and Theory
for Vogue

Vogue.com Redesign
Vogue tapped Code and Theory to develop an online experience as compelling as the iconic print magazine. Advancing its distinctive voice and authoritative positioning, the new Vogue.com presents a highly insightful perspective that no other source can offer. The site maximises Vogue's stunning photography, typography and video content to give the audience an editor's eye view of fashion culture. Over a five-month period, Code and Theory collaborated with Vogue to develop a new approach to narrative form and engagement, rich with custom sponsorship opportunities. The revitalised experience launched for New York's autumn fashion week in 2010.

Designer
Christina Rinaldi
Art Director
Stephane Elbaz
Creative Director
Chenta Yu
Executive Creative Director
Brandon Ralph
Chief Technical Officer
Nicholas Daniel-Richards
Senior User Experience Designer
Anthony Besada
Executive Director of User Experience
Dan Gardner
Lead Developers
Joseph Jorgensen
Vincent Tuscano
Developers
Ed Burnett
Chris Ewen
Aleksandr Fuzaylov
Gregg Meluski
Jon Rogoff
Producer
John Sampogna
Digital Innovation Agency
Code and Theory
Vice President of Strategy & Market Development
Suzanne Hader
Client Services Director
Mike Brady
Client
Vogue

VOGUE
McQUEEN AT THE MET
SEE THE PREVIEW OF "SAVAGE BEAUTY"
VOGUE.COM
LOGIN | REGISTER
SUBSCRIBE FASHION COLLECTIONS PARTIES CULTURE VIDEOS MAGAZINE PROMOTIONS
JUST IN
VOGUE DAILY
SUBSCRIBE
GIVE A GIFT
RENEW
INTERNATIONAL
VOGUE
Givenchy by Riccardo Tischi: Satin panther-print mini minaudière, $1,490, Barneys New York; 888.222.7639. Available August 2011.
Photo: Courtesy of Givenchy
CLOSE
"Evening Roar"
SHARE ADD TO LIGHTBOX
GIVENCHY
COLLECTIONS
just IN
PARTIES
ALT on Grace Coddington's 70th Birthday Party
FALL 2011 RTW
TIFFANY & CO.

Nomination in Digital Design

Websites
faberNovel & Les 84 for the RMN (La Réunion des Musées Nationaux)

Monet 2010
For the largest exhibition ever to be dedicated to Claude Monet at the Grand Palais in Paris, La Réunion des Musées Nationaux and faberNovel asked the studio Les 84 to relay the event online and create a genuine opportunity to dive into the heart of the impressionist master's incredible work. In order to best respond to the challenge of producing a site that is informative, but also one of playful discovery, it is divided into two major parts: a digital gallery and an interactive experience.

Art Directors
Hervé Bienaime
Olivier Bienaime
Creative Directors
Hervé Bienaime
Olivier Bienaime
Benoit Talabot
Technical Director
Jean-Vincent Roger
Copywriter
Nicolas Navarro
Agency Producers
Arnaud Depaul
Marie-Caroline Lanfranchi
Aurélien Pasquier
Sound Designer
Jean Pascal Travier
Digital Agencies
faberNovel
Les 84
Brand Managers
Virginie D'Allens
Axelle Beth
Henri Bovet
Pascale Sillard
Client
RMN (La Réunion des Musées Nationaux)

MONET
GALERIES NATIONALES, GRAND PALAIS, PARIS
22 SEPTEMBER 2010 – 24 JANUARY 2011
HOME
GALLERY
JOURNEY
WEB TV & TWITTER
PRACTICAL INFORMATIONS
Practical Informations
GALLERY
Discover the paintings on show in the "Claude Monet (1840-1926)" exhibition, Galeries nationales, Grand Palais.
JOURNEY
Monet's work at a glance through a unique digital experience
Web TV & Twitter
YOUTH SPACE
ONLINE SHOP
ALL RIGHTS RESERVED © RMN

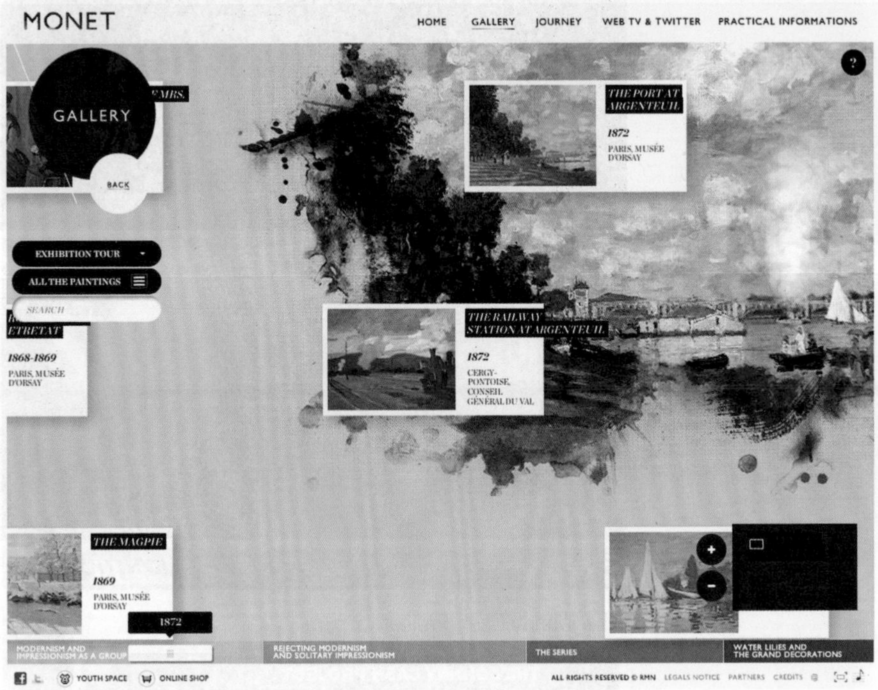
MONET
HOME
GALLERY
JOURNEY
WEB TV & TWITTER
PRACTICAL INFORMATIONS
GALLERY
BACK
THE PORT AT ARGENTEUIL
1872
PARIS, MUSÉE D'ORSAY
EXHIBITION TOUR
ALL THE PAINTINGS
SEARCH
ETRETAT
1868-1869
PARIS, MUSÉE D'ORSAY
THE RAILWAY STATION AT ARGENTEUIL
1872
CERGY-PONTOISE, CONSEIL GÉNÉRAL DU VAL
THE MAGPIE
1869
PARIS, MUSÉE D'ORSAY
1872
MODERNISM AND IMPRESSIONISM AS A GROUP
REJECTING MODERNISM AND SOLITARY IMPRESSIONISM
THE SERIES
WATER LILIES AND THE GRAND DECORATIONS
YOUTH SPACE
ONLINE SHOP
ALL RIGHTS RESERVED © RMN

MONET
THE MAGPIE

MONET
IN NORWEGIAN
NEXT

Nomination in Digital Design

Websites
Milk+Koblin for American Recordings & Lost Highway Records

The Johnny Cash Project
This project was a global collective artwork. Beginning with a single video frame as a template, and using a custom drawing tool embedded in the site, viewers create their own personal portraits of the Man in Black. Their work is combined with art from participants around the world, and integrated into a collective whole: a crowd-sourced, interactive music video for the song 'Ain't No Grave'. Strung together and played in sequence over the song, the portraits create a moving, evolving homage to a beloved musical icon. As people discover and contribute to the project, this living portrait continues to transform and grow.

Creative Directors
Aaron Koblin
Chris Milk
Design Director
James Spindler
Technical Director
Aaron Koblin
Interactive Designer
Frank Campanella
Lead Flash Developer
Jesse Freeman
Lead Developer
Mr.doob
Lead Software Engineer
Avery Brooks
Director
Chris Milk
Producers
Aaron Koblin
Chris Milk
Senior Interactive Producer
James Calhoun
Executive Producers
Jennifer Heath
Jon Kamen
Rick Rubin
Evan Schechtman
Associate Producer
Naomi Gilbert
Visual Effects Designer
Simon Brewster
Editor
Akiko Iwakawa
Digital Creative Agency
Milk+Koblin
Production Companies
@radical.media
Milk+Koblin
Record Companies
American Recordings
Lost Highway Records
Video Commissioner
Retta Harvery
Clients
American Recordings
Lost Highway Records

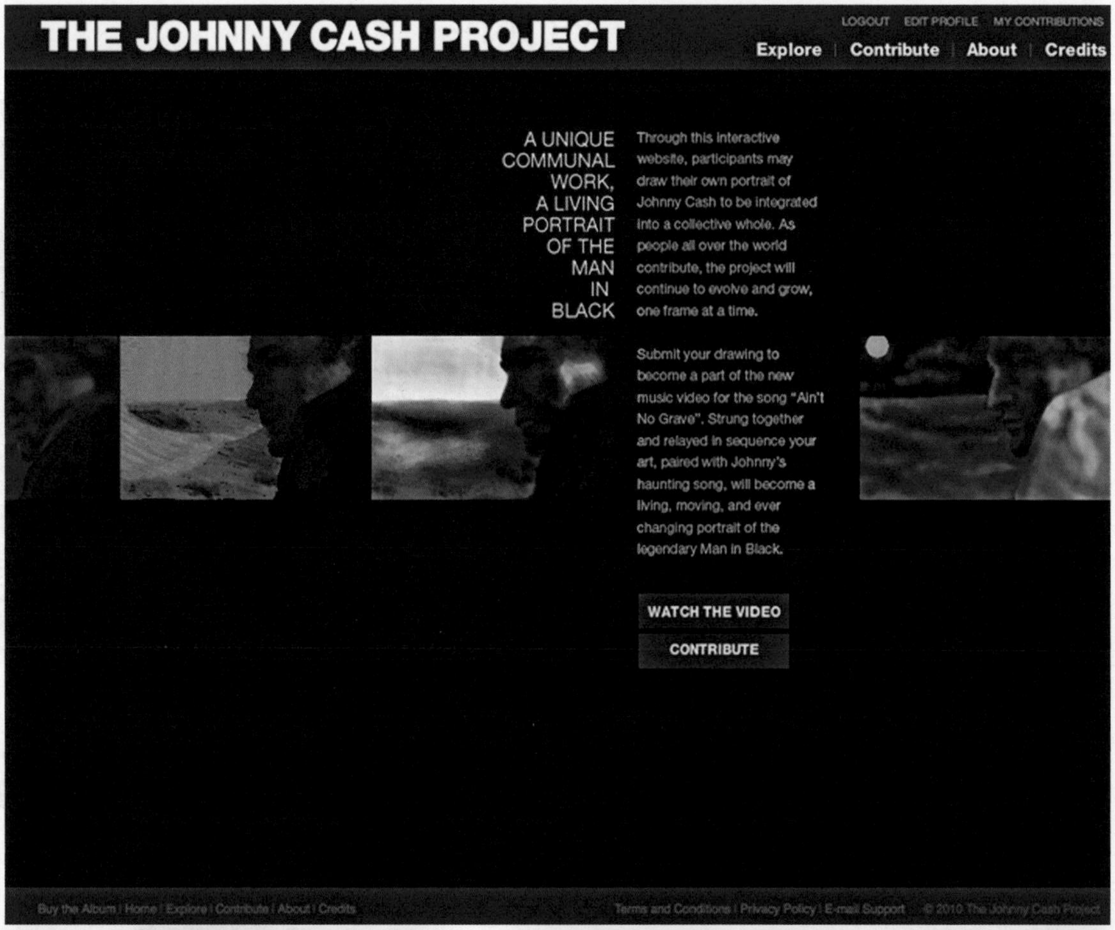
THE JOHNNY CASH PROJECT
LOGOUT EDIT PROFILE MY CONTRIBUTIONS
Explore | Contribute | About | Credits
A UNIQUE COMMUNAL WORK, A LIVING PORTRAIT OF THE MAN IN BLACK
Through this interactive website, participants may draw their own portrait of Johnny Cash to be integrated into a collective whole. As people all over the world contribute, the project will continue to evolve and grow, one frame at a time.
Submit your drawing to become a part of the new music video for the song "Ain't No Grave". Strung together and relayed in sequence your art, paired with Johnny's haunting song, will become a living, moving, and ever changing portrait of the legendary Man in Black.
WATCH THE VIDEO
CONTRIBUTE
Buy the Album | Home | Explore | Contribute | About | Credits
Terms and Conditions | Privacy Policy | E-mail Support © 2010 The Johnny Cash Project

FWA
AWARDS DOCK JOBS EDITORIAL SUBMIT YOUR PROJECT
IGNITIO
The Johnny Cash Project
SITE OF THE DAY MAY 21 2010
THE JOHNNY CASH PROJECT
Explore Contribute About
Frame #721
PREV FRAME
NEXT FRAME
BACK TO VIDEO
DRAW THIS FRAME

CASH PROJECT
REGISTER / SIGN IN
Explore | Contribute | About | Credits
Frame #583
Artist: Fin Cramb
Location: Edinburgh (Scotland), United Kingdom
Style: Realistic
Drawing Time: 01 : 16 : 24
Brush Stroke Count: 4324
Rating:
PREV FRAME
NEXT FRAME
BACK TO VIDEO
DRAW THIS FRAME
SHARE
FRAME: 583

Nomination in Digital Design

Interface & Navigation for Websites
Grip Limited

Grip Limited Website
The Grip Limited site presents the work of this Toronto based advertising agency in a playful and engaging way. Gracefully scaling up to fill large displays, the site combines campaign case studies and agency information with an eccentric mix of odd facts populated by real-time employee survey data. The content is arranged in a series of collapsible columns, with many navigation options available to ensure the unorthodox structure is as intuitive and easy to use as possible. From the bizarre facts, to the dense typography, rambling copy, and scratchable radio spots, the site rewards a spirit of exploration.

Interactive Designer
Jason Pearl
Art Director
Colin Craig
Creative Director
Colin Craig
Flash Developer
Heung Lee
Technical Director
Ben Huxley
Technical Developers
Brian Ayzenman
Jeremy Keston
Copywriters
Jeff Collins
Colin Craig
Agency Producer
Ruby Zagorskis
Advertising Agency
Grip Limited
Client
Grip Limited

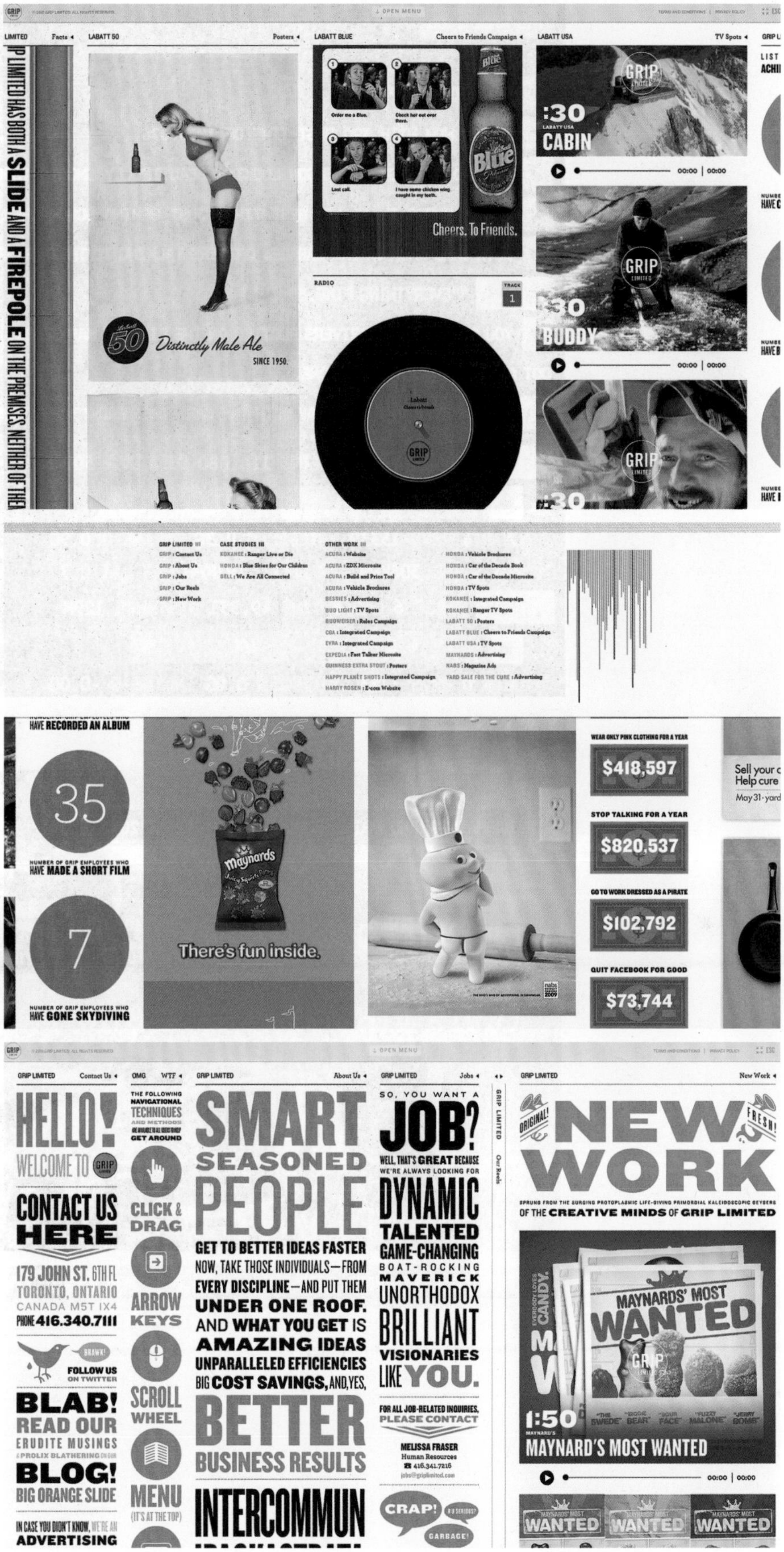
GRIP LIMITED HAS BOTH A SLIDE AND A FIREPOLE ON THE PREMISES. NEITHER OF THEM
LABATT 50
LABATT BLUE
Cheers to Friends Campaign
LABATT USA
TV Spots
Distinctly Male Ale
SINCE 1950.
Cheers. To Friends.
RADIO
:30
CABIN
:30
BUDDY
HAVE RECORDED AN ALBUM
35
NUMBER OF GRIP EMPLOYEES WHO HAVE MADE A SHORT FILM
7
NUMBER OF GRIP EMPLOYEES WHO HAVE GONE SKYDIVING
There's fun inside.
WEAR ONLY PINK CLOTHING FOR A YEAR
$418,597
STOP TALKING FOR A YEAR
$820,537
GO TO WORK DRESSED AS A PIRATE
$102,792
QUIT FACEBOOK FOR GOOD
$73,744
HELLO!
WELCOME TO
CONTACT US HERE
179 JOHN ST. 6TH FL
TORONTO, ONTARIO
CANADA M5T 1X4
PHONE 416.340.7111
FOLLOW US ON TWITTER
BLAB! READ OUR ERUDITE MUSINGS
BLOG!
BIG ORANGE SLIDE
IN CASE YOU DIDN'T KNOW, WE'RE AN ADVERTISING
THE FOLLOWING NAVIGATIONAL TECHNIQUES AND METHODS
GET AROUND
CLICK & DRAG
ARROW KEYS
SCROLL WHEEL
MENU
(IT'S AT THE TOP)
SMART SEASONED PEOPLE
GET TO BETTER IDEAS FASTER
NOW, TAKE THOSE INDIVIDUALS—FROM EVERY DISCIPLINE—AND PUT THEM UNDER ONE ROOF.
AND WHAT YOU GET IS AMAZING IDEAS
UNPARALLELED EFFICIENCIES
BIG COST SAVINGS, AND, YES,
BETTER BUSINESS RESULTS
INTERCOMMUN
SO, YOU WANT A JOB?
WELL, THAT'S GREAT BECAUSE WE'RE ALWAYS LOOKING FOR
DYNAMIC
TALENTED
GAME-CHANGING
BOAT-ROCKING
MAVERICK
UNORTHODOX
BRILLIANT
VISIONARIES
LIKE YOU.
FOR ALL JOB-RELATED INQUIRIES, PLEASE CONTACT
MELISSA FRASER
Human Resources
416.341.7216
CRAP!
GARBAGE!
NEW WORK
OF THE CREATIVE MINDS OF GRIP LIMITED
MAYNARDS' MOST WANTED
1:50
MAYNARD'S MOST WANTED
WANTED

● Nomination in Digital Design

Work Club for Vodafone McLaren Mercedes

McLaren F1 Racing Team: The Race 1.0b
Formula 1 is an exclusive sport, closely tied up with TV broadcasting agreements, but fans are always desperate to know more. The brief was to bring fans closer to the team, so 'The Race 1.0b' was created: a live status update from the cars and team. Direct from behind the scenes at McLaren, wherever they are. Now you know exactly what they know, to the 100th of a second. It's the perfect second screen to enhance the live broadcast; it looks just like McLaren's pit screens, but is simple enough for a fan to follow. Come along for The Race.

Designer
Kristian Saliba
Art Director
Fabian Braun
Creative Directors
Eduardo de Felipe
Ben Mooge
Andy Sandoz
Technical Director
Adrian Rowbotham
Copywriter
Simon Bird
Agency Producer
Josh Tenser
Digital Agency
Work Club
Digital Production Company
Pirata
Client Head of Digital
Derek Harbinson
Client
Vodafone McLaren Mercedes

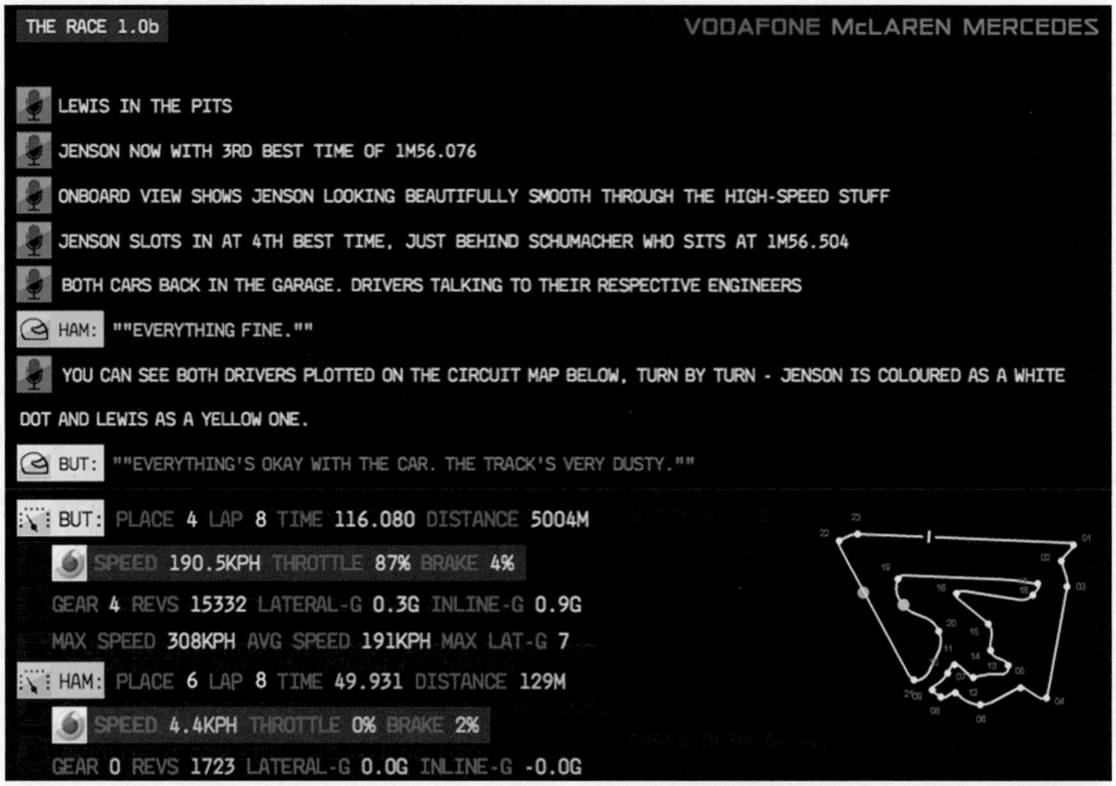
THE RACE 1.0b
VODAFONE McLAREN MERCEDES
LEWIS IN THE PITS
JENSON NOW WITH 3RD BEST TIME OF 1M56.076
ONBOARD VIEW SHOWS JENSON LOOKING BEAUTIFULLY SMOOTH THROUGH THE HIGH-SPEED STUFF
JENSON SLOTS IN AT 4TH BEST TIME, JUST BEHIND SCHUMACHER WHO SITS AT 1M56.504
BOTH CARS BACK IN THE GARAGE. DRIVERS TALKING TO THEIR RESPECTIVE ENGINEERS
HAM: ""EVERYTHING FINE.""
YOU CAN SEE BOTH DRIVERS PLOTTED ON THE CIRCUIT MAP BELOW, TURN BY TURN - JENSON IS COLOURED AS A WHITE DOT AND LEWIS AS A YELLOW ONE.
BUT: ""EVERYTHING'S OKAY WITH THE CAR. THE TRACK'S VERY DUSTY.""
BUT: PLACE 4 LAP 8 TIME 116.080 DISTANCE 5004M
SPEED 190.5KPH THROTTLE 87% BRAKE 4%
GEAR 4 REVS 15332 LATERAL-G 0.3G INLINE-G 0.9G
MAX SPEED 308KPH AVG SPEED 191KPH MAX LAT-G 7
HAM: PLACE 6 LAP 8 TIME 49.931 DISTANCE 129M
SPEED 4.4KPH THROTTLE 0% BRAKE 2%
GEAR 0 REVS 1723 LATERAL-G 0.0G INLINE-G -0.0G

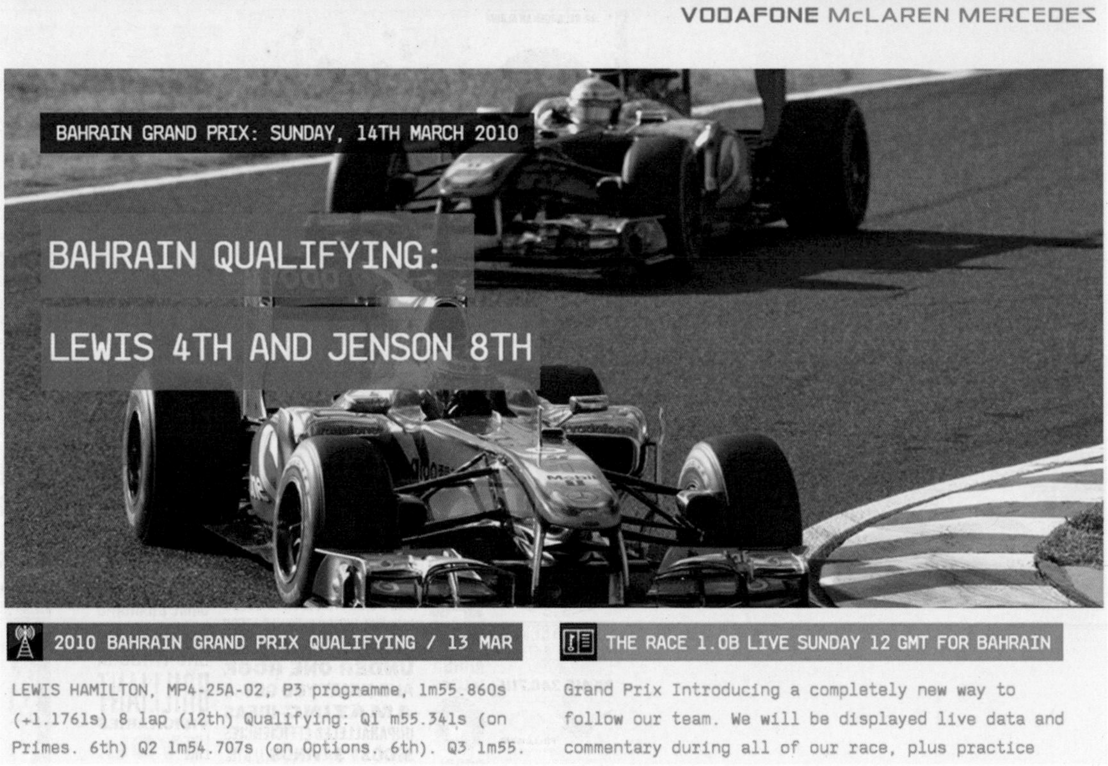
VODAFONE McLAREN MERCEDES
BAHRAIN GRAND PRIX: SUNDAY, 14TH MARCH 2010
BAHRAIN QUALIFYING:
LEWIS 4TH AND JENSON 8TH
2010 BAHRAIN GRAND PRIX QUALIFYING / 13 MAR
LEWIS HAMILTON, MP4-25A-02, P3 programme, 1m55.860s (+1.1761s) 8 lap (12th) Qualifying: Q1 m55.341s (on Primes. 6th) Q2 1m54.707s (on Options. 6th). Q3 1m55.
THE RACE 1.0B LIVE SUNDAY 12 GMT FOR BAHRAIN
Grand Prix Introducing a completely new way to follow our team. We will be displayed live data and commentary during all of our race, plus practice

Nomination in Digital Design

DDB Paris for the INPES

Attraction

Attraction is an anti-smoking interactive anime commissioned by the French health education institute INPES, to raise awareness about tobacco companies manipulating today's youth. As France is the second largest market in the world for Japanese animation, Attraction speaks in a familiar voice to French adolescents, without being a patronising or stern government communication. To meet the expectations of teens who grew up with anime, we worked with Koji Morimoto, one of the directors of 'The Animatrix' and animation director of the infamous film 'Akira'.

Art Directors
Alexander Kalchev
Siavosh Zabeti
Creative Directors
Alexander Kalchev
Siavosh Zabeti
Executive Creative Director
Alexandre Hervé
Technical Director
Yates Buckley
Lead Developer
David Hartono
Interactive Directors
Anrick Bregman
Takayoshi Kishimoto
Copywriters
Alexander Kalchev
Siavosh Zabeti
Director
Koji Morimoto
Integrated Producer
Guillaume Cossou
Executive Producers
Piero Frescobaldi
Eiko Tanaka
Music Composer
Fred Avril
Sound Mixer
Raphael Fruchard
Voice Director
Clement Reynaud
Advertising Agency
DDB Paris
Animation Studio
Studio 4°C
Interactive Production Company
unit9
Sound Production Company
THE
Music Composition
Danger
Account Executive
Mathieu Roux
Board Account Director
Orane Faivre de Condé
Client
INPES

PRÉSENTEZ UN OBJET DE LA COULEUR DEMANDÉE À LA CAMÉRA.
注意

Nomination in Digital Design

Herraiz Soto & Co
for Camper

Have a Camper Day for iPad
Why are weather applications so boring? 'Extraordinary craft' is how Camper understands technology: half imagination, half craft. To communicate this concept in a friendly, original and non-intrusive way, we reconsidered how we receive weather forecasts today (boring and lifeless interfaces and icons). As a result we created new meteorological elements made from prêt-à-porter materials and we turned them into musical instruments that react to touch. Haven't got an iPad? Enjoy it on the web!

Designers
Sergio Puertas
Esteve Traveset
Vicky Walker
Art Director
Esteve Traveset
Creative Directors
Vicente Reyes
Rafa Soto
Esteve Traveset
Technical Director
Cay Garrido
Copywriter
Vicente Reyes
Sound Designer
Carlos Torrecilla
Advertising Agency
Herraiz Soto & Co
Planner
Oliver Henares
Account Handler
Robert Aran
Account Executive
Paulina Arana
Marketing Manager
Pere Quintana
Client
Camper

HAVE A CAMPER DAY

Have a Camper day
Barcelona
14°

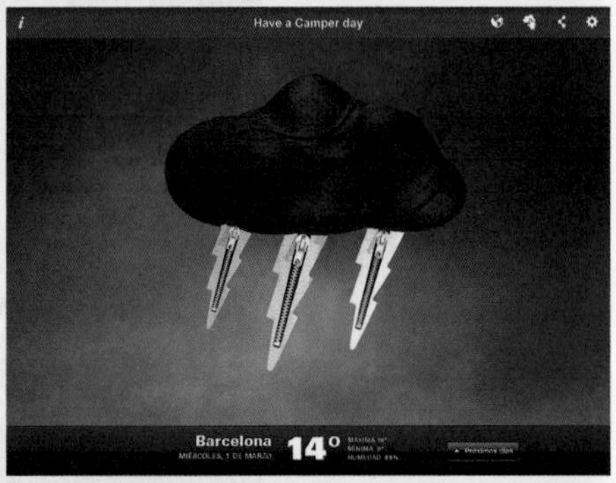
Have a Camper day
Barcelona
14°

Have a Camper day
Barcelona
MIÉRCOLES, 1 DE MARZO
14°
MÁXIMA 18°
MÍNIMA 9°
HUMEDAD 66%
Próximos días

Websites
Modernista! for Boulder Digital Works

Boulder Digital Works
The Boulder Digital Works website is both informative and social, a place where students, faculty and top industry professionals post their favourite websites, work and comments. It is a destination for like-minded creatives and students to find the latest in digital innovation and conversations from a real industry community, while also giving prospective students or professionals the opportunity to learn more about the digital training and education the school has to offer.

Interactive Designer Matt St Gelais
Art Director Brian Leech
Creative Director Gary Koepke
Interactive Creative Director Xavier Teo
Technical Director Matt Howell
Programmer Dee Blake
Developer Michael Jordan
Copywriter Samantha Gutglass
Agency Producer Ryan Harms
Advertising Agency Modernista!
Brand Manager David Slayden
Client Boulder Digital Works

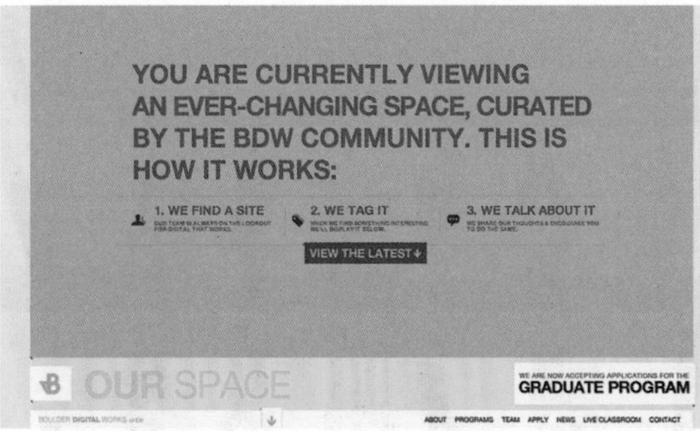
YOU ARE CURRENTLY VIEWING AN EVER-CHANGING SPACE, CURATED BY THE BDW COMMUNITY. THIS IS HOW IT WORKS:
1. WE FIND A SITE
2. WE TAG IT
3. WE TALK ABOUT IT
VIEW THE LATEST
OUR SPACE
GRADUATE PROGRAM

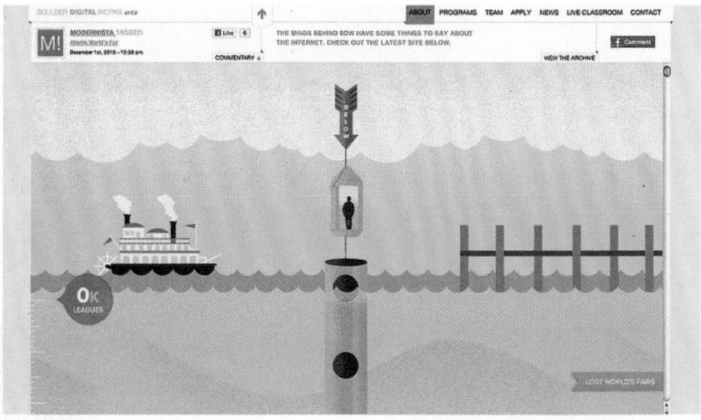

ISLE OF TUNE
What?
How?
View Islands
Create Island

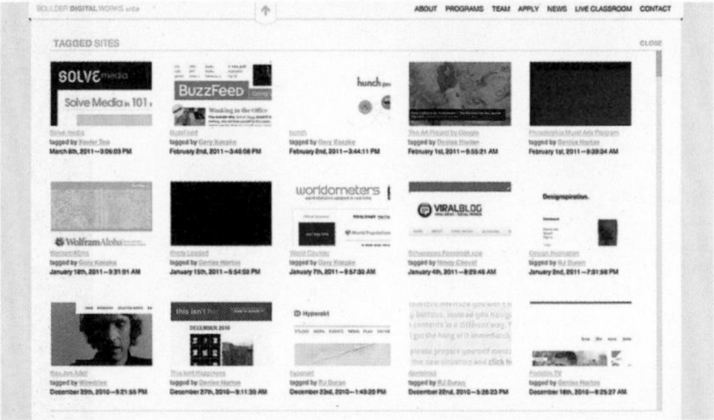
TAGGED SITES

Websites
Soon in Tokyo for Elisava

I Am Not an Artist
'I Am Not an Artist' is an animated .gif paranoia about nonstop design workers. A platform to engage with and spread fun and content to young designers and creatives all over the world. It was conceived for the Barcelona design school Elisava, for future design workers to communicate the school's philosophy of hard daily work, challenging the perception that designers live out their inspirations.

Designer Thiago Monteiro
Art Director Javi Donada
Creative Directors Javi Donada, Angelo Palma
Developer Jesus Gollonet
Copywriter Angelo Palma
Animation Directors Matt Cooper, Johnny Kelly
Sound Designer Cristiano Nicollini
Advertising Agency Soon in Tokyo
Account Handler Nuria Guinovart
Brand Manager Anna Salvador
Marketing Manager Martha Carrio
Client Elisava

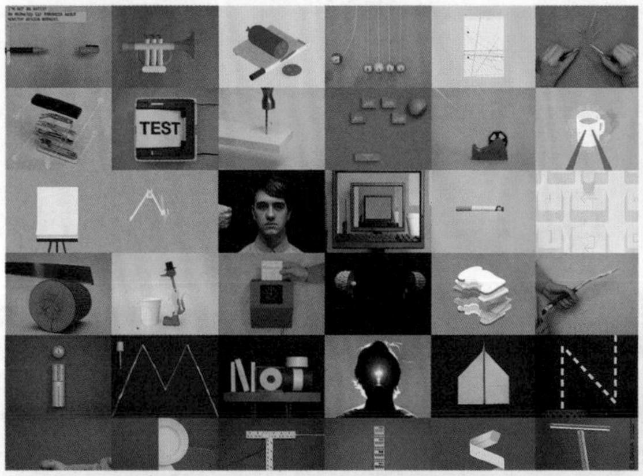
TEST

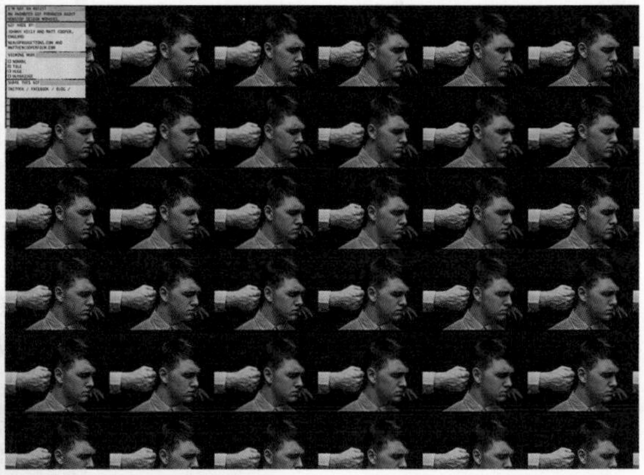

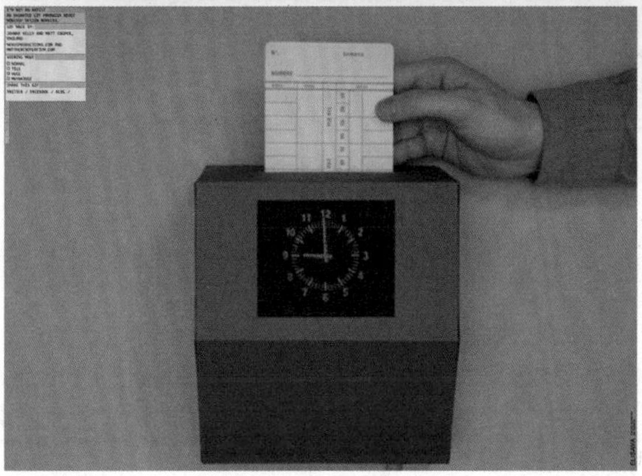

Interface & Navigation
for Websites
altima° for Jules

Jules Online Shop
The French casual menswear brand Jules launched its online shop. The website offers sleek and stylish graphic design, large and creatively presented product shots, and a sophisticated yet simple merchandising plan. Overall, a seamless and exceptional shopping experience.

Design Director
Thomas Tonder
Art Director
Anne Prenelle
Creative Director
Stéphane Lecouturier
Digital Agency
altima°
Technical Project Manager
Jean-Christophe Roussel
Project Managers
Emilie Hornac
Jonathan Speissegger
Account Director
Yann Puslecki
Account Manager
Adeline Lamblin
Client
Jules

Jules
LA MODE BY JULES
PRODUITS
OFFRES DU MOMENT
CLUB JULES
SERVICES
MAGASINS
mon Panier
LIVRAISON EN MAGASIN OFFERTE pour toute commande
//COLLECTION PRINTEMPS-ÉTÉ11//
PRÉSENTATION DES SILHOUETTES PHARES DE L'ENTRÉE DE SAISON.
DU STYLE, DU FUN ET TOUJOURS PLUS DE MODE.
EN SAVOIR PLUS SUR JULES
TOUT LE CATALOGUE JULES
LA PLAYLIST JULES
NOS AUTRES SITES

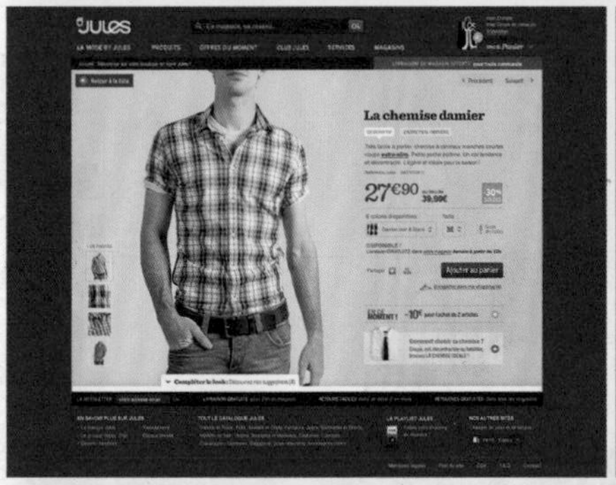
La chemise damier

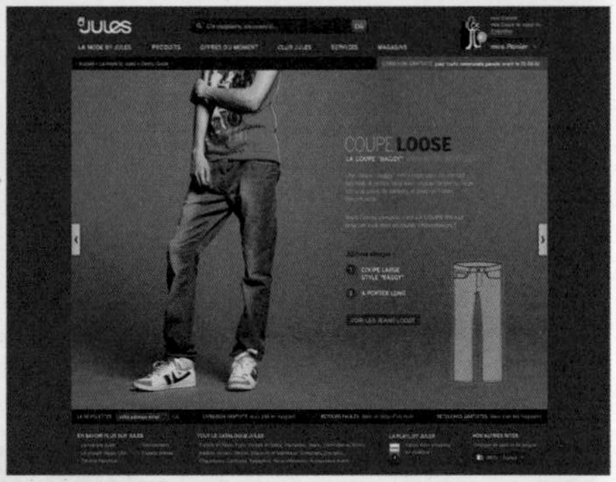
COUPE LOOSE

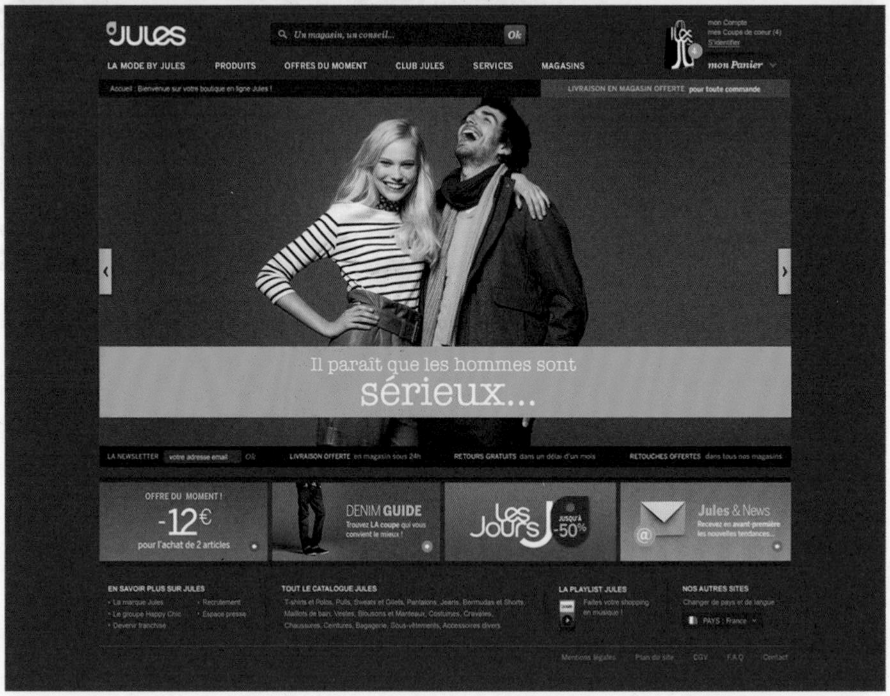
Jules
LA MODE BY JULES
PRODUITS
OFFRES DU MOMENT
CLUB JULES
SERVICES
MAGASINS
mon Panier
LIVRAISON EN MAGASIN OFFERTE pour toute commande
Il paraît que les hommes sont
sérieux...
OFFRE DU MOMENT !
-12€
pour l'achat de 2 articles
DENIM GUIDE
Les Jours J
-50%
Jules & News
EN SAVOIR PLUS SUR JULES
TOUT LE CATALOGUE JULES
LA PLAYLIST JULES
NOS AUTRES SITES

Interface & Navigation for Websites
AID-DCC & Katamari for Asher Roth

AsherRothMusic.com
American Hip Hop artist Asher Roth wanted to connect with his fans, so a website was created that he could take with him wherever he goes. Literally. The interface of his website is printed on a wallet-sized card. When Asher or his friends take a photo displaying that card, that photo gets uploaded to become the top page of AsherRothMusic.com. Using an advanced image recognition program created specifically for the site, all of the site's features then emerge from the surface of the card, seamlessly merging Asher's offline world with his online presence.

Designers
Yuri Morimoto
Masayuki Nishimu
Art Directors
Masa Kawamura
Hal Kirkland
Flash Programmers
Kenji Mori
Saqoosha
Programmers
Masaru Kinoshita
Saqoosha
Creative Directors
Masa Kawamura
Hal Kirkland
Technical Director
Saqoosha
Agency Producers
Yusuke Tominaga
David Wilsher
Illustrators
Yuri Morimoto
Yumi Yamada
Digital Agencies
AID-DCC
Katamari
Creative Agency
Hal & Masa & Brad & Lindsay & Dave
Account Handlers
Brad Haugen
Lindsay Kopec
Project Managers
David Wilsher
Yoko Yamazaki
Client
Asher Roth

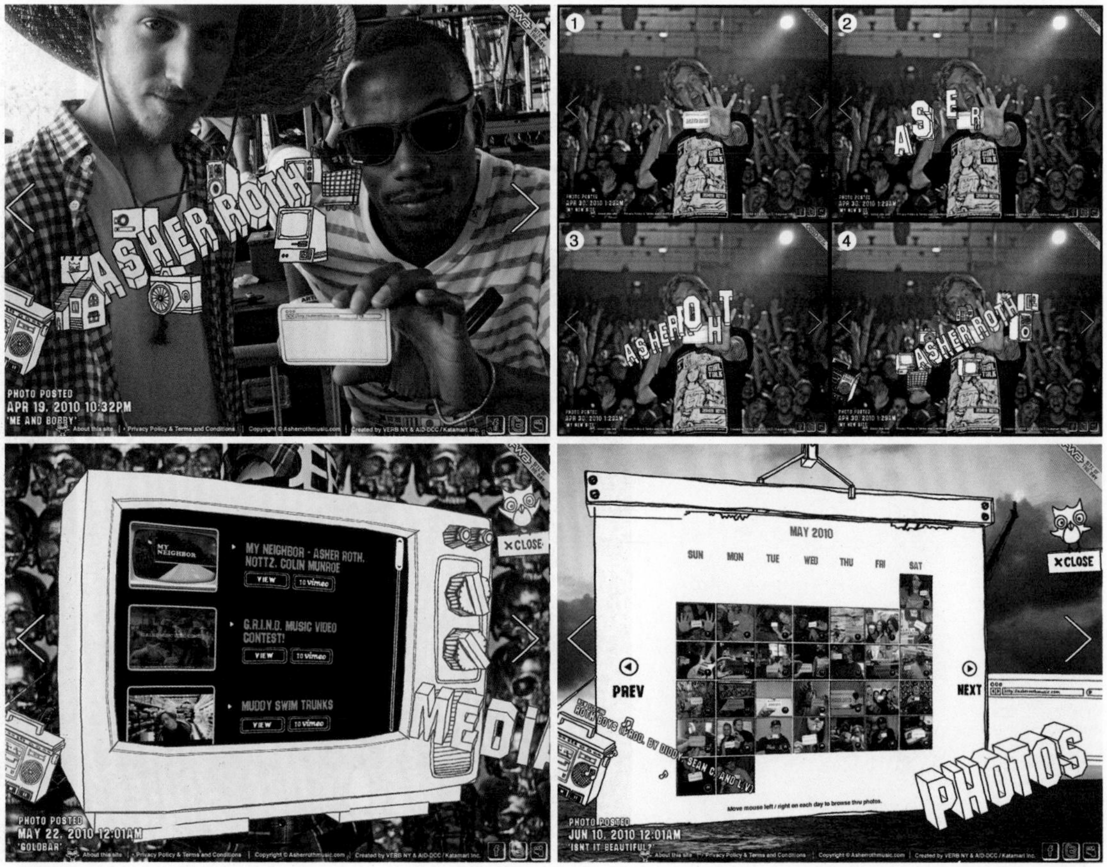
ASHER ROTH
PHOTO POSTED
APR 19. 2010 10:32PM
'ME AND BOBBY'
MY NEIGHBOR - ASHER ROTH, NOTTZ, COLIN MUNROE
G.R.I.N.D. MUSIC VIDEO CONTEST!
MUDDY SWIM TRUNKS
×CLOSE
MEDIA
PHOTO POSTED
MAY 22. 2010 12:01AM
MAY 2010
SUN MON TUE WED THU FRI SAT
PREV
NEXT
PHOTOS
PHOTO POSTED
JUN 10. 2010 12:01AM
'ISNT IT BEAUTIFUL'

Interface & Navigation for Websites
Grimm Gallun Holtappels

The Grimm Gallun Holtappels Website
This is our advertising agency's new homepage. It all begins in our pub, like in real life. The content is concealed behind beer mats with a design based on our logo. What's new is the combination of tracked camera pans and Flash interface in 3D. We want our online appearance to delight our customers and our colleagues in the industry, and champion our capabilities in online creation.

Art Director
Matthias Netzberger
Creative Director
Matthias M Mueller
Motion Designer
Matthias Schulz
Programmer
Matthias Schulz
Advertising Agency
Grimm Gallun Holtappels
Client
Grimm Gallun Holtappels

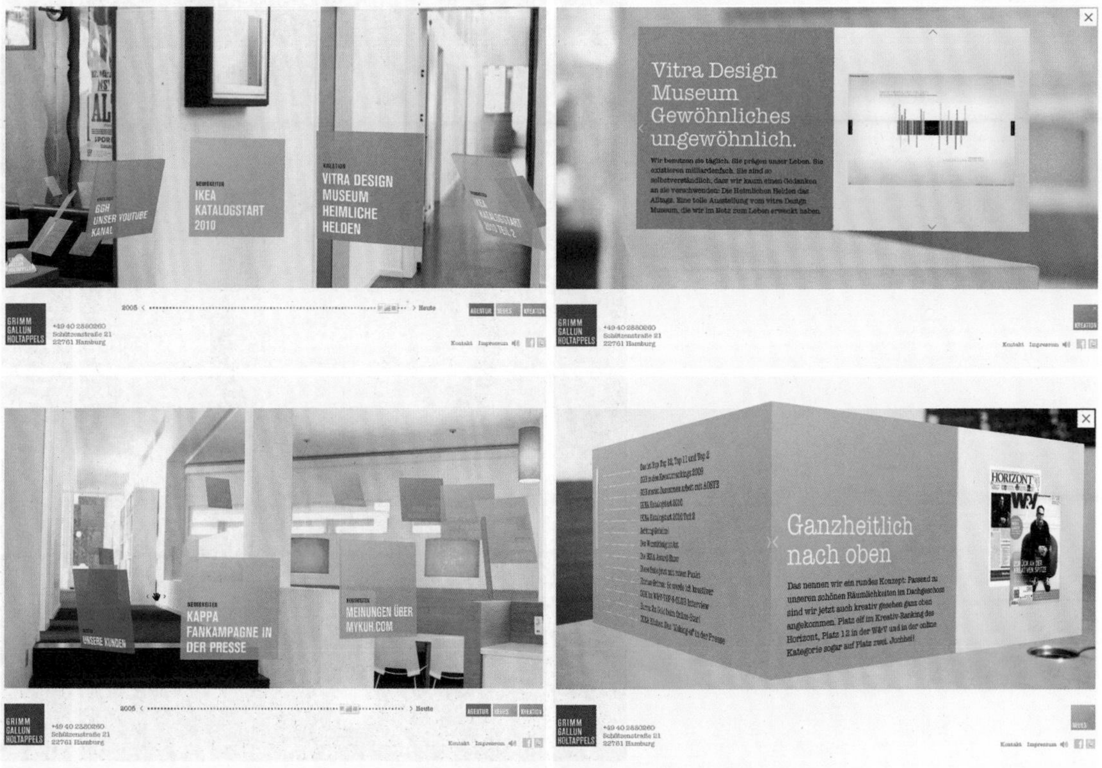
IKEA KATALOGSTART 2010
VITRA DESIGN MUSEUM HEIMLICHE HELDEN
Vitra Design Museum Gewöhnliches ungewöhnlich.
GRIMM GALLUN HOLTAPPELS
KAPPA FANKAMPAGNE IN DER PRESSE
MEINUNGEN ÜBER MYKUH.COM
UNSERE KUNDEN
Ganzheitlich nach oben

Digital Design
Dare for Penguin Books

myFry
To launch the second instalment of Stephen Fry's autobiography, we created an iPhone app giving readers a new way of reading a book. The app takes the traditional art of reading and transforms it for the 21st century. Instead of reading the book from front to back, readers can use a tagged index to select chunks of the book according to subject matter, and read in a non-linear manner. Called myFry, it went to the top of the UK App Store and remains in the all-time top 30 paid-for apps.

Design Director
Ron Siemerink
Designer
Stefanie Posavec
Creative Director
Flo Heiss
Developers
James Mitchell
Joe Nash
Information Architect
John Gibbard
Advertising Agency
Dare
Account Handlers
Seth Campbell
Liza Wostmann
Brand Manager
Anna Rafferty
Client
Penguin Books

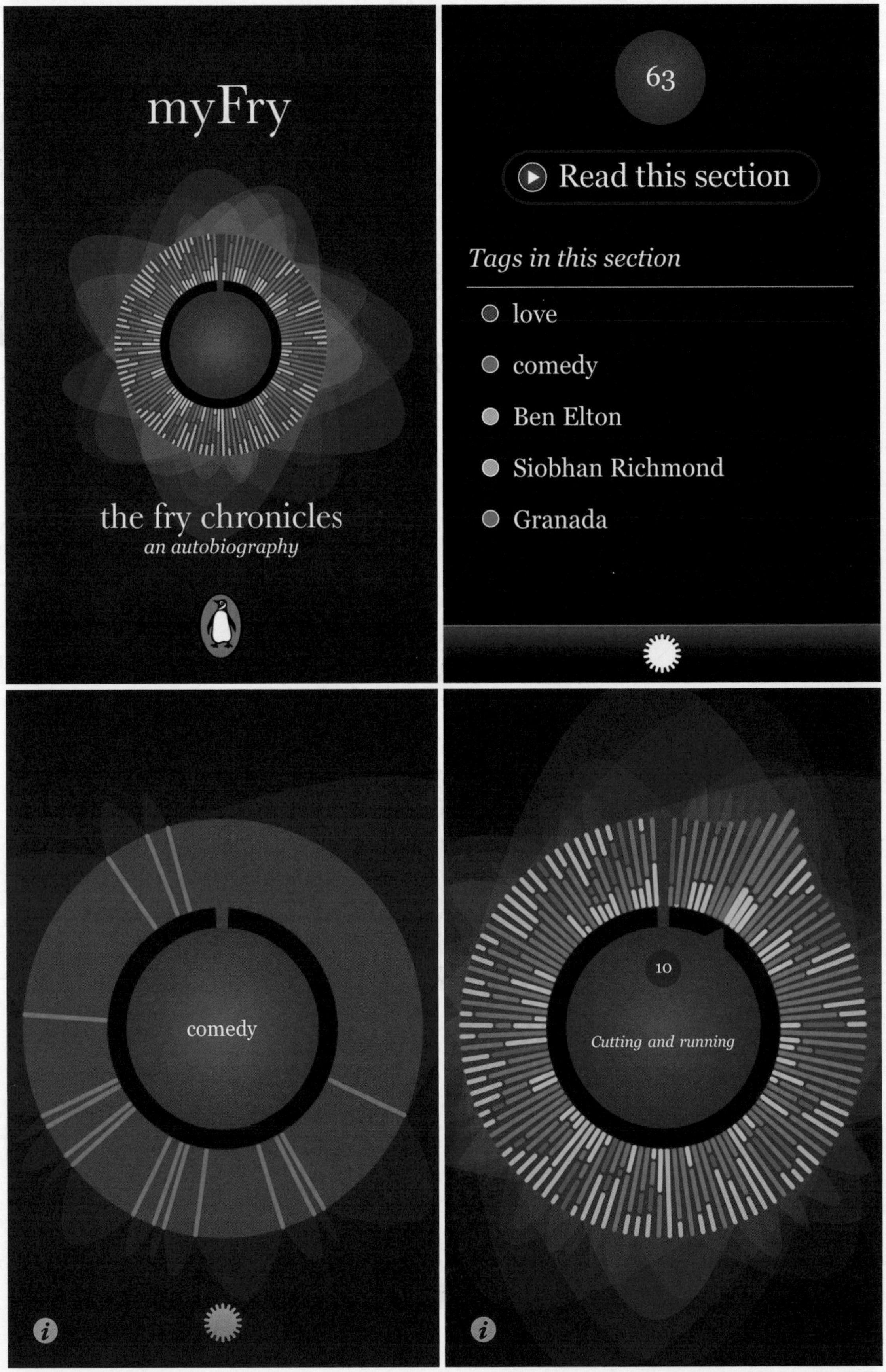
myFry
the fry chronicles
an autobiography
63
Read this section
Tags in this section
love
comedy
Ben Elton
Siobhan Richmond
Granada
comedy
10
Cutting and running

Digital Design
Masashi+Qanta
+Saqoosha+Hiroki
for Zenith Co

SOUR/MIRROR
This is an interactive music video for Japanese band SOUR. The song 'Mirror' is about the fact that everything around you is a mirror that reflects who you are. This gave us the idea of a journey to find yourself through your connections with people online. By connecting via their Facebook, Twitter and webcam, the video is customised for every viewer, based on their personal data and social networking status. We also raised the production budget through Kickstarter, and allowed @SOUR_official's Twitter followers to become part of the colour pixels in the video.

Designer
Masashi Kawamura
Art Director
Masashi Kawamura
Creative Director
Masashi Kawamura
Technical Director
Qanta Shimizu
Flash Programmers
Yuma Murakami
Saqoosha
Qanta Shimizu
Directors
Masashi Kawamura
Hiroki Ono
Saqoosha
Qanta Shimizu
Film Producers
Hisaya Kato
Yasuhito Nakae
Artist
SOUR
Digital Agency
Masashi+Qanta
+Saqoosha+Hiroki
Record Company
Zenith Co
Film Project Manager
Hidetoshi Nagamine
Client
Zenith Co
Brand
SOUR

SOUR / MIRROR
facebook
Hiroki Ono

Digital Design
Jung von Matt/next
for WWF Deutschland

Save as WWF
Millions of square metres of rain forest are cleared every year, for paper on which pointless documents are printed out. To raise global awareness of the destruction this causes, we invented the WWF – a file format that cannot be printed out. Every individual, company and organisation can join in by simply downloading, using and sharing WWF files. Our message: save as WWF, save a tree. After four weeks, 200,000 users from 183 countries had visited the website and downloaded the software over 30,000 times.

Art Directors
Michael Kittel
Alexander Norvilas
Michael Seifert
Creative Directors
Sven Loskill
Jan Rexhausen
Doerte Spengler-Ahrens
Web Designer
Tom Schallberger
Technical Directors
Simone Bitzer
Susanne zu Eicken
Programmers
Lana Nugent
Florian Paul
Copywriters
Lisa Glock
Henning Müller-Dannhausen
Agency Producer
Lana Nugent
Editor
Florian Panier
Sound Engineers
Klaas Nocken
Rose Tribble
Gerrit Winterstein
Digital Agency
Jung von Matt/next
Advertising Agency
Jung von Matt/Fleet
Account Handler
Benjamin Wenke
Brand Manager
Dr Dirk Reinsberg
Client
WWF Deutschland

WWF
Think before you print
A new green file format:
WWF
The WWF format is a PDF that cannot be printed out. It's a simple way to avoid unnecessary printing. So here's your chance to save trees and help the environment. Decide for yourself which documents don't need printing out – then simply save them as WWF.
SAVE AS WWF, SAVE A TREE
Click here to learn all about the WWF format...
Download WWF software for free now
For Mac OS X 10.4+
For Windows ab XP
How can I participate?
1. Download free software to support the WWF format.
2. Save your document as WWF and send it out.
Information for individual users
Information for companies/organisations
Who`s already involved?
More than 53,000 companies, organizations and individuals have already downloaded the WWF software – all over the world.
Read more
Save as wwf – save ressources – save a tree
WWF has long worked with companies and consumers to promote responsible paper use and the option to "Save as WWF" compliments and reinforces other well-established campaigns – most notably the "Think Before You Print" initiative.
Read more
Save as WWF, Save a Tree
auf Facebook
Gefällt mir 13,137
Share the new WWF format!
WWF buttons for your website

Digital Design
Bascule for Japan's Ministry of Education, Culture, Sports, Science and Technology

Programin
On the website of Japan's Ministry of Education, Culture, Sports, Science and Technology (MEXT), we created a place where digitally native children, our future generation, can deepen their understanding of information technology. It was to be the first point of contact for finding new ways to use technology creatively and to learn actively, instead of merely using it passively. We created an environment where children can develop and operate a program intuitively, by using a simple GUI based programming language. Although it was promotional content, it is being used as educational material in homes and classrooms.

Designer
Yoshimi Kawai
Art Director
Yoshimi Kawai
Creative Director
Kampei Baba
Flash Programmers
Takahiro Abe
Kampei Baba
Programmer
Ayumi Ugawa
Illustrator
Ai Tanaka
Agency Producer
Kenichiro Tanaka
Video Editors
Chiho Araki
Tomoyasu Hazaki
Sound Developers
Tomomi Motose
Shojiro Nakaoka
Digital Agency
Bascule
Production Companies
Bascule
bitztream
CLOQUE
Planner
Kampei Baba
Client
Japan's Ministry of Education, Culture, Sports, Science and Technology

プログラミン
文部科学省
プログラミン
プログラムをつくる
おてほんであそぶ
使い方をおぼえる
© Ministry of Education, Culture, Sports, Science and Technology.

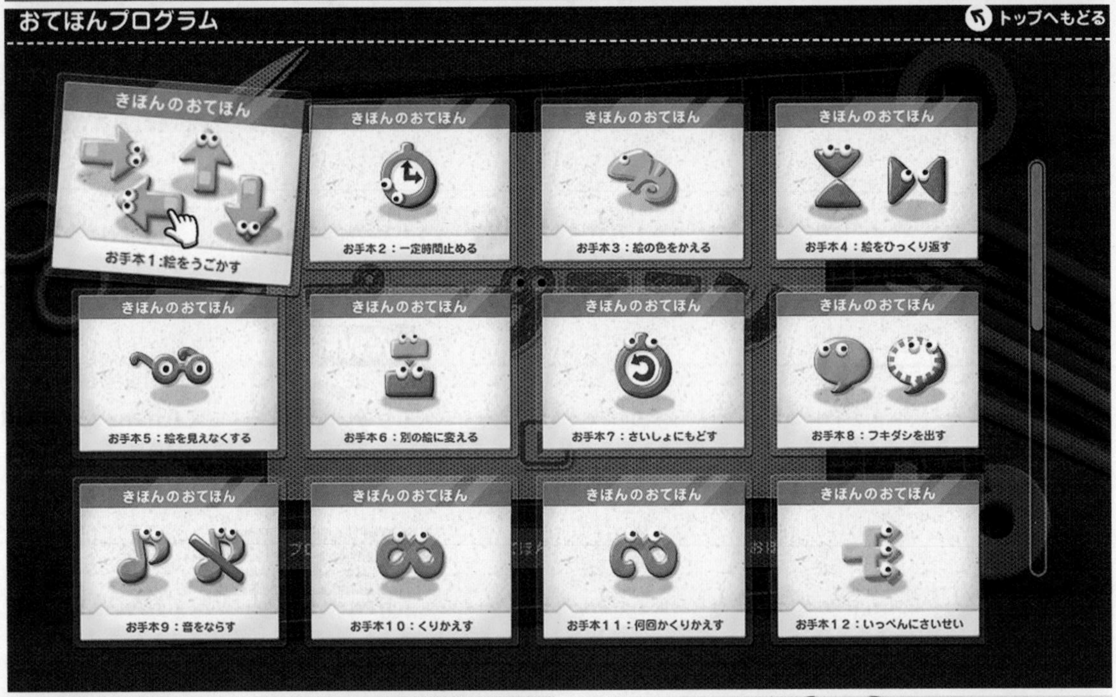
おてほんプログラム
トップへもどる
きほんのおてほん
お手本1：絵をうごかす
お手本2：一定時間止める
お手本3：絵の色をかえる
お手本4：絵をひっくり返す
お手本5：絵を見えなくする
お手本6：別の絵に変える
お手本7：さいしょにもどす
お手本8：フキダシを出す
お手本9：音をならす
お手本10：くりかえす
お手本11：何回かくりかえす
お手本12：いっぺんにさいせい

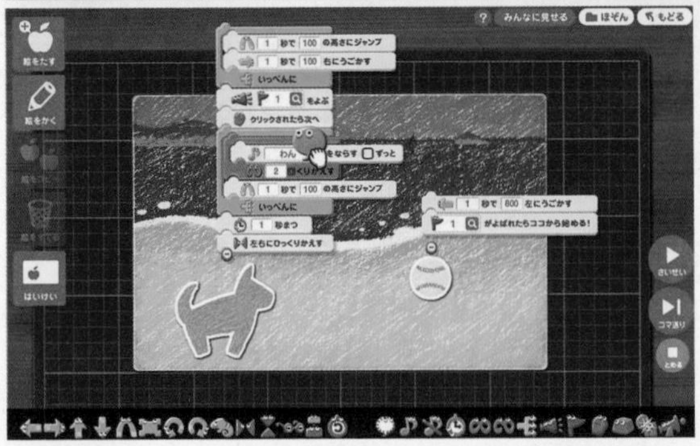

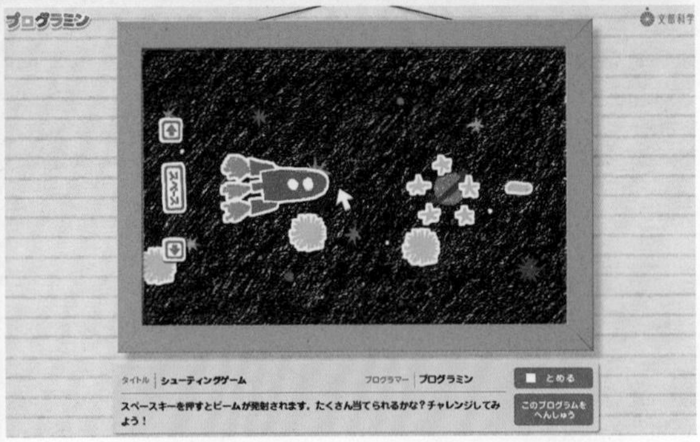
プログラミン
シューティングゲーム
プログラミン
とめる
スペースキーを押すとビームが発射されます。たくさん当てられるかな？チャレンジしてみよう！

Digital Design
OgilvyOne Frankfurt
for Moto Waganari

Directing Shadows
The Japanese artist Moto Waganari asked us to build a virtual show- and salesroom to showcase his filigree polygon sculptures to a worldwide audience of art lovers. But the beautiful sculptures only come to life when they interact with light and shadow. We wanted viewers to experience the sculptures at their best, so turned the presentation of the pieces into a spatial installation. We built 'Directing Shadows', an interactive light gallery where light, sound and voice bring these objects to life and increase the desire to buy.

Designer
Uwe Jakob
Interactive Designer
Ralf Zimmermann
Art Director
Uwe Jakob
Creative Directors
Uwe Jakob
Dr Ulf Schmidt
Executive Creative Director
Michael Kutschinski
Flash Programmer
Jens Steffen
Developer
Isabell Grasshoff
Copywriter
Dr Ulf Schmidt
Music & Sound
Lars Kellner
Advertising Agency
OgilvyOne Frankfurt
Account Handler
Uwe Jakob
Brand Manager
Lutz Wagner
Client
Moto Waganari

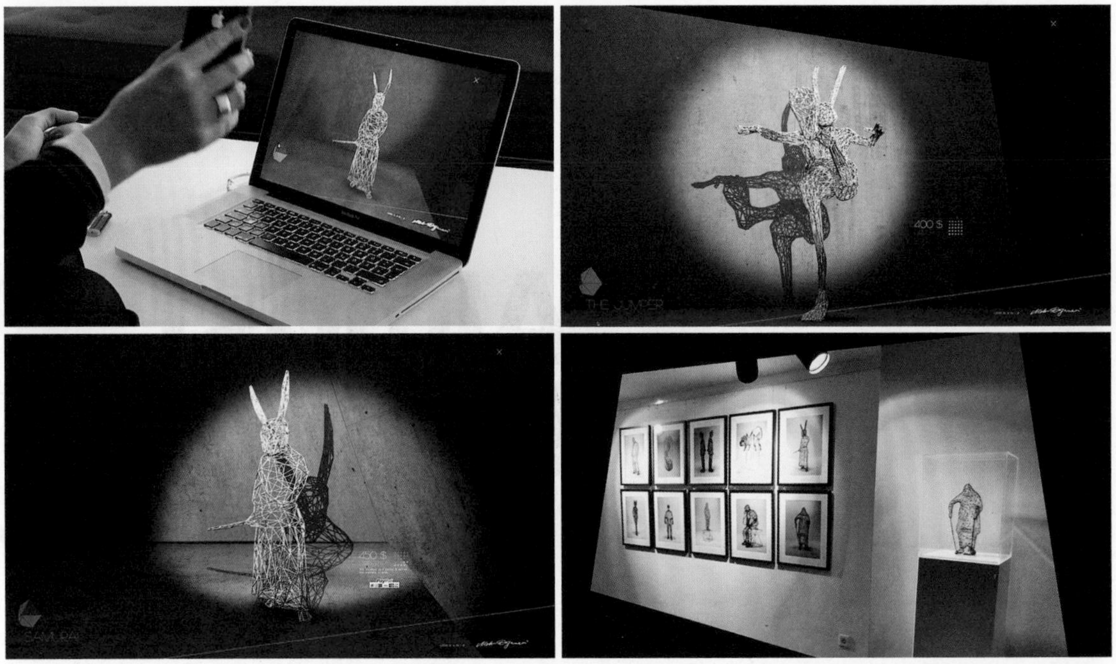

Digital Design
R/GA New York for Nike

Nike+ GPS
Since the launch and success of Nike+, Nike's vision has always been to evolve the platform. Now runners can join the world's largest running club by simply downloading the Nike+ GPS app, whether laced in Nike shoes or not. Nike+ is in your pocket, ready for a run anytime. Running outdoors, GPS tracks your run; indoors, the accelerometer detects movement. The app instantly uploads your run to Nike+, where you can review your runs, set and manage goals, and challenge others.

Design Director
Cesar Marchetti
Senior Interactive Designer
Andrew Mercando
Interactive Design Director
Stephen Kob
Senior Visual Designer
Ray Sison
Art Director
Adam Jesberger
Associate Creative Directors
Masha Ioveva
Joo Youn Paek
Executive Creative Director for Mobile & Social Platforms
Ian Spalter
Technical Director
Sune Kaae
Senior Software Engineer
Robert Carlsen
Software Engineer
Ilya Rivkin
Technical Team Leads
Josh Stephenson
Chris Thorwarth
Senior Copywriter
Ross Weythman
Producer
Allen Yeh
Group Director of Production
James Kuo
Digital Agency
R/GA New York
Executive Director of Quality Assurance
Michael Shagalov
Quality Assurance Engineer
Tim King
Solution Architect
Robert Carlsen
Analyst
Will Sandwick
Managing Director
Sean Lyons
Agency Vice President
Sean Lyons
Client
Nike

3G 9:30 AM
Welcome to Nike+
0 RUNS
0'00" AVG PACE
0:00:00 DURATION
0 cal CALORIES
Start a New Run
Play Nike+ Tag
Take the Tour
Home
History
Settings
Done
Summary
Your Run on 4/22/09 at 11:55am
25
5.27mi
8'56"/mi
1:02:06
431cal
Play Nike+ Tag
Share Run
Route Info
How was your run?
Done
Distance
Pace
7'32" FASTEST
SLOWEST 9'15"
Finish
5.27mi
8'35"/mi
45:15
Google

Yellow Pencil in
Graphic Design

Calendars
The Chase for the BBC

Almost Extinct
The BBC Wildlife Fund raises money to support wildlife projects around the world. We were briefed to convey the serious issue of the large numbers of species becoming extinct each year. A calendar was developed to keep the fund at the front of stakeholders' minds each day, while also directly showing the effect mankind is having on the planet. Sent out with a red pen on 1 January, the calendar prompts the recipient to cross out a different species every day of the year.

Designers
Adam Cartwright
Chris Challinor
Dulcie Cowling
Rebecca Low
Creative Director
Oliver Maltby
Design Company
The Chase
Client
BBC
Brand
BBC Wildlife Fund

Almost
Extinct
Every day, hundreds
of endangered species
get closer to extinction.
By working together,
we can help save them.
BBC
Wildlife
Fund
January
Mon
Tue
Wed
Thur
Fri
Sat
Sun

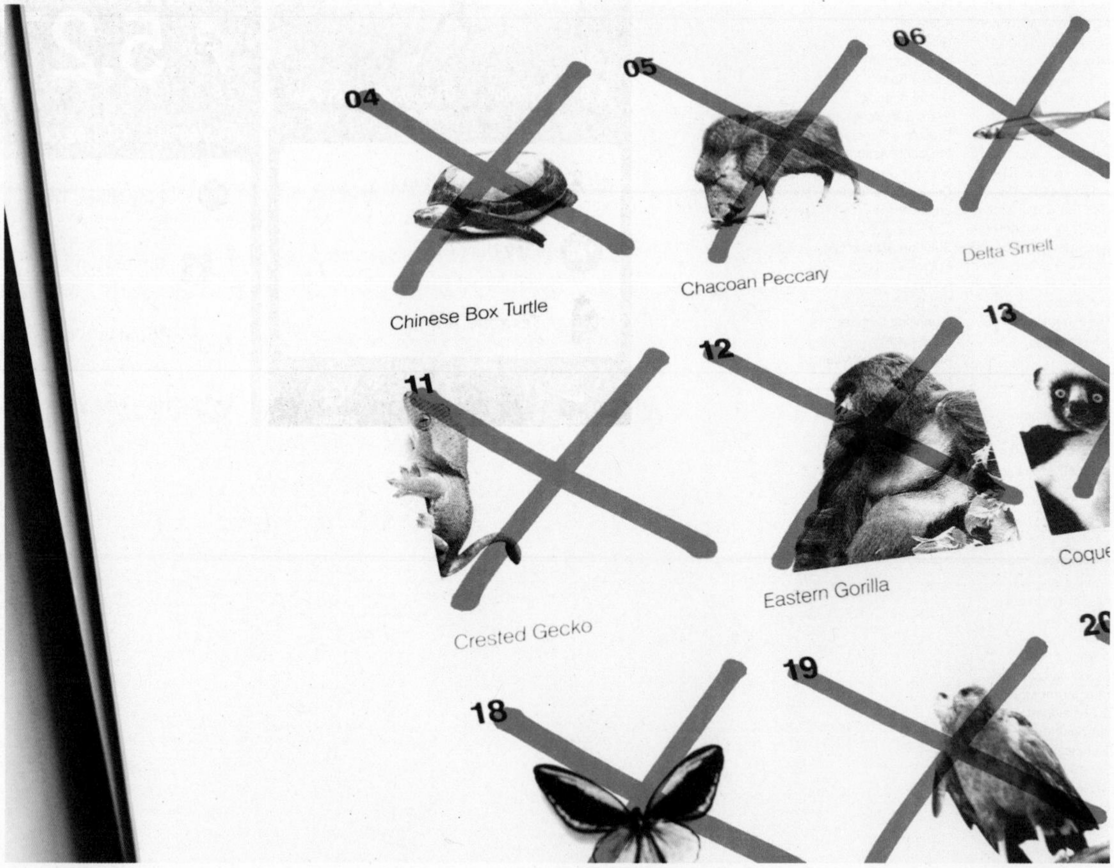
04
Chinese Box Turtle
05
Chacoan Peccary
06
Delta Smelt
11
Crested Gecko
12
Eastern Gorilla
13
18
19

Yellow Pencil in
Graphic Design

Catalogues & Brochures
Jäger & Jäger for Nils Holger Moormann

Moormann in Simple Terms
The 2010 brochure for Moormann furniture portrays Moormann in simple terms. The furniture is presented together with hard facts, insights and perspectives that remain true to scale. The little book reflects the loving detail invested in the furniture, from the typewritten text to the frequent punched holes in the pages.

Designers
Olaf Jäger
Regina Jäger
Design Group
Jäger & Jäger
Marketing Manager
Nicole Christof
Client
Nils Holger Moormann

Moormann in einfachen Verhältnissen

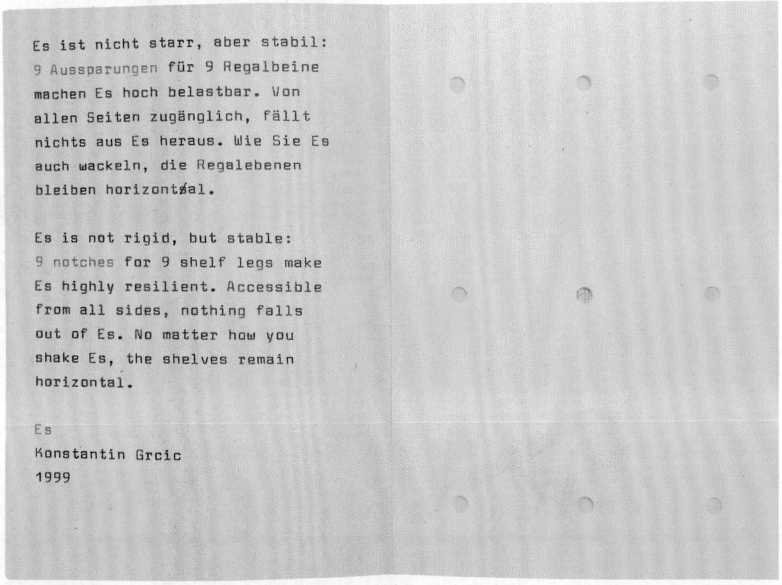
Es ist nicht starr, aber stabil:
9 Aussparungen für 9 Regalbeine
machen Es hoch belastbar. Von
allen Seiten zugänglich, fällt
nichts aus Es heraus. Wie Sie Es
auch wackeln, die Regalebenen
bleiben horizontal.
Es is not rigid, but stable:
9 notches for 9 shelf legs make
Es highly resilient. Accessible
from all sides, nothing falls
out of Es. No matter how you
shake Es, the shelves remain
horizontal.
Es
Konstantin Grcic
1999

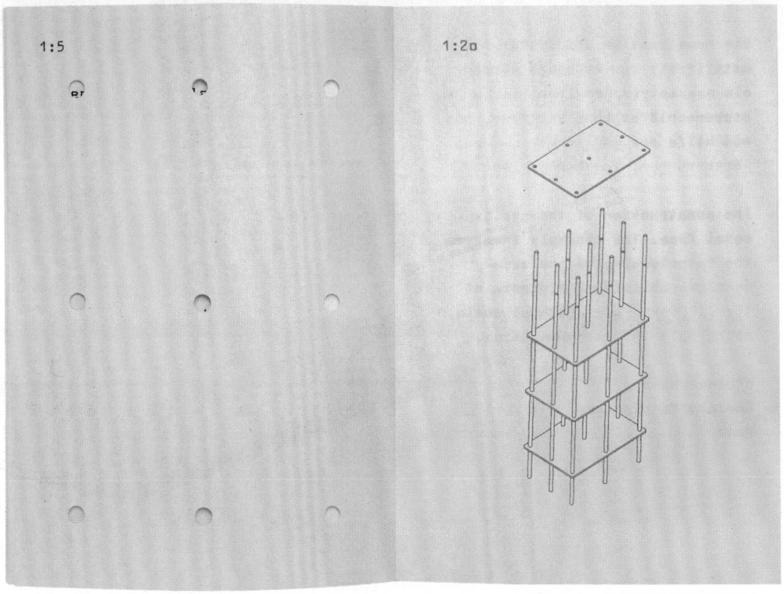
1:5
1:20

Yellow Pencil in Graphic Design

Wayfinding & Environmental Graphics
Cartlidge Levene for the Bristol Museum & Art Gallery

Signage, Wayfinding & Furniture for the Bristol Museum & Art Gallery
The signage for the Bristol Museum & Art Gallery takes the form of leaning timber panels that have minimum impact on the listed building stonework and provide a contemporary layer in the Edwardian interior. To improve understanding of the split level arrangement, wording such as 'up to' and 'through to' was introduced, creating an intuitive flow through the building and avoiding awkward terminology such as first upper and first lower. A map and directory are provided in prominent positions, and threshold panels help visitors negotiate the individual galleries. An information desk, leaflet rack and display panels were also designed as part of the overall language.

Designers
Matt Busher
Ian Cartlidge
Melissa Price
Ben Tibbs
Design Director
Ian Cartlidge
Design Studio
Cartlidge Levene
Client
Bristol Museum & Art Gallery

Up to
Art Galleries
Natural Sciences
Down to
Egypt
Assyria
South West Wildlife
Curiosity
Exhibition Gallery 1
Shop
Workshop Space

French Art

Art Galleries
Natural Sciences

Up to
Art Galleries
Natural Sciences

- Nomination in Graphic Design

Applied Print Graphics
Dentsu Tokyo for the Japan Ministry of Foreign Affairs

Top Lapel Pin
Lapel pins were needed for the attendees of APEC Japan 2010. For security, the pins had to show each class clearly, making the Prime Minister, Cabinet Minister, or their partners easily recognisable. We designed the pin, which is easily identifiable, to be suggestive of the spirit of Japanese hospitality, making it work as a gift for attendees. The 'koma' (spinning top) motif represents our wish for the meeting to move forward smoothly, and the five colours traditionally mean good health in Japan. We designed six types of pins in total.

Designers
Ai Ishimatsu
Yo Kimura
Kana Nakao
Yoichi Takigami
Yoshihiro Yagi
Art Director
Yoshihiro Yagi
Creative Director
Kuranari Hidetoshi
Copywriter
Haruko Tsutsui
Producers
Nadja Kirillova
Kana Koyama
Tadashi Nakamura
Advertising Agency
Dentsu Tokyo
Account Handler
Oshio Masami
Marketing Manager
Takeshi Hikihara
Client
Japan Ministry of Foreign Affairs
Brand
APEC Japan 2010

APEC JAPAN 2010

In Japan, tops have traditionally been favored as an auspicious gift, carrying a message of "May things turn out well for you." Red, black, yellow, green, and white. These five colors - traditionally and currently believed to bring longevity and prevent misfortune - are presented in the pins. May this pin bring you fulfillment and prosperity for our common future.
With compliments,
APEC JAPAN 2010
APEC JAPAN 2010

Nomination in Graphic Design

Applied Print Graphics
DesignStudio for
The Royal Mint

King James Bible Two Pound Coin
The coin celebrates the 400th anniversary of the King James Bible – one of the most significant moments in publishing history – by replicating the process of the printing press and the bible's distribution. The aptly chosen quote, 'In the beginning was the Word' (John 1:1) was used as the basis of the design. In a single entity, the letters of the printing press and the print from the King James Bible are aligned and mirrored on the coin horizontally and three-dimensionally. The reversed text protrudes, representing the printing block, and the correct text is recessed, representing the printed word.

Designers
Luke Alexander
Rich Lyons
Creative Directors
Paul Stafford
Ben Wright
Design Studio
DesignStudio
Client Head of Historical Services
Dr Kevin Clancy
Client
The Royal Mint

KING JAMES BIBLE
In the
beginning
was the
Word
1611—2011

Nomination in Graphic Design

Catalogues & Brochures
Christopher Doyle
& Elliott Scott

This Year I Will Try Not to

Most designers are seduced by design trends. They're easy to appropriate, and even easier to imitate. The challenge is to innovate. To be new. We decided the best (and most enjoyable) approach was to identify and document the most common trends we felt we had to avoid. Before long we found ourselves with a checklist of Don'ts and a new aim: to try to be new. We may fail, but we will try.

Designers
Christopher Doyle
Elliott Scott
Typographer
Christopher Doyle
Photographers
Christopher Doyle
Elliott Scott
Copywriters
Christopher Doyle
Elliott Scott
Image Manipulator
Elliott Scott
Client
Christopher Doyle
& Elliott Scott

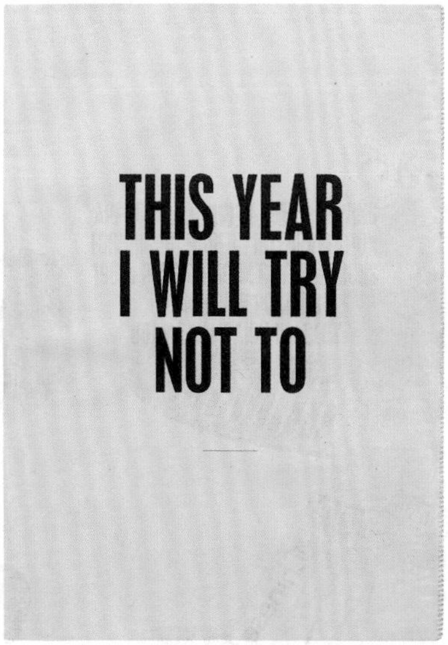
THIS YEAR
I WILL TRY
NOT TO

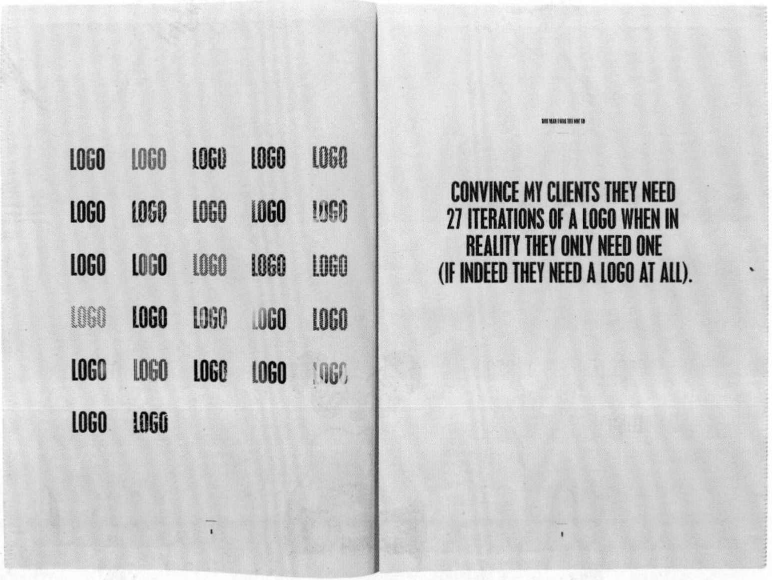
LOGO LOGO LOGO LOGO LOGO
LOGO LOGO LOGO LOGO LOGO
LOGO LOGO LOGO LOGO LOGO
LOGO LOGO LOGO LOGO LOGO
LOGO LOGO LOGO LOGO LOGO
LOGO LOGO
CONVINCE MY CLIENTS THEY NEED
27 ITERATIONS OF A LOGO WHEN IN
REALITY THEY ONLY NEED ONE
(IF INDEED THEY NEED A LOGO AT ALL).

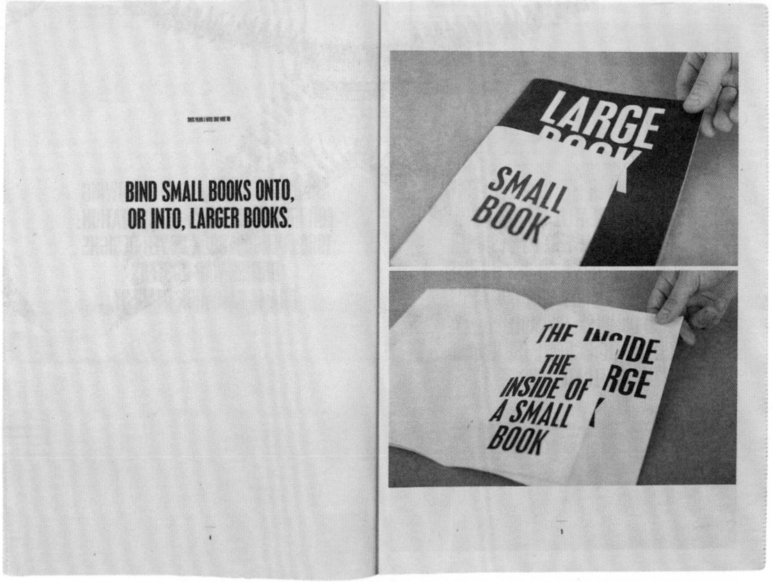
BIND SMALL BOOKS ONTO,
OR INTO, LARGER BOOKS.
LARGE
SMALL
BOOK
THE
INSIDE OF
A SMALL
BOOK

Integrated Graphics
Dentsu Tokyo for
The Yoshida Hideo
Memorial Foundation

China High!
We were asked to launch the 16th China International Advertising Festival Exhibition, to be held in Japan, as well as design the exhibition venue. The theme was 'China High!' which expresses the vibrancy and power of China. Using the traditional Chinese kite as a motif, we explored various designs that best expressed contemporary China. We kept the distinctive designs and forms of Chinese kites, and created four new kites. The mated pair of swallows symbolises city and traffic; the green dragon, body and sports; the panda, food culture; and the red goldfish, fashion and design. The campaign was also selected in Graphic Design Posters.

Designers
Minami Otsuka
Kazuaki Takai
Art Director
Yoshihiro Yagi
Executive Creative Director
Yuya Furukawa
Copywriter
Haruko Tsutsui
Producer
Tatsuro Aono
Print Producer
Takeshi Arimoto
Advertising Agency
Dentsu Tokyo
Clients
Advertising Museum Tokyo
The Yoshida Hideo Memorial Foundation

第16回
中国国際
広告祭展
5.11(TUE.)▷
6.6(SUN.)
Chinese High!
THE 16th
CHINA INTERNATIONAL ADVERTISING FESTIVAL EXHIBITION
ADVERTISING MUSEUM TOKYO

THE 16TH
CHINA
INTERNATIONAL
ADVERTISING
FESTIVAL
5.11
6.6
ADVERTISING MUSEUM TOKYO
ADMISSION FREE
CHINESE HIGH!
THE 16th
CHINA INTERNATIONAL ADVERTISING FESTIVAL EXHIBITION
ADVERTISING MUSEUM TOKYO

第16回
中国国際
広告祭展
5.11(TUE.)–
6.6(SUN.)
CHINESE HIGH!
THE 16th
CHINA INTERNATIONAL ADVERTISING FESTIVAL EXHIBITION
ADVERTISING MUSEUM TOKYO

第16回
中国国際
広告祭展
5.11(TUE.)
6.6(SUN.)
Chinese High!
THE 16th
CHINA INTERNATIONAL ADVERTISING FESTIVAL EXHIBITION
ADVERTISING MUSEUM TOKYO

Integrated Graphics
This is Real Art for
the Musicians' Union

Musicians' Union
This is a rebrand, web design, magazine design and advertising for the Musicians' Union, a trade union for UK musicians.

Designers
Rick Banks
Paul Belford
Matt Judge
Art Director
Paul Belford
Creative Director
Paul Belford
Copywriters
Paul Belford
Richard Foster
Design Group
This is Real Art
Project Manager
Natalie Wetherell
Account Handler
George Lee
Marketing Manager
Horace Trubridge
Client
Musicians' Union

Musicians'
Union

The Musician. Will the BBC bow to pressure and save 6 Music? How might this happen and at what cost? Is Radio1 safe? Or the five regional orchestras? This year sees the 30th anniversary of the historic eight week strike by the Musicians' Union at the BBC. We examine its lasting legacy and ask if such drastic action will ever again be necessary.
Summer 2010.
Journal of the Musicians' Union
theMU.org

Wales & South West
England Region
Spring 2010
—
theMU.org
The Musician, Extra.
Regional Events Diary.
MU Songwriters' Circle.
Member FAQs.
Roving Safety Reps.

20
21
19A
20A
'Free public liability insurance. Because some musicians can be a bit of a liability.'
—
'Trust me. A lot can go wrong at a gig. Especially ours. So it's reassuring to know that I get free public liability insurance with my Musicians' Union membership. Join us at theMU.org'
—
Mark Greenway, Napalm Death
Musicians'
Union

Integrated Graphics
Rose Design for Art on the Underground

Dryden Goodwin Linear
Art on the Underground invited us to collaborate with artist Dryden Goodwin on a project celebrating 30 years of the Jubilee line. We created a billboard installation outside Southwark station and further installations along the Jubilee line, using the 60 pencil studies he had created from interviews with Jubilee line staff. To connect people to the work, posters and leaflets were used across the Underground and a microsite was placed on the Transport for London website. We also used video escalator panels to show films of Dryden's drawings coming to life, and promotional pencils to further raise awareness of the project.

Designer
Rupert Gowar-Cliffe
Design Director
Simon Elliott
Creative Directors
Garry Blackburn
Simon Elliott
Design Group
Rose Design
Client Curator
Louise Coysh
Client Director
Tamsin Dillon
Client
Art on the Underground

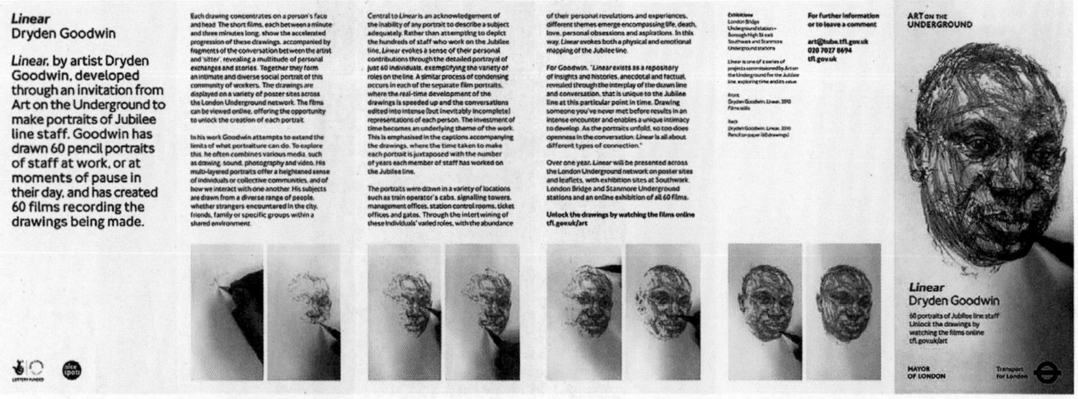
Linear
Dryden Goodwin
Linear, by artist Dryden Goodwin, developed through an invitation from Art on the Underground to make portraits of Jubilee line staff. Goodwin has drawn 60 pencil portraits of staff at work, or at moments of pause in their day, and has created 60 films recording the drawings being made.
ART ON THE UNDERGROUND
Linear
Dryden Goodwin

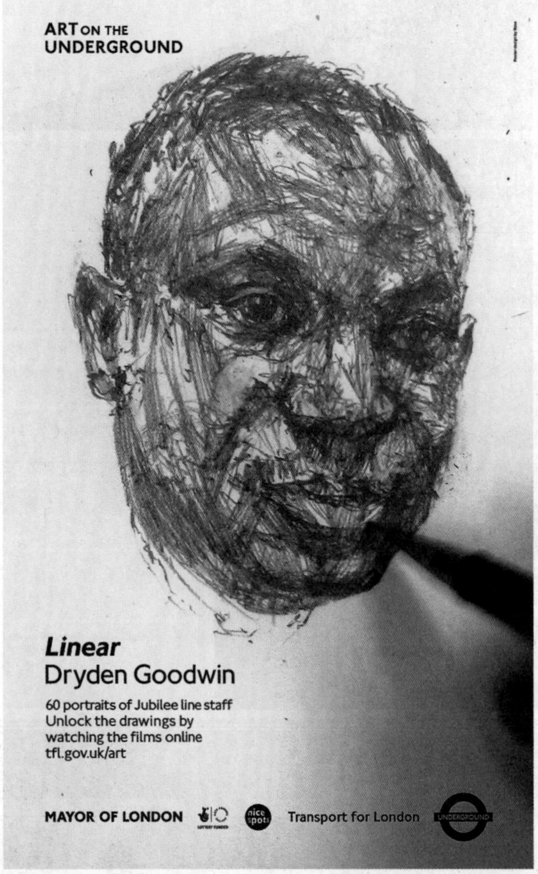
ART ON THE UNDERGROUND
Linear
Dryden Goodwin
60 portraits of Jubilee line staff
Unlock the drawings by watching the films online
tfl.gov.uk/art
MAYOR OF LONDON
Transport for London
UNDERGROUND

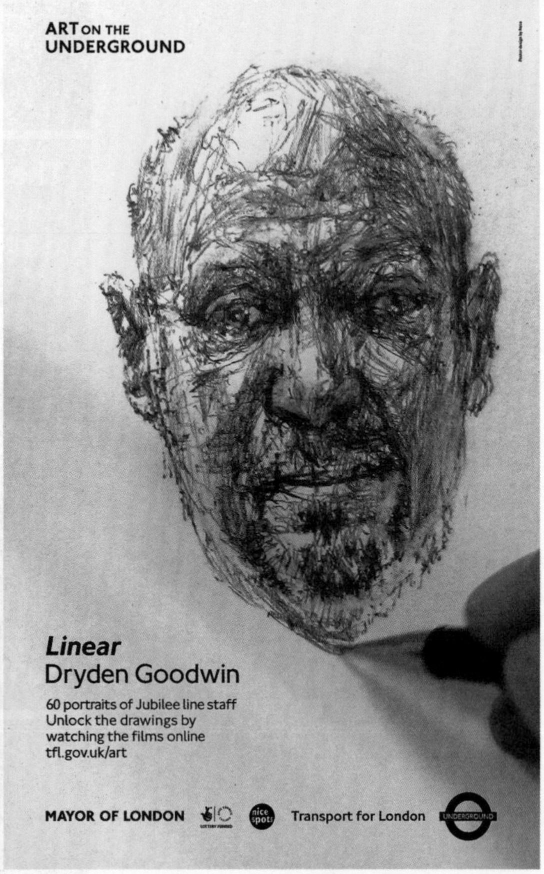
ART ON THE UNDERGROUND
Linear
Dryden Goodwin
60 portraits of Jubilee line staff
Unlock the drawings by watching the films online
tfl.gov.uk/art
MAYOR OF LONDON
Transport for London
UNDERGROUND

Linear Dryden Goodwin

Integrated Graphics
NB for the Museum of London

You are Here
The spectacular new £20million Galleries of Modern London opened on 28 May 2010, telling the story of London and its people from 1666 to the present day. Three years in the making, five new galleries show how the vibrant and unflagging energy of Londoners has shaped this global city. 'You Are Here' is a bold cross-London campaign to launch the new Galleries of Modern London and to relaunch the Museum of London as a relevant and exciting destination for Londoners and tourists.

Designer
Ed Wright
Art Director
Alan Dye
Creative Directors
Alan Dye
Nick Finney
Typographer
Ed Wright
Copywriters
Alan Dye
Ed Wright
Design Group
NB
Photography
Museum of London Archive
Account Handler
Jules Anderson
Client
Museum of London

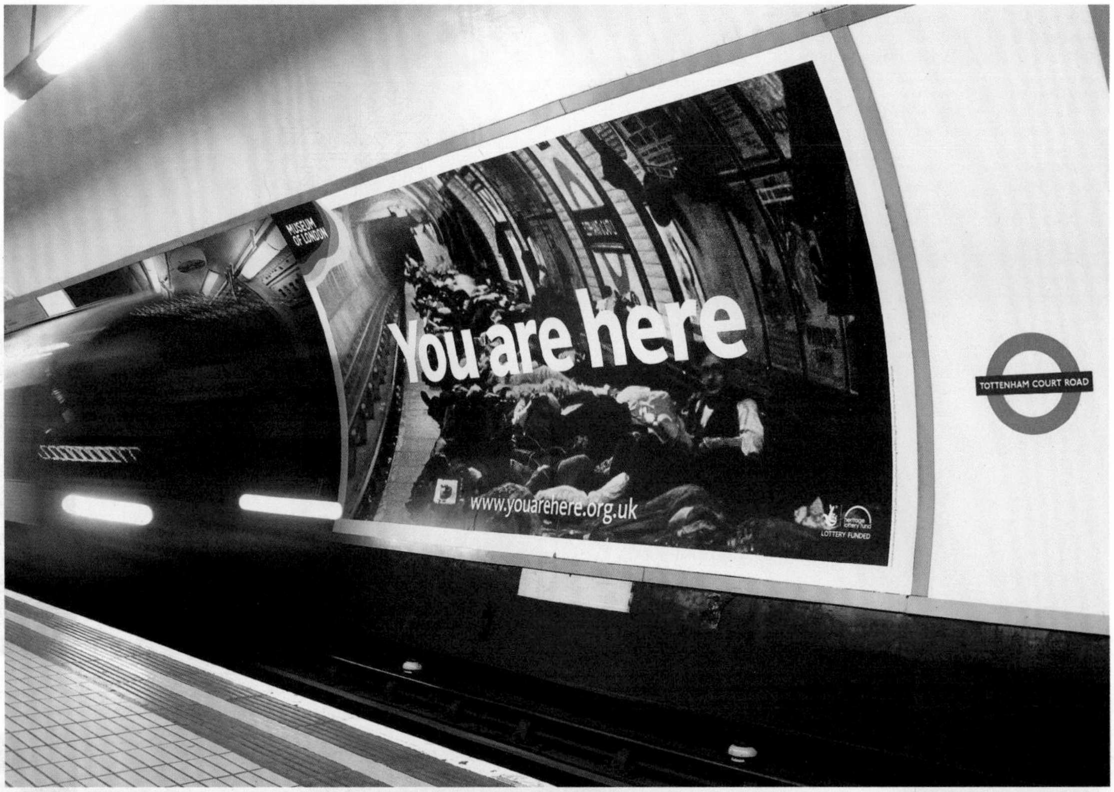
MUSEUM OF LONDON
You are here
www.youarehere.org.uk
LOTTERY FUNDED
TOTTENHAM COURT ROAD

You are here

You are here

You are here
Be here
Join the celebrations

You are here
www.youarehere.org.uk

Moving Image
This is Real Art
for SES Astra

Space Clips
This is a series of animated short films for the satellite operator SES Astra. They explain how satellites are launched and operated. The films are designed to make complex science engaging and understandable.

Designers
Paul Belford
Chris Perry
Sam Renwick
Animator
Chris Perry
Creative Director
Paul Belford
Copywriter
Gideon Todes
Design Group
This is Real Art
Project Manager
Kate Nielsen
Account Handler
George Lee
Marketing Manager
Paul Freeman
Client
SES Astra

Moving Image
Saatchi & Saatchi
Sydney for the Sydney Writers' Festival

Signs of Change
The world of publishing is facing massive change. Is this the end of literature or the dawn of a new golden age? Roadside warning signs were used to express succinct messages emotionally and eloquently. The signs were used at venues during the Sydney Writers' Festival, for the trailer, online and as posters.

Designers
Sharon Lee
Julian Melhuish
Design Creative Director
Julian Melhuish
Director
Ingvar Kenne
Copywriter
Oliver Wingate
Advertising Agency
Saatchi & Saatchi
Sydney
Client
Sydney Writers' Festival

CAUTION: CHANGE AHEAD
THERE'S WAR
AND PEACE
I JUST NEED A LITTLE TIME
TIME TO READ
TIME TO RETHINK
TIME TO RESPOND

Logos
The Stone Twins
for Design
Academy Eindhoven

Design Academy Eindhoven
Design Academy Eindhoven, one of the world's foremost design schools, required a new visual identity to reflect its inclusive, progressive and dynamic nature. The idea behind the bold graphic signature began with the 'E' of Eindhoven, and was conceived to be customised by students and staff. By hand writing the words 'Design Academy Eindhoven' within the three blank bars, there are infinite permutations of the logo. In addition, users are also invited to employ different messages or slogans depending on context, for example, 'Kiss the Future' and 'Dare to Dream'.

Designers
Declan Stone
Garech Stone
Creative Directors
Declan Stone
Garech Stone
Photographer
Åsmund Sollihøgda
Copywriters
Declan Stone
Garech Stone
Design Group
The Stone Twins
Brand Manager
Annemieke Eggenkamp
Marketing Manager
René van Binsbergen
Client
Design Academy Eindhoven

DESIGN ACADEMY EINDHOVEN
DESIGN ACADEMY EINDHOVEN
DESIGN ACADEMY EINDHOVEN
DESIGN ACADEMY EINDHOVEN
Design Academy Eindhoven
Design Academy Eindhoven
DARE TO DREAM
HANDLE WITH CARE
SMELL THE COFFEE

Logos
Leftloft for the
Museum Fredericianum

dOCUMENTA (13)
dOCUMENTA (13) was an event organised by the Museum Fredericianum in Germany. We designed a flexible visual grammar, a non-identity, which does not rely on the repetition of a single graphic element, but fixes a 'rule' for writing the word itself. A series of 13 non-logos has been designed, but any combination is possible following three simple instructions: the 'd' is always written in lowercase, while the rest of the letters are uppercase; the word 'dOCUMENTA' is followed by '13' in brackets; and any font in black is allowed.

Creative Direction
Leftloft
Design Company
Leftloft
Client
Museum Fredericianum
Brand
dOCUMENTA (13)

dOCUMENTA (13)
dOCUMENTA (13)
dOCUMENTA (13)
dOCUMENTA (13)
dOCUMENTA (13)
dOCUMENTA (13)
dOCUMENTA (13)
dOCUMENTA (13)
dOCUMENTA (13)
dOCUMENTA (13)
dOCUMENTA (13)
dOCUMENTA (13)
dOCUMENTA (13)

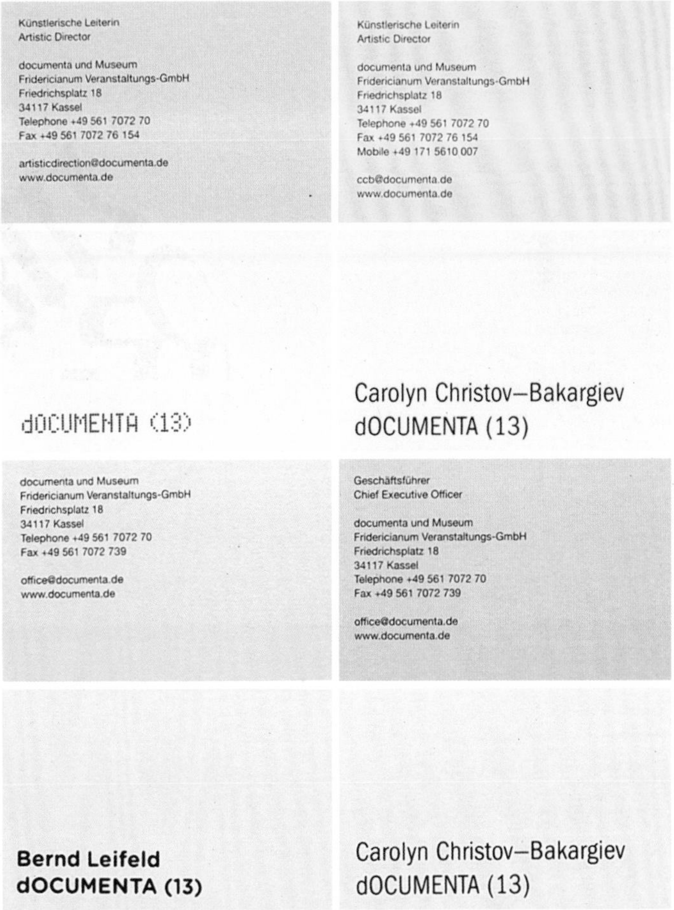
Künstlerische Leiterin
Artistic Director
documenta und Museum
Fridericianum Veranstaltungs-GmbH
Friedrichsplatz 18
34117 Kassel
Telephone +49 561 7072 70
Fax +49 561 7072 76 154
artisticdirection@documenta.de
www.documenta.de
Künstlerische Leiterin
Artistic Director
documenta und Museum
Fridericianum Veranstaltungs-GmbH
Friedrichsplatz 18
34117 Kassel
Telephone +49 561 7072 70
Fax +49 561 7072 76 154
Mobile +49 171 5610 007
ccb@documenta.de
www.documenta.de
dOCUMENTA (13)
Carolyn Christov–Bakargiev
dOCUMENTA (13)
documenta und Museum
Fridericianum Veranstaltungs-GmbH
Friedrichsplatz 18
34117 Kassel
Telephone +49 561 7072 70
Fax +49 561 7072 739
office@documenta.de
www.documenta.de
Geschäftsführer
Chief Executive Officer
documenta und Museum
Fridericianum Veranstaltungs-GmbH
Friedrichsplatz 18
34117 Kassel
Telephone +49 561 7072 70
Fax +49 561 7072 739
office@documenta.de
www.documenta.de
Bernd Leifeld
dOCUMENTA (13)
Carolyn Christov–Bakargiev
dOCUMENTA (13)

Logos
OCD | The Original Champions of Design for the Girl Scouts of the USA

Rebranding the Girl Scouts of the USA
The GSUSA (Girl Scouts of the USA) is more than three million strong. The organisation recently revised its programming to better engage girls today. To support this shift, the identity also needed to be reassessed. For such a large and unregulated organisation to embrace it, the new identity had to live and die by just a few rules and be sensitive to GSUSA's rich history. The trefoil has always played a key role in the GSUSA brand. For consistency, the brand identity has been consolidated to one iconic trefoil shape, creating a design element that inspires limitless brand expression.

Designers
Jennifer Kinon
Bobby C Martin Jr
Illustrators
Joe Finocchiaro
Jasper Goodall
Design Group
OCD | The Original Champions of Design
Client
Girl Scouts of the USA

girl scouts
girl scouts
girl scouts
Building girls of courage, confidence, and character, who make the world a better place.

Logos
StudioLR for The Mary Rose Trust

The Mary Rose Logo
The logo brief was to better represent and manage visitors' expectations of The Mary Rose prior to the opening of an iconic museum in Portsmouth in 2012 – a dynamic attraction rich with narrative and emotion. The logo design emphasises all that makes the museum special, and quickly communicates the potentially complex tale of a Tudor ship whose sinking led to a story that continues today. The logo will bring the story of this famous vessel to life – it will be seen by people across the world as the key image for The Mary Rose and its new museum.

Typographer
Chris Weir
Designers
Richy Lamb
Dave Thompson
Design Director
Mark Wheeler
Creative Director
Lucy Richards
Illustrator
Chris Mitchell
Design Group
StudioLR
Brand Strategist
Scott Sherrard
Business Development Director
Andy Gray
Brand Manager
Charles Barker
Client
The Mary Rose Trust
Brand
The Mary Rose

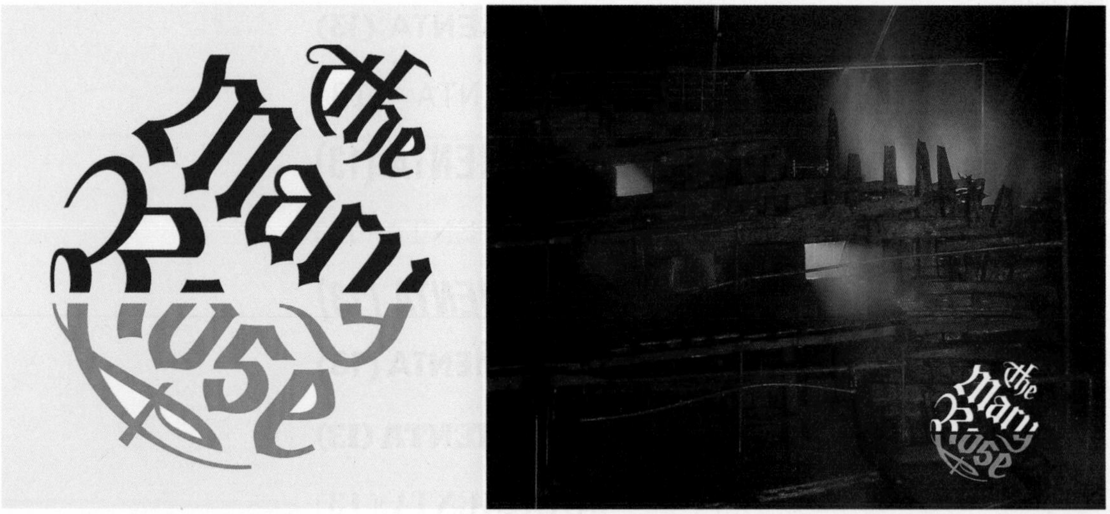
The Mary Rose

Logos
Neumeister Strategic Design for the Swedish Institute

Swedish Fashion Goes Berlin
Sweden is exporting more fashion, music, literature and design than ever before. In order to promote Sweden as a land of creativity, a communication strategy was put together and the platform 'Swedish creativity goes worldwide' was created. The visual identity is easy to adapt for various fields like fashion, film and music, with the circles creating the 's' representing two cultures coming together with all their differences and similarities. The very first event was 'Swedish Fashion Goes Berlin' at the Mercedes-Benz Fashion Week in Berlin, an event that turned the German capital into one enormous catwalk for Swedish fashion.

Designer
Serhat Ferat
Creative Director
Peter Neumeister
Design Agency
Neumeister Strategic Design
Account Handler
Sofia Törling
Client
Swedish Institute
Brand
Swedish Fashion Goes Berlin

SWEDISH
CREATIVITY GOES WORLDWIDE
SWEDISH
FASHION GOES BERLIN
Swedish Fashion Goes Berlin
Auf der Mercedes-Benz Fashion Week Berlin im Januar 2011 heißt es SWEDISH FASHION GOES BERLIN. Drei Designer, zwei Fashion Lectures, eine Fotoausstellung und mehrere Stunden mit Avantgarde-Modefilmen stehen für die gesamte Vielfältigkeit und Breite schwedischer Mode.
Fashion Filmfestival mit schwedischen Modefilmen
Fashion! Fotografien von Camilla Åkrans in der Galerie Swedish Photography
Fashion talks

Logos
Rocío Martinavarro for Matías Nadal

Matías Nadal, Composer
This is the identity for Matías Nadal, a music composer working in film, advertising, television and diverse artistic projects. His initials in stencil, MN, form the black keys of a musical keyboard, his main tool for expression. Five logos aligned together form a whole keyboard and can be used to further develop the graphic system. This conceptually powerful icon is made to last; it is trend-free and neutral enough to represent a wide variety of musical styles.

Designer
Rocío Martinavarro
Client
Matías Nadal

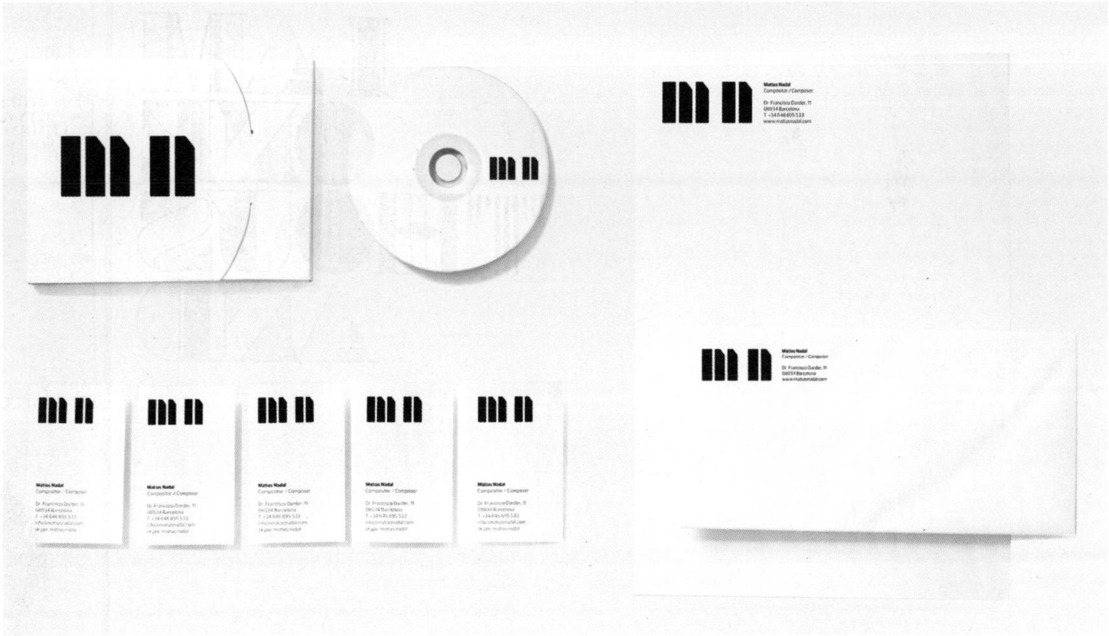

Annual Reports
Roberto Beretta
for Awards for Young Musicians

Giving Talent a Chance
A simple circular die cut highlights the name of a talented young musician funded by Awards for Young Musicians (AYM), a charitable organisation that supports children by giving them a chance to fulfil their musical potential. Once the page is turned the die cut becomes part of one of the instruments that they're playing, transforming their lives.

Designer
Roberto Beretta
Art Director
Roberto Beretta
Illustrator
Roberto Beretta
Photographer
Edward Webb
Copywriter
Ria Hopkinson
Image Manipulator
Roland Wood
Communications Director
Hester Cockcroft
Client
Awards for Young Musicians

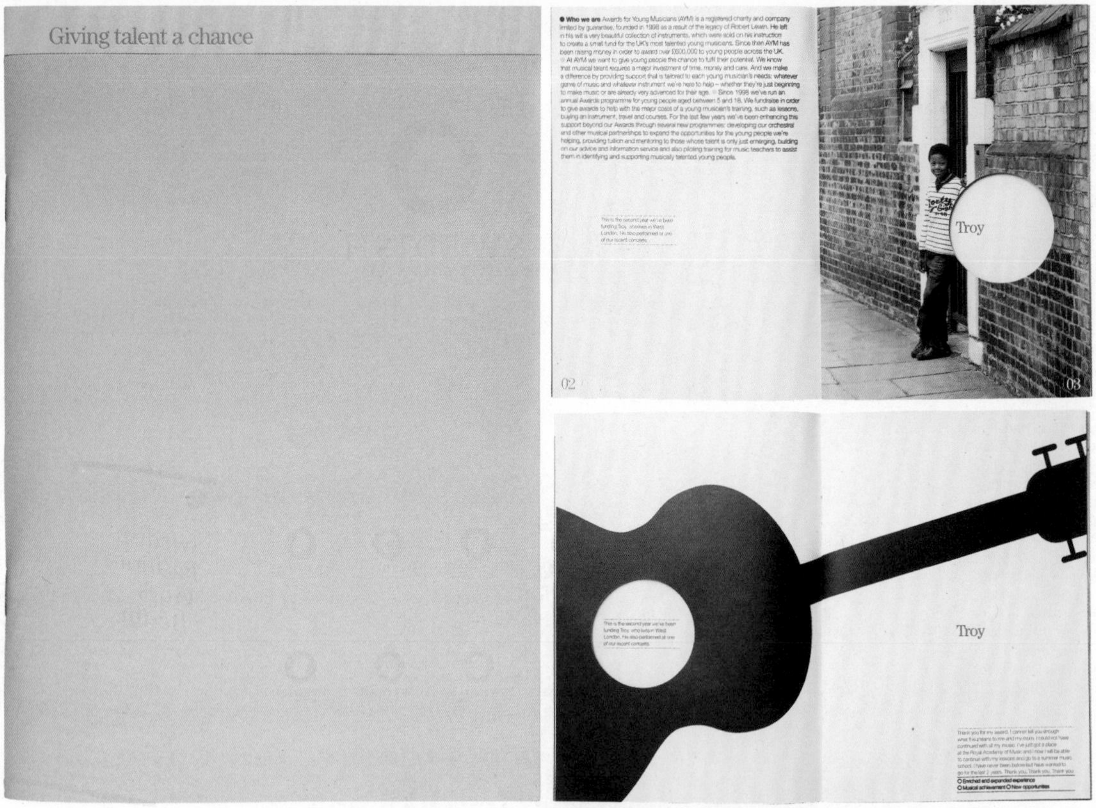
Giving talent a chance
Troy
Troy

Annual Reports
Cossette for Enablis

I Am One Thousand
Enablis is a Canadian Organisation founded by Charles Sirois. It aims to provide financial and professional support to entrepreneurs in West and South Africa, through its members' network. 'I Am One Thousand' evokes strength in numbers and the uniqueness of everyone. Each member is important and brings something distinct to the group. To illustrate this point, we put together a series of various papers and used different graphic styles portraying today's Africa in a postive way.

Designers
Nathalie Boucher
Daniel Cartier
Art Director
Richard Bélanger
Typographer
Richard Bélanger
Illustrator
Richard Bélanger
Design Director
Barbara Jacques
Creative Directors
Barbara Jacques
Michel De Lauw
Copywriter
Patricia Doiron
Advertising Agency
Cossette
Photography
Enablis
Client Chief Executive Officer
Charles Sirois
Client
Enablis

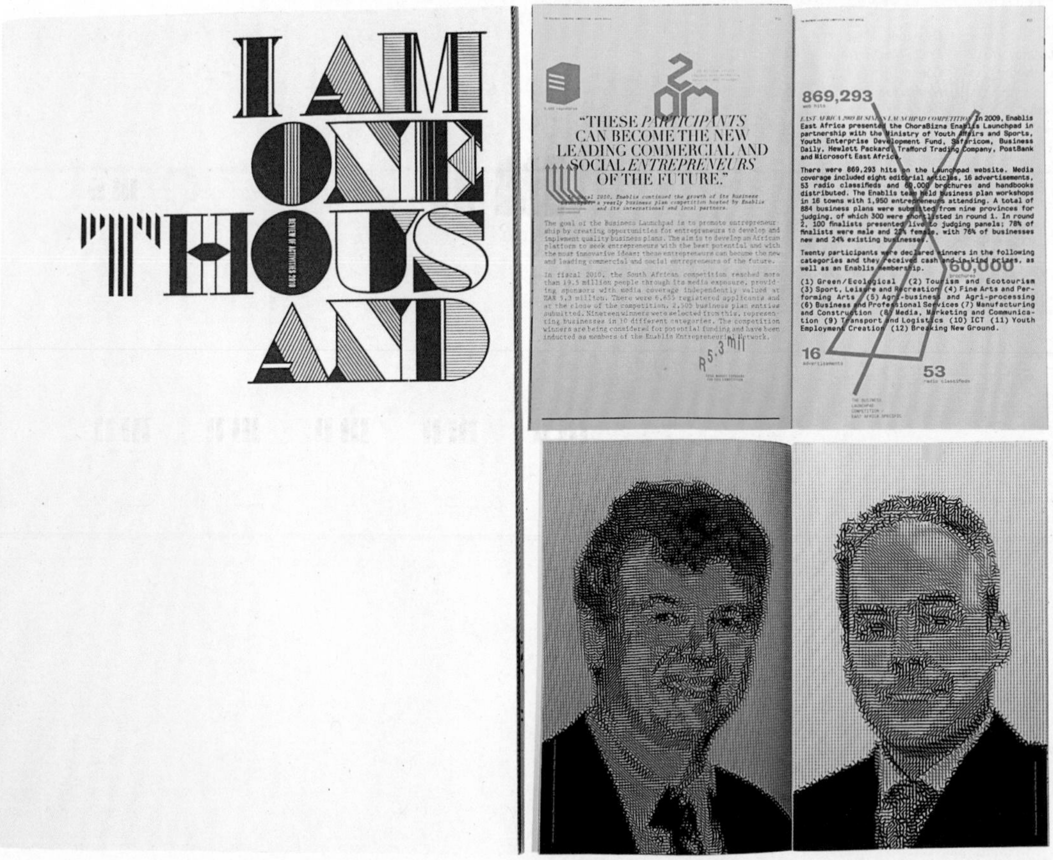
I AM ONE THOUSAND
"THESE PARTICIPANTS CAN BECOME THE NEW LEADING COMMERCIAL AND SOCIAL ENTREPRENEURS OF THE FUTURE."
869,293

Annual Reports
Jung von Matt Hamburg
for LemonAid Beverages

2010's Fairest Annual Report

LemonAid is the first soft drink manufacturer that not only follows fair trade and sustainable sourcing principles, but also pursues a policy of active social engagement. To do justice to this philosophy, we created an annual report that took the concept of fairness to new extremes.

Designer
Katja Kirchner
Art Director
Annika Frey
Creative Directors
Wolf Heumann
Peter Kirchhoff
Photographers
Stefanie Buetow
Johann Cohrs
Copywriter
Christina Drescher
Advertising Agency
Jung von Matt Hamburg
Account Handler
Antje Lindenberg
Brand Manager
Berndt Jakob
Client
LemonAid Beverages
Brand
LemonAid

2010'S FAIREST ANNUAL REPORT
ALL YOU NEED TO KNOW ABOUT FAIRNESS, IN 33 PAGES.
LEMONAID BEVERAGES GMBH

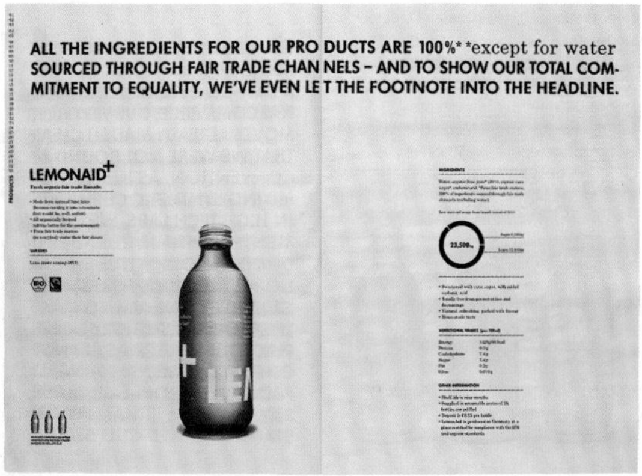
ALL THE INGREDIENTS FOR OUR PRO DUCTS ARE 100%* *except for water SOURCED THROUGH FAIR TRADE CHAN NELS – AND TO SHOW OUR TOTAL COM-MITMENT TO EQUALITY, WE'VE EVEN LE T THE FOOTNOTE INTO THE HEADLINE.
LEMONAID+

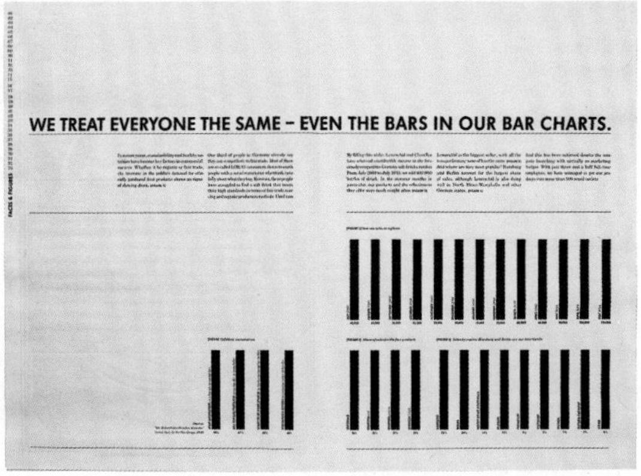
WE TREAT EVERYONE THE SAME – EVEN THE BARS IN OUR BAR CHARTS.

Annual Reports
Rahofer for Palfinger

We Saved Wherever We Could

The economic crisis dealt a severe blow to Palfinger, the market leader for hydraulic knuckle boom cranes and leading manufacturer of hydraulic lifting, loading and handling systems. The logical consequence for Palfinger was to economise wherever possible. It is precisely this sentiment that is expressed in the 2009 Annual Report. The 'economy' concept is a central theme running throughout the report: simple presentation, rough layout, old-fashioned typewriter typeface, cheaply stapled binding, quick scribbles, blacked-out text, even handwritten corrections. The initial impression: that which is being held is merely a draft.

Designer
Katharina Lassnig
Art Director
Katharina Lassnig
Creative Director
Jo Nussbaumer
Illustration
Illunet
Copywriting
Scholdan & Company
Advertising Agency
Rahofer
Marketing Manager
Hannes Roither
Chief Executive Officer
Christian Rahofer
Client
Palfinger

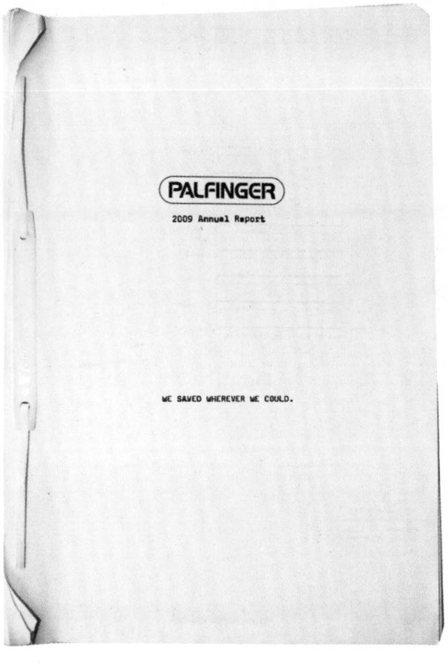
PALFINGER
2009 Annual Report
WE SAVED WHEREVER WE COULD.

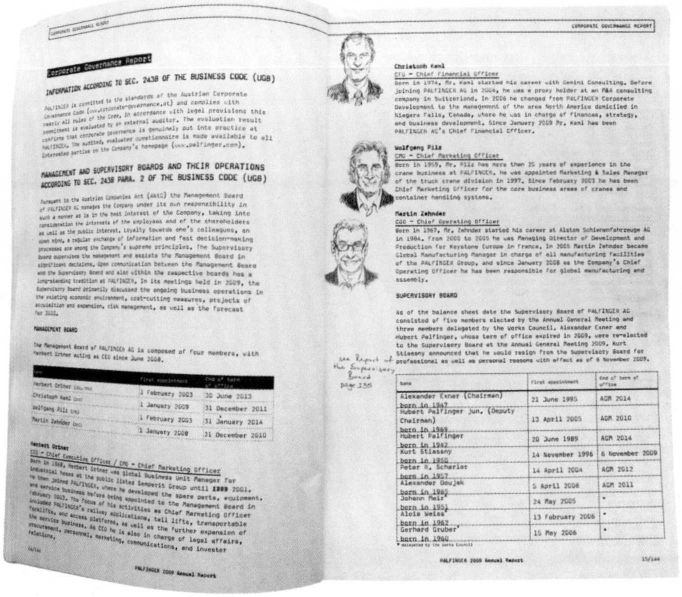
Corporate Governance Report
INFORMATION ACCORDING TO SEC. 243B OF THE BUSINESS CODE (UGB)
MANAGEMENT AND SUPERVISORY BOARDS AND THEIR OPERATIONS ACCORDING TO SEC. 243B PARA. 2 OF THE BUSINESS CODE (UGB)
SUPERVISORY BOARD
PALFINGER 2009 Annual Report

Annual Reports
Interabang for
Cardboard Citizens

Cardboard Citizens Big Annual Review 09–10
Cardboard Citizens is the UK's only homeless people's professional theatre company. The annual review is the most comprehensive document of its work, and as such needs to excite current stakeholders, engage the interest of new supporters and reflect its year of excellence. The review adopts a 'big' theme to encompass Cardboard Citizens' massive year and achievements. This theme is also reflected in the format and tightly cropped imagery, with loose binding suggesting the language of newspapers and important issues. A small format, tipped-in donation form points towards a little help going a long way.

Design Directors
Adam Giles
Ian McLean
Design Group
Interabang
Marketing Manager
Petia Tzanova
Client
Cardboard Citizens

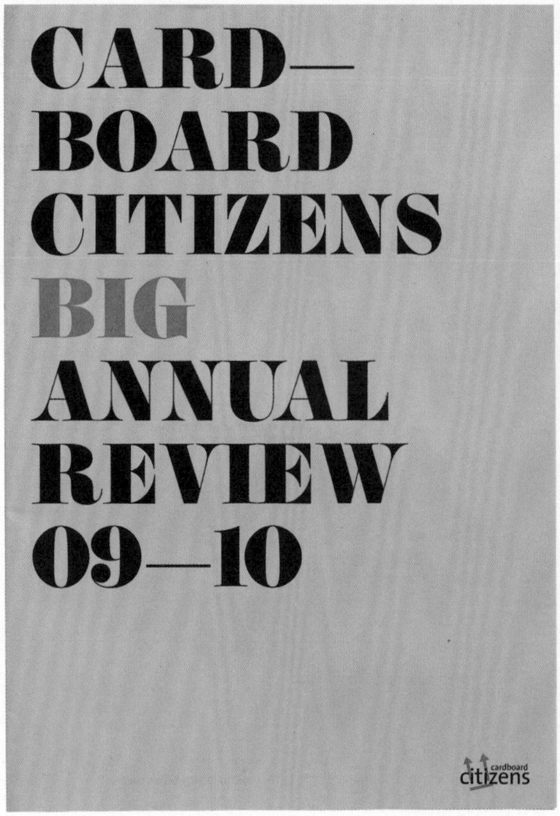
CARD—
BOARD
CITIZENS
BIG
ANNUAL
REVIEW
09—10
cardboard citizens

07
BIG
TALENT
SMALL
HELP
BIG
AMBITION
18
£189,513
£101,618
£155,731
£3,116
£72,060
£61,129
£647,197
£9,982

Annual Reports
Eduardo del Fraile
for Hefame

Pack Annual
The leading distributor of pharmaceutical products, Hefame, needed to publish their annual report. They sought a low-cost solution which they would implement alongside a more comprehensive online report. The proposal was to fit the annual report into a small container, an idea inspired by a simple box of aspirin. The content of the report was produced in the standard information leaflet format using 60gm folded paper. The balance sheets and information were reproduced in a single ink. The annual report was widely distributed to over 3,000 pharmacists and members.

Designer
Manuel Quílez Yufera
Creative Director
Eduardo del Fraile
Design Studio
Eduardo del Fraile
Marketing Manager
Almudena Egea Avilés
Client
Hefame

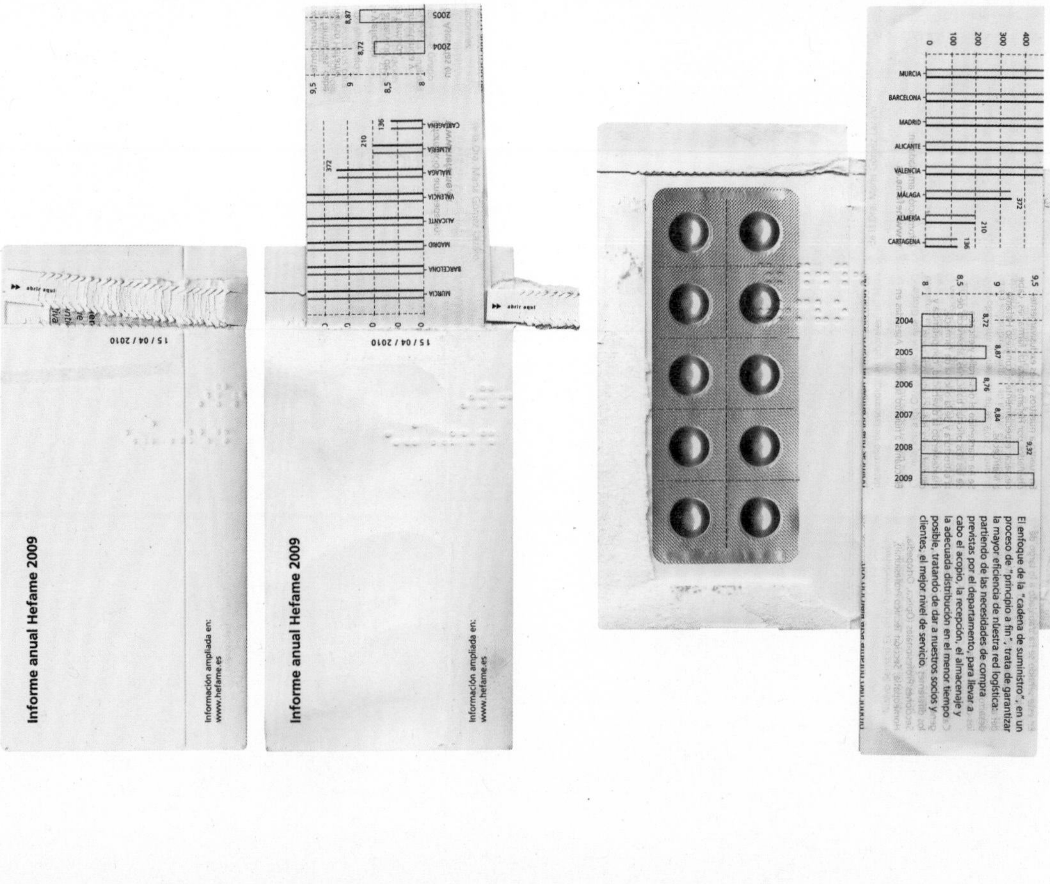
Informe anual Hefame 2009
Información ampliada en:
www.hefame.es
15 / 04 / 2010
MURCIA
BARCELONA
MADRID
ALICANTE
VALENCIA
MALAGA
ALMERIA
CARTAGENA
2004
2005
2006
2007
2008
2009

Annual Reports
1508

X Years of Design in Love with Technology
This is 1508's bespoke annual report, reflecting 10 years of design in love with technology.
X = ten years =
ten statements =
ten chapters.

Designer
Tore Rosbo
Assistant Designer
Jakob Juul Omdahl
Design Director
Line Rix
Creative Director
Rene Christoffer
Illustrator
Tore Rosbo
Copywriter
Jonas Breum
Design Agency
1508
Client
1508

PRIMA DONNAEN

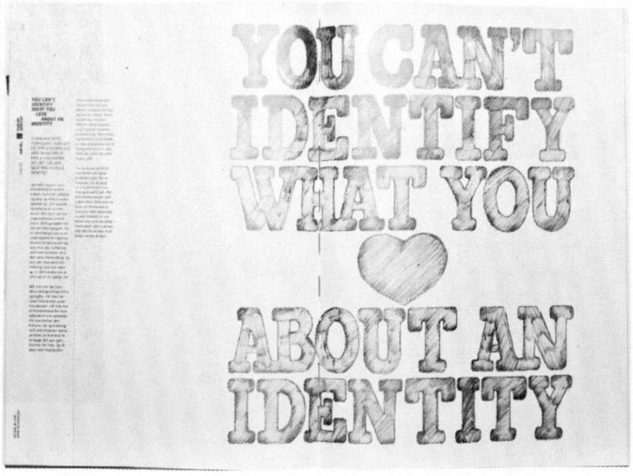
YOU CAN'T
IDENTIFY
WHAT YOU
ABOUT AN
IDENTITY

Annual Reports
Music for Manchester City FC

Manchester City FC CSR Report
After developing a new format for Manchester City's 08/09 CSR report, this year we wanted to take the project one stage further. With sustainability very much in mind, we have created a dedicated microsite to showcase the breadth of community and environmental initiatives in which the club is involved. The site is built around a dynamic cityscape of Manchester, which was created in 3D with the club at the heart of the city. You can see it for yourself at csr.mcfc.co.uk.

Designer
Jordan Stokes
Creative Director
David Simpson
3D Illustrator
Nick Harrison
Flash Developer
Matt Booth
Design Group
Music
Consumer Marketing Manager
Ian Howard
Client
Manchester City FC

Corporate and Social Responsibility Report

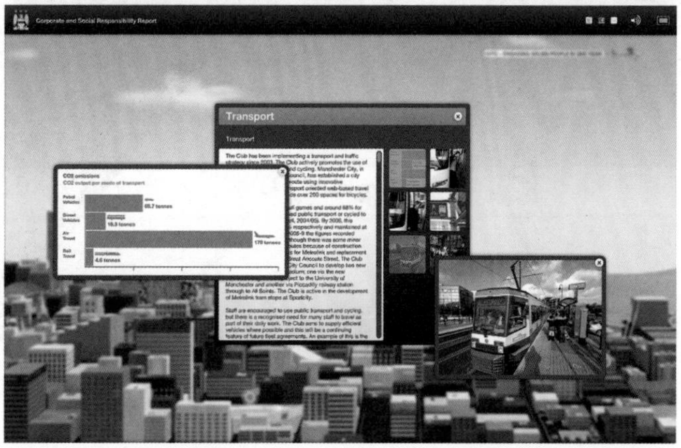
Corporate and Social Responsibility Report
Transport

Annual Reports
Addison for
Neenah Paper

What We Believe
To succeed in a challenging year, it was important for Neenah Paper to build on its firmly held values. This annual report is a clear and honest statement of what Neenah considers most important. The piece is organised into a number of visually eclectic chapters, each embodying a different core belief of the company. The steadfast tone of the content is underscored by the hardcover binding.

Designer
Jason Miller
Creative Director
Richard Colbourne
Illustrators
Micah Lidberg
Jo Ratcliffe
Photographer
Dwight Eschliman
Copywriter
Edward Nebb
Image Manipulator
Joe Kester
Design Group
Addison
Account Handler
Michelle Steg Faranda
Brand Manager
Thomas R Wright
Client
Neenah Paper

What We Believe

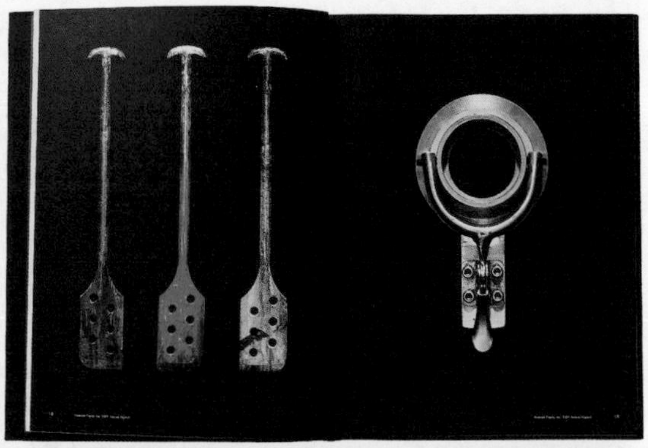

Applied Print Graphics
Happy F&B

Happy Wrapping 2010
Each year at Christmas, Happy creates a collection of wrapping paper as a gift to clients and friends. This year's design might be especially suited for round packages, but makes interesting square ones too. Three variants of double-sided wrapping paper come with 34 stickers. To add an extra fruity dimension, the papers are printed with scented ink. Once all the presents are wrapped up, you have a pile of oranges, bananas and watermelons under the Christmas tree.

Illustrator
Fredrik Persson
Art Direction
Happy F&B
Design Agency
Happy F&B
Client
Happy F&B

HAPPY X-MAS
HAPPY
HAPPY HOLIDAYS
HAPPY

Applied Print Graphics
Magpie Studio for
Gavin Martin
Colournet Limited

Job Bags
Having joined forces in 2010, Gavin Martin Associates and Colournet wanted to raise their new profile without breaking the joint bank account. We suggested making use of an unused canvas: the humble proof bag. Used by printers to deliver wet proofs to their clients, the bags were screen printed with a life-sized collection of eccentric objects. Tucked under the arm, the proof bags act as walking billboards en route, and a talking point when dropped off. Low cost, high impact and with the promise of raising a smile.

Designers
Ben Christie
Tim Fellowes
Creative Directors
David Azurdia
Ben Christie
Jamie Ellul
Design Agency
Magpie Studio
Brand Manager
Phil Le Monde
Client
Gavin Martin
Colournet Limited

Hand delivered by
Gavin Martin Colournet Limited

PLAYBOY
NATIONAL LITHOGRAPHIC

Hand delivered by
Gavin Martin Colournet Limited

Applied Print Graphics
Y&R Malaysia for
Penguin Books

Pause Bookmark
Bookmarks are typically used to remind readers which page they last read. As such Penguin Audiobooks designed bookmarks with the audio symbol for pause, to graphically remind book lovers that Penguin also has a range of audiobooks. Distributed as a free gift with all books, the pause bookmark is a marketing tool with a practical function.

Designer
Toh Han Ming
Art Director
Toh Han Ming
Creative Directors
Mark Fong
Edward Ong
James Procter
Marcus Rebeschini
Copywriter
Mark Fong
Image Manipulator
Sam Ng
Advertising Agency
Y&R Malaysia
Account Handler
Anthony Khoo
Group Chief Executive Officer
Tanuj Philip
Brand Manager
Chung Yaw Hwa
Client
Penguin Books
Brand
Penguin Audiobooks

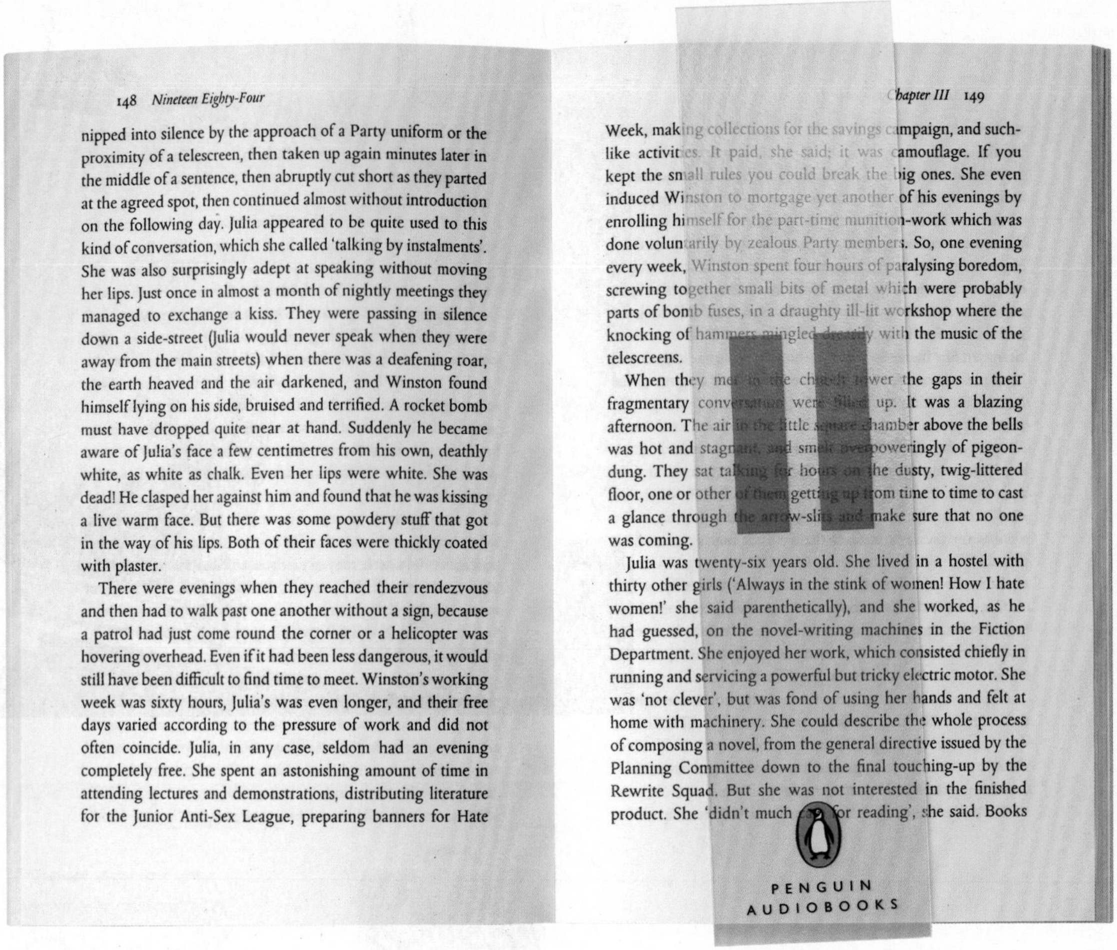
148 Nineteen Eighty-Four
nipped into silence by the approach of a Party uniform or the proximity of a telescreen, then taken up again minutes later in the middle of a sentence, then abruptly cut short as they parted at the agreed spot, then continued almost without introduction on the following day. Julia appeared to be quite used to this kind of conversation, which she called 'talking by instalments'. She was also surprisingly adept at speaking without moving her lips. Just once in almost a month of nightly meetings they managed to exchange a kiss. They were passing in silence down a side-street (Julia would never speak when they were away from the main streets) when there was a deafening roar, the earth heaved and the air darkened, and Winston found himself lying on his side, bruised and terrified. A rocket bomb must have dropped quite near at hand. Suddenly he became aware of Julia's face a few centimetres from his own, deathly white, as white as chalk. Even her lips were white. She was dead! He clasped her against him and found that he was kissing a live warm face. But there was some powdery stuff that got in the way of his lips. Both of their faces were thickly coated with plaster.
There were evenings when they reached their rendezvous and then had to walk past one another without a sign, because a patrol had just come round the corner or a helicopter was hovering overhead. Even if it had been less dangerous, it would still have been difficult to find time to meet. Winston's working week was sixty hours, Julia's was even longer, and their free days varied according to the pressure of work and did not often coincide. Julia, in any case, seldom had an evening completely free. She spent an astonishing amount of time in attending lectures and demonstrations, distributing literature for the Junior Anti-Sex League, preparing banners for Hate
hapter III 149
Week, making collections for the savings campaign, and such-like activities. It paid, she said; it was camouflage. If you kept the small rules you could break the big ones. She even induced Winston to mortgage yet another of his evenings by enrolling himself for the part-time munition-work which was done voluntarily by zealous Party members. So, one evening every week, Winston spent four hours of paralysing boredom, screwing together small bits of metal which were probably parts of bomb fuses, in a draughty ill-lit workshop where the knocking of ham with the music of the telescreens.
When they ower the gaps in their fragmentary conv up. It was a blazing afternoon. The air ttle r above the bells was hot and stag oweringly of pigeon-dung. They sat ta he dusty, twig-littered floor, one or other gett om time to time to cast a glance through w-sl make sure that no one was coming.
Julia was twenty-six years old. She lived in a hostel with thirty other girls ('Always in the stink of women! How I hate women!' she said parenthetically), and she worked, as he had guessed, on the novel-writing machines in the Fiction Department. She enjoyed her work, which consisted chiefly in running and servicing a powerful but tricky electric motor. She was 'not clever', but was fond of using her hands and felt at home with machinery. She could describe the whole process of composing a novel, from the general directive issued by the Planning Committee down to the final touching-up by the Rewrite Squad. But she was not interested in the finished product. She 'didn't much for reading', she said. Books
PENGUIN
AUDIOBOOKS

Applied Print Graphics
Neil Wolfson for
The Royal Mint

Olympic Football 50p
The Royal Mint held a national competition, seeking 50p coin-face designs for each Olympic sport. To represent football, I applied some lateral thinking to explain the offside rule. After researching FIFA's 'Laws of the Game', I drafted a scale diagram of a 75m x 105m football pitch. My tripartite copy, 'Offside explained'/ 'Offside'/ 'Not offside', works like a one-liner, making this possibly the world's first amusing legal tender. It's probably also the world's only coin to be designed on Microsoft Paint. The design was approved by the Chancellor of the Exchequer and Her Majesty the Queen.

Designer
Neil Wolfson
Creative Director
Neil Wolfson
Copywriter
Neil Wolfson
Client
The Royal Mint

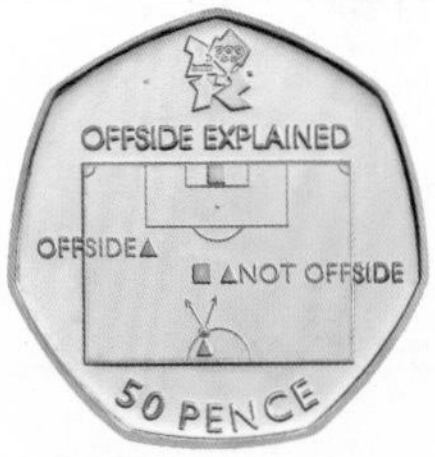
OFFSIDE EXPLAINED
OFFSIDE
NOT OFFSIDE
50 PENCE

Calendars
Sandy Choi Associates
for Antalis Hong Kong

Antalis Calendar 2011
Sandy Choi Associates gave visual expression to time, the theme of the oversized 2011 Antalis Calendar (605 x 825mm), and revived the memory of a time in Hong Kong when calendars were large, prized, and held pride of place on the wall of each household. Beginning in January with Stephen Hawking's lecture on 'The Beginning of Time', to the display of Hong Kong's flag as a British colony to illustrate the significance of our past to the present, the Antalis Calendar reveals the common thread that unites all of us in our perception of time.

Designers
Sandy Choi
Toby Ng
Lau Sui Wah
Design Director
Sandy Choi
Photographer
Ringo Tang
Design Group
Sandy Choi Associates
Brand Manager
Miranda Hui
Marketing Manager
Jovy Tong
Client
Antalis Hong Kong

Marılyn
Monroe
March

May

Calendars
Heye & Partner for FIT Delivery & Shipping

FIT Calendar
We were asked to create a calendar for FIT Delivery & Shipping, known for its reliable service and on-schedule delivery. We showed their reliable 365-day service by means of a calendar delivered by an FIT employee, looking like a regular shipment. Turning the envelope, the recipient can see 12 straps and the statement: 'Delivery by your desired deadline – FIT Delivery & Shipping'. Every month a strap can be pulled off until the envelope is opened in December and reveals an order form for the 2012 calendar. Of course, 'Delivery by your desired deadline' is guaranteed.

Designer
Marcus Feil
Art Director
Marcus Feil
Creative Directors
Fabian Hinzer
Jan Okusluk
Zeljko Pezely
Copywriter
Christina Meister
Advertising Agency
Heye & Partner
Account Handler
Christian Scharrel
Marketing Manager
Alexander Grelck
Client
FIT Delivery & Shipping
(FIT Logistik & Transportmanagement)

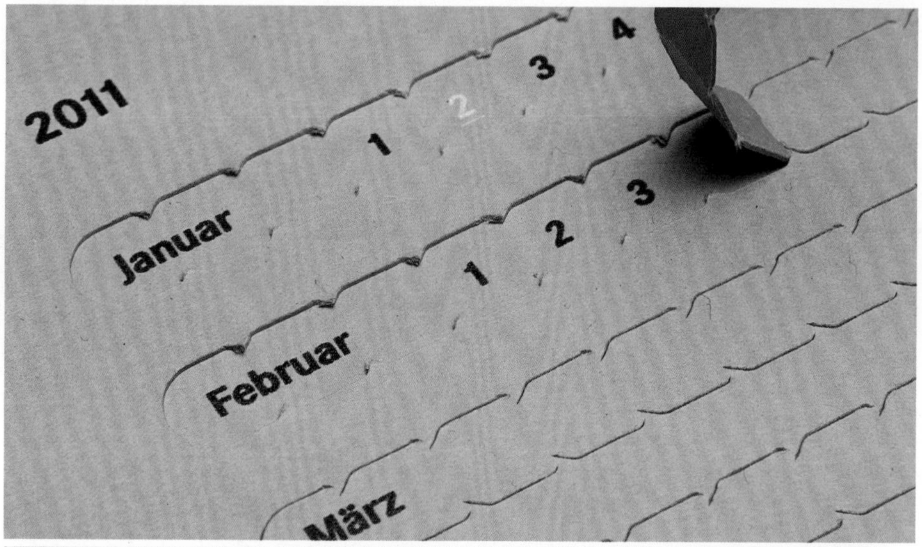
2011
Januar
Februar
März

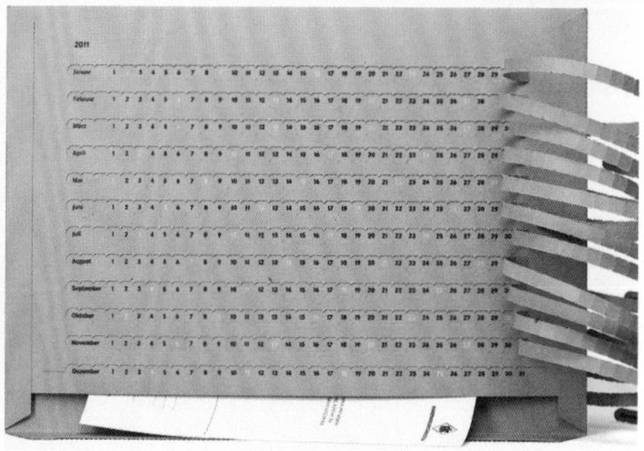

Calendars
TBWA\India for
Yatra Online India

Immigration Stamps
Yatra.com is India's leading online travel portal. The goal was to make 2011 a year when people locked up their houses and headed out. Shown with a calendar of 365 immigration stamps, the message was simple: for the next 365 days, go out and explore places most people haven't even heard of.

Designers
Rishi Chanana
Akash Swami
Design Director
Rishi Chanana
Creative Director
Rishi Chanana
National Creative Director
Rahul Sen Gupta
Illustrators
Rishi Chanana
Akash Swami
Copywriters
Rishi Chanana
Kingshuk Dey
Anish Nath
Advertising Agency
TBWA\India
Account Handler
Aditi Kaushik
Brand & Marketing Manager
Pratik Mazumder
Client
Yatra Online India

yatra.com
go travel

Calendars
Draftfcb Germany for DOM Sicherheitstechnik

Burglarproof Advent Calendar
The task was to use the annual Christmas mailing for regular and potential new clients to draw attention to DOM's expertise in safety engineering. Draftfcb Germany developed the first burglar proof advent calendar. At first glance, the advent calendar looked like a typical promotional gift. But the doors couldn't be opened because they were not die cut as usual. So the chocolate stayed safe. This allowed DOM to demonstrate – and the recipient to experience – its superior safety engineering in a simple and surprising way.

Art Director
Senjel Gazibara
Creative Director
Bill Biancoli
Executive Creative Director
Dirk Haeusermann
Illustrators
Thomas Färber
Vitali Nazarenus
Copywriter
Alexandra Beck
Advertising Agency
Draftfcb Germany
Account Handler
Lea Faupel
Marketing Manager
Andrea Magnor
Client
DOM Sicherheitstechnik
Brand
DOM

DOM
SECURITY LOCKS

Catalogues & Brochures
Magpie Studio for the Parliament's Education Service

Speaker's School Council Awards: The Year Book
The Speaker's School Council Awards recognise excellence in school councils nationwide. Parliament's Education Service ran a pilot competition to highlight a democratic approach in school council projects. The competition was hugely successful and a full identity system and yearbook were commissioned to commemorate the winning projects. The identity needed to appeal to three audiences: students (ages ranging from four to 19), their teachers, and politicians. Our solution focuses on the idea of group participation, one of the key messages. We collaborated with illustrator Tom Gauld. His work, with both a childlike quality and sophistication, appealed to all audiences.

Designer
Will Southward
Creative Directors
David Azurdia
Ben Christie
Jamie Ellul
Typographer
Will Southward
Illustrator
Tom Gauld
Photographers
Kwame Lestrade
Terry Moore
Design Agency
Magpie Studio
Client Project Manager
Lauren Hyams
Client
Parliament's Education Service
Brand
Speaker's School Council Awards

PARLIAMENT
EDUCATION SERVICE
The Year Book
2009—2010
Celebrating school councils and their achievements
4—7 Age Category:
Shared Learning
7—11 Age Category:
Reaching Out
11—16 Age Category:
Identity and Including People
16—19 Age Category:
Taking Control
SPEAKER'S SCHOOL COUNCIL AWARDS

IDEAS!

Catalogues & Brochures
WORK

WERK No.17: Eley Kishimoto
A collaboration between Eley Kishimoto and WERK magazine, this issue visually documents the personal journeys and work by Eley Kishimoto's founders – Mark Eley and Wakako Kishimoto. Presented using photographs, sketches, musings and print designs, it echoes their code of conduct – one that does not succumb to trends and fads. The end result combines iconic Eley Kishimoto prints and fabric bundles with WERK's artisanal perfect-imperfect craftsmanship. Featuring a cover that is made of four randomly selected fabrics secured with staples and tailor pins, WERK No.17 embodies the idea and inspiration of a textile work in progress.

Designers
Sharon Goh
Joanne Lim
Design Director
Theseus Chan
Design Group
WORK
Printing & Construction
alsoDominie
Account Handler
Thida Hawkins
Client
WORK
Brand
WERK Magazine

WARNING: KEEP OUT OF REACH OF CHILDREN AND PETS. PINS AND FASTENINGS USED ARE SHARP AND WILL DETACH WITH HANDLING. PLEASE HANDLE WITH CARE.
CAUTION: THE CONSTRUCTION OF THIS MAGAZINE HAS BEEN HAND-ASSEMBLED. THE FABRIC ATTACHMENTS WILL FRAY WITH HANDLING. THE IMPERMANANCE IS PART OF THE PROCESS OF THE DESIGN. WEAR AND TEAR WILL OCCUR.
WERK No.17:
ELEY KISHIMOTO
336 pages, Colour,
approx 220mm x 305mm
Edition: 1000 copies

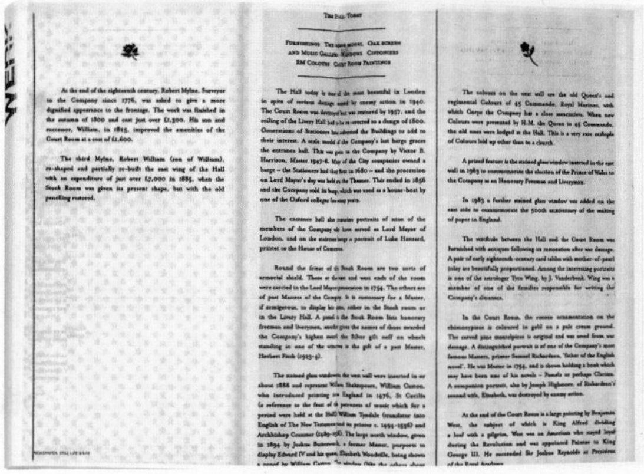

Catalogues & Brochures
Jäger & Jäger for Nils Holger Moormann

Moormann Complete Catalogue
'Complete Catalogue Volume 3' by Nils Holger Moormann presents the current product range from the Chiemgau furniture manufacturer with minimalist ambient pictures and a completely photographed product typology. An exclusive insight into life behind the scenes in the company is provided in the inserted thumbnail pages. Each copy is individually numbered on the cover label, ensuring that each address receives its own personal copy, and underlining the manufactured character of the furniture.

Designers
Olaf Jäger
Regina Jäger
Design Group
Jäger & Jäger
Marketing Manager
Nicole Christof
Client
Nils Holger Moormann

7289 /7.500

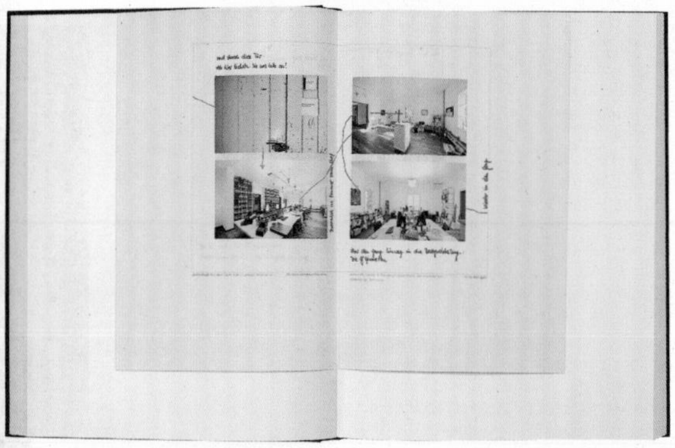

Catalogues & Brochures
Browns for Jonathan Ellery & Mulberry

Worldly Cares and Love Affairs
In autumn 2010, Jonathan Ellery was commissioned by Mulberry to produce a sculptural piece for its new flagship store at 50 New Bond Street in London. The piece consists of 25 circular, machined, solid brass pieces that have been embedded into the concrete floor of the store at specific locations. This catalogue shows the sequential narrative and reveals where the pieces can be found within the store.

Designer
Sabrina Grill
Creative Director
Jonathan Ellery
Design Group
Browns
Publishers
Browns Editions
Clients
Jonathan Ellery
Mulberry

Worldly Cares and Love Affairs
A Catalogue
Jonathan Ellery

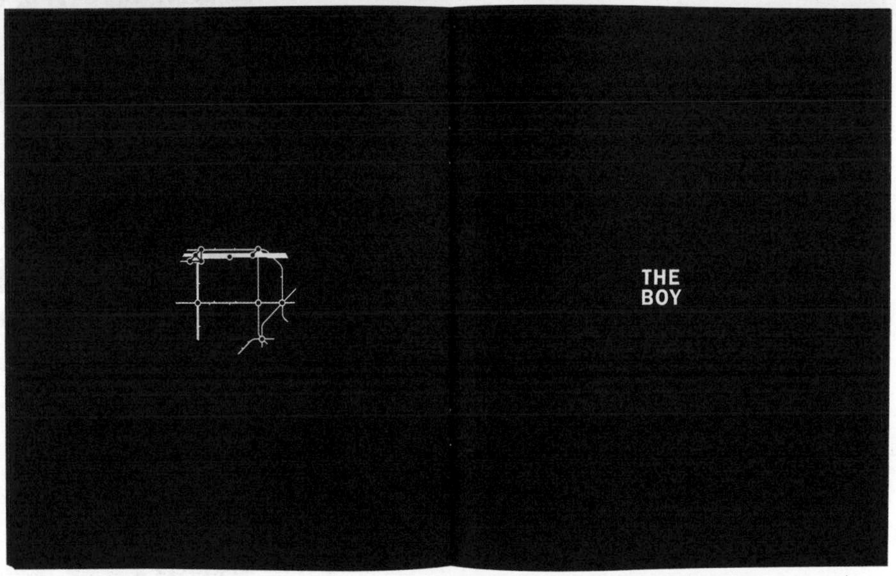
THE
BOY

Catalogues & Brochures
Pentagram Design
for the London Design Festival

Max Lamb – The Vermiculated Ashlar
This publication celebrates the completion of a piece by designer Max Lamb for the St James office of HSBC Private Bank. The piece was commissioned in collaboration with the London Design Festival. This publication charts the journey of the piece, a plaster bench called the Vermiculated Ashlar, from concept to completion.
The debossed cover replicates the vermiculated stonework of the plinth, while the monochrome grey and cream paper refers to the plaster in both its polished and rough forms. The pace of the interior of the booklet is varied through the use of large and small images and type, referencing the scale of the project.

Designer
Jeremy Kunze
Design Director
Domenic Lippa
Typographer
Jeremy Kunze
Copywriters
Jonathan Bell
Suzanne Trocme
Design Group
Pentagram Design
Account Handler
Kate Shepherd
Marketing Manager
Alessandra Canavesi
Head of Marketing & Communications
John Dore
Festival Director
Ben Evans
Clients
HSBC Private Bank
London Design Festival

MAX
LAM
B
HSBC Private Bank
HSBC

PROP
O
SAL
CAS
TING
1.
00
M3

Catalogues & Brochures
The Workshop
for Roundabout

Roundabout Annual Report 2010
Roundabout provides shelter and support to young homeless people in Sheffield. The annual report comes in two parts: a photographic, oversized brochure, and a wraparound booklet containing facts and figures. The photography gets up close and personal with a number of the young people Roundabout supports. They are shown on roundabouts in a playground setting that contrasts with the seriousness of their circumstances.
The wraparound booklet shares some of the young people's stories and reports on the charity's activities. Its smaller format illustrates how the problem of homeless young people in Sheffield is larger than Roundabout's resources.

Designer
Andrew Turner
Art Director
Andrew Turner
Creative Director
Colin Scott
Photographer
Nigel Barker
Design Group
The Workshop
Printing Company
ProCo
Client
Roundabout

ROUND
ABOUT

Catalogues & Brochures
Why Not Smile

Why Not Smile Inventory
This booklet represents the portfolio of Why Not Smile, a graphic design studio in New York. Instead of a traditional way to present work, it employs the concept of inventory by providing a list of work, listed work images, and text describing the studio's thoughts. In order to emphasise the inventory idea, all images were scanned.

Designer
Hyo Kwon
Creative Director
Hoon Kim
Copywriter
Erica Yujin Choi
Design Studio
Why Not Smile
Client
Why Not Smile

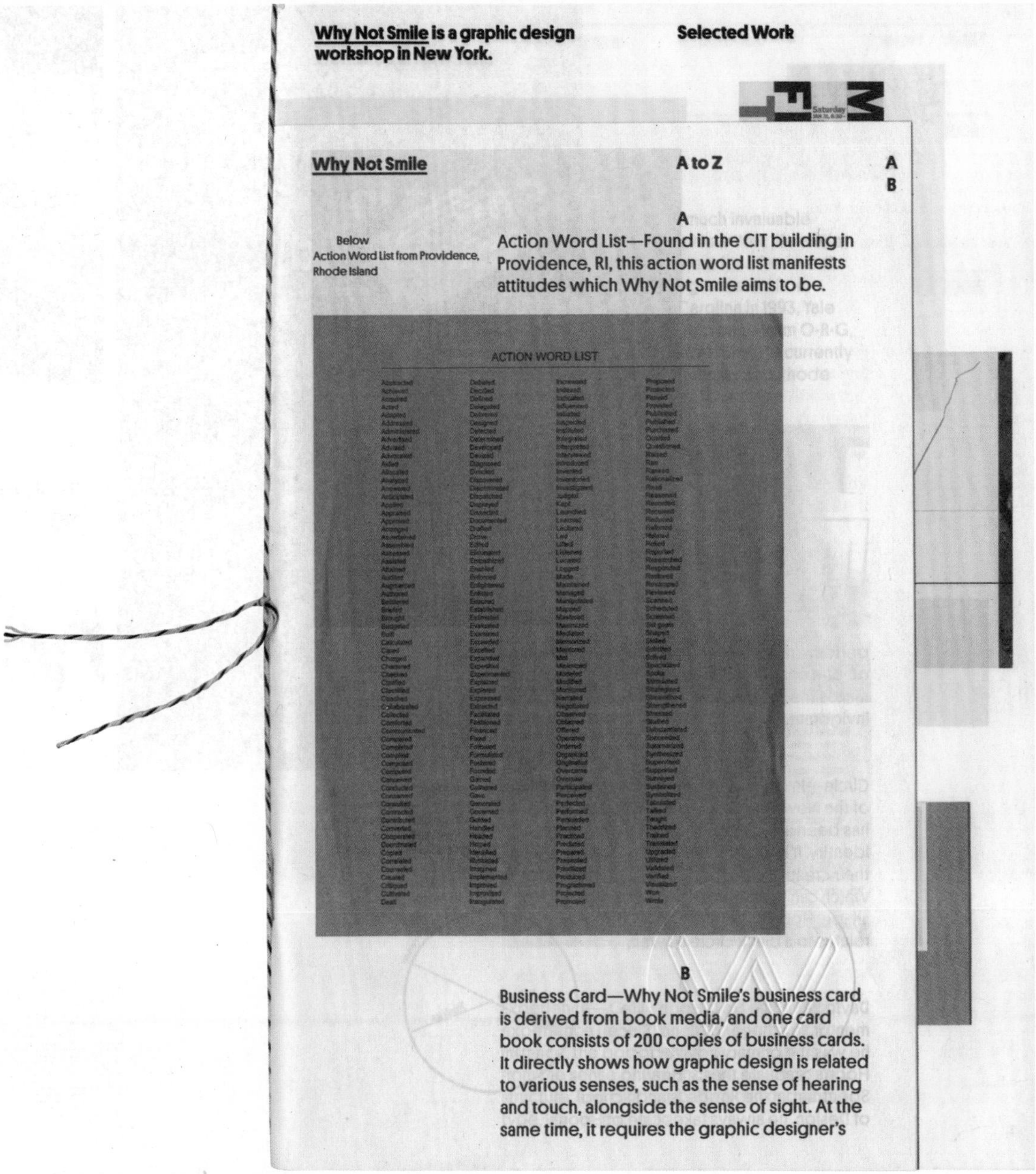
Why Not Smile is a graphic design workshop in New York.
Selected Work
Why Not Smile
A to Z
A
B
Below
Action Word List from Providence, Rhode Island
A
Action Word List—Found in the CIT building in Providence, RI, this action word list manifests attitudes which Why Not Smile aims to be.
ACTION WORD LIST
B
Business Card—Why Not Smile's business card is derived from book media, and one card book consists of 200 copies of business cards. It directly shows how graphic design is related to various senses, such as the sense of hearing and touch, alongside the sense of sight. At the same time, it requires the graphic designer's

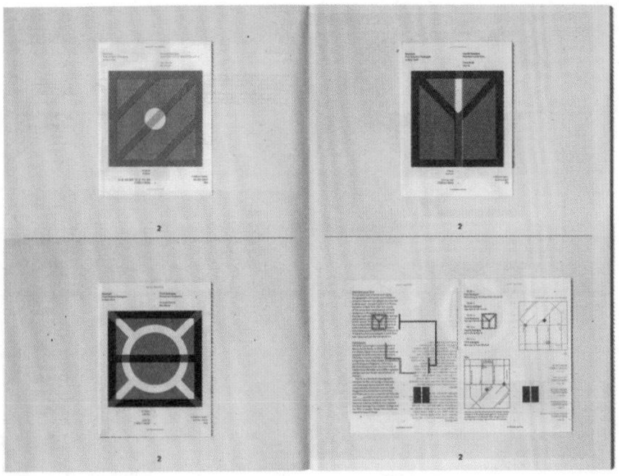

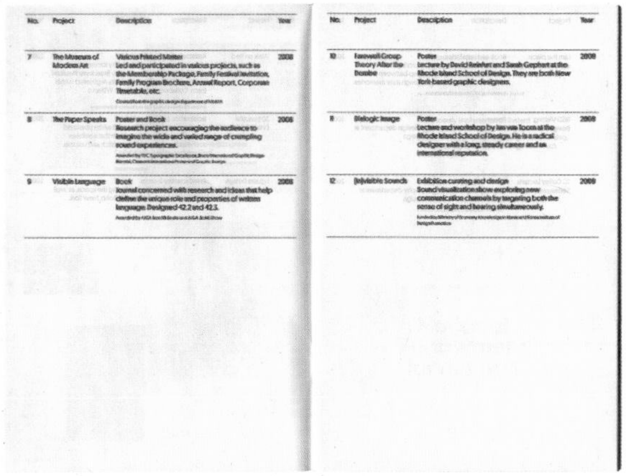

Catalogues & Brochures
Design Army for
Arent Fox

Smart in Your World
'Smart in Your World' is the tagline used by law firm Arent Fox, but it's more than a tagline – it's the culture of the company. The 'Smart in Your World' brochure takes a look at some the most compelling cases and clients the firm has taken on in recent years, but not in a traditional law firm manner. Oversized and simplified, the report uses the key brand colours of the firm, as well as a slick cover with white foil embossing. The brochure stands out in the crowd, and is definitely smart in your world.

Designer
Charles Calixto
Art Director
Pum Lefebure
Creative Directors
Jake Lefebure
Pum Lefebure
Illustrator
Tim Madle
Copywriter
Steven Harras
Design Group
Design Army
Marketing Manager
Denise Delorey
Client
Arent Fox

Smart In
Your World
Aiming
High
THE VISOR SHOT. Buzz Aldrin is an American legend – Astronaut. Scientist. Explorer. In 1969, Dr. Aldrin, along with his colleagues Neil Armstrong and Michael Collins bravely piloted into the unknown for the Apollo 11 lunar expedition. During that historic mission, Dr. Aldrin became one of only a dozen members of humanity to walk on the surface of the moon. His training and survival skills as an Air Force pilot who flew 66 combat missions in Korea and as an astronaut had allowed him to survive treacherous journeys through some of the most hostile environments on and beyond our planet.
Thinking
Big
A SURPRISING PHONE CALL. Arent Fox's Carol Connor Cohen, head of the firm's ERISA litigation practice, was in her Washington, DC office in October, 2004, preparing for a meeting with the senior benefits counsel of W. R. Grace & Co., a premier specialty chemicals and construction materials company, which conducts business in 41 countries and more than 20 currencies, employing approximately 6,500 full-time people worldwide. Grace's top ERISA lawyer was on his way to discuss defense strategy for a class action lawsuit recently filed in federal court in Massachusetts by two former employees who claimed the company's 401(k) plan had breached its duty to retirees by failing to sell Grace stock before the price dropped.

Catalogues & Brochures
Sigi Mayer for Zettl

Liebe Freunde des Guten Geschmacks
The annually released catalogue by local vendor Brigitta Zettl addresses her loyal customers. They visit her deli as people of taste, and expect particularly appetising advertising thanks to Brigitta's well-known passion for her business. The creative challenge was to compose a new and extraordinary catalogue year after year, always focusing on the specialities sold, and inviting customers to savour the delicacies right away.

Creative Director
Sigi Mayer
Photographer
Horst Stasny
Copywriter
Rosa Haider Merlicek
Marketing Manager
Brigitta Zettl
Client
Zettl

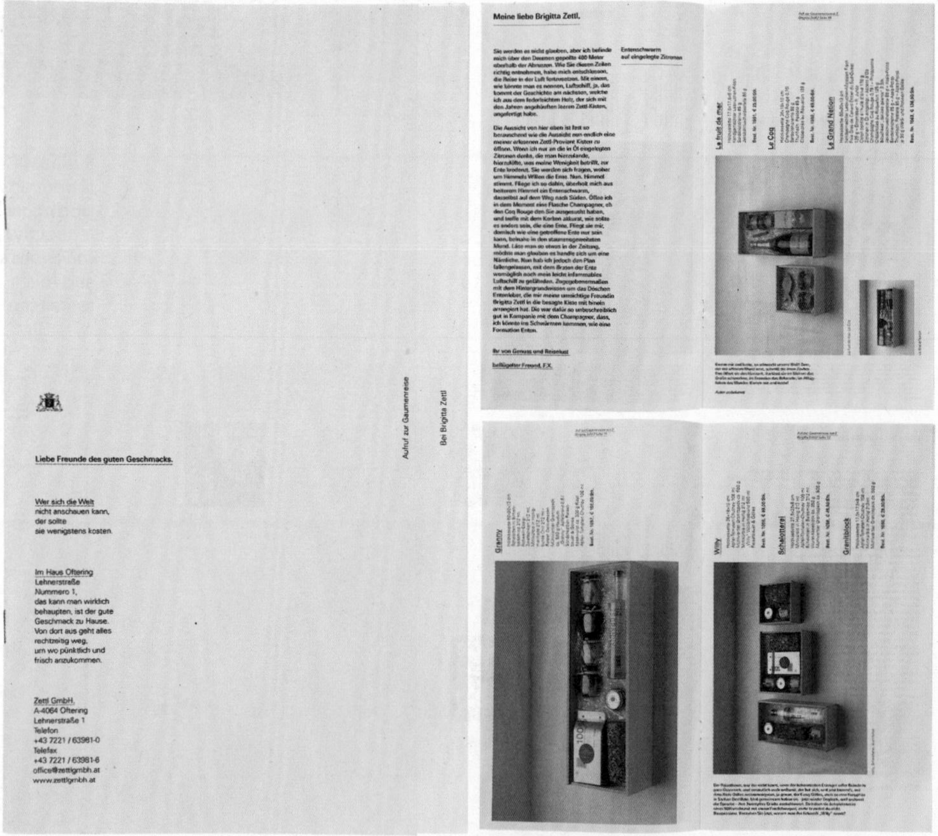
Liebe Freunde des guten Geschmacks.
Wer sich die Welt
nicht anschauen kann,
der sollte
sie wenigstens kosten.
Im Haus Oftering
Lehnerstraße
Nummero 1,
das kann man wirklich
behaupten, ist der gute
Geschmack zu Hause.
Von dort aus geht alles
rechtzeitig weg,
um wo pünktlich und
frisch anzukommen.
Zettl GmbH,
A-4064 Oftering
Lehnerstraße 1
Telefon
+43 7221 / 63981-0
Telefax
+43 7221 / 63981-6
office@zettlgmbh.at
www.zettlgmbh.at
Aufruf zur Gaumenreise
Bei Brigitta Zettl
Meine liebe Brigitta Zettl.

Catalogues & Brochures
Sigi Mayer for The Room

Mr Simon Tyrrell – Works by The Room Inside the Sixties
The Room is a showroom for vintage furniture and decorative arts of the 20th Century. At the inauguration designed for a clientele with an affinity to the 60s, a catalogue was provided highlighting furniture, glassware, pottery and lighting in an unusual ambience. The email correspondence between Simon Tyrrell and his friends while establishing The Room is reproduced, to illustrate the passion he has for his commodities.

Creative Director
Sigi Mayer
Photographers
Ditz Fejer
Horst Stasny
Copywriters
Pete Carty
Simon Tyrrell
Marketing Manager
Simon Tyrrell
Client
The Room

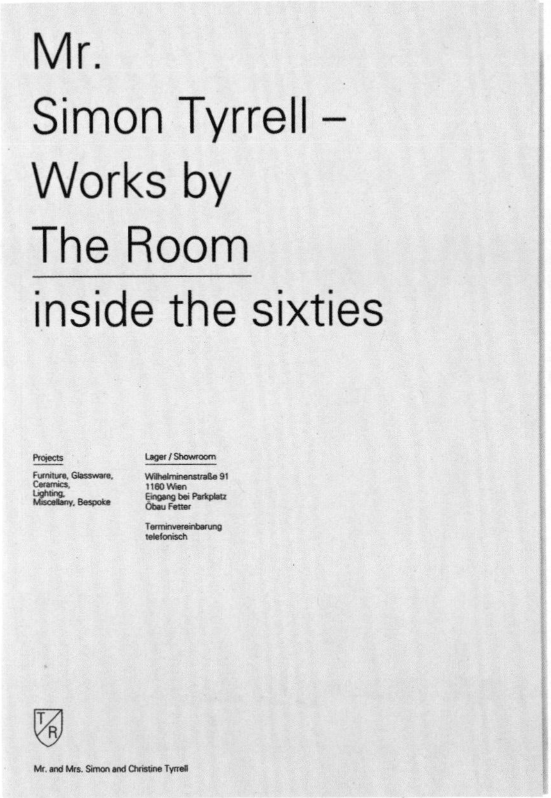
Mr.
Simon Tyrrell –
Works by
The Room
inside the sixties
Projects
Furniture, Glassware, Ceramics, Lighting, Miscellany, Bespoke
Lager / Showroom
Wilhelminenstraße 91
1160 Wien
Eingang bei Parkplatz
Öbau Fetter
Terminvereinbarung telefonisch
Mr. and Mrs. Simon and Christine Tyrrell

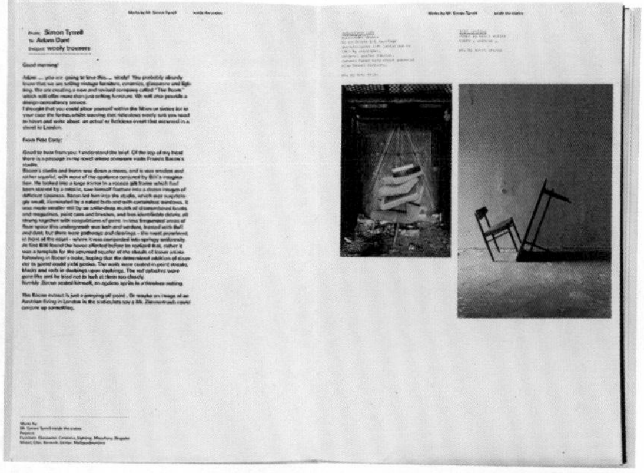

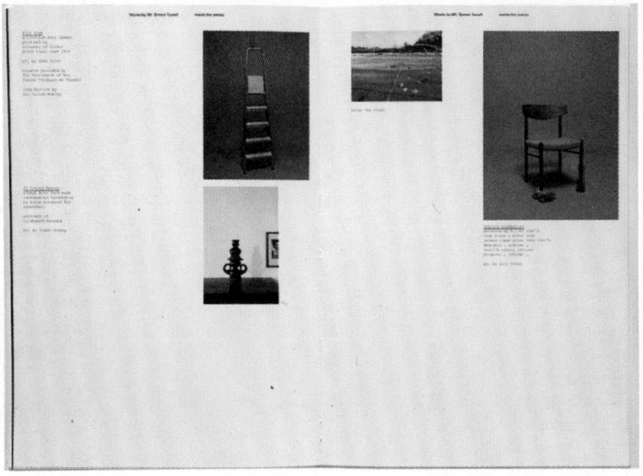

Catalogues & Brochures
MARK for the Manchester Literature Festival

Manchester Literature Festival 2010
The campaign for the 2010 Manchester Literature Festival saw a number of cryptic posters go up around Manchester, each featuring a short quote from authors involved in the event. These were then photographed in situ and used in the festival programme.

Designers
Ben Harisson
Mark Lester
Creative Director
Mark Lester
Photographer
Henry Iddon
Design Group
MARK
Brand Manager
Cathy Bolton
Marketing Manager
Jon Atkin
Client
Manchester Literature Festival

MANCHESTER
LITERATURE
FESTIVAL
14—25
OCTOBER
2010

BEFORE THE SCREAMING STARTS THE NIGHT SILENCE OF THE CONVENT IS ALIVE WITH ITS OWN PARTICULAR SOUNDS...

MY LIFE HAD STOOD A LOADED GUN IN CORNERS...
MIGUELANXO PRADO
Read

Catalogues & Brochures
So Design Consultants
for the Auschwitz-Birkenau Foundation

Auschwitz-Birkenau Fundraising Brochure
Auschwitz-Birkenau is currently in desperate need of preservation and conservation. So Design Consultants conceived and created a fundraising brochure aimed at generating a €120million perpetual fund for the ongoing work at the Auschwitz-Birkenau site. The sensitively designed brochure includes bespoke imagery along with powerful typographic statements to deliver the hard facts of the cause. The aim was to reach out to governments, corporate institutions and private donors in order to generate funds to preserve, educate and inform.

Designer
Steve Haskins
Art Director
Steve Haskins
Photographer
Peter Thorpe
Design Company
So Design Consultants
Client
Auschwitz-Birkenau Foundation

THE PRESERVATION OF AUSCHWITZ-BIRKENAU
OUR RESPONSIBILITY FOR FUTURE GENERATIONS

THE FOUNDATION
THE MISSION
THE STRUCTURE

'THERE IS ONLY ONE THING WORSE THAN AUSCHWITZ ITSELF...AND THAT IS IF THE WORLD FORGETS THERE WAS SUCH A PLACE'

Catalogues & Brochures
Ligalux for fischerAppelt relations

Dek 21
Under the central theme of 'sharpening instead of smoothing', fischerAppelt relations promote a change in thinking and present 21 ideas for sharper communications. Each of the 21 ideas has been individually designed and has its own content and look. The neon yellow of the brochure cover provides a contrast to the environmentally friendly paper used for the brochure itself. The main characteristic of the design is the use of various fonts that underpin the individual nature of each idea. The pixelated Gothic script on the cover combines a bold concept with modern design.

Designer
Tobias Heidmeier
Typographer
Tobias Heidmeier
Creative Director
Jan Kruse
Design Group
Ligalux
Account Handler
Jan Kuruse
Brand Manager
Bernhard Fischer-Appelt
Client
fischerAppelt relations

Deklaration für einen Kurswechsel in der Meinungslandschaft
| Dek 21

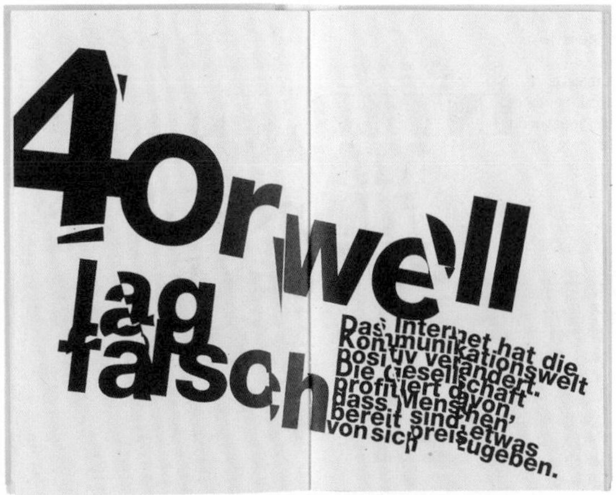
4 Orwell lag falsch
Das Internet hat die Kommunikationswelt positiv verändert. Die Gesellschaft profitiert davon, dass Menschen bereit sind, etwas von sich preiszugeben.

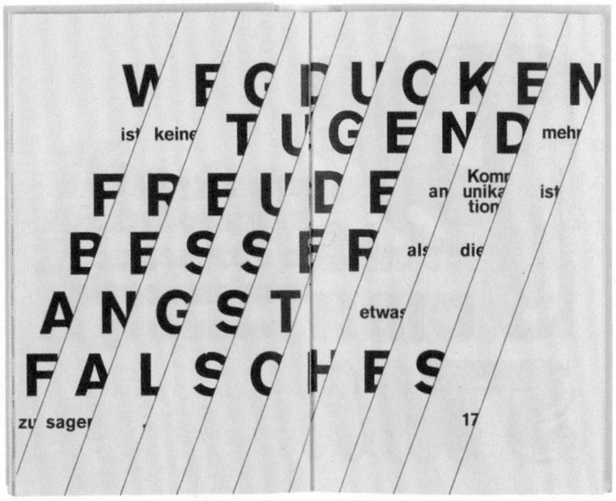
17

Catalogues & Brochures
Visual Arts Press for the School of Visual Arts

Proof
The objective of the School of Visual Arts' undergraduate catalogue, 'Proof', is to show prospective students why SVA is the preeminent training ground for the next generation of artists. Our solution was to present visual and factual evidence, first by giving dozens of facts about NYC, SVA and its students, then by presenting hundreds of examples of student work throughout the book. We also employed an innovative heat-responsive ink on the cover; with the application of heat (such as from a hand) a map of the school is revealed.

Designers
Suck Zoo Han
Brian E Smith
E Patrick Tobin
Art Director
Michael J Walsh
Creative Director
Anthony P Rhodes
Design Group
Visual Arts Press
Client
School of Visual Arts

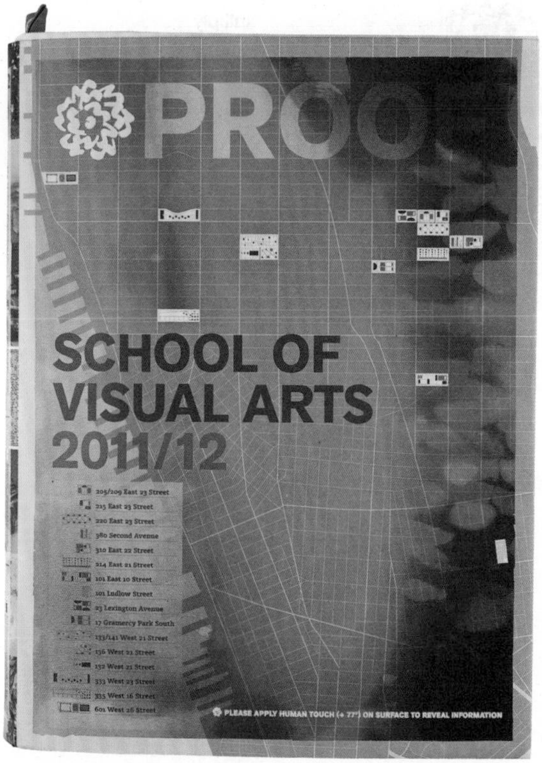
SCHOOL OF VISUAL ARTS 2011/12
PLEASE APPLY HUMAN TOUCH (+ 77°) ON SURFACE TO REVEAL INFORMATION

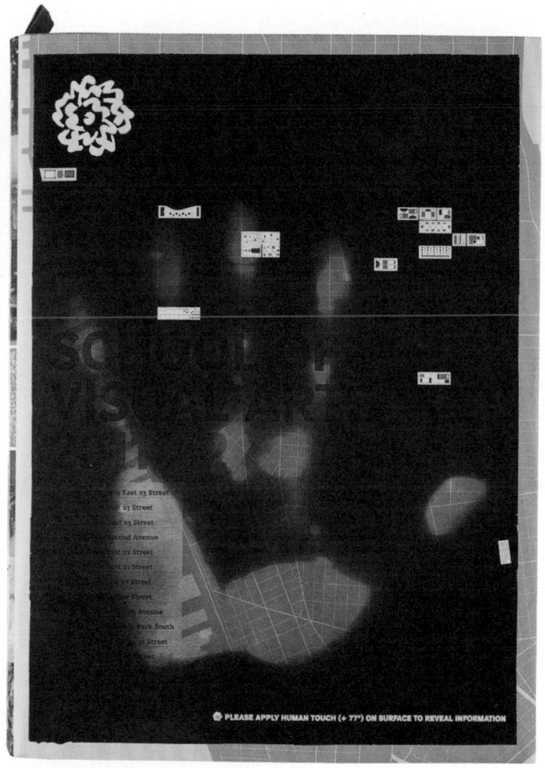
PLEASE APPLY HUMAN TOUCH (+ 77°) ON SURFACE TO REVEAL INFORMATION

Catalogues & Brochures
The Stone Twins

A Catalogue of Curiosities, Relics, Art & Propaganda
'A Catalogue of Curiosities, Relics, Art & Propaganda' (or CRAP for short) is an irreverent trawl through the world of The Stone Twins, a creative partnership based in Amsterdam. The booklet celebrates various aspects of their life and inspirations, and is accompanied by a gummed sheet of images that adds further colour to the stories.

Designers
Declan Stone
Garech Stone
Creative Directors
Declan Stone
Garech Stone
Typographer
Declan Stone
Copywriter
Garech Stone
Design Group
The Stone Twins

A CATALOGUE OF CURIOSITIES, RELICS, ART & PROPAGANDA – THE STONE TWINS – © 2010
+dd
–tract
xultiply
div÷de
A CATALOGUE OF CRAP
THE STONE TWINS

+dd
–tract
xultiply
div÷de
SACRAMENTAL WINE, VINTAGE
1980. One sealed bottle of ruby-red, full-bodied and dry burgundy; better known as 'Blood of Christ'.
This wine received daily ecclesiastical approbation by the Priests of St. Marks Parish, Dublin. Through transubstantiation, the wine became the body, blood, soul and divinity of Christ. Once cornered in the sacristy, we are eternally grateful that the Reverend Father Noone only introduced us to cheap alcohol. No happy hour for him then.*
* Lord, have mercy on us. Christ, have mercy on us. Lord, have mercy on us. Christ, hear us. Christ, graciously hear us.
36
EYE NO. 4 (VOL. 1)
1991. 96pp plus cover, 297 x 237 mm, coated and uncoated sections. A rare and highly collectable item.
For nearly 20 years, the thud of 'Eye Magazine' popping through our letter box triggers eager anticipation. Offering more than eye-candy, it's the only publication with a serious critique and review of the world of graphic design. This bumper issue introduced us to the idiosyncratic talent of Robert Brownjohn and the typographic anarchy of Wolfgang Weingart.
37
AER LINGUS AIRLINE TICKET
1996, used. Routing: Amsterdam – Dublin. Printed on carbon paper. With minor staple holes in front and some slight creasing.
This ticket offered a visit 'home' to see our family and keep tabs on the birth of the now extinct Celtic Tiger, and it's bastard offspring Riverdance and Boyzone. Nowadays, we don't have to pay exorbitant airfares – thanks to a liberalized market and Michael O'Leary. Besides, who misses the rubbery Irish breakfast sealed in a sweaty plastic tub?
24
HAIRY MIDGET
2000. Homo floresiensis with hypertrichosis (male). Discovered on the Belgian border. Good at complimenting strangers.
At least once a year, The Stone Twins attempt to incorporate a hairy midget into their assignments. He has made successful appearances in all of the MassiveMusic events in Cannes, and a proposal for the 'Nationaal Historisch Museum'. We guess the fascination was born in the '80s television schedule of Fantasy Island, Different Strokes and ZZ-Top.
25

Catalogues & Brochures
Music for University College Falmouth

10 Penneth
'10 Penneth' (penneth meaning a personal thought or opinion on what to do about a certain situation or dilemma – although suggesting that it may not be worth much) is an accompaniment to a lecture series given to design students. It takes the form of ten maxims. These maxims title ten short essays, each being an important point or lesson, effectively 'sold' to the students to help them become better designers, and for them to better understand the profession into which they are entering.

Designer
Craig Oldham
Illustrators
Craig Oldham
Chris White aka 3D Glasses
Copywriter
Craig Oldham
Design Group
Music
Production Manager
Shelley Wood
Client
University College Falmouth

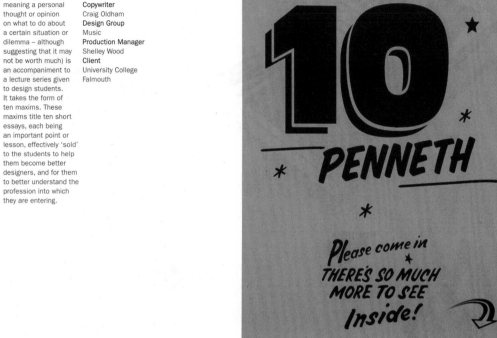

10
PENNETH
Please come in
THERE'S SO MUCH MORE TO SEE
Inside!

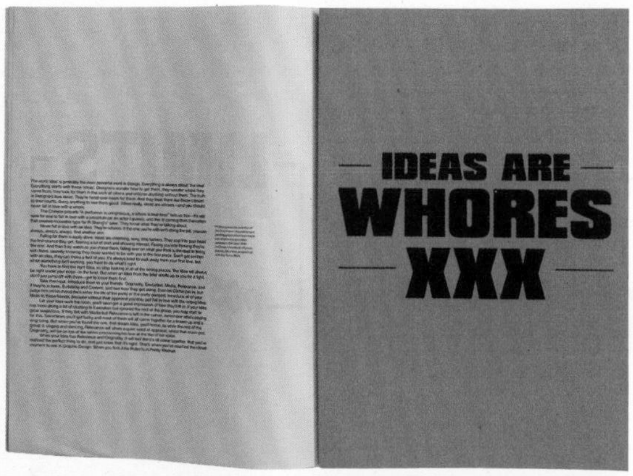
IDEAS ARE
WHORES
XXX

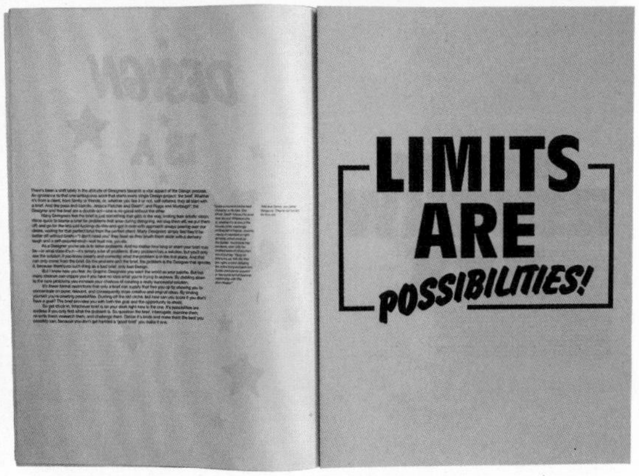
LIMITS
ARE
POSSIBILITIES!

Catalogues & Brochures
Halle34 for Hotel Altes Kloster

Ein Tag
Altes Kloster is a new hotel opened on historic grounds in Hainburg, where in the year 1235 a monastery was founded. Because the conceptual design of the catalogue took place alongside the hotel's construction, we decided to develop it in two parts. This is the first part of the catalogue, called 'Ein Tag'. It illustrates the surroundings of Hainburg, amongst the oldest cultural sites in Austria. These images feature alongside a short story: Otto, a commercial traveller, is actually heading for Vienna, but his navigation device shows unexpected personality and leads him away from his stressful working life.

Art Directors
Sigi Mayer
Emanuela Sarac
Photographer
Lukas Gansterer
Copywriter
Alexander Rabl
Advertising Agency
Halle34
Planner
Marcus Arige
Account Handler
Marcus Arige
Marketing Manager
Michaela Gansterer
Client
Hotel Altes Kloster

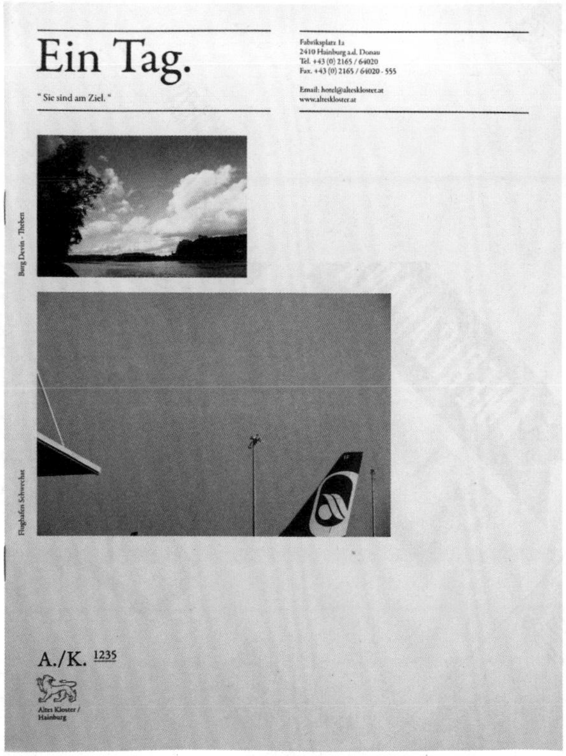
Ein Tag.
A./K. 1235

West.
West.

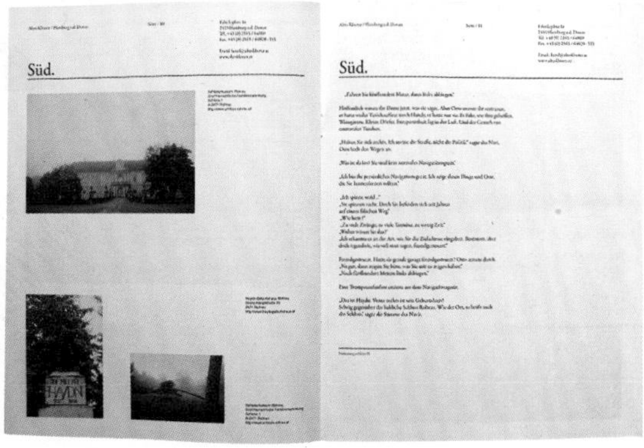
Süd.
Süd.

Catalogues & Brochures
c/c for Hunter College

Americanana
The title of the group exhibition 'Americanana' playfully references the use of the past in the present, as contemporary artists draw from traditional American sources. Hunter College tasked us to design a catalogue that captured the spirit of the show. We explored the theme by considering contrasts and connections between early Americana and post-1960 American art. Printed on textured lightweight French butcher paper, the poster/catalogue progresses from a dense B+W type-filled page to a minimal 4C poster in a mash-up homage to Civil War broadsides, Pop Art silkscreened posters and 80s downtown DIY catalogues.

Designer
Emily Kowzan
Creative Directors
Chen Chieh Ni
Cynthia Pratomo
Design Group
c/c
Client
Hunter College
Brand
Bertha & Karl Leubsdorf Art Gallery

IMAGE CHECKLIST
EDWARDS
GOBER
HALVORSON
JUDD
McCOLLUM
REICHEK
RINGGOLD
TURRELL

AMERICANANA
INTERVIEW
JOSE-PHINE HALVORSON

Catalogues & Brochures
Tayburn for
Edinburgh Printmakers

Edinburgh Printmakers
Edinburgh Printmakers is a world-class, innovative printmaking studio. It needed to tell its story to a number of different audiences, from heads of funding councils to people walking in off the street wanting to learn more about printmaking. To achieve this, Tayburn produced two documents: a cost-effective brochure and a limited edition packaged set of hand-printed loose-leaf prints. Both documents showcase the five main print techniques used in the studio, merged with photography that captures a 'day in the life' at Edinburgh Printmakers.

Designers
Michael O'Shea
Jack Shaw
Design Director
Michael O'Shea
Creative Director
Malcolm Stewart
Photographer
David Boni
Copywriters
Jessica Owen
Sarah Price
Master Printmaker
Alastair Clark
Design Group
Tayburn
Client
Edinburgh Printmakers

edinburgh
printmakers

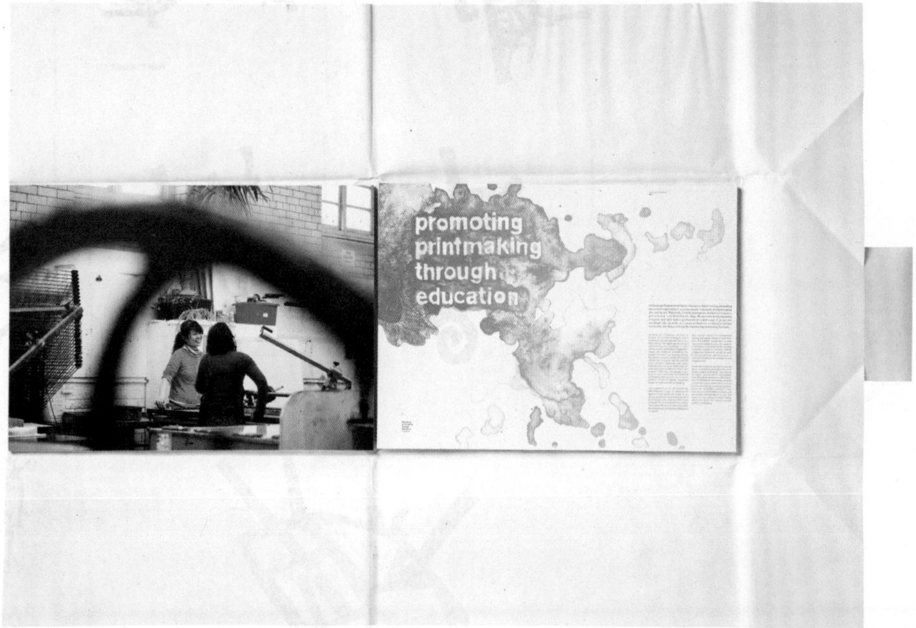
promoting
printmaking
through
education

HORSES

CD, DVD &
Record Sleeves
Dinamomilano
for Die Schachtel

Musica Improvvisa
Musica Improvvisa by Die Schachtel is a ten-CD box featuring ten groundbreaking Italian improv/ electronic/jazz bands and artists. The challenge was to create an innovative visual language, able to convey the sense of vibrant energy and aural displacement provided by the radical music. Both design and typography have been achieved through an 'improvisation' technique. We started with hand-drawn sketches done outside of any structured framework, in unusual places or contexts. The sketches were then assembled by looking for spontaneous juxtapositions, which eventually generated the final designs. The hand-drawn typography was created in a similar fashion.

Designer
Bruno Stucchi
Illustrators
Bruno Stucchi
Riccardo Stucchi
Copywriter
Giulia Capotorto
Design Studio
Dinamomilano
Client
Die Schachtel

MUSICA IMPROVVISA
THAU
AN EXPERIMENT IN NAVIGATION
OSSATURA
XUBUXUE
WINTERMUTE
AMULETO
TUMBLE
A SPIRALE
AMP 2
LIGATURA
MUSICA IMPROVVISA

musica
improvvisa
die Schachtel

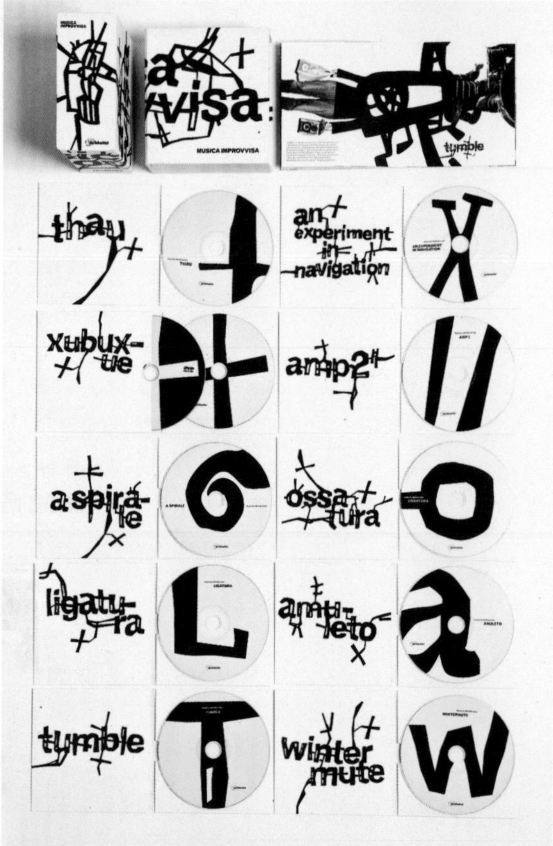
MUSICA IMPROVVISA
tumble
thau
an experiment in navigation
xubux-ue
amp2
a spira-le
ossa-tura
ligatu-ra
amu-leto
tumble
winter mute

CD, DVD &
Record Sleeves
Big Active for Mark Ronson & Sony Music

Mark Ronson – The Record Collection
This album signals a new direction for Mark Ronson and features a diverse showcase of musical collaborators. The challenge was to convey this eclectic spirit while creating an integrated identity. Individual styles of record covers can be recombined in several ways to create imagery for the album release and subsequent singles. Creatively, our solution also aims to be appropriate to alternative new album formats. A seven-inch boxed version features individually printed sleeves housed in a vintage leatherette record carry case. The iTunes format allows interactive access to additional music, image and video content while browsing through the entire record collection.

Designer
Mat Maitland
Art Directors
Mat Maitland
Gerard Saint
Creative Director
Gerard Saint
Illustrators
Jesse Auersalo
Jasper Goodall
Markus Karlsson
Mat Maitland
Parra
Will Sweeney
Photographer
Alexie Hay
Design Group
Big Active
Marketing Manager
Lee Jensen
Clients
Mark Ronson
Sony Music

MARK RONSON
& THE BUSINESS INTL

MARK RONSON & THE BUSINESS INTL "HEY BOY"
MARK RONSON & THE BUSINESS INTL
THE BIKE SONG
MARK RONSON AND THE BUSINESS INTL
MARK RONSON & THE BUSINESS INTL "YOU GAVE ME NOTHING"
"SELECTOR"

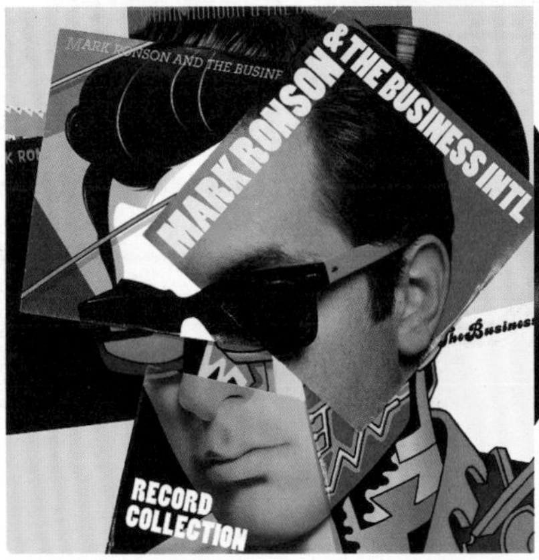
MARK RONSON & THE BUSINESS INTL
RECORD COLLECTION

MARK RONSON & THE BUSINESS INTL
THE BIKE SONG

Direct Mail
NB for the University of Oxford

Oxford Thinking. And Doing.
In collaboration with Michael Wolff, NB relaunched the University of Oxford's fundraising campaign report, 'Oxford Thinking. And Doing'. The report was distributed to a global audience of over 180,000 alumni. The university aims to raise £1.25billion to fund everything from roofs to bursaries. The report is a chance for the university to reach out to its alumni and remind them what makes Oxford thinking so unique. We produced a report that got to the heart of the matter: 'Where the money's going. Where the thinking's going'. The report raised £250,000 in the first two weeks.

Designer
George Adams
Art Director
Alan Dye
Creative Directors
Alan Dye
Nick Finney
Michael Wolff
Typographer
George Adams
Illustrator
Paul Davis
Photographer
Matt Stuart
Copywriters
Howard Fletcher
Michael Wolff
Design Group
NB
Account Handler
Anoushka Rodda
Client
University of Oxford

Oxford Thinking.
And Doing.
Where the money's going.
Where the thinking's going.
A report on the Campaign
for the University of Oxford.
At 31 January 2010
OXFORD THINKING:
TRYING to UNDERSTAND
EVERYTHING

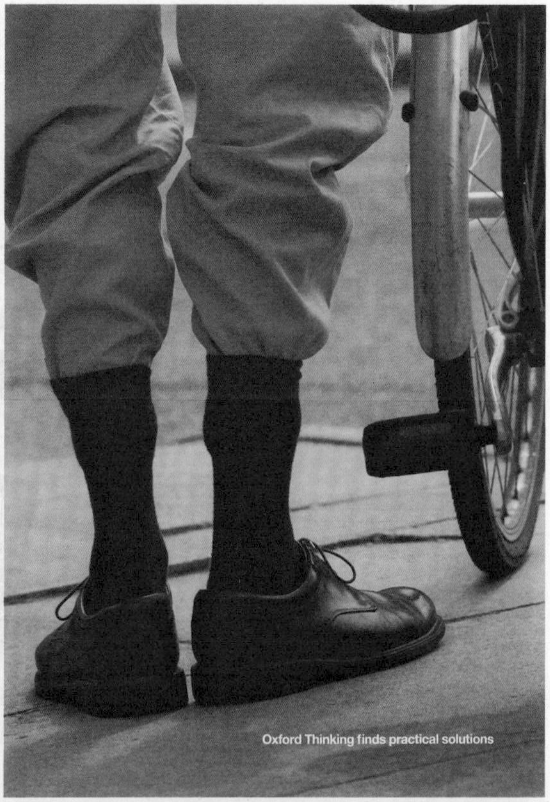
Oxford Thinking finds practical solutions

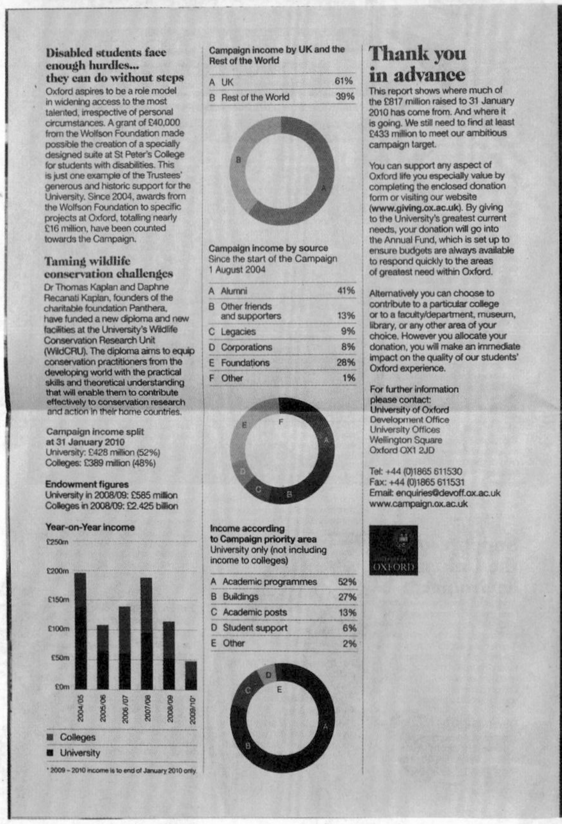

Disabled students face enough hurdles... they can do without steps
Oxford aspires to be a role model in widening access to the most talented, irrespective of personal circumstances. A grant of £40,000 from the Wolfson Foundation made possible the creation of a specially designed suite at St Peter's College for students with disabilities. This is just one example of the Trustees' generous and historic support for the University. Since 2004, awards from the Wolfson Foundation to specific projects at Oxford, totalling nearly £16 million, have been counted towards the Campaign.

Taming wildlife conservation challenges
Dr Thomas Kaplan and Daphne Recanati Kaplan, founders of the charitable foundation Panthera, have funded a new diploma and new facilities at the University's Wildlife Conservation Research Unit (WildCRU). The diploma aims to equip conservation practitioners from the developing world with the practical skills and theoretical understanding that will enable them to contribute effectively to conservation research and action in their home countries.

Campaign income split at 31 January 2010
University: £428 million (52%)
Colleges: £389 million (48%)

Endowment figures
University in 2008/09: £585 million
Colleges in 2008/09: £2.425 billion

Year-on-Year income
£250m, £200m, £150m, £100m, £50m, £0m
2004/05, 2005/06, 2006/07, 2007/08, 2008/09, 2009/10*
Colleges
University
* 2009 – 2010 income is to end of January 2010 only

Campaign income by UK and the Rest of the World

A	UK	61%
B	Rest of the World	39%

Campaign income by source
Since the start of the Campaign 1 August 2004

A	Alumni	41%
B	Other friends and supporters	13%
C	Legacies	9%
D	Corporations	8%
E	Foundations	28%
F	Other	1%

Income according to Campaign priority area
University only (not including income to colleges)

A	Academic programmes	52%
B	Buildings	27%
C	Academic posts	13%
D	Student support	6%
E	Other	2%

Thank you in advance
This report shows where much of the £817 million raised to 31 January 2010 has come from. And where it is going. We still need to find at least £433 million to meet our ambitious campaign target.

You can support any aspect of Oxford life you especially value by completing the enclosed donation form or visiting our website (**www.giving.ox.ac.uk**). By giving to the University's greatest current needs, your donation will go into the Annual Fund, which is set up to ensure budgets are always available to respond quickly to the areas of greatest need within Oxford.

Alternatively you can choose to contribute to a particular college or to a faculty/department, museum, library, or any other area of your choice. However you allocate your donation, you will make an immediate impact on the quality of our students' Oxford experience.

For further information please contact:
University of Oxford
Development Office
University Offices
Wellington Square
Oxford OX1 2JD

Tel: +44 (0)1865 611530
Fax: +44 (0)1865 611531
Email: enquiries@devoff.ox.ac.uk
www.campaign.ox.ac.uk

OXFORD

Oxford Thinking stands out

Direct Mail
The Chase for Blackpool and The Fylde College

Blackpool School of Arts Promotional Poster
Historically, Blackpool and The Fylde College had distanced itself from the stereotypical views of Blackpool. For this piece of direct mail, we opted to embrace everything Blackpool stood for, creating an identity that was 'Blackpool', and making the college instantly recognisable among the national competition. This poster was mailed as a teaser to prospective students before they received a prospectus. It also served as a promotional piece at the national student enrolment fairs. The poster uses the stripes from the new identity and is rolled and wrapped to mimic a traditional stick of Blackpool rock. A summer treat for students to take away as a souvenir.

Designer David Thompson
Creative Director Peter Richardson
Design Company The Chase
Account Handler Paul Waters
Client Blackpool and The Fylde College

FINE ART
DESIGN
PHOTOGRAPHY
PERFORMING ARTS
FASHION
SCHOOL OF ARTS

SCHOOL OF ARTS
BLACKPOOL

Greeting Cards & Invitations
TBWA\Hunt\Lascaris Johannesburg for City Lodge Hotels

Cassette
To celebrate City Lodge's 25th anniversary as the agency's client, we took their customer-focused promise of 'Feel at Home' a step further and made City Lodge feel like we're all one family. We collected memories the same way a family would have 25 years ago – on home video. A scuffed and aged VHS sleeve contained a moulded cassette, which opened up to reveal two DVDs containing a reel of all the ads we'd done together, plus old, embarrassing photos from parties and other interactions the agency and client had had over the years.

Designer Bronwen Bridgeford
Art Director Adam Weber
Creative Director Adam Weber
Executive Creative Director Damon Stapleton
Copywriter Kamogelo Sesing
Videographer Fausto Becatti
Agency Producer Sandra Gomes
Advertising Agency TBWA\Hunt\Lascaris Johannesburg
Account Handler Jenny Trenchard
Marketing Manager Peter Schoeman
Client City Lodge Hotels

HLCL
HUNT LASCARIS CITY LODGE
HIGH QUALITY VIDEO
CITY LODGE
25 YEARS OF MEMORIES
E-180
VHS
Magnum P.I.
City Lodge 1985

HLCL
HUNT LASCARIS CITY LODGE
E-180
25 YEARS OF MEMORIES
HIGH QUALITY VIDEO
VHS
E-180
HISTORY REEL
HIGH QUALITY VIDEO
VHS

Greeting Cards
& Invitations
Hari & Jen for
Harinderpal Bajwa
& Jennifer Bajwa

Commemorative Plate
The wedding invite. Surely one of the toughest briefs ever to land on a creative's desk. And in a cruel twist of fate, there's the added complication of the fiancée being an account handler. 'It needs to be personal yet all-embracing, striking but subtle, irreverent though sincere, cheap as well as premium…' I vow never to remarry.

Designer
Rory Sutherland
Illustrator
Gillian Flint
Copywriter
Harinderpal Bajwa
Design Group
Hari & Jen
Account Handler
Jennifer Bajwa
Clients
Harinderpal Bajwa
Jennifer Bajwa

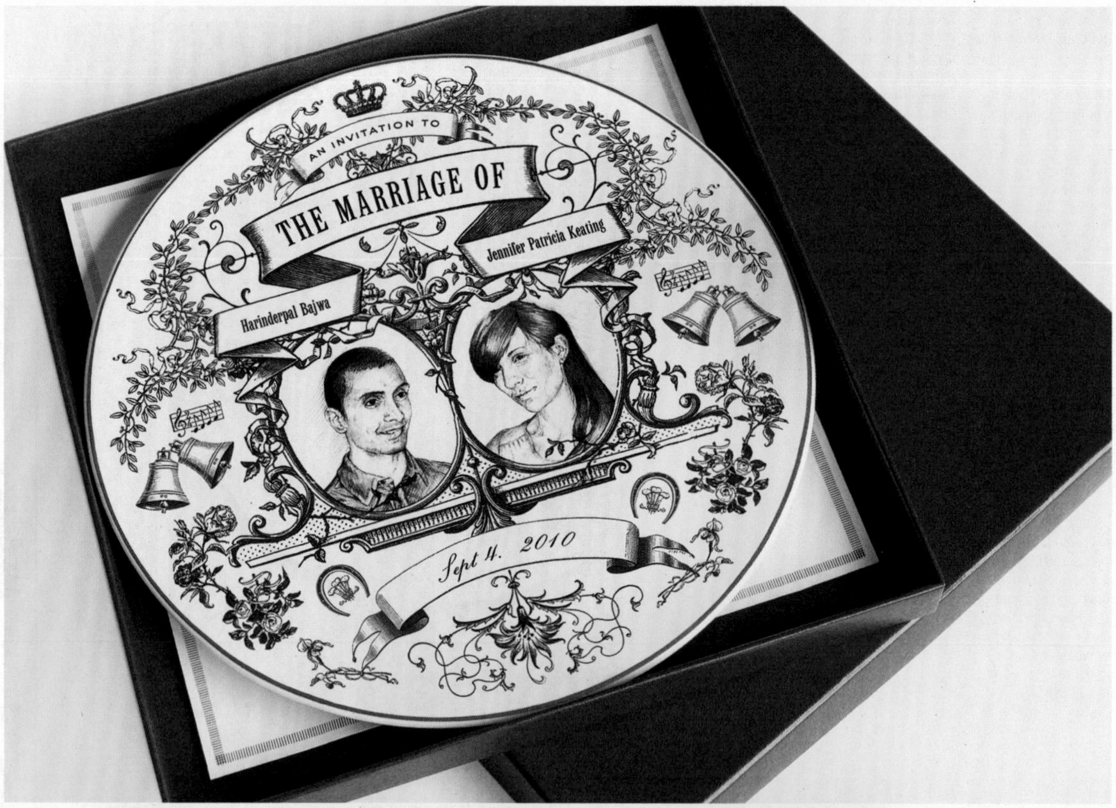
AN INVITATION TO
THE MARRIAGE OF
Harinderpal Bajwa
Jennifer Patricia Keating
Sept 4. 2010

CERTIFICATE OF AUTHENTICITY
Dear Richard Pearson
It is hereby certified that this commemorative plate is your official invitation to the wedding of
HARINDERPAL BAJWA & JENNIFER PATRICIA KEATING
Please use the following contact details to confirm your attendance and preference of either meat or vegetarian menu, by the 11th June 2010.
HARINDER.BAJWA@GMAIL.COM / JENKEATS28@HOTMAIL.COM
TEL. 0161 237 5015
Harinderpal Bajwa
Groom
IN YOUR POSSESSION IS PLATE
26
OF A LIMITED RUN OF 35
Jennifer Patricia Keating
Bride
The couple have chosen not to set-up a gift list as your company is gesture enough. However if you'd like to make a contribution, a donation to their honeymoon would be greatly appreciated.

Greeting Cards
& Invitations
DHM

The Instant Kudos Xmas Card
This is a box of Christmas cards to make desks and mantelpieces more impressive. Each card has a hand-written personal message inside from an iconic figure: 'Sorry we missed each other at Frieze. Laters, Damien' from Damien Hirst; 'Great to see you had such a splendid year. John' from John Hegarty; 'Beerz soon? Smithy' from Paul Smith; 'I must get that egg recipe from you in the New Year. Charlie' from Charles Saatchi and Nigella Lawson; 'Merry Christmas from the office of Sir Martin Sorrell' from Martin Sorrell.

Art Director
Christopher Bowsher
Design Assistant
Rob Corey
Creative Director
Dave Dye
Typographer
Andy Dymock
Copywriter
Dave Dye
Advertising Agency
DHM
Client
DHM

THE INSTANT KUDOS CHRISTMAS CARD SET

MERRY CHRISTMAS
FROM THE OFFICE OF
SIR MARTIN SORRELL

SEASONS GREETINGS
Beerz Soon?
Smithy x

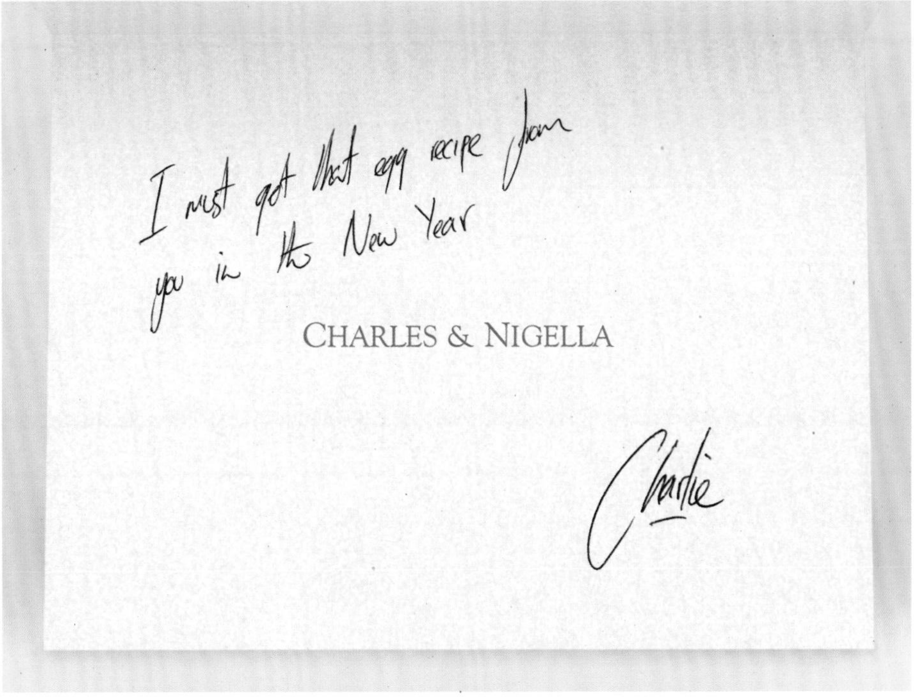
I must get that egg recipe from you in the New Year
CHARLES & NIGELLA
Charlie

Point of Sale
Saatchi & Saatchi New Zealand for the Breast Cancer Research Trust

Pick One
One in nine women will get breast cancer. Unless you've been affected in some way, this is just a number. So we designed a point of sale piece to look like an ordinary government form, then distributed it amongst other paperwork in medical clinics. The readers were asked to pick a family member before they even realised why. When it was revealed in the fine print, we were able to prove that someone close to them could get breast cancer.

Designers
Carolyn Davis
Matthew Page
Art Director
Carolyn Davis
Copywriter
Matthew Page
Advertising Agency
Saatchi & Saatchi New Zealand
Account Manager
Alina Godfrey
Group Account Director
Natasja Barclay
Marketing Manager
Phillipa Green
Client Chief Executive Officer
Tony Moffatt
Client
Breast Cancer Research Trust

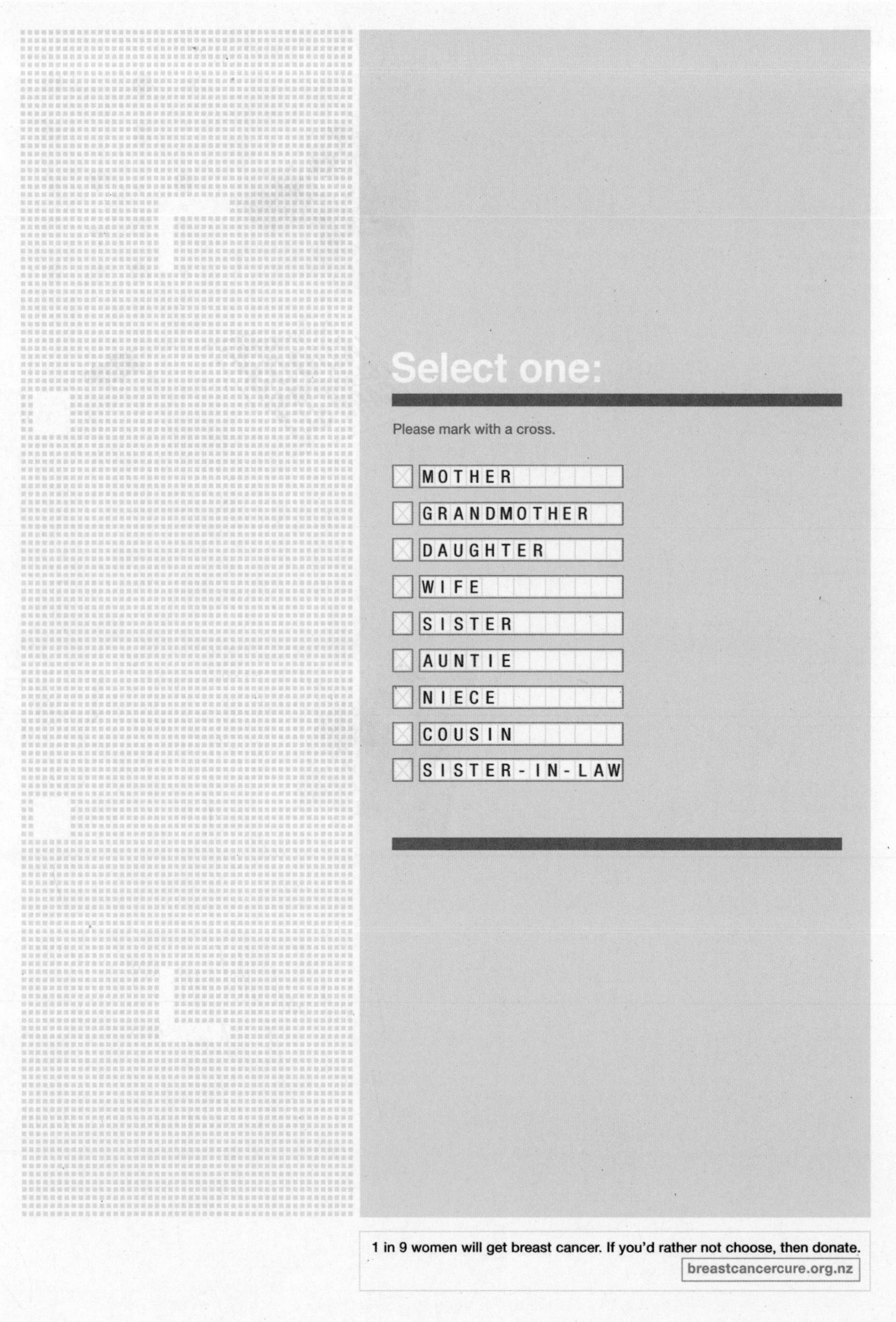
Select one:
Please mark with a cross.
MOTHER
GRANDMOTHER
DAUGHTER
WIFE
SISTER
AUNTIE
NIECE
COUSIN
SISTER-IN-LAW
1 in 9 women will get breast cancer. If you'd rather not choose, then donate.
breastcancercure.org.nz

Point of Sale
Ogilvy Brasil for Bar Aurora & Boteco Ferraz

$73,000 Bar Tab
How do you convince drunk people to take a taxi instead of driving? We added the real costs of drunk driving to people's bar tabs. When customers went to pay their bar tabs, they were in for a shock. Their tabs were extremely expensive, with totals as high as 79,000 Brazilian Reais. Items such as 'Ambulance', 'Day in ICU', 'X-ray', 'Amputation', and 'Wheelchair' were listed among their drink purchases. At the bottom of the bar tab, customers read: 'Driving home could be very expensive. Don't Drink and Drive. Bar Aurora and Boteco Ferraz'.

Art Director
Bruno Ribeiro
Creative Directors
Rubens Filho
Anselmo Ramos
Copywriter
Megan Farquhar
Advertising Agency
Ogilvy Brasil
Brand Manager
Pedro Costa
Clients
Bar Aurora
Boteco Ferraz

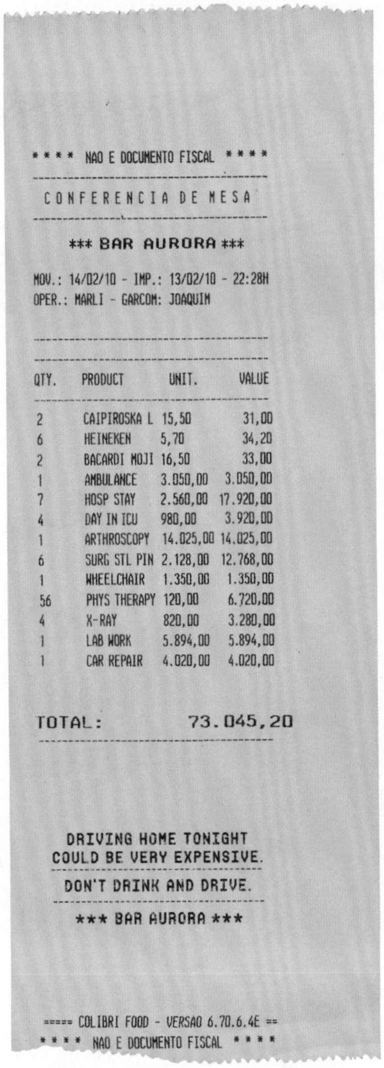
**** NAO E DOCUMENTO FISCAL ****
CONFERENCIA DE MESA
*** BAR AURORA ***
MOV.: 14/02/10 - IMP.: 13/02/10 - 22:28H
OPER.: MARLI - GARCOM: JOAQUIM
QTY. PRODUCT UNIT. VALUE
2 CAIPIROSKA L 15,50 31,00
6 HEINEKEN 5,70 34,20
2 BACARDI MOJI 16,50 33,00
1 AMBULANCE 3.050,00 3.050,00
7 HOSP STAY 2.560,00 17.920,00
4 DAY IN ICU 980,00 3.920,00
1 ARTHROSCOPY 14.025,00 14.025,00
6 SURG STL PIN 2.128,00 12.768,00
1 WHEELCHAIR 1.350,00 1.350,00
56 PHYS THERAPY 120,00 6.720,00
4 X-RAY 820,00 3.280,00
1 LAB WORK 5.894,00 5.894,00
1 CAR REPAIR 4.020,00 4.020,00
TOTAL: 73.045,20
DRIVING HOME TONIGHT
COULD BE VERY EXPENSIVE.
DON'T DRINK AND DRIVE.
*** BAR AURORA ***
===== COLIBRI FOOD - VERSAO 6.70.6.4E ==
**** NAO E DOCUMENTO FISCAL ****

**** NAO E DOCUMENTO FISCAL ****
CONFERENCIA DE MESA
*** BAR AURORA ***
MOV.: 15/03/10 - IMP.: 15/03/10 - 03:51H
OPER.: MARLI - GARCOM: MATHEUS
MESA: 12 SEQ: 81
QTDE. DESCRICAO UNIT. VALOR
5 VODKA SMIRNO 11,50 57,50
3 ENERGETICO 11,00 33,00
1 AMBULANCIA 3.050,00 3.050,00
18 INTERNACAO 2.560,00 46.080,00
1 EQUIP.MEDICA 14.675,00 14.675,00
4 DIARIA UTI 980,00 3.920,00
1 ARTROSCOPIA 14.025,00 14.025,00
1 CAD DE RODA 1.350,00 1.350,00
6 RADIOGRAFIA 820,00 4.920,00
TOTAL: 88.110,50
TEMPO DE PERMANENCIA: 04:24:20
DIRIGIR PARA CASA HOJE
PODE SAIR CARO.
SE BEBER, NAO DIRIJA.
*** BAR AURORA ***
===== COLIBRI FOOD - VERSAO 6.70.6.4E ==
**** NAO E DOCUMENTO FISCAL ****

**** NAO E DOCUMENTO FISCAL ****
CONFERENCIA DE MESA
BOTECO FERRAZ
BOTECO FERRAZ
MOV.: 12/03/10 - IMP.: 12/03/10 - 01:08H
OPER.: EDSON - GARCOM: LEONARDO
MESA: 814 SEQ: 183
QTDE. DESCRICAO UNIT. VALOR
1 AGUA MINERAL 3,50 3,50
1 CAIPIROSKA L 15,50 15,50
1 SAKERITA LIC 16,50 16,50
1 CAIPIROSKA L 15,50 15,50
1 DIARIA DE IN 2.560,00 2.560,00
1 PINO DE PLAT 2.128,00 2.128,00
1 PROTESE 6.080,00 6.080,00
3 AMBULANCIA 3.050,00 9.150,00
3 FISIOTERAPIA 120,00 360,00
4 EQ. MEDICA 14.675,00 58.700,00
SUBTOT. : 79.029,00
TX OPCIONAL : 5,10
TOTAL: 79.034,10
****
DIRIGIR PARA CASA HOJE PODE SAIR CARO.
SE BEBER, NAO DIRIJA.
BOTECO FERRAZ
****
====: COLIBRI FOOD - VERSAO 6.70.6.4E ==
**** NAO E DOCUMENTO FISCAL ****

Posters
Pentagram Design for the Haiti Poster Project

Haiti Poster
This poster was designed for the Haiti Poster Project in aid of Doctors Without Borders. The overall goal was to reach a donation level of $1million through the sale of limited edition posters created by designers from around the world. Apart from the money donated, the aim was also to increase social awareness and to highlight the role design can play in conveying important messages. Harry Pearce describes his work as simply trying to capture the weight of the sadness: 'A city as a body beneath a sheet. It's still, silent and the plain facts say it all'.

Designer
Harry Pearce
Photographer
Richard Foster
Printers
Gavin Martin
Design Group
Pentagram Design
Client Project Organiser
Leif Steiner
Client
Haiti Poster Project

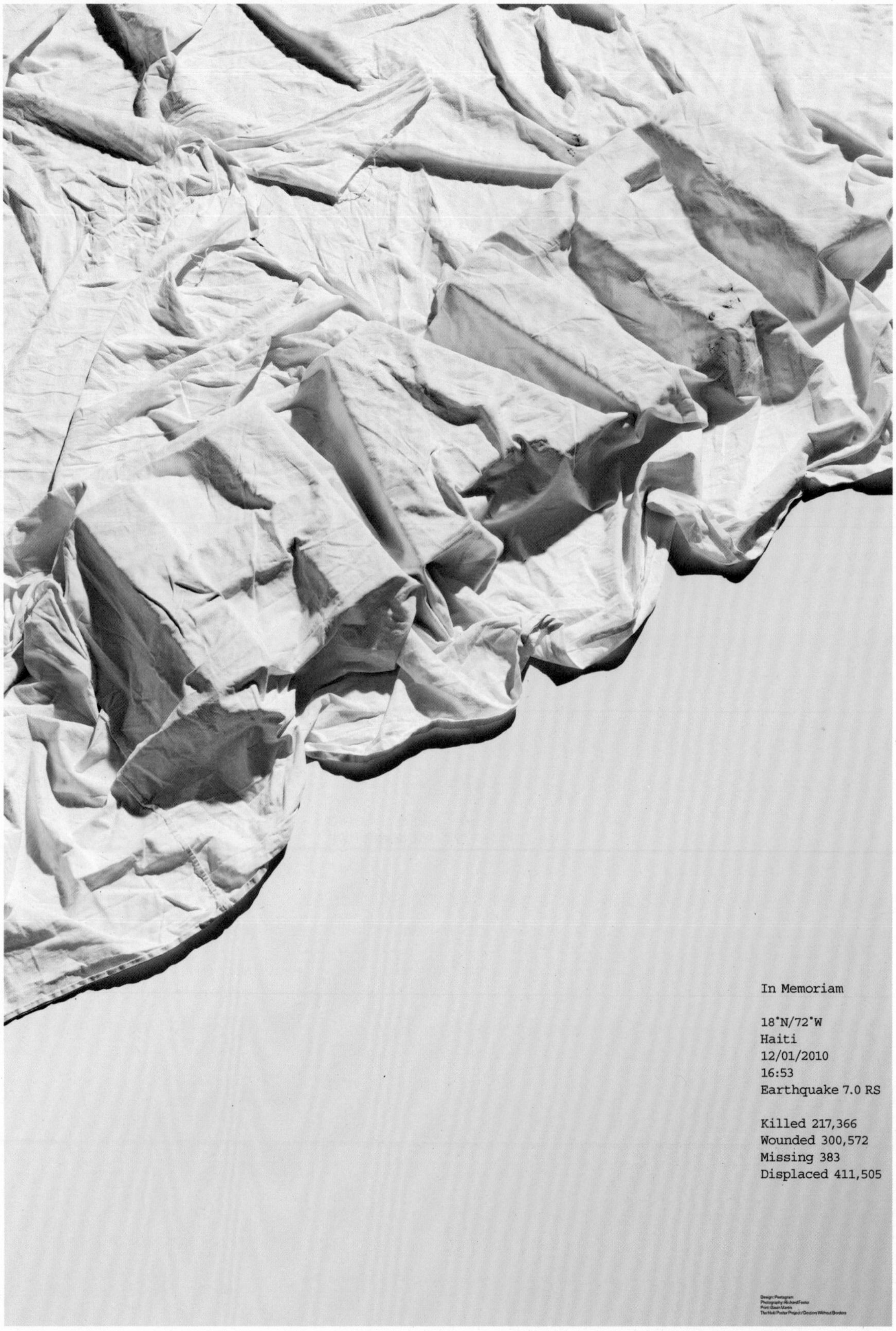
In Memoriam
18°N/72°W
Haiti
12/01/2010
16:53
Earthquake 7.0 RS
Killed 217,366
Wounded 300,572
Missing 383
Displaced 411,505
Design: Pentagram
Photography: Richard Foster
Print: Gavin Martin
The Haiti Poster Project / Doctors Without Borders

Posters
The Leith Agency
for the Scottish
Chamber Orchestra

Mozart at the Usher Hall
The Scottish Chamber Orchestra's 2010 season launch needed a promotional poster for its season of Mozart, played at Edinburgh's renowned Usher Hall. Using Barbara Krafft's famous image of Mozart as our reference, we noticed the seating plan for the Upper Circle perfectly reflected the shape of Mozart's wig – something that would instantly communicate both the event and the venue where it would take place.

Designer
Matthew Robinson
Creative Director
Alan Ainsley
Typographer
Matthew Robinson
Copywriter
David Amers
Image Manipulator
Iain Winning
Advertising Agency
The Leith Agency
Account Handler
Brieanna Tahere
Brand Manager
Ann Monfries
Client
Scottish Chamber Orchestra

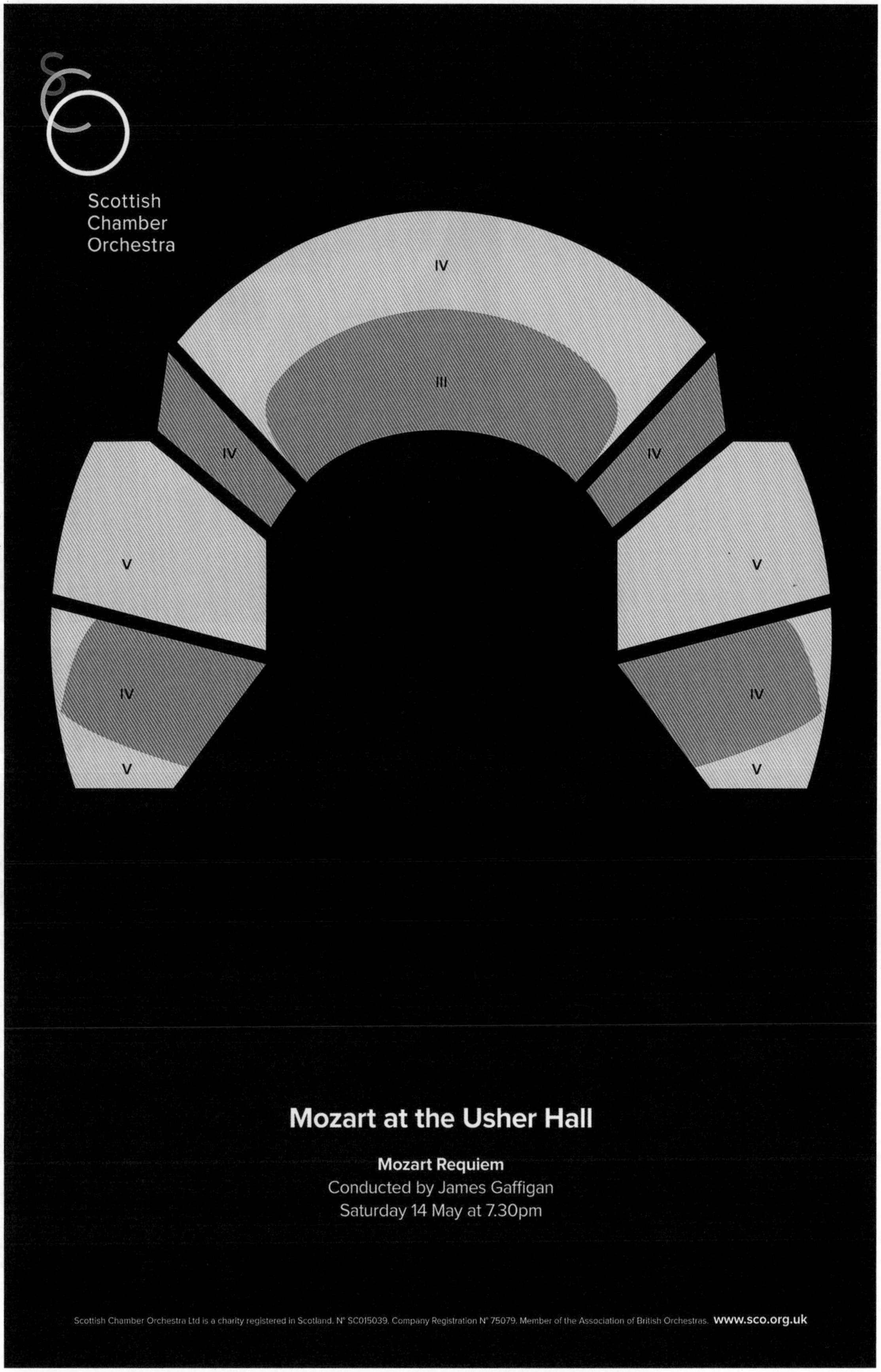
Scottish
Chamber
Orchestra
IV
III
IV
IV
V
V
IV
IV
V
V
Mozart at the Usher Hall
Mozart Requiem
Conducted by James Gaffigan
Saturday 14 May at 7.30pm
Scottish Chamber Orchestra Ltd is a charity registered in Scotland. Nº SC015039. Company Registration Nº 75079. Member of the Association of British Orchestras.
www.sco.org.uk

Posters
wortwerk for the Ars Electronica Center

AEC Nightline Posters
The Ars Electronica Festival is about Electronic music that goes under the skin. Sense organs were photographed like art objects. With the words 'Listen', 'Watch', 'Feel' and 'Think', we invited viewers to sharpen their senses on the music and visuals of the year's nightline.

Art Director
Verena Panholzer
Photographer
Peter Garmusch
Design Studio
wortwerk
Client
Ars Electronica Center
Brand
AEC Festival

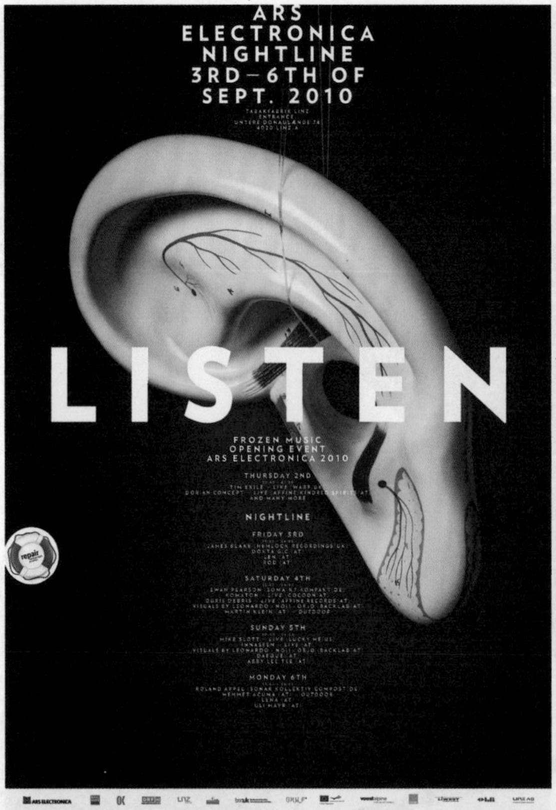
ARS
ELECTRONICA
NIGHTLINE
3RD–6TH OF
SEPT. 2010
LISTEN
FROZEN MUSIC
OPENING EVENT
ARS ELECTRONICA 2010
THURSDAY 2ND
NIGHTLINE
FRIDAY 3RD
SATURDAY 4TH
SUNDAY 5TH
MONDAY 6TH

ARS
ELECTRONICA
FACADES FESTIVAL
3RD–6TH OF
SEPT. 2010
WATCH

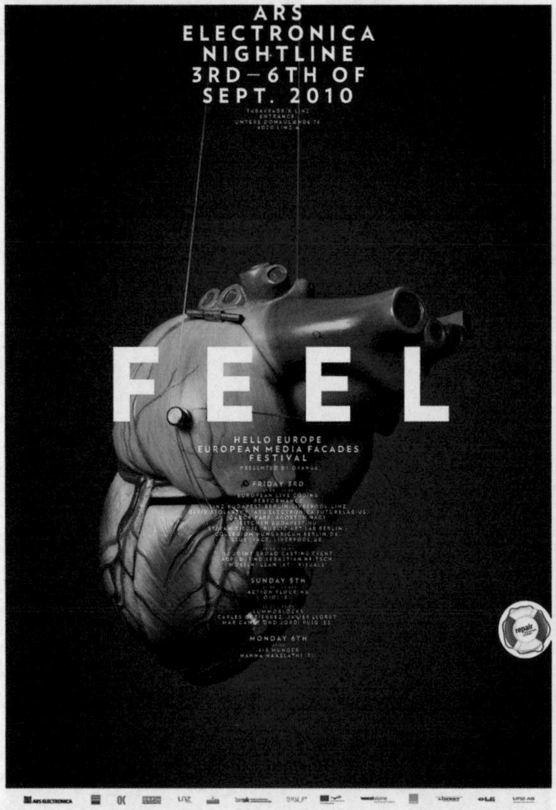
ARS
ELECTRONICA
NIGHTLINE
3RD–6TH OF
SEPT. 2010
FEEL
HELLO EUROPE
EUROPEAN MEDIA FACADES
FESTIVAL
FRIDAY 3RD
SUNDAY 5TH
MONDAY 6TH

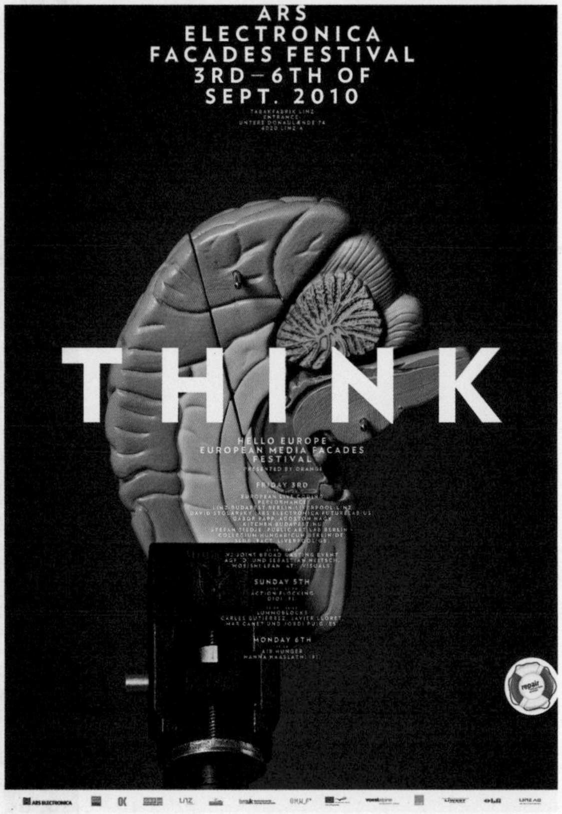
ARS
ELECTRONICA
FACADES FESTIVAL
3RD–6TH OF
SEPT. 2010
THINK
HELLO EUROPE
EUROPEAN MEDIA FACADES
FESTIVAL
FRIDAY 3RD
SUNDAY 5TH
MONDAY 6TH

Posters
Office for IBM

IBM Smarter Planet, Business Services
Office partnered with Ogilvy & Mather New York to develop a series of ads for IBM's business services. More than 43,000 gigabytes of data are generated by trillions of objects every day. And IBM's advanced analytics help businesses use this data not just to see what's happening today, but also to predict what's coming next. Office illustrated this concept of spotting patterns and crystallising trends to make smarter decisions. These ads, now running in selected publications, are part of IBM's 'Smarter Planet' campaign, which Office has been supporting since November 2008.

Designers
Rob Alexander
Will Ecke
Jason Schulte
Art Directors
Jason Schulte
Lew Willig
Illustrators
Rob Alexander
Will Ecke
Copywriter
Rob Jamieson
Executive Creative Directors
Tom Godici
Greg Ketchum
Worldwide Executive Creative Director
Susan Westre
Vice Chairman of Creative
Chris Wall
Design Studio
Office
Advertising Agency
Ogilvy & Mather New York
Client
IBM

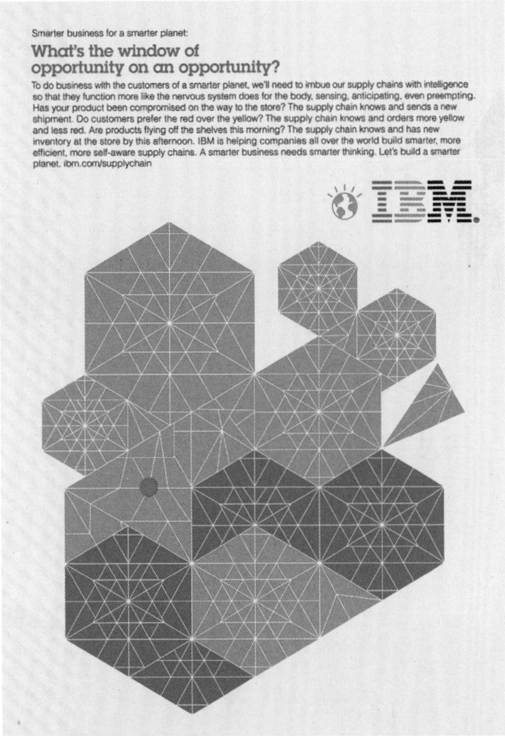
Smarter business for a smarter planet:
What's the window of opportunity on an opportunity?
To do business with the customers of a smarter planet, we'll need to imbue our supply chains with intelligence so that they function more like the nervous system does for the body, sensing, anticipating, even preempting. Has your product been compromised on the way to the store? The supply chain knows and sends a new shipment. Do customers prefer the red over the yellow? The supply chain knows and orders more yellow and less red. Are products flying off the shelves this morning? The supply chain knows and has new inventory at the store by this afternoon. IBM is helping companies all over the world build smarter, more efficient, more self-aware supply chains. A smarter business needs smarter thinking. Let's build a smarter planet. ibm.com/supplychain

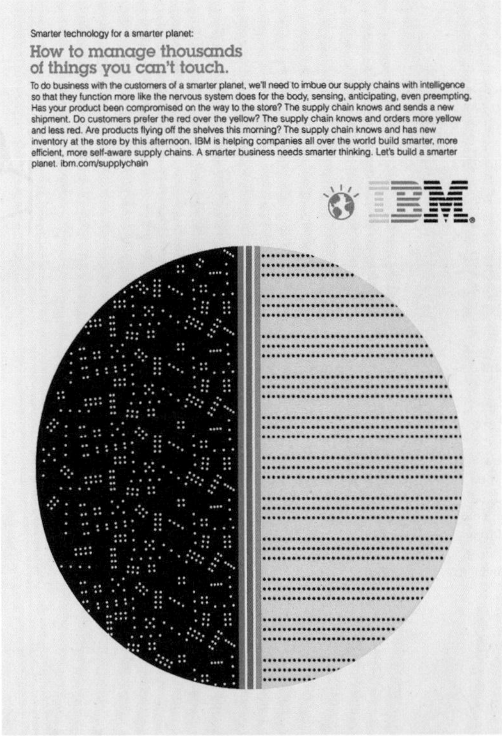
Smarter technology for a smarter planet:
How to manage thousands of things you can't touch.
To do business with the customers of a smarter planet, we'll need to imbue our supply chains with intelligence so that they function more like the nervous system does for the body, sensing, anticipating, even preempting. Has your product been compromised on the way to the store? The supply chain knows and sends a new shipment. Do customers prefer the red over the yellow? The supply chain knows and orders more yellow and less red. Are products flying off the shelves this morning? The supply chain knows and has new inventory at the store by this afternoon. IBM is helping companies all over the world build smarter, more efficient, more self-aware supply chains. A smarter business needs smarter thinking. Let's build a smarter planet. ibm.com/supplychain

Smarter business for a smarter planet:
Can an entire business be given a nervous system?

Smarter technology for a smarter planet:
Can an entire business be given a nervous system?

Smarter technology for a smarter planet:
How to manage thousands of things you can't touch.

Smarter business for a smarter planet:
What's the window of opportunity on an opportunity?

Smarter business for a smarter planet:
What if your supply chain saw what you needed before you did?

Smarter business for a smarter planet:
What if your supply chain saw what you needed before you did?

Posters
Dentsu Tokyo for
Dentsu London

Japan Bullet Zing!Thunk!
Tokyo Innovation was an exhibition held for the opening of Dentsu's London office. The design motif was the shuriken, a small star-shaped throwing weapon used by ninjas, aiming to 'pierce' the hearts of visitors with 'sharp' creative ideas. The simple black and white image of an origami shuriken was used to communicate speed, sharpness and precision, like a bullet. Made of two pieces of paper, it symbolised a powerful weapon in the world of advertising, to be achieved by combining two elements, Tokyo and London, through Japan's craftsmanship and technology.

Designers
Katsutoshi Hanada
Yo Kimura
Yoshihiro Yagi
Art Director
Yoshihiro Yagi
Creative Directors
Naoto Oiwa
Yasuharu Sasaki
Copywriter
Haruko Tsutsui
Printing Director
Takeshi Arimoto
Advertising Agency
Dentsu Tokyo
Account Handlers
Wendy Colman
Keiko Furuichi
Hiroki Takasaki
Client
Dentsu London
Brand
Tokyo Innovation

Tokyo
Innovation
Wednesday 21st April 2010 19:00 to 22:00

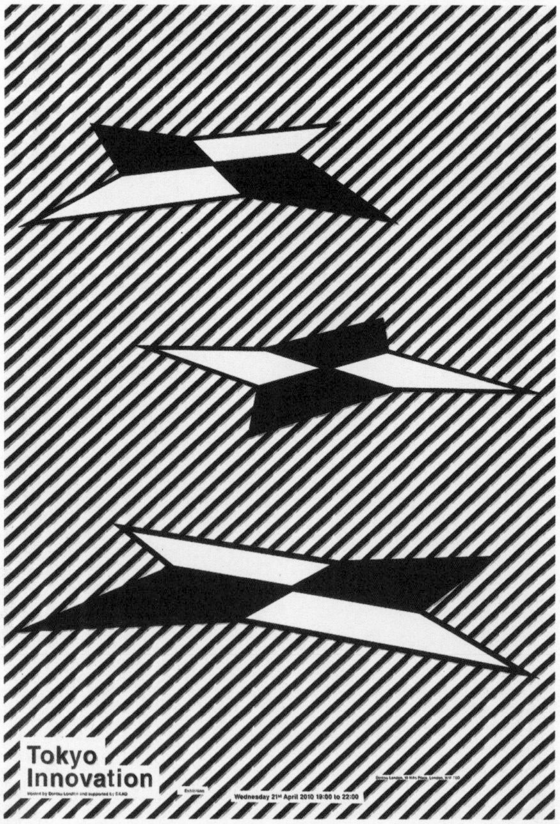
Tokyo
Innovation
Wednesday 21st April 2010 19:00 to 22:00

Tokyo
Innovation
Wednesday 21st April 2010 19:00 to 22:00

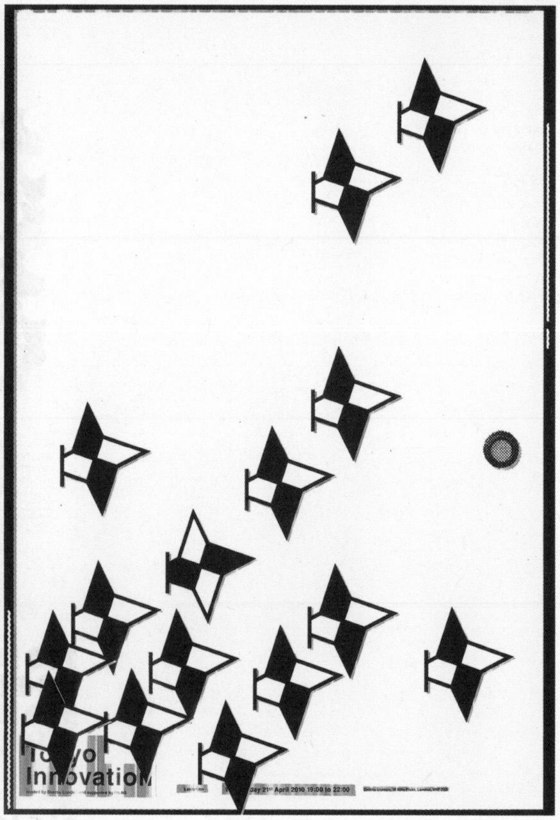

Posters
Ogilvy & Mather Singapore for
Faber Castell

Self Portrait / Girl with a Pearl Earring / Mona Lisa
We could go on and on about the Faber Castell artist pen's precision and control, but we thought we'd just show you.

Art Directors
Chan Hwee Chong
Fajar Kurnia
Eric Yeo
Creative Director
Eric Yeo
Executive Creative Directors
Eugene Cheong
Robert Gaxiola
Illustration
Cue Art
Copywriter
Jeremy Chia
Image Manipulation
Pro Colour
Advertising Agency
Ogilvy & Mather Singapore
Account Handler
Jamie Tang
Client
Faber Castell

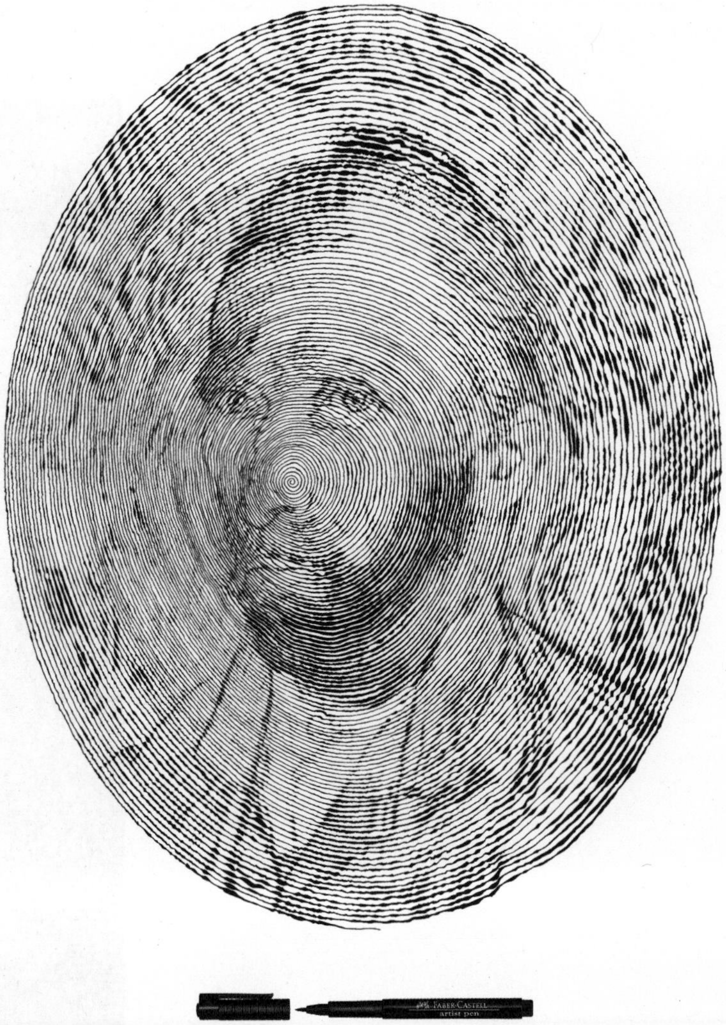
FABER-CASTELL
artist pen

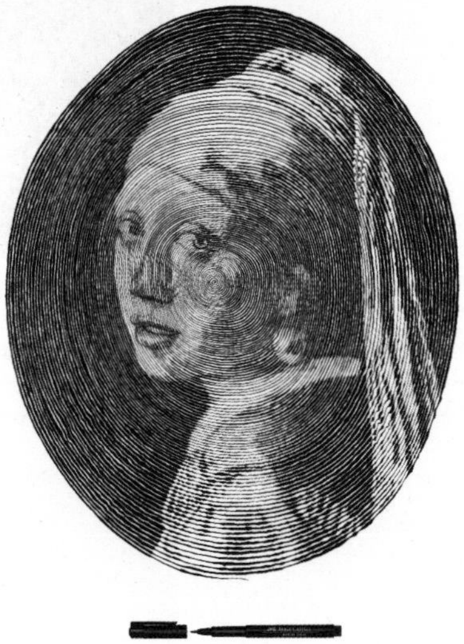

Posters
The Partners

Please God...
The poster was created in reaction to events that unfolded at the 2010 World Cup. Two abject performances had put England on the brink of a humiliating elimination. The nation had lost faith in the manager, the players, and even Wayne Rooney. There seemed to be nothing left to do but plead for divine intervention. Please God...

Designers
Leon Bahrani
Sam Griffiths
Design Agency
The Partners
Client
The Partners

Prayers begin at 3pm
Congregate at the big screen
Bread and wine provided
Please God...

Posters
Scandinavian DesignLab
for Republique Theatre

Republique Theatre
Season 02 Posters
Republique is a theatre that challenges creative boundaries. The theatre is more than its repertoire, and the repertoire more than a collection of performances. The task was to create a simple yet visually powerful poster concept, expressing both the vision of the theatre and the individual performance, plus attracting attention on the street. The circle is placed in the exact same place and at the exact size on all posters. This ensures recognition, while allowing changes in artistic expression from season to season. Copenhagen's copper roofs inspired the corporate colour. Fluorescent orange was used for the season 02 posters, to create a powerful, visual synergy between image and performance posters.

Designers
Per Madsen
Robert Daniel Nagy
Creative Director
Per Madsen
Photographer
Per Morten Abrahamsen
Design Agency
Scandinavian DesignLab
Account Handler
Christina Orth
Account Director
Anne-Mette Højland
Marketing Managers
Hans Christian Gimbel
Charlotte Sejer Pedersen
Client
Republique Theatre
Brand
Republique

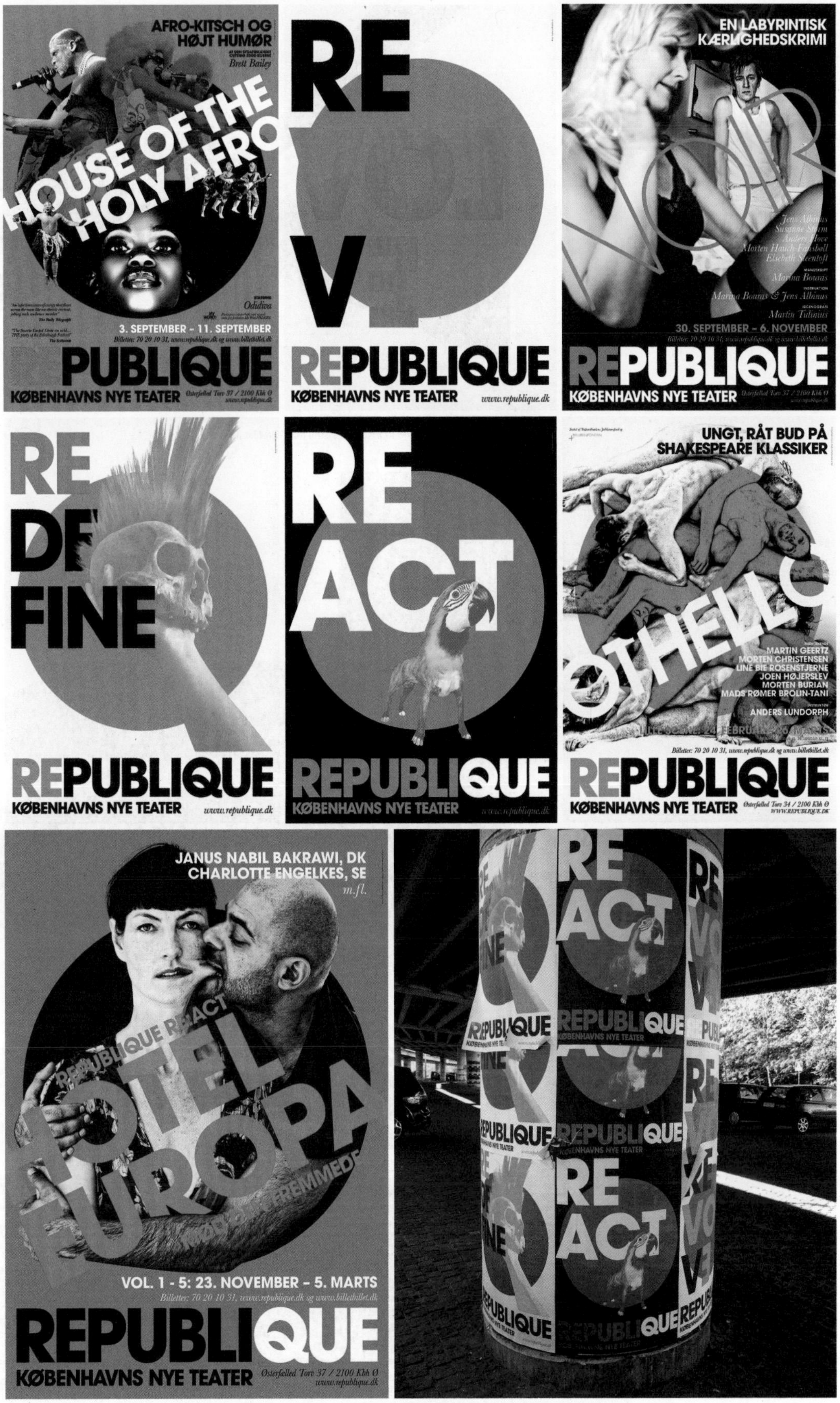
AFRO-KITSCH OG HØJT HUMØR
Brett Bailey
HOUSE OF THE HOLY AFRO
3. SEPTEMBER - 11. SEPTEMBER
PUBLIQUE
KØBENHAVNS NYE TEATER
RE
V
REPUBLIQUE
KØBENHAVNS NYE TEATER
www.republique.dk
EN LABYRINTISK KÆRLIGHEDSKRIMI
30. SEPTEMBER - 6. NOVEMBER
REPUBLIQUE
KØBENHAVNS NYE TEATER
RE
DF
FINE
REPUBLIQUE
KØBENHAVNS NYE TEATER
www.republique.dk
RE
ACT
REPUBLIQUE
KØBENHAVNS NYE TEATER
UNGT, RÅT BUD PÅ SHAKESPEARE KLASSIKER
OTHELLO
MARTIN GEERTZ
MORTEN CHRISTENSEN
LINE BIE-ROSENSTJERNE
JOEN HØJERSLEV
MORTEN BURIAN
MADS RØMER BROLIN-TANI
ANDERS LUNDORPH
REPUBLIQUE
KØBENHAVNS NYE TEATER
JANUS NABIL BAKRAWI, DK
CHARLOTTE ENGELKES, SE
m.fl.
REPUBLIQUE REACT
HOTEL EUROPA
VOL. 1 - 5: 23. NOVEMBER - 5. MARTS
Billetter: 70 20 10 31, www.republique.dk og www.billetlugen.dk
REPUBLIQUE
KØBENHAVNS NYE TEATER
Østerfælled Torv 37 / 2100 Kbh Ø
www.republique.dk

Posters
Jung von Matt
for Daimler

Comand APS
The Comand APS navigation system from Mercedes-Benz presents all street views in 3D. This realistic display makes it much easier for drivers to find their way. Mercedes-Benz wanted to communicate this benefit in an eye-catching print campaign. The solution was to show the national flags of various countries in 3D, from a driver's perspective. The target audience was the self-employed, freelancers and managers between 30 and 60 years of age.

Art Director
Jochen-Patrick Winker
Creative Director
Michael Ohanian
Copywriter
Tassilo Gutscher
Illustration
The Scope
Advertising Agency
Jung von Matt
Brand Manager
Damir Maric
Marketing Manager
Lueder Fromm
Client
Daimler
Brand
Mercedes-Benz

Navigating through the U.S. just became easier.
COMAND APS. The 3D navigation system from Mercedes-Benz.
Mercedes-Benz
The best or nothing.

Navigating through the UK just became easier.
COMAND APS. The 3D navigation system from Mercedes-Benz.
Mercedes-Benz
The best or nothing.

Navigating through South Africa just became easier.
COMAND APS. The 3D navigation system from Mercedes-Benz.
Mercedes-Benz
The best or nothing.

Posters
The Chase for Paul Thompson Photography

A Picture Speaks a Thousand Words
Tired of receiving predictable direct mail from photographers, we thought it was time for a change. We developed an idea which wouldn't feature any photographs, just beautiful and engaging descriptions, encouraging the recipient to visit Paul Thompson's website and discover the photographs described. Each description was exactly 1,000 words and set to exactly the proportions of the original image. The aim was to convey more about Paul's personality rather than just his work, as the relationship between art director, client and photographer is key.

Creative Directors
Ben Casey
Peter Richardson
Typographers
Lionel Hatch
Harry Heptonstall
Peter Richardson
Artworker
Rachel Pratt
Copywriter
Nick Asbury
Design Company
The Chase
Account Handler
Paul Waters
Client
Paul Thompson Photography

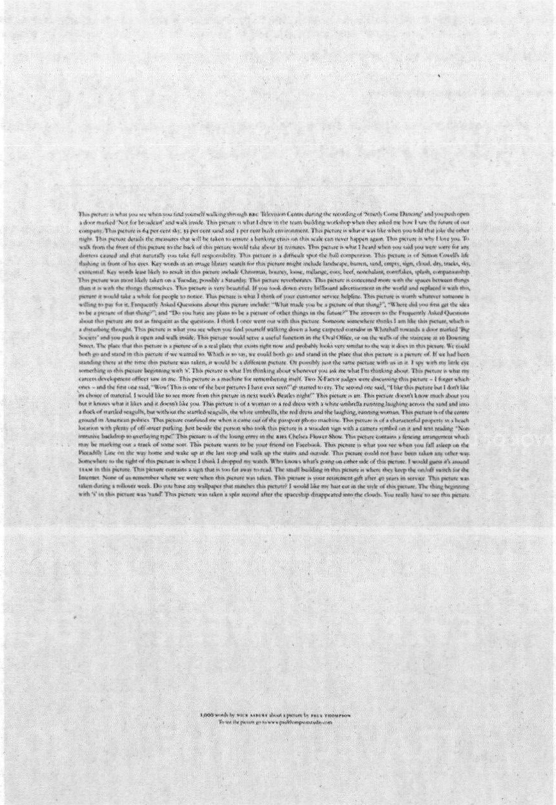
1,000 words by Nick Asbury about a picture by Paul Thompson

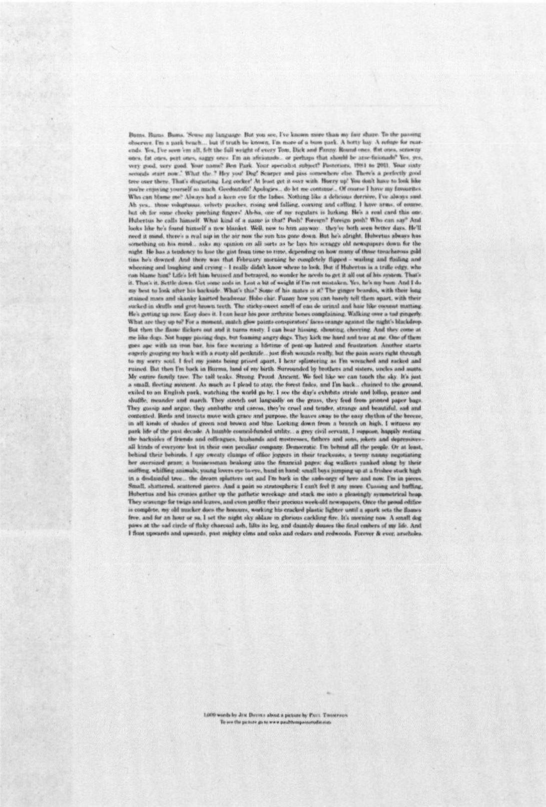

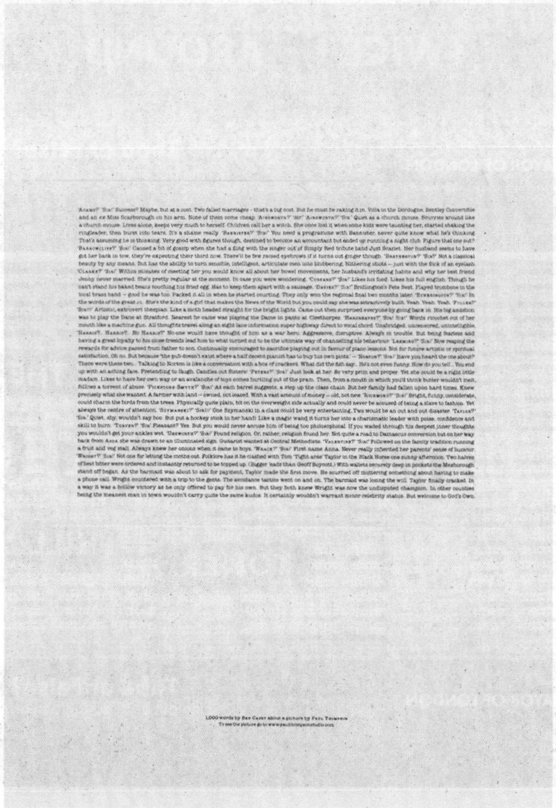

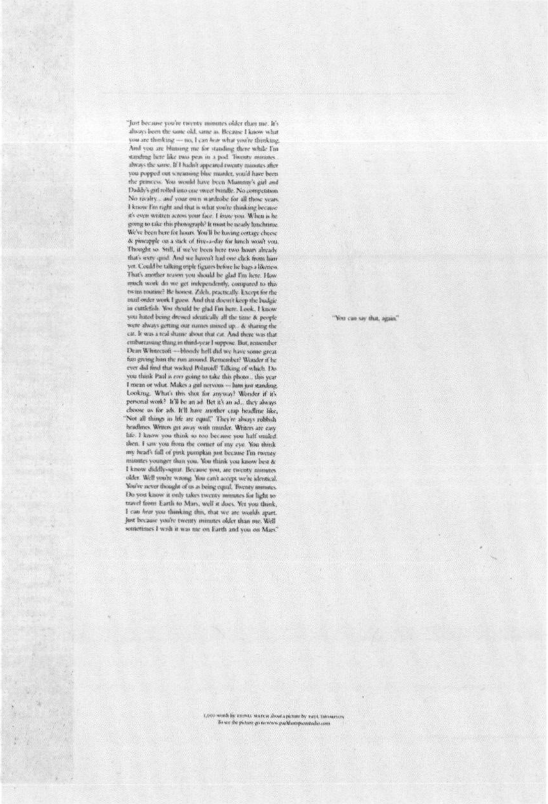

Posters
M&C Saatchi London
for Transport for London

Heritage Campaign
There are hundreds of interesting stories about the tube. Our brief was to bring a few of them to life. We did this by weaving facts (and a bit of fiction) into the designs of historical seat covers. We then asked passengers to guess: Tube or False?

Art Director
Ned Corbett-Winder
Typographer
Gareth Davies
Executive Creative Director
Graham Fink
Copywriter
Martin Latham
Image Manipulator
Mark Petty
Advertising Agency
M&C Saatchi London
Account Handler
Tom Vaughan
Director of Group Marketing
Chris MacLeod
Group Marketing & Communications Manager
Nigel Hanlon
Client
Transport for London
Brand
London Underground

The ghost of actor
William Terris is thought to
haunt Covent Garden station
MAYOR OF LONDON
Tube or False?
Find out at tfl.gov.uk/tubeorfalse
Transport for London
UNDERGROUND

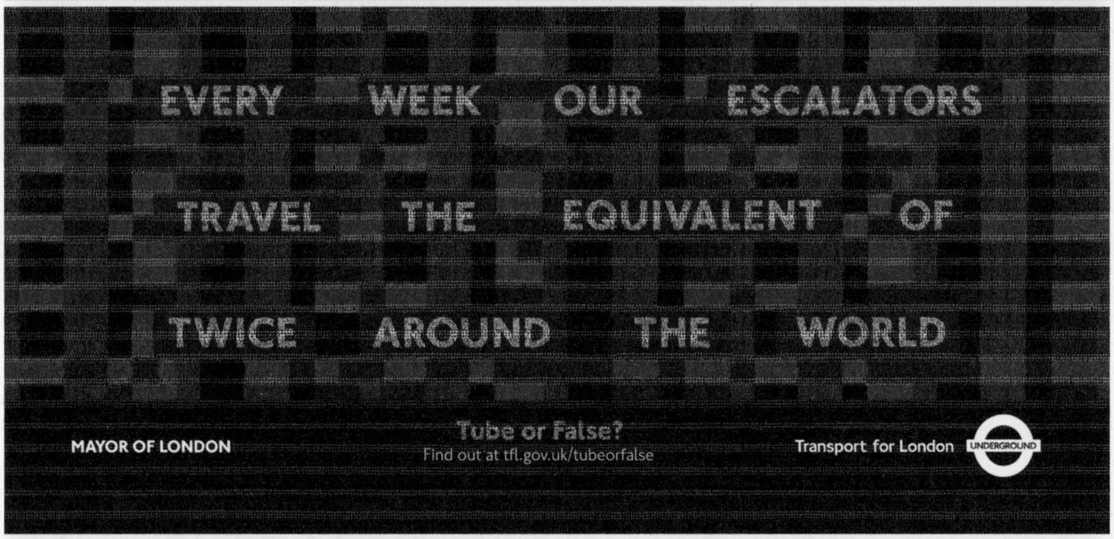
EVERY WEEK OUR ESCALATORS
TRAVEL THE EQUIVALENT OF
TWICE AROUND THE WORLD
MAYOR OF LONDON
Tube or False?
Find out at tfl.gov.uk/tubeorfalse
Transport for London
UNDERGROUND

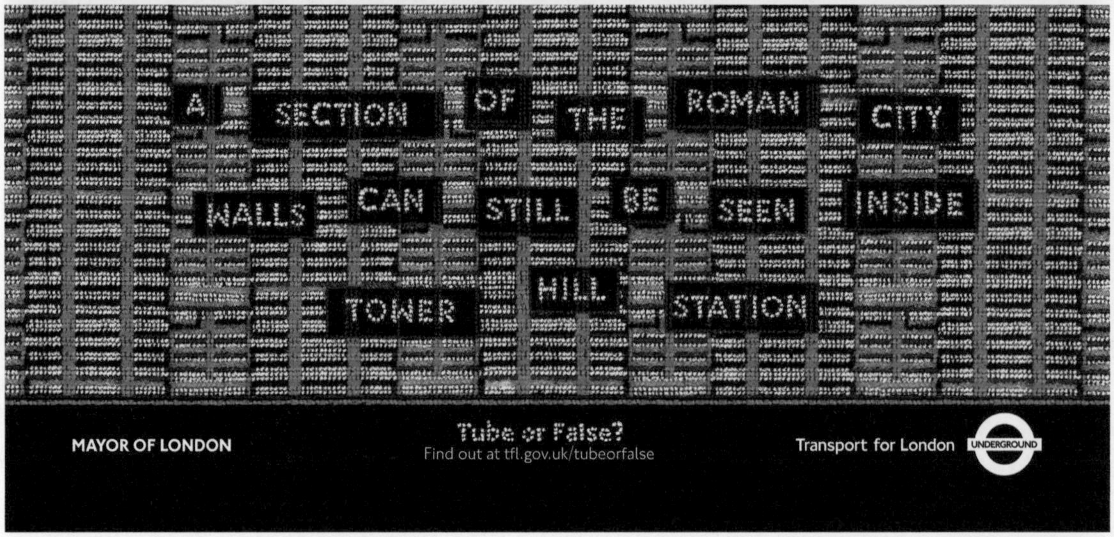
A SECTION OF THE ROMAN CITY
WALLS CAN STILL BE SEEN INSIDE
TOWER HILL STATION
MAYOR OF LONDON
Tube or False?
Find out at tfl.gov.uk/tubeorfalse
Transport for London
UNDERGROUND

Posters
Ogilvy France for IBM

Outcomes
To the naked eye, our world seems very much the same. But IBM is making everything from roads, to trains, to food smarter: cutting congestion, delays, food waste and more. With simple, universally understood graphics, we created a global campaign that explains these stories and their outcomes, inspiring government leaders and forward thinkers to join in and help us build a smarter planet.

Designer
Sid Tomkins
Art Director
Ginevra Capece
Creative Director
Susan Westre
Executive Creative Director
Chris Garbutt
Illustrator
Noma Bar
Copywriter
Fergus O'Hare
Advertising Agency
Ogilvy France
Account Handlers
Ben Messiaen
Eleonore Di Perno
Client Manager
Suzanne Assaf
Client
IBM

Now food can tell you how fresh it is.
While the world wastes 25% of its food, a smart supply chain ensures Norway's arrives fresh. ibm.com/smarterplanet
IBM

Drivers now see traffic jams before they happen.
IBM

Now every doctor knows you personally.
IBM helped Servicio Extremeño de Salud offer more personalised care and raise efficiency 30% by sharing patient files in all its clinics. ibm.com/smarterplanet
IBM

Data now catches tax dodgers.
Smarter analytics helped New York State save over $1.2 billion in lost taxes.
ibm.com/smarterplanet
IBM

Now trains keep passengers on track.
IBM helps the Taiwan High Speed Rail Corporation predict repairs in advance, letting 99.15% of trains run on time. ibm.com/smarterplanet
IBM

Shirts can pick a tie for you.
IBM

Posters
4creative for Channel 4

Big Brother R Eye P
2010 saw the last outing of 'Big Brother' on Channel 4. The brief was to create an arresting piece of communication to mark the final episode. We thought it appropriate to respectfully lay the series to rest. We used the iconic 'Big Brother' eye logo as the 'I' in R.I.P. So iconic was the eye, and so linked to Channel 4 was the programme, that we were able to pare it right back to a striking funereal black-and-white palette and run the graphic as a poster without any Channel 4 branding or programme information.

Designers
Jack Newman
Kevin Price
Art Director
Molly Manners
Design Director
Tom Tagholm
Creative Director
Tom Tagholm
Illustrators
Jack Newman
Kevin Price
Producer
Edward Webster
Design Group
4creative
Advertising Agency
4creative
Account Handler
Stephen Johnstone
Brand Manager
Sarah Owen
Marketing Manager
Rufus Radcliffe
Client
Channel 4

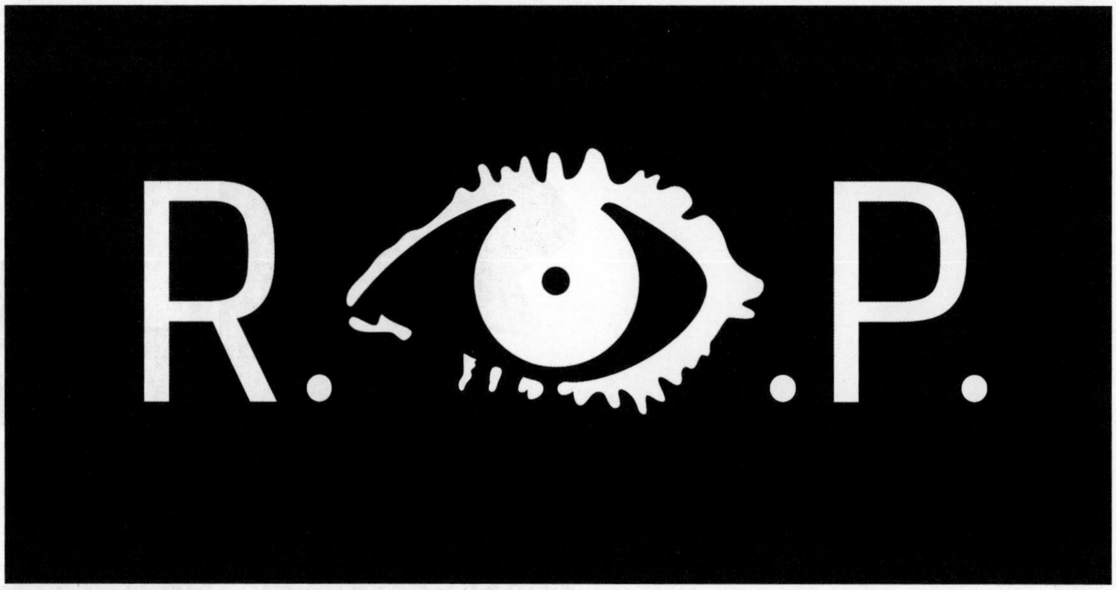
R.
.P.

Posters
The Jupiter Drawing Room Cape Town for Hyundai South Africa

No. 58 / No. 36
With its sportier design and 105kW engine with 186Nm torque, the Hyundai i30 2.0 GLS offers drivers an exhilarating, high performance experience. To communicate this to its predominantly male market, we designed a poster made of race car decals, incorporating the branding of the car.

Art Director
Lucas van Vuuren
Creative Directors
Joanne Thomas
Livio Spazone Tronchin
Typographer
Lucas van Vuuren
Copywriter
Jonathan Commerford
Advertising Agency
The Jupiter Drawing Room Cape Town
Account Handler
Rowan Eva
Brand Manager
Albrecht Grundel
Client
Hyundai South Africa
Brand
Hyundai i30

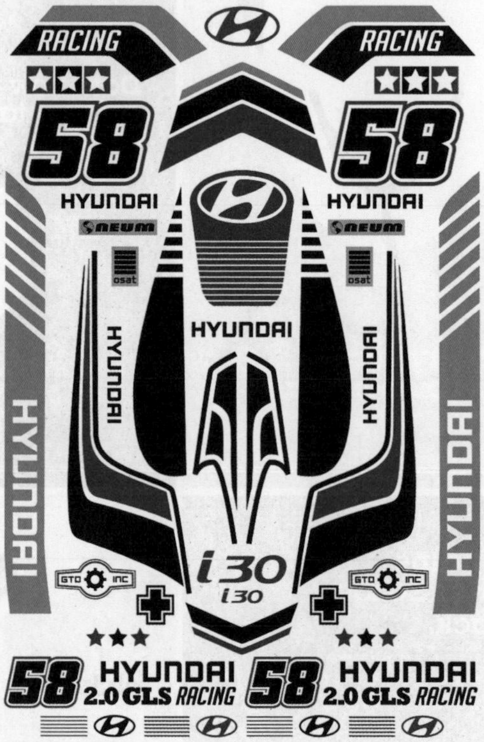
RACING
RACING
58
58
HYUNDAI
HYUNDAI
HYUNDAI
HYUNDAI
HYUNDAI
HYUNDAI
HYUNDAI
i30
58 HYUNDAI 2.0 GLS RACING
58 HYUNDAI 2.0 GLS RACING

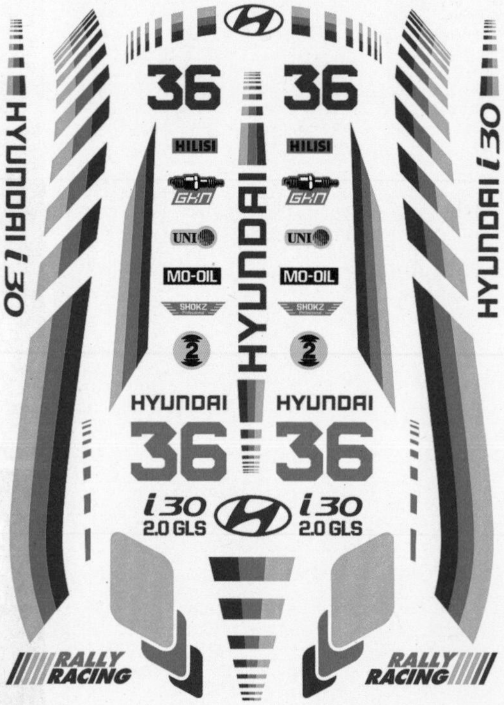
36
36
HYUNDAI i30
HYUNDAI i30
HILISI
HILISI
MO-OIL
MO-OIL
HYUNDAI
HYUNDAI
HYUNDAI
36
36
i30 2.0 GLS
i30 2.0 GLS
RALLY RACING
RALLY RACING

Stamps
Studio Dempsey
for Royal Mail

Classic Album Covers
Royal Mail wanted to celebrate some of the most iconic British album covers. Finding a different way of presenting them, beyond just having the cover artwork, was key to Studio Dempsey. Thumbing through an old collection of albums, it became clear that it was the tactile quality of the vinyl itself that was the appeal – and the answer to the design problem. We gave the stamps a three-dimensional effect and emphasised the vinyl aspect by showing discs partway out of the sleeve. All the albums were sourced in their original form and photographed to show their imperfections for authenticity.

Designers
Mike Dempsey
Stephanie Jerey
Head of Design
Marcus James
Art Director
Mike Dempsey
Photographer
Andy Seymour
Design Group
Studio Dempsey
Design Manager
Clare Shedden
Client
Royal Mail

1ST
blur
PARKLIFE
COLDPLAY A RUSH OF BLOOD TO THE HEAD
DAVID BOWIE
ZIGGY STARDUST
K.WEST
ROLLING STONES LET IT BLEED
The Clash
LONDON CALLING

Stamps
Serviceplan Gruppe
for Reporters Without Borders Austria

Human Rights Postmark
Global organisation Reporters Without Borders fights for and supports the release of innocent journalists who are detained in prisons worldwide. In order to generate charitable donations, we worked with the Post Office and developed an exceptional mailing to get viewers' attention even before they open the envelope, as we confront them with the issue right away.

Designers
Annalena Bottmann
Elena Ressel
Art Director
Alexander Nagel
Creative Director
Christoph Everke
Copywriter
Cosimo Moeller
Design Group
Serviceplan Gruppe
Account Handler
Nadine Wintrich
Marketing Manager
Hanna Ronzheimer
Client
Reporters Without Borders Austria

EYNULLA FATULLAYEV
Journalist
AUSTRIA 55
TAG DER MENSCHEN RECHTE
10.12.2010 · 1010 WIEN
EYNULLA FATULLAYEV
Journalist
AUSTRIA 55

Leaflets
JWT Toronto
for Walmart

Toy Flyer
Walmart, the world's largest retailer, wanted to be seen as the ultimate toy shopping destination for Christmas shoppers, so a clever holiday toy flyer was created. Custom die cuts were used to make it look like a child had used scissors to cut out all their favourite toys for their Christmas wish list. The back page featured the following message: 'Your kids already know what they want for Christmas'. Over 200,000 flyers were distributed.

Art Director
Craig Markou
Creative Directors
Don Saynor
Martin Shewchuk
Paul Wales
Copywriter
Colin Winn
Print Producer
Stacey Towey
Advertising Agency
JWT Toronto
Account Handler
Genevieve Cote
Brand Manager
Jeff Lobb
Client
Walmart

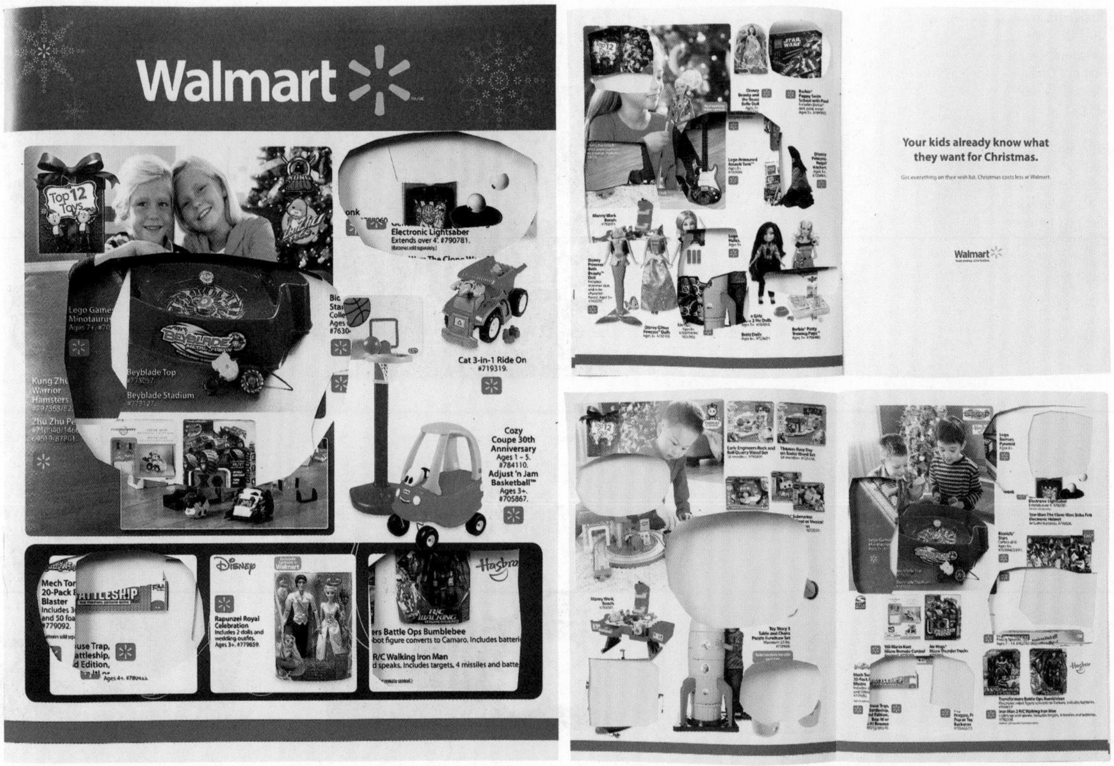
Walmart
Cat 3-in-1 Ride On
Cozy Coupe 30th Anniversary
Your kids already know what they want for Christmas.
Walmart

Leaflets
johnson banks for the Victoria & Albert Museum

V&A and Me
The idea for these leaflets stemmed from a discussion about designers' inspirations. We decided to design personal 'trails' across the museum, based on notable people's selections from the museum's vast array of objects. We had a nice mixture of designers (such as Paul Smith and Stephen Jones), pop stars (Florence from Florence and the Machine), theatre personalities (Cameron Mackintosh), writers (Jacqueline Wilson) and a supermodel (Erin O'Connor). Our early experiments in folding the A2 sized maps revealed an unusual 'map fold' that creates the illusion of many pieces of paper, but emanates from just one single A2 sheet.

Designers
Ed Cornish
Michael Johnson
Bethan Jones
Andy Shrubsole
Julia Woollams
Creative Director
Michael Johnson
Photographer
Leon Steele
Model Maker
Welsey West
Design Group
johnson banks
Client Project Manager
Vicky Broackes
Client
Victoria & Albert Museum

V&A
and me
Sir Paul
Smith
Designer

Sir Paul
Smith
Designer
V&A
and me
Dame
Jacqueline
Wilson
Children's
Author

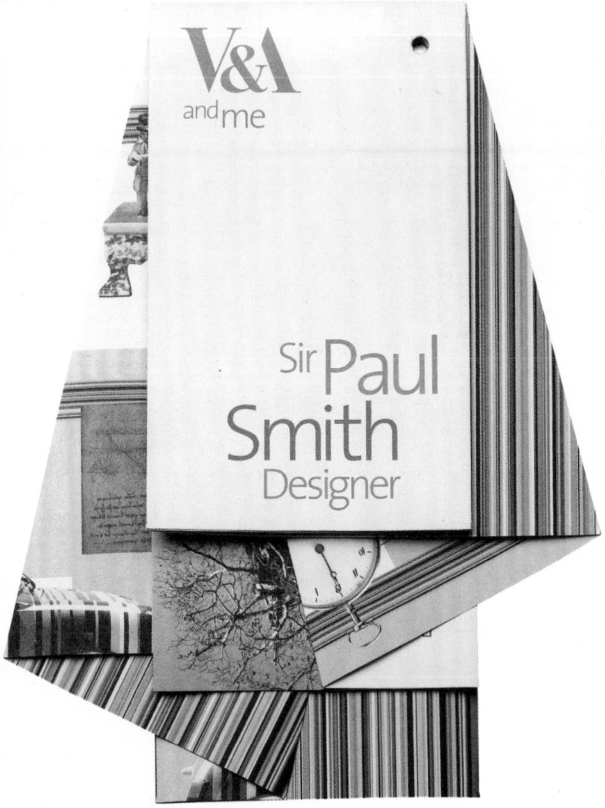
V&A
and me
Sir Paul
Smith
Designer

Stationery
Magpie Studio for
Sarah Grundy

Sarah Grundy
Sarah Grundy is a make-up artist with high standards. With over 30 years' experience in the film and TV industry, Sarah has crafted an expertise in almost every aspect of her trade. She typically picks up new commissions through word-of-mouth, so approached us with a challenge: to broaden her appeal and attract the attention of a younger generation of directors. The identity highlights Sarah's ability to make the unbelievable believable. From bearded ladies to tattooed toddlers, it works as a talking point for Sarah, with every element a demonstration of her skill.

Designer
David Azurdia
Creative Directors
David Azurdia
Ben Christie
Jamie Ellul
Photographer
Patrick Baldwin
Make-up Artist
Sarah Grundy
Design Agency
Magpie Studio
Client
Sarah Grundy

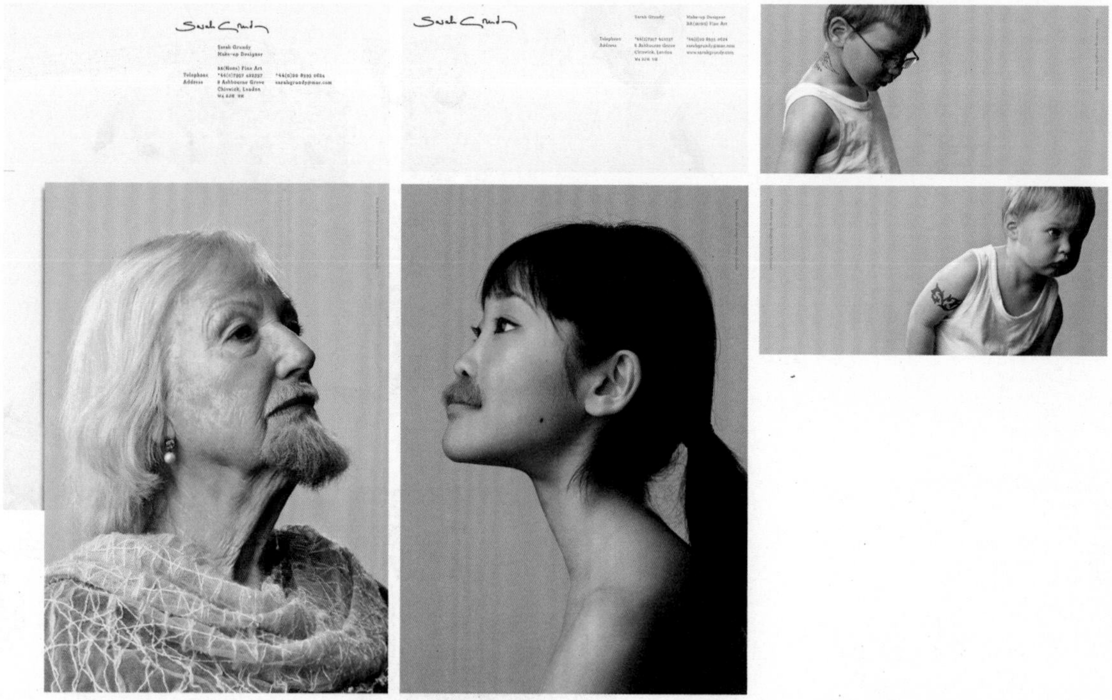

Stationery
Magpie Studio for GLUE

GLUE: Forging Links, Building Bridges, Creating Bonds
GLUE is a new think tank, specialising in connecting brands and policy makers with a largely disaffected youth. The identity, which began with a naming stage, needed to appeal to a demographic of hard-to-reach 16 to 25-year-olds. A graphic language of bold patterns was created to represent the different groups and communities that GLUE brings together. These contrasting patterns are physically joined by a unifying wordmark, to form a simple and memorable identity that sits in stark contrast to the jargon-heavy, grey identities that typify the sector.

Designer
Tim Fellowes
Creative Directors
David Azurdia
Ben Christie
Jamie Ellul
Illustrator
Tim Fellowes
Design Agency
Magpie Studio
Client
GLUE

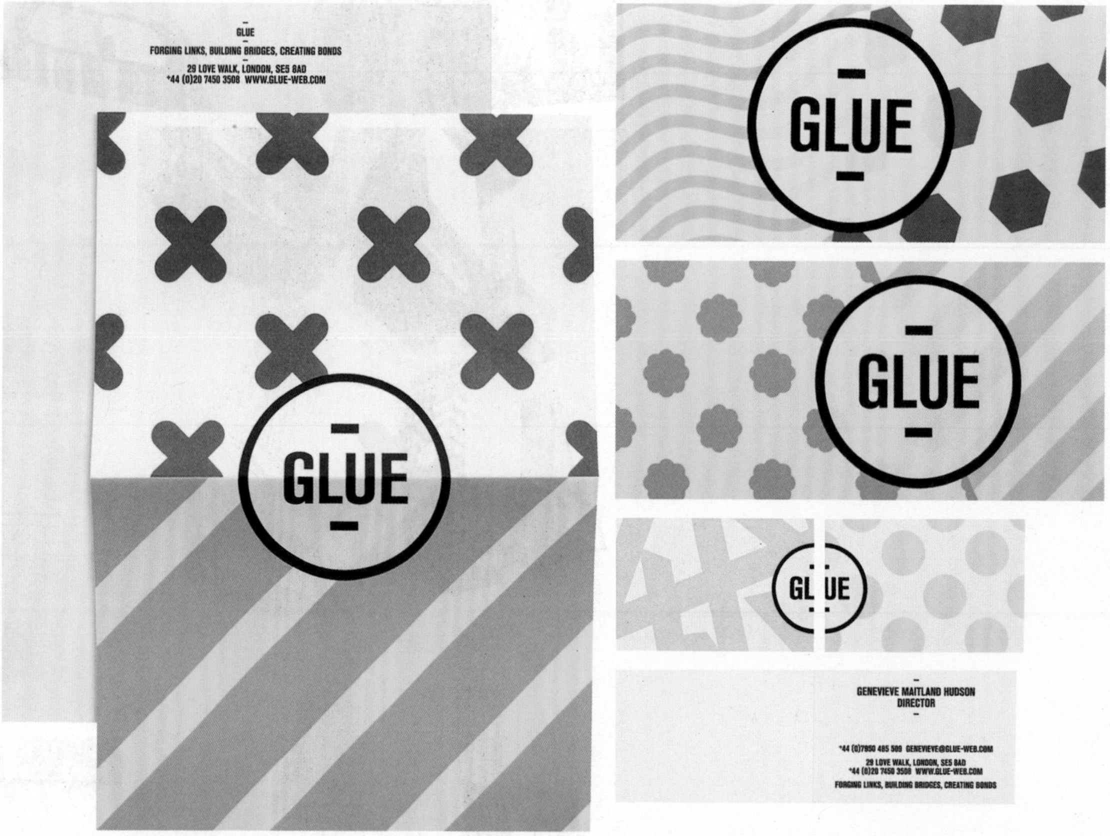
GLUE
FORGING LINKS, BUILDING BRIDGES, CREATING BONDS
29 LOVE WALK, LONDON, SE5 8AD
+44 (0)20 7450 3508 WWW.GLUE-WEB.COM
GLUE
GLUE
GLUE
GENEVIEVE MAITLAND HUDSON
DIRECTOR
+44 (0)7950 485 509 GENEVIEVE@GLUE-WEB.COM
29 LOVE WALK, LONDON, SE5 8AD
+44 (0)20 7450 3508 WWW.GLUE-WEB.COM
FORGING LINKS, BUILDING BRIDGES, CREATING BONDS

Wayfinding & Environmental Graphics
Leo Burnett Hong Kong
for Zoo Records

Hidden Sound Campaign
Zoo Records champions the hidden sound of alternative music. To promote the company, we took 14 local indie bands and embedded their songs into QR codes assembled into the shapes of animals that live hidden in the city. Scanning the codes reveals the songs and allows you to buy the CDs.

Art Directors
Kenny Ip
Leo Yeung
Creative Directors
Brian Ma
Alfred Wong
Executive Creative Director
Connie Lo
Copywriters
Joey Chung
Cyrus Ho
Wen Louie
Advertising Agency
Leo Burnett Hong Kong
Account Handler
Matthew Kwan
Client
Zoo Records

THE CITY IS ALIVE WITH SOUNDS, IF YOU KNOW WHERE TO LOOK.
SCAN THE ANIMAL WITH YOUR MOBILE, AND LISTEN TO THE HIDDEN SOUND OF THE CITY.
ZOO RECORDS

PL 8169
THE CITY IS ALIVE WITH SOUNDS, IF YOU KNOW WHERE TO LOOK.

Wayfinding &
Environmental Graphics
Buro North for
Falls Creek Resort
Management

Falls Creek Wayfinding & Signage Design
Falls Creek required the development of a wayfinding system to help visitors navigate their complex alpine ski resort. A modular system of sign types was created to provide information in a wide variety of directions to suit the complex village layout and changing seasonal functions. The design aims to offer the highest possible visibility of information while retaining the smallest presence of supporting structure. The system is extremely efficient, using a minimum number of elements for a range of sign types, while also minimising the production energy requirements.

Designers
Tom Allnutt
Ante Ljubas
Soren Luckins
David Williamson
Design Director
Finn Butler
Creative Director
Soren Luckins
Design Studio
Buro North
Client
Falls Creek Resort
Management
Brand
Falls Creek

Slalom St.
Christie St.
Slalom St.
Slalom Plaza
Snow Sport School
via Express Lift
Information Centre
Village Bowl
XC Trails 1.4km
via Aqueduct Trail
Post Office
Medical Centre

Christie St.
Christie St.

VILLAGE MAP

Wayfinding &
Environmental Graphics
Taku Satoh Design
Office for
the Musashino
Art University

Signage for the
Musashino Art
University Museum
& Library
This is design work for the academic library of an art university. Architect Sousuke Fujimoto's concept 'Forest of Books' was implemented in the library, thus creating a space where visitors are guided by numeric signs to the books they are looking for. The numbers of the signs represent the content of the classification: the number for the industrial category, six, is made from recycled plastic bottle caps painted white, collected from within the school; number nine indicates the literature section, containing many genres and spanning various languages, and so we created the number from lots of smaller nines in different typefaces, in order to show the diversity of literature.

Designer
Shingo Noma
Art Director
Taku Satoh
Design Studio
Taku Satoh Design
Office
Client
Musashino Art
University

5
7
9 1 2 3 4 0
8 5 6
7

Wayfinding &
Environmental Graphics
hat-trick design for
Land Securities

Illuminating London
The brief was to use a big prominent hoarding space in London's Victoria to promote the area. A typeface of illuminated letters was designed. Each told a different story for passers-by to discover. We wanted to end up with a visually rich and eclectic set of letters to sum up the area, a mix of past, present and future, heritage, culture, art, green spaces and wildlife. The style of each letter was inspired by the particular story being told. We decided the execution could be photographic, illustrative or graphic; depending on what best communicated it in a visually engaging way.

Designers
Laura Bowman
Tim Donaldson
Adam Giles
Gareth Howat
Alexandra Jurva
Jim Sutherland
Alex Swatridge
Creative Directors
Gareth Howat
Jim Sutherland
Typographers
Tim Donaldson
Gareth Howat
Jim Sutherland
Illustrator
Rebecca Sutherland
Photographers
Paul Grundy
John Ross
Copywriter
Nick Asbury
Design Group
hat-trick design
Brand Manager
Anna Chapman
Client
Land Securities

Parliament Square

Illuminating Victoria
A

Wayfinding & Environmental Graphics
Bostock and Pollitt for European Land

5 Merchant Square Marketing Suite
Merchant Square, a new development in London Paddington by European Land, needed to sell its vast floor space to property agents and potential tenants. Using our proposition 'A bright future for Paddington', the challenge was to engage visitors and enable them to see the potential of the space. We created a number of installations and transformed the space into a gallery, with each piece communicating a key benefit of the building, its specification or location.

Designers
Martin Brown
Kari Smith
Creative Director
Nick Pollitt
Design Group
Bostock and Pollitt
Account Handler
Jo Thorpe
Client
European Land
Brand
Merchant Square

Wayfinding & Environmental Graphics
Skidmore, Owings & Merrill for the Oakland Museum of California

Donor Wall
The donor wall was the key element of a comprehensive graphic programme created to revitalise the Oakland Museum of California. Located along the central staircase that connects all levels of the museum, the donor wall animates an important circulation space. When viewed in its entirety, the donor wall appears as an abstract representation of ivy, enlivening the concrete walls of the staircase and referencing nearby gardens. The non-hierarchical organisation of the donor wall showcases the collective contributions of the community, rather than highlighting individual donors.

Designers
Lonny Israel
Alan Sinclair
Brad Thomas
Design Studio
Skidmore, Owings & Merrill
Architectural Studio
Mark Cavagnero Associates
Manufacturer
Thomas-Swan Sign Company
Client
Oakland Museum of California

TICKETS ENTRADAS

IN RECOGNITION OF OUR
COMMUNITY OF DONORS TO THE
MUSEUM OF CALIFORNIA CAMPAIGN
社區 COMMUNITY
COMUNIDAD

Wayfinding &
Environmental Graphics
good design company
for the Museum of
Contemporary Art Tokyo

Signs at the Museum of Contemporary Art Tokyo
The idea for these signs was inspired by the shape of the museum building. The signs consist of three types: all uppercase letters for places of prime importance, such as the exhibition rooms; upper and lowercase letters for places of secondary importance; and lowercase letters only for other places, such as the restrooms. We decided to use this notation to give people an idea of the importance of each place in the museum simply by glancing at the signs. This method of display is rather uncommon in Japan, although often used in other countries.

Designer
Manabu Mizuno
Art Director
Manabu Mizuno
Design Group
good design company
Client
Museum of
Contemporary Art Tokyo

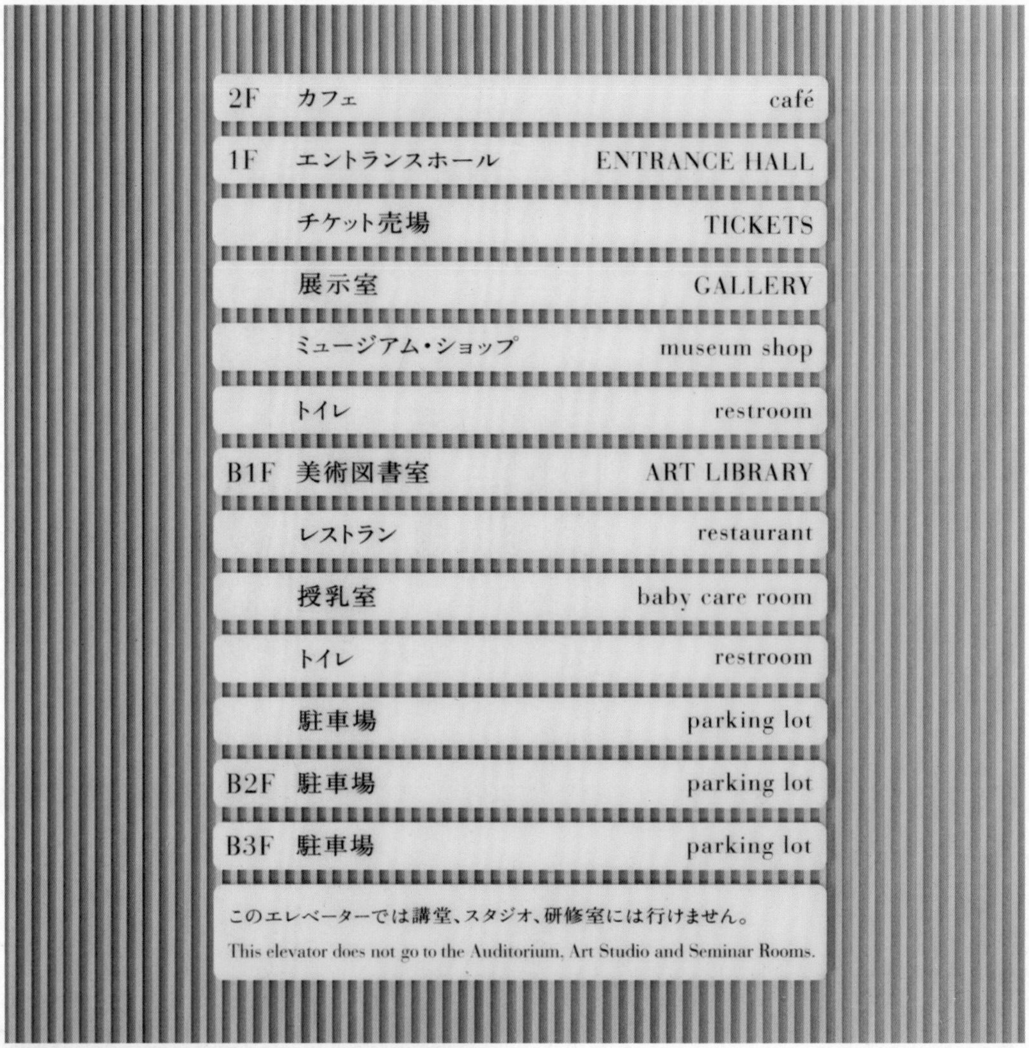
2F カフェ café
1F エントランスホール ENTRANCE HALL
チケット売場 TICKETS
展示室 GALLERY
ミュージアム・ショップ museum shop
トイレ restroom
B1F 美術図書室 ART LIBRARY
レストラン restaurant
授乳室 baby care room
トイレ restroom
駐車場 parking lot
B2F 駐車場 parking lot
B3F 駐車場 parking lot
このエレベーターでは講堂、スタジオ、研修室には行けません。
This elevator does not go to the Auditorium, Art Studio and Seminar Rooms.

the following
and during year-end
and New Year's holidays.

トイレ restroom

Wayfinding & Environmental Graphics
Adi Stern Design for the Design Museum Holon

Design Museum Holon – Signage & Wayfinding System
The signage and wayfinding system for the Design Museum Holon challenges common approaches by using white arrows on white walls, primarily discernible by the shadows they cast on the wall. The challenge was to create a system that is visible and easy to use, while not competing with Ron Arad's dynamic architecture. The shape of the arrows echoes the flow and movement of the steel bands that surround the museum building, creating a unity of design throughout the museum. The system holds three scripts – Hebrew, Arabic and Latin – and includes a custom proprietary Hebrew font.

Designer
Adi Stern
Art Director
Adi Stern
Design Group
Adi Stern Design
Brand Managers
Galit Gaon
Alon Sapan
Marketing Manager
Tamar Zadok
Client
Design Museum Holon

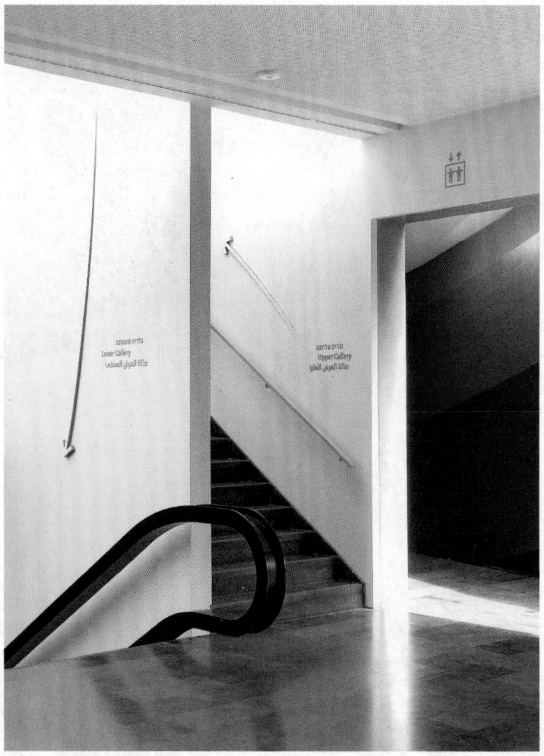
Lower Gallery
Upper Gallery

מעבדת עיצוב
Design Lab
مختبر تصميم
אבגדהוזחטיכל
מנסעפצקרשת

Wayfinding & Environmental Graphics
Colenso BBDO for Auckland Council

Beautify Your City – a Rubbish Idea
Rubbish is never going to disappear, but we've found a way to make it beautiful. We turned the ordinary rubbish bag into a bushy hedge, which formed garden beds when placed kerbside. The 'Beautify Your City' campaign was a 360-degree project to make Auckland a more beautiful city. We prevented illegal dumping by placing flowerbeds in targeted areas, and educated businesses with a kit delivered by council ambassadors.

Designer
Renee Lam
Art Directors
Lisa Fedyszyn
Zoe Hawkins
Kia Heinnen
Creative Director
Levi Slavin
Executive Creative Director
Nick Worthington
Copywriters
Zoe Hawkins
Kia Heinnen
Jonathan McMahon
Retoucher
Kevin Hyde
Agency Producer
Gabrielle Buckle
Advertising Agency
Colenso BBDO
Account Directors
Marcelle Baker
Celeste Pulman
Group Account Director
Lou Kuegler
Client Chief Executive Officer
Alex Swney
Client
Auckland Council

mag nation
SOUVENIRS

SOUVENIRS

● Yellow Pencil in Magazine & Newspaper Design

Entire Magazines
New York Magazine

Spring & Fall Fashion Issues
New York Magazine's annual spring and fall fashion issues provide an in-depth look at the trends and ideas from the seasons' fashion shows in Paris, Milan and New York. The magazine also includes fashion related essays, and an extensive photo portfolio by a documentary photographer who spent time at the shows in all three cities.

Art Director
Randy Minor
Deputy Art Director
Hitomi Sato
Associate Art Director
Josef Reyes
Designers
Raul Aguila
Hilary Fitzgibbons
Design Director
Chris Dixon
Publisher
Larry Burstein
Photographers
Lauren Greenfield
Marco Grob
Hannah Whitaker
Photography Director
Jody Quon
Photo Editors
Lea Golis
Caroline Smith
Editor in Chief
Adam Moss
Publishers
New York Media
Client
New York Magazine

New York
The Blazing Darkness of ALEXANDER McQUEEN p.90
FEBRUARY 22–MARCH 1, 2010
INCLUDING
Lorenzo Martone: MARRYING MARC JACOBS
BY TIM MURPHY
The Rebranding of KATE & ANDY SPADE
BY AMY LAROCCA
ALSO
Christina Hendricks and the return of the Voluptuous
Underwear As Outerwear, the Little White Dress, Froth, Office Shorts, and 11 other signs of a new season.
By HARRIET MAYS POWELL
Spring Fashion
Fashion Scions
Vlad & Julia Restoin Roitfeld in New York
WHAT'S GILT GROUPE Doing to Fashion?
BY ANDREW RICE
AND
SCORSESE Directs DiCAPRIO
Is 59 Obama's Lucky Number?
BY JOHN HEILEMANN
$4.99 USA/CANADA
NYMAG.COM

New York
INCLUDING
Naomi Campbell: WHERE TO BEGIN?
The FABULOUS FACES OF FASHION
ALSO
This Season's Look-by-Look Playbook
+ WHY DO TWEENS DRESS LIKE STRIPPERS?
MICHAEL KORS, The Happiest Man in Fashion
DAPHNE GUINNESS, Lady Gaga's Spiritual Godmother
Johnny Weir REALLY DOESN'T CARE WHAT YOU THINK
By AMY LAROCCA
Fall Fashion
AND
Katie Holmes as JACKIE O.

1
DREAM Complex
Charm OFFENSIVE
Ring
SHAPE
Gilt Groupe,
ALEXANDER McQUEEN'S

Capes!

Yellow Pencil in Magazine & Newspaper Design

Entire Magazines
Bloomberg Businessweek

2010 Year in Review
Bloomberg Businessweek's 2010 'Year in Review' is not only a reappraisal of the year but a rethinking of the institution of the year-end issue. Organised around six words that informed the year – currency, jobs, spills, gaga, normal, and stuck – the issue takes each word literally, then flips it. 'Jobs' starts with a look at the crisis in the labour force and ends with 365 days in the life of Apple's Steve Jobs. 'Spills' dissects the effects of BP's Gulf of Mexico disaster then looks at the year's professional tumbles.

Art Director
Robert Vargas
Designers
Evan Applegate
Jennifer Daniel
Patricia Kim
Gina Maniscalco
Maayan Pearl
Kenton Powell
Lee Wilson
Design Director
Cynthia Hoffman
Creative Director
Richard Turley
Photo Editors
Donna Cohen
Emily Keegin
Myles Little
Tania Pirozzi
Diana Suryakusuma
Director of Photography
David Carthas
Senior Photo Editor
Karen Frank
Editor in Chief
Josh Tyrangiel
Redesign Consultant
Mark Leeds
Art Manager
Emily Anton
Client
Bloomberg Businessweek

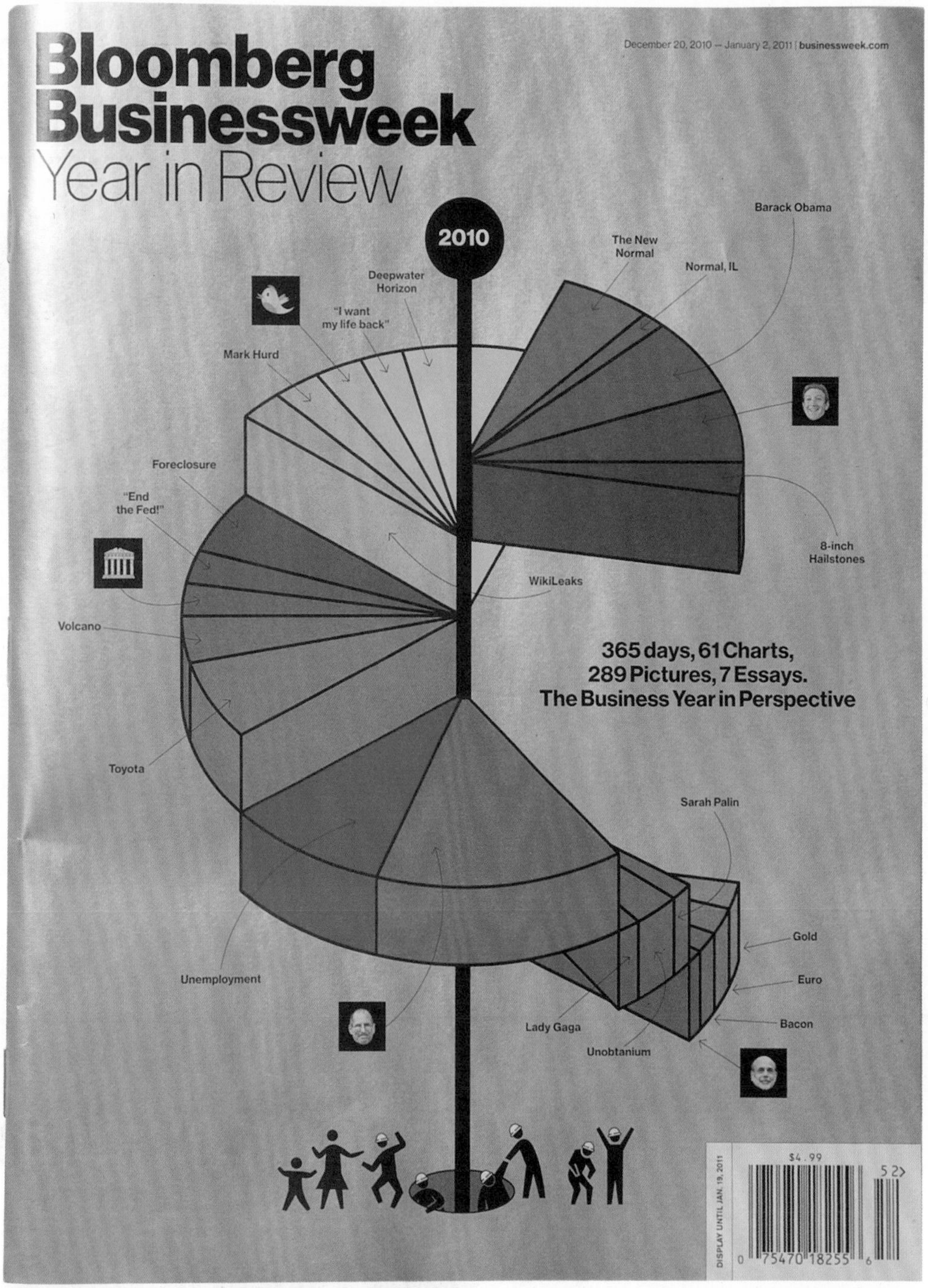
Bloomberg Businessweek
Year in Review
December 20, 2010 – January 2, 2011 | businessweek.com
2010
Barack Obama
The New Normal
Normal, IL
Deepwater Horizon
"I want my life back"
Mark Hurd
Foreclosure
"End the Fed!"
8-inch Hailstones
WikiLeaks
Volcano
365 days, 61 Charts, 289 Pictures, 7 Essays. The Business Year in Perspective
Toyota
Sarah Palin
Gold
Euro
Bacon
Unemployment
Lady Gaga
Unobtanium
$4.99
DISPLAY UNTIL JAN. 19, 2011

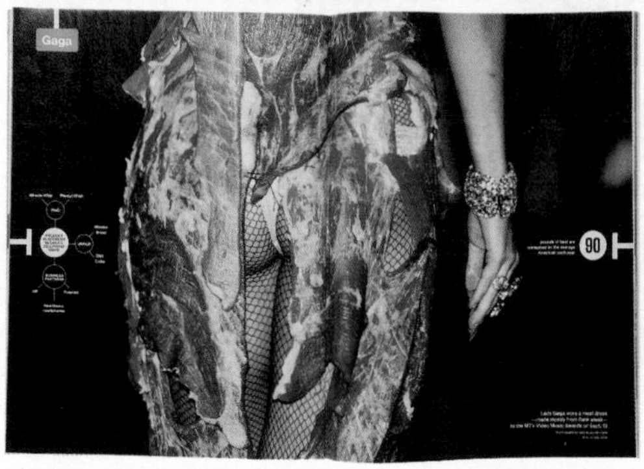
Gaga
90

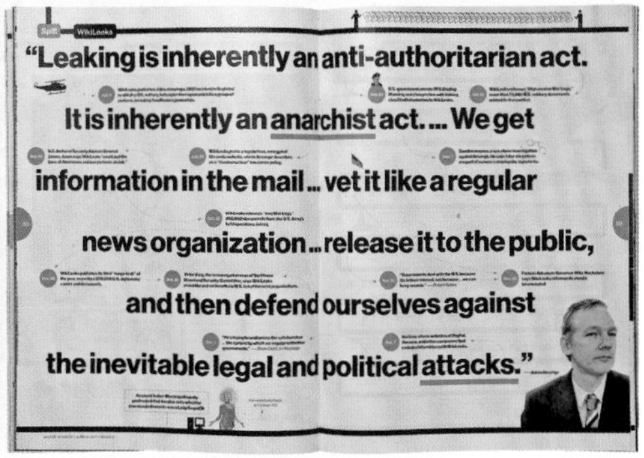
WikiLeaks
"Leaking is inherently an anti-authoritarian act. It is inherently an anarchist act.... We get information in the mail... vet it like a regular news organization... release it to the public, and then defend ourselves against the inevitable legal and political attacks."

Yellow Pencil in Magazine & Newspaper Design

Magazine Front Covers
Wallpaper*

Wallpaper* Custom Covers
Wallpaper* magazine's custom covers project was the showpiece of its August 2010 Handmade Issue. The issue featured over 100 collaborations and products – from yachts to coffee blends, kitchens to crisps. Interactive designers Kin produced an online application enabling readers to design their own cover, using elements supplied by artists and illustrators Anthony Burrill, James Joyce, Nigel Robinson, Kam Tang and Hort. Readers then received the issue with the cover they designed themselves in the post. Over 21,000 unique covers were printed, bound and delivered, making this project a showcase for the positive integration of online and print.

Art Director
Meirion Pritchard
Designer
Matt Wade
Illustrators
Anthony Burrill
Hort
James Joyce
Nigel Robinson
Kam Tang
Editor in Chief
Tony Chambers
Interactive Design & Programming
Kin
Client
Wallpaper*

Wallpaper*
UK £4.50
US $9.50
AUSTRALIA $ 10.50
CANADA $ 10.50
DENMARK DKK 75.00
FRANCE € 8.50
GERMANY € 10.50
HOLLAND € 8.50
ITALY € 9.00
JAPAN ¥ 1740
SINGAPORE $ 18.20
SPAIN € 8.50
SWEDEN SEK 75.00
SWITZERLAND CHF 16.00
UAE AED 45.00
AUGUST 2010
*DESIGNINTERIORSFASHIONARTLIFESTYLE
TOUCH
ME
WALLPAPER*
BLUE FIN BUILDING
110 SOUTHWARK STREET
LONDON
SE1 0SU
UNITED KINGDOM
my_test09

Wallpaper*
AUGUST 2010
*DESIGNINTERIORSFASHIONARTLIFESTYLE
THE
HANDMADE
ISSUE

Wallpaper*
AUGUST 2010
*DESIGNINTERIORSFASHIONARTLIFESTYLE
HANDLE
WITH
CARE
THE
HANDMADE
ISSUE

● Nomination in Magazine & Newspaper Design

Entire Magazines
New York Magazine

The Neighborhoods Issue
This issue is about the best neighbourhoods in New York City. The feature provides varying levels of information about New York boroughs, through dense, multi-page information graphics, a story on the branding of New York neighbourhoods, a photo essay on the locals, and more.

Art Director
Randy Minor
Deputy Art Director
Hitomi Sato
Associate Art Director
Josef Reyes
Designer
Hilary Fitzgibbons
Design Director
Chris Dixon
Publisher
Larry Burstein
Photographers
Andreas Laszlo Konrath
Hannah Whitaker
Photography Director
Jody Quon
Editor in Chief
Adam Moss
Publishers
New York Media
Client
New York Magazine

the NEIGHBORHOODS issue
NEW YORK
APRIL 19, 2010
the best place to live in new york is
turn to p.34
INCLUDING
Hasids Vs. Hipsters in Williamsburg p.44
What to Eat in Flushing, Red Hook + 58 Other Neighborhoods p.84
Soho, Dumbo, Fidi...Now NoMad? p.52
Is Murray Hill Morphing Into the Upper East Side? p.66
The Bird Man of Fort Greene p.58
The Gayest, Most Atheistic, Most Republican Nabes p.64
Mayberry in The Rockaways p.70
Realtor: Next Big Thing Is West Harlem p.66
Plus, a 5-Borough, 5,000-Person Poll: A Third of All New Yorkers Would Rather Live in the West Village; The Happiest People Live in Cobble Hill p.64
Nate Silver's Empirical Rankings of the City's Most Livable Neighborhoods
$4.99 USA/CANADA
NYMAG.COM

The Locals
A neighborhood is nothing without its characters.

What the Neighbors Think
A five-borough, 5,000-person poll.
West Village
Astoria
Tribeca
Upper East Side
Lower East Side
East Village
Williamsburg
Financial District
Upper West Side
Morningside Heights
Staten Island
Melrose
Harlem
Chelsea
87
Harlem
86
Tribeca
97
36
Most immigrants
43
Fewest immigrants
10

Nomination in Magazine & Newspaper Design

Newspaper Supplements
The Times

Eureka
Eureka is the monthly science and environment magazine produced by The Times. Introduced in October 2009, the magazine seeks to bring the wonders of science to a wider audience. Eureka has tackled complex subjects from string theory to the Large Hadron Collider, making them accessible with clear and distinctive art direction.

Art Director
Matt Curtis
Designer
Fraser Lyness
Picture Editor
Madeleine Penny
Publishers
Times Newspapers
Client
The Times

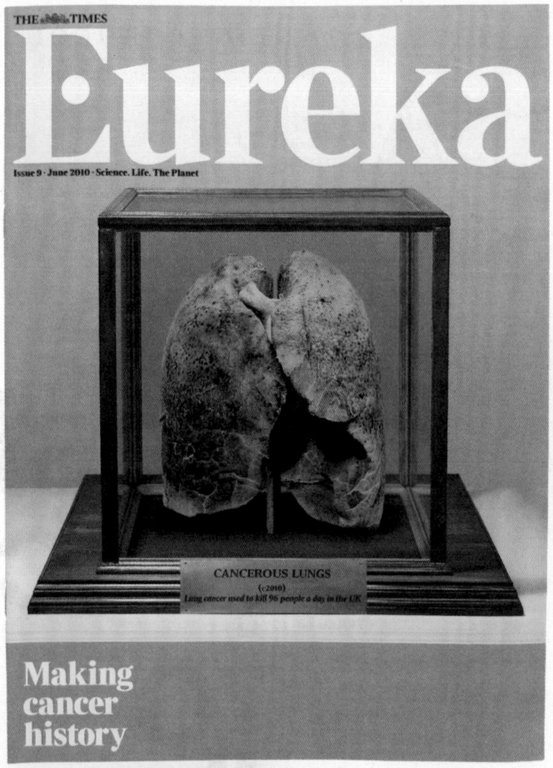
THE TIMES
Eureka
Issue 9 · June 2010 · Science. Life. The Planet
CANCEROUS LUNGS
(c2010)
Lung cancer used to kill 96 people a day in the UK
Making cancer history

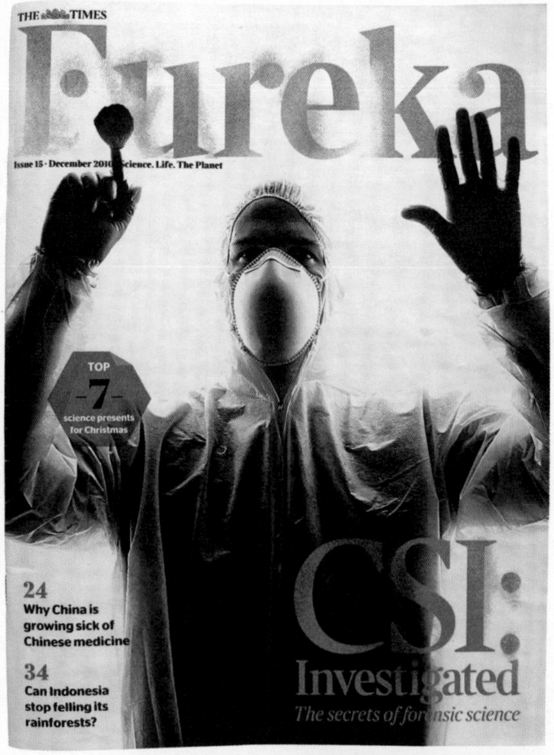
THE TIMES
Eureka
Issue 15 · December 2010 · Science. Life. The Planet
TOP
7
science presents for Christmas
24
Why China is growing sick of Chinese medicine
34
Can Indonesia stop felling its rainforests?
CSI:
Investigated
The secrets of forensic science

A FOREST CLEARING

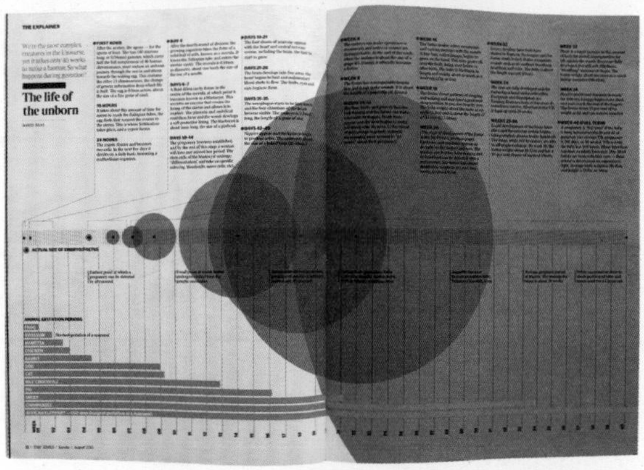
The life of the unborn

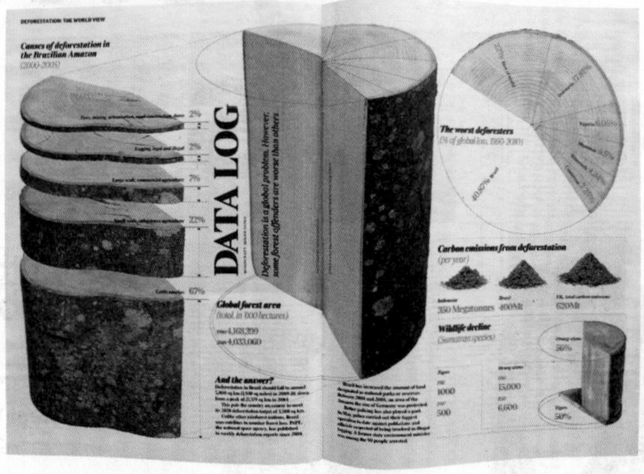
DATA LOG
Causes of deforestation in the Brazilian Amazon
The worst deforesters
Carbon emissions from deforestation
Global forest area
Wildlife decline
And the answer?

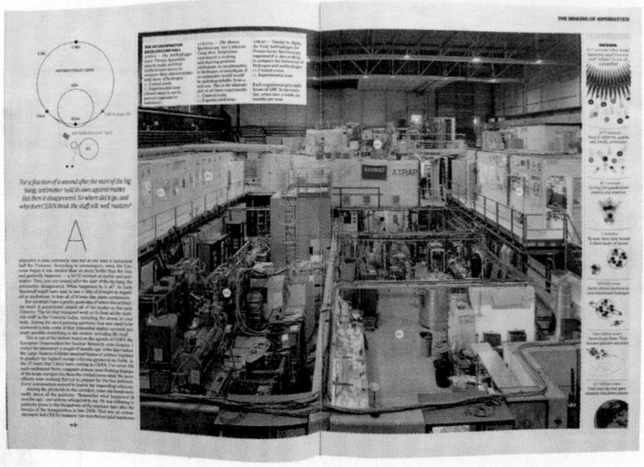

Entire Magazines
Studio8 Design for
Frame Publshing

Elephant Magazine
Issue 5
The fifth issue of art and culture magazine Elephant includes four bespoke headline typefaces and one bespoke numeral set.

Designer
Matt Willey
Publisher
Peter Huiberts
Typographer
Matt Willey
Cover Illustrator
Valero Doval
Editor in Chief
Marc Valli
Design Studio
Studio8 Design
Client
Frame Publishing

ELEPHANT
THE ART & VISUAL CULTURE MAGAZINE
RAYMOND PETTIBON
BERLIN GUIDE
THOMAS DEMAND
MAYA GOLD
THE ART OF COLLAGE
MONICA NARANJO URIBE
WOLFE VON LENKIEWICZ
THE MIKE MEIRÉ FACTORY
TOM HINGSTON
WINTER 2010-11
KIM HIORTHØY

THE
MIKE MEIRÉ
FACTORY

RAYMOND
PETTIBON

Entire Magazines
RUBBISH INK

RUBBISH Two and a Half
Issue Two and a Half from cult fashion read RUBBISH is an oversized celebration of playfulness. Limited to a run of 1,000 copies, the publication follows on from the success of the annual format of issues one and two. Creative director Jenny Dyson commissioned long time collaborator and art director Bianca Wendt to design this issue, with contributions from many fashionable creatives including Henry Holland, Holly Fulton, illustrators Ruth Clifford, Anthony Zinonos and Blue Bushell, writer and co-founder Jack Dyson and philosopher Alain de Botton. Contributors' portraits were created by Dot Jones, aged seven. Theme: playfulness. Lots of fun for all.

Art Director
Bianca Wendt
Creative Director
Jenny Dyson
Editor in Chief
Jenny Dyson
Design Agency
RUBBISH INK
Production Manager
George Ryan
Publishers
RUBBISH INK
Client
RUBBISH INK

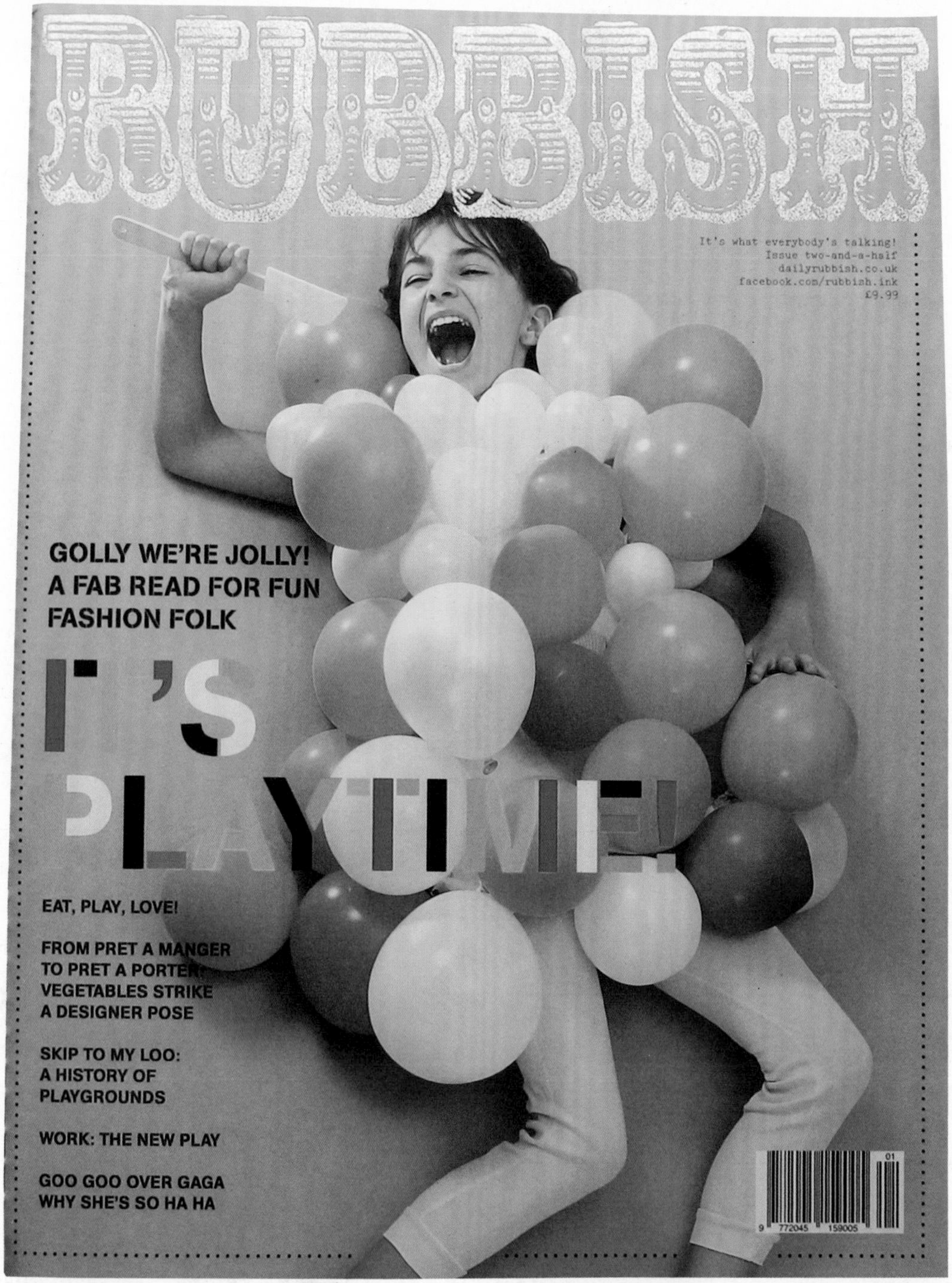
RUBBISH
It's what everybody's talking!
Issue two-and-a-half
dailyrubbish.co.uk
facebook.com/rubbish.ink
£9.99
GOLLY WE'RE JOLLY!
A FAB READ FOR FUN
FASHION FOLK
IT'S
PLAYTIME!
EAT, PLAY, LOVE!
FROM PRET A MANGER
TO PRET A PORTER:
VEGETABLES STRIKE
A DESIGNER POSE
SKIP TO MY LOO:
A HISTORY OF
PLAYGROUNDS
WORK: THE NEW PLAY
GOO GOO OVER GAGA
WHY SHE'S SO HA HA

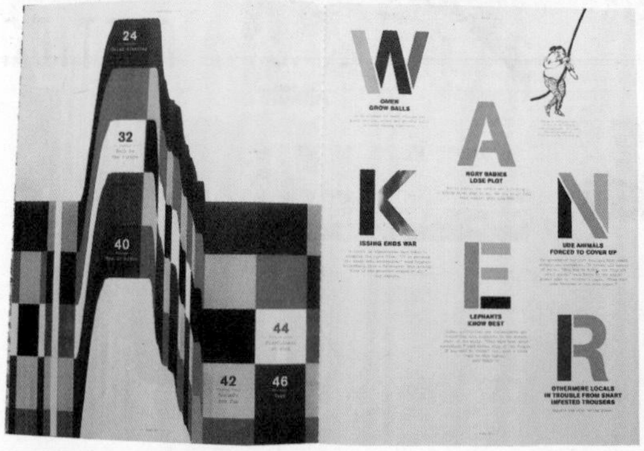
24
32
40
44
42
46
W
A
K
N
E
R

J O I
T H E
F A
C L U B

Entire Magazines
Il Sole 24 Ore

IL – Intelligence in Lifestyle, Issue 21
'IL – Intelligence in Lifestyle' is the monthly news magazine from publishers Il Sole 24 Ore. IL is dedicated to contemporary trends and consumer interests, and uses current events as the key to understanding changes in lifestyle. Its market is a contemporary audience that looks for unconventional and reflective content. The idea is to give readers 'soft' news as if it were 'hard' news: in a serious, journalistic style. It's a publication that always tries to reinvent itself, creating and designing different modules in every issue. The design takes inspiration from the magazines printed in the 60s.

Art Director
Francesco Franchi
Designer
Ilaria Tomat
Executive Editor
Roberto Napoletano
Editor in Chief
Walter Mariotti
Publishers
Il Sole 24 Ore
Client
Il Sole 24 Ore

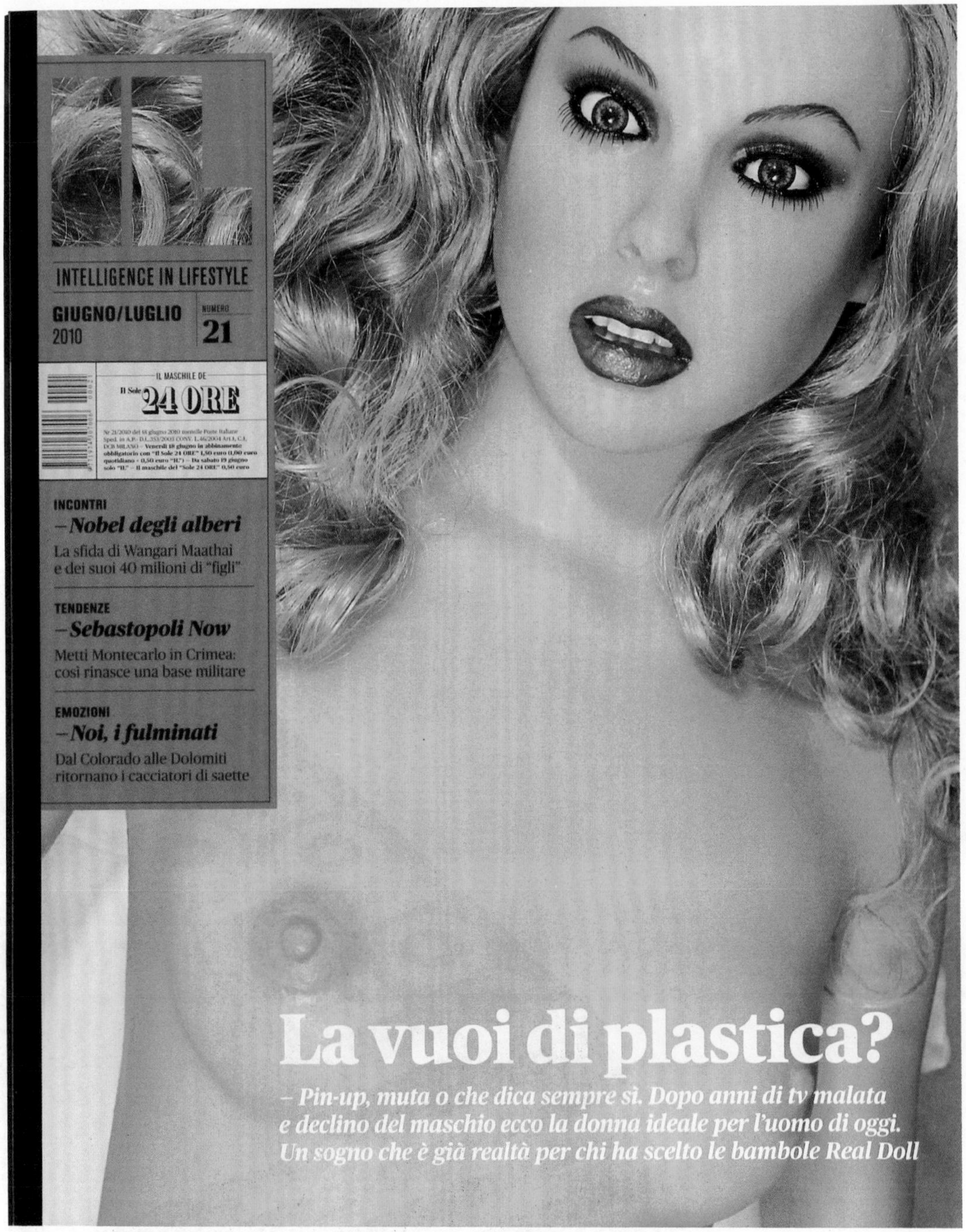
INTELLIGENCE IN LIFESTYLE
GIUGNO/LUGLIO 2010
NUMERO 21
IL MASCHILE DE
Il Sole 24 ORE
INCONTRI
–Nobel degli alberi
La sfida di Wangari Maathai e dei suoi 40 milioni di "figli"
TENDENZE
–Sebastopoli Now
Metti Montecarlo in Crimea: così rinasce una base militare
EMOZIONI
–Noi, i fulminati
Dal Colorado alle Dolomiti ritornano i cacciatori di saette
La vuoi di plastica?
– Pin-up, muta o che dica sempre sì. Dopo anni di tv malata e declino del maschio ecco la donna ideale per l'uomo di oggi. Un sogno che è già realtà per chi ha scelto le bambole Real Doll

La babele delle birr

E L'UOMO CREÒ LA BAMBOLA

Entire Magazines
Fabrica

Colors Collector
In the year of its 20th anniversary, Colors dedicated the winter 2010-2011 edition to collectors: those who amass, categorise and catalogue objects of the same type. These may be works of art or, in most cases, everyday objects which, because they are rare, distinctive or represent something special, become extraordinary cult objects, steeped in memories that feed passions and obsessions. True to its tradition as a 'magazine about the rest of the world', Colors Collector celebrates the diversity of local cultures and of creativity, casting a contemporary eye on tradition and crossing the boundaries between ordinary and extraordinary, reality and representation.

Art Directors
Magdalena Czarnecki
Brian Wood
Designer
Namyoung An
Creative Director
Sam Baron
Photographers
Carolina Amoretti
Jesse Marlow
James Mollison
Michael Winokur
Image Manipulator
Mauro Bedoni
Executive Editor
Giulia De Meo
Managing Editor
Erica Fusaro
Editor in Chief
Carlos Mustienes
Press Officer
Angela Quintavalle
Publishers
Fabrica

PRESIDENT OF THE UNITED STATES
BARACK OBAMA
44th
YES W
CHANGE
AIR
OBAMA
RICOMPENSA
CAN O. BIN LADEN
COUNTRY STEW

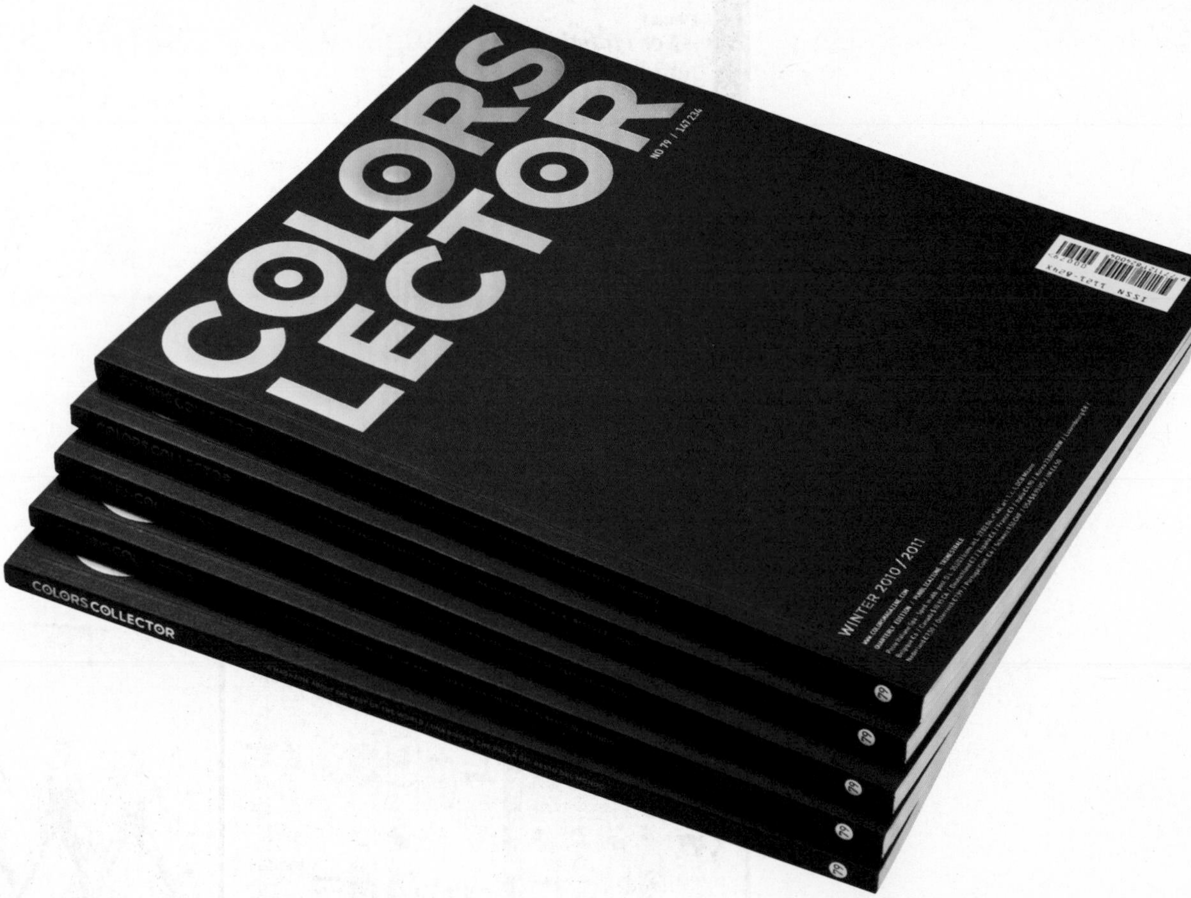
COLORS
LECTOR
NO 79 | 147234
WINTER 2010 / 2011
COLORS COLLECTOR

Entire Magazines
Mash for Meat & Livestock Australia

Chef's Special
The latest issues of Chef's Special aim to give chefs the tools and know-how to become less wasteful and more sustainable. In these times of concern over energy and climate change, it is important for chefs to be more creative with red meat by thinking further than the fillet, and to use Australian beef, veal, lamb and goat responsibly. Mash creatively directs ever-changing typographic landscapes to garnish hand-created illustrations and a raw style of realist photography.

Art Director
James Brown
Designer
Darren Song
Illustrators
Andrew McIntyre
Minka Sicklinger
Typographer
Darren Song
Photographer
John Laurie
Food Stylist
Simon Bajada
Design Studio
Mash
Client
Meat & Livestock Australia

- WINTER 2010 - JOURNAL #70 -
CHEF'S SPECIAL
A BEAST OF A JOB with Justin North pg.04 • MASTER CLASS pg.08
ON THE INTERNATIONAL STAGE: The World Association of
Chefs Societies 2010 Congress pg.12 • ADD TWO TABLESPOONS OF
COGNITIVE DISSONANCE AND STIR... pg.16 • BEEF MASTERPIECES -
Make Your Magnum Opus pg.20 • AGING GRACEFULLY - The Life
And Times Of A Dry Aged Steak pg.22 • ON THE MENU pg.26
ONE CUT WONDERS pg.34 • BITE SIZED pg.44
MOMENTARY - 2:34Pm With Romeo Baudouin pg.46
MEAT & LIVESTOCK AUSTRALIA

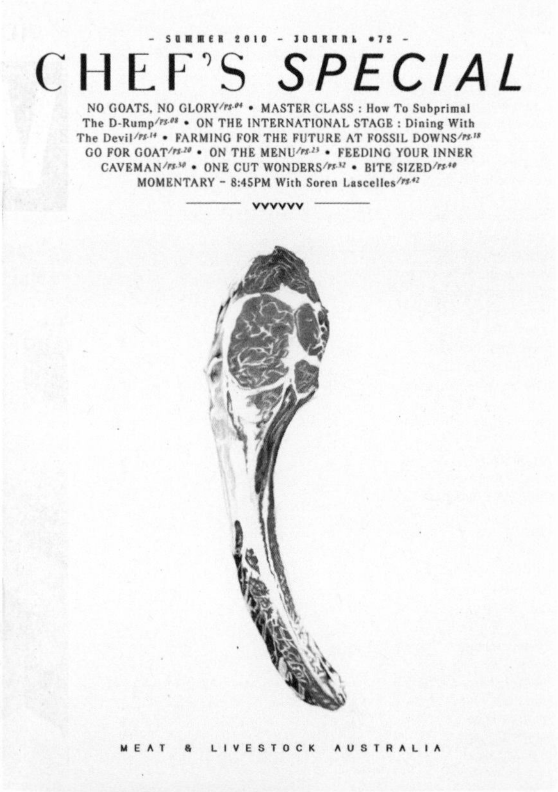
- SUMMER 2010 - JOURNAL #72 -
CHEF'S SPECIAL
NO GOATS, NO GLORY/pg.04 • MASTER CLASS : How To Subprimal
The D-Rump/pg.08 • ON THE INTERNATIONAL STAGE : Dining With
The Devil/pg.14 • FARMING FOR THE FUTURE AT FOSSIL DOWNS/pg.18
GO FOR GOAT/pg.20 • ON THE MENU/pg.25 • FEEDING YOUR INNER
CAVEMAN/pg.30 • ONE CUT WONDERS/pg.32 • BITE SIZED/pg.40
MOMENTARY - 8:45PM With Soren Lascelles/pg.42
MEAT & LIVESTOCK AUSTRALIA

- SPRING 2010 - JOURNAL #71 -
CHEF'S SPECIAL
KEEPING IT REAL : Auditing The System Which Guarantees
You Tender Beef pg.04 • ON THE INTERNATIONAL STAGE pg.06
VISIONS OF GREENER PASTURES pg.12 • SPRING LAMB pg.14
ON THE MENU : Bar Menus pg.16 • ONE CUT WONDERS pg.24
BITE SIZED pg.30 • MOMENTARY - 3:15PM With Naomi
Stephenson pg.33 • THE MSA CHAIN REACTION pg.34
MEAT & LIVESTOCK AUSTRALIA

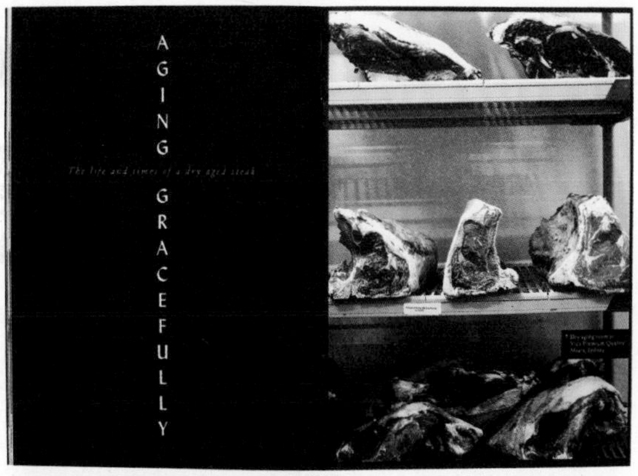
AGING GRACEFULLY

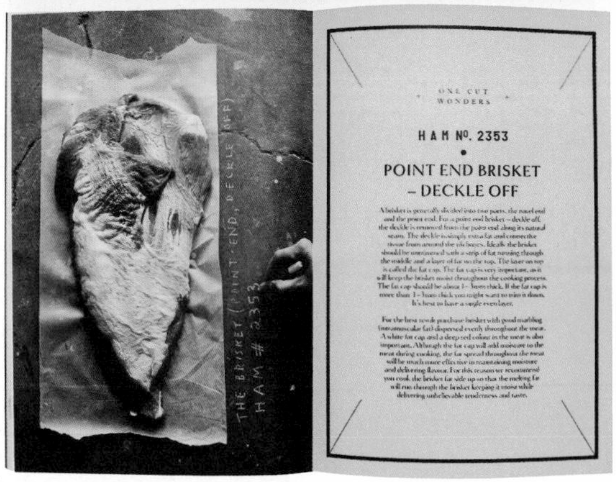
ONE CUT WONDERS
HAM No. 2353
POINT END BRISKET
– DECKLE OFF

Entire Magazines
Wired

Wired
Wired is the UK's leading monthly magazine about ideas, technology, design and business. It has carved out a niche for itself as the authoritative voice on the people and themes that are changing the world. Wired is at the forefront of magazine design. From fluorescent special colours to innovative cover treatments, it sets a standard that other magazines aspire to, not only in the UK but worldwide.

Art Director
Andrew Diprose
Deputy Art Director
Gary Cadogan
Designer
Ben Fraser
Illustrators
Ben Oliver
Harry Pearce
Diogo Soares
Photographers
James Day
Jill Greenberg
Brent Humphreys
Spencer Lowell
Brad Swonetz
Picture Editor
Steve Peck
Editor
David Rowan
Writers
David Baker
Joshuah Bearman
Duncan Graham-Rowe
Guy Martin
Neal Pollack
James Silver
Illustration
ITO
Pentagram
Photography
Diver & Aquilar
Publishers
Condé Nast
Client
Wired

IDEAS TECHNOLOGY CULTURE BUSINESS
WIRED
WHY THE iPAD REALLY MATTERS P.120
UK MAGAZINE LAUNCH OF THE YEAR
100
WHO'S SHAPING THE DIGITAL WORLD?
FROM VIRAL HIT-MAKERS TO V.C. TITANS: THE WIRED 100 P.86
MAY 10 £3.99 wired.co.uk
THE FUTURE AS IT HAPPENS
BATTLE OF THE BROWSERS! MOZILLA VS GOOGLE P.112
DUCK! WE TEST BULLET-PROOF VESTS P.132

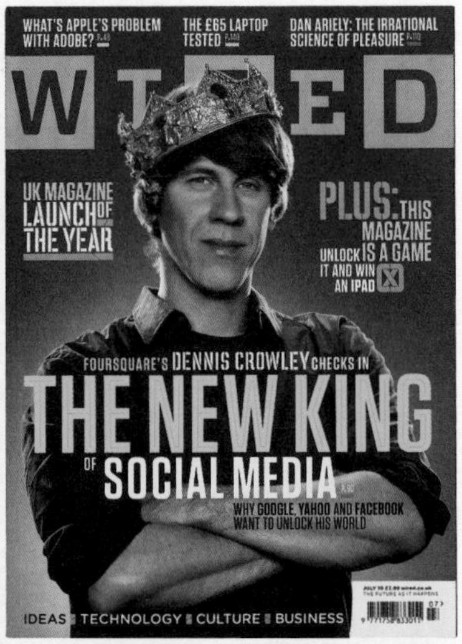
WHAT'S APPLE'S PROBLEM WITH ADOBE?
THE £65 LAPTOP TESTED
DAN ARIELY: THE IRRATIONAL SCIENCE OF PLEASURE
WIRED
UK MAGAZINE LAUNCH OF THE YEAR
PLUS: THIS MAGAZINE IS A GAME UNLOCK IT AND WIN AN IPAD
FOURSQUARE'S DENNIS CROWLEY CHECKS IN
THE NEW KING OF SOCIAL MEDIA
WHY GOOGLE, YAHOO AND FACEBOOK WANT TO UNLOCK HIS WORLD
IDEAS TECHNOLOGY CULTURE BUSINESS

IDEAS / TECHNOLOGY / CULTURE / BUSINESS
WIRED
UK MAGAZINE LAUNCH OF THE YEAR
THE HOW TO ISSUE
CREATE NEW LIFE
BUILD A DRONE
MAKE MONEY ON THE IPAD
HACK CHEAP FLIGHTS
PLUS:
BLINDNESS CURED!
THE BIONIC IMPLANT P.112
"HOW TO KEEP YOUR #*#!ING JOB
WE RATE:
SMARTER PHONES
FUEL-CELL CARS
SEA SCOOTERS
THE THICK OF IT'S OLLIE AND MALCOLM ON SURVIVING A NEW REGIME P.84

The ART of the STEAL

DATA
INFORMATION

Entire Magazines
Winkontent

Monocle Issue 39
Monocle is a news, current affairs, business and design journal, printed on various stocks throughout and published ten times a year.

Art Director
Izabella Bielawska
Designer
James Melaugh
Creative Director
Richard Spencer Powell
Publishers
Winkontent

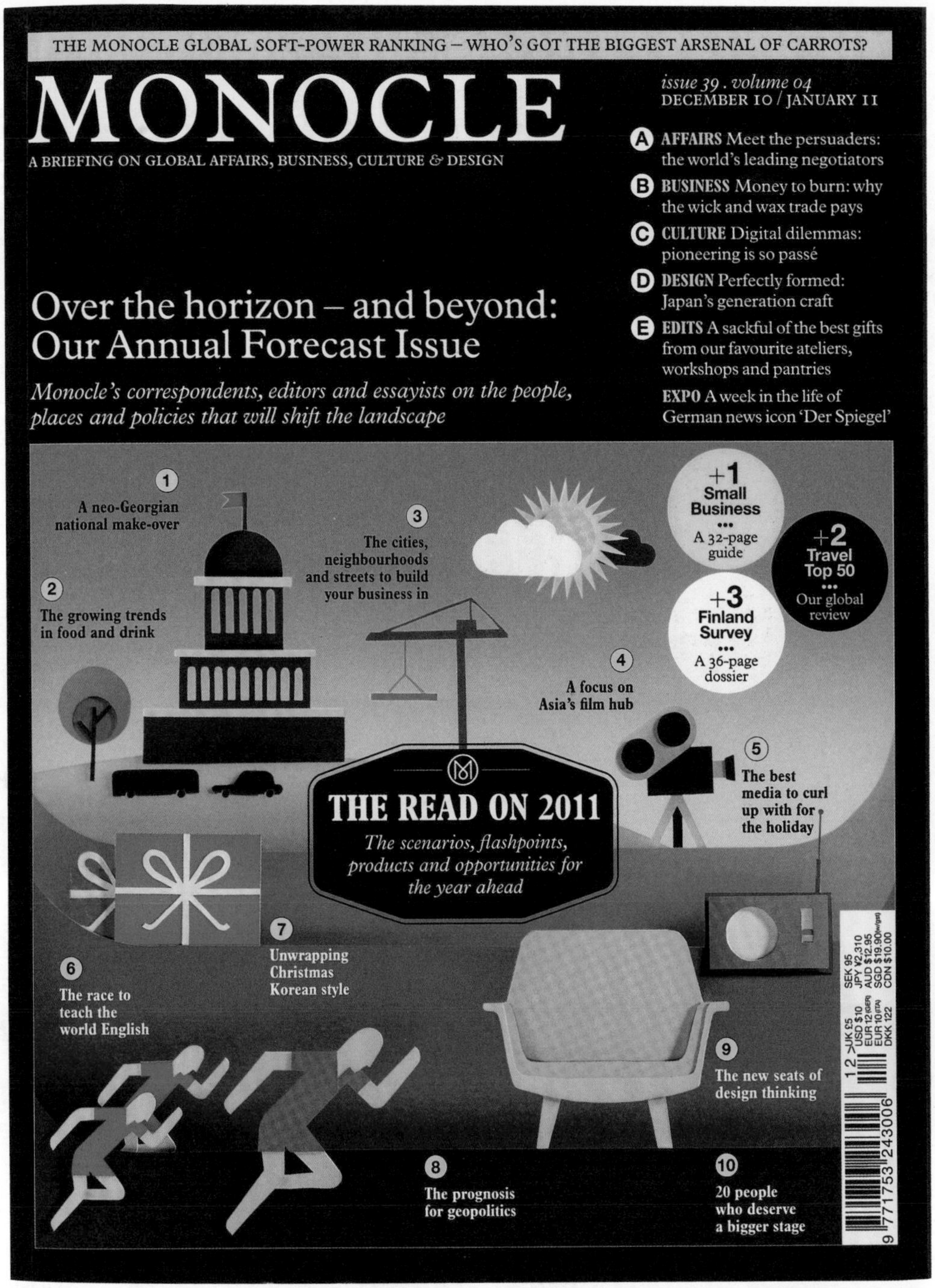
THE MONOCLE GLOBAL SOFT-POWER RANKING – WHO'S GOT THE BIGGEST ARSENAL OF CARROTS?
MONOCLE
A BRIEFING ON GLOBAL AFFAIRS, BUSINESS, CULTURE & DESIGN
issue 39 . volume 04
DECEMBER 10 / JANUARY 11
A AFFAIRS Meet the persuaders: the world's leading negotiators
B BUSINESS Money to burn: why the wick and wax trade pays
C CULTURE Digital dilemmas: pioneering is so passé
D DESIGN Perfectly formed: Japan's generation craft
E EDITS A sackful of the best gifts from our favourite ateliers, workshops and pantries
EXPO A week in the life of German news icon 'Der Spiegel'
Over the horizon – and beyond: Our Annual Forecast Issue
Monocle's correspondents, editors and essayists on the people, places and policies that will shift the landscape
1 A neo-Georgian national make-over
2 The growing trends in food and drink
3 The cities, neighbourhoods and streets to build your business in
4 A focus on Asia's film hub
5 The best media to curl up with for the holiday
6 The race to teach the world English
7 Unwrapping Christmas Korean style
8 The prognosis for geopolitics
9 The new seats of design thinking
10 20 people who deserve a bigger stage
+1 Small Business ••• A 32-page guide
+2 Travel Top 50 ••• Our global review
+3 Finland Survey ••• A 36-page dossier
THE READ ON 2011
The scenarios, flashpoints, products and opportunities for the year ahead
UK £5 USD $10 EUR 12 DKK 122
SEK 95 JPY ¥2,310 AUD $12.95 SGD $19.90 CDN $10.00
9 771753 243006

THE PRINT MEISTER
—Hamburg

BURNING BRIGHT
—Normandy

Entire Newspapers
Leterme Dowling
for Counter-Print

Eight:48
Eight:48 is a new publication launched as a sister newspaper to online stores Counter-Print and Counter-Objects, which sell books, graphic art and product design. The purpose of the newspaper was threefold: to provide a printed context in which the clients could promote their contributing designers; to offer a platform where they could tackle issues relevant to their audience; and to provide inspiring content.

Art Directors
Jon Dowling
Celine Leterme
Illustrator
Robert Hanson
Design Agency
Leterme Dowling
Client
Counter-Print

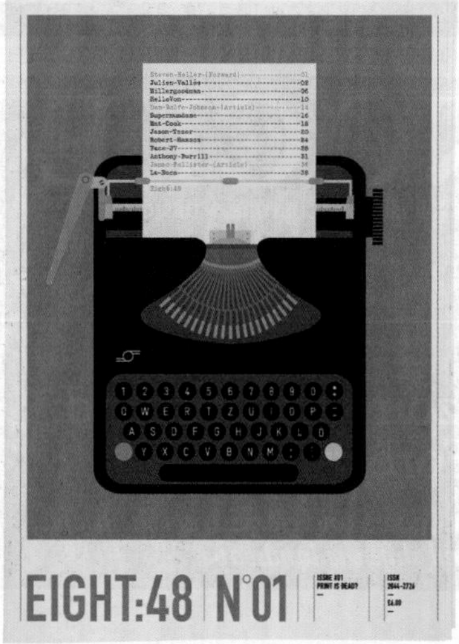
EIGHT:48 N°01

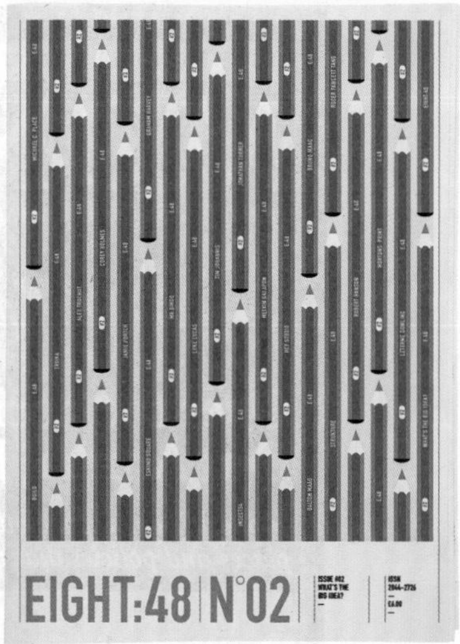
EIGHT:48 N°02

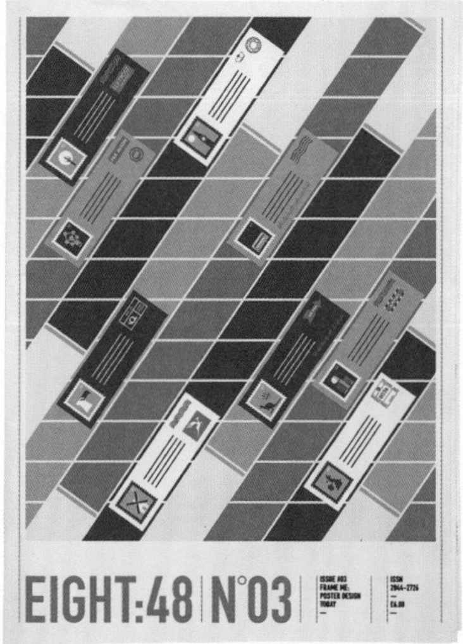
EIGHT:48 N°03

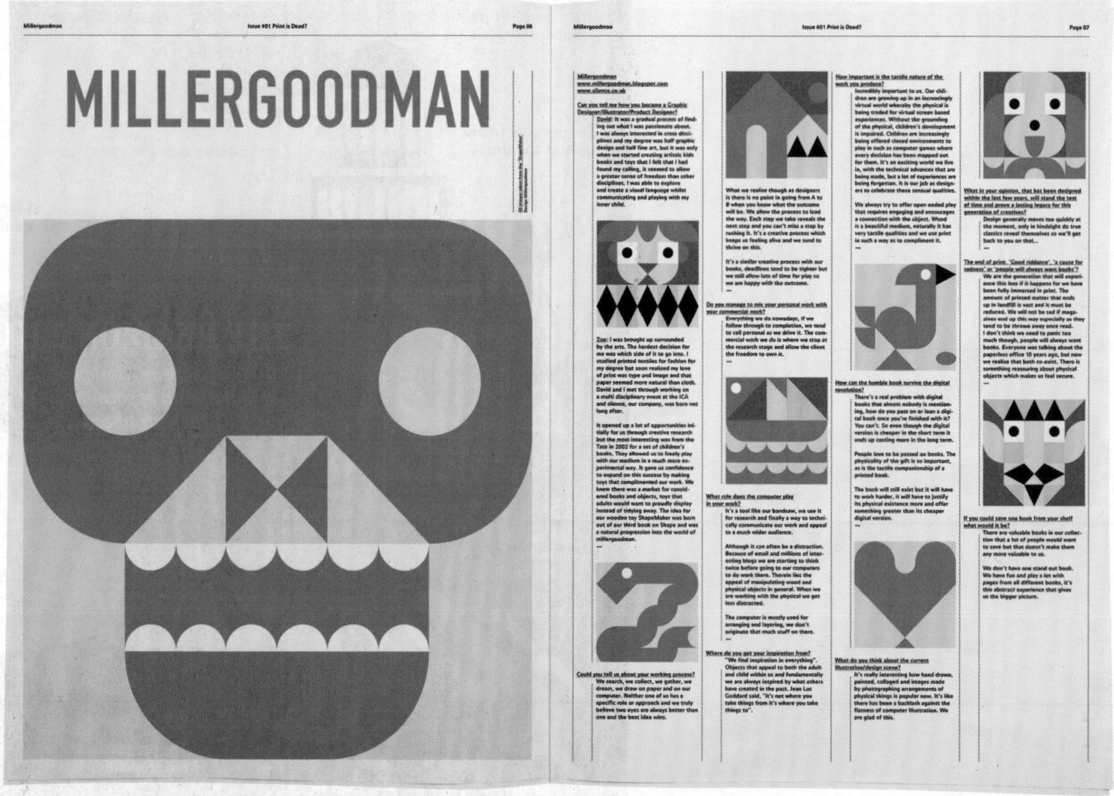
MILLERGOODMAN

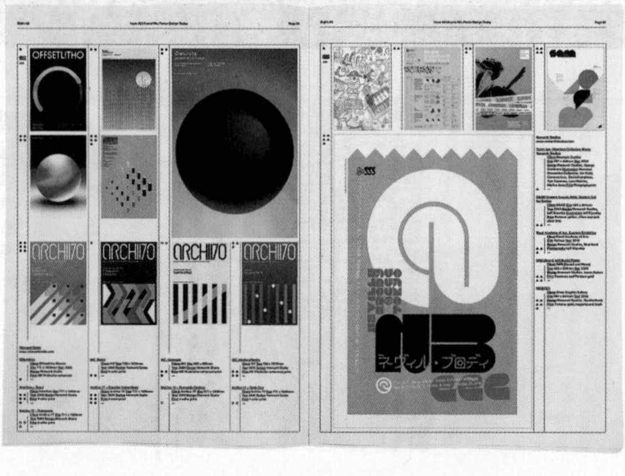
OFFSETLITHO
ARCHI170

JULIEN VALLÉE P04
MILLERGOODMAN P08
HELLOVON P12
SUPERMUNDANE P18
MAT COOK P20
JASON TOZER P22
ROBERT HANSON P26
FACE 37 P30
ANTHONY BURRILL P33
LA BOCA P38
STEVEN HELLER

Entire Newspapers
Wlinkontent

Monocle Alpino
The Monocle Alpino newspaper is the sister publication of Monocle. It covers news, current affairs, business and design. It is printed twice a year over the seasonal holiday periods in summer and winter.

Art Director
Izabella Bielawska
Designer
James Melaugh
Creative Director
Richard Spencer Powell
Publishers
Winkontent

••• 72 PAGES OF OPINION, OBSERVATIONS, ESSAYS, REPORTAGE, INTERVIEWS AND INSPIRATION •••

MONOCLE
ALPINO

ISSUE 02 WINTER 2010/11

A completely sun, ice, ski wax and snow-friendly print media product from the editors of Monocle

A AFFAIRS The politics of hosting mountainside summits and forming high-altitude alliances
B BUSINESS Carving out a profitable future on two planks
C CULTURE Why Reykjavik wants to be a cool media capital, and the film that changed the Alps
D DESIGN A selection of solid craft from the peaks of Europe
E EDITS The essentials to help you escape, imbibe and entertain on a winter's night

1 Swiss rescue agency – The team you can depend on when accidents happen
55 Resolutions – A new regime for sharpening your form in 2011
50 Media choices – For listening, watching and lazing around with

Germany takes the high ground in defence
Monocle goes on snow patrol with the Federal Republic's Gebirgsjägerbrigade, the traditional Alpine troops with a very modern mission

Monocle *in the* Alps
Monocle Alpino is the second super-premium newspaper from the London-based Monocle media stable. As we slide into 2011 our editors and correspondents have traversed from Vorarlberg to Hokkaido and most peaks in between. To keep your holiday media buffet stocked, we also have a toasty audio series for download and smart new series on Bloomberg Television.
Our audio show, The Monocle Winter Series, goes live every Friday on iTunes and at monocle.com

Small and perfectly formed: *With its traditional industries under threat, is the statelet of Andorra feeling the squeeze and can it find a prince to save the day?*

Retreats on high: *Three high-minded residences for keeping snug and cosy*

Weather guard: *Thermals, sweaters and outerwear for attaining piste performance*

Radio: *Four modern alternatives to Alpine horn blowing*

Food: *Hearty dishes from top tables in Italy, Korea and Sweden. Warning: reindeer should make themselves scarce*

Essays: *Dispatches to provoke, inspire, contemplate and even warm the heart*

A MONOCLE SPECIAL EDITION
£4.00
EUR 6
USD 8

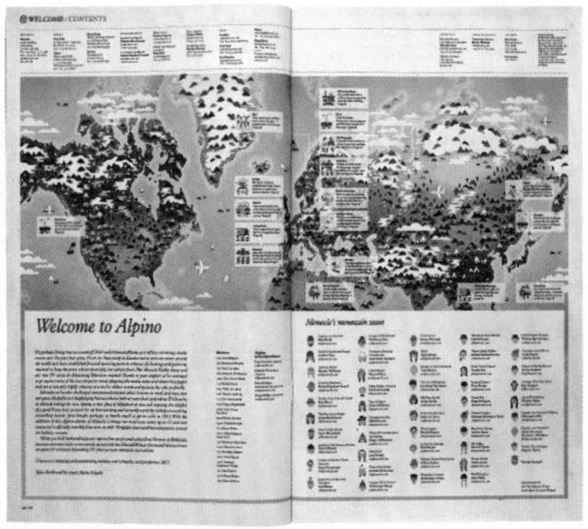
Welcome to Alpino

Magazine Front Covers
Bloomberg
Businessweek

Bloomberg
Businessweek
Cover Series

Bloomberg Businessweek covers come together quickly. We are published weekly, so we try to make the solution current and dynamic, placing the idea at the heart of the concept. The aim is for the finished product to have a sense of urgency. We strive for something that looks a little removed from what people traditionally perceive an American business magazine to look like; something accessible to anyone passing a newsstand.

Art Director
Robert Vargas
Creative Director
Richard Turley
Illustrator
Nick White
Photographer
Fredrik Broden
Director of Photography
David Carthas
Photo Editor
Diana Suryakusuma
Senior Photo Editor
Karen Frank
Editor in Chief
Josh Tyrangiel
Client
Bloomberg
Businessweek

Policy
NASA: Laid Off From Outer Space
Etc.
Christopher Buckley on Glenn Beck
Markets
Goodbye to California's Pot Cowboys?
Plus
Bloomberg Businessweek
Coke
In Africa

Opening Remarks
The Delusion of Income Inequality
Technology
STEVE JOBS' LAST BOSS TELLS ALL
Imports
Tilapia: Chinese Chicken of the Sea
Plus
Bloomberg Businessweek
Shredded
Who owns your house?
A $1 trillion crisis of faith

Management
Stephen Miles, The CEO Whisperer
Peeking at The Lingerie Football League
Plus
Bloomberg Businessweek
THE GREAT COPPER HEIST
WITH PRICES NEAR RECORD HIGHS, THIEVES ARE SELLING AMERICA FOR SCRAP

Real Estate
Why Your Mortgage Can't Be Found
Technology
Microsoft Gets Mobile Right. Finally
Etc.
Millennials: The New Office Morons
Plus
Bloomberg Businessweek
WHY BUSINESS DOESN'T TRUST THE TEA PARTY

Magazine Front Covers
ELLE UK

ELLE Collections
Autumn/Winter 2010
For the autumn/winter 2010 issue of Elle Collections, colour was the basis of the cover design. Building on the strength of the issue's pull-out section featuring the season's colour trends, we used hundreds of catwalk images to create strong bands of colour that blended into one another, rather like a magic eye picture. The result is a strong cover that had a big impact on the shop shelves.

Art Director
Tom Meredith
Senior Designer
Lisa Rahman
Creative Director
Marissa Bourke
Publisher
Rita Lewis
Catwalk Photographer
Anthea Simms
Image Manipulator
Noel Allen
Picture Editor
Charlie Hall
Editor
Avril Mair
Editor in Chief
Lorraine Candy
Publishers
Hachette Filipacchi UK
Client
ELLE UK
Brand
ELLE Collections

ELLE
COLLECTIONS
THE ONLY GUIDE TO THE NEW SEASON
AUTUMN WINTER 2010
£6
9 771751 457016
09
OFF SALE 7 SEPTEMBER 2010

Magazine Front Covers
Granta Publications

Granta 110: Sex
Granta magazine tackles numerous themes through literature and art. In this issue, we address the toughest topic of all – sex – from an array of angles. Granta 110 provides an example of how we try to use cover art to initiate dialogue and as the catalyst for branding universal topics. The cover was printed on a tactile, velveteen stock, playing on our sense of touch. We created three moving illustrations with the Institute for Eyes from stories in the issue. They're housed in a breathing website by Theo Tillberg (www.thisisnotapurse.com), which makes further use of the cover art.

Art Director
Michael Salu
Photographer
Billie Segal
Deputy Editor
Ellah Allfrey
Editor in Chief
John Freeman
Web Designer
Theo Tillberg
Filmmakers
Joseph Bull
Luke Seomore
Publishers
Granta Publications

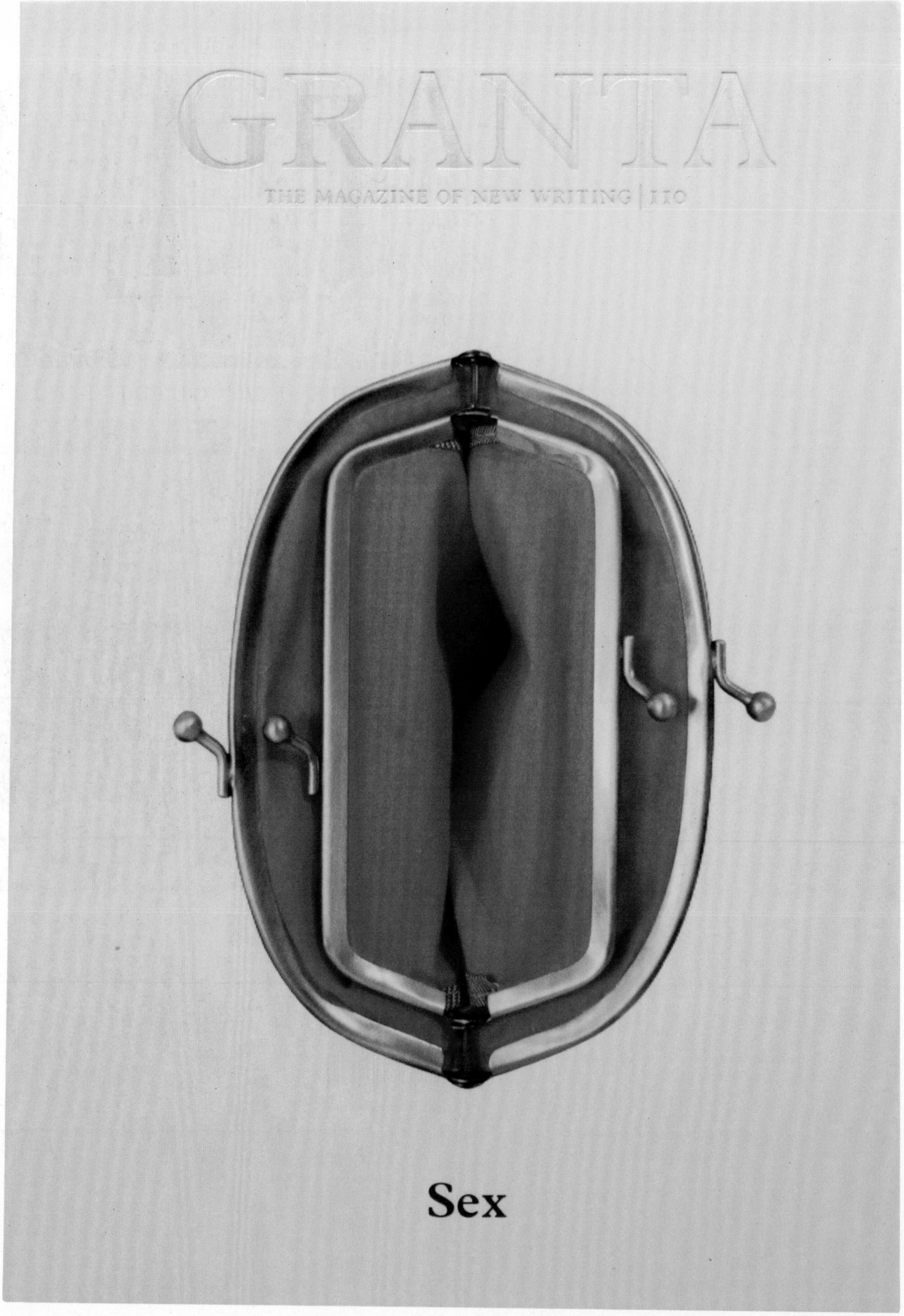
GRANTA
THE MAGAZINE OF NEW WRITING | 110
Sex

Magazine Front Covers
The Jupiter Drawing Room Cape Town
for Interactive Africa

Design Indaba Superstars Cover
Design Indaba welcomed delegates to the 'Creative Playing Field', the concept for their 2010 design conference and expo. We teamed up conference speakers as the touring All Stars, and invited South Africans to try out for our country's first ever national creative team, the hosting Design Indaba Superstars. In keeping with this concept, we designed March's 'Design Indaba' magazine cover to present every reader with their very own playing field. On this field they could pop up 11 players who'd tried out for the Superstars team and, essentially, let the Design Indaba games begin.

Designers
Brandt Botes
Alex Hayn
Creative Director
Joanne Thomas
Copywriter
Annabel Slingsby
Design Group
The Jupiter Drawing Room Cape Town
Marketing Manager
Ravi Naidoo
Client
Interactive Africa
Brand
Design Indaba

DESIGN INDABA
WINNER OF 12 INTERNATIONAL & 6 NATIONAL AWARDS
DESIGN INDABA MAGAZINE
Q1
1ST QUARTER '10
10

CLEVER LITTLE BAG
CLEVER LITTLE BAG
CLEVER LITTLE BAG
350734 01

Yellow Pencil in Packaging Design

GBH for PUMA

Clever Little Bag
Clever Little Bag is a reusable bag that eliminates the need for a separate PUMA shoebox and carrier bag. Shoes are transported from factory to store in the reusable bag using a protective card inner, which is retained by PUMA for recycling, while the customer takes the shoes home in the bag. It is classic PUMA, with its looks and language delivering a serious message with trademark wit. Replacing the shoebox reduces paper usage by 65 per cent and carbon emissions by ten tonnes each year, while eliminating the shopping bag saves 275 tonnes of plastic per year.

Graphic Designers
Sophie Paynter
Jacob Vanderkar
Graphic Design Director
Jason Gregory
Structural Designers
Nick Cronan
Josh Morenstein
Seth Murray
Structural Chief Designer
Yves Behar
Creative Directors
Mark Bonner
Jason Gregory
Peter Hale
Graphic Design Studio
GBH
Structural Design Studio
fuseproject
Brand Manager
Antonio Bertone
Client
PUMA

Nomination in Packaging Design

Packaging Design
GBH for PUMA International

PUMA Phone Packaging
The packaging for the PUMA phone highlights the eco credentials of the world's first solar powered mobile phone. The one-piece moulded pulp container is made from 30 per cent recycled newspaper and 70 per cent corrugated cardboard off-cuts, air dried to minimise energy in production. It even has a handle so you won't need a bag, and you don't have to worry about it getting wet as it is completely waterproof too. The minimal band uses vegetable inks and recycled paper stock. The packaging is the antithesis to the usual and supports the phone's claim to be 'not like all those other phones'.

Designers
Phil King
Russell Saunders
Jacob Vanderkar
Design Director
Peter Hale
Creative Directors
Mark Bonner
Jason Gregory
Peter Hale
Copywriters
Peter Hale
Russell Saunders
Design Studio
GBH
Brand Managers
Antonio Bertone
Nina Wolf
Director of Marketing & User Experience
Jerome Nadel
Clients
PUMA International
Sagem Wireless

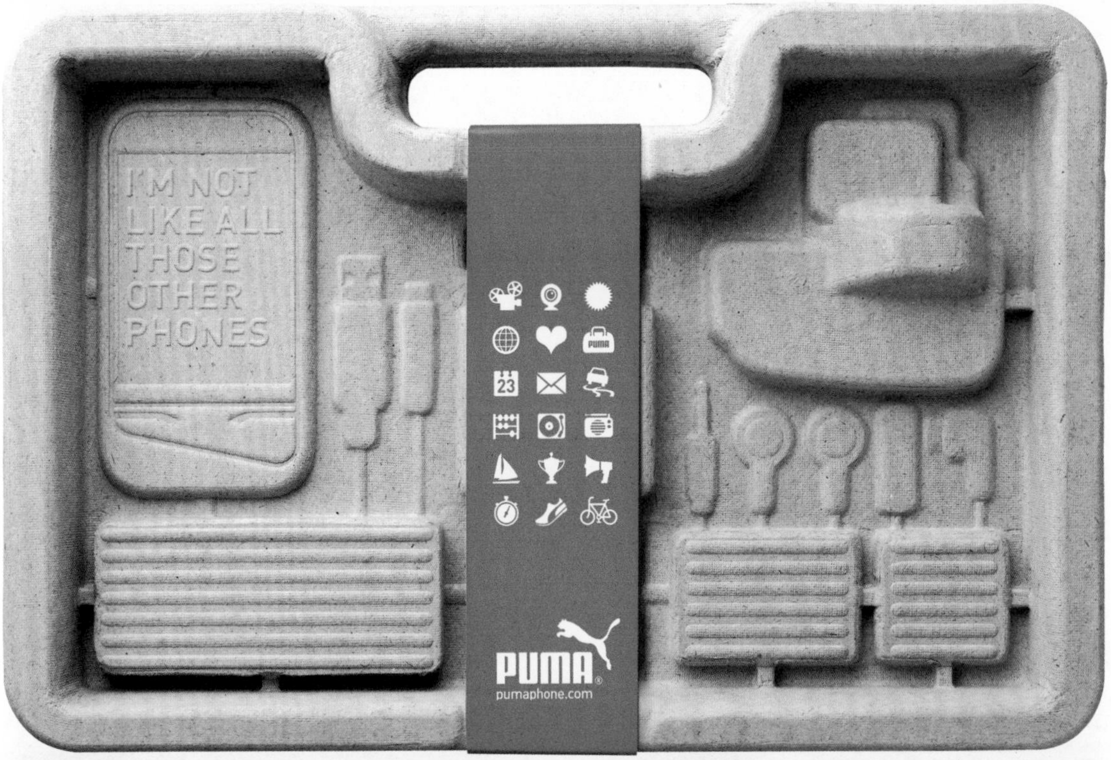
I'M NOT LIKE ALL THOSE OTHER PHONES
PUMA
pumaphone.com

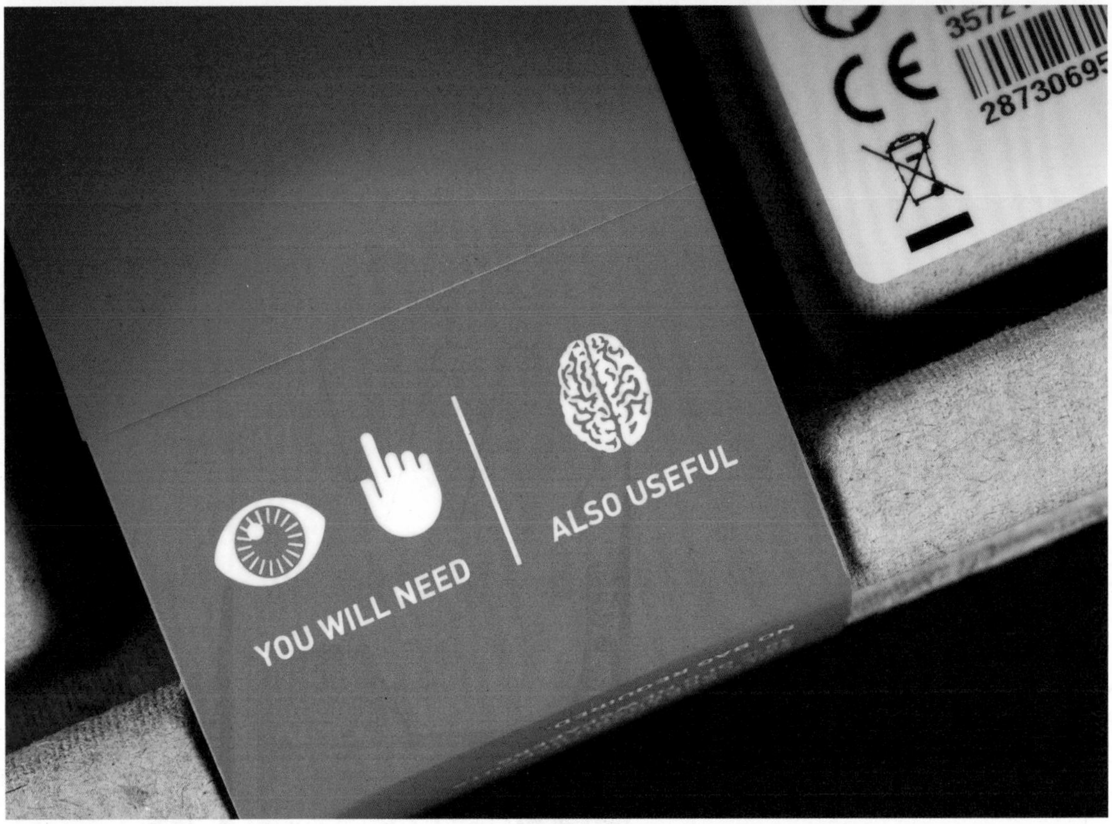
YOU WILL NEED
ALSO USEFUL

Packaging Design
Marc Atlan Design
for Kjaer Weis

Kjaer Weis
Makeup Collection
In this makeup collection for Kjaer Weis, the compacts are shaped to mirror the features they will be used to enhance: slim and long for the lips, large and square for the cheeks, small and round for the eyes. These compacts are designed to be conserved rather than recycled. Cast in white bronze and monogrammed in glossy white enamel, each object conveys the substance of a valuable keepsake. The line fuses an understated and timeless classicism with the crisp minimal lines of modern jewellery.

Designer
Marc Atlan
Art Director
Marc Atlan
Copywriter
Marc Atlan
Design Studio
Marc Atlan Design
Client
Kjaer Weis

KW
Kjaer Weis
KW
Kjaer Weis
KW
Kjaer Weis

Packaging Design
Bendita Gloria
for Casa Mariol

Casa Mariol
Casa Mariol is a family-owned winery that has been producing wines in Terra Alta for over 100 years. They defend what is natural in the broadest sense of the word and are not at ease with the luxury that often goes with the wine industry. For example, the bottles clearly call a spade a spade, describing the wines by their grape variety and their age, avoiding romantic, cheesy names. Mariol makes homemade wines, so the design has also been resolved using 'homemade' tools such as WordArt, Excel and Clipart.

Graphic Designers
Santi Fuster
Alba Rosell
Creative Directors
Santi Fuster
Alba Rosell
Design Studio
Bendita Gloria
Brand Manager
Miquel Àngel Vaquer
Client
Casa Mariol

GARNA-TXA BLANCA
BLANC
JOVE
CASA MARIOL
GARNA-TXA NEGRA
NEGRE
JOVE
CASA MARIOL
ULL DE LLEBRE
CRIANÇA
12 MESOS
CASA MARIOL
MERLOT
CRIANÇA
12 MESOS
CASA MARIOL
CABERNET SAU-VIG-NON
RESERVA
26 MESOS
CASA MARIOL
SYRAH
RESERVA
22 MESOS
CASA MARIOL
BLANC
CASA MARIOL
VI DE COLLITA

Packaging Design
Landor Associates
for SKYY Spirits

Espolón
Espolón is an award-winning tequila with little brand awareness in the US. The goal was to reintroduce the brand in a crowded premium segment. We learned that consumers wanted a product that felt real. The new brand was inspired by the original Posada engravings, which told real stories of the struggles and social injustice in Mexico. The name Espolón refers to the spur of a rooster, so to give it relevance, we created a rooster, Ramon, named after the master distiller. Espolón is a living identity that depicts stories of real life in Mexico.

Designer
Tony Rasstatter
Design Director
Cameron Imani
Art Director
Anastasia Laksmi
Creative Director
Nicolas Aparicio
Branding Consultancy
Landor Associates
Account Handler
Deborah Crudo
Client
SKYY Spirits
Brand
Espolón

100% PURO AGAVE
EL ESPOLÒN
TEQUILA BLANCO
750 ML (80 PROOF)
100% PURO AGAVE
EL ESPOLÒN
TEQUILA REPOSADO
750 ML (80 PROOF)

Packaging Design
Jun Kuroyanagi
for Mitaniseitou
Hanesanuki Honpo

Wasanbon: Song of the Sea
The Wasanbon sugar recipe was established 300 years ago at the Mitani sugar factory in Japan by using selected sugarcane and complicated hand-work. The challenge was to represent this excellent material through the sweets' shape and packaging. We chose to focus on the idea of blessings of nature. Each sweet is a cone formed by dropping sugar particles, and the arranged sweets seem to ripple.

Designer
Jun Kuroyanagi
Box Maker
Masakazu Yamane
Print Director
Masakazu Yamane
Wooden Confectionery Mould Maker
Takeyuki Tanaka
Project Managers
Chiaki Hayashi
Fram Kitagawa
Kosuke Kuwabara
Masako Maeda
Brand Manager
Shoji Mitani
Client
Mitaniseitou
Hanesanuki Honpo

和三盆
うみのうた

Packaging Design
Jun Kuroyanagi for
Udon-no-sho Kanaizumi

Sanuki Udon:
Sanuki-no-yume 2000
Sanuki Udon noodles are a favourite in Kagawa in Shikoku, Japan, and they are widely acknowledged as high-quality udon. Kanaizumi is the leading manufacturer of the noodles. The company wanted new packaging for the Setouchi International Art Festival 2010 and to promote sales of Sanuki Udon as souvenirs and gifts. The multi-sided outer box with curved slits is a visual reminder of udon, while the colour and feel of the packaging arouses the consumers' imagination. It's an ultimately simple solution that conveys the values of the company and product.

Designer
Jun Kuroyanagi
Box Maker
Akiyoshi Yamada
Print Director
Akiyoshi Yamada
Project Managers
Chiaki Hayashi
Fram Kitagawa
Kosuke Kuwabara
Masako Maeda
Marketing Manager
Hiroshi Kodaka
Client
Udon-no-sho Kanaizumi

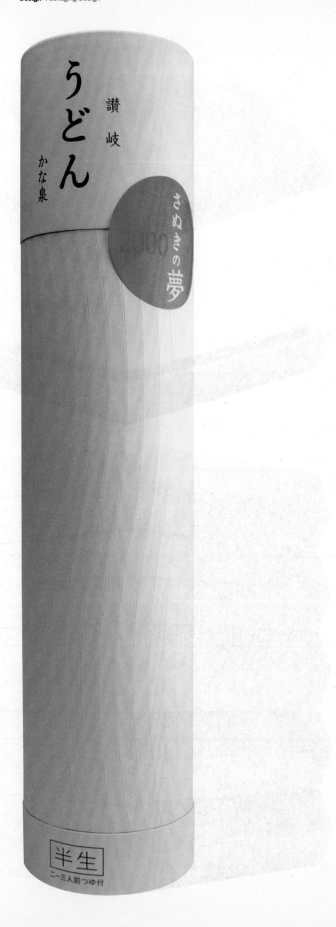

讃岐
うどん
かな泉
さぬきの夢
2000
半生
二~三人前つゆ付

Packaging Design
Turner Duckworth: London & San Francisco
for The Coca-Cola Company North America

Coca-Cola Summer 2010 Packaging
The Coca-Cola Summer 2010 packaging evolves the approach from the previous year to celebrate the joy and optimism of summer and Coke's authentic connection to the season. The graphic designed by Turner Duckworth was featured on packaging, in-store displays and select TV spots. The design was also used for summer premiums on everything from T-shirts and bags to beach towels, all in celebration of summer's favourite beverage, Coca-Cola.

Designers
Emily Charette
Josh Michels
Brian Steele
Design Director
Sarah Moffat
Creative Directors
Bruce Duckworth
David Turner
Design Studios
Turner Duckworth: London & San Francisco
Account Handler
Jessica Rogers
Client
The Coca-Cola Company North America
Brand
Coca-Cola

Coca-Cola

Packaging Design
guertlerbachmann
for Görtz

Shoelace Birds
The colourful Görtz world of birds presented itself in all the Görtz sales areas set aside for children's shoes. Simple shoelaces were transformed into small colourful worms in the beaks of five lovingly designed bird characters. This eye-catching packaging shows different types of native birds, inviting play and collection.

Designer
Merle Schroeder
Design Director
Uli Guertler
Art Director
Merle Schroeder
Creative Director
Uli Guertler
Illustrator
Merle Schroeder
Copywriter
Claudia Oltmann
Advertising Agency
guertlerbachmann
Marketing Manager
Michael Jacobs
Client
Görtz

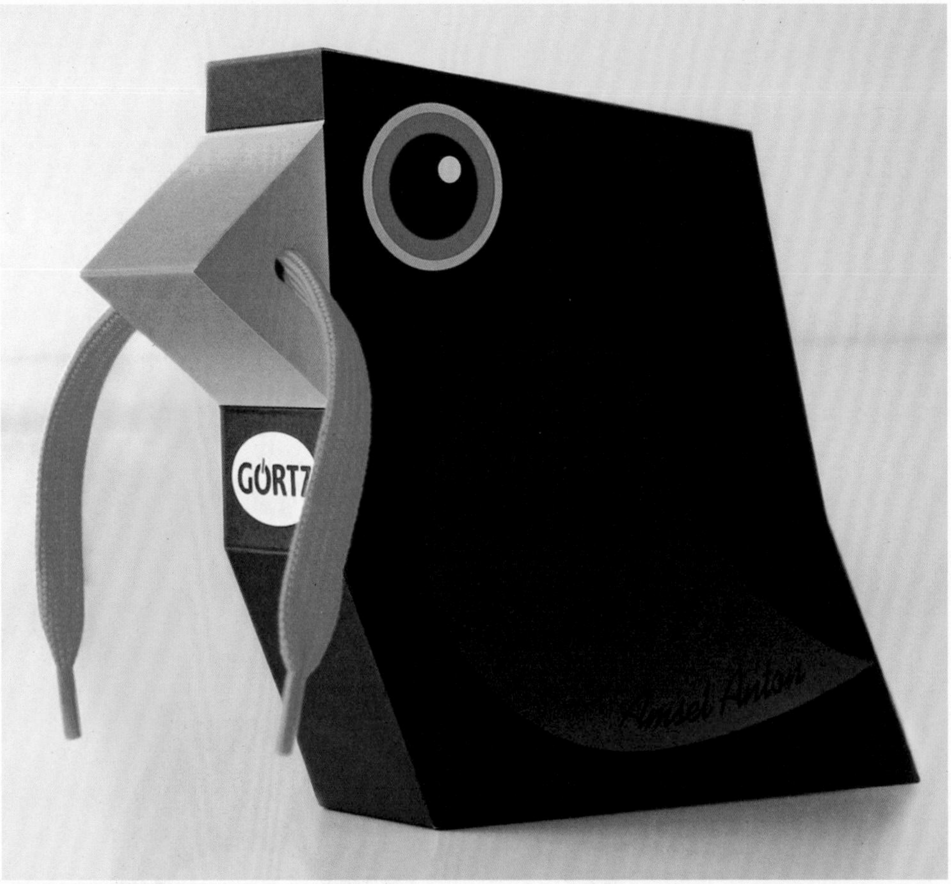
GÖRTZ
Amsel Anton

GÖRTZ
GÖRTZ
GÖRTZ
GÖRTZ

Packaging Design
Magpie Studio for
Gavin Martin
Colournet Limited

Job Bags
Having joined forces in 2010, Gavin Martin Associates and Colournet wanted to raise their new profile without breaking the joint bank account. We suggested making use of an unused canvas: the humble proof bag. Used by printers to deliver wet proofs to their clients, the bags were screen printed with a life-sized collection of eccentric objects. Tucked under the arm, the proof bags act as walking billboards en route, and a talking point when dropped off. Low cost, high impact and with the promise of raising a smile.

Designers
Ben Christie
Tim Fellowes
Creative Directors
David Azurdia
Ben Christie
Jamie Ellul
Design Agency
Magpie Studio
Brand Manager
Phil Le Monde
Client
Gavin Martin
Colournet Limited

Hand delivered by
Gavin Martin Colournet Limited
PLAYBOY
NATIONAL LITHOGRAPHIC

Hand delivered by
Gavin Martin Colournet Limited

Hand delivered by
Gavin Martin Colournet Limited

Nomination in Product Design

Consumer
Product Design
Gavin Thomson Design
for Stellar

Eazistore Cookware
Eazistore is a patent-pending, space-saving cookware solution, combining three saucepans with respective handles and lids within the footprint of the largest pan. Following the Russian doll principle and without any need for moving elements, the smallest saucepan (16cm), complete with lid and handle, fits into the medium-sized saucepan (18cm), which in turn is stored inside the largest saucepan (20cm). Lids rotate to close handle vents when in use. Initially launched in a stainless steel substrate, the range also extends to frying pans and casseroles, and has inherent transportation advantages.

Designer
Gavin Thomson
Design Agency
Gavin Thomson Design
Main License Holder
Imperial International
Client
Gavin Thomson Design
Brand
Stellar

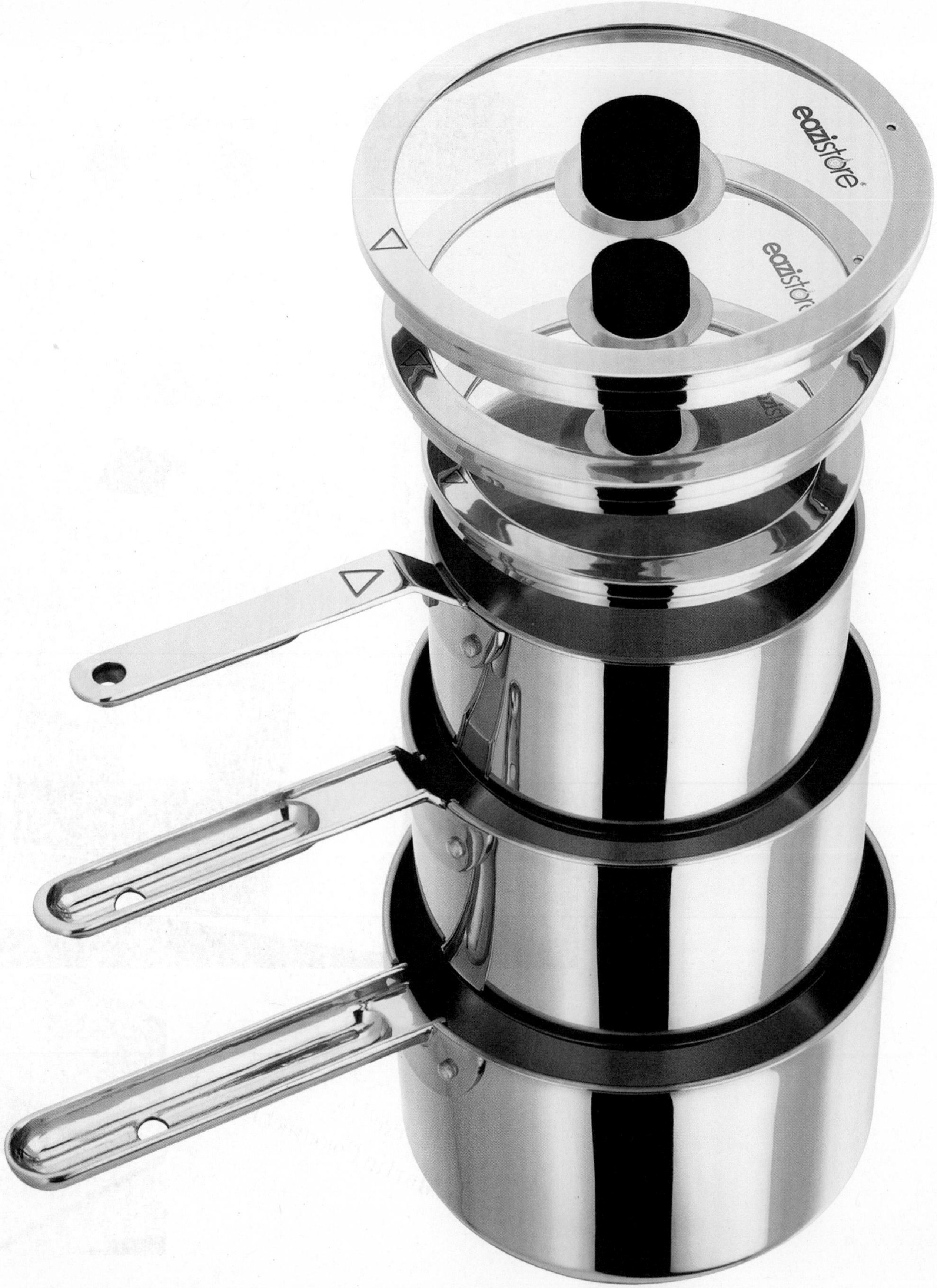
eazistore
eazistore

Nomination in Product Design

Consumer Product Design
DesignWright for Joseph Joseph

Pie Kitchen Timer
This striking 60-minute kitchen timer takes some of the guesswork out of cooking. Simply twist the top half of the unit to gradually reveal an easy-to-read analogue dial, stopping when you reach the required number of minutes and seconds. Release the bezel and the unit begins counting down, leaving you free to concentrate on other tasks. The graphic dial allows you to monitor progress at a glance, even from a distance. When the time is up, a classic alarm bell sounds to attract your attention.

Designers
Adrian Wright
Jeremy Wright
Design Studio
DesignWright
Manufacturer
Joseph Joseph

15
5
25
20
15

5
10
15
20
25
30
35

Nomination in Product Design

Consumer
Product Design
CASE-REAL for EK Japan

The 22 Hybrid Tube Amplifier
In order to represent the simple beauty of the amplifier tube as it is, we used only two beautiful tubes on the top, and two big operation dials on the front to match. These two elements make up the form of the amplifier. The concept was to wipe out the existing ideas of valve amplifiers, while the design aims to fit smoothly into a variety of lifestyles by both physically and aesthetically slimming down.

Designer
Koichi Futatsumata
Design Group
CASE-REAL
Manufacturer
EK Japan
Brand & Marketing Manager
Hidemi Iguchi
Client Director
Hidemi Iguchi
Client
EK Japan
Brand
22

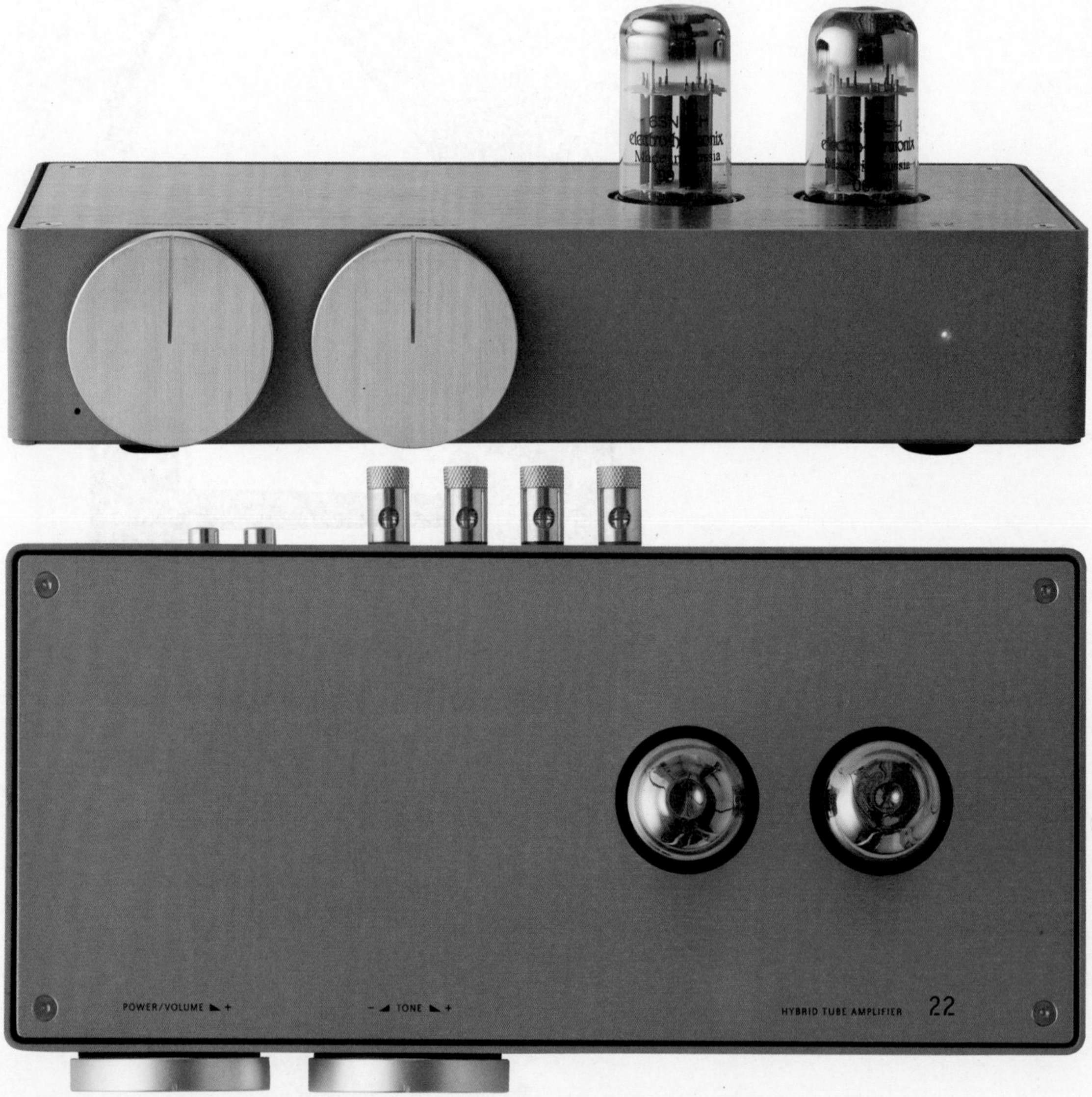
POWER/VOLUME +
– TONE +
HYBRID TUBE AMPLIFIER
22

Nomination in Product Design

Furniture Design
Factorydesign for
Acro Aircraft Seating

Superlight Aircraft Seat
Designed for short-haul single aisle aircraft, the Superlight is the lightest airline seat in its class. The design is motivated by reduction and simplicity, using as few parts as possible. It reveals the qualities of the materials rather than hiding them. Machined details such as the armrest are declared, resulting in an honest simplicity of form, while the considered ergonomics make the seat extremely comfortable. The backrest creates more legroom by transferring unused space to the passenger behind and, with fewer than sixty parts per triple, the modular construction allows any component to be replaced in under two minutes.

Designers
Lee Bazalgette
Matthew Fiddimore
James Tanner
Design Directors
Adrian Berry
Adam White
Manufacturer
Acro Aircraft Seating
Design Group
Factorydesign
Client Managing Director
Chris Brady
Client
Acro Aircraft Seating

● **Nomination in Product Design**

Furniture Design
Studio 7.5 for
Herman Miller

Setu Chair
Setu is an innovative family of multipurpose chairs for meeting, training and relaxing. The key feature is the kinematic spine, allowing the user freedom of movement without the need for a tilt. Made with a breathable membrane, it also offers thermal comfort and even pressure distribution. The design was conceived around a change in office work patterns; we now simply grab a chair that's available. Setu bridges the gap between simple chairs that aren't comfortable and comfortable chairs that aren't simple. It combines ergonomic benefits in a simple, instantly comfortable chair that fits many applications.

Designers
Claudia Plikat
Burkhard Schmitz
Carola Zwick
Roland Zwick
Manufacturer
Herman Miller
Design Studio
Studio 7.5
Client
Herman Miller

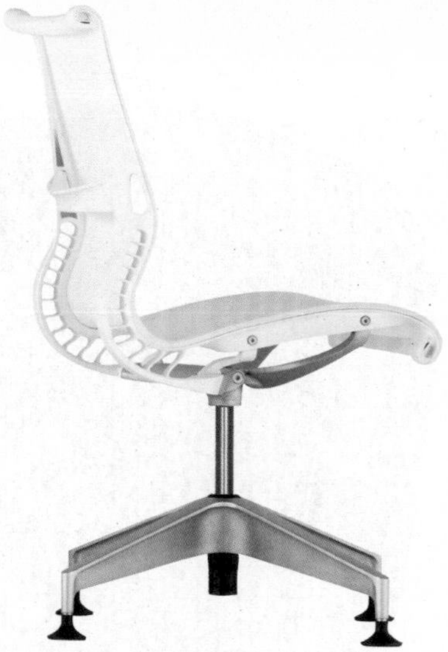

Nomination in
Product Design

Furniture Design
therefore for Bednest

The Bednest Crib
Bednest helps mother and baby bond in the first precious months. By attaching to the parents' bed, it provides unparalleled closeness when sleeping and resting yet keeps the baby safe and secure in his or her own crib. Bednest can be adjusted to fit almost any parent bed and has a folding side for access when feeding and comforting. The stand can attach to the parent bed or be decoupled for use as a standalone crib; it can also be angled to ease congestion or reflux. Bednest folds neatly for travel, and is the only bed the baby needs whether at home or away, equally suited to nursery or bedroom.

Designers
Andrew Clift
Jim Reeves
Martin Riddiford
Design Group
therefore
Project Manager
Jim Fullalove
Client Managing Director
Nigel Whitaker
Client
Bednest

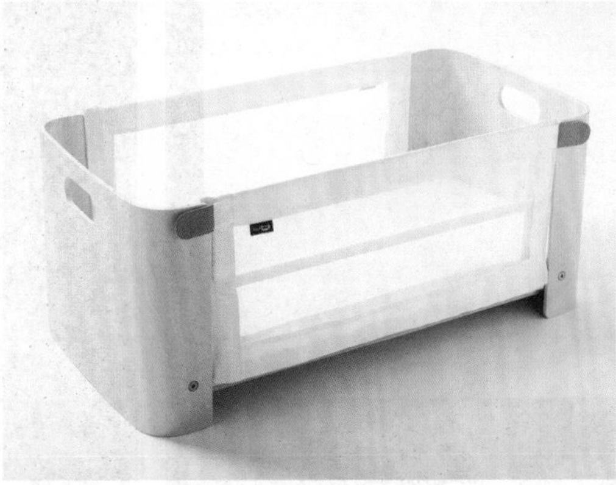

Consumer
Product Design
Apple Industrial Design Team for Apple

iPhone 4
The iPhone 4 is the thinnest smartphone ever – 9.3mm – featuring FaceTime video calling and Apple's stunning new Retina display. The front and back are made of aluminosilicate glass, chemically strengthened to be 30 times harder than plastic. Encircling the iPhone 4 is a stainless steel band made of a custom alloy, forged to be five times stronger than standard steel.

Designers
Jody Akana
Bart Andre
Jeremy Bataillou
Daniel Coster
Evans Hankey
Julian Hönig
Richard Howarth
Daniele De Iuliis
Jonathan Ive
Steve Jobs
Duncan Kerr
Shin Nishibori
Matthew Rohrbach
Peter Russell-Clarke
Christopher Stringer
Eugene Whang
Rico Zörkendörfer
Manufacturer
Apple
Design Group
Apple Industrial Design Team
Client
Apple

3G
9:41 AM
Monday
7
Messages
Calendar
Photos
Camera
280
73°
YouTube
Stocks
Maps
Weather
Notes
Utilities
iTunes
App Store
Settings
Phone
Mail
Safari
iPod
iPhone

Consumer
Product Design
fuseproject for Jawbone

Jambox
The Jambox is a breakthrough Bluetooth wireless audio speaker and speakerphone that employs the latest noise-cancelling technology for which Jawbone headsets are famous. Jambox is a chic, portable, audio powerhouse that allows users to express themselves by offering a compelling package of compact technology and iconic design. In addition to delivering full spectrum audio, Jambox quickly and easily connects with mobile phones, computers, tablets, iPods or any other Bluetooth devices, allowing consumers to seamlessly stream and share music, movies, games, phone and conference calls anywhere – wirelessly, all in the palm of your hand.

Designer
Gabe Lamb
Design Director
Yves Behar
Design Studio
fuseproject
Client
Jawbone

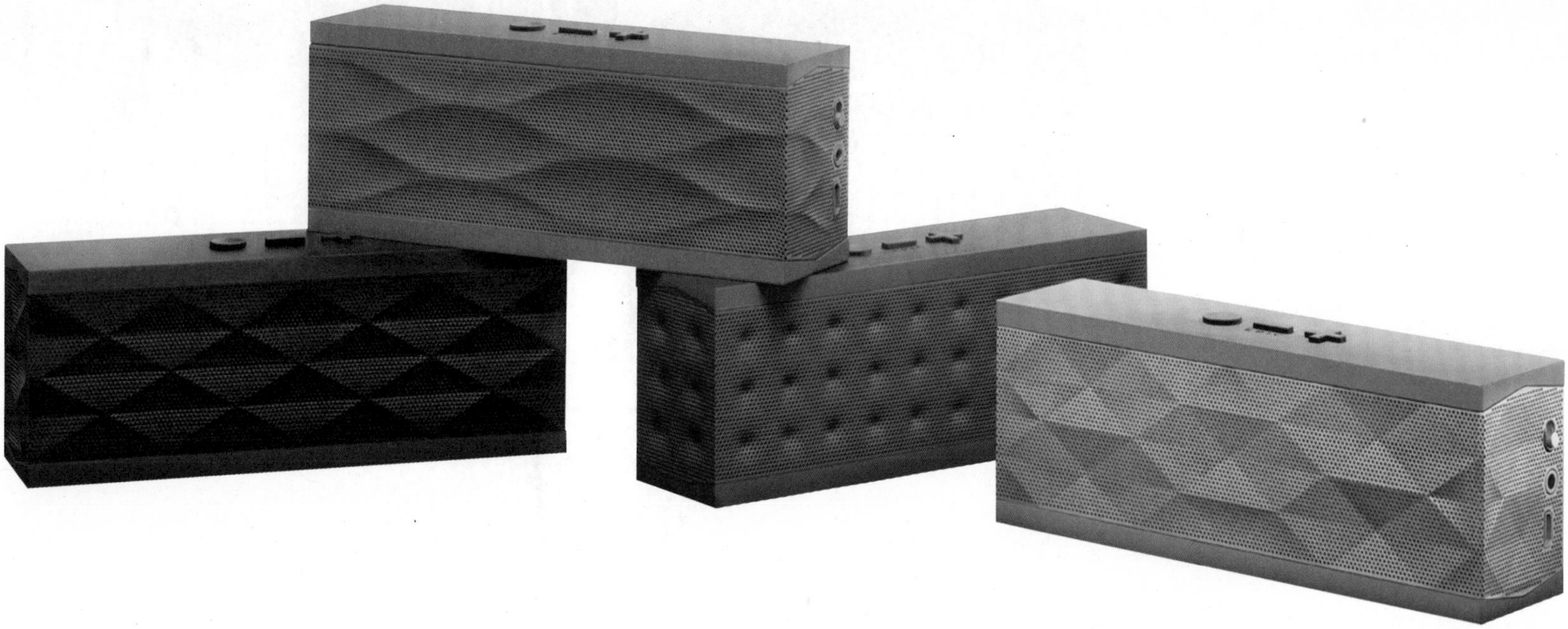

Consumer
Product Design
fuseproject for PUMA

Clever Little Bag
Clever Little Bag is a reusable bag by PUMA that eliminates the need for a separate PUMA shoebox and carrier bag. Shoes are transported from factory to store in the reusable bag using a protective card inner, which is retained by PUMA for recycling, while the customer takes the shoes home in the bag. It is classic PUMA, with its looks and language delivering a serious message with trademark wit. Replacing the shoebox reduces paper usage by 65 per cent and carbon emissions by ten tonnes each year, while eliminating the shopping bag saves 275 tonnes of plastic per year.

Structural Designers
Nick Cronan
Josh Morenstein
Seth Murray
Structural Chief Designer
Yves Behar
Graphic Designers
Sophie Paynter
Jacob Vanderkar
Graphic Design Director
Jason Gregory
Creative Directors
Mark Bonner
Jason Gregory
Peter Hale
Structural Design Studio
fuseproject
Graphic Design Studio
GBH
Brand Manager
Antonio Bertone
Client
PUMA

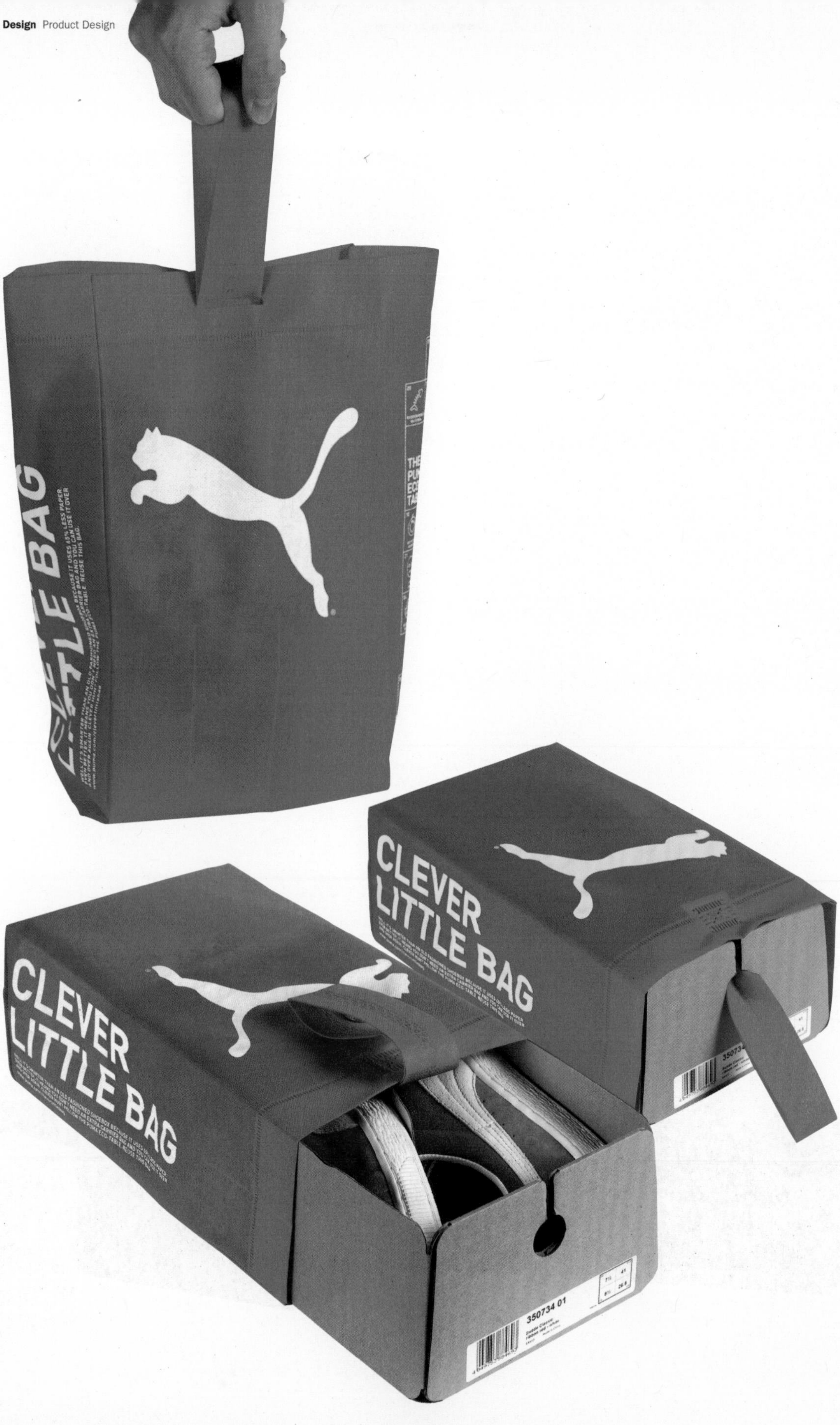
CLEVER LITTLE BAG
CLEVER LITTLE BAG
CLEVER LITTLE BAG
350734 01

Consumer
Product Design
Magmatic for Trunki

BoostApak
With the law requiring all children under 12 years or 135cm in height to use a booster seat, it's important to have one to hand at all times. Carrying one around often isn't convenient though. BoostApak is the ideal solution, a spacious, hand-luggage approved rucksack which doubles as a booster seat, ideal for holidays abroad, public transport and car-pooling. The hard plastic shell protects contents in both modes, and the removable cover enables easy cleaning. BoostApak is certified to regulation ECE R44.04 for Group 2 and 3 car seats.

Designer
Rob Law
Technical Designer
Derrick Barker
Design Studio
Magmatic
Client
Magmatic
Brand
Trunki

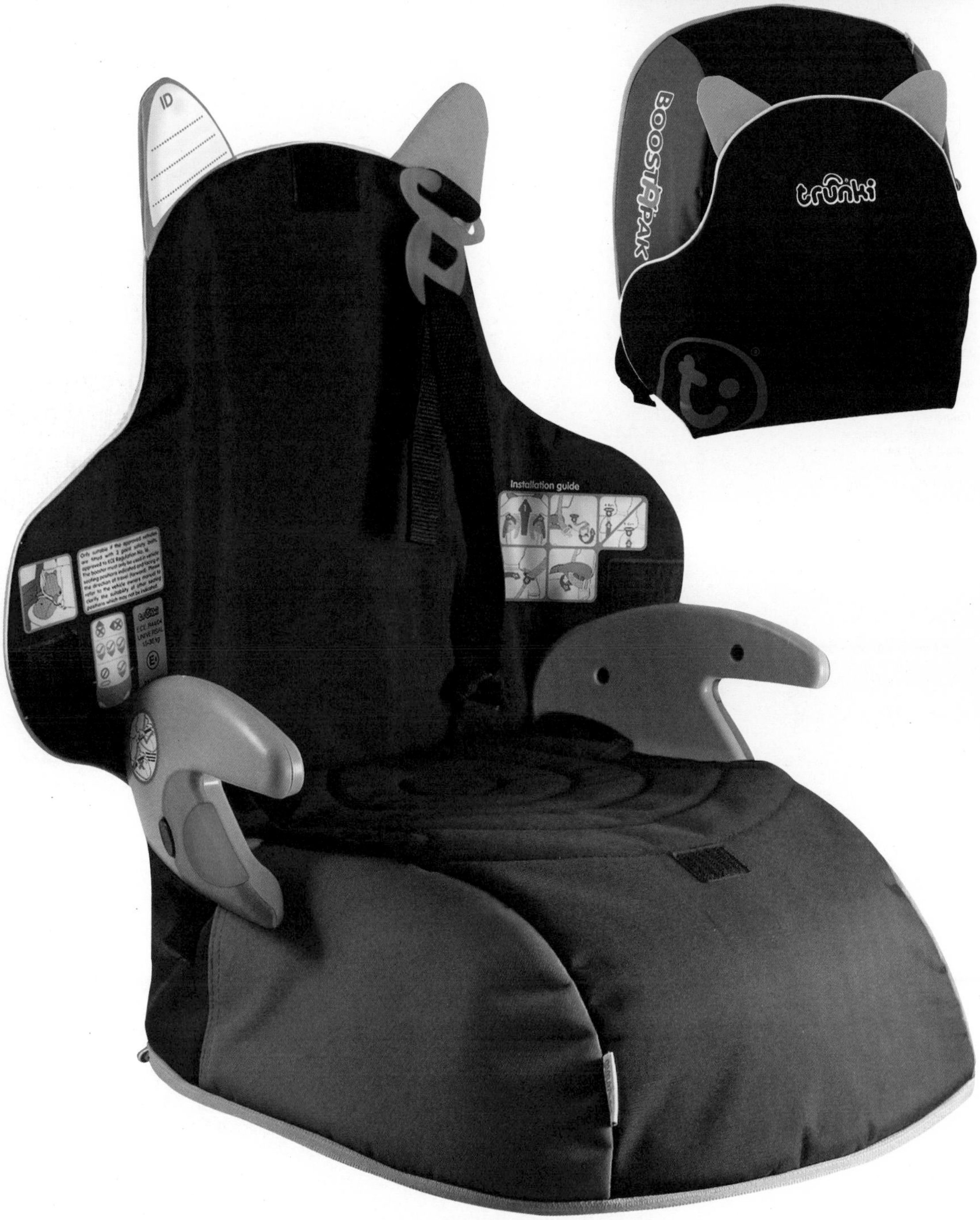
BOOSTAPAK
trunki
ID
Installation guide

Consumer
Product Design
Ammunition for Monster
Cable Products

Beats Pro
Beats Pro is the latest addition to the globally successful Beats by Dr Dre headphone line, delivering incredible audio performance paired with iconic design. The headphones are built from strong yet lightweight aluminium for durability. They feature an innovative folding mechanism for compact storage and carrying. Flip-up ear cups allow users to easily free one ear to hear outside noise, while dual input/output jacks make it possible to share music by daisy-chaining devices. The oversized ear cushions fit snugly over the ear for superior sound isolation, and are removable for cleaning.

Designers
Kenny Sweet
Gregoire
Vandenbussche
Design Director
Robert Brunner
Mechanical Engineer
Chris Fruhauf
Manufacturer
Monster Cable Products
Product Manager
David Leung
Design Group
Ammunition
Brand Manager
Susan Paley
Client
Monster Cable Products
Brand
Beats by Dr Dre

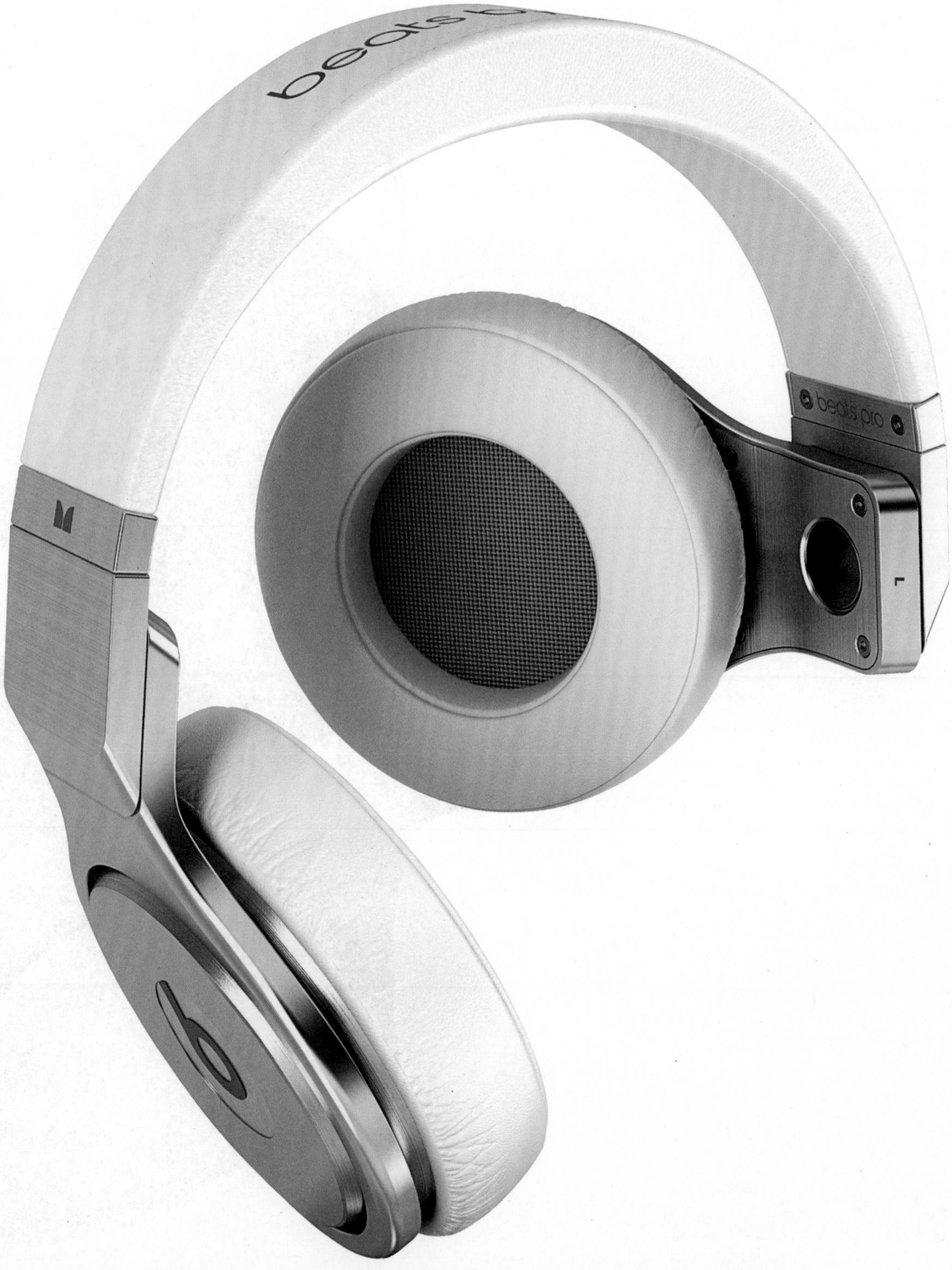
beats pro
L

Furniture Design
Andrea Ruggiero Design
for Lammhults

Mobi
Mobi is an innovative mobile workstation that allows users to redefine their workspace on demand. Developed specifically for today's flexible work environments, Mobi consists of a work surface and a sound-absorbing partition on locking wheels. Therefore it can be easily moved and intuitively reconfigured by one person. Combining two or more units can create a variety of ever-changing configurations, from collaborative team-based arrangements to individual workstations. However, unlike traditional partition-based systems, Mobi can be rapidly assembled onsite. It does not require a costly installer or any special tools.

Designer
Andrea Ruggiero
Manufacturer
Abstracta
Design Group
Andrea Ruggiero Design
Client
Lammhults
Brand
Abstracta

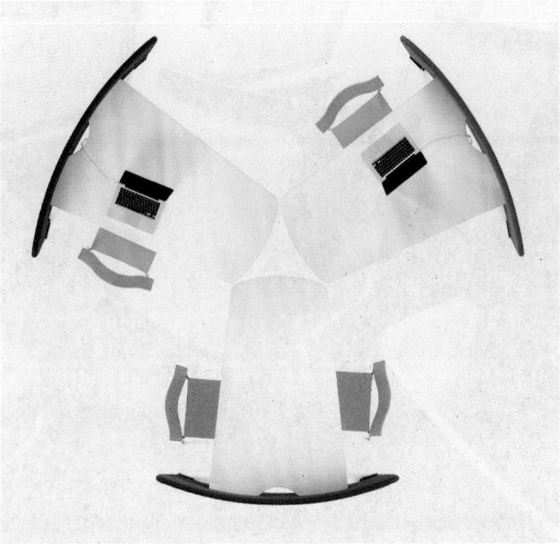

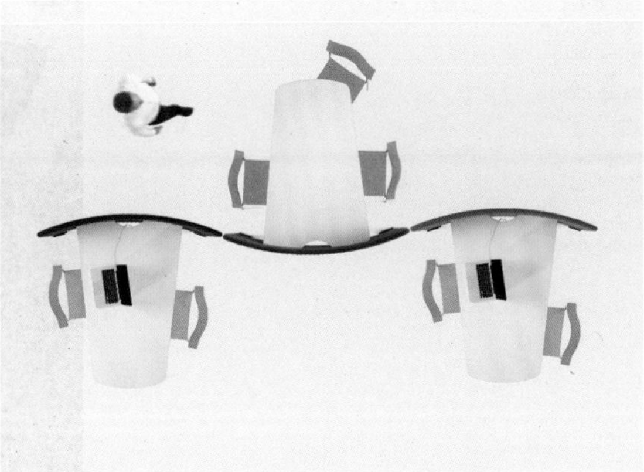

Furniture Design
Forpeople & Tangerine
for British Airways

British Airways
First Cabin
British Airways First defines a new level of style, service and comfort for the world's travelling elite. Design consultants Forpeople and Tangerine worked together with British Airways' in-house design experts on every aspect of the new BA First experience. They drew on BA's rich heritage to create an exclusive experience based on timeless design and understated luxury. Every feature of the cabin was extensively researched and meticulously designed to ensure customer satisfaction and create an intimate private jet experience on board. Gadgets and gimmicks were resisted in favour of simplicity and quality.

Designers
Roland Boal
Matt Garwood
Paul Grader
Richard Lawson
Alistair Roots
David Summerfield
Michael Tropper
Design Directors
Peter Cooke
Martin Darbyshire
Fiona Hurst
Richard Stevens
Technical Designers
Nick McKinley
Matt Round
Manufacturers
Dave Anana
Doug Rasmussen
Design Groups
BA Design Team
Forpeople
Tangerine
Marketing Manager
Abigail Comber
Client
British Airways

Furniture Design
IDEO for Steelcase

Node Chair
The Steelcase Node Chair is a highly mobile and flexible classroom chair. Node was designed in response to a changing educational environment where classrooms and classroom furniture need to respond to a more collaborative and active learning style. It allows for quick, easy transitions from one teaching mode to the next; a classroom can switch from lecture-based mode to team-based mode, and back again, without interruption.

Designers
Steve Bishop
Thomas Brisebras
Larry Cheng
Sean Corcorran
Tim Elms
Jim Feuhrer
Jesse Fourt
Derek Goodwin
Jon Kaplan
James Ludwig
Peter Macdonald
Afshin Mehin
Nacho Mendez
Elger Oberwelz
Thomas Overthun
Annetta Papadopoulos
Lukas Scherrer
Joerg Student
Nathan Whipple
Design Groups
Steelcase
IDEO
Client
Steelcase

ANNIE LEIBOVITZ

Furniture Design
Inga Sempé
for Ligne Roset

Ruché Sofa
Ruché brings together the unusual and the traditional. Inspired by swing seats, Ruché is made from a solid beech frame with a distinctive quilted pad. Alternately flattened by the stitches then set free, the quilting can 'curl' in places, giving rise to its distinctive appearance. The combination of its rangy uprights and the undulations of its duvet offers a harmonious union of rigorous straight lines and soft, welcoming curves. Slender and fine in appearance, Ruché is nonetheless soft and inviting, allying comfort and compactness.

Designer
Inga Sempé
Manufacturer
Ligne Roset
Client
Ligne Roset

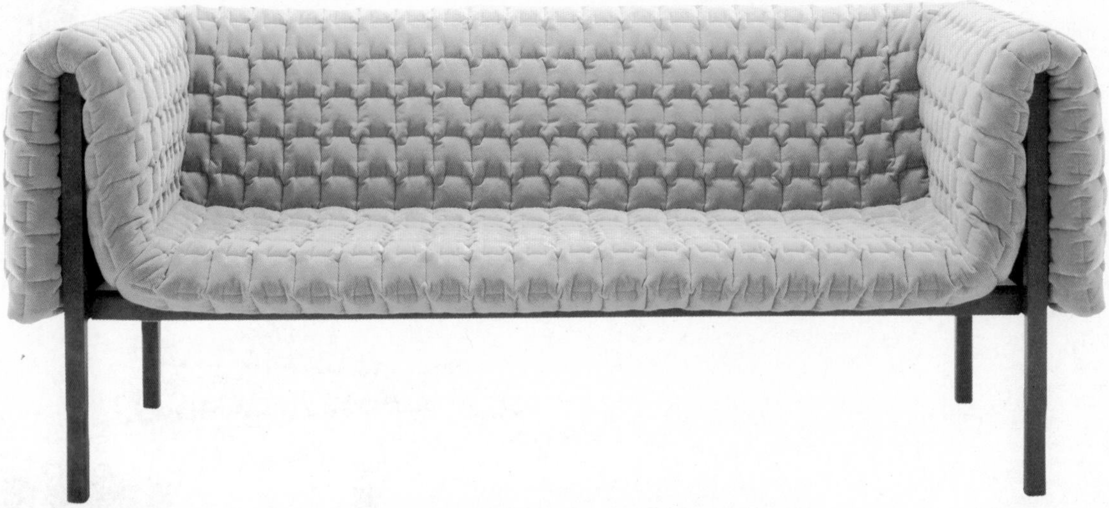

Interactive Design
for Products
IDEO for BBVA

Custom-designed Automated Teller Machine
Driven by the desire to make self-service banking more intuitive, BBVA and IDEO redesigned the ATM from the ground up. The new machines offer improved privacy, ease of use, and simplicity. The customer stands at 90 degrees to anyone else who may be waiting, shielded by a frosted panel. All operations, including PIN entry, are completed on a 19-inch touch screen that displays only the information relevant to the transaction at hand. All cash, statements and receipts are handed in and out through a single slot.

Designers
Jesús Alejano
Elena Alfaro
Vicky Arndt
Robin Bigio
Martin Frey
Alexander Grots
Judith Hufnagel
Beatriz Lara
Julio Pérez
Andrés Retortillo
Jorge Rodriguez Palomar
Matteo Signorini
Pascal Soboll
Design Group
IDEO
Implementation Partners
Fujitsu
NCR
Client
BBVA

BBVA
?
20
20
10
20
50
50

Cajero automático

Yellow Pencil in Spatial Design

Carmody Groarke
for Bistrotheque & Westfield Stratford City

Studio East Dining
Built on top of a 35m high multi-storey car park in a live construction site, this temporary pavilion hosted a pop-up restaurant, Studio East Dining, during summer 2010. Its translucent form contained a large dining room, made from a cluster of interlocking timber-lined spaces, which related to key elevated views across London's 2012 Olympic site. The project was designed and built within ten weeks from initial briefing to opening night, and with a life-span of only three weeks. The 800m lightweight structure was built with 100 per cent recyclable materials borrowed from the surrounding construction site.

Architects
Kevin Carmody
Tomohiro Fujisawa
Andy Groarke
Lewis Kinneir
Engineer
Bob Young
Architectural Studio
Carmody Groarke
Main Contractors
Benchmark Scaffolding
Services Contractors
Imtech Media
Cladding Contractors
SCA Group
Chef
Tom Collins
Restaurateurs
Pablo Flack
David Waddington
Clients
Bistrotheque
Westfield Stratford City

Yellow Pencil in Spatial Design

Installations
Troika for the Victoria & Albert Museum

Palindrome
Troika's 'Palindrome' is a kinetic object that recognises the rich collection of the V&A with over 3,000 years' worth of cultural artefacts from the world's most established cultures. At the centre of Palindrome is the iconic V&A monogram, originally designed by Alan Fletcher. It is made of three independently revolving parts. The logo deconstructs and reconnects itself with each half turn forming a playful palindrome legible from either side, while the wheels produce a gentle ticking sound reminiscent of Victorian automaton clockwork.

Designers
Conny Freyer
Sebastian Noel
Eva Rucki
Design Group
Troika
Client
Victoria & Albert Museum

platform art
LIFE
IS A
LAUGH
BRIAN GRIFFITHS
South Kensington Station
Science Museum
Royal Albert Hall

Nomination in Spatial Design

Exhibition Design
Carmody Groarke for the Barbican Art Gallery

The Surreal House
'The Surreal House' exhibition at the Barbican Art Gallery created an extraordinary journey into the 'mind of the house'. Featuring a wide collection of surrealist art, film, sculpture and architecture, the double-height gallery was transformed with a cluster of archetypal 'house' installations. Downstairs, they disorientated visitors in a labyrinth of dark corridors, shadowy corners and brooding chambers. Upstairs, the 'houses' became an abstract roof-scape that drew on the familiar, the subconscious and the sublime. Composed apertures for physical and visual connections between rooms and exhibits blurred the subject/object relationship of the surrealist art, gallery, and visitors.

Architects
Lukas Barry
Kevin Carmody
Andy Groarke
Exhibition Graphic Designer
Angus Hyland
Architectural Studio
Carmody Groarke
Exhibition Fit Out
Benchworks
Curator
Jane Alison
Assistant Curator
Alona Pardo
Client
Barbican Art Gallery

Nomination in Spatial Design

Installations
Jason Bruges Studio
for Nexus

Platform 5
Platform 5 is a 144m long and 3m tall glass light wall in an underground train station in Sunderland. Shadows of passengers seem to be visible through the glass, like ghosts waiting for their own train. Orchestrated by passing trains, characters appear gradually and a crowd gathers, waiting for a train to arrive. Each time a train arrives and leaves, some of the characters appear to board. Each character has its own behaviour; ones that are friends often stand together in conversation, others are anti-social and stand away from the crowd, one or two bring their dogs, a few have musical instruments and some read newspapers. We thank the 35 local volunteers who were filmed as if waiting for a train; their movements were digitally deconstructed and reassembled to create the animated characters that appear on the light wall.

Lighting Designer
Jonathon Hodges
Electronic Design Engineer
Stefan Dzisiewski-Smith
Mechanical Designer
Wanju Kim
Computational Designer
Karsten Schmidt
Architect
David Benison
Creative Director
Jason Bruges
Project Engineers
Richard Eakin
Jennifer Hewett
Metalworker
David Hopton
Mechanical & Electrical Installation
Peter Read
Glass Block Supplier
Pietro Guarino
Lighting Equipment Suppliers
Phil Grice
Lee Shields
Design Studio
Jason Bruges Studio
Art Consultant
Andrew Knight
Studio Manager
Sam Hoey
Clients
Graham Campbell
Nexus

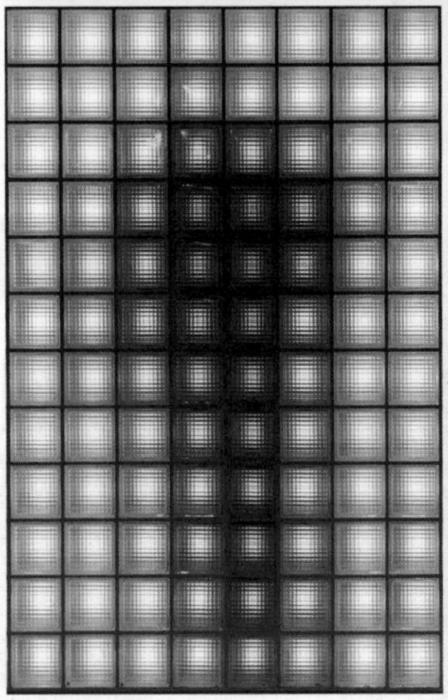

Nomination in Spatial Design

Yuusuke Karasawa Architects for Kenichi Karasawa

Villa Kanousan
This is a weekend house built high in the mountains near Tokyo. The house has four rooms on the first floor and four on the second, which divide the house's rectangular solid into eight spaces. The partition walls and ceilings of these eight spaces are interrupted by six small cubes that create gaps in the walls and ceilings, providing visual connections between the various rooms. The angles of inclination of each of these cubes are determined by an algorithm.

Architect
Yuusuke Karasawa
Architectural Design Studio
Yuusuke Kárasawa Architects
Mechanical Design
GH9
Manufacturer
Eiger
Client
Kenichi Karasawa

● Nomination in Spatial Design

Heatherwick Studio
for the UK Foreign & Commonwealth Office

Seed Cathedral: UK Pavilion at Shanghai Expo 2010
Heatherwick Studio led the winning team in the competition to design the UK Pavilion for the Shanghai 2010 Expo. The Expo was the largest ever, with 200 countries taking part and over 70 million visitors expected. The theme was: 'Better City, Better Life'. The Seed Cathedral was constructed from 66,000 transparent 7.5-metre long optical strands, each with a seed embedded within its tip. It acted as a platform to show the work of the Kunming Institute of Botany, a partner of Kew's Royal Botanic Gardens' Millennium Seed Bank.

Designers
Peter Ayres
Romona Becker
Katerina Dionysopoulou
Chiara Ferrari
Jem Hanbury
Thomas Heatherwick
Ingrid Hu
Jaroslav Hulin
Andrew Taylor
Robert Wilson
Stuart Wood
Structural Engineer
Adams Kara Taylor
Design Studio
Heatherwick Studio
Supporting Architects
RHWL
Local Design Institute
Architectural Design & Research Institute of Tongji University
Walkway Exhibition Design
Troika
Environmental Engineers
Atelier Ten
Fire & Risk Engineers
Safe Consulting
Project Management
Mace Group
Client
UK Foreign & Commonwealth Office

Exhibition Design
P-06 Atelier for MUDE (Museum of Design & Fashion, Lisbon)

Creative Lab Signed by Tenente
'Creative Lab' was the starting point for the interaction between all involved (MUDE, José António Tenente, SAMI Arquitectos and P-06 Atelier). The exhibition aimed to be a continuity of the aesthetic of the fashion designer José António Tenente. It consisted of a piece of black fabric, alternating between linear walls and curved pleats, opaque and translucent elements, in a bare scene. There were mirrored letters under the black voile as well as lettering made of light. Extra care was taken in the balance between natural and artificial lighting, reinforcing the scenic environment.

Architects
Miguel Vieira
Inês Vieira da Silva
Designers
Giuseppe Greco
Vanda Mota
Design Director
Nuno Gusmão
Architectural Studio
SAMI Arquitectos
Design Group
P-06 Atelier
Client
MUDE (Museum of Design & Fashion, Lisbon)
Brand
José António Tenente

ASSINADO POR
TENENTE

Installations
P-06 Atelier for the Pavilion of Knowledge

Skin – Pavilion of Knowledge
This is an environmental project for a multipurpose room, the foyer of the Pavilion of Knowledge in Lisbon. The intention was to create the texture for a perforated wall for acoustic and lighting purposes. The theme, ASCII (American Standard Code for Information Interchange), refers to the museum's aim of sharing information. By creating different texture densities with bigger or smaller cuts, acoustic percentages and the openings in the window areas of the rear rooms were controlled. White LED lighting between the wall and the 'skin' was balanced with natural light.

Architect
João Luís Carrilho da Graça
Designers
Giuseppe Greco
Vera Sacchetti
Design Director
Nuno Gusmão
Architectural Studio
JLCG Architects
Design Group
P-06 Atelier
Manufacturers
ACF (Arlindo Correia & Filhos)
Demetro a Metro
Client
Pavillion of Knowlege

EXPOSIÇÕES
EXHIBITIONS

Installations
Julius Popp for SAP Germany & the Victoria & Albert Museum

bit.code
SAP was looking for an impressive way to demonstrate how software helps us to get a grip on our daily 'information overkill'. In partnership with the Victoria & Albert Museum, SAP commissioned bit.code, a work by German artist Julius Popp, for the exhibition 'Decode: Digital Design Sensations'. With a large screen comprising spinning black and white tracks representing ones and zeros, bit.code engages the viewer with its movement and mechanical noise. Frequently, bit.code aligns to display relevant keywords from the internet, extracted in real-time using SAP software.

Designer
Julius Popp
Creative Director
Peter Strauss
Advertising Agency
Ogilvy Frankfurt
Account Handler
Veronika Sikvoelgyi
Marketing Manager
Barbara Windisch
Clients
SAP Germany
Victoria & Albert Museum

Nomination in Art Direction

Art Direction for Poster Advertising
Team Saatchi for the Ethnic Multicultural Media Academy (EMMA) Trust

Keep the Far Right, Right Out
To combat growing support for racist, far right parties in the UK, we created a campaign encouraging people to think twice about whom to vote for in the upcoming General Election. Posters ran in the London area of Barking, where the British National Party was gathering support and was expected to win its first seat in Parliament. Executions consisted of graphic illustrations intended to create the look of modern day propaganda posters. Through the use of negative space, viewers saw graphic symbols of fascism such as the swastika emerge from innocent election imagery. We helped inflict a humiliating defeat on the BNP on election night.

Art Director
Ajab Samrai
Designers
Roger Kennedy
Ajab Samrai
Copywriters
David Fowle
John Pallant
Ajab Samrai
Illustrator
Noma Bar
Typographer
Roger Kennedy
Creative Director
Ajab Samrai
Advertising Agency
Team Saatchi
Account Handlers
Sophie Hooper
Gemma Morris
Tom Rudge
Brand Manager
Bobby Syed
Client
Ethnic Multicultural Media Academy (EMMA) Trust

THE BALLOT BOX HIDES
AN UGLY FACE. BE CAREFUL WHO
YOU VOTE FOR ON MAY 6th.
Keep the far right, right out. www.emmatrust.com

BE CAREFUL WHO'S CANVASSING FOR YOUR VOTE ON MAY 6th.
Keep the far right, right out. www.emmatrust.com

IT'S DECISION TIME. BE CAREFUL WHO YOU VOTE FOR ON MAY 6th.
Keep the far right, right out. www.emmatrust.com

BE CAREFUL WHO YOU HAND YOUR VOTE TO ON MAY 6th.
Keep the far right, right out. www.emmatrust.com

BE CAREFUL WHERE YOU MARK YOUR VOTE ON MAY 6th.
Keep the far right, right out. www.emmatrust.com

Art Direction for
Poster Advertising
Leo Burnett Hong Kong
for Greenpeace

Melt
Cars are a major source of climate-warming greenhouse gases. As the Earth gets hotter, extreme weather events will become more common, threatening lives around the world. Every year, Greenpeace promotes Car Free Day, trying to change people's behaviour by getting them to stop driving for a day. To help people realise that driving and climate change go hand in hand, we used a visual consisting of parallel tyre tracks. In one, we show a story of the fun that driving can bring. In the other, we show the death and destruction caused by the resulting climate change.

Art Directors
Kenny Ip
Nicky Sun
Designers
Matt Johnstone
Nicky Sun
Copywriters
Joey Chung
Wen Louie
Illustrator
Matt Johnstone
Creative Directors
Brian Ma
Alfred Wong
Executive Creative Director
Connie Lo
Advertising Agency
Leo Burnett Hong Kong
Account Handler
Sherona Mak
Client
Greenpeace
Brand
Car Free Day

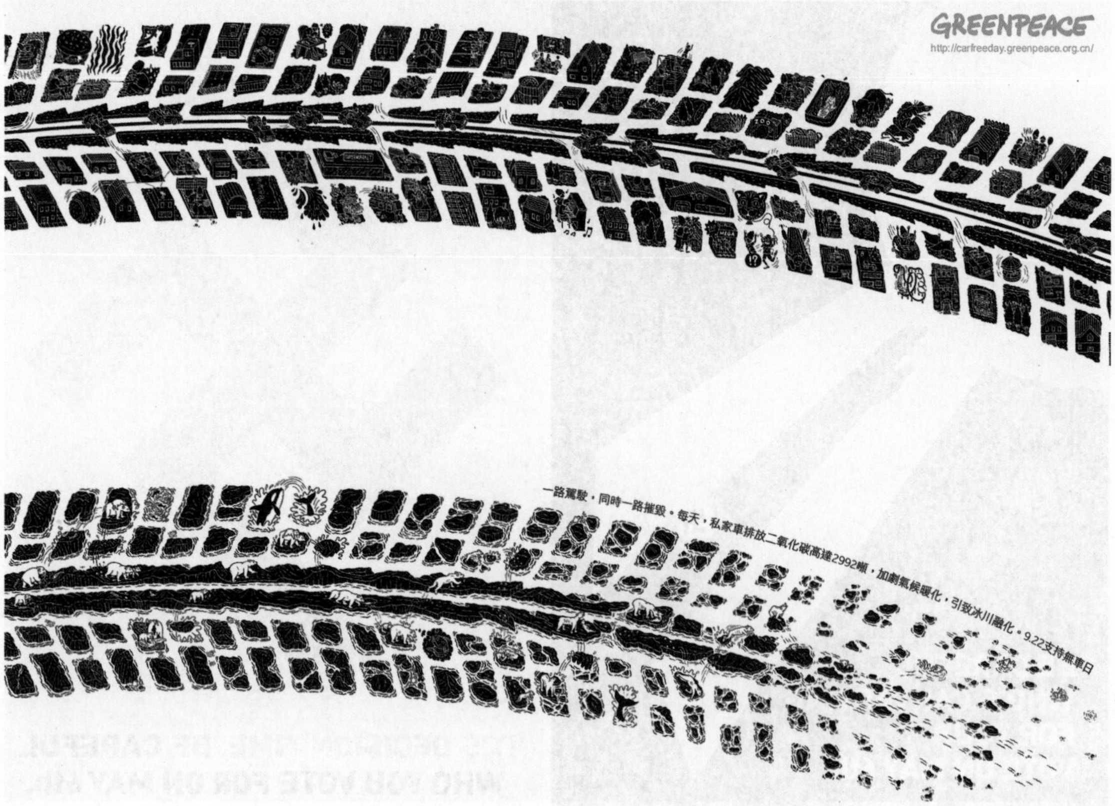
GREENPEACE
http://carfreeday.greenpeace.org.cn/
一路駕駛，同時一路摧毀。每天，私家車排放二氧化碳高達2992噸，加劇氣候暖化，引致冰川融化。9.22支持無車日

Art Direction for
Poster Advertising
Ogilvy Malaysia
for GlaxoSmithKline

Pain Overload – Noisy Neighbours / Traffic Blues / Hyper Kid
New Panadol Extra provides more effective relief for severe headaches compared to regular Panadol. The brief was to highlight this benefit to differentiate it from other variants, so we dramatised the effects of hard-hitting pain. The campaign carries the message that despite a pain overload, relief can be found with Panadol Extra. It appeared in national dailies and was placed in environments that typified stressful situations, such as noisy transit areas and busy roads, to bring out the relevance of the message.

Art Directors
Yee Wai Khuen
Gavin Simpson
Julian Yap
Copywriters
Adam Chan
Donevan Chew
Photographers
Quah Kwan Guan
Lim Sok Lin
David Lok
Typographers
Anne Yong
Yusrizal Yusof
Image Manipulator
Simon Ong
Creative Director
Daniel Comar
Executive Creative Director
Gavin Simpson
Advertising Agency
Ogilvy Malaysia
Account Handler
Melanie Mei
Client Head of Marketing
Vong Yuit Meng
Client
GlaxoSmithKline
Brand
Panadol Extra

Find your Calm
Panadol EXTRA

Find your Calm
Panadol EXTRA

Panadol EXTRA
Find your Calm

Art Direction for Poster Advertising
Dentsu Brasil for CEATA (Acupuncture Studies & Alternative Therapy Centre)

Needles
Brazil has a large Chinese community, which means there are many acupuncture centres in the country. To differentiate our client's business, we focused on the high quality of its services, showing that CEATA's professionals find exactly where the pain is.

Art Directors
Rodrigo Burdman
Estefânio Holtz
Copywriter
Gabriel Schmitt
Print Producer
Ricardo Lopez
Creative Directors
Felipe Cama
Alexandre Lucas
Illustration
Vetor Zero
Advertising Agency
Dentsu Brasil
Planner
Flavia Faust
Account Handler
Tiago Lara
Art Buyer
Ana Luiza Rodrigues
Brand Manager
Dr Wu Tow Kwang
Client
CEATA (Acupuncture Studies & Alternative Therapy Centre)

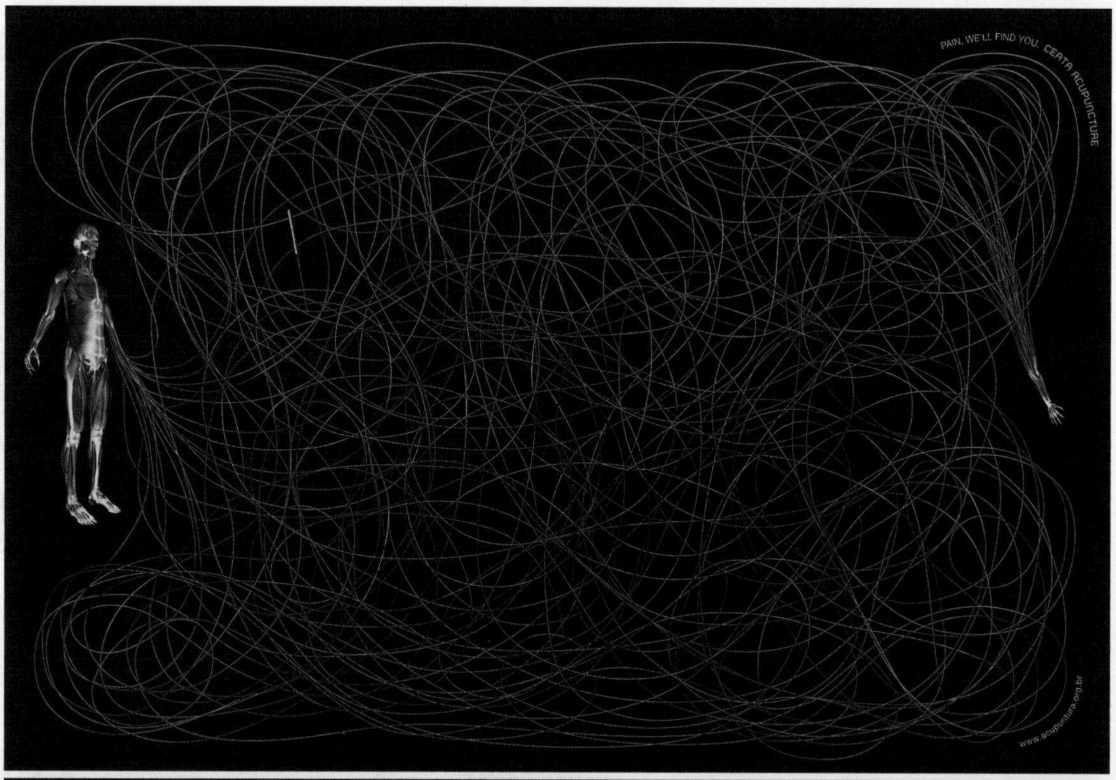
PAIN. WE'LL FIND YOU. CERTA ACUPUNCTURE
www.acupuntura.org.br

PAIN. WE'LL FIND YOU. CERTA ACUPUNCTURE
www.acupuntura.org.br

Art Direction for
Poster Advertising
Fallon London for
French Connection

French Connection Spring/Summer 2010
This campaign launched French Connection's new Spring/Summer 2010 collection, highlighting the brand's design credentials and the quality of its clothes. The campaign was also selected in Art Direction for Press Advertising.

Art Director
Selena McKenzie
Copywriter
Toby Moore
Photographer
Tariel Meliava
Creative Directors
Dirk van Dooren
Richard Flintham
Advertising Agency
Fallon London
Account Handler
Katharine Easteal
Brand Manager
Stephen Marks
Client
French Connection

"MAN SHOULD
BE BRAVE."
FRENCH CONNECTION FOR MAN

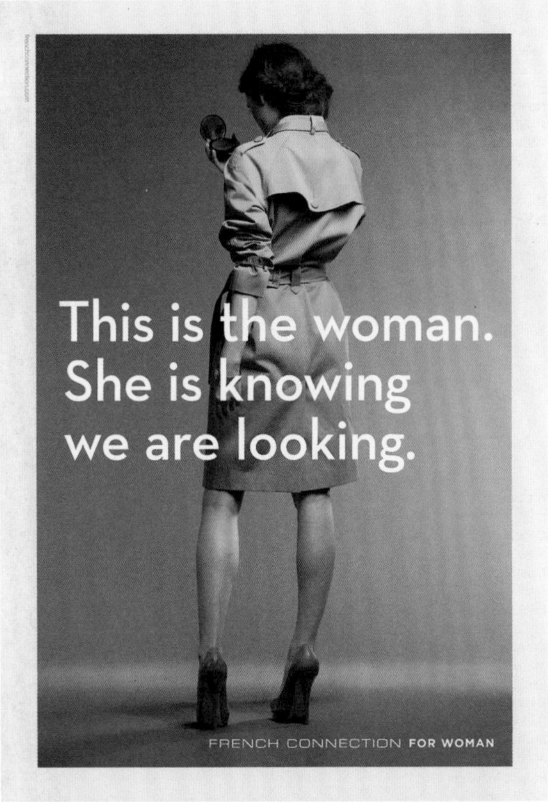
This is the woman.
She is knowing
we are looking.
FRENCH CONNECTION FOR WOMAN

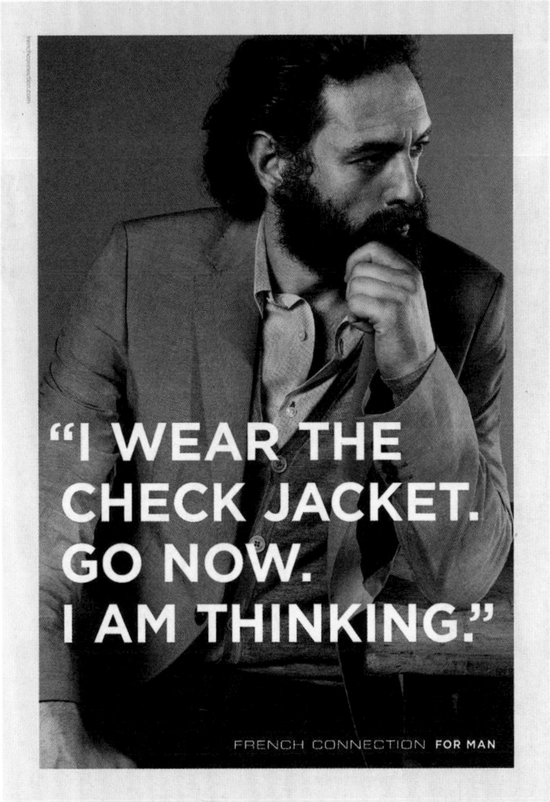
"I WEAR THE
CHECK JACKET.
GO NOW.
I AM THINKING."
FRENCH CONNECTION FOR MAN

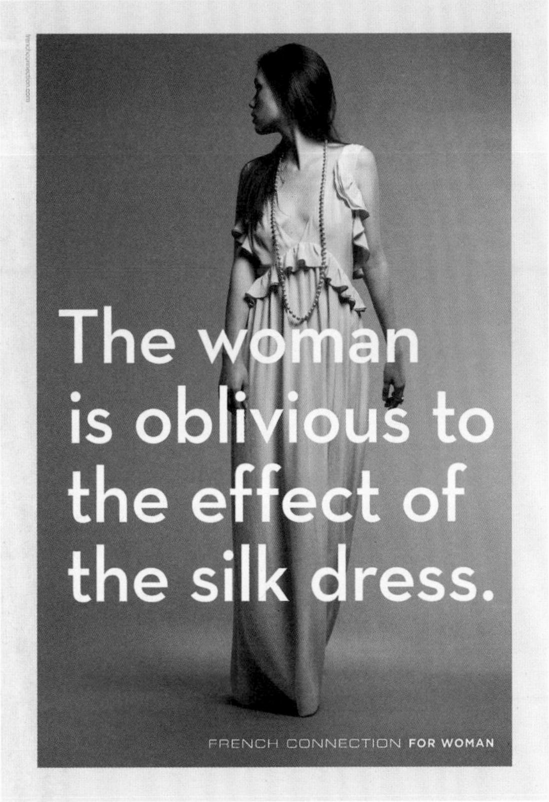
The woman
is oblivious to
the effect of
the silk dress.
FRENCH CONNECTION FOR WOMAN

Art Direction for
Press Advertising
AMV BBDO for the V&A
Museum of Childhood

Nostrils / Minds / Plasticine / Playtime
We were asked to come up with a campaign that brought to life the idea that play isn't just mucking about, but actively helps us to learn. We came up with a series of four print ads that highlight this very thought. Each uses an iconic childhood toy or game, from Meccano to LEGO, alongside headlines that humorously answer the brief. The illustrative style has a beautiful, childlike quality.

Art Director
Mark Fairbanks
Copywriter
Mark Fairbanks
Illustrator
Mick Marston
Print Producer
Kirstie Johnstone
Creative Director
Mark Fairbanks
Executive Creative Director
Paul Brazier
Advertising Agency
AMV BBDO
Project Manager
Linda Carlos
Planner
Martin Beverley
Account Handler
James Drummond
Marketing Manager
Joanne Bolitho
Client
V&A Museum of Childhood

Museum of Childhood
Bethnal Green
museumofchildhood.org.uk
V&A
kids soon discover fingers aren't just for sticking up nostrils.

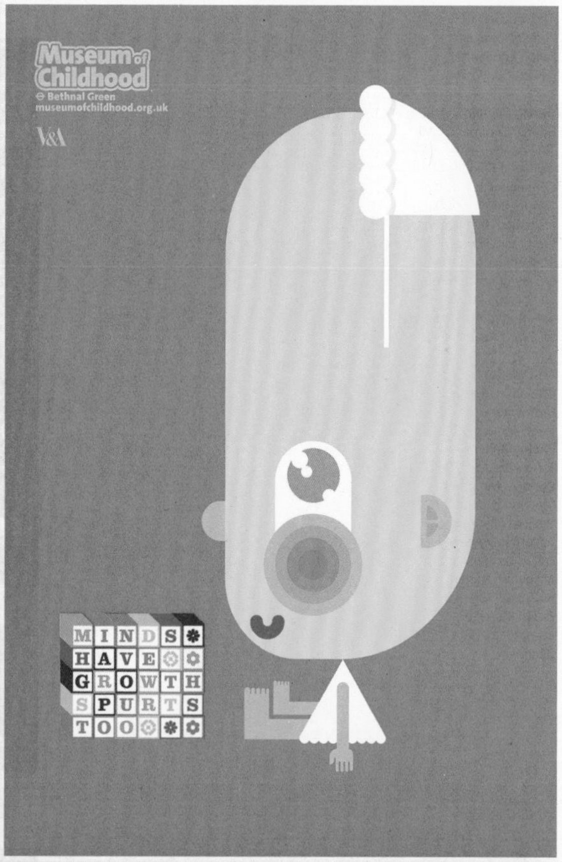
Museum of Childhood
Bethnal Green
museumofchildhood.org.uk
V&A
MINDS HAVE GROWTH SPURTS TOO

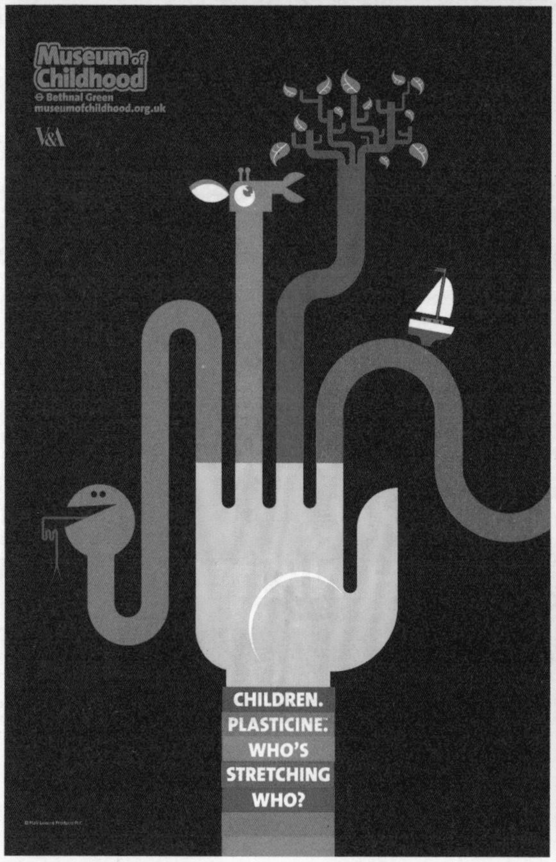
Museum of Childhood
Bethnal Green
museumofchildhood.org.uk
V&A
CHILDREN. PLASTICINE. WHO'S STRETCHING WHO?

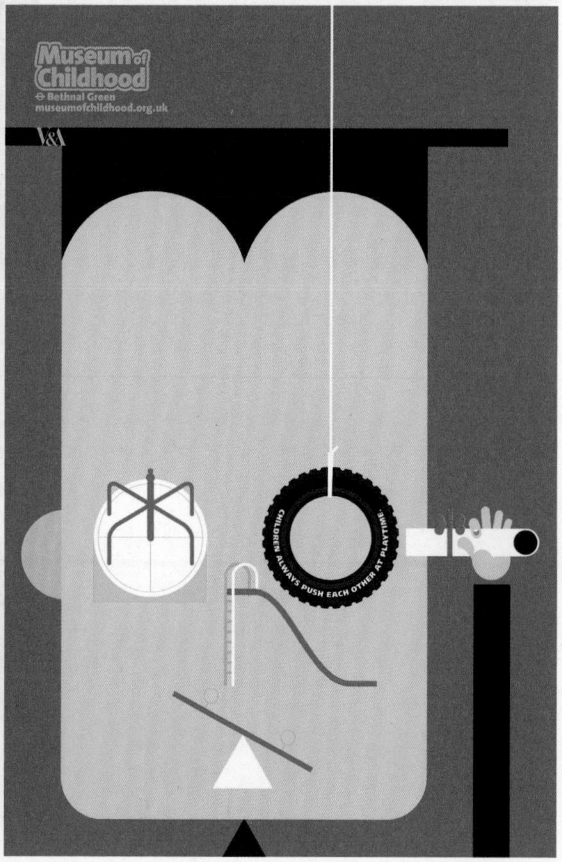
Museum of Childhood
Bethnal Green
museumofchildhood.org.uk
V&A
CHILDREN ALWAYS PUSH EACH OTHER AT PLAYTIME.

Art Direction for Press Advertising
Marcel Paris for Editions Points

Famous Speeches Collection
Some speeches have deeply influenced the world we live in. They have helped to bring about revolutions, wars or peace. In a word, they have changed history. Editions Points, a French publishing house, has published the Famous Speeches Collection to underline the important role they have played in our past and, consequently, in our present. We created posters with speech titles on. Each letter has been designed to illustrate an event, so that by reading the entire title we chronologically view what the speech has changed in our history.

Art Directors
Romain Galli
Souen Le Van
Copywriters
Romain Galli
Souen Le Van
Illustrator
K.I.M. aka
Florence Lucas
Typographer
K.I.M. aka
Florence Lucas
Creative Directors
Anne de Maupeou
Frederic Témin
Advertising Agency
Marcel Paris
Account Handler
Michel Kowalski
Brand Manager
Emmanuelle Vial
Client
Editions Points
Brand
Famous Speeches

"I HAVE A DREAM"
Words that changed the world. Famous speeches in pocket book collection. POINTS

APOLOGY FOR SLAVERY

"BLOOD, TOIL, TEARS AND SWEAT"

"NON-VIOLENCE IN PEACE AND WAR"

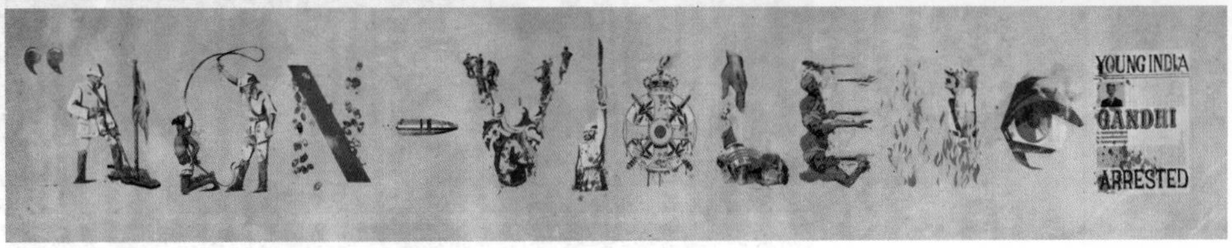
YOUNG INDIA
GANDHI
ARRESTED

Art Direction for
Press Advertising
This is Real Art for
the Musicians' Union

Mark / Don / Billy / Abram / Jimmy
The Musicians' Union (MU) is a trade union for UK musicians, with over 30,000 members. This campaign is designed to encourage even more musicians to become members. It features testimonials from some well-known members from different music genres.

Art Director
Paul Belford
Copywriters
Paul Belford
Richard Foster
Photographers
Jørgen Angel
Paul Belford
Boogie
Donald Christie
Martin Cohen
Laurie Haskell
Andrew Whitton
Typographer
Paul Belford
Creative Director
Paul Belford
Advertising Agency
This is Real Art
Project Manager
Natalie Wetherell
Account Handler
George Lee
Marketing Manager
Horace Trubridge
Client
Musicians' Union

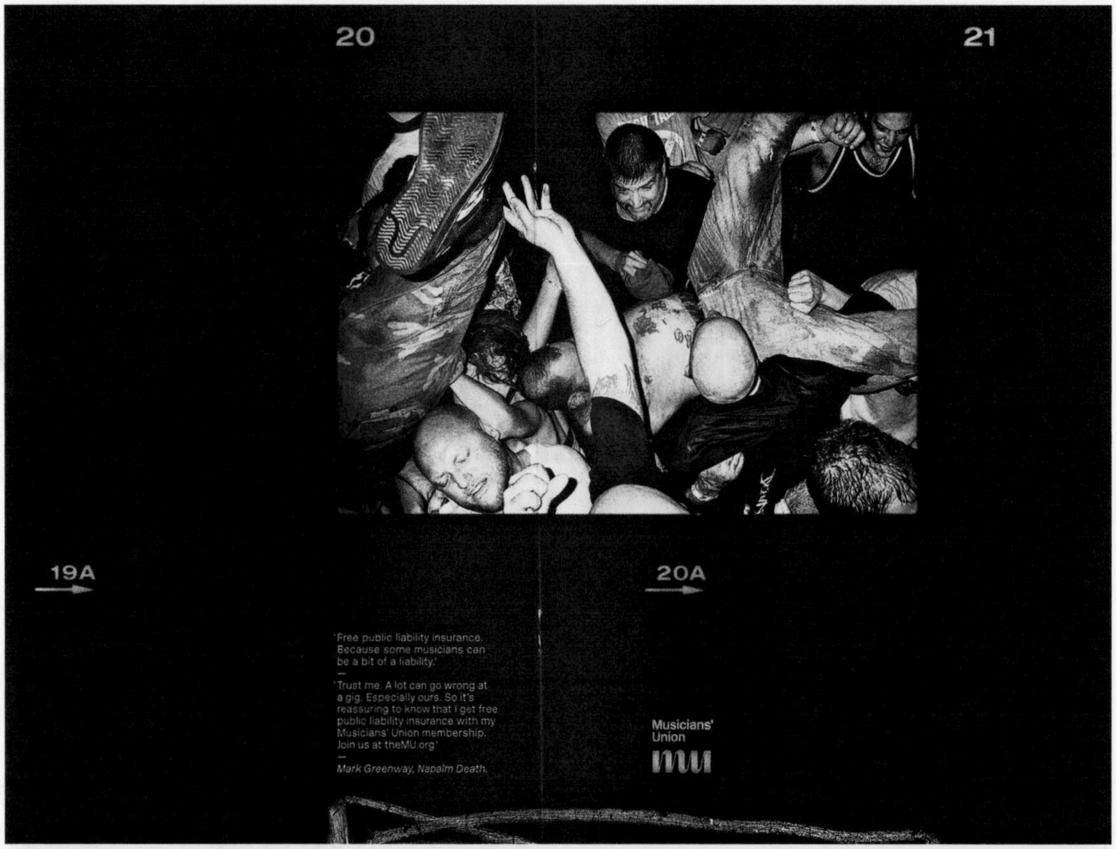
20
21
19A
20A
'Free public liability insurance. Because some musicians can be a bit of a liability.'
—
'Trust me. A lot can go wrong at a gig. Especially ours. So it's reassuring to know that I get free public liability insurance with my Musicians' Union membership. Join us at theMU.org'
—
Mark Greenway, Napalm Death.
Musicians' Union
mu

16A
17A
16
17
mu

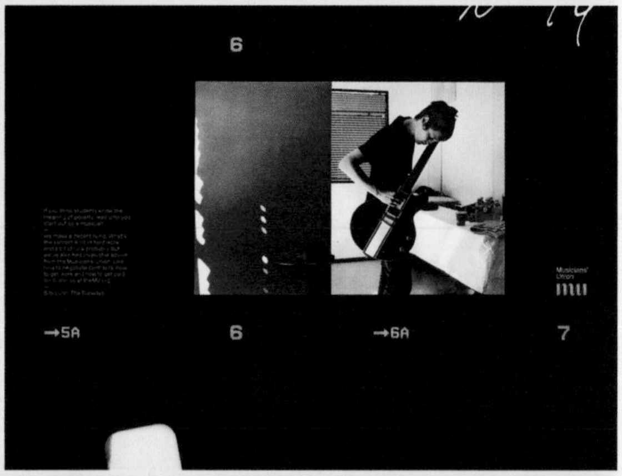
6
5A
6
6A
7
mu

6 3 3 6
400
13
14
mu
6 3 3 6

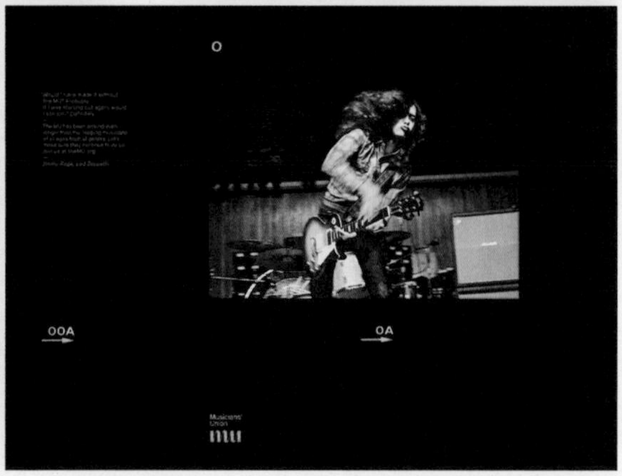
0
00A
0A
mu

Art Direction for
Press Advertising
This is Real Art for
the Musicians' Union

Graffiti
This ad helped launch
a campaign to promote
debate about the future
of the music industry.

Art Director
Paul Belford
Copywriter
Paul Belford
Typographer
Paul Belford
Creative Director
Paul Belford
Graffiti Artist
Fred Birdsall
Design Group
This is Real Art
Project Manager
Natalie Wetherell
Account Handler
George Lee
Marketing Manager
Horace Trubridge
Client
Musicians' Union
Brand
Music Supported Here

Money and music. The debate.
MusicSupportedHere.com
Music
7 471926 950524 >

Art Direction for
Press Advertising
This is Real Art

Web Developer Ad
This is a recruitment ad for a web developer, written in a language that the successful applicant would understand.

Art Director
Paul Belford
Copywriter
Andy Mathieson
Typographer
Paul Belford
Creative Director
Paul Belford
Design Group
This is Real Art
Project Manager
Natalie Wetherell
Client
This is Real Art

```
<?php
class WebDeveloper extends ThisisRealArt {

    const constant   = 'opportunities';

    public  $company = 'This is Real Art';
    public  $address = '2 Sycamore St, London, EC1Y 0SF';
    public  $phone   = '020 7253 2181';
    private $email   = 'info@thisisrealart.com';

    public function getRecruit(){

        // What do we require?
        $this->db->select('webDeveloper');

        // From where are we selecting?
        $this->db->from('peopleWhoLoveIdeas');

        // Select criteria
        $where = "'PHP OOP & mySQL'  = 'strong'
                   AND 'XHTML & CSS' = 'strict'
                   AND ('jQuery'     = 'bonus'
                        OR 'linux'   = 'bonus'
                        OR 'flash'   = 'bonus') ";
        $this->db->where($where);

        // How should we prioritize?
        $orderBy = array(
                        'ability'=>'DESC',
                        'hardWorking'=>'DESC',
                        'sociable'=>'DESC',
                        'davidBowieFan'=>'DESC',
                        'ManUtdSupporter'=>'ASC'
        );
        $this->db->orderBy($orderBy);

        // How many results do we need?
        $this->db->limit(1);

        // Run the search
        $this->db->get();
    }

    protected function _setBenefits(){
        $this->daysHoliday = 28;
        $this->fun         = 'guaranteed';
        $this->salary      = 'negotiable';

    }
}
?>
```

Art Direction for Press Advertising
Saatchi & Saatchi Brussels for the University of Gent

Bookcase
This print ad for the University of Gent brings its 'Dare to think' credo to life.

Art Directors
Arnaud Bailly
Ross McCurrach
Copywriters
Arnaud Bailly
Ross McCurrach
Creative Director
Jan Teulingkx
Photography
354 photographers
Image Manipulation
Beefactory
Advertising Agency
Saatchi & Saatchi Brussels
Account Handler
Nicolas Pignatelli
Client
University of Gent

UNIVERSITEIT GENT
DURF DENKEN

Art Direction for
Press Advertising
BBH London for
St John Ambulance

Life Lost
This campaign launched the new positioning of St John Ambulance: 'The Difference'. The 'Lives Lost' executions demonstrate day-to-day situations where first aid could have made a difference, but didn't. The role of this campaign was to create a reappraisal of first aid, and consequently of St John Ambulance, positioning it as a life saving charity.

Art Directors
Victoria Daltrey
Mark Reddy
Adrian Rossi
Designer
Rich Kennedy
Copywriters
Will Bingham
Alex Grieve
Photographer
Nadav Kander
Typographer
Dave Wakefield
Retouchers
Antony Crossfield
Gary Meade
Print Producer
Sarah Pascoe
Creative Directors
Alex Grieve
Adrian Rossi
Advertising Agency
BBH London
Account Planner
Jude Lowson
Account Handlers
Lou Addley
Mehdi Benali
Art Buyer
Sarah Pascoe
Brand Manager
Scott Jacobson
Client
St John Ambulance

A grape stuck in my throat. I couldn't breathe. It was really scary. But I knew a grown-up would help me. Who was clever at first aid. Who knew that all I needed was some hard slaps on the back. Because grown-ups always know what to do. Don't they?
Abigail West
You can be the difference between life. And death. To find out how text 'free guide' to 82727.
St John Ambulance
The difference.

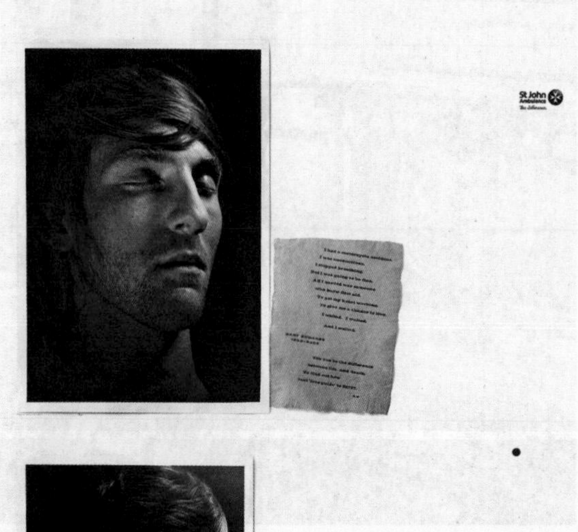

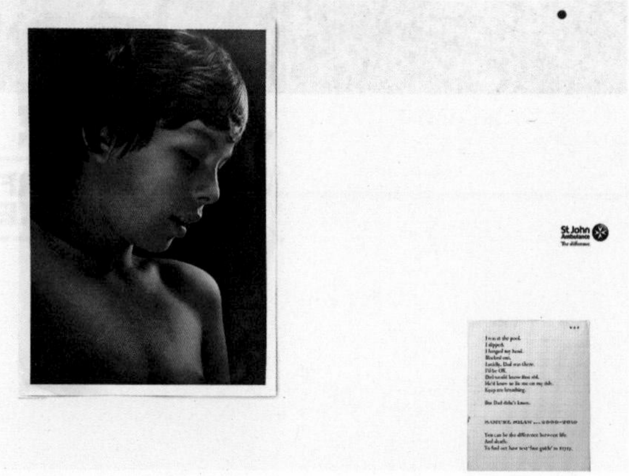

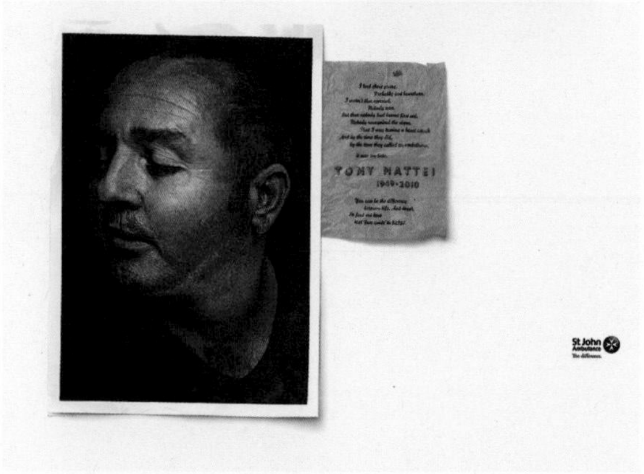
TONY MATTEI

Art Direction for Press Advertising **Young & Rubicam Paris** for the Surfrider Foundation Europe

Ocean Initiatives 2010
Each year, the Surfrider Foundation invites volunteers to clean beaches around the world during a three-day operation called Ocean Initiatives. This year, the Surfrider Foundation wanted to remind people that even the smallest pieces of trash (macro-waste) are just as toxic for the environment as oil spills, which are greater in scale and receive much more media coverage.

Art Director
Sebastien Guinet
Copywriter
Josselin Pacreau
Photographer
Ben Stockley
Creative Directors
Jorge Carreno
Robin De Lestrade
Advertising Agency
Young & Rubicam Paris
Account Handler
Aure Tessandier
Brand Manager
Stéphane Latxague
Client
Surfrider Foundation Europe

THERE'S NO SUCH THING AS A LITTLE MARINE POLLUTION
www.surfrider.eu

THERE'S NO SUCH THING AS A LITTLE MARINE POLLUTION
www.surfrider.eu

THERE'S NO SUCH THING AS A LITTLE MARINE POLLUTION
www.surfrider.eu

Art Direction for
Press Advertising
Ogilvy Frankfurt
for Axel Springer
Mediahouse Berlin

Copy On
Today, for every legal music download, there are six illegal downloads. Internet piracy and illegal copying are destroying musicians' livelihoods. Young artists in particular are concerned about the impact on their income, as well as their entire existence as musicians. We took covers of legendary music albums and copied them with a standard photocopier – over and over again – until the well-known album covers were only barely recognisable. This technique demonstrates the effect of copying: the more you copy, the more music will disappear.

Art Director
Eva Stetefeld
Copywriters
Taner Ercan
Dr Stephan Vogel
Creative Director
Helmut Meyer
Advertising Agency
Ogilvy Frankfurt
Account Handler
Dr Stephan Vogel
Account Consultants
Georg Fechner
Peter Heinlein
Marketing Manager
Rainer Schmidt
Client
Axel Springer
Mediahouse Berlin
Brand
Rolling Stone Magazine

Copy on.
And one day all those legendary albums will disappear. And the great bands. And all the gifted young musicians. How are they supposed to make a living when everyone downloads their work for free? Support us: money-for-music.de
Rolling Stone

Copy on.

Copy on.

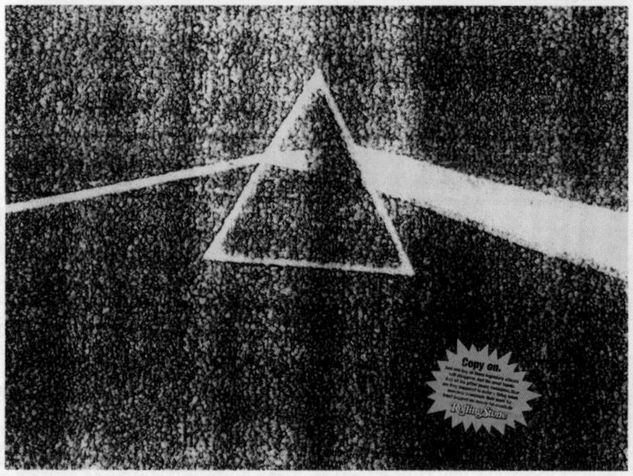
Copy on.

Copy on.

Art Direction for Press Advertising
F/Nazca Saatchi & Saatchi for the Pinacoteca do Estado de São Paulo

Almeida Junior Code
This is part of a campaign that publicises the library of art books at the Pinacoteca de São Paulo. This execution shows codes of letters and numbers that correspond to a painting by the great Brazilian artist Almeida Junior.

Art Director
Bruno Oppido
Designer
Bruno Oppido
Copywriter
Romero Cavalcanti
Head of Art
João Linneu
Creative Directors
Fabio Fernandes
Eduardo Lima
Advertising Agency
F/Nazca Saatchi & Saatchi
Planners
Fernand Alphen
José Porto
Account Handler
Marcela Paiva
Account Manager
Camila Hamaoui
Media Managers
Lica Bueno
Andre Gramorelli
Marketing Managers
Marcelo Araujo
Camila Sampaio
Client
Pinacoteca do Estado de São Paulo

TRANSLATING A®T WITH LETTERS ◆ WALTER WEY A®T LIBRARY ◆ PINACOTECA'S LIBRARY
Largo General Osório, 66 . Centro . Tuesdays to Fridays from 10 a.m to 5:30 p.m . Saturdays and Holidays from 10 a.m to 5:00 p.m . Free Admission

Art Direction for Press Advertising
F/Nazca Saatchi & Saatchi for the Pinacoteca do Estado de São Paulo

Tarsila do Amaral Code
This is part of a campaign that publicises the library of art books at the Pinacoteca de São Paulo. This execution shows codes of letters and numbers that correspond to a painting by the great Brazilian artist Tarsila do Amaral.

Art Director
Bruno Oppido
Designer
Bruno Oppido
Copywriter
Romero Cavalcanti
Head of Art
João Linneu
Creative Directors
Fabio Fernandes
Eduardo Lima
Advertising Agency
F/Nazca Saatchi & Saatchi
Planners
Fernand Alphen
José Porto
Account Handler
Marcela Paiva
Account Manager
Camila Hamaoui
Media Managers
Lica Bueno
Andre Gramorelli
Marketing Managers
Marcelo Araujo
Camila Sampaio
Client
Pinacoteca do Estado de São Paulo

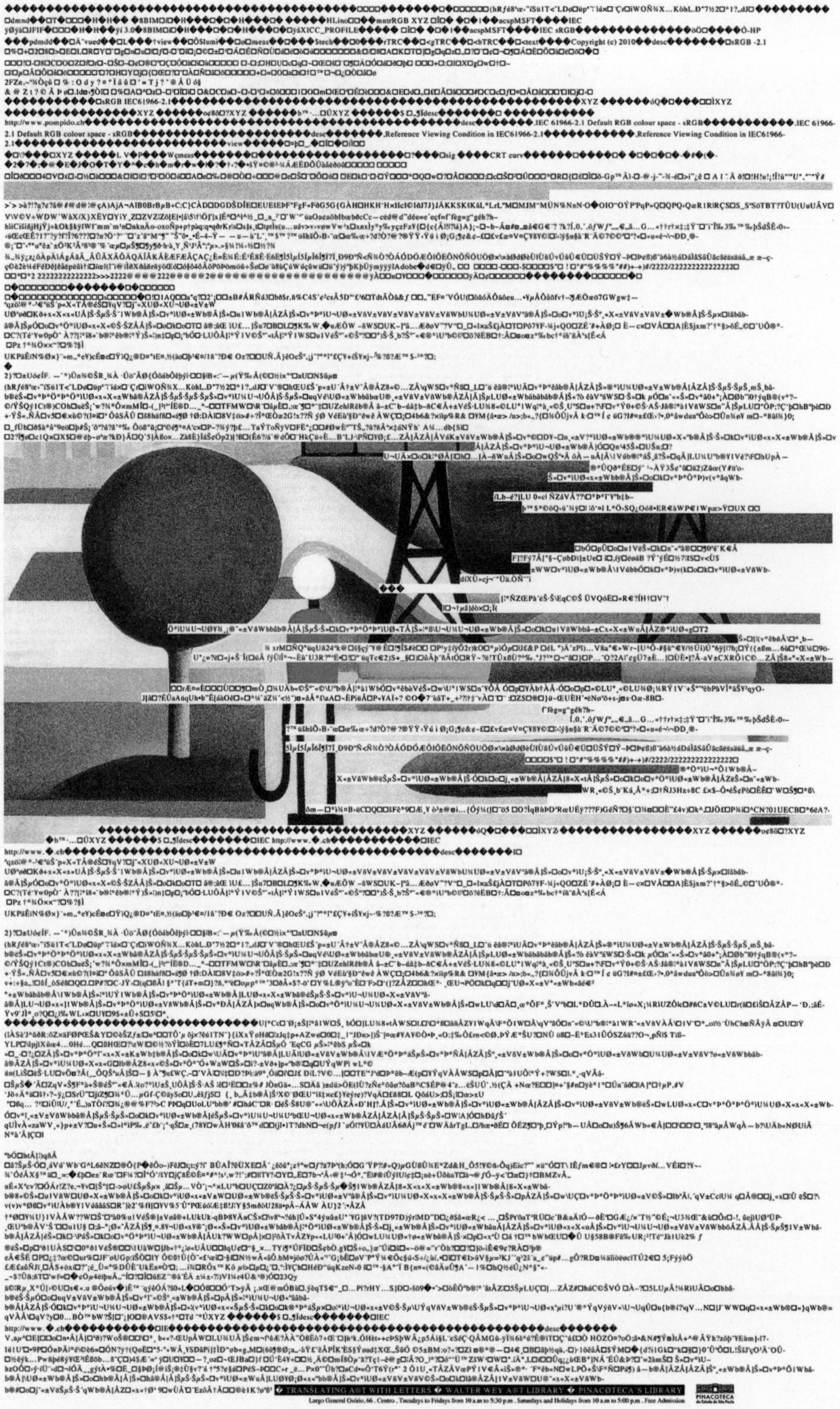
TRANSLATING ART WITH LETTERS ◆ WALTER WEY ART LIBRARY ◆ PINACOTECA'S LIBRARY
Largo General Osório, 66 . Centro . Tuesdays to Fridays from 10 a.m to 5:30 p.m . Saturdays and Holidays from 10 a.m to 5:00 p.m . Free Admission
PINACOTECA

Art Direction for Press Advertising
F/Nazca Saatchi & Saatchi for the Pinacoteca do Estado de São Paulo

Portinari Code
This is part of a campaign that publicises the library of art books at the Pinacoteca de São Paulo. This execution shows codes of letters and numbers that correspond to a painting by the great Brazilian artist Portinari.

Art Director
Bruno Oppido
Designer
Bruno Oppido
Copywriter
Romero Cavalcanti
Head of Art
João Linneu
Creative Directors
Fabio Fernandes
Eduardo Lima
Advertising Agency
F/Nazca Saatchi & Saatchi
Planners
Fernand Alphen
José Porto
Account Handler
Marcela Paiva
Account Manager
Camila Hamaoui
Media Managers
Lica Bueno
Andre Gramorelli
Marketing Managers
Marcelo Araujo
Camila Sampaio
Client
Pinacoteca do Estado de São Paulo

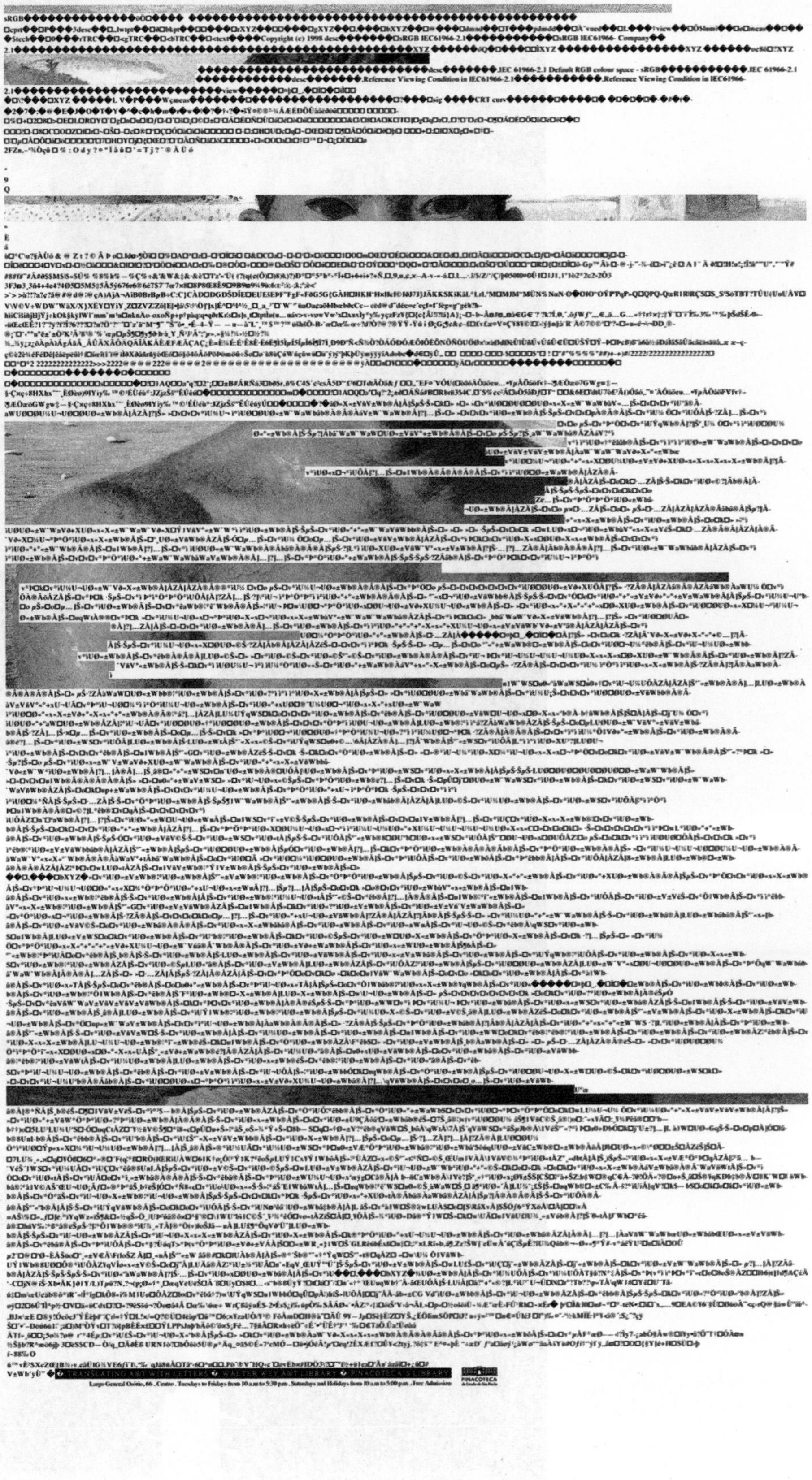

Yellow Pencil in
Film Advertising Crafts

Animation for
Film Advertising
Pleix for
Amnesty International

Death Penalty
In a chiaroscuro mood, a firing squad is pointing guns at a prisoner. The characters, made of candle wax, start to melt down. As a reveal, the strapline 'Death to the death penalty', formed from candle wax, is followed by the Amnesty candle logo, explaining that Amnesty is fighting against the death penalty and that its own flame is melting down executioners.

Animation
Pleix
Direction
Pleix
Art Director
Philippe Taroux
Copywriter
Benoit Leroux
Creative Directors
Eric Holden
Remi Noel
Agency Producer
Maxime Boiron
Production Companies
Gang Films
Warm & Fuzzy
Post Production Companies
Digital District
Mecanique Generale
Advertising Agency
TBWA\Paris
Art Buyers
Barbara Chevalier
Dorothee Dupont
Account Handlers
Anne-Laure Brunner
Anne Vincent
Communications Director
Sylvie Haurat
Client
Amnesty International

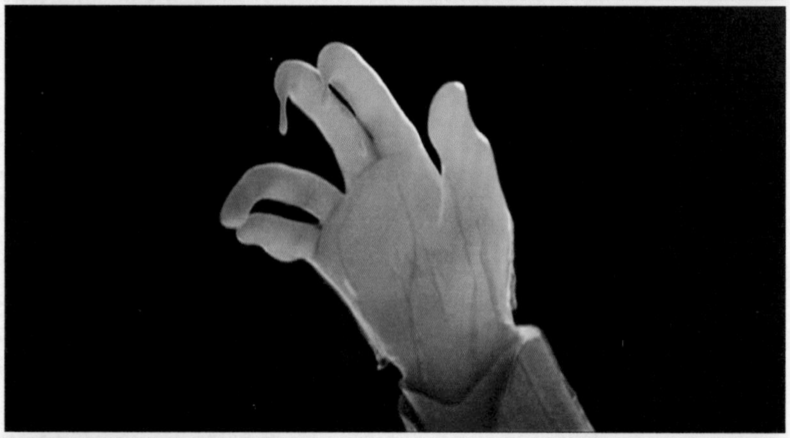

DEATH TO
THE DEATH PENALTY

139 COUNTRIES HAVE WIPED OUT THE DEATH PENALTY.
ONLY 58 ARE LEFT TO CONVINCE.

Yellow Pencil in Film Advertising Crafts

Animation for
Film Advertising
Studio AKA for the BBC

Winter Olympics
This is the story of an Inuit warrior who has been tasked with rescuing a piece of an ancient ceremonial Inukshuk statue, which has been stolen by an evil bear spirit. The warrior braves death-defying arctic conditions and uses his sporting prowess to recapture the missing stone, thus restoring peace and balance to the world.

Animators
Norm Konyu
Florian Mounie
Max Stoehr
Lucas Vigroux
Director
Marc Craste
Art Directors
Freddy Mandy
Tim McNaughton
Copywriters
Freddy Mandy
Tim McNaughton
Creative Director
Damon Collins
Producers
Deborah Stewart
Sharon Titmarsh
Editor
Nic Gill
Sound Designer
Anthony Austin
Production Companies
Red Bee Media
Studio AKA
Advertising Agency
RKCR/Y&R
Planner
Ben Kay
Account Handler
David Pomfret
Client
BBC
Brand
BBC Sport

Yellow Pencil in Film Advertising Crafts

Cinematography for Film Advertising
Great Guns for the BBC

Local Radio
This spot for the BBC encourages us all to not only appreciate our locality, but also get involved by listening to our local radio station. People who really love where they live are depicted getting physically affectionate with what they love about their home town.

Lighting Cameraperson
Natasha Braier
Director
Olly Blackburn
Art Director
Jules Chalkley
Copywriter
Nick Simons
Creative Director
Damon Collins
Producer
Ella Littlewood
Editor
Andy Phillips
Production Companies
Great Guns
Red Bee Media
Post Production
The Mill London
Advertising Agency
RKCR/Y&R
Client
BBC

PALACE

Yellow Pencil in
Film Advertising Crafts

Direction for
Film Advertising
Independent Films
for Nike

Write the Future

Every four years, the keys to football heaven are dangled in front of the international elite. One goal, one pass, one game saving tackle can be the difference between fame and forgotten. Nike's epic film 'Write the Future' showed us what the players were really playing for, in their own lives and in the lives of those who follow them. Our goal was to weave the brand into conversations about this major tournament in a way that celebrated the participating teams and athletes, and engaged football fans around the world. This ad was also awarded a Yellow Pencil in Editing for Film Advertising, and selected in Cinematography for Film Advertising and Sound Design for Film Advertising.

Director
Alejandro González Iñárritu
Art Directors
Stuart Harkness
Freddie Powell
Copywriters
Stuart Harkness
Freddie Powell
Creative Directors
Mark Bernath
Eric Quennoy
Executive Creative Director
Jeff Kling
Producers
Greg Cundiff
Dominic Freeman
Agency Producers
Olivier Klonhammer
Elissa Singstock
Executive Producers
Jani Guest
Richard Packer
Post Executive Producer
Jane Dilworth
Visual Effects Executive Producer
Stephen Venning
2D & 3D Designer
Tom Busel
2D & 3D Artist
Neil Davies
Editors
Ben Jordan
Stephen Mirrione
Charlie Moreton
Rick Orrick
Lighting Cameraperson
Emmanuel Lubezki
Director of Photography
Jeroen van der Poel
Sound Designer
Raja Sehgal
Production Company
Independent Films
Advertising Agency
Wieden+Kennedy
Amsterdam
Digital Agency
AKQA Amsterdam
Visual Effects
The Mill London
& New York
Editing
Mirrione
Work
Sound Design
Grand Central Studios
Phaze UK
Music Remix
MassiveMusic
Amsterdam
Planners
Graeme Douglas
Dan Hill
Account Handlers
David Anson
Jordi Pont
Head of Broadcast
Erik Verheijen
Brand Communications Director
Enrico Balleri
Global Brand Communications Director
Todd Pendleton
Global Advertising & Content Manager
Colin Leary
Client
Nike

RONALDO
7

Yellow Pencil in
Film Advertising Crafts

Direction for
Film Advertising
Made in Valby for
the Danish Road
Safety Council

The Family: The Party
This ad was part
of a traffic campaign
targeted at young men.
It shows that even
the Mafia take road
safety seriously and
find traffic the most
stupid place to die.

Director
Adam Hashemi
Copywriters
Brian Lykke
Jesper Rofelt
Creative Director
Jesper Rofelt
Producer
Tanja Paik
Set Designer
Peter Grant
Cinematographer
Lasse Frank
Production Company
Made in Valby
Advertising Agency
Made in Valby
Client
Danish Road
Safety Council

Yellow Pencil in
Film Advertising Crafts

Sound Design for
Film Advertising
HEIMAT, Berlin
for Hornbach

Faces
It's not about, 'I have to do it myself to save money'. It's about, 'Yes, I wanna do it! I wanna improve my home, my house, my garden – whatever it takes! Give me a sledgehammer, a spade, a million litres of paint. You think I'm crazy?' How much madness are you made of? This ad was also selected in Editing for Film Advertising.

Sound Designer
Viktor Ekrt
Director
Martin Krejci
Art Directors
Susanne Fill
Teresa Jung
Copywriters
Guido Heffels
Mirjam Kundt
Creative Directors
Guido Heffels
Matthias Storath
Producer
Jan Dressler
Agency Producer
Kerstin Heffels
Line Producer
Eva Pèrez
Editor
Guido Notari
Lighting Cameraperson
Stepan Kucera
Telecine
Seamus O'Kane
Production Company
Stink Berlin
Advertising Agency
HEIMAT, Berlin
Strategic Planner
Matthias von Bechtolsheim
Account Handlers
Mark Hassan
Nicole Varga
Marketing Manager
Frank Sahler
Client
Hornbach

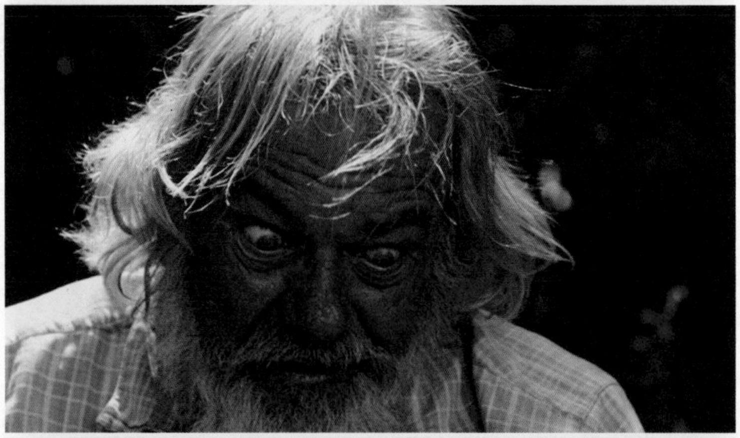

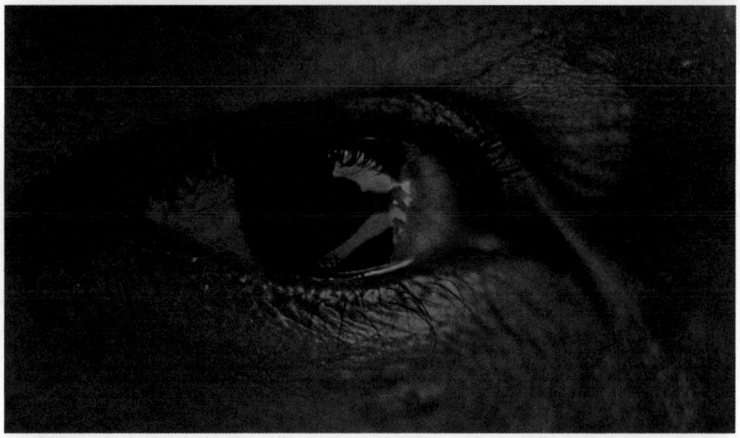

Nomination in
Film Advertising Crafts

Direction for
Film Advertising
Academy Films
for Match.com

Piano
The online dating market has a tendency to come over all scientific, functional and logical. But we all know it's not about that. For Match.com, it had to be about an unequivocal belief in love. We wanted to inspire people to start their own love stories; to shift Match.com from a technical position to an emotional one. To stay away from the cliché of Hollywood happy ever afters and to capture the indescribable moment when you both just know. This is 'boy meets girl' the way we really dream about it happening. 'Piano' was also nominated in Use of Music for Film Advertising.

Direction
Si & Ad
Art Directors
Nick Hallbery
Erik Nordenankar
Copywriters
David Colman
Daniel Mencak
Creative Directors
Stephen Butler
Al MacCuish
Robert Saville
Mark Waites
Ed Warren
Producer
Lucy Gossage
Agency Producer
Kirsten Kates
Set Designer
Cat Meredydd
Editor
Jonnie Scarlet
Lighting Cameraperson
Lasse Frank
Music Composers
Lauren Balthrop
Steve Salett
Music Arranger
Lara Meyerratken
Sound Designer
Sam Robson
Production Company
Academy Films
Advertising Agency
Mother London
Brand Manager
Karl Gregory
Client
Match.com

Nomination in
Film Advertising Crafts

Direction for
Film Advertising
RSA Films for Philips

The Gift
This sci-fi thriller, Podarok (The Gift), introduces us to a dystopian future. An experienced KGB agent is on his way to deliver a special gift. Expressionless and seemingly empty, the lone man makes his way across the city. As the secret of the gift is unveiled to the receiver, the agent's desire for the object becomes evident. He must have it. Even at the cost of a man's life. A high octane chase through Moscow ensues as the murdered man's robotic butler tries to rescue the precious gift. This ad was also selected in Cinematography for Film Advertising and Special Effects for Film Advertising.

Director
Carl Erik Rinsch
Art Directors
Denis Lischenko
Shishir Patel
Copywriter
Sam Oliver
Creative Director
Jeremy Craigen
Producer
Margo Mars
Agency Producers
Lucinda Ker
Natalie Powell
Production Designer
Denis Lischenko
Special Effects
Jeff Julian
J J Palomo
Editors
Dan Swietlik
Dayn Williams
Lighting Cameraperson
Roman Vas'yanov
Music Arrangers
Eddie Kim
Rommel Molina
Andrew Tracy
Sound Designers
Eddie Kim
Rommel Molina
Andrew Tracy
Production Company
RSA Films
Advertising Agency
DDB London
Account Handler
Zoë Hinckley
Client
Philips

● Nomination in
Film Advertising Crafts

Editing for Film Advertising
The Quarry
for Volkswagen

Last Tango in Compton
Shot in north London, Last Tango in Compton stars two of the world's best tango dancers: Gaspar Godoy, Argentinean tango world champion, and partner Manuella Rossi, the world number two. The pair dance a specially choreographed routine overseen by one of the world's foremost choreographers with a simultaneous set-up of over 20 different cameras following their every move. The pair dance a sensual and beautiful tango to a tough urban hip-hop track (Don't Stop by rapper Roc C), creating a surprising and stunning contrast.

Editor
Paul Watts
Director
Jonathan Glazer
Art Director
Richard Denny
Copywriter
Dave Henderson
Creative Director
Jeremy Craigen
Producer
Ben Link
Agency Producer
Sarah Browell
Lighting Cameraperson
Dan Landin
Music Composer
Roc C
Editing
The Quarry
Production Company
Academy Films
Advertising Agency
DDB London
Music Arrangement
Soundtree
Wave
Account Handler
Matt Delahunty
Brand Manager
Sarah Clayton-Jones
Client
Volkswagen
Brand
Polo

Nomination in
Film Advertising Crafts

Sound Design for
Film Advertising
Kouz Production
for CANAL+

Tick

This trailer begins with a car bomb explosion. As the clip goes backwards in time, we discover that the scene takes place in the middle of a tranquil Paris street. Ending with a familiar ticking sound, the trailer is designed to intrigue the viewer to watch the series and find out more about the person behind the bomb, Carlos, the terrorist who threatened the world. The agency and CANAL+ wanted to pitch the right tone, a suitably sober approach across all media, to avoid falling into the trap of eulogising a character who is, after all, a murderer. The trailer was also selected in Special Effects for Film Advertising.

Sound Designers
Gregoire Couzinier
Thomas Couzinier
Director
Wilfrid Brimo
Art Director
Viken Guzel
Copywriter
Charles Lefort
Creative Directors
Olivier Apers
Stéphane Xiberras
Agency Producer
David Green
Sound Design
Kouz Production
Special Effects
Wanda Productions
Production Company
Wanda Productions
Advertising Agency
BETC Euro RSCG
Client
CANAL+

MONSIEUR CH

MONSIEUR CHARLES

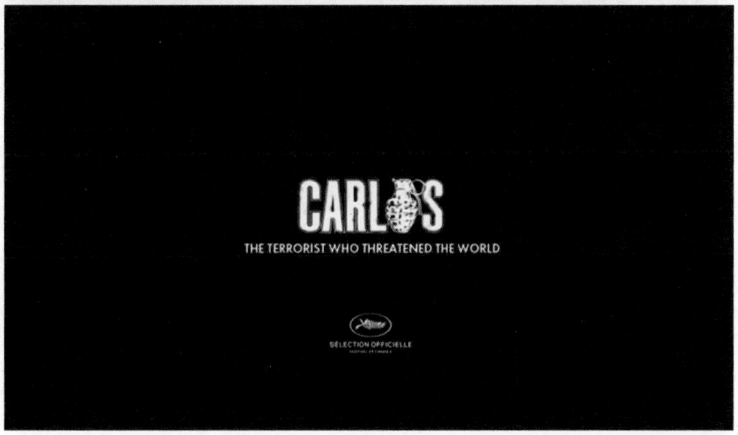
CARLOS
THE TERRORIST WHO THREATENED THE WORLD
SÉLECTION OFFICIELLE

Nomination in
Film Advertising Crafts

Special Effects for
Film Advertising
MPC for Drench

Cubehead
Cubehead features a puzzled man trying to solve his own Rubik's cube style puzzle head. MPC created the puzzle head by combining live action elements.

Visual Effects Supervisor
Matthew Unwin
Director
Ulf Johansson
Creative Directors
Ed Edwards
Dave Masterman
Ewan Paterson
Producer
Philippa Smith
Agency Producer
Kate Bailey
Post Production Producer
Chris Allen
Director of Telecine
Jean-Clement Soret
Editor
John Smith
Special Effects
MPC
Production Company
Smith & Jones
Post Production
MPC
Advertising Agency
CHI & Partners
Brand Manager
Laura Watson
Client
Drench

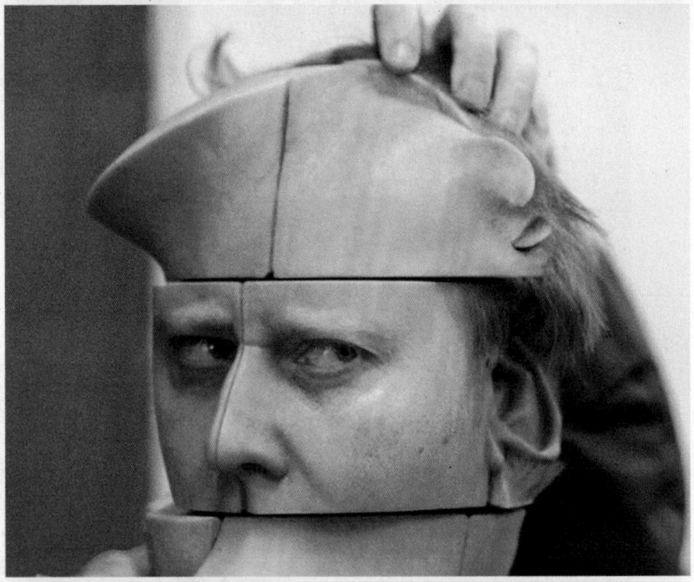

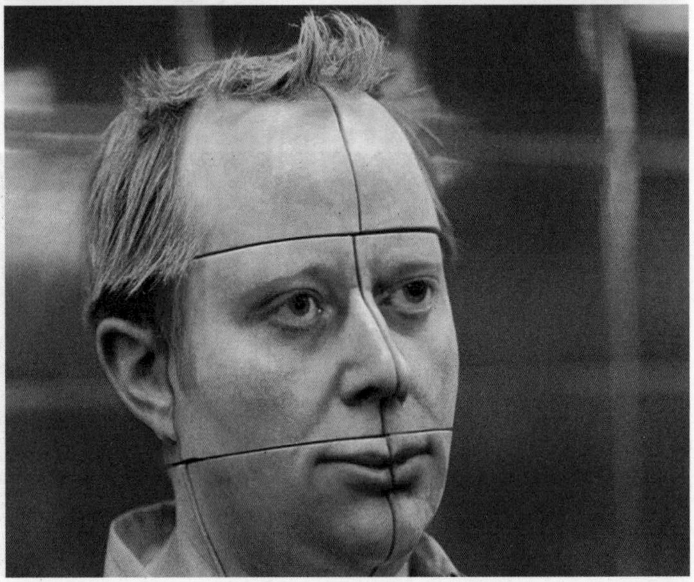

Nomination in
Film Advertising Crafts

Use of Music for
Film Advertising
BBH London for
Heineken UK

Slow the Pace
A new positioning for Kronenbourg saw the launch of 'Slow the Pace'. It takes Lemmy and his band Motorhead to a French bar, where, inspired by the laid-back atmosphere and a slow, cold Kronenbourg 1664, they play their legendarily manic song, 'Ace of Spades', at half the normal speed.

Music Composers
Lemmy / Clark / Taylor
Directors
Will Lovelace
Dylan Southern
Art Director
Matt Doman
Copywriter
Ian Heartfield
Creative Directors
Matt Doman
Ian Heartfield
Producer
Mark Harbour
Agency Producer
Michelle Kendrick
Editor
Leo Scott
Post Production
Producer
Lisa Vaughan
Lighting Cameraperson
Manel Ruiz
Sound Designer
Jack Sedgwick
Production Company
Pulse Films
Post Production
Absolute Post
Advertising Agency
BBH London
Planner
Agathe Guerrier
Account Handler
Helen James
Account Manager
Mehdi Benali
Account Director
Paisley Wright
Senior Brand Manager
Lucas Bergmans
Brand Director
Bruce Reinders
Client
Heineken UK
Brand
Kronenbourg 1664

Kronenbourg
1664
Slow the pace

Nomination in Film Advertising Crafts

Use of Music for Film Advertising
Goodby, Silverstein & Partners for the NBA

Stepping Up / Unity
Jay-Z owns a portion of the New Jersey Nets. Marvin Gaye sang the greatest version of the US national anthem at the 1983 NBA all-star game. And Shaq likes to rap... well... sorta. Most NBA players use music to pump themselves up or focus before every game. Music and the NBA just seem to go really well together. We officially embraced this musical synergy and partnered with DJ Steve Porter to produce a TV campaign of 'mashups'. These songs have celebrity singers; the vocals are actual sound bites of players and coaches from the NBA put to beats.

Music Composer
DJ Steve Porter
Art Director
Devin Sharkey
Copywriter
Craig Mangan
Creative Director
Jamie Barrett
Associate Creative Directors
Paul Charney
Stefan Copiz
Post Producer
Tony Joo
Assistant Post Producer
Ana Orrach
Agency Producer
Jake Grand
Editor
Jack Bibbo
Assistant Editor
Nat Fuller
Post Production
GSP eLevel
Advertising Agency
Goodby, Silverstein & Partners
Account Handler
Tanin Blumberg
Client
NBA

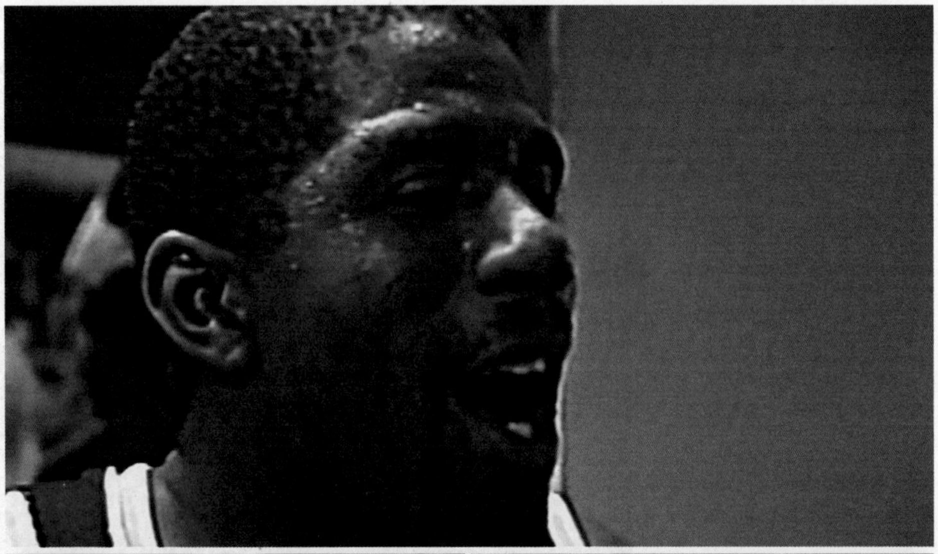

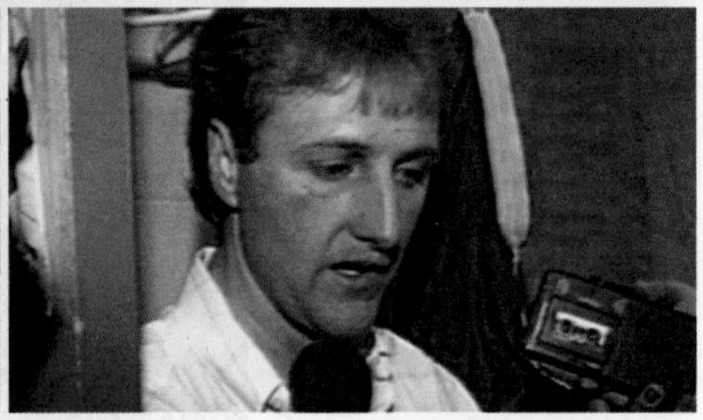

Stepping Up

PLAYOFFS
NBA.com

Unity

Animation for
Film Advertising
BL:ND for Audi UK

Imagination
We take a journey into the mind of the Audi designer and see that his vision for the A7 Sportback is almost identical to the finished vehicle.

Lead Animators
Hatem Ben Abdallah
Jason Kim
Lawrence Wyatt
Animators
Ehren Addis
Eli Guerron
Ben Lopez
Director
Vanessa Marzaroli
Art Directors
Andy Clough
Richard McGrann
Copywriters
Andy Clough
Richard McGrann
Creative Directors
Nick Kidney
Kevin Stark
Agency Producer
Glenn Paton
Director of Photography
Alex Barber
Music Composers
Felix Buxton
Simon Ratcliffe
Production Company
BL:ND
Post Production
Framestore
Advertising Agency
BBH London
Editing
BL:ND
Strategist
Bill Scott
Account Director
Simon Coles
Account Manager
Polly Knowles
Brand Manager
Eve Tyers
Marketing Director
Peter Duffy
Client
Audi UK
Brand
Audi A7 Sportback

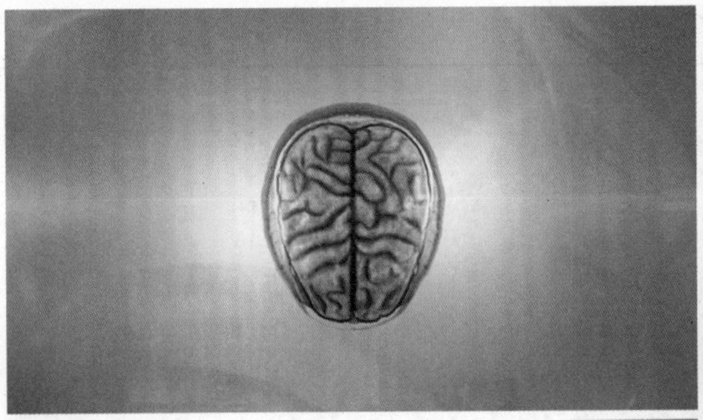
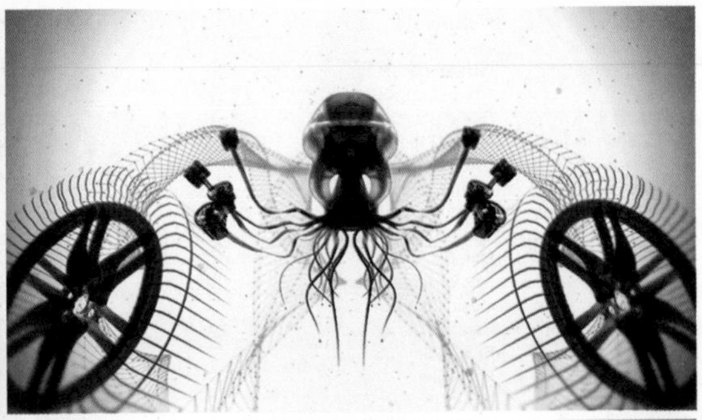
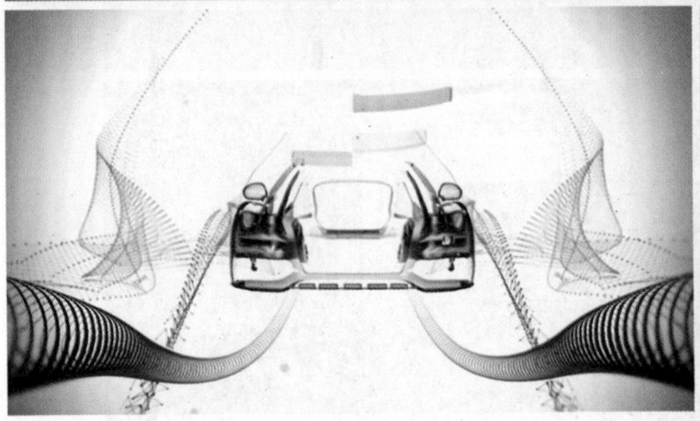

Animation for
Film Advertising
Mikros for Citroën

The Dog
This commercial presents a little dog composed of different objects: a bag, glasses, shoes. The dog is lost – its owners have disappeared. We see the dog walking around on the beach, in the street, trying to find new people. Then a super appears: 'Don't leave the things you love behind'. The Citroën C3 Picasso stops in front of the dog, who is very happy to see the car and climbs in. The name for the Citroën C3 Picasso concept is 'The Spacebox'.

Animators
Anne Chatelain
Gregory Mougne
Michael Nauzin
Cedric Nicolas
Morgan Sagel
Director
Sebastien Strasser
Art Director
Luca Cinquepalmi
Copywriter
Marco Venturelli
Creative Directors
Luca Cinquepalmi
Gilbert Scher
Marco Venturelli
Producer
Jérome Denis
Agency Producer
Christopher Thiery
Special Effects
Julien Meesters
Computer Graphics Supervisor
Manuel Souillac
Editor
Nils Landmark
Music Composers
Bruce Hart
Joseph Raposo
Animation
Mikros
Production Company
Wanda Productions
Advertising Agency
H
Music Arrangement
Sesame Street
Account Handler
Eric Britton
Brand Manager
Jean Marc Savigne
Client
Citroën
Brand
C3 Picasso

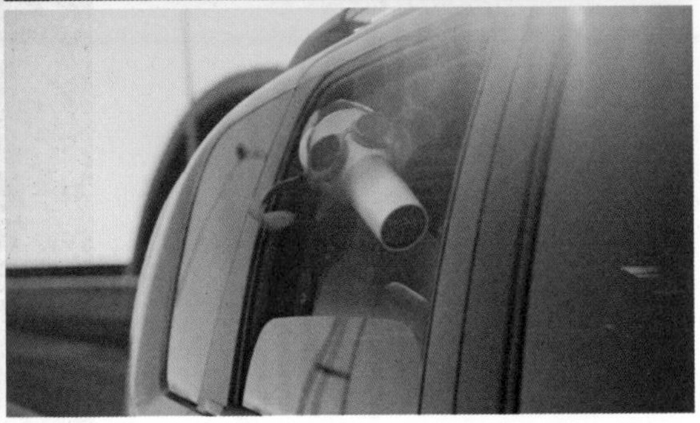

Animation for
Film Advertising
Mikros for AIDES

Graffiti
AIDES is the leading association fighting the spread of AIDS in France. It leads the way against discrimination, and promotes tolerance and open-mindedness. Despite preventative actions in the field, mass communication remains essential. Assertive yet hilarious, Graffiti delivers the message in the most efficient manner. This commercial celebrates happy sex – as long as it is safe. It's also a reminder that condoms can be seen as an asset.

2D Animator
Yves Bigerel
3D Animators
Mickael Nauzin
Morgan Sagel
Director
Yoann Lemoine
Art Director
Ingrid Varetz
Copywriter
Ingrid Varetz
Creative Directors
Eric Holden
Remi Noel
Producer
Jerome Denis
Post Producers
Pascal Giroux
Olivier Glandais
Agency Producers
Maxime Boiron
Virginie Chalard
Designer
Barthelemy Maunoury
Editor
Nicolas Larrouquere
Music Composers
Pascal Bonifay
Fabrice Smadja
Animation
Mikros
Production Company
Wanda Productions
Advertising Agency
TBWA\Paris
Sound Design
Attention O Chiens
Account Handler
Anne Vincent
Communications Director
Floriane Cutler
Client
AIDES

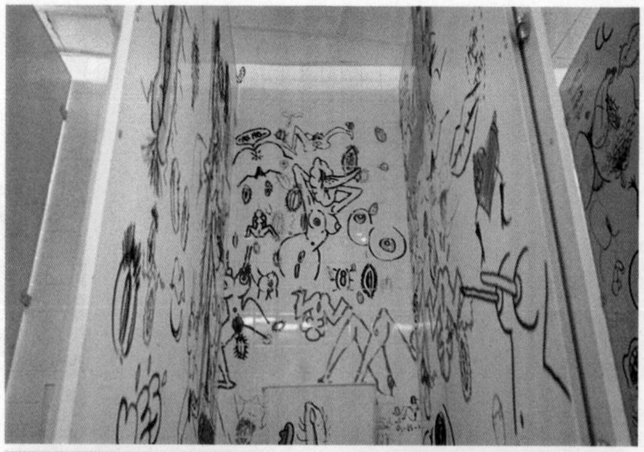
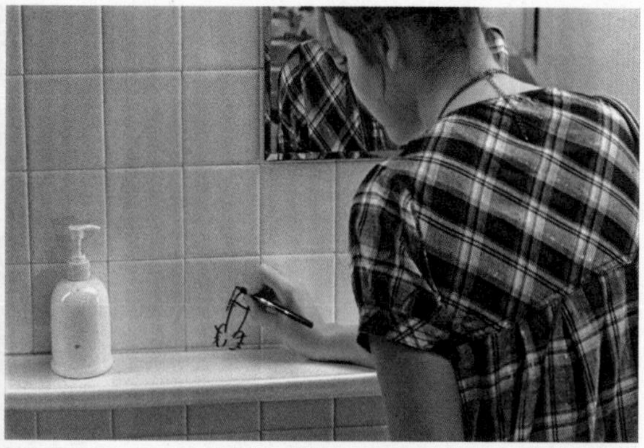
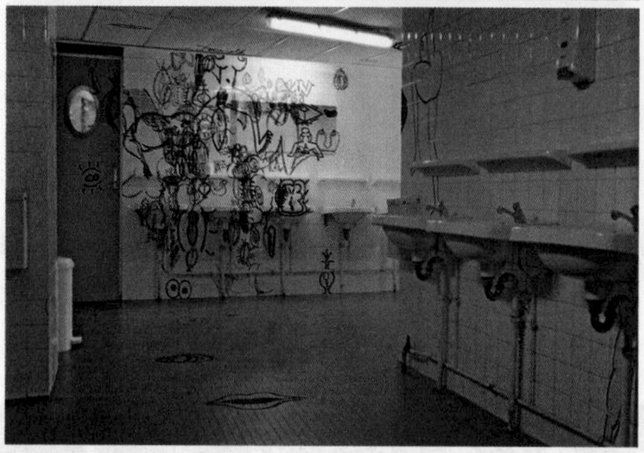

AIDES
www.aides.org

Animation for
Film Advertising
Psyop Los Angeles
for Xbox

Revolution
Taking the life and death struggle for freedom and staging it in a theatrical, classical manner, we filled the screen with drama and detail. We looked to the masters – Rembrandt, Caravaggio, Delacroix – for inspiration. The backgrounds were painted like backdrops, the clouds of revolution boiling overhead in an El Greco style. We used the same techniques the Dutch Masters used to guide the viewer through the frame: controlling the lighting and manipulating the vanishing point while playing with depth and perspective. In the end we created something beautiful, artistic and theatrical while staying true to the spirit of the game.

Lead Animator
David Bosker
Animators
Alejandro Castro
Victor Garza
Chris Meek
Direction
Psyop Los Angeles
Computer Graphics Lead Artist
David Chontos
Art Directors
Steve Couture
Jeremy Diessner
Aramis Israel
Copywriter
Michael Illick
Creative Director
Laurent Ledru
Executive Creative Directors
Scott Duchon
John Patroulis
Producer
Alyssa Evans
Executive Producer
Neysa Horsburgh
Agency Producer
Alex Spahr
Director of Integrated Production
Tom Wright
Special Effects
Ben Fiske
Allan McKay
Visual Effects Supervisor
David Chontos
Editor
Brett Nicoletti
Production Company
Psyop Los Angeles
Advertising Agency
agencytwofifteen
Client
Xbox
Brand
Fable III

Animation for
Film Advertising
Aardman Animations
for Nokia

The World's Smallest Stop-Motion Character Animation

Our brief was to position the Nokia N8 as a powerful tool for creativity by focusing on its 12mp camera and HD video features. We created a magical, microscopic animation with an intricately crafted 9mm heroine. Shot entirely on the N8, the film used and celebrated CellScope technology, an innovative life-saving microscope.

Animator
Ed Patterson
Direction
Sumo Science
Producers
Jason Bartholomew
Laura Pepper
Agency Producers
Lucie Georgeson
Lucy Russell
Executive Producer
Heather Wright
Creative Directors
Richard Dorey
Scott Dungate
Mark McCall
Executive Creative Directors
Tony Davidson
Kim Papworth
Lead Flame Artist
Will Studd
Assistant Flame Artist
Fincher Trist
Editor
Nikk Fielden
Director of Photography
Mark Chamberlain
Sound Designer
Aaron Reynolds
Music Supervisor
Simon Robinson
Animation
Aardman Animations
Advertising Agencies
Aardman Animations
Wieden+Kennedy
London
Account Director
Toby Hussey
Account Manager
Natasha Markley
Client
Nokia

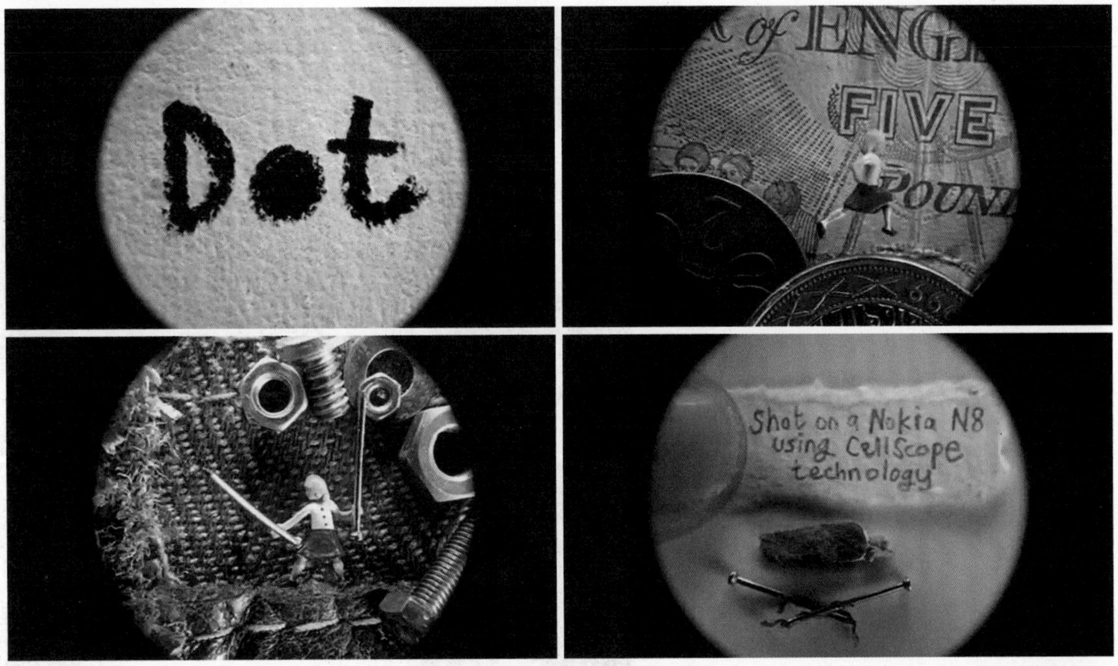
Dot
FIVE
POUND
Shot on a Nokia N8 using CellScope technology

Animation for
Film Advertising
Mekanism for PepsiCo

Brisk Machete

To revamp the 'That's Brisk, baby' campaign, Mekanism worked with PepsiCo to create web films that reimagined the message of Lipton Brisk Iced Tea through a new lens. We continued the brand's legacy of replicating iconic celebrities through stop-motion puppet animation, but we livened up the look and feel with new technology. We also decided to take the brand's iconic tagline rather literally in the messaging. In this spot we condensed the movie 'Machete' into a 60-second online film, with Danny Trejo narrating at rapid-fire speed. That's Brisk, baby!

Animators
Amy Adamy
Webster Colcord
Justin Kohn
Scott Kravitz
Richard Zimmerman
Assistant Animator
Matt Manning
Animation Director
Misha Klein
Art Directors
Pierre Maurer
Dieter Wiechmann
Copywriter
Andre Ricciardi
Creative Director
Andre Ricciardi
Executive Creative Director
Ian Kovalik
Producer
Tim Rayel
Executive Producer
Jason Harris
Agency Producer
Bud Johnston
Head of Production
Mat Lundberg
Set Designer
Pierre Maurer
Design Director
Emmett Feldman
Production Designer
Fon Davis
Effects Supervisor
Colin Miller
Computer Graphics Modeller
Seryong Kim
Lead NUKE Artist
Ben Hawkins
Production Company
Mekanism
Advertising Agency
Mekanism
Director of Client Strategy
Michael Zlatoper
Brand Manager
Jamal Henderson
Marketing Managers
Eric Fuller
Marisol Tamaro
Client
PepsiCo
Brand
Lipton Brisk

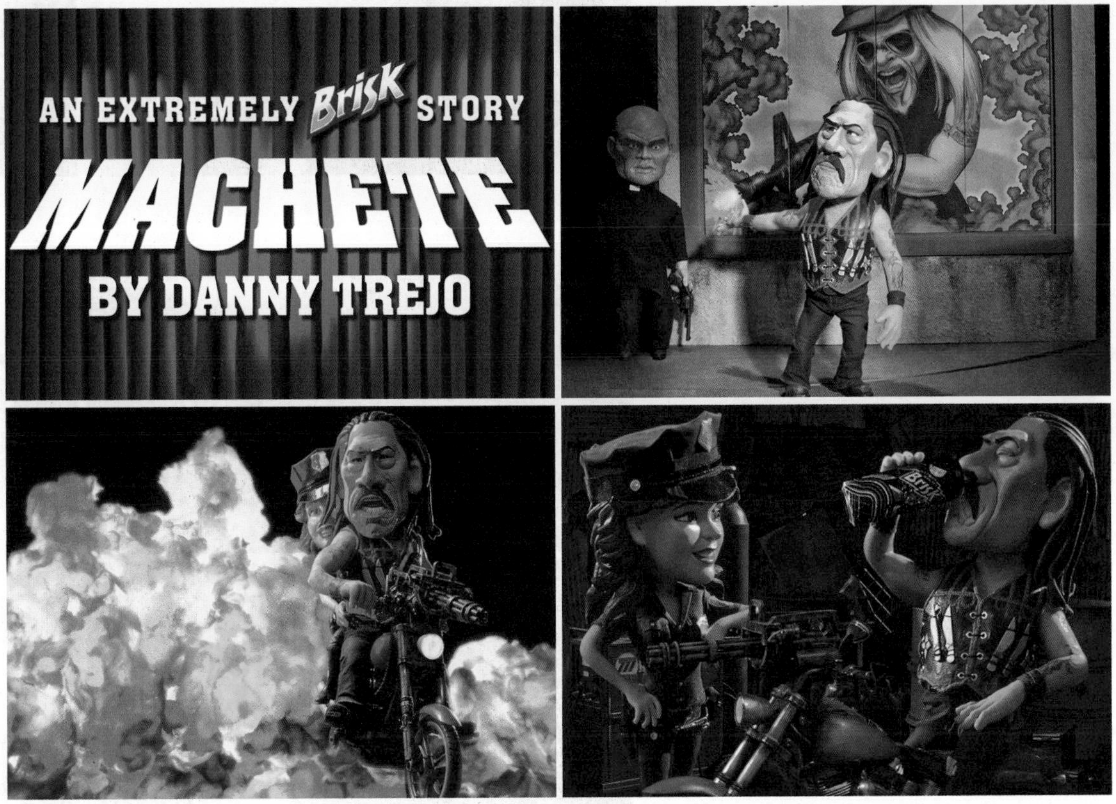
AN EXTREMELY Brisk STORY
MACHETE
BY DANNY TREJO

Animation for
Film Advertising
Psyop New York for LG

Something's Lurking
How do you show the dangers of the hidden dirt and allergens that lurk in carpets in a way people might actually watch and share? That was the challenge with LG's Kompressor Elite, a powerful vacuum cleaner with technology we knew would appeal to savvy viewers online. So we made a video that feels more like an epic, scary film. The dirt and allergens are represented as shark fins menacing a group of toys. We're right there with them, in the fibres and carnage until, eventually, they're saved. And viewers are hopefully intrigued to find out more.

Lead 3D Artist
Christian Bach
Lead 2D Artist
Nick Tanner
Direction
Psyop New York
Art Director
Gabriel Hoskins
Copywriter
Cheryl Chapman
Creative Directors
Marie Hyon
Marco Spier
Executive Creative Directors
Ian Reichenthal
Scott Vitrone
Global Creative Directors
Stuart Harricks
Andrew McKechnie
Producers
Michael Neithardt
Sean Sullivan
Editor
Cass Vanini
Director of Photography
Fred Elmes
Executive Music Producer
Eric David Johnson
Senior Content Producer
Tennille Teague
Executive Directors of Content Production
Nathy Aviram
Lora Schulson
Production Companies
Psyop New York
Smuggler
Visual Effects
Psyop New York
Advertising Agency
Y&R New York
Sound Design
Q Department
Marketing Manager
Markus Werner
Client Senior Manager
Lucas Oh
Client
LG
Brand
Kompressor Elite

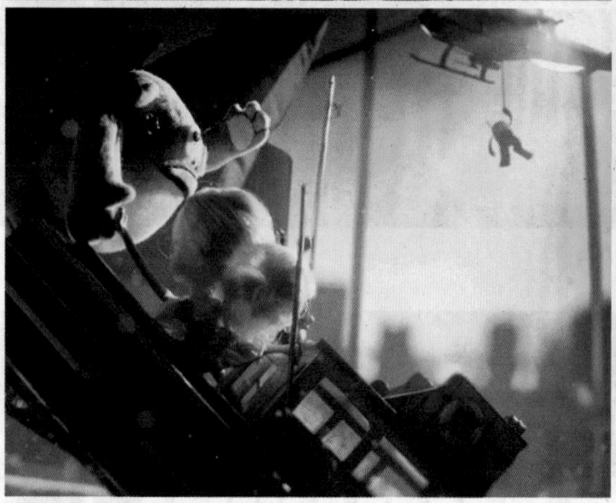

Cinematography
for Film Advertising
Net#work BBDO
for Nedbank

Fish
In the current economic climate, investment banks need to be ingenious, quick-witted and resilient. This depiction of a true natural phenomenon perfectly demonstrates these qualities in the most extraordinary of times.

Lighting Cameraperson
Timothy Pike
Director
Terence Neale
Art Directors
Byron Liatos
Brent Singer
Copywriter
Jenny Glover
Creative Directors
Rob McLennan
Mariana O'Kelly
Producer
Rozanne Rocha-Gray
Agency Producer
Maggie Post
Set Designer
Elmi Badenhorst
Animator
Tracy-Lee Portnoi
Special Effects
Tracy-Lee Portnoi
Editor
Saki Bergh
Sound Designer
Lorens Persson
Production Companies
Egg Films
Humanoid
Animation
Black Ginger
Advertising Agency
Net#work BBDO
Music Composition & Arrangement
Q Department
Account Handler
Stuart Gormley
Marketing Manager
Rochelle Grove
Client
Nedbank

Cinematography for Film Advertising
Exit Films Melbourne for Coca Cola

Ride
This film tells the story of real-life characters from Distreeto, a street skateboarding collective in Mexico City. The film follows them from dawn till dusk on their journey across the urban landscape, catching fire as they pick up speed, performing tricks and stunts. It sets out to capture the sense of both community and individualism synonymous with the pursuit. Shot by director Garth Davis, the film was made in collaboration with Los Angeles skate legend Steve Berra and created alongside two other Burn productions. The approach involved existing communities in the creation and distribution of key campaign material.

Lighting Cameraperson
Greig Fraser
Director
Garth Davis
Art Director
Andrew Ostrom
Copywriter
Ian Williamson
Creative Director
Micah Walker
Producer
Karen Sproul
Agency Producer
Philippa Smart
Special Effects
Colin Renshaw
Editor
Jack Hutchings
Music Composers
James Cecil
Django Django
Cornel Wilczek
Music Supervisor
Karl Richter
Production Company
Exit Films Melbourne
Advertising Agency
Publicis Mojo Sydney
Sound Design
GASinc Melbourne
Account Handlers
John Flood
Simon Ludowyke
Marketing Manager
Francesco Cibo
Client
Coca Cola
Brand
Coke Burn

Direction for Film Advertising
Mojo Films for Celestial Movies

Break Up
This TV commercial opens in a restaurant. A couple is about to break up. A waiter interrupts and starts giving the girlfriend tips on breaking up. First, he asks her to weep a little while keeping the anger within. Then, he gets her to splash water over and slap her boyfriend. The woman does as he says and dumps the boyfriend. Satisfied, the waiter then turns to the camera and says: 'I'm good because I watch good movies'. It ends with the line: 'Only Celestial Movies has the best Chinese blockbusters'.

Director
Barney Chua
Art Director
Wong Shu Kor
Copywriters
Raphael Ang
Ted Lim
Kimberley Yap
Creative Director
Ted Lim
Producer
Tan Leng Ean
Agency Producer
Sharon De Silva
Editor
Shahrol Esham Bin Shalim
Lighting Cameraperson
Jordan Chiam Wei Meng
Production Company
Mojo Films
Advertising Agency
Naga DDB Malaysia
Music Arrangement
Two AM
Account Handlers
Michelle Chong
Liew Wai Fun
Gyn Gan
Client Senior Vice President
Andy Chang
Client
Celestial Movies

天映頻道
CELESTIAL MOVIES
Only CELESTIAL MOVIES has the best Chinese blockbusters.

Direction for
Film Advertising
Gorgeous for Hovis

Miss Chief
Our little girl Mary is naughty, getting up to all the things mischievous girls do. She was bad, but now she's good, and it's good to be good. Hovis is as good today as it's always been. The spot is set to the track 'Ça Plane Pour Moi' by Plastic Bertrand.

Director
Vince Squibb
Creative Director
Danny Brooke-Taylor
Producer
Spencer Dodd
Agency Producer
Hannah Boase
Editor
Russell Icke
Lighting Cameraperson
Jess Hall
Production Company
Gorgeous
Post Production
The Mill London
Editing
The White House
Advertising Agency
Dare
Sound Studio
Grand Central Studios
Client
Hovis

Direction for
Film Advertising
The Glue Society
for CANAL+

iPhone La Bascule
CANAL+ is now available on iPhone. In this spot, a television show couple prepare to embrace in the midst of a romantic moment, when their entire world is literally turned on its side. The whole scene is tilted and the couple falls from their set and into the next room. As the set is tipped back again, we learn that this is the work of a viewer watching CANAL+ on an iPhone and tilting the device left and right.

Direction
The Glue Society
Art Director
Raphael Halin
Copywriter
Benjamin Sanial
Creative Director
Stéphane Xiberas
Producer
Gaspard Chevance
Executive Producer
Jackie Kelman Bisbee
Agency Producer
Fabrice Brovelli
Set Designer
Teresa Carriker-Thayer
Editor
Carlos Arias
Production Company
Moonwalk Films
Production Services Agency
Park Pictures
Advertising Agency
BETC Euro RSCG Paris
Account Handler
Alice Cheron
Brand Manager
Coline Andre
Client
CANAL+

Direction for
Film Advertising
Gorgeous for VISA

Football Evolution
This ad promotes VISA's sponsorship of the 2010 World Cup. A chubby football fan, inspired by a goal on telly, legs it all the way from his flat in Europe to the World Cup Football event in South Africa, just in time to score the winning goal. This ad was also selected in Editing for Film Advertising.

Director
Chris Palmer
Art Director
Jonathan Santana
Copywriter
Xander Smith
Creative Directors
Paul Silburn
Kate Stanners
Producer
Rupert Smythe
Agency Producer
Rebecca Williams
Editor
Paul Watts
Lighting Cameraperson
Ian Foster
Production Company
Gorgeous
Post Production
Framestore
Prime Focus
Advertising Agency
Saatchi & Saatchi
London
Music Composition
Thompson
Sound Design
Wave
Group Account Director
Michelle Greenhalgh
Client Executive Vice President
Mariano Dima
Client
VISA

VISA
VISA

Direction for
Film Advertising
Gorgeous for Honda

Red Green Blue
The thing about this hybrid is that it's fantastic to drive. You can choose to engage with the road and the world around you in three distinct ways. That's essentially what the film is all about.

Director
Frank Budgen
Creative Directors
Chris Groom
Sam Heath
Producer
Rupert Smythe
Agency Producers
Lucy Russell
Danielle Stewart
Editor
Paul Watts
Lighting Cameraperson
Dan Landin
Production Company
Gorgeous
Advertising Agency
Wieden+Kennedy
London
Client
Honda

Direction for
Film Advertising
Partizan for
Virgin Atlantic

001
From the very first frame, Traktor's Virgin Atlantic 001 is a hyper glamorous celebration of Richard Branson's transatlantic airline. From scarlet-suited stewardesses and dashing pilots to martinis and mirrorballs, from pole-dancing passengers to somersaulting cabin crew and cloud duvets for the sleepy, it's an epic feast with a wiggle in its walk and a tongue in its cheek. What more could you want from an airline, or indeed a commercial for one?

Direction
Traktor
Art Director
Chris Hodgkiss
Copywriter
Pip Bishop
Creative Director
Mark Roalfe
Producer
David Stewart
Agency Producer
Jody Allison
Set Designer
Robin Brown
Editor
Rick Russell
Lighting Cameraperson
Stephen Blackman
Production Company
Partizan
Advertising Agency
RKCR/Y&R
Client
Virgin Atlantic

Virgin

Direction for
Film Advertising
Blink Productions
for John Lewis

Always a Woman
This ad for UK department store John Lewis is shot in a single, seamless camera move, which charts the life of a woman from birth through to old age. It shows that John Lewis provides a lifelong commitment to its customers. The ad was also selected in Use of Music for Film Advertising.

Director
Dougal Wilson
Copywriters
Emer Stamp
Ben Tollett
Steve Wioland
Matt Woolner
Creative Directors
Ben Priest
Emer Stamp
Ben Tollett
Producer
Matthew Fone
Agency Producer
Leila Bartlam
Editor
Joe Guest
Lighting Cameraperson
Dan Landin
Music Arranger
Abi Leland
Music Supervisor
Mat Goff
Sound Designer
James Saunders
Production Company
Blink Productions
Advertising Agency
adam&eve
Account Handler
Tammy Einav
Marketing Director
Craig Inglis
Client
John Lewis

John Lewis
johnlewis.com

Direction for
Film Advertising
Gorgeous for the
British Film Institute

Dialogue
This film plays on the London Film Festival's rich heritage of bringing the world's best new films to the capital. It depicts a series of everyday London scenarios in which the dialogue has been lifted directly from iconic movies that have been shown at the festival over the years. Because of the festival's target audience of avid cinemagoers and hardcore film buffs, dialogue was chosen from a wide range of films in order to give the piece real depth and make it something they will want to watch repeatedly in order to figure out every reference.

Director
Chris Plamer
Art Directors
Richard Brim
Rob Tenconi
Copywriters
Daniel Fisher
Mark Franklin
Creative Directors
Jim Bolton
John Burley
Producer
Michaela Johnson
Agency Producers
Ben Catford
Kirsten Kates
Editor
Johnny Scarlett
Lighting Cameraperson
Bruno Delbonnel
Sound Designers
Tom Dedenham
Jack Sedgwick
Production Company
Gorgeous
Advertising Agency
Leo Burnett London
Account Handlers
Stephen Attree
Richard Bookey
Brand Manager
Gail Cohen
Marketing Manager
Tim Platt
Client
British Film Institute
Brand
London Film Festival

Editing for
Film Advertising
Work for PUMA

After Hours Athlete
PUMA has released this spot championing the 'after hours athlete' – the adventures of the average Joe on a night out with his mates.

Editor
Rich Orrick
Director
Ringan Ledwidge
Art Directors
Amanda Clelland
Jesse Juriga
Copywriters
Kevin Brady
Tim Gordon
Executive Creative Director
Ted Royer
Creative Chairman
David Droga
Producer
Sally Humphries
Agency Producer
Dana May
Head of Integrated Production
Sally-Ann Dale
Director of Photography
Ben Seresin
Music Composer
Phil Kay
Sound Designer
Jay Nierenberg
Sound Mixer
Philip Loeb
Voice Over Artist
Nash Kato
Editing
Work
Production Company
Smuggler
Post Production
The Mill New York
Advertising Agency
Droga5 New York
Planner
Chet Gulland
Client
PUMA

PUMA
puma.com

Editing for
Film Advertising
Spot Welders for Nike

LeBron Rising
After his summer as a free agent, and his declaration on a live ESPN special, 'The Decision', that he would leave his hometown team for Miami Heat, American basketball star LeBron James' character was under fire. It became a necessity to wipe the slate clean and reframe the conversation. To do so, we created a 90 second TV spot addressing LeBron's critics head on. The result was a thought-provoking piece that fueled discussion and ultimately caused the public to reevaluate the expectations they had placed upon LeBron.

Editor
Robert Duffy
Director
Stacy Wall
Art Director
Taylor Twist
Copywriter
Caleb Johnson
Creative Directors
Ryan O'Rourke
Alberto Ponte
Executive Creative Directors
Mark Fitzloff
Susan Hoffman
Executive Producer
Doug Halbert
Agency Producer
Erika Madison
Agency Executive Producer
Ben Grylewicz
Special Effects
Tony Smoller
Lighting Cameraperson
Sal Totino
Sound Designer
Gus Koven
Editing
Spot Welders
Production Company
Imperial Woodpecker
Advertising Agency
Wieden+Kennedy
Portland
Music & Sound Design
Stimmung
Client
Nike

Blah Blah
blah blah

Production Design
for Film Advertising
RSA Films for Philips

Darkroom

Set in a retro future Shanghai, 'Darkroom' opens on a covert surveillance operative as he searches for his criminal quarry. Scanning a polluted city skyline, we see through his technology as he zooms ever deeper into a distant apartment. Through the imaginative use of reflections and technology he begins to unravel a sinister secret. Through this voyeuristic journey we are led to a climax with dramatic consequences.

Production Designer
Alex Marden
Director
Johnny Hardstaff
Art Director
Shishir Patel
Copywriter
Sam Oliver
Creative Director
Jeremy Craigen
Producer
Caspar Delaney
Agency Producers
Lucinda Ker
Natalie Powell
Animator
Michael Gilbert
Special Effects
Paul McGeoch
Editor
JD Smyth
Lighting Cameraperson
Mark Patten
Music Composers & Arrangers
Simon Elms
Colin Smith
Sound Designers
Simon Elms
Colin Smith
Production Company
RSA Films
Advertising Agency
DDB London
Account Handler
Zoë Hinckley
Client
Philips

Production Design
for Film Advertising
4creative for Channel 4

Airplane Monument / Blackpool Beach / Recycling
This new and engaging set of channel idents was created to support and advance the Channel 4 brand.

Production Designers
Patrick Lyndon-Stanford
Adam Zoltowski
Director
Brett Foraker
Creative Director
Brett Foraker
Producer
Gwilym Gwillim
3D Supervisor
Ashley Bernes
Editor
Adam Rudd
Lighting Cameraperson
Doug Holgate
Sound Designer
Rich Martin
Production Company
4creative
Special Effects
Method New York
Marketing Manager
Rufus Radcliffe
Client
Channel 4

Airplane Monument

Blackpool Beach

Recycling

Special Effects for Film Advertising
Legacy & MPC Los Angeles for DirecTV

Robots
DirecTV needed to move from 'just another box in a sea of boxes' to 'the ultimate entertainment experience'. Robots were used to engage viewers in a narrative of filmic proportions. Creating a story that looked and felt like a movie allowed us to brilliantly showcase a DVR feature DirecTV's competitors were also advertising. Elevating the brand offering to a level usually only seen on the big screen solidified the brand's higher standard in consumers' minds.

Special Effects
Legacy
Visual Effects
MPC Los Angeles
Director
Rupert Sanders
Creative Directors
Tor Myhren
Denise O'Bleness
Todd Tilford
Digital Executive Creative Director
Perry Fair
Producers
Lynne Mannino
Eric Stern
Agency Producer
Andrew Chinich
Editor
Neil Smith
Director of Photography
Greg Fraser
Music Composer
Atticus Ross
Music Producers
Lee Brooks
Josh Rabinowitz
Sound Designer
Jay Jennings
Production Company
MJZ Los Angeles
Advertising Agency
Grey New York
Strategic Planner
Pele Cortizo-Burgess
Account Handlers
Beth Culley
Alison Monk
Client
DirecTV

Sound Design for Film Advertising
Jafbox Sound for Google

Google Chrome Speed Tests
Since there is no benchmark for speed on the internet, we created one and dubbed it 'Chrome Fast'. To demonstrate how fast 'Chrome Fast' really is, we created the 'Chrome Speed Test' films, comparing the rendering speed of Google's Chrome browser against extremely fast things in real life: a potato gun, sound waves, and lightning. We filmed everything in slow motion with no CG effects, capturing them as live science experiments. The result was an engaging way to visualise speed and prove that Google Chrome is a very fast browser indeed.

Sound Designer
Joseph Fraioli
Director
Aaron Duffy
Art Director
Steve Peck
Copywriter
Jared Elms
Executive Creative Directors
Calle Sjoenell
Pelle Sjoenell
Robert Wong
Chief Creative Officer
Kevin Roddy
Executive Producer
Sam Penfield
Agency Producer
Orlee Tatarka
Editor
Charlie Johnston
Sound Design
Jafbox Sound
Audio Post Production
Plush New York City
Production Company
1st Avenue Machine
Online Production House
Black Hole
Editing
Lost Planet
Telecine
Katabatic
Advertising Agencies
BBH New York
Google Creative Lab
Account Handler
Rossa Hsieh
Head of Broadcast
Lisa Setten
Client
Google
Brand
Chrome

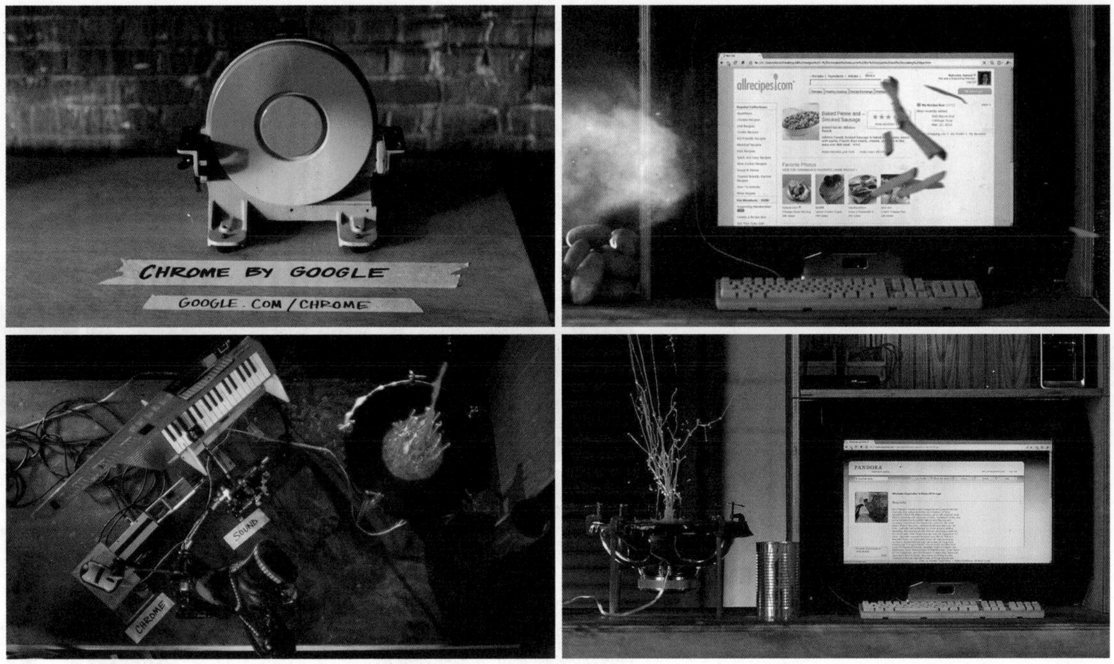
CHROME BY GOOGLE
GOOGLE.COM/CHROME
allrecipes.com
SOUND
CHROME

Use of Music for Film Advertising
Mother London for IKEA

Kitchen Party
IKEA isn't known for kitchens in the UK. We needed to change this and make IKEA kitchens famous. We looked for a cultural truth that we could use, that would fit with our 'happy inside' campaign idea. This truth was that you always end up in the kitchen at parties; this is immortalised by Jona Lewie's 80s hit song, 'You'll always find me in the kitchen at parties'.

Music Composer
Jona Lewie
Music Arranger
Anthony Moore
Director
Kim Gehrig
Art Directors
Erik Nordenankar
Julia Stenius
Copywriters
Erik Hedman
Daniel Mencak
Creative Directors
Stephen Butler
Robert Saville
Feh Tarty
Mark Waites
Producer
Laura Hegarty
Agency Producer
Craig Keppler
Set Designer
Serban Rotariu
Editor
Joe Guest
Lighting Cameraperson
Florian Hoffmeister
Sound Designer
Arthur Baker
Production Company
Academy Films
Advertising Agency
Mother London
Marketing Manager
Anna Crona
Client
IKEA

Use of Music for Film Advertising
Saatchi & Saatchi London for T-Mobile

Welcome Back
On 27 October 2010, thousands of unsuspecting passengers arriving at Heathrow's Terminal Five were given a welcome home to remember. They were greeted by a 300-strong choir and vocal orchestra singing a medley of songs, completely a cappella, to welcome them back into the country.

Music Arranger
Shai Fishman
Music Director
Shai Fishman
Director
Henry-Alex Rubin
Art Director
Rick Dodds
Copywriter
Stephen Howell
Creative Directors
Paul Silburn
Kate Stanners
Producer
Ray Leakey
Agency Producer
James Faupel
Editors
Spencer Ferzst
Patric Ryan
Lighting Cameraperson
Brett Turnbull
Sound Designer
Ben Leeves
Production Company
Smuggler
Advertising Agency
Saatchi & Saatchi London
Account Managers
Anna Mills
Laura Mills
Account Director
Sarah Galea
Senior Account Director
Charles Pym
Head of Brand & Advertising
Lynne Ormrod
Brand Manager
Kelly Engstrom
Client
T-Mobile

Use of Music for
Film Advertising
Y&R Chicago
for DieHard

DieHard Battery
vs. Gary Numan

How do you demonstrate that a DieHard Platinum battery performs in just about any situation? There are a lot of ways. We chose to use a single DieHard Platinum to power 80s avant-garde electro-pop rocker Gary Numan, his keyboards, lights, and a custom organ made of 24 cars. After Gary played his 1979 hit 'Cars', using the horns and headlights of the 24 cars, the same battery started all 24 cars.

Music Composer
Gary Numan
Director
James Frost
Art Director
Jamie Overkamp
Copywriter
Todd Taber
Creative Directors
Ken Erke
Jamie Overkamp
Todd Taber
Producer
Gower Frost
Agency Producers
Jayson Miller
Luke Rzewnicki
Brian Smego
Editor
Ruben Vela
Production Company
Zoo Film Productions
Advertising Agency
Y&R Chicago
Brand Manager
Kris Malkoski
Client
DieHard

Yellow Pencil in Illustration

Illustration for Press & Poster Advertising
Ogilvy & Mather Singapore
for Faber Castell

Self Portrait / Girl with a Pearl Earring / Mona Lisa
We could go on and on about the Faber Castell artist pen's precision and control, but we thought we'd just show you.

Illustration
Cue Art
Art Directors
Chan Hwee Chong
Fajar Kurnia
Eric Yeo
Copywriter
Jeremy Chia
Creative Director
Eric Yeo
Executive Creative Directors
Eugene Cheong
Robert Gaxiola
Image Manipulation
Pro Colour
Advertising Agency
Ogilvy & Mather Singapore
Account Handler
Jamie Tang
Client
Faber Castell

FABER-CASTELL
artist pen

● Nomination in Illustration

Illustration for Press & Poster Advertising
AMV BBDO for the V&A Museum of Childhood

Nostrils / Minds / Plasticine / Playtime
We were asked to come up with a campaign that brought to life the idea that play isn't just mucking about, it also actively helps us to learn. We came up with a series of four print ads that highlight this very thought. Each uses an iconic childhood toy or game, from Meccano to Lego, alongside headlines that humorously answer the brief. The illustrative style has a beautiful, childlike quality. The campaign was also nominated in Illustration for Design.

Illustrator
Mick Marston
Art Director
Mark Fairbanks
Copywriter
Mark Fairbanks
Print Producer
Kirstie Johnstone
Creative Director
Mark Fairbanks
Executive Creative Director
Paul Brazier
Advertising Agency
AMV BBDO
Project Manager
Linda Carlos
Account Handler
James Drummond
Marketing Manager
Joanna Bolitho
Client
V&A Museum of Childhood

Museum of Childhood
Bethnal Green
museumofchildhood.org.uk
V&A
kids soon discover fingers aren't just for sticking up nostrils.

Museum of Childhood
Bethnal Green
museumofchildhood.org.uk
V&A
MINDS HAVE GROWTH SPURTS TOO

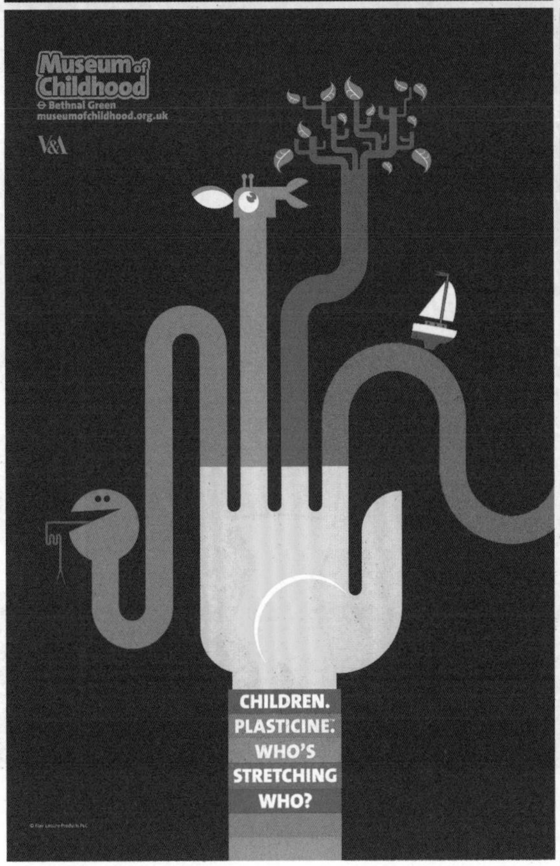
Museum of Childhood
Bethnal Green
museumofchildhood.org.uk
V&A
CHILDREN. PLASTICINE. WHO'S STRETCHING WHO?

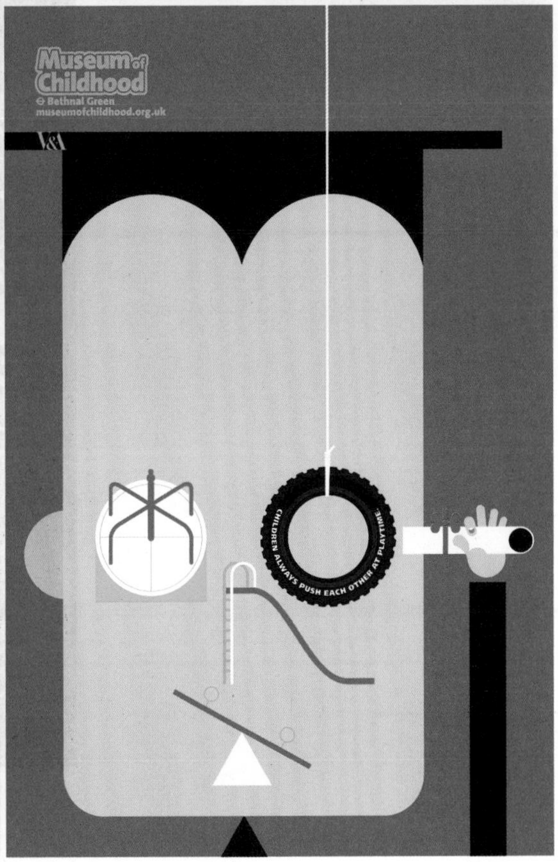
Museum of Childhood
Bethnal Green
museumofchildhood.org.uk
V&A
CHILDREN ALWAYS PUSH EACH OTHER AT PLAYTIME

● Nomination in Illustration

Illustration for Press & Poster Advertising
358 Helsinki
for Hartwall

Tastebuddies
Tastebuddies by Heineken is an event concept created at the Flow Festival in Helsinki. Two top designers with conflicting tastes were locked in a container. They were given a brief and 30 minutes to solve the problem. At the festival the container was placed next to the main stage with a bar in front of it, so people could sip beer and see the designers inside the container. A multi-camera broadcast unit shot footage for the event and online documentaries. Dutch illustrator Parra depicted the ideas of the designer pairs in these posters created during the sessions.

Illustrator
Parra
Art Director
Maria Fridman
Designer
Ville Kovanen
Copywriter
Valtteri Väkevä
Typographer
Parra
Producer
Peggy Petrell
Creative Directors
Erkki Izarra
Antero Jokinen
Advertising Agency
358 Helsinki
Account Handler
Sami Alppiranta
Brand Manager
Ossi Ahto
Client
Hartwall
Brand
Heineken

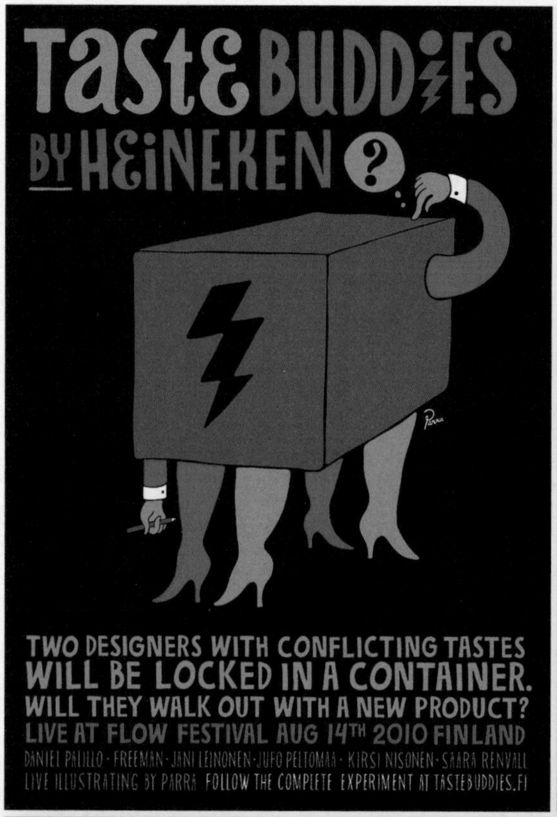
TASTEBUDDIES
BY HEINEKEN
TWO DESIGNERS WITH CONFLICTING TASTES
WILL BE LOCKED IN A CONTAINER.
WILL THEY WALK OUT WITH A NEW PRODUCT?
LIVE AT FLOW FESTIVAL AUG 14TH 2010 FINLAND
DANIEL PALILLO · FREEMAN · JANI LEINONEN · JUFO PELTOMAA · KIRSI NISONEN · SAARA RENVALL
LIVE ILLUSTRATING BY PARRA FOLLOW THE COMPLETE EXPERIMENT AT TASTEBUDDIES.FI

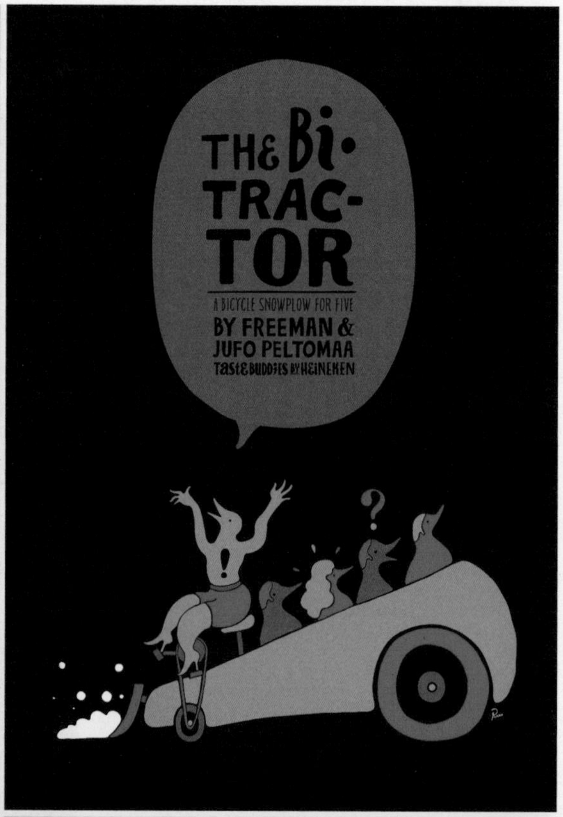
THE BI-TRACTOR
A BICYCLE SNOWPLOW FOR FIVE
BY FREEMAN & JUFO PELTOMAA
TASTEBUDDIES BY HEINEKEN

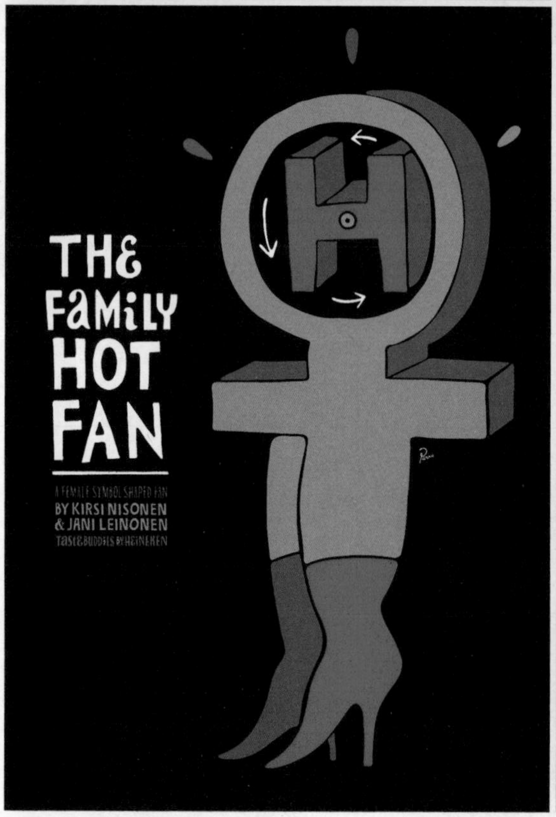
THE FAMILY HOT FAN
A FEMALE SYMBOL SHAPED FAN
BY KIRSI NISONEN & JANI LEINONEN
TASTEBUDDIES BY HEINEKEN

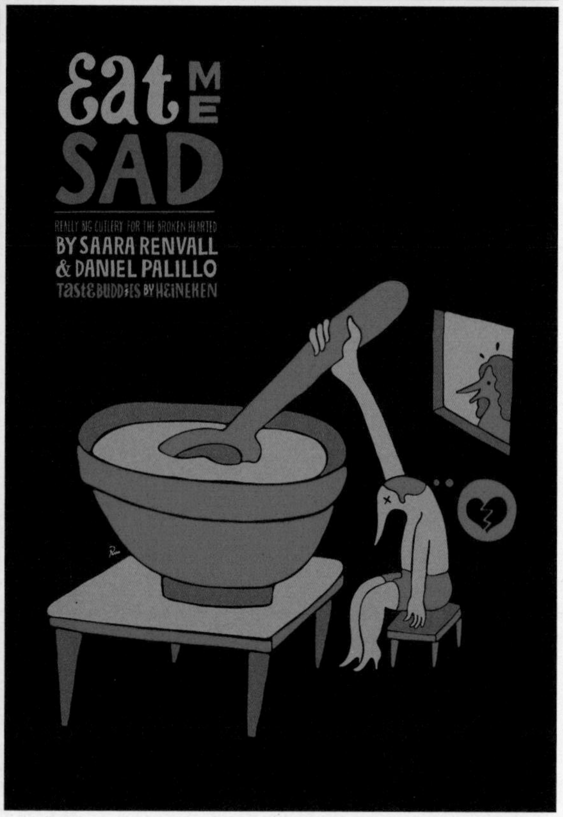
EAT ME SAD
REALLY BIG CUTLERY FOR THE BROKEN HEARTED
BY SAARA RENVALL & DANIEL PALILLO
TASTEBUDDIES BY HEINEKEN

Nomination in Illustration

Illustration for Press & Poster Advertising
Young & Rubicam Buenos Aires
for Kopelco

Apocalypse
A simple idea. Close to the apocalypse, a medieval painting shows us humanity just before doomsday.

Illustrator
Eduardo Torassa
Art Director
Demian Veleda
Copywriters
Matias Varise
Demian Veleda
Image Manipulator
Daniel Romanos
Print Producer
Fernando Costanza
Creative Director
Demian Veleda
Executive Creative Director
Martín Mercado
Advertising Agency
Young & Rubicam Buenos Aires
Account Handler
Gabriela Zecchi
Client
Kopelco
Brand
Tulipan

HURRY, THE WORLD IS COMING TO AN END.
tulipán
condoms

- **Nomination in Illustration**

Illustration for Press & Poster Advertising
Ogilvy & Mather Mumbai
for Perfetti Van Melle

Unbearably Sour
Mentos Sour Marbels is a unique product in the Indian market. While candies are generally associated with sweetness, Marbels broke the mould with their sour taste. The challenge was to get the nation interested in sour candies. Instead of competing with normal sweets, we decided to capitalise on the sour factor by exaggerating the effect Sour Marbels have on people. Our ads suggest that they are so unbearably sour that the only way you can escape them is by resorting to multiple suicides. Or should we say 'sourcides'?

Illustrator
Deelip Khomane
Art Director
Ashish Naik
Designer
Ashish Naik
Copywriters
Anurag Agnihotri
Anupama Sirsalewal
Typographer
Ashish Naik
Creative Directors
Anurag Agnihotri
Ashish Naik
National Creative Directors
Abhijit Avasthi
Rajiv Rao
Advertising Agency
Ogilvy & Mather Mumbai
Account Handler
Antara Suri
Marketing Manager
Namita Gupta
Client
Perfetti Van Melle
Brand
Mentos Sour Marbels

PERFETTI
mentos Marbels Sour
Unbearably Sour

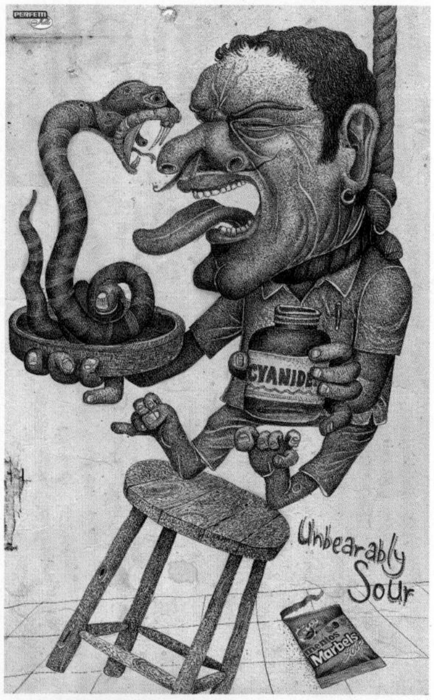
PERFETTI
CYANIDE
Unbearably Sour
mentos Marbels

Unbearably Sour
mentos Marbels

Nomination in Illustration

Illustration for Press & Poster Advertising
Mudra Communication
for Loving Hands Ministries India

Dwarf Depression
The brief was to convey to teenagers and young adults that depression can be combated with the right advice and guidance. To people suffering from depression, it can seem overwhelming, almost as if it is suffocating them or towering over them. This poster was put up in colleges and other places popular with young adults. It uses a graphic representation to convey the power of advice and counselling when it comes to dwarfing the problems of depression.

Illustrator
Shailesh Khandeparkar
Art Director
Shailesh Khandeparkar
Designer
Shailesh Khandeparkar
Copywriter
Shailesh Khandeparkar
Creative Directors
Bobby Pawar
KB Vinod
Advertising Agency
Mudra Communication
Brand Manager
Mera Baboji Rao
Client
Loving Hands Ministries India
Brand
Reach

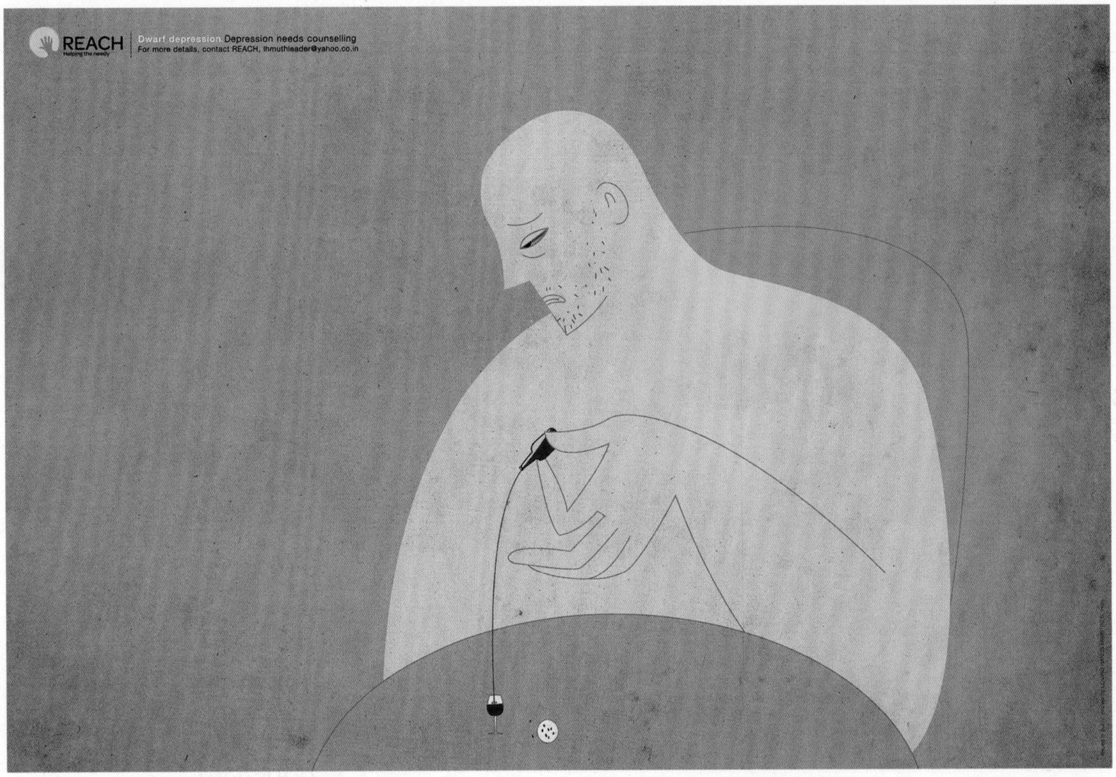
REACH
Helping the needy
Dwarf depression Depression needs counselling
For more details, contact REACH, lhmuthleader@yahoo.co.in

Nomination in Illustration

Illustration for Design
KING for ICA

ICA Good Life
ICA is Sweden's largest grocery store. Its health label, ICA Good Life, contains over 80 products. Our brief was to create a packaging concept and visualise healthy living in a way that would interest all customers, not just the health-conscious ones. We came up with a healthy, playful world with characters and situations relating to a healthy and active lifestyle, without being rigorous, boring or devoid of taste. With friendly, accessible copy, we created something far removed from the complicated technical information usually seen on healthier product lines.

Illustrator
Klas Fahlén
Art Director
Helena Bielke
Assistant Art Director
Eddie Åhgren
Copywriter
Hedvig Bruckner
Creative Director
Jonas Yrlid
Production Manager
Catharina Erlandsson
Advertising Agency
KING
Account Handler
Mattias Bohlin
Head of Account Management
Sunit Mehrotra
Brand Manager
Teddy Falkenek
Client
ICA

FULLKORN
COUSCOUS
FULLKORN
SPAGHETTI
FULLKORNS
FLINGOR
CASHEW
NÖTTER
LÅNGKORNIG
FULLKORNSRIS
FULLKORN
CONCHIGLIE
FULLKORN
GRAHAMSMJÖL
ÄGG

Illustration for Press & Poster Advertising
Ogilvy & Mather London for First Edition Restaurant

Grapes
First Edition has been operating as one of Canary Wharf's finest independent restaurants for 15 years. First Edition wanted a campaign to celebrate this anniversary and raise its profile among its target audience: working professionals within the wharf. A poster/outdoor campaign was designed to pique interest. On first observation the posters looked like ads for first editions of classic books. However they have been cleverly adapted to include illustrations of the restaurant and the restaurateur's name as the author's name.

Illustrator
Jon Morgan
Art Director
Mike Watson
Copywriter
Jon Morgan
Typographer
Steve O'Leary
Creative Director
Paul Smith
Design Group
Room Design
Advertising Agency
Ogilvy & Mather London
Account Handler
Christina Bell
Brand Manager
Pamela Schnieder
Client
First Edition Restaurant

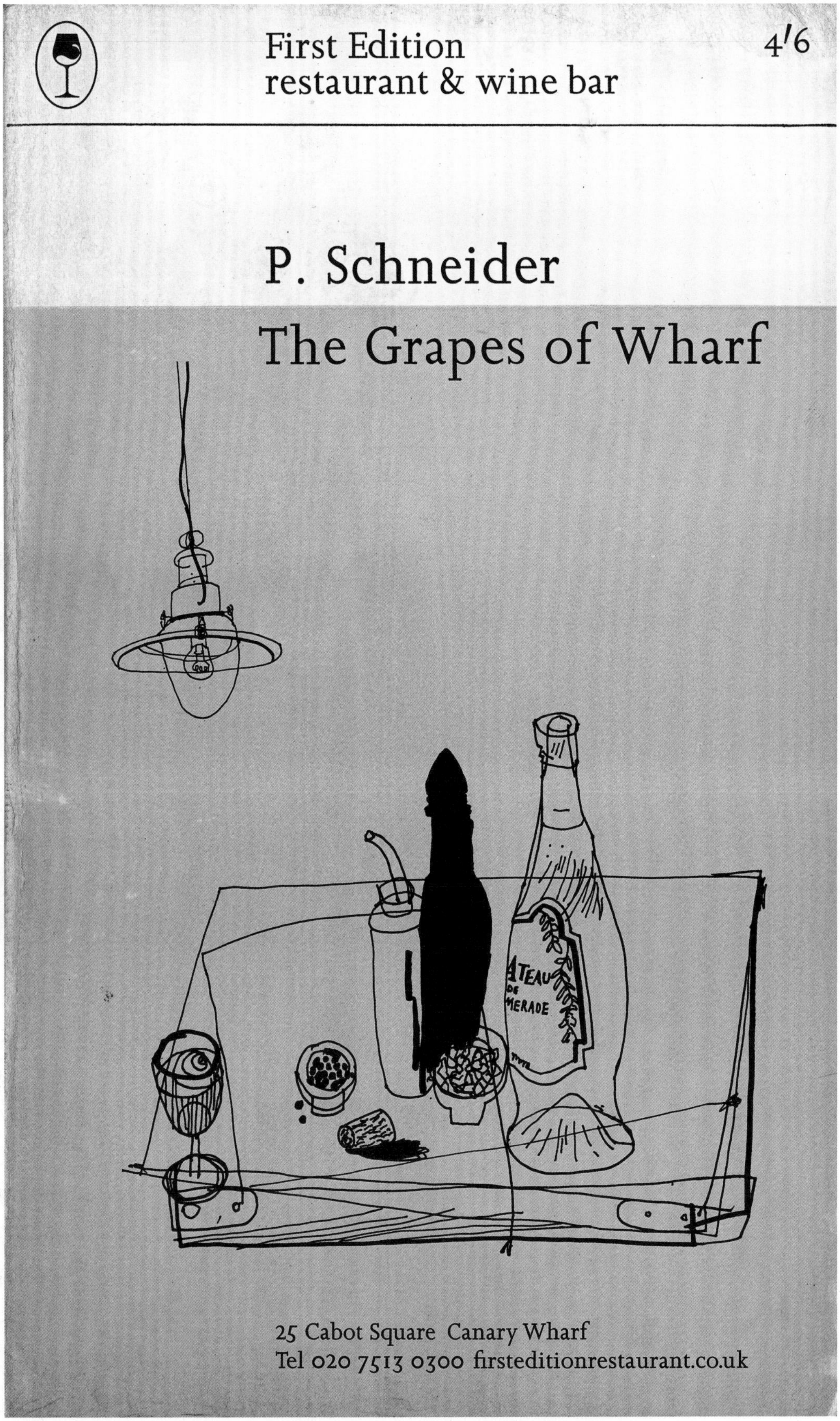
First Edition
restaurant & wine bar
4/6
P. Schneider
The Grapes of Wharf
25 Cabot Square Canary Wharf
Tel 020 7513 0300 firsteditionrestaurant.co.uk

Illustration for Press & Poster Advertising
Ogilvy & Mather Shanghai for Shirley Price Eye Care

Numerous-Sluggo / Tri-Monstro / Multi-Creepo
Gentle on your eyes. These are the words that you want to hear when choosing something to put in your eyes. There are many brands of eye drops to choose from in China, but none of them are as gentle as Shirley Price.

Illustrators
Deng Jing
Ke Weilin
Art Directors
Jordan Dong
Kevin Lee
Zhang Lei
Kelvin Leong
Robin Wu
Minsheng Zhang
Copywriters
Weina Ha
Kit Ong
Print Producer
Gerald Lee
Creative Directors
Kevin Lee
Kelvin Leong
Kit Ong
Retouching
MEETHEPEOPLE
Advertising Agency
Ogilvy & Mather Shanghai
Client
Shirley Price Eye Care

Be CAREFUL
You Only
HAVE TWO
ShirleyPrice
EYE CARE

Be CAREFUL
You Only
HAVE TWO

Be CAREFUL
You Only
HAVE TWO

Illustration for Press & Poster Advertising
DDB UK for Volkswagen Fleet

Sistine Chapel / Acropolis / Hampton Court
The Passat is an important car in the fleet market; Volkswagen wanted to build anticipation ahead of the launch of the new Passat in January. Our solution was a campaign communicating that the Passat would be 'worth the wait'. It drew tongue-in-cheek parallels with other items which, historically, have been worth waiting for: painting the Sistine Chapel, building the Acropolis, and the growth of Hampton Court Maze. The illustrative style used gave us standout in the text-heavy, serious publications aimed at fleet managers and financial directors, and, we hope, raised a smile.

Illustrator
SHOUT
Art Director
Daniel Seager
Copywriter
Steve Hall
Head of Art
Grant Parker
Executive Creative Director
Jeremy Craigen
Advertising Agency
DDB UK
Project Manager
Monika Andexlinger
Planner
Ami Smith
Account Manager
Laura Balfour
Account Director
Amanda Griffiths
Art Buyer
Helen Parker
Client Communications Manager
Josie Taylor
Client
Volkswagen Fleet
Brand
Passat

Some things are worth waiting for.
Fleet Services

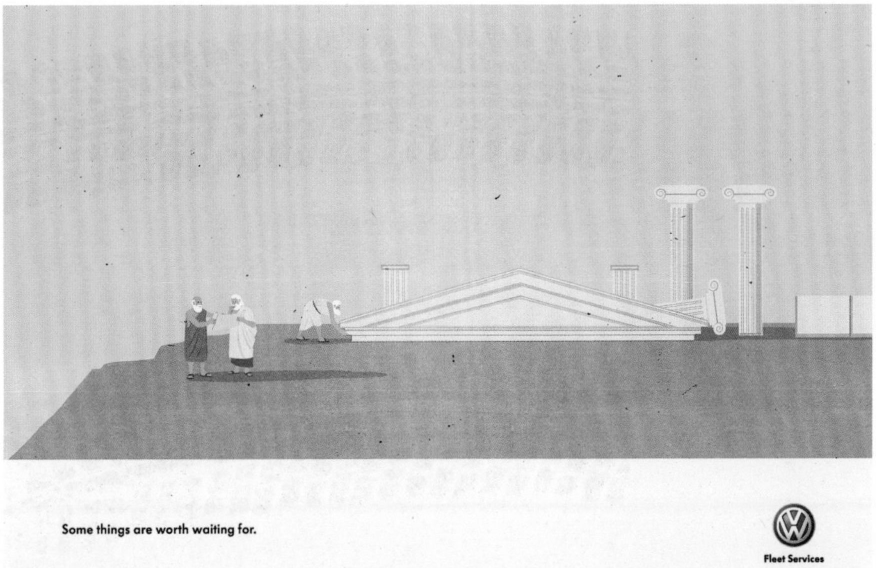
Some things are worth waiting for.
Fleet Services

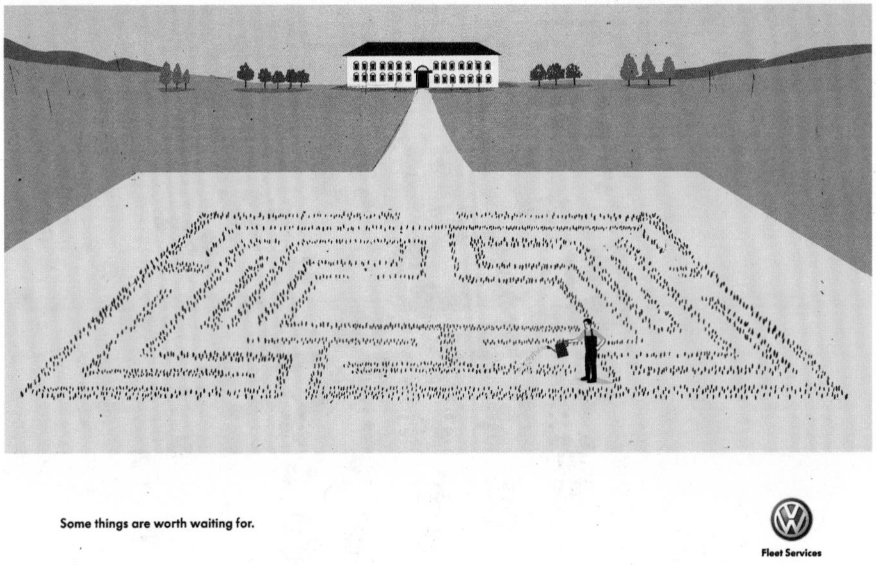
Some things are worth waiting for.
Fleet Services

Illustration for Press & Poster Advertising
Leo Burnett Hong Kong
for Greenpeace

Parallel Consequences Campaign
Cars are a major source of climate-warming greenhouse gases. As the Earth gets hotter, extreme weather events will become more common, and threaten lives around the world. Every year, Greenpeace promotes Car Free Day, trying to change people's behaviour by getting them to stop driving for a day. To help people realise that driving and climate change go hand in hand, we used a visual consisting of parallel tyre tracks. In one, we show a story of the fun that driving can bring. In the other, we show the death and destruction caused by the resulting climate change.

Illustrator
Matt Johnstone
Art Directors
Kenny Ip
Nicky Sun
Designers
Matt Johnstone
Nicky Sun
Copywriters
Joey Chung
Wen Louie
Creative Directors
Brian Ma
Alfred Wong
Executive Creative Director
Connie Lo
Advertising Agency
Leo Burnett Hong Kong
Account Handler
Sherona Mak
Client
Greenpeace
Brand
Car Free Day

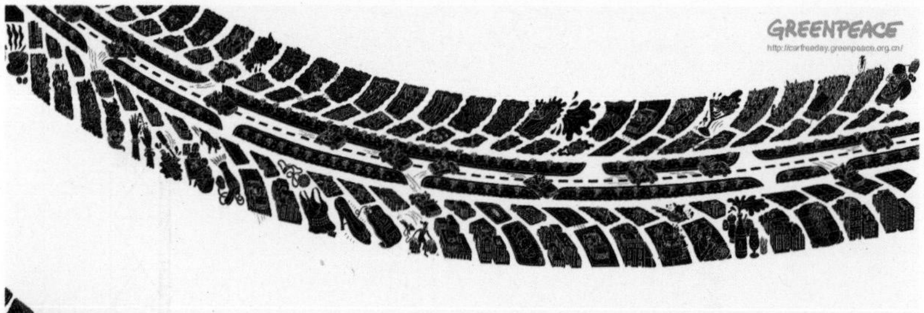
GREENPEACE
http://carfreeday.greenpeace.org.cn/

一路駕駛，同時一路摧毀。每天，私家車排放二氧化碳高達2992噸，加劇氣候暖化，導致乾旱
9.22支持無車日

GREENPEACE
http://carfreeday.greenpeace.org.cn/

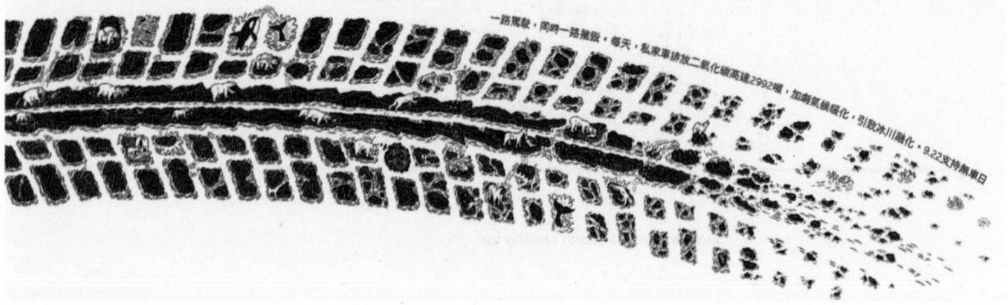
一路駕駛，同時一路摧毀。每天，私家車排放二氧化碳高達2992噸，加劇氣候暖化，引致冰川融化。9.22支持無車日

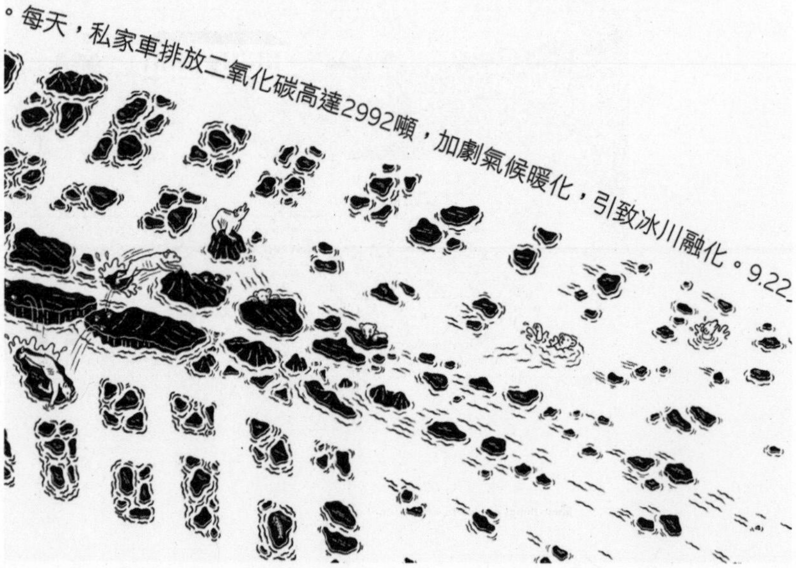
。每天，私家車排放二氧化碳高達2992噸，加劇氣候暖化，引致冰川融化。9.22

Illustration for Press & Poster Advertising
Ogilvy Malaysia for Pet World Marketing

Salmon Odyssey / Tuna Talisman
ProDiet is a range of cat food that is never stingy with its ingredients. It settles for nothing less than the best and purest seafood. A series of posters illustrates the colourful but tragic lives of sea creatures and dramatises ProDiet's commitment that nothing comes between it and getting the best seafood for your cat. These posters were placed in waiting lounges at veterinary clinics, where people could enjoy looking at them and consider purchasing ProDiet.

Illustrator
Jay Lee
Illustration
Sixth Creation
Art Directors
Kit Chen
Tan Chee Keong
Jarrod Reginald
Gavin Simpson
Copywriters
Adam Chan
Michelle Lim
Paul Lim
Darren Winter
Creative Directors
Tan Chee Keong
Gavin Simpson
Group Executive Creative Director
Gavin Simpson
Advertising Agency
Ogilvy Malaysia
Marketing Manager
Lai Kuan
Client
Pet World Marketing
Brand
ProDiet

Salmon Odyssey
PHOOM!
IT'S CAT FOOD!
-END OF STORY-
ProDiet
100% SALMON

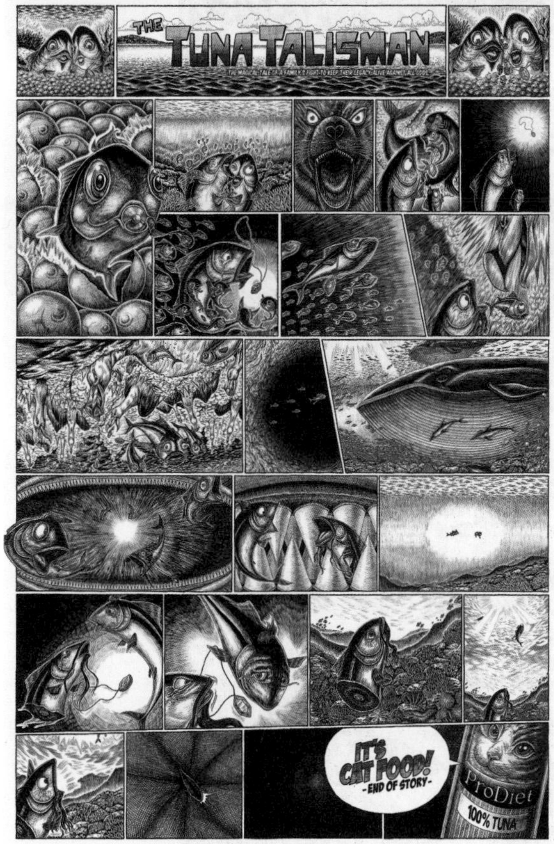
THE TUNA TALISMAN
IT'S CAT FOOD!
-END OF STORY-
ProDiet
100% TUNA

Illustration for Press & Poster Advertising
Think3 Group for Qiaodan Sports

Hell
Qiaodan Sports was popular in China, but facing a crisis of brand aging. In 2010, the brand was badly in need of reshaping. After investigation, we discovered the relationship between our brand belief and the spirit of sport. So we initiated a campaign of advertising with the theme 'Beyond yourself'. The advertising illustrated the simultaneously arduous and exhilarating experience of consumers challenging and recreating themselves. The campaign was released on outdoor and print media in cities in China; it successfully struck a chord with customers and built efficient communication between them and the brand.

Illustrator
Yu Chen
Art Director
Feng Liu
Designer
Oliver Yang
Copywriter
Renato Zhao
Print Producer
Yan Xin
Creative Director
Perry Zheng
Advertising Agency
Think3 Group
Account Handlers
Dong Huilai
Sherry Luo
Stone Yang
Brand Manager
Xiaoyan Hu
Client
Qiaodan Sports

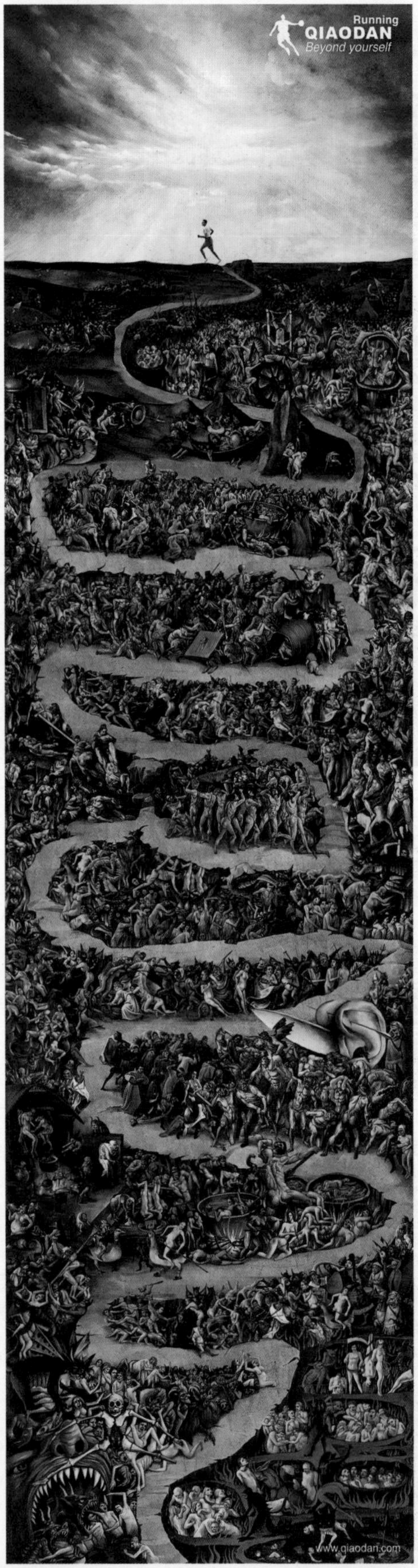
Running
QIAODAN
Beyond yourself
www.qiaodan.com

Illustration for Press & Poster Advertising
Team Saatchi for the Ethnic Multicultural Media Academy (EMMA) Trust

Keep the Far Right, Right Out
To combat growing support for racist, far right parties in the UK, we created a campaign promoting multicultural Britain, encouraging people to think twice about whom to vote for in the upcoming General Election. Posters ran in Barking, where the British National Party was gathering support and was expected to win its first seat in Parliament. Executions consisted of graphic illustrations intended to create the look of modern day propaganda posters. Through the use of 'negative' space, viewers saw graphic symbols of fascism emerge from innocent election imagery. We helped to inflict a humiliating defeat on the BNP on election night.

Illustrator
Noma Bar
Art Director
Ajab Samrai
Designers
Roger Kennedy
Ajab Samrai
Copywriters
David Fowle
John Pallant
Ajab Samrai
Typographer
Roger Kennedy
Creative Director
Ajab Samrai
Advertising Agency
Team Saatchi
Account Handlers
Sophie Hooper
Gemma Morris
Tom Rudge
Brand Manager
Bobby Syed
Client
Ethnic Multicultural Media Academy (EMMA) Trust

THE BALLOT BOX HIDES
AN UGLY FACE. BE CAREFUL WHO
YOU VOTE FOR ON MAY 6th.
Keep the far right, right out. www.emmatrust.com

BE CAREFUL
WHO'S CANVASSING
FOR YOUR
VOTE ON MAY 6th.
Keep the far right, right out. www.emmatrust.com

Illustration for Press & Poster Advertising
DDB Singapore
for the Breast Cancer Foundation

Pimple
Each year, over 280 Singaporean women succumb to breast cancer. In the majority of cases, the tragedy could have been avoided with early detection. Superficial things like spa treatments take approximately 45 minutes, while mammograms take just 20 minutes. To encourage women to get their breasts screened and to promote early detection, we challenged them to rethink their priorities. What is more deserving of your time: a pimple or breast cancer? We brought this insight to life with a novel body painting technique.

Illustrator
Andy Yang
Art Directors
Andrea Kuo
Thomas Yang
Copywriters
Joji Jacob
Khairul Mondzi
Photographer
Allan Ng
Typographer
Andrea Kuo
Creative Directors
Joji Jacob
Neil Johnson
Thomas Yang
Advertising Agency
DDB Singapore
Image Manipulation
Digitalist
Account Handlers
Rowena Bhagchandani
Ng Ling Kai
Dominic Lee
Brand Manager
Elaine Tan
Client
Breast Cancer Foundation

Are you obsessed with the right things?
When we last checked, pimples weren't life-threatening at all. But breast cancer surely was. The fatal disease affects at least 280 Singaporean women each year. That's 280 valuable lives that could have been saved with a simple 30-minute screening. Please get your breasts examined today.
BREAST CANCER FOUNDATION
www.bcf.org.sg

Illustration for Press & Poster Advertising
Young & Rubicam Paris for the Surfrider Foundation Europe

Marine Animals
In 2010, the Surfrider Foundation launched the petition 'notonourbeaches.com'. With this campaign, it illustrated the devastating impact our waste can have on aquatic life.

Illustrator
John Paul Thurlow
Art Director
Gregory Jeanjacquot
Copywriter
Nicolas Gerard
Creative Directors
Jorge Carreno
Robin De Lestrade
Advertising Agency
Young & Rubicam Paris
Account Handler
Aure Tessandier
Brand Manager
Stephane Latxague
Client
Surfrider Foundation Europe

EACH YEAR,
MILLIONS OF MARINE ANIMALS
ARE KILLED BY OUR RUBBISH.
SIGN THE PETITION AGAINST MARINE DEBRIS
AT NOTONOURBEACHES.COM

EACH YEAR,
MILLIONS OF MARINE ANIMALS
ARE KILLED BY OUR RUBBISH.
SIGN THE PETITION AGAINST MARINE DEBRIS
AT NOTONOURBEACHES.COM

EACH YEAR,
MILLIONS OF MARINE ANIMALS
ARE KILLED BY OUR RUBBISH.
SIGN THE PETITION AGAINST MARINE DEBRIS
AT NOTONOURBEACHES.COM

Illustration for Press
& Poster Advertising
AlmapBBDO for Bayer

Beware of the Evil Food
This campaign demonstrates that a heavy meal can be harmful when not properly digested. We employed a playful approach to advertise Alka-Seltzer as an effective solution against indigestion.

Illustrator
Marco Patini Furtado
Art Directors
Denis Peralta
Guilherme Sakosigue
Copywriter
André Kassu
Typographer
José Roberto Bezerra
Creative Director
Luiz Sanches
Advertising Agency
AlmapBBDO
Marketing Manager
Luiza Dias
Client
Bayer
Brand
Alka-Seltzer

BEWARE OF THE EVIL FOOD.

BEWARE OF THE EVIL FOOD.

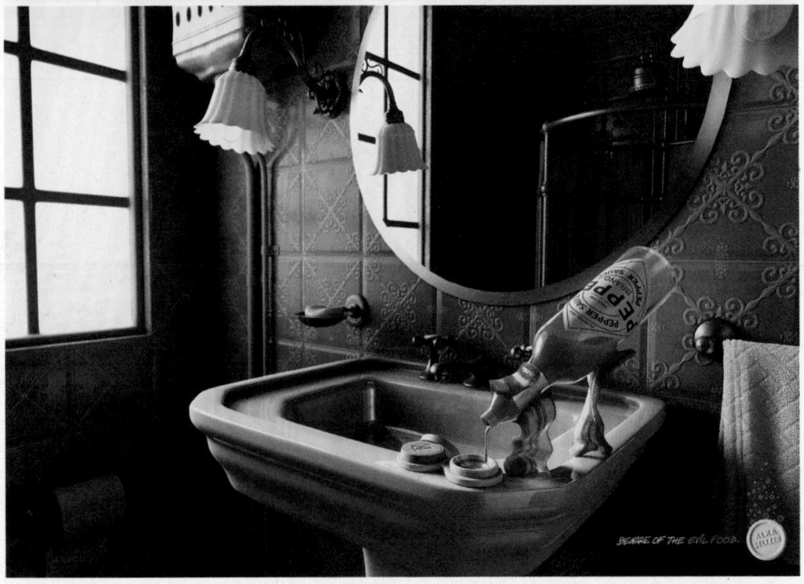
BEWARE OF THE EVIL FOOD.

Illustration for Press
& Poster Advertising
Y&R New York for
Colgate-Palmolive

2 Minutes
Our mission was to make brushing their teeth for two minutes a part of a child's daily routine. We came up with the concept that brushing for two minutes is healthy for everyone.

Illustrator
Andrey Gordeev
Art Director
Alexander Nowak
Copywriter
Feliks Richter
Typographer
Jessica Hische
Retoucher
Raul Pardo
Creative Directors
Icaro Doria
Menno Kluin
Guillermo Vega
Executive Creative Directors
Ian Reichenthal
Scott Vitrone
Global Creative Director
Meg Rogers
Advertising Agency
Y&R New York
Art Buyer
Helen O'Neill
Client Consumer Marketing Director
Thais Bruce
Client
Colgate-Palmolive
Brand
Colgate

BRUSHING FOR 2 MINUTES
WILL BE
HEALTHY
FOR
EVERYONE
Colgate

BRUSHING FOR 2 MINUTES
WILL BE
HEALTHY
FOR
EVERYONE
Colgate

BRUSHING FOR 2 MINUTES
WILL BE
HEALTHY
FOR
EVERYONE
Colgate

Illustration for Press
& Poster Advertising
Y&R New York for VH1

**The Wonderful
World of VH1**
The wonderful world of television network VH1 is music and culture in a blender. The more extreme the artist becomes, the more popular they are.

Illustrator
Eamo
Art Director
Alexander Nowak
Designer
Mihail Aleksandrov
Copywriter
Feliks Richter
Typographer
Mihail Aleksandrov
Creative Directors
Icaro Doria
Menno Kluin
**Executive Creative
Directors**
Ian Reichenthal
Guillermo Vega
Scott Vitrone
Advertising Agency
Y&R New York
Art Buyers
Bill Gastinger
Helen O'Neill
Client Creative Director
Juan Frontini
Client
VH1

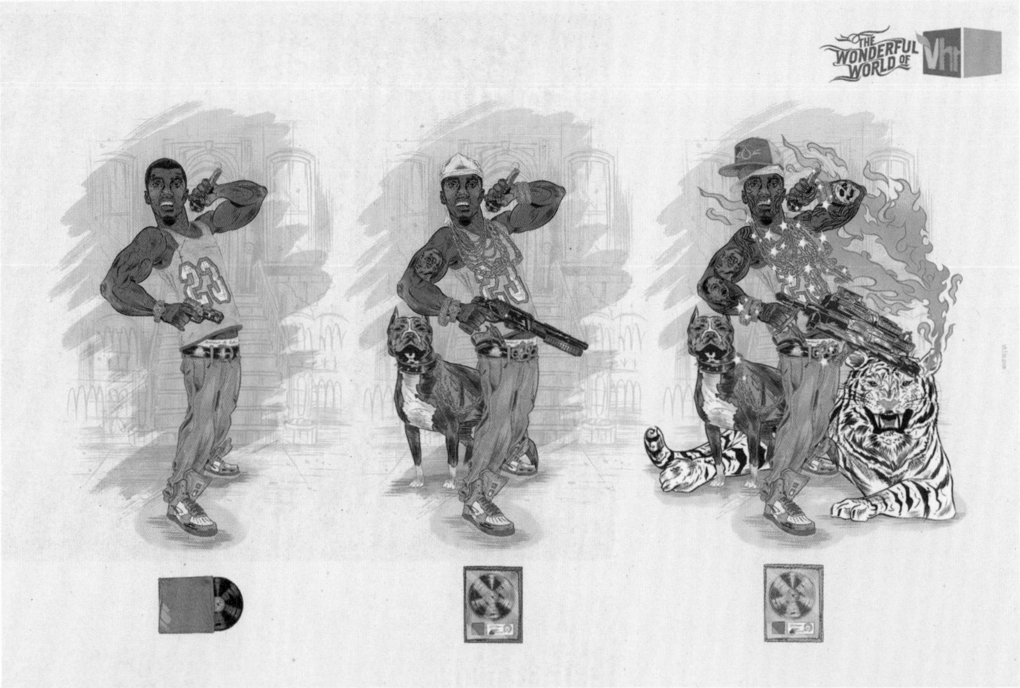
THE WONDERFUL WORLD OF VH1

THE WONDERFUL WORLD OF VH1
MOM
DAD
BROTHER
MOM
SISTER

THE WONDERFUL WORLD OF VH1

THE WONDERFUL WORLD OF VH1

Illustration for Press
& Poster Advertising
Kinetic Singapore for
www.alzheimersdisease.sg

Marriage / Celebrations / Childhood / Motherhood
Alzheimer's disease robs victims of all that matters to them. Due to the nature of the disease, there is no stopping it from taking indiscriminately, and victims are helpless against it. There are few ways victims can safeguard themselves against the disease, let alone preserve their precious memories.

Illustrator
Ng Xiao Yan
Art Directors
Gian Jonathan
Pann Lim
Ng Xiao Yan
Designer
Gian Jonathan
Copywriter
Eugene Tan
Creative Director
Pann Lim
Advertising Agency
Kinetic Singapore
Client
www.alzheimersdisease.sg

Alzheimer's Disease Robs.
For volunteer work or donations, visit www.alzheimersdisease.sg

Alzheimer's Disease Robs.
For volunteer work or donations, visit www.alzheimersdisease.sg

Alzheimer's Disease Robs.
For volunteer work or donations, visit www.alzheimersdisease.sg

Alzheimer's Disease Robs.
For volunteer work or donations, visit www.alzheimersdisease.sg

Illustration for Press & Poster Advertising
Kinetic Singapore for Mentholatum Singapore

Wrestle / Doctor / Wedding / Prison
A pimple-ridden face is the curse of many people, especially youngsters. It causes them to be socially awkward and to shy away from day-to-day encounters and even important occasions. They need help, and Oxy Maximum Strength is here to turn things around for them.

Illustrator
Linus Chen
Art Directors
Linus Chen
Pann Lim
Designer
Linus Chen
Creative Director
Pann Lim
Advertising Agency
Kinetic Singapore
Client
Mentholatum Singapore
Brand
Oxy

Maximum Strength
OXY10

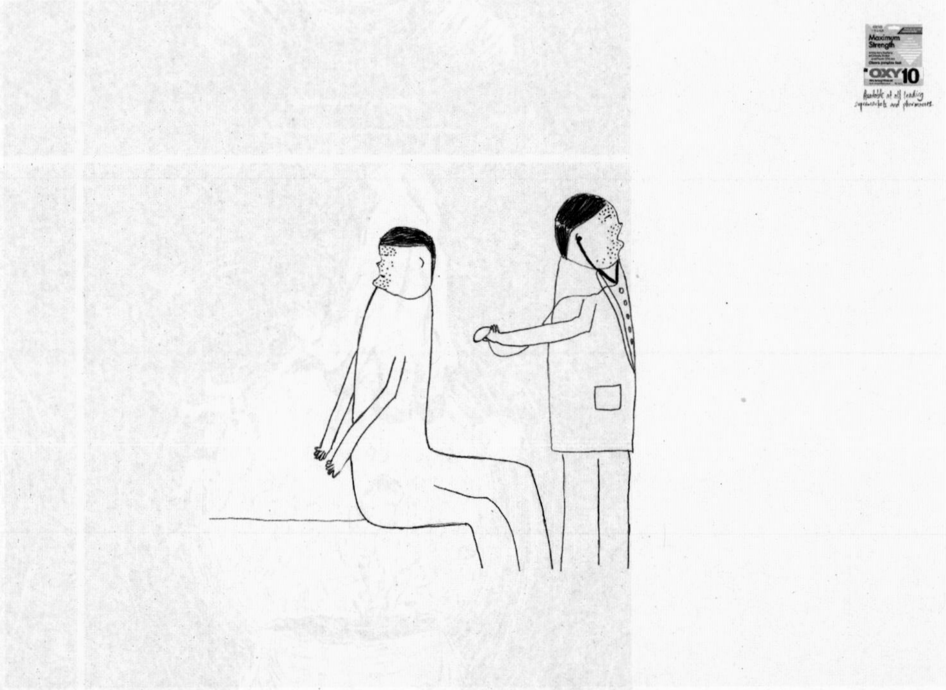
Maximum Strength
OXY10

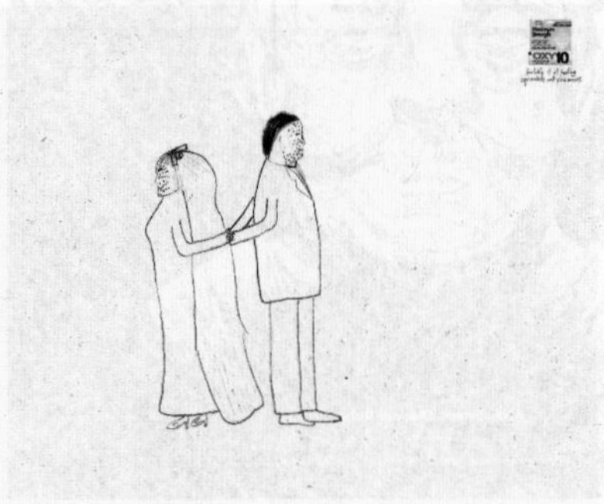

Illustration for Press & Poster Advertising
Peppermill Berlin for BUND (Friends of the Earth Germany)

Time Up, Life Over
Friends of the Earth Germany (BUND) asked us to raise awareness of the extinction crisis facing many species. The key message was that man-made climate catastrophes and environmental disasters, shrinking wildlife habitats, and unscrupulous hunting were leading to many endangered species running out of time. The challenge was to illustrate this dramatic situation in an easily understandable yet arresting and emotional way.

Illustration
Peppermill Berlin
Art Directors
Rene Gebhardt
Bjoern Kernspeckt
Ksenia Slavcheva
Graphic Designer
Sebastian Frese
Creative Directors
Martin Pross
Mathias Rebmann
Florian Schwalme
Matthias Spaetgens
Advertising Agency
Scholz & Friends Berlin
Account Handlers
Susanne Kieck
Christine Scharney
Brand Manager
Mark Hoerstermann
Marketing Manager
Norbert Franck
Client
BUND (Friends of the Earth Germany)

EVERY 60 SECONDS A SPECIES DIES OUT.
EACH MINUTE COUNTS, EACH DONATION HELPS: BUND.NET
BUND
FRIENDS OF THE EARTH

EVERY 60 SECONDS A SPECIES DIES OUT.
EACH MINUTE COUNTS, EACH DONATION HELPS: BUND.NET
BUND
FRIENDS OF THE EARTH

EVERY 60 SECONDS A SPECIES DIES OUT.
EACH MINUTE COUNTS, EACH DONATION HELPS: BUND.NET
BUND
FRIENDS OF THE EARTH

Illustration for Press & Poster Advertising
Leo Burnett Manila
for The Coca-Cola Export Corporation

Night Watchman
We drew inspiration from apocalyptic illustrations of good versus the myriad forces of evil. In this ad, a night watchman is about to patrol a village alley. He faces an assortment of characters: the drunks, the thieves, the prostitutes, the gamblers, the electricity pilferers, the cranky vendor, and even the rabid stray dog. Not to worry, he's armed with Samurai.

Illustrator
Rey Macutay
Art Directors
Angela Arches
Mike dela Cuesta
Mon Pineda
Copywriters
Sheila dela Cuesta
Therese Endriga
Nino Gupana
Raoul Panes
Creative Directors
Mike dela Cuesta
Sheila dela Cuesta
Executive Creative Director
Raoul Panes
Image Manipulator
Robert Perez
Advertising Agency
Leo Burnett Manila
Account Handlers
Cathy Nicolay
Ben Reyes
Kandice Ting
Client
The Coca-Cola Export Corporation
Brand
Samurai

Illustration for Press & Poster Advertising
Leo Burnett Manila
for The Coca-Cola Export Corporation

Cook
We drew inspiration from apocalyptic illustrations of good versus the myriad forces of evil. In this ad, a lone cook faces an army of hungry and impatient customers. Not to worry, he's armed with Samurai.

Illustrator
Joel Cotejar
Art Directors
Angela Arches
Mike dela Cuesta
Dante Dizon
Mon Pineda
Copywriters
Sheila dela Cuesta
Therese Endriga
Nino Gupana
Raoul Panes
Creative Directors
Mike dela Cuesta
Sheila dela Cuesta
Dante Dizon
Executive Creative Director
Raoul Panes
Image Manipulator
Robert Perez
Advertising Agency
Leo Burnett Manila
Account Handlers
Cathy Nicolay
Ben Reyes
Kandice Ting
Client
The Coca-Cola Export Corporation
Brand
Samurai

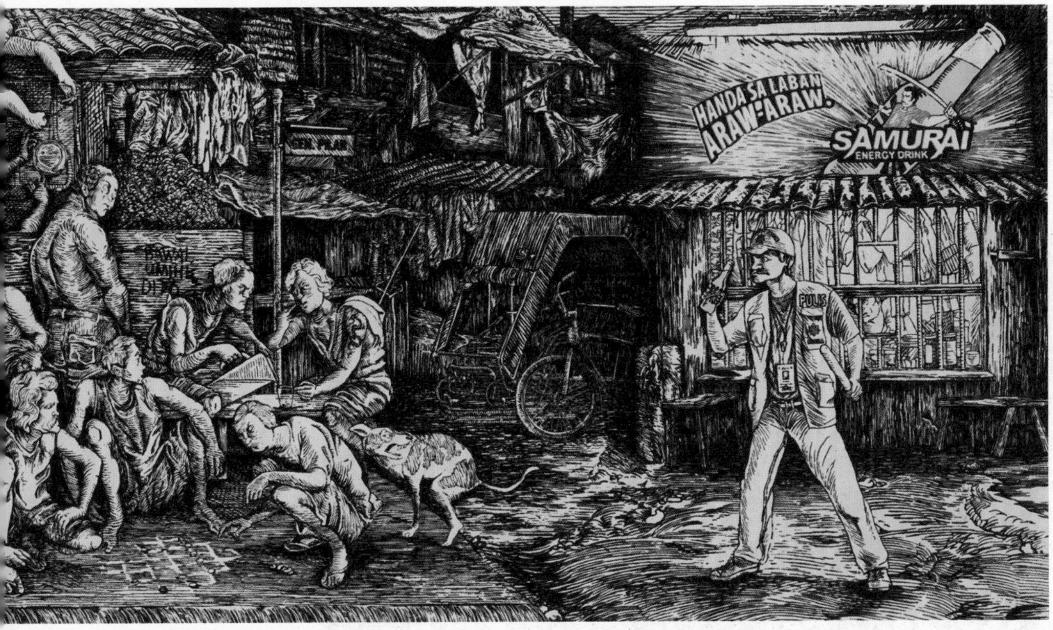
HANDA SA LABAN
ARAW-ARAW.
SAMURAI
ENERGY DRINK

HANDA SA LABAN
ARAW-ARAW.
SAMURAI
ENERGY DRINK

Illustration for Press & Poster Advertising
Taproot India for Transasia Papers

Colours of India
Conqueror Paper, a premium paper manufacturing brand, was celebrating its first decade in India. It wanted to take the opportunity to pay tribute to a culture and market that had supported it all these years. Bridging the core category – all forms of base paper – and the vibrant, colourful country called India, we created an incredible though painstaking visual illustration that involved hundreds of rolled-up mini paper scrolls embedded on a flat surface. The size and colour of each scroll combined to create a breathtaking, colourful mosaic of iconic Indian characters: the Kathakali dancer, the royal Rajput and the spiritual guru.

Illustrator
Anant Nanaware
Art Director
Santosh Padhi
Copywriter
Agnello Dias
Photographer
Amol Jadhav
Creative Director
Santosh Padhi
Advertising Agency
Taproot India
Account Handler
Manan Mehta
Brand Manager
Rajesh Kejriwal
Client
Transasia Papers
Brand
Conqueror Paper

CELEBRATING
A DECADE IN THE
LAND OF
A MILLION HUES
conqueror
paper

CELEBRATING
A DECADE IN THE
LAND OF
A MILLION HUES
conqueror
paper

CELEBRATING
A DECADE IN THE
LAND OF
A MILLION HUES
conqueror
paper

Illustration for Design
FHV BBDO for
ReclameArsenaal

Advertisement Classics – Reclame Klassiekers
These posters promoted an exhibition of classic Dutch advertising held by ReclameArsenaal, a foundation curating the Netherlands' advertising heritage. How do you capture the rich history of Dutch advertising in a single uniform campaign? With this challenge in mind, we developed a concept that became a tribute to advertising classics in Dutch history. The campaign we developed addressed the collective memory of a nation, taking you back to the time when, for instance, women still sat on the hoods of cars. The art direction was inspired by traditional cultural museum posters, creating a healthy mix between advertising and art. Because advertising is worth exhibiting!

Illustrator
Christian Borstlap
Art Director
Christian Borstlap
Copywriter
André Dammers
Advertising Agency
FHV BBDO
Client Managing Director
Jan Knaap
Client
ReclameArsenaal

TOEN
ZWANEN
NOG
STRAAL
MOTOREN
HADDEN
reclameArsenaal presenteert
reclameklassiekers.nl
100 JAAR
Reclame
Klassiekers
Beurs van Berlage
18-12-10 t/m 27-02-11
Amsterdam

Toen
Olifanten
nog
jongetjes
Sloegen
reclameArsenaal presenteert
reclameklassiekers.nl
100 JAAR
Reclame
Klassiekers
Beurs van Berlage
18-12-10 t/m 27-02-11
Amsterdam

Toen
Vrouwen
nog op de
Motorkap
lagen
reclameArsenaal presenteert
reclameklassiekers.nl
100 JAAR
Reclame
Klassiekers
Beurs van Berlage
18-12-10 t/m 27-02-11
Amsterdam

reclameArsenaal presenteert
reclameklassiekers.nl
100 JAAR
Reclame
Klassiekers
Beurs van Berlage
18-12-10 t/m 27-02-11
Amsterdam
TOEN
MANNEN
OP
PAARDEN
NOG
ROOKTEN

Illustration for Design
Visual Arts Press
for the School
of Visual Arts

David Sandlin
Subway Posters
The School of Visual Arts' now iconic posters have been serving as an advertising and recruiting vehicle for the college since the 1950s. Seen by millions of commuters in the NYC subway system, past posters have been designed by distinguished illustrators and designers including Milton Glaser, Paula Scher, George Tscherny and James Victore. The posters have come to represent the collective history, innovation and talent of SVA. The 2010 posters were designed by David Sandlin, renowned painter, printmaker and cartoonist who has published and exhibited widely both in Europe and the United States.

Illustrator
David Sandlin
Art Director
Michael J Walsh
Creative Director
Anthony P Rhodes
Design Group
Visual Arts Press
Client
School of Visual Arts

SVA
SCHOOL of VISUAL ARTS
WWW. SVA.EDU
NEWS

DEEPER... DEEPER... INTO THE DARK NIGHT
SEARCHING FOR...
GAS
SOMETHING THERE... IN THE MIST...
SVA SCHOOL of VISUAL ARTS
WWW.SVA.EDU

SVA SCHOOL of VISUAL ARTS
WWW.SVA.EDU
SO... SO... CLOSE...
YES... YES... AT LAST... LONG LAST...
GAS
I THINK... I CAN... MAKE IT
SVA

Illustration for Design
Ogilvy Shanghai for the Public Health Bureau of Fengxian, Shanghai

The 70-metre Spit
Spitting is a national habit in China. The Public Health Bureau of the Fengxian district in Shanghai wanted an anti-spitting public awareness campaign targeting migrant workers in Shanghai. Most migrant workers have learnt that sputum in spit contains germs that spread diseases. But many do not know that the wind also helps to carry germs that are in the spray of the spit further away. According to the bureau, germs can spread to as far as 70 metres depending on wind conditions. How do we make workers see this? The solution is simple: make the germs visible.

Illustrators
Huang Haibo
Nial O'Connor
Bao Siwen
Xu Xueyong
Hui Yao
Minsheng Zhang
Art Directors
Deng Hua
Xiao Kun
Kevin Lee
Zhang Lei
Kelvin Leong
Robin Wu
Copywriters
Adams Fan
Kit Ong
Executive Creative Director
Kevin Lee
Producers
Hon Foong
Aywei Wong
Chye Yee
Advertising Agency
Ogilvy Shanghai
Client
Public Health Bureau of Fengxian, Shanghai

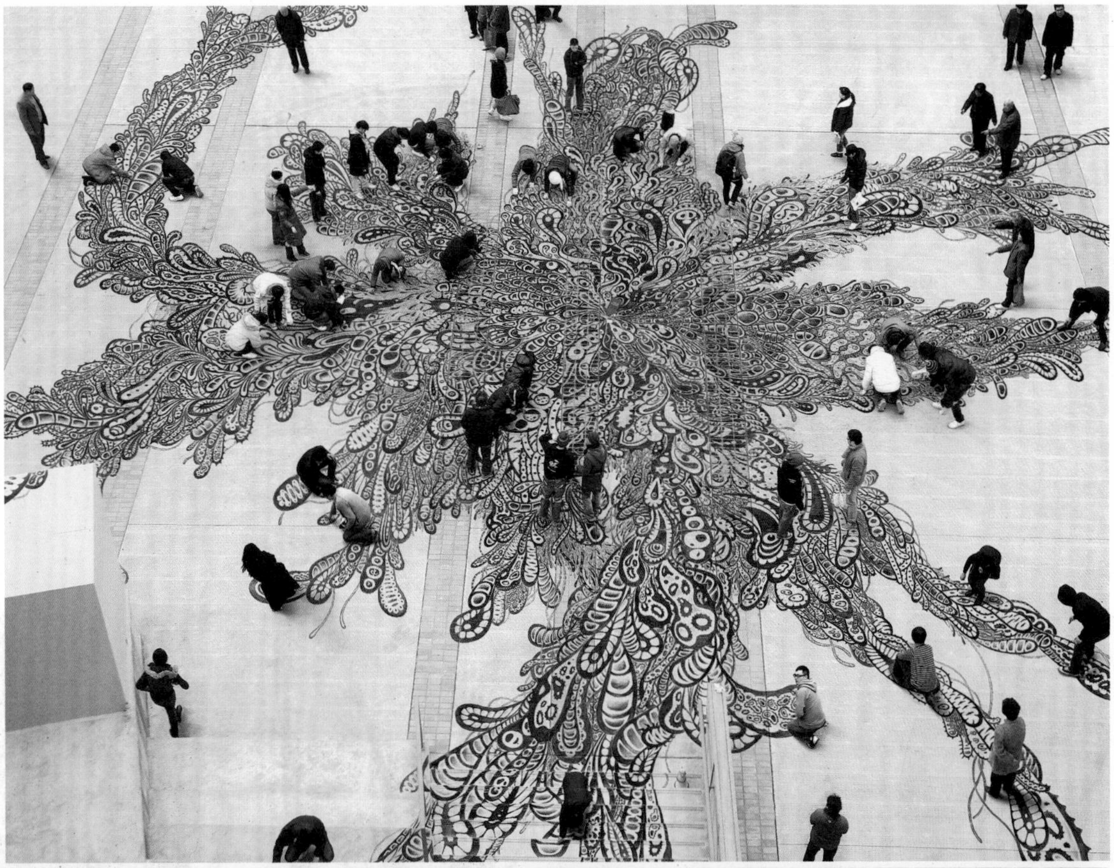

一口痰的危害
可以达到70米
痰液中的病原体
可以通过空气传播。
为他人健康，
请不要随地吐痰。

Illustration for Design
WORK

WERK No.18: Keiichi Tanaami, Psychedelic Visual Master
Keiichi Tanaami is a Japanese artist and graphic designer whose work has transcended various art mediums. His radical artistic creations, which are influenced by his dreams and memories, have often been the source of inspiration for young contemporary artists. WERK No.18 visually documents his psychedelic visions with more than 200 illustrations from his personal collection. The cover of each issue is hand coloured with different forms of powdered pigment such as chalk, crayon, granite and pastel, emulating Keiichi Tanaami's colouring methods.

Illustrator
Keiichi Tanaami
Designers
Sharon Goh
Joanne Lim
Design Director
Theseus Chan
Design Group
WORK
Printing & Construction
alsoDominie
Account Handler
Taka Nakanishi
Client
WORK
Brand
WERK

CAUTION:
WARNING
WERK No.18:
KEIICHI
TANAAMI
PSYCHEDELIC VISUAL MASTER
336 pages, Colour,
approx 220mm × 305mm
Edition: 1000 copies

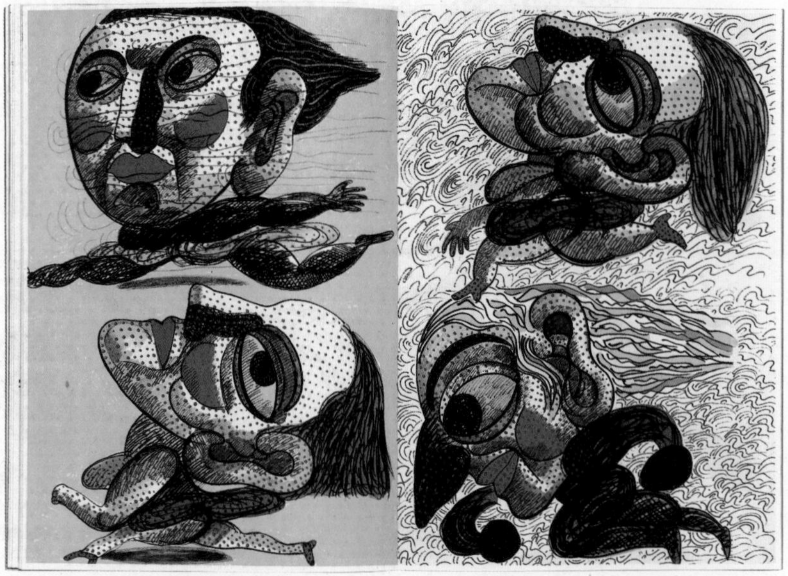

Illustration for Design
Bruketa&Zinic OM
for the Igepa Group

Spam Jam
The agency Bruketa&Zinic OM is speaking about spam in an anti-spam manner. 'Spam Jam' is the limited edition designers' picture book published by Igepa. The book, printed on expensive paper with various luxury finishing and hand-drawn illustrations, speaks about the cheapest, most aggressive, vulgar and usually fake means of human communication.

Illustrator
Nebojsa Cvetkovic
Art Director
Nebojsa Cvetkovic
Designer
Nebojsa Cvetkovic
Image Manipulator
Marko Ostrez
Print Producer
Marko Stritof
Creative Directors
Davor Bruketa
Nikola Zinic
Advertising Agency
Bruketa&Zinic OM
Account Handler
Ana Sutic
Marketing Manager
Mirna Despot
Client
Igepa Group

Spam Jam
Inbox
Picture Book

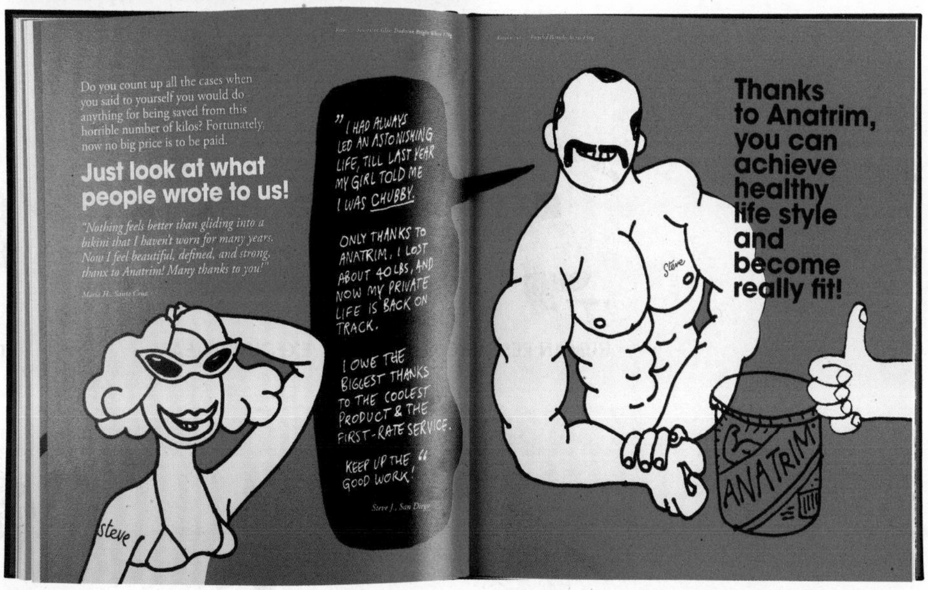
Do you count up all the cases when you said to yourself you would do anything for being saved from this horrible number of kilos? Fortunately, now no big price is to be paid.
Just look at what people wrote to us!
"Nothing feels better than gliding into a bikini that I haven't worn for many years. Now I feel beautiful, defined, and strong, thanx to Anatrim! Many thanks to you!"
" I HAD ALWAYS LED AN ASTONISHING LIFE, TILL LAST YEAR MY GIRL TOLD ME I WAS CHUBBY.
ONLY THANKS TO ANATRIM, I LOST ABOUT 40 LBS, AND NOW MY PRIVATE LIFE IS BACK ON TRACK.
I OWE THE BIGGEST THANKS TO THE COOLEST PRODUCT & THE FIRST-RATE SERVICE.
KEEP UP THE GOOD WORK! "
Steve J., San Diego
Thanks to Anatrim, you can achieve healthy life style and become really fit!
ANATRIM

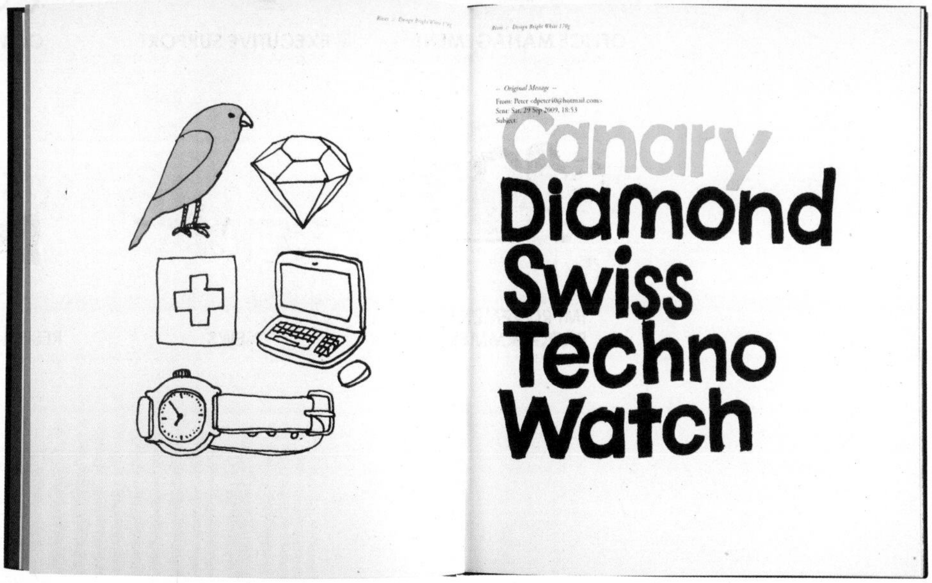
– Original Message –
Sent: Sat, 29 Sep 2009, 18:53
Subject:
Canary
Diamond
Swiss
Techno
Watch

Illustration for Design
Together Design for
The Health Foundation

The Hub Intranet
As part of its rebrand of the Health Foundation, Together Design was asked to design an intranet interface. We needed to engage users by giving it personality and making it unique to the organisation. Jochen Schievink was selected as the illustrator, chosen for the tone and style of his work, which carries through the illustrated approach in the core identity. Illustrations were developed for each of the departments, with seasonal embellishments for the Hub logo. Staff were central in developing the illustration concepts, which were launched with a competition to name the 'news dog', now known as Rupert.

Illustrator
Jochen Schievink
Design Group
Together Design
Client
The Health Foundation

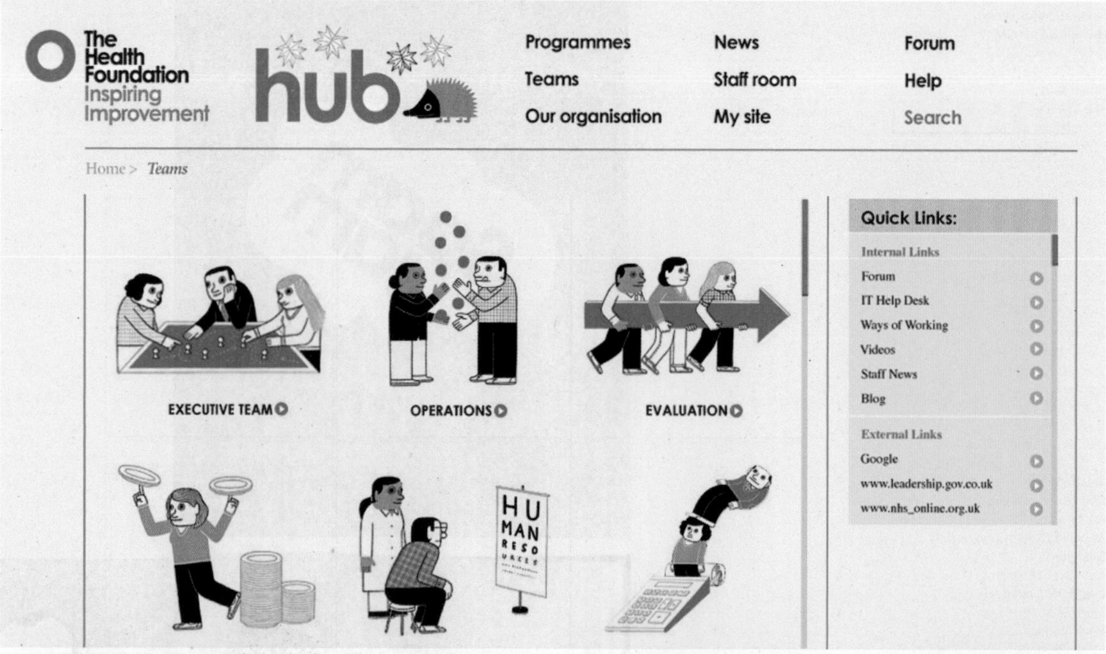
The Health Foundation
Inspiring Improvement
hub
Programmes
Teams
Our organisation
News
Staff room
My site
Forum
Help
Search
Home > Teams
EXECUTIVE TEAM
OPERATIONS
EVALUATION
HU MAN RESO URCES
Quick Links:
Internal Links
Forum
IT Help Desk
Ways of Working
Videos
Staff News
Blog
External Links
Google
www.leadership.gov.co.uk
www.nhs_online.org.uk

HUMAN RESOURCES
EXECUTIVE TEAM
OPERATIONS
RESPONSIBILITY
OFFICE MANAGEMENT
EXECUTIVE SUPPORT
COMMUNICATIONS
EVALUATION
IMPROVEMENT PROGRAMMES
NEWS
RESEARCH DEVELOPMENT
FINANCE

Illustration for Design
The Partners for the
Richard House
Children's Hospice

Going Going Gone Red!
The Richard House Children's Hospice requires £1.9million a year to operate. 'Go Red!' is its largest annual fundraiser. Inspired by the children's game Consequences, the identity combines multiple images and words to create examples of how to 'Go Red!' To get our industry involved, we asked 120 brilliant illustrators to play Consequences in aid of the charity. With 64,000 different combinations of heads, bodies and legs, and the potential to raise £3.8million, visitors to the website can create and order their own beautiful giclée print. But be quick – there's only one of each combination. Although we cannot name them all here, we would like to thank all 120 illustrators who contributed to the project. Please head over to www.goinggoinggone-red.org to see the full list of kind participants.

Designers
Tim Brown
Sean Rees
Senior Designer
Sam Griffiths
Junior Designer
Henry Hadlow
Artworkers
Bernadette Feely
Alex John
Design Director
Michael Paisley
Creative Director
Jack Renwick
Design Agency
The Partners
Project Manager
Suzanne Neal
Client
Richard House
Children's Hospice

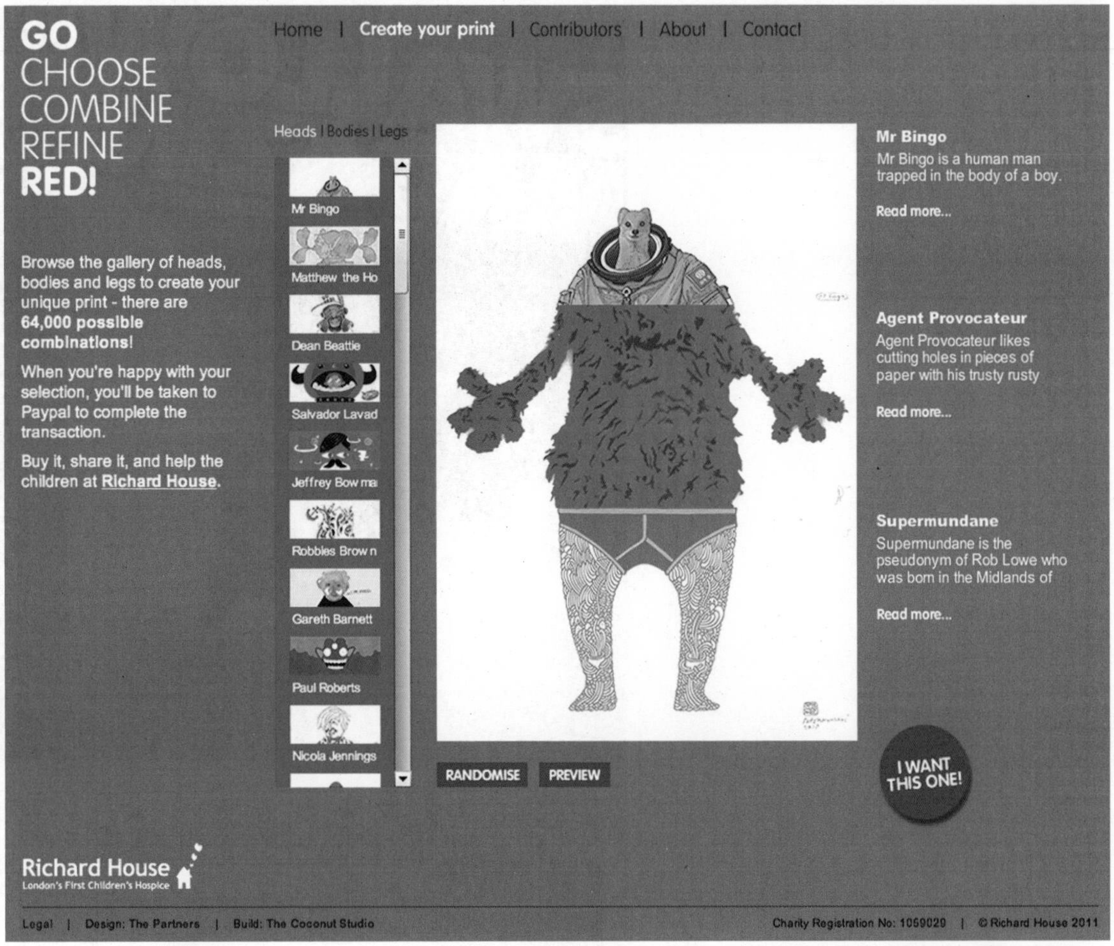
GO
CHOOSE
COMBINE
REFINE
RED!
Home | Create your print | Contributors | About | Contact
Heads | Bodies | Legs
Mr Bingo
Matthew the Ho
Dean Beattie
Salvador Lavad
Jeffrey Bow ma
Robbies Brow n
Gareth Barnett
Paul Roberts
Nicola Jennings
Browse the gallery of heads, bodies and legs to create your unique print - there are 64,000 possible combinations!
When you're happy with your selection, you'll be taken to Paypal to complete the transaction.
Buy it, share it, and help the children at Richard House.
Mr Bingo
Mr Bingo is a human man trapped in the body of a boy.
Read more...
Agent Provocateur
Agent Provocateur likes cutting holes in pieces of paper with his trusty rusty
Read more...
Supermundane
Supermundane is the pseudonym of Rob Lowe who was born in the Midlands of
Read more...
RANDOMISE
PREVIEW
I WANT THIS ONE!
Richard House
London's First Children's Hospice
Legal | Design: The Partners | Build: The Coconut Studio
Charity Registration No: 1059020 | © Richard House 2011

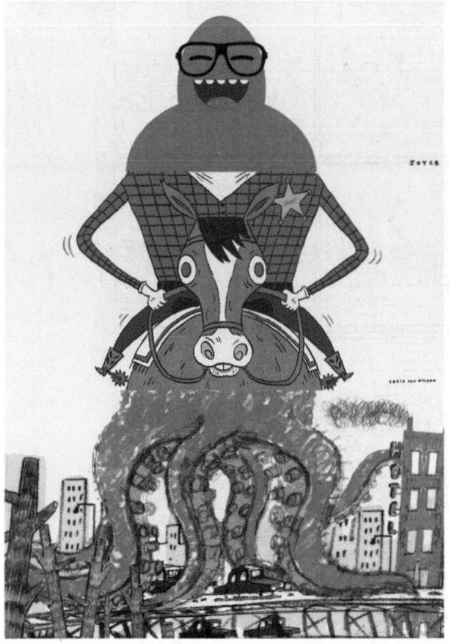

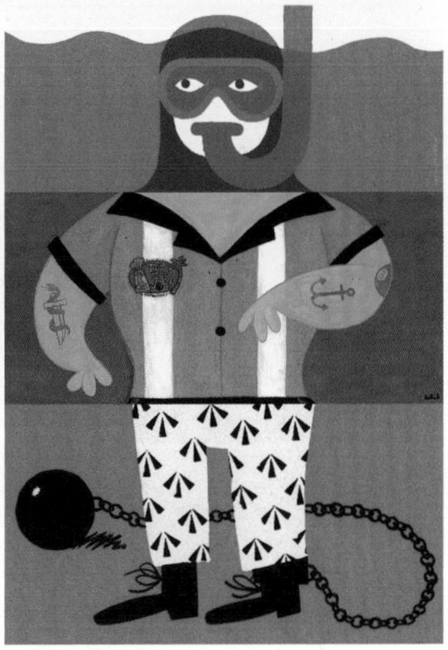

Illustration for Design
Swallow Magazine

Swallow Magazine: Devil in the Details Comic
Swallow Magazine is a food and travel magazine unlike any other. Presented as a bi-annual hardbound book, the magazine avoids the usual foodie clichés, showcasing compelling content, both visual and written, from a completely uncommon perspective. Instead of running a conventional travel disaster story about losing a passport while travelling across Russia's interior, illustrator Andrew Rae and creative director James Casey created a 20-page comic that drew on Casey's first-hand experiences, with more than a touch of magical realism thrown in for good measure (sleazy cops, romantic fantasies, and diabolical cats abound!).

Illustrator
Andrew Rae
Copywriter
James Casey
Creative Director
James Casey
Publishers
Swallow Publications
Client
Swallow Magazine

SWALLOW MAGAZINE
THE TRANS-SIBERIAN ISSUE

DEVIL IN
THE DETAILS
BY ANDREW RAE AND JAMES CASEY

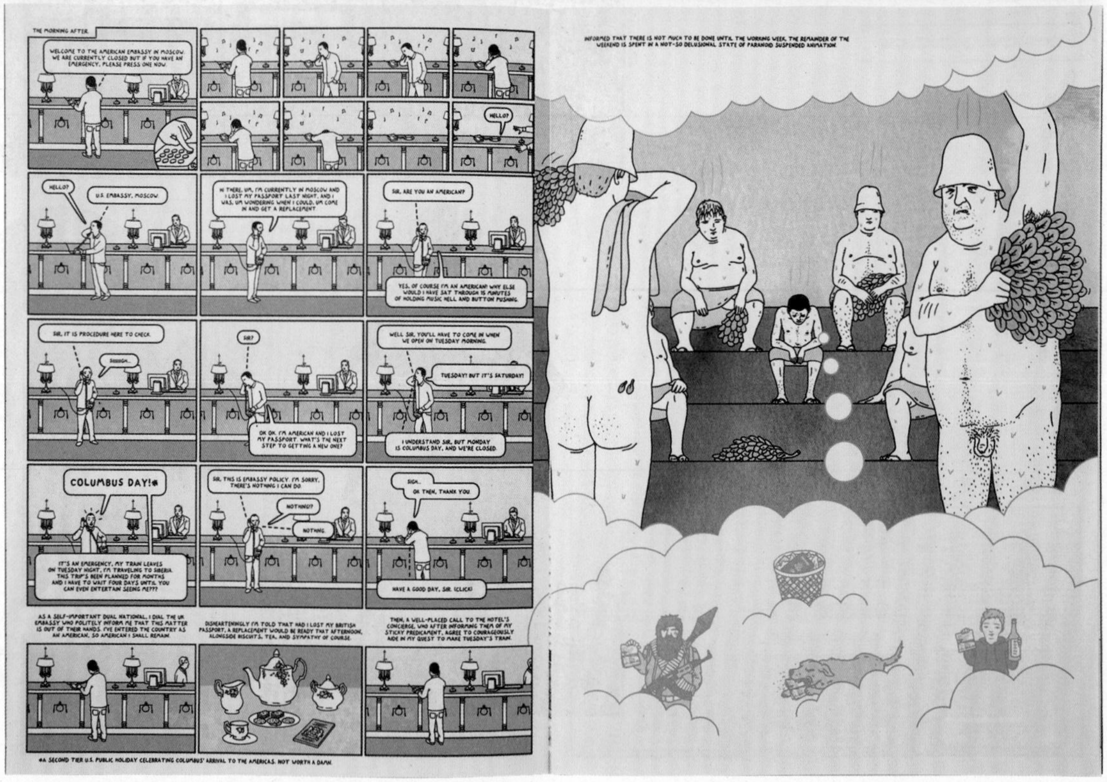
COLUMBUS DAY!*

Illustration for Design
Viva & Co. for
Condé Nast

Great Expectations
The cyclist is on his way to declare his love to a current or hoped-for girlfriend; the dog may be a gift. The night is gloomy, but the young man's great expectations illuminate his face and create a cheerful scene.

Illustrator
Frank Viva
Art Director
Françoise Mouly
Design Firm
Viva & Co.
Client
Condé Nast
Brand
The New Yorker

PRICE $5.99
THE NEW YORKER
JAN. 18, 2010
minx
VIVA

Illustration for Design
Craig & Karl
for Nowness

Darcel Disappoints & Fashion Week(s)
The blog Darcel Disappoints follows the illustrated life of Darcel, a mostly miserable character who traverses New York observing the small moments of everyday life in a big city. Commissioned by LVMH's online magazine Nowness to cover the spring/summer fashion week cycle, Darcel traipsed from New York to London, Milan and Paris capturing his experiences in illustration form, from the runway to backstage, from crowded after-parties to introspective moments alone. Twenty-eight illustrations, posted daily to the Nowness site, and four animations introducing the beginning of each city's fashion week, allowed viewers to experience the fashion industry from an outsider's perspective, almost in real time; one where getting turned away at the door was as common as fighting for a front row seat inside.

Illustrator
Craig Redman
Art Director
Craig Redman
Design Agency
Craig & Karl
Brand Manager
Claudia Donaldson
Clients
LVMH
Nowness

Going to Shoreditch House to escape fashion week was not a very well thought-out idea.

Soho Chanel reopening + Karl + booze + a dash of Assume Vivid Astro Focus & Richard Woods? Yes thanks!

Louis Vuitton is giving me a Siegfried & Roy on a glittery ride through China vibe, and that's a trip I'd like to be on.

Refused entry at Burberry, I can't figure out why?

A runway? Nope. A mega screen, Kristen McMenamy, Parc de Bercy and Gareth Pugh will do just nicely thanks.

AnOther
10
VOGUE

Fashion weak.

Illustration for Design **Studio Tipi** for the Art Gallery of Alberta & Pigeon Post

The Art of Animation
These postcards were created exclusively for a collaboration between paper goods brand Pigeon Post and the Art Gallery of Alberta to celebrate their exhibition 'The Art of Animation'. The series is inspired by some of the most recognised characters in modern cartoon history, and looks behind the scenes of traditional animation production.

Illustrators
Judi Chan
Keith-Yin Sun
Art Directors
Judi Chan
Keith-Yin Sun
Illustration Studio
Studio Tipi
Design Group
Vanguard Works
Clients
Art Gallery of Alberta
Pigeon Post

WABBIT SEASON
ACME

Nomination in Photography

Photography for Press & Poster Advertising
Young & Rubicam Paris
for the Surfrider Foundation Europe

Ocean Initiatives 2010
Each year, the Surfrider Foundation invites volunteers to clean beaches around the world during a three-day operation called Ocean Initiatives. This year, the Surfrider Foundation wanted to remind people that even the smallest pieces of trash (macro-waste) are just as toxic for the environment as oil spills, which are greater in scale and receive much more media coverage. The impact of macro-waste is much larger than we think.

Photographer
Ben Stockley
Art Director
Sebastien Guinet
Copywriter
Josselin Pacreau
Creative Directors
Jorge Carreno
Robin De Lestrade
Advertising Agency
Young & Rubicam Paris
Account Handler
Aure Tessandier
Brand Manager
Stephane Latxague
Client
Surfrider Foundation Europe
Brand
Ocean Initiatives 2010

THERE'S NO
SUCH THING
AS A LITTLE MARINE
POLLUTION
www.surfrider.eu

THERE'S NO
SUCH THING
AS A LITTLE MARINE
POLLUTION
www.surfrider.eu

THERE'S NO
SUCH THING
AS A LITTLE MARINE
POLLUTION
www.surfrider.eu

Nomination in Photography

Photography for Press & Poster Advertising
Publicis Conseil
for Samusocial

Asphaltisation
For Samusocial, the French emergency service helping the homeless, Publicis Conseil created a shock press and display campaign based on the concept of 'asphaltisation'. The word means all the physical and mental symptoms developed by people living on the street: loss of orientation in time and space, loss of identity, etc. Publicis Conseil created this campaign to breathe life into the word and get everyone to understand that urgent action is needed, as the street sucks a little more life from the homeless every day.

Photographer
Marc Paeps
Art Director
Alexandra Offe
Copywriter
Veronique Sels
Print Producers
Gael Cheval
Charly Forin
Creative Director
Veronique Sels
Head of Art
Frederic Royer
Advertising Agency
Publicis Conseil
Account Handlers
Debora Guarachi
Emmanuelle Henry
Art Buyer
Jean-Luc Chirio
Client Founding President
Xavier Emmanuelli
Client Chief Executive Officer
Stefania Parigi
Client
Samusocial

THE LONGER YOU LIVE ON THE STREET
THE HARDER IT IS TO GET OFF IT
samusocial
SUPPORT US AT WWW.SAMUSOCIAL.FR

THE LONGER YOU LIVE ON THE STREET
THE HARDER IT IS TO GET OFF IT
samusocial

THE LONGER YOU LIVE ON THE STREET
THE HARDER IT IS TO GET OFF IT
samusocial

Nomination
in Photography

Photography for Design
Clay Weiner

Try-ons
This book chronicles Clay Weiner's attempts to 'be somebody' through living the lives of an eccentric array of real and imaginary characters. 'Growing up, I was always told to be somebody. In an attempt to find myself, I tried 85 personas. I'm still confused.'

Photographer
Clay Weiner
Designer
Hans Seeger
Stylist
Jenna Wright
Client
Clay Weiner

TRY-ONS
TRY-ONS
Clay Weiner
Clay Weiner

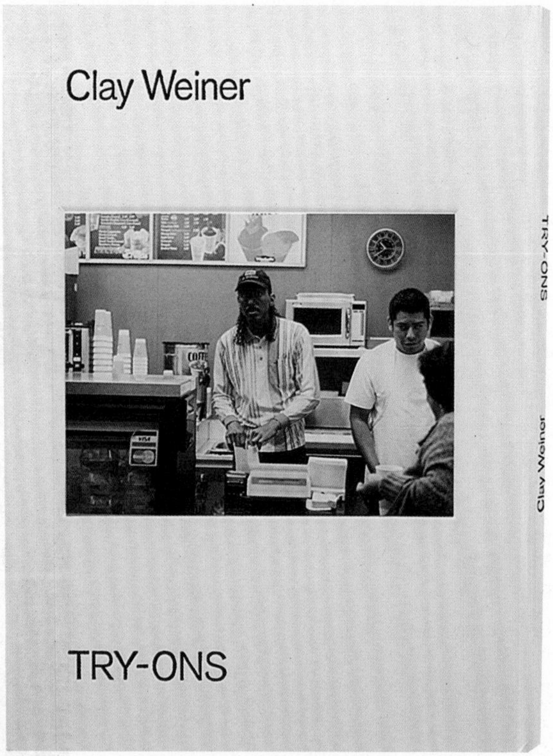
Clay Weiner
TRY-ONS
Clay Weiner
TRY-ONS

AVOCADO LOVER
9 AM TO 6 PM

Photography for Press & Poster Advertising
BBH London for
St John Ambulance

Life Lost
This campaign launched the new positioning of St John Ambulance: The Difference. The 'Life Lost' executions demonstrate day-to-day situations where first aid could have made a difference, but didn't. The role of this campaign was to create a reappraisal of first aid, and consequently of St John Ambulance, positioning it as a life saving charity.

Photographer
Nadav Kander
Retouchers
Antony Crossfield
Gary Meade
Art Directors
Victoria Daltrey
Mark Reddy
Adrian Rossi
Designer
Rich Kennedy
Copywriters
Will Bingham
Alex Grieve
Typographer
Dave Wakefield
Print Producer
Sarah Pascoe
Creative Directors
Alex Grieve
Adrian Rossi
Advertising Agency
BBH London
Account Planner
Jude Lowson
Account Handlers
Lou Addley
Mehdi Benali
Art Buyer
Sarah Pascoe
Brand Manager
Scott Jacobson
Client
St John Ambulance

A grape stuck in my throat. I couldn't breathe. It was really scary. But I knew a grown-up would help me. Who was clever at first aid. Who knew that all I needed was some hard slaps on the back. Because grown-ups always know what to do. Don't they?
Abigail West 2005-2010
You can be the difference between life. And death. To find out how text 'free guide' to 82727.
St John Ambulance
The difference.

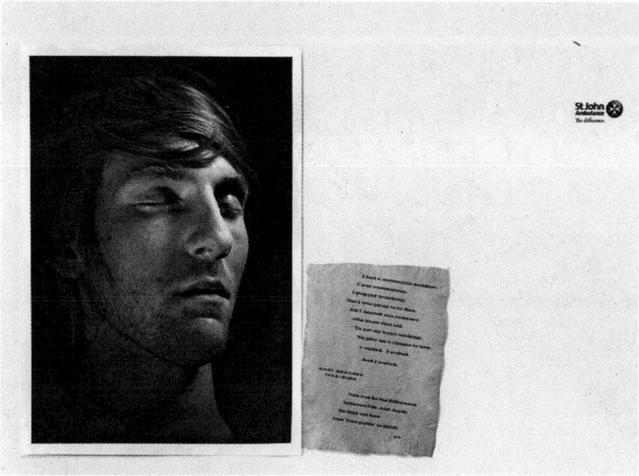

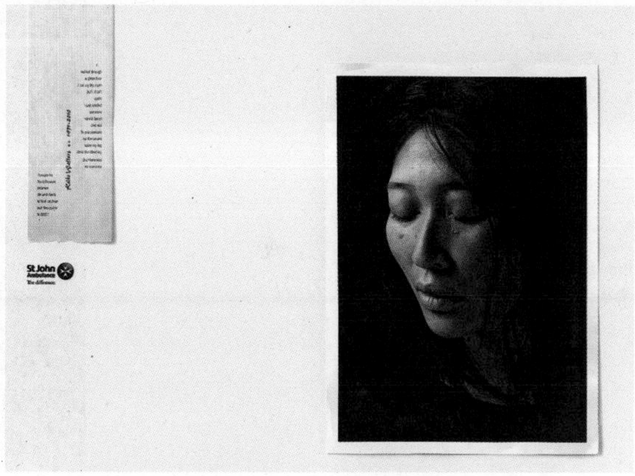

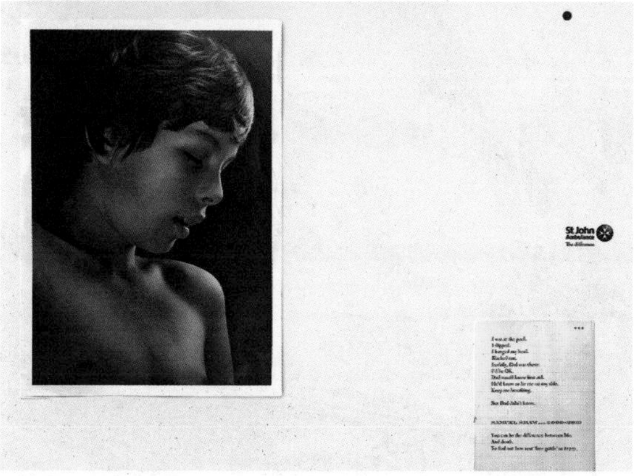

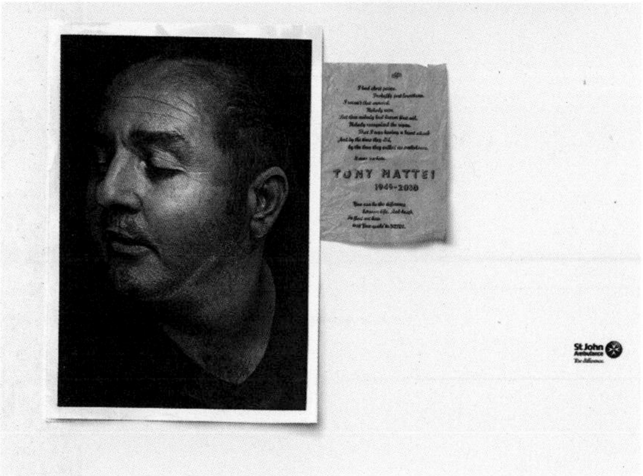

Photography for Press & Poster Advertising
TBWA\Hunt\Lascaris Johannesburg for The Endangered Wildlife Trust

Bottle Top / Golf Ball / Lighter / Rope
The Endangered Wildlife Trust wanted to take preventative action against increased littering during the 2010 World Cup. To alert South Africans and tourists to the plight of coastal birds due to excessive littering, TBWA\Hunt\Lascaris created a press campaign highlighting the effect of this pollution. The advertisements show birds that have been killed by litter they have ingested. The images carry the line: 'If you don't pick it up they will'. The birds' bodies are decaying around the rubbish inside them, demonstrating how litter outlasts wildlife. Readers were driven to visit www.ewt.org.za to find out more.

Photographer
Chris Jordan
Art Director
Wihan Meerholz
Copywriter
Jared Osmond
Creative Director
Adam Weber
Executive Creative Director
Damon Stapleton
Advertising Agency
TBWA\Hunt\Lascaris Johannesburg
Account Handler
Bridget Langley
Brand Manager
Vanessa Bezuidenhout
Client
The Endangered Wildlife Trust

IF YOU DON'T PICK IT UP THEY WILL.
(Image unaltered and courtesy of Chris Jordan)
ENDANGERED WILDLIFE TRUST
www.ewt.org.za

IF YOU DON'T PICK IT UP THEY WILL.
(Image unaltered and courtesy of Chris Jordan)
ENDANGERED WILDLIFE TRUST
www.ewt.org.za

F YOU DON'T PICK IT UP THEY WILL.
mage unaltered and courtesy of Chris Jordan)
ENDANGERED WILDLIFE TRUST
www.ewt.org.za

YOU DON'T PICK IT UP THEY WILL.
age unaltered and courtesy of Chris Jordan)
ENDANGERED WILDLIFE TRUST
www.ewt.org.za

Photography for Press
& Poster Advertising
TBWA\Paris for
Amnesty International

Death Penalty
In a chiaroscuro mood, an electric chair, a firing squad, and hangmen are depicted made of candle wax that has started to melt down. The strapline 'Death to the death penalty' is also shaped in candle wax. It is followed by the Amnesty candle logo, to express that Amnesty is fighting against the death penalty and that its own flame is melting down executioners.

Photographer
Antoine Magnien
Art Director
Philippe Taroux
Copywriter
Benoit Leroux
Creative Directors
Eric Holden
Remi Noel
Advertising Agency
TBWA\Paris
3D Imaging Studio
Mécanique Général
Account Handlers
Anne-Laure Brunner
Anne Vincent
Art Buyers
Barbara Chevalier
Dorothee Dupont
Communications Director
Sylvie Haurat
Client
Amnesty International

DEATH TO THE DEATH PENALTY
139 COUNTRIES HAVE WIPED OUT THE DEATH PENALTY. ONLY 58 ARE LEFT TO CONVINCE. JOIN US AT WWW.AMNESTY.FR
AMNESTY INTERNATIONAL

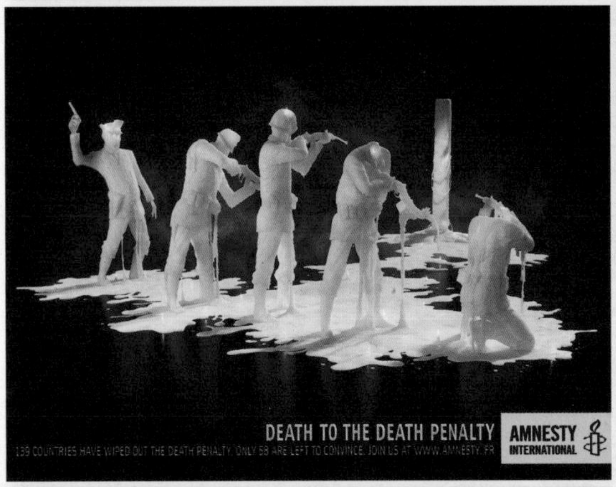
DEATH TO THE DEATH PENALTY
139 COUNTRIES HAVE WIPED OUT THE DEATH PENALTY. ONLY 58 ARE LEFT TO CONVINCE. JOIN US AT WWW.AMNESTY.FR
AMNESTY INTERNATIONAL

DEATH TO THE DEATH PENALTY
139 COUNTRIES HAVE WIPED OUT THE DEATH PENALTY. ONLY 58 ARE LEFT TO CONVINCE. JOIN US AT WWW.AMNESTY.FR
AMNESTY INTERNATIONAL

DEATH TO THE DEATH PENALTY
139 COUNTRIES HAVE WIPED OUT THE DEATH PENALTY. ONLY 58 ARE LEFT TO CONVINCE. JOIN US AT WWW.AMNESTY.FR
AMNESTY INTERNATIONAL

Photography for Press
& Poster Advertising
Publicis Mojo Sydney for
The Coca Cola Company

Flame / Snow / Skate
Burn already has a brand identity in the flame – we wanted to imbue it with more meaning, central to our core idea: when you fiercely express your creativity, you leave behind a signature that challenges and inspires. The aim wasn't to take the perfect image but to portray the aesthetic of our chosen communities and tell a story, making something true to the people we were talking to, rather than using typical advertising imagery. Print and outdoor ads used images from behind-the-scenes reportage to performances captured for the medium, ensuring everything we did was a published part of the campaign.

Photographer
Ben Stockley
Image Manipulator
Inness Robins
Art Director
Andrew Ostrom
Copywriter
Ian Williamson
Print Production Manager
Oscar Birken
Creative Director
Micah Walker
Advertising Agency
Publicis Mojo Sydney
Account Handler
Simon Ludowyke
Art Buyer
Alison Dunlop
Brand Manager
Francesco Cibo
Client
The Coca Cola Company
Brand
Burn

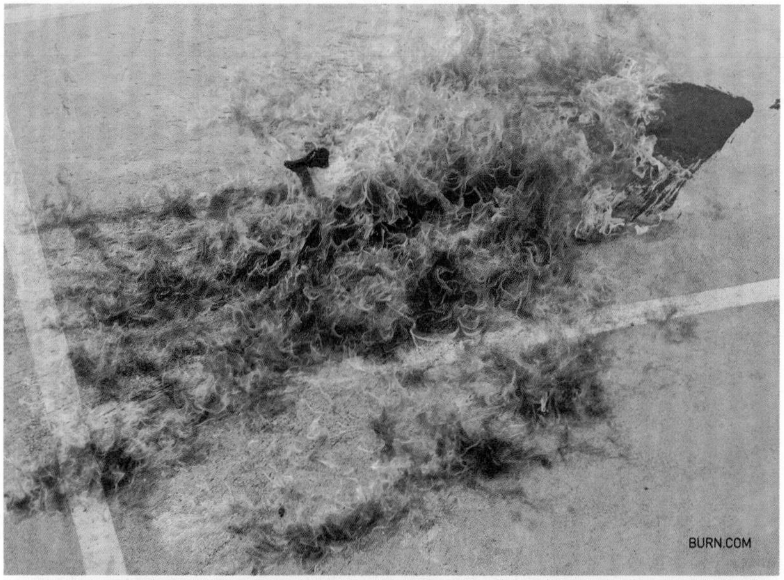
BURN.COM

BURN.COM

BURN.COM

Photography for Press
& Poster Advertising
Leo Burnett Sydney
for WWF

Icefield
WWF wanted to remind people of the fragile beauty of the world around them and encourage them to have a more conservational perspective. This is a continuation of a new brand focus for WWF around sustainability, based on the fact that humans are currently consuming the Earth's resources as if we have three planets instead of one. To convey the aesthetic beauty of these settings, poems were written, bringing to life the feeling someone would get from actually being in the different environments, and providing a sombre warning for the consequences of inaction.

Photographer
Simon Harsent
Art Director
Cameron Harris
Designer
Cameron Harris
Copywriter
David Harsent
Typographer
Masataka Kawano
Creative Director
Andy DiLallo
Advertising Agency
Leo Burnett Sydney
Account Handlers
Paul Everson
Jodi McLeod
Marketing Manager
Lawrence Hennessy
Client
WWF

'Our planet's voice', by David Harsent.
A place of ice over ice, of white over white
and beauty in absences. There was a time when the only sound
was the wind calling its ghosts, when the skyline was set
clean as a scar on glass, when your heartbeat slowed
with the cold, when your dreams brought in a white bird
on a white sky and music that could only be heard
from time to time on the other side of night.
Now the horizon's dark, now there's a terrible weight
in the air and a stain cut hard and deep in the permafrost.
Breakage and slippage, the rumble of some vast
machine cranking its pistons, of everything on the slide,
and the water rising fast, and the music lost.
Lend us your voice.
WWF

Photography for Press & Poster Advertising
George Logan Photography for the Born Free Foundation

Homeless Animals
This campaign highlights the habitat loss that is affecting endangered species.

Photographer
George Logan
Image Manipulator
Dave Jewell
Art Director
Katy Hopkins
Copywriter
Steve Hawthorne
Creative Directors
Yan Elliott
Luke Williamson
Photographic Agency
George Logan Photography
Advertising Agency
WCRS
Account Handler
Paul Johnson
Brand Manager
Anne Tudor
Client
Born Free Foundation

Thousands of animals are made homeless every month
Help keep wildlife in the wild at bornfree.org.uk
BORN FREE

THOUSANDS OF ANIMALS ARE MADE HOMELESS EVERY MONTH

WARNING
SPIRIT
FRIDAYS @ ghost
THOUSANDS OF ANIMALS ARE MADE HOMELESS EVERY MONTH
FREE

Photography for Press & Poster Advertising
Groovy Studio for the Sea Shepherd Conservation Society

Tuna Boat / Tsukiji Market / Wharf
This is a campaign to raise awareness of the plight of the bluefin tuna, which is in great danger of slipping into extinction. Due to four decades of overfishing, levels have dropped to just three per cent of the 1960 population.

Photography
Groovy Studio
Art Director
Anthony Tham
Copywriter
Jagdish Ramakrishnan
Creative Director
Eugene Cheong
Image Manipulation
Procolour
Advertising Agency
Ogilvy & Mather Singapore
Client
Sea Shepherd Conservation Society

When you see tuna, think panda. The bluefin tuna is so endangered, it is likely to entirely disappear from our oceans in just a couple of years. Industrial overfishing has already wiped out 85% of bluefin populations. Act now to save the rest. Don't sell, buy or eat endangered species. Help defend the bluefin tuna by supporting Operation Blue Rage. www.seashepherd.org
SEA SHEPHERD CONSERVATION SOCIETY

2
When you see tuna, think panda. The bluefin tuna is now on the brink of extinction, thanks to industrial overfishing and corporate greed. Breeding populations could disappear from our oceans as early as 2012. Act now to end this trade. Don't sell, buy or eat endangered species. Help defend the bluefin tuna by supporting Operation Blue Rage. www.seashepherd.org

When you see tuna, think panda. The bluefin tuna is now critically endangered to the point of extinction. Industrial overfishing, fueled by the voracious appetite for tuna in Asia, is killing off all breeding populations. Act quickly to save what's left. Don't sell, buy or eat endangered species. Help defend the bluefin tuna by supporting Operation Blue Rage. www.seashepherd.org

Photography for Press
& Poster Advertising
Elephant Cairo for
Sima Food Industries

Out of this World
All three images in
this campaign were
shot in one day, using
one Chinese strobe
light that we had
at the agency.

Photographer
Ali Ali
Art Directors
Ali Ali
Maged Nassar
Copywriters
Ali Ali
Maged Nassar
Advertising Agency
Elephant Cairo
Client
Sima Food Industries
Brand
Lika Gum

LIKA GUM
OUT OF THIS WORLD

OUT OF THIS WORLD

OUT OF THIS WORLD

Photography for Design
NB for D&AD

Sorry Old Blood, the New Blood Has Arrived
This ad was created to promote New Blood, D&AD's graduate talent show. It is part of a campaign that features portraits of prominent members of the creative community who are at the point of ending it all, because of the quality of the new blood on the horizon.

Photographer
David Stewart
Art Directors
Alan Dye
Nick Finney
Designer
Ed Wright
Copywriters
David Fowle
Ajab Samrai
Typographer
George Adams
Design Group
NB
Marketing Director
Rob Eves
Client
D&AD
Brand
D&AD New Blood

NB: Alex Taylor was not harmed during the making of this poster and continues to Art Direct at the very highest level.
Sorry old blood, the new blood has arrived.
View the work of the best advertising, design, graphics and digital media graduates from across the UK.
New Blood 2010
Thurs 24 — Mon 28 June
Old Truman Brewery
15 Hanbury Street
London E1 6QR
www.dandad.org/newblood

Photography for Design
Laurence Haskell
Photography

Out of a Box
'Out of a Box' is an exploration of the aesthetic and conceptual potential of the most seemingly mundane of objects. Through skilful manipulation, ordinary waste items of empty packaging appear to have taken on new forms. The result is a collection of images that is as visually striking as it is thought-provoking.

Photographer
Laurence Haskell
Image Manipulator
Victoria Frances Smith
Art Directors
Laurence Haskell
Victoria Frances Smith
Designer
Victoria Frances Smith
Photographic Agency
Laurence Haskell Photography
Design Group
Tell Tale Studios
Brand Manager
Henry Newman
Client
Laurence Haskell Photography

Two
Apple Time Capsule, expanded polystyrene foam.

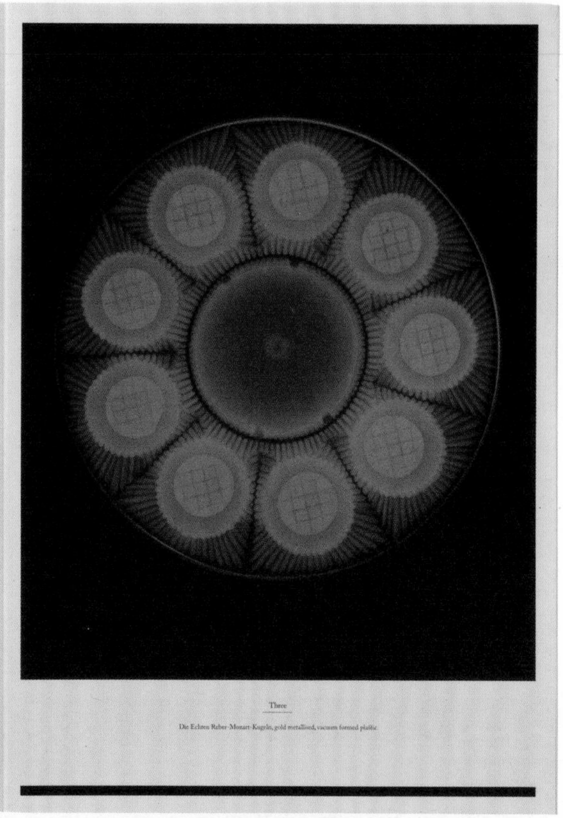
Three
Die Echten Reber-Mozart-Kugeln, gold metallised, vacuum formed plastic.

Four
Above, main image, American Express 'Titanium' mailer, coated cardboard. Top, Chocolate box, vacuum formed plastic. Bottom, M&S chocolate biscuits, vacuum formed plastic.
Lower left & right images, Apple Mighty Mouse, high density fibre board.
Page five, main image, Epson 7900 printer, expanded polystyrene foam. Top, American Express 'Titanium' mailer, coated cardboard.

Yellow Pencil in Typography

Typefaces
Mucho for the Fundación Arte y Mecenazgo

Art Out
Our task was to create the graphics for a foundation sponsoring the arts. The foundation is geared mainly towards patrons, collectors and gallery owners, but also towards artists. As an important part of the identity, we presented this typeface with a classic but contemporary appearance. This allowed us to communicate with a traditional audience without discouraging the younger or more experimental. The design takes its proportions from the Didone font. To present the typeface, we created a type specimen that includes the details of its design.

Typographer
Carles Rodrigo
Design Director
Pablo Juncadella
Creative Directors
Marc Català
Pablo Juncadella
Tilman Solé
Design Group
Mucho
Print Production
Leicrom
Client
Fundación Arte y Mecenazgo (AYM)

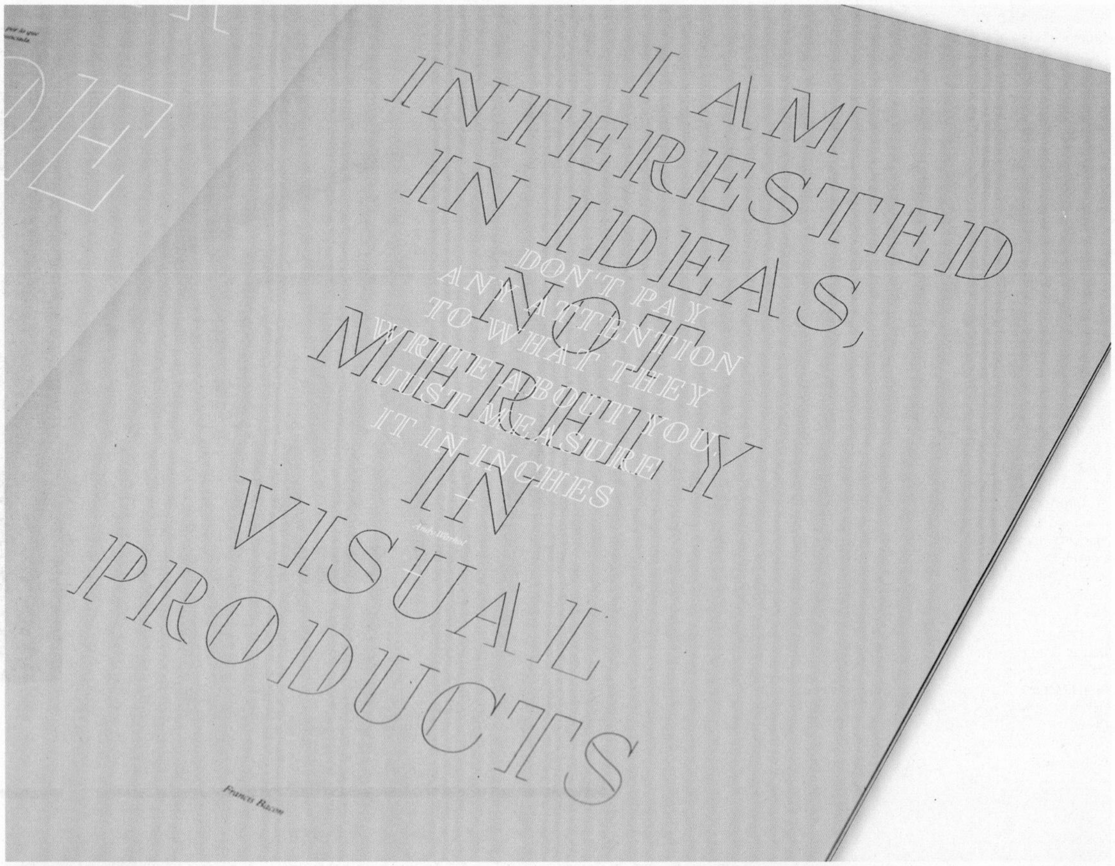
I AM INTERESTED IN IDEAS, NOT MERELY IN VISUAL PRODUCTS
DON'T PAY ANY ATTENTION TO WHAT THEY WRITE ABOUT YOU JUST MEASURE IT IN INCHES

Fundación Arte y Mecenazgo
COLECCIONISMO Y MECENAZGO EN EL SIGLO XXI
GLENN LOWRY
PREMIOS ARTE Y MECENAZGO
PRIMERA EDICION

Nomination in Typography

Typography for Design
Studio8 Design for
Frame Publshing

Elephant Magazine
Issue 5
The fifth issue of art and culture magazine Elephant includes four bespoke headline typefaces and one bespoke numeral set.

Typographer
Matt Willey
Designer
Matt Willey
Illustrator
Valero Doval
Design Studio
Studio8 Design
Publisher
Peter Huiberts
Editor in Chief
Marc Valli
Client
Frame Publishing
Brand
Elephant Magazine

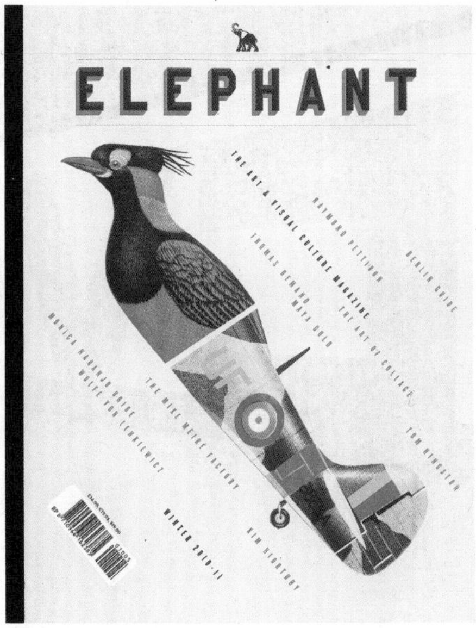
ELEPHANT

AN
INTERVIEW
WITH
RAYMOND
PETTIBON
ANOTHER EDITED
FICTION
BY
KATYA TYLEVICH

MY OWN PRIVATE BAUHAUS:
THE
MIKE MEIRÉ
FACTORY
BY
KATYA TYLEVICH
PHOTOGRAPHS
BY
ALEXEI TYLEVICH

Nomination in Typography

Typography for Press & Poster Advertising
Serviceplan Gruppe
for BMW Deutschland

Reflection – The BMW Light Wall
BMW asked us to develop an idea for the BMW M3 Coupé for a very special billboard at Hamburg airport – a 50 x 2m light wall in the middle of the arrivals hall. For a car that exceeds limits, we created a billboard that exceeded limits. We designed a headline out of half letters. To complete them we used their reflection on the shiny floor. The result: we doubled the media space for free; we doubled the attention for free.

Typographer
Andreas Schriewer
Graphic Designer
Savina Mokreva
Art Directors
Roman Becker
Manuel Wolff
Creative Directors
Maik Kaehler
Christoph Nann
Chief Creative Officer
Alexander Schill
Advertising Agency
Serviceplan Gruppe
Account Handler
Michael Falkensteiner
Marketing Manager
Manfred Braeunl
Client
BMW Deutschland
Brand
BMW M3 Coupé

EXCEED

BMW M.
Das BMW M3 Coupé:
309 kW (420 PS)
0-100 km/h: 4,8 Sekunden
M CY 4547
BMW M3
www.bmw.de/M3
Freude am Fahren

EXCEED

Typography for Design
Creative Juice\Bangkok
for Siam Tamiya

Tamiya Business Card
This is a business card for the Bangkok office of model kit manufacturers Tamiya. When something as simple as characters on a name card can be turned into a miniature model, it triggers the consumers' curiosity and makes them want to try it out.

Art Directors
Manasit Imjai
Tienchutha Rukhavibul
Designers
Manasit Imjai
Tienchutha Rukhavibul
Creative Directors
Tienchutha Rukhavibul
Thirasak Tanapatanakul
Chief Creative Officer
Thirasak Tanapatanakul
Advertising Agency
Creative Juice\Bangkok
Marketing Manager
Chayada Bangkaew
Client
Siam Tamiya

TAMIYA
SHOP DIRECT
21/23 BLOCK B SOI SOONVICHAI RAMA IX ROAD,
BANGKAPI, HUAY KWANG, BANGKOK 10320
OFFICE TEL:0-2203-0081-4 www.tamiya.co.th
TAMIYA

SHOP DIRECT
21/23 BLOCK B SOI SOONVICHAI RAMA IX ROAD,
BANGKAPI, HUAY KWANG, BANGKOK 10320
OFFICE TEL:0-2203-0081-4 www.tamiya.co.th

Typography for Design
Kolle Rebbe / KOREFE
for T.D.G. Vertriebs

Stop the Water While Using Me!
'Stop the Water While Using Me!' is a high-quality range of toiletries that meets the increasing requirements of an ecologically aware society. The products set new standards in environmental protection. The range is thoroughly eco-friendly, from the manufacturing through to the design of the packaging, right up to the finished product.

Art Director
Christian Doering
Graphic Designer
Ana Magalhães
Copywriter
Till Grabsch
Creative Director
Katrin Oeding
Advertising Agency
Kolle Rebbe / KOREFE
Account Handler
Marie Steinhoff
Art Buyer
Emanuel Mugrauer
Marketing Manager
Felix Negwer
Client
T.D.G. Vertriebs
Brand
Stop the Water While Using Me!

STOP
THE WATER
WHILE
USING ME!
250 ML ORGANI
SHAMPOO
STOP
THE WATER
WHILE
USING ME!
250 ML ORGANIC
SHOWER GEL
STOP
THE WATER
WHILE
USING ME!
75 ML ORGANIC
TOOTHPASTE

Typography for Design
design hoch drei
for the Christian-Wagner-Gesellschaft

Warmbronner Schriften 21
The 21st volume of the 'Warmbronn Scriptures' focuses on the literary significance of poet Christian Wagner's impressions from travels in Italy around the year 1900, and forms the prelude to the newly redesigned journal series. The personal, historical and current aspects of Wagner's work – his progressive and modern ideas – are portrayed in an unconventional manner. Large headings act like old newspaper mastheads and organise the volume into three chapters. The scientific, documentary style of the book is consistently eased on a written and pictorial level. Expressive poem sketches and illustrated postcards remind the reader of a travel diary.

Designer
Lisa Jung
Art Director
Helmut Kirsten
Copywriter
Prof Dr Burckhard Dücker
Creative Director
Tobias Kollmann
Editor
Harald Hepfer
Design Group
design hoch drei
Client
Christian-Wagner-Gesellschaft (Christian Wagner Society)

Warmbronner Schriften
21
W
Wohin nun anders als nach

Warmbronner Schriften
21
W
Wohin nun anders als nach
ITALIEN?
Burckhard Dücker

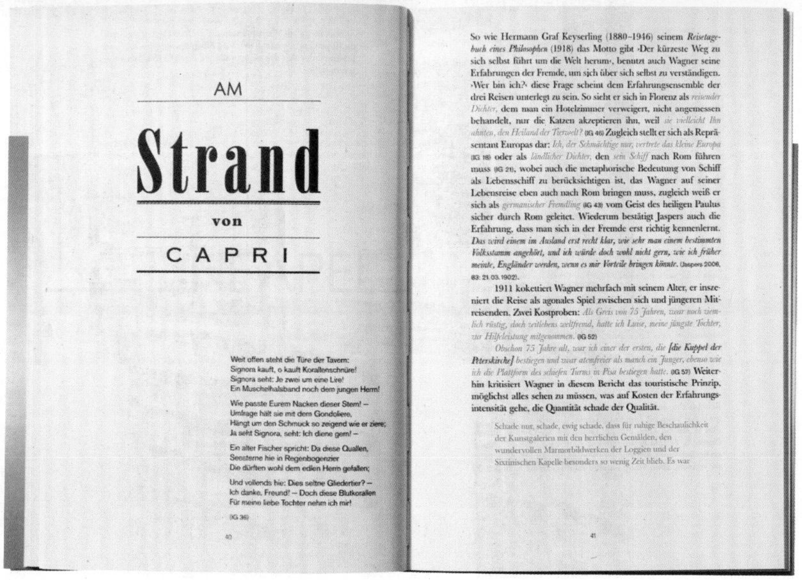
AM
Strand
von
CAPRI
Weit offen steht die Türe der Tavern:
Signora kauft, o kauft Korallenschnüre!
Signora seht: Je zwei um eine Lire!
Ein Muschelhalsband noch dem jungen Herrn!
Wie passte Eurem Nacken dieser Stern! –
Umfrage hält sie mit dem Gondoliere,
Hängt um den Schmuck so zeigend wie er ziere;
Ja seht Signora, seht: Ich diene gern! –
Ein alter Fischer spricht: Da diese Quallen,
Seesterne hie in Regenbogenzier
Die dürften wohl dem edlen Herrn gefallen;
Und vollends hie: Dies seltne Gliedertier? –
Ich danke, Freund! – Doch diese Blutkorallen
Für meine liebe Tochter nehm ich mir!
(IG 36)
40
So wie Hermann Graf Keyserling (1880–1946) seinem Reisetagebuch eines Philosophen (1918) das Motto gibt ›Der kürzeste Weg zu sich selbst führt um die Welt herum‹, benutzt auch Wagner seine Erfahrungen der Fremde, um sich über sich selbst zu verständigen. ›Wer bin ich?‹ diese Frage scheint dem Erfahrungsensemble der drei Reisen unterlegt zu sein. So sieht er sich in Florenz als reisender Dichter, dem man ein Hotelzimmer verweigert, nicht angemessen behandelt, nur die Katzen akzeptieren ihn, weil sie vielleicht Ihn ahnten, den Heiland der Tierwelt? (IG 46) Zugleich stellt er sich als Repräsentant Europas dar: Ich, der Schmächtige nur, vertrete das kleine Europa (IG 18) oder als ländlicher Dichter, den sein Schiff nach Rom führen muss (IG 21), wobei auch die metaphorische Bedeutung von Schiff als Lebensschiff zu berücksichtigen ist, das Wagner auf seiner Lebensreise eben auch nach Rom bringen muss, zugleich weiß er sich als germanischer Fremdling (IG 43) vom Geist des heiligen Paulus sicher durch Rom geleitet. Wiederum bestätigt Jaspers auch die Erfahrung, dass man sich in der Fremde erst richtig kennenlernt. Das wird einem im Ausland erst recht klar, wie sehr man einem bestimmten Volksstamm angehört, und ich würde doch wohl nicht gern, wie ich früher meinte, Engländer werden, wenn es mir Vorteile bringen könnte. (Jaspers 2006, 63: 21.03.1902).
1911 kokettiert Wagner mehrfach mit seinem Alter, er inszeniert die Reise als agonales Spiel zwischen sich und jüngeren Mitreisenden. Zwei Kostproben: Als Greis von 75 Jahren, zwar noch ziemlich rüstig, doch zeitlebens weltfremd, hatte ich Luise, meine jüngste Tochter, zur Hilfeleistung mitgenommen. (IG 52)
Obschon 75 Jahre alt, war ich einer der ersten, die [die Kuppel der Peterskirche] bestiegen und zwar atemfreier als manch ein Junger, ebenso wie ich die Plattform des schiefen Turms in Pisa bestiegen hatte. (IG 57) Weiterhin kritisiert Wagner in diesem Bericht das touristische Prinzip, möglichst alles sehen zu müssen, was auf Kosten der Erfahrungsintensität gehe, die Quantität schade der Qualität.
Schade nur, schade, ewig schade, dass für ruhige Beschaulichkeit der Kunstgalerien mit den herrlichen Gemälden, den wundervollen Marmorbildwerken der Loggien und der Sixtinischen Kapelle besonders so wenig Zeit blieb. Es war
41

Typography for Design
Taku Satoh Design Office for the Musashino Art University

Signage for the Musashino Art University Museum & Library
This is design work for the academic library of an art university. The concept 'The Forest of Books' by architect Sousuke Fujimoto was implemented in the library. The result is a space where visitors are guided by numeric signs to the books they are looking for. The numbers of the signs represent the content of the classification: the number seven is made from the letters spelling 'art'; and for the technology category, fives have been arranged like the cogwheels of a clock in order to represent the concept of technology.

Designer
Shingo Noma
Art Director
Taku Satoh
Design Studio
Taku Satoh Design Office
Client
Musashino Art University

Typography for Design
Happiness Brussels for the Coalition to Restore Coastal Louisiana

Oil & Water Do Not Mix
After the Gulf of Mexico oil spill, creatives from ad agency Happiness Brussels went to the region and collected oil from the polluted beaches. The oil was used to print a limited edition of 200 posters that sold out in less than 48 hours. All profits went towards the Coalition to Restore Coastal Louisiana, to fund its clean-up campaign on the Louisiana beaches.

Graphic Designer
Anthony Burrill
Art Directors
Ramin Afshar
Cecilia Azcarate Isturiz
Tom Galle
Copywriters
Ramin Afshar
Cecilia Azcarate Isturiz
Tom Galle
Screen Printers
Quitin Good
Michael Shoemaker
Creative Directors
Karen Corrigan
Gregory Titeca
Agency Producer
Bart Vande Maele
Advertising Agency
Happiness Brussels
Client
Coalition to Restore Coastal Louisiana

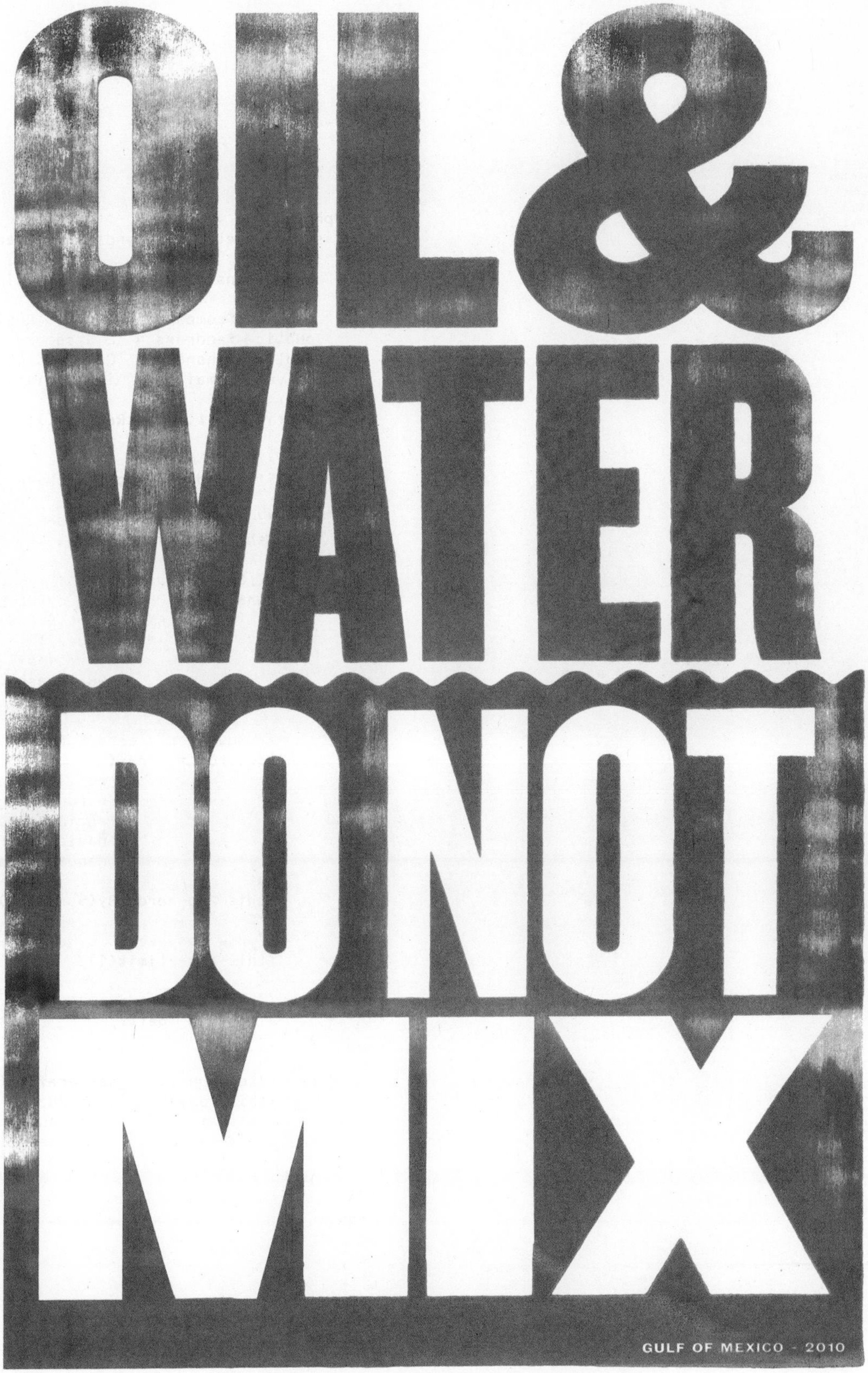
OIL &
WATER
DO NOT
MIX
GULF OF MEXICO - 2010

Typography for Design
This is Real Art

Web Developer Ad
This is a recruitment ad for a web developer job, written in a language that the successful applicant would understand.

Typographer
Paul Belford
Art Director
Paul Belford
Copywriter
Andy Mathieson
Creative Director
Paul Belford
Design Group
This is Real Art
Project Manager
Natalie Wetherell
Client
This is Real Art

```
<?php
class WebDeveloper extends ThisisRealArt {

    const constant   = 'opportunities';

    public  $company = 'This is Real Art';
    public  $address = '2 Sycamore St, London, EC1Y OSF';
    public  $phone   = '020 7253 2181';
    private $email   = 'info@thisisrealart.com';

    public function getRecruit(){

        // What do we require?
        $this->db->select('webDeveloper');

        // From where are we selecting?
        $this->db->from('peopleWhoLoveIdeas');

        // Select criteria
        $where = "'PHP OOP & mySQL'  = 'strong'
                  AND 'XHTML & CSS' = 'strict'
                  AND ('jQuery'     = 'bonus'
                       OR 'linux'   = 'bonus'
                       OR 'flash'   = 'bonus') ";
        $this->db->where($where);

        // How should we prioritize?
        $orderBy = array(
                        'ability'=>'DESC',
                        'hardWorking'=>'DESC',
                        'sociable'=>'DESC',
                        'davidBowieFan'=>'DESC',
                        'ManUtdSupporter'=>'ASC'
        );
        $this->db->orderBy($orderBy);

        // How many results do we need?
        $this->db->limit(1);

        // Run the search
        $this->db->get();
    }

    protected function _setBenefits(){
        $this->daysHoliday = 28;
        $this->fun         = 'guaranteed';
        $this->salary      = 'negotiable';

    }
}
?>
```

Typography for Design
C Plus C Workshop
for the Hong Kong
Taekwondo Federation

The 19th ITF Taekwondo
Championship
The ITF Taekwondo championship is a famous Taekwondo competition held every year in Hong Kong. We presented the visual identity of the competition by creating posters for media promotion. Each poster captures competitors in different scenarios and movements, forming the nine letters of the word 'Taekwondo'. The typographic approach created a strong visual impact and demonstrated the passion and professionalism of Taekwondo practitioners.

Typographer
Kim Hung Choi
Designer
Kim Hung Choi
Print Producer
Simon Chung
Creative Director
Kim Hung Choi
Design Agency
C Plus C Workshop
Client
Hong Kong Taekwondo Federation

26/09/SUN/9AM-7PM
Date 比賽日期
TAE
Tung Chung
Man Tung Road Sports Centre
東涌文東路體育館
Venue 比賽地點
KWO
G/F., Tung Chung Municipal Services Building,
39 Man Tung Road, Tung Chung
東涌文東路39號,東涌市政大樓地下
NDO
THE 19TH
ITF TAEKWONDO
CHAMPIONSHIP
第十九屆ITF跆拳道大賽
Organization 主辦機構
INTERNATIONAL TAEKWON-DO FEDERATION
HKTF (China)
designed by www.cplusc-workshop.com

Typography for Design
hat-trick design for
Land Securities

Illuminating London
The brief was to use a big, prominent hoarding space in Victoria, London, to promote the area. A typeface of illuminated letters was designed, with each letter telling a different story for passers-by to discover. We wanted to end up with a visually rich and eclectic set of letters to sum up the area: a mix of past, present and future, heritage, culture, art, green spaces and wildlife. The style of each letter was inspired by the particular story being told. We decided the execution could be photographic, illustrative or graphic, depending on what best communicated it in a visually engaging way.

Typographers
Tim Donaldson
Gareth Howat
Jim Sutherland
Designers
Laura Bowman
Tim Donaldson
Adam Giles
Gareth Howat
Alexandra Jurva
Jim Sutherland
Alex Swatridge
Copywriter
Nick Asbury
Illustrator
Rebecca Sutherland
Photographers
Paul Grundy
John Ross
Creative Directors
Gareth Howat
Jim Sutherland
Design Group
hat-trick design
Brand Manager
Anna Chapman
Client
Land Securities

Illuminating Victoria
A

Typography for Design **300million** for the Orchestre de Paris

Orchestre de Paris 2010/2011 Season Brochure
Orchestre de Paris is a renowned orchestra based in the heart of Paris with a rich history of world-class conductors. For the redesign of its season brochure, we were asked to acknowledge this heritage while also appealing to a younger, more diverse local audience. We used Hoefler & Frere-Jones's modern revival of the iconic typeface Didot for its historical context and scaling feature, which allowed us to use it expressively throughout while maintaining a relative consistency in the serif weight. This detail aimed to express a sense of the precision, craft and passion evident in the performances.

Designer
Tom Mesquitta
Design Director
Graeme Rodrigo
Creative Director
Matt Baxter
Design Group
300million
Account Handler
Adam Stuart
Marketing Managers
Florence Alibert
Nadine Deldyck
Client
Orchestre de Paris

Orchestre de Paris
Saison 2010 2011
Salle Pleyel
Paavo Järvi Directeur musical

4 Concerts symphoniques
24 Musique de chambre
28 Jeune public
34 Tournées
38 En savoir plus
42 Nous soutenir
46 Réserver S'abonner

Typography for Design
David Pearson Design
for Penguin Books

The Wolfman
Our objective was to produce a book cover for Sigmund Freud's 'The Wolfman' that adheres to the fixed parameters of Penguin's Great Ideas series: using type as image, only two colours, and a debossed element.

Designer
David Pearson
Design Director
Jim Stoddart
Design Agency
David Pearson Design
Client
Penguin Books

PENGUIN
BOOKS
GREAT
IDEAS
SIGMUND
FREUD
THE
olf
an
WHY
ARE
THE
WOLVES
WHITE?

Typography for Design
A2/SW/HK for
Faber & Faber

Samuel Beckett:
Complete Works
Each cover design features a custom-made type treatment printed in a minimal palette of two or three colours. A2/SW/HK designed A2 Beckett, a bespoke type family consisting of five weights. It is used to ensure each cover has an individual character but is still clearly identifiable as part of a larger collection. A neutral grey background has been chosen as a counterpoint to the Pantone colours selected for each of the 18 titles. This choice is also a playful reference to Samuel Beckett's directive that his gravestone be 'any colour, so long as it's grey'.

Typographers
Henrik Kubel
Scott Williams
Designers
Henrik Kubel
Scott Williams
Design Group
A2/SW/HK
Client
Faber & Faber

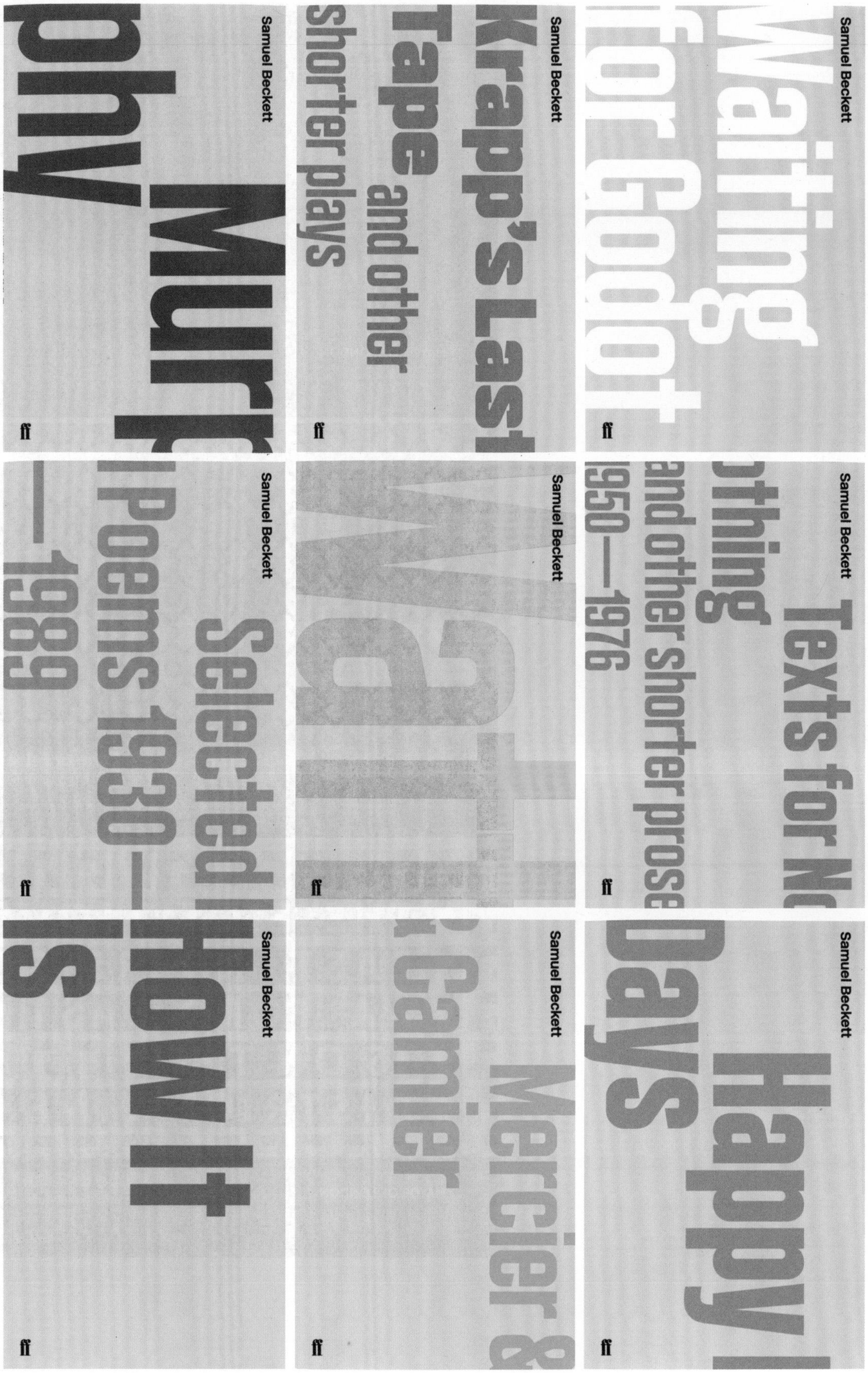
Samuel Beckett
Waiting for Godot
Samuel Beckett
Krapp's Last Tape and other shorter plays
Samuel Beckett
Samuel Beckett
and other shorter prose
1950—1976
Samuel Beckett
Samuel Beckett
Samuel Beckett
Days
Samuel Beckett
Samuel Beckett

Typography for Design
M&C Saatchi London
for Transport for London

Heritage Campaign
There are hundreds of interesting stories about the tube. Our brief was to bring a few of them to life. We did this by weaving facts (and a bit of fiction) into the designs of historical seat covers. We then asked passengers to guess: Tube or False?

Typographer
Gareth Davies
Art Director
Ned Corbett-Winder
Copywriter
Martin Latham
Image Manipulator
Mark Petty
Print Producer
Ray Price
Executive Creative Director
Graham Fink
Advertising Agency
M&C Saatchi London
Account Handler
Tom Vaughan
Group Marketing & Communications Manager
Nigel Hanlon
Director of Group Marketing
Chris MacLeod
Client
Transport for London
Brand
London Underground

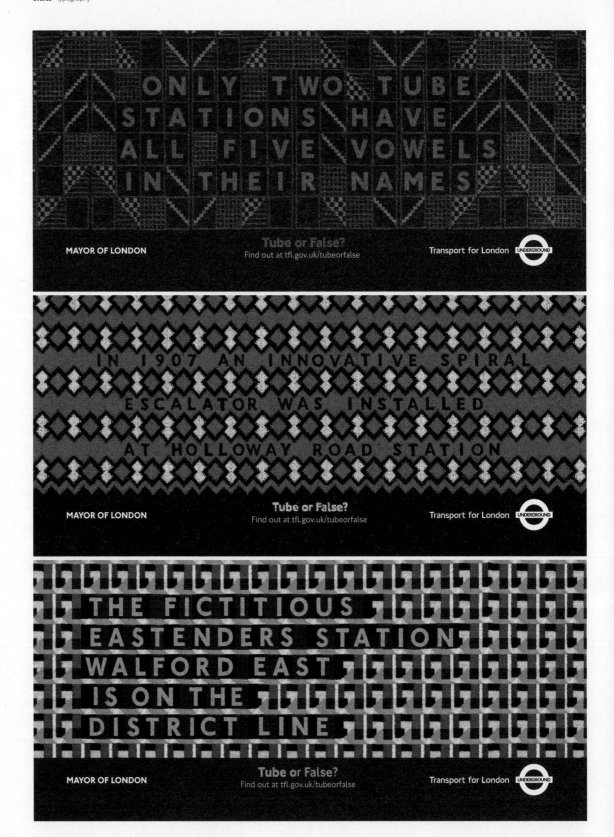

ONLY TWO TUBE STATIONS HAVE ALL FIVE VOWELS IN THEIR NAMES
MAYOR OF LONDON
Tube or False?
Find out at tfl.gov.uk/tubeorfalse
Transport for London
UNDERGROUND

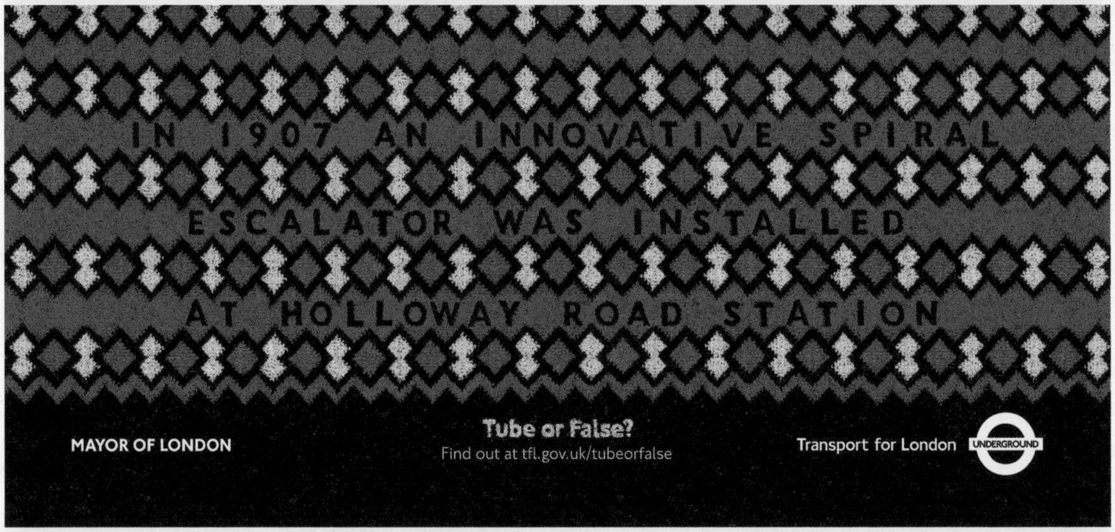
IN 1907 AN INNOVATIVE SPIRAL ESCALATOR WAS INSTALLED AT HOLLOWAY ROAD STATION
MAYOR OF LONDON
Tube or False?
Find out at tfl.gov.uk/tubeorfalse
Transport for London
UNDERGROUND

THE FICTITIOUS EASTENDERS STATION WALFORD EAST IS ON THE DISTRICT LINE
MAYOR OF LONDON
Tube or False?
Find out at tfl.gov.uk/tubeorfalse
Transport for London
UNDERGROUND

Typography for Design
Julius Popp for SAP Germany & the Victoria & Albert Museum

bit.code
SAP wanted to demonstrate how software helps us to get a grip on our daily 'information overload' – and found an unusual and spectacular way to do so. In partnership with the Victoria & Albert Museum, SAP commissioned bit.code, a work by German artist Julius Popp, for the exhibition 'Decode: Digital Design Sensations'. With a large screen comprising spinning black and white tracks representing ones and zeros, bit.code engages the viewer with its movement and mechanical noise. Frequently, bit.code aligns to display relevant keywords from the internet, extracted in real-time using SAP software.

Designer
Julius Popp
Creative Director
Peter Strauss
Advertising Agency
Ogilvy Frankfurt
Account Handler
Veronika Sikvoelgyi
Marketing Manager
Barbara Windisch
Clients
SAP Germany
Victoria &
Albert Museum

Typography for Design
FLAME for the
Naoshima Fukutake Art
Museum Foundation

Fukutake House 2010
This is the third
instalment of an
initiative to mount
exhibition signage
on an old elementary
school building. We
took into consideration
that the signage would
be altered by the wind,
rain and the passage
of time.

Typographer
Masayoshi Kodaira
Designer
Yukiharu Takematsu
Art Director
Masayoshi Kodaira
Producer
Soichiro Fukutake
Design Group
FLAME
Client
Naoshima Fukutake Art
Museum Foundation
Brand
The Setouchi
International Art Festival

FUKUTAKE HOUSE
SHUGOARTS
CREATIVE SPACE
GALLERY
KURIMANZUTTO
JAMES COHAN GALLERY
KOYAMA GALLERY
GALERIE THADDAEUS ROPAC
SCAI
注意

Typography for Press
& Poster Advertising
Ogilvy Beijing
for Greenpeace

Chopsticks Posters
Greenpeace wanted to create awareness about the destruction of forests and encourage people to stop using disposable chopsticks. Posters were created and placed in busy urban areas, around and inside restaurants. Poster headlines were made from used (and sanitised) chopsticks. Copy drove people to the campaign website where they could make a pledge not to use disposable chopsticks.

Typographers
Shiyang He
Shujie Qi
Art Directors
Shiyang He
Shujie Qi
Copywriter
Lianhui Hao
Illustrator
Shujie Qi
Creative Director
Shiyang He
Executive Creative Directors
Bill Chan
Wilson Chow
Doug Schiff
Advertising Agency
Ogilvy Beijing
Account Handlers
Cara Fan
Vivian Guo
Yoyo Liu
Raymond Tao
Client
Greenpeace

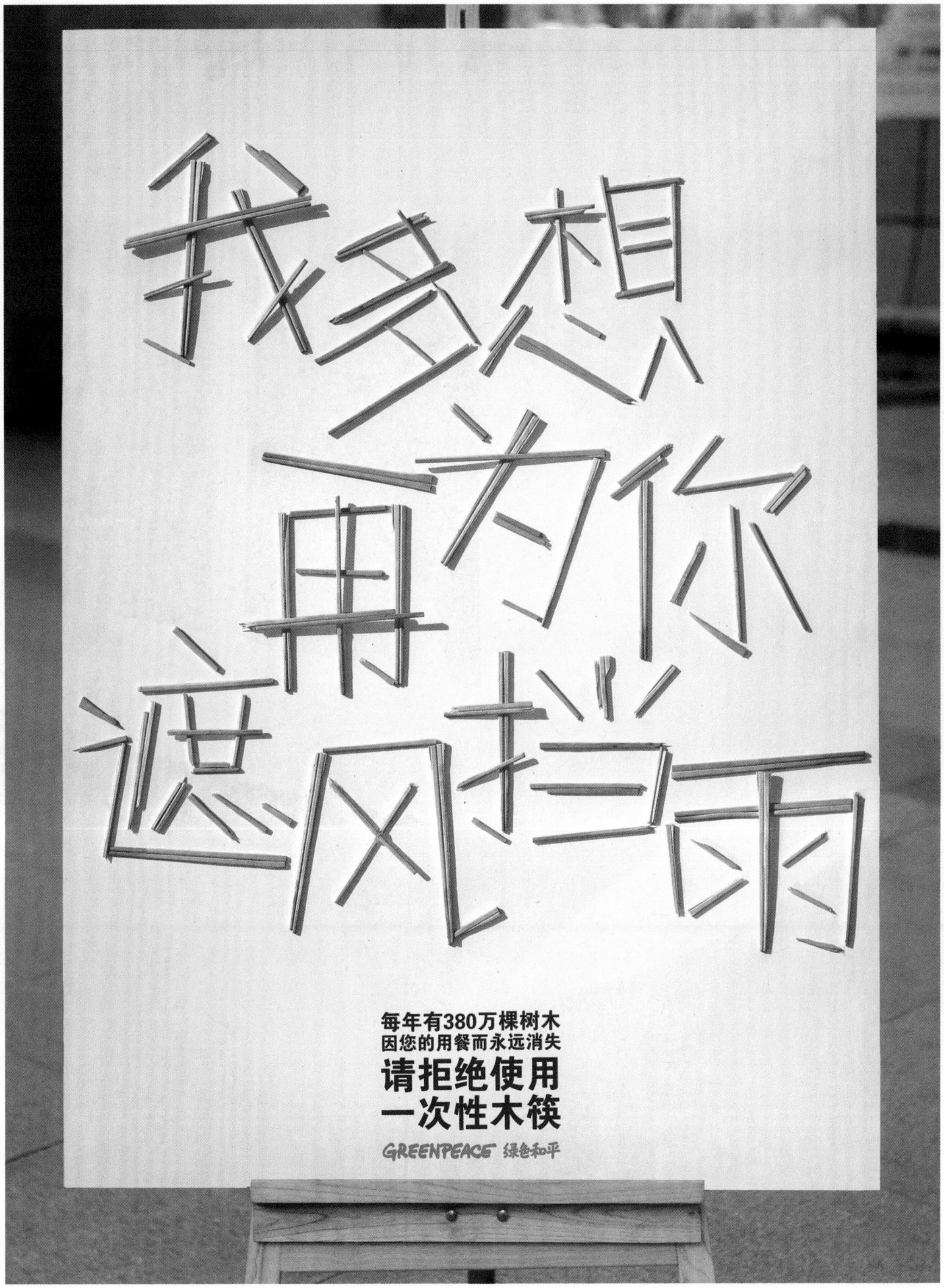
我多想
再为你
遮风挡雨
每年有380万棵树木
因您的用餐而永远消失
请拒绝使用
一次性木筷
GREENPEACE 绿色和平

Typography for Press & Poster Advertising
The Partners for The Injured Jockeys Fund

The Injured Jockeys Fund: HELP
Since 1964, The Injured Jockeys Fund has helped jockeys whose careers have been affected by serious injury. Traditionally supported by the racing establishment and celebrities within the sport, the charity wanted to raise its profile amongst younger race-goers. We created a typeface with each letter composed from details of UK regulation racing silk patterns. When produced as individual posters and arranged appropriately, the typeface allows the charity to communicate to race-goers in a bold, refreshingly colourful way. The first example spells 'HELP', identifying the charity as care providers while subtly appealing for support.

Typographers
Leon Bahrani
James Titterton
Designers
Leon Bahrani
James Titterton
Design Director
Michael Paisley
Seamstresses
Lisa Menzel
Alice Speak
Photographer
Toby Edwards
Design Agency
The Partners
Client
The Injured Jockeys Fund

Typefaces
Oded Ezer Typography
for Mota Italic

Rutz (aka Vesper Hebrew)
This font was designed as a Hebrew version of Rob Keller's Vesper. Matching the Latin Vesper, Rutz, which means 'running' in Hebrew (the same as in 'running text'), includes five different weights: light, regular, medium, bold and heavy. This is the first Hebrew serif text font family that consists of five weights.

Typographer
Oded Ezer
Design Studio
Oded Ezer Typography
Client
Mota Italic

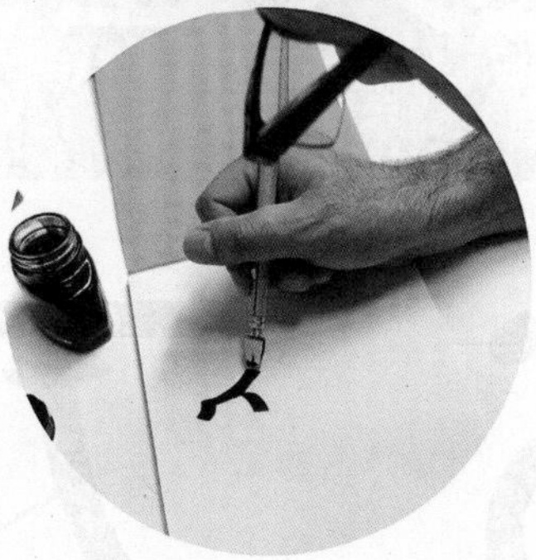

העברית
טקסט (מלטינית: Textum), הוא מונח שמקורו בתחום הבלשנות, המתאר רצף מילים, משפטים ופסקאות היוצרים יחד מכלול, שהוא הטקסט. המונח ומשמעויותיו התרחבו במהלך הדורות, כדי להתאים לניתוח התנהגויות אנושיות שונות במסגרת מדעי החברה.
גופנים
במסגרת תורות הניתוח של הטקסט, ניתן למצוא גם את תורת חקר השיח ואת תורת הרטוריקה. תורות הניתוח השונות מבצעות את ניתוח הטקסט במסגרת הקונטקסט - תוך התחשבות גם במוען, בנמען, באופן הפרסום וביחסים בין כל אלו. במסגרת מדעי החברה התרחבה מאד משמעות המושג.
פונט

Typefaces
VISUAL DESIGN LABORATORY

KyoSensha
KyoSensha is a boldface, handwritten brush-style typeface based on the Edomoji Senja script. Edomoji are Japanese lettering styles that were used for advertising and popular culture, such as sumo and kabuki, in the Edo period (1603–1868). The challenge was to develop these Senja characters, originally written with thick brushes, into 6 weights, from fine-brush to thick-brush styles, something no one had tried before. By emphasising the characteristics of a brush-style script, we created a vivid, dynamic and sophisticated typeface.

Typographers
Kyoko Katsumoto
Shigeru Katsumoto
Design Director
Kyoko Katsumoto
Design Studio
VISUAL DESIGN LABORATORY
Client
VISUAL DESIGN LABORATORY

魅惑大陸アフリカ

あ　ア　漢

あいうえお　アイウエオ　亜娃阿哀愛
かきくけこ　カキクケコ　逢葵悪渥鯵
さしすせそ　サシスセソ　虻絢或伊以
たちつてと　タチツテト　位帷意為易
なにぬねの　ナニヌネノ　維衣謂井遺
はひふへほ　ハヒフヘホ　亥域育郁壱
まみむめも　マミムメモ　溢稲鰯因胤
わゐんゑを　ワヰンヱヲ　淫隠烏羽雨
がぎぐげご　ガギグゲゴ　炎迂緒瓜渦
ざじずぜぞ　ザジズゼゾ　永泳蚊縁燕

Typefaces
Willerstorfer
Font Foundry

Acorde
Acorde is a reliable workhorse for large, demanding design projects. It was designed to be perfectly suited to all different sizes, from small continuous text to large headlines and signage. The typeface's name is derived from 'a' 'cor'porate 'de'sign typeface, however Acorde is suitable for information design and editorial design purposes as well. Acorde's characterful details give it a distinctive appearance in large sizes and contribute to its high legibility in small sizes. It comes in 14 styles – seven weights in Roman and Italic each.

Designer
Stefan Willerstorfer
Design Studio
Willerstorfer Font Foundry
Client
Willerstorfer Font Foundry

Acorde
a corporate design typeface
suitable for all sizes from small text to headlines and big signage
humanist sans
14 styles with 925 glyphs per font
Acorde's characterful details are found within all styles
workhorse
unique appearance
Acorde is available in seven weights
in Roman and Italic each,
from Regular to Extrablack – that is
14 styles with 925 glyphs per font,
suitable for all sizes from small
text to headlines and big signage.
Various OpenType features allow
for a sophisticated typography
in corporate design, information
design and editorial design.
The huge character set supports
a vast range of languages,
so trust this high quality product
and order your package now.
Regular
Italic
Medium
Medium Italic
Semibold
Semibold Italic
Bold
Bold Italic
Extrabold
Extrabold Italic
Black
Black Italic
Extrablack
Extrablack Italic
→ www.willerstorfer.com

Yellow Pencil in Writing for Advertising

Writing for Film Advertising
Wieden+Kennedy Portland for Old Spice

Old Spice Response Campaign
'The Man Your Man Could Smell Like' made a big splash in early 2010, but we wanted to leverage the success to have a more direct, engaging conversation with fans. The result was the 'Response' campaign, an experiment in real-time branding in which the Old Spice guy personally responded to fans online. Over 186 messages were created in just over two-and-a-half days of production; the work would go on to record more than 65 million views, making it one of the fastest growing and most popular online campaigns in history.

Copywriters
Craig Allen
Jason Bagley
Eric Baldwin
Eric Kallman
Art Directors
Craig Allen
Eric Kallman
Creative Directors
Jason Bagley
Eric Baldwin
Executive Creative Directors
Mark Fitzloff
Susan Hoffman
Global Interactive Creative Director
Iain Tait
Producer
Ann-Marie Harbour
Developers
John Cohoon
Trent Johnson
Interactive Designer
Matthew Carroll
Advertising Agency
Wieden+Kennedy Portland
Production Company
Don't Act Big
Digital Strategist
Josh Millrod
Senior Digital Strategist
Dean McBeth
Account Handler
Diana Gonzalez
Brand Manager
James Moorhead
Assistant Brand Manager
Shanan Sabin
Client
Old Spice

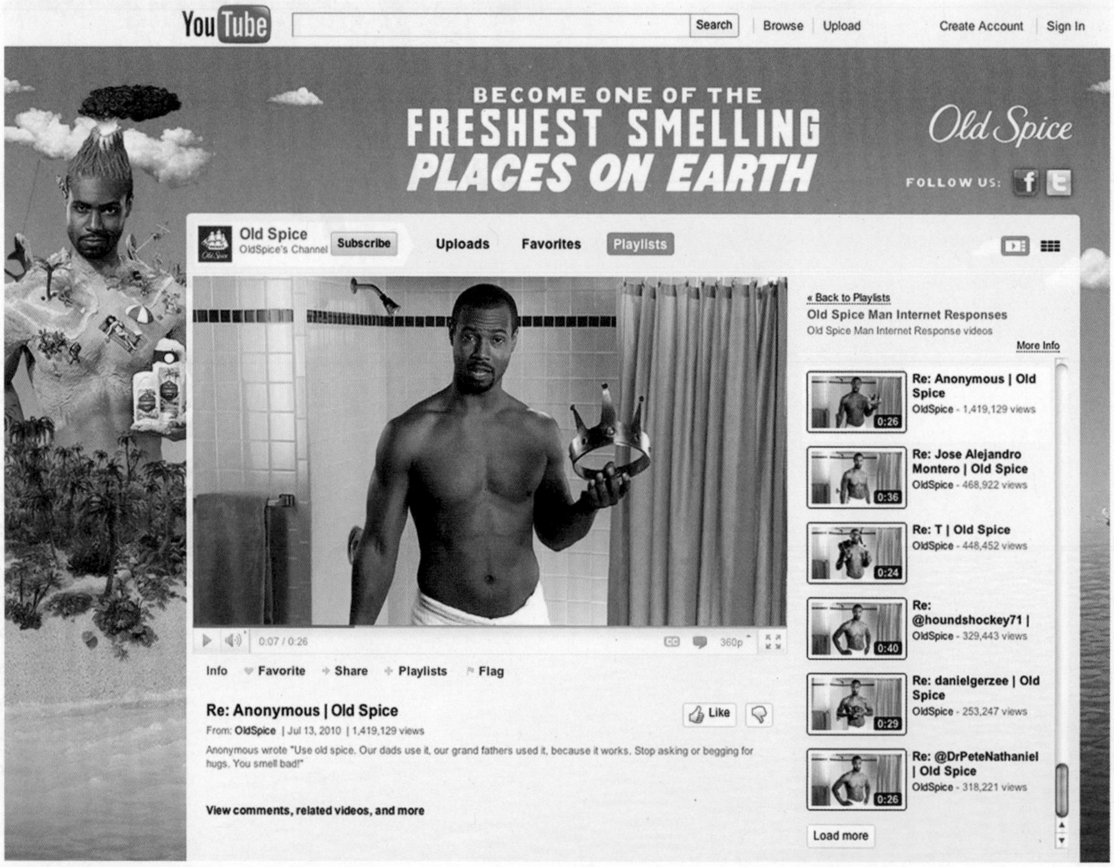
YouTube
Search
Browse
Upload
Create Account
Sign In
BECOME ONE OF THE
FRESHEST SMELLING
PLACES ON EARTH
Old Spice
FOLLOW US:
Old Spice
OldSpice's Channel
Subscribe
Uploads
Favorites
Playlists
« Back to Playlists
Old Spice Man Internet Responses
Old Spice Man Internet Response videos
More Info
Re: Anonymous | Old Spice
OldSpice - 1,419,129 views
0:26
Re: Jose Alejandro Montero | Old Spice
OldSpice - 468,922 views
0:36
Re: T | Old Spice
OldSpice - 448,452 views
0:24
Re: @houndshockey71 |
OldSpice - 329,443 views
0:40
Re: danielgerzee | Old Spice
OldSpice - 253,247 views
0:29
Re: @DrPeteNathaniel | Old Spice
OldSpice - 318,221 views
0:26
Load more
0:07 / 0:26
360p
Info
Favorite
Share
Playlists
Flag
Re: Anonymous | Old Spice
From: OldSpice | Jul 13, 2010 | 1,419,129 views
Like
Anonymous wrote "Use old spice. Our dads use it, our grand fathers used it, because it works. Stop asking or begging for hugs. You smell bad!"
View comments, related videos, and more

Nomination in
Writing for Advertising

Writing for Film
Advertising
Y&R New York
for Land Rover

Sword Collector
When a manager has to tell his samurai sword-carrying employee that Human Resources doesn't want him stockpiling swords and knives in his office anymore, he makes sure he is safe inside a Land Rover LR4 in order to give his psychotic employee the bad news.

Copywriter
Brandon Henderson
Art Director
Dan Treichel
Director
Jim Jenkins
Creative Directors
Icaro Doria
Dan Morales
Guillermo Vega
Executive Creative Directors
Ian Reichenthal
Scott Vitrone
Global Creative Director
Graham Lang
Producers
Devon Clark
Toni Lipari
Executive Producer
Marc Grill
Editor
Jason Macdonald
Director of Photography
Robert Yeoman
Executive Directors of Content Production
Nathy Aviram
Lora Schulson
Advertising Agency
Y&R New York
Production Company
O Positive
Editing
Number Six
Sound Design
Henryboy
Vice President of Marketing
Finbar McFall
Client
Land Rover
Brand
LR4

YOU'LL FEEL SAFE INSIDE.

Nomination in Writing for Advertising

Writing for Film Advertising
Saatchi & Saatchi Los Angeles for the Toyota Motor Corporation

Sienna 'Swagger Wagon' Music Video
Minivans are the laughing stock of the automotive world. It was a huge challenge for Toyota to get parents to want its redesigned Sienna, much less make it a vehicle people talk about. With this insight, the agency developed a campaign called 'The Sienna Family' and later a music video called 'Swagger Wagon', which would serve as a rally for proud parents everywhere. As a result of the campaign, the 'Swagger Wagon' video has garnered close to nine million views. But more importantly, the Sienna exceeded yearly sales expectations by almost 20 per cent.

Copywriters
David J Evans V
Donnell Johnson
Art Director
Stephan Baik
Director
Jody Hill
Creative Director
Erich Funke
Executive Creative Director
Mike McKay
Associate Creative Director
Donnell Johnson
Executive Integrated Producer
David J Evans V
Broadcast Producer
Karena Dacker
Senior Broadcast Producer
Gil DeCuir
Director of Integrated Production
Tanya LeSieur
Telecine Colourist
Siggy Fersti
Editor
Teddy Gersten
Sound Mixer
Peter Rincon
Advertising Agency
Saatchi & Saatchi Los Angeles
Production Company
Caviar Los Angeles
Editing
Butcher
Music Composition
Black Iris
Planner
Ginny Kollewe
Account Director
Steven Sluk
Client
Toyota Motor Corporation
Brand
Sienna

Nomination in Writing for Advertising

Writing for Press & Poster Advertising
AMV BBDO for PepsiCo

Pat
Brands have been asking consumers to make their TV ads for some time. But are these ads any good? Doritos challenged us to run a campaign that would ensure a great commercial at the end of the process. To generate a higher standard of entries for our branded TV show, called 'Doritos King of Ads', we developed provocative press executions that begged aspiring creatives to outdo the handful of hacks who often win such competitions.

Copywriter
Paul Knott
Art Director
Tim Vance
Designer
Aaron Moss
Photographer
David Stewart
Typographer
Aaron Moss
Creative Director
Mark Fairbanks
Executive Creative Director
Paul Brazier
Print Producer
Chloe Robinson
Advertising Agency
AMV BBDO
Planners
Nicky Davies
Tom White
Account Handlers
Ben Griffiths
Philip Lloyd
Adam Tucker
Brand & Marketing Manager
Sam Hinchcliffe
Client
PepsiCo
Brand
Doritos

A low-flying crop duster started it all. You know, the one in North By Northwest?
As a young man, Patrick (or Pat to his only pal) went doolally for that scene. If he shut his eyes, he was Cary Grant, taking cover in that cornfield. It gave him butterflies.
It helped him understand – he was born to act.
Eventually, it would also become a metaphor for his career: Pat, the swooping barnstormer discharging gallons of raw, thespian pesticide. And ducking for cover? Horrified relatives, agents and producers alike.
Consider his first casting. Pat read somewhere that
"Acting is like standing up naked & turning around, very slowly."
Sadly, he took this literally. Pat would never audition in his hometown again.
"Auditions schmauditions" as he would say. Unbowed, he formed a dramatic society called The Galloping Swans. Their first project, Yentl, was to be staged for the local retirement home.
One evening, Pat turned up to rehearsals in his Y-fronts, three sheets to the wind. This upset the old folk, so management pulled the plug.
But the show must go on.
By chance, he landed a role in a toupee commercial for one of those shopping channels. Pat loved his costume, a ginger hairpiece, which gave him an "aura of untold elegance". Surely this would be his big break?
A gig at the Sunderland Empire followed. Admittedly, it was pushing a mop. But he doesn't tell people that, why should he? The run came to an end when Pat slipped on a half-eaten pasty during the triumphant finale of an imagined King Lear, fracturing his fibula.
After that? Pat turned his talents to Youtube. A two-hour performance of Equus had thirteen hits before it was taken down by request of animal welfare. He saw this as a runaway success, the highlight of his career.
Until now.
Pat wants to make the next Doritos TV ad & win £200k.
Please.
Win it before he does.
Doritos
For more information visit doritos.co.uk

A low-flying crop duster started it all. You know, the one in North By Northwest?
As a young man, Patrick (or Pat to his only pal) went doolally for that scene. If he shut his eyes, he was Cary Grant, taking cover in that cornfield. It gave him butterflies.
It helped him understand – he was born to act.
Eventually, it would also become a metaphor for his career: Pat, the swooping barnstormer discharging gallons of raw, thespian pesticide. And ducking for cover? Horrified relatives, agents and producers alike.
Consider his first casting. Pat read somewhere that
"Acting is like standing up naked & turning around, very slowly."
Sadly, he took this literally. Pat would never audition in his hometown again.
"Auditions schmauditions" as he would say. Unbowed, he formed a dramatic society called The Galloping Swans. Their first project, Yentl, was to be staged for the local retirement home.
One evening, Pat turned up to rehearsals in his Y-fronts, three sheets to the wind. This upset the old folk, so management pulled the plug.
But the show must go on.
By chance, he landed a role in a toupee commercial for one of those shopping channels. Pat loved his costume, a ginger hairpiece, which gave him an "aura of untold elegance". Surely this would be his big break?
A gig at the Sunderland Empire followed. Admittedly, it was pushing a mop. But he doesn't tell people that, why should he? The run came to an end when Pat slipped on a half-eaten pasty during the triumphant finale of an imagined King Lear, fracturing his fibula.
After that? Pat turned his talents to Youtube. A two-hour performance of Equus had thirteen hits before it was taken down by request of animal welfare. He saw this as a runaway success, the highlight of his career.
Until now.

Writing for Film Advertising
BMF Sydney for Meat & Livestock Australia

Lambassador 2010
If you don't eat lamb on Australia Day, you're un-Australian – that's what Sam Kekovich has been telling Aussies for years. His annual address to the nation has made lamb our national meat – lamb is to Australia Day what turkey is to Christmas. So after conquering Australia, it was time to take on the world, by having Sam appointed as Australia's first official Lambassador.

Copywriters
Dennis Koutoulogenis
Jake Rusznyak
Art Director
Jake Rusznyak
Directors
Trent O'Donnell
Scott Pickett
Creative Directors
Warren Brown
Dennis Koutoulogenis
Producer
Nicola Patterson
Agency Producer
Jenny Lee-Archer
Sound Designer
Paul Taylor
Advertising Agency
BMF Sydney
Production Company
Jungleboys
Special Effects
Emerald City
Account Handler
Rebecca Booth
Brand Manager
Janice Byrnes
Client
Meat & Livestock Australia

CHINA
ERIA
We love our Lamb

Writing for Film Advertising
Y&R New York for Land Rover

Cat Sitter
When a couple returning from holiday enquire as to the whereabouts of their beloved cat, the cat sitter waits until he is safely behind the wheel of a Land Rover LR4 to tell them that he neglected to give their sick cat its daily medicine.

Copywriter
Brandon Henderson
Art Director
Dan Treichel
Director
Jim Jenkins
Creative Directors
Icaro Doria
Dan Morales
Guillermo Vega
Executive Creative Directors
Ian Reichenthal
Scott Vitrone
Global Creative Director
Graham Lang
Producers
Devon Clark
Toni Lipari
Executive Producer
Marc Grill
Editor
Jason Macdonald
Director of Photography
Robert Yeoman
Executive Directors of Content Production
Nathy Aviram
Lora Schulson
Advertising Agency
Y&R New York
Production Company
O Postive
Editing
Number Six
Sound Design
Henryboy
Vice President of Marketing
Finbar McFall
Client
Land Rover
Brand
LR4

YOU'LL FEEL SAFE INSIDE.
LAND ROVER

Writing for Film Advertising
Wong, Doody, Crandall, Wiener for the Washington State Department of Health

Dear Me: Robert
Despite declining smoking rates, tobacco use among Washington State's working poor remained relatively unchanged. And as the US faced a deep recession, the idea of convincing smokers to give up what is often their only stress-relief tool became almost ridiculous. So we stepped aside and let them convince themselves. We followed genuine smokers as they read aloud 'Dear Me' letters they'd written to themselves describing how they felt about their habit.

Copywriter
Matt McCain
Art Director
Tony Zimney
Director
David Turnley
Creative Director
Matt McCain
Executive Creative Director
Tracy Wong
Agency Producer
Steph Huske
Editor
Alan Nay
Sound Designer
John Buroker
Advertising Agency
Wong, Doody, Crandall, Wiener
Production Company
Furlined
Client
Washington State Department of Health

No one can make me quit but me.

Writing for Film Advertising
Goodby, Silverstein & Partners for Logitech

Ivan Cobenk
The Logitech Revue uses Google TV to bring shows, movies, web videos and more right to your television. So who better to represent the enormous breadth of content available than the ubiquitous Kevin Bacon? With a little effects magic, we turned him into Ivan Cobenk, a Kevin-obsessed super fan, and created an amusing demo of the Revue and its ability to instantly access all the Kevin that Ivan could ever want.

Copywriter
Nat Lawlor
Art Director
Croix Gagnon
Director
Ringan Ledwidge
Creative Director
David Kolbusz
Producer
Alison Kunzman
Agency Producer
Elizabeth O'Toole
Editor
Rich Orrick
Director of Photography
Alwin Kuchler
Advertising Agency
Goodby, Silverstein & Partners
Production Company
Smuggler
Visual Effects Company
Woodshop
Special Effects Make-Up
Legacy Effects
Account Handler
Leslie Barrett
Client
Logitech
Brands
Google TV
Logitech Revue

TREMORS

Writing for Film
Advertising
JWT Melbourne
for the Melbourne
Writers Festival

Writer's Block
This is a 45-second cinema and online commercial that was created as part of the 'Stories from Every Angle' campaign for the 2010 Melbourne Writers Festival. The idea for the spot is based around the musings of a writer's inner voice as he debates the different angles of his story, with comedic results.

Copywriter
Jim Ritchie
Art Director
Hannah Smit
Direction
Sferrazza
Creative Director
Richard Muntz
Producer
Catherine Warner
Agency Producer
Justine Kubale
Editor
Dave Wade
Sound Designer
Stevo Williams
Advertising Agency
JWT Melbourne
Production Company
Plush Films
Sound Design
Flagstaff Studios
Planner
Anuj Mehra
Account Handlers
Melissa Benavides
Prue Tehan
Marketing Manager
Juliette Kringas
Client
Melbourne Writers
Festival

STORIES
from
EVERY
ANGLE
MELBOURNE
WRITERS
FESTIVAL
27 AUG - 5 SEPT 2010 WWW.MWF.COM.AU

Writing for Film Advertising
Red Bee Media
for the BBC

Precision Engineered Comedy
BBC Two star Peter Capaldi gives us a rare insight into the precision engineering and craft required to make great comedy. In a behind the scenes interview he describes the research, thought and effort that goes into a joke... before swearing for a laugh.

Copywriter
Chris Balmond
Director
Oliver Parsons
Creative Director
James de Zoete
Executive Creative Director
Charlie Mawer
Group Creative Director
Frazer Jelleyman
Producers
Bridie Harrison
Caroline Hicks
Designers
Simon Graham
Teak Tse
Production Manager
Jane Hunt
Creative Agency
Red Bee Media
Planner
John Jones
Account Handler
Elinor Jones
Account Director
Richard Stuart
Brand Executive
Bimala Devi
Brand Manager
Felicity Williams
Head of Marketing
Ash Makkar
Client
BBC
Brand
BBC Two

Precision engineered comedy
bbc.co.uk/comedy
BBC TWO

Writing for Film Advertising
Three Drunk Monkeys
for the BBC

Honk if You're Human
'Honk if You're Human' takes the viewer on a humorous journey through some of mankind's great and not-so-great achievements, ending on the BBC Knowledge brand positioning of 'A little knowledge goes a long way'. It's a follow-up to the much lauded 'Eat Up Brain' and 'Moon Week' ads.

Copywriter
Damian Fitzgerald
Art Director
Matt Heck
Director
Sean Pecknold
Creative Director
Noah Regan
Executive Creative Directors
Justin Drape
Scott Nowell
Producer
Brian Waldrop
Executive Producer
Aaron Ball
Agency Producers
Thea Carone
John Ruggiero
Animators
Britta Johnson
Sean Pecknold
Sound Designer
Justin Braegelmann
Mixer
Justin Braegelmann
Sound Producer
Virginia Welsh
Advertising Agency
Three Drunk Monkeys
Production Company
Grandchildren
Planner
Fabio Buresti
Account Director
Kristen Hardeman
Group Account Director
Dan Beaumont
Marketing Manager
Amanda McGregor
Client
BBC
Brand
BBC Knowledge

Writing for Film
Advertising
Leo Burnett Chicago
for Allstate

Mayhem Campaign
All the other insurance companies want to talk about is saving money. But what about the protection you get? When you cut your price, you cut your coverage. And if you don't have Allstate, you might not be protected… from mayhem. All four spots in this campaign were also separately selected as single executions in this category.

Copywriters
Matt Miller
Josh Mizrachi
Art Directors
Greg Nobles
Chris Rodriguez
Director
Phil Morrison
Creative Directors
Britt Nolan
Jo Shoesmith
Executive Creative Directors
Jeanie Caggiano
Charley Wickman
Chief Creative Officer
Susan Credle
Producers
Charlie Cocuzza
Martha Davis
Suzanne Hargrove
Executive Producer
Lisa Margulis
Agency Producer
Bryan Litman
Agency Executive Producer
Veronica Puc
Visual Effects Producers
Angela Bowen
Nancy Nina Hwang
Luisa Murray
Jamie Scott
Kyle Write
Editors
Haines Hall
Matthew Wood
Directors of Photography
Peter Donahue
Toby Irwin
Wally Pfister
Sound Designer
John Binder
Advertising Agency
Leo Burnett Chicago
Production Company
Epoch Films
Visual Effects Company
Mass Market
Client
Allstate

GO STATE!

Teen Driver

Flag

Douglas Fir

Lawn Game

Writing for Press
& Poster Advertising
AMV BBDO for PepsiCo

Iain / Eunice / Simone
Brands have been asking consumers to make their TV ads for some time. But are these ads any good? Doritos challenged us to run a campaign that would ensure a great commercial at the end of the process. To generate a higher standard of entries for our branded TV show, called 'Doritos King of Ads', we ran provocative press ads in creative titles including 'Creative Review', 'Dazed & Confused' and 'Campaign'. These executions begged aspiring creatives to outdo the handful of hacks who often win such competitions.

Copywriter
Paul Knott
Art Director
Tim Vance
Designer
Aaron Moss
Photographer
David Stewart
Typographer
Aaron Moss
Creative Director
Mark Fairbanks
Executive Creative Director
Paul Brazier
Print Producer
Chloe Robinson
Advertising Agency
AMV BBDO
Planners
Nicola Davies
Tom White
Marketing Manager
Sam Hinchcliffe
Client
PepsiCo
Brand
Doritos

"Wanna listen to my *gateaux blaster*? I baked it myself."
Lock up your daughters, that's the sound of Iain on the pull.
You see, Iain's email signature reads *Punmeister General*. "All puns blazing!" he likes to explain. Ask him. He might even tell you about his *No nest for the wicked* bedspread. Good one mate.
Iain has puns for every problem. He's aiming to sell t-shirt slogans for extra cash. *Pie Hard, Ale along the Watchtower, Keep off the Grass* and *Men Who Stare at Moats* are all his. Impressed?
He is. Which might explain why he says "skill" so much.
Consider his mum's coffee shop, which he attempted to rebrand.
Home of the Milfshake wasn't exactly what she had in mind.
Iain insists he used "a typeface only mothers would love." Strangely, it didn't fly.
Never outgunned, Iain went on to enter an advertising competition for an ice cream start up. He designed a special layout using photos of roadkill. The headline? *Rocky Road. Best served stone cold.* He didn't even place. Obviously the judging was rigged.
But hey ho, backwards and downwards. Iain's still huge on Twitter. Mostly because his screen resolution is set to 640x480. That said, he does have two followers. One is a pretty young lady (he thinks she's real). And there's always "the satisfaction of a *Quality Tweet*."
Skill.
You see? Iain's hellbent on *"pushing the envelope, with my pen."* And if you don't count a short-lived obsession with urban poetry (whatever that is), he's been desperate to find his next challenge.
Until now.
Iain wants to make the next Doritos TV ad & win £200k.
Please.
Win it before he does.
Doritos
For more information visit doritos.co.uk

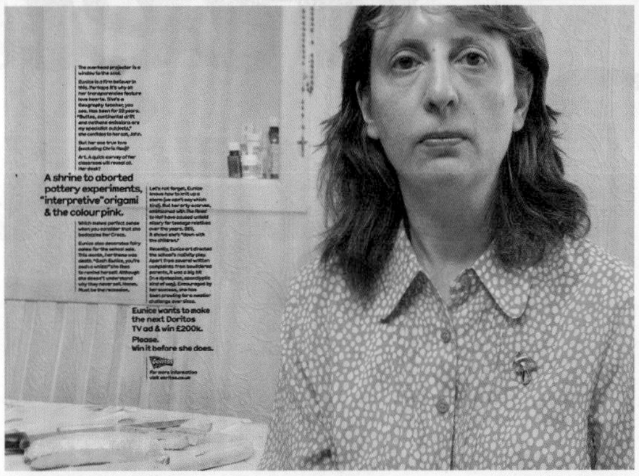
A shrine to aborted pottery experiments, "interpretive" origami & the colour pink.
Eunice wants to make the next Doritos TV ad & win £200k.
Please.
Win it before she does.

"My gonzo health and safety video came first."
Simone wants to make the next Doritos TV ad & win £200k.
Please.
Win it before she does.

The overhead projector is a window to the soul.
Eunice is a firm believer in this. Perhaps it's why all her transparencies feature love hearts. She's a Geography teacher, you see. Has been for 22 years. "Buttes, continental drift and methane emissions are my specialist subjects," she confides to her cat, John.
But her one true love (excluding Chris Rea)?
Art. A quick survey of her classroom will reveal all. Her desk?
A shrine to aborted pottery experiments, "interpretive" origami & the colour pink.
Which makes perfect sense when you consider that she bedazzles her Crocs.
Eunice also decorates fairy cakes for the school sale. This month, her theme was death. "Gosh Eunice, you're such a whizz!" she likes to remind herself. Although she doesn't understand why they never sell. Hmmm. Must be the recession.
Let's not forget, Eunice knows how to knit up a storm (we can't say which kind). But her arty scarves, emblazoned with *The Road to Hell* have caused untold misery for teenage relatives over the years. Still, it shows she's "down with the children."
Recently, Eunice art directed the school's nativity play. Apart from several written complaints from bewildered parents, it was a big hit (in a dystopian, apocalyptic kind of way). Encouraged by her success, she has been prowling for a meatier challenge ever since.
Eunice wants to make the next Doritos TV ad & win £200k.
Please.
Win it before she does.

Writing for Press & Poster Advertising
McCann Erickson Malaysia for the National Cancer Society Malaysia

Hello
The HPV viral infection causes a large majority of cases of cervical cancer. A Pap smear, an early detection screening test, can reduce the risks. But the uptake is poor. Why? Lack of knowledge and social taboo. This ad encourages urban Malaysian women aged 21–50 to have their Pap smears through direct and light-hearted long copy in a tongue-in-cheek manner, turning a serious matter into something more accessible and acceptable. Apart from national newspapers, posters were placed in ladies' rooms in nightclubs, gyms, and food and drink hang-outs in town.

Copywriters
Jennie Ban
Szu-Hung Lee
Art Directors
Ean-Hwa Huang
Jerome Ooi
Designer
Sze-Mei Chan
Creative Directors
Ean-Hwa Huang
Szu-Hung Lee
Print Producer
Jimmy Ong
Advertising Agency
McCann Erickson Malaysia
Account Handler
JB Ling
Client Managing Director
Rubi-Ain Dahlan
Client
National Cancer Society Malaysia

A GUIDE TO KNOWING YOUR PRIVATES BETTER.

There's a lot that you may know about yourself. But girl, how well do you *really* know your southern sister?

Vaginas generally look alike
Inside or out, it's the same. The size of the clitoris, however, varies and so do those butterfly wings, formally known as labia. One side usually flaps lower than the other.

Mission: Orgasm
Your G-spot is only an inch within your vadge and the reason sex feels so amazing with all the OOH-AH stimulation is thanks to those feel-good hormones your body produces. Reaching the big fat O, however, is a bonus.

It can handle a giant member. Really.
Bring on the big guns as the vagina is incredibly elastic and can fit a well-hung guy, yet it always returns to its usual tightness after sex (just think, rubber band).

A good workout benefits both ways
Regular sweat sessions at the gym keep your abs in shape. So it should come as no surprise that you can tone up your vagina just as well. *Psst*, it may make it easier to climax besides giving you (and him) a tighter grip. So, do your *Kegels* (that's vaginal exercises to any lads who may be reading this).

Things lost inside, can be found.
It isn't a black hole. If you can't retrieve stuff while squatting or standing up and inserting two fingers inside, check-in with your gynae. But that doesn't give you the licence to experiment, either. Just saying.

Discharge changes throughout your cycle
When your discharge is clear like egg white, it means you're ovulating. Creamy and thick texture means you're about to get your period.

Its aroma changes according to the lunar cycle
A healthy vagina emits a slightly different odour depending on where you are in your cycle. It tends to be pungent after your period and after workouts because of sweat glands; and during sex, thanks to the natural lubrication you produce.

It's loaded with microbes
Chill. Just like yoghurt they make sure you don't get an infection.

Too much sex is whack
While regular action can relax you, too much in a short period of time may leave you chafed or inflamed or even give you a lovely case of urinary-tract infection.

Hello Vagina

Having cobwebs won't make you a virgin again
There's a rumour out there that if you find yourself in a long dry spell, your vagina will become so tight that getting back in the saddle will hurt. It's a myth.

It's self-cleaning. Like an oven.
Your vagina cleanses itself with discharge. Yes, that icky-sticky stuff has a function. The secretions flush out cells from the vaginal wall, excess water and bad bacteria.

A gentle probe once a year keeps you safe
Calm down, we mean getting a Pap smear.

You see, if you're sexually active you might have an unlucky encounter with the *Human Papillomavirus* (HPV), the virus that can lead to cervical cancer.

The HPV is so common that 8 out of 10 women will get infected once in their life.

Thankfully, cervical cancer caused by the HPV can be cured if detected early with a Pap smear. So routine screening once a year with your gynaecologist or family doctor is highly recommended.

Don't worry, it only needs a few minutes, isn't painful and takes a week or less to get the results.

It's a little much-needed discomfort for a whole lot of vaginal peace of mind.

National Cancer Society Malaysia
Giving Hope Celebrating Life

FOR MORE INFORMATION, COUNSELLING OR GUIDANCE REGARDING THE HPV, PAP SMEAR OR CERVICAL CANCER, PLEASE VISIT WWW.CANCER.ORG.MY, CALL 03-2698 7300 OR EMAIL CONTACT@CANCER.ORG.MY

Writing for Press & Poster Advertising
Ogilvy & Mather Singapore for the Global Alliance for Preserving the History of World War II in Asia

Hideki Tojo
The objective of this campaign was to tell the ugly but historical truth of World War II in Asia to a new generation. Unlike the war in Europe, history remains a very sensitive subject in the Asia Pacific region. Our aim was to create a stir by exaggerating our own propaganda to such a point that it made people doubt it. By making people question history we started a dangerous but necessary debate.

Copywriter
Eugene Cheong
Art Directors
Chan Hwee Chong
Chris Soh
Eric Yeo
Photographer
Jeremy Wong
Typographer
Chris Soh
Creative Director
Eric Yeo
Executive Creative Director
Robert Gaxiola
Regional Creative Director
Eugene Cheong
Illustration
Magic Cube
Advertising Agency
Ogilvy & Mather Singapore
Client
Global Alliance for Preserving the History of World War II in Asia

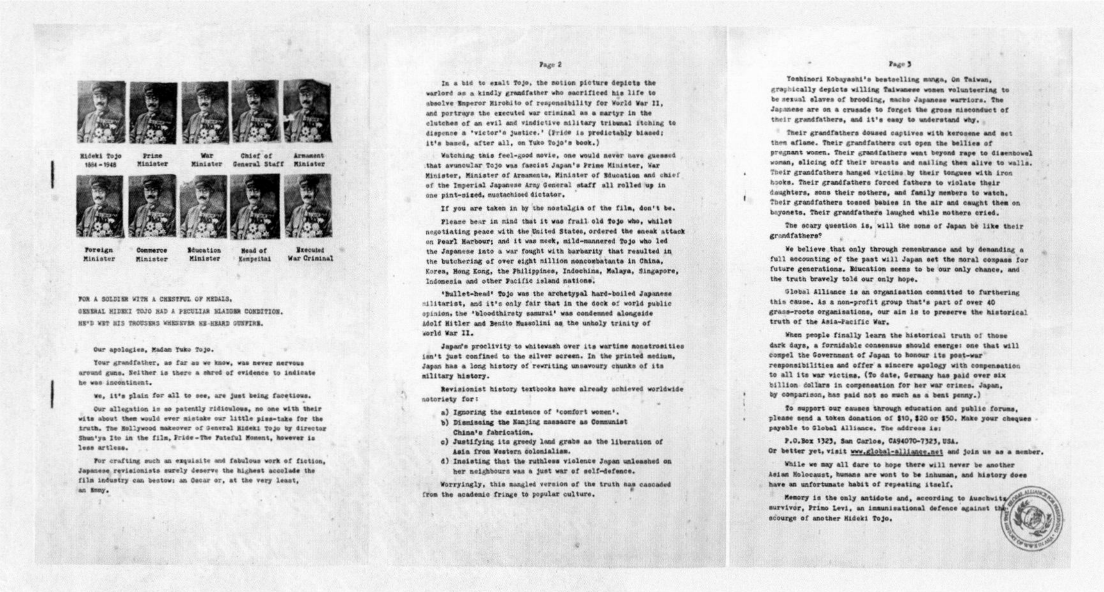

Hideki Tojo 1884-1948 | Prime Minister | War Minister | Chief of General Staff | Armament Minister

Foreign Minister | Commerce Minister | Education Minister | Head of Kempeitai | Executed War Criminal

FOR A SOLDIER WITH A CHESTFUL OF MEDALS,
GENERAL HIDEKI TOJO HAD A PECULIAR BLADDER CONDITION.
HE'D WET HIS TROUSERS WHENEVER HE HEARD GUNFIRE.

Our apologies, Madam Yuko Tojo.

Your grandfather, as far as we know, was never nervous around guns. Neither is there a shred of evidence to indicate he was incontinent.

We, it's plain for all to see, are just being facetious.

Our allegation is so patently ridiculous, no one with their wits about them would ever mistake our little piss-take for the truth. The Hollywood makeover of General Hideki Tojo by director Shun'ya Ito in the film, Pride-The Fateful Moment, however is less artless.

For crafting such an exquisite and fabulous work of fiction, Japanese revisionists surely deserve the highest accolade the film industry can bestow: an Oscar or, at the very least, an Emmy.

Page 2

In a bid to exalt Tojo, the motion picture depicts the warlord as a kindly grandfather who sacrificed his life to absolve Emperor Hirohito of responsibility for World War II, and portrays the executed war criminal as a martyr in the clutches of an evil and vindictive military tribunal itching to dispense a 'victor's justice.' (Pride is predictably biased; it's based, after all, on Yuko Tojo's book.)

Watching this feel-good movie, one would never have guessed that avuncular Tojo was fascist Japan's Prime Minister, War Minister, Minister of Armaments, Minister of Education and chief of the Imperial Japanese Army General staff all rolled up in one pint-sized, mustachioed dictator.

If you are taken in by the nostalgia of the film, don't be.

Please bear in mind that it was frail old Tojo who, whilst negotiating peace with the United States, ordered the sneak attack on Pearl Harbour; and it was meek, mild-mannered Tojo who led the Japanese into a war fought with barbarity that resulted in the butchering of over eight million noncombatants in China, Korea, Hong Kong, the Philippines, Indochina, Malaya, Singapore, Indonesia and other Pacific island nations.

'Bullet-head' Tojo was the archetypal hard-boiled Japanese militarist, and it's only fair that in the dock of world public opinion, the 'bloodthirsty samurai' was condemned alongside Adolf Hitler and Benito Mussolini as the unholy trinity of World War II.

Japan's proclivity to whitewash over its wartime monstrosities isn't just confined to the silver screen. In the printed medium, Japan has a long history of rewriting unsavoury chunks of its military history.

Revisionist history textbooks have already achieved worldwide notoriety for:

a) Ignoring the existence of 'comfort women'.
b) Dismissing the Nanjing massacre as Communist China's fabrication.
c) Justifying its greedy land grabs as the liberation of Asia from Western colonialism.
d) Insisting that the ruthless violence Japan unleashed on her neighbours was a just war of self-defence.

Worryingly, this mangled version of the truth has cascaded from the academic fringe to popular culture.

Page 3

Yoshinori Kobayashi's bestselling manga, On Taiwan, graphically depicts willing Taiwanese women volunteering to be sexual slaves of brooding, macho Japanese warriors. The Japanese are on a crusade to forget the gross misconduct of their grandfathers, and it's easy to understand why.

Their grandfathers doused captives with kerosene and set them aflame. Their grandfathers cut open the bellies of pregnant women. Their grandfathers went beyond rape to disembowel woman, slicing off their breasts and nailing them alive to walls. Their grandfathers hanged victims by their tongues with iron hooks. Their grandfathers forced fathers to violate their daughters, sons their mothers, and family members to watch. Their grandfathers tossed babies in the air and caught them on bayonets. Their grandfathers laughed while mothers cried.

The scary question is, will the sons of Japan be like their grandfathers?

We believe that only through remembrance and by demanding a full accounting of the past will Japan set the moral compass for future generations. Education seems to be our only chance, and the truth bravely told our only hope.

Global Alliance is an organisation committed to furthering this cause. As a non-profit group that's part of over 40 grass-roots organisations, our aim is to preserve the historical truth of the Asia-Pacific War.

When people finally learn the historical truth of those dark days, a formidable consensus should emerge: one that will compel the Government of Japan to honour its post-war responsibilities and offer a sincere apology with compensation to all its war victims. (To date, Germany has paid over six billion dollars in compensation for her war crimes. Japan, by comparison, has paid not so much as a bent penny.)

To support our causes through education and public forums, please send a token donation of $10, $20 or $50. Make your cheques payable to Global Alliance. The address is:

P.O.Box 1323, San Carlos, CA94070-7323, USA.
Or better yet, visit www.global-alliance.net and join us as a member.

While we may all dare to hope there will never be another Asian Holocaust, humans are wont to be inhuman, and history does have an unfortunate habit of repeating itself.

Memory is the only antidote and, according to Auschwitz survivor, Primo Levi, an immunisational defence against the scourge of another Hideki Tojo.

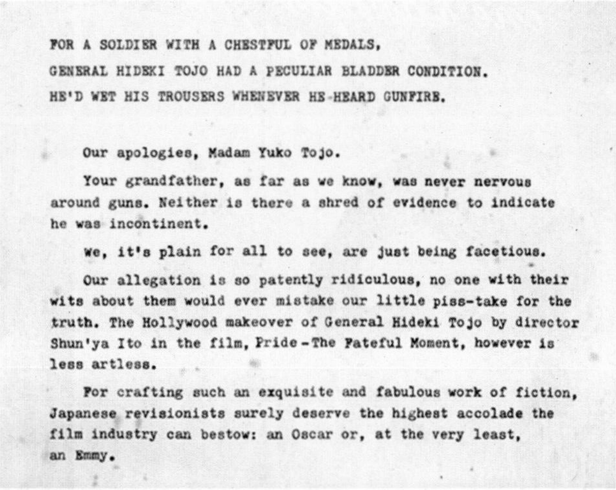

FOR A SOLDIER WITH A CHESTFUL OF MEDALS,
GENERAL HIDEKI TOJO HAD A PECULIAR BLADDER CONDITION.
HE'D WET HIS TROUSERS WHENEVER HE HEARD GUNFIRE.

Our apologies, Madam Yuko Tojo.

Your grandfather, as far as we know, was never nervous around guns. Neither is there a shred of evidence to indicate he was incontinent.

We, it's plain for all to see, are just being facetious.

Our allegation is so patently ridiculous, no one with their wits about them would ever mistake our little piss-take for the truth. The Hollywood makeover of General Hideki Tojo by director Shun'ya Ito in the film, Pride-The Fateful Moment, however is less artless.

For crafting such an exquisite and fabulous work of fiction, Japanese revisionists surely deserve the highest accolade the film industry can bestow: an Oscar or, at the very least, an Emmy.

Writing for Press
& Poster Advertising
DHM for Penhaligon's

Merchants of Attraction
The aim of this campaign was to reposition Penhaligon's as a contemporary perfumer without ignoring the brand's 100-year-old heritage.

Copywriter
Frances Leach
Art Director
Christopher Bowsher
Typographer
Andy Dymock
Creative Director
Dave Dye
Advertising Agency
DHM
Head of Marketing
Emily Maben
Client
Penhaligon's

PENHALIGON'S
MERCHANTS of ATTRACTION
since 1870
Orange Blossom
Should it meet the nostrils of a gentleman he will be eyeing one's ankles forthwith.

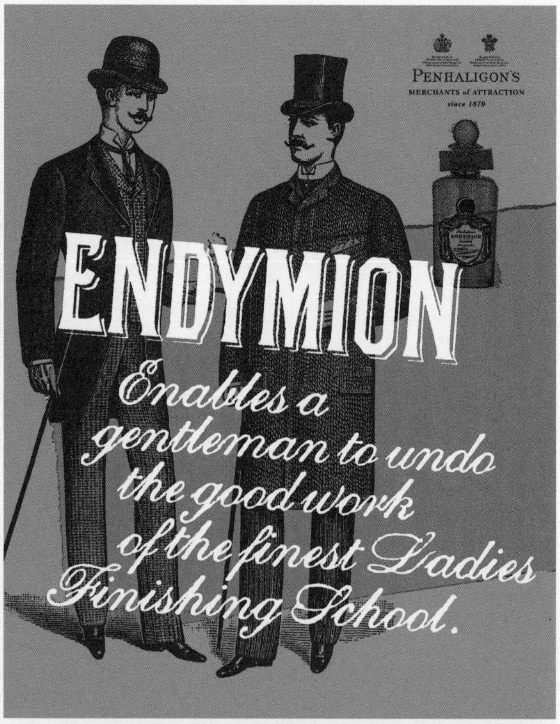
PENHALIGON'S
MERCHANTS of ATTRACTION
since 1870
ENDYMION
Enables a gentleman to undo the good work of the finest Ladies Finishing School.

PENHALIGON'S
MERCHANTS of ATTRACTION
since 1870
MALABAH
Perfect for any young lady looking to find herself compromised.

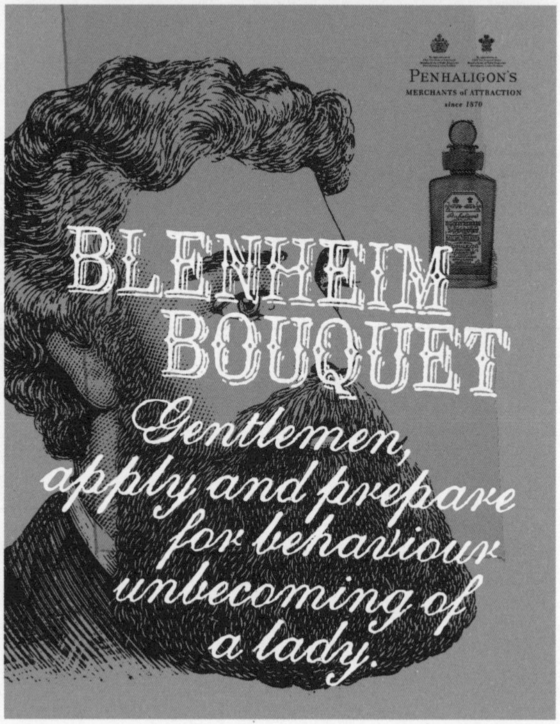
PENHALIGON'S
MERCHANTS of ATTRACTION
since 1870
BLENHEIM BOUQUET
Gentlemen, apply and prepare for behaviour unbecoming of a lady.

Writing for Press
& Poster Advertising
Three Drunk Monkeys
for the BBC

A Little Knowledge Goes a Long Way – Africa
BBC Knowledge programmes are informative and entertaining. This ad highlights the benefits of the acquired knowledge for those who choose to watch one of its shows, reinforcing the brand positioning line, 'A little knowledge goes a long way'.

Copywriter
Damian Fitzgerald
Art Directors
Terry Chisholm
Matt Heck
Photographer
Matt Heck
Creative Director
Noah Regan
Executive Creative Directors
Justin Drape
Scott Nowell
Print Producer
Tom Harrison
Advertising Agency
Three Drunk Monkeys
Planner
Fabio Buresti
Group Account Director
Dan Beaumont
Marketing Manager
Amanda McGregor
Client
BBC
Brand
BBC Knowledge

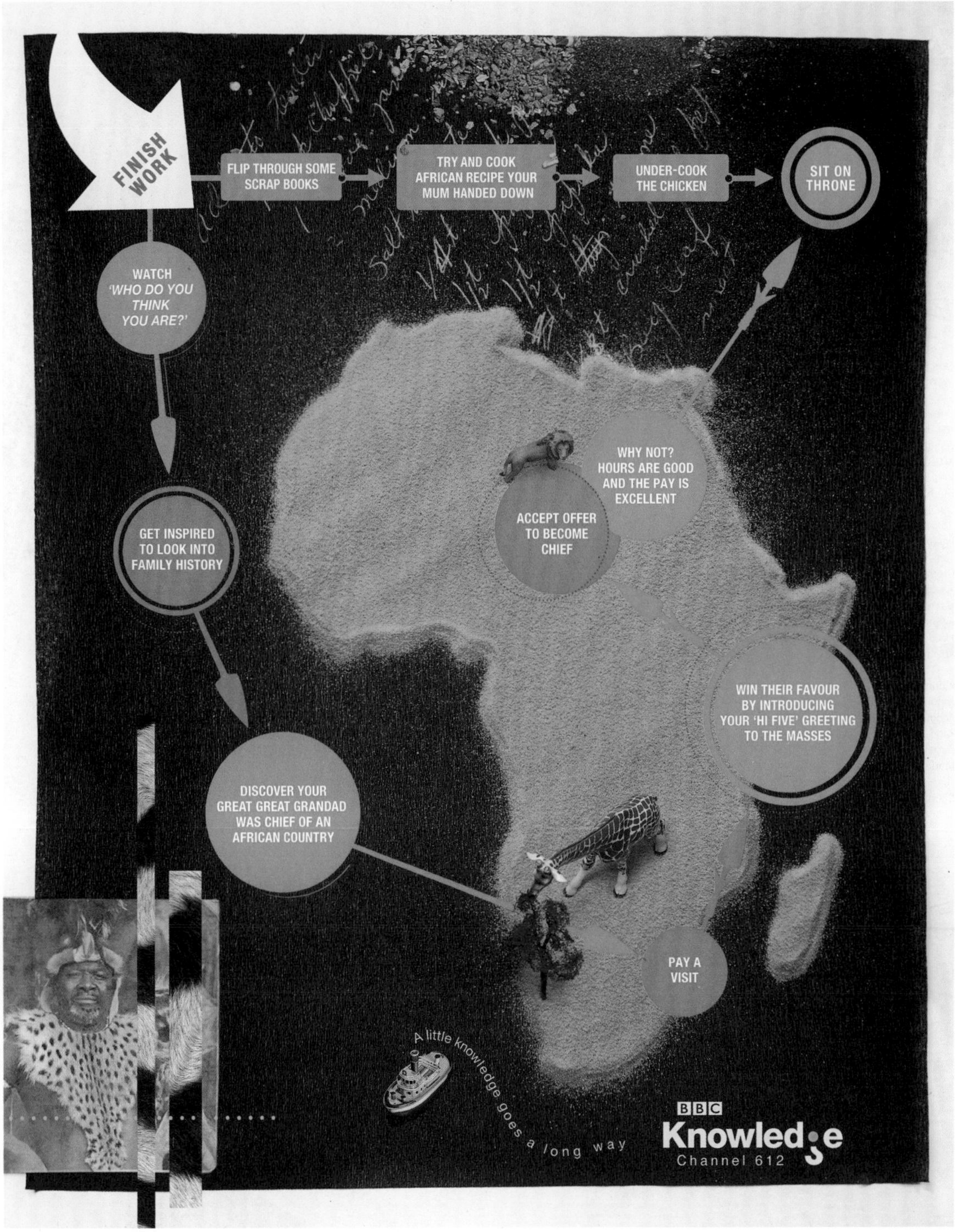
FINISH WORK
FLIP THROUGH SOME SCRAP BOOKS
TRY AND COOK AFRICAN RECIPE YOUR MUM HANDED DOWN
UNDER-COOK THE CHICKEN
SIT ON THRONE
WATCH 'WHO DO YOU THINK YOU ARE?'
GET INSPIRED TO LOOK INTO FAMILY HISTORY
DISCOVER YOUR GREAT GREAT GRANDAD WAS CHIEF OF AN AFRICAN COUNTRY
PAY A VISIT
ACCEPT OFFER TO BECOME CHIEF
WHY NOT? HOURS ARE GOOD AND THE PAY IS EXCELLENT
WIN THEIR FAVOUR BY INTRODUCING YOUR 'HI FIVE' GREETING TO THE MASSES
A little knowledge goes a long way
BBC
Knowledge
Channel 612

Writing for Press
& Poster Advertising
Y&R Dubai for
Land Rover

Rare
To promote and instil the classic adventure spirit of Land Rover in the next generation of prospective owners, this brand campaign portrays Land Rover drivers as a group of people with an unconventional point of view. For them, there is nothing special about rare creatures found in hidden places around the globe. They are merely food, camping tools or even toilet paper.

Copywriters
Kalpesh Patankar
Shahir Zag
Art Directors
Kalpesh Patankar
Shahir Zag
Designer
Kalpesh Patankar
Illustrator
Jomy Varghese
Creative Directors
Kalpesh Patankar
Shahir Zag
Agency Producer
Amin Soltani
Advertising Agency
Y&R Dubai
Planner
Nadine Ghossoub
Account Handlers
Farid Hobeiche
Sarah Locke
Marketing Manager
Jean Atik
Client
Land Rover

FOR BOTANISTS:
Yakla Snow Lotus (Sassurea yakla)
This rare lotus is only found at altitudes of 3,500 to 4,300 metres.
The leaves of this beautiful plant are arranged in a rosette pattern on the ground.
Has a multitude of medicinal properties.
Yakla Pass: 27° 22' N, 88° 48' E.
FOR LAND ROVER OWNERS:
Handy substitute to toilet paper.
LAND-ROVER
www.landrover.com

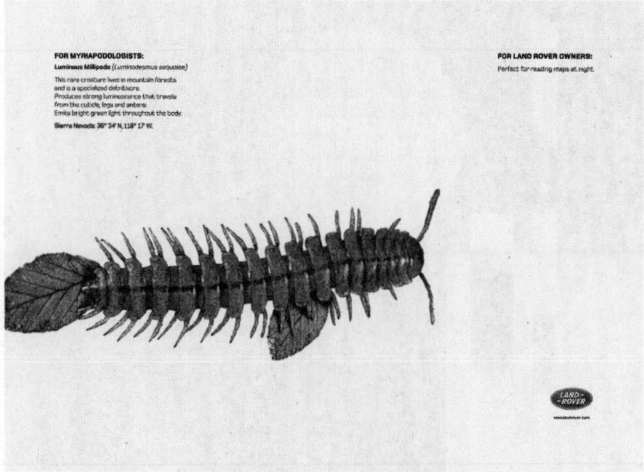
FOR MYRIAPODOLOGISTS:
Luminous Millipede
FOR LAND ROVER OWNERS:
Perfect for reading maps at night.

FOR HERBOLOGISTS:
Snow Mountain Garlic
FOR LAND ROVER OWNERS:
Applying juice on skin makes an effective mosquito repellent.

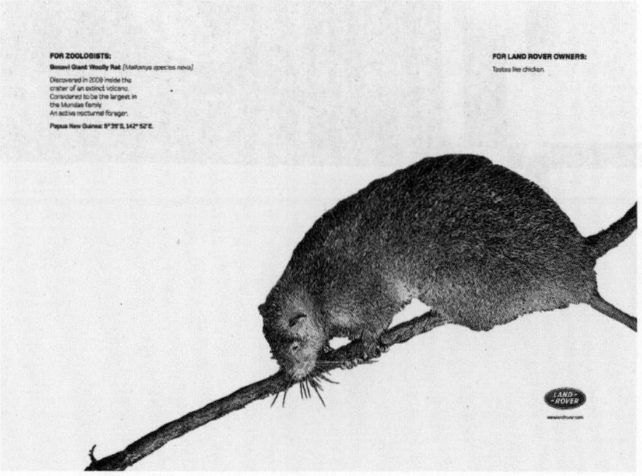
FOR ZOOLOGISTS:
Bosavi Giant Woolly Rat
Discovered in 2009 inside the crater of an extinct volcano.
An active nocturnal forager.
FOR LAND ROVER OWNERS:
Tastes like chicken.

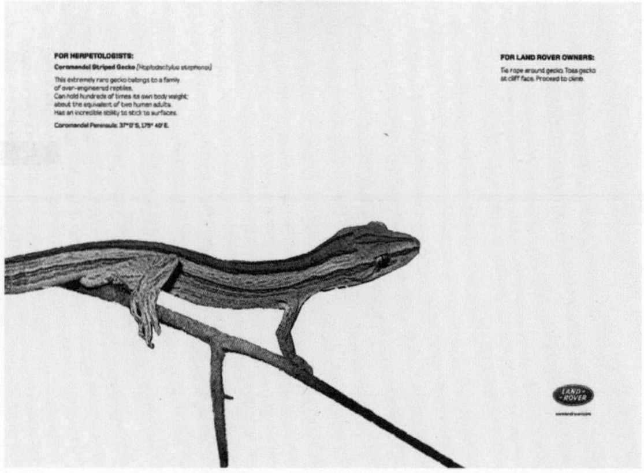
FOR HERPETOLOGISTS:
Coromandel Striped Gecko
This extremely rare gecko belongs to a family of over-engineered reptiles.
Can hold hundreds of times its own body weight; about the equivalent of two human adults.
Has an incredible ability to stick to surfaces.
FOR LAND ROVER OWNERS:
Tie rope around gecko. Toss gecko at cliff face. Proceed to climb.

Writing for Press
& Poster Advertising
George Patterson Y&R for the Alliance Française

Free Yourself from the Formula
This campaign was produced to launch the 2011 Alliance Française French Film Festival. The festival is organised annually by the Alliance Française to promote French culture in Australia. It runs across seven states and 300 cinemas.

Copywriter
Bart Pawlak
Art Directors
Chris Crawford
David Joubert
Typographer
Chris Crawford
Creative Director
Julian Watt
Print Producer
Matthew Commensoli
Advertising Agency
George Patterson Y&R
Account Handler
Emma Boyle
Marketing Manager
Frederic Dart
Client
Alliance Française
Brand
French Fim
Festival 2011

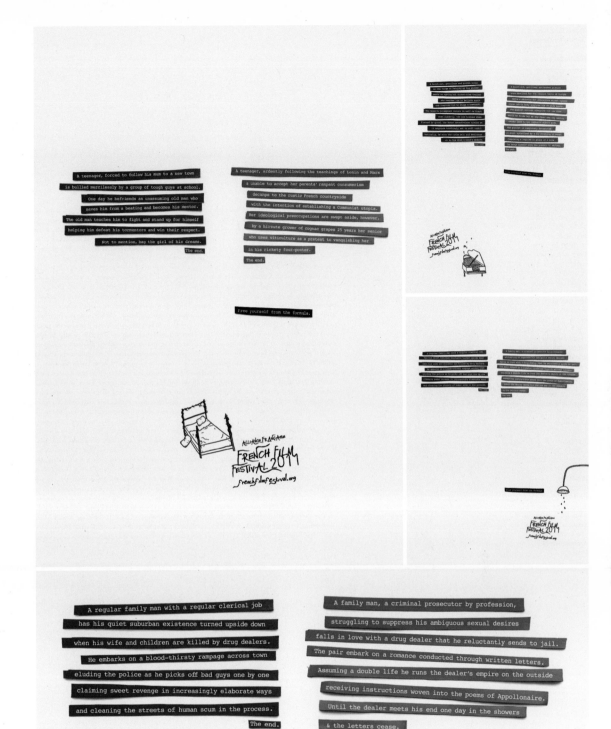

A teenager, forced to follow his mum to a new town
is bullied mercilessly by a group of tough guys at school.
One day he befriends an unassuming old man who
saves him from a beating and becomes his mentor.
The old man teaches him to fight and stand up for himself
helping him defeat his tormentors and win their respect.
Not to mention, bag the girl of his dreams.
The end.
A teenager, ardently following the teachings of Lenin and Marx
& unable to accept her parents' rampant consumerism
decamps to the rustic French countryside
with the intention of establishing a Communist utopia.
Her ideological preoccupations are swept aside, however,
by a hirsute grower of cognac grapes 25 years her senior
who uses viticulture as a pretext to vanquishing her
in his rickety four-poster.
The end.
Free yourself from the formula.
Alliance Française
French Film Festival 2011
frenchfilmfestival.org

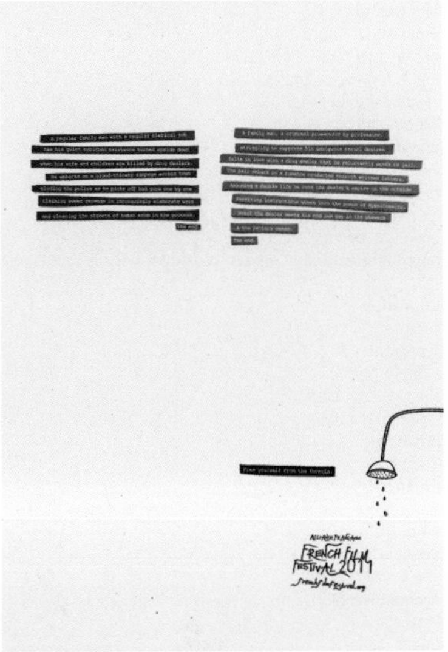

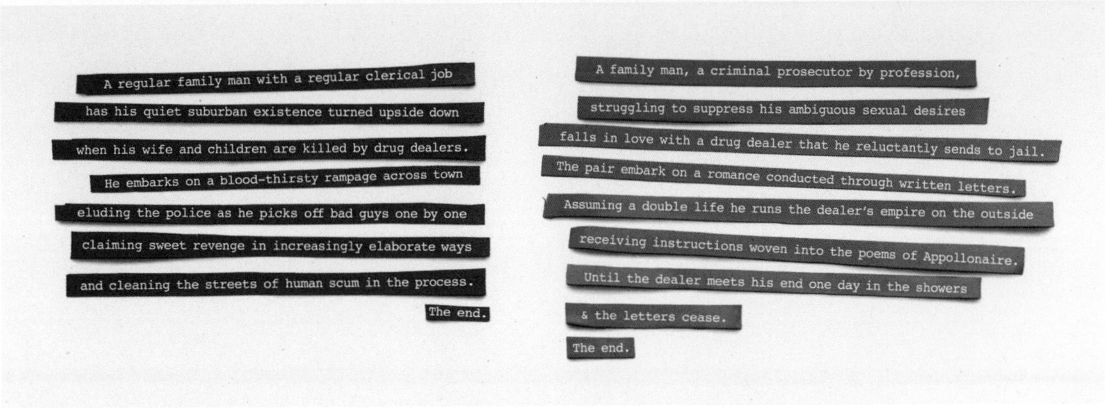
A regular family man with a regular clerical job
has his quiet suburban existence turned upside down
when his wife and children are killed by drug dealers.
He embarks on a blood-thirsty rampage across town
eluding the police as he picks off bad guys one by one
claiming sweet revenge in increasingly elaborate ways
and cleaning the streets of human scum in the process.
The end.
A family man, a criminal prosecutor by profession,
struggling to suppress his ambiguous sexual desires
falls in love with a drug dealer that he reluctantly sends to jail.
The pair embark on a romance conducted through written letters.
Assuming a double life he runs the dealer's empire on the outside
receiving instructions woven into the poems of Appollonaire.
Until the dealer meets his end one day in the showers
& the letters cease.
The end.

Yellow Pencil in Writing for Design

Nick Asbury for Paul Thompson Photography

A Picture Speaks a Thousand Words
Tired of receiving predictable direct mail from photographers, we thought it was time for a change. We developed an idea which wouldn't feature any photographs, just beautiful and engaging descriptions, encouraging the recipient to visit Paul Thompson's website and discover the pictures described. Each description was exactly 1,000 words and set to exactly the proportions of the original image. The aim was to convey more about Paul's personality rather than just his work, as the relationship between art director, client and photographer is key. Paul hand delivered the posters; this gave him an opportunity to speak to existing and potential clients.

Copywriter
Nick Asbury
Typographers
Lionel Hatch
Harry Heptonstall
Peter Richardson
Artworker
Rachel Pratt
Creative Directors
Ben Casey
Peter Richardson
Design Company
The Chase
Account Handler
Paul Waters
Client
Paul Thompson Photography

This picture is what you see when you find yourself walking through BBC Television Centre during the recording of 'Strictly Come Dancing' and you push open a door marked 'Not for broadcast' and walk inside. This picture is what I drew in the team-building workshop when they asked me how I saw the future of our company. This picture is 64 per cent sky, 33 per cent sand and 3 per cent built environment. This picture is what it was like when you told that joke the other night. This picture details the measures that will be taken to ensure a banking crisis on this scale can never happen again. This picture is why I love you. To walk from the front of this picture to the back of this picture would take about 25 minutes. This picture is what I heard when you said you were sorry for any distress caused and that naturally you take full responsibility. This picture is a difficult spot-the-ball competition. This picture is of Simon Cowell's life flashing in front of his eyes. Key words in an image library search for this picture might include landscape, barren, sand, empty, sign, cloud, dry, tracks, sky, existential. Key words least likely to result in this picture include Christmas, bouncy, loose, mélange, cosy, beef, nonchalant, cornflakes, splash, companionship. This picture was most likely taken on a Tuesday, possibly a Saturday. This picture reverberates. This picture is concerned more with the spaces between things than it is with the things themselves. This picture is very beautiful. If you took down every billboard advertisement in the world and replaced it with this, picture it would take a while for people to notice. This picture is what I think of your customer service helpline. This picture is worth whatever someone is willing to pay for it. Frequently Asked Questions about this picture include: "What made you be a picture of that thing?"; "Where did you first get the idea to be a picture of that thing?"; and "Do you have any plans to be a picture of other things in the future?" The answers to the Frequently Asked Questions about this picture are not as frequent as the questions. I think I once went out with this picture. Someone somewhere thinks I am like this picture, which is a disturbing thought. This picture is what you see when you find yourself walking down a long carpeted corridor in Whitehall towards a door marked 'Big Society' and you push it open and walk inside. This picture would serve a useful function in the Oval Office, or on the walls of the staircase at 10 Downing Street. The place that this picture is a picture of is a real place that exists right now and probably looks very similar to the way it does in this picture. We could both go and stand in this picture if we wanted to. Which is to say, we could both go and stand in the place that this picture is a picture of. If we had been standing there at the time this picture was taken, it would be a different picture. Or possibly just the same picture with us in it. I spy with my little eye something in this picture beginning with 's'. This picture is what I'm thinking about whenever you ask me what I'm thinking about. This picture is what my careers development officer saw in me. This picture is a machine for remembering itself. Two X-Factor judges were discussing this picture – I forget which ones – and the first one said, "Wow! This is one of the best pictures I have ever seen!" & started to cry. The second one said, "I like this picture but I don't like its choice of material. I would like to see more from this picture in next week's Beatles night!" This picture is art. This picture doesn't know much about you but it knows what it likes and it doesn't like you. This picture is of a woman in a red dress with a white umbrella running laughing across the sand and into a flock of startled seagulls, but without the startled seagulls, the white umbrella, the red dress and the laughing, running woman. This picture is of the centre ground in American politics. This picture confused me when it came out of the passport photo machine. This picture is of a characterful property in a beach location with plenty of off-street parking. Just beside the person who took this picture is a wooden sign with a camera symbol on it and text reading "Non-intrusive backdrop to overlaying type." This picture is of the losing entry in the RHS Chelsea Flower Show. This picture contains a fencing arrangement which may be marking out a track of some sort. This picture wants to be your friend on Facebook. This picture is what you see when you fall asleep on the Piccadilly Line on the way home and wake up at the last stop and walk up the stairs and outside. This picture could not have been taken any other way. Somewhere to the right of this picture is where I think I dropped my watch. Who knows what's going on either side of this picture. I would guess it's around 11AM in this picture. This picture contains a sign that is too far away to read. The small building in this picture is where they keep the on/off switch for the Internet. None of us remember where we were when this picture was taken. This picture is your retirement gift after 40 years in service. This picture was taken during a rollover week. Do you have any wallpaper that matches this picture? I would like my hair cut in the style of this picture. The thing beginning with 's' in this picture was 'sand'. This picture was taken a split second after the spaceship disappeared into the clouds. You really have to see this picture.

1,000 words by NICK ASBURY about a picture by PAUL THOMPSON
To see the picture go to www.paulthompsonstudio.com

● Nomination in Writing for Design

Christopher Doyle & Elliott Scott

This Year I Will Try Not to

Most designers are seduced by design trends. They're easy to appropriate, and even easier to imitate. The challenge is to innovate. To be new. We decided the best (and most enjoyable) approach was to identify and document the most common trends we felt we had to avoid. Before long we found ourselves with a checklist of Don'ts and a new aim: to try to be new. We may fail, but we will try.

Copywriters
Christopher Doyle
Elliott Scott
Art Directors
Christopher Doyle
Elliott Scott
Designers
Christopher Doyle
Elliott Scott
Typographer
Christopher Doyle
Image Manipulator
Elliott Scott
Clients
Christopher Doyle
& Elliott Scott

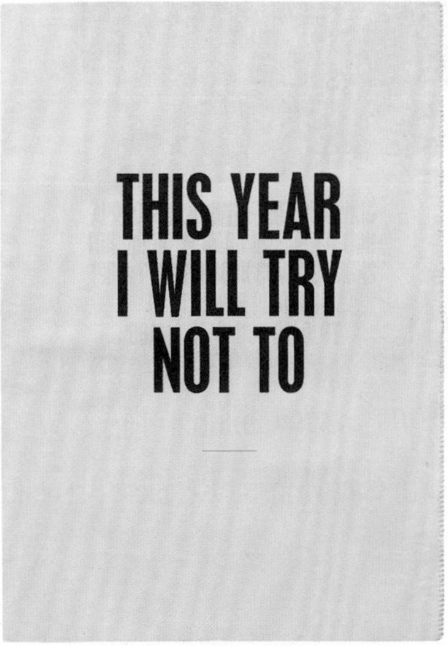
THIS YEAR
I WILL TRY
NOT TO

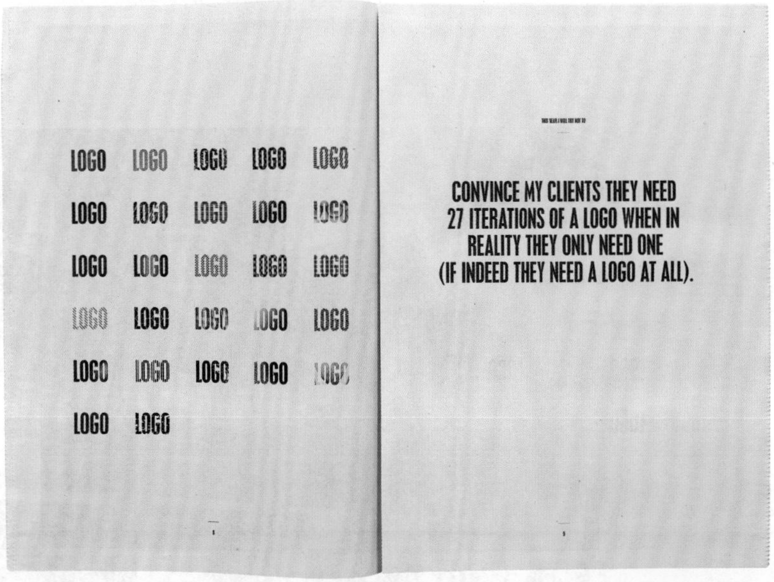
LOGO LOGO LOGO LOGO LOGO
LOGO LOGO LOGO LOGO LOGO
LOGO LOGO LOGO LOGO LOGO
LOGO LOGO LOGO LOGO LOGO
LOGO LOGO LOGO LOGO
LOGO LOGO
CONVINCE MY CLIENTS THEY NEED
27 ITERATIONS OF A LOGO WHEN IN
REALITY THEY ONLY NEED ONE
(IF INDEED THEY NEED A LOGO AT ALL).

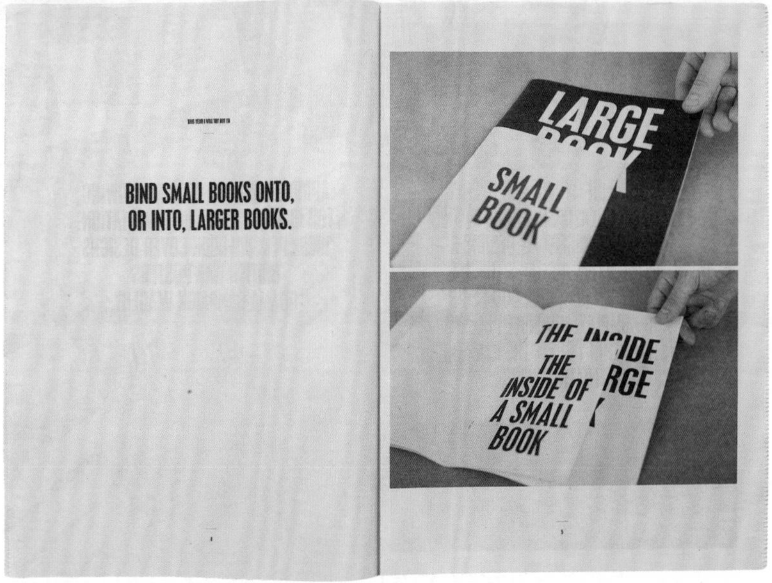
BIND SMALL BOOKS ONTO,
OR INTO, LARGER BOOKS.
LARGE
SMALL
BOOK
THE INSIDE OF
A SMALL
BOOK

Nomination in Writing for Design

Writing for Design
We Made This for the Ministry of Stories

Hoxton Street Monster Supplies
Based on the brilliant 826 programme in the USA, Hoxton Street Monster Supplies is the fantastical shop front for the Ministry of Stories, a pioneering children's writing workshop. The story is that the shop was established in 1818 to serve the daily needs of London's monster community. Inside you'll find a whole range of products for monsters, including Tinned Fears, Human Preserves, Neck Bolt Tighteners and Death Certificates (to prove you really are dead). But the most important part is that the shop shelves hide a secret – the disguised entrance to the Ministry of Stories.

Copywriters
Mikey Bennett
Joe Dunthorne
Alistair Hall
Martin Jackson
Alex Myers
Tom Raphael Eaves
Designers
Alistair Hall
Matt Roden
Creative Director
Alistair Hall
Design Group
We Made This
Client Directors
Lucy Macnab
Ben Payne
Client
Ministry of Stories
Brand
Hoxton Street Monster Supplies

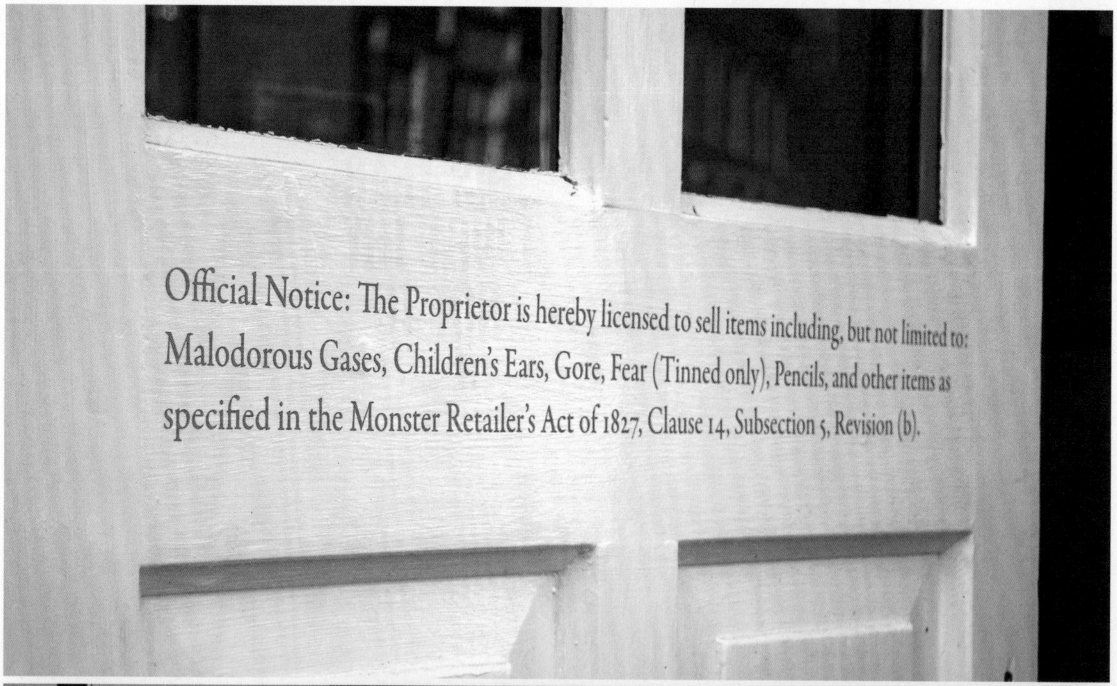
Official Notice: The Proprietor is hereby licensed to sell items including, but not limited to:
Malodorous Gases, Children's Ears, Gore, Fear (Tinned only), Pencils, and other items as
specified in the Monster Retailer's Act of 1827, Clause 14, Subsection 5, Revision (b).

NECK-BOLT TIGHTENER

ONLY ONE GIANT IN THE SHOP AT A TIME
•
CUSTOMERS ARE POLITELY REQUESTED TO REFRAIN FROM EATING THE STAFF
•
NOCTURNAL OPENING (BY APPOINTMENT) FOR VAMPIRE CUSTOMERS ONLY

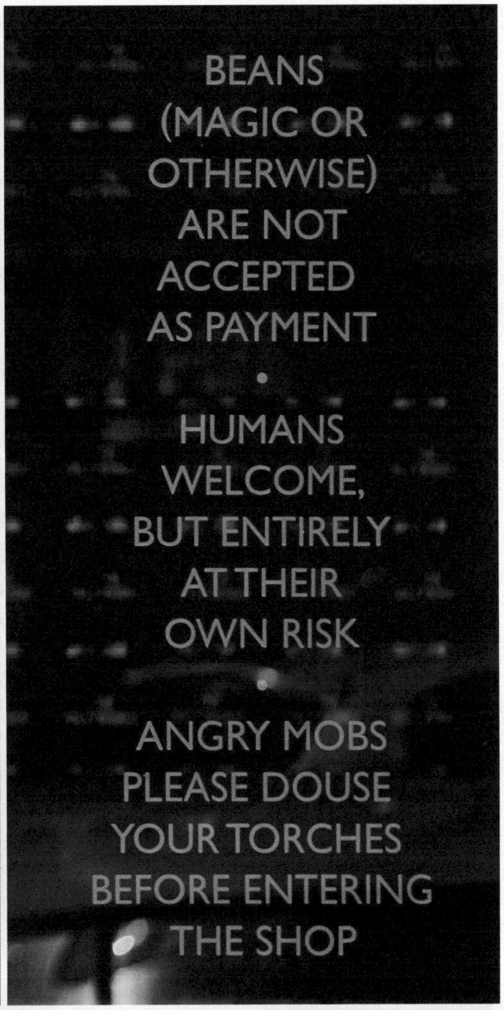
BEANS (MAGIC OR OTHERWISE) ARE NOT ACCEPTED AS PAYMENT
•
HUMANS WELCOME, BUT ENTIRELY AT THEIR OWN RISK
•
ANGRY MOBS PLEASE DOUSE YOUR TORCHES BEFORE ENTERING THE SHOP

Hoxton Street Monster Supplies
ESTD 1818
~ Purveyor of Quality Goods for Monsters of Every Kind ~
THICKEST HUMAN SNOT
The ultimate delicacy at any self-respecting monster's table. Our free-range snivelling humans are fed on a diet of milk and misery for the very thickest snot.

Hoxton Street Monster Supplies
ESTD 1818
~ Purveyor of Quality Goods for Monsters of Every Kind ~
CASH ONLY
We are tragically unable to accept the following forms of payment:
Credit Cards
Beans (Magic or Otherwise)
Pre-Decimal Pound Sterling
Human Sacrifice

Hoxton Street Monster Supplies
ESTD 1818
~ Purveyor of Quality Goods for Monsters of Every Kind ~
TINNED FEAR
THE COLLYWOBBLES
PREPARED ACCORDING TO THE MONSTROUS PHARMACOPŒIA
Effects a gradual but most certain sensation of The Collywobbles. Corrects and relieves all symptoms of Comfort, Confidence and Contentment. Most useful in countering cases of Unbearable Smugness. Peculiarly unpleasant to taste.

Writing for Design
Quietroom

Santa Brand Book
Christmas Card
There are brands. There are super-brands. And then there's this brand. You can imagine how smug we were when Santa Claus Global Enterprises invited us to hew from our raw imagination its brand guidelines. Frankly, we wept. We hope that when you read it, you weep too.

Copywriters
Vincent Franklin
Simon Grover
Designers
Tommy Taylor
Bob Young
Brand Language Consultancy
Quietroom
Client
Quietroom
Brand
Santa

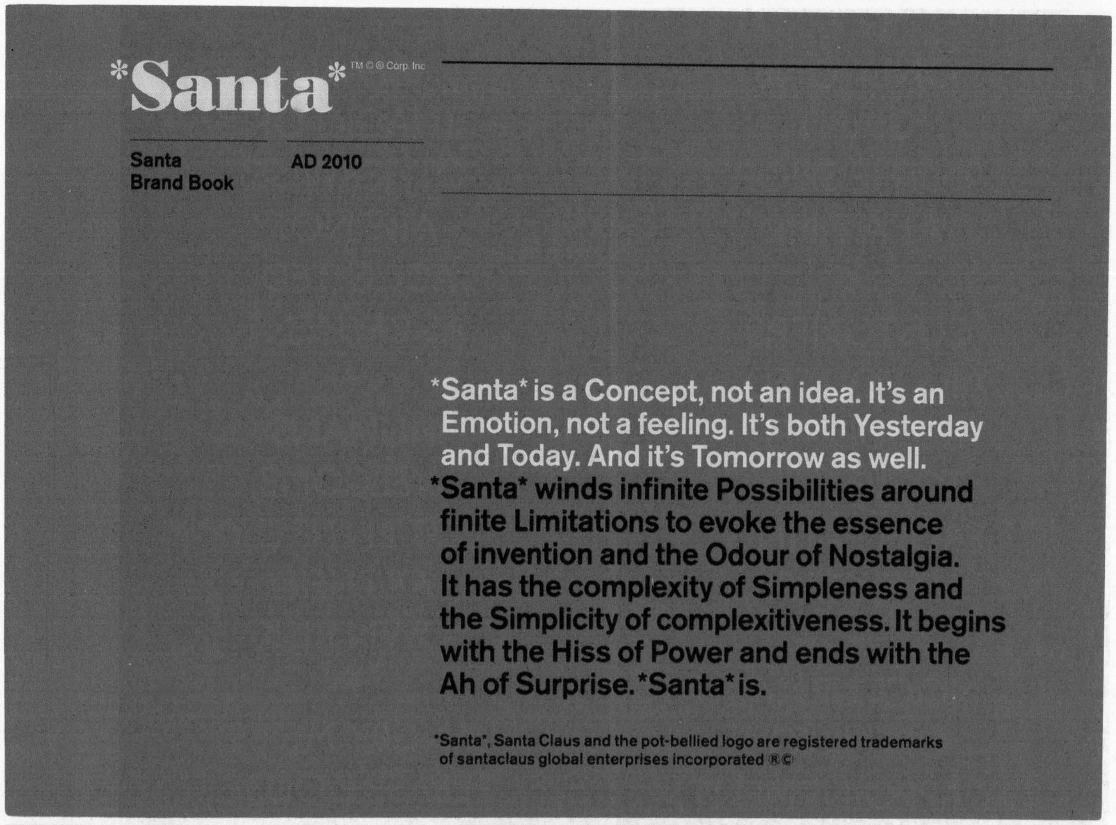
Santa TM © ® Corp. Inc
Santa
Brand Book
AD 2010
Santa is a Concept, not an idea. It's an Emotion, not a feeling. It's both Yesterday and Today. And it's Tomorrow as well.
Santa winds infinite Possibilities around finite Limitations to evoke the essence of invention and the Odour of Nostalgia. It has the complexity of Simpleness and the Simplicity of complexitiveness. It begins with the Hiss of Power and ends with the Ah of Surprise. *Santa* is.
Santa, Santa Claus and the pot-bellied logo are registered trademarks of santaclaus global enterprises incorporated ®©

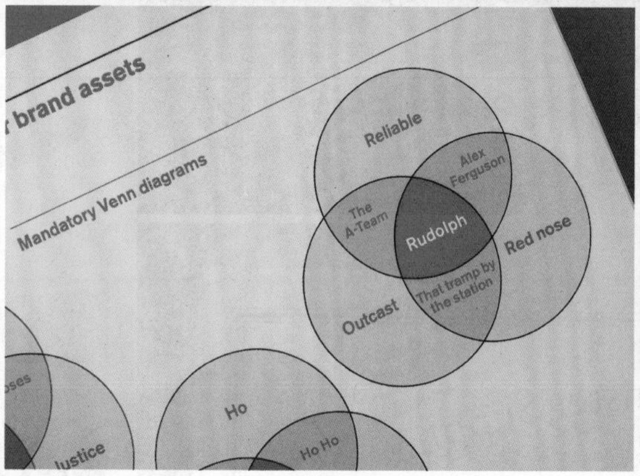
brand assets
Mandatory Venn diagrams
Reliable
Alex Ferguson
The A-Team
Rudolph
Red nose
That tramp by the station
Outcast
Ho
Ho Ho
Justice

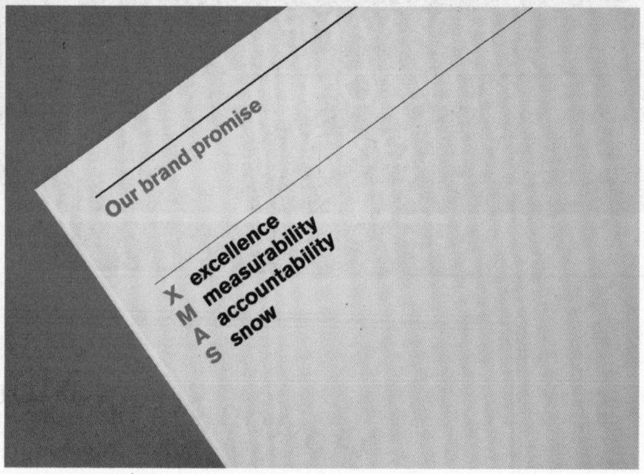
Our brand promise
X excellence
M measurability
A accountability
S snow

Writing for Design
Jung von Matt Hamburg
for Daimler

Tramp a Benz
For over 125 years Mercedes-Benz has stood for a certain ambition: the best or nothing. Last year this principle of the founder Gottlieb Daimler became the new claim of the brand. The brief was to make this principle come alive. What does this ambition feel like today? What does 'the best or nothing' mean on the road, where it has to prove itself every day? In one of the coldest Decembers Berlin has ever witnessed, street photographer and performance artist Stefan Gbureck set out on a journey with no destination but one goal: to travel with 'the best or nothing'.

Copywriter
Georg Baur
Art Director
Tilman Gossner
Designer
Daniel Gumbert
Typographer
Daniel Gumbert
Photographer
Stefan Gbureck
Creative Director
Thimoteus Wagner
Advertising Agency
Jung von Matt Hamburg
Account Handler
Sven Dörrenbächer
Brand Manager
Anders-Sundt Jensen
Marketing Manager
Damir Maric
Client
Daimler
Brand
Mercedes-Benz

DAY 08

WALK THE LINE

AFTER EIGHT DAYS ON THE ROAD, I GOT TO KNOW WHAT THE "NOTHING" MEANT IN "THE BEST OR NOTHING".
THERE WAS NO MERCEDES TO BE FOUND SO I HAD TO WALK THE 18 KILOMETRES FROM VENTIMIGLIA TO MONTE CARLO.
WHEN I ARRIVED AT THE ESPLANADE, I WAS SOAKING AND STARVING. I TUCKED INTO THE MOST EXPENSIVE PASTA OF MY LIFE, BUT AT LEAST THE SPAGHETTI CAME NOT ONLY WITH SEAFOOD BUT ALSO SEA VIEW.
FULL, DRY AND BROKE, I WASN'T IN THE MOOD FOR CHASING CARS.
SO I WENT CHASING THE FORMULA 1 FEELING INSTEAD AND FOLLOWED THE RACE TRACK FROM THE CASINO TO THE PORT.
BY THE WAY, I DIDN'T QUITE MANAGE TO BEAT MICHAEL SCHUMACHER'S FASTEST LAP OF 2004.

DAY 10

MY FAIR LADY

AT A MOTORWAY SERVICE STATION IN AVIGNON, I SAW A SILVER SLK ROLLING OUT OF THE CAR WASH. I ASKED FOR A LIFT BUT THE LADY MUST HAVE MISUNDERSTOOD ME AND HANDED OVER TWO EUROS.

- NON, NON, MADAME. J'AIMERAIS BIEN VOUS ACCOMPAGNER DANS VOTRE VOITURE!
- AH OUI? EH BEN, MONTEZ ALORS.

LATER THAT DAY, I REALISED I SHOULD HAVE TAKEN THE MONEY. MY LAPTOP HAD GIVEN UP THE GHOST.
IT MUST HAVE GOT DAMP WHEN I WAS SLEEPING OUTSIDE IN THE FOREST THE OTHER DAY. YOU WIN SOME, YOU LOSE SOME.

ANYWAY, THE FRENCH LADY HAD FLOWERS ON THE BACK SEAT AND WAS DRIVING TO A FRIEND'S BIRTHDAY PARTY. SHE TOLD ME ABOUT HER HUSBAND'S BUSINESS AND THAT SHE WAS QUITE LUCKY NOT TO HAVE TO WORK ANY MORE. I DIDN'T BOTHER ASKING IF SHE HAD EVER WORKED IN HER LIFE.
AT THE END OF OUR "DATE" SHE INVITED ME TO JOIN HER AND "THE GIRLS." IT SOUNDED TEMPTING BUT FOR ONCE I DECIDED TO SKIP THE CHAMPAGNE PARTY.

MERCEDES-BENZ ONLY!

DAY 03

EXCUSE MY FRENCH

THE SWISS OBVIOUSLY KNOW A THING OR TWO ABOUT MONEY, I THOUGHT, WHEN ONE OF THOSE NICE NEW CLS MODELS PICKED ME UP NEAR ZURICH. THE DRIVER WAS THE "BUSY BUSINESSMAN" TYPE AND GOT A LITTLE IMPATIENT WHEN I TOOK PICTURES OF MYSELF CLAMBERING INTO HIS CLS.

- HURRY UP, WE'VE GOT TO GO!

AS WE FOLLOWED THE WINDING ROAD TO ZURICH, HE GOT A PHONE CALL FROM HIS WIFE. MY FRENCH ISN'T THE BEST BUT HERE IS WHAT I REMEMBER.

- HEY, DARLING, I PICKED UP A GUY FROM THE ROADSIDE.
- WHAT?
- HE'S AN ARTIST AND ONLY WANTS TO TRAVEL IN MERCEDES CARS.
- AN ARTIST?
- YEAH, FROM BERLIN.
- HONEY, I'M NOT SURE THIS IS A VERY GOOD IDEA.
- TRAVELLING IN MERCEDES CARS?
- NO, TAKING ALONG SOME CRAZY ARTIST. DOES HE SPEAK FRENCH?
- DON'T THINK SO, WE SPEAK ENGLISH TOGETHER.
- SO TELL HIM YOU HAVE AN IMPORTANT APPOINTMENT.

IMAGINE MY SUPRISE WHEN HE TOLD ME ABOUT HIS IMPORTANT APPOINTMENT. THANKS FOR THE NICE RIDE, ANYWAY.
BACK TO THE OLD-SCHOOL HITCHHIKING STYLE: WAITING, LIFTING MY SIGN AND - VERY IMPORTANT - SMILING.

Writing for Design
Waldo Pancake
for Really Good

Waldo Pancake
Greeting Cards
These are three greeting cards from the Waldo Pancake product range.

Copywriter
Jim Smith
Designer
Jim Smith
Typographer
Jim Smith
Design Agency
Waldo Pancake
Client
Really Good

You mean so much to me that I got you this bit of folded in half paper.

Get well soon so I can stop being so nice.

Ditto last year.

Writing for Design
This is Real Art for the Musicians' Union

Spring / Summer / Autumn / Winter
This is a redesign of 'The Musician', the magazine for Musicians' Union members. The design reflects a more serious tone for the magazine.

Copywriter
Paul Belford
Designers
Rick Banks
Paul Belford
Typographer
Paul Belford
Creative Director
Paul Belford
Design Group
This is Real Art
Project Manager
Natalie Wetherell
Account Handler
George Lee
Marketing Manager
Horace Trubridge
Client
Musicians' Union

The Musician. What does the future hold for the funding of the Arts? Will the outcome of the next general election lead to a bleak period for the cultural life of the nation? Or do we have nothing to fear? In this issue we talk to the politicians, the major stakeholders and commentators to find out if an ailing economy really leads to a dead culture.
Spring 2010. Journal of the Musicians' Union theMU.org

The Musician. Will the BBC bow to pressure and save 6 Music? How might this happen and at what cost? Is Radio 1 safe? Or the five regional orchestras? This year sees the 30th anniversary of the historic eight week strike by the Musicians' Union at the BBC. We examine its lasting legacy and ask if such drastic action will ever again be necessary.
Summer 2010. Journal of the Musicians' Union theMU.org

The Musician. Noise can seriously damage hearing. But how much noise and who is most affected? The Noise at Work regulations were introduced back in 2008 but have they really helped musicians better protect their hearing? Do we need more complex legislation to limit noise levels? Or is this perhaps another example of the workings of a nanny state?
Autumn 2010. Journal of the Musicians' Union theMU.org

The Musician. According to an announcement by the coalition government, there is to be yet another review of copyright. Could this benefit writers and performers? Or will the law be relaxed to allow the greater use of copyright works without an owner's permission? Will this new review merely serve the interests of the ISPs, the telecoms and Google?
Winter 2010. Journal of the Musicians' Union theMU.org

Writing for Design
Lemon scented tea
for K-Swiss

You Gotta Know Your Classics
The 'You Gotta Know Your Classics' campaign is, as far as global campaigns go, a low-key affair. K-Swiss purposely avoided creating a tedious tome or overly designed catalogue, and instead worked with Amsterdam storytelling agency Lemon scented tea and a handful of highly credible international designers to visualise the story on the front and back of limited-edition posters. The chapter names provide historic and cultural context to 'The Classic'. Each poster is a stand-alone illustration, underscoring the lack of hierarchy in the story of 'The Classic'.

Copywriter
John Weich
Art Director
Fabian Jenny
Creative Director
John Weich
Advertising Agency
Lemon scented tea
Design Group
Cobbenhagen Hendriksen
Account Handler
Miranda Smit
Brand Manager
Dian Verkooijen
Marketing Manager
Edward Knol
Client
K-Swiss
Brand
K-Swiss Classic

K•SWISS
YOU GOTTA KNOW YOUR CLASSICS.
kswiss.com

CHAPTER 4/8

WE KILLED CANVAS. SORRY.

We killed canvas on the tennis court. Sorry.

It's hard to fathom, but there was actually a time when elite athletes won grand slams in flimsy plimsoll canvas sneakers. No longer. The launch of The Classic in 1966 ushered in a whole new era of tennis. The game accelerated. Athletes became swifter, their rackets lighter, the balls they hit faster. And The Classics they wore were high-performance leather, not canvas.

While designed in California, the first Classics were manufactured in Switzerland, in a factory that specialized in football shoes. In those days football was the only sport that idolized leather shoes; every other athlete chased records in canvas. When Art and Ernie came to California they brought with them this leather expertise, and even when they moved the manufacturing to their Los Angeles garage they retained that Swiss simplicity and precision. The Classic has always been about nuances, and always will be.

Turns out The Classic didn't just kill canvas on the tennis court but also on just about every court. Soon after its launch, athletic shoes across the globe were following The Classic's lead and going all leather. And by the early 1970s, The Classic was being adopted as a leisure shoe on upscale urban streets in California and Tokyo. The Classic wasn't meant to be a street shoe; it just became one. In fact, you could even argue that every leather tennis shoe walking around your neighborhood today can be traced back to The Classic.

Design Poster Front: Non-Format

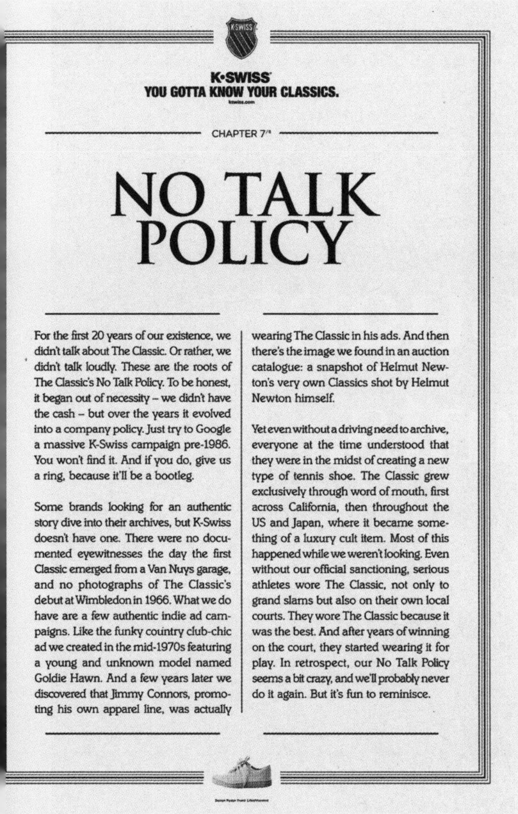

K•SWISS
YOU GOTTA KNOW YOUR CLASSICS.
kswiss.com
CHAPTER 7TH
NO TALK POLICY
For the first 20 years of our existence, we didn't talk about The Classic. Or rather, we didn't talk loudly. These are the roots of The Classic's No Talk Policy. To be honest, it began out of necessity – we didn't have the cash – but over the years it evolved into a company policy. Just try to Google a massive K-Swiss campaign pre-1986. You won't find it. And if you do, give us a ring, because it'll be a bootleg.
Some brands looking for an authentic story dive into their archives, but K-Swiss doesn't have one. There were no documented eyewitnesses the day the first Classic emerged from a Van Nuys garage, and no photographs of The Classic's debut at Wimbledon in 1966. What we do have are a few authentic indie ad campaigns. Like the funky country club-chic ad we created in the mid-1970s featuring a young and unknown model named Goldie Hawn. And a few years later we discovered that Jimmy Connors, promoting his own apparel line, was actually wearing The Classic in his ads. And then there's the image we found in an auction catalogue: a snapshot of Helmut Newton's very own Classics shot by Helmut Newton himself.
Yet even without a driving need to archive, everyone at the time understood that they were in the midst of creating a new type of tennis shoe. The Classic grew exclusively through word of mouth, first across California, then throughout the US and Japan, where it became something of a luxury cult item. Most of this happened while we weren't looking. Even without our official sanctioning, serious athletes wore The Classic, not only to grand slams but also on their own local courts. They wore The Classic because it was the best. And after years of winning on the court, they started wearing it for play. In retrospect, our No Talk Policy seems a bit crazy, and we'll probably never do it again. But it's fun to reminisce.

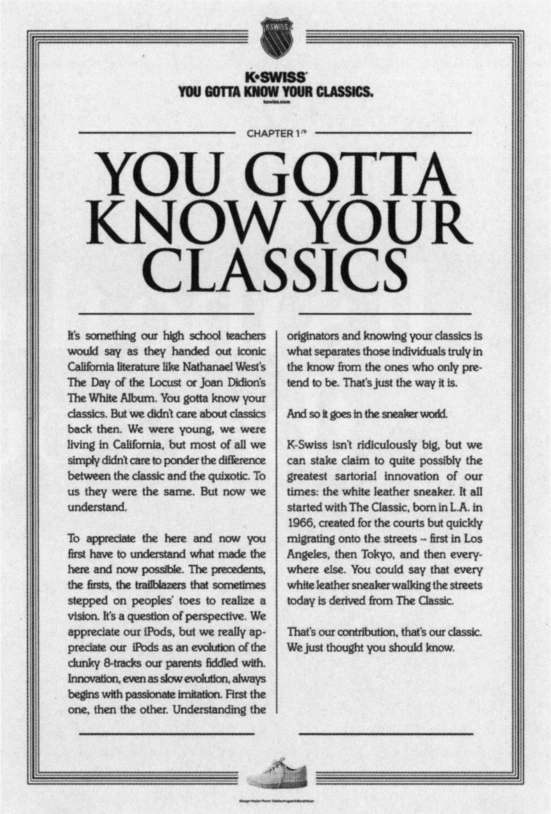

K•SWISS
YOU GOTTA KNOW YOUR CLASSICS.
kswiss.com
CHAPTER 1ST
YOU GOTTA KNOW YOUR CLASSICS
It's something our high school teachers would say as they handed out iconic California literature like Nathanael West's The Day of the Locust or Joan Didion's The White Album. You gotta know your classics. But we didn't care about classics back then. We were young, we were living in California, but most of all we simply didn't care to ponder the difference between the classic and the quixotic. To us they were the same. But now we understand.
To appreciate the here and now you first have to understand what made the here and now possible. The precedents, the firsts, the trailblazers that sometimes stepped on peoples' toes to realize a vision. It's a question of perspective. We appreciate our iPods, but we really appreciate our iPods as an evolution of the clunky 8-tracks our parents fiddled with. Innovation, even as slow evolution, always begins with passionate imitation. First the one, then the other. Understanding the originators and knowing your classics is what separates those individuals truly in the know from the ones who only pretend to be. That's just the way it is.
And so it goes in the sneaker world.
K-Swiss isn't ridiculously big, but we can stake claim to quite possibly the greatest sartorial innovation of our times: the white leather sneaker. It all started with The Classic, born in L.A. in 1966, created for the courts but quickly migrating onto the streets – first in Los Angeles, then Tokyo, and then everywhere else. You could say that every white leather sneaker walking the streets today is derived from The Classic.
That's our contribution, that's our classic. We just thought you should know.

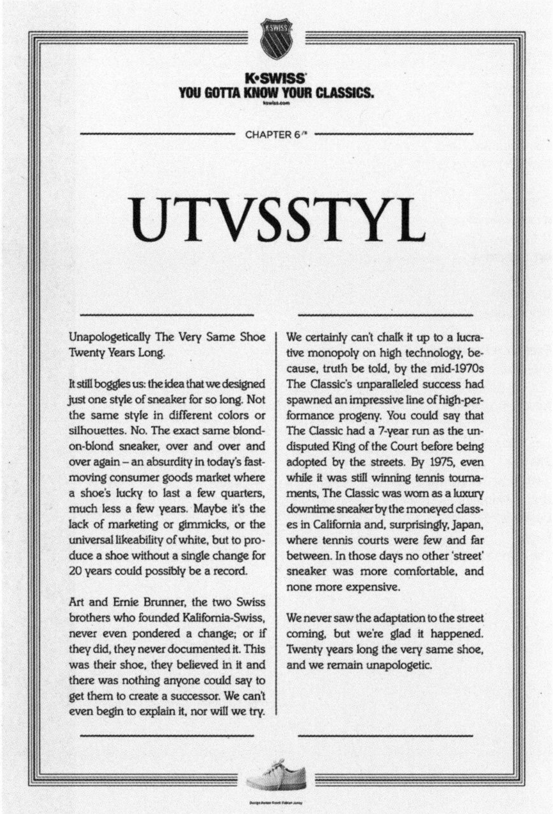

K•SWISS
YOU GOTTA KNOW YOUR CLASSICS.
kswiss.com
CHAPTER 6TH
UTVSSTYL
Unapologetically The Very Same Shoe Twenty Years Long.
It still boggles us: the idea that we designed just one style of sneaker for so long. Not the same style in different colors or silhouettes. No. The exact same blond-on-blond sneaker, over and over and over again – an absurdity in today's fast-moving consumer goods market where a shoe's lucky to last a few quarters, much less a few years. Maybe it's the lack of marketing or gimmicks, or the universal likeability of white, but to produce a shoe without a single change for 20 years could possibly be a record.
Art and Ernie Brunner, the two Swiss brothers who founded Kalifornia-Swiss, never even pondered a change; or if they did, they never documented it. This was their shoe, they believed in it and there was nothing anyone could say to get them to create a successor. We can't even begin to explain it, nor will we try. We certainly can't chalk it up to a lucrative monopoly on high technology, because, truth be told, by the mid-1970s The Classic's unparalleled success had spawned an impressive line of high-performance progeny. You could say that The Classic had a 7-year run as the undisputed King of the Court before being adopted by the streets. By 1975, even while it was still winning tennis tournaments, The Classic was worn as a luxury downtime sneaker by the moneyed classes in California and, surprisingly, Japan, where tennis courts were few and far between. In those days no other 'street' sneaker was more comfortable, and none more expensive.
We never saw the adaptation to the street coming, but we're glad it happened. Twenty years long the very same shoe, and we remain unapologetic.

NO
TALK
POL-
ICY
You gotta know your classics.
K•SWISS

K•SWISS
IN 1966 WE BROKE ALL THE RULES. THAT'S OUR CONTRIBUTION, THAT'S OUR CLASSIC.

U T V S S T Y L
YOU GOTTA KNOW YOUR K•SWISS CLASSICS
UNAPOLOGETICALLY THE VERY SAME SHOE TWENTY YEARS LONG

Writing for Design
Ogilvy & Mather Singapore for
The Economist

Thoughts
Subscriptions to The Economist can now be given as a gift.

Copywriters
Ross Fowler
Greg Rawson
Art Directors
Mo Chong
Chris Soh
Typographer
Eric Yeo
Executive Creative Director
Robert Gaxiola
Advertising Agency
Ogilvy & Mather Singapore
Planner
Sonal Narain
Brand Manager
Bala Shetty
Client
The Economist

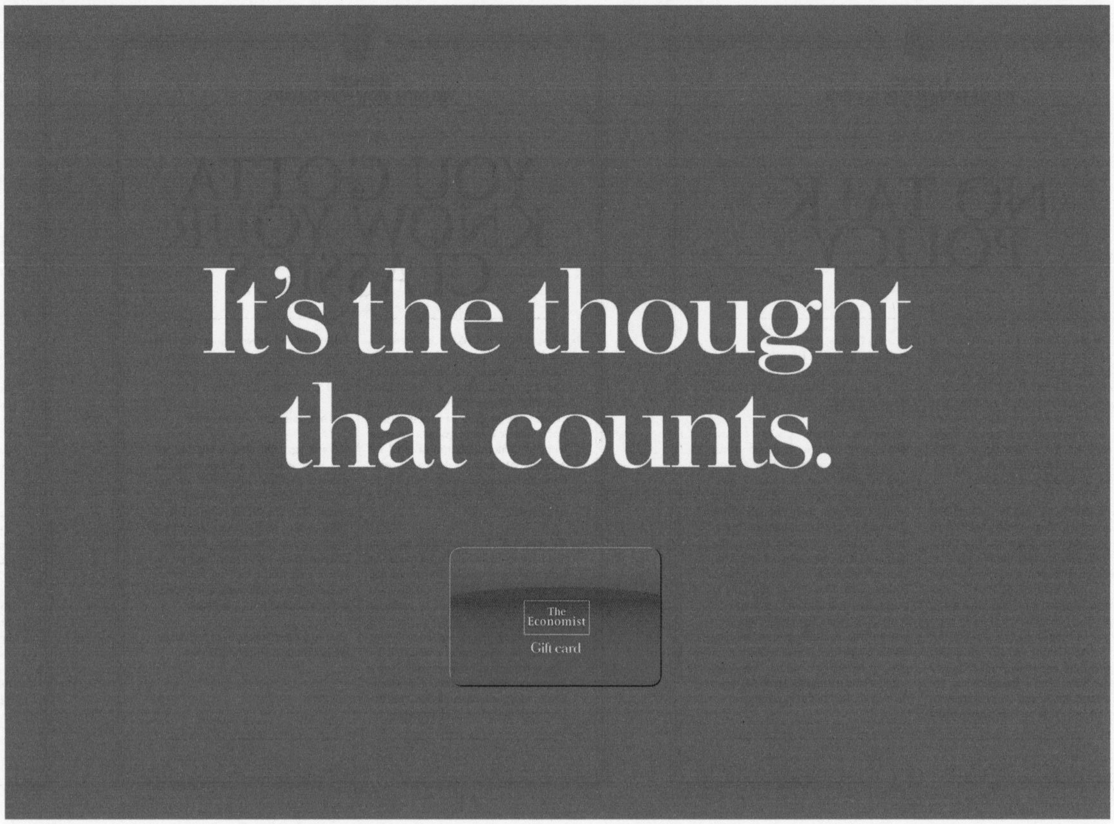
It's the thought that counts.
The Economist
Gift card

Writing for Design
Interbrand Australia
for Stephen Bland

The Great Blandini
The objective was to create an identity for the highly skilled retoucher Stephen Bland. He wanted a fun solution that would appeal to the creative industry. Stephen is a retoucher extraordinaire, multi-skilled in the mysterious ways of Photoshop, and a true Mac wizard. So it was that Stephen Bland revealed himself to be The Great Blandini. An engaging, Victorian-inspired typographic look and feel unfolded, referencing an era when magic was still truly magical. Together we developed a distinct tone of voice based around an amusing combination of modern day, technical terminology and Victorian English.

Copywriters
Mike Reed
Mike Rigby
Designers
Andrew Droog
Malin Holmstrom
Artworker
Oliver Kendal
Creative Director
Mike Rigby
Design & Branding Agency
Interbrand Australia
Client
Stephen Bland
Brand
The Great Blandini

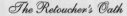

WONDER at Phantasmagorical PHOTO-SHOPPE Phenomena
GASP AS BLANDINI VANISHES ELEMENTS OF YOUR CHOICE
THE GREAT BLANDINI
LAYER UPON LAYER OF INTRIGUE AND SORCERY!
APPROACH AND BE AMAZED! MESMERISING! MARVELLOUS! MAC-NIFICENT!
FANTASTIC FILTERS
THE MASTER OF MASKS
ASTONISHING ADJUSTMENTS
For Personal Appearances STEVE BLAND Telephone +44 (0)7854 434 428
THE GREAT BLANDINI
IMAGE MANIPULATION AND PHOTO-SHOPPE TRICKERY
The Retoucher's Oath
As a Retoucher I promise never to reveal the secret of any Transformation to a Non-Retoucher, unless that one swears to uphold the Retoucher's Oath in turn.
I promise never to perform any Transformation for any Non-Retoucher without first practising the effect until I can perform it well enough to achieve the transformation of retouching.
ROLL-UP! ROLL-UP!
THE GREAT BLANDINI
IMAGE MANIPULATION AND PHOTO-SHOPPE TRICKERY
THE VANISHING ACT
Beware: frail women may swoon as elements disappear before your very eyes!
For Personal Appearances
STEVE BLAND
+44 (0)7854 434 428
THE RABBIT FROM THE HAT
Blandini renders countless wonders, in the briefest time and from the meanest purse!
For Personal Appearances
STEVE BLAND
+44 (0)7854 434 428
THE TRANSPOSITION OF ELEMENTS
Marvel as that which appeared fixed is transported into new configurations!
For Personal Appearances
STEVE BLAND
+44 (0)7854 434 428
THE RESTORATION ACT
New life for pallid colour! The dull made sharp! Imperfection vanquished!
For Personal Appearances
STEVE BLAND
+44 (0)7854 434 428

Writing for Design
johnson banks
for More Th>n

Little Green Book
Ten years after launch, More Th>n wanted a revised brand manual. But that felt a bit formal, so we set about writing a pocket-sized 'Little Green Book' that would only take two minutes to read but would quickly sum up the More Th>n brand without resorting to cliché or jargon.

Copywriter
Michael Johnson
Designers
Michael Johnson
Julia Woollams
Typographer
Michael Johnson
Design Group
johnson banks
Brand Manager
Heather Watson
Client
More Th>n

Our little green book

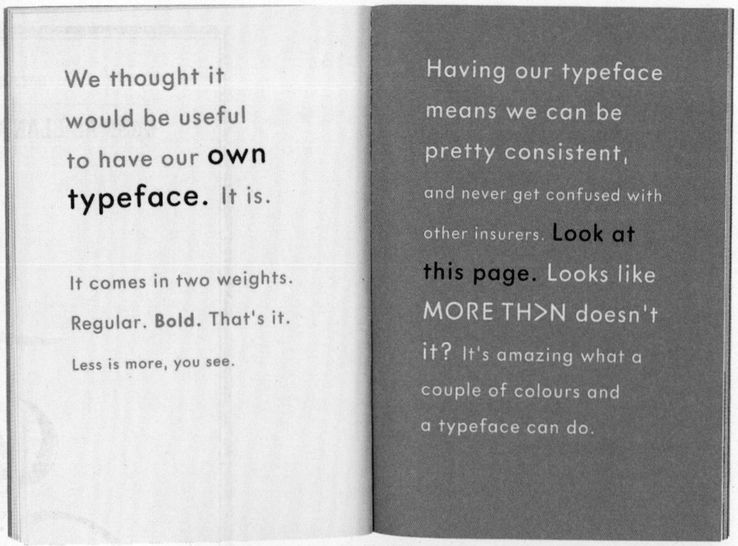
We thought it would be useful to have our own typeface. It is.
It comes in two weights.
Regular. Bold. That's it.
Less is more, you see.
Having our typeface means we can be pretty consistent, and never get confused with other insurers. Look at this page. Looks like MORE TH>N doesn't it? It's amazing what a couple of colours and a typeface can do.

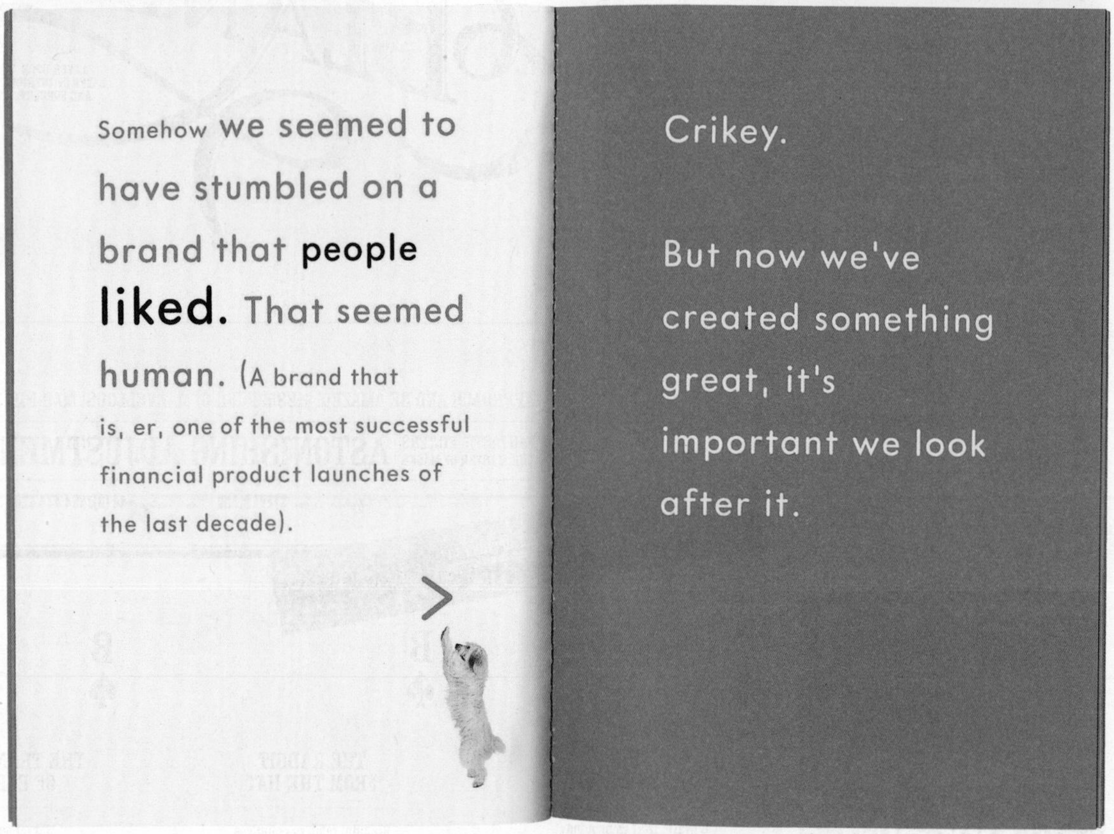
Somehow we seemed to have stumbled on a brand that people liked. That seemed human. (A brand that is, er, one of the most successful financial product launches of the last decade).
Crikey.
But now we've created something great, it's important we look after it.

Writing for Design
Leo Burnett Chicago
for Symantec

This Book is a Weapon
A trusted leader in security software, Norton has a new brand purpose: to protect people's rights online. Today's hackers are far more dangerous than they were before. They are real criminals who don't just ruin computers; they ruin lives. To introduce the new brand book, we changed the job description of every Norton employee. They no longer work for a security software company. They fight cybercrime and this book is their weapon. Using typography and imagery, we illustrated the magnitude of the cybercrime problem and armed them with the tools they need to fight cybercrime.

Copywriters
Dave Loew
Tohru Oyasu
Molly Scanlon
Art Directors
Chris von Ende
Rainer Schmidt
Photographer
James Day
Creative Directors
Dave Loew
Jon Wyville
Chief Creative Officer
Susan Credle
Agency Producer
Laurie Gustafson
Retouching
Core Digital
Advertising Agencies
Arc Worldwide Chicago
Leo Burnett Chicago
Account Director
Antoniette Wico
Senior Account Executive
CJ Nielsen
Client
Symantec
Brand
Norton

IN YOUR HANDS, THIS BOOK IS A WEAPON.

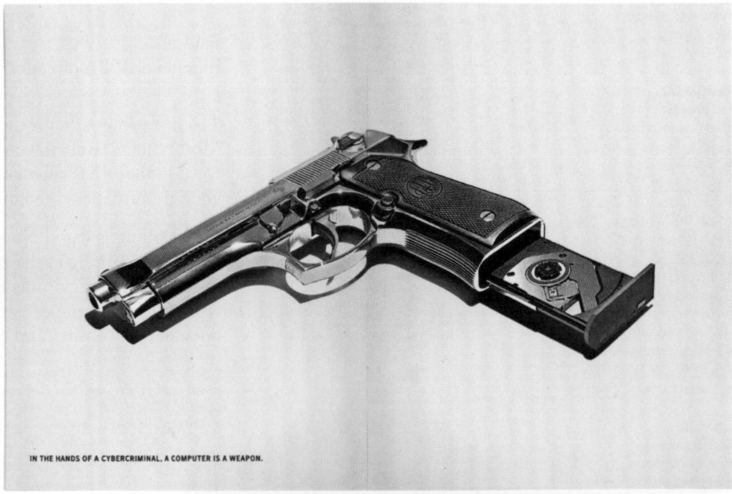
IN THE HANDS OF A CYBERCRIMINAL, A COMPUTER IS A WEAPON.

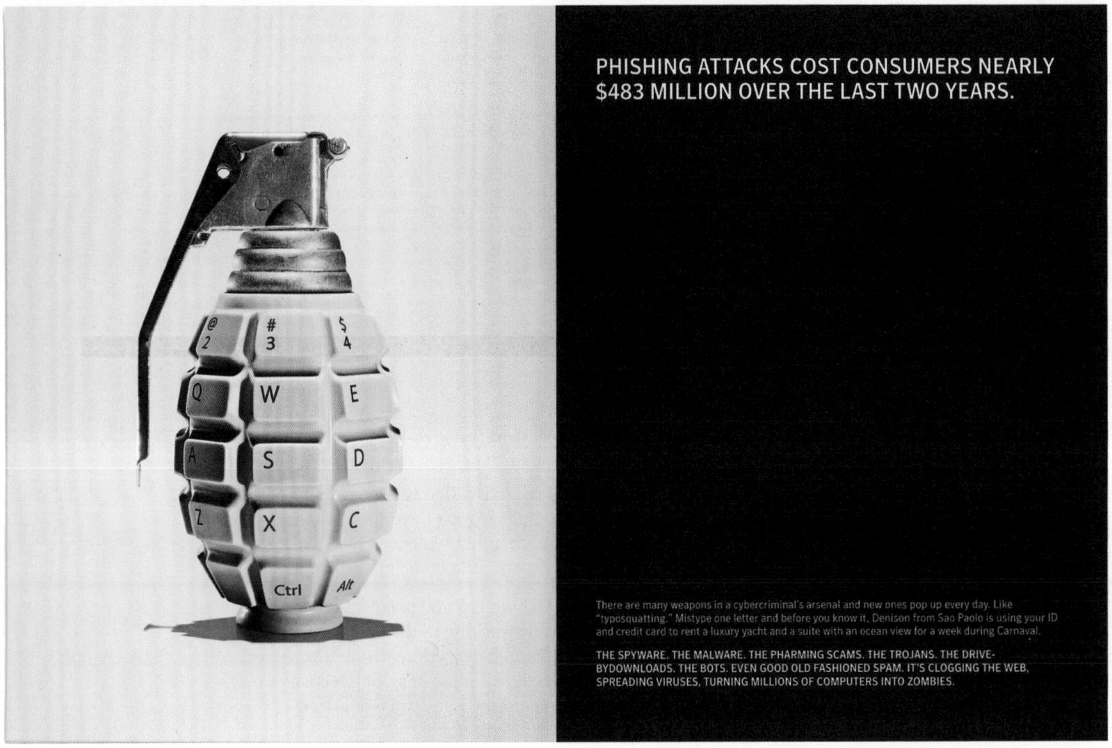
PHISHING ATTACKS COST CONSUMERS NEARLY $483 MILLION OVER THE LAST TWO YEARS.
There are many weapons in a cybercriminal's arsenal and new ones pop up every day. Like "typosquatting." Mistype one letter and before you know it, Denison from Sao Paolo is using your ID and credit card to rent a luxury yacht and a suite with an ocean view for a week during Carnaval.
THE SPYWARE. THE MALWARE. THE PHARMING SCAMS. THE TROJANS. THE DRIVE-BYDOWNLOADS. THE BOTS. EVEN GOOD OLD FASHIONED SPAM. IT'S CLOGGING THE WEB, SPREADING VIRUSES, TURNING MILLIONS OF COMPUTERS INTO ZOMBIES.

Writing for Design
Nick Asbury
for Paul Dalling

Paul Dalling, Proofreader
This is a promotional website for proofreader Paul Dalling, aiming not only to promote Paul himself, but also to persuade people of the importance of proofreading in general. The site practises what it preaches – clarity and attention to detail – using witty copy and a simple navigational device to highlight the deliberate errors.

Copywriter
Nick Asbury
Creative Director
Mark Wheatcroft
Design Group
Wheatcroft&Co
Client
Paul Dalling

Paul Dalling
Independent Proofreader

"To be or to be: that is the question." Or is it? Most readers won't have spotted the missing word in that first sentence. That's where a good proofreader come in.

Paul Dalling is a god proofreader. He's spent a lifetime working in the print industry, proofreading everything from goverment reports to exam paper's, high security documents, websites and colanders.

Proofreading
Proofreading covers the usual checking for spelling, typographical, punctuation, and grammatical errors. (Spell-check has its uses but it only catch so mulch and will thin a sentience like this is fine.)

Editing
As well as proofreading, Paul will check the text from a stylistic point of view to introduce an enhanced reader experience in terms of clarity and consistency issues.

Fact checking
Wherever necessary, Paul will check the factual accuracy and relevance of your content and suggest rewording. He is one of the best in the world at this.

Service
Paul will work on hard copy manuscripts sent by post or e-mailed files using the 'track changes' function in Microsoft Word®.

Fees
Fees are negotiable and reflect the nature of the work. Straight forward proofreading starts at £7 per 1000 words. Bear in mind that the cost of not proofreading (reprints, lost custom, damaged crudibility) is often much greater.

To call or to email
01332 664439
typo@pauldalling.co.uk

CLICK TO VIEW THE TYPOS... p.d.

Paul Dalling
Independent Proofreader

"To be or to be: that is the question." Or is it? Most readers won't have spotted the missing word in that first sentence. That's where a good proofreader come in. s

Paul Dalling is a god proofreader. He's spent a lifetime working in the print industry, proofreading everything from goverment reports to exam paper's, high security documents, websites and ~~colanders~~. o n calendars.

Proofreading
Proofreading covers the usual checking for spelling, typographical, punctuation, and grammatical errors. (Spell-check has its uses but it only catch so mulch and will thin a sentience like this is fine.) es k

Editing
As well as proofreading, Paul will check the text from a stylistic point of view to introduce ~~an enhanced reader experience in terms of clarity and consistency issues.~~ greater clarity and consistency.

Fact checking
Wherever necessary, Paul will check the factual accuracy and relevance of your content and suggest rewording. ~~He is one of the best in the world at this.~~ STET

Service
Paul will work on hard copy manuscripts sent by post or e-mailed files using the 'track changes' function in Microsoft Word®.

Fees
Fees are negotiable and reflect the nature of the work. Straight forward proofreading starts at £7 per 1000 words. Bear in mind that the cost of not proofreading (reprints, lost custom, damaged ~~crudibility~~) is often much greater. credibility

To call or to email
01332 664439
typo@pauldalling.co.uk

← GO BACK TO THE ORIGINAL COPY

Advertising Agencies

Animation

Architectural Studios

Brands

Clients

Contractors

Design Groups

Developers

Digital Agencies

Editing

Events & Events Marketing Agencies

Illustration

Image Manipulation

Manufacturers

Media Agencies

Music

Photography

Printing & Print Production

Post Production Companies

Production Companies

Public Relations Agencies

Publishers

Record Companies

Recording Studios

Retouching

Sound Design & Production

Special Effects

Visual Effects

Writing Agencies

Printed in Italy by Printer Trento
The first printer in Italy to have been awarded the certification FSC (Forest Stewardship Council) – Chain of Custody. Also ISO 14001 certified.

Paper: Recystar Polar
100% recycled, woodfree uncoated paper made by Lenzing, Austria.

Cover board: Eskaboard FSC 100% recycled

Cover paper: Gardagloss FSC, 10% PCW

Lamination: Clarifoil cellulose diacetate film
The compostable alternative to the usual plastic coating.

Weight: 1.6kg
By reducing the weight of all 2011 Annuals printed by a total of 12,330kg compared to last year, we have made a 40% saving on paper stock and also reduced our use of fuel for transportation.

CO2e emissions per copy: 0.8kg
This is an 82% reduction compared to 2010.

Harry, Sanky, Nat

9 Graphite Square, Vauxhall Walk
London SE11 5EE
+44 (20) 7840 1111
www.dandad.org

Art Direction
Pentagram
Design
Harry Pearce
Diogo Soares
Jason Ching
Cover Photography
Richard Foster
Group Shot & Sanky's Portrait
Nicholas Turner
Sustainable Design Consultant
Nat Hunter
Awards Director
Holly Hall
Coordination & Editing
Jana Labaki
Artworkers
Kim Browne
Laura Mingozzi
Senior Editorial Assistant
Bethan Morris
Editorial Assistance
Chris Berry
Lina Soblyte
Barbara Torres
Image Production
Donal Keenan
Guy Porter
Nagore Gonzalez
Matthew Mitchell-Camp
Naqeeb Popal
Production Consultant
Martin Lee
Origination
DawkinsColour, London

Hohenzollernring 53, D-50672 Köln
www.taschen.com

Editor in Charge
Julius Wiedemann
Editorial Coordination
Daniel Siciliano Bretas
German Translation
Jürgen Dubau
French Translation
Aurélie Daniel
for Equipo de Edición

ISBN: 978-3-8365-2884-9

MIX
Paper from responsible sources
FSC® C015829